Dark Age of Camelot™

Prima's Official Strategy Guide

An Incan
Monkey God Studios
Production

Prima Games
A Division of Random House, Inc.
3000 Lava Ridge Court
Roseville, CA 95661
(916) 787-7000

For valuable updates to this book, check out our website!
www.primagames.com

IMGS Writer: Melissa Tyler
Statistics and Editing: Beth Loubet, David Ladyman
Interior Graphic Design: Sharon Freilich and Raini Madden

Interior Layout: Sharon Freilich, Raini Madden, Melissa Tyler, Tuesday Frase, David Ladyman, Beth Loubet

Border Knotwork Art: Cari Buziak

Nearly Holy Team Warriors

Matt Firor, Lori Silva, Eugene Evans, Jim Montgomery, Chris Rabideau

Valiant Team Knights

CJ Grebb, Colin Hicks, Dave Rickey, Erik Krebs, Lisa Krebs, Spyke Alexander, Maurice Nelson, Brian Axelson, Mark Jacobs, and Aryn Pennington

Friends Indeed: Mike Luer, Jed Norton (Realm maps), Rusel de Maria, Mark Warrington, Jared Warrington, Chris Treloar, Eric Penn, Joseph Vantiem, Aglavalin, Avira, Ayden, Forlon, Gelain, Groog, Hvines, Innovations, Lamorak, Lord PrydeKell, Mirianne, Rungar, Timil, Turbo

Utterly Incomparable Panelists

Ethan "Esis" Kidhardt
Eric "Bubski" Bramblett
Steve "LarianLeQuella" Lundquist
Monica "Seraphym" Hayes
Marc "Biggs" Quesnel
Ted "Falryx" Wallace
Harold "Mindeater" Pontious
Joe "Varnarok" Bayley
Nate "Stylean" Nieman
Adam R. "Prior Tuck" Fritz
Bob "Rambler" Sleys
Heather "Orlena" Rothwell
Cory "Bonham" Magel
Doug "Kaiser" Fernandes
Jim "Oaklief" Rothwell
Robin "Maia" Harris
Shelby "Garthlik" Cardozo
Joe "Sevith" Ascani
Kevin "Morgan" McLaughlin
DJ "Aphexplotz" Larkin
Andrew "3DKnight" Knight
Brian "MrMoose" Beck
Todd "Jubal" Wharton
Dave "i3ullseye" Maynor
Mary "Scarlet" Scheffler
Andrea "Flower" Pontius
Dan "Ghalun" Dean
Jennifer "Ellyndria" Beaulieu
Lauren "Plio" Hanlon
Katharine "Rhiannon" Beach
Matt "Kyle" Shirley
Michelle "lilwitch" Tune
Mike "Muse" Swiernik
Ian "Iain ap Conlan" Wright
Jim "Skam" Skamarakas
Dana "Lepidus" Massey
Jeff "Deg" Royle

Product Manager: Sara E. Wilson

Project Editor: Terri Stewart

ISBN: 07615-3945-X

Library of Congress Catalog Card Number: 2002103850

Printed in the United States of America

03 04 BB 10 9 8 7 6 5 4 3

Table of Contents

Front Matter

Player Characters

Overview (Tips for New Players)

Realm of Albion

Realm of Hibernia

Realm of Midgard

Realm vs. Realm

Appendices

How to Use this Guide

Well, you've probably noticed this is a big guide. Believe me, that's not because we added pages and then stretched the information out to cover it. In fact, it's the opposite. We've squeezed probably 600 pages of information into the 408-page book you're holding. It's because *Dark Age of Camelot* is a big game. In fact, it's a huge game. As far as information is concerned, it's really three and a half games … each realm — Albion, Hibernia and Midgard — has its own set of weapons, spells, monsters, towns, etc. The Realm vs. Realm area makes up the last "half game." It has its own data, but not quite as much as a full-fledged realm. What's more, the team at *Mythic* has generously offered to share the nuts and bolts of the game with our readers. It was our goal, in writing this book, to stuff as much data into this book as *Mythic* was willing to give us.

However, we didn't just rely on the team for information. That works for some sorts of games, but not Massive Online Games. No, we went straight to the players and amassed a Panel of Experts. Some are team leads who have played *DAoC* since it was in early Beta testing; many are avid and devoted gamers who wanted to help make a guide as complete and accurate as possible; one or two are relatively new players who didn't want other newbies to have to go through the stages of uncertainty that they had gone through. Each gave excellent advice and then read what other people had to say to double-check for accuracy. Their opinions may not be consistent with every players', but they are valid opinions. Any outright mistakes should be assumed to be the fault of rewriting, mistranslating or inaccurate editing on the part of the writers/editors.

Please, as you read this book, remember two things.

1) *DAoC* is a constantly growing, ever-changing game. We're filling this guide to the brim with good advice and helpful information, and most of it will remain rock-solid through upcoming changes … but some things will change. Changes will be announced in the Patch Updates you'll occasionally see as you log in. For instance, right now Realm Abilities have started being tested. Rather than leave them out, we've put them in as they originally appeared on the test server … but any changes that will occur as the result of this major addition are not reflected in the Class Discussions.

2) This is a game where the experience is directly influenced by the player. It will be a different game for you than it is for anyone else. Take the advice we give as valid, but then adjust it to your own experience.

FINDING WHAT YOU WANT

We've divided the book into six major sections. There's an "Overview" section, designed to introduce new players to the basics of *DAoC*. The section for Albion includes all the Albion-specific information. Likewise there are sections for Hibernia and Midgard. (No, we aren't playing favorites by always placing Albion first. That's just the way they fall alphabetically.) There's a section for Realm vs. Realm — this is where the Darkness Falls map is — and at the end there's an Appendix for all the details that have to do with the game in general, not just one particular area.

Overview

If you've played *Dark Age of Camelot* already, you probably don't need to read this section at all … but if you're new to *DAoC*, it's definitely worth a good going-over. It explains the very basics of character creation — a quick recap of what's in the manual, with more detailed discussions in each class's write-up — and also gives some advice to new players. Massive Online Games have developed a culture of their own, with each game, *DAoC* included, developing a unique sub-culture. The Overview section helps eliminate some of the shock of stepping into an entirely alien environment.

Albion, Hibernia, Midgard

Each realm covers all the things that are unique to that realm.

Horse Routes. Kind of like the medieval version of the public transportation system, in *DAoC* you can always hire a horse to take you to another location. Also similar to public transportation, you don't get to steer. You go where you go, and this list tells you what your options are.

Merchants Table. We've assembled a chart of what is sold where by whom. We hope it helps the serious shopper … although items made by crafters should also be considered.

Player Classes. For the new player the most important part of the section is the class descriptions. These discuss what a player should know about each class, to establish a character who can go the farthest with the least frustration. This is also the section most vulnerable to personal bias … so remember, this is friendly advice, nothing more.

Quests. You'll find a table that outlines the available quests in that realm. The location and quest-giver are listed, as well as what level or other prerequisites you must meet in order to be given the quest. We don't list the rewards for each because they change frequently.

Item Stats. The statistics for all weapons, armor, shields, musical instruments, etc. that can be made or found are listed here. There are tons of 'em.

Crafting Recipes. Yep, we've got them.

Monsters. Here's a list of the NPC opponents that roam the lands, listed by type. In this case, we're following the advice of our player panel — certain types of classes and weapons do much better against certain types of monsters. The dedicated player prefers to go after those things that are most vulnerable to his attack. If you can't find a monster you're looking for, you can find its realm and type in the Monster Cross-Reference, beginning on page 375.

Maps. Here are the city maps (with NPCs called out), realm region maps (with landmarks and terrain features detailed) and dungeon maps (with general monster locations noted).

Realm vs. Realm

DAoC is a fun game even if you never venture outside the secure areas, but the *real* excitement is when you seek out and destroy the marauders from enemy realms. The famed adventurer Esis the Intrepid has boldly gone where none could follow, and has given us advice based on his adventures and explorations. He notes monster locations to a certain extent, advises on the best hunting areas, and — please take note — outlines areas of greater and lesser danger of meeting up with those pesky enemy marauders.

Darkness Falls is given in full, monster-detailed glory. Please excuse that we don't have specifics on the boss-monsters of *DF*. *Mythic* was very forthcoming about information, but they were understandably disinclined to give us the nuts-and-bolts mechanics of the big baddies of DF. However, we can and have told you who they are and where to find them.

Appendices

A. Explanations. If our thumbnail explanation of what's going on in our many tables is a little confusing, we explain the method to our madness here.

B. Crafting. We've included Brian "Falaanla" Beck's personal narrative of a career in crafting. It explains the process step-by-step.

C. Roles. The finer points of being an archer or rogue are explained here. These can be particularly difficult careers, and we thought they warranted some further explanation. The master for this invaluable tutorial is Jim "Oaklief" Rothwell.

D. Glossary. If you haven't played Massive Online Games, you probably don't know the lingo. Read this glossary through just once, and suddenly the local chatter will make sense.

E. Slash Commands. Yes, most of the slash commands are in the manual — but not all! We've gathered the full set by perusing the patch updates, talking to players, and checking underneath the sofa cushions at *Mythic*.

F. Websites. These are the ones recommended by panelists or the team, or the ones that seem to keep their sites up-to-date and accurate.

Player Characters

First, let's take some of the pressure off. Making a character is not like volunteering for the army. It's not a decision that you're going to have to live and die with for the next few years. It's more like trying to find a good pair of shoes. There are questions to be answered, some research to be done, and a little bit of an investment — but in the end it's just a matter of trying on different styles until you find the one that's right for you.

First of all, relax!

Adjust your mindset. If you have played a massive multiplayer game before, you at least know the fundamentals of what to expect. If not, you're in for a real treat.

First and foremost, DAoC is a game. It's not trading on the stock market, or deciding whether to have children. It's not even as serious as coming up with a grocery list for the week. It's just a way for a lot of people to get together and have a good time. Wearing armor and swinging a sword, casting spells, swapping combat stories in a tavern … when you come right down to it, it's all just plain fun.

Just because someone writes a guide on how he plays his character, it doesn't mean it's any sort of bible. It's *your* character … do what you want! You should listen to the advice of those who have been there before, but it's still your game and your character!

Most people talk about leveling and getting to be a master craftsman or whatever. One of the most successful and well-known characters in all of Hibernia is in Guinevere — and is only a 3rd level magic user! He logs on and talks to everyone! He is now the Mayor of Mag Mell (no one remembers the election, but we are assured it was a landslide). Have fun, get to know folks, and enjoy yourself. There is no big rush to get to Level 50 or over 1000 in a tradeskill.

Now, that being said ….

Who Are You, Really?

Who are you? The first step in developing a character that you're going to enjoy playing is to think about your personality. Are you comfortable being a quiet person, or are you more outspoken? Do you like interacting with other people, or do you prefer to spend more time accomplishing things on your own? Do think you'll prefer combat against other players, or would you rather stay with the slightly more predictable and controllable in-realm world?

There are lots of roles that you can take on, from solo player (which is, by the way, the most difficult way to play the game) to healer to melee combat specialist. Read the pros and cons for each class (Albion, pp. 38-79, Hibernia, pp. 138-177, Midgard, pp. 232-267.) and decide which one sounds the most appealing. Then give it a try for a while. See if you like it. If not, try something else.

RACE AND CLASS COMBINATIONS

	Brit	High	Aval	Sara	Celt	Luri	Firb	Elf	Nors	Kobo	Trol	Dwarf
Armsman (2x)	√	√	√	√								
Cabalist (1x)	√		√	√								
Cleric (1x)	√	√	√									
Friar (1.5x)	√											
Infiltrator (2.5x)	√			√								
Minstrel (1.5x)	√	√		√								
Paladin (2x)	√		√	√								
Scout (2x)	√	√		√								
Sorcerer (1x)	√		√	√								
Theurgist (1x)	√		√									
Wizard (1x)			√									
Bard (1.5x)					√		√					
Blademaster (2x)					√		√					
Champion (2x)					√	√		√				
Druid (1x)					√		√					
Eldritch (1x)						√		√				
Enchanter (1x)						√		√				
Hero (2x)					√		√					
Mentalist (1x)					√	√		√				
Nightshade (2.5x)						√		√				
Ranger (2x)					√	√		√				
Warden (1.5x)					√		√					
Berserker (2x)									√		√	√
Healer (1x)									√			√
Hunter (2x)									√	√		√
Runemaster (1x)									√	√		√
Shadowblade (2.5x)									√	√		
Shaman (1x)										√	√	
Skald (1.5x)									√	√	√	√
Spiritmaster (1x)									√	√		
Thane (1.5x)									√		√	√
Warrior (2x)									√	√	√	√

BASIC RACE ABILITIES

	Brit	High	Aval	Sara	Celt	Luri	Firb	Elf	Nors	Kobo	Trol	Dwar
Strength	60	70	45	50	60	40	90	40	70	50	100	60
Constitution	60	70	45	50	60	40	60	40	70	50	70	80
Dexterity	60	50	60	80	60	80	40	75	50	70	35	50
Quickness	60	50	70	60	60	80	40	75	50	70	35	50
Intelligence	60	60	80	60	60	60	60	70	60	60	60	60
Charisma	60	60	60	60	60	60	60	60	60	60	60	60
Empathy	60	60	60	60	60	60	70	60	60	60	60	60
Piety	60	60	60	60	60	60	60	60	60	60	60	60

Important Class Attributes

STRENGTH

Affects weapon damage for crushing/slashing weapons. Affects 50% of thrusting weapon damage. Affects how much you can carry: you are unencumbered up to your Strength (if it is an even number, or one less than your Strength if it is odd). After that you become more encumbered (you slow down). If you have a Strength of less than 50 you have a penalty applied to your encumbrance for every point less than 50.

Maximum encumbrance is twice your normal encumbrance weight. After maximum, you can't move at all.

Beware the Debuff. While you can rely on magical items to buff your Strength, it's dangerous to rely on them too much. In Realm vs. Realm, some of your opponents have serious Debuff spells. A heavily laden character hit by a Debuff spell is an immobile character.

CONSTITUTION

Adjusts maximum hit points.

DEXTERITY

Dexterity is the one attribute that affects archery ability.

It determines weapon damage for thrusting weapons (along with Strength). It also determines all eogue/Stealth skills.

Also, a high Dexterity can reduce the xasting speed of a spell by up to 25%.

QUICKNESS

Quickness gives a bonus to attack speed.

INTELLIGENCE

Intelligence determines maximum spell points for Intelligence (Way of Magic) casters.

EMPATHY

Empathy determines max spell points for naturalist (Way of Nature) casters.

PIETY

Piety determines max spell points for priest/cleric (Mystic, Seer) casters.

CHARISMA

Charisma determines the effectiveness of Skald/Minstrel/Bard songs.

Choosing Realms

While classes are similar in different realms, the "feel" of the world is dramatically different. Choosing a realm comes down to a number of things.

Friends. This is the obvious but best thing to base your decision on. Do you have friends who play *DAoC*? If so, start off on whatever server they're on. Games are twice as much fun if you have a "native guide" to show you the ropes.

Profession/race. Decide what you want to do, and then decide which race will do the job best. (This takes research, so read up on the information on classes for each realm.) Do you want to be a nuker or a melee-tank? Do you want to heal? Do you feel sneaky? Be aware that not every race can do everything in each realm. Figure out which race has the best advantages, and then choose your realm accordingly.

Just plain race. Many races are realm-based. So, if you've gotta be an Elf, you've gotta be in Hibernia. Sometimes it's just that straightforward.

Atmosphere. The three realms have radically different environments, but the goal of the team is to have them all equally balanced with opportunities and population.

Albion is the "Olde England" realm. It has the classes and races most familiar to the average player. A lot of people start off there … and a lot of people stay there. Historically, Albion has been considered the "teacher's pet" realm, and was the realm finished earliest in the beta, but that's not so much the case anymore.

Hibernia is pretty … a fitting home for Elves and anyone who loves a lush environment. It has a lot of class choices and is bright and airy. Gaelic names are tricky for a lot of people to remember or pronounce, though. "Tír na Nog" means "Land of Youth" in old Irish, in case you wondered.

Midgard is dark and foreboding, a great place for people who don't want to be cheerful 24/7. It's primarily a priest/melee realm. There's less magic, more combat, and some very versatile, powerful classes. It's good for someone who wants something a little different. Historically it's been harder to get to higher levels than in other realms, but with significant rewards at the end of your labors. Mythic has been balancing Midgard assiduously, and now it is home to just about as many people as the other realms.

Play around. If you aren't sure — or don't have friends to lure you onto any particular server — go ahead and make a character in each realm. (You need to pick different servers … you can't play multiple realms on the same server.)

Experience Points

How You Get Them

Here's a rough explanation of what brings in experience points.

Killing. The higher the Monster's level, the more XP it gives. This is adjusted by the age of the monster (more XP) and how heavily its spawn site gets hunted (fewer XP).

It's pretty safe to say that 1 yellow = 2 blues, and 1 blue = 3 greens. 1 yellow is often far more difficult to kill than 2 blues …but at low levels you get twice as many XP. (It's easier to recover from killing a blue, so there is less downtime.) 1 blue is often more economical to kill than 3 greens, but they are harder to find.

But it's more complicated than that.

Questing. Finish a task or a quest assigned to you by an NPC, and you'll rack in not only XP but some hard-earned cash.

Delivering. Similar to a quest, but it usually takes you farther afield. If you were already headed that way, it makes a great traveling bonus. If not … it gives you a reason to explore places past your own back gate. However, don't think that they only send you to safe places! Be on your guard, and group when you can.

Healing. To even up the playing field between fighters and healers, you can get XP for healing people outside your group who are fighting a monster (if it's a higher level than they are).

Leaching. Be careful on this one! Leaching is doing damage spells on a high-level (to them) monster that someone else is fighting. You should never fight someone else's monster without being invited. In a very important way, Leaching is different from the healing or debuffing methods of getting experience points — it's stealing. What you get, they lose. That can earn you a really bad reputation really quickly.

Debuffing. Similar to the healing method of getting experience, debuffing a high-level monster that's chomping on a stranger (i.e., someone who isn't in your group) will give you experience points. It will not leach XP, which makes it okay to use on people who have not asked — you're not stealing any of their experience. And it might be just enough to help a newbie win that fight!

Who's Got Them

Experience points are important to anyone who's interested in gaining levels.

Group bonus. Group bonus is for monsters who are linked together. It's a reward for fighting a lot of creatures at once, not a bonus for being in a party.

XP bonus. A creature who remains unkilled over a period of time begins to amass additional experience points. If you go hunting in largely unexplored regions, the same monster who would net you 600 points in a populated area might earn you 650.

XP degradation. Monsters from a heavily hunted area (meaning people pounce on it as soon as it spawns) will gradually give fewer and fewer XP per kill. For example, imagine an untouched pristine camp that spawns monsters worth 150 XP. Someone comes along and starts killing them soon after each spawn. The first three spawns are normal: 150 XP. But after a serious hunting season the return might be diminished by 23 or possibly 30 percent. That means that a creature that would normally net you 150 points would give only 120 XP.

This is to keep people from sitting in one place and just killing whatever pops up. Know what? There are still hour-long "waiting lists" for some places! (If you get on a waiting list, stay close enough that other players don't have to wait on *you* when your time comes. Parking nearby is safest, but with a little experience, you may be able to wander just a bit and solo while you wait.)

Allocation

XP can get tricky in groups, because dividing up the XP equally can be unfair.

The game figures how much experience points each player gets by working the numbers. It looks at how close each member of the group's level is to the highest-ranking member. Then it works out how the experience points are divided accordingly.

4 EQUAL CHARACTERS

Points are divided equally.

Equal players mean that everyone's close enough in level that the monster is the same color to all of them. Since it would be unfair to count up how much damage each character did to the monster (which would cut out a support character like a Healer), it's assumed that equal-level characters participated to the same level, and everyone gets the same XP. For example: Out of a total of 80 points, each character would gain 20.

1 BUFF, 3 WIMPS

Nobody gets anything.

If the highest-ranking person is fighting a gray (to her) monster, it's no challenge for her at all. If it's no challenge at all for someone in the group, then no one really had to do much at all. Therefore no one gets any experience.

3 REGULAR WITH 1 KINDA-WIMPY

3 get 25% apiece, the fourth one gets less.

Say there are three characters who are fighting a monster that cons yellow to them. They have a buddy who sees it as red. They're all working as hard as they can, and the monster goes down.

If the fourth character's level is within 75% of the others' levels, he'll get experience ... he just won't get as much as the others. (If the other players are at level 16, the fourth one needs to be within four levels of them to get experience.) He'll get whatever his level cap says he can. The rest of the experience points? Nobody gets 'em.

For example: Out of a total of 80 points, each of the three higher-level characters gets 20. The fourth one has a cap of 12, and that's what he gets. The last 8 points disappear.

3 REGULAR WITH 1 REALLY-WIMPY

3 get 25% apiece, the fourth one gets a percentage of his XP cap.

Three characters are facing a blue monster. Their buddy sees it as a purple. (In other words, he's not within 75% of the others.) Everybody fights, monster is killed.

Because the monster was only 80% of the highest player's level, the lowest-leveled player only gets 80% of his XP cap. If the big boys had been facing something equal to him, the lowest-level guy would get his full cap. But they weren't really challenged, and it's the lowbie who's going to pay for it.

For example: The big three get 20 apiece ... their full share. The lowbie gets 80% of his cap. If his cap is 12, he gets around 10. The last 10 points just disappear.

Specialization

Special thanks to Jim and Heather Rothwell, who have an excellent article on specialization, and have given us permission to run it here. More information can be found at http://rothwellhome.org/camelot.html.

The material in this article applies to all classes, and is drawn from experiences with different characters during all of beta testing and various developer comments. The two principle authors of this guide held the position of Cleric Team Leader and Scout Team Leader during beta, and had closer contact with developers than many of the beta testers. That is offered by way of credentials, but you are more than welcome to ignore the advice offered here.

Initial Levels

All characters in the game initially start out as a generic class, near their class trainer. At fifth level, all characters choose an advanced class that will determine their specific career path, and give them a different trainer.

All generic classes get one specialization point per level each time they level. That is, two points when you attain second level, three points at third level, etc. You begin the game with some skills that you cannot specialize in, and some that you can specialize in. You can choose to receive extra training in a skill, start it with first rank specialization.

When you level, extra training in a specializable skill costs the next rank in specialization points. So, to raise one of your initial skills to the 2nd rank in specialization costs two specialization points (which happens to be all that you get at second level). When you attain third level, you can use your three specialization points two different ways. You can raise the skill that was at 2nd rank to 3rd rank and use all of your new points, or you can raise a different skill to 2nd rank by using two specialization points and leaving one extra point for the next time you level and visit your trainer again. All training in skills happens at your class trainer before you choose an advanced class, or at your advanced class trainer after that.

You should also be aware that skills often determine success or other attributes (like range, radius or damage) based on a comparison of specialization level to character level, opponent level, base level of effect, or some combination of the above. So a 5th rank skill is much more effective for a sixth level character, but not much more effective than an untrained skill when a character is 30th level.

One Times (1x) Specialization

Classes with only three or four specializable skills always receive specialization points equal to their attained level. These tend to be the pure caster classes.

Classes with this type of specialization scheme have enough specialization points to fully spec in one line, keeping all other lines at the 1st rank (until you reach Level 40-50 Bonus Points — see p. 17). It will make you very strong in one area but it may hurt your ability to solo, and you might be less adaptable in groups. This *can* gimp your character, so ask around before you choose a pure path. (Now, 100% Fire Wizards, for example, aren't gimped at all by pure specialization. Neither are Air Theurgists.)

Sometimes the best thing to do is specialize in one area until you reach Levels 40-50, and then branch out.

The methods that the developers have said are preferable for these classes to spend their specialization points are of two suggested styles. Of course, depending on actual points at a particular level, and the way numbers round, you will sometimes be able to do more and sometimes do a bit less.

1) Two skills at two-thirds your level and the rest at minor levels.

2) One skill at two-thirds your level and two skills at one-half your level.

One-and-a-Half (1.5x) Times Specialization

Classes with five or six specializable skills usually receive specialization points equal to one-and-a-half times their attained level. These tend to be some of the tank and rogue classes.

Classes with this type of specialization scheme have enough specialization points to fully spec in one line and have enough points left over to train a second skill to half-level (until you reach Level 40-50 Bonus Points — see p. 17). Please note that the developers have stated repeatedly that this is not the recommended way to spend your specialization points, but the choice isn't as bad as fully specializing in one skill is for one times classes. Again, the choice is yours to make. It will make you very strong in one area but overall it will hurt your ability to solo and you'll be much less adaptable in groups.

The method that the developers have said is preferable for these classes to use in spending their specialization points is to aim for one of several suggested styles. Of course, depending on actual points at a particular level, and the way numbers round, you will sometimes be able to do more and sometimes do a bit less.

1) Two skills at two-thirds your level, one at one-half your level, and the rest at minor levels.

2) One skill at two-thirds your level and three skills at one-half your level.

3) All skills at just over one-half your level.

Two Times (2x) Specialization

Classes with more than six specializable skills usually receive specialization points equal to two times their attained level. These tend to be some of the tank and rogue classes.

Classes with this type of specialization scheme have enough specialization points to fully spec in two lines, keeping all other lines at the 1st rank (until you reach Level 40-50 Bonus Points — see p. 17). Please note that the developers have stated that this is not the recommended way to spend your specialization points. Again, the choice is yours to make.

The developers have recommended these classes to use one of the styles below in spending their specialization points. Of course, depending on actual points at a particular level, and the way numbers round, you will sometimes be able to do more and sometimes do a bit less.

1) One skill equal to your level, two skills at two-thirds your level, and the rest at minor levels.

2) One skill equal to your level, one skill at two-thirds your level and two skills at one-half your level.

3) Two skills at two-thirds your level, two at one-half your level, and the rest at minor levels.

4) One skill at two-thirds your level and the rest at one-half your level.

Two-and-a-Half (2.5x) Times Specialization

Infiltrators now have 2.5 times points. That gives a wealth of choices, and has beefed up the Infiltrator class significantly since the early months of the game. Nightshades and Shadowblades have also gone up, and now have 2.2 times points.

Bonus Points

From Levels 40 to 50, you get extra points. This is to give characters the chance to investigate skills they wouldn't otherwise be able to afford.

Every level you receive the points you would normally receive, and then at the mid-way mark to the next level, you receive an additional half-set of points.

In other words, for a class that receives 1x spec points:

40th level	40 points
40.5	20 points
41st level	41 points
41.5	20 points
42nd level	42 points
42.5	21 points
…	
50th level	50 points
50.5	nothing (the magic's over)
51st level	51 points

Effects of Specialization

This can get very complicated with melee, so I'll describe the effects for spells and most rogue abilities, and then mention briefly how it gets modified for melee skills. Note that this is what we have figured out, with some developer input, but the inner workings were not laid bare for us.

First, you will notice on the casting classes guides that there are two spell lists for each type of style. The first list is the basic spells that are granted as you go up levels. Each time you level, you automatically get the spells on these lists, no matter what your specializations are. The advanced spell lists are specialization dependent, you get the spells from them when you train high enough in those types of spells. Those advanced spells are appropriate at all levels, as they do damage or healing based on a percentage of your target's scores.

Let's look at a cleric's spells as an example; others are similar to this. Basically, for heals and smites, it compares your specialization level to the level of the spell. The closer your spec level is to the level of the spell, the closer to 125% you do. If you have no specialization (minimum), the range goes from 25-125%. If you have half the specialization of the spell you do from 75-125% (average 100%), and if your spec level is equal to or over the level of the spell, you do 125% reliably. It also appears to have some mitigating effect on the resist rate.

Special combat styles are gained as you add specialization points into an ability. For instance, as an archer trains with her bow more, she gets faster versions of critical shot, then longshot, and eventually volley.

Those who train in melee weapons get special attacks that can add to damage, cause bleeding damage for the next few rounds, stun their opponents, get the mob's attention or help divert its attention to others, etc.

Rogue skills have variables such as range (for Stealth) that are dependent on your specialization vs. your level. When it comes time to check your effectiveness though, your specialization is compared to either a set number (like picking locks), your opponent's level (mobs and most characters seeing through Stealth), or your opponent's skill level (enemies using perception to see through Stealth). This comparison affects the chances of success or failure.

Melee skills are also dependent on your specialization level compared to your level. If you have no specialization (minimum), the range of damage goes from 50% to 100%. If your specialization is half your level, the range of damage is 75% to 125%. And if you are fully specialized, that is, your specialization level is equal to your character level, you do 100% to 150%. Now, here is where it gets very confusing. The advanced weapon skills, like Polearm and 2-Handed in Albion, are further modifiers on this, and overall damage relies on both that skill, and the basic weapon type skill. Dual Wield specialization affects how often and for what amount you hit with the second weapon.

Starting Locations

ALBION

Fighters	
Avalonian	Avalon Marsh
Briton	Camelot Hills
Highlander	Black Mountains South
Saracen	Campacorentin Station
Rogues	
Briton	Camelot Hills
Highlander	Black Mountains South
Saracen	Campacorentin Station
Acolytes	
Avalonian	Avalon Marsh
Briton	Camelot Hills
Highlander	Black Mountains South
Elementalists	
Avalonian	Camp Forest
Briton	Camelot Hills
Mages	
Avalonian	Camp Forest
Briton	Avalon Marsh
Saracen	Ludlow Village

HIBERNIA

Guardians	
Celt	Shannon
Elf	Silvermine
Firbolg	Ardee
Lurikeen	Mag Mell
Stalkers	
Celt	Silvermine
Elf	Mag Mell
Lurikeen	Ardee
Naturalists	
Celt	Shannon
Firbolg	Ardee
Magicians	
Celt	Silvermine
Elf	Mag Mell
Lurikeen	Shannon

MIDGARD

Vikings	
Dwarf	Mularn
Kobold	Gotar
Norseman	East Svealand
Troll	Myrkwood
Rogues	
Dwarf	Mularn
Kobold	Gotar
Norseman	East Svealand
Seers	
Dwarf	East Svealand
Kobold	Mularn
Norseman	Gotar
Troll	Myrkwood
Mystics	
Dwarf	Mularn
Kobold	Gotar
Norseman	East Svealand

Overview Or: Tips for New Players

Dark Age of Camelot is big — really, really big. In fact, it's so big that it's impossible to say "this is the way you should do it." It's large and complex, not to mention constantly changing as Mythic adds and removes things, or tweaks various systems to try and keep the game balanced. The good news is that there are a lot of people who have been playing this game since the beta started. There are people who knew what was what even before the game went live, or who have devoted quite a significant chunk of their lives to learning and playing DAoC. We went to these people and asked them to become a part of our panel of experts … and when asked what they wished they had known at the outset, this is what they had to say.

Essentials

Dying

Go ahead and die in Levels 1-5. You lose nothing in Levels 1-5 by dying. Nothing, nothing, nothing. Not experience, not items, not a single coin. *Don't be afraid of dying.* It's a sure sign you're a newbie.

Go ahead and die in Levels 6-10. You lose almost nothing in Levels 6-10 when you die. Especially if you just leveled, all you lose is a little experience and some Constitution (temporarily). It's worth it for the knowledge you gain. *Don't be afraid of dying.*

Well, try not to die over Level 20. After Level 20 or so, you lose a lot of time and effort. It's not the end of the world, but it's just not fun. Don't even sweat it if you can't get resurrected … all that saves you is a trip back to your gravesite and a little Constitution (that you can get back from a town healer). Go ahead and type /release if there's no one near who's inclined to resurrect you. *Don't be afraid of dying.*

Don't get angry if a Priest, Bard, Warden or Paladin says he can't/won't rez you. First, once you type /release, no one can resurrect you. Second, there's a timer on resurrection … if someone says she can't make it to where you are in time, she's probably right. Third, someone far below your level just can't rez you. Last, you can never tell when someone's too busy, too far away, too low on Power, or having a really bad day … if you ask and get told "no," be polite. Don't blow a gasket, don't swear eternal enmity, and don't call anyone names. Just type /release and go on with living.

Interface

Shift C is how you check your compass and find out where you are.

/Stick vs. /Follow. /Stick is a very useful command. You can stay close to friends or foes by typing /stick. It keeps you on target during combat, or simply together during travel.

Hint: If you /stick to a target and get the "target out of range" message (as often happens on steep slopes or with huge foes), just move, retarget and type /stick again. That's all it takes.

/Follow is usually a good way to stay with your buddies during regular travel.

In complicated places, however — thick woods, twisty dungeons or busy cities — it's actually easier for everyone if you use the /stick command. People don't get stuck behind things as often.

Basics

Type /help. You can always type /help and scroll through the text for basic information. It's a pretty good online manual.

Ask advisors for advice. Players who have been in the game for a long time can "sign up" to act as advisors for the newer players. (They do this by typing in /advise.)

New players can get a list of the advisors who are logged in by typing /advice.

You can ask any of the advisors a question by typing /advice <advisor name> <question>. The advisor will respond.

Make use of this feature. It's friendly, it's free, and it's specific to whatever is confusing you. Advisors are people who are eager to have others enjoy the experience; they really *want* to help.

Don't ask advisors for help! Advisors are not Customer Service representatives. All they can do is tell you what they've learned from their own experiences. They can't unstick you, or clear a quest, or do any of the other "nuts and bolts" things that an actual CRS can.

Know the plusses. *DAoC* uses colors to show you what level an item or creature is in relation to your character. Unfortunately, that leaves the color-blind players a little confused … and possibly a little dead. So Mythic has implemented a *symbol equivalent* of the colors. (Note this is not a gradation of the color, it's just an equivalent. A red with a ++ is a red, not a super-duper red.)

Gray	- - -	Utterly harmless
Green	- -	Below you
Blue	-	A bit below you
Yellow	<none>	Equal to you (ideal)
Orange	+	Above you
Red	++	Dangerously above you
Purple	+ + +	Lethal

Don't waste spec points. Pick a specialization based on your playing style and map out a plan for spending your training points. Specializing heavily in one area might pay off at lower levels, but at higher levels you might have to spread out a bit more to be more "rounded" over all. You may also want to wait until you join your advanced class at Level 5 to use any of your specialization points, because new areas for specialization are given then that you don't have in your starter class.

Take tasks. Yes, you can eventually reach a decent level just by killing critters, but that's hardly the best way to get started. Ask around and get some low-level quests. Local guard needs a message delivered? Volunteer with a glad cry. On your way there, kill the little critters that are unlucky enough to cross your path. Getting started is faster and a lot more fun when you do the tasks. (Some say it goes faster if you solo until Level 4 and then do all your tasks.) There is a cap to how much XP you can gain per level, and once you reach Level 20 you won't be given any more tasks.

Sometimes you can even get a weapon. Look around for a task that will get you a better-than-basic dagger. Some people mention a good way to get a small (but nice) weapon if you bring them something. Do it!

Cheap XP boost. Take a task right before you level to 20, then level up normally. Then go and finish the task. You'll get more experience points for finishing a task at Level 21 than you do at Level 20.

Go afield. Look around and see if you can find some newbie fields farther from your starting point. You can recognize them because they'll have blues and greens, yes? Not only are they less crowded, but sometimes the monsters give more experience … and when you're trying to get to Level 5, more experience is a good thing. Remember, when you're starting out, it's okay to die. That makes looking around a lot easier.

If you already know where you want to go, see if you can get lucky with a task that's in that direction. For instance, if you're in Salisbury and want to head back to Camelot, try asking /help to the NPCs in the west part of town. Chances are good you'll get a task to either Cotswold or Prydwen Keep. Same is true for Cotswold to Humberton or Ludlow — and you might get another task for Camelot.

Binding. When you bind your soul to an area, you don't have to be standing right next to a bind stone. At Level 6 and above, you should almost always bind yourself next to a healer if you can find one within the acceptable radius around the bind stone.

Baby groups. It's fun to group, and it's important to know how to group, but grouping at low levels isn't the fastest way to level up. That's because you have to share the experience points among more people, so you have to kill that many more creatures. If you group with other players who aren't low-level, you still won't get more points because you'll have a cap on your experience gain. (See **Experience Point Allocation**, p. 13.) So until you reach Level 5, group if you want the fun and social exposure … but not for quick experience points.

Watch where you're going. Always try to keep track of your location when in a group. It's surprising how easy it is to follow someone across the landscape, log out for the night … and log back in completely unaware of where you are.

Watch where you've been. Keep an eye out for guard posts. When you're being chased by a big baddie, you're going to want to know where those guards are. They also make a nice, safe location to log out!

Figure out why you're not working up to snuff. If your character seems to be lagging, you can check your packet loss with Shift P.

Check your spells. If you're a magic user, check out your spells whenever you level up. Some spells appear automatically, some you get after you visit your trainer.

Save sprint power. If you're going to try a yellow (or higher) and think you might not win, don't make a lot of style attacks. They drain Endurance, and you just might want that extra minute of sprinting!

Using guards. If you're being pestered by reds and oranges in your happy hunting grounds, you can always try tagging them and running to a guard. As long as you can make it to the guard, they'll take care of the problem for you.

Remember to have fun. If what you're doing in any way turns into a chore, do something else. Remember this is a game.

Equipment

Buy a better weapon at Level 2 or 3. It is really important for new characters to get something a little less worthless at Level 2 or 3. If you're playing with the equivalent of a butter knife or an old stick, you're going to hate the game because it will take you ages to level up.

Don't buy a better weapon at Level 4 if you don't have to. When you hit Level 5, some guilds will give you a very nice new weapon, based on your class and combat skill specialization. So it's a waste of good money to upgrade when you reach Level 4. If you have extra cash, put it into some nicer armor.

Now, not all guilds will give weapons. Some give armor or trinkets. Just ask around and find out what you can expect … and plan on not buying prematurely.

Treat your equipment with respect. Try to keep your weapons and armor repaired to above 80% if possible. If necessary, learn a trade skill and use the /repair command.

When an item degrades in durability, it is usually time to get a new one.

Note, though, that being good at repair can also make you good money, as well as keep your stuff working well!

Look for leather. If you don't have armor, and a monster drops some tattered armor, wear it! It's amazingly better than nothing. When you can afford better, buy better.

Sell or trade what you can't wear. This goes double for magic items (you'll have to ask around to see what's "hot"). Put what you want to keep in the "bottom" of your bag.

Color My Stuff

Ideally, you want all your stuff … weapons, armor, magic items … to show up as yellow to you. This means that the item exactly matches your level, and you're getting the absolute best you can out of it in terms of damage, speed, protection or whatever.

If an item is too high for you – orange, red or purple – you won't get much more benefit (if any) from it than if it were an item of your level. For example, an 8th level character wielding a 15th level sword will get no better damage or speed than they would from an 8th level sword.

There is a penalty for using an object far above your level – they deteriorate much faster than normal. Since higher-level items are more valuable, and therefore more expensive to repair, this can represent a significant drain on your resources.

The deterioration penalty for high-level items ranges from 2 times normal for reds, to 4 times normal for "low" purples, to a whopping 8 times normal for "high" purples far above your level. (And some very high purple items may not be usable at all.) Oranges are a bit of a special case. Depending on your level, "low" oranges may not have a penalty at all, while "high," almost-red items will fall into the 2-times deterioration category. The exact "breaking point" is that items 10% or more above your level will carry a deterioration penalty. So, if you're Level 40, a Level 43 item won't deteriorate when you use it, but a Level 44 item will.

Now, that doesn't mean you *can't* use jewelry, etc. that's higher than your level. It will probably be better to wear it for as long as it lasts than to destroy it. It's just not the best use of the item.

As for lower-level items, the drawbacks are

pretty obvious. There are no arbitrary penalties; they're just far inferior to the best items you could be using for your level. A lower level item will always do the best it can for you … even gray armor is better than no armor at all … but remember you're fighting far below your potential.

Monsters

Please be aware that color "con" is relative to your type of character. For a tank (high Strength and Constitution) orange is ideal … for a Rogue (lower STR and DEX), yellow is death.

Yellows. In general, yellows will kill a low-level or weak character. However, if you're close to home, you can often run back and attack the same yellow monster while it's still wounded from your last attack. This is good if it drops better equipment … if it doesn't, you're better off fighting greens and blues.

Ideal yellow. All classes are supposed to have an "ideal" yellow. Clerics and Undead, for instance. It will certainly help if the type of monster is particularly vulnerable to your kind of attack (for instance, a skeleton is vulnerable to Crush attacks).

Kill greenies, too. When you're a low-level character, you'll be faced with a lot of green and blue critters around your starting area. While blue monsters give more XP per kill, they take longer to kill, plus they'll take a bite out of you each battle. If you kill green Monsters, you kill them faster and you don't have to rest to recuperate your Hit Points. In other words, don't hesitate to kill greenies just because they're "beneath you." You can actually level up pretty quickly on greens.

Multi-Monsters for beginners. At higher levels you can try taking on a blue with one or two greens, all together. You get more loot than if you tackled a yellow, and it's not that difficult.

Big one? Buff! If you think you're going up against a tough enemy, recast your Buff spells. There's nothing worse than a shielding/Buff spell fading in the middle of battle.

Monster scouts. Sometimes it doesn't take much to bite off more than you can chew. When you target a monster you'll get a message letting you know its aggression level. Sometimes you'll also see "and is a scout." That means if you make it angry, it'll turn around, get its entire camp, and the whole gang will come and reduce you to jam. Occasionally some monsters won't even wait for you to do anything hostile … the Tomb Raiders will gang up on you if they so much as see you hanging around.

Inventory Control

Don't litter! If you have things that you don't want anymore, don't just take them out and drop them. That's because what you drop, everyone else will target … even though they can't pick it up! When you want to clear up inventory space, the polite thing to do is ask your friends or guild-mates if they want anything you have, and then destroy anything that's left over. (A lot of people map V to "destroy item.")

Watch what you've got. See if anything stacks.

You might as well just keymap Delve (a useful place is F2), to save the wear and tear on your fingers. You use Delve *all the time* to identify items.

It's better to keep all the things you are intending to sell in the same bag. It makes it faster to get rid of them when you start dealing with a merchant.

Keep what you're going to sell up front — it's where the game automatically puts things (Bag 1 first, 2 second, etc.), and also it's where you won't have to dig around to find them.

More than that, it's far too easy to pick up and accidentally drop an item when you're trying to get something repaired. Even that's not too big of an issue, since no one else can pick it up … but it doesn't take too long on the ground before it starts to decay, so don't get distracted when you're clicking around in your backpack.

Put your valuable items in your last bag, just to be sure you don't click on something important accidentally.

Take it off. If you want to give someone something that you're wearing — like armor — you need to remove it and put it in your inventory bag, then hand it over to them.

Sort your arrows. (Sorting arrows is only necessary or useful until a quiver system is in place. In the meantime, this is a useful system.) Arrows placed in Bag 1/Slot 1 are used first, followed by those in Bag 1/Slot 2, and so on. After you go through all the arrows in Bag 1, you continue to those in Bag 2.

A good way to sort your arrows is to keep a few slots in Bag 1 reserved for arrows, but don't keep any other arrows in Bag 1 at all. Keep your regular, "everyday" arrows in Bag 2. Keep your expensive, special arrows in Bag 8. If you need them in a hurry, you can just grab them, click forward one bag to Bag 1, and drop them in the slots. Badaboom! You're good to go.

Muscle Power

This section is intended for the weaker characters, not for the strong of arm. If you signed up for a fighting class or are a Troll, Dwarf, or any other naturally strong race, you won't need this. Pure casters and frail races need to think about this at the outset.

Let's face it. Life's just a little bit more complicated when you have to constantly keep track of all your worldly possessions. Some people can get along just fine carrying just a few things … but then it usually turns out that the "few things" those people actually want are pretty heavy. A big, tough Berserker might feel he can get by with only the armor on his loins and the sword in his hand … but you know, that's a lot right there. Meanwhile, the slender Scout who wouldn't want to wear a Berserker's outfit even if she could, is left wondering how she could possibly travel while carrying enough arrows to survive a stint in enemy territory.

Carrying too much means being encumbered, which means that you run more slowly even with Sprint, which means that the monsters can catch you more easily … and that's just plain bad.

Give yourself a head start. Initial attributes are good in establishing Strength, but there are many Strength-buffing items in the games that you can rely on to improve your natural abilities.

It's a good idea to increase your initial Strength to 50 regardless of who you are, because at 50 STR the formula changes. Someone with a Strength of 50 can carry a lot more than someone with 49 STR.

Check. If you can't move, first check spells/lag and *then* check Encumbrance.

Don't overdress. Take care when choosing your armor. It's usually better to wear lighter armor and not be encumbered than to wear heavy armor, be too slow, and have to spend all of your free time running like a sloth to the nearest merchant to sell things.

Don't over-pack. Okay, if you're as strong as Atlas, you don't have to worry about carrying too much. But you still only have so much room you can devote to stuff, so you might want to think about what to carry and how. And if you aren't covered in muscles, you definitely want to think about what to carry and what to toss.

Don't carry extra armor. Either it's good enough to wear, or it isn't.

The same goes for weapons. Don't be a collector. Keep a different or extra weapon as a backup, but keep your best and sell the rest.

Buff. If you must pack to the point of Encumbrance just to walk around, try to find some magic Strength items. Ask around, do favors for friends, until you can at least keep up with carrying your own inventory.

Pick your fights. Some monsters drop a lot of low-value loot, some drop less stuff — but what they do drop is more valuable. Obviously, it's better to get quality over quantity.

Get a mule. Currently each person has a personal account (one per character) that can be accessed from a Vault Keeper. Vault Keepers are in the main building of each Realm's capitol city, and also located in places far away from the capitol. However, some people — especially crafters — need more space than the vault allows. One way to get around this is to keep a mule.

Mules are characters that you've created entirely for their ability to carry a lot of stuff — things you want to keep, but don't need to have readily available. Since the strong can usually carry whatever they want, mules are mostly (but not entirely) a caster/crafter issue.

Mules need to be as strong as possible (Highlanders/Trolls/Firbolgs are popular) because their only purpose is to carry as many items as possible. When creating one, put the maximum points into Strength.

Set their bindpoint somewhere convenient to where you spend much of your time.

Currently you cannot drop an item and have anyone else pick it up … even if that other person is you, only playing a different character. So what you do is give the items to a friend, log out, log back in as your mule, go to where your friend is waiting, get the items (or give them to your friend), then have your mule pick a fight with a tough critter nearby. Don't resist, so that the mule is killed. That way when you return to your mule, later, it will respawn back at the original bindpoint.

Then log back out and in again as your "regular" persona, and go get your stuff from where your friend is holding it.

Oftentimes friends or guilds will have their mules concentrated in a convenient area, somewhere they will often be: their HQ, or a specific location such as a Tavern/Inn or a bind stone. Just let a friend know what you're up to.

Archers need Strength Buff items. Characters whose primary combat ability is archery (usually Scout, Ranger, Hunter) have an instant inventory problem. They have to carry their weapons with them — in bulk — to be much use. Be reasonable in your inventory. It doesn't take 1,000 arrows to be effective. You'll survive just fine with 400.

Don't refuse to wear armor. Okay, wizards in movies and books don't usually walk around in good armor. In fact, they usually only wear a robe and a felt hat. Well, that may be fine for Merlin, but as you face rougher, tougher monsters, you'll probably want a little extra protection.

Buff to your armor-comfort level. With low Strength you cannot carry much or wear much armor. Keep an eye out for Strength-enhancing items, and then judge whether the Strength-buffing item will allow you to upgrade your armor. Some sort of armor is a priority.

You can mix and match your armor, putting the toughest armor in the most frequently hit spots. Put on a plate breastplate, perhaps some chain on your arms and legs, then some sort of leather for the gloves, boots and helm. As you get stronger you can swap out some of the leather for chain, and then some of the chain for plate.

Weaklings need weapons, too. Thrusting weapons are the lightest in the game and everyone needs some sort of melee weapon. Therefore, thrusting weapons are often the preferred choice of the weaker classes.

Immigrating (Coming in From Other Games)

There are many Massive Online Games available to the public today, and there's no law that says you can only play one. In fact, a lot of the new players in *Dark Age of Camelot* come directly from other MOGs. Usually they like what they see, and if they don't, they tend to just disappear from the landscape, and go back to the world they're more familiar with.

It's important to remember that different games have surprisingly different cultures. It's a lot like moving from one country to another: things that you used to take for granted as "natural" will suddenly get you laughed at — or worse, in trouble.

Don't be afraid of dying. We've said it before, we'll say it again: Don't sweat getting killed. It's not a bad thing. *DAoC* is much more forgiving about death than some games, and there's no reason at all to be afraid of making fatal mistakes before Level 10. All that happens is that you wind up back at your trainer. So go forth and tackle the big monsters, just to see what happens. Get a feel for the game, learn the interface, and find out what happens when you take on an orange or a red monster.

Even at higher levels, death only means a loss of some experience and constitution points. You'll *never* lose so much experience that you drop in level. You can get half of your experience back by praying at the gravestone where you died, which helps. Also, you get two "discount" death per level — the first time you die, you only lose half the experience points you normally would have. The second time you lose more, but not as many as normal.

Death means buying back your con. Dying will remove some of your Constitution (unless you're resurrected by another player). The way to get it back is to go to an NPC healer and pay to have your CON recovered.

Interface. Take about 20 minutes to get comfortable with the new interface before you try anything trickier than stabbing a snake.

Split window woes. It can take a while to get used to the "system" messages being overhead and separate from the "chat" messages which are at the bottom of the screen. There's not much you can do about it, it just takes time to get used to it.

Don't help unless asked. Even if someone looks like he's about to die in a tough solo fight, *if they don't ask you for help, don't jump in.* Ask if they need help. If you want to be nice, buff them, or wait around until the fight is over to resurrect them (if you can rez) or heal them. Helping someone kill something will decrease the amount of XP they get ... sometimes significantly. You don't want to be seen as stealing/blocking xp, so don't do anyone favors unless they're asking for it.

Just for the record, kill stealing *is not* tolerated. If you get reported enough times, it can get you booted from the game.

Don't hog a camp. In DAoC, no one "owns" a spawn site. In some other games, when you and your buddies settle down at a spawn spot, it's all yours until you leave — anyone who comes in and pulls monsters from a "taken" camp spot is being really rude. That's not the way it works in DAoC. Mythic really discourages long-term camping in general (over-hunting an area will tend to drive the XP of the local monsters down, for instance), so the culture is distinctly different.

If you and your group are pulling from a spawn site, and someone else comes up, you need to take turns. The only monsters you "own" are the ones that you're current pulling, currently fighting, or have mezzed. It's okay to pull from the same spawn site as someone else, but it's not okay to take something someone has targeted.

Same name, different class. Just because a class has the same name as a class in another game, doesn't mean the class will perform the same function. A Bard in *EverQuest* isn't the same thing as a Bard in *DAoC* ... or a Minstrel, or anything else.

In fact, even within DAoC, same-name classes will have decidedly different abilities. This is because different people use their specialization points differently. It's possible to have a Cleric who is a lousy healer, for example, even though another Cleric is a healing whiz.

Repair your equipment. Don't wait too long to repair your equipment. Several days of battles will leave your things with lousy condition.

Don't refuse to try. It can be especially difficult for an *EverQuest* melee player to learn to take risks.

In DAoC, it's possible to fight and win against a monster that's higher in level than you are. Don't go out of your way to take on a red, but don't refuse to try if your buddies are eager to give it a go.

Gang up. *EverQuest* people understand ganging up on one monster at a time, with the magic users keeping the others safely mezzed. *Asheron's Call* immigrants are a little less familiar with the concept of "assisting" in combat. In general the way combat works is the magic users keep the monsters asleep while the tanks pick them off one by one.

A trick in helping you fight the correct monster is to target it, and then type /stick. That will keep you on the right track.

Mages need to be people-people. Players who are used to being magic users in *Asheron's Call* may have an especially difficult time learning how to function in a group. In *AC*, Area-Effect spells and multiple tanks on separate targets are the way combat works, but in *DAoC* that will get you killed.

It's a matter of control. Magic users from *EverQuest* have a good understanding of the use of DoTs (Damage over Time spells), Mezzes (mesmerization spells), aggro management (keeping the monster focused on the tanks) and group communication. Magic users don't wade into battle very much, but they're always paying very close attention to what's going on.

Things that a mage needs to know:

Kiting — the art of keeping the deadly monsters out of range.

Ping ponging — keeping a monster confused by swapping attacks back and forth, so it doesn't focus on killing one person.

Assisting the prime tank — letting your lead fighter declare the target, then everyone fights that one, as the magic users keep the other monsters under control.

Crowd control (large scale) — keeping a ton of monsters under spells to keep them from eating you and your friends.

Group etiquette — calling out your target, Power level, or anything else of interest to others.

Pets — how to use your pets in combat.

Don't ask for Buffs. In other online games, casting enhancement spells on strangers is a good way to earn magical experience points. In those worlds, it's acceptable to ask for Buffs, because both parties benefit. In *DAoC*, however, Buffs cost the casters Power and they get nothing in return. So in *DAoC* it's not very polite to ask without offering something in return ... or at least being extraordinarily complimentary.

Appreciate the group dynamic. In some games, certain classes perform certain roles in a group. That's the way they were designed, and that's the way people play those games. Try to find the "must have" class to build the "perfect" group, and each class performs a precisely defined role. In *DAoC*, player ingenuity defines what happens. Having a unique play style is possible, and adds to the experience. (For instance, one successful group contained three Healers, only one of which actually spent much time healing!) Characters evolve at the discretion of the player. Therefore it is not necessarily a sign that someone is a twinked-up newbie who doesn't know how to group if he doesn't perform a role in an exact manner.

Watch the way your group works. Some groups do better with having multiples of lower-level monsters, some do better with having a single very-high level monster.

Power-leveling. It does not, repeat *does not*, help you level to have a higher level character kill with you. If they help you kill a monster — even if they are not grouped with you — your experience gain will diminish accordingly. (Check out **Experience Points**, p. 12.)

Now, having someone of high level cast Buffs on you has a huge impact.

That being said, the quickest way to get through Level 20 is by doing "kill tasks." The good thing is that you learn a lot about the local creatures. The bad thing would be that you don't learn the *game* quite as well as you would by regular hunting. If you want kill tasks and the local named NPC won't give you any, go to another town and ask around.

KEYBOARD INTERFACE

Redefine your keyboard. The *DAoC* keyboard interface is completely customizable. Go ahead and make it as similar to your old game as you'd like. There's no reason to suffer through relearning everything … no one can see what keys you press.

Keyboard shortcut advice:

Change the camera control keys to the ones you are used to.

"Auto-attack" (or "Combat Mode") should be what you're familiar with.

Move "Target nearest enemy" to a key near the hotkeys you use for combat styles.

Assign "Target nearest item" and "Pick up item" to adjacent keys.

Player Guilds

Why are Player Guilds Important?

- A high-level character can have trouble finding a well-balanced group of the appropriate level. A guild, especially a large guild or one that is dedicated to leveling together, can make this easier.
- Tradeskills are usually available to guild members at an enormous discount. Some hand-me-downs are free, but other things you can get for cost (plus sometimes a little extra cash for a "thank you").
- It makes socialization easier … and for most people playing an online game the social aspect is the factor that most largely determines how enjoyable the experience is. Other players are an excellent source of advice and support, and make *DAoC* less of a game and more of a world.
- RvR is designed for group combat. Groups that work together often learn how to communicate, anticipate and use tactics. This gives them an enormous advantage over other groups. Guilds provide a place to discuss tactics (sometimes via email) and practice teamwork and communication.
- A strong guild gives you a greater good in which to participate and be proud. A server will develop a history, and participating in an active guild gives you a better chance to be part of that history.
- Some guilds have made informal RvR networks to keep informed of enemy invasions. It's the best way to stay in the thick of things.

Finding a Guild

Player guilds play a large part in the overall experience of the game, especially when players need to be organized enough to really make waves playing Realm-versus-Realm. While it's not a once-in-a-lifetime decision (you can always quit and join another), you can save yourself some aggravation by doing a little research.

Remember, you can't get along with everyone … and there's no reason to join a guild you don't enjoy.

- Don't just ask the world at large if there are any guilds that will let you join. There are … but they usually won't be what you're looking for. "Anyone can join" guilds tend to be chat rooms with a little game wrapped around it.
- Ask if they ever group with non-members — they almost always do. If they invite you for a hunt, hang out with them for a day and see if you have a good time. Sometimes they'll have low-level characters just for running around with recruits. If you don't have fun hunting with a guild, you're not going to have fun doing RvR with them.

Even tightly knit groups eventually add new members … and most guilds don't mind even a never-played-before newbie.

- Ask if they have a website that you could check out. (Some have websites that only members can see.)
- Ask what the goal/mission/charter of the guild is.
- Ask what the guild is like.
- Figure out what you'd want out of a guild, and ask them if they're good at that.
- Ask around to see what other people say about the guild.
- Ask what time of day they get together (real time).

After you've grouped with them for a day and know what they're like …

- Ask what the prerequisites are for joining. (This kind of information is often on a website.)
- Ask what their rules are. (Do they require dues? Do you have to group with a certain number of members? Etc.)

Making a Guild Happy

Playing a Massive Online Game isn't rocket science; it's a game. Just about anyone can learn how to play, although of course some people pick up the tricks and commands faster than others. The valuable players are the people who want to make the game fun for everyone. They pay attention during outings, don't leave the keyboard (and the group) frequently, or for long periods of time. So really, it doesn't matter if you have experience, as long as you're polite and considerate to the people you group with.

A player who's paying attention to what's going on is a good player and useful to group with. A player who gets distracted — even if they're excellent when they're "on" — is a liability. If your group gets frustrated because you're doing your own thing, or looking after yourself first, or just not responding, they're not going to ask you back. They *certainly* won't ask you to join their guild.

If you give priority to the guild, then priority to the group, and lastly look after your own interests, guildspeople will enjoy grouping with you. It's that easy.

Guild Commands

/gc invite Invites a targeted player into the guild.

/gc invite <name> Invites named player into the guild.

/gc info Lists the settings for all rank levels, and displays information such as Total Guild Realm Points, Artifacts Captured and similar data.

/gc cancel Cancels any previously executed guild command such as /gc form or /gc invite.

/gc claim Claims a frontier keep as belonging to your guild. Several conditions must be met for **/gc claim** to work. (See **Realm vs. Realm**, p. 318.)

/gc quit Removes you from a guild.

/gc motd Sets a special message-of-the-day for the guild. *This is a Guild Master-only command.*

/gc promote <#> The promote command followed by a rank (##) 1-9, allows a user (with promote ability) to promote the target to the said level. You must have the person whom you wish to promote targeted with your cursor.

/gc demote <#> The demote command followed by a rank (##)1-9, allows the user (if they have demote ability) to demote the target to the said level. You must have the person whom you wish to demote targeted with your cursor.

/gc emblem Chooses your guild's emblem via the selection device — insignia, pattern, and primary and secondary colors. (After selecting the emblem, you'll need to go to a Guild Emblemeer to have your cloak or shield modified.)

/gc release Releases a frontier keep from the control of your guild. The "releaser" must be of a rank given Release privileges.

/gc remove Removes the targeted person from the guild.

/gc who Lists what members of your guild are online.

/gu <message> Send a message to all online guild members.

/osend or /os Send a message to the Officer's Channel, if you have access.

/gc webpage <guild website URL>
Sets URL that will be displayed in The Herald, and whenever a member types **/gc info**. Only the Guild Master can set the webpage.

/gc email <contact@guildpage.com>
Sets the contact email address that will be displayed in the Herald, and whenever a member types **/gc info**. Only the Guild Master can set the contact email address.

/gc omotd	Sends an Officer Message Of The Day. Appears to officers (or those who have Officers' Channel Hear clearance) when they log in. Only the Guild Master can set by the omotd.
/gc upgrade	Upgrades the keep (and thereby the guards, archers, patrollers and Keep Lord's combat strength). It requires more daily Guild Points to maintain an upgraded keep. (See **Realm vs. Realm**, p. 318.)
/webdisplay nopoints (toggle)	If this flag is set to yes, realm points are displayed on the Herald. Type /webdisplay nopoints to toggle the command off, and the realm points are not displayed. *The default is yes.*
/webdisplay trades (toggle)	If this flag is set to yes, tradeskill levels are displayed on The Herald. Type /webdisplay trades to toggle the command on and off. *The default is no.*
/gc displayofficers <y or n>	If this flag is set to yes, a hierarchy of the guild from ranks 0-9 is displayed. *The default is yes.*

Guild Structure Commands

/gc leader	Hand over leadership to the player targeted. *This is a Guild Master-only command.*
/gc edit <#> ranklevel <#>	Assigns rank to a certain slot. The first <#> indicates the slot that will be reranked, the second <#> changes the rank level.
/gc edit <#> title <titlename>	Assigns a title to a certain slot. The <#> indicates the slot that will have a title assigned to it. <Titlename> is the new title.

SUBCOMMANDS

These commands are all yes/no options.

Follow each command with a [space] y (for yes) or a [space] n (for no) to specify whether the action is permitted. You need to edit each slot/rank so that they can/cannot perform certain actions.

/gc edit <#> alli	Allow a rank to enter/leave alliances This essentially creates a diplomatic officer.
/gc edit <#> motd	Allow a rank to edit the guild motd. You must be a Guild Master to do this.
/gc edit <#> invite	Can invite others to join guild.
/gc edit <#> ochear	Can hear the Officers' Channel.

/gc edit <#> ocspeak	Can speak on the Officers' Channel.
/gc edit <#> gchear	Can hear the Guild Channel.
/gc edit <#> gspeak	Can speak on the Guild Channel.
/gc edit <#> release	Can release the guild's keep from guild control.
/gc edit <#> remove	Can remove guild members of lower rank.
/gc edit <#> promote	Can promote guild members.
/gc edit <#> emblem	Can wear the guild's emblem.
/gc edit <#> view	Can see the Guild Chat screen.
/gc edit <#> deposit	Can deposit money into the guild bank.
/gc edit <#> withdraw	Can withdraw money from the guild bank.
/gc edit <#> achear	Can hear the Alliance Channel.
/gc edit <#> acspeak	Can speak on the Alliance Channel.

Alliance Commands

Only Guild Masters can use these commands.

/gc ainvite	Invite another guild to alliance.
/gc aaccept	Accept invitation.
/gc adecline	Declines an invitation to join an alliance.
/gc acancel	Cancels guild alliance to another guild.
/gc amotd <message>	Send/edit an Alliance Message Of The Day. This is viewed by all members of the alliance when they log in. Setting up a guild amotd does nothing unless your guild is the Alliance Leader. Only the Alliance Leader can set the amotd.
/gc aremove <#>	Removes the follower # from your guild alliance group.
/gc aremove leader	Removes your guild from an alliance with another guild.

A strong guild gives you a greater good in which to participate and be proud. A server will develop a history, and participating in an active guild gives you a better chance to be part of that history.

Template. An organization can be as tightly or loosely organized as its members (or rather, as its founding leaders) want it to be. Some larger guilds might want many tiers of hierarchy, so that when the guild goes out in squads or companies, it's easy to see who the most experienced are. In RvR play, a unified strategy is key.

One thing to consider when setting up a guild: how many ranks do you actually need? A basic guild only needs a Leader, a few Officers and the rest just regular members. Once the guild gets larger than a few dozen members, though, it might need to expand its ranks. Keeping this in mind, place your main officers at the high ranks (ranklevel 1) and your lowest members at the bottom (ranklevel 9) so that you have room in between to create new ranks.

Below is a template of "slash edits" that shows the commands entered by a Guild leader to establish a six-rank guild. The top rank is given access to all chat and privileges while the lowest level — intended for emergency troops — has only basic chat capabilities ... and the ability to deposit funds. (Does anyone ever tell people they can't donate to the cause?)

Following the template will give you a solid basic rank system for your guild. Don't forget to assign your people ranks!

Guild Creation Template

```
/gc edit 1 ranklevel 1
/gc edit 2 ranklevel 2
/gc edit 3 ranklevel 3
/gc edit 4 ranklevel 4
/gc edit 5 ranklevel 5
/gc edit 9 ranklevel 9

/gc edit 0 title Head Honcho
/gc edit 1 title General
/gc edit 2 title Captain
/gc edit 3 title Group Leader
/gc edit 4 title Trusted Follower
/gc edit 5 title Spear Carrier
/gc edit 9 title Temp Help

/gc edit 1 invite y
/gc edit 1 promote y
/gc edit 1 demote y
/gc edit 1 remove y
/gc edit 1 deposit y
/gc edit 1 withdraw y
/gc edit 1 view y
/gc edit 1 achear y
/gc edit 1 acspeak y
/gc edit 1 gchear y
/gc edit 1 gcspeak y
/gc edit 1 ochear y
/gc edit 1 ocspeak y

<repeat for ranks 2-5 >

/gc edit 9 invite n
/gc edit 9 promote n
/gc edit 9 demote n
/gc edit 9 remove n
/gc edit 9 deposit y
/gc edit 9 withdraw n
/gc edit 9 view y
/gc edit 9 achear n
/gc edit 9 acspeak n
/gc edit 9 gchear y
/gc edit 9 gcspeak y
/gc edit 9 ochear y
/gc edit 9 ocspeak n
```

Realm of Albion

Albion is the land of Arthurian legend. Fighters vie for honor and search for glory in the defense of their land, magic-users build reputations with spectacular and deadly displays, and Rogues rule the shadows.

Races & Classes

ACOLYTE

Acolytes are dedicated to the Church of Albion, the only religion in the Realm. Saracens cannot become Acolytes.

Briton Acolyte

As a devotee of the Church, at fifth level you must choose to be a Cleric or a Friar. Clerics receive healing and protective magic that helps their realmmates. By joining the Defenders of Albion, Friars gain the ability to fight with the quarterstaff, but are limited to leather armors. Friars get limited spellcasting ability to complement their fighting skills. Britons are the only race that are allowed to be Friars.

As a Briton, you will make an average Cleric, and a good Friar.

Highlander Acolyte

As a devotee of the Church, at fifth level you will become a Cleric, receiving healing and protective magic that helps your realmmates. The Clerical profession is the only path open to Highlander Acolytes.

With your innately high Strength and Constitution, Highlanders make good solid Clerics — although they must make sure not to neglect their Piety.

Avalonian Acolyte

As a devotee of the Church, at fifth level you become a Cleric, receiving healing and protective magic that helps your realmmates. The Clerical profession is the only path open to Avalonian Acolytes.

Clerics are able to fight (with the right specializations), but are extremely valuable in their roles as group healers.

ELEMENTALIST

Elementalists are experts at the handling of fire, ice, air and earth. To further specialize your training, at fifth level you must choose your guild.

You may join the Defenders of Albion and become a Theurgist, specializing in the element of earth. Earth magic gives you the ability to both protect and destroy forts and keeps, as well as summon earth elementals to protect you.

By joining the Academy you become a Wizard, which teaches you to master the element of air, creating powerful cloud spells that can affect wide areas of a battlefield.

Highlanders cannot become Elementalists.

Avalonian Elementalist

With your inherently high Intelligence, Avalonians make the best Elementalists in the Realm of Albion.

Briton, Saracen Elementalists

As a Briton or Saracen, you will make an average Elementalist.

Really, Britons and Saracens should not become Elementalists, since the frustration of not advancing in your chosen profession will easily outweigh the other factors, such as extra Strength (or perhaps facial features) that might have influenced the decision to choose one of those races.

FIGHTER

As a Fighter, you use the force of arms to vanquish your enemies and advance in level.

At fifth level, you must choose which career path to take: Mercenary, Armsman or Paladin. (Avalonians can only become Paladins.) Mercenaries are specialists in dual-wielding and evasive defense, while Armsmen, as members of the Defenders of Albion, receive the ability to wear plate armor and use polearm weapons. Paladins dedicate their life to the Church of Albion, and receive combat-enhancing prayers to complement their plate armor and two-handed weapon abilities.

Briton Fighter

Briton Fighters are good at most aspects of melee combat, but are not outstanding at any one aspect.

An even distribution of stats is not a bad thing in a Fighter, it just means you will not be as strong or as dexterous as Fighters of other races. Many people choose this combination.

Highlander Fighter

Highlanders are naturally stronger and have higher Constitutions than the other races in the Realm, which make you a good choice to be a Fighter.

Saracen Fighter

Saracens can make effective Fighters, although be aware that your base Strength and Constitution are lower than that of other Fighters. However, your natural Dexterity and Quickness make up a lot of the difference, making you better at defensive maneuvers.

Avalonian Fighter

As an Avalonian, the only Fighter career path that is open to you is that of the Paladin. Avalonians do not inherently make good Paladins, since your Strength and Constitution are lower than that of other races. Choosing to be an Avalonian Paladin is a difficult choice, but can be done.

MAGE

Mages use mastery of magical essence to cast spells that harm your enemies. At fifth level, you choose to become a Sorcerer or a Cabalist, to continue your training. Sorcerers specialize in destructive magic, and also may charm and control semi-intelligent creatures. Cabalist can build creatures, imbue them with magical life and command them to do their bidding.

Highlanders cannot become Mages.

Avalonian Mage

With their inherently high Intelligence, Avalonians make the best Mages in the Realm of Albion.

Briton, Saracen Mages

As a Briton or Saracen, you will make an average Mage. "Average," in this context, does not mean that you will be better than some and worse than others. Since most people try to create a character that will excel in its field, an "average" Mage will be worse than most Mages ... which will almost inevitably lead to frustration. The only reason to choose a Briton or Saracen Mage would be because of role-play reasons, or because you like the facial features.

ROGUE

Rogues use a mix of subterfuge and other Dexterity-based skills to accomplish your aims. At fifth level, you'll be able to specialize by choosing to join the Defenders of Albion as a Scout, the Academy as a Minstrel, or the Guild of Shadows as an Infiltrator. (Avalonians and Highlanders cannot become Infiltrators.) Scouts learn tracking and bow skills, Minstrels learn songs that encourage your groupmates to fight more effectively, and Infiltrators learn hiding and sneaking.

Saracen Rogue

Saracens are naturally quick and dextrous, making you an outstanding choice to become any Rogue.

Briton Rogue

Briton Rogues are good at what they do, although not as innately skilled as Saracens.

Avalonian Rogue

Avalonians can become good Scouts and Minstrels. However, the Guild of Shadows does not accept Avalonian Rogues, so you cannot become an Infiltrator.

Highlander Rogue

While Highlanders can become Rogues, be aware that you do not have a naturally high Dexterity, and suffer some penalties because of it. Also, the Guild of Shadows does not accept Highlander Rogues, so you cannot become an Infiltrator.

HORSE ROUTES

For a description of how to rent and ride a horse, see Horse Routes, page 37.

STABLE	STABLE MASTER	TICKETS TO
Adribard's Retreat (Avalon Marsh)	Grank	West Downs (Salisbury Plain) Castle Sauvage
Caer Ulfwych (Campacorentin Forest)	Idian	Cornwall Station
Caer Witrin (Avalon Marsh)	Jhular	Western Cornwall
Camelot Hills (Nob's Farm)	Haruld	North Camelot Gates
East Camelot Gates	Vuloch	Snowdonia Station Campacorentin Station
North Camelot Gates	Bombard	Camelot Hills (Nob's Farm)
Camelot Hills (Gronyr's Farm)	Fluvon	Campacorentin Forest
Campacorentin Station	Ridder	Camelot Hills (Gronyr's Farm) East Camelot Gates
Castle Sauvage	Uliam	Ludlow Avalon Marsh (Adribard's Retreat) Snowdonia Fortress
Castle Snowdonia	Flambon	Castle Sauvage
Cornwall Station	Pethos	Caer Ulfwych (Campacorentin Forest)
Humberton Village	Gracchus	Snowdonia Fortress
Ludlow Village	Yaren	Castle Sauvage
Snowdonia Station	Trachon	East Camelot Gates
Western Cornwall (Stable)	Addard Yardly	Caer Witrin (Avalon Marsh)
West Downs (Salisbury Plain)	Edarg	Avalon Marsh (Adribard's Retreat)

Armsman

Races

Briton / Highlander / Avalonian / Saracen

Titles

Level	Title
5	Enlistee
10	Footsoldier
15	Infantryman/woman
20	Soldier
25	Legionnaire
30	Sergeant
35	Lieutenant
40	Centurian
45	Captain
50	General

Skills

Level	Skill
1	Crushing
1	Slashing
1	Thrusting
5	Polearm
5	Shields
10	Parry
10	Two Handed
15	Crossbow

Abilities

Level	Ability
1	Staves
1	Cloth Armor
1	Leather Armor
1	Studded Armor
1	Small Shields
1	Sprint
4	Medium Shields
5	Chain Armor
5	Polearms
10	Large Shields
11	Protect I
12	Intercept
15	Plate Armor
20	Protect II
27	Protect III

Styles

Crushing
Slashing
Thrusting
Polearm
Shields

You get up close and personal with the bad guys. You stand in the thick of battle, blocking and parrying incoming attacks. Dishing out damage faster than it can be healed is your bread and butter. In PvE, you're the point man for the group. You get to stand toe to toe with the monsters, and make sure they stay focused on you. You get the armor, the weaponry, and the melee skills to back it up.

The Best Part: Watching an enemy caster crumple under your melee assault.

The Worst Part: Falling victim to one of the many "hold" spells that render your player immobile for a duration.

Race Choices:

Britons. Nice, evenly distributed stats — and no ugly kilt!

Highlanders. Higher CON (gives more HP at higher levels) and STR, but DEX and QUI suffer.

Saracen or Avalonian. Fast, agile and quick, although you only get a small increase in melee speed. Not worth it, really.

Stat Choices: STR, then CON and DEX. An even spread of 10 points each is probably best.

Weapon Choices: Everything in Albion except short bow, longbow, and quarterstaves, though you can't specialize in all of them (e.g., Staves).

Spec Paths:

- *Defensive:* Highly specialized in Shields/Parry along with pure specialization in one weapon or split between two weapons utilizing autotraining. Common Templates: 50 Slash, 42 Shields, 30 Parry, 26 Crossbow; or 35 Slash, 35 Thrust, 42 Shield, remainder split between Parry and Crossbow. These Armsmen are geared towards longevity and tanking for groups. Groups at higher levels have a hard time surviving while earning fast XP without defensive tanks.
- *Offensive:* Highly specialized in Polearms/2-Handed along with backup damage type and some Parry. Common Templates: 50 Polearms, 35 Slash/Crush/Thrust, 35 Parry, 28 Crossbow; or 39 Polearms, 35 Slash/Crush, 35 Thrust, 35 Parry, remainder in Crossbow. These Armsmen are geared towards hard hitting. They sacrifice defense for offense. These Armsmen fare well in RvR due to maximum damage hits during chaos. They do not fare as well in PvE due to minimal defense and rely more on groups to back them up.
- *Crossbow:* The crossbow is a very important part of any Armsman's arsenal. The recommended level of specialization is 50% of your level. (Don't start spec'ing until higher levels.) A single crossbow shot with 50% spec hits harder than your best Polearm style, and it takes very little Endurance to shoot. The benefits for specialization stop around 2/3 of your level, so it serves you best to keep your skill at 50% and use items and/or realm ranks to boost yourself to the 2/3 range. Specialization only grants additional damage per shot.
- *Advanced Spec:* Specializing in 2-Handed/Polearm grants combat styles as well as adding a damage bonus to your attacks with the advanced weapon. If specializing in an advanced weapon, you should keep your skill to at least 2/3 of your level.

- *Base Spec:* Base damage type specializing affects your damage range, along with granting combat styles. 0 to 1/3 level is 25-75% damage. 1/3 to 1/2 level is 50-100% damage. 1/2 to 2/3 level is 75-125%. 2/3 to full level is 100-150%. The percentages scale up as you raise your specialization. The sweet spot is 2/3 level. Full specialization grants the 100-150% damage bracket, but you can reach this level with magic items and don't need to waste your spec points.

Big Mistakes to Avoid in Character Creation:

- *Spread Specialization:* You must focus on one or two damage types (training the second only at high levels — 40+). If you choose to use an advanced weapon, do not train in both 2-Handed and Polearms because you cannot use both at the same time.
- *Slashing Damage:* Slashing damage is supreme for PvE, but extremely poor in RvR. If you choose to specialize in Slashing, allow points in your high levels for Thrust training or you may be disappointed with the endgame.
- Spread your starting attribute points across your three primary stats: STR, CON and DEX. Anything else results in lost points without benefit.

Deciding what you want your role to be:

- *Defensive:* Shields allow an Armsman to absorb damage for themselves and other group members. With added shield skills, a defensive Armsman has more options available and will be a prime PvE group member. Low damage with 1-handed weapons has caused some frustration in RvR combat but shield stun styles make up for a lot, along with the Guard ability that helps keep your casters safe from archers.
- *Offensive:* Advanced weapons can be a lot of fun. If you like to rush into battle and yell, "SMACK!", then this is your subclass. Defense is sacrificed for pure damage potential. Your strongest asset is the ability to do massive damage in a single hit, along with a few useful side effects from mid-high level combat styles. Offensive Armsmen excel at RvR, but fall short in PvE.

Plotting Your Future: Stick to one damage type at low levels with a defensive ability close behind. After your mid levels (25+), you can start to spread your specialization out a little more while fleshing out your template. Additional damage types should not be added until you have hit maximum autotraining level (13 spec level for free!) in order to max out effectiveness of your points for the endgame.

Grouping:

- Take damage and deal it out. Keep monsters focused on you.
- Defensive Armsmen make the best PvE group members due to the Guard, Engage, Protect and Intercept abilities along with shield stuns and their keen ability to absorb damage without overworking the healer. PvE groups are where this subclass shines.
- Offensive Armsmen take more damage than other tanks so they are better off being a secondary tank in a group. Pairing a defensive Armsman along with an offensive Armsman is quite deadly due to the Guard ability absorbing damage for the offensive Armsman (making up for lost defense).

Combining your skills with others: This depends on your skills. Pay attention to what's going on around you and react accordingly.

Soloing:

- Your class' ability: Heavy melee damage and damage absorption. You can specialize in offense or defense, and you can fire a crossbow.
- Best things to solo: Whatever sad, sorry creature crosses your path. Do learn which creatures are more vulnerable to your primary weapon/damage type. As you level it becomes harder to kill monsters that are strong against your damage type, especially if they get a bonus against your armor.
- Sensible tactics: Stay away from casters. Armsmen need to be close to their targets. If you have to attack a caster from a distance, use your crossbow to disrupt their spells. Use styles until your Endurance runs out — Endurance regenerates very quickly, and Health is much slower, so anytime you can save the latter by exhausting the former, go for it.

Realm Versus Realm:

- Your job as a tank is to defend your casters and engage archers while identifying enemy healers and casters. If you can, take any kill you can get, but don't allow enemy casters and healers to kite you around or they'll single you out and you will quickly die. Your primary job as a tank in RvR is to be the brute force of keep and relic raids.
- During keep raids, heavy tanks play a key role in dealing with the guards along with bashing down the keep doors. Casters aid in attack and defense while archers and rogues give warning and engage enemy defenders. Heavy tanks are necessary to defeat the Keep Lord.
- Roaming RvR is difficult for a melee due to "hold" spells. Always group with a speed enhancing class so you can get into melee range quicker. Never go into RvR solo or you'll be a very easy target.

Beginner's Tips:

- Seek out quests. Find the mobs that drop "flint cherts". Grab these cherts and turn them in by Level 2 or 3 and get a free weapon from a stonecutter in Cotswold. That should hold you until you get your initiate's weapon at Level 5. Quests outfit you well into your 30s and Albion is packed with them!
- If you plan on advanced weapon training, put it off until later in your career. Focus on your base damage type and some defensive ability at least until Level 15-17. After that point, you'll be in prime shape for the heavy hitting advanced weapons.
- As soon as you can afford it, purchase a suit of Bronze Mail Armor from a merchant. This is the cheapest chainmail you can get and will work wonders until you can find some rare drops or afford a better suit.
- Focus all of your finances on saving for a good suit of plate at Level 15. Do not purchase alloy. It wears out too quickly. Instead, attempt to purchase fine alloy plate, which will last you until Level 24. Use quest drops and find rare drops to get you by until that time. Don't forget to talk to your local friendly armorcrafters. They're cheaper than the store!

Advanced Techniques:

- Group, group, group! Unless you have two accounts or know a Cleric who will heal you after every fight, the fastest way to Level 50 is by grouping.
- As a tank, you may end up pulling. Do it, but pay attention to mana bars. Get a feel for the group, then once you're comfortable, establish a pulling pace and stick to it. Consistency is the key.

Armsman Styles

Abbreviations. *Headers:* **F**atigue **C**ost / **B**onus **D**amage / **B**onus **t**o **H**it. *In table:* **L**ow / **M**edium / **H**igh / **V**ery **H**igh / **D**efensive **B**onus (for you, on next round) / **D**efensive **P**enalty (to you, on next round) / **A**ttack **S**peed **R**eduction / **M**ovement **R**eduction (for target)

Crush

See the Mercenary's styles, page 43, for this style.

Thrust

See the Mercenary's styles, page 43, for this style.

Slash

See the Mercenary's styles, page 43, for this style.

Shields

See the Mercenary's styles, page 43, for this style.

Polearm

Lvl	Style	FC	BD	BtH	Prerequisites / Other Notes
2	Impale	H	M	–	
4	Defender's Cross	M	M	M	Prereq: beside target / Low MR
6	Deflect	M	–	–	Attempt to turn away target; High DB
8	Defender's Faith	H	M	L	Low Bleed; Low DP
10	Executioner	M	M	L	Prereq: target parried by anyone / ASR
12	Distract	M	L	L	Attempt to taunt target; Med DP
15	Defender's Courage	M	M	M	Prereq: Defender's Faith / Med ASR
18	Crippling Blow	M	M	M	Med MR
21	Disabler	L	M	–	Prereq: Crippling Blow / Low ASR
25	Phalanx	M	M	M	Prereq: behind target
29	Mangle	M	H	–	Prereq: Crippling Blow
34	Defender's Rage	L	VH	H	Prereq: target fumbled / Med Bleed
39	Poleaxe	H	M	–	
44	Defender's Revenge	L	–	VH	Prereq: Defender's Rage / High Stun
50	Defender's Aegis	M	–	H	Prereq: Phalanx / High MR; Low DB

Mercenary

Races		Abilities	
Briton / Highlander / Saracen		1	Staves
		1	Cloth Armor
Titles		1	Leather Armor
5	Strong-Arm	1	Studded Armor
10	Pugilist	1	Small Shields
15	Escalader	1	Sprint
20	Swashbuckler	5	Medium Shields
25	Soldier of Fortune	10	Chain Armor
30	Blackguard	10	Shortbows
35	Veteran	10	Evade I
40	Warrior	15	Protect I
45	Master Warrior	19	Intercept
50	Mercenary Master	20	Dirty Tricks
Skills		23	Protect II
1	Crushing	32	Protect III
1	Slashing	**Styles**	
5	Thrusting		Crushing
5	Dual Wield		Slashing
5	Shield		Thrusting
17	Parry		Dual Wield
			Shields

You are the lightweight tank of Albion and have the hit points to prove it. Chain mail and Evade help you compete with any Armsman or Paladin until they get plate (level 15-20). Training Parry helps defensively, and the short bow makes you an excellent puller.

The Best Part: Fast attacks, and lots of them! Damage buff plus Dual Wield do lots of damage, sans styles. You're a great puller.

The Worst Part: You undoubtedly feel the pain of chain sometimes, but it does not rule out tanking.

Race Choices: Most Mercenaries choose Highlander and Briton. The only stats that matter there are STR, CON, DEX and QUI. Saracens can become Mercenaries, but it's not really advisable.

Briton. Base race; no strengths or weaknesses.

Highlander. Popular choice, since STR and CON are important. If you're making a Thrust Mercenary, DEX matters more.

Saracen. Clearly lacking STR and CON. High DEX might not make up for it.

Stat Choices: Consider the following fighter base stats for each race (STR/CON/DEX/QUI before bonus points):

Briton	60/60/60/60
Highlander	70/70/50/50
Saracen	50/50/80/60

For a Mercenary, you get 30 bonus points to add to STR, CON and DEX. Go 10/10/10 or any combination of 10/5/15 or 12/13/15. STR increases the fastest as you level.

- *STR*: Affects damage from Slashing and Crushing weapons, and, to a point, Thrusting weapons. Changes how much you can carry (although weight limits are rarely a problem with Mercenaries).
- *CON:* Affects hit points.
- *DEX:* Affects defensive abilities and how much Thrust damage you do.

Weapon Choices:

- *Slash:* Gives the most weapon choices (many drops/quests award them, even left-handed ones). Many mobs are susceptible to Slash (like Trees), but some are resistant (Undead). It is a "safe" choice. Not as good as Thrust against enemy realm tanks in RvR.
- *Crush:* Mercs find Crushing advantageous at lower levels against mobs. Fewer drops and quests exist for Crushing weapons. Weaponsmiths can always make whatever you can't find.
- *Thrust:* Best choice against enemy realm tanks in RvR. Not commonly dropped or awarded, but you can visit a Weaponsmith. Many PvE mobs can resist Thrust.

Big Mistakes to Avoid in Character Creation:

- Don't make a Saracen unless it is for role-playing reasons.
- Don't dump all your points into one stat. Try to spread them between STR, CON and DEX (or at least two of the three).

Deciding What You Want Your Role To Be: Undoubtedly, you'll be up front hitting mobs or players, or perhaps using Dual Wield styles. You may need to assume the role of a main or secondary tank, or become a puller.

Plotting Your Future: Using your Spec Points: As a Mercenary, you get 2x skill points and 6 trainable skills (Slash, Crush, Thrust, Dual Wield, Shield, Parry). Pick one weapon and max it out, along with Dual Wield at level 5. Put a few points into Parry (half your level). Some Mercs put a few into Shield for its related skills, but if you Dual Wield a lot, that may be a waste for you.

Grouping: Assess your role according to the group. Think about three things — protecting, pulling and tanking.

- *Protecting:* With Protect, your first decision is to figure out who to use it on. Protect the Cleric or main healer. If that's not needed, protect a Wizard or other caster.
- *Pulling:* You make an excellent puller by level 10 (short bow). Bring lots of flight arrows to increase range.
- *Tanking:* If grouping with an equal or higher level Armsman or Paladin, let them be the main tank and make yourself a secondary tank. If you're of higher level, take the main tank role. Level counts a lot when it comes to taking and dealing damage.

Combining Your Skills With Others:

- Talk to the other tanks. Decide who is going to protect who if there's more than one Cleric, Friar or caster. Get all healers protected, then decide which casters to protect.
- Got a Shield spec'ed Armsman or Paladin? Ask them to Guard you.

Being All You Can Be:

- Keep your eyes open. Even as secondary tank, you must take hits when the main tank is injured and the Cleric is low on power. Use Taunt styles to knock mobs off.
- If your group has no crowd control, hit extra mobs once or twice to keep them off healers and casters before you focus on the main mob.
- Intercept can deflect a hit for a Cleric or caster who is aggro'd and close to dying.
- Use styles that work from the back or side when you can; they may do more damage. But for long fights, don't spend all your Endurance using styles on the first mob. Reserve some in case you need to pull an aggro'd enemy off a friend later in the fight.
- Use increased fumbles wisely (long timer). Save it for a difficult mob and when Power and Health are low.
- If you find yourself aggro'd too much even with a main tank, you have two options. First, space out your styles to slow down aggro intensity. Second, turn off your attack for one or two rounds while another tank in the group regains aggro. Then, turn your attack back on.

Soloing: Mercs do OK soloing, although you may find yourself sitting a lot to regain HP. Keep yourself in armor and weapons that are best for your level (blue con is ok, but yellow is best). With good gear for your level, you should be able to solo yellow mobs.

- Look for mobs that can't resist your weapon type. Slashing is good against Tree mobs, and Crushing against Insect mobs.
- Solo mobs with no bonuses against your armor.
- Stay away from human mobs that use polearms or 2-handed weapons — those hurt.
- Keep yourself in the best armor and weapons possible for your level. Yellow is great; a few blue pieces are okay.
- Use styles, but watch Health and Endurance. If you're more injured than the mob, don't be afraid to sprint away at half Health. (Reserve enough Endurance to sprint; about half a bar is usually sufficient.)

Realm Versus Realm:

- Get up close and hit people. You won't make as many solo kills, but you can keep healers and casters busy.
- From afar, use your bow. You cannot train your bow skill, so you won't do a lot of damage. But, drawing a bow against a caster or healer can stop them from casting.
- Stick close enough to the group to receive heals, but far enough away to avoid an Area Effect stun or mez.
- Melee range gives the best damage. Dual Wield can stop other realms' healers and casters. Kill them first, then concentrate on tanks. Watch for tanks beating on your own Cleric or caster.
- If you're with someone who can mez or stun the opposing realms' players, team up to take down enemies one at a time.

Beginner's Tips:

- Keep your primary weapon and Dual Wield (when it becomes available) maxed.
- Thrusting/Dual Wield can be devastating at mid-to-high levels, but Slashing and Crushing also work well with Dual Wield, and they're friendlier at lower levels.
- 30% chance to block same-level enemy archers' arrows. Modified by Shield spec, quality and condition of shield, and Engage skill.

- Make Shields your primary defensive specialization. You can get some decent styles, and it greatly enhances your survivability when you have to tank.
- Never allow yourself to get pinned between two enemies.
- Ability Dirty Tricks. Target your enemy, and throw dirt in his face. The effect lasts for 30 seconds. The enemy misses you 25% more often, and when they miss, they fumble 50% more often than their base fumble rate. Usable once every 30 minutes. Higher-level players and monsters have a chance to resist.

Advanced Techniques:

- Your styles are your main edge in combat, but try to use them sparingly because of the energy drain.
- Look for ways to combine your styles creatively. Don't assume that the heaviest hit is always the most effective.
- You're the thinking man's tank. You're too vulnerable to just wade in and take damage, so use strategy to optimize your damage and keep yourself alive.
- A stealthed archer is visible when he fires; when he nocks his arrow, if he fails his Stealth check. Stealth spec % (-20% on Critical Shots) = % chance to stay hidden.

Mercenary Styles

Abbreviations. *Headers:* **F**atigue **C**ost / **B**onus **D**amage / **B**onus **t**o **H**it. *In table:* **L**ow / **M**edium / **H**igh / **V**ery **H**igh / **D**efensive **B**onus (for you, on next round) / **D**efensive **P**enalty (to you, on next round) / **A**ttack **S**peed **R**eduction / **M**ovement **R**eduction (for target)

Crush

Lvl	Style	FC	BD	BtH	Prerequisites / Other Notes
2	Daze	H	M	–	
4	Back Crush	L	M	M	Prereq: behind target / Low Stun
6	Maul	H	H	H	Small DP
8	Bludgeon	M	M	–	Prereq: Maul / Attempt to taunt target; DP
10	Bruiser	M	M	M	Prereq: Back Crush / Low Bleed
12	Concussion	M	M	L	ASR
15	Contusions	M	M	M	Prereq: Bludgeon / Med Stun
18	Blackjack	–	M	M	Prereq: Maul / Low Stun
21	Protector	M	–	–	Attempt to turn away target; DB
25	Divine Hammer	M	M	M	Prereq: behind target
29	Skull Breaker	L	M	H	Prereq: target blocked by anyone /Low DP
34	Side Crush	M	M	M	Prereq: beside target / Med Bleed
39	Bone Crusher	L	M	M	Prereq: parried target / High MR; Med DB
44	Body Masher	M	M	M	Prereq: Skull Breaker / High ASR
50	Devastate	H	H	H	Prereq: Side Crush / High Stun; Med DP

Slash

Lvl	Style	FC	BD	BtH	Prerequisites / Other Notes
2	Ruby Slash	H	M	–	
4	Cross Slash	L	M	M	Prereq: beside target / Med DB
6	Uppercut	M	M	L	
8	Enrage	M	L	–	Attempt to taunt target; Med DP
10	Bloodletter	M	–	H	Prereq: Cross Slash / Low Bleed; Med DB
12	Reflect	M	–	–	Attempt to turn away target; DB
15	Opal Slash	M	M	M	Prereq: Uppercut / Low Bleed
18	Riposte	L	H	M	Prereq: block target / Med DB
21	Side Slicer	L	L	–	Prereq: beside target / MR
25	Cleave	L	M	M	Prereq: Uppercut
29	Amethyst Slash	M	L/M	H	
34	Befuddler	M	M	M	Prereq: Riposte / Med Stun
39	Back Slash	H	M	H	Prereq: behind target
44	Sapphire Slash	L	M	M	Prereq: Enrage / Med Bleed; High DP
50	Diamond Slash	H	H	VH	Prereq: Amethyst Slash

Shields

Lvl	Style	FC	BD	BtH	Prerequisites / Other Notes
3	Numb	M	M	–	Low Stun
8	Stun	M	M	–	Prereq: blocked target / Low Stun
13	Disable	M	M	–	Prereq: beside target / Med Stun
18	Incapacitate	H	M	–	Prereq: blocked target / Med Stun; Med DB
23	Paralyze	M	M	–	Prereq: behind target / Med Stun
29	Bash	M	M	–	Prereq: blocked target / Med Stun
35	Mangle	M	M	–	Prereq: beside target / High Stun
42	Slam	VH	M	–	High Stun
50	Brutalize	L	M	–	Prereq: blocked target / High Stun

Thrust

Lvl	Style	FC	BD	BtH	Prerequisites / Other Notes
2	Thistle	H	M	–	
4	Ratfang	L	M	M	Prereq: evaded target / Low Stun; Low DB
6	Puncture	M	M	M	Low Bleed
8	Sting	M	L	M	Attempt to taunt target; High DP
10	Wolftooth	M	H	M	Prereq: Ratfang / Low MR
12	Bloody Dance	M	M	M	Prereq: puncture / Med Bleed; Low DP
15	Beartooth	L	M	H	Prereq: blocked target / Med Stun
18	Tranquilize	M	–	–	Attempt to turn away target; High DB
21	Lunge	M	M	H	Prereq: Puncture
25	Ricochet	L	–	H	Prereq: target blocked by anyone / Med Bleed; Med DP
29	Pierce	M	M	H	Prereq: behind target / Med Bleed; Med DP
34	Liontooth	L	M	M	Prereq: Wolftooth / High Bleed; Low DB
39	Basiliskfang	M	M	L	Prereq: beside target / High ASR; Low DB
44	Wyvernfang	L	M	M	Prereq: Beartooth / High MR
50	Dragonfang	L	M	H	Prereq: evaded target / High Stun; Low DP

Dual Wield

See the Infiltrator's styles, page 55, for this style.

Paladin

Races	
Briton / Avalonian / Saracen	
Titles	
5	Neophyte
10	Tyro/Tyress
15	Protector/Protectress
20	Defender
25	Guardian
30	Benefactor/Benefactress
35	Crusader
40	Justicator
45	Champion
50	Templar
Skills	
1	Crushing
1	Slashing
1	Thrusting
4	Chants (Magic)
5	Two Handed
5	Shield
15	Parry

Abilities	
1	Staves
1	Cloth Armor
1	Leather Armor
1	Studded Armor
1	Small Shields
1	Sprint
4	Medium Shields
9	Protect I
10	Chain Armor
10	Large Shields
10	Intercept
14	Protect II
19	Protect III
20	Plate Armor
Styles	
	Crushing
	Thrusting
	Two Handed
	Shields

Paladins are fighters, great in a group or solo. You get to use all melee weapons except polearms and wear all types of armor (as well as self-buff). You're a great tank and you look good in plate mail. Finally, Paladins are the "motivational speaker" for most groups.

The Best Part: You're welcome in any group due to tanking skills and chants that you're able to instantaneously cast on yourself and groups.

The Worst Part: No ranged attack or unique class ability. Less effective than an Armsman in solo play or RvR.

Race Choices:

Briton. Good all-around race, but no real defining stats. Keep it all at an even 60.

Highlander. Good base STR and CON, but lower-than-average DEX and QUI. You don't move very fast.

Saracen. Agile (good DEX and QUI), but STR and CON suffer slightly.

Avalonian. Not very popular, but good if you want a different look and can live without STR. You also get (much later) lightweight fluted plate armor.

Stat Choices: Concentrate on STR, CON, DEX, QUI and PIE. Try 10 points in three stats most needed for your race and playing style (e.g., 10 points for Saracen or Avalonian).

- *STR:* Improves weapon skills/encumbrance.
- *CON:* Improves HP.
- *DEX:* Improves Thrusting and chance to hit.
- *QUI:* Improves weapon speed.
- *PIE:* Helps Power (mana).
- If you plan on using spells that don't require much mana, PIE is probably less important.
- DEX and QUI never rise later, while CON improves with leveling.

Weapon Choices:

- *Slash:* Lots of available weapons to choose from, good styles. But, weakness against chain and scale armor keep it from being highly damaging in RvR.
- *Crush:* Plenty of monsters are susceptible to Crush. Gives good damage, but not a lot of Crush quests exist.
- *Thrust:* Good for RvR, as scale and chain are susceptible. But, not a lot of quests, and many monsters have good resistance against Thrust.
- *2-Handed:* High damage, but slow re-swing rate. For the most punch, combine 2-Handed Weapon skill with a base skill (Slash, Crush, Thrust). Remember that base skill combat moves don't work with advanced weapons.
- For emphasis on damage, not defense, or for grouping with tanks, go 2-handed. A shield is still a good idea for rushing ranged foes.
- For effective tanking and damage absorption, go with a 1-handed weapon and shield.
- Thrust is best for RvR play, given opponents in Midgard and Hibernia.
- Crushing is best for Albion's mobs, followed by Slashing, then Thrusting.
- A shield can be a handicap in mid-sized to large RvR battles, where max damage is more important. It also doesn't protect against a large number of foes.

Spec Paths:

- Pick a defensive or offensive path, and don't toy with the other one. Concentrate to remain effective. You have two basic paths — a) Chants, base weapon (Slash/Thrust/Crush), Shield and Parry, or b) Chants, 2-handed weapon, base weapon and Parry.
- Chants aren't optional; they give increasing power at higher levels. Three lines exist —

Refreshment battle chants invoke a group heal, but nearly guarantee you'll get aggro'd. Battle chants give damage add to your group's missile or ranged weapons. Crusader chants boost the group's armor factor.

Big Mistakes To Avoid In Character Creation: Don't put all your starting points into one stat. Spread them out. Don't put any into Piety, as only your Resurrection spell uses it.

Deciding What You Want Your Role To Be: Not a lot to decide here. You're a tank, so stand up front and hit monsters.

Plotting Your Future:

- Paladins get 2x skill points per level, and have seven skills to raise, but you only need four (see above).
- Keep Chants close to two-thirds of your current level, along with base weapon and/or 2-handed weapon or Parry.

Grouping:

- You're a tank, or sometimes a secondary tank (due to lower damage than Mercs or Armsmen). Using chants, you can make the group perform better (with extra damage and armor). If things go bad, use Refresh to taunt the monster off other injured tanks.
- Damage add works best when one person gets aggro'd a lot and you have multiple tanks. (Healing chants only work on the one damaged person.) But, a group healing chant may be best if the group only has one tank.
- Monitor the battle and group, and change chants during a fight if needed.
- To find your role, talk to the group to see who they want you to Protect, or additionally, Guard if you're Shield-specialized. Ask what chants they prefer you to use; as main tank, running Refreshment full time will guarantee that you keep the aggro.
- If pulling, be careful not to pull too many. Look for less aggressive mobs. A Shield stun works rather well.
- Remain aware of nearby monsters that may join the fight. Be ready to swap chants as needed for the fight (turning on Refreshment for aggro or damage add).

Soloing:

- You can solo well at most levels. Just keep armor and weapons in tiptop condition and level-appropriate (yellow with a bit of blue).
- Blue cons and most yellows are fine. Just don't fight things that resist your weapon.
- Don't roam too close to archers and casters.
- Keep yourself in the best armor and weapons for your level.
- Use styles, but watch HP and END. There's no lost honor in running away at 1/2 Health.
- Damage add makes a good first chant, especially if the mob is susceptible to your weapon. Also, if the mob isn't damaging you very much with each hit, try a healing chant but no damage add to conserve END.

Realm Versus Realm:

- Don't expect to get realm points playing solo. Having no ranged attack makes that nearly impossible. Instead, find a good group and attack the enemy with melee combat.
- Stay with your group, but not within mez/stun range.
- Most archers and assassins will avoid you because of the shiny plate you're wearing, but watch for them around casters.

Paladin Styles

Abbreviations. *Headers:* **F**atigue **C**ost / **B**onus **D**amage / **B**onus **t**o **H**it. *In table:* **L**ow / **M**edium / **H**igh / **V**ery **H**igh / **D**efensive **B**onus (for you, on next round) / **D**efensive **P**enalty (to you, on next round) / **A**ttack **S**peed **R**eduction / **M**ovement **R**eduction (for target)

Crush, Thrust

See the Mercenary's styles, page 43, for these styles.

Shields

See the Mercenary's styles, page 43, for this style.

Two Handed

Lvl	Style	FC	BD	BtH	Prerequisites / Other Notes
2	Half Moon	H	M	–	
4	Double Back	M	M	M	Prereq: behind target / Low Stun
6	Rile	M	L	L	Attempt to taunt target; Med DP
8	Pacify	M	–	–	Attempt to turn away target; DB
10	Two Fists	M	M	M	Prereq: Double Back / Low Bleed
12	Bone Bruiser	M	M	L	Med ASR
15	Double Recovery	L	H	M	Prereq: you fumbled / Med MR
18	Fury	L	M	M	Prereq: target parried by anyone / Low Bleed; High DP
21	Bone Splitter	M	M	L	Prereq: Bone Bruiser / Med MR
25	Recenter	L	M	L	Prereq: Fury / High DB
29	Bone Breaker	M	M	L	Prereq: Bone Bruiser / Low Stun
34	Obfuscate	M	M	M	Prereq: Fury / High ASR
39	Doubler	H	M	L	
44	Two Moons	L	M	H	Prereq: Double Recovery / High Stun
50	Sun and Moon	M	–	L	Prereq: Bone Breaker / High Bleed

Beginner's Tips:

- Fight mobs that are weak against your weapon.
- It's often better to group with other players — that's what a Paladin does best.
- 30% chance to block same-level enemy archers' arrows. Modified by Shield spec, quality and condition of shield, and Engage skill.

Advanced Techniques: "Twisting" – running multiple chants simultaneously, re-casting every eight seconds when one runs out. Some use this tactic and some don't, but there's no denying that it makes you very effective, either solo or in a group. Set up Chants on the Hotbar and rattle off one right after another. Wait until they are useable again and repeat. This consumes Endurance, so Paladins wait until they run out of Endurance from styles, then twist (you can do this with zero Endurance).

Paladin Spells

Chants

Buffs Caster's AF.

Skill.....Chants Casting Time.....4 sec.
Duration.....10 min.

Lvl	Spell	Cost	Buff
1	Aura of Protection*	3P	14
6	Aura of Deflection*	6P	19
11	Aura of Safety*	9P	24
17	Aura of Defense*	12P	30
24	Aura of Indestructibility*	17P	37
33	Aura of Invincibility*	23P	46
43	Aura of Salvation	30P	56

Heals groupmates in combat by (Heal) HP every 6.5 sec. You must wait 8 seconds before casting one of these spells again.

Skill.....Chants Cost.....0P
Casting Time.....Shout Range.....700
Duration.....Chant

Lvl	Spell	Heal
2	Minor Refreshment*	3
5	Lesser Refreshment*	5
8	Refreshment*	8
12	Major Refreshment*	11
16	Greater Refreshment*	14
20	Crusader's Refreshment*	17
26	Saint's Refreshment*	22
35	Angel's Refreshment*	29
45	Archangel's Refreshment	37

Groupmates' damage/sec buffed (stacks as group 2). You must wait 8 seconds before casting one of these spells again.

Skill.....Chants Dmg Type.....Body
Cost.....0P Casting Time.....Shout
Range.....1500 Duration.....Chant + 6

Lvl	Spell	Buff
3	Battle Fervor*	1
7	Greater Battle Fervor*	1.6
10	Battle Vigor*	2.1
15	Greater Battle Vigor*	2.8
21	Battle Fury*	3.7
28	Greater Battle Fury*	4.8
36	Battle Zeal*	6
46	Greater Battle Zeal	7.5

Buffs Groupmates' AF. You must wait 8 seconds before casting one of these spells again.

Skill.....Chants Cost.....0P
Casting Time.....Shout Range.....1500
Duration.....Chant + 6

Lvl	Spell	Buff
4	Crusader's Ward*	24
9	Crusader's Shield*	33
13	Crusader's Guard*	40
18	Crusader's Barrier*	51
23	Crusader's Defense*	61
29	Crusader's Shelter*	75
38	Crusader's Protection*	99
48	Crusader's Mantle	127

Resurrects corpse; target is resurrected with a percentage of its original Power and/or HP.

Skill.....Chants Duration.....Inst.
Casting Time.....4 sec. Range.....1500
Cost.....Power cost based on corpse (see p. 368)

Lvl	Spell	Power	HP
30	Revive	No Power	10%

Buffs Groupmates' Body resistance. You must wait 8 seconds before casting a Groupmate resistance buff spell again.

Skill.....Chants Cost.....0P
Casting Time.....Shout Range.....1500
Duration.....Chant + 5

Lvl	Spell	Buff
25	Body Ward*	10
44	Body Shield	20

Buffs Groupmates' Spirit resistance. You must wait 8 seconds before casting a Groupmate resistance buff spell again.

Skill.....Chants Cost.....0P
Casting Time.....Shout Range.....1500
Duration.....Chant + 5

Lvl	Spell	Buff
26	Mind Ward*	10
45	Mind Shield	20

Buffs Groupmates' Energy resistance. You must wait 8 seconds before casting a Groupmate resistance buff spell again.

Skill.....Chants Cost.....0P
Casting Time.....Shout Range.....1500
Duration.....Chant + 5

Lvl	Spell	Buff
27	Energy Ward*	10
46	Energy Shield	20

Buffs Groupmates' Heat resistance. You must wait 8 seconds before casting a Groupmate resistance buff spell again.

Skill.....Chants Cost.....0P
Casting Time.....Shout Range.....1500
Duration.....Chant + 5

Lvl	Spell	Buff
28	Heat Ward*	10
47	Heat Shield	20

Buffs Groupmates' Cold resistance. You must wait 8 seconds before casting a Groupmate resistance buff spell again.

Skill.....Chants Cost.....0P
Casting Time.....Shout Range.....1500
Duration.....Chant + 5

Lvl	Spell	Buff
29	Cold Ward*	10
48	Cold Shield	20

Buffs Groupmates' Matter resistance. You must wait 8 seconds before casting a Groupmate resistance buff spell again.

Skill.....Chants Cost.....0P
Casting Time.....Shout Range.....1500
Duration.....Chant + 5

Lvl	Spell	Buff
30	Earth Ward*	10
49	Earth Shield	20

Scout

Races		Abilities	
Briton / Highlander / Saracen		1	Staves
Titles		1	Cloth Armor
5	Apprentice Scout	1	Leather Armor
10	Bowman/woman	1	Studded Armor
15	Tracker	1	Small Shields
20	Watcher	1	Evade I
25	Reconnoiterer	1	Sprint
30	Pathfinder	5	Small Shields
35	Hawkeye	10	Studded Armor
40	Sentinel	12	Evade II
45	Ranger	20	Evade III
50	Master Scout	**Styles**	
Skills			Thrusting
1	Slashing		
1	Stealth		
5	Thrusting		
5	Longbow		
5	Shields		

Scouts are proficient with their deadly ranged weapon, and also skilled in melee combat. In solo play, they can easily track down an enemy and hit it with the longbow, then finish it off with a swift round of melee. In groups, Scouts can often use themselves as bait and attack at range with arrows, pull a creature, or use Stealth to scout out RvR enemies. Some Scouts take on the duty of protector, shielding casters and healers from the harm of enemy blows. The main strengths of this class are the longbow, quick moves, hiding and evasive tactics.

The Best Part: You have the farthest reaching, most damaging ranged weapon in the game., and you're nearly always on the move and doing something as you fight with the tanks, shoot from a distance, pull for a group, defend the casters or stand guard during down time.

The Worst Part: There are no special abilities other than the incredible power and range of the longbow and your proficiency with a shield. Scouts have no spells, and their bows aren't as fast or powerful as the bows of some of the other archers. You also have to pay for arrows.

Race Choices:

Briton. Most well-rounded choice. Able to use and switch easily between longbow and melee.

Saracen. Clearly excellent with the longbow, but are correspondingly weaker at melee.

Highlander. Better at melee, and slower than usual with the longbow. Very few Highlanders become Scouts, as they reason that the short bow of the Mercenary gives up little in range for much better armor and dual-wielding weapons.

Stat Choices:

- *STR:* Affects how many arrows you can carry; never have Strength below 50, 60 is better. (Slashing Highlanders might want a bit more.)
- *CON:* Affects total Health; this never raises as you level, except through magical spells or items.
- *DEX:* Affects longbow damage, and raises one point every level starting at level 6. As Scouts are weak at melee, doing as much damage with the longbow as possible is highly desired.
- *QUI:* Affects longbow speed, and for those interested in RvR, speed is king.
- *INT*, *EMP*, *PIE* and *CHA* have no bearing on Scouts, so don't spend any of your 30 discretionary points on these skills.

Weapon Choices: Weapon choice revolves on whether you want to spec in Thrust or Slash.

- *Thrusting*: Faster than Slashing weapons, but do less damage per hit. For Thrusting weapons, increase your Strength and Dexterity.
- *Slashing:* Contributes more to the group per hit. For Slash, only increase your Strength, and ignore Dexterity.

The choice between *longbow*, *regular bow* or *hunter's bow* comes in around Level 10 or 12, when the gifted huntsman's longbow needs to be replaced with a new bow.

- The *hunter's bow* is much faster, but does less damage per hit and has the same range as Midgard's bows.
- The *regular bow* has speed and damage in between the hunter's bow and the longbow, again, with the same range as Midgard's bows.
- The *longbow* has the longest draw time, but hits significantly harder with each hit and has 4 paces of longer range than Midgard's bows – the longest ranged attack in the game.
- PvE hunting and sniping should be done with longbows, while the hunter's bow is better for group RvR and for killing casters.

Spec Paths:

- *Longbow:* Primary specialization (see Archery 101 and Archery 102). Keep it maxed out using both equipment and specialization points spent in training. Going over your level does not gain you anything.
- *Melee specialization:* (Thrusting or Slashing) Discussed under Weapon Choices; train to at least half your level.
- *Shield specialization:* Improves your block rate, and also gives you shield bashes which stun your opponent and do crushing damage. In addition, there are some additional abilities tied to shield specialization.
- *Guard ability (shield spec):* Allows you to defend another character if you are in close proximity to them by using your shield to block attacks aimed at either one of you; tanks using 2-handed weapons (so they can't use a shield) are particularly pleased for you to use this skill near them.
- *Engage ability (shield spec):* Only works in PvE, and is a crowd control ability; you must have the mob's attention in order for Engage to do any good, but with it you will block almost all of the time at the expense of not being able to attack. Engage is also particularly useful against other archers and assassins in RvR.
- *Stealth specialization:* Mostly useful for hiding. It's recommended that you only put extra specialization points into the skill up to level 25 or 30. In order to get better, use other skills until you are closer to going into RvR. At that point dump as many points into Stealth as you desire, depending on your chosen role of longbowman or sniper.

  With any bow, Stealth specialization gives an equal chance of staying hidden while nocking an arrow. So, 50% spec'd gives a 50% chance, and 100% spec'd gives 100% chance (20% less for a critical shot). But, you always turn visible after firing an arrow. Also, END doesn't regenerate while you're aiming an arrow.

Big Mistakes To Avoid In Character Creation: Forgetting to boost STR — you have to carry lots of arrows with you!

Deciding What You Want Your Role To Be:

- *Sniper:* The conventional RvR Scout — 50 Longbow, 50 Stealth, miscellaneous others. Their role is almost always striking from hiding, then trying to fade away before the enemy gathers sufficient force to hunt them down, and is a difficult path. Snipers have the hardest time leveling in PvE, and are often the Scouts you hear complaining the most about changes to the class.
- *Longbowman:* A combat-oriented Scout that can generally provide artillery support, as well as be a bodyguard for other support troops in an engagement.
- Both variations have you train to over two-thirds in all your skills, with items boosting them even closer to max. Currently this seems to be the ideal spec path for a Scout — good scouting, good bow damage, easy leveling in PvE, and surprising punch in RvR.

Plotting Your Future: Take a good, hard look at your long-term goals and develop your playing style by spec'ing the things you think you'll be using most.

Grouping: Your role depends on your skills and abilities — there's a variety of options. You can help tanks, protect casters, pull monsters, protect 2-handed melee fighters....

- Lay yourself out as bait and help the party surprise a mob, or pull a single critter with your longbow and sprint back to the group. Alternately, stand up front and dodge hits while swinging your melee weapon. Or, hang back and guard your group's casters and healers using your Shield ability.
- Your most excellent group contribution is your ranged Longbow attack. Damaging the mob at range weakens it so that your casters or fighters can easily finish it off. The more people in your group, the better your chance of hitting a mob (also true for meleeing).

Soloing: Stealth and a strong long-distance attack make soloing possible. You can attack at range and do most of your damage, and if the creature manages to close, you can quickly switch to your melee weapon and finish it off.

Best things to solo (most arrows do Thrust damage): Fleshy Undead, Furry Animals, chainmail.

Sensible Tactics:

- Begin firing from your bow's farthest range, and whittle them down until you can finish them off with your sword.
- Learn to love Stealth, never take on more than one, and run when you need to.
- Hunt mobs that con blue and green, noting that green ones usually hand over more loot.
- Early on, hunt skeletons so that you can acquire a full set of armor.
- Use your costlier, long-range arrows to bring a Monster in, then switch to cheaper, shorter-range ones. You can also finish off a closing mob with melee, if you choose to.
- Your Shield's stun ability is useful when you're trying to run away from an opponent. Stun, then run!

Realm Versus Realm: It depends on your spec path. Your role varies widely depending on what you've trained to do.

- *Wait.* The primary tip for all archers in RvR is patience. He who comes out of Stealth first to shoot a target of opportunity usually falls to another archer or assassin who hadn't yet emerged from Stealth.
- *Keep moving.* Hidden assassins can detect you much further away than you can detect them, and the only way to keep from being prey is to make it very hard for them to get into position to backstab you.
- *Stun.* If you are being shot or attacked, hit Engage and then after a block you can use one of your Shield styles to stun your opponent. At that point you can run away, attack, or back up and loose a few arrows at them.
- You get Climb at your 25th train in Stealth. Scale those keep walls!

Beginner's Tips:

- Fletching is an invaluable trade skill, since arrows don't come cheaply, and the free training arrows you get don't work as well as ones you make or buy.
- In order to be as proficient as possible with the bow, Scouts need the greater mobility afforded by leather and studded leather armors; so don't try to stand toe-to-toe in the infantry line next to your heavily armored shieldmates.
- Learn your ranges and your arrow types. You should be using freebie arrows from your trainer up to level 9 to 12. After that, you should be using arrows that cost no more than 5 times the loot that the mob you are hunting drops.
- A stealthed archer is visible when he fires; when he nocks his arrow, if he fails his Stealth check. Stealth spec % (-20% on Critical Shots) = % chance to stay hidden.

Note: Please see *Archery 101* (p. 386) and *Archery 102* (pp. 387-388).

- You can use a DoT poison, and be able to rehide while continuing to do damage.
- Ability Danger Sense. Tells when a scout notices your party. Always on. 8 Stealth trains.

Advanced Techniques:

- You can use your shield as a weapon if you're specialized in it.
- A failed Shield style will still deal out damage. If you want to hurt something, try the lower-Endurance higher styles.
- If the situation looks grim, stun the creature in front of you, turn off autoattack so you don't accidentally hit it and break the stun, then sprint like mad.
- No Stealth usable when carrying a Relic.

Scout Styles

Abbreviations. *Headers:* **F**atigue **C**ost / **B**onus **D**amage / **B**onus **t**o **H**it. *In table:* **L**ow / **M**edium / **H**igh / **V**ery **H**igh / **D**efensive **B**onus (for you, on next round) / **D**efensive **P**enalty (to you, on next round) / **A**ttack **S**peed **R**eduction / **M**ovement **R**eduction (for target)

Thrust

Lvl	Style	FC	BD	BtH	Prerequisites / Other Notes
2	Thistle	H	M	–	
4	Ratfang	L	M	M	Prereq: evaded target / Low Stun; Low DB
6	Puncture	M	M	M	Low Bleed
8	Sting	M	L	M	Attempt to taunt target; High DP
10	Wolftooth	M	H	M	Prereq: Ratfang / Low MR
12	Bloody Dance	M	M	M	Prereq: puncture / Med Bleed; Low DP
15	Beartooth	L	M	H	Prereq: blocked target / Med Stun
18	Tranquilize	M	–	–	Attempt to turn away target; High DB
21	Lunge	M	M	H	Prereq: Puncture
25	Ricochet	L	–	H	Prereq: target blocked by anyone / Med Bleed; Med DP
29	Pierce	M	M	H	Prereq: behind target / Med Bleed; Med DP
34	Liontooth	L	M	M	Prereq: Wolftooth / High Bleed; Low DB
39	Basiliskfang	M	M	L	Prereq: beside target / High ASR; Low DB
44	Wyvernfang	L	M	M	Prereq: Beartooth / High MR
50	Dragonfang	L	M	H	Prereq: evaded target / High Stun; Low DP

Minstrel

Races	
Briton / Highlander / Saracen	
Titles	
5	Balladeer
10	Sonneteer
15	Versesmith
20	Lyricist
25	Troubadour
30	Rhapsodist
35	Elegist
40	Soloist
45	Master Soloist
50	Virtuoso/Virtuosa

Skills	
1	Slashing
1	Thrusting
1	Stealth
5	Instruments
Abilities	
1	Staves
1	Cloth Armor
1	Leather Armor
1	Evade I
5	Small Shields
10	Studded Armor
15	Evade II
20	Chain Armor
Styles	
	Thrusting

Minstrels are jacks-of-all-trades. They can fight, stealth, mesmerize, stun and cast spells. A Minstrel is useful in any situation, whether as a tank, power source for casters, or crowd controller. Versatile class, with the ability to both group and fly solo.

The Best Part: Minstrels are wanted by groups everywhere for their instrument line of group-friendly songs.

The Worst Part: The Minstrel is well-rounded, but a master of nothing. Mez and stun spells have short duration and range. Though Minstrels can train in a weapon, bear a shield and wear chain, HP are still low.

Race Choices:

Highlander. Best HP and best soloing race. Well suited for Slashing weapons. High STR means you hit harder and can wear chain while carrying lots of loot. Low DEX hinders evasion and blocking. For soloing, take 10 STR, CON and CHA.

Briton. Across-the-board character. All stats start at 60. Medium STR and DEX, equally suited for either Slashing or Thrusting weapons. Can block and evade relatively well. For Thrusting, put 10 CHA, CON and DEX. For Slashing, put 10 in STR instead and sacrifice something else.

Saracen. Naturally high DEX (good for evades/blocks). Low HP and STR, so armor and loot feel very heavy. Try 10 CHA, 10 CON and 10 STR.

Stat Choices: The primary statistics are CHA, DEX and STR, in that order.

- *CHA:* Determines song resistances and power. Put at least 10 points into this at the start.
- *PIE/INT/EMP:* Don't bother with these.
- *QUI:* Not really needed, but some points here can add "oomph" to melee.
- *STR:* Rises slowly. Vital for carrying armor/weapons/loot and melee damage.

Weapon Choices: You can't really call instruments weapons, but they are your best choice. Other than that, Slashing and Thrusting, Slashing and Thrusting. Rinse and repeat.

Spec Paths:

- *Instruments:* Gives songs and shouts; melee line of either Slashing or Thrusting, plus Stealth. Keep all three around two-thirds your level. With 44 in Instruments you get final damage shout, necessary for melee damage.
- *Melee Weapon:* Melee weapon choice should also be at two-thirds level, especially for soloing or hard battle. You get decent styles and good chain. At less skill, even DD shouts don't do much damage.
- *Stealth:* Also worth keeping at two-thirds level. Any lower, and you move too slowly to be effective. Rate of stealthy movement directly relates to Stealth and your character level. At Level 10 with 8 Stealth, you run faster than at Level 20 with 10 Stealth.
- The only other Stealth advantage is hiding (no Detect Hidden or Safe Fall). Don't bother putting points in Stealth until you're ready for RvR. Stealth accomplishes little in PvE. Spend points instead on Instrument and melee skills. If you want Stealth, start at level 20.
- All spec lines can be raised through items, but no higher than your character skill.
- Bonus items don't give the next skill or spell.
- Keep Instrument even with level until Level 12 to get the base song in each type. Any lower, and crowd control suffers. For meleeing, keep that skill at your level instead.

Big Mistakes To Avoid In Character Creation: Putting points into categories that don't matter, like Intelligence. It controls Power for casters, but not Minstrels. CHA fulfills that function for you.

Deciding What You Want Your Role To Be: Decide whether you want to group or solo. This affects where you put the most points (Instrument or melee). Either way, reserve Stealth for RvR and leave it alone until Level 20.

Plotting Your Future:

- Early levels are pretty easy. Your biggest decision is to go with Instruments or melee. For RvR, Stealth can be devastating. Obviously, you can't keep all three maxed out. Try raising Instruments to just over two-thirds level and stop at 45. Split other points between Stealth and melee, or just melee if you don't RvR.
- Keeping melee weapon skill at just under two-thirds level makes you a proficient killer, with enough points left for Instrument.

Grouping:

- Find groups early. Lower levels are hard for crowd control, but your Song of Power is in demand by casters.
- For a passive game, group with casters to keep power up. Use Stun and Confuse shouts for damage.
- For an active game, fight with melee and Direct Damage shouts. During downtime, play Song of Power/Healing.
- For both, engage in melee fights, Stun, and use DD shouts and mezzes on the crowd.
- Song of Power (and Song of Healing) only work at 50% efficiency in combat.

Combining your skills with others: With tanks, do crowd control. With casters, be a tank or power booster. With rogues, soak up damage until a rogue makes a critical hit.

Soloing: You can solo alone, or with a pet.

- *Soloing alone.* Solo blues and prime yellows. Your chain armor and innate ability to block and evade keep you alive. Use Direct Damage shouts often; pull the mob with them and run a bit to help refresh time.
- *Soloing with a pet:* Use a blue pet for high experience. Yellows often resist, and if it breaks the charm (higher spec lessens the chance), your pet may attack you. Either send the pet to attack and occasionally use a DD shout (letting the pet do the most damage) or jump in and have it help. The more damage you do, the more XP you get. Your pet can only go where a normal player can go.

Best things to solo: With Thrusting, kill reptiles. With Slashing, kill animals. Stay away from ghosts.

Note: Instruments degrade with use.

Realm Versus Realm:

- Get your part of the army to battle with Motivational Anthem. Pick up stragglers or escapees.
- Stealth up and attack people at the edge of battle. Use two DD shouts and Stun for good results.
- Songs don't work while Stealthed. Shouts break Stealth. No Stealth with Relics.
- Charm the highest possible pet and send it into battle. Stun and join the attack.
- Stay on the edge of the battle and keep the drum handy for Motivational Anthem.
- If you see an escapee, run them down and Stun, then melee.
- Keep your flute out during battle. Stun and mez people as they run past tanks.
- Target and mez on the move. If you see someone in trouble, Stun. Or swap the flute for your drum and sing Motivational Anthem as you run down an enemy for a Realmmate.
- Use your sword to kill assassins, archers, and hybrids. Stun tanks for someone stronger.

Minstrel Styles

Abbreviations. *Headers:* **F**atigue **C**ost / **B**onus **D**amage / **B**onus **t**o **H**it. *In table:* **L**ow / **M**edium / **H**igh / **V**ery **H**igh / **D**efensive **B**onus (for you, on next round) / **D**efensive **P**enalty (to you, on next round) / **A**ttack **S**peed **R**eduction / **M**ovement **R**eduction (for target)

Thrust

Lvl	Style	FC	BD	BtH	Prerequisites / Other Notes
2	Thistle	H	M	–	
4	Ratfang	L	M	M	Prereq: evaded target / Low Stun; Low DB
6	Puncture	M	M	M	Low Bleed
8	Sting	M	L	M	Attempt to taunt target; High DP
10	Wolftooth	M	H	M	Prereq: Ratfang / Low MR
12	Bloody Dance	M	M	M	Prereq: puncture / Med Bleed; Low DP
15	Beartooth	L	M	H	Prereq: blocked target / Med Stun
18	Tranquilize	M	–	–	Attempt to turn away target; High DB
21	Lunge	M	M	H	Prereq: Puncture
25	Ricochet	L	–	H	Prereq: target blocked by anyone / Med Bleed; Med DP
29	Pierce	M	M	H	Prereq: behind target / Med Bleed; Med DP
34	Liontooth	L	M	M	Prereq: Wolftooth / High Bleed; Low DB
39	Basiliskfang	M	M	L	Prereq: beside target / High ASR; Low DB
44	Wyvernfang	L	M	M	Prereq: Beartooth / High MR
50	Dragonfang	L	M	H	Prereq: evaded target / High Stun; Low DP

Beginner's Tips:

- Try many configurations of Hotbars until you find one that works best.
- Don't let armor fall too far behind your level. With gray and green armor, you find yourself flattened quickly.
- Keep your weapon blue or better. If you fall behind the curve, solo greens.
- Drop instruments in your ranged weapons slot.
- Ability Danger Sense. Tells when a scout notices your party. Always on. 8 Stealth trains.

Advanced Techniques:

- If you are pulling reds, be prepared to be attacked by a would-be pet. Remember those extra mez attempt seconds can save the party or let your rezzer escape.
- When a pull goes bad, charm one critter in the mob and fight with it. Release and kill it at the end of the fight.
- Let an Infiltrator pull with a crossbow, then run away. Direct Damage the mob to gain aggro as the Infiltrator gets out of range, Stealths up, and makes a critical strike.
- Running with a pet involves twisting. Start the Run song, stop almost immediately, toggle Charm on and off, and start Run again before the pulse dies. This takes practice, but can be handy in RvR.

Minstrel Spells

Instruments

Group Speed Buff Song: buffs by (Speed %); requires drum.

Skill............Instruments Cost............................0P
Casting Time........3 sec. Range....................2000
Duration..........Song + 6

Lvl	Spell	Speed %
3	Motivational Chant*	44%
11	Motivational Song*	56%
23	Motivational Hymn*	74%
33	Motivational Strains*	89%
43	Motivational Anthem	104%

Buffs groupmates' health regeneration by (Buff) every cycle; requires lute.

Skill............Instruments Cost............................0P
Casting Time........3 sec. Range.......................700
Duration..........Song + 6

Lvl	Spell	Buff
1	Song of Minor Renewal*	2
8	Song of Renewal*	3
14	Song of Minor Healing*	4
19	Song of Healing*	5
25	Song of Minor Regeneration*	7
31	Song of Regeneration*	8
37	Song of Minor Rejuvenation*	9
47	Song of Rejuvenation	11

Buffs Groupmates' power regeneration by (Buff) every cycle; requires drum.

Skill............Instruments Cost............................0P
Casting Time........3 sec. Range.......................700
Duration..........Song + 6

Lvl	Spell	Buff
10	Song of Power*	1
21	Song of Energy*	2
30	Song of Clarity*	3
39	Song of the Mind*	4
50	Song of Empowering	5

DD. You must wait 15 seconds before casting a Dischordant, Stunning or Cant spell again.

Skill............Instruments Dmg Type..............Body
Casting Time........Shout Range.......................700
Duration..................Inst.

Lvl	Spell	Cost	Dmg
2	Dischordant Note*	3P	7
7	Dischordant Tone*	9P	21
17	Dischordant Wail*	19P	47
35	Dischordant Shriek	43P	92

DD. You must wait 15 seconds before casting one of these spells again.

Skill............Instruments Dmg Type..............Body
Casting Time........Shout Range.......................700
Duration..................Inst.

Lvl	Spell	Cost	Dmg
4	Lesser Cacophony*	5P	13
12	Cacophony*	15P	33
26	Greater Cacophony*	31P	69
44	Major Cacophony	55P	115

Charms creature up to 70-110% of Caster's level (depending on level of specialization); target has chance to resist and break the charm every 4.75 sec. You must wait 5 seconds before casting one of these spells again.

Skill............Instruments Cost............................0P
Casting Time........Shout Range....................2000
Duration.......Chant + 10

Lvl	Spell	Targets
6	Captivating Melodies*	Humanoids
13	Enchanting Melodies*	Above + animals
20	Attracting Melodies*	Above + insects
27	Pleasurable Melodies*	Above + magical creatures
34	Enticing Melodies*	Same as above
41	Alluring Melodies	Same as above

Stuns target, making him unable to move or perform actions. You must wait 10 seconds before casting a Dischordant, Stunning or Cant spell again.

Skill............Instruments Dmg Type..............Body
Casting Time........Shout Range.......................700

Lvl	Spell	Cost	Dur
5	Stunning Yell*	7P	2 sec.
15	Stunning Shout*	17P	3 sec.
28	Stunning Screech*	33P	4 sec.
40	Stunning Bellow	49P	6 sec.

Mesmerize: target halts all movement and is unable to attack or cast spells; the effect breaks when the target is healed or takes damage; pulse every 5 sec; requires flute. (There are no PvE/RvR limitations.)

Skill............Instruments Dmg Type..............Spirit
Cost............................0P Casting Time........3 sec.
Range....................1500

Lvl	Spell	Dur
9	Compelling Cadence*	Song + 12
18	Constraining Cadence*	Song + 17
24	Coercing Cadence*	Song + 20
36	Compulsory Cadence*	Song + 26
42	Commanding Cadence	Song + 29

Confusion: (Switch %) chance to switch targets; (Ally %) chance to attack own ally. You must wait 30 seconds before casting a Dischordant, Stunning or Cant spell again.

Skill............Instruments Dmg Type..............Spirit
Cost............................0P Casting Time........Shout
Range.......................700 Duration.............20 sec.

Lvl	Spell	Switch %	Ally %
5	Cant of Befuddling*	70%	0%
15	Cant of Bewilderment*	85%	0%
25	Cant of Confusion*	100%	0%
35	Cant of Discord*	100%	15%
45	Cant of Perplexity	100%	30%

Infiltrator

Races		Abilities	
Briton / Saracen		1	Staves
Titles		1	Cloth Armor
5	White Hand	1	Leather Armor
10	Lurker	1	Sprint
15	Blue Hand	1	Evade I
20	Spy	4	Small Shields
25	Red Hand	4	Evade II
30	Assassin	5	Crossbows
35	Master Spy	5	Distraction
40	Black Hand	8	Danger Sense
45	Infiltrator	10	Evade III
50	Master Infiltrator	10	Safe Fall I
Skills (& Styles)		16	Detect Hidden
1	Slashing	20	Evade IV
1	Thrusting (& Styles)	20	Safe Fall II
1	Stealth	25	Climb Walls
4	Critical Strike (& Styles)	30	Evade V
5	Dual Wield (& Styles)	30	Safe Fall III
5	Envenom	40	Evade VI
		40	Safe Fall IV
		50	Evade VII

The Infiltrator hides, sneaks up on enemies, and executes deadly Critical Strikes to do a lot of damage. They then use a combination of combat styles to finish off the enemy. They can Envenom their weapons to do more damage, and each has a ranged attack that they can use as well. The focus on the Infiltrator is RvR, much like the focus of the Cleric is healing. This class isn't the easiest to play, and requires a bit of patience. The Infiltrator is designed for speed and stealth, spying and assassination.

The Best Part: The Infiltrator is the king of soloing in the RvR world. Stealth allows you to survive without protection in the frontiers. They also have the highest Evade in the game, giving a very nice defense bonus to make up for low armor. They debuff, snare and damage their enemies using poisons.

The Worst Part: In RvR and Solo, it requires real patience to play this class. It's not uncommon to wait 20 real-world minutes before executing a kill. Also, being restricted to leather armor means low armor protection.

Race Choices:

Briton. Slightly stronger than Saracen, but considerably less dexterous. You can get an advantage in Slashing by choosing this race and increasing STR.

Saracen. Holds a 20-point DEX advantage, but lacks the STR and CON of a Briton. If you're going to primarily serve as a spy, you can really get a high DEX by putting even more points into that stat. That will help your speed and evasion. For Thrusting, the Saracen class with the higher DEX is the better choice.

Stat Choices: Allocate your stat points to make up for any racial differences and to cater to your specs and weapons. Balance out any DEX disadvantages, since that's your most critical attribute, and base your choices around the race you choose and the weapon type you want. The Infiltrator's main stats are Dexterity (primary), Quickness (secondary) and Strength (tertiary).

- *STR:* More critical if you plan on soloing and Slashing. Affects Slashing damage and the amount of loot you can carry. For a slashing Infiltrator, put more extra Strength into your Briton rogue — it will only raise 1 point every 3rd level as opposed to every level as Dexterity does.
- *DEX:* This is your vital stat, since you often Sprint and Evade. Put at least 10 or 15 points here. DEX also affects your Thrusting damage and chance to hit your enemy.
- *QUI:* Your 2nd most important stat, which determines how fast you swing your weapon — the higher your QUI, the more swings you get.
- *CON:* Affects how many HP you gain per level. If you're going to try soloing, put points here.

Weapon Choices:

- You can use Slashing or Thrusting styles, as well as a crossbow, for pulling a creature from a group at range.
- Your best "weapon" is often the poison you apply using Envenom abilities. Then, you get the initial strike damage, plus the slow effects of the poison. Your main asset is Backstab, followed by special attacks.
- Use ranged weapons to pull a critter from a group. The larger your group, the better your chance to hit.
- Your main attack is the Backstab line. Try poisoning your weapons beforehand and using a Critical Strike or Dual Wield style to deliver a big damage punch.

Spec Paths: You can basically choose whether to melee or be a stealthy spy. Since RvR combat is one of the best uses for this class, determine what you plan to do there.

- *Slash/Thrust:* Base weapon path. Training in this opens up styles and normalizes your damage output. Training in this is important. It raises the minimum damage you do, and raises the maximum later on as well.
- *Dual Wield*: Worth paying attention to. Every Infiltrator can dual-wield weapons without training. However, putting points in the track increases the chance to hit with both weapons and also opens up styles. Infiltrators always have a base % chance to hit with both weapons, so it isn't required that you train this to do it, but it increases your chances dramatically.
- *Envenom:* Envenom is like "magic." To use poisons, train up to the level of the poison you buy. There are four types that become available (and increase in power and cost) as you train higher in Envenom. There's a DoT, a Strength/Constitution debuff, a Snare, and a Disease (which prevents hit point regeneration).
- The Infiltrator is a melee class, so training in your weapon type is important, but don't go too overboard. You will need Stealth and Critical Strike to function at your full potential. The CS/Weapon/Dual Wield combination makes for a good assassination Infiltrator. High Stealth in conjunction with your bow gives a better chance of hiding while nocking an arrow.

Big Mistakes To Avoid In Character Creation:

- Spreading points too thinly will gimp your character. That's really the only big mistake.
- Decide what weapon type you want to use before spending your points. Stick to boosting STR and CON for Slashing, and DEX and QUI for Thrusting.

Deciding What You Want Your Role To Be: Do you want to be a melee-heavy class? If so, train high in Weapon, Critical Strike and Dual Wield … adding in enough in Stealth to be useful. Do you want to be an assassin, dealing a lot of damage in the first few hits? Keep your Stealth and CS up and focus on your Weapon more. Are you interested in poisons? Carrying 5 pre-poisoned daggers, you can be a virtual walking Area-Effect DoT.

Plotting Your Future: Save your spec points until Level 5.

Grouping: In a PvE group, your role is to bring extra damage into a fight. You can't do this without a "tank" class in the group to take the hits.

- Deliver backstabs to monsters while they're engaged, or use poison to debuff. The trick to the Infiltrator is to "kill before being killed". Using your Backstab styles and poisons, you can easily out-damage an equal level Armsman, but be careful — your defenses are low!
- The Infiltrator's main skill is Stealth. In RvR, Infiltrators are primarily a mage/archer/assassin killer, and it's fun!
- Climb up the walls of relic keeps and strike at the archers or mages (or try stealing the relic itself!). You get Climb at your 25th train in Stealth.
- Relay enemy positions back to the main force — trying not to be discovered — or get close up and personal in the skirmish with fast-hitting weapons.
- Beware though, once an Infiltrator is discovered and set upon he will not have much of a chance without backup. Leather armor has low defense, so don't get overconfident.
- Be wary of enemy Assassin classes though — they also have detect hidden and may uncover you.
- Hiding works much better when you're behind a critter.
- You can act as a puller if your group has a tank that can absorb aggro (something you yourself must avoid at all costs). Use the crossbow, but don't pull off more than you can outrun.
- Your Critical Strike styles work well in group combat. If you happen to draw the aggro, just stop attacking and let your tank taunt the monster off you. Stay still as long as you can to make this easier and yell for the healer.
- In less hectic battles, take the time to use more poison-laced Backstabs. You can now hide after delivering DoT poison damage!
- Wait for the tank(s) to get aggro before you make your attack.
- A stealthed archer is visible when he fires; when he nocks his arrow, if he fails his Stealth check. Stealth spec % (-20% on Critical Shots) = % chance to stay hidden.

Soloing: Soloing isn't really for you, but if you decide to do it, don't attack mobs that can cast. Look for critters most susceptible to Thrusting or Slashing weapons. Find an area in which you can easily hide without running into other mobs. Pull with your crossbow, fight, retreat and regroup, then repeat the process.

Realm Versus Realm:

- By using Stealth, you can infiltrate the keep, Backstab archers and casters or get to relics. No Stealth while carrying relics, though.
- Your light armor won't do much to protect you if you're discovered.
- If your job's to assassinate, look for casters and archers, preferably far from the battle's edge.
- If your job is to distract, concentrate your crossbow efforts on casters.
- Don't attack everything you see! A living Infiltrator is much more useful for scouting enemy positions and movements.
- Avoid attacking tanks unless they're alone.

Beginner's Tips:

- Wait for the right time to strike.
- After your first "Backstab" attack combo, melee attacks should be low and fast-hitting.
- Spend Endurance freely before you start a fight to take advantage of styles.
- Poison weapons before combat.
- Experiment with your character — you get quite a few points along the way.
- Ability Danger Sense. Tells when a scout notices your party. Always on. 8 Stealth trains.
- Ability Detect Hidden. See hidden enemy players at increased range. 16 Stealth trains.

Advanced Techniques:

- Have three weapons ready. Keep your two strongest weapons in your left and right slots, and your weakest one in your 2 hand. Start with your left-handed and weaker 2-handed slot weapon wielded. If the 2-handed weapon procs its poison during your backstab combo, use your Hotkeys to switch back to your main weapons. If you're lucky, all 3 poisons hit the mob.
- Avoid Snare poison in PvE, until you think you're losing the fight. Switch to it when you're ready to run; it doesn't last long at lower levels. However, in RvR, Snare poisons are great. Backstab, Snare, then finish the job.

Infiltrator Styles

Abbreviations. *Headers:* **F**atigue **C**ost / **B**onus **D**amage / **B**onus **t**o **H**it. *In table:* **L**ow / **M**edium / **H**igh / **V**ery **H**igh / **D**efensive **B**onus (for you, on next round) / **D**efensive **P**enalty (to you, on next round) / **A**ttack **S**peed **R**eduction / **M**ovement **R**eduction (for target)

Thrust

Lvl	Style	FC	BD	BtH	Prerequisites / Other Notes
2	Thistle	H	M	–	
4	Ratfang	L	M	M	Prereq: evaded target / Low Stun; Low DB
6	Puncture	M	M	M	Low Bleed
8	Sting	M	L	M	Attempt to taunt target; High DP
10	Wolftooth	M	H	M	Prereq: Ratfang / Low MR
12	Bloody Dance	M	M	M	Prereq: puncture / Med Bleed; Low DP
15	Beartooth	L	M	H	Prereq: blocked target / Med Stun
18	Tranquilize	M	–	–	Attempt to turn away target; High DB
21	Lunge	M	M	H	Prereq: Puncture
25	Ricochet	L	–	H	Prereq: target blocked by anyone / Med Bleed; Med DP
29	Pierce	M	M	H	Prereq: behind target/Med Bleed; Med DP
34	Liontooth	L	M	M	Prereq: Wolftooth / High Bleed; Low DB
39	Basiliskfang	M	M	L	Prereq: beside target / High ASR; Low DB
44	Wyvernfang	L	M	M	Prereq: Beartooth / High MR
50	Dragonfang	L	M	H	Prereq: evaded target / High Stun; Low DP

Dual Wield

Lvl	Style	FC	BD	BtH	Prerequisites / Other Notes
2	Twin Spikes	M	VH		
4	Twin Return	L	M	M	Prereq: evaded target / Low Bleed; Low DB
6	Shadow's Edge	M	H	H	Prereq: behind target
8	Inflame	M	L	–	Attempt to taunt target; Med DP
10	Orbit	M	M	M	Prereq: Twin Return / Low MR
12	Eclipse	M	M	M	Prereq: Shadow's Edge / Low ASR
15	Misty Gloom	H	M	L	
18	Obscure	M	–	–	Attempt to turn away target; High DB
21	Penumbra	M	H	H	Prereq: Shadow's Edge
24	Reflection	L	M	L	Prereq: target parried by anyone / Low DB
29	Flank	M	M	–	Prereq: beside target / Med MR; Med DB
34	Dark Tendrils	L	M	M	Prereq: evaded target / High Bleed
39	Shadows Rain	M	M	M	Prereq: Flank / High ASR; Low DB
44	Hypnotic Darkness	M	M	H	Prereq: Reflection / Med Stun
50	Dual Shadows	M	M	M	Prereq: in front of target/High Bleed;Med DP

Critical Strikes

Lvl	Style	FC	BD	BtH	Prerequisites / Other Notes
2	Backstab	M	M	M	Prereq: behind target, hidden / Med DP
4	Eviscerate	M	H	L	Prereq: Backstab / Low ASR; Low DP
6	Kidney Rupture	L	VH	L	Prereq: Eviscerate / Low Bleed; Med DP
8	Pincer	M	M	H	Prereq: beside target / High DP
10	Backstab 2	H	M	H	Prereq: behind target, hidden / Med DP
12	Hamstring	L	M	M	Prereq: evaded target / Med Bleed; Med DB
15	Thigh Cut	M	VH	M	Prereq: Backstab 2 / Low DP
18	Garrote	H	M	M	Med MR; Med DP
21	Perforate Artery	M	M	H	Prereq: in front of target, hidden / High Bleed; Med DP
25	Achilles Heel	M	H	M	Prereq: Garrote / High ASR
29	Leaper	L	M	H	Prereq: Hamstring / High Bleed; Low DB
34	Creeping Death	L	VH	H	Prereq: Perforate Artery / Med Stun
39	Stunning Stab	L	VH	VH	Prereq: Creeping Death / Low DB
44	Rib Separation	M	H	H	Prereq: Leaper / High MR
50	Ripper	M	VH	H	Prereq: Rib Separation/High Bleed; Low DB

Friar

Races		Abilities	
Briton / Avalonian		1	Staves
Titles		1	Crushing
5	Friar Acolyte	1	Cloth Armor
10	Lesser Chaplain	1	Leather Armor
15	Fanatic	1	Small Shields
20	Zealot	1	Sprint
25	Ecstatic	5	Evade I
30	Chaplain	10	Evade II
35	Inquisitor	15	Evade III
40	Greater Chaplain	22	Evade IV
45	Master Inquisitor	33	Evade V
50	Chaplain Primus	**Styles**	
Skills			Staff
1	Enhancement (Magic)		
1	Rejuvenation (Magic)		
5	Enhancement Spec.		
5	Rejuvenation Spec.		
5	Staff		
10	Parry		

A Friar is part healer, part fighter, capable of solo play or grouping. You'll never be bored playing this class, as you get melee with your staff and some magical skills. While you never entirely conquer either one, your versatility and ability to resurrect fallen comrades will earn you a standing place in any group.

The Best Part: You're versatile, and you get to play with magic as you heal and resurrect.

The Worst Part: Because you're skilled in many things, you're never outstanding. Plus, your magic skills start paling at higher levels in a group, and you're limited to light armor.

Race Choices:

Briton. Not much to discuss. Be a Briton!

Stat Choices: Allocate your 30 points to areas that most benefit your long-term plan.

- *STR:* Good for more melee damage.
- *PIE:* Affects Power. Boost if you plan to heal.
- *CON:* Boosts HP. More important for melee types than healers.
- *DEX:* Put in at least 10 for Evasion purposes.
- *QUI:* Helps with melee weapon speed.

Weapon Choices: You can melee using a 2-handed staff, which hits for considerable damage but doesn't allow you to also wield a shield. The good thing is that, once trained, you can use your staves to inflict painful hits on mobs while soloing. You can also train in Parry, but the majority of your points should go into Staff.

- *Staff:* Primary melee skill for Friar class. By keeping this at about two-thirds of your character level, you'll get the best use out of it. You also get special combat styles at various skill levels, so investing points heavily in Staves is recommended if you like to fight.
- *Parry:* Helps block hits from mobs or enemy players. This is important, as you can't carry a shield while swinging a staff. Each point you put here starting at level 10 gives you more of a chance of blocking a hit. You still want to put most of your points into Staves, but a few here can't hurt.

Spec Paths: You get a matching number of skill points each time you progress a level (i.e., 20 points for level 20). You can specialize in either Rejuvenation or Enhancement. You can go for pure soloing with high emphasis on Enchantment, then some on Parry and Staff. Or, you can concentrate on healing by devoting points to Rejuvenation and some to Staff. Many Friars play as a hybrid, with high emphasis on Staff, medium emphasis on Rejuvenation, and a small bit of Enchantment for Armor Factor. For the latter, concentrate on Staff, then keep either Enhancement or Rejuvenation (and perhaps Parry) at about one-quarter to one-third of weapon skill level.

- *Enhancement:* Buffing line of spells and chants. You share the basic line of spells early on with the Cleric. If you plan to solo, you probably want to spec this instead of Rejuvenation. If you try to use your armor buffs in a group, they don't work in conjunction with those from other classes. For grouping, don't waste more than a few points to get your first Armor Factor boost.
- *Rejuvenation:* Base skills are the same as a Cleric's. Keep this at about half of your level so that you reserve enough spec points for Staff. Go only as far as you need to for the spells you want. Most people stop at 15 (after you get a resurrect spell and two cures) or 25 (when you get a major healing spell). The higher your Rejuvenation, the more you can heal, but this comes at the expense of your Staff skill.

Big Mistakes to Avoid in Character Creation: Trying to spread spec points out too thinly.

Deciding What You Want Your Role to Be: Your first choice, which you should make prior to level 5, is whether to focus on solo or group play. That determines your spell spec line. Also, decide whether to focus on healing or melee; this determines whether you concentrate more on spell spec lines or your weapon.

Plotting Your Future: Figure out what specific styles and skills you want out of the spec lines available to you. Spend points according to plan, and don't go further than you need to in any one area. If you're developing two different things, don't neglect one of them for five or 10 levels; split points up accordingly as you go along.

Grouping:

- You can perform Cleric functions for a group early on — buffing, healing and rezzing. But, unlike a Cleric, you can also deliver measurable damage to PvE mobs.
- If you're playing a Cleric role, hang back. You don't want to be taking damage if you're responsible for healing. Also, heal people before they drop to half their HP.
- You're a good backup healer and rezzer who can also move to the front lines and evade hits while banging a mob with a staff.
- Split healing with a Cleric. Let the Cleric heal during battle while you fight, and then take over healing duties between battles to give the Cleric resting time.
- Before combat, apply the basic buffs and let the Cleric reserve power for the higher-level buffs you can't give.
- If you move to the front lines, keep an eye on the Cleric and assist if necessary.

Soloing:

- Remember that chants use Power. Be judicious about using them while alone in battle.
- Enhancement mostly includes self-buffs useful in solo play. Your Staff does damage, stat and speed buffs help, you're good at Evading, and you can heal between battles.
- Buff and strike with your best shots first.
- Evasion is your best defense. Parry helps, but your main dodging ability comes from the Evade skill you develop at higher level.

Realm Versus Realm:

- The Briton base race provides sufficient STR.
- Your potential to deliver damage makes you a good candidate for hunting down casters. But, don't tangle with a dedicated fighter bearing a 2-handed weapon — at least not alone!
- In RVR, battles happen fast. Don't worry so much about conserving mana — buff your speed and do your best damage early on.

Beginner's Tips:

- Even if you *don't* particularly like fighting, you'll often need a weapon (especially at higher levels) with which to defend yourself.
- Avoid attracting the attention of really social mobs. Otherwise, you'll get more than you bargained for.

Advanced Techniques:

- Keep Enhancement and Parry at around 20-25% of Staff. They're handy, but not as useful as Staff, Rejuvenation and Evade.
- Choose your fights wisely. You're an excellent anti-caster shock troop, and your Crushing attacks are great for squishing bugs and disconnecting skeletons. Your substantial damage penalty against zombie types and air or ghost Monsters, though, make them less than desirable targets.

Friar Styles

Abbreviations. *Headers:* **F**atigue **C**ost / **B**onus **D**amage / **B**onus **t**o **H**it. *In table:* **L**ow / **M**edium / **H**igh / **V**ery **H**igh / **D**efensive **B**onus (for you, on next round) / **D**efensive **P**enalty (to you, on next round) / **A**ttack **S**peed **R**eduction / **M**ovement **R**eduction (for target)

Staff

Lvl	Style	FC	BD	BtH	Prerequisites / Other Notes
2	Spinning Staff	M	M	–	Low DB
4	Figure Eight	L	H	M	Prereq: parried target / Low DB
6	Friar's Ally	M	M	M	Prereq: Figure Eight / Low Stun
8	Defender's Fury	M	M	L	Med ASR
10	Quick Strike	M	M	–	Prereq: Defender's Fury
12	Friar's Redress	M	–	–	Attempt to turn away target; Very High DB
15	Double Strike	L	M	M	Prereq: Figure Eight / Low Bleed; Low DB
18	Friar's Friend	H	H	M	Prereq: beside target / Med Stun
21	Counter Evade	L	H	L	Prereq: evaded target / Med MR; Med DB
25	Banish	L	VH	M	Prereq: Quick Strike / Med DB
29	Friar's Boon	M	M	–	Med DB
34	Holy Staff	H	M	L	
39	Friar's Fury	L	M	M	Prereq: Counter Evade / Med Bleed; Low DB
44	Stunning Wrath	M	–	H	Prereq: Banish / High Stun; Med DB
50	Excommunicate	M	H	M	Prereq: evaded target / Low DB

Friar Spells

Rejuvenation

Heals damage by (Heal) HP to Friend.
Skill...........Rejuvenation Casting Time ...2.25 sec.
Range....................1350 Duration..................Inst.

Lvl	Spell	Cost	Heal
1	Minor Rejuvenation*	1P	6
3	Minor Regeneracy*	2P	11
5	Minor Relief*	3P	16
8	Minor Restoration*	4P	23
11	Minor Recuperation*	6P	31
14	Minor Renewal*	7P	38
18	Minor Revival*	9P	48
23	Minor Resuscitation*	11P	60
29	Minor Reviction*	14P	75
37	Minor Refection*	19P	95
47	Minor Refocillation	24P	119

Resurrects corpse; target is resurrected with a percentage of its original Power and/or HP.
Skill...........Rejuvenation
Cost . . . . .Power cost based on corpse (see p. 368)
Casting Time ....4 sec. Range....................1500
Duration..................Inst.

Lvl	Spell	Power	HP
10	Revive	No Power	10%

Heals damage to Groupmates by (Heal) HP.
Skill...........Rejuvenation Casting Time ....3 sec.
Range....................1200 Duration..................Inst.

Lvl	Spell	Cost	Heal
15	Angelic Commendation*	29P	33
25	Angelic Benediction*	48P	53
35	Angelic Blessing*	69P	73
45	Angelic Approbation	91P	93

Heals damage to Friend by (Heal) HP.
Skill...........Rejuvenation Casting Time ...2.75 sec.
Range....................1350 Duration..................Inst.

Lvl	Spell	Cost	Heal
4	Regeneracy*	5P	26
6	Relief*	6P	36
9	Restoration*	9P	50
12	Recuperation*	12P	65
16	Renewal*	15P	85
21	Revival*	20P	109
27	Resuscitation*	26P	138
31	Reviction*	30P	158
36	Refection*	36P	183
46	Refocillation	47P	231

Revival

Heals damage to Friend by (Heal) HP.
Skill...........Rejuvenation Casting Time ...3.25 sec.
Range....................1350 Duration..................Inst.

Lvl	Spell	Cost	Heal
5	Major Restoration*	11P	55
8	Major Recuperation*	16P	82
11	Major Renewal*	21P	109
14	Major Revival*	27P	136
18	Major Resuscitation*	34P	172
25	Major Reviction*	48P	235
33	Major Refection*	65P	307
43	Major Refocillation	87P	396

Resurrects corpse; target is resurrected with a percentage of its original Power and/or HP.
Skill...........Rejuvenation CostPower cost based on corpse (see page 368)
Casting Time ....7 sec. Range....................1500
Duration..................Inst.

Lvl	Spell	Power	HP
15	Raise Fallen	10%	30%

Cures Friend.
Skill...........Rejuvenation Casting Time .....3.2 sec.
Range....................1500 Duration..................Inst.

Lvl	Spell	Cost
6	Cure Poison	6%P
7	Cure Disease	6%P

Enhancement

Buffs Friend's STR.
Skill ....Enhancements Casting Time ....3 sec.
Range....................1000 Duration...........Concent.

Lvl	Spell	Cost	Buff
3	Blessed Strength**	1C	12
7	Blessed Potency**	3C	15
14	Blessed Power**	5C	21
20	Holy Strength**	7C	26
30	Holy Potency**	11C	34
41	Holy Power	15C	42
50	Holy Might	19C	50

Buffs Friend's AF.
Skill ....Enhancements Casting Time ....3 sec.
Range....................1000 Duration...........Concent.

Lvl	Spell	Cost	Buff
2	Aura of Shielding**	1C	12
5	Greater Aura of Shielding**	2C	15
10	Aura of Defense**	4C	20
16	Greater Aura of Defense**	6C	26
22	Aura of Guarding**	8C	32
31	Greater Aura of Guarding	11C	41
42	Aura of Deflection	15C	52

Buffs Friend's DEX.
Skill ....Enhancements Casting Time ....3 sec.
Range....................1000 Duration...........Concent.

Lvl	Spell	Cost	Buff
8	Blessed Dexterity**	3C	16
13	Blessed Agility**	5C	20
19	Blessed Coordination**	7C	25
28	Holy Dexterity**	10C	32
38	Holy Agility	14C	40
48	Holy Coordination	18C	48

Buffs Friend's CON.
Skill ....Enhancements Casting Time ....3 sec.
Range....................1000 Duration...........Concent.

Lvl	Spell	Cost	Buff
6	Blessing of Health**	2C	14
11	Benison of Health**	4C	18
15	Benediction of Health**	5C	22
24	Blessing of Fortitude**	8C	29
33	Benison of Fortitude	12C	36
43	Benediction of Fortitude	16C	44

Faithful Shield

Buffs Caster's AF.
Skill ....Enhancements Cost......................10%P
Casting Time ....4 sec. Duration.............10 min.

Lvl	Spell	Buff
1	Shield of Faith*	14
3	Shield of Piety*	16
7	Shield of Devotion*	20
11	Shield of Grace*	24
16	Shield of Justice*	29
24	Shield of Zeal*	37
33	Shield of Holiness*	46
45	Shield of the Sanctified	58

Buffs Caster's fatigue regeneration by (Buff) every cycle.
Skill ....Enhancements Cost 2P/1.5s
Casting Time ....Shout Duration ....Chant + 5

Lvl	Spell	Buff
2	Saint's Vigor	2

Reduces Caster's fatigue cost by (Bonus %).
Skill ....Enhancements Cost......................10%P
Casting Time ....3 sec. Duration.............10 min.

Lvl	Spell	Bonus %
12	Saint's Energy*	10%
22	Saint's Stamina*	15%
32	Saint's Persistence*	20%
42	Saint's Tenacity	25%

Buffs Caster's attack speed by (Speed %). You must wait 3 minutes before casting one of these spells again.
Skill ....Enhancements Cost 10%P
Casting Time ....Shout Duration ....30 sec.

Lvl	Spell	Speed %
5	Speed of the Angel*	26%
10	Haste of the Angel*	32%
15	Alacrity of the Angel*	38%
23	Speed of the Archangel*	46%
30	Haste of the Archangel*	56%
38	Alacrity of the Archangel*	64%
47	Alacrity of the Heavenly Host	76%

Buffs Friend's Heat resistance.
Skill ....Enhancements Casting Time ....3 sec.
Range.....................1000 Duration...........Concent.

Lvl	Spell	Cost	Buff
21	Resilience of the Wanderer**	7C	8
31	Fortitude of the Wanderer	11C	16
46	Piety of the Wanderer	17C	24

Buffs Friend's Cold resistance.
Skill ....Enhancements Casting Time ....3 sec.
Range.....................1000 Duration...........Concent.

Lvl	Spell	Cost	Buff
25	Hearth's Blessing**	9C	8
35	Hearth's Benison	12C	16
48	Hearth's Gift	18C	24

Buffs Friend's Matter resistance.
Skill ....Enhancements Casting Time ....3 sec.
Range.....................1000 Duration...........Concent.

Lvl	Spell	Cost	Buff
27	Attunement to Creation**	9C	8
37	Blessing of Creation	13C	16
49	Oneness with Creation	18C	24

Non-magical damage to Caster reduced by (Bonus %).
Skill ....Enhancements Cost 10%P
Casting Time ....3 sec. Duration ....10 min.

Lvl	Spell	Bonus %
26	Blessing of Resilience*	5%
34	Blessing of Absorption*	10%
44	Blessing of Dissipation	15%

Cleric

Races

Briton / Highlander / Avalonian

Titles

Lvl	Title
5	Initiate
10	Novice
15	Curate
20	Prelate
25	Deacon
30	Ecclesiastic
35	Abbot/Abbess
40	Bishop
45	Cardinal
50	Pontifex

Skills

Lvl	Skill
1	Enhancement (Magic)
1	Rejuvenation (Magic)
5	Enhancement Spec.
5	Rejuvenation Spec.
5	Smiting (Magic)
5	Smiting Spec.

Abilities

Lvl	Ability
1	Staves
1	Crushing
1	Cloth Armor
1	Leather Armor
1	Small Shields
10	Studded Armor
10	Medium Shields
20	Chain Armor

While not the "hammer of the Church" that Friars are, Clerics of Albion are good all-around characters that can heal, solo, group, and provide support. The Cleric acts with others in the Realm to defend against those that would attempt to bring turmoil to the peaceful lands of Albion.

The Best Part: The ability to "buff" physical stats, as well as heal yourself or others. You also get the unique ability to mesmerize, stun and smite foes with magic — useful both in solo and group combat — and you know how to use a mace or staff.

The Worst Part: Can you say meditation and service to others? You must give your life over to charity and enlist the help of Realmmates to overthrow heavy foes. Plus, your melee and damage abilities are only average. You're limited to leather armor early on, and only progress to chain at higher levels.

Race Choices:

Briton. The other races all have some lower-than-average ability, so the balanced Briton is the choice of many. Small, and good for hiding.

Highlander. Strength gives a boost to melee ability and makes soloing easier. Big, strong, but not that attractive.

Saracen. Nimble movements give a bonus to speed during casting and attacks.

Avalonian. This race is often chosen for good looks or roleplaying more than racial abilities.

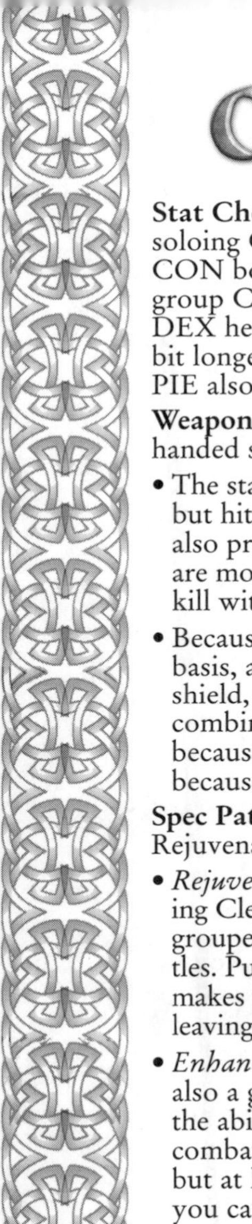

Stat Choices: If you intend to be primarily a soloing Cleric, increasing STR, DEX and CON boosts melee ability. If you plan to be a group Cleric, then increasing PIE, CON and DEX helps you cast spells quickly and live a bit longer when a nasty mob turns on you. PIE also gives you more mana.

Weapon Choices: Clerics can choose a 2-handed staff or mace and shield.

- The staff hits for more damage per contact, but hits less frequently than a mace. The staff also prevents you from using a shield. Staves are most useful in solo play, when you can kill with a nuke and then a whack or two.
- Because damage add occurs on a per-hit basis, and because of the ability to hold a shield, most Clerics choose the mace/shield combination. You'll take less damage because of the shield and do more damage because of damage add.

Spec Paths: Clerics can specialize in Rejuvenation, Enhancement or Smite.

- *Rejuvenation:* Rejuvenation makes for a healing Cleric. You'll use spells primarily when grouped with others to help them survive battles. Putting more points into Enhancement makes you even more desirable to a group, leaving "leftover" points for Smite.
- *Enhancement:* The Enhancement Cleric is also a grouping template, as you don't have the ability to self-heal or smite very well in combat. Buffs let you solo blue con enemies, but at higher levels, the percentage of blues you can solo decreases. Combining Smite with Enhance makes for a very powerful Cleric, either solo or in a group.
- *Smite:* A Smite-specialized Cleric is the most "solo friendly" template. You can do damage at range, gain crowd control ability, and even have decent melee skills. You won't, however, be the best healer.
- *Balanced:* The most versatile template is the balanced Cleric. Putting slightly more points into one path but evenly balancing the others gives you the ability to solo or group as the opportunity arises. Healing and Enhancement is a good combination for grouping. For soloing, concentrate on Smiting and balance the other two. Taking Rejuvenation a little above two-thirds and splitting the other two evenly gives crowd control, buffing and some healing.

Big Mistakes to Avoid in Character Creation:

- Don't put all of your ability points into one area. This hurts in two ways — you don't get a 1:1 ratio (as you would with 10 points into 3 different areas), and the increase after 10 points is negligible, output-wise. Putting all points into CON, for example, isn't going to increase HP by that much at any level. Clerics need a wide range of abilities, so spread out your points.
- Don't put points into anything that isn't a default for this class.
- Not knowing where you're going with your character (see PlottingYour Future).

Deciding What You Want Your Role To Be:

- Know how you plan to gain levels and what you want to do in RvR. Specializing healing or buffing gets you into group RvR sooner than Smiting (heals and buffs aren't "resisted" the way Smites are). On the other hand, the Smite-specialized Cleric is powerful at high levels in RvR with area damage and single-target Smites.
- In a group, you either Smite and do crowd control, or heal. So, knowing how you want to play and in what style is going to make a big difference in how you specialize your character.

Plotting Your Future:

- Even if your choice is to be a Smite-spec'ed Cleric at level 50, neglecting Rejuvenation and Enhancement until level 40 (when you get "extra" points) hurts. If your plan calls for 11 Rejuvenation, then go ahead and get 11 as you gain levels so you have Insta-cast heal.
- Know your "critical levels" spell-wise on each specialization path and use them to figure out what points to spend where, and when.

Grouping:

- If you're balanced, you will be able to fill in for any missing class in a pinch — you can nuke, heal and provide crowd control.
- Stick close to your group regardless of your role, and you will stay busy. Don't let the enemy close in with melee. You're probably going to die and won't have done much in the process.

Soloing: Soloing for a Cleric is plausible, especially with Smite. You can pull from a distance, manage mobs with area-effect mez spells, and heal yourself. With the right skills, you can easily solo yellows, with a rare orange.

Realm Versus Realm:

- RvR and PvE roles are similar, except that going solo in RvR isn't quite as easy. The solo Cleric is an easy target for a stealthy archer or assassin. Your best defense is then your mez spell. Find stealthed enemies fast and hit with mez, followed by normal attacks.
- Clerics work best in RvR at range, whether that's smiting or healing. Make it hard for the enemy to find you, and when they do, make it harder for them to stick with you by mezzing and stunning them when you can.

Beginner's Tips:

- Look for undeads vulnerable to blunt and who dislike chain armor.
- Get Smite at level 5 and learn your maximum distance.
- When fighting a group, using an AoE Direct Damage spell on a mezzed mob breaks your own mez. Mez, and then back up so that mob is out of range for the DD spell.
- 30% chance to block same-level enemy archers' arrows with your shield. Modified by Shield spec, quality and condition of shield, and Engage skill.

Advanced Techniques:

- Stun won't be useful until higher levels, when you can stun a mob long enough to get off an extra Smite on the pull. Learn the range on your spells. Most Clerics pull with a Smite spec spell, followed by a base line Smite, a Stun (at higher levels) and another base line Smite until the mob closes.
- Before pulling, make sure damage add (the "Hammer" line of spells) doesn't drop in mid-combat. You'll end up making melee take forever. Learn the timer on the "Drive Evil" line of spells — know just how long that time is, either in melee swings or by watching a timer, so that you can use it as soon as it's available.

Cleric Spells

Rejuvenation

Heals damage by (Heal) HP to Friend.

Skill...........Rejuvenation Casting Time ...2.25 sec.
Range.....................1350 Duration..................Inst.

Lvl	Spell	Cost	Heal
1	Minor Rejuvenation*	1P	6
3	Minor Regeneracy*	2P	11
5	Minor Relief*	3P	16
8	Minor Restoration*	4P	23
11	Minor Recuperation*	6P	31
14	Minor Renewal*	7P	38
18	Minor Revival*	9P	48
23	Minor Resuscitation*	11P	60
29	Minor Reviction*	14P	75
37	Minor Refection*	19P	95
47	Minor Refocillation	24P	119

Resurrects corpse; target is resurrected with a percentage of its original Power and/or HP.

Skill...........Rejuvenation
Cost .....Power cost based on corpse (see p. 368)
Casting Time ....4 sec. Range.....................1500
Duration..................Inst.

Lvl	Spell	Power	HP
10	Revive	No Power	10%

Heals damage to Groupmates by (Heal) HP.

Skill...........Rejuvenation Casting Time ....3 sec.
Range.....................1200 Duration..................Inst.

Lvl	Spell	Cost	Heal
15	Angelic Commendation*	29P	33
25	Angelic Benediction*	48P	53
35	Angelic Blessing*	69P	73
45	Angelic Approbation	91P	93

Heals damage to Friend by (Heal) HP.

Skill...........Rejuvenation Casting Time ...2.75 sec.
Range.....................1350 Duration..................Inst.

Lvl	Spell	Cost	Heal
4	Regeneracy*	5P	26
6	Relief*	6P	36
9	Restoration*	9P	50
12	Recuperation*	12P	65
16	Renewal*	15P	85
21	Revival*	20P	109
27	Resuscitation*	26P	138
31	Reviction*	30P	158
36	Refection*	36P	183
46	Refocillation	47P	231

Rebirth

Heals damage to Friend by (Heal) HP.
Skill...........Rejuvenation Casting Time ...3.25 sec.
Range.....................1350 Duration..................Inst.

Lvl	Spell	Cost	Heal
5	Major Restoration*	11P	55
8	Major Recuperation*	16P	82
11	Major Renewal*	21P	109
14	Major Revival*	27P	136
18	Major Resuscitation*	34P	172
25	Major Reviction*	48P	235
33	Major Refection*	65P	307
43	Major Refocillation	87P	396

Cures Friend.
Skill...........Rejuvenation Casting Time .....3.2 sec.
Range.....................1500 Duration..................Inst.

Lvl	Spell	Cost
6	Cure Poison	6%P
7	Cure Disease	6%P

Heals damage to Friend by (Heal) HP.
Skill...........Rejuvenation Casting Time ...3.75 sec.
Range.....................1350 Duration..................Inst.

Lvl	Spell	Cost	Heal
10	Greater Recuperation*	29P	145
14	Greater Renewal*	40P	197
19	Greater Revival*	54P	263
25	Greater Resuscitation*	71P	341
32	Greater Reviction*	94P	432
41	Greater Refection*	123P	549
50	Greater Refocillation	154P	667

Heals damage to Groupmates by (Heal) HP.
Skill...........Rejuvenation Casting Time ....4 sec.
Range.....................1350 Duration..................Inst.

Lvl	Spell	Cost	Heal
15	Heaven's Commendation*	29P	65
26	Heaven's Benediction*	50P	109
36	Heaven's Blessing*	71P	149
46	Heaven's Approbation	93P	189

Heals damage to Friend by (Heal % HP) once every 15 min. You must wait 15 minutes before casting one of these spells again.
Skill...........Rejuvenation Cost............................0P
Casting Time ....Shout Range.....................1350
Duration..................Inst.

Lvl	Spell	Heal %
11	Gift of the Heavens*	40%
21	Boon of the Heavens*	60%
33	Favor of the Heavens*	80%
42	Blessing of the Heavens	100%

Heals damage to Groupmates by (Heal % HP) once every 20 min. You must wait 20 minutes before casting one of these spells again.
Skill...........Rejuvenation Cost............................0P
Casting Time ....Shout Range.....................1350
Duration..................Inst.

Lvl	Spell	Heal %
23	Beautified Remedy*	50%
35	Glorious Remedy*	75%
45	Magnificent Remedy	100%

Resurrects corpse; target is resurrected with a percentage of its original Power and/or HP.
Skill...........Rejuvenation CostPower cost based on corpse (see page 368)
Range.....................1500 Duration..................Inst.

Lvl	Spell	Cast	Power	HP
15	Raise Fallen	7 sec.	10%	30%
24	Reincarnate	9 sec.	25%	50%
40	Resurrection	14 sec.	50%	100%

Enhancement

Buffs Friend's STR.
Skill ....Enhancements Casting Time ....3 sec.
Range.....................1000 Duration...........Concent.

Lvl	Spell	Cost	Buff
3	Blessed Strength**	1C	12
7	Blessed Potency**	3C	15
14	Blessed Power**	5C	21
20	Holy Strength**	7C	26
30	Holy Potency**	11C	34
41	Holy Power	15C	42
50	Holy Might	19C	50

Buffs Friend's AF.
Skill ....Enhancements Casting Time ....3 sec.
Range.....................1000 Duration...........Concent.

Lvl	Spell	Cost	Buff
2	Aura of Shielding**	1C	12
5	Greater Aura of Shielding**	2C	15
10	Aura of Defense**	4C	20
16	Greater Aura of Defense**	6C	26
22	Aura of Guarding**	8C	32
31	Greater Aura of Guarding	11C	41
42	Aura of Deflection	15C	52

Buffs Friend's DEX.
Skill ....Enhancements Casting Time ....3 sec.
Range.....................1000 Duration...........Concent.

Lvl	Spell	Cost	Buff
8	Blessed Dexterity**	3C	16
13	Blessed Agility**	5C	20
19	Blessed Coordination**	7C	25
28	Holy Dexterity**	10C	32
38	Holy Agility	14C	40
48	Holy Coordination	18C	48

Buffs Friend's CON.
Skill ....Enhancements Casting Time ....3 sec.
Range.....................1000 Duration...........Concent.

Lvl	Spell	Cost	Buff
6	Blessing of Health**	2C	14
11	Benison of Health**	4C	18
15	Benediction of Health**	5C	22
24	Blessing of Fortitude**	8C	29
33	Benison of Fortitude	12C	36
43	Benediction of Fortitude	16C	44

Guardian Angel

Buffs Friend's AF.
Skill ....Enhancements Casting Time ....3 sec.
Range.....................1000 Duration...........Concent.

Lvl	Spell	Cost	Buff
6	Blessed Shield**	4C	20
12	Blessed Guard**	8C	27
18	Blessed Barrier**	12C	35
25	Holy Shield**	17C	43
34	Holy Guard	24C	55
44	Holy Barrier	32C	67

Buffs Friend's STR and CON.
Skill ....Enhancements Casting Time ....3 sec.
Range.....................1000 Duration...........Concent.

Lvl	Spell	Cost	Buff
5	Angelic Strength**	4C	21
9	Angelic Potency**	6C	25
13	Angelic Power**	9C	30
19	Archangel's Strength**	13C	37
26	Archangel's Potency**	18C	45
35	Archangel's Power	24C	57
46	Archangel's Might	33C	69

Buffs Friend's DEX and QUI.
Skill ....Enhancements Casting Time ....3 sec.
Range.....................1000 Duration...........Concent.

Lvl	Spell	Cost	Buff
7	Angelic Dexterity**	5C	22
14	Angelic Agility**	9C	31
20	Angelic Coordination**	13C	39
30	Dexterity of the Archangel**	21C	51
40	Agility of the Archangel	28C	63
50	Coordination of the Archangel	37C	75

Buffs Friend's health regeneration by (Buff) every cycle.
Skill ....Enhancements Casting Time ....3 sec.
Range.....................1000 Duration...........Concent.

Lvl	Spell	Cost	Buff
10	Renewal**	4C	3
21	Regeneration**	7C	5
32	Revitalization	11C	7
43	Heavenly Infusion	16C	9

Buffs Friend's INT, EMP and PIE.

Skill ....Enhancements Casting Time ....3 sec.
Range.....................1000 Duration...........Concent.

Lvl	Spell	Cost	Buff
11	Acuity of the Seer**	4C	21
22	Acuity of the Prophet**	8C	32
31	Acuity of the Sage	11C	41
42	Acuity of the Magi	15C	52

Buffs Friend's Spirit resistance.

Skill ....Enhancements Casting Time ....3 sec.
Range.....................1000 Duration...........Concent.

Lvl	Spell	Cost	Buff
24	Spiritual Shield**	8C	8
36	Spiritual Guard	13C	16
47	Spiritual Barrier	17C	24

Buffs Friend's Energy resistance.

Skill ....Enhancements Casting Time ....3 sec.
Range.....................1000 Duration...........Concent.

Lvl	Spell	Cost	Buff
27	Energy Shield**	9C	8
37	Energy Guard	13C	16
48	Energy Barrier	18C	24

Buffs Friend's Body resistance.

Skill ....Enhancements Casting Time ....3 sec.
Range.....................1000 Duration...........Concent.

Lvl	Spell	Cost	Buff
23	Shield of Health**	8C	8
33	Guard of Health	12C	16
45	Barrier of Health	16C	24

Smiting

DD.

Skill ....Smiting Dmg Type ....Spirit
Casting Time ....3 sec. Range.....................1350
Duration..................Inst.

Lvl	Spell	Cost	Buff
5	Minor Smite*	4P	17
7	Lesser Smite*	5P	24
9	Smite*	7P	31
13	Major Smite*	9P	41
16	Greater Smite*	11P	52
21	Minor Judgement*	15P	65
27	Lesser Judgement*	19P	85
34	Judgement*	24P	106
42	Greater Judgement*	30P	130
50	Supreme Judgement	37P	153

Stuns target, making him unable to move or perform actions.

Skill ....Smiting Dmg Type ....Spirit
Casting Time .....2.5 sec. Range.....................1000

Lvl	Spell	Cost	Dur
6	Stunning Flash*	4P	3 sec.
15	Stunning Flare*	9P	5 sec.
26	Stunning Glare*	16P	6 sec.
36	Stunning Halo*	23P	8 sec.
46	Stunning Aura	30P	9 sec.

Terrible Hammer

Caster's damage/sec buffed (stacks as group 1).

Skill ....Smiting Dmg Type ....Spirit
Casting Time ....3 sec. Duration.............10 min.

Lvl	Spell	Cost	Buff
1	Hammer of Faith*	2P	1
4	Hammer of the Pious*	3P	1.6
9	Hammer of Devotion*	6P	2.7
14	Hammer of Grace*	9P	3.7
18	Hammer of Justice*	11P	4.6
24	Hammer of Zeal*	15P	5.8
31	Hammer of the Martyr*	19P	7.3
40	Hammer of Holiness*	25P	9.2
50	Hammer of the Sanctified	33P	11.3

AoE DD, centered on Caster, radius 200. You must wait 20 seconds before casting one of these spells again.

Skill ....Smiting Dmg Type ....Spirit
Casting Time ....Shout Duration..................Inst.

Lvl	Spell	Cost	Buff
6	Drive Evil*	5P	21
11	Repel Evil*	9P	34
17	Repulse Evil*	14P	55
22	Dispel Evil*	18P	68
32	Banish Evil*	26P	99
42	Annihilate Evil	35P	130

DD.

Skill ....Smiting Dmg Type ....Spirit
Casting Time ....4 sec. Range.....................1350
Duration..................Inst.

Lvl	Spell	Cost	Buff
5	Holy Anger*	4P	26
8	Greater Holy Anger*	6P	41
12	Holy Rage*	9P	57
16	Greater Holy Rage*	11P	77
21	Holy Wrath*	15P	97
27	Greater Holy Wrath*	19P	128
35	Holy Fury*	25P	164
48	Greater Holy Fury	35P	225

AoE Mesmerize: centered on Caster; target halts all movement and is unable to attack or cast spells; the effect breaks when the target is healed or takes damage; radius 200 wu. You must wait 30 seconds before casting one of these spells again (see p. 367 for Pve/RvR limitations).

Skill ....Smiting Dmg Type ....Spirit
Casting Time ....Shout

Lvl	Spell	Cost	Dur
3	Heavenly Visions*	3P	9 sec.
7	Heavenly Images*	5P	11 sec.
15	Heavenly Mirage*	9P	15 sec.
23	Heavenly Dreams*	14P	19 sec.
34	Heavenly Imagination*	21P	25 sec.
44	Theophany	28P	30 sec.

AoE DD.

Skill ....Smiting Dmg Type ....Spirit
Casting Time ....4 sec. Range.....................1350
Duration..................Inst.

Lvl	Spell	Cost	Dmg	Radius
10	Heavenly Strike*	10P	31	150
20	Heavenly Blast*	21P	62	200
30	Heavenly Bolt*	31P	92	250
39	Heavenly Force*	42P	122	300
49	Heavenly Detonation	54P	153	350

Theurgist

Races

Briton / Avalonian

Titles

Level	Title
5	Theurgist Recruit
10	Journeyman Theurgist
15	Summoner
20	Sapper
25	Engineer
30	Summoner Prime
35	Engineer Prime
40	Combat Engineer
45	Master Summoner
50	Master Theurgist

Skills

Level	Skill
1	Earth Magic
1	Cold Magic
5	Wind Magic
5	Earth Magic Spec.
5	Cold Magic Spec.
5	Wind Magic Spec.

Abilities

Level	Ability
1	Staves
1	Cloth Armor
1	Sprint
5	QuickCast

The Theurgist is a magic user who temporarily summons elemental creatures to battle at his or her beck and call. This, along with an array of magical Enhancement spells, makes the Theurgist a force to be reckoned with.

The Best Part: You have the ability to summon around nine pets to do battle for you. Talk about a helping hand! Also, minor Speed spells make traveling easier, and a pulsing Bladeturn spell comes in handy. All of these are great plusses to being a Theurgist.

The Worst Part: You're pretty fragile. With such low HP, it's not uncommon for Theurgists to be dropped with a single shot in RvR combat.

Race Choices:

Avalonian. Really, Avalonians are generally the best choice for any class that casts spells. Having a naturally high INT gives extra casting power. On the negative side, this race has low STR and CON... but then again, why do you need those? Find yourself a few strong buddies, and you're set.

Stat Choices:

- *CON:* Increasing your constitution as a Theurgist may make you last a bit longer in combat. Remember, though, that any points put into CON are points you can't spend elsewhere. In the life of a Theurgist, this stat really doesn't make that much of difference, anyway.
- *DEX:* Adding more DEX points definitely improves your casting time. If you concentrate on this, make sure you specialize enough in Earth to get the pulsing Bladeturn.
- *INT:* This is where your real power to cast stems from. Any extra points you can spare for INT give you more magical power overall. But, since summoning a pet costs a fixed percentage of your Power, regardless of how much Power you have, extra Power won't give you the ability to summon more pets.

Weapon Choices: Your "weapon" is your magic.

Spec Paths: As a Theurgist, you have 3 different paths from which to choose — Earth, Ice and Wind. You get a base spell line in each area, but you can also acquire a specialization line of spells in each. That's where you get your pets.

- The Earth path is melee-friendly. Your magical enhancements include a damage add spell, and a Bladeturn (which nullifies hits against you). Earth Elementals use melee against their targets, so they are the best pets for this spec.
- The Ice path spells are Direct Damage spells, as well as movement reduction spells. The pets for this spec — Ice Elementals — are somewhat flexible in combat. They can cast spells, but they also have the ability to melee if the target moves close enough to them. These pets offer a decent mixture of both casting and melee. Their melee skills don't quite stack up to those of the Earth Elementals. Nor can Ice Elementals cast as well as the Air Elementals... but it has been rumored that they cast better than they can melee.
- The Wind path includes an Area Effect Mesmerize spell and an insta-cast Direct Damage spell. The Air Elemental pets are casters, plain and simple.

Big Mistakes To Avoid On Character Creation:

- The number one rule: Don't put stat points into stats that you don't use (PIE, EMP, CHA) or into stats you will get very little use from (STR). While putting points into STR might make you hit a little bit harder when you have to go into hand-to-hand combat, you shouldn't have to resort to that very often. If you do, you should have played a tank.
- Not picking a primary path to specialize in will leave you with sub-par pets. Don't try to spread yourself too thinly into too many different areas.

Deciding What You Want Your Role To Be:
As a Theurgist, your main role is inherently to cast spells that summon up pets. You also get a nice line of magical enhancements, or buffs. These allow you to support the tank classes with your buffs, while directly backing up the offense with pets or DD nuke spells.

Plotting Your Future:
Like any other class, know where you want to end up five to ten more levels down the line. Don't concentrate too much on any one thing at the expense of something else.

Grouping:

- Your focus in a group should be to keep your fellow group members buffed.
- Truly, one of your best assets in a group is your pet-summoning ability. Since you can often solo orange and red con mobs, the group can pull mobs they're not really sure about, and if things turn bad, fall back on your summoning ability and use pets to help defeat the mob.
- Don't forget about other players — remember if they die, then you're probably next. Keep an eye on your protectors and try to assist them however you can.
- The ability to AoE mesmerize with the Wind specialization can make a group pretty deadly. This is especially true when you have missile-like pets to send after helpless victims.

Soloing:

- Pets are your best friends if you're a solo Theurgist. You can pull up to red con mobs with the help of many pets. But, you still have to be careful because pets do not hold aggros very well. If they are overcome and the mob comes after you, you'd better get out of the way because your low HP curse is about to haunt you.
- One strategy that is pretty common is to cast three pets, move back, cast three more pets, and move back yet again (depending on mob level). When the mob switches aggro from your pets to you, start nuking it.

Realm Versus Realm:

- Eliminate the enemy by any means necessary. If you're defending a keep, you can buff the guards with haste and damage add, as well as casting nuke spells or sending pets in from the battlements.
- During the takeover of an enemy's keep, casting haste on friendly players can help them take the doors down faster. Also, don't forget your pets — you can set them onto the door to lend a helping hand.
- Sending all your pets at one target can almost ensure death for the enemy, but you may have to worry about the numerous players who are out for revenge.
- Distributing your pets evenly among different targets who are casters can cause confusion, as well as prevent them from casting

Beginner's Tips:

- Your pets will die in about 30 seconds regardless of being hit. For this reason, make sure you put enough points into Earth and INT to acquire the pulsing Bladeturn spell.
- Your pet can't go anywhere that a normal player can't go.
- Remember, your job is to cast spells.

Advanced Techniques:

- Keep your group buffed with Bladeturns and Earthen Burst, while slowing your opponents' attack speeds.
- Planning and coordination. Coordinate with your group first, then let the other guys have it! And you've got it all, if you can plan it right: buffs, debuffs, mezzes, pets and DD all in one glorious package.

Theurgist Spells

Path of Earth

Buffs Caster's AF.
Skill ....2/3 Spec Dmg Type...........Matter
Casting Time ....3 sec. Duration............15 min.

Lvl	Spell	Cost	Buff
1	Amethyst Shield	2P	13
3	Amethyst Shield (Enhanced)	3P	22
5	Ruby Shield	4P	32
9	Ruby Shield (Enhanced)	6P	51
13	Cobalt Shield	8P	71
18	Cobalt Shield (Enhanced)	11P	95
24	Emerald Shield	15P	124
31	Emerald Shield (Enhanced)	19P	158
40	Diamond Shield	25P	201
50	Diamond Shield (Enhanced)	33P	250

Friend's damage/sec buffed (stacks as group 1).
Skill ....Earth Dmg Type...........Matter
Casting Time ....3 sec. Range.....................1000
Duration.............10 min.

Lvl	Spell	Cost	Buff
4	Minor Earthen Power	3P	1.6
8	Earthen Power	5P	2.5
11	Greater Earthen Power	7P	3.1
15	Minor Earthen Burst	9P	3.9
20	Earthen Burst	12P	5
26	Great Earthen Burst	16P	6.3
34	Earthen Fury	21P	7.9
44	Greater Earthen Fury	28P	10

Non-magical damage to Caster reduced by (Bonus %).
Skill ....Earth Dmg Type...........Matter
Casting Time ....3 sec. Duration............15 min.

Lvl	Spell	Cost	Bonus %
30	Buffer of Earth	19P	5%
41	Buffer of Stone	26P	10%

Abrasion

Calls temporary pet (Earth), up to 88% of Caster's level.
Skill ....Earth Casting Time ....3 sec.
Range.....................1875 Duration ....30 sec.

Lvl	Spell	Cost	Max Lvl
1	Call Minor Earth Elemental	15%P	10
7	Call Lesser Earth Elemental	12%P	15
12	Call Earth Elemental	12%P	25
20	Call Potent Earth Elemental	12%P	37
32	Call Mighty Earth Elemental	12%P	50

Bladeturn: Absorbs damage of single hit.
Skill ....Earth Dmg Type...........Matter
Casting Time ....4 sec. Range.....................1250 (except Lvl 2)

Lvl	Spell	Cost	Dur	Target
2	Skin of Dust	8%P	Until Hit	Self
10	Skin of Sand	8%P	Until Hit	Friend
18	Skin of Earth	12%P	Until Hit	Group
26	Skin of Rock[1]	16P, 4P/10s	Chant+10	Group
35	Skin of Stone[2]	22P, 5P/8s	Chant+8	Group
45	Skin of Diamond[3]	29P, 7P/6s	Chant+6	Group

[1] Absorbs first hit every 10 sec.
[2] Absorbs first hit every 8 sec.
[3] Absorbs first hit every 6 sec.

Debuffs attack speed by (Debuff %).
Skill ....Earth Dmg Type ....Spirit
Casting Time .....3.5 sec. Range.....................1500
Duration...............2 min.

Lvl	Spell	Cost	Debuff %
3	Minor Friction	3P	5.5%
8	Lesser Friction	5P	7%
14	Friction	9P	9%
21	Major Friction	13P	11%
28	Greater Friction	17P	13%
37	Superior Friction	23P	16%
47	Paralyzing Friction	30P	19%

Path of Ice

DD.
Skill.........................Cold Dmg Type................Cold
Casting Time .....2.6 sec. Range.....................1500
Duration.................Inst.

Lvl	Spell	Cost	Dmg
1	Ice Cloud (Minor)	2P	5
2	Ice Cloud	2P	9
3	Ice Cloud (Greater)	3P	14
6	Ice Cloud (Potent)	4P	26
9	Glittering Ice Cloud (Lesser)	6P	37
13	Glittering Ice Cloud	8P	49
17	Glittering Ice Cloud (Major)	10P	65
24	Ice Blast (Minor)	15P	89
33	Ice Blast	21P	120
41	Ice Blast (Potent)	26P	148
50	Ice Blast (Major)	33P	180

Root: Enemy speed debuffed to 1% of original movement.
Skill.........................Cold Dmg Type................Cold
Casting Time .....2.5 sec. Range.....................1500

Lvl	Spell	Cost	Dur
5	Cold's Bitter Grip (Lesser)	4P	16 sec.
10	Cold's Bitter Grip	6P	23 sec.
16	Cold's Bitter Grip (Greater)	10P	30 sec.
22	Fingers Of Ice (Lesser)	13P	38 sec.
30	Fingers Of Ice	19P	49 sec.
39	Fingers Of Ice (Greater)	25P	60 sec.
49	Anchor Of Ice	32P	73 sec.

Refrigeration

DD, Snare: enemy's speed debuffed to 65% of original movement.
Skill.........................Cold Dmg Type................Cold
Casting Time ....3 sec. Range.....................1500
Duration ....30 sec.

Lvl	Spell	Cost	Dmg
2	Frost Blast	2P	9
5	Chilling Blast	4P	21
9	Frigid Blast	6P	37
12	Snow Blast	8P	49
17	Ice Blast	10P	65
24	Winter Blast	15P	89
33	Auroral Blast	21P	120
41	Hibernal Blast	26P	148
50	Arctic Blast	33P	180

Calls temporary pet (Ice), up to 88% of Caster's level.
Skill.........................Cold Casting Time ....3 sec.
Range.....................1875 Duration ....25 sec.

Lvl	Spell	Cost	Max Lvl
1	Summon Minor Ice Spirit	15%P	10
7	Summon Lesser Ice Spirit	12%P	15
13	Summon Ice Spirit	12%P	25
18	Summon Aged Ice Spirit	12%P	37
25	Summon Elder Ice Spirit	12%P	50

AoE Root: Enemy speed debuffed to 1% of original movement, radius of 350 wu.
Skill.........................Cold Dmg Type................Cold
Casting Time .....2.5 sec. Range.....................1500

Lvl	Spell	Cost	Dur
4	Field of Frost	3P	15 sec.
10	Field of Slush	6P	23 sec.
16	Field of Snow	10P	30 sec.
20	Field of Ice	12P	36 sec.
30	Floe of Snow	19P	49 sec.
39	Floe of Ice	25P	60 sec.
49	Expanse of Ice	32P	73 sec.

Path of Air

Buffs friend's attack speed by (Buff %).

Skill .... Wind Dmg Type .... Spirit
Casting Time ..... 3.5 sec. Range 1500
Duration .... 10 min.

Lvl	Spell	Cost	Buff %
5	Bolstering Gust (Minor)	4P	13%
9	Bolstering Gust	6P	15%
14	Bolstering Gust (Major)	9P	18%
21	Bolstering Storm (Minor)	13P	22%
28	Bolstering Storm	17P	26%
38	Bolstering Storm (Major)	24P	32%
49	Bolstering Storm (Greater)	32P	39%

Group Speed Buff by (Speed %).

Skill .... Wind Dmg Type .... Spirit
Cost .... none Casting Time .... 3 sec.
Range .... 2000 Duration .... Chant + 6

Lvl	Spell	Speed %
6	Brisk Wind (Minor)	24%
16	Brisk Wind	32%
26	Lissome Wind (Minor)	39%
36	Lissome Wind	47%
46	Lissome Wind (Major)	54%

Vapormancy

Calls temporary pet (Air), up to 88% of Caster's level.

Skill .... Wind Casting Time .... 3 sec.
Range .... 1875 Duration .... 20 sec.

Lvl	Spell	Cost	Max Lvl
1	Call Lesser Air Sprite	15%P	10
7	Call Minor Air Sprite	12%P	15
12	Call Air Sprite	12%P	25
20	Call Potent Air Sprite	12%P	37
32	Call Mighty Air Sprite	12%P	50

AoE Mesmerize: target halts all movement and is unable to attack or cast spells; the effect breaks when the target is healed or takes damage (see page 367 for PvE/RvR limitations).

Skill .... Wind Dmg Type .... Spirit
Casting Time .... 3 sec. Range 1250
Radius 300

Lvl	Spell	Cost	Dur
4	Confusing Gust (Minor)	3P	10 sec.
13	Confusing Gust	8P	14 sec.
21	Confusing Gust (Major)	13P	18 sec.
30	Confusing Wind (Minor)	19P	23 sec.
39	Confusing Wind	25P	27 sec.
49	Confusing Storm	32P	32 sec.

DD.

Skill .... Wind Dmg Type .... Spirit
Casting Time ..... 2.8 sec. Range 1500
Duration .... Inst.

Lvl	Spell	Cost	Dmg
2	Blasting Breeze	2P	11
5	Blasting Gust	4P	26
8	Blasting Winds	5P	41
11	Blasting Gale	7P	51
16	Blasting Squall	10P	77
22	Blasting Storm	13P	103
28	Blasting Cyclone	17P	133
35	Blasting Tempest	22P	164
45	Blasting Maelstrom	29P	210

Sorcerer

Races

Briton / Avalonian / Saracen

Skills

Level	Skill
1	Matter Magic
1	Body Magic
5	Mind Magic
5	Matter Magic Spec.
5	Body Magic Spec.
5	Mind Magic Spec.

Abilities

Level	Ability
1	Staves
1	Cloth Armor
1	Sprint
5	QuickCast

Titles

Level	Title
5	Apprentice Sorcerer/Sorceress
10	Journeyman Sorcerer/Sorceress
15	Befuddler
20	Charmer
25	Confuser
30	Malefice
35	Entrancer
40	Enigmatic
45	Sorcerer/Sorceress
50	Sorcerer Primus/ Sorceress Prime

Sorcerers are perhaps the most feared class in the game. Swords and bows? Who needs them, when a Sorcerer can mez an entire group at twenty paces and let the fighters whale away while the tanks absorb all the damage? The Sorcerer is a highly viable soloing class and a welcome addition to any group. Disposable charmed pets, character longevity, okay melee skills for most of the game and the ability to exert a mesmerizing influence on a crowd make this an enjoyable and functional class.

The Best Part: Regardless of all else, you wield some of the most powerful abilities in all the lands. The class has many abilities, so whether solo, in a group, or in the frontier hunting other players, you always have skills to bring to the table. You also don't have to fork over a lot of cash for armor, weapons or arrows.

The Worst Part: As a caster, you are everyone's number one target. Plus, many of your abilities (Charm, Confusion, etc.) have NO effect on enemy players. Though you wield much power, a group must learn to follow your guidelines in hunting or your abilities could be wasted.

Race Choices:

Briton. Possesses more STR and CON than either of the other two races. Better for characters you intend to take into melee more often, or if you just want more HP.

Avalonian. Most INT (a casting advantage), but low STR and CON/HP. Also very tall.

Saracen. High DEX, but less INT, and thus, lesser casting power.

- You can acquire bonus items to offset your race's weaknesses if you don't want to put more points into a particular attribute.

Stat Choices: Of utmost importance are INT and CON. INT earns you Power, and Power is what makes a spellcaster shine. CON earns you HP. These two attributes are normally inversely related. If you have high INT, your CON is likely to be low.

- *INT:* Vital stat, since INT affects casting mana. Put at least 10 points into this, perhaps even 15 for a weaker race.
- *DEX:* Important — affects casting time.
- *QUI:* Helps you swing a staff for those occasional melee fights.

Weapon Choices:

- *Staff:* No debate here. You will take your staff and (not) like it!
- Your "other weapons" are spells and pets.

Spec Paths: As a sorcerer, you get to experiment with three different types of magic.

- *Body:* Draining the life of others, debilitating their body and doing raw damage.
- *Matter:* Slowly destroying a target with Damage-over-Time (DoT) spells.
- *Mind:* The real mark of the Sorcerer; destruction and control of an enemy's mental faculties.

The Mind line is unique to the Sorcerer. One common strategy is to choose Body for damage spells and rooting spells, or Mind for charming pets and Mez capabilities. Focus on one of your two choices fairly heavily and dump all remaining points into the other until you break at least 30 in each. This is not the ONLY path, but it is safe and reliable. The playstyles are quite a bit different depending on which you focus on, but in the end they all even out. The thing to do is keep in mind the general playstyle you can expect from each of the lines and choose accordingly.
(Body: stop the enemy in their tracks and blast them with high damage spells. Mind: charm a pet and send it to your foes, then assist it with your other abilities. Matter: cast a spell on your opponent that does damage each combat round until the spell ends.) Currently, Matter can somewhat enhance either of the other 2 lines, but really cannot stand on its own as a primary focus of the character.

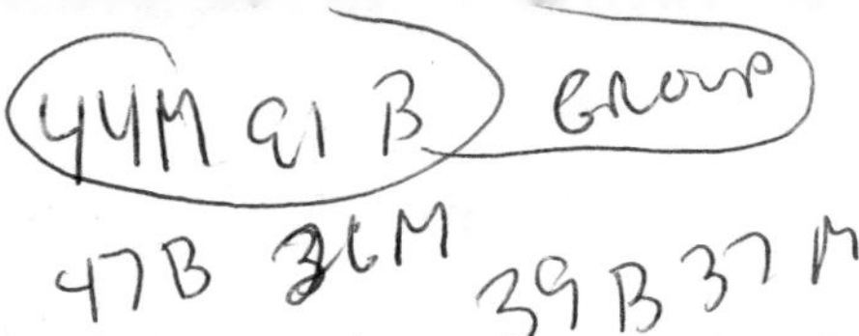

Big Mistakes To Avoid On Character Creation:

- *Body Spec:* Don't forget basic abilities. Use all your tools and you'll be more than a Root and Blast Wizard with weak damage capability.
- *Mind Spec:* Spec wisely and always charm a pet up to your level. If you let your Mind spec slip and it's your primary, you could have pets a few levels lower than you, and not enough firepower in other lines to compensate.
- *Matter Spec:* You'll have a rough ride with this as your primary focus. This may change, but for now, Matter is just not enough to depend on.
- Whatever you do, do NOT 100% spec in one line. It's harmful to the Power level of the class, and takes away a lot of the variety this class brings with it. A balanced approach across all three ensures you can do a bit of just about everything. Sorcerers are not specialist casters, but the supreme generalists!

Deciding What You Want Your Role To Be: Pet caster or not? To hunt reliably with pets, you must give major focus to your Mind spec throughout your career. If you make this decision late (level 8 or above), you could play a major game of catch-up for even level pets.

Plotting Your Future: Again, even level pets or not? Everything else is pure preference, but acquiring even pets requires a very strict adherence and dedication to the Mind spec path.

Grouping: You are the MASTER of crowd control. Groups love your ability to control the crowd and confuse enemy creatures. Control the mob and manage aggro. Then the fighters and damage-dealing casters can do their jobs (with your damaging spells).

- All group encounters can be turned into single encounters with your abilities.
- You only see your fullest potential if others learn to work within the rules you create for encounters. No one is more suited to call the shots than the Sorcerer. You can select what enemy to fight and when, since you can best control the pace of that enemy. To see your real power, take charge, or be with people who are well versed in your abilities and how not to hinder them.

Soloing: One of the best solo hunters in the game.

- The target to hunt is anything you can charm.
- Body DD spells used to get bonus damage on most Undead. They may again someday....
- If you're Mind spec, hunt where your pets can be recycled quickly. They are disposable!
- Unlike most other classes, pulling groups is preferable to the Sorcerer, even when solo. Grouped and linked enemies provide bonus experience since you must deal with more than one at a time. (But we can single them out for sequential solo encounters!)
- If your pet gets too injured, release him and charm another monster in the group instead.
- If a creature turns on you, cast Amnesia on it and let your pet make a few attacks to gain the aggro. Then, attack the creature to attract its attention. Cast Amnesia again and let the pet attack. This way, both of you have time to recover.
- If you have to make a run for your life, leave your pet behind to fight. AoE root spell, Amnesia on the group, and an AoE mez. Your pet earns XP while you make a break for it.
- You can't heal your pet or make it rest.
- With a pet, mobs often summon friends to help.
- Pets run faster with a speed buff.

Realm Versus Realm: Pets are powerful in RvR, and there are other things you bring to the table.

- There's a welcome group run Song.
- Amnesia has one of the longest ranges in the game, and can interrupt casters and archers.
- Mez is the single most potent battle tool.
- Sorcerers die, and they die FAST. Sometimes you don't even get one Mez off. But when you do, it can sway the tide of battle.
- Confusion does not work on PCs, but it DOES work on their pets.
- The only thing more devastating than a well-placed Mez is a stealthed Rogue. Always watch your back.

Beginner's Tips:

- Hunt lots of humanoid monsters. Especially if you can charm them.
- Pets can only go where normal players can.
- Do NOT forget to get decent armor, and swing that staff from time to time. Through level 10 or so, you can dish out about as much damage in melee as many grunt types, especially after you land some debuffs on them.
- Don't cast any DoT spell immediately after Amnesia. The monster may aggro on you.

- If many of your spells are being resisted, you may want to abandon the fight. Several resists in row can spell disaster for you.
- You may not want to use life drain spells if you're healthy. They do damage, but cost a bit more Mana compared to other DD spells.
- Even though you're limited to cloth armor, don't neglect armor. Some attacks are affected by armor levels. And grey con armor leaves you vulnerable, even if it has bonuses.

Advanced Techniques: Too many to list. The only real advice is to constantly experiment. With the tools available, the combinations and strategies you can put together are amazing.

Sorcerer's Spells

Body Destruction

DD, with (Drain %) of damage drained from target to Caster.

Skill........................Body Dmg Type...............Body
Casting Time .....2.5 sec. Range.....................1500
Duration..................Inst.

Lvl	Spell	Cost	Dmg	Drain %
1	Minor Vitality Drain	2P	5	30%
2	Lesser Vitality Drain	2P	8	30%
3	Vitality Drain	3P	12	30%
5	Greater Vitality Drain	4P	18	30%
7	Major Vitality Drain	5P	25	30%
10	Minor Essence Consumption	6P	32	30%
14	Lesser Essence Consumption	9P	45	30%
18	Essence Consumption	11P	59	40%
23	Greater Essence Consumption	14P	73	40%
28	Major Essence Consumption	17P	90	50%
35	Increased Essence Consumption	22P	110	50%
45	Superior Essence Consumption	29P	141	60%

STR debuff.

Skill........................Body Dmg Type...............Body
Casting Time ....2 sec. Range.....................1500
Duration ....60 sec.

Lvl	Spell	Cost	Debuff
4	Fatigue Body	3P	6.5
8	Debilitate Body	5P	8
12	Weaken Body	8P	9.5
17	Deteriorate Body	10P	11.5
22	Enfeeble Body	13P	13.5
29	Degenerate Body	18P	16.5
37	Cripple Body	23P	19.5
46	Dilapidate Body	30P	23

Root: Enemy speed debuffed to 1% of original movement.

Skill........................Body Dmg Type...............Body
Casting Time .....2.5 sec. Range.....................1500

Lvl	Spell	Cost	Dur
3	Minor Crippling*	2P	9 sec.
6	Lesser Crippling*	3P	13 sec.
13	Cripple*	6P	23 sec.
19	Major Crippling*	9P	31 sec.
26	Greater Crippling*	12P	41 sec.
31	Leg Twist*	15P	48 sec.
40	Greater Leg Twist*	20P	61 sec.
49	Superior Leg Twisting	25P	73 sec.

Disorientation

DD.

Skill........................Body Dmg Type..............Spirit
Casting Time .....2.8 sec. Range.....................1500
Duration..................Inst.

Lvl	Spell	Cost	Dmg
1	Lesser Mind Jolt	2P	5
4	Mind Jolt	3P	21
8	Lesser Mind Blast	5P	41
12	Mind Blast	8P	57
16	Lesser Mind Scream	10P	77
22	Mind Scream	13P	103
28	Lesser Mind Shriek	17P	133
35	Mind Shriek	22P	164
45	Mind Flay	29P	210

AoE DEX/QUI debuff, radius 250 wu.

Skill........................Body Dmg Type...............Body
Casting Time ....3 sec. Range.....................1500
Duration...............2 min.

Lvl	Spell	Cost	Debuff
3	Minor Imbalance	2P	9
7	Lesser Imbalance	4P	11
15	Imbalance	7P	16.5
21	Greater Imbalance	10P	19.5
29	Major Imbalance	14P	24.5
37	Critical Imbalance	18P	29
47	Superior Imbalance	24P	35

Root: Enemy speed debuffed to 1% of original movement.

Skill........................Body Dmg Type...............Body
Casting Time .....2.5 sec. Range.....................1500 (except Lvl 20: (1))

Lvl	Spell	Cost	Dur	Area
20	Lesser Body Lock	12P	36 sec.	(1)
30	Body Lock	19P	49 sec.	Radius 350
39	Greater Body Lock	25P	60 sec.	Radius 350
49	Superior Body Lock	32P	73 sec.	Radius 350

Heat resistance debuff.

Skill........................Body Casting Time ....2 sec.
Range.....................1500 Duration ....15 sec.

Lvl	Spell	Cost	Debuff %
23	Illusions of Flame	11P	7.5%
33	Visions of Flame	16P	15%
44	Dreams of Flame	22P	25%

Cold resistance debuff.

Skill........................Body Casting Time ....2 sec.
Range.....................1500 Duration ....15 sec.

Lvl	Spell	Cost	Debuff %
24	Illusions of Winter	12P	7.5%
34	Visions of Winter	16P	15%
46	Dreams of Winter	24P	25%

Matter resistance debuff.

Skill........................Body Casting Time ....2 sec.
Range.....................1500 Duration ....15 sec.

Lvl	Spell	Cost	Debuff %
27	Illusions of the Wastes	13P	7.5%
36	Visions of the Wastes	18P	15%
48	Dreams of the Wastes	24P	25%

Core Matters

Buffs Caster's AF.

Skill ....2/3 Spec Dmg Type............Matter
Casting Time ....4 sec. Duration.............15 min.

Lvl	Spell	Cost	Buff
1	Ward Blow	2P	13
4	Fend Blow	3P	27
6	Dampen Blow	4P	37
9	Deflect Blow	6P	51
14	Ward Offense	9P	75
20	Fend Offense	12P	104
28	Dampen Offense	17P	143
38	Deflect Offense	24P	191
48	Nullify Offense	31P	240

Non-magical damage to Caster reduced by (Bonus %).

Skill.....................Matter Dmg Type............Matter
Casting Time ....3 sec. Duration.............15 min.

Lvl	Spell	Cost	Bonus %
30	Dampening Ward	19P	5%
41	Nullifying Ward	26P	10%

DoT: inflicts (Dmg) every 5 seconds.
Skill.....................Matter   Dmg Type............Matter
Casting Time ....3 sec.   Range.....................1500
Duration ....20 sec.

Lvl	Spell	Cost	Dmg
2	Corrosive Mist	3P	4
3	Corrosive Fog	4P	6
5	Corrosive Cloud	6P	9
7	Corrosive Smoke	7P	13
10	Dissolving Mist	10P	17
13	Dissolving Fog	13P	23
16	Dissolving Cloud	15P	29
21	Dissolving Smoke	20P	37
27	Disintegrating Fog	26P	49
35	Disintegrating Cloud	35P	63
44	Disintegrating Smoke	45P	79

Bladeturn: Absorbs damage of single hit.
Skill.....................Matter   Dmg Type............Matter
Casting Time ....4 sec.   Duration.............10 min.

Lvl	Spell	Cost	Target
19	Barrier of Warding	8%P	Self

DEX debuff.
Skill.....................Matter   Dmg Type..............Spirit
Casting Time ....2 sec.   Range.....................1500
Duration ....60 sec.

Lvl	Spell	Cost	Debuff
8	Mystic Web	5P	8
12	Mystic Trap	6P	9.5
17	Mystic Net	9P	11.5
23	Magical Web	11P	14
29	Magical Trap	14P	16.5
36	Magical Net	17P	19
46	Sorcerous Web	22P	23

Telekinesis

DoT: inflicts (Dmg) every 4 seconds.
Skill.....................Matter   Dmg Type............Matter
Casting Time ....3 sec.   Range.....................1500
Duration ....24 sec.

Lvl	Spell	Cost	Dmg
1	Lesser Abrasive Force	2P	2
3	Abrasive Force	4P	6
5	Lesser Grinding Force	6P	9
7	Grinding Force	7P	13
10	Lesser Pounding Force	10P	17
13	Pounding Force	13P	23
16	Lesser Crushing Force	15P	29
21	Crushing Force	20P	37
27	Lesser Pulverizing Force	26P	49
35	Pulverizing Force	35P	63
44	Lesser Disintegrating Force	45P	79
50	Disintegrating Force	52P	89

DEX/QUI debuff.
Skill.....................Matter   Dmg Type..............Spirit
Casting Time ....2 sec.   Range.....................1500
Duration ....60 sec.

Lvl	Spell	Cost	Debuff
4	Minor Mesh of Force	3P	9.5
8	Mesh of Force	5P	12
9	Major Mesh of Force	5P	12.5
14	Minor Net of Force	7P	15.5
19	Net of Force	9P	18.5
25	Major Net of Force	12P	22.5
36	Minor Web of Force	17P	28.5
46	Major Web of Force	22P	34.5

Mind Twisting

Confusion: (Switch %) chance to switch targets; (Ally %) chance to attack own ally.
Skill ....Mind   Dmg Type ....Spirit
Casting Time .....2.5 sec.   Range.....................1500

Lvl	Spell	Cost	Dur	Switch %	Ally %
2	Confuse Mind	1P	14 sec.	70%	0%
7	Befuddle Mind	4P	24 sec.	85%	0%
13	Obscure Mind	6P	36 sec.	100%	0%
20	Mystify Mind	9P	50 sec.	100%	15%
27	Muddle Mind	13P	64 sec.	100%	30%
34	Perplex Mind	16P	78 sec.	100%	45%
41	Darken Mind	20P	1.5 min.	100%	60%
48	Paradox Mind	24P	1.8 min.	100%	75%

Mesmerize: target halts all movement and is unable to attack or cast spells; the effect breaks when the target is healed or takes damage (see page 367 for PvE/RvR limitations).
Skill ....Mind   Dmg Type ....Spirit
Casting Time ....3 sec.   Range.....................1500

Lvl	Spell	Cost	Dur
1	Minor Mesmerization	2P	16 sec.
5	Lesser Mesmerization	3P	21 sec.
9	Mesmerization	5P	26 sec.
15	Major Mesmerization	8P	34 sec.
23	Greater Mesmerization	11P	44 sec.
31	Fascination	15P	55 sec.
40	Greater Fascination	19P	67 sec.
50	Superior Fascination	23P	80 sec.

Amnesia: Enemies in area have (Forget %) chance to forget they hate each person on their hate list.
Skill ....Mind   Dmg Type ....Spirit
Casting Time ....2 sec.   Range.....................2300
Duration ....Inst.

Lvl	Spell	Cost	Forget %	Area
8	Inflict Minor Forgetfulness	4P	70%	(1)
17	Inflict Forgetfulness	8P	77%	100 radius
28	Inflict Minor Amnesia	16P	84%	175 radius
37	Inflict Amnesia	27P	91%	250 radius
49	Inflict Oblivion	37P	100%	325 radius

Group Speed Buff: buffs by (Speed %).
Skill ....Mind   Dmg Type ....Spirit
Cost...........................0P   Casting Time ....3 sec.
Range.....................2000   Duration ....Chant + 6

Lvl	Spell	Speed %
6	Amplify Movement	24%
16	Amplify Running	32%
26	Amplify Coordination	39%
36	Amplify Equilibrium	47%
46	Amplify Balance	54%

Domination

Charms creature up to 100% of Caster's level.
Skill ....Mind   Dmg Type ....Spirit
Cost......................25%P   Casting Time ....4 sec.
Range.....................1000   Duration ....Until Neg.

Lvl	Spell	Max Lvl	Targets
1	Persuade Will	10	Human-like
7	Coerce Will	15	Above + animals
12	Compel Will	26	Above + insects
20	Control Will	40	Above + magical creatures
32	Wrest Will	50	Same as above

AoE STR/CON debuff, radius 250 wu.
Skill ....Mind   Casting Time ....3 sec.
Range.....................1500   Duration...............2 min.

Lvl	Spell	Cost	Debuff
2	Banish Will	1P	8
6	Banish Motivation	3P	10.5
11	Banish Conviction	5P	13.5
18	Banish Dedication	8P	18
25	Banish Faith	12P	22.5
33	Banish Confidence	16P	27
43	Banish Hope	21P	33

AoE Mesmerize: each target halts all movement and is unable to attack or cast spells; the effect breaks when the target is healed or takes damage (see page 367 for PvE/RvR limitations).
Skill ....Mind   Dmg Type ....Spirit
Casting Time ....3 sec.   Range.....................1500

Lvl	Spell	Cost	Dur	Radius
4	Fog of Senility	3P	20 sec.	200
14	Blanket of Senility	7P	33 sec.	250
24	Cloud of Senility	12P	46 sec.	300
34	Veil of Senility	16P	59 sec.	350
44	Shroud of Senility	21P	72 sec.	400

Wizard

Race		Skills	
Avalonian		1	Earth Magic
Titles		1	Cold Magic
		5	Fire Magic
5	Apprentice Wizard/Wizardress	5	Earth Magic Spec.
		5	Cold Magic Spec.
10	Wizard/Wizardress Adept	5	Fire Magic Spec.
15	Elementalist	**Abilities**	
20	Spellbinder		
25	Magus/Magess	1	Staves
30	Invoker	1	Cloth Armor
35	Thaumaturge	1	Sprint
40	Master Elementalist	4	QuickCast
45	Master Spellbinder		
50	Magus/Magess Prime		

The Wizard is primarily a Direct-Damage-dealing class. Spells are your livelihood, and your physical skills are your bane.

The Best Part: You get to deal pure, undiluted damage rapidly, with devastating effect. Tanks and other casters are constantly in awe of your damage-dealing capabilities. Best nuker in the realm.

The Worst Part: You have an incredible lack of versatility. Your ability to do damage is your sole purpose in life.

Race Choices:

Avalonian. Most Intelligence of any race by 20 points. Low STR/CON. Tall.

Saracen. High DEX (big plus), but less STR and CON than Britons.

Briton. More STR/CON than Avalonian or Saracen.

Stat Choices:

- *INT:* Very important for casting; put as many points into this stat as you can spare.
- *DEX:* Higher DEX reduces casting time.
- *STR:* Good for Staves and for carrying loot, but not as important as INT or DEX.
- *CON:* Good for more HP (good for survival).
- For Avalonians, put 20 points into INT and 10 into DEX (higher DEX reduces casting time). Or, try 10 INT, 10 DEX and 10 in either STR or CON.
- For Saracen or Briton, put at least 20 points into Intelligence and balance out DEX.

Weapon Choices:

- *Staff:* Only weapon of choice as a Wizard, and you can't train in it. So, melee skills are obsolete around level 20 (if not earlier). Focus staves, though, significantly reduce the mana cost of spells if level-appropriate.
- If you primarily spec in Fire or Ice, you want the best staff you can get for that sphere of magic. It should con orange to you — if not red for an odd level (current decay rates mean that the condition will not deteriorate too fast even if red). When it gets below 90% Condition (85% minimum, repair it).

Spec Paths:

- *Fire:* Main damage line. Comes with two bolts on separate timers, good damage and ranged Area of Effect spell (Pyromancy).
- *Ice:* Great DD spells, including one with a snare. Potent point blank (centered on caster) is good as well. Respectable damage line, but not quite as good as Fire.
- *Earth:* Biggest drawback is that you don't get any DD spells. Shielding spells no longer depend on this specification. The best thing you get out of Earth is a few weapon damage buffs (keeps damage variance at a minimum).
- Max out Fire or Ice (not both), and put half-level spec points into Earth at levels 40 to 50.

Big Mistakes To Avoid On Character Creation: Starting with low Intelligence, putting points into Empathy or Charisma, or failing to choose Elementalist as a starting profession.

Deciding What You Want Your Role To Be: Little choice here — you are a damage dealer!

Plotting Your Future: Your path is well-mapped since you don't specialize in multiple things until after level 40.

- Keep pumping points into either Fire or Ice.
- The only thing to really think about before level 40 is what armor you want to wear in RvR for resist modifier purposes.
- Hold off on buying armor as long as you can, save your money, and buy something that's player crafted.
- Estimate when your focus staff will con blue. Know how much a replacement costs, or where to find a good drop. Just bear in mind you don't get bonuses with items until later.

Grouping: Your role is to deal damage — large amounts of it through DD spells.

- You partner well with most classes, except for Clerics.
- Damage you do to a mob can draw aggro. Make sure you aren't hurting the mob the most. Stand back as far back as you can and find a tank to protect you.
- If you're higher in level than others in the group, try lower-level DD spells early, finishing off with big blasts. Forget Bolts in large battles, since they'll often be blocked.

Combining your skills with others:

- If you can't manage aggro, the group is at a disadvantage. It's hard to monitor Health/healing spells; but, if you aggro too early, you either die or waste healers' mana.
- With a decent root spell, you can perform partial crowd control if the mob doesn't have spells or ranged weapons.
- Weapon damage add and damage shield cost a lot of mana and don't last long. Keep these up on one person, but not everyone, for the benefit of the group.
- Keep Shield spells up at all times, including Bladeturn (gained at 19).
- When not casting, sit down and regain mana. Don't try to melee.
- Watch for roamers and rest in safe places.

Soloing: Soloing can be easy and quick if you keep the target(s) out of melee range. In the case of casters or archers, don't let them interrupt your casting. The rule is, don't let the enemy get to you.

- Bolt, Blast, Root, Run, Blast, Blast... if a mob isn't dead at the end of this sequence, you had better be able to outrun it.
- Use your external camera to look back as you run. Don't run too far, or the critter will go "home" and possibly return with friends.

Best things to solo: Everything depends on what element you're casting. Learn what's vulnerable to Ice or Fire — e.g., snakes and basilisks don't like Cold damage. You can tackle much higher mobs relative to your level if they are weak to your strengths.

Realm Versus Realm:

- Bolts are nice and have range, but are reduced by armor absorption. Good for caster battles, but ineffective for melee or against chainmail.
- Area of Effect spells are nice, but if they hit rooted or mezzed opponents, the opponents re-enter combat.
- DD spells are your mainstay — hit fast and hit hard.
- Stay within casting range of healers.
- Aggro rules do not apply in RvR. If enemy tanks aren't after healers, they're after you.
- RvR is a team system. Again, your purpose is to do maximum damage without worrying about NPC aggro. Out of mana means out of the fight.
- Keep Bladeturn up at all times.

Beginner's Tips:

- Forget dungeon exploration — even a green mob can take you down fast.
- Your Liquification line has a lot of DD spells that damage and snare a mob.
- If mana drops to about one-third, regeneration takes longer.
- To learn spell ranges, practice on a guard. Face him and try to cast a spell. Keep backing off casting until you get a message saying the target is out of range. Pinning down range can mean getting off extra spells before the enemy closes.

Advanced Techniques:

- Aggroing is a very real threat. Except in very early levels, a Wizard can't take much damage due to their low Armor Factor, absorption and HP.
- If you've spec'ed Fire, Fireball is the best way to attract Monsters from the maximum possible distance. Then throw your highest damage spell and finish them off with another, or freeze them and run for another round.
- If a Monster doesn't have many HP left, you can melee by keeping your best shield up and buffing your weapon with Earth Magic *at all times.*

Wizard Spells

Path of Earth

Buffs Caster's AF.
Skill ....2/3 Spec Dmg Type............Matter
Casting Time ....3 sec. Duration.............15 min.

Lvl	Spell	Cost	Buff
1	Amethyst Shield	2P	13
3	Amethyst Shield (Enhanced)	3P	22
5	Ruby Shield	4P	32
9	Ruby Shield (Enhanced)	6P	51
13	Cobalt Shield	8P	71
18	Cobalt Shield (Enhanced)	11P	95
24	Emerald Shield	15P	124
31	Emerald Shield (Enhanced)	19P	158
40	Diamond Shield	25P	201
50	Diamond Shield (Enhanced)	33P	250

Friend's damage/sec buffed (stacks as group 1).
Skill ....Earth Dmg Type............Matter
Casting Time ....3 sec. Range......................1000
Duration.............10 min.

Lvl	Spell	Cost	Buff
4	Minor Earthen Power	3P	1.6
8	Earthen Power	5P	2.5
11	Greater Earthen Power	7P	3.1
15	Minor Earthen Burst	9P	3.9
20	Earthen Burst	12P	5
26	Great Earthen Burst	16P	6.3
34	Earthen Fury	21P	7.9
44	Greater Earthen Fury	28P	10

Non-magical damage to Caster reduced by (Bonus %).
Skill ....Earth Dmg Type............Matter
Casting Time ....3 sec. Duration.............15 min.

Lvl	Spell	Cost	Bonus %
30	Buffer of Earth	19P	5%
41	Buffer of Stone	26P	10%

Calefaction

Damage Shield: On Friend (stacks as group 1).
Skill ....Earth Dmg Type...............Heat
Casting Time ....4 sec. Range......................1000
Duration.............10 min.

Lvl	Spell	Cost	Dmg
1	Minor Shield of Magma	2P	0.7
5	Shield of Magma	4P	1.1
9	Greater Shield of Magma	6P	1.4
14	Minor Shell of Magma	9P	1.9
22	Shell of Magma	13P	2.6
33	Greater Shell of Magma	21P	3.6
44	Exalted Magma Shield	28P	4.6

Bolt (ranged DD). You must wait 20 seconds before casting one of these spells again.
Skill ....Earth Dmg Type...............Heat
Casting Time ....4 sec. Range......................1875
Duration..................Inst.

Lvl	Spell	Cost	Dmg
2	Bolt of Lava	2P	16
4	Bolt of Lava (Enhanced)	3P	30
7	Lava Strike	5P	52
12	Lava Strike (Enhanced)	8P	82
17	Lava Force	10P	118
24	Lava Force (Enhanced)	15P	163
31	Lava Strike	19P	207
38	Lava Strike (Enhanced)	24P	259
46	Lava's Fury	30P	309

DD, AoE Snare: enemy's speed debuffed to 65% of original movement; radius 350 wu.
Skill ....Earth Dmg Type...............Heat
Casting Time ....4 sec. Range......................1500
Duration.............30 sec.

Lvl	Spell	Cost	Dmg
8	Molten Earth	7P	25
11	Lava Field	9P	31
15	Expanse of Magma	12P	44
20	Molten Puddle	16P	57
28	Molten Pool	23P	81
36	Molten Lake	30P	103
47	Molten Ocean	40P	134

Path of Ice

DD.
Skill..........................Cold Dmg Type................Cold
Casting Time .....2.6 sec. Range......................1500
Duration..................Inst.

Lvl	Spell	Cost	Dmg
1	Ice Cloud (Minor)	2P	5
2	Ice Cloud	2P	9
3	Ice Cloud (Greater)	3P	14
6	Ice Cloud (Potent)	4P	26
9	Glittering Ice Cloud (Lesser)	6P	37
13	Glittering Ice Cloud	8P	49
17	Glittering Ice Cloud (Major)	10P	65
24	Ice Blast (Minor)	15P	89
33	Ice Blast	21P	120
41	Ice Blast (Potent)	26P	148
50	Ice Blast (Major)	33P	180

Root: Enemy speed debuffed to 1% of original movement.
Skill..........................Cold Dmg Type................Cold
Casting Time .....2.5 sec. Range......................1500

Lvl	Spell	Cost	Dur
5	Cold's Bitter Grip (Lesser)	4P	16 sec.
10	Cold's Bitter Grip	6P	23 sec.
16	Cold's Bitter Grip (Greater)	10P	30 sec.
22	Fingers Of Ice (Lesser)	13P	38 sec.
30	Fingers Of Ice	19P	49 sec.
39	Fingers Of Ice (Greater)	25P	60 sec.
49	Anchor Of Ice	32P	73 sec.

Liquifaction

AoE DD centered on Caster, radius 300 wu.

Skill.........................Cold Dmg Type................Cold
Casting Time ....3 sec. Duration..................Inst.

Lvl	Spell	Cost	Dmg
7	Burst of Steam (Minor)	5P	52
11	Burst of Steam	7P	74
15	Steaming Blast (Minor)	9P	104
20	Steaming Blast	12P	134
26	Steaming Blast (Major)	16P	177
32	Steaming Wind (Minor)	20P	215
39	Steaming Wind	25P	265
48	Steaming Wind (Major)	31P	325

DD, Snare: enemy's speed debuffed to 65% of original movement.

Skill.........................Cold Dmg Type................Cold
Casting Time ....3 sec. Range.....................1350
Duration ....30 sec.

Lvl	Spell	Cost	Dmg
1	Ensnaring Haze (Minor)	2P	5
5	Ensnaring Haze (Lesser)	4P	21
9	Ensnaring Haze	6P	37
13	Ensnaring Haze (Greater)	8P	49
17	Ensnaring Haze (Potent)	10P	65
24	Entangling Haze (Minor)	15P	89
33	Entangling Haze	21P	120
41	Entangling Haze (Greater)	26P	148
50	Entangling Haze (Potent)	33P	180

Cold DD with 5% resistance debuff.

Skill.........................Cold Dmg Type................Cold
Casting Time ....3 sec. Range.....................1500
Duration ....20 sec.

Lvl	Spell	Cost	Dmg
3	Searing Wind (Minor)	3P	14
6	Searing Wind (Lesser)	4P	26
12	Searing Wind	8P	45
16	Searing Gust (Minor)	10P	61
21	Searing Gust	13P	77
27	Searing Wave (Minor)	17P	100
37	Searing Wave	23P	136
47	Searing Blast	30P	172

AoE Heat DD with 5% resistance debuff; radius 350.

Skill.........................Cold Dmg Type ....Heat
Casting Time ....4 sec. Range.....................1500
Duration ....20 sec.

Lvl	Spell	Cost	Dmg
8	Simmering Cloud	7P	25
14	Broiling Cloud	11P	41
22	Sweltering Cloud	18P	63
29	Burning Cloud	24P	84
36	Torrid Cloud	30P	103
46	Boiling Cloud	39P	131

Path of Fire

DD.

Skill..........................Fire Dmg Type ....Heat
Casting Time ....3 sec. Range.....................1500
Duration..................Inst.

Lvl	Spell	Cost	Dmg
3	Summon Fire	3P	14
5	Fire Wind	4P	21
7	Circle Of Flames	5P	29
10	Fiery Orbs	6P	37
13	Fire Storm (Minor)	8P	49
17	Fire Storm	10P	65
23	Fire Storm (Major)	14P	85
30	Fiery Maelstrom (Minor)	19P	108
37	Fiery Maelstrom	23P	136
47	Fiery Maelstrom (Major)	30P	172

Bolt (ranged DD). You must wait 20 seconds before casting one of these spells again.

Skill..........................Fire Dmg Type ....Heat
Casting Time ....4 sec. Range.....................1875
Duration..................Inst.

Lvl	Spell	Cost	Dmg
2	Fire Bolt	2P	13
4	Fiery Bolt	3P	24
6	Fireball	4P	36
9	Reign of Fire (Minor)	6P	53
14	Reign of Fire	9P	75
18	Reign of Fire (Major)	11P	98
22	Flaming Rocks (Minor)	13P	115
28	Flaming Rock	17P	149
36	Flaming Rocks (Greater)	23P	188
46	Flaming Rocks (Major)	30P	239

Bladeturn: Absorbs damage of single hit.

Skill..........................Fire Dmg Type ....Heat
Casting Time ....4 sec. Duration.............10 min.

Lvl	Spell	Cost	Target
19	Aura of Incineration	8%P	Self

Pyromancy

DD.

Skill..........................Fire Dmg Type ....Heat
Casting Time ....3 sec. Range.....................1500
Duration..................Inst.

Lvl	Spell	Cost	Dmg
1	Minor Combustion	2P	5
3	Lesser Combustion	3P	16
6	Combustion	4P	32
10	Greater Combustion	6P	47
13	Major Combustion	8P	62
17	Minor Conflagration	10P	82
23	Lesser Conflagration	14P	108
30	Conflagration	19P	138
37	Greater Conflagration	23P	174
47	Major Conflagration	30P	220

AoE DD, radius 350.

Skill..........................Fire Dmg Type ....Heat
Casting Time ....4 sec. Range.....................1500
Duration..................Inst.

Lvl	Spell	Cost	Dmg
2	Explosive Blast (Minor)	2P	8
5	Explosive Blast	4P	20
7	Explosive Burst (Minor)	5P	28
12	Explosive Burst	8P	44
18	Concussive Blast (Minor)	11P	68
24	Concussive Blast	15P	88
32	Ebullient Blast (Minor)	20P	116
44	Ebullient Blast	28P	159

Bolt (ranged DD). You must wait 20 seconds before casting one of these spells again.

Skill..........................Fire Dmg Type ....Heat
Casting Time ....4 sec. Range.....................1875
Duration..................Inst.

Lvl	Spell	Cost	Dmg
4	Minor Fire Streak	3P	30
8	Fire Streak	5P	60
14	Minor Flame Streak	9P	96
19	Flame Streak	12P	134
25	Minor Incendiary Lance	15P	170
33	Incendiary Lance	21P	221
41	Minor Flame Spear	26P	273
50	Flame Spear	33P	332

Cabalist

Races		Skills	
Briton / Avalonian / Saracen		1	Matter Magic
Titles		1	Body Magic
5	Apprentice Cabalist	5	Spirit Magic
10	Journeyman Cabalist	5	Matter Magic Spec.
15	Imbuer	5	Body Magic Spec.
20	Creater	5	Spirit Magic Spec.
25	Veteran Cabalist	**Abilities**	
30	Spiritist	1	Staves
35	Animator	1	Cloth Armor
40	Master Spiritist	1	Sprint
45	Master Imbuer	5	QuickCast
50	Cabalist Prime		

Cabalists are masters of Body, Matter and Spirit magic, capable of creating golems to fight by their side. This is a fun class to play, since you also have Direct Damage, Damage-over-Time, debuff and healing spells. You can hit the enemy quickly, slowly, or simply slow him down for a long, torturous death at the hands of your pet. While shunned by some classes, your skills can be a valuable asset to a group, especially against caster mobs.

The Best Part: Striking someone down with your oversized pet and getting to do a little bit of everything magic-wise.

The Worst Part: You don't do a whole lot of damage while casting. Playing this class well requires some patience and dedication.

Race Choices:

Briton. Average race, with no outstanding or deficient stats.

Avalonian. Least CON and STR of any Cabalist race, but excellent starting INT at 80.

Saracen. More CON and STR than Britons, but less than Avalonians. This race's biggest advantage is in DEX.

Stat Choices:

- *INT:* This is your most critical stat, since INT affects your casting mana. Put at least 10 points into this, perhaps even 15 if you're not Avalonian.
- *DEX:* Saracens start with a big advantage here. DEX affects your casting time and ranks second to INT in importance. With enough DEX, you can shave one quarter off your casting time.
- *QUI:* Not really related to magic, but QUI can help you wield a staff if you opt to do so.

Weapon Choices: Your golem pet is your best weapon, preceded by a good combat debuff. You won't carry any weapons, save a staff if you choose.

Spec Paths: As a Cabalist, you have access to destroy Matter, Spirit and Body and must choose a primary focus. Train your chosen combat line to two-thirds of your level, as well as Spirit Twisting. The pet buffs you get from Spirit grow more and more valuable as you progress in level.

- *Quick Cast:* Skill that lets you cast a spell twice as fast... but for twice as much mana. Mostly, you'll find this useful in situations of desperation where every second counts.
- *Body Magic:* Base spells include snares, debuffs and STR drains. Spec'ing gives you Health transfers (vital for RvR play), attack speed debuffs to use on enemies, and disease spells.
- *Matter Manipulation:* Base spell line provides self-armor buffs and DoT spells. By specializing in Matter, you also get pet damage shields and AoE DoTs.
- *Spirit Twisting:* This is the most important line of spells, since the base spells give you pets and STR pet buffs. The specialized spells include pet speed and damage adds, plus, at higher levels, root spells.

Big Mistakes to Avoid in Character Creation: Failing to make up for race-related deficiencies and picking an incompatible main damage line by spec'ing too early.

Deciding What You Want Your Role to Be: With a slightly dark bent, you're one of the few classes that can summon pets. However, unless you've taken the road less traveled and invested in Staff, you won't be doing any meleeing. Your job is to keep the enemy debuffed and occasionally, transfer Health to a Realmmate. Your pet will do most of the dirty work if you keep it present, buffed and boosted.

Plotting Your Future: Remember that your pet and its buffs are your primary weapon. Keep this in mind when you're spending points. Of course, if your goal is to be an RvR

master at healing, you'll probably want to develop Body Magic more than Spirit Twisting. Take a look at the spell charts and see what you want, and when.

Grouping:

- Some groups may not appreciate your pet fighting because your pet "steals" some of the experience. Be prepared to provide other services if this happens. (Your buffed pet can help the group take down mobs that otherwise might overcome the group.) Use the pet to back up front-line fighters and protect any members that really need it.
- Your primary job will usually be to debuff the mob, occasionally throwing out a DoT spell for good measure. Sometimes, you may even have to heal.

Soloing:

- Send out a Fatigue Body or Inflict Malaise on a mob target, then send your pet off to attack. Throw your strongest DoT at the monster, then drain it as your pet finishes the kill.
- Look for lone monsters so that your mana doesn't get wasted on an entire group. You can most easily kill caster monsters, but they're not always easy to find.

Realm Versus Realm: You are an adept RvR class, although the fact that you die easily and do your damage slowly is a hindrance.

- Realm battles are usually over and done with pretty quickly, so you may not have time for many of your strongest DoTs.
- Talk to your Realmmates and see what they want you to accomplish. Your pet can help hold a keep door, or you can stay busy debuffing enemies while tanks and front-line fighters whale away at them.

Beginner's Tips:

- You can't wear any real armor, so you're very vulnerable to attacks by multiple monsters. Make sure you fight only one at a time, especially while soloing.
- Buff your pet prior to sending it in for attack.
- Your pet can only go where normal players can go.

Advanced Techniques:

- If you've spec'ed in Matter, your AoE DoT spells work well. For a Body spec'ed Cabalist, disease spells can often be the best way to help.
- With your Body Magic line of spells, you can perform emergency heals on your realm buddies as needed. Watch your healer's status and help accordingly.

Cabalist Spells

Body Destruction

DD, with (Drain %) of damage drained from target to Caster.

Skill........................Body Dmg Type...............Body
Casting Time.....2.5 sec. Range.....................1500
Duration..................Inst.

Lvl	Spell	Cost	Dmg	Drain %
1	Minor Vitality Drain	2P	5	30%
2	Lesser Vitality Drain	2P	8	30%
3	Vitality Drain	3P	12	30%
5	Greater Vitality Drain	4P	18	30%
7	Major Vitality Drain	5P	25	30%
10	Minor Essence Consumption	6P	32	30%
14	Lesser Essence Consumption	9P	45	30%
18	Essence Consumption	11P	59	40%
23	Greater Essence Consumption	14P	73	40%
28	Major Essence Consumption	17P	90	50%
35	Increased Essence Consumption	22P	110	50%
45	Superior Essence Consumption	29P	141	60%

STR debuff.

Skill........................Body Dmg Type...............Body
Casting Time........2 sec. Range.....................1500
Duration.............60 sec.

Lvl	Spell	Cost	Debuff
4	Fatigue Body	3P	6.5
8	Debilitate Body	5P	8
12	Weaken Body	8P	9.5
17	Deteriorate Body	10P	11.5
22	Enfeeble Body	13P	13.5
29	Degenerate Body	18P	16.5
37	Cripple Body	23P	19.5
46	Dilapidate Body	30P	23

Root: Enemy speed debuffed to 1% of original movement.

Skill........................Body Dmg Type...............Body
Casting Time.....2.5 sec. Range.....................1500

Lvl	Spell	Cost	Dur
3	Minor Crippling*	2P	9 sec.
6	Lesser Crippling*	3P	13 sec.
13	Cripple*	6P	23 sec.
19	Major Crippling*	9P	31 sec.
26	Greater Crippling*	12P	41 sec.
31	Leg Twist*	15P	48 sec.
40	Greater Leg Twist*	20P	61 sec.
49	Superior Leg Twisting	25P	73 sec.

Essence Manipulation

DD, with (Drain %) of damage drained from target to Caster.

Skill........................Body Dmg Type...............Body
Casting Time .....2.5 sec. Range.....................1500
Duration..................Inst.

Lvl	Spell	Cost	Dmg	Drain %
1	Remove Lifeforce	2P	5	70%
5	Snatch Lifeforce	4P	22	70%
7	Pilfer Lifeforce	5P	30	70%
10	Drain Lifeforce	6P	39	70%
14	Siphon Lifeforce	9P	56	70%
18	Absorb Lifeforce	11P	73	80%
23	Steal Lifeforce	14P	90	80%
28	Seize Lifeforce	17P	111	80%
35	Capture Lifeforce	22P	137	90%
45	Abduct Lifeforce	29P	175	90%

Transfers HP from Caster to Friend.

Skill........................Body Casting Time ....3 sec.
Range....................1350 Duration.................Inst.

Lvl	Spell	Cost	Max HP
4	Shift Health	3P	22
6	Shift Vigor	3P	30
9	Shift Essence	5P	42
12	Shift Vitality	6P	54
16	Shift Spirit	8P	71
21	Transplace Health	10P	91
27	Transplace Vigor	13P	116
31	Transplace Essence	15P	132
36	Transplace Vitality	18P	152
46	Transplace Spirit	24P	193

Debuffs attack speed by (Debuff %).

Skill........................Body Dmg Type..............Spirit
Casting Time ....3 sec. Range.....................1500

Lvl	Spell	Cost	Dur	Debuff %
2	Inflict Malaise	1P	33 sec.	5.5%
8	Inflict Greater Malaise	4P	44 sec.	7%
13	Inflict Suffering	6P	52 sec.	8.5%
19	Inflict Greater Suffering	9P	63 sec.	10.5%
25	Inflict Misery	12P	73 sec.	12.5%
32	Inflict Greater Misery	16P	86 sec.	14.5%
39	Inflict Excruciation	20P	1.6 min.	16.5%
47	Inflict Greater Excruciation	24P	1.9 min.	19%

Debuffs STR by 7.5% and movement speed by 15%; halves effect of any healing spell cast on target.

Skill........................Body Dmg Type................Cold
Casting Time ....3 sec. Range.....................1500

Lvl	Spell	Cost	Dur	Radius
3	Cursed Vigor	3P	60 sec.	(1)
15	Cursed Spirit	9P	1.5 min.	250
24	Cursed Soul	15P	2 min.	300
34	Cursed Vitality	21P	2.5 min.	350
44	Cursed Essence	28P	3 min.	400

Core Matters

Buffs Caster's AF.

Skill ....2/3 Spec Dmg Type............Matter
Casting Time ....4 sec. Duration.............15 min.

Lvl	Spell	Cost	Buff
1	Ward Blow	2P	13
4	Fend Blow	3P	27
6	Dampen Blow	4P	37
9	Deflect Blow	6P	51
14	Ward Offense	9P	75
20	Fend Offense	12P	104
28	Dampen Offense	17P	143
38	Deflect Offense	24P	191
48	Nullify Offense	31P	240

DoT: inflicts (Dmg) every 5 seconds.

Skill.....................Matter Dmg Type............Matter
Casting Time ....3 sec. Range.....................1500
Duration ....20 sec.

Lvl	Spell	Cost	Dmg
2	Corrosive Mist	3P	4
3	Corrosive Fog	4P	6
5	Corrosive Cloud	6P	9
7	Corrosive Smoke	7P	13
10	Dissolving Mist	10P	17
13	Dissolving Fog	13P	23
16	Dissolving Cloud	15P	29
21	Dissolving Smoke	20P	37
27	Disintegrating Fog	26P	49
35	Disintegrating Cloud	35P	63
44	Disintegrating Smoke	45P	79

Bladeturn: absorbs damage of single hit.

Skill.....................Matter Dmg Type............Matter
Casting Time ....4 sec. Duration.............10 min.

Lvl	Spell	Cost	Target
19	Barrier of Warding	8%P	Self

Non-magical damage to Caster reduced by (Bonus %).

Skill.....................Matter Dmg Type............Matter
Casting Time ....3 sec. Duration.............15 min.

Lvl	Spell	Cost	Bonus %
30	Dampening Ward	19P	5%
41	Nullifying Ward	26P	10%

DEX debuff.

Skill.....................Matter Dmg Type..............Spirit
Casting Time ....2 sec. Range.....................1500
Duration ....60 sec.

Lvl	Spell	Cost	Debuff
8	Mystic Web	5P	8
12	Mystic Trap	6P	9.5
17	Mystic Net	9P	11.5
23	Magical Web	11P	14
29	Magical Trap	14P	16.5
36	Magical Net	17P	19
46	Sorcerous Web	22P	23

Matter Manipulation

DoT: inflicts (Dmg) every 4 seconds.

Skill.....................Matter Dmg Type............Matter
Casting Time ....3 sec. Range.....................1500
Duration ....24 sec.

Lvl	Spell	Cost	Dmg
2	Lesser Decrepify	3P	4
3	Decrepify	4P	6
5	Lesser Deterioration	6P	9
7	Deterioration	7P	13
10	Lesser Contamination	10P	17
13	Contamination	13P	23
16	Lesser Devolution	15P	29
21	Devolution	20P	37
27	Lesser Degeneration	26P	49
35	Degeneration	35P	63
44	Lesser Delaceration	45P	79
49	Delaceration	51P	89

Pet Focus Dmg Shield: Pet's damage/sec buffed until Caster interrupted or out of power (stacks as group 2).

Skill.....................Matter Dmg Type............Matter
Casting Time .....2.5 sec. Range.....................1350
Duration................Focus

Lvl	Spell	Cost	Buff
1	Reflect Attack	1P/6s	0.7
4	Reflect Blow	3P/6s	3
6	Reflect Damage	3P/6s	4.5
9	Reflect Offense	5P/6s	6.8
15	Channel Attack	8P/6s	10.5
22	Channel Blow	11P/6s	15.1
30	Channel Damage	15P/6s	20.3
40	Channel Offense	20P/6s	27.1
50	Reflective Backlash	26P/6s	33.9

AoE DoT: inflicts (Dmg) every 5 seconds, radius 350 wu.

Skill.....................Matter Dmg Type............Matter
Casting Time ....3 sec. Range.....................1500
Duration ....20 sec.

Lvl	Spell	Cost	Dmg
18	Puncture Spirit	17P	33
24	Perforate Spirit	23P	43
29	Bore Spirit	28P	53
36	Drill Spirit	36P	65
46	Lance Spirit	47P	83

Reduces range on ranged attacks by (Debuff %).

Skill.....................Matter Dmg Type............Matter
Casting Time ....2 sec. Range.....................2300
Duration...............2 min.

Lvl	Spell	Cost	Debuff %
11	Encrust Eyes	5P	25%
19	Obscuring Dust	9P	35%
25	Clouded Sight	12P	45%
32	Darkened Cloud	16P	55%
41	Persistent Obscuration	20P	65%

Spirit Animation

Calls pet, up to 88% of Caster's level.
Skill ....Spirit Dmg Type ....Spirit
Cost ....25%P Casting Time ....6 sec.
Duration ....Until Neg.

Lvl	Spell	Max Lvl
1	Amber Simulacrum	50
7	Ruby Simulacrum	50
12	Sapphire Simulacrum	50
20	Emerald Simulacrum	50
32	Jade Simulacrum	50

Buffs Pet's STR.
Skill ....Spirit Dmg Type ....Spirit
Casting Time ....3 sec. Range........1000
Duration........10 min.

Lvl	Spell	Cost	Buff
3	Strengthen Spirit	2P	12
6	Enhance Spirit	3P	14
11	Imbue Spirit	5P	18
18	Amplify Spirit	8P	24
24	Intensify Spirit	12P	29
31	Magnify Spirit	15P	34
41	Empower Spirit	20P	42

Heals damage by (Heal) HP to Pet.
Skill ....Spirit Dmg Type ....Spirit
Casting Time ....3 sec. Range........1350
Duration........Inst.

Lvl	Spell	Cost	Heal HP
5	Mend Simulacrum	4P	31
9	Patch Simulacrum	6P	51
13	Repair Simulacrum	8P	71
19	Restore Simulacrum	12P	101
28	Reconstruct Simulacrum	17P	146
35	Reanimate Simulacrum	22P	181
44	Rebuild Simulacrum	28P	226

Buffs Pet's DEX.
Skill ....Spirit Dmg Type ....Spirit
Casting Time ....3 sec. Range........1000
Duration........10 min.

Lvl	Spell	Cost	Buff
4	Improve Dexterity	2P	13
8	Develop Dexterity	4P	16
14	Increase Dexterity	7P	21
21	Enhance Dexterity	10P	26
33	Amplify Dexterity	16P	36
38	Augment Dexterity	19P	40
48	Magnify Dexterity	24P	48

Vivification

Pet's damage/sec buffed (stacks as group 2).
Skill ....Spirit Dmg Type ....Spirit
Casting Time ....3 sec. Range........1000
Duration........10 min.

Lvl	Spell	Cost	Buff
1	Detect Flaw	1P	1.2
4	Find Flaw	2P	1.9
7	Discover Flaw	4P	2.6
10	Expose Flaw	4P	3.3
15	Pinpoint Flaw	7P	4.5
20	Illuminate Flaw	9P	5.7
26	Unveil Flaw	12P	7.2
34	Pierce Flaw	16P	9.1
44	Exploit Flaw	22P	11.5

Buffs pet's attack speed by (Speed %).
Skill ....Spirit Dmg Type ....Spirit
Casting Time ......3.5 sec. Range........1000
Duration........10 min.

Lvl	Spell	Cost	Speed %
2	Encourage Aggression	2P	11%
8	Enhance Aggression	5P	14%
14	Amplify Aggression	9P	17%
21	Increase Aggression	13P	20%
27	Excite Aggression	17P	23%
32	Magnify Aggression	20P	26%
40	Overcharge Aggression	25P	30%

Kills pet, transferring 10% of pet's HP to Caster.
Skill ....Spirit Dmg Type ....Spirit
Casting Time ....3 sec. Range........1000
Duration........Inst.

Lvl	Spell	Cost
3	Convert Spirit	5%P

Snare: Enemy's speed debuffed to 60% of original movement.
Skill ....Spirit Dmg Type ....Spirit
Casting Time ......2.5 sec. Range........1500

Lvl	Spell	Cost	Dur	Area
23	Constrict Spirit	14P	70 sec.	(1)
30	Encase Spirit	19P	82 sec.	Radius 350
38	Imprison Spirit	24P	1.6 min.	Radius 350
48	Shackle Spirit	31P	1.9 min.	Radius 350

Body resistance debuff.
Skill ....Spirit Casting Time ....2 sec.
Range........1500 Duration ....15 sec.

Lvl	Spell	Cost	Debuff %
22	Diminish Immunities	10P	7.5%
33	Dissipate Immunities	16P	15%
46	Banish Immunities	24P	25%

Spirit resistance debuff.
Skill ....Spirit Casting Time ....2 sec.
Range........1500 Duration ....15 sec.

Lvl	Spell	Cost	Debuff %
24	Diminish Will	12P	7.5%
36	Dissipate Will	18P	15%
47	Banish Will	24P	25%

Energy resistance debuff.
Skill ....Spirit Casting Time ....2 sec.
Range........1500 Duration ....15 sec.

Lvl	Spell	Cost	Debuff %
28	Diminish Conductivity	13P	7.5%
37	Dissipate Conductivity	18P	15%
49	Banish Conductivity	25P	25%

Buffs Pet's STR and CON.
Skill ....Enchantments Dmg Type ....Spirit
Casting Time ....3 sec. Range........1000
Duration........10 min.

Lvl	Spell	Cost	Buff
11	Strengthen Golem	9P	18
18	Invigorate Golem	15P	24
29	Fortify Golem	24P	33
39	Empower Golem	33P	41
50	Vivify Golem	43P	50

Buffs Pet's DEX and QUI.
Skill ....Enchantments Dmg Type ....Spirit
Casting Time ....3 sec. Range........1000
Duration........10 min.

Lvl	Spell	Cost	Buff
12	Hurry Golem	10P	19
19	Animate Golem	15P	25
31	Quicken Golem	25P	34
41	Accelerate Golem	35P	42

Classes & Races

	Briton	Highlander	Avalonian	Saracen
Armsman (2x)	√	√	√	√
Mercenary (2x)	√	√		√
Paladin (2x)	√		√	√
Scout (2x)	√	√		√
Minstrel (1.5x)	√	√		√
Infiltrator (2.5x)	√			√
Friar (1.5x)	√			
Cleric (1x)	√	√	√	
Theurgist (1x)	√		√	
Sorcerer (1x)	√		√	√
Wizard (1x)			√	
Cabalist (1x)	√		√	√

Starting & Final Classes

Guild: *Class*	Defenders of Albion	Church of Albion	The Guild of Shadows	The Academy
Fighter	Armsman	Paladin	Mercenary	
Rogue	Scout		Infiltrator	Minstrel
Acolyte	Friar	Cleric		
Elementalist	Theurgist			Sorcerer
Mage			Cabalist	Wizard

Basic Racial Attributes

	Briton	Highlander	Avalonian	Saracen
Strength	60	70	45	50
Constitution	60	70	45	50
Dexterity	60	50	60	80
Quickness	60	50	70	60
Intelligence	60	60	80	60
Charisma	60	60	60	60
Empathy	60	60	60	60
Piety	60	60	60	60

Innate Racial Resistances

	Briton	Highlander	Avalonian	Saracen
Crushing	+2	+3	+2	–
Slashing	+3	+2	+3	+2
Thrusting	–	–	–	+3
Body	–	–	–	–
Cold	–	+5	–	–
Heat	–	–	–	+5
Spirit	+5	–	+5	–

Merchants

Armor/Clothing

Armor/Clothing (various)
- Camelot — Elzbet Sable
- Llyn Barfog — Gwalter ap Trevis, Thomas ap Seyton, Tewdwr ap Greid, Twm ap Gusg

Armor (Mithril)
- Camelot — Jeffrey Kenric

Chain
- Caer Ulfwych — Stephan Fall
- Caer Witrin — Azrael Mucto
- Camelot — Serena Muftar
- Campac. St. — Junger Gannon
- Cornwall Station — Sar Aldar
- Cotswold Village — Col Aldar
- Snowdonia Station — Aelda

Chain (Mithril)
- Camelot — Lora Theomund

Cloaks
- Camelot — Radek Silven

Cloth (Quilted)
- Adribard's Retreat — Anga Weaver
- Camelot — Raggart Bruce
- Cotswold Village — Farma Hornly
- Humberton Village — Bline Tengit
- Ludlow Village — Seamstress Marie
- Snowdonia Station — Guyon
- West Downs — Erwin Holdyn

Cloth (Quilted (Sylvan))
- Camelot — Meccus Yrre

Leather
- Camelot — Edmee Heolstor, Jeffrey Kenric, Lara Weathers

Leather (Cymric)
- Camelot — Geor Nadren
- Campac. St. — Fluitha Sufron

Leather (Roman)
- Adribard's Retreat — Morin Davem
- Camelot — Yoren Shazra
- Cotswold Village — Lundeg Tranyth
- Prydwen Keep — Hugh Gallen

Leather (Siluric)
- Camelot — Warren Gibson
- Ludlow Village — Fost Mra
- Snowdonia Station — Boc

Plate
- Adribard's Retreat — Tathan
- Camelot — Hafgan Corley
- Cornwall Station — Jack Weyland
- Prydwen Keep — Karn Graem
- Snowdonia Station — Cranly

Plate (Mithril)
- Camelot — Torr Upton

Plate (Steel, Alloy)
- Cotswold Village — Gill Hoxley

Robes
- Adribard's Retreat — Tersa Weaver
- Camelot — Radek Silven
- Cotswold Village — Jon Smythe
- Humberton Village — Siom Felanis
- Lethantis Assoc. — Epin Lemut
- Ludlow Village — Seamstress Lynnet
- West Downs — Aric Barlow

Studded Leather
- Cotswold Village — Ellyn Weyland
- Outland Wharf — Leshorn Hael
- West Downs — Garvyn Kensington

Scale
- Camelot — Fuston Talgurt
- Humberton Village — Gert Elm

Studded Leather (Boned)
- Camelot — Jana Hickey, Lan
- Humberton Village — Dun Mra
- Snowdonia Station — Aldys Meccus

Studded Leather (Lamellar)
- Caer Witrin — Geofram Hael
- Campac. St. — Rundeg Faerweth

Weapons

Weapons (various)
- Camelot — G. Egesa, Tait Nerian, Cigolin Dalston, Colby Dalston, Heostor Wyman, Holt Finan, Iden Wissan, Landry Woden, Larcwide Wirt, Lynna Lang, Odella Cerdic, Olaevia Wyman, Ordra Yaney, Pedrith Edyn
- Llyn Barfog — Adwr ap Even
- Outland Wharf — William Oswy
- Snowdonia Station — Osric

Weapons (Mithril)
- Camelot — Wyne Scead

Arrows
- Caer Ulfwych — Fellya Fletcher
- Camelot — Jana Fletcher
- Campac. St. — Falin Fletcher, Goodwin Fletcher
- Castle Sauvage — Lenia Fletcher
- Cornwall Station — Iohannes Aldar
- Cotswold Vill. — Braenwyn Fletcher, Yetta Fletcher
- Huginfell — Alden Fletcher
- Humberton Village — Nelda Fletcher, Tria Ellowis
- Llyn Barfog — Duncan Curan
- Ludlow Village — Gillery Fletcher, Nulb Pew
- Outland Wharf — Allyn Fletcher
- Snowdonia Station — Edrea Fletcher, Gleda Fletcher
- Swanton Keep — Agrakor Fletcher, Dwira Fletcher
- West Downs — Ainsley Fletcher

Bows
- Caer Ulfwych — Elger Leafblade
- Camelot — Sara Graston
- Campac. St. — Flaudin Bowman
- Cotswold Village — Grum Bowman
- Humberton Village — Feren Erimen
- Ludlow Village — Angus Bowman
- Outland Wharf — Epheria Brighteye
- Snowdonia St. — Staeven Bowman
- Swanton Keep — Lynd Moidg
- West Downs — Aldrin Collyer

Bow Materials
- West Downs — Farley Daegal

Crossbows & Bolts
- Cornwall Station — Heylyn Aldar
- West Downs — Radella Fletcher

Crossbow Bolts
- Caer Ulfwych — Eiddin Walelden
- Camelot — Sasha Fletcher
- Outland Wharf — Boudron Fletcher

Crushing Weapons
- Adribard's Retreat — Theois Gwynf
- Caer Ulfwych — Ellard Gram
- Caer Witrin — Gregor Lannis

Camelot Fash
Humberton Village Stephon Bash
Prydwen Keep Barric Camber
Snowdonia Station Elwyn

Piercing Weapons
Outland Wharf Swyno

Polearms
Camelot Moira Camber
Campac. St. Balthazar Encambion
Cotswold Village Rayn Olwyc
Swanton Keep Ley Manton

Slashing Weapons
Adribard's Retreat Tyngyr Blade
Camelot Ethan Farley, Joffrey
Cotswold Village Grannis Ynos
Humberton Village Ban Ronem
Prydwen Keep Alburn Hale
Snowdonia Station Ember

Slashing Weapons (Axes, Swords)
Caer Ulfwych Langston Fall

Staves
Adribard's Retreat Nai Whit
C. Ulfwich G. Dalston, G. Bermorn
Camelot Marius Caestus
Campac. St. Archibald Oakheart
Cotswold Village Samwell Hornly
Humberton Village Mif Feit
Ludlow Village Sals Pew
Swanton Keep Nia Leof

Thrusting Weapons
Camelot Fenris Blakely
Campac. St. Geston Lurger
Cotswold Village John Weyland
Humberton Village Alhrick Duglas
Ludlow Village Crep Pew
Prydwen Keep Elvar Tambor
Snowdonia Station Jonalyn

Two Handed Weapons
Adribard's Retreat Tathal
Camelot Dougal Heathis
Campac. St. Malin Cullan
Cotswold Village Bedamor Routh
Swanton Keep Jerad

Shields

Adribard's Retreat Devyn Godric
Caer Ulfwych Grindag Halig
Camelot C. Denisc, Ver Nuren
Cotswold Village Lar Rodor
Humberton Vill. Heorot Kenway
Prydwen Keep Ryce Scrydan
Snowdonia St. Cedd Aethelbert

Focus Items

Cabalist Staves
Caer Witrin Wina Wyman
Cotswold Village Odelia Wyman
Lethantis Assoc. Elga Wyman
Ludlow Village Andrya Wyman

Sorcerer Staves
Adribard's Retreat Wylie Edyn
Cotswold Village Cauldir Edyn
Lethantis Assoc. Norvel Edyn
Ludlow Village Calldir Edyn

Theurgist Staves
Adribard's Retreat Graeme Dalston
Cotswold Village Cudbert Dalston
Ludlow Village Farl Dalston

Wizard Staves
Adribard's Retreat Daisi Egesa
Cotswold Village Doreen Egesa
Lethantis Assoc. Loretta Agesa
Ludlow Village Eabae Egesa

Instruments

Adribard's Retreat Trill
Cotswold Village Eileen Morton
Lethantis Assoc. Sleria
Ludlow Village Greta Blandish

Other Goods

Merchant
Camelot C. Bordin, Corley Nodens, Hector Darian, Kedoenad, Velmis, Willa Dalston

Cloth
Cornwall Station Adaliae Ruthic

Dyes
Adribard's Retreat Blueheart, Dyemaster Camdene
Caer Ulfwych Dyemasters Druce, Eldred, Esme, Nedda
Camelot Bren, Edare, Emma, Kael, Lendand, Mara, Vandras
Campac. St. Gwendolyn Arlington
Cotswold Village Dyemaster Alwin, Eowyln Astos
Humberton Village Dyemaker Bal, Dyemaster Brun
Ludlow Village Dyemaster Cor
Outland Wharf Dyemasters Carye, Earh, Godric, Kaly
Prydwen Keep Arleigh Penn, Dyemaster Arthw

Dyes (Cloth)
Ludlow Village Aileen Wyatt

Dyes (Enamel)
Cotswold Vill. Dyemstrs. Edra, Octe

Dyes (Leather)
Campac. St. Dyemaster Esme
Cotswold V. Dmstrs. Leax, Wanetta

Poisons
Caer Witrin Etie
Campac. St. Linidd
Castle Sauvage Melannon, Onyg
Cotswold Village Unendalden
Humberton Village Nydomath
Outland Wharf Wiceit
Swanton Keep Glaeric

Tailoring Equipment
Swanton Keep Yorel Anbidian

Wood
Camelot Brach Leof
Cornwall Station Thule Ruthic

Various expensive trade skill items
Ludlow Village Ochan Aethelhere

Services

Blacksmith
Caer Ulfwych Ellard Fall
Llyn Barfog Olvryn Wynford

Enchanter
Adribard's Ret. Enchanter Braesia
Camelot Enchanter Evala
Cotswold V. Enchanter Grumwold
Humberton V. Enchanter Haephus

Healer
Adribard's Retreat Sister Endri
Caer Ulfwych Brother Eurius
Caer Witrin Sister Lilly
Camelot Brother Michel; Penric
Cornwall Station Eva Aldar
Humberton Village Brother Demay, Brother Sabutai
Prydwen Keep Brother Maynard
Snowdonia Station Odaro Hengist
West Downs Master Gerol

Master Stonemason
Cotswold Vill. Stonemason Glover

Realm Gate
Castle Sauvage Sall Fadri

Scout
Swanton Keep Lieutenant Fisra
Caer Witrin Fread Gramley
Camelot J. Hammerfel
Campac. St. Dafyd Graham
Cornwall Station Seysild Aldar
Cotswold Village Elvar Ironhand
Humberton Village Parisch Ealyn
Ludlow Village Master Sceley
Outland Wharf Erstal Furlan
Prydwen Keep Gram Ironhand
Snowdonia Station Thol Dunnin
West Downs Lillian Brydger

Vault Keeper
Adribard's Retreat Trulion Vrundon
Castle Sauvage Earl Grael

Trainers

Armsman Trainer
Caer Ulfwych Captain Falron
Camelot Captains Alphin, Rion
Swanton Keep Captain Presan

Cabalist Trainer
Caer Witrin Magus Dimos
Camelot Magi Agufen, Isen
Lethantis Assoc. Magus Sacyn
Swanton Keep Magus Jeril

Cleric Trainer
Adribard's Retreat Lady Lynn
Caer Ulfwych Collen Blist
Camelot Ladies Fridwulf, Winchell

Elementalist Trainer
Cotswold Village Master Stearn
Lethantis Assoc. Mistress Trethia

Fighter Trainer
Adribard's Retreat Master Dyrin
Campac. St. Master Lorik
Humberton Village Master Torr
Prydwen Keep Master Graent

Fletching Trainer
Camelot Acey Dalston

Friar Trainer
Adribard's Retreat Brother Caun
Caer Ulfwych Brother Spilr
Camelot Brs. Ethelbald, Sterlyn
Swanton Keep Brother Daniel

Infiltrator Trainer
Caer Witrin Master Noijan
Camelot Masters Eadig, Edric
Lethantis Assoc. Master Qilith
Swanton Keep Master Brignun
Outland Wharf Bruna

Mage Trainer
Adribard's Retreat Magus Saloc
Cotswold Village Magus Aelle
Lethantis Assoc. Magus Oreal
Ludlow Village Magus Aldred

Master Trainer
Camelot Grummond Attor, Hephas Elgen, Runthal Devyn

Mercenary Trainer
Caer Witrin Master Dohajan
Camelot Masters Almund, Arenis
Campac. St. Master Astyp
Swanton Keep Master Kel

Minstrel Trainer
Adribard's Retrt. Master Liennon
Camelot Masters Berwick, Dubri
Lethantis Assoc. Master Glorous
Swanton Keep Master Hanis

Paladin Trainer
Adribard's Retreat Lord Adribard
Caer Ulfwych Lord Ulfwych
Camelot Lady Triss, Lord Prydwen

Rogue Trainer
Campac. St. Master Hadis
Cotswold Village Master Sorac
Ludlow Village Master Odon

Scout Trainer
Adribard's Retreat Lt. Crosean
Caer Ulfwych Lt. Mhoudi
Camelot Lts. Kaherdin, Rydderac

Sorcerer Trainer
Adribard's Retreat Magus Edaev
Camelot Magess Tena, Magus Cormac
Lethantis Assoc. Magus Crystolos
Swanton Keep Magus Sarun

Tailoring Trainer
Camelot Arliss Eadig

Theurgist Trainer
Adribard's Ret. Mistress Jeryssa
Caer Ulfwych Mistress Frina
Camelot Mastr. Cear, Mistr. Welss
Swanton Keep Mistress Cessa

Wizard Trainer
Adribard's Retreat Master Traoyr
Camelot Master Grundelth, Mistress Ladriel
Lethantis Assoc. Master Arbaedes
Swanton Keep Mistress Alarisa

Quests

Quests are only available once you've reached the appropriate Level. When only specific races or classes can receive a quest, they are mentioned in the Restrictions column. Similarly, sometimes you must have finished a lower-level quest before you can advance to the next one; these prerequisite quests are also listed, in parentheses, in the Restrictions column.

L Quest	Source / Restrictions
1 Immediate Resolution	Varies: trainer
1 Wolf Pelt Cloak	Humberton Keep: Steward Willie
2 Commencement	Varies: trainer
3 Association	Prydwen Keep: Master Graent
4 Guild Preparation	Varies: trainer
4 Hunt For Slith	North Camelot Gates: Commander Burcrif
5 Cleric Mulgrut	Prydwen Keep: Hugh Gallen
5 Ripper	Camelot West Tower Outpost: Lt. Jursen
5 Simple Request	Snowdonia Fortress: Lt. Brude
6 Camdene's Components	Adribard's Retreat: Camdene
6 Outcast Ormgarth	Campacorentin Station: Olorustos
7 Goblin Hunting	Cear Ulfwych: Huntress Lenna
7 Heart of Sephucoth	Cotswold: Eowyln Astos
7 Search For Sil	Outside Cotswold: Nob the Stableboy
8 Father Hugrath	Cotswold: Frip
8 Lady Leana	Prydwen Keep: Sir Quait
9 Dunan's Bear Tooth	Ludlow: Dunan
9 Thinking Cap	Snowdonia Station: Cranly
9 Tyngyr's Daughter	Adribard's Retreat: Blade
10 Departed Hero	Snowdonia Fortress: Lt. Brude
10 Dragon Ant Charm	Snowdonia Station: Ember
10 Intervention	Fort Snowdonia: Sir Defi / Church
10 Nenet's Research	Lethantis Association: Nenet
11 Cloak of Shades Part 1	Cotswald: Leridia / Rogue
11 Cloak of Shades Part 2	/ Rogue
11 Niea's Missing Brother	Humberton Keep: Niea
11 Sals' Jar	Ludlow: Sals Pew
11 Sir Gleran's Lost Necklace	West Downs: Andryn / (Niea's Missing Brother)
11 Staff of Life	Behind Prydwen Keep: Llewellyn Camber
12 Bandit Camp	Camelot: Sir Kenley / Fighter, Rogue
12 Guarding the Stone	Prydwen Keep: Sir Jerem
13 Barnett's Shield	Humberton Keep: Sir Gleran / (Sir Gleran's Lost Necklace)
13 Growler Mace	Campacorentin Forest: Growler / Fighter, Cleric
13 Growler's Necklace	Campacorentin: Growler/Fighter, Cleric (Growling Ghost)
13 Lady Judith's Circlet	Cam.: Gaevin Sebryn or Aonghas Prirerd / Fighter,Rogue
13 Mathien's Metal	Snowdonia Station: Mathien / (The Growling Ghost)
13 Slythcur Cloak	Adribard's Retreat: Anga Weaver
13 The Captured Courier	Camelot: Sister Rhigwyn / Armsman, Paladin
13 The Growling Ghost	Prydwyn Keep Bridge: Sgt. Alain / Fighter, Cleric
14 Oaken Boots	Caer Ulfwych: Cayla / Fighter
14 Siom's Staff	Humberton Keep: Siom Felanis
14 The Hunt For Arachneida	Campecorentin Station: Kealan
15 Bedelia's Grief	Camelot: Bedelia / (Barnett's Shield)
15 Supplies For Lillian	West Downs: Beria
16 Amulet of the Planes	Lethantis: Mairi Ralilden / Mage, Elementalist
16 Ivy Weave Gloves	Adribard's Retreat: Brother Onoloth / Church
16 The Walelden's Pendant	Caer Ulfwych: Fianya Waleldan/Armsman, Paladin
17 Contyth's Hammer	Humberton Keep: Contyn
17 Kindred of the Fallen	Forest Sauvage: Lt. Kuebler
17 Lord Aryon's Box	Camelot: Sister Elaydith
17 The Stolen Spells	Camelot: Vadri Pade
18 Druid Medicine	Salisbury Guard Tower: Landon Huntington
19 Bishop Burhoff's Curse	Camelot: Brother Lensar / (Lord Aryon's Box)
19 Dugan's Magic Totem	Caer Witrin: Dugan Advien
20 Escaped Bandits	Salisbury Plain S. Guard Tower, or W. Downs: Guard Synon
21 The Heretical Hermit	Adribard's Retreat: Aiellana
30 Long Lion Fang	Camelot: Laurenna / Fighter, Rogue, Cleric
32 Wizard's Demand	Swanton Keep: Yorel Anbidian/Fighter, Cler., Infil., Scout
33 Impossible Mission	Camelot gates: Albion runner / Fighter, Acolyte
39 Crushed Faith	Sister Rhigwyn / Fighter, Acolyte
40 The Forest Plot	Forest Sauvage: Rob Ria/Scout (+ faction with Mist Hunters)
41 Secret Orders	Swanton Keep: Heather Barclay / Fighter, Rogue, Cleric
45 Prelude to War	Cotswold: Master Kless

Guild Track

You may only undertake the quests for your own guild. You must complete each quest before undertaking the next.

The Academy

7 Traveler's Way: Stones of Power	Varies: trainer
11 Wisdom	Camelot: trainer
15 Scura Tragedia	Camelot: trainer
20 La Morti Parla	Camelot: Vismer
25 Animare Il Morti	Camelot: Vismer
30 Legione Perso	Camelot: Vismer
40 Arc of Ages	Camelot: Vismer
43 Symbol of the Broken: 43,45,48,50	Camelot: trainer

Church of Albion

7 Traveler's Way: Church Aid	Varies: trainer
11 List of Denial	Camelot: trainer
15 Abolishment of Sacrifice	Camelot: trainer
20 Deserter Amano	Black Mountains North: Amano
25 Point of Reason	Camelot: trainer
30 Chains of Death	Camelot: trainer
40 Departed Fellowship	Camelot: Lady Triss
43 Passage to Eternity: 43,45,48,50	Camelot: trainer

The Defenders of Albion

7 Traveler's Way: Dwarf Raid	Varies: trainer
11 Fortune of Few	Camelot: trainer
15 Legend of the Lake 15, 20, 25	Avalon Marsh: Lady Nimue
30 Hands of Fate	Camelot: trainer
40 The Craft of Retribution	Camelot: trainer
43 Feast of the Decadent: 43,45,48,50	Camelot: trainer

The Guild of Shadows

7 Traveler's Way: Supply Run	Varies: trainer
11 Entry Into Tomorrow	Camelot: trainer
15 Rebellion Accepted	Camelot: trainer
20 The Renegade	Snowdonia Forest: Captain Rhodri
25 Regal Nobility: 25, 30	Snowdonia: Captain Rhodri
40 Hidden Insurrection	Camelot: Magus Agyfen
43 Lord of Deceit: 43,45,48,50	Camelot: trainer

Standard (Craftable) Weapons

Standard (craftable) weapons are sorted by the skill needed to wield them. For **Arrow** stats, see page 363. For unique weapons (including unique arrows), see page 84. For **Siege Equipment**, see page 324. For a general discussion of weapons and weapon stats, see page 361.

Headings. Delay = time between blows, in seconds / **Dam (M# 1)** = damage per hit, using a Material Level 1 weapon / **Incr**ement = additional damage per hit, with each improvement in Material / **Base DPS** = damage per second using a Material Level 1 weapon / **Wt.** = weight of the weapon / **Sec. Skill** = secondary skill that influences damage / **Range** = range of weapon, in world units / * = this weapon can be used as a second weapon with Hibernia's Celtic Dual skill.

Standard (Craftable) Weapons

Bow

Lvl	Weapon	Delay (sec.)	Dam (M# 1)	Incr	Base DPS	Wt.	Range
1	Short Bow	4.0	5.9	6.0	1.5	2.6	1200

Crossbow

Lvl	Weapon	Delay (sec.)	Dam (M# 1)	Incr	Base DPS	Wt.	Range
5	Crossbow	5.0	10.5	7.5	2.1	4	1200

Crush

Lvl	Weapon	Delay (sec.)	Dam (M# 1)	Incr	Base DPS	Wt.
1	Hammer *	3.1	4.6	4.6	1.5	2.4
2	Mace *	3.3	6	5.0	1.8	2.8
3	Flanged Mace	3.5	7.3	5.2	2.1	3.2
4	Spiked Mace	3.8	9.1	5.7	2.4	3.6
5	War Hammer	4.3	11.6	6.4	2.7	4
6	War Mace *	3.0	9	4.5	3.0	2

Longbow

Lvl	Weapon	Delay (sec.)	Dam (M# 1)	Incr	Base DPS	Wt.	Range
5	Hunter Bow	4.0	10.8	6.0	2.7	2.6	1600
5	Bow	4.7	12.7	7.1	2.7	3.1	1600
5	Long Bow	5.4	14.6	8.1	2.7	3.6	1760

Polearm

Lvl	Weapon	Sec.	Dam (M# 1)	Incr	Base DPS	Wt.
1	Pike (Thrust)	4.4	6.6	6.6	1.5	4.5
2	Lochaber Axe (Slash)	4.8	8.7	7.2	1.8	5
3	Bill	5.2	11	7.9	2.1	5.5
4	Lucerne Hammer (Crush)	5.6	13.5	8.4	2.4	6
5	Halberd	6.0	16.2	9.0	2.7	6.5
6	Bardiche (Slash)	5.5	16.7	8.3	3.0	5.5
6	Partisan (Thrust)	5.5	16.5	8.3	3.0	5
6	Poleaxe (Slash)	5.8	17.5	8.7	3.0	5.5
6	Spiked Hammer (Crush)	5.9	17.8	8.9	3.0	6.5

Slash

Lvl	Weapon	Delay (sec.)	Dam (M# 1)	Incr	Base DPS	Wt.
1	Dagger *	2.4	3.6	3.6	1.5	0.8
1	Short Sword *	2.8	4.2	4.2	1.5	1.8
2	Broadsword *	3.2	5.8	4.8	1.8	2
2	Hand Axe	2.9	5.2	4.3	1.8	1
3	Scimitar	3.3	6.9	4.9	2.1	2.2
4	Long Sword	3.6	8.7	5.4	2.4	2.3
5	Bastard Sword	3.9	10.6	5.9	2.7	3
6	Jambiya *	2.6	8	3.9	3.1	1.3
6	Sabre	3.6	10.8	5.4	3.0	1.9

Staff

Lvl	Weapon	Sec.	Dam (M# 1)	Incr	Base DPS	Wt.
1	Staff	4.5	6.7	6.8	1.5	4.5
1	Shod Staff	5	10.5	7.5	2.1	4.5
1	Focus Staff	4.5	6.7	6.7	1.5	4.5
1	Quarterstaff	3.1	4.6	4.6	1.5	4.5
3	Shod Quarterstaff	4.2	8.9	6.4	2.1	4.5

Thrust

Lvl	Weapon	Delay (sec.)	Dam (M# 1)	Incr	Base DPS	Wt.
1	Dirk *	2.3	3.4	3.4	1.5	0.8
2	Stiletto *	2.5	4.5	3.8	1.8	1.1
3	Main Gauche *	2.8	5.9	4.2	2.1	1.4
4	Rapier	3.2	7.7	4.8	2.4	1.7
5	Gladius	3.7	10	5.6	2.7	2
6	Guarded Rapier	3.5	10.6	5.3	3.0	2.1

Two-Handed

Lvl	Weapon	Delay (sec.)	Dam (M# 1)	Incr	Base DPS	Wt.	Sec. Skill
1	War Mattock	3.8	5.7	5.7	1.5	4	Crush
2	Two-Handed Sword	4.3	7.8	6.5	1.8	4.4	Slash
3	War Axe	4.4	9.3	6.6	2.1	4.8	Slash
3	Great Hammer	4.8	10.1	7.2	2.1	4.8	Crush
4	Battle Axe	4.9	11.8	7.4	2.4	5.2	Slash
4	Great Sword	5.1	12.3	7.7	2.4	5.6	Slash
5	Great Axe	5.2	14	7.8	2.7	6	Slash
6	Arch Mace	5.1	15.3	7.7	3.0	5.5	Crush
6	Great Scimitar	4.8	14.6	7.2	3.0	4	Slash
6	War Pick	5.0	15	7.5	3.0	5	Thrust

Weapon Drops & Rewards

Note: Polearms and two-handed weapons in Albion use two skills to determine damage. The main skill (Polearm or Two-Handed) determines the maximum possible damage. The secondary skill (based on damage type: Slash, Crush or Thrust) determines the minimum possible damage. The closer the secondary skill is to the main skill, the higher your minimum possible damage with each hit.

Abbreviations

Headings. PL = Power Level / **M#** = Material (M) and Material Level (#) / **Ql** = Quality / **Spd** = Speed, or weapon delay (the time between successive swings) / **Dam** = Damage with each hit / **DPS** = Damage per second / **Type** = Type of damage (**Cr**ush, **Sl**ash or **Thr**ust) / **Range** = basic range of the bow or crossbow, in world units (1 pace ≈ 60 world units ≈ 1 yard).

Stats. Resistance, **S**kill, Focus / **Cha**risma, **Con**stitution, **Emp**athy, **Dex**terity, **Int**elligence, **Pie**ty, **Qui**ckness, **Str**ength / **C**loth, **L**eather, **M**etal, **W**ood. The first positive percentage in any bonus indicates your increased chance to hit with the weapon.

* There is more than one weapon with this same name. This happens most often with casters' focus staffs, where up to four can have the same name but significantly different stats.

Crush Skill (Club, Cudgel, Hammer, Mace, Scepter)

Weapon	Bonus	PL	M#	Ql	Spd	Dam	DPS	Type	Generic
Training Mace		0	M1	90	2.7	3	1.2	Cr	Mace
Fellwood Cudgel (birch)		2	W	89	3.7	7	1.8	Cr	Cudgel
Flinthead Club		5	M2	100	2.7	7	2.7	Cr	Club
Mace of the Initiate	Crush S. +1	6	M2	90	3.1	9	3.0	Cr	Mace
Old Sledge		8	M2	80	4.3	15	3.6	Cr	Hammer
Bloody Scepter		8	M2	70	3.5	13	3.6	Cr	Scepter
Hammer of Smiting	+5%; Smiting S. +2	10	M2	90	4	17	4.2	Cr	Hammer
Hammer of the Plains	+5%; Str +4	13	M3	89	3.8	19	5.1	Cr	Hammer
Arm-Bone Scepter	+5%; Smiting S. +2	13	M3	89	3.5	18	5.1	Cr	Scepter
Slaver Hammer	+5%; Crush S. +1; Qui +1; Spirit R. +2	14	M3	89	2.7	15	5.5	Cr	Hammer
Growler	+5%; Crush S. +2; Str +3	14	M3	100	4	22	5.4	Cr	Mace
Mithrian Mace	+5%; Pie +4	14	M3	89	3.5	19	5.4	Cr	Mace
Bushwack Mace	+5%; Crush S. +1; Body R. +4	15	M3	89	3.3	19	5.7	Cr	Mace
Deathscent Mace	+5%; Crush S. +2	15	M3	89	3.5	20	5.7	Cr	Mace
Ogre King's Decider	+10%; Crush S. +1; Str +1	16	M4	89	4.3	26	6.0	Cr	Hammer
Breaker	+10%; Crush S. +2; Pie +4	18	M4	100	3	20	6.6	Cr	Hammer
War Hammer	+10%; Crush S. +2; Pie +4	20	M4	100	4.3	31	7.2	Cr	Hammer
Mace of the Meek	+10%; Crush S. +2	20	M4	89	3.7	27	7.2	Cr	Mace
Goblin War Hammer	+10%; Str, Dex +3; Con +1	23	M5	89	4.3	35	8.1	Cr	Hammer
Dark Mace	+10%; Str +3; Pie +4	23	M5	89	3.5	28	8.1	Cr	Mace
Hoarde Hammer	+10%; Crush, Parry S. +1; Slash R. +2	24	M5	89	3	25	8.4	Cr	Hammer
Hammer of Wrath	+15%; Smiting S. +3; Str +6	26	M6	100	4.4	40	9.0	Cr	Hammer
Goblin Crusher	+15%; Dual Wield S. +1; Qui +4	28	M6	89	3	29	9.6	Cr	Hammer
Mithril Building Hammer	+10%; Crush S. +2; Con +3; Qui +4	30	M6	89	3	31	10.2	Cr	Hammer
Despoiled Flanged Mace	+15%; Crush S. +2; Con +3	30	M6	100	3.5	36	10.2	Cr	Mace
Despoiled Mace	+15%; Crush S. +2; Str +3	30	M6	89	3.1	32	10.2	Cr	Mace
Eye-Studded Mace	+15%; Power +1; Crush S. +1; Spirit R. +4; Body R. +2	32	M7	89	3.3	36	10.8	Cr	Mace
Deathward	+15%; HP +9; Crush R. +8; Pie +3	35	M7	89	3.7	43	11.7	Cr	Mace
Morvel Mauler	+15%; Str +4; Con +6	35	M7	89	3.5	41	11.7	Cr	Mace
Spiked War Scepter	+20%; Crush S. +2; Str, Pie +3	35	M7	89	3.7	43	11.7	Cr	Mace
Yog's Iron Fist	+15%; Crush S. +2; Pie +10; Str +6	35	M7	100	4.2	49	11.7	Cr	Mace
Worn Asterite Hammer	Crush S. +2	37	M8	80	4	49	12.3	Cr	Hammer
Clergyman's Mace	+20%; Power +2; Pie +3; Con +4	38	M8	89	3.3	42	12.6	Cr	Mace
Unforgiving Mace	+20%; Crush S. +1; Con +6; Dex +3	40	M8	89	3.8	50	13.2	Cr	Mace
Glacial Hammer	+20%; Crush S. +2; Str +9; Qui +4; Pie +6	41	M8	100	4	54	13.5	Cr	Hammer

Weapon	Bonus	PL	M#	Ql	Spd	Dam	DPS	Type	Generic
Beater's Bludgeon	+20%; Crush S. +3; Str +4	42	M8	89	4.2	58	13.8	Cr	Hammer
Hammer of Deliverance	+20%; Rejuvenation S. +4; Str +13	43	M8	100	4.4	62	14.1	Cr	Hammer
Hammer of Faithful Might	+20%; Enhancements S. +4; Str +13	43	M8	100	4.4	62	14.1	Cr	Hammer
Hammer of Judgment	+20%; Smiting S. +4; Str +13	43	M8	100	4.4	62	14.1	Cr	Hammer
Light Asterite Hammer	+20%; Crush S. +3; Str +4	43	M8	89	4	56	14.1	Cr	Hammer
Arcing Bludgeoner	+20%; Crush, Parry, Dual Wield S. +2; Qui +9	43	M8	100	2.8	39	14.1	Cr	Mace
Glitter	+20%; Crush, Dual Wield S. +4	43	M8	100	3.5	49	14.1	Cr	Mace
Mace of the Cherub	+20%; Crush S. +4; HP +27	43	M8	100	3.5	49	14.1	Cr	Mace
Mace of Retribution	+20%; Crush S. +4; HP +27	43	M8	100	3.5	49	14.1	Cr	Mace
Pygmy Needle Mace	+20%; Crush S. +3; Str +6	44	M8	89	3	43	14.4	Cr	Mace
Smoldering Sable Mace	+25%; Crush S. +2; Pie +7	47	M8	89	3.4	52	15.3	Cr	Mace
Stone Breaker	+25%; Crush S. +3; Pie +6	48	M8	89	3.3	51	15.6	Cr	Mace
Darkened Sledge	+25%; Smiting S. +4; Pie +10	50	M8	90	4.4	71	16.2	Cr	Hammer
Doomcaller	+30%; Crush S. +6; Str +9; Body R. +10	50	M8	93	3	49	16.2	Cr	Hammer
Ellyll Hammer	+20%; Crush S. +3; Pie +7	50	M8	89	4	65	16.2	Cr	Hammer
Feather Light Granite Hammer	+25%; Crush S. +4; Dual Wield S. +3; Body R. +2	50	M8	90	2.3	37	16.2	Cr	Hammer
Fiery Pious Bludgeoner	+25%; Pie +9; Con, Str +7	50	M8	90	4.3	70	16.2	Cr	Hammer
Granite Pulverizer	+25%; HP +18; Pie +7; Con +6	50	M8	90	3.8	62	16.2	Cr	Hammer
Hammer of Crushing Might	+25%; Crush S. +3; Str, Qui +4; Parry S. +2	50	M8	90	4.3	70	16.2	Cr	Hammer
Sulfurous Basher	+25%; Crush S. +3; Str +7; Slash R. +8	50	M8	90	3.8	62	16.2	Cr	Hammer
Toad Thumper	+25%; Crush S. +6; Dex +4	50	M8	90	4.2	68	16.2	Cr	Hammer
Cailiondar Mace	+25%; Crush S. +3; Pie +10; Con, Str +4	50	M8	91	3.6	58	16.2	Cr	Mace
Diamond Mace	+25%; Parry S. +4; Slash, Matter, Cold R. +6	50	M8	90	3.5	57	16.2	Cr	Mace
Hair Wrapped Mace	+25%; Crush S. +6; Str +7	50	M8	90	3.3	53	16.2	Cr	Mace
Tooth Studded Mace	+30%; Crush S. +7; Str +11; Crush R. +8; Body R. +6	50	M8	93	3.8	62	16.2	Cr	Mace

Polearm Skill (Axe, Bardiche, Bill, Halberd, Hammer, Pike)

Weapon	Bonus	PL	M#	Ql	Spd	Dam	DPS	Type	Generic
Pike of the Initiate	Polearm S. +1	6	M2	100	3.3	10	3.0	Thr	Pike
Old Lucerne Hammer		8	M2	80	5.7	21	3.6	Cr	Hammer
Ogre Forged Cleaver	+5% to hit	13	M3	89	5	26	5.1	Sl	Axe
Mithrian Barbed Pike	+5%; Dex +3; Str +1	14	M3	89	4.6	25	5.4	Thr	Pike
Night's Fall Halberd	+5%; Polearm S. +2	15	M3	89	6	34	5.7	Sl	Halberd
Night's Fall Hammer	+5%; Polearm S. +2	15	M3	89	5.6	32	5.7	Cr	Hammer
Skullcracker	+5%; Crush S. +2; Str +4	16	M4	90	5	30	6.0	Cr	Hammer
Night's Edge Bill	+10%; Polearm S. +1; Str +1	17	M4	89	5.2	33	6.3	Thr	Bill
Lifetaker	+10%; Polearm S. +2; Str +4	18	M4	100	5.8	38	6.6	Sl	Axe
Night's Edge Axe	+10%; Polearm S. +1; Str +1	18	M4	89	4.8	32	6.6	Sl	Axe
Night's Edge Pike	+10%; Polearm S. +2	19	M4	89	4.4	30	6.9	Thr	Pike
Keltoi Honed Halberd	+10%; Polearm, Parry S. +1	21	M5	89	5.9	44	7.5	Sl	Halberd
Hob Hunter Hammer	+10%; Polearm S. +1; Str +4	23	M5	89	5.6	45	8.1	Cr	Hammer
Dark Lucerne Hammer	+10%; Str +7	24	M5	89	5.5	46	8.4	Cr	Hammer
Fire-Forged Pike	+15%; Polearm S. +1; Str +3; Dex +1	28	M6	89	4.4	42	9.6	Thr	Pike
Despoiled Lochaber Axe	+15%; Polearm S. +2; Con +3	31	M7	89	5	53	10.5	Sl	Axe
Despoiled Bill	+15%; Polearm S. +2; Qui +3	31	M7	89	5.4	57	10.5	Thr	Bill
Despoiled Lucerne Hammer	+15%; Polearm S. +2; Str +3	31	M7	89	5.8	61	10.5	Cr	Hammer
Goblin-Forged Lochaber Axe	+15%; Polearm S. +1; Str +3; Qui +4	32	M7	89	4.8	52	10.8	Sl	Axe
Arawnite Serrated Halberd	+15%; Polearm S. +3; Str +4	35	M7	89	6	70	11.7	Sl	Halberd
Worn Asterite Lochaber Axe	Polearm S. +2	37	M8	80	4.9	60	12.3	Sl	Axe
Worn Asterite Lucerne Hammer	Polearm S. +2	37	M8	80	5.5	68	12.3	Cr	Hammer
Worn Asterite Pike	Polearm S. +2	37	M8	80	4.4	54	12.3	Thr	Pike
Deathly Lochaber Axe	+15%; Polearm S. +4	39	M8	89	4.8	62	12.9	Sl	Axe
Dash's Long Hammer	+20%; Polearm, Crush S. +2; Str +9; Qui +4	39	M8	100	5.6	72	12.9	Cr	Hammer
Dead Warrior's Pike	+15%; Dex, Qui +3; Polearm S. +2	39	M8	89	4.4	57	12.9	Thr	Pike
Danaoin Harpoon	+20%; Thrust, Polearm S. +1; Con, Qui +3	40	M8	89	4.8	63	13.2	Thr	Pike
Glacial Long Hammer	+20%; Polearm, Crush S. +2; Str +9; Qui +4	41	M8	100	5.6	76	13.5	Cr	Hammer
Keen Asterite Lochaber Axe	+20%; Slash S. +1; Polearm S. +2; Str +4	43	M8	89	4.9	69	14.1	Sl	Axe
Bardiche of Retribution	+20%; Polearm S. +6; Parry S. +3	43	M8	100	5.6	79	14.1	Sl	Bardiche
Fiery Impaler	+20%; Polearm S. +3; Dex, Str +9	43	M8	100	5	71	14.1	Thr	Bill
Cerulean Rime	+20%; Polearm S. +3; Str, Qui +9	43	M8	100	5.5	78	14.1	Cr	Hammer
Light Asterite Lucerne Hammer	+20%; Crush S. +1; Polearm S. +2; Con +4	43	M8	89	5.5	78	14.1	Cr	Hammer
Keen Asterite Pike	+20%; Thrust S. +1; Polearm S. +2; Heat R. +4; Thrust R. +2	43	M8	89	4.4	62	14.1	Thr	Pike
Fallen Soldier's Axe	+20%; Slash, Polearm S. +2; Str +3	45	M8	89	4.5	66	14.7	Sl	Axe

Weapon	Bonus	PL	M#	QI	Spd	Dam	DPS	Type	Generic
Fallen Soldier's Hammer	+20%; Crush, Polearm S. +2; Str +3	45	M8	89	5.5	81	14.7	Cr	Hammer
Fallen Soldier's Pike	+20%; Thrust, Polearm S. +2; Str +3	45	M8	89	4.3	63	14.7	Thr	Pike
Grim Impaler	+25%; Polearm S. +2; Str +4; Energy R. +4	47	M8	89	5.2	80	15.3	Thr	Bill
Halberd of the Covetous	+25%; Polearm S. +2; Str +7	47	M8	89	5.9	90	15.3	Sl	Halberd
Hammer of the Yearning Soul	+25%; Polearm S. +2; Str +7	47	M8	89	5.5	84	15.3	Cr	Hammer
Diamond Lochaber	+25%; Polearm S. +3; Matter R. +8; Body, Energy R. +6	50	M8	90	4.8	78	16.2	Sl	Axe
Stonewatch Bill	+25%; Polearm S. +4; Thrust S. +2; Parry S. +1; Body R. +4	50	M8	90	5.3	86	16.2	Thr	Bill
Toad Bill	+25%; Parry S. +3; Body, Slash R. +6; HP +12	50	M8	90	5.2	84	16.2	Thr	Bill
Bloodied Halberd	+30%; Polearm, Parry S. +4; Qui +6; HP +9	50	M8	91	6	97	16.2	Sl	Halberd
Halberd of the Stonewatch	+25%; Polearm S. +4; Slash S. +3; Parry S. +1; Body R. +2	50	M8	90	5.6	91	16.2	Sl	Halberd
Hammer of the Stonewatch	+25%; Polearm S. +4; Crush S. +3; Parry S. +1; Body R. +2	50	M8	90	5.6	91	16.2	Cr	Hammer
Royal Scepter	+30%; Polearm S. +5; Str +7; HP +21	50	M8	93	5.5	89	16.2	Cr	Hammer
Diamond Pike	+25%; Polearm S. +7; Con +4	50	M8	90	4.4	71	16.2	Thr	Pike
Raven Clan Skewer	+25%; Polearm S. +5; Dex +7	50	M8	90	4.6	75	16.2	Thr	Pike

Slash Skill (Axe Claw Dagger Falchion Fang Knife Lightbringer Scimitar Sword Talon Tooth Tusk)

Weapon	Bonus	PL	M#	QI	Spd	Dam	DPS	Type	Generic
Training Axe		0	M1	90	2.5	3	1.2	Sl	Axe
Practice Long Sword		0	M1	90	3.7	3	0.7	Sl	Sword
Practice Sword		0	M1	90	2.5	3	1.2	Sl	Sword
Sharp Claw		5	M2	95	2.3	6	2.7	Sl	Claw
Flint Knife		5	M2	100	2.3	6	2.7	Sl	Knife
Old Iron Dagger	+5%; Dex +1	6	M2	89	2.4	7	3.0	Sl	Dagger
Tarnished Dagger		6	M2	71	2.3	7	3.0	Sl	Dagger
Sword of the Initiate	Slash S. +1	6	M2	90	2.5	8	3.0	Sl	Sword
Parrying Falchion	Parry S. +1	7	M2	100	2.5	8	3.3	Sl	Falchion
Ceremonial Scimitar		8	M2	80	3.4	12	3.6	Sl	Scimitar
Gem Studded Dagger	Slash S. +2	10	M2	90	2	8	4.2	Sl	Dagger
Gem Studded Long Sword	Slash S. +2	10	M2	90	3.3	14	4.2	Sl	Sword
Carrion Drake Talon		10	M3	71	2.3	10	4.2	Sl	Talon
Sharp Tusk		10	M3	95	2.3	10	4.2	Sl	Tusk
Small Tusk		10	M2	100	2.7	11	4.2	Sl	Tusk
Sacrificial Dagger		11	M3	71	2.5	11	4.5	Sl	Dagger
Lightbringer	+5%; Chants S. +2	13	M3	89	3	15	5.1	Sl	Lightbringer
Barker	+5%; Slash S. +2; Str +3	13	M3	100	3.6	18	5.1	Sl	Sword
Blade of Etheric Mist	+1%; Cold R. +2; Slash S. +1	13	M3	90	3.5	18	5.1	Sl	Sword
Ogre Forged Slicer	+5% to hit	13	M3	89	3.5	18	5.1	Sl	Sword
Roman Short Sword		13	M3	80	2.5	13	5.1	Sl	Sword
Jagged Axe	+1%; Str +3; Slash S. +1	14	M3	100	2.7	15	5.4	Sl	Axe
Mithrian Longsword	+5%; Str +4	14	M3	89	3.7	20	5.4	Sl	Sword
Bloody Short Sword	+5%; Slash S. +2; Str +3	16	M4	100	2.5	15	6.0	Sl	Sword
Golden Inlaid Sword	+5%; Slash S. +2; Str +3	16	M4	90	3.6	22	6.0	Sl	Sword
Well-Used Long Sword		16	M4	71	4	24	6.0	Sl	Sword
Endearment Dagger	+10%; Slash S. +1; Qui +1	17	M4	89	2.4	15	6.3	Sl	Dagger
Long Animal Fang	+10%; Slash S. +1; Str +1	17	M4	100	3	19	6.3	Sl	Fang
Snakehead Axe	+10%; Slash S. +1; Dex +1	18	M4	89	2.5	17	6.6	Sl	Axe
Warden's Sword	+10%; Slash S. +1; Cold, Matter R. +2	19	M4	89	2.8	19	6.9	Sl	Sword
Decorated Roman Dagger	+5%; Slash S. +2; Dex +3	20	M4	89	2.3	17	7.2	Sl	Dagger
Hound Tooth	+15% to hit	20	M4	89	2.5	18	7.2	Sl	Tooth
Dark Scimitar	+10%; Str, Qui +3	21	M5	89	3.2	24	7.5	Sl	Scimitar
Dark Short Sword	+10%; Slash S. +2	21	M5	89	2.7	20	7.5	Sl	Sword
Lion Etched Sword	+10%; Slash S. +2; Spirit R. +8	21	M5	89	4	30	7.5	Sl	Sword
Razor Bone Edge	+10%; Slash S. +1; HP +6	21	M5	89	3.5	26	7.5	Sl	Sword
Salisbury Dagger	+10%; Slash S. +1; Str, Dex +3	21	M5	90	3.2	24	7.5	Sl	Sword
Death Sliver	+10%; Slash S. +2; Str +1	22	M5	89	3.9	30	7.8	Sl	Sword
Nature's Charm	+10%; Slash S. +3	22	M5	89	4.3	34	7.8	Sl	Sword
Goblin Reaver	+10%; Slash S. +1; Str +4	23	M5	89	3.6	29	8.1	Sl	Sword
Hunter's Broadsword	+10%; Qui +6; Slash S. +1	24	M5	89	3.2	27	8.4	Sl	Sword
Knifeman's Crystal Dagger	+5%; Dex +12	26	M6	89	2.2	20	9.0	Sl	Dagger
Knifeman's Gold Dagger	+5%; Slash S. +2; Dex +6	26	M6	89	2.4	22	9.0	Sl	Dagger
Knifeman's Silver Dagger	+5%; Slash S. +4	26	M6	89	2.5	23	9.0	Sl	Dagger
Frosted Scimitar	+5%; Slash S. +2; Dex +3	26	M6	100	3.1	28	9.0	Sl	Scimitar

Weapon	Bonus	PL	M#	Ql	Spd	Dam	DPS	Type	Generic
Shadow-Slicer	+15%; Slash, Parry S. +1; Dex +4	26	M6	90	2.2	20	9.0	Sl	Sword
Golden-Alloy Sword	+15%; Slash S. +3; Parry S. +2; Str +9	27	M6	100	3	28	9.3	Sl	Sword
Sheer Ruby Blade	+15%; Slash S. +5; Dex +10	27	M6	100	2.5	23	9.3	Sl	Sword
Goblin Cleaver	+15%; Dual Wield S. +1; Qui +4	28	M6	89	2.7	26	9.6	Sl	Axe
Despoiled Short Sword	+15%; Slash S. +2; Qui +3	29	M6	89	2.9	29	9.9	Sl	Sword
Despoiled War Sword	+15%; Slash S. +2; Qui +3	29	M6	89	3.6	36	9.9	Sl	Sword
Serrated Lion Fang	+15%; Slash, Dual Wield S. +2; Str +7	32	M7	100	2.6	28	10.8	Sl	Fang
Sheer Ruby Defender	+15%; Parry S. +4; Dual Wield S. +2; Crush, Slash R. +5	33	M6	100	2	22	11.1	Sl	Sword
Singular War Sword	+20%; Slash S. +3	33	M7	89	3.8	42	11.1	Sl	Sword
Arawnite Longsword	+15%; Qui +4; Slash S. +3	35	M7	89	3.5	41	11.7	Sl	Sword
Director's Devastator	+15%; Slash S. +2; Str +6	35	M7	89	3	35	11.7	Sl	Sword
Worn Asterite Blade	Slash S. +2	37	M8	80	3.5	43	12.3	Sl	Sword
Diamond Scimitar	+25%; Slash S. +3; Qui +6; Body R. +6; HP +12	38	M8	90	3.3	42	12.6	Sl	Scimitar
Great Hound Tooth	+20%; Slash S. +1; HP +18	38	M8	89	2.7	34	12.6	Sl	Tooth
Huge Sharpened Boar Tusk	+20%; Slash S. +3; Slash R. +6; Qui, Str +4	38	M8	100	2.7	34	12.6	Sl	Tusk
Sword of Avengement	+20%; Slash S. +1; Dex +6; Str +3	39	M8	89	3.6	46	12.9	Sl	Sword
Tusker's Old Wound	+20%; Slash, Parry S. +2; Body, Energy R. +8	40	M8	100	3.4	45	13.2	Sl	Sword
Claw of the Rending	+20%; Body R. +6; Qui, Str +4	42	M8	89	2.7	37	13.8	Sl	Claw
Long Drake Talon	+20%; Slash S. +3; Cha +4	42	M8	89	3.5	48	13.8	Sl	Talon
Danaoin Bladeblocker	+20%; Parry S. +2; HP +18	43	M8	89	3	43	14.2	Sl	Scimitar
Dazzle	+20%; Slash, Dual Wield S. +4	43	M8	100	3.6	51	14.1	Sl	Sword
Death Dancer	+20%; Slash, Dual Wield S. +4	43	M8	100	3.6	51	14.1	Sl	Sword
Deathtale	+20%; Slash S. +4; HP +27	43	M8	100	3.7	52	14.1	Sl	Sword
Keen Asterite Blade	+20%; Slash S. +1; Parry S. +2; Qui +4	43	M8	89	3.5	49	14.1	Sl	Sword
Longsword of Retribution	+20%; Slash S. +4; HP +27	43	M8	100	3.7	52	14.1	Sl	Sword
Shadow Cutter	+20%; Slash S. +6; Str +7	43	M8	100	3.7	52	14.1	Sl	Sword
Spark of Midnight	+20%; Slash, Parry, Dual Wield S. +2; Qui +9	43	M8	100	2.8	39	14.1	Sl	Sword
Sword of the Seraph	+20%; Slash S. +6; Str +7	43	M8	100	3.7	52	14.1	Sl	Sword
Timber Walker's Defender	+15%; Parry S. +5	43	M8	89	2.2	31	14.1	Sl	Sword
Timber Walker's Slicer	+15%; Slash S. +5	43	M8	89	2.9	41	14.1	Sl	Sword
Fiery Hound Tooth	+20%; HP +21; Dual Wield S. +1	43	M8	89	3	42	14.1	Sl	Tooth
Fallen Archer's Dagger	+20%; Slash, Parry S. +1; Str +6	45	M8	89	2.4	35	14.7	Sl	Dagger
Caller Shard	+20%; Slash, Parry S. +2; Str +3	45	M8	89	3.6	53	14.7	Sl	Sword
Fallen Guardsman's Sword	+20%; Slash S. +2; Parry S. +1; Spirit, Body R. +4	45	M8	89	3.3	49	14.7	Sl	Sword
Longsword of Rancor	+20%; Slash S. +1; Con +6; Str +3	45	M8	89	3.6	53	14.7	Sl	Sword
Ancient Ebony Scimitar	+25%; Slash S. +2; Qui +7	47	M8	89	3	46	15.3	Sl	Scimitar
Shard of the Stonewatch	+25%; Slash, Parry S. +2; Con +3	47	M8	89	3.6	55	15.3	Sl	Sword
Sheer Ruby Scale-Splitter	+25% to hit	48	M8	89	3.2	50	15.6	Sl	Sword
Molten Magma Sword	+25%; Slash S. +3; Dex +6	49	M8	89	2.8	45	15.9	Sl	Sword
Feather Light Granite Axe	+25%; Slash S. +4; Dual Wield S. +3; Body R. +2	50	M8	90	2.4	39	16.2	Sl	Axe
Frenzy Axe	+25%; Parry S. +3; Cold, Energy R. +8; Qui +6	50	M8	90	2.7	44	16.2	Sl	Axe
Diamond Dagger	+25%; Envenom S. +3; Body R. +12; Qui +6	50	M8	90	2.7	44	16.2	Sl	Dagger
Facimil	+25%; Slash S. +4; Dex, Qui +9	50	M8	91	3.3	53	16.2	Sl	Scimitar
Cailiondar Bastard Sword	+25%; Slash S. +4; Parry S. +2; Str +10	50	M8	91	3.8	62	16.2	Sl	Sword
Darksword of Granite	+25%; Slash S. +4; Str +9; Body R. +10	50	M8	90	3.9	63	16.2	Sl	Sword
Diamond Bastard	+25%; Parry S. +3; Con +6; Crush R. +6; HP +6	50	M8	90	3.9	63	16.2	Sl	Sword
Doom Sword	+30%; Slash S. +3; Parry S. +4; Body R. +8; Dex +7	50	M8	91	2.8	45	16.2	Sl	Sword
Ellyll Sword	+20%; Slash S. +3; Str +7	50	M8	89	3.3	53	16.2	Sl	Sword
Gorged Blade	+25%; Parry S. +4; Matter, Cold, Body R. +6	50	M8	90	3	49	16.2	Sl	Sword
Lava Forged Sword	+25%; Slash S. +4; Qui, Dex +7	50	M8	90	2.8	45	16.2	Sl	Sword
Longsword	+25% to hit	50	M8	100	3	49	16.2	Sl	Sword
Toad Bane	+25%; Power +2; Slash S. +3; Con +7; Parry S. +1	50	M8	90	3.5	57	16.2	Sl	Sword

Staff Skill (Scepter, Staff)

Weapon	Bonus	PL	M#	Ql	Spd	Dam	DPS	Type	Generic
Trimmed Branch		0	W	90	2.7	3	1.2	Cr	Staff
Ashen Fellwood Staff (birch)		1	W	89	4.5	7	1.5	Cr	Staff
Ebony Fellwood Staff		1	W	89	4.5	7	1.5	Cr	Staff
Heartwood Staff		1	W	89	4.5	7	1.5	Cr	Staff
Shambler Staff (birch)	+1% to hit	2	W	89	2.5	5	1.8	Cr	Staff
Petrified Branch	Cold Magic, Earth Magic, Body Magic, Matter Magic F. +2	4	W1	90	4.4	11	2.4	Cr	Staff
Cabalist Staff of Alteration *	Cabalist spells F. +4	6	W2	85	4.5	14	3.0	Cr	Staff

Weapon	Bonus	PL	M#	QI	Spd	Dam	DPS	Type	Generic
Cabalist Staff of Body *	Body Magic F. +5; other Cabalist spells F. +2	6	W2	85	4.5	14	3.0	Cr	Staff
Cabalist Staff of Focus	Cabalist spells F. +4	6	W2	90	4.5	14	3.0	Cr	Staff
Cabalist Staff of Matter *	Matter Magic F. +5; other Cabalist spells F. +2	6	W2	85	4.5	14	3.0	Cr	Staff
Cabalist Staff of Spirit *	Spirit Magic F. +5; other Cabalist spells F. +2	6	W2	85	4.5	14	3.0	Cr	Staff
Old Otherworldly Staff	+1%; Mage spells F. +5	6	W2	80	4.5	14	3.0	Cr	Staff
Sorcerer Staff of Alteration *	Sorcerer spells F. +4	6	W2	85	4.5	14	3.0	Cr	Staff
Sorcerer Staff of Body *	Body Magic F. +5; other Sorcerer spells F. +2	6	W2	85	4.5	14	3.0	Cr	Staff
Sorcerer Staff of Focus	Sorcerer spells F. +4	6	W2	90	4.5	14	3.0	Cr	Staff
Sorcerer Staff of Matter *	Matter Magic F. +5; other Sorcerer spells F. +2	6	W2	85	4.5	14	3.0	Cr	Staff
Sorcerer Staff of Mind *	Mind Magic F. +5; other Sorcerer spells F. +2	6	W2	85	4.5	14	3.0	Cr	Staff
Theurgist Staff of Earth *	Earth Magic F. +5; other Theurgist spells F. +2	6	W2	85	4.5	14	3.0	Cr	Staff
Theurgist Staff of Elements *	Theurgist spells F. +4	6	W2	85	4.5	14	3.0	Cr	Staff
Theurgist Staff of Focus	Theurgist spells F. +4	6	W2	90	4.5	14	3.0	Cr	Staff
Theurgist Staff of Ice *	Cold Magic F. +5; other Theurgist spells F. +2	6	W2	85	4.5	14	3.0	Cr	Staff
Theurgist Staff of Wind *	Wind Magic F. +5; other Theurgist spells F. +2	6	W2	85	4.5	14	3.0	Cr	Staff
Wizard Staff of Earth *	Earth Magic F. +5; other Wizard spells F. +2	6	W2	85	4.5	14	3.0	Cr	Staff
Wizard Staff of Elements *	Wizard spells F. +4	6	W2	85	4.5	14	3.0	Cr	Staff
Wizard Staff of Fire *	Fire Magic F. +5; other Wizard spells F. +2	6	W2	85	4.5	14	3.0	Cr	Staff
Wizard Staff of Focus	Wizard spells F. +4	6	W2	90	4.5	14	3.0	Cr	Staff
Wizard Staff of Ice *	Cold Magic F. +5; other Wizard spells F. +2	6	W2	85	4.5	14	3.0	Cr	Staff
Staff of Winds	+5%; Cold Magic F. +5; other Theurgist spells F. +2	7	W2	89	4.5	15	3.3	Cr	Staff
Old Quarterstaff		8	W2	80	3.1	11	3.6	Cr	Staff
Old Staff of Elements	+1%; Elementalist spells F. +5	8	W2	80	4.6	17	3.6	Cr	Staff
Cabalist Staff of Alteration *	Cabalist spells F. +7	11	W3	85	4.5	20	4.5	Cr	Staff
Cabalist Staff of Body *	Body Magic F. +9; other Cabalist spells F. +5	11	W3	85	4.5	20	4.5	Cr	Staff
Cabalist Staff of Matter *	Matter Magic F. +9; other Cabalist spells F. +5	11	W3	85	4.5	20	4.5	Cr	Staff
Cabalist Staff of Spirit *	Spirit Magic F. +9; other Cabalist spells F. +5	11	W3	85	4.5	20	4.5	Cr	Staff
Imbued Staff	+5%; Staff S. +2	11	W3	100	4.5	20	4.5	Cr	Staff
Mithrian Otherworldly Staff	+5%; Mage spells F. +11	11	W3	89	4.5	20	4.5	Cr	Staff
Sorcerer Staff of Alteration *	Sorcerer spells F. +7	11	W3	85	4.5	20	4.5	Cr	Staff
Sorcerer Staff of Body *	Body Magic F. +9; other Sorcerer spells F. +5	11	W3	85	4.5	20	4.5	Cr	Staff
Sorcerer Staff of Matter *	Matter Magic F. +9; other Sorcerer spells F. +5	11	W3	85	4.5	20	4.5	Cr	Staff
Sorcerer Staff of Mind *	Mind Magic F. +9; other Sorcerer spells F. +5	11	W3	85	4.5	20	4.5	Cr	Staff
Staff of Life	+5% to hit	11	W3	100	5	23	4.5	Cr	Staff
Theurgist Staff of Earth *	Earth Magic F. +9; other Theurgist spells F. +5	11	W3	85	4.5	20	4.5	Cr	Staff
Theurgist Staff of Elements *	Theurgist spells F. +7	11	W3	85	4.5	20	4.5	Cr	Staff
Theurgist Staff of Ice *	Cold Magic F. +9; other Theurgist spells F. +5	11	W3	85	4.5	20	4.5	Cr	Staff
Theurgist Staff of Wind *	Wind Magic F. +9; other Theurgist spells F. +5	11	W3	85	4.5	20	4.5	Cr	Staff
Wizard Staff of Earth *	Earth Magic F. +9; other Wizard spells F. +5	11	W3	85	4.5	20	4.5	Cr	Staff
Wizard Staff of Elements *	Wizard spells F. +7	11	W3	85	4.5	20	4.5	Cr	Staff
Wizard Staff of Fire *	Fire Magic F. +9; other Wizard spells F. +5	11	W3	85	4.5	20	4.5	Cr	Staff
Wizard Staff of Ice *	Cold Magic F. +9; other Wizard spells F. +5	11	W3	85	4.5	20	4.5	Cr	Staff
Gnarled Staff	Int +4; Dex –5	12	W3	89	4.5	22	4.8	Cr	Staff
Michaelian Staff	+5%; Enhancements S. +1; Pie +3	12	W3	89	2.2	11	4.8	Cr	Staff
Ebony Staff	+5%; Power +1; Int +4	13	M3	90	5	26	5.1	Cr	Staff
Ogre Forged Quarterstaff	+5% to hit	13	M3	89	3	15	5.1	Cr	Staff
Staff of Melting	+10%; Fire Magic F. +15; other Wizard spells F. +10; Power +2	13	W3	89	3.5	18	5.1	Cr	Staff
Ponderer	+5%; Int +4; Cabalist spells F. +10	13	W3	89	5	26	5.1	Cr	Staff
Mithrian Staff of Elements	+5%; Elementalist spells F. +11	14	W3	89	4.6	25	5.4	Cr	Staff
Staff of Forgotten Ways	+5%; Qui +4	14	W3	89	3.4	18	5.4	Cr	Staff
Charred Bone Staff	+5%; Staff S. +2	15	W3	100	4.5	26	5.7	Cr	Staff
Alloy Shod Staff	+5%; Staff S. +1; Qui +4	16	W4	90	5	30	6.0	Cr	Staff
Ashen Spirit Staff	+10%; Spirit Magic S. +1; Int +1; Spirit Magic F. +16	16	W4	89	5	30	6.0	Cr	Staff
Cabalist Staff of Alteration *	Cabalist spells F. +11	16	W4	85	4.5	27	6.0	Cr	Staff
Cabalist Staff of Body *	Body Magic F. +13; other Cabalist spells F. +7	16	W4	85	4.5	27	6.0	Cr	Staff
Cabalist Staff of Matter *	Matter Magic F. +13; other Cabalist spells F. +7	16	W4	85	4.5	27	6.0	Cr	Staff
Cabalist Staff of Spirit *	Spirit Magic F. +13; other Cabalist spells F. +7	16	W4	85	4.5	27	6.0	Cr	Staff
Elder Staff of Earthen Fire	+10%; Fire, Earth Magic S. +1; Fire, Earth Magic F. +16	16	W4	89	5	30	6.0	Cr	Staff
Elder Staff of Wintry Winds	+10%; Cold, Wind Magic S. +1; Cold, Wind Magic F. +16	16	W4	89	5	30	6.0	Cr	Staff
Scepter of Intellect	+5%; Fire Magic, Matter Magic S. +1; Int +4	16	M4	90	4	24	6.0	Cr	Scepter
Sorcerer Staff of Alteration *	Sorcerer spells F. +11	16	W4	85	4.5	27	6.0	Cr	Staff
Sorcerer Staff of Body *	Body Magic F. +13; other Sorcerer spells F. +7	16	W4	85	4.5	27	6.0	Cr	Staff
Sorcerer Staff of Matter *	Matter Magic F. +13; other Sorcerer spells F. +7	16	W4	85	4.5	27	6.0	Cr	Staff

Weapon	Bonus	PL	M#	Ql	Spd	Dam	DPS	Type	Generic
Sorcerer Staff of Mind *	Mind Magic F. +13; other Sorcerer spells F. +7	16	W4	85	4.5	27	6.0	Cr	Staff
Theurgist Staff of Earth *	Earth Magic F. +13; other Theurgist spells F. +7	16	W4	85	4.5	27	6.0	Cr	Staff
Theurgist Staff of Elements *	Theurgist spells F. +11	16	W4	85	4.5	27	6.0	Cr	Staff
Theurgist Staff of Ice *	Cold Magic F. +13; other Theurgist spells F. +7	16	W4	85	4.5	27	6.0	Cr	Staff
Theurgist Staff of Wind *	Wind Magic F. +13; other Theurgist spells F. +7	16	W4	85	4.5	27	6.0	Cr	Staff
Wizard Staff of Earth *	Earth Magic F. +13; other Wizard spells F. +7	16	W4	85	4.5	27	6.0	Cr	Staff
Wizard Staff of Elements *	Wizard spells F. +11	16	W4	85	4.5	27	6.0	Cr	Staff
Wizard Staff of Fire *	Fire Magic F. +13; other Wizard spells F. +7	16	W4	85	4.5	27	6.0	Cr	Staff
Wizard Staff of Ice *	Cold Magic F. +13; other Wizard spells F. +7	16	W4	85	4.5	27	6.0	Cr	Staff
Oaken Mind Staff	+10%; Mind Magic S. +1; Int +1; Mind Magic F. +17	17	W4	89	5	32	6.3	Cr	Staff
Holy Oaken Quarterstaff	+10%; Pie +4	18	W4	89	4.2	28	6.6	Cr	Staff
Runed Elm Staff	+10%; Cabalist spells F. +14; Int +6	18	W4	89	4.5	30	6.6	Cr	Staff
Cabalist Staff of Alteration *	Cabalist spells F. +14	21	W5	85	4.5	34	7.5	Cr	Staff
Cabalist Staff of Body *	Body Magic F. +18; other Cabalist spells F. +9	21	W5	85	4.5	34	7.5	Cr	Staff
Cabalist Staff of Matter *	Matter Magic F. +18; other Cabalist spells F. +9	21	W5	85	4.5	34	7.5	Cr	Staff
Cabalist Staff of Spirit *	Spirit Magic F. +18; other Cabalist spells F. +9	21	W5	85	4.5	34	7.5	Cr	Staff
Dark Shod Staff	+10%; Str, Qui +3	21	W5	89	4	30	7.5	Cr	Staff
Elder Fellwood Staff	+10%; HP +6; Pie +7	21	W5	89	5	38	7.5	Cr	Staff
Elemental Staff of Wonders	+5%; Theurgist spells F. +18; Power +6	21	W5	100	4.5	34	7.5	Cr	Staff
Sorcerer Staff of Alteration *	Sorcerer spells F. +14	21	W5	85	4.5	34	7.5	Cr	Staff
Sorcerer Staff of Body *	Body Magic F. +18; other Sorcerer spells F. +9	21	W5	85	4.5	34	7.5	Cr	Staff
Sorcerer Staff of Matter *	Matter Magic F. +18; other Sorcerer spells F. +9	21	W5	85	4.5	34	7.5	Cr	Staff
Sorcerer Staff of Mind *	Mind Magic F. +18; other Sorcerer spells F. +9	21	W5	85	4.5	34	7.5	Cr	Staff
Theurgist Staff of Earth *	Earth Magic F. +18; other Theurgist spells F. +9	21	W5	85	4.5	34	7.5	Cr	Staff
Theurgist Staff of Elements *	Theurgist spells F. +14	21	W5	85	4.5	34	7.5	Cr	Staff
Theurgist Staff of Ice *	Cold Magic F. +18; other Theurgist spells F. +9	21	W5	85	4.5	34	7.5	Cr	Staff
Theurgist Staff of Wind *	Wind Magic F. +18; other Theurgist spells F. +9	21	W5	85	4.5	34	7.5	Cr	Staff
Wizard Staff of Earth *	Earth Magic F. +18; other Wizard spells F. +9	21	W5	85	4.5	34	7.5	Cr	Staff
Wizard Staff of Elements *	Wizard spells F. +14	21	W5	85	4.5	34	7.5	Cr	Staff
Wizard Staff of Fire *	Fire Magic F. +18; other Wizard spells F. +9	21	W5	85	4.5	34	7.5	Cr	Staff
Wizard Staff of Ice *	Cold Magic F. +18; other Wizard spells F. +9	21	W5	85	4.5	34	7.5	Cr	Staff
Boneshaper's Spine	+5%; Cabalist spells F. +18; Power +6	22	M5	100	4.5	35	7.8	Cr	Staff
Staff of the Clear Mind	+1%; Staff S. +2; Pie +4; Rejuvenation S. +1	22	W5	100	2.5	20	7.8	Cr	Staff
Goblin Quarterstaff	+10%; Staff S. +1; Dex +4	23	W5	89	3	24	8.1	Cr	Staff
Goblin Staff of Body Magic	+10%; Body Magic F. +23; Int +4; Dex +3	23	W5	89	4.5	36	8.1	Cr	Staff
Goblin Staff of Matter Magic	+10%; Matter Magic F. +23; Int +4; Dex +3	23	W5	89	4.5	36	8.1	Cr	Staff
Cabalist Staff of the Imposter	+10%; Cabalist spells F. +18; HP +15	24	W5	89	4.4	37	8.4	Cr	Staff
Sorcerer Staff of the Imposter	+10%; Sorcerer spells F. +18; HP +15	24	W5	89	4.4	37	8.4	Cr	Staff
Theurgist Staff of the Imposter	+10%; Theurgist spells F. +18; HP +15	24	W5	89	4.4	37	8.4	Cr	Staff
Wizard Staff of the Imposter	+10%; Wizard spells F. +18; HP +15	24	W5	89	4.4	37	8.4	Cr	Staff
Bwgan Fishing Pole	+15%; Power +2; HP +6	26	M6	89	4.7	42	9.0	Cr	Staff
Cabalist Staff of Alteration *	Cabalist spells F. +17	26	W6	85	4.5	41	9.0	Cr	Staff
Cabalist Staff of Body *	Body Magic F. +21; other Cabalist spells F. +11	26	W6	85	4.5	41	9.0	Cr	Staff
Cabalist Staff of Matter *	Matter Magic F. +21; other Cabalist spells F. +11	26	W6	85	4.5	41	9.0	Cr	Staff
Cabalist Staff of Spirit *	Spirit Magic F. +21; other Cabalist spells F. +11	26	W6	85	4.5	41	9.0	Cr	Staff
Sorcerer Staff of Alteration *	Sorcerer spells F. +17	26	W6	85	4.5	41	9.0	Cr	Staff
Sorcerer Staff of Body *	Body Magic F. +21; other Sorcerer spells F. +11	26	W6	85	4.5	41	9.0	Cr	Staff
Sorcerer Staff of Matter *	Matter Magic F. +21; other Sorcerer spells F. +11	26	W6	85	4.5	41	9.0	Cr	Staff
Sorcerer Staff of Mind *	Mind Magic F. +21; other Sorcerer spells F. +11	26	W6	85	4.5	41	9.0	Cr	Staff
Theurgist Staff of Earth *	Earth Magic F. +21; other Theurgist spells F. +11	26	W6	85	4.5	41	9.0	Cr	Staff
Theurgist Staff of Elements *	Theurgist spells F. +17	26	W6	85	4.5	41	9.0	Cr	Staff
Theurgist Staff of Ice *	Cold Magic F. +21; other Theurgist spells F. +11	26	W6	85	4.5	41	9.0	Cr	Staff
Theurgist Staff of Wind *	Wind Magic F. +21; other Theurgist spells F. +11	26	W6	85	4.5	41	9.0	Cr	Staff
Wizard Staff of Earth *	Earth Magic F. +21; other Wizard spells F. +11	26	W6	85	4.5	41	9.0	Cr	Staff
Wizard Staff of Elements *	Wizard spells F. +17	26	W6	85	4.5	41	9.0	Cr	Staff
Wizard Staff of Fire *	Fire Magic F. +21; other Wizard spells F. +11	26	W6	85	4.5	41	9.0	Cr	Staff
Wizard Staff of Ice *	Cold Magic F. +21; other Wizard spells F. +11	26	W6	85	4.5	41	9.0	Cr	Staff
Zealot's Staff of the Pious	+10%; Staff S. +3; Enhancements S. +2; Pie +6	26	W6	100	2.9	26	9.0	Cr	Staff
Goblin Staff of Cold Magic	+15%; Cold Magic F. +28; Int +4; Dex +3	28	W6	89	4.5	43	9.6	Cr	Staff
Goblin Staff of Earth Magic	+15%; Earth Magic F. +28; Int +4; Dex +3	28	W6	89	4.5	43	9.6	Cr	Staff
Goblin Staff of Wind Magic	+15%; Wind Magic F. +28; Int +4; Dex +3	28	W6	89	4.5	43	9.6	Cr	Staff
Earthen Staff	+15%; Earth Magic F. +34; Earth Magic S. +2; Int +4	29	W6	89	4.8	48	9.9	Cr	Staff
Frozen Staff	+15%; Cold Magic F. +34; Cold Magic S. +2; Int +4	29	W6	89	4.8	48	9.9	Cr	Staff

Weapon	Bonus	PL	M#	QI	Spd	Dam	DPS	Type	Generic
Shepherd's Shod Staff	+15%; Staff, Enhancements, Rejuvenation, Parry S. +1	29	W6	89	4	40	9.9	Cr	Staff
Leg Bone Quarterstaff	+15%; Staff S. +2; Pie +3	30	W6	89	3	31	10.2	Cr	Staff
Fiery Staff	+15%; Fire Magic F. +36; Fire Magic S. +2; Int +4	31	W7	89	4.7	49	10.5	Cr	Staff
Haze	+15%; Staff S. +4; Qui +6	31	M7	100	3	32	10.5	Cr	Staff
Knotted Hamadryad Staff	+20%; Staff S. +4	31	W7	89	5.4	57	10.5	Cr	Staff
Magus Battlest.	+15%; Body, Matter Magic F. +14; Spirit, Mind Magic F. +22	31	M7	90	5	53	10.5	Cr	Staff
Staff of Compliance	+15%; Sorcerer spells F. +26; Int +10	31	M7	100	4	42	10.5	Cr	Staff
Staff of Enlightenment		31	W7	100	4.5	47	10.5	Cr	Staff
Staff of the Blazing Inferno	+10%; Fire Magic F. +26; other Wizard spells F. +17; Power +5	31	M7	90	5	53	10.5	Cr	Staff
Staff of the Fire Tempest	+15%; Wizard spells F. +26; Int +10	31	M7	100	4	42	10.5	Cr	Staff
Staff of the Tempest Wind	+15%; Theurgist spells F. +26; Int +10	31	M7	100	4	42	10.5	Cr	Staff
Staff of Winter	+10%; Cold Magic F. +26; other Theurgist spells F. +17; Power +5	31	W7	90	5	53	10.5	Cr	Staff
Visage of Death	+15%; Cabalist spells F. +26; Int +10	31	M7	100	4	42	10.5	Cr	Staff
Windy Staff	+15%; Wind Magic F. +36; Wind Magic S. +2; Int +4	31	W7	89	4.7	49	10.5	Cr	Staff
Goblin Staff of Fire Magic	+15%; Fire Magic F. +33; Int +6; Dex +4	32	W7	89	4.5	49	10.8	Cr	Staff
Goblin Staff of Mind Twisting	+15%; Mind Magic F. +33; Int +6; Dex +4	32	W7	89	4.5	49	10.8	Cr	Staff
Goblin Staff of Spirit Animation	+15%; Spirit Magic F. +33; Int +6; Dex +4	32	W7	89	4.5	49	10.8	Cr	Staff
Tribunus Staff of the Damned	+15%; Power +2; Int +6;	32	W7	89	4	43	10.8	Cr	Staff
+32 Focus for a single spell type* (* = Earth, Cold, Fire, Wind, Matter, Body, Mind or Spirit)									
Bloody Staff	+20%; Body Magic F. +38; Body Magic S. +2; Int +4	33	W7	89	4.8	53	11.1	Cr	Staff
Dissolution Staff	+20%; Matter Magic F. +38; Matter Magic S. +2; Int +4	33	W7	89	4.8	53	11.1	Cr	Staff
Wisened Staff of the Enforcer	+15%; Parry S. +2; Pie +4	33	W7	89	4	44	11.1	Cr	Staff
Mind Staff	+20%; Mind Magic F. +40; Mind Magic S. +2; Int, Dex +3	35	W7	89	4.7	55	11.7	Cr	Staff
Spirit Staff	+20%; Spirit Magic F. +40; Spirit Magic S. +2; Int, Dex +3	35	W7	89	4.7	55	11.7	Cr	Staff
Staff of Defense	+5%; Staff, Parry S. +2; Dex +7	36	W7	100	2.2	26	12.0	Cr	Staff
Worn Asterite Cabalist Staff	Cabalist spells F. +28	37	M8	80	4	49	12.3	Cr	Staff
Worn Asterite Shod Staff	Staff S. +2	37	M8	80	5	62	12.3	Cr	Staff
Worn Asterite Sorcerer Staff	Sorcerer spells F. +28	37	M8	80	4	49	12.3	Cr	Staff
Worn Asterite Theurgist Staff	Theurgist spells F. +28	37	M8	80	4	49	12.3	Cr	Staff
Worn Asterite Wizard Staff	Wizard spells F. +28	37	M8	80	4	49	12.3	Cr	Staff
Whirling Defender	+10%; Parry S. +2; Staff S. +1; Dex +7	38	W8	89	3.3	42	12.6	Cr	Staff
Jagged Granite Staff	+20%; Staff S. +2; Dex +7	41	W8	89	4.5	61	13.5	Cr	Staff
Staff of the East	+20%; Cabalist spells F. +30; Int +13	41	W8	89	4	54	13.5	Cr	Staff
Staff of the North	+20%; Wizard spells F. +30; Int +13	41	W8	89	4	54	13.5	Cr	Staff
Staff of the South	+20%; Theurgist spells F. +30; Int +13	41	W8	89	4	54	13.5	Cr	Staff
Staff of the West	+20%; Sorcerer spells F. +30; Int +13	41	W8	89	4	54	13.5	Cr	Staff
Gnarled Branch of Grovewood	+20%; Con, Pie, Str +4	43	W8	89	4.2	59	14.1	Cr	Staff
Great Asterite Shod Staff	+20%; Staff S. +3; Crush, Slash, Thrust R. +2	43	M8	89	5	71	14.1	Cr	Staff
Polished Ilmenite Staff	+20%; Staff S. +4; Con +1	43	W8	89	4.5	63	14.1	Cr	Staff
Slender Asterite Cabalist Staff	+20%; Cabalist spells F. +32; HP +24	43	M8	89	4	56	14.1	Cr	Staff
Slender Asterite Sorcerer Staff	+20%; Sorcerer spells F. +32; HP +24	43	M8	89	4	56	14.1	Cr	Staff
Slender Asterite Theurgist Staff	+20%; Theurgist spells F. +32; HP +24	43	M8	89	4	56	14.1	Cr	Staff
Slender Asterite Wizard Staff	+20%; Wizard spells F. +32; HP +24	43	M8	89	4	56	14.1	Cr	Staff
Staff of Arctic Elderwood	+20%; Theurgist spells F. +33; HP +33	43	M8	100	4	56	14.1	Cr	Staff
Staff of Body Manipulation	+20%; Body Magic F. +43; other Sorcerer spells F. +33; HP +33	43	M8	100	4	56	14.1	Cr	Staff
Staff of Earthen Delight	+20%; Earth Magic F. +43; other Wizard spells F. +33; HP +33	43	M8	100	4	56	14.1	Cr	Staff
Staff of Earthen Fury	+20%; Earth Magic F. +43; other Theurgist spells F. +33; HP +33	43	M8	100	4	56	14.1	Cr	Staff
Staff of Enhancements	+20%; Staff S. +4; Qui +6; Enhancements S. +3	43	M8	100	3	42	14.1	Cr	Staff
Staff of Eternal Channeling	+20%; Matter Magic F. +43; other Cabalist spells F. +33; HP +33	43	M8	100	4	56	14.1	Cr	Staff
Staff of Eternal Lifeforce	+20%; Body Magic F. +43; other Cabalist spells F. +33; HP +33	43	M8	100	4	56	14.1	Cr	Staff
Staff of Frozen Tears	+20%; Cold Magic F. +43; other Wizard spells F. +33; HP +33	43	M8	100	4	56	14.1	Cr	Staff
Staff of Matter Manipulation	+20%; Matter Magic F. +43; other Sorcerer spells F. +33; HP +33	43	M8	100	4	56	14.1	Cr	Staff
Staff of Mind Manipulation	+20%; Mind Magic F. +43; other Sorcerer spells F. +33; HP +33	43	M8	100	4	56	14.1	Cr	Staff
Staff of Rejuvenation	+20%; Staff S. +4; Qui +6; Rejuvenation S. +3	43	M8	100	3	42	14.1	Cr	Staff
Staff of Spirit Consumption	+20%; Spirit Magic F. +43; other Cabalist spells F. +33; HP +33	43	M8	100	4	56	14.1	Cr	Staff
Staff of the Leaping Flame	+20%; Fire Magic F. +43; other Wizard spells F. +33; HP +33	43	M8	100	4	56	14.1	Cr	Staff
Staff of the Maelstrom	+20%; Wind Magic F. +43; other Theurgist spells F. +33; HP +33	43	M8	100	4	56	14.1	Cr	Staff
Deathly Cabalist Staff	+20%; Cabalist spells F. +38; Power +10	45	W8	100	4	59	14.7	Cr	Staff
Deathly Sorcerer Staff	+20%; Sorcerer spells F. +38; Power +10	45	W8	100	4	59	14.7	Cr	Staff
Deathly Theurgist Staff	+20%; Theurgist spells F. +38; Power +10	45	W8	100	4	59	14.7	Cr	Staff
Deathly Wizard Staff	+20%; Wizard spells F. +38; Power +10	45	W8	100	4	59	14.7	Cr	Staff
Cabalist Slender Ebony Staff	+25%; Cabalist spells F. +35; Cold R. +18	47	M8	89	4.8	73	15.3	Cr	Staff
Crackling Ebony Sunderer	+25%; Staff S. +3; Energy R. +6	47	M8	89	5.5	84	15.3	Cr	Staff

Weapon	Bonus	PL	M#	QI	Spd	Dam	DPS	Type	Generic
Sorcerer Slender Ebony Staff	+25%; Sorcerer spells F. +35; Body R. +18	47	M8	89	4.8	73	15.3	Cr	Staff
Theurgist Slender Ebony Staff	+25%; Theurgist spells F. +35; Energy R. +18	47	M8	89	4.8	73	15.3	Cr	Staff
Wizardly Slender Ebony Staff	+25%; Wizard spells F. +35; Cold R. +18	47	M8	89	4.8	73	15.3	Cr	Staff
Bitten Staff	+25%; Cold Magic F. +50; Power +6; HP +21	50	W8	90	4.5	73	16.2	Cr	Staff
Chewed Staff	+25%; Matter Magic F. +50; Power +6; HP +21	50	W8	90	4.5	73	16.2	Cr	Staff
Festering Staff	+30%; Spirit Magic F. +50; Power +8; HP +18; Slash R. +8	50	W8	93	4	65	16.2	Cr	Staff
Gnarled Witherwood Staff	+25%; Staff, Enhancements, Rejuvenation, Parry S. +2	50	W8	90	4	65	16.2	Cr	Staff
Gnawed Staff	+25%; Body Magic F. +50; Power +6; HP +21	50	W8	90	4.5	73	16.2	Cr	Staff
Mouldering Staff	+30%; Fire Magic F. +50; Power +8; HP +18; Slash R. +8	50	W8	93	4	65	16.2	Cr	Staff
Nibbled Staff	+25%; Earth Magic F. +50; Power +6; HP +21	50	W8	90	4.5	73	16.2	Cr	Staff
Pillar of Might	+20%; Parry S. +2; Staff S. +2; Dex, Str +6	50	W8	90	3.2	52	16.2	Cr	Staff
Polished Granite Staff of Body	+25%; Power +6; Body Magic F. +50; Body Magic S. +3; Dex +7	50	W8	91	4.5	73	16.2	Cr	Staff
Polished Granite Staff of Cold	+25%; Power +6; Cold Magic F. +50; Cold Magic S. +3; Dex +7	50	W8	91	4.5	73	16.2	Cr	Staff
Polished Granite Staff of Earth	+25%; Power +6; Earth Magic F. +50; Earth Magic S. +3; Dex +7	50	W8	91	4.5	73	16.2	Cr	Staff
Polished Granite Staff of Fire	+25%; Power +6; Fire Magic F. +50; Fire Magic S. +3; Dex +9	50	W8	91	4.5	73	16.2	Cr	Staff
Polished Granite Staff of Matter	+25%; Power +6; Matter Magic F. +50; Matter Magic S. +3; Dex +7	50	W8	91	4.5	73	16.2	Cr	Staff
Polished Granite Staff of Mind	+25%; Power +6; Mind Magic F. +50; Mind Magic S. +3; Dex +9	50	W8	91	4.5	73	16.2	Cr	Staff
Polished Granite Staff of Spirit	+25%; Power +6; Spirit Magic F. +50; Spirit Magic S. +3; Dex +9	50	W8	91	4.5	73	16.2	Cr	Staff
Polished Granite Staff of Wind	+25%; Power +6; Wind Magic F. +50; Wind Magic S. +3; Dex +9	50	W8	91	4.5	73	16.2	Cr	Staff
Putrid Staff	+30%; Wind Magic F. +50; Power +8; HP +18; Slash R. +8	50	W8	93	4	65	16.2	Cr	Staff
Rift Sealer	+25%; Staff S. +5; Pie +10	50	W8	90	3.1	50	16.2	Cr	Staff
Rotting Staff	+30%; Mind Magic F. +50; Power +8; HP +18; Slash R. +8	50	W8	93	4	65	16.2	Cr	Staff
Stately Quarterstaff	+30%; Staff S. +4; Rejuvenation S. +3; Power +3; Pie +6	50	W8	91	4.2	68	16.2	Cr	Staff
Stonesoul Staff	+20%; Staff S. +4; Pie +3	50	W8	89	4.5	73	16.2	Cr	Staff

Thrust Skill (Dirk, Fang, Gauche, Gladius, Rapier, Shard, Spear, Stiletto, Sword, Tooth)

Weapon	Bonus	PL	M#	QI	Spd	Dam	DPS	Type	Generic
Practice Dirk		0	M1	90	2.3	3	1.2	Thr	Dirk
Fencer's Rapier	+1%; HP +6	4	M1	90	3.2	8	2.4	Thr	Rapier
Flint Dirk		5	M2	100	2.3	6	2.7	Thr	Dirk
Sharp Snake Fang	+5%; HP +6	5	M2	89	2.3	6	2.7	Thr	Fang
Rapier of the Initiate	Thrust S. +1	6	M2	90	3.2	10	3.0	Thr	Rapier
Spined Fish-Sticker	Thrust S. +1	7	M2	90	3	10	3.3	Thr	Gauche
Raiders Blade	Thrust S. +1	7	M2	90	2.8	9	3.3	Thr	Rapier
Ornamental Rapier		8	M2	80	3.3	12	3.6	Thr	Rapier
Stinging Gauche	+5%; Thrust S. +2	13	M3	89	2.6	13	5.1	Thr	Gauche
Roman Gladius		13	M3	80	3.2	16	5.1	Thr	Gladius
Ogre Forged Impaler	+5% to hit	13	M3	89	3.4	17	5.1	Thr	Spear
Battleworn Gladius	+5%; Parry S. +2	13	M3	90	2.7	14	5.1	Thr	Sword
Cutter	+5%; Thrust S. +2; Dex +3	14	M3	100	2.8	15	5.4	Thr	Rapier
Mithrian Gladius	+5%; Dex +4	14	M3	89	3.8	21	5.4	Thr	Sword
Lost Soul's Gauche	+5%; Thrust S. +1; Dex +1; Thrust R. +2	15	M3	89	2.9	17	5.7	Thr	Gauche
Leaper Gut Rapier	+5%; Thrust S. +2	15	M3	89	3.2	18	5.7	Thr	Rapier
Heart Piercer	+5%; Thrust S. +1; Qui +1; Cold R. +2	15	M3	89	2.3	13	5.7	Thr	Stiletto
Jeweled Rapier	+5%; Thrust S. +2; Dex +4	16	M4	90	2.8	17	6.0	Thr	Rapier
Spear of the Legions	+5%; Thrust S. +3	16	M4	90	3.8	23	6.0	Thr	Spear
Ruined Roman Gladius	+10%; Con +4	16	M4	89	3.6	22	6.0	Thr	Sword
Forgotten Roman Gladius	+10%; Thrust S. +1; Dex +1	18	M4	89	3.7	24	6.6	Thr	Sword
Death Spark	+10%; Thrust S. +1; Heat, Body R. +2	20	M4	89	2.2	16	7.2	Thr	Dirk
Decorated Roman Stiletto	+10%; Thrust S. +2; Qui +3	20	M4	89	2.4	17	7.2	Thr	Stiletto
Cythraul's Dirk	+10%; Dex, Qui +1; Heat, Cold R. +2	21	M5	89	2.3	17	7.5	Thr	Dirk
Keltoi Defender	+10%; Parry S. +1; Dex +3	21	M5	89	2.8	21	7.5	Thr	Gauche
Giants Toothpick	+10%; Thrust S. +4; Cha –6	21	M5	90	2.4	18	7.5	Thr	Rapier
Embossed Bone Gladius	+10%; Thrust S. +3; Dex +4	23	M5	100	3.6	29	8.1	Thr	Gladius
Cornwall Hunter's Rapier	+10%; Thrust S. +2; Dex +1	23	M5	89	3	24	8.1	Thr	Rapier
Goblin Rapier	+10%; Thrust S. +1; Dex +4	23	M5	89	3.2	26	8.1	Thr	Rapier
Bwgan Skinning Dirk	+10%; Thrust S. +2; Body R. +2	24	M5	89	2.8	24	8.4	Thr	Dirk
Hunter's Rapier	+10%; Dex +6; Thrust S. +1	24	M5	89	2.5	21	8.4	Thr	Rapier
Keen Dark Gladius	+10%; Qui +7	24	M5	89	3.7	31	8.3	Thr	Sword
Shadow-Slinkers Blade	+15%; Qui +10	26	M6	90	3.6	32	9.0	Thr	Sword
Goblin Gauche	+15%; Dual Wield S. +1; Dex +4	28	M6	89	2.8	27	9.6	Thr	Gauche
Despoiled Gauche	+15%; Thrust S. +2; Dex +3	29	M6	89	2.9	29	9.9	Thr	Gauche

Weapon	Bonus	PL	M#	Ql	Spd	Dam	DPS	Type	Generic
Despoiled Gladius	+15%; Thrust S. +2; Dex +3	29	M6	89	3.6	36	9.9	Thr	Sword
Long Lion Fang	+15%; Thrust, Parry S. +2; Dex +7	32	M7	100	2.4	26	10.8	Thr	Fang
Praetorian Gladius	+20%; Thrust S. +3	33	M7	90	3.3	37	11.1	Thr	Sword
Assassin's Blade	+15%; Critical Strike S. +4; Thrust S. +3	34	M7	100	2.7	31	11.4	Thr	Gauche
Glyne Gladius	+15%; Thrust S. +2; Dex +4	34	M7	89	3.7	42	11.4	Thr	Sword
Worn Asterite Main Gauche	Parry S. +2	37	M8	80	2.7	33	12.2	Thr	Gauche
Long Drake Fang	+20%; Thrust S. +2; Dex, Str +3	40	M8	89	3	40	13.2	Thr	Fang
Basher's Finger	+20%; Thrust S. +2; Dual Wield S. +2; Cold R. +2	42	M8	89	2.7	37	13.8	Thr	Dirk
Ghoulish Viper Fang	+20%; Body R. +6; Dex, Qui +4	42	M8	89	2.6	36	13.8	Thr	Fang
Crackling Impaler	+20%; Thrust, Parry, Dual Wield S. +2; Qui +9	43	M8	100	2.8	39	14.1	Thr	Gauche
Keen Asterite Main Gauche	+20%; Parry S. +3; Dex +4	43	M8	89	2.8	39	14.1	Thr	Gauche
Ivory Handled Rapier	+20%; Thrust S. +3; Dex +4	43	M8	89	3.2	45	14.1	Thr	Rapier
Shard of Grovewood	+20%; Thrust S. +3; Parry S. +2	43	W8	89	3.4	48	14.1	Thr	Shard
Ivory Handled Stiletto	+20%; Dual Wield S. +3; Qui +4	43	M8	89	2.3	32	14.1	Thr	Stiletto
Death's Touch	+20%; Thrust S. +5; Dual Wield S. +4	43	M8	100	3.2	45	14.1	Thr	Sword
Rapier of Retribution	+20%; Thrust S. +4; HP +27	43	M8	100	3.7	52	14.1	Thr	Sword
Shadow Piercer	+20%; Thrust S. +6; Dex +7	43	M8	100	3.7	52	14.1	Thr	Sword
Songsworn	+20%; Thrust S. +4; HP +30	43	M8	100	3.7	52	14.1	Thr	Sword
Spark	+20%; Thrust, Dual Wield S. +4	43	M8	100	3.7	52	14.1	Thr	Sword
Sword of Eternal Faith	+20%; Thrust S. +6; Dex +7	43	M8	100	3.7	52	14.1	Thr	Sword
Stone Cutter	+25%; Thrust, Parry S. +2; Body R. +2	45	M8	89	2.8	41	14.7	Thr	Gauche
Rift Finder	+20%; Thrust, Stealth S. +2; Dex +3	45	M8	89	3.2	47	14.7	Thr	Rapier
Fallen Archer's Stiletto	+20%; Thrust S. +2; Dual Wield S. +1; Dex +6	45	M8	89	2.4	35	14.7	Thr	Stiletto
Sheer Granite-Slicer	+25%; Thrust S. +4; Dex +9	47	M8	89	3.2	49	15.3	Thr	Rapier
Stone Splitter	+25%; Thrust S. +2; Dex, Qui +4	47	M8	89	2.5	38	15.3	Thr	Stiletto
Frozen Heart-Piercer	+25%; Thrust S. +2; Dex +7	47	M8	89	3.6	55	15.3	Thr	Sword
Rancid Black Tooth	+25%; Parry, Dual Wield S. +2; Qui +10	47	M8	100	2.5	38	15.3	Thr	Tooth
Powder Maker	+25%; Thrust S. +2; Str +4; Body R. +6	49	M8	89	3.7	59	15.9	Thr	Sword
Stone Gutter	+25%; Thrust, Parry S. +2; Str +3	49	M8	89	3.7	59	15.9	Thr	Sword
King's Nail	+30%; Thrust S. +5; Dual Wield S. +4; Qui +6	50	M8	93	2.9	47	16.2	Thr	Dirk
Feather Light Granite Gauche	+25%; Thrust S. +2; Dual Wield S. +5; Body R. +4	50	M8	90	2.4	39	16.2	Thr	Gauche
Mouth's Tooth	+30%; Thrust, Dual Wield S. +5; Dex +4	50	M8	93	2.8	45	16.2	Thr	Gauche
Gladius of the Battlelord	+20%; Thrust S. +2; HP +21	50	M8	89	3.5	57	16.2	Thr	Gladius
Ellyll Rapier	+20%; Thrust S. +3; Qui +7	50	M8	89	2.4	39	16.2	Thr	Rapier
Gorged Rapier of Smiting	+25%; Thrust, Parry S. +3; Thrust R. +6; Cold R. +4	50	M8	90	3.2	52	16.2	Thr	Rapier
Thrusting Frenzy	+25%; Envenom S. +4; Thrust, Body R. +6; Dex +6	50	M8	90	2.7	44	16.2	Thr	Stiletto
Cailiondar Rapier	+25%; Thrust S. +3; Parry S. +2; Dex +7; Qui +6	50	M8	91	3.5	57	16.2	Thr	Sword
Flycatcher	+25%; Thrust S. +5; Dex +6; Qui +4	50	M8	90	3.6	58	16.2	Thr	Sword

Two Handed Skill (Axe, Hammer, Mattock, Pick, Sword)

Weapon	Bonus	PL	M#	Ql	Spd	Dam	DPS	Type	Generic
Digging Mattock		0	M1	100	3.4	4	1.2	Thr	Mattock
Practice Great Sword		0	M1	100	4.8	3	0.6	Sl	Sword
Greatsword of the Initiate	Two Handed S. +1	6	M2	90	4.7	14	3.0	Sl	Sword
Great Iron Sword	+1%; Two Handed S. +1; Str +1	7	M2	90	5.5	18	3.3	Sl	Sword
Old Headsman's		8	M2	80	5.3	19	3.6	Sl	Axe
Ogre Forged Cutter	+5% to hit	13	M3	89	4.5	23	5.1	Sl	Sword
Mithrian Great Hammer	+5%; Con +4	14	M3	89	5	27	5.4	Cr	Hammer
Splitter	+5%; Two Handed S. +2; Qui +3	14	M3	100	4.8	26	5.4	Sl	Sword
Slaver Axe	+5%; Two Handed S. +2	15	M3	89	4.4	25	5.7	Sl	Axe
Kearcs' Mattock	+5%; Two Handed S. +2	15	M3	89	3.8	22	5.7	Thr	Mattock
Sword of the Unruly	+5%; Two Handed S. +2	15	M3	89	4.3	25	5.7	Sl	Sword
Blackened Hammer	+10%; Two Handed S. +3	16	M4	100	4.5	27	6.0	Cr	Hammer
Ogre King's Demolisher	+10%; Two Handed S. +1; Str +1	16	M4	89	4.8	29	6.0	Cr	Hammer
Head Slicer	+10%; Two Handed S. +2	21	M5	89	5.2	39	7.5	Sl	Axe
Dark Spine-Breaker	+10%; HP +12	21	M5	89	4.9	37	7.5	Cr	Hammer
Lost Sword of the Eternals	+10%; Two Handed S. +2; Dex +1	22	M5	89	5.1	40	7.8	Sl	Sword
Dark Sheer Great Sword	+10%; Two Handed S. +1; Qui +4	24	M5	89	5	42	8.4	Sl	Sword
Corpsecleaver	+15%; Two Handed S. +2; Str +6	26	M6	90	5.6	50	9.0	Sl	Sword
Despoiled Great Hammer	+15%; Two Handed S. +2; Str +3	31	M7	89	5	53	10.5	Cr	Hammer
Despoiled Mattock	+15%; Two Handed S. +2; Con +3	31	M7	89	4	42	10.5	Thr	Mattock
Sebian War Mattock	+15%; Str +4; Qui +6	31	M7	89	3.8	40	10.5	Thr	Mattock

Weapon	Bonus	PL	M#	Ql	Spd	Dam	DPS	Type	Generic
Despoiled Two-Handed Sword	+15%; Two Handed S. +2; Str +3	31	M7	89	4.6	48	10.5	Sl	Sword
Battlesword of Command	+10%; Two Handed S. +2; Con, Str +4	31	M7	90	4.6	48	10.5	Sl	Sword
Farmer's Stump Cutter	+15%; Slash, Two Handed S. +1; Con +4	32	M7	89	4	43	10.8	Sl	Axe
Sarel Sebian Smasher	+15%; Two Handed S. +2; Qui +4	32	M7	89	4.8	52	10.8	Cr	Hammer
Goblin War Mattock	+15%; Two Handed S. +1; Str +3; Dex +4	32	M7	89	3.8	41	10.8	Thr	Mattock
Goblin Demolisher	+15%; Two Handed S. +1; Qui +3; Con +4	32	M7	89	5.1	55	10.8	Sl	Sword
Goblin Great Hammer	+15%; Str +3; HP +15	33	M7	89	4.8	53	11.1	Cr	Hammer
Whisperer of Death	+15%; Two Handed S. +2; Qui +6	35	M7	89	5.1	60	11.7	Sl	Sword
Point of the Infidel	+20%; Slash S. +1; Str +4; Dex +3	36	M8	89	4.3	52	12.0	Sl	Sword
Worn Asterite War Axe	Two Handed S. +2	37	M8	80	4.5	55	12.3	Sl	Axe
Worn Asterite Great Hammer	Two Handed S. +2	37	M8	80	4.6	57	12.3	Cr	Hammer
Worn Asterite Mattock	Two Handed S. +2	37	M8	80	3.8	47	12.3	Thr	Mattock
Cyclops Headsman's Axe	+15%; Str, Qui +4; Two Handed S. +2	42	M8	89	5	69	13.8	Sl	Axe
Broad Asterite War Axe	+20%; Two Handed S. +1; Parry S. +2; Str +4	43	M8	89	4.5	63	14.1	Sl	Axe
Great Axe of Retribution	+20%; Two Handed S. +6; Parry S. +3	43	M8	100	5.2	73	14.1	Sl	Axe
Ivy Avenger	+20%; Str, Qui +6; Two Handed S. +4; Body R. +4	43	M8	100	4.8	68	14.1	Cr	Hammer
Light Asterite Great Hammer	+20%; Two Handed S. +1; Parry S. +2; Con +4	43	M8	89	4.6	65	14.1	Cr	Hammer
Cobalt Void-Rifter	+20%; Two Handed S. +4; Qui, Str +6; Spirit R. +4	43	M8	100	4.2	59	14.1	Thr	Mattock
Light Asterite Mattock	+20%; Two Handed S. +1; Parry S. +2; Qui +4	43	M8	89	3.8	54	14.1	Thr	Mattock
Greatsword of Eternal Virtue	+20%; Two Handed S. +6; Parry S. +3	43	M8	100	5.2	73	14.1	Sl	Sword
Lesser Telamon Scimitar	+20% to hit	45	M8	89	5	74	14.7	Sl	Sword
Fiery Headsman's Axe	+25%; Parry, Two Handed S. +2; Heat R. +2	47	M8	89	5.4	83	15.3	Sl	Axe
Golden Tree-Cleaver	+25%; Two Handed, Parry S. +2; Str +10; Spirit R. +6	47	M8	100	5.3	81	15.3	Sl	Axe
Solemn Destroyer	+25%; Parry, Two Handed S. +2; Spirit R. +2	47	M8	89	4.8	73	15.3	Cr	Hammer
Ancient Ebony Mattock	+25%; Parry, Two Handed, Cold R. +2	47	M8	89	4	61	15.3	Thr	Mattock
Black Ash Soul Slayer	+25%; Two Handed S. +4; Cold R. +6; Qui +12	47	M8	100	5	77	15.3	Sl	Sword
Avenging Knight's Hammer	+25%; Crush S. +1; Two Handed S. +2; Str +6	49	M8	89	4.5	72	15.9	Cr	Hammer
Axe of Smiting	+25%; Two Handed S. +3; Cold, Energy R. +6; Qui +7	50	M8	90	5.2	84	16.2	Sl	Axe
Stately Axe	+30%; Two Handed, Parry S. +4; Crush R. +6; HP +9	50	M8	91	4.4	71	16.2	Sl	Axe
Danaoin Great Hammer	+25%; HP +21; Crush S. +1; Two Handed S. +3	50	M8	90	4.7	76	16.2	Cr	Hammer
Malevolent Hammer	+30%; Crush, Two Handed S. +5; Str +6	50	M8	93	4.8	78	16.2	Cr	Hammer
Polished Hammer of Eldspar	+25%; Two Handed S. +4; Crush, Parry S. +2; Body R. +2	50	M8	90	4.8	78	16.2	Cr	Hammer
Dark Crystal Mattock	+25%; Two Handed S. +4; Thrust, Parry S. +2	50	M8	90	3.8	62	16.2	Thr	Mattock
Diamond Mattock	+25%; Two Handed S. +3; Con, Qui +3; HP +15	50	M8	90	3.8	62	16.2	Thr	Mattock
Danaoin War Pick	+25%; HP +21; Thrust S. +1; Two Handed S. +3	50	M8	90	5	81	16.2	Thr	Pick
Crush Born Sword	+25%; Two Handed S. +4; Slash S. +3; Parry S. +2; Body R. +2	50	M8	90	4.3	70	16.2	Sl	Sword
Danaoin Two-Handed Sword	+25%; HP +21; Slash S. +1; Two Handed S. +3	50	M8	90	4.5	73	16.2	Sl	Sword
Frenzied Blade	+25%; Two Handed S. +4; Con +7; Matter R. +6; Spirit R. +4	50	M8	90	4.3	70	16.2	Sl	Sword
Greater Telamon Scimitar	+25%; Two Handed S. +5; Str +10	50	M8	90	5	81	16.2	Sl	Sword
Kraggon Sword	+25%; Two Handed S. +3; Str +9	50	M8	90	4	65	16.2	Sl	Sword
Malevolent Great Sword	+30%; Two Handed, Parry S. +4; Power +3; Body R. +6	50	M8	91	5.1	83	16.2	Sl	Sword
Raven Clan Battle Sword	+25%; Two Handed S. +4; Str +10	50	M8	90	5	81	16.2	Sl	Sword
Raven Clan Meat Cleaver	+15%; Two Handed S. +6	50	M8	89	4.6	75	16.2	Sl	Sword

Crossbow Skill (Crossbow)

Weapon	Bonus	PL	M#	Ql	Spd	Dam	DPS	Range	Generic
Embossed Crossbow	+5%; Crossbow S. +1; Qui +4	12	W3	100	5	24	4.8	1200	Crossbow
Finely Crafted Crossbow	+10%; Crossbow S. +2	16	W4	90	4	24	6.0	1200	Crossbow
Sure Shot Crossbow	+10%; Dex +4	17	W4	89	5	32	6.3	1200	Crossbow
Dark Embossed Crossbow	+10%; Dex +4; Qui +3	24	W5	89	5.5	46	8.4	1200	Crossbow
Antiquated Crossbow	+15%; Dex +10	33	W7	89	4	44	11.1	1200	Crossbow
Goblin Archer Crossbow	+15%; Crossbow S. +1; Dex +4; Con +3	33	W7	89	5	56	11.1	1200	Crossbow
Worn Asterite Shod Crossbow	Crossbow S. +2	37	M8	80	5	62	12.3	1200	Crossbow
Fine Asterite Shod Crossbow	+20%; Crossbow S. +4	43	M8	89	5	71	14.1	1200	Crossbow
Oversized Pygmy Crossbow	+20%; Crossbow S. +2; Dex +9	45	W8	89	5.2	76	14.7	1200	Crossbow
Crossbow of the Blackheart	+25%; Crossbow S. +4	47	M8	100	5.2	80	15.3	1200	Crossbow
Defender's Crossbow	+20%; Crossbow S. +2; Dex +10	50	W8	89	4.9	79	16.2	1200	Crossbow
Eldspar Crafted Crossbow	+25%; Crossbow S. +4; Dex +12	50	W8	90	5	81	16.2	1200	Crossbow
Ilmenite Crafted Crossbow	+25%; Crossbow S. +7; Str +3	50	W8	90	5	81	16.2	1200	Crossbow
Mordacious Crossbow	+30%; Cold, Energy, Thrust R. +8; Dex +12	50	W8	93	4.6	75	16.2	1200	Crossbow

Bow Skill (Bow)

Weapon	Bonus	PL	M#	QI	Spd	Dam	DPS	Range	Generic
Spirit Crafted Shortbow	+10%; Dex +6	20	W4	89	4	29	7.2	1200	Bow
Heavy Pull Short Bow	+5%; Bow S. +3; Qui +6	21	W5	100	4.1	31	7.5	1200	Bow
Goblin Archer Short Bow	+10%; Bow S. +1; Dex +4	23	W5	89	4	32	8.1	1200	Bow
Snowdonian Bandit Bow	+10%; Dex +9	27	W6	89	3.9	36	9.3	1200	Bow
Antiquated Bow	+15%; Dex +10	33	W7	89	3.8	42	11.1	1200	Bow
Worn Asterite Shod Short Bow	Bow S. +2	37	M8	80	4	49	12.3	1200	Bow
Fine Asterite Shod Short Bow	+20%; Bow S. +4	43	M8	89	4	56	14.1	1200	Bow
Short Bow of the Blackheart	+25%; Dex +9; Cold, Heat, Spirit R. +2	47	M8	89	4.2	64	15.3	1200	Bow
Bloodied Bow	+30%; Dex +11; Cold, Energy, Heat R. +8	50	W8	93	3.9	63	16.2	1200	Bow
Bow of the Stonewatch	+25%; Dex, Str +12	50	W8	90	4	65	16.2	1200	Bow

Longbow Skill (Bow)

Weapon	Bonus	PL	M#	QI	Spd	Dam	DPS	Range	Generic
Huntsman's Longbow	Longbow S. +1	6	W2	90	5.4	16	3.0	1760	Bow
Worn Mithrian Bow		10	W2	80	4.8	20	4.2	1600	Bow
Ancient Mithrian Bow	+5%; Dex +4	14	W3	89	5.6	30	5.4	1760	Bow
Slaver Longbow	+5%; Longbow S. +2	15	W3	89	5.4	31	5.7	1760	Bow
Ancient Oak Bow	+5%; Longbow S. +2	16	W4	90	5.2	31	6.0	1760	Bow
Silver Oak Longbow	+10%; Longbow S. +2; Dex +3	21	M5	90	5.3	40	7.5	1760	Bow
Natures Blessing	+10%; Longbow S. +3	22	W5	89	5.4	42	7.8	1760	Bow
Bwgan's Hunting Bow	+10%; Crush R. +2; Longbow S. +1; HP +6	23	W5	89	4	32	8.1	1600	Bow
Carved Keltoi Bow	+10%; Longbow S. +1; Qui +4	24	W5	89	5.3	45	8.4	1760	Bow
Hunter's Great Bow	+10%; Dex +6; Longbow S. +1	25	W5	89	5.3	46	8.7	1760	Bow
Light Hunter's Bow	+10%; Longbow S. +2; Dex +3	25	W5	89	4.3	37	8.7	1600	Bow
Shadow-Oak Longbow	+10%; Longbow S. +2; Dex +6; Str +4	26	W6	100	5.3	48	9.0	1760	Bow
Goblin Archer Long Bow	+15%; Longbow S. +1; Dex +4	28	W6	89	5.4	52	9.6	1760	Bow
Golden Oak Bow	+15%; Longbow S. +2; Dex +9	31	W7	90	5.5	58	10.5	1760	Bow
Bow of the Decaying Legions	+15%; Dex +10	33	W7	89	4.8	53	11.1	1600	Bow
Worn Asterite Shod Bow	Longbow S. +2	37	M8	80	5.4	66	12.3	1760	Bow
Bow of the Forest Lord	+20%; Longbow S. +2; HP +15; Dex +9; Qui +6	42	W8	100	5.3	73	13.8	1760	Bow
Fine Asterite Shod Bow	+20%; Longbow S. +3; Body R. +4; Thrust R. +2	43	M8	89	5.4	76	14.1	1760	Bow
Prey Seeker	+20%; Dex +10	43	W8	89	5.2	73	14.1	1760	Bow
Fallen Archer's Great Bow	+20%; Longbow S. +2; Dex, Qui +4	45	W8	89	5	74	14.7	1760	Bow
Runed Bow of Ill Omen	+25%; Longbow S. +3; Crush, Thrust, Slash R. +2	47	M8	89	5.5	84	15.3	1760	Bow
Bow of Doom	+30%; Longbow S. +7; Dex +13	50	W8	93	5.3	86	16.2	1760	Bow
Enlicimun	+25%; Longbow S. +6; Stealth S. +2; Dex +1	50	W8	90	5.2	84	16.2	1760	Bow
Radiant Moonclipper	+25%; Longbow S. +3; Dex +10; Qui +6	50	M8	90	5.3	86	16.2	1760	Bow
Cailiondar Longbow	+25%; Longbow S. +5; Qui +13	51	W8	91	5.2	86	16.5	1760	Bow

Arrows

Weapon	Bonus	QI	Dam	Type	Generic
Arrow of the Bwgan	+10% to hit	89	x1	Thr	Arrow
Arrows of the Fallen	+20% to hit	100	x1.25	Sl	Arrow
Barbed Elven Arrows	+20% to hit	89	x1.35	Sl	Arrow
Elven Arrows	+5% to hit	89	x1.25	Sl	Arrow
Sureflight Arrows		90	x1	Thr	Arrow

When firing an arrow or bolt, the speed of the bow determines how rapidly you can fire, and the shot's base damage. The arrow or bolt determines the type of damage (Crush, Slash or Thrust) and provides a multiplier to the base damage (indicated by "x1", "x1.25", and so forth).

Miscellaneous Drops & Rewards

Item	Bonus	PL	QI
Antler: Broken Antler			100
Fang: Sharp Cwn Annwn Fang			100
Totem: Stick-Figure Totem	Power +3		89
Metal: Chewed Asterium Metal		0	80
Globe: Glowing Globe of Blue Mist	Power +2	7	89
Stone: Spirit Stone	Power +2	7	89
Stone: Demon Soul Gem	Int +4	8	100
Stone: Stone Heart of the Earth Spirit	Con +3; Pie +1	9	89

Item	Bonus	PL	QI
Ball: Glowing Ball of Mud	Matter R. +6; Con +3	14	89
Idol: Cold Clay Idol	Matter R. +4; Str +4	18	89
Totem: Skull-Shaped Totem	Con +9; Str +3	20	100
Fruit: Petrified Elder Beech Fruit	Pie, Int +6	27	89
Tail: Diseased Rat Tail	Body R. +8; HP +21	38	89
Hook: Virulent Fishing Hk.	Enven. S. +2; Body R. +4; Dex, Qui +4	40	89
Goblet: Ancient Sacrif. Goblet	Pie +6; Smit., Enhan., Rejuv. S. +2	46	90
Stone: Stone of Evil Emanations	HP +27; Heat, Energy, Spirit R. +4	50	89

Armor

For a brief discussion of how armor and armor stats work in *Dark Age of Camelot*, see page 362.

Abbreviations. Mat = Base Material / **A**rmor **F**actor (per piece) / **ABS**orption / **Cl**oth / **L**ea**t**her / **St**udded Leather / **Ch**ain / **Pl**ate.

Standard (Craftable) Armor Stats

Armor	Mat	Power Levels	AF	ABS
Quilted	Cl	1,6,11, etc.	4,9,14, etc.	0%
Robe	Cl	1,6,11, etc.	4,9,14, etc.	0%
Roman	Lt	1,6,11, etc.	4,14,24, etc.	10%
Cymric	Lt	2,7,12, etc.	6,16,26, etc.	10%
Siluric	Lt	4,9,14, etc.	10,20,30, etc.	10%
Studded	St	1,6,11, etc.	4,14,24, etc.	19%
Boned	St	2,7,12, etc.	6,16,26, etc.	19%
Lamellar	St	4,9,14, etc.	10,20,30, etc.	19%
Chainmail	Ch	1,6,11, etc.	4,14,24, etc.	27%
Mail	Ch	3,8,13, etc.	8,18,28, etc.	27%
Platemail	Pl	13, etc.	20,30,40, etc.	34%
Scaled Platemail	Pl	13, etc.	24,34,44, etc.	34%
Fluted Platemail	Pl	14, etc.	40,50,60, etc.	34%

Note that plate armor cannot be worn by anyone before level 15, and the lowest quality available is steel. There is no bronze or iron plate armor.

Armor Weights

Location	Cl	Lt	St *	Ch	Pl *
Cap/Helm	0.8	1.6	2.4	3.2	4.0
Vest/Jerkin/Breastplate	2.0	4.0	6.0	8.0	10.0
Sleeves	1.2	2.4	3.6	4.8	6.0
Gloves/Gauntlets	0.8	1.6	2.4	3.2	4.0
Pants/Leggings	1.4	2.8	4.2	5.6	7.0
Boots	0.8	1.6	2.4	3.2	4.0
Robe	2.0				

** Fluted plate weighs the same as studded armor.*

Armor Drops & Rewards

Armor is sorted by type (Cloth, Leather, etc.), then by location (Head, Torso, Arms, Hands, Legs, Feet, Robes), then by Power Level.

Abbreviations

Headings. Power Level / Armor Factor / **M** = Material and Material Level / Quality.

The first negative percentage in any bonus indicates your opponent's reduced chance of hitting you when you are wearing the item.

Stats. **R**esistance, **S**kill / **Cha**risma, **Con**stitution, **Emp**athy, **Dex**terity, **Int**elligence, **Pie**ty, **Qui**ckness, **Str**ength / **C**loth, **L**eather, **M**etal.

Cloth

Head

Item	Bonus	P	A	M	Q
Cap of the Intuit	-1%; Int +1; Body Magic S. +1; Power +1	7	7	C2	100
Cap of the Quickthinker	Int +4; Power +1	7	7	C2	100
Aged Mithrian Cloth Cap		9	9	C2	100
Thinking Cap	-5%; Int +4; Power +1	10	10	C3	100
Ancient Mithrian Cloth Cap	-5%; Int +4; Power +1	13	13	C3	89
Cap of the Lost	-5%; Int +4; Energy R. +4	14	14	C3	89
Cap of the Keen Mind	-10%; Cha +1; Int +9	19	19	C4	89
Resolute Cap	-10%; Int +6; Body R. +8	20	20	C5	89
Insurgent's Cap	-10%; Enchant., Mental., Void Magic S. +2; Int +6	24	24	C5	89
Hob Hunter Cap	-10%; Int +6; Dex +3; Energy R. +4	24	24	C5	89
Ifor's Headband	-15%; Power +2; Int, Dex, Qui +3	28	28	C6	89
Antiquated Noble's Cap	-15%; Power +4; Int +6	31	31	C7	89
Aqueous Cap	-15%; HP +15; Int +7	32	32	C7	89
Glittering Netherite Cap	-10%; Int +12; Mind Magic S. +2	34	34	C7	89
Glittering Arcanite Cap	-10%; Int +12; Wind Magic S. +2	34	34	C7	89
Faded Cap of the Risen	-1%; Power +2	36	36	C8	80
Cap of the Risen	-20%; Spirit, Crush, Cold R. +4; Int +7	37	37	C8	89
Stonepin Woven Cap	-20%; Int +12; Dex +4; Energy, Heat R. +2	41	41	C8	89
Cap of Delusional Power	-20%; HP +18; Int +10	42	42	C8	89
Frozen Quilted Cap	-25%; Body R. +6; Power +6; Int +9; Str +7	46	46	C8	100
Ancient Ebony Cap	-25%; Spirit, Cold, Heat R. +4; Int +12	46	46	C8	89
Woven Spirit Cap	-20%; Int +10; Spirit Magic S. +3	49	49	C8	89
Woven Elemental Cap	-20%; Int +10; Fire Magic S. +3	49	49	C8	89
Granite Seer's Cap of the:					
Spirit	-25%; Int +12; Cold, Spirit R. +8; Spirit Magic S. +3	49	49	C8	91
Mind	-25%; Int +12; Cold, Spirit R. +8; Mind Magic S. +3	49	49	C8	91
Fire Imbued Cap	-25%; Int +12; Cold, Matter R. +8; Fire Mg. S. +3	49	49	C8	91
Wind Imbued Cap	-25%; Int +12; Cold, Mat. R. +8; Wind Mg. S. +3	49	49	C8	91
Ichor-Lined Cap	-30%; Int +12; Body Mg., Earth Mg. S. +3; HP +15	49	49	C8	91
Cursed Malcontent's Cap	-25%; HP +18; Dex, Int +9; Crush R. +6	49	49	C8	90

Torso

Item	Bonus	P	A	M	Q
Mildewed Tunic	Int +1; HP +6	6	6	C2	90
Aged Mithrian Cloth Vest		9	9	C2	80
Ancient Mithrian Cloth Vest	-5%; HP +6; Int +3; Dex +1	13	13	C3	89
Vest of the Lost	-10%; Power +4	20	20	C5	89
Vest of the Resolute	-10%; HP +6; Power +2; Dex +3	20	20	C5	89
Insurgent's Vest	-10%; HP +9; Slash R. +6; Int +4	24	24	C5	89
Hob Hunter Vest	-10%; HP +12; Dex +3; Heat R. +4	24	24	C5	89
Spellhurler's Vest	-15%; HP +12; Cold, Heat R. +2; Int +6	25	25	C6	90
Fish Scale Vest	-15%; Int +6; Dex, Qui +3	26	26	C6	89
Eye-Studded Tunic	-15%; Power +2; Int +3; Con +4; Slash R. +4	31	31	C7	89
Antiquated Noble's Vest	-15%; HP +30	31	31	C7	89
Aqueous Vest	-15%; Con, Int +6; Power +2	32	32	C7	89
Glittering Netherite Vest	-10%; Int +6; HP +12; Matter Magic S. +2	34	34	C7	89
Glittering Arcanite Vest	-10%; Int +6; HP +12; Earth Magic S. +2	34	34	C7	89
Faded Vest of the Risen	-1%; Power +2	36	36	C8	80
Vest of the Risen	-20%; HP +15; Int +6; Slash R. +4	37	37	C8	89
Vest of Delusional Power	-20%; Con +6; Int +10; Crush R. +4	42	42	C8	89
Stonepin Woven Vest	-20%; HP +18; Power +4; Energy, Heat R. +2	43	43	C8	89
Ancient Ebony Vest	-25%; HP +24; Crush, Slash, Thrust R. +4	46	46	C8	89
Woven Spirit Vest	-20%; HP +30; Body Magic S. +3	49	49	C8	89
Woven Elemental Vest	-20%; HP +30; Cold Magic S. +3	49	49	C8	89
Granite S's Vest o.t. Body	-25%; HP +36; Power +6; Body Mg. S. +3	49	49	C8	91
Lava Imbued Vest	-25%; HP +36; Power +6; Earth Magic S. +3	49	49	C8	91
Ichor-Drenched Vest	-30%; Con +10; Power +8; Heat, Cold R. +10	49	49	C8	91
Cursed Malcontent's Vest	-25%; HP +21; Power +4; Dex, Int +6	49	49	C8	90

Arms

Item	Bonus	P	A	M	Q
Mildewed Sleeves	Power +1	3	3	C1	90
Aged Mithrian Cloth Sleeves		9	9	C2	80
Ancient Mithrian Cloth Sleeves	-5%; HP +6; Dex, Str +3	13	13	C3	89
Resilient Sleeves	-10%; HP +3; Heat, Cold R. +4	15	15	C4	89
Sleeves of the Lost	-10%; Int +6; Energy R. +4	18	18	C4	89
Sleeves of the Resolute	-10%; Str +3; Int +6; Cold R. +4	20	20	C5	89
Trimmed Pelt Sleeves	-10%; Int +4; Dex +3; Power +3	21	21	C5	100
Insurgent's Sleeves	-10%; HP +9; Str +4; Int +3	24	24	C5	89
Hob Hunter Sleeves	-10%; Str, Dex +3; HP +6; Matter R. +4	24	24	C5	89
Antiquated Noble's Sleeves	-15%; HP +15; Int +4; Dex +3	31	31	C7	89
Aqueous Sleeves	-15%; Str, Dex, Int +3; Power +2	32	32	C7	89
Glittering Netherite Sleeves	-10%; Str, Int +6; Spirit Magic S. +2	34	34	C7	89
Glittering Arcanite Sleeves	-10%; Int, Str +6; Cold Magic S. +2	34	34	C7	89
Faded Sleeves of the Risen	-1%; Power +2	36	36	C8	80
Sleeves of the Risen	-20%; Str, Int +4; Dex +3; HP +9	37	37	C8	89
Sleeves of Del. Power	-20%; Power +2; Energy R. +4; Int +7; Str +3	42	42	C8	89
Stonepin Woven Sleeves	-20%; Int +6; Heat, Energy R. +3; Str +10	44	44	C8	89
Ancient Ebony Sleeves	-25%; Power +3; Cold, Heat R. +4; Int +6	46	46	C8	89
Woven Spirit Sleeves	-20%; Str +6; Int +9; Matter Magic S. +3	49	49	C8	89
Woven Elemental Sleeves	-20%; Str +6; Int +9; Wind Magic S. +3	49	49	C8	89
Granite Seer's Sleeves of Matter	-25%; Str, Con +10; Matter Magic S. +3; Spirit R. +2	49	49	C8	91
Cold Imbued Sleeves	-25%; Str, Con +10; Cold Mg. S. +3; Mat. R. +2	49	49	C8	91
Ichor-Lined Sleeves	-30%; Str +7; Body, Cold R. +12; HP +36	49	49	C8	91
Cursed Malcontent's Sleeves	-25%; HP +21; Str, Int +7; Thrust R. +8	49	49	C8	90

Hands

Item	Bonus	P	A	M	Q
Resilient Gloves	-10%; Power +1; Matter, Spirit R. +4	15	15	C4	89
Gloves of the Lost	-10%; Power +4	19	19	C4	89
Gloves of the Resolute	-10%; Dex +3; Power +3	20	20	C5	89
Insurgent's Gloves	-10%; Power +2; Dex +6	24	24	C5	89
Hob Hunter Gloves	-10%; Qui, Int, Con +3; Spirit R. +4	24	24	C5	89
Antiquated Noble's Gloves	-15%; Power +4; Dex, Int +3	31	31	C7	89
Aqueous Gloves	-15%; HP +21; Int +4	32	32	C7	89
Glittering Netherite Gl.	-10%; Int +6; Power +2; Body Mg. S. +2	34	34	C7	89
Glittering Arcanite Gloves	-10%; Int +6; Power +2; Fire Mg. S. +2	34	34	C7	89
Faded Gloves of the Risen	-1%; Power +2	36	36	C8	80
Gloves of the Risen	-20%; HP +9; Power +2; Int +6	37	37	C8	89
Gloves of Delus. Power	-20%; Body R. +6; Thrust R. +4; Qui, Int +6	42	42	C8	89
Stonepin Woven Gloves	-20%; Int +6; Heat, Energy R. +3; Qui +10	44	44	C8	89
Ancient Ebony Gloves	-25%; Power +3; Dex +7; Int +4	46	46	C8	89
Woven Spirit Gloves	-20%; Dex, Int +6; Qui +3; Mind Mg. S. +3	49	49	C8	89
Woven Elemental Gl.	-20%; Dex, Int +6; Qui +3; Earth Mg. S. +3	49	49	C8	89
Granite Seer's Gloves of the Spirit	-25%; Int +10; Cold, Spirit R. +8; Spirit Magic S. +4	49	49	C8	91
Granite Seer's Gloves of the Mind	-25%; Int +10; Cold, Spirit R. +8; Mind Magic S. +4	49	49	C8	91
Fire Imbued Gl.	-25%; Int +12; Cold, Matter R. +8; Fire Mg. S. +3	49	49	C8	91
Wind Imbued Gl.	-25%; Int +12; Cold, Matter R. +8; Wind Mg. S. +3	49	49	C8	91
Ichor-Drenched Gl.	-30%; Dex +12; Power +4; Int +7; Matter R. +12	49	49	C8	91
Cursed Malcontent's Gloves	-25%; Str, Dex, Int +7; Energy R. +10	49	49	C8	90

Legs

Item	Bonus	P	A	M	Q
Aged Mithrian Cloth Pants		9	9	C2	80
Ancient Mithrian Cloth Pants	-5%; Power +2; Con +3	13	13	C3	89
Pants of the Lost	-5%; HP +15	14	14	C3	89
Leggings of the Resolute	-10%; Con +6; Power +2	20	20	C5	89
Insurgent's Pants	-10%; Crush R. +6; Con +6; Power +1	24	24	C5	89
Hob Hunter Pants	-10%; Con, Dex +4; Cold R. +4	24	24	C5	89
Antiquated Noble's Pants	-15%; HP +21; Dex +4	31	31	C7	89
Aqueous Pants	-15%; Con +9; Power +3	32	32	C7	89
Glittering Netherite Pants	-10%; Con, Dex +9	34	34	C7	89
Glittering Arcanite Pants	-10%; Con, Dex +9	34	34	C7	89
Faded Pants of the Risen	-1%; Power +2	36	36	C8	80
Pants of the Risen	-20%; Con +7; Energy R. +8; Body R. +4	37	37	C8	89
Pants of Delusional Power	-20%; Power +4; Dex +7	42	42	C8	89
Ancient Ebony Pants	-25%; HP +12; Power +2; Con +6; Int +3	46	46	C8	89
Stonepin Woven Pants	-25%; Con +10; Dex +3; Energy, Heat R. +2	46	46	C8	89
Woven Spirit Pants	-20%; Str +3; Con, Dex +6; Int +9	49	49	C8	89
Woven Elemental Pants	-20%; Str +3; Con, Dex +6; Int +9	49	49	C8	89
Granite Seer's Pants	-25%; Con +10; Dex +9; Power +6; Spirit R. +2	49	49	C8	91
Matter Imbued Pants	-25%; Con +10; Dex +9; Power +6; Mat. R. +2	49	49	C8	91
Ichor-Lined Pants	-30%; Dex +12; HP +27; Slash R. +14; Con +7	49	49	C8	91
Cursed Malcontent's Pants	-25%; Con +12; Dex +10; Power +4	49	49	C8	90

Feet

Item	Bonus	P	A	M	Q
Boots of the Lost	-5%; Dex +7	14	14	C3	89
Boots of the Resolute	-10%; Dex +6; Cold R. +8	20	20	C5	89
Insurgent's Boots	-10%; Dex +6; Power +2	24	24	C5	89
Hob Hunter Boots	-10%; Dex, Str, Int +3; Body R. +4	24	24	C5	89
Antiquated Noble's Boots	-15%; Con, Dex +6; Body R. +4	31	31	C7	89
Aqueous Boots	-15%; Dex, Con +6; Thrust R. +4	32	32	C7	89
Glittering Netherite Boots	-10%; Str, Qui +3; Dex +9; HP +6	34	34	C7	89
Glittering Arcanite Boots	-10%; Str, Qui +3; Dex +9; HP +6	34	34	C7	89
Faded Boots of the Risen	-1%; Power +2	36	36	C8	80
Boots of the Risen	-20%; HP +12; Dex +4; Power +2	37	37	C8	89
Boots of Delusional Power	-20%; Cold, Heat R. +6; Con +3; Dex +7	42	42	C8	89
Ancient Ebony Boots	-25%; HP +15; Con, Dex +9	46	46	C8	89
Stonepin Woven Boots	-25%; Dex +13; Heat, Energy R. +2	48	48	C8	89
Woven Spirit Boots	-20%; Con +3; Dex +10; Power +2; HP +9	49	49	C8	89
Woven Elemental Boots	-20%; Con +3; Dex +10; Power +2; HP +9	49	49	C8	89
Granite Seer's Boots	-25%; Dex +10; Qui +13; Power +4; Mat. R. +2	49	49	C8	91
Matter Imbued Boots	-25%; Dex +10; Qui +13; Power +4; Mat. R. +2	49	49	C8	91
Ichor-Coated Boots	-30%; Dex +10; Con +12; HP +21; Body R. +8	49	49	C8	91
Cursed Malcontent's Boots	-25%; HP +18; Dex +7; Power +5	49	49	C8	90

Robes

Item	Bonus	P	A	M	Q
Robe of Chance	-5%; Power +1; Int +1	6	6	C2	89
Rotting Robes	-5%; Power +2; Int +1; Cha -3	12	12	C3	89
Spider Silken Robe	-5%; HP +6; Int, Dex +4	14	14	C3	100
Robe of the Lost	-5%; Power +2; Int +3	14	14	C3	89
Deathrune Robes	-10%; Int +7; Power +1; Body Magic S. +1	20	20	C5	90
Invoker's Robes	-10%; Int +10; HP +12	20	20	C5	100
Robes of Scintilation	-10%; Int +7; Power +3	20	20	C5	100
Robes of the Resolute	-10%; Dex +3; Power +2; HP +6	20	20	C5	89
Emissary's Robe	-10%; HP +12; Int +6	24	24	C5	89
Silken Hob Hunter Robe	-10%; HP +12; Dex +3; Heat R. +4	24	24	C5	89
Bonelord's Robe	-15%; Spirit, Body, Matter Mg. S. +2; Cold R. +5	25	25	C6	100
Smoldering Robes	-10%; Fire Magic, Wind Magic S. +1; Int +7	27	27	C6	89
Netherworldly R.	-10%; Matter Magic, Body Magic S. +1; Int +7	27	27	C6	89
Antiquated Robe	-15%; Con +3; Dex, Int +6	32	32	C7	89
Robe of the Abyss	-20%; Int +9; Dex +6; Matter R. +6	32	32	C7	90
Glittering Arcanite Robes	-10%; Int +6; HP +12; Earth Magic S. +2	34	34	C7	89
Glittering Netherite R.	-10%; Int +6; HP +12; Matter Magic S. +2	34	34	C7	89
Robe of the Overseer	-20%; HP +9; Dex +4; Int +6	35	35	C8	89
Faded Robes of the Risen	-1%; Power +2	36	36	C8	80
Robes of the Risen	-20%; HP +15; Int +6; Slash R. +4	37	37	C8	89
Robes of Delusional Power	-20%; Con +6; Int +10; Crush R. +4	42	42	C8	89
Ancient Ebony Robes	-25%; HP +24; Crush, Slash, Thrust R. +4	46	46	C8	89
Emerald Dusted Robe	-25%; Int +10; Power +3; HP +12	49	49	C8	90
Ruby Dusted Robe	-25%; Int +10; HP +30	49	49	C8	90
Sapphire Dusted Robe	-25%; Int +10; Power +5	49	49	C8	90
Diamond Dusted Robe	-25%; Int, Dex +10	49	49	C8	90
R. o.t. Sp. Stone	-25%; HP +30; Power +6; Spir. Mg. S. +3; Thr. R. +4	49	49	C8	91
R. o.t. Eter. Wind	-25%; HP +30; Power +6; Wind Mg. S. +3; Thr. R. +4	49	49	C8	91
R. o. Stn. Speak.	-25%; HP +30; Power +6; Mind Mg. S. +3; Thr. R. +4	49	49	C8	91
Lava Imb. R.	-25%; HP +30; Power +6; Fire Mg. S. +3; Thr. R. +4	49	49	C8	91
Ichor-Coated R.	-30%; Power +10; HP +21; Heat R. +6; Cold R. +8	49	49	C8	93
Mystic Robes of Bedazzlement	-25%; HP +24; Int +12; Dex +6	49	49	C8	90

Item	Bonus	P	A	M	Q
Celestial Cailiondar R.	-25%; HP +36; Thrust R. +10; Dex, Int +12	50	50	C8	94
Bernor's Numinous Robes	-25%; HP +24; Power +14; Cold R. +4	50	50	C8	100

Leather

Head

Item	Bonus	P	A	M	Q
Emult Helm	Int +1	5	10	L2	100
Headband of Focus	-5%; Enhancements S. +1	6	12	L2	89
Cracked Leather Helm		9	18	L2	80
Musty Leather Helm	-5%; Pie +4; Power +1	13	26	L3	89
Wormskin Helm	-5%; Pie +4; Spirit R. +4	14	28	L3	89
Bloodied Leather Helmet	-10%; Cold R. +8; Qui +6	21	42	L5	89
Observer's Helm	-10%; Stealth S. +2; Dex, Qui +3	24	48	L5	89
Molded Leather Helm	-15%; Con, Dex +4; Spirit R. +6	29	58	L6	89
Goblinskin Helm	-15%; Str, Con +4; Energy R. +6	30	60	L7	89
Deluged Kelp H.	-15%; Parry, Rejuvenation, Enhance. S. +1; Pie +6	34	68	L7	89
Faded Helm of the Dejected	-1%; Cha +3; Cold R. +4	36	72	L8	80
Helm of the Dejected	-20%; Spirit, Heat R. +4; Str +6; Dex +4	37	74	L8	89
Magma Hardened Leather H.	-20%; Dex, Qui +7; Energy, Spirit R. +2	38	76	L8	89
Bounder Fur Helmet	-15%; Dex, Qui +6; Heat R. +4; Stealth S. +1	39	78	L8	89
Sable Helm of Dementia	-20%; Spirit R. +8; HP +12; Dex +4; Str +3	42	84	L8	89
Frozen Leather Helm	-25%; Body R. +6; HP +18; Qui +13; Str +7	46	92	L8	100
Helm of the Ghostly Light	-25%; HP +24; Con, Dex, Qui +3	46	92	L8	89
Magmas Imbued Helm	-25%; Pie +10; Con +6; Cold R. +2	47	94	L8	89
Helm of Opposition	-25%; Dex +9; Qui +7; Stealth S. +2	47	94	L8	89
Regal Helm	-30%; Con, Qui +13; HP +24; Cold R. +8	49	98	L8	93
Danaoin Nightwatcher H.	-25%; HP +27; Pie +12; Crush, Slash R. +4	49	98	L8	90

Torso

Item	Bonus	P	A	M	Q
Supple Hide Jerkin	-1%; Qui +3	4	8	L1	90
Ripper Jerkin	HP +9	5	10	L2	100
Pilfered Jerkin	Con, Str +4; Cha -2	9	18	L2	90
Cracked Leather Jerkin		9	18	L2	80
Boar Hide Jerkin		10	20	L3	89
Troll Hide Jerkin		10	20	L3	95
Hard Leather Vest	-1%; Dex, Qui +1	12	24	L3	80
Musty Leather Jerkin	-5%; Dex, Qui +3; Str +1	13	26	L3	89
Spider Emblazoned Tunic	-5%; Str +3; Pie +4; HP +9	14	28	L3	100
Embossed Spider Tunic	-5%; Dex, Str +3; HP +12	14	28	L3	100
Wormskin Jerkin	-10%; HP +6; Spirit R. +4	15	30	L4	89
Bloodied Leather Jerkin	-10%; Str, Qui +3; HP +12	21	42	L5	89
Observer's Jerkin	-10%; HP +15; Dex +4	24	48	L5	89
Vest of the Infamous Blade	-10%; Dual Wield S. +4; Str, Qui +4	25	50	L6	100
Black Lion-Hide Jerkin	-15%; Qui +9; Con +6	29	58	L6	89
Molded Leather Breastplate	-15%; HP +18; Qui +4	29	58	L6	89
Spiderweave Jerkin	-10%; HP +42	30	60	L7	90
Goblinskin Jerkin	-15%; HP +12; Dex +4; Heat R. +4	30	60	L7	89
Deluged Kelp Jerkin	-15%; HP +24; Slash, Thrust R. +2	34	68	L7	89
Ghost Wolf Hide Jerkin	-20%; HP +24; Stealth S. +2; Dex +6	36	72	L8	100
Faded Jerkin of the Dejected	-1%; HP +12	36	72	L8	80
Jerkin of the Dejected	-20%; Con, Dex, Qui +4; Str +3	37	74	L8	89
Bounder Fur Jerkin	-15%; Dex +9; HP +21	39	78	L8	89
Magma Hard. Leat. J.	-20%; HP +18; Con +7; Energy, Spirit R. +2	40	80	L8	89
Sable Jerkin of Dementia	-20%; HP +39	42	84	L8	89
Jerkin of Ghostly Light	-25%; HP +21; Dex +4; Qui, Str +3	46	92	L8	89
Jerkin of Opposition	-25%; HP +36; Dex +12; Heat R. +2	49	98	L8	90
Regal Jerkin	-30%; Dex, Pie +12; HP +18	49	98	L8	93
Danaoin Nightwatcher J.	-25%; Con, Dex, Qui +9; Thrust R. +6	49	98	L8	90
Celestial Cailiondar J.	-25%; HP +42; Crush R. +10; Dex +10; Str +9	50	100	L8	94

Arms

Item	Bonus	P	A	M	Q
Emult Sleeves	Str +4	5	10	L2	100
Cracked Leather Sleeves		9	18	L2	80
Hard Leather Sleeves		12	24	L3	80
Troll Hide Sleeves	-5%; Con +6	12	24	L3	89
Musty Leather Sleeves	-5%; Dex +3; Str +4	13	26	L3	89
Wormskin Sleeves	-10%; Str +6	15	30	L4	89
Soft Drake Hide Sleeves	-5%; Qui +6; Str +4	20	40	L5	100
Bloodied Leather Sleeves	-10%; Str +6; Dex, Qui +3	21	42	L5	89
Observer's Sleeves	-10%; Qui, Str +6	24	48	L5	89
Molded Leather Armplates	-15%; HP +18; Str +4	29	58	L6	89
Goblinskin Sleeves	-15%; Str, Qui +3; HP +9; Matter R. +4	30	60	L7	89
Deluged Kelp Sleeves	-15%; Str, Pie +7	34	68	L7	89
Faded Sleeves of the Dejected	-1%; Str, Dex +3	36	72	L8	80
Sleeves of the Dejected	-20%; Body, Slash R. +6; Str +7	37	74	L8	89
Bounder Fur Sleeves	-15%; Str +10; Con +3; Dex +6	39	78	L8	89
Sable Sl. of Dementia	-20%; Cold, Spirit R. +4; Str +9; Qui +4	42	84	L8	89
Magma Hardened Leather Sl.	-20%; Str, Dex +9; Energy, Spirit R. +2	42	84	L8	89
Sleeves of Ghostly Light	-25%; Str +10; Dex +6; Qui +4	46	92	L8	89
Magmas Imbued Sleeves	-25%; Str +12; Con, Pie +9; Cold R. +2	49	98	L8	90
Sleeves of Opposition	-25%; Str +18; Qui +12; Heat R. +2	49	98	L8	90
Regal Sleeves	-30%; Str, Con, Qui +13; Cold R. +6	49	98	L8	93
Danaoin Nightwatcher Sl.	-25%; Str +13; Pie +9; Energy, Cold R. +6	49	98	L8	90

Hands

Item	Bonus	P	A	M	Q
Farmers Gloves	HP +6	3	6	L1	90
Emult Gloves	Dex +4	5	10	L2	100
Aged Mithrian Cloth Gloves		9	18	L2	80
Cracked Leather Gloves		9	18	L2	80
Troll Hide Gloves		10	20	L3	95
Hard Leather Gloves		12	24	L3	80
Herb Gatherer's Gloves	-5%; Pie +1; Power +1	12	24	L3	100
Ancient Mithrian Cloth Gloves	-5%; Dex +4; Int +3	13	26	L3	89
Musty Leather Gloves	-5%; HP +9; Pie +3	13	26	L3	80
Wormskin Gloves	-10%; Dex +6	15	30	L4	89
Shadowhands Gloves	-10%; Slash, Thrust S. +1; Str +7	20	40	L5	90
Bloodied Leather Gloves	-10%; Str +3; Qui, Dex +4	21	42	L5	89
Observer's Gloves	-10%; Slash, Thrust S. +1; Qui +6	24	48	L5	89
Molded Leather Gloves	-15%; Con, Str +6; Crush R. +2	29	58	L6	89
Goblinskin Gloves	-15%; Qui, Dex, Con +3; Spirit R. +6	30	60	L7	89
Frog Rider's Riding Gl.	-15%; Slash, Thrust S. +2; Dex +6; Str +4	33	66	L7	100
Deluged Kelp Gloves	-15%; Qui +9; Pie +6	34	68	L7	89
Faded Gloves of the Dejected	-1%; Dex, Qui +3	36	72	L8	80
Gloves of the Dejected	-20%; Energy, Crush R. +6; Qui +7	37	74	L8	89
Bounder Fur Gl.	-15%; Str +7; Qui +4; Body R. +4; Crit. Strike S. +1	39	78	L8	89
Sable Gloves of Dementia	-20%; HP +12; Dex, Qui, Str +4	42	84	L8	89
Magma Hard. Leather Gl.	-20%; Str, Qui +9; Energy, Spirit R. +2	42	84	L8	89
Gloves of Ghostly Light	-25%; HP +18; Dex, Qui +6	46	92	L8	89
Magmas Imbued Gloves	-25%; Qui +12; Con, Str +4; Cold R. +2	47	94	L8	89
Gloves of Opposition	-25%; Dex +7; Qui +10	47	94	L8	89
Regal Gloves	-30%; Envenom, Parry S. +3; Str, Qui +13	49	98	L8	93
Danaoin Nightwatcher Gloves	-25%; HP +18; Str, Qui, Pie +7	49	98	L8	90

Legs

Item	Bonus	P	A	M	Q
Emult Leggings	Con +4	5	10	L2	100
Wolf Hide Leggings		5	10	L2	89
Filthy Hide Pants		5	10	L2	70
Pilfered Leather Leggings	Con, Dex +3; Cha -2	6	12	L2	90
Svelte Armor Leggings	-1%; Cha +4; Dex +3	7	14	L2	100
Cracked Leather Leggings		9	18	L2	80
Hard Leather Leggings		12	24	L3	80
Wormskin Leggings	-5%; Con +7	13	26	L3	89
Musty Leather Leggings	-5%; Con +7	13	26	L3	89
Soft Leather Traveler's Leg.	-5%; Con +4; Qui +3; Matter R. +8	15	30	L4	100
Bloodied Leather Leggings	-10%; Con +6; Body R. +8	21	42	L5	89
Observer's Leggings	-10%; Dex, Con +6	24	48	L5	89
Molded Leather Greaves	-15%; HP +18; Dex +4	29	58	L6	89
Spiderweave Leggings	-10%; Con +10; Body R. +8	30	60	L7	90

Item	Bonus	P	A	M	Q
Goblinskin Leggings	-15%; Con, Qui +4; Cold R. +6	30	60	L7	89
Deluged Kelp Leggings	-15%; Con +10; Dex +4	34	68	L7	89
Faded Leggings of the Dejected	-1%; Con +3; Body R. +4	36	72	L8	80
Leggings of the Dejected	-20%; HP +15; Dex, Qui +4	37	74	L8	89
Magma Hard. Leat. Leg.	-20%; Con +12; Qui +3; Energy, Spirit R. +2	38	76	L8	89
Bounder Fur Leggings	-15%; Con +12; Dex +7	39	78	L8	89
Sable Leggings of Dementia	-20%; Con +10; Dex, Str +4	42	84	L8	89
Leg. of Ghostly Light	-25%; Con +12; Cold, Matter, Heat R. +4	46	92	L8	89
Magmas Imbued Leggings	-25%; Con +10; Dex +12; Cold R. +4	49	98	L8	90
Leggings of Opposition	-25%; Con +10; Dex +6; Qui +9	49	98	L8	90
Regal Leggings	-30%; Str, Con +10; HP +21; Slash R. +6	49	98	L8	93
Danaoin Nightwatch. Leg.	-25%; Con +10; Dex, Qui +6; Energy R. +6	49	98	L8	90

Feet

Item	Bonus	P	A	M	Q
Emult Boots	Qui +4	5	10	L2	100
Aged Mithrian Cloth Boots		5	10	L2	80
Forest Runners Boots	Con, Qui +3; Dex +1	9	18	L2	90
Cracked Leather Boots		9	18	L2	80
Hard Leather Boots		12	24	L3	80
Ancient Mithrian Cloth Boots	-5%; Dex +4; Qui +3	13	26	L3	89
Musty Leather Boots	-5%; Evade S. +1; Dex +4	13	26	L3	89
Wormskin Boots	-5%; Qui +7	14	28	L3	89
Lightfoot Boots	-5%; Qui +7; Stealth S. +1	15	30	L4	90
Soft Doeskin Boots	-10%; Evade S. +3; Dex +4; Qui +3	20	40	L5	100
Bloodied Leather Boots	-10%; Dex +6; Qui +3; Evade S. +1	21	42	L5	89
Observer's Boots	-10%; Evade S. +1; Dex +6; Qui +3	24	48	L5	89
Cat Hide Boots	-10%; Stealth S. +2; Dex +13	25	50	L6	100
Molded Leather Boots	-15%; Dex, Qui +6; Matter R. +2	29	58	L6	89
Goblinskin Boots	-15%; Dex, Str +4; Body R. +6	30	60	L7	89
Deluged Kelp Boots	-15%; Dex +12; Cold, Energy R. +2	34	68	L7	89
Faded Boots of the Dejected	-1%; Con, Dex +3	36	72	L8	80
Boots of the Dejected	-20%; HP +12; Dex +10	37	74	L8	89
Bounder Fur Boots	-15%; Dex +3; Qui +13; Evade S. +1	39	78	L8	89
Magma Hard. Leat. B.	-20%; Qui +4; Dex +12; Energy, Spirit R. +2	40	80	L8	89
Sable Boots of Dementia	-20%; Body R. +8; Dex +13	42	84	L8	89
Boots of Ghostly Light	-25%; Dex +12; Crush, Energy, Slash R. +4	46	92	L8	89
Magmas Imbued Boots	-25%; Dex +10; Con, Str +7	49	98	L8	90
Boots of Opposition	-25%; Dex +14; Stealth S. +2; Heat R. +4	49	98	L8	90
Regal Boots	-30%; Stealth, Rejuvenation S. +3; Dex, Qui +13	49	98	L8	93
Danaoin Nightwatcher Boots	-25%; HP +18; Dex +10; Qui +7	49	98	L8	90

Robes

Item	Bonus	P	A	M	Q
Friar Robes		0	0	L1	100
Robes of the Novice	Evade S. +1	5	10	L2	100
Robes of the Neophyte	-1%; Evade S. +2	11	22	L3	100
Robes of the Journeyman	-5%; Evade S. +3	15	30	L4	100
Robes of Battle	-5%; HP +24	15	30	L4	100
Robes of the Adept	-5%; Evade S. +4	20	40	L5	100
Spirit-Fighters Robes	-1%; Evade S. +1; HP +12; Qui +7	20	40	L5	89
Keltoi Infiltrators Disguise	-10%; HP +12; Qui, Pie +3	24	48	L5	89
Robes of the Master	-10%; Evade S. +5	25	50	L6	100
Ghost Robes	-15%; Rejuvenation, Enhancements S. +2; Pie +1	29	58	L6	89
War Torn Robe	-15%; Con, Qui +7	32	64	L7	89
Shepherd's Robes	-15%; HP +33	33	66	L7	89
Robe of Deft Movement	-15%; HP +18; Dex, Str +4	37	74	L8	100
Faded Robes of the Dejected	-1%; HP +12	38	76	L8	80
Robes of the Dejected	-20%; HP +15; Str +6; Qui +4	39	78	L8	89
Sable Robes of Dementia	-25%; HP +18; Str +9	42	84	L8	89
Robes of Ghostly Light	-25%; Con, Dex +6; Str +7	46	92	L8	89
Robes of Celerity	-25%; HP +30; Evade S. +3; Dex +7	49	98	L8	90
Magmas Imbued Robe	-25%; HP +24; Power +2; Pie +10	49	98	L8	90
Putrefied Robes	-30%; Pie, Con +10; Dex +13	49	98	L8	93
Restless Robes	-25%; HP +30; Str, Pie +7	49	98	L8	90
Cailiondar Battle Robe	-25%; HP +36; Slash R. +10; Qui, Pie +12	50	100	L8	94

Studded Leather

Head

Item	Bonus	P	A	M	Q
Helm of Vision	-5%; Cold R. +1; Qui +1	6	12	M2	89
Worn Studded Helm		9	18	M2	80
Helm of the Observant	-5%; Power +2; Pie +4	11	22	M3	100
Faded Helm		12	24	M3	80
Resounding Helm	-1%; Pie +6	12	24	M3	89
Shimmering Etheric Helm	-5%; Pie +6; Rejuvenation S. +1	12	24	M3	90
Preserved Studded Helm	-5%; Pie +4; Cha +3	13	26	M3	89
Spirit Spun Helm	-10%; Dex +6	15	30	M4	89
Forester's Helmet	-10%; Evade S. +1; Cold R. +8; Dex +3	21	42	M5	89
Hunter's Helm	-15%; HP +21	23	46	M5	89
Prey-Stalker's Helm	-10%; Stealth S. +2; Qui, Dex +3	24	48	M5	89
Rigid Roman Helm	-15%; Str +6; Dex +6; Cold R. +2	30	60	M7	89
Woebegone Miner Helm	-15%; Dex, Str +6; Energy R. +4	32	64	M7	89
Worn Helm of the Blackheart	-1%; Cold, Heat R. +4	36	72	M8	80
Helm of the Blackheart	-20%; Dex +4; Qui +6; Slash, Cold R. +4	37	74	M8	89
Runic Ravenbone Helm	-20%; Con, Str +4; Dex +10	42	84	M8	89
Studded Fae H.	-15%; Dex +7; Qui +7; Slash R. +4; Stealth S. +1	43	86	M8	89
Aqueous Coral Studded Helm	-20%; Dex, Str +7; Cold R. +8	44	88	M8	89
Stonecrush Helm	-20%; Qui +12; Con +7; Thrust R. +2	44	88	M8	89
Frozen Boned Helm	-25%; Body R. +8; HP +18; Dex +10; Str +9	46	92	M8	100
Helm of the Baleful Dead	-25%; Body R. +16; Stealth S. +3	46	92	M8	89
Ageless Telamon H.	-25%; HP +30; Cold, Heat R. +8; Stealth S. +2	49	98	M8	90
Bloodied Helm	-30%; Qui +7; Con +10; Crush R. +12; HP +27	49	98	M8	91
Dark Crystalline Helm	-25%; Qui +12; Dex, Str +9; Energy R. +2	49	98	M8	90

Torso

Item	Bonus	P	A	M	Q
Preserved Studded Vest	-1%; Pie +3; Str +4	9	18	M2	90
Worn Studded Vest		9	18	M2	80
Faded Tunic	-1%; Pie, Con +1	12	24	M3	80
Preserved Studded Vest	-5%; HP +15	13	26	M3	89
Spirit Spun Vest	-5%; Str +6; Spirit R. +2	13	26	M3	89
Studded Spider Eye Vest	-5%; HP +9; Pie +3; Qui +4	14	28	M3	100
Vest of the Valiant	-10%; Body, Slash R. +4; Pie +6	20	40	M5	100
Forester's Jerkin	-10%; Str, Qui +3; HP +12	21	42	M5	89
Prey-Stalker's Vest	-10%; HP +12; Dex, Qui +3	24	48	M5	89
Hunter's Vest	-15%; HP +18; Qui +3	25	50	M6	89
Light Chain Tunic	-10%; Slash R. +2; Qui +9; HP +12	25	50	M6	100
Shadowhunter's Vest	-15%; HP +21; Str +4	25	50	M6	90
Rigid Roman Vest	-15%; Con, Qui +6; Body R. +2	30	60	M7	89
Studded Green Jerkin	-15%; HP +30; Crush, Slash R. +4	30	60	M7	100
Woebegone Miner Vest	-15%; HP +12; Dex +4; Heat R. +6	32	64	M7	89
Worn Vest of the Blackheart	-1%; Con, Dex, Qui, Str +1	36	72	M8	80
Vest of the Blackheart	-20%; HP +21; Dex, Str +3	37	74	M8	89
Runic Ravenbone Vest	-20%; HP +21; Crush, Thrust, Energy R. +4	42	84	M8	89
Studded Fae Vest	-15%; Str +3; Con +4; Slash R. +4; HP +21	43	86	M8	89
Aqueous Coral Studded Vest	-20%; HP +42	44	88	M8	89
Stonecrush Vest	-25%; HP +24; Dex +7; Thrust R. +2	46	92	M8	89
Vest of the Baleful Dead	-25%; HP +24; Dex, Str, Qui +3	46	92	M8	89
Ageless Telamon Vest	-25%; Con, Str +12; Cold R. +6; Slash R. +4	49	98	M8	90
Bloodied Vest	-30%; Con, Qui +12; HP +27; Thrust R. +10	49	98	M8	91
Dark Crystalline Vest	-25%; HP +36; Dex, Con +7; Energy R. +2	49	98	M8	90
Celestial Cailiondar Vest	-25%; HP +42; Slash R. +10; Dex +13	50	100	M8	94

Arms

Item	Bonus	P	A	M	Q
Sleeves of Might	-1%; Str +4; HP +6	7	14	M2	100
Worn Studded Sleeves		9	18	M2	80
Faded Sleeves		12	24	M3	80
Preserved Studded Sleeves	-5%; Str +4; Qui +3	13	26	M3	89
Spirit Spun Arms	-5%; Str +7	14	28	M3	89
Forester's Sleeves	-10%; Str +6; Body R. +8	21	42	M5	89
Tooth Studded Sleeves	-10%; Str +12; HP +9	21	42	M5	100

Item	Bonus	P	A	M	Q
Prey-Stalker's Sleeves	-10%; HP +6; Str +6; Dex +3	24	48	M5	89
Hunter's Sleeves	-15%; Str +9; Body R. +4	25	50	M6	89
Rigid Roman Arms	-15%; Str, Qui +6; Energy R. +2	30	60	M7	89
Woebegone Miner Sleeves	-15%; Str, Dex +6; Matter R. +4	32	64	M7	89
Worn Arms of the Blackheart	-1%; HP +6; Str +3	36	72	M8	80
Sleeves of the Blackheart	-20%; Str +7; Con +6; Energy R. +4	37	74	M8	89
Runic Ravenbone Arms	-20%; HP +15; Con, Dex +6	42	84	M8	89
Studded Fae Sleeves	-15%; Str +12; Qui +6; Slash R. +4	43	86	M8	89
Aqueous Coral Studded Arms	-20%; Str +10; Longbow S. +2	44	88	M8	89
Arms of the Baleful Dead	-25%; HP +15; Str +10; Qui +3	46	92	M8	89
Stonecrush Arms	-25%; Str +12; Dex +9; Thrust R. +2	48	96	M8	89
Ageless Telamon Sleeves	-25%; HP +18; Str +11; Qui +6	49	98	M8	90
Bloodied Arms	-30%; Body, Cold R. +12; Str +12; Qui +10	49	98	M8	91
Dark Crystalline Arms	-25%; Str +18; Dex +13; Energy R. +2	49	98	M8	90

Hands

Item	Bonus	P	A	M	Q
Worn Studded Gauntlets		9	18	M2	80
Faded Gloves		12	24	M3	80
Preserved Studded Gauntlets	-5%; Str, Pie +3; Qui +1	13	26	M3	89
Spirit Spun Gauntlets	-5%; Dex +6; Thrust R. +2	14	28	M3	89
Gauntlets of Archery	-5%; Longbow S. +2; Qui +3; Dex +4	15	30	M4	100
Ivy-Weave Gloves	-10%; Pie +9; Qui +3	16	32	M4	100
Forester's Gloves	-10%; Qui, Dex +4; Longbow S. +1	21	42	M5	89
Hunter's Gauntlets	-15%; Dex, Qui +4; Cold R. +2	23	46	M5	89
Prey-Stalker's Gauntlets	-10%; Longbow S. +1; Qui, Str +4	24	48	M5	89
Rigid Roman Gauntlets	-15%; Str, Dex +6; Body R. +2	30	60	M7	89
Woebegone Miner G.	-15%; Qui, Dex +4; Con +3; Spirit R. +4	32	64	M7	89
Worn Gloves of the Blackheart	-1%; Qui +6	36	72	M8	80
Gauntlets of the Blackheart	-20%; Str +7; Qui +6; Crush R. +4	37	74	M8	89
Runic Ravenbone G.	-20%; Body R. +4; Slash R. +2; Str +12; Qui +3	42	84	M8	89
Studded Fae Gl.	-15%; Str, Dex +7; Slash R. +4; Longbow S. +1	43	86	M8	89
Aqueous Coral Studded Gloves	-56%; Qui +10; Crush, Slash R. +2	44	88	M8	89
Gauntlets of the Baleful Dead	-25%; Body R. +8; Qui, Dex +7	46	92	M8	89
Stonecrush Gauntlets	-25%; Dex, Qui +10; Thrust R. +2	48	96	M8	89
Ageless Telamon G.	-25%; Longbow S. +3; Dex, Qui, Str +7	49	98	M8	90
Bloodied G.	-30%; Thrust S. +4; Dex +12; Shield S. +3; Body R. +8	49	98	M8	91
Dark Crystalline G.	-25%; Qui +11; Str +12; Longbow S. +2	49	98	M8	90

Legs

Item	Bonus	P	A	M	Q
Worn Studded Leggings		9	18	M2	80
Faded Leggings		12	24	M3	80
Preserved Studded Leggings	-5%; Con +4; Str +3	13	26	M3	89
Spirit Spun Leggings	-10%; Con +4; Thrust R. +2	15	30	M4	89
Forester's Leggings	-10%; Con +9; Str +3	21	42	M5	89
Prey-Stalker's Leggings	-10%; HP +6; Con, Qui +4	24	48	M5	89
Hunter's Leggings	-15%; Con +9; Dex +3	25	50	M6	89
Rigid Roman Legs	-15%; Con, Dex +6; Heat R. +2	30	60	M7	89
Woebegone Miner Leggings	-15%; Con, Qui +6; Cold R. +4	32	64	M7	89
Worn Leggings of the Blackheart	-1%; HP +6; Body R. +4	36	72	M8	80
Leggings of the Blackheart	-20%; Con +7; Qui +6; Body R. +4	37	74	M8	89
Runic Ravenbone Leggings	-20%; HP +21; Str, Dex +4	42	84	M8	89
Studded Fae Leggings	-15%; Str +3; Con +10; Slash R. +4	43	86	M8	89
Aqueous Coral Studded Legs	-20%; Con +10; Stealth S. +2	44	88	M8	89
Stonecrush Leggings	-20%; Con +12; Dex +7; Thrust R. +2	44	88	M8	89
Leg. of the Baleful Dead	-25%; Con +12; Dex, Str +3; Energy R. +4	46	92	M8	89
Ageless Telamon Leg.	-25%; Con +10; Qui, Dex +4; Energy R. +10	49	98	M8	90
Bloodied Leg.	-30%; Str +10; Energy R. +14; Spirit R. +12; HP +21	49	98	M8	91
Dark Crystalline Legs	-25%; Con +12; Dex, Qui +9; Energy R. +4	49	98	M8	90

Feet

Item	Bonus	P	A	M	Q
Worn Studded Boots		9	18	M2	80
Faded Boots		12	24	M3	80
Preserved Studded Boots	-5%; Dex +7	13	26	M3	89
Spirit Spun Boots	-10%; Qui +6; Spirit R. +2	16	32	M4	89
Forester's Boots	-10%; Dex, Qui +4; Energy R. +4	21	42	M5	89
Hunter's Boots	-15%; Dex +9; Energy R. +2	23	46	M5	89
Prey-Stalker's Boots	-10%; Dex +9; Qui +3	24	48	M5	89
Rigid Roman Boots	-15%; Con, Dex +6; Body R. +2	30	60	M7	89
Woebegone Miner Boots	-15%; Dex, Str +6; Body R. +4	32	64	M7	89
Worn Boots of the Blackheart	-1%; Dex, Con +3	36	72	M8	80
Boots of the Blackheart	-20%; Dex +10; Str +3; Body R. +4	37	74	M8	89
Faded Boots of Blessing	-20%; HP +10; Str +4; Con +6; Cold R. +8	42	84	M8	100
Faded Boots of Glory	-20%; Str +10; Cold R. +10; Body R. +5	42	84	M8	100
Faded Boots of Honor	-20%; HP +8; Cold R. +4; Dex, Qui +7	42	84	M8	100
Runic Ravenbone Boots	-20%; Energy, Cold R. +4; Qui +13	42	84	M8	89
Splendid B. of Blessing	-20%; HP +15; Str +7; Con +9; Cold R. +12	42	84	M8	100
Splendid Boots of Glory	-20%; Str +10; Cold R. +16; Body R. +8	42	84	M8	100
Splendid B. of Honor	-20%; HP +12; Cold R. +6; Dex +12; Qui +10	42	84	M8	100
Studded Fae Boots	-15%; Dex +10; Qui +6; Evade S. +2	43	86	M8	89
Aqueous Coral Studded Boots	-20%; Dex +10; Body R. +4	44	88	M8	89
Boots of the Baleful Dead	-25%; Cold, Heat R. +6; Dex +12	46	92	M8	89
Stonecrush Boots	-25%; Qui +9; Dex +12; Thrust R. +2	46	92	M8	89
Ageless Telamon Boots	-25%; HP +21; Str +10; Energy R. +10	49	98	M8	90
Bloodied B.	-30%; Stealth S. +4; Dex +12; Heat R. +10; HP +21	49	98	M8	91
Dark Crystalline B.	-25%; Qui +9; Dex +10; Stealth S. +2; En. R. +2	49	98	M8	90

Chain

Head

Item	Bonus	P	A	M	Q
Corroded Chainmail Coif		9	18	M2	80
Helm of the Forlorn	-5%; HP +9; Qui +3	13	26	M3	89
Ruined Roman Helm	-10%; Pie +3; Crush, Spirit R. +2	15	30	M4	89
Skull of Aer'ambor	-10%; Body R. +4; Pie +4	17	34	M4	89
Chain Coif of Disparity	-10%; Dex +6; Thrust R. +4	18	36	M4	89
Dusk-Walker's Coif	-10%; Dex, Qui +3; Pie +4	21	42	M5	89
Fire-Forged Coif	-10%; Str, Con +3; Energy R. +4	21	42	M5	89
Mithril Chain Coif	-15%	25	50	M6	80
Goblin Goldminer Coif	-15%; Pie, Dex +4; Energy R. +4	28	56	M6	89
Despoiled Coif	-15%; Cha, Pie +6; Con +3	31	62	M7	89
Arawnite Coif	-15%; Pie +9; Dex, Qui +3; Crush R. +4	34	68	M7	89
Worn Coif of Dissolution	-1%; Pie, Str +3	36	72	M8	80
Coif of Dissolution	-20%; Pie +10; Heat, Cold R. +4	37	74	M8	89
Scarlet Coif of the Covetous	-20%; HP +12; Dex, Con, Pie +4	42	84	M8	89
Banded Coral Coif	-20%; Cha, Pie +7; Crush R. +4	43	86	M8	89
Banded Coral Coif	-20%; Smiting, Rejuv., Enhanc. S. +1; Pie +12	43	86	M8	89
Corrupt Greatheart Coif	-25%; HP +18; Pie +12	46	92	M8	89
Frozen Stone H.	-25%; Body R. +6; Smiting S. +4; Pie +13; Str +4	46	92	M8	100
Coif of the Stoneharvest	-25%; Qui +12; Con +9; Crush R. +2	47	94	M8	89
Danaoin Lightwatcher C.	-25%; Cha, Pie +9; Parry S. +3; Sl. R. +6	49	98	M8	90
Doom Helm	-30%; Cha, Pie +13; Smiting S. +4; Power +3	49	98	M8	93
Ilmenite Laced Chain Coif	-25%; Pie +12; Con +10; Slash R. +4	49	98	M8	90
Ircon Bound Chain C.	-25%; Cha, Dex +12; Instr. S. +3; Thr. R. +4	49	98	M8	90
Polished Coif of Eldspar	-25%; Qui, Dex +12; Str +9; Slash R. +4	49	98	M8	90

Torso

Item	Bonus	P	A	M	Q
Corroded Chainmail Hauberk		9	18	M2	80
Footman's Chainmail	-1%; Con, Str +1	12	24	M3	80
Hauberk of the Forlorn	-5%; HP +9; Str +3	13	26	M3	89
Ringed Spider Chitin Tunic	-5%; HP +9; Str +4; Qui +3	14	28	M3	100
Chain Hauberk of Disparity	-10%; HP +12	15	30	M4	89
Chitin Mail	-10%; HP +12; Str +6	16	32	M4	100
Ruined Roman Hauberk	-10%; HP +15	18	36	M4	89
Hauberk of the Valiant	-10%; HP +18; Slash, Crush R. +2	20	40	M5	100
Dusk-Walkers Hauberk	-10%; HP +21	21	42	M5	89
Fire-Forged Hauberk	-10%; HP +9; Dex +1; Heat R. +4	21	42	M5	89
Chain Shirt of Comfort	-15%; HP +12; Str +7; Con +6	25	50	M6	100
Mithril Chain Hauberk	-15%	25	50	M6	80
Keltoi Battlemail	-15%; HP +48	27	54	M6	100
Goblin Goldminer Hauberk	-15%; HP +12; Dex +3; Heat R. +4	28	56	M6	89

Item	Bonus	P	A	M	Q
Despoiled Mail	-15%; Con, Str +6; Energy R. +4	31	62	M7	89
Arawnite Deathmail	-15%; Pie +4; HP +21; Slash R. +4	34	68	M7	89
Worn Mail of Dissolution	-1%; Body R. +8	36	72	M8	80
Mail of Dissolution	-20%; HP +21; Pie, Str +3	37	74	M8	89
Scarlet Mail of the Covetous	-20%; Con +6; Pie, Qui, Str +4	42	84	M8	89
Banded Coral Hauberk	-20%; HP +24; Cha, Pie +4	43	86	M8	89
Banded Coral Hauberk	-20%; HP +27; Str +7	43	86	M8	89
Corrupt Greatheart Mail	-25%; HP +15; Dex, Pie, Str +4	46	92	M8	89
Danaoin Lightwatcher Hauberk	-25%; HP +36; Str +9; Cha, Pie +3	49	98	M8	90
Hauberk of Doom	-30%; HP +21; Pie +12; Con +10; Matter R. +12	49	98	M8	93
Hauberk of the Stoneharvest	-25%; HP +33; Str +12; Crush R. +2	49	98	M8	90
Ilmenite Laced Ch. Hbk.	-25%; HP +39; Power +2; Pie +13; Sl. R. +2	49	98	M8	91
Ircon Bound Ch. Hbk.	-25%; HP +33; Power +4; Dex +12; Thr. R. +2	49	98	M8	91
Polished Hbk. of Eldspar	-25%; HP +24; Str +10; Qui +9; Sl. R. +4	49	98	M8	91
Celestial Cailiondar Hbk.	-25%; HP +45; Cha, Pie +10; Str +10	50	100	M8	94

Arms

Item	Bonus	P	A	M	Q
Armsman Sleeves	-1%; Str +4; HP +6	7	14	M2	100
Corroded Chainmail Sleeves		9	18	M2	80
Footman's Chain Sleeves		12	24	M3	80
Sleeves of the Forlorn	-5%; Str +7	13	26	M3	89
Chain Sleeves of Disparity	-5%; Str +7	14	28	M3	89
Ruined Roman Sleeves	-10%; Str +6; Cold R. +2	18	36	M4	89
Dusk-Walkers Sleeves	-10%; Str +7; Pie +3	21	42	M5	89
Fire-Forged Sleeves	-10%; Str, Qui +3; Matter R. +4	21	42	M5	89
Mithril Chain Sleeves	-15%	25	50	M6	80
Goblin Goldminer Sleeves	-15%; Str, Dex +4; Matter R. +4	28	56	M6	89
Despoiled Sleeves	-15%; Str +9; Cha, Pie +3	31	62	M7	89
Arawnite Sleeves	-15%; Str +9; Power +2; Slash R. +4	34	68	M7	89
Worn Sleeves of Dissolution	-1%; HP +12	36	72	M8	80
Sleeves of Dissolution	-20%; Str +9; Qui +4; Pie +3	37	74	M8	89
Scarlet Sleeves of the Covetous	-20%; HP +15; Str, Pie +6	42	84	M8	89
Banded Coral Sleeves	-20%; Str +18; Qui +3	43	86	M8	89
Banded Coral Sleeves	-20%; Str +13; Cha, Pie +4	43	86	M8	89
Corrupt Greatheart Sleeves	-25%; Str +12; Pie +9	46	92	M8	89
Arms of Doom	-30%; Dex +11; Qui +10; HP +15; Body R. +10	49	98	M8	93
Danaoin Lightwatcher Sleeves	-25%; Str +18; Pie +12; Cha +3	49	98	M8	90
Ilmenite Laced Chain Sl.	-25%; Str +10; Pie +12; Con +9; Slash R. +2	49	98	M8	90
Ircon Bound Chain Sl.	-25%; Str, Cha +10; Dex +6; Thrust R. +2	49	98	M8	90
Polished Sl. of Eldspar	-25%; Str +10; Dex +9; Con +12; Slash R. +2	49	98	M8	90
Sleeves of the Stoneharvest	-25%; Str, Dex +10; Crush R. +2	49	98	M8	90

Hands

Item	Bonus	P	A	M	Q
Corroded Chainmail Mittens		9	18	M2	80
Skull-Embossed Gauntlets	-5%; Str +3	10	20	M3	89
Footman's Chain Gauntlets		12	24	M3	80
Drakescale Gauntlets	-5%; HP +6; Dex, Str +3	12	24	M3	90
Chain Gloves of Disparity	-5%; Dex +7	13	26	M3	89
Gauntlets of the Forlorn	-5%; Qui +7	13	26	M3	89
Ruined Roman Gauntlets	-10%; Cha, Dex +3	15	30	M4	89
Ivy-Weave Gloves	-10%; Pie +9; Qui +3	16	32	M4	100
Dusk-Walkers Gauntlets	-10%; Dex, Str +3; Pie +4	21	42	M5	89
Fire-Forged Mittens	-10%; Qui, Dex +3; Spirit R. +4	21	42	M5	89
Gauntlets of Celerity	-15%; Dual Wield S. +3; Qui +6	25	50	M6	90
Mithril Chain Mittens	-15%	25	50	M6	80
Goblin Goldminer Mittens	-15%; Qui, Pie +4; Spirit R. +4	28	56	M6	89
Gauntlets of Blinding Speed	-15%; Str, Qui +6; Dual Wield S. +4	31	62	M7	100
Despoiled Gloves	-15%; Dex, Qui +4; Cold, Heat R. +4	31	62	M7	89
Arawnite Chain Gl.	-15%; Str, Qui +6; Pie +3; Instruments S. +1	34	68	M7	89
Worn Gloves of Dissolution	-1%; Con +6	36	72	M8	80
Gauntlets of Dissolution	-20%; Qui, Dex +6; Pie +4	37	74	M8	89
Scarlet Gloves of the Covetous	-20%; Qui +7; Str, Pie +6	42	84	M8	89
Banded Coral G.	-20%; Dual Wield S. +2; Parry S. +1; Qui +12	43	86	M8	89
Banded Coral Gauntlets	-20%; Instruments S. +2; Qui, Pie +7	43	86	M8	89
Corrupt Greatheart G.	-25%; Cold, Body R. +4; Qui +9; Pie +6	46	92	M8	89
Danaoin Ltw. G.	-25%; HP +18; Qui +12; Dual Wd. S. +3; Thr. R. +4	49	98	M8	90
Gl. of Doom	-30%; Dex +13; Dual Wield, Slash S. +3; Power +4	49	98	M8	93
Gloves of the Stoneharvest	-25%; Qui, Dex +10; Crush R. +2	49	98	M8	90
Ilmenite Laced Chain Mittens	-25%; Dex, Str +18; Slash R. +4	49	98	M8	91
Polished Mittens of Eldspar	-25%; Dex +10; Str +7; HP +33	49	98	M8	91

Legs

Item	Bonus	P	A	M	Q
Corroded Chainmail Leggings		9	18	M2	100
Footman's Chain Legs		12	24	M3	80
Leggings of the Forlorn	-5%; Con +7	13	26	M3	89
Redoubled Leggings	-10%; Pie +4; Con +7	15	30	M4	100
Chain Leggings of Disparity	-10%; Con +4; Thrust R. +4	17	34	M4	89
Ruined Roman Leggings	-10%; Con +6; Body R. +2	18	36	M4	89
Leggings of Comfort	-10%; Qui +7; Con +6; Energy R. +4	20	40	M5	100
Dusk-Walker's Leggings	-10%; Con +10	21	42	M5	89
Fire-Forged Leggings	-10%; Con, Qui +3; Cold R. +4	21	42	M5	89
Mithril Chain Leggings	-15%	25	50	M6	80
Goblin Goldminer Leggings	-15%; Con, Dex +4; Cold R. +4	28	56	M6	89
Despoiled Legs	-15%; Con +9; Cha, Dex +3	31	62	M7	89
Arawnite Leggings	-15%; Con +12; Dex +3; Slash R. +4	34	68	M7	89
Worn Leggings of Dissolution	-1%; HP +12	36	72	M8	80
Leggings of Dissolution	-20%; Con +9; Dex +4; Str +3	37	74	M8	89
Scarlet L. o.t. Covetous	-20%; Mat. R. +4; Sl. R. +2; Con +12; Str +3	42	84	M8	89
Banded Coral Leggings	-20%; Con +10; Cha +6	43	86	M8	89
Banded Coral Leggings	-20%; Con +13; Dex +7	43	86	M8	89
Corrupt Greatheart Leggings	-25%; HP +30; Body, Crush R. +4	46	92	M8	89
Danaoin Lightwatcher Leggings	-25%; Con +10; Cha, Dex +9	49	98	M8	90
Doom Leggings	-30%; Con +13; Cold R. +12; HP +21; Heat R. +10	49	98	M8	93
Ilmenite Laced Chain Legs	-25%; Con +10; Dex +12; Pie +9	49	98	M8	90
Ircon Bd. Ch. L.	-25%; Cha +12; Con +10; Stealth S. +2; Thrust R. +4	49	98	M8	90
Leg. o.t. Stoneharvest	-25%; Dex +7; Qui, Con +12; Crush R. +2	49	98	M8	90
Polished Leggings of Eldspar	-25%; Con, Dex, Qui +12	49	98	M8	90

Feet

Item	Bonus	P	A	M	Q
Corroded Chainmail Boots		9	18	M2	80
Boots of the Forlorn	-5%; Dex +7	12	24	M3	89
Footman's Chain Boots		12	24	M3	80
Ruined Roman Boots	-10%; Dex, Con +3	15	30	M4	89
Chain Boots of Disparity	-10%; Qui +7	16	32	M4	89
Dusk-Walker's Boots	-10%; Dex +7; Qui +3	21	42	M5	89
Fire-Forged Boots	-10%; Dex, Str +3; Body R. +4	21	42	M5	89
Mithril Chain Boots	-15%	25	50	M6	80
Goblin Goldminer Boots	-15%; Dex, Str +4; Body R. +4	28	56	M6	89
Despoiled Boots	-15%; Con, Dex +6; Body R. +4	31	62	M7	89
Arawnite Boots	-15%; Dex, Qui +7; Crush R. +4	34	68	M7	89
Worn Boots of Dissolution	-1%; Energy R. +4; Dex +3	36	72	M8	80
Boots of Dissolution	-20%; Dex +7; Cold, Body R. +6	37	74	M8	89
Scarlet B. o.t. Covetous	-20%; Cold, Energy R. +4; Dex +10; Con +3	42	84	M8	89
Banded Coral Boots	-20%; Con, Qui +4; Dex +12	43	86	M8	89
Banded Coral Boots	-20%; HP +24; Body R. +8; Energy R. +4	43	86	M8	89
Corrupt Greatheart B.	-25%; Energy, Matter R. +4; Dex +9; Qui +6	46	92	M8	89
Boots of Doom	-30%; Dex +11; Body R. +22; Str +13	49	98	M8	93
B. of the Stoneharvest	-25%; Dex, Qui +12; Con +9; Crush R. +2	49	98	M8	90
Danaoin Lightwatcher Boots	-25%; Dex, Qui +13; Cold R. +8	49	98	M8	90
Ilmenite Laced Chain Boots	-25%; Qui +13; Str +9; Dex +10	49	98	M8	90
Polished B. of Eldspar	-25%; Qui +10; Dex +12; Str +9; Slash R. +2	49	98	M8	90

Plate

Head

Item	Bonus	P	A	M	Q
Ghoul Knight Helm	-10%; Pie +7	16	32	M4	89
Lion Embossed Full Helm	-10%; Cha +3; Pie +6; Chants S. +1	20	40	M5	89
Vindicator's Helm	-10%; HP +9; Con, Str +3	21	42	M5	89
Goblin-Forged Plate Helm	-15%; Str +4; Con +3; Energy R. +4	26	52	M6	89
Ancient Helmet	-15%; Str, Pie +4; Heat R. +4	26	52	M6	89

Item	Bonus	P	A	M	Q
Legions Scaled H.	-15%; Chants S. +2; Con +6; Cold, Body R. +2	31	62	M7	89
Stonewatch Helm	-20%; Dex +12; Qui +3; Slash R. +2	35	70	M8	89
Worn Helm of Mortification	-1%; HP +12	36	72	M8	80
Helm of Mortification	-20%; Con, Dex, Str +4; Qui +3	37	74	M8	89
Hollow Helm	-20%; Dex, Qui, Pie +6; Crush R. +4	39	78	M8	89
Ebony Helm of the Corrupt	-20%; HP +21; Heat R. +4; Cold R. +8	42	84	M8	89
Adamant Coral H.	-20%; Chants S. +3; Con +6; Crush, Thrust R. +4	44	88	M8	89
Frosted Plate H.	-25%; Body R. +6; Chants S. +4; Pie +6; Str +12	46	92	M8	100
Helm of Eternal Midnight	-25%; HP +24; Spirit, Heat, Cold R. +6	46	92	M8	89
Cailiondar Helm	-25%; Con, Dex, Str +7; Chants S. +3	49	98	M8	90
Crushed Helm	-25%; Qui +10; Str +9; Dex +7; Crush R. +2	49	98	M8	90
H. o.t. Malevolent	-30%; Pie +9; Str +18; Crush S. +5; Cold R. +6	49	98	M8	93
Hollow Telamon Head	-25%; HP +30; Slash, Crush R. +6; Str +9	49	98	M8	90
Kraggon Worm H.	-25%; Pie +7; Qui +13; Chants S. +2; Body R. +4	49	98	M8	90

Torso

Item	Bonus	P	A	M	Q
Wight-Scarred Breastplate	-10%; HP +15	12	24	M3	89
Ancient Red Steel Hauberk	-1%; HP +9; Dex, Str +3	12	24	M3	90
Ghoul Knight Breastplate	-10%; HP +12; Spirit R. +4	18	36	M4	89
Lion Embossed Breastplate	-10%; Str +4; HP +15	20	40	M5	89
Vindicator's Breastplate	-10%; HP +12; Str +4	21	42	M5	89
Blade-Stopper	-15%; HP +15; Con, Str +4	25	50	M6	100
Breastplate of the Depths	-15%; Con, Str +7	25	50	M6	90
Master of Arms Platemail	-15%; HP +21; Dex, Str +4	25	50	M6	100
Ancient Breastplate	-15%; HP +15; Dex +3; Str +4	26	52	M6	89
Goblin-Forged Breastplate	-15%; HP +9; Dex +3; Heat R. +4	26	52	M6	89
Breastplate of the Legion	-15%; HP +24; Str +6; Con +3	31	62	M7	100
Legions Scaled Breastplate	-15%; Con +9; Str +6	31	62	M7	89
Worn Plate of Mortification	-1%; HP +12	36	72	M8	80
Plate of Mortification	-20%; Con +9; Str +4; Qui +3	37	74	M8	89
Stonewatch Breastplate	-20%; HP +21; Str +6; Slash R. +2	37	74	M8	89
Hollow Breastplate	-20%; Str, Con +3; Dex +3; HP +24	39	78	M8	89
Ebony Plate of the Corrupt	-20%; HP +39	42	84	M8	89
Adamant Coral Breastplate	-20%; HP +30; Str +6	44	88	M8	89
Plate of Eternal Midnight	-25%; HP +24; Crush R. +4; Body R. +8	46	92	M8	89
Cailiondar Breastplate	-25%; HP +45; Str, Qui +7	49	98	M8	90
Holy Crushed Breastplate	-25%; HP +42; Chants S. +2; Str +9	49	98	M8	90
Kraggon Worm Breastplate	-25%; HP +45; Con +6; Body R. +4	49	98	M8	90
Malevolent Breastplate	-30%; Str, Con +12; HP +21	49	98	M8	93
Sturdy Crushed Breastplate	-25%; HP +45; Str +9; Qui +4	49	98	M8	90
Celestial Cailiondar Bpl.	-25%; HP +51; Str +10; Cr., Sl. R. +4	50	100	M8	94

Arms

Item	Bonus	P	A	M	Q
Sleeves of the Stoic	-10%; Str +9; Qui +3	15	30	M4	100
Ghoul Knight Arms	-10%; Str +7	17	34	M4	89
Vambraces of the Defender	-10%; Str +6; Dex +4; Power +2	20	40	M5	100
Lion Embossed Vambraces	-10%; Str +6; Dex, Qui +3	20	40	M5	89
Vindicator's Sleeves	-10%; Str +10	21	42	M5	89
Sleeves of Deflection	-15%; Str +12	25	50	M6	90
Goblin-Forged Plate Vambraces	-15%; Str +7; Matter R. +4	26	52	M6	89
Ancient Vambraces	-15%; Str +9; Qui +3; Heat R. +4	26	52	M6	89
Legions Scaled Armplates	-15%; Str +10; Con +3; Crush R. +2	31	62	M7	89
Worn Arms of Mortification	-1%; HP +12	36	72	M8	80
Sleeves of Mortification	-20%; Str +13; Slash R. +4	37	74	M8	89
Hollow Arms	-20%; Str +12; Con +6; Slash R. +4	39	78	M8	89
Stonewatch Arms	-20%; Str +12; Dex +4; Slash R. +2	39	78	M8	89
Ebony Arms of the Corrupt	-20%; Str +10; Body R. +6	42	84	M8	89
Adamant Coral Vambraces	-20%; HP +30; Str +6	44	88	M8	89
Vambraces of Eternal Midnight	-25%; Slash, Energy R. +4; Str +10	46	92	M8	89
Crushed Sleeves	-25%; Str, Con +11; Crush R. +2	49	98	M8	90
Kraggon Worm Arms	-25%; Str +16; Body R. +8	49	98	M8	90
Malevolent Arms	-30%; Str, Dex +10; HP +21; Crush R. +8	49	98	M8	93
Cailiondar Vambraces	-25%; HP +24; Str +14; Thrust R. +6	49	98	M8	90

Hands

Item	Bonus	P	A	M	Q
Ghoul Knight Gauntlets	-10%; Dex +7	17	34	M4	89
Lion Embossed Gauntlets	-10%; Dex, Qui +3; Slash R. +8	20	40	M5	89
Vindicator's Gauntlets	-10%; Qui +10	21	42	M5	89
Ancient Gauntlets	-15%; Dex +9; Parry, Slash S. +1	26	52	M6	89
Goblin-Forged Plate Gauntlets	-15%; Qui +7; Spirit R. +4	26	52	M6	89
Blessed Vindicators	-15%; Parry S. +3; Cold, Body R. +4; Str +9	31	62	M7	100
Gauntlets of Battle	-15%; Con +7; Str +10; Slash, Thrust R. +4	31	62	M7	100
Legions Scaled G.	-15%; Parry S. +3; Thrust, Crush, Slash R. +2	31	62	M7	89
Worn Mortification Gauntlets	-1%; HP +12	36	72	M8	80
Gauntlets of Mortification	-20%; Str +4; Qui +6; Cold R. +8	37	74	M8	89
Stonewatch Gauntlets	-20%; Dex +12; Pie +4; Slash R. +2	38	76	M8	89
Hollow Gauntlets	-20%; Str +12; Dex +3; HP +6; Thrust R. +4	39	78	M8	89
Ebony Corrupt Gauntlets	-20%; Qui +9; Str +6; Heat R. +6	42	84	M8	89
Adamant Coral Gauntlets	-20%; Str +6; Dex, Qui +9	44	88	M8	89
G. of Eternal Midnight	-25%; Thrust R. +4; Dex, Qui, Str +6	46	92	M8	89
Cailiondar Gauntlets	-25%; Qui +11; Dex, Str +6; Parry S. +3	49	98	M8	90
Holy Crushed G.	-25%; Dex +12; Chants S. +3; Qui +7; Cr. R. +2	49	98	M8	90
Kraggon Worm G.	-25%; Str +12; Body R. +8; Shield, Parry S. +2	49	98	M8	90
Malevolent G.	-30%; Dex +12; Slash, Thrust S. +5; Energy R. +6	49	98	M8	93
Sturdy Crushed G.	-25%; Dex +11; Str +10; Con +7; Crush R. +2	49	98	M8	90

Legs

Item	Bonus	P	A	M	Q
Ghoul Knight Leggings	-10%; Con +7	16	32	M4	89
Lion Embossed Greaves	-10%; Con +6; Cha +3; HP +6	20	40	M5	89
Hardened Leggings	-10%; Con +13; Crush R. +6	20	40	M5	100
Vindicator's Greaves	-10%; Con +10	21	42	M5	89
Ancient Greaves	-15%; Con +9; Heat R. +8	26	52	M6	89
Goblin-Forged Plate Legs	-15%; Con +7; Cold R. +4	26	52	M6	89
Legions Scaled Greaves	-15%; Con +12; Body R. +4	31	62	M7	89
Worn Leggings of Mortification	-1%; HP +12	36	72	M8	80
Leggings of Mortification	-20%; Con +10; Heat, Energy R. +4	37	74	M8	89
Hollow Greaves	-20%; Con +10; Qui +6; HP +9	39	78	M8	89
Stonewatch Leggings	-20%; Con +10; Dex +3; Slash R. +2	40	80	M8	89
Ebony Legs o.t. Corrupt	-20%; Con +10; Crush, Slash, Thrust R. +2	42	84	M8	89
Adamant Coral Leggings	-20%; HP +30; Qui +6	44	88	M8	89
Leggings of Eternal Midnight	-25%; Con +12; Dex +3; Qui +6	46	92	M8	89
Kraggon Worm Greaves	-25%; Con +15; Body R. +10	49	98	M8	90
Cailiondar Leggings	-25%; Con +15; Energy, Cold R. +10	49	98	M8	90
Crushed Leggings	-25%; Con +11; Dex +10; Str +6; Crush R. +2	49	98	M8	90
Legs of the Malevolent	-30%; Con, Qui +10; HP +21; Heat R. +8	49	98	M8	93

Feet

Item	Bonus	P	A	M	Q
Oaken Boots	-5%; Qui +9; Dex +3	14	28	M3	100
Ghoul Knight Boots	-10%; Qui +6; Spirit R. +4	18	36	M4	89
Lion Embossed Boots	-10%; Dex, Qui, Str +3; Energy R. +4	20	40	M5	89
Vindicator's Boots	-10%; Dex +10	21	42	M5	89
Ancient Boots	-15%; Qui +10; Con +4	26	52	M6	89
Goblin-Forged Plate Boots	-15%; Dex +7; Body R. +4	26	52	M6	89
Legions Scaled Boots	-15%; Con +6; Dex, Qui +4	31	62	M7	89
Worn Boots of Mortification	-1%; HP +12	36	72	M8	80
Boots of Mortification	-20%; Dex +7; Qui +3; Energy, Body R. +4	37	74	M8	89
Hollow Boots	-20%; Con +4; Dex +9; Qui +3; HP +9	39	78	M8	89
Dull Boots of Blessing	-20%; HP +6; Str, Con +3; Cold R. +4	42	84	M8	100
Dull Boots of Glory	-20%; Str +6; Cold R. +6; Body R. +3	42	84	M8	100
Dull Boots of Honor	-20%; HP +4; Cold R. +2; Dex, Dex +3	42	84	M8	100
Ebony Boots of the Corrupt	-20%; Dex +9; Qui +6; Energy R. +6	42	84	M8	89
Stonewatch Boots	-20%; Qui +4; Dex +10; Slash R. +2	42	84	M8	89
Adamant Coral Boots	-20%; Dex +10; Con +4; Cold, Spirit R. +4	44	88	M8	89
Boots of Eternal Midnight	-25%; Con, Dex +7; Qui +6	46	92	M8	89
Cailiondar Boots	-25%; HP +24; Dex +12; Body, Cold R. +6	49	98	M8	90
Crushed Boots	-25%; Qui +11; Dex +10; Str +4; Crush R. +2	49	98	M8	90
Kraggon Worm Boots	-25%; Dex, Qui +12; Body R. +8	49	98	M8	89
Malevolent Boots	-30%; Dex +12; Qui +10; HP +18; Cold R. +6	49	98	M8	93

Shield Drops & Rewards

For Standard (Craftable) Shields, see page 361.

For more information on what the various stats mean, see **Armor** (p. 362), **Weapons** (p. 361) and **Material** (p. 360).

Abbreviations

The first negative percentage in any bonus indicates your opponent's reduced chance of hitting you when you are wearing the item.

Headings. Power Level / **A**rmor Factor / **M#** = Material (M) and Material Level (#) / **Q**uality / **Sp**eed, or weapon delay (the time between bashes) / **D**amage with each hit / **DpS** = Damage per second.

The first positive percentage in any bonus indicates your increased chance to block with the shield and (if it can be used as a weapon), your increased chance to hit with it.

Stats. Resistance, **S**kill / **Cha**risma, **Con**stitution, **Dex**terity, **Pie**ty, **Qui**ckness, **Str**ength / **C**loth, **L**eather, **M**etal, **W**ood.

Small

Shield	Bonus	P	A	M#	Q	Sp	D	DpS
Bark Sh.	HP +5	3	6	W1	90	3	6	2.1
Old Banded Sh.		8	16	M2	80	2.8	10	3.6
Sh. of Uln	+5%; Sh. S. +1; Str +3	12	24	M3	89	5	24	4.8
Spirit Crafted Sh.	+5%; Str +7	15	30	M3	89	2.9	16	5.5
Branded Keltoi Sh.	+10%; Con, Str, Qui +3	21	42	M5	89	2.8	21	7.5
Goblin Protector	+15%; Pie, Str, Dex, Qui +3	28	56	M6	89	4.3	41	9.6
Sh. of Swirl. Notes	+15%; Sl. R. +8; Cha, Dex, Qui +6	31	62	M7	100	4.3	45	10.5
Decaying Legions Sh.	+15%; HP +30	32	64	M7	89	3	32	10.8
Worn Asterite Round Sh.	Sh. S. +2	37	74	M8	80	3	37	12.3
Prot. o.t. Harvest	+20%; Sh. S. +4; Dex +4; Thr. R. +4	41	82	M8	89	2.8	39	13.8
Blood Bd. Sh.	+20%; HP +33; Heat, Spir. R. +6; Str +7	43	86	M8	100	3	42	14.1
Fine Asterite Rd. Sh.	+20%; Sh. S. +2; Dex +7; Con +6	43	86	M8	89	3	42	14.1
Prot. o.t. St. Elders	+20%; Sh. S. +4; Str +6; Thr. R. +4	43	86	M8	88	4.5	65	14.4
Jet Bone Sh.	+25%; Cr., Ener. R. +4; Str +7; HP +15	47	94	M8	89	3	46	15.3
Smok. Sable Prot.	+25%; Str, Pie, Qui +7; Spir. R. +8	47	94	M8	89	4.6	70	15.3
Doomsayer	+30%; Sh. S. +4; Heat, Sl. R. +6; Con +13	50	100	M8	91	2.7	44	16.2
Ellyll Round Sh.	+20%; Cold, Heat R. +6; Qui, Dex +7	50	100	M8	89	3	49	16.2
Prot. o.t. St. Lords	+25%; Sh. S. +6; Dex +10; Thr. R. +6	50	100	M8	90	4.3	70	16.2
Prot. o.t. St. Oracles	+25%; Smit., Rejuv., Enhan. S. +4	50	100	M8	90	4	65	16.2

Medium

Shield	Bonus	P	A	M#	Q	Sp	D	DpS
Ancient Body Sh.	+5%; Sh. S. +2; Sl., Body, Cr. R. +2	13	26	M3	90	3	15	5.1
Footman's Kite Sh.		13	26	M3	80	4.3	22	5.1
Hard Leather Sh.		13	26	L3	80	2.8	14	5.1
Sh. of the Abandoned	+5%; HP +9; Qui +3	14	28	M3	89	4.5	24	5.4
Faithbound Sh.	+10%; Power +2; Str, Con +3	16	32	M4	100	4.3	26	6.0
Sh. of Spirit Might	+10%; Str +9	20	40	M4	89	4.3	31	7.2
Animal Skin Sh.	+10%; Sh. S. +2; Dex +4; Body R. +2	23	46	M5	89	4.3	36	8.4
Goblin Defender	+10%; Sh. S. +2; Con +4	23	46	M5	89	2.8	23	8.1
Symb. of Faith	+15%; Cr. R. +6; HP +15; Pie +7; Con +4	30	60	M7	100	4.3	45	10.5
Despoiled War Sh.	+15%; Con, Str +6; Pie +3	32	64	M7	89	4	43	10.8
Sh. of Scorn	+20%; Str +9; Dex +6; Con +4	36	71	M8	89	4.3	58	13.5
Worn Asterite Kite Sh.	Sh. S. +2	37	74	M8	80	4.3	53	12.3
Clergyman's Sh.	+20%; Smiting S. +2; Pie, Str +6	38	76	M8	89	4	50	12.6
Fine Asterite Kite Sh.	+20%; Sh. S. +2; Pie +7; Str +6	43	86	M8	89	4.3	61	14.1
Sh. of Grovewd. Bk.	+20%; Sh. S. +2; Con, Pie, Str +4	43	86	W8	89	4.3	61	14.1
Anc. Witherwd. Bark	+25%; Con, Pie +13; Cold R. +12	50	100	M8	90	4	65	16.2
Sh. of Malevolence	+30%; Sh. S. +8; Crush R. +8; Cold R. +6; Con +9	50	100	M8	91	4.3	70	16.2

Large

Shield	Bonus	P	A	M#	Q	Sp	D	DpS
Iron-Strapped Sh.		6	12	M2	89	3.8	11	3.0
Roman Sh.		13	26	M3	80	4	20	5.1
Scraek's Crusher	+5%; Sh. S. +2	13	26	M3	89	3.8	19	5.1
Well-Used Sh.		16	32	M4	71	4.2	25	6.0
Heraldic Keltoi Sh.	+10%; Sh. S. +1; Dex, Str +3	21	42	M5	89	3.8	29	7.5
Sing. Fellwd. Sh.	+10%; Sh. S. +2; Str, Con +3; Ht. R. +2	21	42	M5	90	4.3	32	7.5
Lion Faced Sh.	+15%; Sh. S. +2; Str, Con +4	26	52	M6	90	4.3	39	9.0
Sheet of Aged Beech Bark	+15%; Con +4; Str +3; Body, Cold R. +4	30	60	M7	89	3.8	39	10.2
Goblin Tower Sh.	+15%; Sh. S. +2; Str, Con +4	32	64	M7	89	4.5	49	10.8
Large Despoiled War Sh.	+15%; Sh. S. +2; Str +9	33	66	M7	89	4	44	11.1
Worn Asterite Tower Sh.	Sh. S. +2	37	74	M8	80	4.5	55	12.3
Flttnd. Eye Sh.	+20%; Sh. S. +3; Con +4; Cr., Mat. R. +4	42	84	M8	89	3.5	48	13.8
Fine Asterite Tower Sh.	+20%; Sh. S. +2; Str +7; Crush, Heat R. +4	43	86	M8	89	4.5	63	14.1
Fall. Grdsmn's Sh.	+20%; Sh. S. +2; Str +9; Cr., En. R. +4	45	90	M8	89	3.8	56	14.7
Crims. Blade-Stop.	+25%; Thr., Sl. R. +4; Con, Qui +7	47	94	M8	89	4.9	75	15.3
Frenz. Sh.	+25%; Sh. S. +4; Body R. +6; HP +27; Con +6	50	100	M8	90	3.8	62	16.2

Musical Instruments

Like most other items in the game, musical instruments vary in quality. All current instruments begin at Level 1 (which means that higher-grade instruments are available at Levels 6, 11, 16, 21 and so forth). The higher the level of your instrument, the more effective your magical Songs. Recipes are on page 362.

Abbreviations

Headings. Power Level / **M#** = Material (M) and Material Level (#) / Quality.

Stats. Skill, Resistance / **Cha**risma, **Con**stitution, **Dex**terity.

Drums (weight 2.0)

Instrument	Bonus	PL	M#	Ql
Drum (standard)		1,6,11, etc.	W	100
Deluged Drum	Instruments S. +5	26	W6	89
Goblin Excavator's Drum	Instruments S. +1; Cha +4	26	W6	89
Despoiled Drum	HP +30	31	W7	89
Drum of Fading Valor	HP +24; Cold, Energy, Spirit R. +4	36	M8	89
Ellyll Drum	Instruments S. +3; HP +21	36	W8	89
Fine Asterite Drum	HP +39	36	M8	89
Granite Drum	Instruments S. +2; Cha +3; Spirit R. +2	36	W8	88
Worn Asterite Drum	Instruments S. +2	36	M8	80

Flutes (weight 1.0)

Instrument	Bonus	PL	M#	Ql
Flute (standard)		1,6,11, etc.	W	100
Flute of Displacement	Instruments S. +2; Evade S. +2	16	W4	100
Goblin Excavator's Flute	Instruments S. +1; Cha +4	21	W5	89
Deluged Flute	Instruments S. +2; HP +18	26	W6	89
Despoiled Flute	HP +30	31	W7	89
Ellyll Flute	Instruments S. +3; Cha +12	36	W8	89
Fine Asterite Flute	Instruments S. +3; Cha +10	36	M8	89
Flute of Dementia	Instruments S. +5; Spirit R. +10	36	M8	89
Polished Granite Flute	Instruments S. +2; Cha +4; Spirit R. +4	36	W8	89
Worn Asterite Flute	Instruments S. +2	36	M8	80

Lutes (weight 1.5)

Instrument	Bonus	PL	M#	Ql
Lute (standard)		1,6,11, etc.	W	100
Lute of the Initiate		6	W2	100
Melodic Lute	Instruments S. +2; Cha +1	11	W3	90
Deluged Lute	Instruments S. +2; HP +15	26	W6	89
Despoiled Lute	HP +30	31	W7	89
Goblin Excavator's Lute	Instruments S. +1; Cha +4; Con +3	31	W7	89
Ellyll Lute	Instruments S. +3; Dex +12	36	W8	89
Fine Asterite Lute	Instruments S. +3; HP +21	36	M8	89
Lute of Haunting Melody	HP +42	36	M8	89
Polished Granite Lute	Instruments S. +2; Cha +4; Spirit R. +4	36	W8	88
Worn Asterite Lute	Instruments S. +2	36	M8	80

Jewelry Drops & Rewards

Abbreviations

Headings. Power Level / Quality.

Stats. **R**esistance, **S**kill / **Cha**risma, **Con**stitution, **Emp**athy, **Dex**terity, **Int**elligence, **Pie**ty, **Qui**ckness, **Str**ength.

Item	Bonus	PL	Ql
Amulet			
Bonecharm Amulet	Str +1; HP +2	4	90
Porcine Amulet	Body Magic S. +1	5	71
Wisp Heart Amulet	Wind Magic S. +1; Power +1; Int +1	13	90
Amulet of the Planes	Int +3; Power +2	15	100
Armband			
Wristband of the Eye	Spirit R. -4; Cold, Body R. +2; HP +12	36	89
Belts			
Aged Leather Baldric	Str +1	4	90
Scaled Belt	Con +1	4	90
Belt of Animation	HP +6	5	100
Bone Studded Belt	Str +3	8	89
Girdle of Stalwart Spirit	Pie +1; HP +6	8	100
Garnet Belt	Power +2; Int +1	11	100
Belt of Battle	Str +6; Slash R. +2	12	100
Belt of Acuity	Dex +7	13	90
Thick Hide Belt	Str +3; Body R. +1	13	89
Gilded Golden Belt	Int, Dex +3	14	89
Belt		20	100
Hob Hunter Belt	Dex +6; Int +4	23	89
Keltoi Belt of Agility	Dex +6; Qui +4	24	89
Wanderer's Belt	Str +6; Pie +4	24	89
Cythrian Baldric	Str +6; HP +15	26	90
Sturdy Keeper	HP +15; Int +4	28	89
Tactician's Belt	Int +9; Body R. +6	29	89
Belt of Arcane Protection	Energy, Heat, Spirit R. +4; Int +6	31	90
Goblinskin Belt	Dex, Con +4; Str +6	32	89
Restless Centurion Belt	Str +10; Cold R. +2; Body R. +4	32	89
Studded Farmer's Belt	HP +24; Body, Slash R. +2	32	89
Belt of Deathly Might	HP +21; Str +9	42	89
Girdle of Cat-Like Movement	Dex +7; Qui +6; Evade S. +2	43	89
Oaken Girdle	HP +21; Str +9	43	89
Belt of Granite Enhancement	Str +12; Crush, Slash, Thrust R. +4	47	89
Runic Belt of Arcane Might	Cold, Heat R. +4; Power +3; Int +6	47	89
Belt of Etheric Mist	Stealth S. +3; Dex, Qui +6	48	89
Belt of the Protector	Pie +9; HP +33; Power +4	50	90
Netherite Dusted Belt	Power +4; Dex +6; Slash R. +6	50	89
Runic Troll-Hide Belt	Body, Thrust R. +6; HP +27	50	89

Bracelets

Item	Bonus	PL	QI
Netherworld Bracelet	Spirit Magic S. +1; Int +3	10	90
Minor Elemental Insight	Power +1; Int +4	12	100
Bracelet of Matter Manipulation	Matter Magic S. +1; Power +2	16	100
Bracelet of the Arctic	Cold Magic S. +3; Cold R. +6; Int +9	50	89
Bracelet of Bonded Matter	Matter Mg. S. +3; Matter R. +6; Int +9	50	89
Shaped Bone Bracelet	Body Magic S. +3; Body R. +6; Int +9	50	89
Woven Reed Bracelet	Earth Magic S. +3; Matter R. +6; Int +9	50	89

Bracers (Br)

Item	Bonus	PL	QI
Gornax Brs.	Str +3	7	89
Bone Studded Br.	Qui, Dex +1	8	89
Quicksilver Br.	Parry S. +1; Qui +3	9	100
Br. of Deftness	Dex +4; Qui +3	12	100
Br. of the Stoic Defender	Con +4; HP +6	12	100
Might	Str +7	12	100
Ancient Battle Br.	Slash S. +1; Dex +4	13	90
Tacticians Ornamental Honor	Int, Dex +1; HP +6	13	80
Thick Hide Br.	Con +4; Slash R. +3	13	89
Golden Br.	HP +12	14	89
Fury	Dual Wield S. +2; HP +6	16	100
Br. of Arms	Slash, Crush, Thrust S. +1	21	89
Br. of Magic	Fire, Wind, Spirit, Mind Magic S. +2	21	89
Crypt Robbers Br.	Stealth S. +1; Dex +3; Str +4	21	90
Roman Tactician Br.	Int, Dex +3; HP +6	21	89
Bowmasters Br.	Longbow S. +2; Dex +3; Qui +4	26	90
Goblin-Forged Br. of Speed	Qui +6; Str +3; HP +6	28	89
Decaying Legion Battle Br.	Dual Wield, Parry S. +1; Str +7	29	89
Br. of the Pious Defender	Pie +10; Body R. +6	32	89
Goblinskin Br.	Int, Pie +4; Dex, Con +3	32	89
Br. of Martial Skill	Parry S. +1; Qui +6; HP +12	34	89
Symbiotic Leech Br.	HP -21; Power +6; Int +9	38	89
Br. of Shaved Bone	Cold R. +6; Pie, Int +3; Dex +7	41	89
Veiled Br. of Eyes	Cold R. +16; Body R. +8; HP +15	43	100
Angled Bone Br.	Body, Matter, Earth, Cold Magic S. +4	45	100
Br. of Dauntless Courage	Spirit, Matter R. +4; Con +9; Str +6	46	89
Cailiondar Br. of Battle	Cha +9; Con, Dex, Str +7	50	90
Cailiondar Br. of Piety	HP +36; Pie +13	50	90
Stonewatch Br.	Pie, Str +12; Dex +7	50	90

Cape

Item	Bonus	PL	QI
Rancid Fur Cape	Cold R. +3	7	70

Chain

Item	Bonus	PL	QI
Silver Chain	Power +1; HP +3	8	100

Charms

Item	Bonus	PL	QI
Snake Charm	Con +3	6	100
Snake's Head Charm	Body R. +2	7	70
Dragon Ant Charm	Con +4	8	100
Blessed Planter's Necklace	Enhanc., Rejuv., Smit. S. +1; Power +6	45	89

Choker

Item	Bonus	PL	QI
Grass Choker	Int +3	8	89

Clasp

Item	Bonus	PL	QI
Falconheaded Cloak Pin	Con, Dex, Qui +1	8	100

Cloak (Cl)

Item	Bonus	PL	QI
Wolf Pelt Cloak	Qui +1; Cha -1	3	100
Cloak of the Old Defender	Dex +3	7	90
Gyrg's Cloak	Qui +4	8	100
Molded Cloak	Pie +3	8	89
Apprentice Cloak	Qui +1; Power +2	12	100
Cloak of Shades	Stealth S. +2; HP +3	13	100
Velvet Lined Cloak	Power +1; Str +3	13	89
Regal Mithrian Cloak	Cha, Con +3	14	89
Slythcur Cloak	Evade S. +1; Body R. +2	14	100
Bounder Fur Mantle	Evade S. +1; Dex +6	16	90
Hide Cloak	Pie, Dex +3	20	89
Shadowhands Cloak	Evade, Stealth S. +1; Dex +4	21	90
Hob Hunter Cloak	Dex +6; Pie +4	23	89
Light Hunter's Cloak	HP +9; Cha, Dex +3	23	89
Keltoi Mantle of Insight	HP +9; Int, Pie +3	24	89
Resplendent Mantle	Con +4; Dex, Str +3	24	89
Fire Threaded Cloak	Fire Magic S. +1; Power +2; Dex +6	26	100
Furlined Cloak	Cold R. +8; Cha +6	26	89
Spirit Threaded Cloak	Spirit Magic S. +1; Power +2; Dex +6	26	100
Thought Threaded Cloak	Mind Magic S. +1; Power +2; Dex +6	26	100
Wind Threaded Cloak	Wind Magic S. +1; Power +2; Dex +6	26	100
Black Lion-Skin Cloak	Dex +9; Cha +4	30	89
Antiquated Cloak	Pie +6; Str +4; Body R. +4	31	89
Mantle of the Bowmaster	Longbow S. +2; Qui +6; Dex +7	31	100
Shadowbinder's Mantle	Stealth S. +2; Dex +13	31	100
Windbound Cloak	Evade, Stealth S. +1; Dex +10	31	90
Goblin Mine Cloak	Str, Con +4; Cha +6	32	89
Mantle of Resplendence	Con +9; Cha +4; Body R. +4	35	89
Morbid Mantle	Str +4; Dex, Qui +6	35	89
Cloak of the Blackheart	HP +15; Pie, Int +4	38	89
Clergyman's Pious Mantle	HP +18; Rejuvenation S. +1; Pie +6	38	89
Gwyllgi's Hide	HP +15; Cold R. +8; Dex, Pie +4	38	100
Magma Imbued Cloak	Str, Dex +6; Con, Qui +3	38	89
Ghost Wolf Hide Cloak	Body R. +12; Con, Str +4	40	89
Basher's Sash	Crush R. +6; Power +2; Dex, Cha +4	42	89
Conquerer's Cloak	Str, Con, Dex +4	42	89
Bernor's Well-Used Cloak	Int, Dex +7; Power +6	47	100
Cape of Corruscating Harmony	Str, Dex, Cha +7; Energy R. +8	47	100
Cape of the Iron Will	Qui, Str +9; Pie +6	47	100
Cape of Vigilant Defense	Dex, Qui +12; Spirit R. +6	47	100
Cloak of Defiant Soul	Pie +10; Power +4; Spirit R. +6	47	100
Cloak of Mental Acuity	Int, Dex +7; Power +6	47	100
Cloak of the Shadowy Embers	Qui, Str +7; HP +18; Cold R. +4	47	100
Cloak of the Stalwart Arm	Con, Dex +12; Spirit R. +6	47	100
Ignuixs' Portable Shadow	Con, Qui +12; Cold R. +6	47	100
Prayer-Bound Vestments	Con +12; Power +6; Crush R. +4	47	100
Shielding Dweomer	Int +7; Power +6; Dex +7	47	100
Warm Construct Cloak	Int, Dex +7; Power +6	47	100
Immolated Hound Skin Cloak	HP +18; Heat R. +6; Str +9	48	89
Avenging Knight's Cloak	Body R. +12; Con +7; Str +6	49	89
Majestic Mantle of the Eternal	Spirit, Cold R. +8; Pie +10	49	89
Afanc Hide Cloak	Stealth S. +3; Con, Dex +12; Cha +9	50	93
Afanc Scale Cloak	Con, Str +13; Slash, Thrust R. +8	50	93
Afanc Tooth-Edged Cloak	Polearm , Two Handed, Shield S. +4; Str +3	50	93
Embroidered Afanc Eye Cloak	Stealth, Longbow, Shield S. +4; Dex +3	50	93
Enchanted Afanc Cloak	Con +12; Power +4; Dex +7; Int +10	50	93
Holy Afanc Cloak	Rejuvenation, Enhancements S. +2; Pie, Con +12	50	93
Kraggon Cloak	Body R. +16; Dex +10	50	90
Mantle of the Champion	Str +7; Pie +6; HP +12; Body R. +4	50	89
Sage's Rune Stitched Cloak	Dex +9; Int +7; Power +3	50	90
Shadowy Afanc Cloak	Dual Wield, Crit. Strike, Stealth S. +4; Dex +3	50	93
Shining Aura Cloak	Chants S. +2; Str, Con +13; Power +3	50	93

Collar

Item	Bonus	PL	QI
Ebony Collar of the Dead	(Slash R. +4; Str, Int, Pie +4) *or* (none)	27	100

Eyes

Item	Bonus	PL	QI
Hidden Eye	Power +1; Int +3	8	100
Jeweled Left Eye	Int +6; Matter Magic S. +1; Spirit R. +4	28	89
Jeweled Right Eye	Str, Con +4; Cold R. +4	28	89
Tunneler Eye	Cold, Heat R. +4; Con +6; Str +4	37	89
Beater's Poked Eye	Power +4; HP +9	42	89
Cyclop's Pupil	Rejuven. S. +2; Chants, Cold Magic S. +1; Con +6	42	89

Item	Bonus	PL	QI
Gems			
Gem of Shadowy Intentions	Stealth, Critical Strike S. +1; HP +6	16	100
Goblin Gem of Resistance	Cold, Heat R. +4; Str +6	28	89
Hob Hunter Gem	Power +2; Con +6	32	89
Jewels & Jewelry			
Pulsing Ruby	Power +1; HP +6	12	89
Jewel of the Prowler	Stealth S. +2; Dex +4	24	89
Jewel of the Resilient	HP +21	24	89
Prismatic Jewel	Dex, Int, Str +4	26	90
Ancient Roman Signet	HP +12; Body R. +4; Str +4	31	89
Forgotten Jewel	Dex +10; Body R. +6	35	89
Jewel of Dark Beauty	Stealth, Critical Strike S. +3	39	89
Cyclops Eye	Heat, Cold R. +6; Cha +10	42	89
Pulsing Gem	Instruments S. +2; Cha +6; Body R. +8	42	89
J. of Insight into Undeath	Body, Matter, Spirit, Mind Magic S. +2	43	89
J. of Elemental Biding	Earth, Cold, Wind, Fire Magic S. +2	45	89
Jewel of Enticement	Mind Magic S. +2; Power +3; HP +15	50	89
Locket			
Muck Crusted Ruby Locket	Instruments S. +2; Con +3; Cha +4	30	89
Medallion			
Macabre Medallion	HP +12; Stealth S. +2; Qui, Dex +6	41	100
Medallion of Albion	Str +4; Dex +3	43	89
Necklaces (N)			
Fingerbone Necklace	HP +4	3	89
Faerie Charm Necklace	Cha +3; Int +1; Str -1	7	90
Beartooth Charm	Str +4	8	100
Bone Necklace	Int +3	8	89
Fiery Crystal Pendant	Fire Magic S. +1; Int +1	8	100
Amulet of Feline Graces	Dex +4; Qui +3	12	100
Golden Mithrian Necklace	Pie, Str +3	14	89
N. of Elemental Influence	Cold, Earth, Wind Magic S. +1	16	100
Vine Necklace	Power +2; Pie +4	17	100
Troll Bone Necklace	Str +4; HP +6	18	89
Band of Fellwood Leaves	Dex +7; Qui +4	20	100
Earthen Necklace of Fellwood	Int +9; Matter R. +4	20	100
Fellwood Charm of Purity	Int +9; Body R. +4	20	100
Grail Shaped Charm of Fellwood	Pie +9; Matter R. +2	20	100
Twisted Fellwood Necklace	Str +7; Con +4	20	100
Necklace of Brilliance	Int +9	21	89
Necklace of Fortitude	Thrust R. +4; HP +9; Str +4	21	100
Necklace of the Pious	Pie +9	21	89
Goblin-Forged Chain of Strength	Str +7; HP +6	23	89
Guardian's Necklace	Con, Str +4; Longbow S. +1	25	89
Snowdonian Bandit Warmer	Cold, Spirit R. +4; Con +6	26	89
Hob Hunter Necklace	Power +2; Dex +3	28	89
Islwyn's Bead Necklace	Instruments, Stealth S. +2; Thrust R. +2	29	89
Decaying Roman Necklace	Con +6; Str +4; Body R. +4	30	89
Werewolf Tooth Necklace	Pie, Int +6; HP +9	31	90
Resplendent Necklace	Int +10; Body R. +6	33	89
Bwcan Beads	Power +2; Pie, Int +4	35	89
Human Tooth Necklace	Qui, Str, Dex +6	40	89
Necklace of the Dark Soul	Power +3; Int +9	40	89
Necklace of Glowing Ebony	HP +18; Dex, Pie +6	45	89
Bwcan Colored Beads	Power +2; Int, Pie +7	46	89
Pendants			
Blessed Pendant	Chants S. +1; Str +1	8	100
Pendant of Twisting	Body Magic S. +1; Int +4	12	100
Pins			
Harping Pin	Cha +3	5	89
Fey Jewelry	Con, Pie +1	7	90
Stonewatch Pin	Pie +1; Smiting, Rejuv., Enhancements S. +2	43	89
Opposition Pin	Dex +6; Qui +4; Stealth S. +4	50	90
Polished Granite Pin	Int +12; Power +3; Body R. +4	50	90

Item	Bonus	PL	QI
Rings (R)			
Faithbound Ring	Pie +1	4	90
Signet Ring	Cha, Dex +1	6	90
Slith's Tail	Dex +3	7	100
Bone Ring	Str, Con +1	8	89
Ring of Flight	Dex +4	8	100
Ring of Rejuvenation	Rejuvenation S. +1; Pie +1	8	100
Brimstone Ring	Str +4	10	89
Elven Ring	Dex +1; Pie +3	10	90
Ring of Longevity	HP +12	10	90
Band of Ice	Cold Magic S. +1; Power +2	12	100
Bookworm's Ring	Matter Magic S. +1; Int +4	12	100
Ring of Clarity	Enhancements S. +1; Dex +4	12	100
Ring of Prestige	Cha +3; Dex +4	12	100
Ring of Inspiration	Cha +6	13	89
Ruby Encrusted Ring	Int +6	13	89
Golden Mithrian Ring	Int +3; HP +6	14	89
Ring of Arawn	Str, Con +3	14	89
Band of Earth	Earth Magic S. +1; Int +6	16	100
Boneshaper's Ring	Body Magic S. +1; Power +2	16	100
Ring of the Empire	HP +15	16	89
Ring of Alteration	Body Magic, Matter Magic S. +1; Power +1	20	89
R. of Elemental Fury	Fire Magic, Wind Magic S. +1; Power +1	20	89
Insurgent's Ring	Cha, Int, Pie +3	21	89
Keltoi Forester's Ring	Dex +6; Str +3	21	89
Majestical Ring	Power +2; Pie +3	21	90
Ring of Insane Might	Str +10	21	90
Goblin-Forged Ring of Health	HP +15; Con +3	23	89
R. of the Leader	Cha +3; Instruments S. +1; Power +1; Cold R. +2	24	89
Hob Hunter Ring	Pie, Con, Dex, Int +3	28	89
Manaweave Ring	Power +3; Int +3	28	89
Decaying Roman Ring	Rejuvenation, Enhancements S. +1; HP +15	30	89
Band of Pious Might	Pie, Str +7	31	90
Knotted Dryroot Band	Int, Pie +4; Power +3	32	89
Resplendent Ring	Con +10; Body R. +6	33	89
Ring of Etiquette	Cha +9; Dex, Str +3	36	89
Ghastly Ring of Bone	Int, Pie, Dex, Str +4	39	89
Ring of the Stonewatch	Pie, Con, Dex +6	39	89
Band of Eldspar	HP +15; Power +4; Dex +3	42	89
Chitin Ring	Cha, Qui, Pie +6; Slash R. +2	43	89
Fire Asterite Ring	Dex, Str, Pie +6; Heat R. +2	43	89
Ring of Secret Intentions	HP +24; Str, Pie, Int +4	43	100
R. of Forgotten Arcane Words	Earth, Cold, Fire, Wind Magic S. +2	44	89
Bernor's Tarnished R.	Fire, Earth, Cold Magic S. +2; Int +9	45	100
Construct Ring	Body, Matter, Spirit Magic S. +2; Int +9	45	100
Ring of Coruscating Harmony	Qui +9; Str +7; Dex +6; Cold R. +6	45	100
Ring of Defiant Soul	Con +12; Dex +10; Crush R. +6	45	100
Ring of the Iron Will	Con +12; Dex, Pie +6; Body R. +4	45	100
R. of Mental Acuity	Mind, Body, Matter Magic S. +2; Int +9	45	100
Ring of Prayers	Dex, Pie +12; Spirit R. +4	45	100
Ring of Shades	Str, Dex +7; Stealth S. +3; Body R. +4	45	100
Ring of Shadowy Embers	Qui +12; Dex +10; Thrust R. +6	45	100
R. of Shielding Power	Wind, Earth, Cold Magic S. +2; Int +9	45	100
Ring of the Stalwart Arm	Str, Dex, Con +7; Slash R. +6	45	100
Ring of Vigilant Defense	Con +12; Dex +6; Qui +4; Thrust R. +6	45	100
Symbol of Loyalty	HP +15; Con, Dex, Str +4	45	89
R. of Granite Enhancement	Slash, Crush, Thrust S. +2; HP +9	49	89
Band of Ilmenite	Int +13; Power +4; Body R. +8	50	91
Band of Ircon	Int +13; Power +4; Body R. +8	50	91
Etheric Ring	Con, Pie, Dex +6; Body R. +6	50	89
Ring of Sturdy Warding	HP +15; Power +4; Crush R. +2	50	89
Torc			
Tarnished Silver Torc	Power +1	4	89

Crafting Recipes

For a more detailed description of these stats, see **Crafting**, page 364.

For **Arrow** crafting, see page 363.

For **Siege Equipment** crafting, see page 324.

For instruments and miscellaneous craftable items, see page 362.

Abbreviations

Time. Time to craft the item at 1st and 10th Material Levels.

Skills. A = Armorcraft / **C** = Clothworking / **F** = Fletching / **L** = Leatherworking / **M** = Metalworking / **T** = Tailoring / **Wd** = Woodworking / **Wp** = Weaponcraft.

Tools. F = Forge / **H** = Smith's Hammer / **K** = Sewing Kit / **L** = Lathe / **P** = Planing Tool.

Components. b = Metal Bars / **c** = Cloth squares / **l** = Leather / **t** = Thread / **w** = Wooden boards.

Costs. Costs are listed in Silver and Copper for Material Level 1. They're listed in Gold and Silver for Material Levels 5 and 10, rounded to the nearest Silver.

Crafting Armor & Clothing

Cloth (+ Secondary: C (all), L (gloves, cap, boots); all at (-15))

Item	Time (sec.)	Skills	Tools	Components	1st (S.C)	5th (G.S)	10th (G.S)
Cloth (Quilted)							
Vest	7-75	T95	K	40c,10t	1.22	7.06	71.44
Pants	5-72	T65+	K	25c,5t	0.73	4.25	43.01
Arms	6-74	T80+	K	16c,4t	0.49	2.82	28.58
Gloves	1-69	T15+	K	4c,3t,2l	0.24	1.40	14.14
Cap	2-70	T30+	K	16c,5t,6l	0.73	4.25	43.01
Boots	3-71	T45+	K	2c,2t,4l	0.24	1.41	14.29
Robes							
Plain	1-69	T15+	K	40c,22t	1.49	8.61	87.19
Dress	1-69	T15+	K	40c,22t	1.49	8.61	87.19
Fancy	1-69	T15+	K	40c,22t	1.49	8.61	87.19

Leather (+ Secondary: L, C at (-15))

Item	Time (sec.)	Skills	Tools	Components	1st (S.C)	5th (G.S)	10th (G.S)
Roman Jerkin	7-75	T95+	K	20l,3t	0.81	4.71	47.68
Leggings	5-72	T65+	K	12l,2t	0.49	2.85	28.87
Sleeves	6-74	T80+	K	8l,1t	0.32	1.86	18.81
Gloves	1-69	T15+	K	3l,2t	0.15	0.91	9.19
Boots	3-71	T45+	K	3l,2t	0.15	0.91	9.19
Helm	2-70	T30+	K	12l,2t	0.49	2.85	28.87
Cymric Jerkin	9-76	T115+	K	29l,3t	1.15	6.65	67.36
Leggings	6-74	T85+	K	17l,2t	0.68	3.93	39.80
Sleeves	8-75	T100+	K	11l,2t	0.45	2.64	26.68
Gloves	3-71	T35+	K	5l,2t	0.23	1.34	13.56
Boots	5-72	T65+	K	5l,2t	0.23	1.34	13.56
Helm	4-71	T50+	K	17l,2t	0.68	3.93	39.80
Siluric Jerkin	13-81	T175+	K	56l,8t	2.28	13.13	132.97
Leggings	11-78	T145+	K	34l,4t	1.36	7.86	79.61
Sleeves	12-80	T160+	K	22l,4t	0.91	5.27	53.36
Gloves	7-75	T95+	K	10l,4t	0.46	2.68	27.12
Boots	9-77	T125+	K	10l,4t	0.46	2.68	27.12
Helm	8-76	T110+	K	34l,4t	1.36	7.86	79.61

Studded (+ Secondary: L, C, M (-15)) (based on Armorcraft or Tailoring; st. = studs)

Item	Time (sec.)	Skills	Tools	Components	1st (S.C)	5th (G.S)	10th (G.S)
Studded							
Vest	7-75	A/T95+	K,H,F	19l,4t,5st	9.55	55.02	557.10
Legs	5-72	A/T65+	K,H,F	12l,2t,3st	5.74	33.09	335.05
Arms	6-74	A/T80+	K,H,F	8l,1t,2st	3.82	22.02	222.93
Gauntlets	1-69	A/T15+	K,H,F	2l,4t,1st	1.91	11.03	111.68
Boots	3-71	A/T45+	K,H,F	2l,4t,1st	1.91	11.03	111.68
Helm	2-70	A/T30+	K,H,F	12l,2t,3st	5.74	33.09	335.05
Boned Vest	9-77	A/T115+	K,H,F	25l,5t,8st	15.05	86.69	877.72
Legs	6-74	A/T85+	K,H,F	12l,7t,5st	9.35	53.90	545.73
Arms	1-69	A/T100+	K,H,F	8l,2t,4st	7.34	42.31	428.36
Gauntlets	3-70	A/T35+	K,H,F	4l,5t,1st	2.01	11.59	117.37
Boots	5-72	A/T65+	K,H,F	4l,5t,1st	2.01	11.59	117.37
Helm	4-71	A/T50+	K,H,F	12l,7t,5st	9.35	53.90	545.73
Lamellar Vest	12-79	A/T155+	K,H,F	50l,10t,16st	30.10	173.38	1755.43
Legs	9-77	A/T125+	K,H,F	24l,14t,10st	18.71	107.80	1091.46
Arms	11-78	A/T140+	K,H,F	16l,4t,8st	14.69	84.61	856.72
Gloves	6-73	A/T75+	K,H,F	8l,10t,2st	4.02	23.18	234.74
Boots	8-75	A/T105+	K,H,F	8l,10t,2st	4.02	23.18	234.74
Helm	7-74	A/T90+	K,H,F	24l,14t,10st	18.71	107.80	1091.46

Chain (+ Secondary: M, L (-15)) (wr = wire; rm., cy. = matching piece of roman, cymric leather)

Item	Time (sec.)	Skills	Tools	Components	1st (S.C)	5th (G.S)	10th (G.S)
Chain Hauberk	7-75	A95+	H,F	15wr,rm.	27.06	155.91	1578.58
Legs	5-72	A65+	H,F	9wr,rm.	16.24	93.57	947.41
Sleeves	6-74	A80+	H,F	6wr,rm.	10.82	62.34	631.17
Mittens	1-69	A15+	H,F	3wr,rm.	5.40	31.15	315.37
Coif	2-70	A30+	H,F	9wr,rm.	16.24	93.57	947.41
Boots	3-71	A45+	H,F	3wr,rm.	5.40	31.15	315.37
Mail Hauberk	10-78	A135+	H,F	29wr,cy.	51.90	298.97	3027.10
Leggings	8-75	A105+	H,F	18wr,cy.	32.18	185.37	1876.88
Sleeves	9-77	A120+	H,F	12wr,cy.	21.45	123.60	1251.40
Mittens	4-72	A55+	H,F	6wr,cy.	10.73	61.82	625.92
Coif	5-73	A70+	H,F	18wr,cy.	32.18	185.37	1876.88
Boots	6-74	A85+	H,F	6wr,cy.	10.73	61.82	625.92

Plate (+ Secondary: M, L, C at (-15)) (st = straps, cl. = matching piece of cloth armor)

Item	Time (sec.)	Skills	Tools	Components	1st (S.C)	5th (G.S)	10th (G.S)
Plate Breastplate	7-75	A95+	H,F	11b,5st,cl.	10.93	63.00	637.88
Legs	5-72	A65+	H,F	8b,1st,cl.	3.18	18.36	185.90
Arms	6-74	A80+	H,F	5b,1st,cl.	2.67	15.42	156.15
Gauntlets	1-69	A15+	H,F	2b,1st,cl.	2.16	12.48	126.41
Helm	2-70	A30+	H,F	8b,1st,cl.	3.18	18.36	185.90
Boots	3-71	A45+	H,F	2b,1st,cl.	2.17	12.50	126.55

Item	Time (sec.)	Skills	Tools	Components	1st (S.C)	5th (G.S)	10th (G.S)
Scaled Plate							
Breastplate	10-78	A135+	H,F	37b,5st,cl.	13.21	76.10	770.55
Legs	8-75	A105+	H,F	22b,3st,cl.	7.91	45.58	461.46
Arms	9-77	A120+	H,F	15b,2st,cl.	5.30	30.54	309.24
Gauntlets	4-72	A55+	H,F	6b,3st,cl.	6.01	34.66	350.94
Full Helm	5-73	A70+	H,F	22b,3st,cl.	7.91	45.58	461.46
Boots	6-74	A85+	H,F	6b,3st,cl.	6.02	34.68	351.09
Fluted Plate (+5)							
Breastplate	43-81	A575+	H,F	50b,6st,cl.	–	92.74	938.95
Legs	41-80	A545+	H,F	29b,4st,cl.	–	59.18	599.24
Arms	42-80	A560+	H,F	20b,3st,cl.	–	43.14	436.82
Gauntlets	37-75	A495+	H,F	9b,3st,cl.	–	36.17	366.25
Full Helm	38-76	A510+	H,F	30b,3st,cl.	–	49.61	502.28
Boots	39-77	A525+	H,F	8b,5st,cl.	–	55.84	565.41

Crafting Weapons

Secondary Skills

+ Unless otherwise noted, completing a finished weapon also requires the skills necessary to craft its two component parts, minus 15. For example, when crafting a dagger at Material Level 2, your primary skill requirement is Weaponcraft 115, but you also must have Leatherworking and Metalworking at 100 (since crafting the blade and hilt require those skills at 115).

* Item will never be part of a consignment order.

Item	Time (sec.)	Skills	Tools	Components	1st (S.C)	5th (G.S)	10th (G.S)
Crushing							
Hammer	1-55	Wp15+	F,H	haft,head	0.98	5.69	57.59
Haft	1-14	Wd15	F,H,P	1b,2w,1l	0.20	1.15	11.66
Head	1-14	M15	F,H	9b	0.78	4.54	45.93
Mace	2-56	Wp35+	F,H	haft,head	1.51	8.71	88.21
Haft	1-14	Wd35	F,H,P	1b,3w	0.20	1.15	11.66
Head	1-14	M35	F,H	15b	1.31	7.56	76.55
Flanged Mace	3-57	Wp55+	F,H	haft,head	1.81	10.44	105.71
Haft	1-14	Wd55	F,H,P	2b,3w,1l	0.32	1.87	18.95
Head	1-14	M55	F,H	17b	1.48	8.57	86.75
Spiked Mace	5-59	Wp75+	F,H	haft,head	2.16	12.46	126.12
Haft	1-15	Wd75	F,H,P	2b,4w	0.32	1.87	18.95
Head	1-15	M75	F,H	21b	1.83	10.58	107.16
War Hammer	6-60	Wp95+	F,H	haft,head	2.81	16.20	164.03
Haft	1-15	Wd95	F,H,P	2b,5w	0.36	2.09	21.14
Head	1-15	M95	F,H	28b	2.45	14.11	142.88
War Mace (5+)*	31-61	Wp515+	F,H	haft,head	–	19.44	196.83
Haft	8-15	Wd515	F,H,P	2b,6w	–	2.30	23.33
Head	8-15	M515	F,H	34b	–	17.14	173.50
Polearm							
Pike	1-55	Wp15+	F,H	shaft,head	1.31	7.56	76.55
Head	1-14	M15	F,H	8b	0.70	4.03	40.82
Shaft	1-14	Wd15	F,H,P	1b,14w	0.61	3.53	35.72
Lochaber Axe	2-57	Wp35+	F,H	shaft,head	1.67	9.65	97.69
Head	1-14	M35	F,H	12b	1.05	6.05	61.24
Shaft	1-14	Wd35	F,H,P	2b,12w	0.62	3.60	36.45

Item	Time (sec.)	Skills	Tools	Components	1st (S.C)	5th (G.S)	10th (G.S)
Bill	3-57	Wp55+	F,H	shaft,head	1.97	11.38	115.18
Head	1-14	M55	F,H	15b	1.31	7.56	76.55
Shaft	1-14	Wd55	F,H,P	2b,13w	0.66	3.82	38.64
Lucerne Hammer	5-59	Wp75+	F,H	shaft,head	2.98	17.21	174.23
Head	1-15	M75	F,H	27b	2.36	13.61	137.78
Shaft	1-15	Wd75	F,H,P	2b,12w	0.62	3.60	36.45
Halberd	6-60	Wp95+	F,H	shaft,head	3.33	19.22	194.64
Head	1-15	M95	F,H	31b	2.71	15.62	158.19
Shaft	1-15	Wd95	F,H,P	2b,12w	0.62	3.60	36.45
Bardiche (5+)*	31-61	Wp515+	F,H	shaft,head	–	22.97	232.55
Head	8-15	M515	F,H	41b	–	20.66	209.22
Shaft	8-15	Wd515	F,H,P	2b,6w	–	2.30	23.33
Partisan (5+)*	31-61	Wp515+	F,H	shaft,head	–	22.97	232.55
Head	8-15	M515	F,H	41b	–	20.66	209.22
Shaft	8-15	Wd515	F,H,P	2b,6w	–	2.30	23.33
Poleaxe (5+)*	31-61	Wp515+	F,H	shaft,head	–	22.97	232.55
Head	8-15	M515	F,H	41b	–	20.66	209.22
Shaft	8-15	Wd515	F,H,P	2b,6w	–	2.30	23.33
Spiked Ham. (5+)*	31-61	Wp515+	F,H	shaft,head	–	22.97	232.55
Head	8-15	M515	F,H	41b	–	20.66	209.22
Shaft	8-15	Wd515	F,H,P	2b,6w	–	2.30	23.33
Slashing							
Dagger	1-55	Wp15+	F,H	hilt,blade	0.81	4.68	47.39
Blade	1-14	M15	F,H	7b	0.61	3.53	35.72
Hilt	1-14	L15	F,H	1b,1w,2l	0.20	1.15	11.66
Short Sword	1-55	Wp15+	F,H	hilt,blade	0.98	5.69	57.59
Blade	1-14	M15	F,H	9b	0.78	4.54	45.93
Hilt	1-14	L15	F,H	1b,1w,2l	0.20	1.15	11.66
Broadsword	2-56	Wp35+	F,H	hilt,blade	1.82	10.51	106.43
Blade	1-14	M35	F,H	18b	1.57	9.07	91.85
Hilt	1-14	L35	F,H	2b,1w,1l	0.25	1.44	14.58
Hand Axe	2-56	Wp35+	F,H	haft,head	1.30	7.49	75.82
Haft	1-14	Wd35	F,H,P	1b,2w	0.16	0.94	9.48
Head	1-14	M35	F,H	13b	1.13	6.55	66.34
Scimitar	3-57	Wp55+	F,H	hilt,blade	2.00	11.52	116.64
Blade	1-14	M55	F,H	20b	1.75	10.08	102.06
Hilt	1-14	L55	F,H	2b,1w,1l	0.25	1.44	14.58
Longsword	5-59	Wp75+	F,H	hilt,blade	2.47	14.26	144.34
Blade	1-15	M75	F,H	25b	2.18	12.60	127.58
Hilt	1-15	L75	F,H	2b,1w,2l	0.28	1.66	16.77
Bastard Sword	6-60	Wp95+	F,H	hilt,blade	2.96	17.06	172.77
Blade	1-15	M95	F,H	31b	2.71	15.62	158.19
Hilt	1-15	L95	F,H	2b,1w,1l	0.25	1.44	14.58
Jambiya (5+)*	31-61	Wp515+	F,H	hilt,blade	–	20.59	208.49
Blade	8-15	M515	F,H	38b	–	19.15	193.91
Hilt	8-15	L515	F,H	2b,1w,1l	–	1.44	14.58
Sabre (5+)*	31-61	Wp515+	F,H	hilt,blade	–	20.59	208.49
Blade	8-15	M515	F,H	38b	–	19.15	193.91
Hilt	8-15	L515	F,H	2b,1w,1l	–	1.44	14.58
Thrusting							
Dirk	1-55	Wp15+	F,H	hilt,blade	0.81	4.68	47.39
Blade	1-14	M15	F,H	7b	0.61	3.53	35.72
Hilt	1-14	L15	F,H	1b,1w,2l	0.20	1.15	11.66
Stiletto	2-56	Wp35+	F,H	hilt,blade	1.16	6.70	67.80
Blade	1-14	M35	F,H	10b	0.87	5.04	51.03
Hilt	1-14	L35	F,H	2b,1w,2l	0.28	1.66	16.77
Main Gauche	3-57	Wp55+	F,H	hilt,blade	1.82	10.51	106.43
Blade	1-14	M55	F,H	18b	1.57	9.07	91.85
Hilt	1-14	L55	F,H	2b,1w,1l	0.25	1.44	14.58

Item	Time (sec.)	Skills	Tools	Components	1st (S.C)	5th (G.S)	10th (G.S)
Rapier	5-59	Wp75+	F,H	hilt,blade	2.17	12.53	126.85
Blade	1-15	M75	F,H	22b	1.92	11.09	112.27
Hilt	1-15	L75	F,H	2b,1w,1l	0.25	1.44	14.58
Gladius	6-60	Wp95+	F,H	hilt,blade	2.78	16.06	162.57
Blade	1-15	M95	F,H	29b	2.53	14.62	147.99
Hilt	1-15	L95	F,H	2b,1w,1l	0.25	1.44	14.58
Grded. Rapier (5+)*	31-61	Wp515+	F,H	hilt,blade	–	19.58	198.29
Blade	8-15	M515	F,H	36b	–	18.14	183.71
Hilt	8-15	L515	F,H	2b,1w,1l	–	1.44	14.58
Staff (+ Secondary: M, Wd, L; all at 0)							
Staff	2-56	F35+	L,H,P	4b,25w,1l	1.32	7.63	77.27
Shod Staff	5-59	F75+	L,H,P	4b,38w,1l	1.81	10.44	105.71
Quarterstaff	2-56	F40+	L,H,P	4b,25w,1l	1.32	7.63	77.27
Shod Quarterstaff	5-59	F80+	L,H,P	14b,24w,1l	2.16	12.46	126.12
Two Handed							
War Mattock	1-55	Wp15+	F,H	haft,head	1.47	8.50	86.02
Haft	1-14	Wd15	F,H,P	1b,9w	0.42	2.45	24.79
Head	1-14	M15	F,H	12b	1.05	6.05	61.24
Two Handed Sword	2-56	Wp35+	F,H	hilt,blade	1.82	10.51	106.43
Blade	1-14	M35	F,H	18b	1.57	9.07	91.85
Hilt	1-14	L35	F,H	2b,1w,1l	0.25	1.44	14.58
War Axe	2-56	Wp35+	F,H	haft,head	2.17	12.53	126.85
Haft	1-14	Wd35	F,H,P	2b,9w	0.51	2.95	29.89
Head	1-14	M35	F,H	19b	1.66	9.58	96.96
Great Hammer	3-57	Wp55+	F,H	haft,head	2.31	13.32	134.87
Haft	1-14	Wd55	F,H,P	2b,8w	0.47	2.74	27.70
Head	1-14	M55	F,H	21b	1.83	10.58	107.16
Battle Axe	5-59	Wp75+	F,H	haft,head	2.83	16.34	165.48
Haft	1-15	Wd75	F,H,P	2b,8w	0.47	2.74	27.70
Head	1-15	M75	F,H	27b	2.36	13.61	137.78
Great Sword	5-59	Wp75+	F,H	hilt,blade	3.17	18.29	185.17
Blade	1-15	M75	F,H	33b	2.88	16.63	168.40
Hilt	1-15	L75	F,H	2b,1w,2l	0.28	1.66	16.77
Great Axe	6-60	Wp95+	F,H	haft,head	3.45	19.87	201.20
Haft	1-15	Wd95	F,H,P	2b,8w	0.47	2.74	27.70
Head	1-15	M95	F,H	34b	2.97	17.14	173.50
Archmace (5+)*	31-61	Wp515+	F,H	haft,head	–	23.98	242.76
Haft	8-15	Wd515	F,H,P	2b,6w	–	2.30	23.33
Head	8-15	M515	F,H	43b	–	21.67	219.43
Grt. Scimitar (5+)*	31-61	Wp515+	F,H	hilt,blade	–	24.05	243.49
Blade	8-15	M515	F,H	44b	–	22.18	224.53
Hilt	8-15	L515	F,H	2b,2w,2l	–	1.87	18.95
War Pick (5+)*	31-61	Wp515+	F,H	haft,head	–	24.05	243.49
Haft	8-15	Wd515	F,H,P	2b,4w	–	1.87	18.95
Head	8-15	M515	F,H	44b	–	22.18	224.53
Bows (+ Secondary: Wd, C; both at 20 below Primary)							
Short Bow	1-55	F15+	P,L	16w,3t	0.66	3.84	38.93
Hunting Bow	2-56	F40+	P,L	24w,4t	0.99	5.70	57.74
Bow	4-58	F65+	P,L	32w,6t	1.33	7.69	77.86
Longbow	5-59	F90+	P,L	44w,8t	1.83	10.54	106.73
Crossbow (+ Secondary: Wd, L, C; all at 20 below Primary)							
Crossbow	3-57	F25+	P,L,H	32w,5t,4b	1.66	9.58	96.96

Monsters

For more complete descriptions of what these stats describe, and a chart of which type of attack works best against each body type, see **Monster Stats**, p. 373.

Abbreviations

Speed. Slow, **M**edium, **F**ast, **2x**, **3x**, **4x** (two, three and four times faster than the average PC).

Aggr. (Aggression). **L**ow, **M**edium, **H**igh (with percent chance that it will attack).

Attack Type. **C**rush, **S**lash, **T**hrust. Information after a slash ("/") is type and percent chance of secondary attack.

Combat Modifier. Monster's modifier to hit / modifier to avoid being hit (defense) / modifier to hit points. When there is just one number, it modifies all three situations.

Social. Social monsters might group; **Call** means it is Social and might call for help.

Body Type. The body types are:

BU	Bony Undead	**EW**	Elemental Water	**Pl**	Plate
Ch	Chain	**FM**	Feeble-Minded	**Rp**	Reptile (Scaled)
Cl	Cloth	**FU**	Fleshy Undead	**Sh**	Shell (Chitin)
DV	Darkness/Void	**FA**	Furry Animal	**Soft**	Soft
EA	Elemental Air	**IU**	Incorporeal Undead	**St**	Studded Leather
EE	Elemental Earth	**Lr**	Leather	**TP**	Tree/Plant
EF	Elemental Fire	**LE**	Light Energy	**Tr**	Troll-like
EI	Elemental Ice	**ME**	Magical Energy		

Animal

Monster	Lvl	Body Type	Spd	Agg	Atk Spd	Atk Type	Ev %	Comb Mod	Soc. Call
Bear	8	FA	M/195	–	4.2	C	–	–	–
Bear Cub	2	FA	M/192	–	4.8	C	–	–	–
Black Bear	16-21	FA	M/200	L/10	3.4	C	–	–	–
Black Dog	9-10	FA	M/205	M/50	4.1	T	–	–	Soc.
Black Lion	30	FA	M/205	L/20	2.6	S/S3	1	–	Soc.
Black Lioness	30	FA	M/205	L/20	2.6	S/S3	1	–	Soc.
Black Wolf	3	FA	M/197	–	4.7	S	–	–	Soc.
Black Wolf Pup	1	FA	S/150	–	4.9	S	–	–	Soc.
Boar Piglet	1	FA	S/150	–	4.9	S	–	–	–
Brown Bear	15	FA	M/200	L/3	3.8	C	–	–	–
Cart Horse	10	FA	F/270	–	4.0	C	–	–	–
Cave Bear	24	FA	M/192	L/10	3.8	S/S5	–	–	Soc.
Cave Bear Cub	16-18	FA	M/192	L/10	3.8	S	–	–	Soc.
Cave Hound	38	FA	M/200	H/80	3.7	T	–	–	Soc.
Cave Lion	24-26	FA	M/192	L/10	3.8	S/S5	–	–	Soc.
Cornish Frog	13	Soft	S/150	–	4.6	C	–	–	–
Corpse-Eating Sow	36	FA	M/200	L/20	3.7	S	–	-20/-20/-	–
Cwn Annwn	20-22	FA	M/200	L/10	3.5	S	–	–	–
Dappled Lynx	2-3	FA	M/195	–	3.8	S	–	–	–
Dappled Lynx Cub	0	FA	S/160	–	4.0	S	–	–	–
Dartmoor Pony	34-36	FA	M/188	–	3.8	C	–	-/-/20	Soc.
Death Stalker	16-27	FA	M/210	M/30	3.4	S	–	–	–
Diamondback Toad	51-55	Rp	F/250	–	4.0	C	–	-/-/20	–
Diseased Rat	38	FA	M/200	H/80	3.5	T	2	-5/-5/-	–
Eel	2	Soft	S/150	–	4.8	S	–	–	–
Faerie Frog	28-30	Soft	F/235	–	4.0	C	–	-20	–
Forest Bear	7-9	FA	M/192	L/10	4.1	C	–	–	–
Forest Bear Cub	3	FA	M/180	–	4.3	C	–	–	–
Forest Cat	16	FA	M/195	L/20	3.6	S/S1	1	–	–
Forest Lion	6	FA	M/195	L/20	3.7	S	–	–	–
Giant Boar	34-35	FA	M/200	L/20	3.5	S	–	–	–
Giant Frog	3-4	Soft	S/150	–	4.3	C	–	–	–
Giant Rooter	30-34	FA	M/210	L/20	3.0	T/S5	–	–	–
Giant Water Leaper	15	Soft	M/188	M/50	3.7	S	–	–	–
Giant Wolf	15-17	FA	F/220	H/75	3.5	S	–	–	–
Gray Warg	9-11	FA	M/192	M/50	3.7	S	–	–	Soc.
Gray Wolf	4	FA	M/190	–	3.6	S	–	–	–
Gray Wolf Pup	1	FA	S/150	–	3.9	S	–	–	–
Great Boar	42-46	FA	M/200	–	3.8	S	–	–	–
Huge Boar	18-19	FA	F/220	H/80	3.2	S	–	–	Soc.
Keltoi Familiar	23-25	FA	M/200	–	3.5	S/S1	1	–	Soc.
Large Rock Bounder	45-46	FA	F/230	H/90	3.5	S/S5	3	–	Soc.
Lone Wolf	20	FA	F/300	H/90	3.0	S	–	–	–
Marrow Leech	38	Soft	M/170	H/80	3.5	T	–	–	–
Marsh Worm	9-11	Soft	M/175	M/40	3.7	S	–	–	–
Moor Den Mother	17	FA	M/205	M/50	3.7	S	–	–	Soc.
Moor Pack Leader	15	FA	M/205	M/33	3.6	S	–	–	Soc.
Moor Wolf	14	FA	M/205	L/13	3.6	S	–	–	Soc.
Mud Worm	0	Soft	S/150	–	3.8	C	–	–	–
Red Lion	3	FA	M/198	–	4.7	S	–	–	–
Rot Worm	5	Soft	S/165	–	3.8	S	–	–	–
Scrawny Red Lion	3	FA	M/205	–	4.1	S	–	–	–
Scum Toad	0	Soft	S/160	–	3.8	C	–	–	–
Shadowhunter	39-41	FA	F/220	H/70	3.5	T/T1	4	–	Call
Shadowh. She-Wolf	42-43	FA	F/220	H/70	3.5	T/T1	4	–	Call
Small Bear	4	FA	M/188	–	4.6	C	–	–	–
Small Gray Wolf	3	FA	M/188	–	3.8	S	–	–	–
Small Rock Bounder	22-23	FA	M/210	L/1	3.6	S/S2	3	–	Soc.
Spiny Eel	3	Rp	S/155	–	4.7	T	–	–	–
Swamp Rat	4	FA	M/200	H/99	1.0	T	–	–	Call
Water Leaper	8-10	Soft	M/185	L/2	3.7	C	2	–	–
Wild Boar	10	FA	F/220	M/30	4.0	S	–	–	–
Wild Mare	9	FA	F/270	–	4.1	C	–	–	Soc.
Wild Sow	2	FA	S/150	–	4.8	S	–	–	–
Wild Stallion	10	FA	F/270	–	4.0	C	–	–	Soc.
Woodeworm	55	Rp	M/175	L/20	3.8	C	–	-10	Soc.
Yell Hound	15-16	FA	F/220	H/75	3.5	T	3	–	Call
Young Boar	6	FA	S/150	H/90	4.4	S	–	–	–
Young Brown Bear	13	FA	M/195	L/20	4.0	C	–	–	–

Demon

Monster	Lvl	Body Type	Spd	Agg	Atk Spd	Atk Type	Ev %	Comb Mod	Soc. Call
Boulder Imp	7	EE	M/188	L/20	4.1	C	–	–	–
Fiery Fiend	41-43	EF	M/170	H/80	3.8	S	–	-10/-10/-	–
Gabriel Hound	40-48	EA	F/230	H/80	2.7	S	–	–	–
Grumoz Demon	10-11	EF	M/192	H/90	3.7	S	–	-20/-/-	Soc.
Impling	0	Soft	M/170	–	3.8	C	–	–	–
Manes Demon	8-7	EF	M/180	H/80	4.2	C	–	-20/-/-	Soc.
Rock Imp	3-5	EE	M/188	–	4.0	C	–	–	–
Scaled Fiend	42	Rp	F/240	H/80	3.2	T/S8	5	–	Soc.
Wind Mephit	14	EA	F/270	M/60	3.6	S	2	-5	Call

Dragon

Monster	Lvl	Body Type	Spd	Agg	Atk Spd	Atk Type	Ev %	Comb Mod	Soc. Call
Brown Drakeling	34	Rp	F/240	–	3.8	S	–	-10	Call
Carrion Drake	8-9	Rp	M/180	–	4.2	T	–	-10	Call
Cornwall Drake	40-44	Rp	M/192	L/20	2.4	S	–	–	Soc.
Draconic Ancilla	50	Rp	2x/350	M/50	2.0	S	8	20/-/-	–
Great Brown Drake	55-59	Rp	2x/500	H/70	3.9	C	–	-10	Soc.
River Drake Hatchling	3	Rp	S/150	–	4.7	T	–	–	Soc.
River Drakeling	5	Rp	S/160	L/5	4.5	T	–	–	Soc.
Young Brown Drake	47	Rp	F/260	M/50	3.8	S	–	-10	Call

Elemental

Monster	Lvl	Body Type	Spd	Agg	Atk Spd	Atk Type	Ev %	Comb Mod	Soc. Call
Boulderling	9	EE	M/192	H/100	4.1	C	–	–	–
Dryad	7-9	Soft	M/188	M/50	3.7	C	–	–	Soc.
Dryad Invert	9	Soft	S/150	M/50	4.1	C	–	–	Soc.
Dryad Twig	1	Soft	M/170	–	3.8	S	–	–	Soc.
Faerie Bell-Wether	5	CI	M/185	–	4.5	S	–	–	Call
Faerie Mischief-Maker	3	CI	M/180	–	4.7	S	–	–	Call
Faerie Wolf-Crier	4	CI	M/185	–	4.6	S	–	–	Call
Large Boulderling	11-12	EE	M/192	H/100	3.9	C	–	–	Call
Mist Monster	16	EW	M/195	H/80	3.6	C	–	–	–
Mist Sprite	6	EW	M/170	M/30	3.5	C	–	–	Call
Mud Golem	14	EE	S/160	M/50	3.6	C	–	–	–
Pixie	6-7	Soft	M/170	M/30	4.3	C	–	–	Soc.
Pixie Imp	0	Soft	S/150	–	4.1	T	–	–	Soc.
Pixie Scout	8	Soft	M/180	M/50	3.7	T	–	–	Soc.
Quicksand	16	EE	F/230	M/50	3.4	C/C2	–	–	–
River Sprite	6	EW	M/170	L/5	4.4	C	–	–	Call
River Spriteling	3-4	EW	S/150	–	4.6	C	–	–	Call
Rock Elemental	11-12	EE	M/192	H/100	3.9	C	–	–	Call
Spriggarn	2	FA	M/175	–	4.8	C	–	–	Soc.
Spriggarn Ambusher	15	FA	F/220	H/99	3.5	S	1	–	Soc.
Spriggarn Elder	3	FA	M/185	L/1	4.7	C	–	–	Call
Spriggarn Howler	16	FA	F/220	H/99	3.4	S	1	–	Soc.
Spriggarn Waylayer	14	FA	F/220	H/99	3.6	S	1	–	Soc.
Stone Sentinel	48-50	EE	S/150	H/80	4.1	C	–	20/20/-	Soc.

Giant

Monster	Lvl	Body Type	Spd	Agg	Atk Spd	Atk Type	Ev %	Comb Mod	Soc. Call
Cornish Giant	40	Lr	F/250	H/99	5.0	C	–	–	–
Cyclops	41-42	FM	M/175	H/90	3.9	C/C1	–	–	Soc.
Cyclops Scout	32	FM	M/175	H/90	3.9	C/C1	–	–	–
Ettin Shaman	11-14	CI	M/192	M/50	3.9	C	–	-20/-20/-	Call
Forest Ettin	12-16	CI	M/192	H/80	3.8	C	–	–	Call
Forest Giant	18-21	FM/CI	F/230	H/99	4.0	C	–	–	–

Monster	Lvl	Body Type	Spd	Agg	Atk Spd	Atk Type	Ev %	Comb Mod	Soc. Call
Granite Giant (GG)	36-40	EE	F/250	H/80	4.0	C	–	5/-10/10	Call
GG Earthmagi	65	EE	3x/600	H/99	3.8	C	–	30/-/10	Soc.
GG Elder	62-64	EE	F/250	H/80	5.4	C/C5	–	5/-15/10	Call
GG Gatherer	42-46	EE	F/250	H/80	4.4	C	–	5/-10/10	Call
GG Herdsman	39-43	EE	F/250	H/80	4.2	C	–	5/-10/10	Call
GG Oracle	62-64	EE	F/250	H/80	5.2	C	–	5/-25/-	Call
GG Outlooker	51-55	EE	F/250	H/80	4.8	C	–	5/-15/10	Soc.
GG Pounder	54-58	EE	F/250	H/80	5.0	C/C4	–	5/-15/10	Soc.
GG Reinforcer	65	EE	3x/600	H/99	3.8	C	–	10/20/10	Soc.
GG Stonecaller	45-49	EE	F/250	H/80	4.4	C	–	5/-25/-	Call
GG Stonelord	57-61	EE	F/250	H/80	5.2	C	8	5/-15/10	Soc.
GG Stonemender	65	EE	3x/600	H/99	3.8	C	–	20/-/20	Soc.
GG Stoneshaper	48-52	EE	F/250	H/80	4.6	C	–	5/-15/10	Soc.
Marsh Scrag	11	Tr	M/180	H/80	3.6	C	–	–	Call
Pogson	42	FM	M/175	H/90	3.9	C/C1	25	–	–
Pygmy Goblin Bombard.	42	FM	M/200	H/90	4.2	C/C1	–	20/-/10	Soc.
Ravenclan Giant	50-51	St	M/175	H/70	4.1	C/C6	–	–	Call
Salisbury Giant	18-21	FM	F/220	H/99	3.2	C	–	–	Call
Scrag	8	Tr	M/170	H/70	3.7	C	–	–	Call
Scragling	6	Tr	S/160	M/60	3.8	C	–	–	Call
Stonecr. Demolisher	51-55	FM/Cl	F/220	H/80	3.4	C/C5	–	–	Soc.
Stonecrush Excavator	45-49	FM/Cl	F/220	H/80	3.8	C	–	–	Soc.
Stonecr. Rockgrinder	48-52	FM/Cl	F/220	H/80	3.6	C/C1	–	–	Soc.
Wood Ogre Berserker	14-15	FM/Cl	M/192	H/100	3.5	C	–	–	Call
Wood Ogre Lord	16	FM/Cl	M/192	H/70	3.4	C	–	–	Call
Wood Ogre Mystic	11	FM/Cl	M/192	H/80	3.9	C	–	-20	Call
Wood Ogre Scourge	12-13	FM/Cl	M/192	H/80	3.6	C	–	–	Call
Wood Ogre Seer	14	FM/Cl	M/192	M/50	3.8	C	–	-20	Call

Human-like

Monster	Lvl	Body Type	Spd	Agg	Atk Spd	Atk Type	Ev %	Comb Mod	Soc. Call
Albion Waylayer	35	Lr	M/192	M/30	3.0	S	–	–	Soc.
Angry Bwca	45-47	FA	M/175	H/70	3.5	C	–	–	–
Apprent. Beastmaster	31	St	M/192	L/10	3.6	C	–	20/-/20	Soc.
Arawnite Headhunter	36-38	Lr	M/175	H/90	3.6	T	–	–	Call
Arawnite Shamaness	34-35	Lr	M/175	H/90	4.0	C	–	-20	Call
Arawnite Warrior	34-35	Lr	M/175	H/90	3.7	S/S4	–	–	Soc.
Bandit	5-6	Lr	M/188	H/100	3.8	S	–	–	Call
Bandit Henchman	9	St	M/188	H/100	3.4	S	–	-5	Call
Bandit Leader	11	St	M/188	H/100	3.7	C	–	–	Call
Bandit Lieutenant	9	St	M/188	H/100	3.8	S	–	–	Call
Bandit Messenger	9	Lr	M/200	–	4.1	S	–	–	Call
Bandit Thaumaturge	8	Cl	M/185	H/100	4.2	C	–	-20	Call
Boggart	45-49	Lr	M/170	–	3.8	S	–	–	Call
Bogman	3-4	Cl	S/160	M/45	4.1	S	–	–	Call
Bogman Fisher	9	Cl	S/150	M/40	3.8	T	–	–	Call
Bogman Gatherer	8	Cl	S/160	M/45	3.8	S	–	–	Call
Bogman Grappler	5	Cl	S/150	M/55	4.5	C	–	–	Call
Bogman Hunter	11	Cl	S/150	M/55	3.7	C	–	–	Call
Bogman Trapper	10	Cl	S/165	M/50	3.7	T	–	–	Call
Brownie	0	FA	M/170	–	5.0	C	–	–	Soc.
Brownie Grassrunner	7	FA	M/195	L/5	4.3	T	–	–	Call
Brownie Nomad	8-9	FA	M/188	L/15	4.2	T	–	–	Call
Brownie Rover	12	FA	M/188	H/70	3.8	T	–	–	Call
Bucca	23-24	FA	M/175	–	3.8	C	–	–	–
Bullyboy	5-6	Cl	M/188	M/50	3.8	S	–	–	Soc.
Bwca	24	FA	M/175	–	3.8	C	–	–	–
Bwgan	22-23	Cl	M/188	L/20	3.8	S	–	–	Soc.
Bwgan Elder	24	Cl	M/188	L/20	3.8	S	–	–	Soc.
Bwgan Fisherman	27-29	Cl	M/192	–	3.8	S	–	–	Soc.
Bwgan Horde	23	Cl	M/188	L/20	3.8	S	–	–	Soc.
Bwgan Horde Leader	24	Cl	M/188	L/20	3.8	S	–	–	Soc.
Bwgan Hunter	22-23	Cl	M/192	L/20	3.7	T	–	–	Soc.

Monster	Lvl	Body Type	Spd	Agg	Atk Spd	Atk Type	Ev %	Comb Mod	Soc. Call
Cornwall Hunter	23-25	Lr	M/192	L/25	2.7	S	–	–	Soc.
Cornwall Leader	25	Lr	M/192	L/25	2.7	S	–	–	Soc.
Cutpurse	4	Lr	M/188	L/5	4.6	T	–	–	Call
Deep Goblin	42	Lr	M/188	H/80	3.6	T/T1	4	–	Call
Deep Goblin Blighter	43	Lr	M/188	H/80	3.6	T/T1	4	–	Call
Devout Filidh	8-9	Cl	M/188	H/90	4.2	C	–	-20/-20/-	Call
Druid	18-19	Cl	M/192	H/90	4.3	C	–	–	Call
Druid	7-8	Cl	M/200	H/90	4.3	T	–	–	Call
Druid Sacrificer	20-21	Cl	M/192	H/90	4.1	C	–	-5	Call
Druid Sacrificer	9	Cl	M/200	H/90	4.1	S	–	-5	Call
Druid Seer	8	Cl	M/192	H/90	4.2	C	–	-/-30/-	Call
Druid Seer	15	Cl	M/192	H/90	4.1	C	–	-/-30/-	Call
Druid Seer	19-21	Cl	M/192	H/90	4.2	C	–	-20/-20/-10	Call
Dwarf Brawler	3-4	Lr	M/170	L/2	3.6	S	–	–	Call
Dwarf Pillager	4-5	Lr	M/170	L/20	3.6	S	–	–	Call
Dwarf Raider	5-6	Lr	M/170	L/20	3.6	S	–	–	Call
Ellyll Champion	53-57	Pl	M/215	H/90	3.8	S/S4	–	–	Call
Ellyll Froglord	51-54	Pl	F/235	H/90	3.3	S/S4	2	–	Call
Ellyll Guard	49-51	Ch	M/215	H/90	3.4	S/S2	2	–	Call
Ellyll Sage	53	Cl	M/200	H/90	4.0	C	–	-20	Call
Ellyll Seer	59	Cl	M/200	H/90	4.0	C	–	-20	Soc.
Ellyll Villager	45	Cl	M/180	M/40	3.9	C	–	–	Call
Ellyll Windchaser	47-50	Lr	F/220	H/90	3.9	C	5	-20	Call
Escaped Bandit	18	Lr	M/192	H/100	4.5	S	–	–	Soc.
Escaped Bandit Leader	19	Ch	M/200	H/100	3.9	C	–	–	Call
Filidh	7-8	Cl	M/188	H/90	4.3	C	–	–	Call
Filidh Sacrificer	9-10	Cl	M/188	H/90	4.1	C	–	–	Call
Fitful Bwca	38-36	FA	M/175	M/50	3.6	C	–	–	–
Forest Chief	19	Lr	M/192	M/50	3.5	S/S3	2	-/-/10	–
Forest Hunter	21-24	St	M/192	–	2.9	S	3	–	Soc.
Forest Messenger	15	Cl	M/192	–	3.5	S	–	–	Soc.
Forest Runner	20	St	M/192	–	3.5	T	–	–	Soc.
Forest Smuggler	17	Lr	M/192	M/50	3.5	S/S2	2	-10/15/-10	–
Forest Stalker	27	St	M/192	–	2.9	T	4	–	Soc.
Forest Tracker	15	Lr	M/192	M/50	3.5	S	–	–	–
Forester	31	St	M/192	–	3.0	S	4	–	Soc.
Forester Merchant	24	St	M/192	–	2.9	S	3	–	Soc.
Freybug	35-38	Lr	M/170	–	3.8	S	1	–	–
Goblin	25-29	Lr	M/192	L/10	3.8	S	–	–	Soc.
Goblin	8-10	Cl	M/188	L/20	3.8	S	–	–	Call
Goblin Apprentice	24-27	St	M/192	H/90	3.7	S	–	–	Soc.
Goblin Beastmaster	31	St	M/192	L/10	3.8	S	–	–	Soc.
Goblin Cleaner	30	Lr	M/192	L/10	3.8	C	–	20/-/20	Soc.
Goblin Crawler	23-24	Lr	M/192	L/10	3.5	S/S5	–	–	Soc.
Goblin Fisherman	4-6	Cl	M/188	L/20	4.2	S	–	–	Call
Goblin Imperator	31	St	M/192	H/90	3.7	S	–	–	Soc.
Goblin Lookout	8	Lr	M/188	L/20	3.8	S	–	–	Call
Goblin Lord	11	Lr	M/188	L/20	4.2	S	–	–	Call
Goblin Monitor	33	St	M/192	H/90	3.7	S	–	–	Soc.
Goblin Patrol Leader	27	St	M/192	H/90	3.7	S/T5	–	40	Soc.
Goblin Scout	7	Lr	M/188	L/20	3.8	T	–	–	Call
Goblin Shaman	9-10	Lr	M/188	L/20	4.4	C	–	-20	Call
Goblin Snatcher	31	St	F/220	H/90	3.7	S	–	–	Soc.
Goblin Warrior	8	Lr	M/188	M/50	3.8	S	–	–	Soc.
Goblin Watcher	20-22	Lr	M/192	L/10	3.8	S	–	–	Soc.
Goblin Whip	30-32	St	M/192	H/90	3.8	S	–	–	Soc.
Granite Knocker	47	Lr	M/188	H/80	2.8	T	–	–	–
Grave Goblin	40	Lr	M/188	H/80	3.6	T/T1	1	–	Call
Grave Goblin Crueler	43	Lr	M/188	H/80	3.6	T/T1	1	–	Call
Grave Goblin Shaman	38	Lr	M/188	H/80	3.6	T/T1	–	-20	Call
Grave Goblin Whelp	28-32	Lr	M/188	L/1	3.6	T/T1	1	–	Call

Monster	Lvl	Body Type	Spd	Agg	Atk Spd	Atk Type	Ev %	Comb Mod	Soc. Call
Greater Boogey	35-41	Tr	M/180	L/20	2.4	T/T5	–	–	Soc.
Greenhorn Poacher	25-31	St	M/188	H/80	3.3	T/T1	1	–	–
Gremlin	20-21	Cl	M/188	M/50	3.8	C	–	–	–
Grove Nymph	10-18	Cl	M/192	H/90	3.8	S	3	-20	Call
Heretical Hermit	20	Cl	M/170	H/80	3.0	C	–	-20	Call
Hibernian Waylayer	35	St	M/192	M/30	3.0	S	–	–	Soc.
Highwayman	7	Cl	M/188	H/75	3.8	S	–	–	Soc.
Hill Avenger	12	St	M/192	H/75	3.5	S/S5	–	-10/20/-10	Call
Hill Chief	14	St	M/192	H/75	3.5	S/S5	3	10/20/10	Call
Hill Guard	11	St	M/192	M/50	3.5	S/S2	2	-/10/10	Call
Hill Scrag	39-41	St	M/175	H/90	3.9	C/C3	–	–	Call
Hill Shaman	12	Cl	S/150	M/50	4.4	C	–	-20	Call
Hill Warrior	10	St	M/192	M/50	3.5	S/S1	2	-/-/20	Call
Hollow Man	39-41	Lr	M/175	H/70	3.7	C	–	-5/-/-	Call
Howling Knifeman	26-27	Cl	M/180	H/90	3.6	S/S1	1	–	Soc.
Howling Maiden	24-26	Cl	M/180	H/90	3.6	S	1	–	Soc.
Isolationist Armsman	47	Pl	M/180	L/20	3.3	S/S5	–	10	Call
Isolationist Cleric	46-48	Ch	M/180	L/20	3.7	C	–	-10	Call
Isolationist Courier	46	Ch	M/180	L/20	3.3	S/S8	2	–	Call
Isolationist Mercenary	46	Ch	M/180	L/20	3.3	S/S8	2	–	Call
Isolationist Paladin	48	Pl	M/180	L/20	3.3	S/S1	–	–	Call
Isolationist Scout	47	St	M/180	L/20	3.3	T/T1	4	–	Call
Isolationist Sorcerer	46	Cl	M/180	L/20	4.0	C	–	-20	Call
Isolationist Wizardess	47	Cl	M/180	L/20	4.0	C	–	-20	Call
Keltoi Banisher	22-23	Cl	M/188	M/50	3.6	S/T1	4	–	Soc.
Keltoi Eremite	21	Cl	M/188	–	4.2	C	–	-20/-20/-	Soc.
Keltoi Initiate	20	Cl	M/188	–	4.0	C	–	-20/-20/-	Call
Keltoi Recluse	22	Cl	M/188	–	4.3	C	–	-20/-20/-	Soc.
Keltoi Ritualist	23	Cl	M/188	L/5	3.8	C	–	-20/-20/-	Soc.
Keltoi Spiritualist	25	Cl	M/188	L/5	3.8	C	–	-20/-20/-	Soc.
Keltoi Visionary	21-22	Cl	M/188	–	3.8	C	–	-20/-20/-	Soc.
Master Hunter	33	St	M/192	–	2.7	S	6	–	Soc.
Merc. Tomb Raider	26-28	St	M/195	H/99	3.0	T	6	–	Call
Midgard Waylayer	35	Ch	M/192	M/30	3.0	S	–	–	Soc.
Mindless Minion	8-10	Cl	S/165	H/95	4.1	C	–	–	Soc.
Moor Boogey	25-30	Tr	M/180	L/20	3.0	C/C5	–	–	Soc.
Nain Dwarf	9	St	M/170	L/20	3.6	S	–	–	Call
Outcast Rogue	1	Lr	M/188	–	3.8	T	–	–	–
Peallaidh	35-41	Lr	M/192	H/80	3.5	S	3	–	Soc.
Pictish Druid	40-42	Cl	M/188	M/30	4.0	C	–	-20	Soc.
Pictish Warrior	40-44	Cl	M/188	M/30	3.7	S/S2	–	–	Soc.
Poacher	4	Lr	M/188	L/5	4.6	S	–	–	Call
Poacher Leader	5	Lr	M/188	L/20	4.5	S	–	–	Call
Priestess	40-44	Ch	S/165	–	4.0	C	–	-10	Soc.
Pygmy Goblin	43	Lr	M/192	H/99	3.0	T	4	-/-/-50	Call
Pygmy Goblin Tangler	45	Lr	M/192	H/99	2.5	T	8	-/-/-50	Call
Red Dwarf Bandit	6-8	Lr	M/180	L/20	3.7	S	1	–	Call
Red Dwarf Chief	10	St	M/180	L/10	3.6	S/S1	–	–	Call
Red Dwarf Matron	6-8	Lr	M/180	L/20	3.6	C	–	–	Call
Red Dwarf Thief	5-7	Lr	M/180	L/20	3.8	T	1	–	Call
Red Dwarf Youth (Fem.)	25	Ch	M/192	L/10	3.6	S	–	–	Soc.
Red Dwarf Youth (Male)	5	Cl	M/180	L/20	3.8	S	–	–	Call
Renegade Guard	19-20	Pl	M/192	L/25	3.1	S	–	–	Soc.
Ruthless Brigand	39-43	St	M/188	H/80	3.3	S/S3	4	–	–
Scorned Bwca	32-34	FA	M/175	L/1	3.7	C	–	–	–
Scrawny Bogman	2	Cl	S/165	–	4.2	T	–	–	Call
Slave	11	Cl	M/180	–	3.9	S	–	–	Soc.
Slave Master	13-15	St	M/188	–	3.7	S	–	–	Call
Slave Master Bodygrd.	15	Ch	M/192	H/99	3.5	S	–	–	Soc.
Slaver	12-15	St	M/192	H/90	3.8	S	–	–	Soc.
Sylvan Goblin	5	Cl	S/165	M/50	4.5	C	–	–	Soc.
Sylvan Goblin Chief	16-17	Ch	M/185	H/75	3.4	S/T4	–	–	Soc.
Sylvan Goblin Hunter	6-8	Lr	M/190	M/50	3.7	T	1	–	Soc.
Sylvan Goblin Magician	10	Cl	S/150	H/75	4.0	C	–	-20/-20/-	Soc.
Sylvan Goblin Warrior	9-12	St	M/180	M/50	3.7	S/S2	–	–	Soc.
Sylvan Goblin Whelp	3	Cl	S/150	–	4.0	C	–	–	Soc.
Templar	50-54	Pl	M/192	M/30	3.2	S/S3	–	–	Soc.
Tomb Raider	16-17	St	M/188	H/99	3.4	S	4	–	Call
Tomb Raider Comm.	18-20	Ch	M/192	H/99	3.2	S	5	–	Call
Tomb Raider Digger	10-13	Lr	M/188	H/99	4.0	S	–	–	Call
Tomb Raider Scout	13-15	St	M/188	H/99	3.7	T	3	–	Call
Tylwyth Teg Huntress	43-45	St	M/190	M/50	3.6	S	4	–	Call
Tylwyth Teg Ranger	46-47	St	M/190	M/50	3.5	S	4	–	Call
Tylwyth Teg Rover	41-42	St	M/190	M/50	3.7	S	4	–	Call
Welsh Hobgoblin	17-19	Cl	M/192	L/20	3.2	S	–	–	Soc.
Welsh Hobgoblin Chief	20	Ch	M/192	L/25	3.0	S	–	–	Soc.
Young Cutpurse	3	Lr	M/188	L/5	4.7	S	–	–	Call
Young Forest Runner	10	Cl	M/192	–	4.0	S	–	–	Soc.
Young Poacher	3	Lr	M/188	L/3	4.7	S	–	–	Call

Insect

Monster	Lvl	Body Type	Spd	Agg	Atk Spd	Atk Type	Ev %	Comb Mod	Soc. Call
Angler	28	Sh	M/192	L/10	3.8	S/T20	–	-/-20/-	Soc.
Ant Drone	2	Sh	S/150	–	3.0	T	–	–	Soc.
Bloated Spider	10-11	Sh	M/170	H/75	4.0	T	–	–	Soc.
Bone Snapper	63	Sh	F/300	H/99	3.3	S/S4	–	-/-/200	–
Carrion Crab	2	Sh	S/150	–	4.8	S	–	–	–
Cave Fisher	22-24	Sh	M/192	L/10	3.6	S/T20	–	-/-20/-	Soc.
Cliff Crawler	42-45	Sh	F/240	–	3.7	T	–	-10/-10/-	Call
Cliff Spider	18	Sh	M/198	M/60	3.1	T	–	-10	Soc.
Cliff Spiderling	14	Sh	M/180	M/40	3.2	T	–	-10	Call
Dragon Ant Drone	8	Sh	M/192	L/20	4.2	T	–	–	Call
Dragon Ant Queen	10	Sh	M/200	L/20	4.0	T	–	–	Call
Dragon Ant Soldier	7	Sh	M/192	L/20	4.3	T	–	–	Call
Dragon Ant Worker	5	Sh	M/192	L/2	4.5	T	–	–	Call
Fisher Hatchling	15-17	Sh	M/192	L/10	3.7	S	–	–	Soc.
Giant Spider	6-8	Sh	M/180	–	4.0	T	–	-/-10/-	–
Large Ant	1	Sh	S/150	–	3.9	T	–	–	Soc.
Plague Spider	0	Sh	S/165	–	5.0	T	–	–	–
Sprawling Arachnid	34-35	Sh	F/240	H/90	3.6	T	–	–	–
Stalker	18-21	Sh	M/192	L/10	3.8	S	–	–	–
Tree Spider	2	Sh	S/150	–	4.8	T	–	–	Soc.
Warrior Ant	3	Sh	M/175	–	3.5	T	–	–	Soc.
Worker Ant	0	Sh	S/150	–	5.0	T	–	–	Soc.

Magical

Monster	Lvl	Body Type	Spd	Agg	Atk Spd	Atk Type	Ev %	Comb Mod	Soc. Call
Bearded Gorger	55	Rp	F/230	H/99	3.0	T/T5	5	–	–
Cailleach Guard	60-66	Pl	M/192	H/80	3.0	S/T3	–	–	Soc.
Cailleach Priest	64-67	Pl	M/192	H/80	3.9	C	–	-20	Soc.
Cave Fairy	40-46	EE	M/188	M/30	3.8	C	–	-10	Soc.
Frenzied Feeder	57	Rp	F/230	H/99	2.0	T/T5	5	–	–
Greater Telamon	54	Pl	2x/450	H/99	4.2	S/S5	–	–	Soc.
Lesser Telamon	44	Pl	F/300	H/99	3.5	S/S5	–	–	Soc.
Medial Telamon	49	Pl	2x/375	H/99	3.8	S/S5	–	–	Soc.
Mineshaft Juggernaut	32	EE	M/192	H/90	3.7	C/C10	–	20	Soc.
Muryan	18-20	Sh	M/188	–	3.8	T	–	–	Soc.
Muryan Emmisary	25	Sh	M/188	–	3.8	T	–	–	Soc.
Muryan Trickster	20-21	Sh	M/188	–	3.8	T	–	–	Soc.
Needletooth Devourer	59	Rp	F/230	H/99	4.0	T/T5	5	–	–
Piper Fairy	52-56	EE	M/188	M/30	3.6	C	–	–	Soc.
Will O' Wisp	9-11	LE	M/180	–	3.7	S	3	-10	Soc.

Reptile

Monster	Lvl	Body Type	Spd	Agg	Atk Spd	Atk Type	Ev %	Comb Mod	Soc. Call
Adder	7	Rp	M/200	–	4.3	T	–	-5	–
Afanc Hatchling	25	Rp	M/192	L/25	2.5	S/C2	–	–	–
Aged Basilisk	19	Rp	S/150	M/50	3.1	T	–	-20	–

Monster	Lvl	Body Type	Spd	Agg	Atk Spd	Atk Type	Ev %	Comb Mod	Soc. Call
Ancient Basilisk	21	Rp	S/150	M/50	3.1	T	–	-20/-20/-	–
Basilisk	15	Rp	S/150	M/50	3.5	T	–	-10/-10/-	–
Cockatrice	42-43	Rp	M/180	H/99	3.3	T	–	-10/-10/-	–
Cornish Hen	24	Rp	M/188	L/5	3.5	S	–	–	–
Emerald Snake	5	Rp	M/185	–	4.5	T	–	–	–
Enraged Cockatrice	12	Rp	F/230	H/99	3.3	T	–	-10/-10/-	–
Forest Adder	16-17	Rp	M/192	M/50	3.4	T	2	-10/-10/-	–
Forest Snake	3	Rp	S/150	–	4.7	T	–	–	–
Giant Lizard	36-38	Rp	M/210	–	3.9	T	–	–	–
Grass Snake	5	Rp	M/188	–	4.5	T	–	–	–
Green Snake	0	Rp	S/150	–	5.0	T	–	–	–
Hoary Worm	53-55	Rp	M/210	M/40	3.9	C	–	–	–
Lake Adder	10	Rp	M/185	L/5	4.0	T	–	–	–
Muck Snake	1	Rp	S/150	–	3.8	T	–	–	–
Pseudo Basilisk	12	Rp	S/150	M/50	3.8	T	–	-5/-5/-	–
Red Adder	10	Rp	M/205	L/10	4.0	T	5	-20	–
River Racer	7	Rp	M/188	–	4.3	T	–	-5/-5/-	–
Slime Lizard	1	Rp	S/160	–	3.8	T	–	–	–
Slith Broodling	0	Rp	S/150	–	5.0	T	–	–	–
Slough Serpent	0	Rp	S/160	–	3.8	T	–	–	–
Small Snake	0	Rp	S/165	–	5.0	T	–	–	–
Snake	3	Rp	S/150	–	4.7	T	–	–	–
Tree Snake	0	Rp	S/160	–	4.9	T	–	–	–
Trimbeak	15	Rp	F/230	H/99	3.3	T	–	-10/-10/-	–
Tunneler	37	Rp	M/175	L/5	3.7	T	–	–	–
Water Snake	0	Rp	S/150	–	5.0	S	–	–	–
Western Basilisk	49-50	Rp	M/200	M/40	3.8	T	–	-20	–
Worm	39-42	Rp	M/210	–	3.8	C	–	–	–

Tree or Plant

Monster	Lvl	Body Type	Spd	Agg	Atk Spd	Atk Type	Ev %	Comb Mod	Soc. Call
Ashen Fellwood	16-17	TP	M/192	M/50	3.4	C	–	–	Soc.
Aspen Fellwood	23	TP	M/192	M/50	4.3	C	–	–	Soc.
Black Poplar Fellwood	24	TP	M/192	M/50	4.3	C	–	–	Soc.
Black Willow Fellwood	20	TP	M/192	M/50	3.8	C	–	–	Soc.
Creeping Crud	2	TP	S/140	–	3.8	S	–	–	–
Death Grip Vines	7	TP	S/130	H/80	3.7	S	–	–	Soc.
Downy Fellwood	24	TP	M/192	M/50	4.3	C	–	–	Soc.
Ebony Fellwood	13-14	TP	M/192	M/50	3.7	C	–	–	Soc.
Elder Beech	23-28	TP	M/200	L/20	4.0	C	–	–	Soc.
Gnarled Fellwood	45-49	TP	M/180	M/50	4.1	C/C1	–	-10	Call
Gold Oaken Fellwood	33	TP	M/192	M/50	4.3	C	–	–	Soc.
Grimwood	46-50	TP	M/174	H/70	4.2	C/C1	–	–	Soc.
Hamadryad	30-38	TP	M/185	H/80	4.0	C	–	–	–
Hornbeam Fellwood	27	TP	M/192	M/50	4.3	C	–	–	Soc.
Knotted Fellwood	43-46	TP	M/180	M/30	4.0	C/C1	–	-10	Call
Oak Man	7-9	TP	M/192	M/30	4.3	C	–	–	–
Oaken Fellwood	18	TP	M/192	M/50	3.2	C	–	–	Soc.
Shambler	12-13	TP	S/140	M/60	3.5	C	–	–	Soc.
Silver Oaken Fellwood	31	TP	M/192	M/50	4.3	C	–	–	Soc.
Swamp Slime	3	TP	S/125	–	3.8	S	–	–	–
White Willow Fellwood	21	TP	M/192	M/50	4.3	C	–	–	Soc.
Witherwoode	57	TP	2x/350	H/99	3.8	C/S6	–	–	Soc.

Undead

Monster	Lvl	Body Type	Spd	Agg	Atk Spd	Atk Type	Ev %	Comb Mod	Soc. Call
Actarius	31	IU	M/188	L/5	4.0	C	–	–	Soc.
Aquilifer	31	IU	M/188	L/5	3.9	T/T1	–	-5/-5/-	Soc.
Archer	45	IU/Pl	M/192	H/80	3.0	S	–	–	Soc.
Barguest	57-58	FA	M/180	M/40	3.5	T	1	–	Soc.
Barrow Wight	43-44	BU	M/190	H/80	3.8	S/S4	–	-20/-/-	Soc.
Bean-Nighe	50-54	IU	M/195	H/80	3.3	S	–	-10/-10/-	Soc.
Bleeder	10	FU	F/220	–	3.0	S	–	–	–
Bloody-Bones	7	Tr	M/188	L/25	3.7	S	–	–	–
Botched Sacrifice	11	FU/Cl	M/188	H/75	3.8	S	–	–	Soc.

Monster	Lvl	Body Type	Spd	Agg	Atk Spd	Atk Type	Ev %	Comb Mod	Soc. Call
Bwgwl	28-29	BU	M/188	L/20	3.3	S	–	–	Soc.
Cait Sidhe	48-56	IU	M/200	M/30	3.0	S	–	-20	Soc.
Celtic Lich	50	FU	M/188	H/80	3.8	C	–	-20	Soc.
Celtic Sepulchre Chieft.	52	FU	M/188	H/80	3.4	S/S6	3	–	Soc.
Celtic Sepulchre Warr.	47	FU	M/188	H/80	3.5	S/S2	1	–	Soc.
Centurio Manipularis	31	IU	M/188	L/5	3.3	T/T4	–	5/5/-	Soc.
Centurio Pilus Posterior	31	IU	M/188	L/5	3.1	T/T5	–	5/5/-	Soc.
Centurio Primus Ordines	31	IU	M/188	L/5	3.1	T/T5	–	5/5/-	Soc.
Centurio Primus Pilus	32	IU	M/188	L/5	3.1	T/T6	–	5/5/-	Soc.
Chilled Presence	10	BU/St	M/188	H/100	3.8	C	–	–	Soc.
Clergyman	36	IU/Cl	M/192	H/80	3.0	S	–	–	Soc.
Cohorstalis	30	IU	M/188	L/5	3.4	T/T2	–	–	Soc.
Creeping Ooze	42	FU	S/140	–	4.0	C	–	-5	–
Cursed Believer	13	IU/Ch	M/188	H/85	2.9	C	–	–	Soc.
Cyhraeth	50-51	IU	M/188	H/70	3.3	S	1	-20	–
Cythraul	20-21	BU	M/192	L/25	3.0	S	–	–	–
Danaoin Clerk	35-39	IU/Lr	M/192	H/80	3.9	C	–	-20/-20/-	Soc.
Danaoin Commander	60	IU/Ch	M/192	H/80	2.8	S/T5	–	–	Soc.
Danaoin Farmer	44-46	IU/Cl	M/192	H/80	3.0	S	–	–	Soc.
Danaoin Fisherman	40-42	IU/Cl	M/192	H/80	3.0	S	–	–	Soc.
Danaoin Lieutenant	58	IU/Ch	M/192	H/80	2.9	S/T3	–	–	Soc.
Danaoin Priest	42-44	IU/Lr	M/192	H/80	3.7	C	–	-20/-20/-	Soc.
Danaoin Sailor	44-46	IU/Cl	M/192	H/80	3.0	S	–	–	Soc.
Danaoin Soldier	50-54	IU/Ch	M/192	H/80	3.0	S	–	–	Soc.
Dark Fire	42	DV	M/188	H/80	3.8	C	–	-20/-20/-	–
Decayed Barbarian	40	FU	M/175	H/80	3.8	C/C1	–	–	Soc.
Decayed Barb. Chieftain	42	FU	M/175	H/80	3.8	C/C3	–	–	Soc.
Decayed Zombie	3	FU	M/175	L/1	4.7	C	–	–	Soc.
Decaying Spirit	8	BU	M/188	M/65	4.2	C	–	–	Soc.
Decaying Tomb Raider	36	FU	M/175	H/80	3.8	S	–	–	Soc.
Decurion	31	IU	M/188	L/5	3.5	T/T3	–	–	Soc.
Devout Follower	9	IU/Cl	M/188	M/65	4.2	S	–	–	Soc.
Disturbed Presence	12-14	IU	M/175	H/75	3.8	S	–	–	–
Doomed Minion	12	IU/St	M/188	H/85	2.9	C	–	–	Soc.
Draconarius	31	IU	M/188	L/5	3.9	T/T1	–	-5/-5/-	Soc.
Dreadful Cadaver	8	FU/Cl	M/188	M/65	4.2	S	–	–	Soc.
Druidic Spirit	21	IU/Cl	M/192	H/90	4.0	C	–	–	Call
Dunter	30-34	FU	M/180	H/80	3.8	S/S1	–	–	–
Dux	32	IU	M/188	L/5	3.3	T/T3	–	5/5/-	Soc.
Echo Of Life	41	IU	M/188	H/80	3.8	C	–	–	–
Ectoplasm	41	FU	M/170	L/1	3.9	C	–	-5	–
Endless Sorrow	9	BU/St	M/188	M/65	4.2	S	–	–	Soc.
Eternal Scream	14	BU/St	M/188	H/70	2.9	S	–	–	Soc.
Fading Spirit	7-8	IU	M/175	M/50	4.3	S	–	–	Soc.
Faint Grim	20-21	IU	M/188	–	3.8	S	–	-5	Soc.
Fallen Cleric	10	IU/St	M/188	H/75	3.8	C	–	–	Soc.
Fallen Paladin	11	IU/St	M/188	H/75	3.8	S	–	–	Soc.
Fallen Warrior	41	Pl	M/188	H/80	3.7	S/S5	2	–	Soc.
Footman	45	IU/Pl	M/192	H/80	3.0	S	–	–	Soc.
Forgotten Emperor	35	IU	M/188	L/5	3.8	T	–	10/10/-	Soc.
Forgotten Promise	9	IU/Cl	M/188	M/65	4.2	C	–	–	Call
Ghost Miner	11-12	IU/Lr	M/192	H/75	3.8	C	–	–	Call
Ghost Wolf	32-34	IU	M/205	H/70	3.1	T	1	–	–
Ghostly Cleric	12	IU/Ch	M/190	L/20	3.8	C	–	-10/-/-	–
Ghostly Knight	8-10	IU/Pl	S/150	H/100	3.7	S	3	–	Soc.
Ghostly Paladin	12-13	IU/Ch	M/190	L/25	3.8	S	–	-5/-/-	–
Ghoul Footman	17	FU	M/188	H/70	3.4	S/S3	2	–	Soc.
Ghoul Knight	18	FU	M/188	H/70	3.3	S/S4	3	–	Soc.
Ghoul Lord	19	FU	M/188	H/70	3.2	S/S5	4	–	Soc.
Ghoulic Viper	42	Rp	M/200	H/80	3.5	T	2	–	–
Giant Skeleton	27-28	BU	S/160	H/90	3.8	S	–	–	–

Monster	Lvl	Body Type	Spd	Agg	Atk Spd	Atk Type	Ev %	Comb Mod	Soc. Call
Glowing Goo	36	FU	S/160	–	3.9	C	–	-5	–
Green Ghast	12-14	IU	M/175	H/80	3.8	S	–	-5	–
Grimwood Keeper	43-47	FU	M/174	H/70	3.5	S/S3	–	-10/-10/-	Call
Guardsman	45	IU/PI	M/192	H/80	3.0	S	–	–	Soc.
Gwr-Drwgiaid	15-17	IU	M/180	L/20	3.5	S	–	–	–
Gytrash	35-38	FA	M/180	M/50	3.8	C	–	–	–
Haunting Gloom	8	IU/Ch	M/188	M/65	4.2	C	–	–	Soc.
Imaginifer	31	IU	M/188	L/5	3.9	T/T1	–	-5/-5/-	Soc.
Immunis	29	IU	M/188	L/5	3.4	T/T2	–	–	Soc.
Insidious Whisper	14	BU/St	M/188	H/70	2.9	S	–	–	Soc.
King's Wight	50	FU	M/190	H/80	3.1	S/S10	5	–	Soc.
Knight	49	IU/PI	M/192	H/80	3.0	S	–	–	Soc.
Large Skeleton	5	BU	M/188	L/10	4.5	C	–	–	Soc.
Last Breath	15	BU/St	M/188	H/90	2.9	C	–	–	Soc.
Legatio	33	IU	M/188	L/5	2.9	T/T3	2	5/5/-	Soc.
Legionarius	29	IU	M/188	L/5	3.5	T/T1	–	–	Soc.
Legionnaire	30-36	BU	S/160	M/30	3.0	S	–	–	Soc.
Lingering Shade	11	IU/CI	M/188	H/75	3.8	C	–	–	Soc.
Living Entombed	11	FU/CI	M/188	H/75	3.8	S	–	–	Soc.
Magister	32	IU	M/188	L/5	3.8	T	–	-20/-20/-	Soc.
Malefic Phantom	47	IU	M/188	H/80	3.8	C	–	-10/-10/-	Soc.
Malevolent Disciple	13	IU/CI	M/188	H/85	2.9	C	–	–	Soc.
Manipularis	30	IU	M/188	L/5	3.3	T/T3	–	–	Soc.
Megalith Wight	46	BU	M/190	H/80	3.8	S/S6	–	-20/-/-	Soc.
Megalithic Terror	49	FU	M/190	H/80	3.2	S/S8	5	–	Soc.
Menacing Presence	8	BU/St	M/188	H/100	4.2	C	–	–	Soc.
Moldy Skeleton	2	BU	S/150	–	4.8	S	–	–	Soc.
Moorlich	48	FU	F/300	H/80	3.8	C	–	-20	–
Mouldering Corpse	3	FU	M/175	–	4.7	C	–	–	Soc.
Mountain Grim	35-39	IU	M/174	H/70	3.8	S	–	–	–
Optio	31	IU	M/188	L/5	3.2	T/T4	–	–	Soc.
Ossuary Guardian	48	FU	M/188	H/80	3.5	C/S4	1	–	Soc.
Padfoot	51-54	FA	M/195	M/50	3.6	T	–	–	–
Pendragon Ardent	48	PI	M/188	H/80	3.5	S/S5	1	–	Soc.
Pendrake	48	Rp	M/199	H/80	3.5	T/S2	–	–	Soc.
Petrified Grovewood	43	EE	S/160	–	3.8	C	–	-10	–
Phantom	2	FU/CI	M/192	–	3.6	S	–	–	Soc.
Phantom Page	4-5	IU/CI	S/160	H/80	4.6	C	–	–	Call
Phantom Squire	6-7	IU/CI	M/170	H/80	3.8	T	–	–	Soc.
Pikeman	45	IU/PI	M/192	H/80	3.0	S	–	–	Soc.
Praefectus	32	IU	M/188	L/5	3.3	T/T3	–	5/5/-	Soc.
Praetor	31	IU	M/188	L/5	3.3	T/T4	–	–	Soc.
Praetorian Guard	33	IU	M/188	L/5	3.5	T/T3	2	10/10/-	Soc.
Princep	32	IU	M/188	L/5	3.2	T/T4	–	–	Soc.
Puny Skeleton	1	BU	S/160	–	5.0	C	–	–	–
Putrid Sacrificer	9	FU/CI	M/188	M/65	4.2	S	–	–	Soc.
Putrid Zombie	4	FU/CI	M/180	L/2	4.6	S	–	–	Soc.
Reanimated Foe	37-38	BU	M/188	H/80	3.8	S/S2	–	–	Soc.
Redbone Skeleton	37	FU	M/188	H/80	3.7	S	3	–	–
Repentant Follower	37	PI	M/188	H/80	3.7	S/S2	–	–	Soc.
Roman Ghost	15	IU	M/180	M/35	4.1	S	–	–	Soc.
Roman Spirit	12	IU	M/180	L/15	4.4	S	–	–	Soc.
Rotting Skeleton	1	BU	S/150	–	5.0	C	–	–	Soc.
Rotting Tombraider	9	IU/CI	M/188	M/65	4.2	C	–	–	Soc.
Rotting Zombie	5-6	FU/CI	M/180	H/70	4.4	C	–	-/-5/-	Soc.
Sacrificed Slave	10	IU/CI	M/188	H/75	3.8	C	–	–	Soc.
Sacrificial Soul	43	IU	M/188	H/80	3.8	S	–	–	–
Saxonbone Skeleton	40	BU	M/188	H/80	3.7	S	–	–	Soc.
Shepherd	34	IU/CI	M/192	H/80	3.0	S	–	–	Soc.
Signifier	31	IU	M/188	L/5	3.9	T/T1	–	-5/-5/-	Soc.
Singular	33	IU	M/188	M/50	2.7	T/T5	7	10/10/-	Soc.
Skeletal Centurion	21	BU/PI	M/198	H/70	3.5	T/S2	–	-5/-5/-10	Soc.
Skeletal Druid	44	BU	M/188	H/80	3.8	S	–	-20	Soc.
Skeletal Druidess	44	BU	M/188	H/80	3.8	S	–	-20	Soc.
Skeletal High Priestess	46	BU	M/188	H/80	3.8	S	–	-20	Soc.
Skeletal Legionnaire	18	BU/PI	M/198	M/50	3.5	S/S1	–	-5/-5/-	Soc.
Skeleton	2	BU	M/180	–	4.8	C	–	–	Soc.
Small Skeletal Centurion	17	BU/PI	M/198	H/70	3.4	T/S1	–	-/-/-5	Soc.
Small Skel. Legionnaire	14	BU/PI	M/198	M/50	3.8	S/S1	–	–	Soc.
Snowdon Grim	36-38	IU	M/188	H/70	3.8	S	–	-5	–
Soul Harvester	41	IU	M/188	H/80	3.4	T/S2	–	–	–
Spectral Essence	46-47	IU	M/188	H/80	3.8	C	–	-10/-10/-	Soc.
Spectral Wizard	47	IU	M/188	H/80	3.8	C	–	-20/-20/-	Soc.
Spirit	6	IU	M/175	M/40	4.4	S	–	–	Soc.
Spirit Hound	0	IU	S/150	–	5.0	S	–	–	–
Spiritual Advisor	48	IU	M/188	H/80	3.8	C	–	-20	Soc.
Spiteful Wraith	10	BU/St	M/188	H/100	3.8	C	–	–	Soc.
Suffering Apparition	12	BU/St	M/188	H/100	2.9	C	–	–	Soc.
Tomb Keeper	41	IU	M/188	H/80	3.8	T	–	–	–
Tomb Wight	42	FU	M/190	H/80	3.5	C/S2	5	–	Soc.
Tortured Soul	9	IU/CI	M/188	M/65	4.2	C	–	–	Soc.
Townsman	30	IU/CI	M/192	H/80	3.0	S	–	–	Soc.
Tree Spirit	6	IU	M/175	M/40	4.4	C	–	-10/-/-	Soc.
Tribune	32	IU	M/188	L/5	3.0	T/T5	–	5/5/-	Soc.
Tribunus Laticlavicus	33	IU	M/188	L/5	3.0	T/T6	–	5/5/-	Soc.
Undead Builder	9	IU/CI	M/188	M/65	4.2	C	–	–	Soc.
Undead Druid	8-10	FU	M/178	H/90	4.2	C	–	-10	Soc.
Undead Filidh	5-7	FU	M/178	H/90	4.5	C	–	–	–
Undead Goblin Chief	6	Lr	M/192	H/85	3.7	C	–	–	Call
Undead Goblin Fisherman	4	BU	M/180	M/50	4.6	S	–	–	Soc.
Undead Goblin Warrior	5	Rp	M/192	H/85	3.7	C	–	–	Soc.
Undead Guardsman	9	IU/PI	M/188	M/65	4.2	C	–	–	Call
Undead Miner	20-23	FU/CI	M/192	L/20	3.7	S	–	–	Soc.
Undead Monk	29-30	BU	M/192	L/20	3.8	S	–	–	Soc.
Undead Poacher	9	IU/CI	M/188	M/65	4.2	C	–	–	Soc.
Undead Retainer	36-37	FU	M/175	H/80	3.8	C	–	–	Soc.
Unfortunate Pragmatic	9	BU	M/188	M/65	4.2	S	–	–	Soc.
Vigilant Soul	46	IU	M/188	H/80	3.5	S	–	–	–
Vigilis	29	IU	M/188	M/50	3.8	T	1	–	Soc.
Wandering Spirit	9-11	IU	M/175	M/55	4.1	S	–	–	–
Weak Skeleton	1	BU	S/150	–	4.9	S	–	–	Soc.
Wicked Cythraul	26-27	BU	M/192	L/25	3.0	S	–	–	–
Wight	23	FU/CI	M/192	–	3.7	S	–	–	Soc.
Wisp Ghoul	0	FU	M/188	–	3.8	S	–	–	–
Zombie Boar	5	FU	M/185	M/50	4.5	S	–	-/-5/-	Call
Zombie Farmer	7	FU	M/188	–	4.3	C	–	-/-20/-	Call
Zombie Sow	4	FU/CI	M/170	L/4	4.6	S	–	–	Call

Camelot

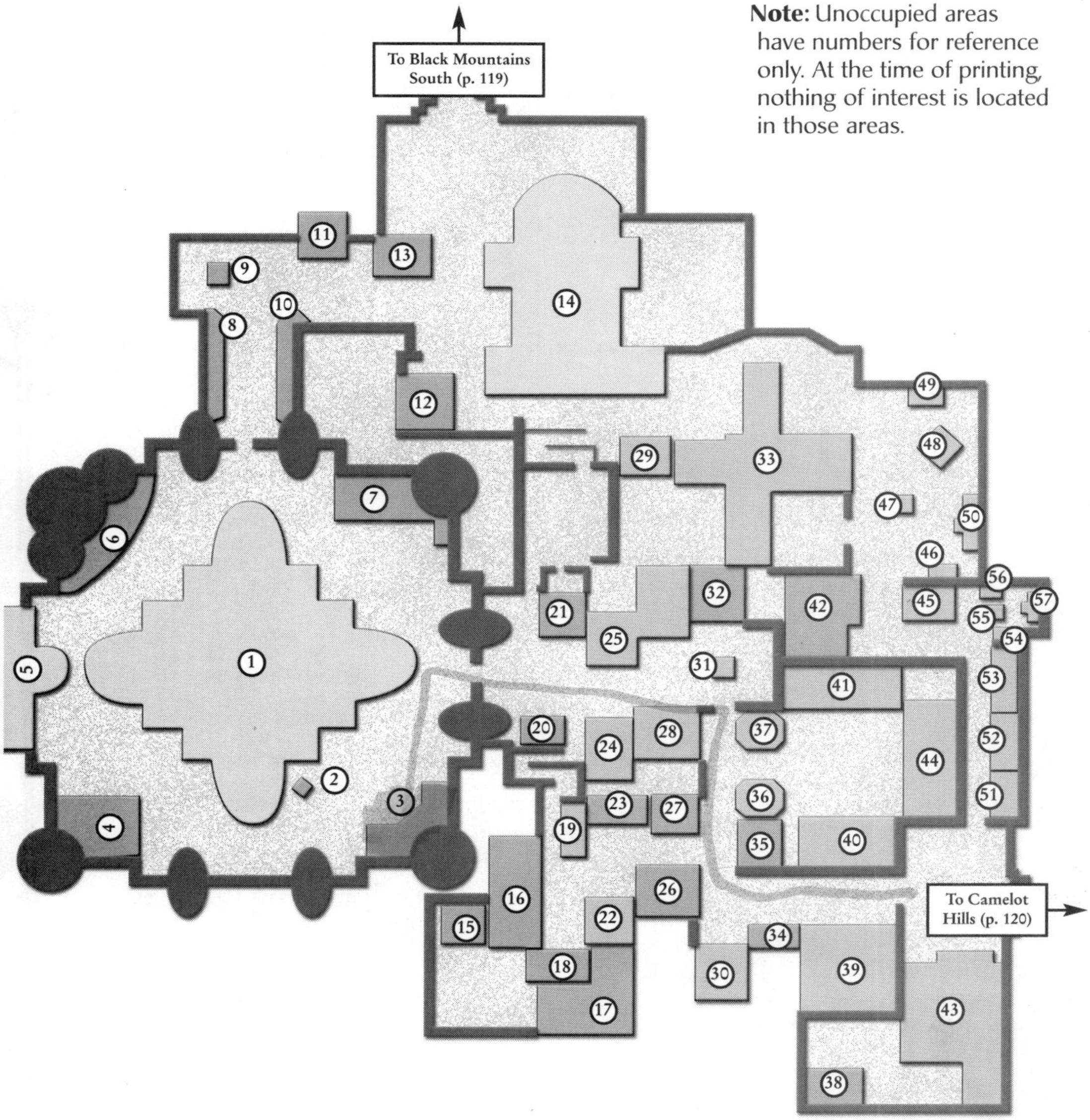

Note: Unoccupied areas have numbers for reference only. At the time of printing, nothing of interest is located in those areas.

To Black Mountains South (p. 119)

To Camelot Hills (p. 120)

1 **Lord Urqhart** Vault Keeper
3 **Edmee Heolstor** Embossed Leather Armor
3 **Grummond Attor** Engineers Master
3 **Hector Darian** Smithing Equipment
3 **Hephas Elgen** Weaponsmiths Master
3 **Jeffrey Kenric** Mithril Armor
3 **Lora Theomund** Mithril Armor
3 **Loraine Elgen** Armorsmith Master
3 **Meccus Yrre** Sylvan Cloth Armor
3 **Runthal Devyn** Fletcher Master
3 **Shallah**
3 **Torr Upton** Mithril Plate Armor
3 **Wyne Scead** Mithril weapons
4 **Lady Charlitte** Name Registrar
4 **Lord Christopher** Guild Registrar
4 **Lord Oachley** Guild Emblemeer
5 **Scribe Veral**
6 **Calldir Edelmar** Bounty
6 **Magess Islia**
13 **Corley Nodens** Tailoring Equipment
13 **Laurenna**
14 **Aklee Edelmar** Bounty
14 **Brother Lensar**
14 **Brother Michel** Healer Trainer
14 **Lady Fridwulf** Cleric Trainer
14 **Lady Triss** Paladin Trainer
14 **Lady Winchell** Cleric Trainer
14 **Lord Prydwen** Paladin Trainer
14 **Lynna Lang** Tanned Cymric Armor, Steel Studded Armor, Bashing Weapons
14 **Sister Elaydith**
14 **Sister Rhigwyn**
14 **Tait Nerian** Iron Studded and Steel Chain Armor, Shields, Swords
15 **Magus Isen** Cabalist Trainer
15 **Master Edric** Infiltrator Trainer
16 **Magus Agyfen** Cabalist Trainer
16 **Master Arenis** Mercenary Trainer
16 **Olaevia Wyman** Cabalist Staves
17 **Freya Edelmar** Bounty
17 **Landry Woden** Armor, Weapons
17 **Larcwide Wirt** Armor, Weapons
17 **Master Almund** Mercenary Trainer
17 **Master Eadig** Infiltrator Trainer
19 **Acey Dalston** Fletcher Master
19 **Jana Fletcher** Arrow
19 **Kedoenad** Poison
19 **Sara Graston** Bows
19 **Sasha Fletcher** Crossbow Bolts
19 **Velmis** Poison
19 **Willa Dalston** Feathers
21 **Berenger Brennar**
21 **Gaevin Sebryn**
25 **Bedelia**
25 **Hamon Sallitt**
26 **Sir Kenley**
28 **Barkeep Broec**
28 **Brother Ethelbald** Friar Trainer
28 **Gamel Platfoot**
30 **Andri**
30 **Barkeep Dwerrav**
30 **Sandre Stanhill**
30 **Sephere Lade**
31 **Master Dubri** Minstrel Trainer
31 **Silura Starish** Bard Instruments
39 **Brother Sterlyn** Friar Trainer
39 **Cigolin Dalston** Theurgist Staves
39 **Colby Dalston** Quilted Armor, Staves
39 **Dare Edelmar** Bounty
39 **Iden Wissan** tanned Cymric, Steel Studded, Maces
39 **Lieutenant Rydderac** Scout Trainer
39 **Master Cear** Theurgist Trainer
39 **Mistress Welss** Theurgist Trainer
39 **Odella Cerdic** Tanned Cymric and Steel Studded Armor, Arrows, Bows, Rapiers
40 **Librarian Ophus**
40 **Maye Edelmar** Bounty
41 **Holt Finan** Bard Instruments, Tanned Siluric Armor, Steel Studded Armor, Pierce Weapons
41 **Mori Godric** Quilted Armor, Staves
41 **Ulyius Feu-Ame**
42 **Enchanter Evala** Enchanter
42 **Marius Caest** Staves
42 **Vadri Pade**
43 **Captain Alphin** Armsman Trainer
43 **Captain Rion** Armsman Trainer
43 **Catelyn Boltar**
43 **Elzbet Sable** Siluric Leather
43 **Heolstor Wyman** Leather
43 **Lieutenant Kaherdin** Scout Trainer
43 **Ordra Yaney** Alloy Weapons (all)
43 **Stephon the Crier**
44 **Gardowen Egesa** Wizard Staves
44 **Loremaster Alain**
44 **Magess Tena** Sorcerer Trainer
44 **Magus Cormac** Sorcerer Trainer
44 **Master Berwick** Minstrel Trainer
44 **Master Grundelth** Wizard Trainer
44 **Master Vismer**
44 **Mistress Ladriel** Wizard Trainer
44 **Pedrith Edyn** Sorcerer Staves
45 **Arliss Eadig** Tailor Master
45 **Coventina Bordin** Tailoring Equipment
45 **Dyemaster Edare** Green/brown/grey/orange/yellow cloth dye
45 **Dyemaster Emma** Blue/turquoise/teal/red/purple leather dye
45 **Dyemaster Kael** Blue/turquoise/teal/red/purple enamel dye
45 **Dyemaster Lendand** Green/brown/grey/orange/yellow leather dye
45 **Dyemaster Mara** Green/brown/grey/orange/yellow enamel dye
45 **Dyemaster Vandras** Blue/turquoise/teal/red/purple cloth dye
45 **Radek Silven** Robes
45 **Raggart Bruce** Quilted Armor
46 **Guardsman Exeter**
46 **Lara Weathers** Studded Armor
46 **Serena Muftar** Chain Armor
46 **Ver Nuren** Shields
48 **Ethan Farley** Alloy/steel Armor
48 **Fenris Blakely** Pierce Weapons
49 **Jana Hickey** Boned Leather Armor
54 **Geor Nadren** Cymric Leather Armor
55 **Dougal Heathis** 2-Handed
55 **Judan Hammerfel** Smith
55 **Yoren Shazra** Roman Leather Armor
56 **Moira Camber** Polearms
57 **Fuston Talgurt** Scaled Plate Armor
57 **Hafgan Corley** Plate/full Armor
57 **Warren Gibson** Siluric Leather Armor

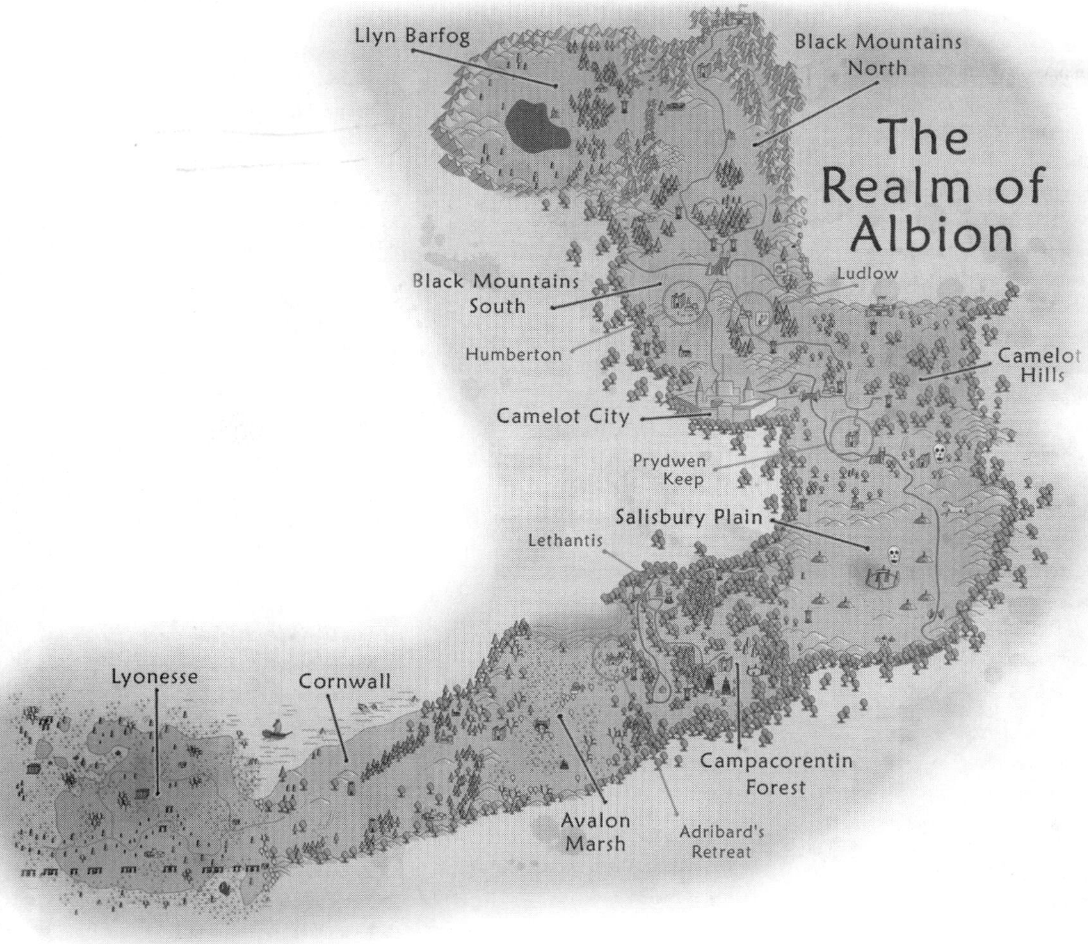

The Realm of Albion

Llyn Barfog

Black Mountains North

Ludlow

Black Mountains South

Humberton

Camelot Hills

Camelot City

Prydwen Keep

Salisbury Plain

Lethantis

Lyonesse

Cornwall

Campacorentin Forest

Avalon Marsh

Adribard's Retreat

AVALON MARSH

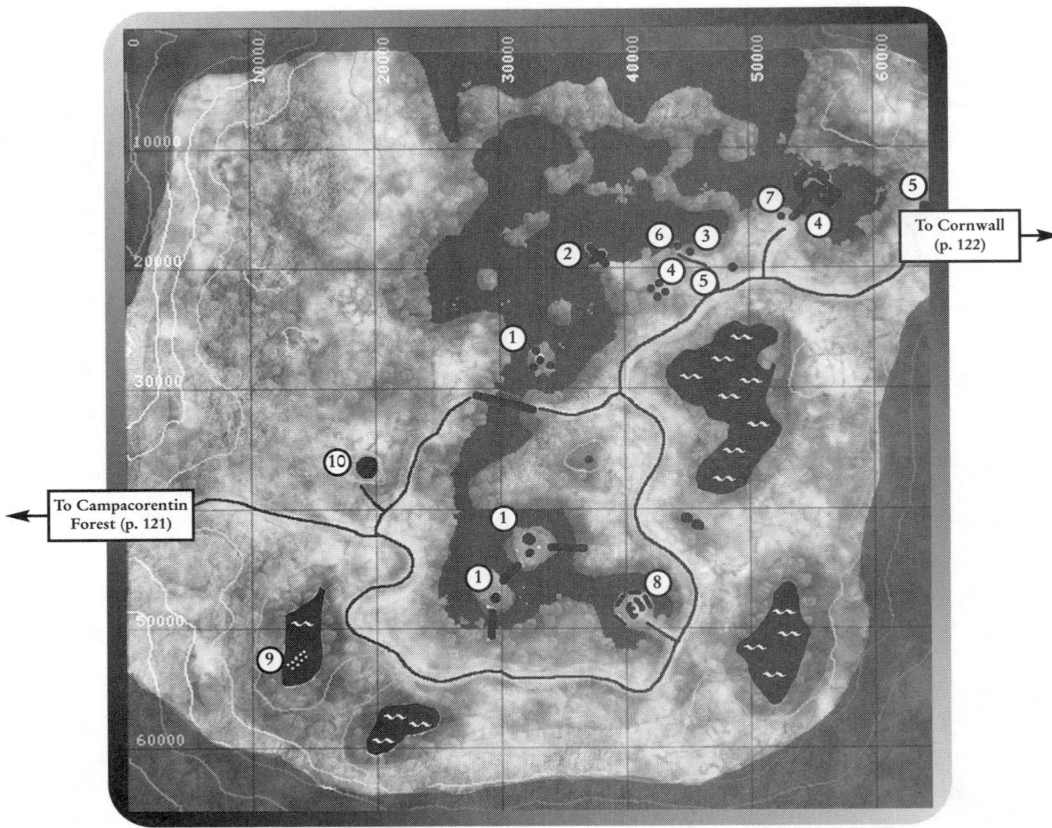

1 Bogman Towers
2 Wharf
3 Undead Stones
4 Bind Stones
5 Towers
6 Dock
7 Adribard's Retreat (p. 127)
8 Haunted Ruins
9 Submerged Columns
10 Caer Witrin & Stables (p. 127)

BLACK MOUNTAINS NORTH

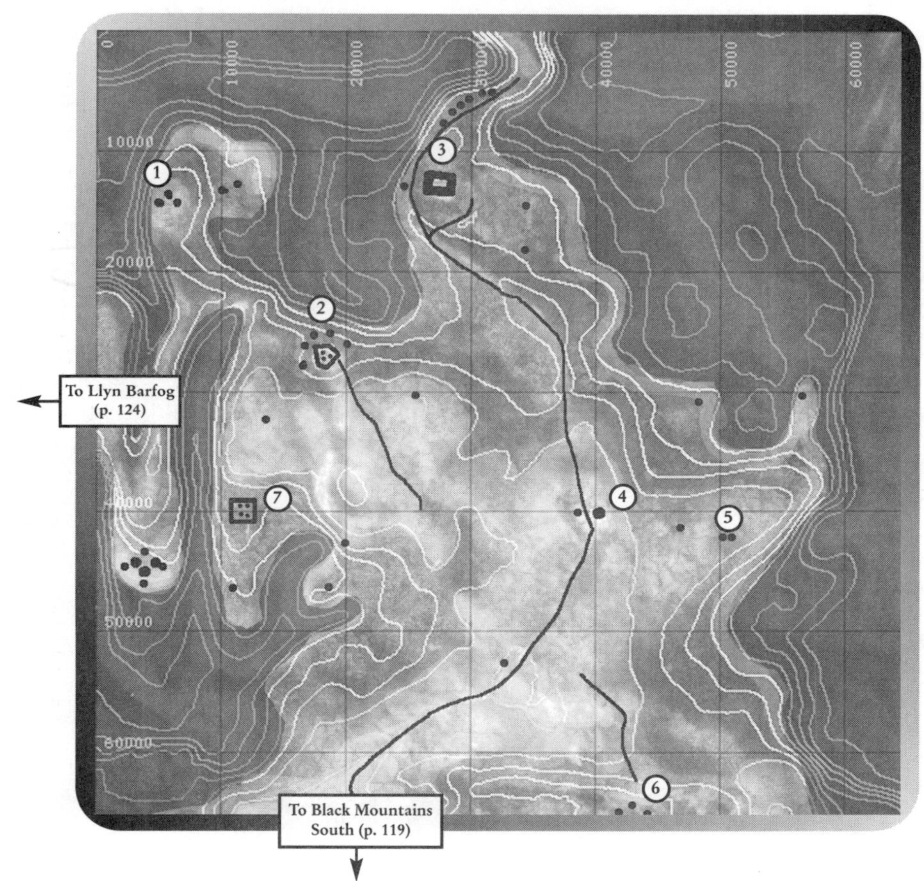

1 Hill Camp
2 Goblin Keep (fort)
3 Swanton Keep (p. 131)
4 Snowdonia Station (p. 131)
5 Forest Camp
6 Stone Circle (Filidh)
7 Skeleton Graveyard

BLACK MOUNTAINS SOUTH

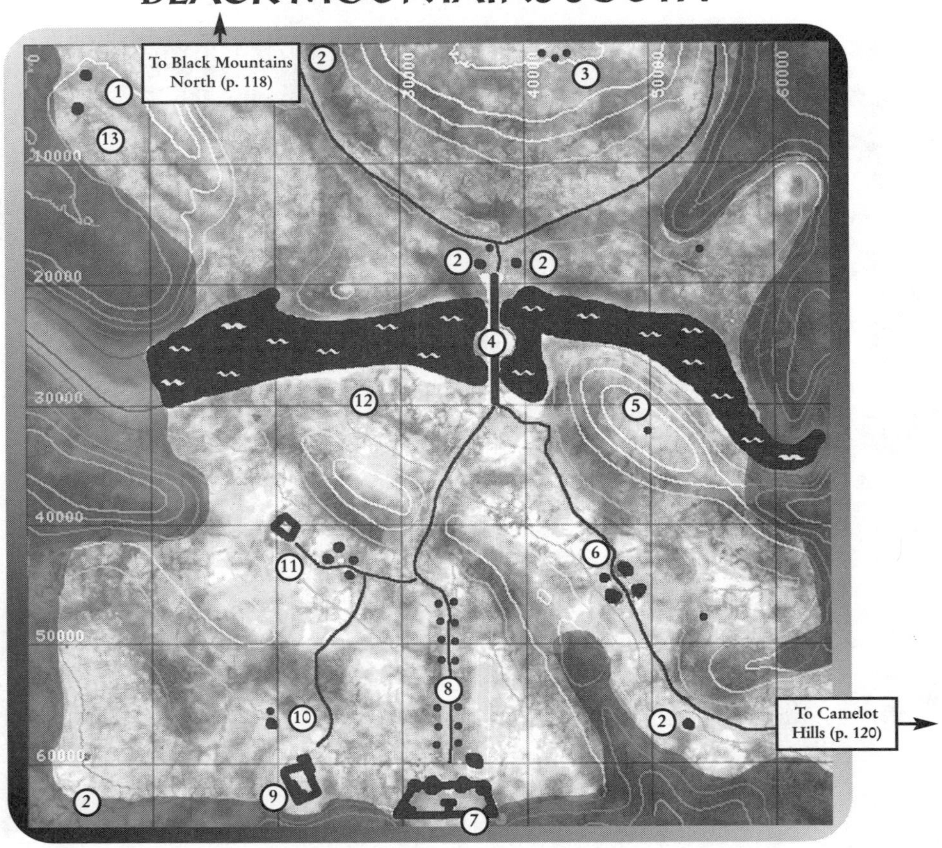

1 Entrance to Tepok's Mine (p. 134)
2 Tower
3 Stone Circle (Filidh)
4 Arched Twin Bridges
5 Crates / Cutpurse Camp
6 Ludlow Village (p. 130)
7 Castle Camelot Entrance (p. 114)
8 Stone Columns
9 Vetusta Abbey
10 Stable
11 Humberton Village (p. 129)
12 Goblin Fishing Camp
13 Goblin Ruins (Grilk's Lair)

CAMELOT HILLS

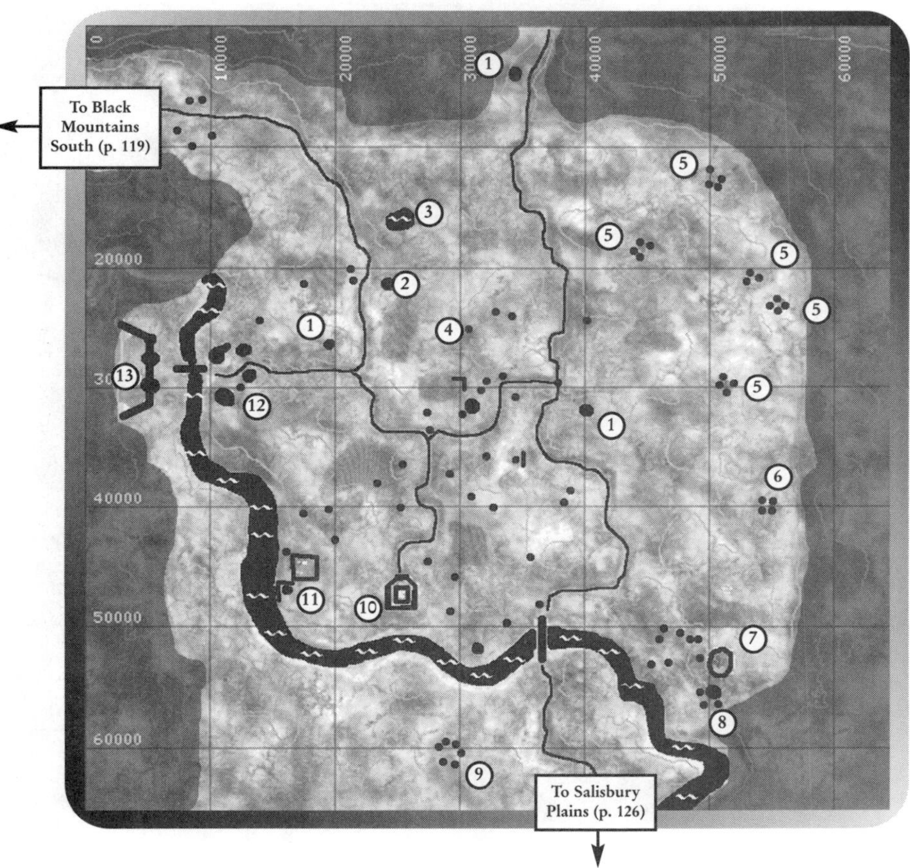

1 Tower
2 Stable
3 Pond with Willows
4 Partially Burned Statue
5 Bandit Camp
6 Undead Stones
7 Large Ruin (Tomb of Mithra) (p. 133)
8 Undead Ruins
9 Large Bandit Camp
10 Prydwen Keep (p. 130)
11 Graveyard
12 Cotswold Village (p. 128)
13 Castle Camelot Entrance (p. 114)

CAMPACORENTIN FOREST

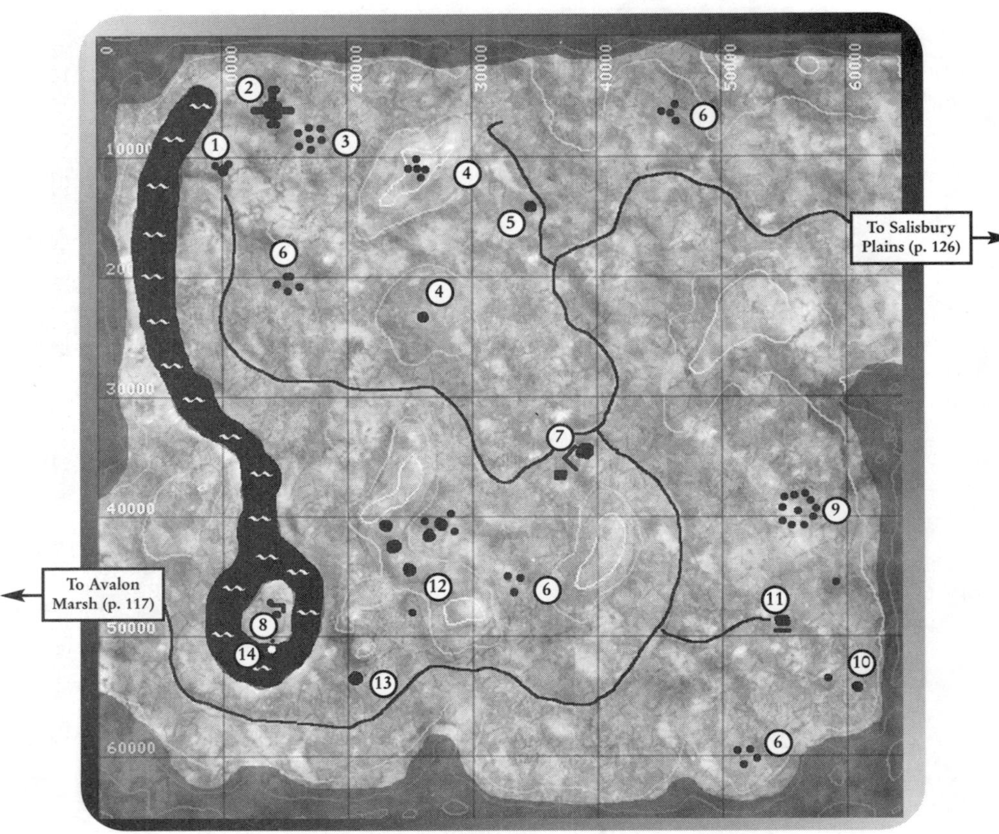

1 Campacorentin Station (Merchant Tower) (p. 128)
2 Lethantis Association (p. 129)
3 Ring of Sentasil
4 Guard Tower
5 Treel Undead Camp
6 Goblin Camp
7 Caer Ulfwych (p. 127)
8 Hermit Ruins
9 Green Witch Altar
10 Keltoi Fogou (p. 134)
11 Disturbed Presence Ruins
12 Ogre Towers
13 Tower
14 Dock

CORNWALL

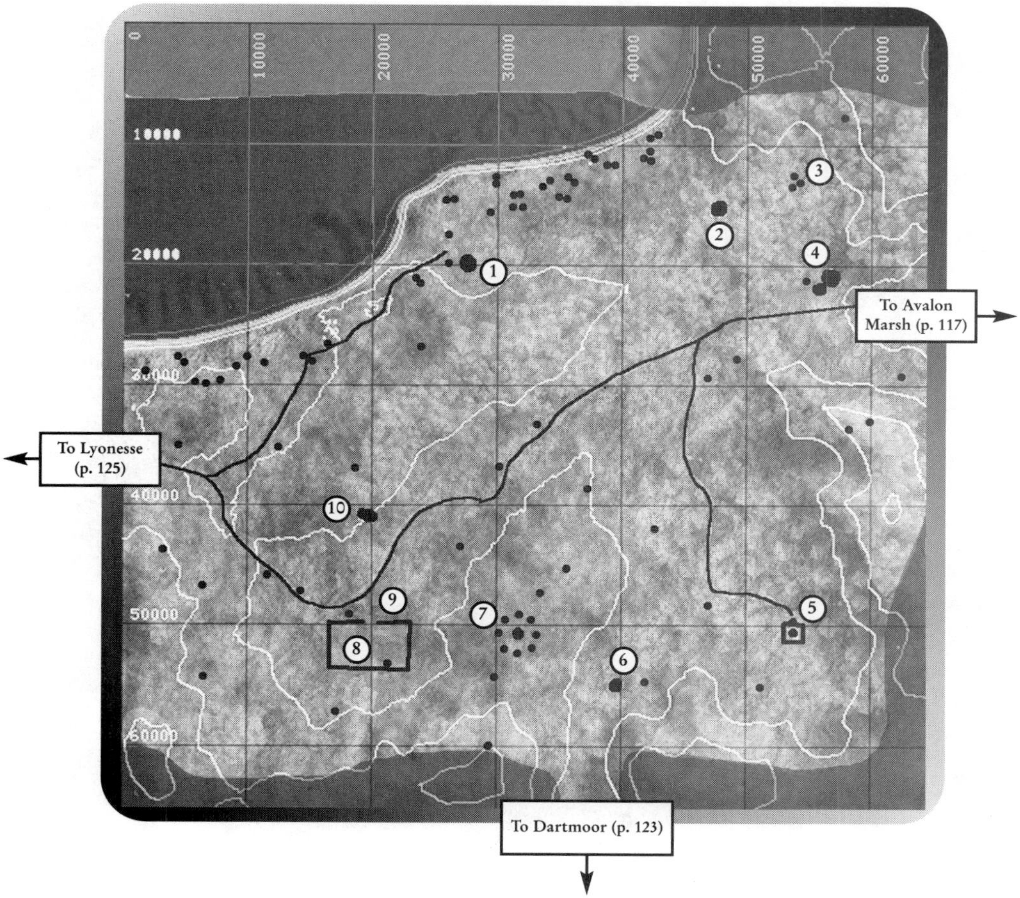

To Avalon Marsh (p. 117)

To Lyonesse (p. 125)

To Dartmoor (p. 123)

1 Boogey Tower
2 Haunted Church Ruins
3 Hunters
4 Cornwall Station & Stables (p. 128)
5 Roman Fort
6 Abandoned Tower
7 Catacombs of Corvoda (p. 133)
8 Rooter Pen
9 Yarley's Stables
10 Tumbled Tower

DARTMOOR

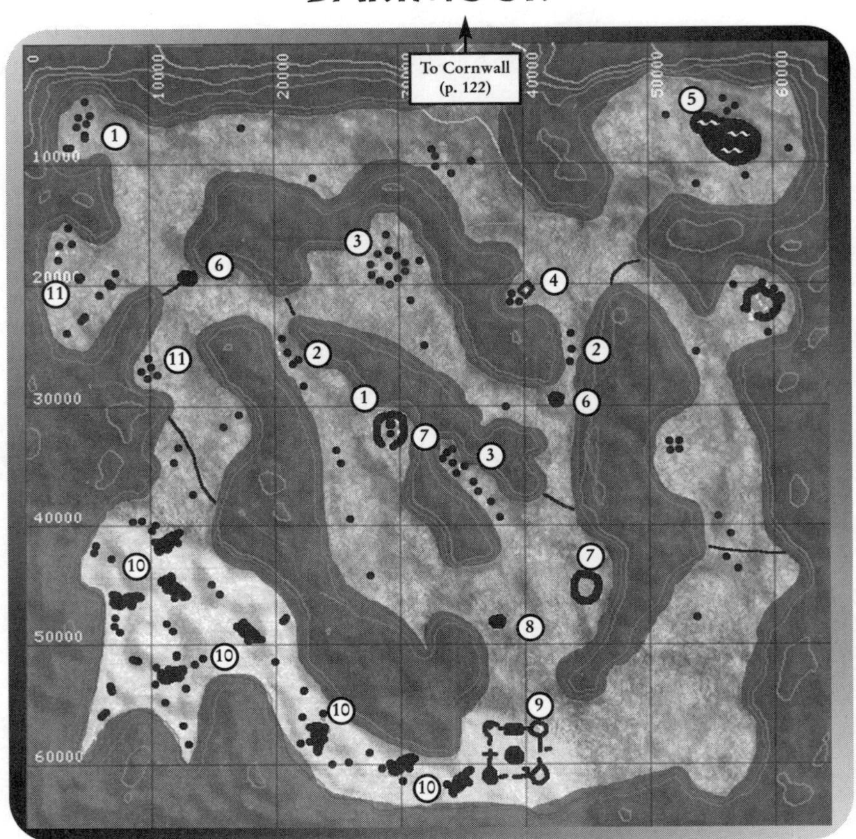

1 Granite Giant Camp
2 Granite Giant Stones
3 Granite Giant Stone Circle
4 Brigand Camp & Ruins
5 Pond
6 Granite Giant Outlook Tower
7 Granite Giant Fort
8 Granite Giant Tower
9 Golestandt & Castle Grounds
10 Granite Formations
11 Stonecrusher Camp

LLYN BARFOG

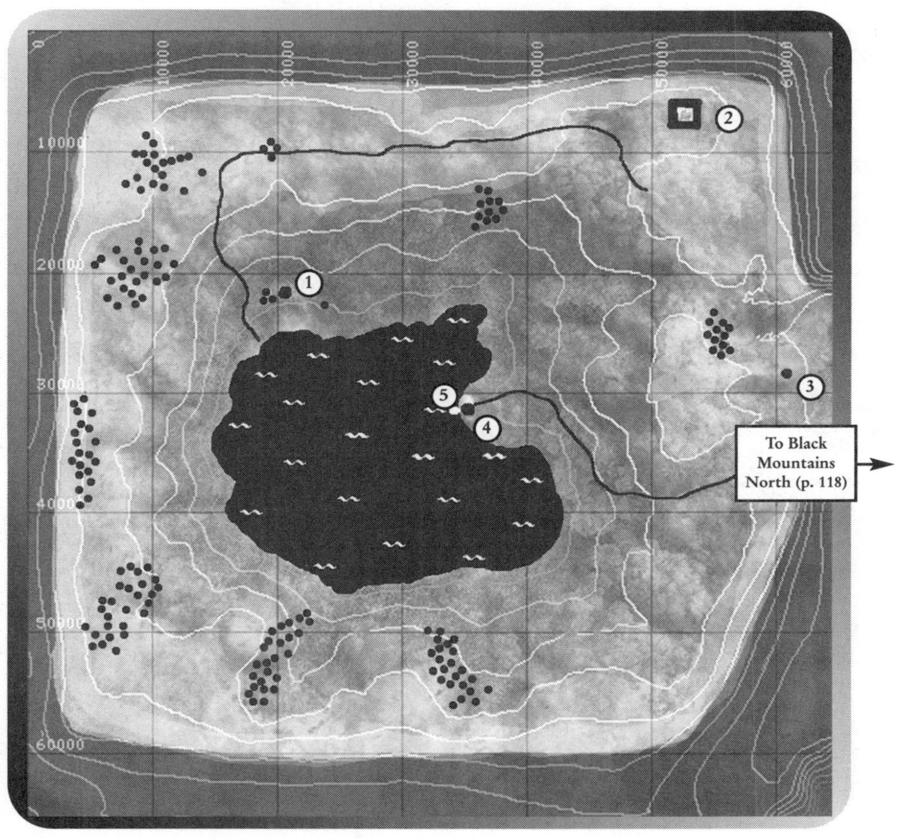

1 Bwgan Fishing Camp
2 Argel Abaty & Undead
3 Tower
4 Llyn Barfog Market (p. 129)
5 Outland Wharf (p. 130)

LYONESSE

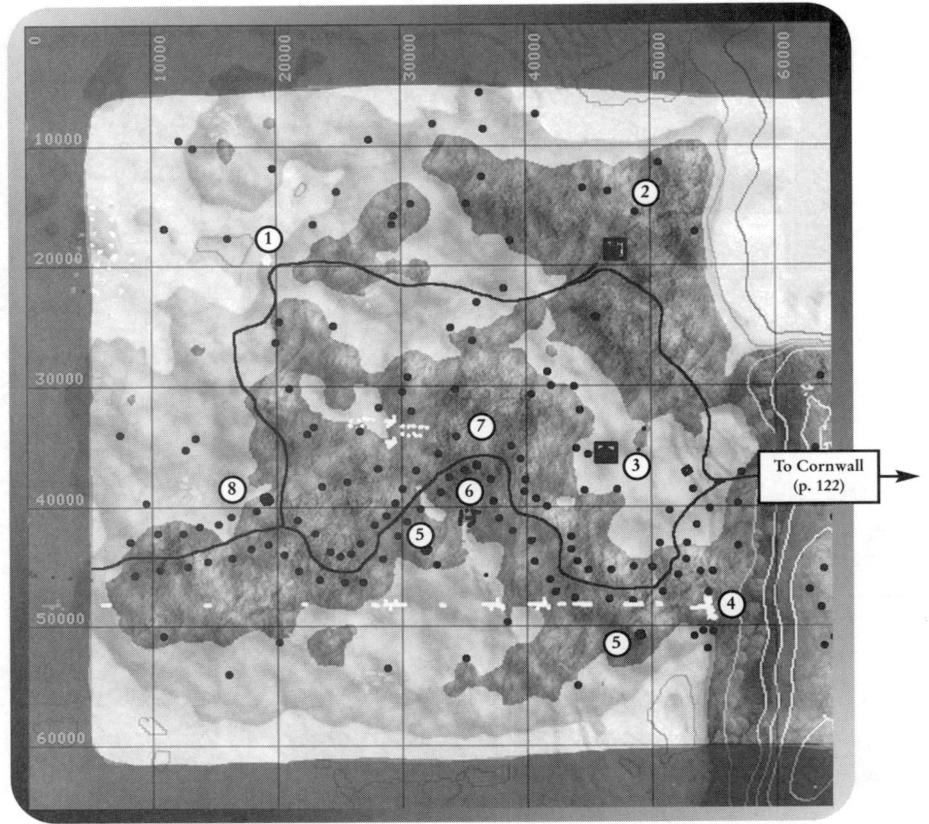

1 Fallen Tower
2 Ruined Danaoin Villa
3 Sunken Danaoin Villa
4 Ghostly Church Service
5 Outpost Ruins
6 Arawn Monastery Ruin
7 Goblin Huts
8 Tower Ruin

SALISBURY PLAINS

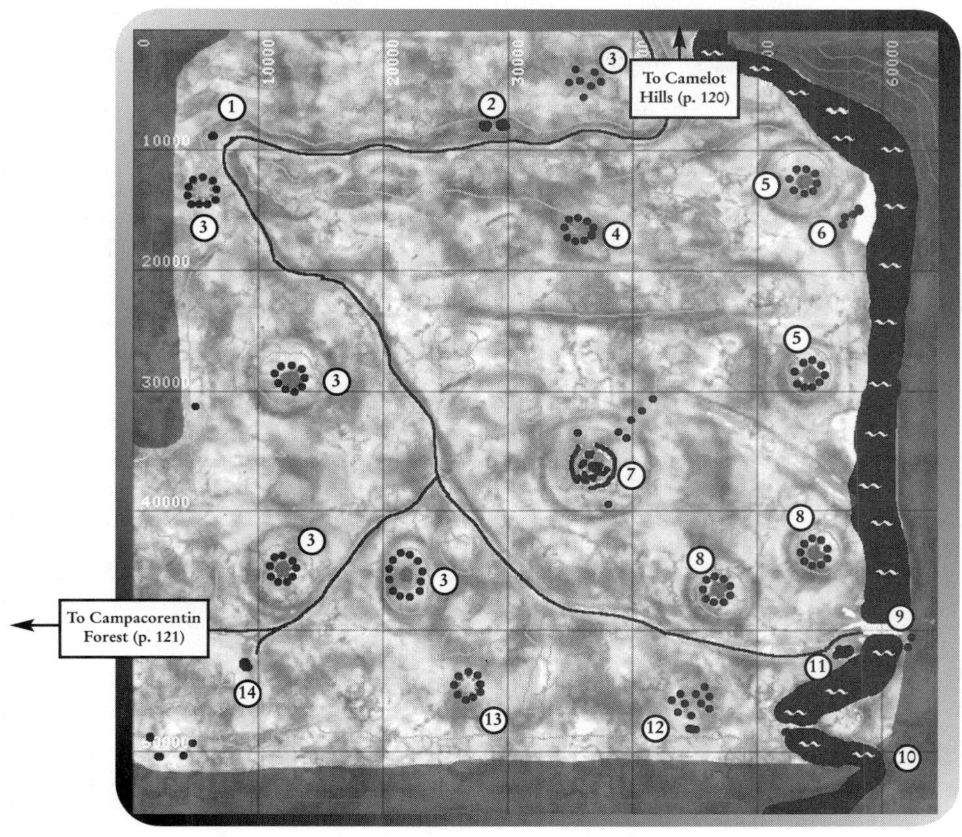

1 Tower
2 West Downs (Merchant Shops & Stable) (p. 131)
3 Stone Circle
4 Stone Circle (Spirits)
5 Stone Circle (Tomb Raiders)
6 Slavemaster Camp
7 Stonehenge Circle / Barrows (p. 132)
8 Skeleton Stone Circles
9 Broken Bridge
10 Stone Ring
11 Skeleton Tower Ruins
12 Tomb Raiders Camp
13 Druid Stone Circle
14 Guard Tower

Adribard's Retreat

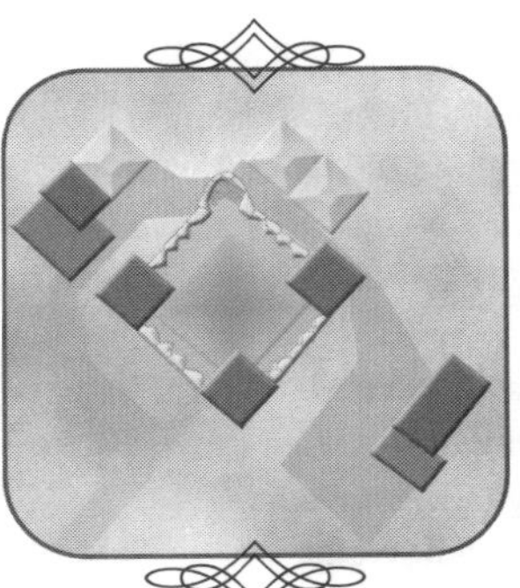

Blueheart Dyes
Dyemstr. Camdene Dyes
Trulion Vrundon Vault Keeper
Enchanter Braesia Enchanter
Tersa Weaver Robes
Anga Weaver Quilted cloth
Nai Whit Staff
Morin Davem Roman leather
Tathal 2-handed weapons
Tathan Plate
Tyngyr Blade Slashing
Trill Bard instruments
Devyn Godric Shields
Theois Gwynf Crushing
Salwis the Crier
Brother Onoloth
Master Liennon Minstrel Trainer
Sister Endri Healer
Sister Chael Acolyte Trainer
Lord Adribard Paladin Trainer
Lady Lynn Cleric Trainer
Master Dyrin Fighter Trainer
Master Traoyr Wizard Trainer
Daisi Egesa Wizard staves
Wylie Edyn Sorcerer staves
Magus Saloc Mage Trainer
Magus Edaev Sorcerer Trainer
Aiellana
Mistress Jeryssa Theurgist Trainer
Graeme Dalston Theurgist staves
Lieutenant Crosean Scout Trainer
Scribe Eril
Brother Caun Friar Trainer

Caer Ulfwych

Calya
Lord Ulfwych Paladin Trainer
Collen Blist Cleric Trainer
Elger Leafblade Bows
Fellya Fletcher Arrows
Brother Spilr Friar Trainer
Brother Eurius Healer
Mistress Frina Theurgist Trainer
Gery Dalston Theurgist staves
Dyemaster Druce Leather dye
Dyemaster Esme Leather dye
Dyemaster Nedda Enamel dye
Dyemaster Eldred Enamel dye
Huntress Lenna
Captain Falron Armsman Trainer
Idian Stable Master
Fianya Walelden
Eiddin Walelden Arrows
Lieutenant Mhoudi Scout Trainer
Ellard Gram Crushing
Stephan Fall Chain armor
Langston Fall Slashing
Ellard Fall Smith
Grindan Halig Shields

Caer Witrin

Jhular Stable Master
Dugan Advien
Tyna Blade
Sister Lilly Healer
Fread Gramley Smith
Gregor Lannis Crushing
Azrael Mucto Chain armor
Magus Dimos Cabalist Trainer
Master Noijan Infiltrator Trainer
Etie Poisons
Master Dohajan Mercenary Trainer
Wina Wyman Cabalist staves

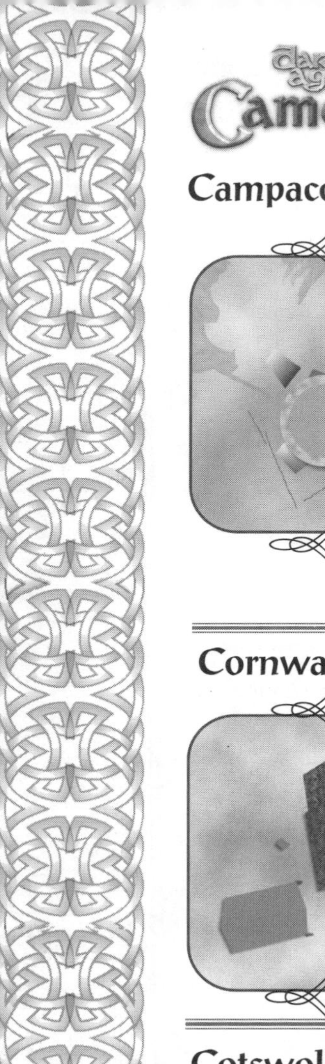

Campacorentin Station

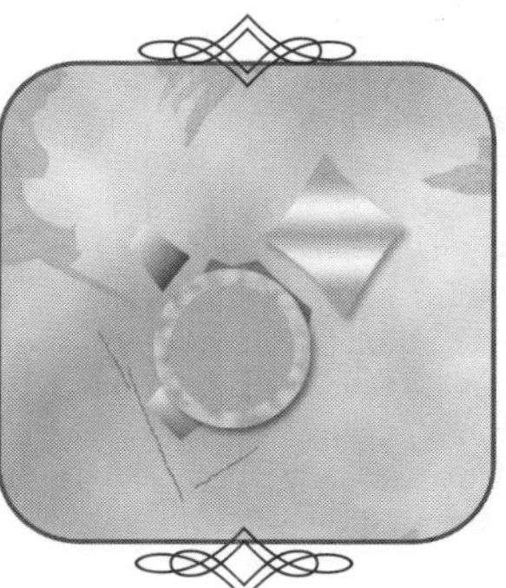

Kealan
Hunter Kenwin
Master Hadis Rogue Trainer
Master Lorik Fighter Trainer
Linidd Poisons
Junger Gannon Chain armor
Grin the Crier
Balthazar Encambion Polearms
Dyemaster Esme Leather dye
Gwendolyn Arlington Cloth dye
Rundeg Faerweth Lamellar studded armor
Geston Lurger Thrusting
Archibald Oakheart Staff
Malin Cullan 2-handed weapons
Fluitha Sufron Cymric leather armor
Master Astyp Mercenary Trainer
Goodwin Fletcher Arrows
Dafyd Graham Smith
Flaudin Bowman Bows
Falin Fletcher Arrows

Cornwall Station

Heylyn Aldar Arrows
Jack Weyland Scaled plate armor
Adaliae Ruthic Tailoring Equipment
Iohannes Aldar Arrows
Sar Aldar Chain Armor
Thule Ruthic Smithing/Tailoring supplies
Seysild Aldar Smith
Eva Aldar Healer
Pethos Stablemaster

Cotswold Village

Enchanter Grumwold Enchanter
Master Sorac Rogue Trainer
Jonathan Lee
Ydenia Philpott
Eileen Morton Bard instruments
Daniel Edwards
Godaleva Dowden
Andrew Wyatt
Dwight Edwards
Unendalden Poisons
Odelia Wyman Cabalist staves
Cullen Smyth
Grum Bowman Bows
Braenwyn Fletcher Arrows
Yetta Fletcher Arrows
Rayn Olwyc Polearms
Gill Hoxley Steel/alloy plate armor
Elvar Ironhand Smith
Lar Rodor Shields
Cudbert Dalston Theurgist staves
Col Aldar Chain armor
Ellyn Weyland Studded armor
Bedamor Routh 2-handed weapons
Grannis Ynos Slashing
John Weyland Thrusting
Pompin the Crier
Master Stearn Elementalist Trainer
Laridia the Minstrel
Master Kless
Doreen Egesa Wizard staves
Dyemaster Wanetta Leather dye
Dyemaster Leax Leather dye
Dyemaster Octe Enamel dye
Dyemaster Edra Enamel dye
Stonemason Glover
Magus Aelle Mage Trainer
Cauldir Edyn Sorcerer staves
Samwell Hornly Staff
Jon Smythe Robes
Lundeg Tranyth Roman armor
Eowyln Astos Cloth dye
Farma Hornly Quilted cloth armor
Dyemaster Alwin Cloth dye

Note. Nob's stable is down the road, across from the guard tower.

Humberton Village

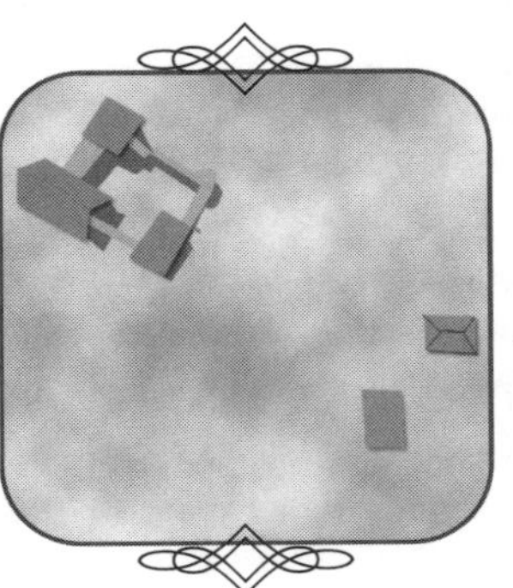

Master Torr Fighter Trainer
Siom Felanis Robes
Mif Feit Staff
Tria Ellowis Arrows
Barnarn the Crier
Dyemaker Bal Cloth dye
Dyemaster Brun Cloth dye
Gert Elm Scaled plate armor
Stephon Bash Crushing
Gracchus Stable Master
Contyth Apprentice smith
Parisch Ealyn Smith
Heorot Kenway Shields
Alhrick Duglas Thrusting
Ban Ronem Slashing
Enchanter Haephus Enchanter
Bline Tengit Quilted cloth armor
Alden Fletcher Arrows
Nelda Fletcher Arrows
Feren Erimen Bows
Brother Demay Healer
Niea
Brother Dupre Acolyte Trainer
Brother Sabutai Healer
Sir Gleran
Dun Mra Boned studded armor
Steward Willie
Sir Ambiz
Mistress Blea
Nydomath Poisons

Lethantis Association

Master Arbaedes Wizard Trainer
Magus Crystolos Sorcerer Trainer
Mistress Trethia Elementalist Trainer
Magus Oreal Mage Trainer
Magus Sacyn Cabalist Trainer
Epin Lemut Robes
Mairi Ralilden
Sleria Bard instruments
Master Glorous Minstrel Trainer
Master Qilith Infiltrator Trainer
Loretta Agesa Wizard staves
Norvel Edyn Sorcerer staves
Elga Wyman Cabalist staves

Llyn Barfog Market

Thomas Seyton Armor
Twm ap Gusg Armor
Gwalter ap Trevis Armor
Olvryn Wynford Blacksmith
Adwr ap Even Weaponsmith
Duncan Curan Arrow
Tewdwr ap Greid Armor
Twr ap Alsig

Ludlow Village

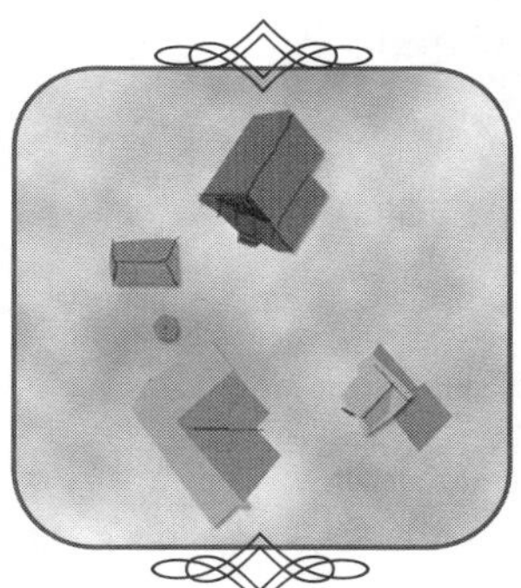

Seamstress Marie Quilted cloth armor
Dyemaster Cor Cloth dye
Aileen Wyatt Cloth dye
Seamstress Lynnet Robes
Yaren Stable Master
Andrya Wyman Cabalist staves
Haskis Mordoo
Guy Reed
Keenar Woedin
Yasminea Dardin
Pebble
Jazzy Piper
Trinny Piper
Greta Blandish Bard instruments
Maggie McClellan
Phyllis Darksky
Graham Mal'toinia
Bouncer Corwin
Master Sceley Smith
Apprentice Dunan
Sals Pew Staff
Farl Dalston Theurgist staves
Calldir Edyn Sorcerer staves
Eabae Egesa Wizard staves
Magus Aldred Mage Trainer
Master Odon Rogue Trainer
Varrin the Crier
Gillery Fletcher Arrows
Angus Bowman Bows
Crep Pew Thrusting
Fost Mra Siluric leather armor
Ochan Aethelhere Expensive various trade skill items
Nulb Pew Arrows
Stonemason Harwin

Outland Wharf

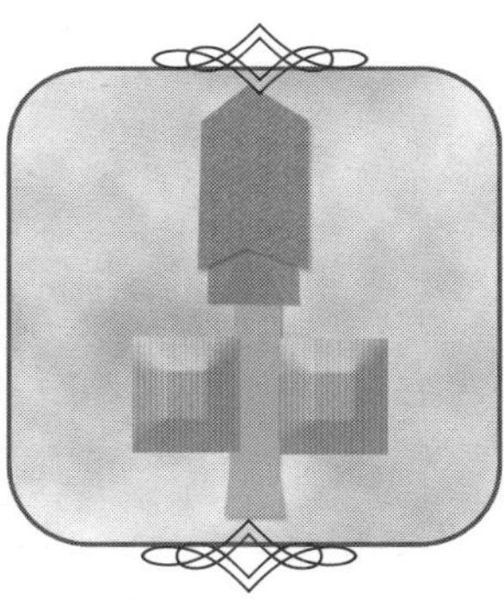

Boudron Fletcher Crossbow bolts
Allyn Fletcher Arrows
Bruna Fletcher Instrument Trainer
Swyno Pierce Weapons
Epheria Brighteye Bows
William Oswy Weapons
Wiceit Poisons
Dyemaster Kaly Dyes
Dyemaster Earh Dyes
Dyemaster Carye Dyes
Dyemaster Godric Dyes
Erstal Furlan Blacksmith
Leshorn Hael Armor

Prydwen Keep

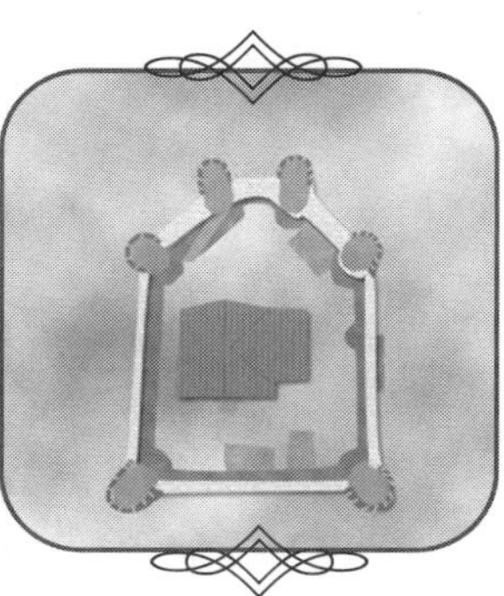

Ryce Scrydan Shields
Alburn Hale Slashing
Elvar Tambor Thrusting
Licrin the Crier
Sir Jerem
Brother Maynard Healer
Sister Gwendolyn Acolyte Trainer
Dyemaster Arthw cloth dye
Arleigh Penn cloth dye
Hugh Gallen Roman leather armor
Karn Graem Plate armor
Gram Ironhand Smith
Meran the Weaver
Atheleys Sy'Lian
Master Graent Fighter Trainer

Snowdonia Station

Blueheart Dyes
Dyemstr. Camdene Dyes
Aldys Meccus Boned studded armor
Staeven Bowman Bows
Edrea Fletcher Arrows
Gleda Fletcher Arrows
Thol Dunnin Smith
Cranly Plate armor
Ember Slashing
Jonalyn Thrusting
Elwyn Crushing
Odaro Hengist Healer
Boc Siluric leather armor
Cedd Aethelbert Shields
Aelda Chain armor
Elrigh

Swanton Keep

Glaeric Poisons
Master Brignun Infiltrator Trainer
Master Hanis Minstrel Trainer
Master Kel Mercenary Trainer
Magus Jeril Cabalist Trainer
Lieutenant Fisra Scout
Agrakor Fletcher Arrows
Dwira Fletcher Arrows
Ley Manton Polearms
Nia Leof Staff
Lynd Moidg Bows
Yorel Anbidian Tailoring Equipment
Brother Daniel Friar Trainer
Captain Presan Armsman Trainer
Jerad 2-handed weapons
Magus Sarun Sorcerer Trainer
Mistress Alarisa Wizard Trainer
Omis
Mistress Cessa Theurgist Trainer

West Downs

Aric Barlow Robes
Garvyn Kensington Studded armor
Lillian Brydger Smith
Radella Fletcher Arrows
Beria apprentice smith
Ainsley Fletcher Arrows
Aldrin Collyer Bows
Erwin Holdyn Quilted cloth armor
Farley Deagal Expensive various trade skill items
Edarg Stable Master
Master Gerol Healer
Stable boy Andryn

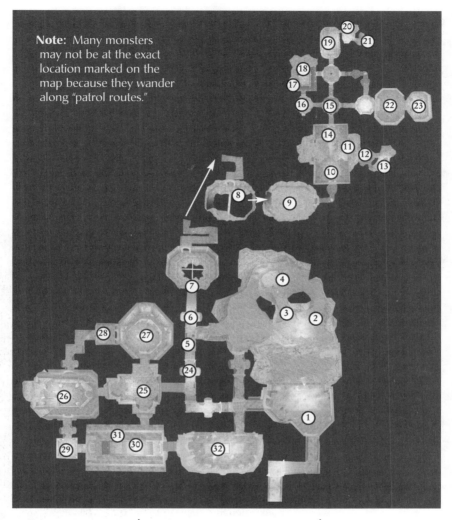

Note: Many monsters may not be at the exact location marked on the map because they wander along "patrol routes."

Stonehenge Barrows

1 Decaying Tomb Raider, Undead Retainer, Grave Goblin Whelp
2 Diseased Rat, Cave Goblin, Tunneler
3 Cave Hound, Diseased Rat, Cave Goblin Shaman
4 Grave Goblin, Grave Goblin Shaman, Cave Hound, Tunneler, Diseased Rat
5 Glowing Goo
6 Repentant Follower
7 Soul Harvester, Ectoplasm
8 Soul Harvester, Ectoplasm
9 Soul Harvester, Ectoplasm
10 Ectoplasm, Echo of Life, Tomb Keeper, Priestess of Purity, Templar Avenger
11 Scaled Fiend
12 Deep Goblin
13 Deep Goblin Blighter, Cave Hound
14 Dark Fire, Tomb Keeper
15 Tomb Wight, Ghoulic Vampire, Tome Wight, Creeping Ooze
16 Ghoulic Viper
17 Barrow Wight
18 Megalith Wight, King's Wight, Barrow Wight
19 Celtic Sepulcher Warrior, Celtic Lich, Ossuary Guardian
20 Celtic Lich
21 Celtic Lich, Ossuary Guardian
22 Sacrificial Soul, Petrified Grovewood, Skeletal Druid
23 Skeletal Druid, Sacrificial Soul
24 Redbone Skeleton, Glowing Goo, Repentant Follower
25 Spectral Essence, Malefic Phantom
26 Stone Sentinel, Pendragon Ardent, Pendrake
27 Spiritual Advisor, Malefic Phantom, Spectral Wizard, Wizard Lichas
28 Spiritual Advisor
29 Repentant Follower
30 Fallen Warrior
31 Vigilant Soul
32 Marrow Leach, Decayed Barbarian, Saxon Bone Skeleton, Reanimated Foe

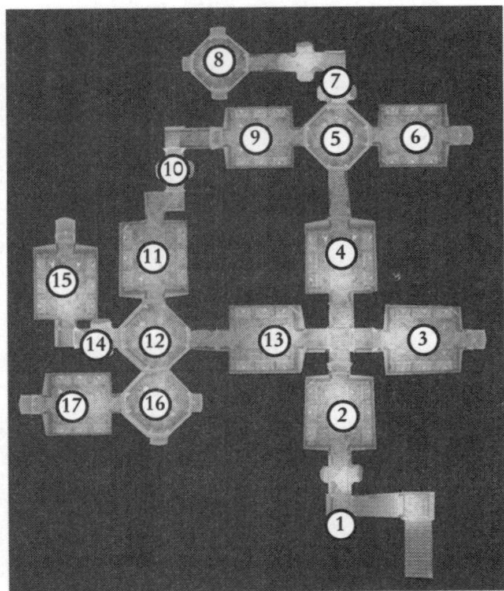

Catacombs of Corvoda

1 Legionarius
2 Legionarius, Decurion
3 Immunis, Vigilis
4 Manipularis, Centurio Manipularis
5 Signifier, Aqualifer, Imaginifer, Draconarius
6 Dux, Legatio, Praefectus, Vigilis
7 Praetorian Guard
8 Forgotten Emperor, Singular, Praetorian Guard
9 Tribune, Tribunus Laticlavicus
10 Cohorstalis
11 Optio, Praetor, Princep
12 Actarius
13 Cohorstalis
14 Cohorstalis
15 Centario Primus Ordines
16 Actarius, Cohorstalis
17 Centario Pilus Posterior, Vigilis

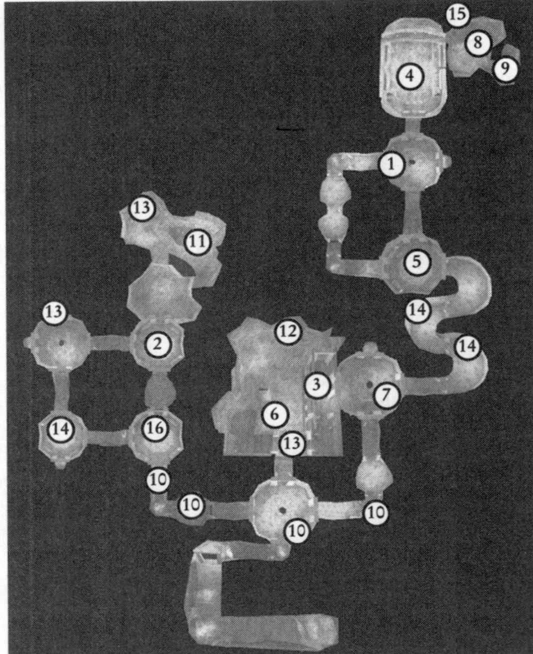

Keltoi Fogou

1 Gremlin, Keltoi Familiar, K. Ritualist
2 Gremlin, K. Visionary, K. Eremite
3 K. Banisher
4 K. Banisher, Gremlin, K. Familiar, Meurig, K. Spiritualist
5 K. Banisher, K. Ritualist, K. Familiar
6 K. Banisher, K. Visionary
7 K. Eremite
8 K. Familiar
9 K. Familiar, K. Spiritualist, Dai
10 K. Initiate, Gremlin
11 K. Recluse, Gwern
12 K. Ritualist
13 K. Visionary
14 K. Visionary, Gremlin
15 Muryan Emissary, K. Familiar
16 Gremlin

Tomb of Mithra

1 Botched Sacrifice, Lingering Shade
2 Cursed Believer, Living Entombed, Eternal Scream
3 Decaying Spirit
4 Doomed Minion, Insidious Whisper
5 Dreadful Cadaver, Putrid Sacrificer, Undead Poacher
6 Favonius Facilis, Malevolent Disciple, Virilis
7 Haunting Gloom
8 Haunting Gloom, Decaying Spirit
9 Lingering Shade
12 Lingering Shade, Undead Builder, Living Entombed, Doomed Minion
13 Menacing Presence
14 Sacrificial Slave, Botched Sacrifice, Undead Builder
15 Spiteful Wraith
16 Suffering Apparition
17 Tortured Soul, Unfortunate Pragmatic, Rotting Tombraider
10 Tortured Souls, Haunting Gloom
11 Undead Builder
18 Undead Guardsman, Forgotten Promise

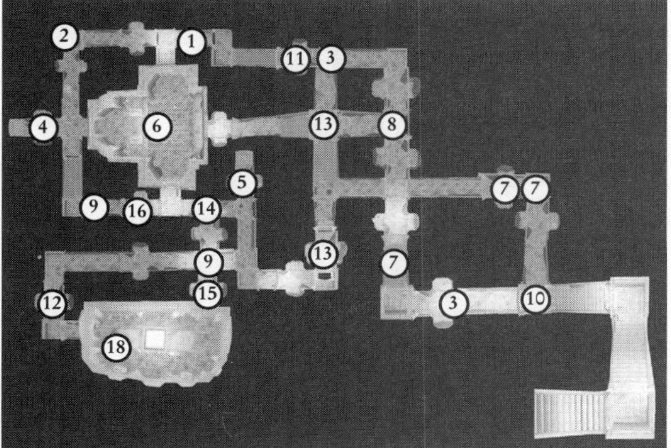

Tepok's Mine

1 Apprentice Beastmaster
2 Cave Fisher
3 Cave Fisher, Goblin, Gob. Crawler, Gob. Patrol Leader
4 Fisher Hatchling, Cave Bear Cub
5 Goblin
6 Goblin Apprentice, Goblin Watcher
7 Goblin Beastmaster, Cave Bear
8 Goblin Beastmaster, Fisher Hatchling, Cave Bear Cub, Angler, Cave Lion, Goblin
9 Goblin Cleaner, Overseer Tepok
10 Goblin Crawler
11 Goblin Watcher, Stalker, Goblin Apprentice
12 Goblin, Cave Lion, Cave Bear
13 Goblin, Goblin Monitor, Juggernaut
14 Juggernaut
15 Morvel Glyne, Tuder Glyne
16 Undead Miner
17 Emissary Sebian, Sarel Sebian
18 Whisperer, Cave Bear, Cave Lion, Goblin

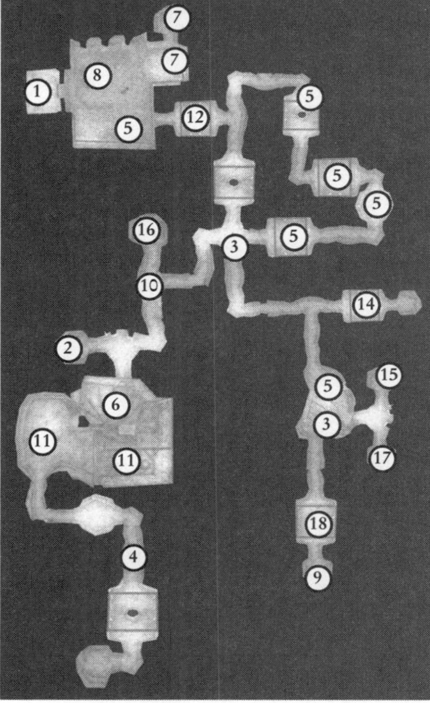

Realm of Hibernia

Hibernia is a beautiful land where valor and wisdom are equally valued. Their brand of civilization relies less on conquering nature and more on learning what it has to teach.

Races & Classes

GUARDIAN

The Way of Arms is the way of the warrior — valiantly wielding your weapons in battle, specializing in melee combat, and protecting the Realm of Hibernia from its foes. As a Guardian, you will be able to learn many weapon skills and styles as well as armor and shield skills.

As a Guardian, at fifth level, you must choose your Path to follow: Focus, to become a Hero; Essence, to become a Champion; or Harmony, to become a Blademaster. Heroes can specialize in almost all weapon types and armors. Champions receive the ability to wield large two-handed weapons and learn the use of magic. Blademasters are specialists in the use of two weapons at once, as well as evasion of enemy attacks.

Celtic Guardian

As a Celtic Guardian, the Way of Arms is a good one for you. You may follow any of the three Paths.

The Celts have a balanced array of abilities. Not the strongest or the quickest, they benefit from having a little of everything.

Firbolg Guardian

Only two Paths are available to Firbolg Guardians: Focus, to become a Hero; or Harmony, to become a Blademaster. The Path of Essence is not open to you. As a Firbolg, the Way of Arms is a good one for you. Your high Strength will give you an advantage in armed combat.

Elven Guardian

As an Elven Guardian, the only Path available to you is that of Essence, to become a Champion. The Way of Arms will be tough for you. Your race, with limited Strength, does not find melee combat easy.

Lurikeen Guardian

As a Lurikeen Guardian, the only Path available to you is that of Essence, to become a Champion. As a Lurikeen, the Way of Arms will be extremely tough for you. Your race, with limited Strength, does not find melee combat easy.

MAGICIAN

The Way of Magic is the way of arcane research, spellcasting, and raw power. Magicians in Hibernia harness the raw forces of primeval power and utilize them in many different ways. Beginning characters on the Way of Magic are known as Magicians.

As a Magician, at fifth level you must choose which Path you wish to follow: the Path of Focus, to become an Eldritch; the Path of Essence, to become an Enchanter; or the Path of Harmony, to become a Mentalist. Eldritches specialize in powerful damage spells that can affect multiple enemies. Enchanters learn spells to enhance friendly players' armor and weapons, as well as a few damage spells. Mentalists learn special mind-control and damage spells.

Firbolg cannot become Magicians.

Elven Magician

As an Elf, you make an outstanding spellcaster, no matter which Path you choose.

Elves have a natural understanding of the ancient ways of magic, but their lack of Strength and Constitution can make it difficult to be a solo Magician.

Lurikeen Magician

As a Lurikeen, you will make an outstanding spellcaster, no matter which Path you choose.

Lurikeens have two main advantages when it comes to embarking on a career as a Magician. They have a naturally high Dexterity, which allows them to cast spells rapidly. They also are so small that from a distance they are difficult to see. In Realm vs. Realm combat, a Magician who can avoid being seen, lives longer.

Celtic Magician

As a Celtic Magician, you must follow the Path of Harmony, where you will become an average Mentalist.

In general, you want to avoid being "average." Since people try to be the best they can be, the "average" character tends to really be the "worst."

NATURALIST

The Way of Nature is the way of the forest, the glen, and the beasts that inhabit them. As a character that chooses this way, blending into and harnessing the primal force that is nature is your primary ability.

As a Naturalist, at fifth level you must choose which Path to follow: the Path of Focus, to become a Warden; the Path of Essence, to become a Bard; or the Path of Harmony, to become a Druid. Wardens are the armed protectors of nature, and as such receive weapon skills and limited bow skills, as well as magic spells that enable them to grasp the power of nature. Bards are the loremasters of the Realm of Hibernia, and as such learn several musical abilities which benefit those around them, as well as basic knowledge of armed combat. Druids are the healers and helpers of the Realm; they receive enhancement spells and their healing spells are unmatched in Hibernia.

Firbolg Naturalist

As a Firbolg, you will make an outstanding Druid and Warden, and an average Bard.

Firbolgs have a natural Strength that makes many aspects of life much easier for them.

However, their size is nothing but a liability when it comes to Realm vs. Realm play. The bigger you are, the harder it is for you to hit. Naturalists, by being jacks-of-all-trades, are more vulnerable to attacks than their brawnier counterparts.

Celtic Naturalist

As a Celt, you will make an average Druid and Warden, and a good Bard.

As always, it's usually less frustrating in the long run to try to build a race/class combination that has the highest potential for advancement. Thus, Bard is the best choice for a Celtic Naturalist. All races start with the same base Charisma, and with the higher DEX and smaller profile, they make better Bards. Smaller targets with faster cast.

STALKER

The Way of Stealth relies on your Dexterity and Quickness to avoid attack, avoid detection and accomplish your tasks; it uses the not-so-obvious methods of distraction and hiding.

As a Stalker, at fifth level you must choose which Path you will follow: the Path of Focus, to become a Ranger, or the Path of Essence, to become a Nightshade. (Celts cannot become Nightshades.) Rangers utilize your skills to become at home in the outdoors by moving undetected, by tracking enemy players, and by mastering the Hibernian recurved bow. Nightshades are Stalkers who learn magic spells to enhance your sneaking and hiding abilities, and become proficient at the art of moving undetected into enemy territory.

Firbolg cannot become Stalkers.

Elven Stalker

As an Elf, you will make an decent Ranger, and with your innate magical affinity, you will make a good Nightshade.

Lurikeen Stalker

As a Lurikeen, with your innate magical affinity and high Dexterity and Quickness, you will make an outstanding Nightshade, and a great Ranger.

Celtic Stalker

As a Celt, you will make an average Ranger.

Unless you have a good reason to want to be a Celt and a Stalker (and role-play is a good reason), it's best to avoid this combination.

HORSE ROUTES

For a description of how to rent and ride a horse, see **Horse Routes**, page 372.

STABLE	STABLE MASTER	TICKETS TO
Ardagh	Edricar	Tir Urphost Connla
Ardee	Freagus	East Lough Derg
Connla	Aelerogh	Druim Ligen Innis Carthaig Culraid
Culraid	Mulgraighy	Innis Carthaig Connla
Druim Cain	Chuchear	Tir na mBeo Druim Ligen
DruimLigen	Ullios	Connla
East Lough Derg	Rheagul	Druim Cain Ardagh
Howth	Pheuloc	Innis Carthaig Mag Mell
Innis Carthaig	Breachus	Tir na mBeo Culraid Druim Cain
Mag Mell	Rumdor	Howth
Tir Urphost	Luergor	Ardagh
Tirn Na mBeo	Truichon	Druim Ligen

Hero

Races	
Celt / Firbolg	

Skills	
1	Blades
1	Blunt
1	Piercing
2	Parry
4	Shields
5	Celtic Spear
10	Large Weaponry

Abilities	
1	Staves
1	Cloth Armor
1	Leather Armor
1	Sprint
1	Small Shields
1	Reinforced Armor
2	Evade I
4	Medium Shields
10	Large Shields
10	Large Weapons
11	Protect I
12	Intercept
15	Scale Armor
15	Shortbows
15	Initiate of the Hunt
20	Protect II
25	Member of the Hunt
27	Protect III
35	Leader of the Hunt
45	Master of the Hunt

Styles
Blades
Blunt
Piercing
Celtic Spear
Large Weapons
Shields

Heroes form the basic fighting class of Hibernia. With this class, there's no doubt that you are a tank, pure and simple. You take damage so that the casters don't have to. You're equally comfortable wielding a long spear, a great 2-handed hammer, or handling a 1-handed weapon and shield. The only downside to playing this class is that you never, ever get to play at magic. The closest you get is being able to use some enhanced weaponry.

The Best Part: You can safely say you know no fear when fighting mobs. Beat on them to get their attention, knock them down, then let them beat on you to give your casters time to kill them with magic.

The Worst Part: It's boring compared to many classes. And having to constantly work to keep your weapons and armor updated is expensive!

Race Choices:

Celtic. Severely lacking in Strength, but quicker and more dexterous than Firbolgs. This means a Celtic Hero hits more often, but for less damage. Slight advantage for PvE play, since more frequent hits help keep aggro.

Firbolg. Massive STR, but a good bit slower, and their lower DEX makes them easier to hit than their Celtic counterparts. Firbolgs outsize Celtics, so they tend to stand out more on the battlefield.

Stat Choices: No matter which race you select, you'll want to boost STR, DEX and CON. The question to answer is whether you want to boost an already-high stat or even out the racial differences.

- *STR:* Affects damage done with your weapon.
- *DEX:* Affects your parry/evade/block.
- *QUI:* Affects how often you land hits and plays a role in how often you evade.
- *CON:* Gives you HP (important for a tank).

Spec/Weapon Choices: Your weapons are your specialty, along with a couple of defensive skills.

- *Blade:* Well-balanced weapons that fall somewhere in between Blunt and Pierce weapons as far as speed and damage go. You get a variety of combat styles — attack speed Debuffs, Stuns, and defense bonuses. Availability of magically enhanced blades is good. Keep in mind that you need high STR to get the full benefit of any damage bonuses.
- *Blunt:* Slow and heavy-hitting. Few magical versions exist, but Blunts tend to be good against many of the creatures you face in this realm, as well as armored foes from other realms. Many of the attacks you get with Blunt have the ability to stun your opponents.
- *Pierce:* Good in conjunction with Shield if you're looking for a 1-handed combination. You'll get a lot of defense bonuses from Piercing weapons, and get more styles early on due to faster attack speeds. DEX also helps your Piercing weapons.
- *Shield:* An all-important, passive defense skill if you're using 1-handed weapons. Shields are also especially effective at blocking archers' arrows and casters' Bolts. You get bonus damage and Stun styles with this spec line. If you get your Shield high, you'll be in great demand for RvR.
- *Guard/Protect:* Gaining some of either skill helps you protect casters in a group or RvR setting. Not really necessary for soloing, though. A person can only be Guarded by one player, but someone can be Protected by multiple players. Protect also helps you maintain aggro instead of someone else who's doing a lot of damage or healing.
- *Intercept:* This is the equivalent of being in the secret service and throwing yourself in front of a bullet. With this skill, you can and take the hit for a friendly target.

- *Parry:* Parrying helps you use your weapon to deflect attacks.
- *Spear:* Spears are a very powerful two-handed weapon which can only effectively be used by Heroes.

If you use Shield, keep it as high as possible. Concentrate your other points mainly on your chosen weapon. It doesn't hurt to give Parry a boost every once in a while, just to deflect a bit more damage. As a tank, you'll see plenty of it. Anything you can do to assist your Healer helps.

Big Mistakes to Avoid in Character Creation: Spending spec points too early. Save them until Level 5, or even Level 10.

Deciding What You Want Your Role to Be: You don't have much leeway here. Your job is to protect the casting classes and knock a few mobs silly in the process.

Plotting Your Future: Decide before Level 10 whether you're going to pursue 2-handed weapons or a 1-handed weapon and shield. This is important, because at 10, you can divert your training points in several different directions.

Grouping:

- Your function as a tank is to soak up the damage and help the mages survive so that they can cast. While they throw magic, you draw aggro.
- Know your attacks and use the best one for any given situation.
- Though you're no spec'ed archer, you can sometimes pull using a short bow.
- You travel well with Bards. They can speed up travel and stitch you up fairly quickly during and in between battles. If you don't want to *take* more damage than you dish out, this is a good pairing.
- Try to join a group that can hunt things that drop what you want, like a specific weapon or armor type.
- If you join a group that hunts high-conning mobs, make sure you've got another melee fighter onboard so that you can team up.
- Keep your weapons and armor in the best condition you can. Weaponsmithing is not a bad side hobby, and it gives you a break from the tedium of combat.
- You and another Hero with Guard can actually Guard each other and save your Healer some time and Power. The one thing to remember is that you need to stick fairly close together. One of you can be the main tank and puller, while the other manages Taunts and helps draw aggro off the main crowd controller.

Soloing:

- You're an awesome soloer right off the bat, as long as you don't fight anything that casts spells or cons too high. Before Level 5, kill anything that cons blue, maybe even green, and loot everything.
- Buy yourself a good weapon as soon as you can, and hunt creatures that drop what you're looking for.
- Try to hunt monsters that travel alone and are most vulnerable to your weapon type.
- Small shields work best for soloing and can stun single opponents on a consistent basis.
- You are better off saving your Endurance and styles as long as possible. At the end, you may be able to chain together several attacks for a kill.

Realm Versus Realm:

- Being very highly spec'ed in Shield is an advantage in RvR play. You can effectively ward off a lot of arrow and bolt damage.
- As in groups, protect your casters.
- Something a little fun and different you can do in RvR is rush the enemy archers and casters. You don't necessarily want to kill them as much as you just want to keep them from drawing arrows or casting spells. Toy with them as long as you can afford to, or as long as you can keep up with their certain retreat.
- Before going into RvR, try to find bonus items that give you resistance to magical attacks.

Beginner's Tips:

- Heater shields are good for battles against multiple enemies, since you can defend against several of them at once.
- You can get scale armor at Level 15. That's a good goal to shoot for.
- With both armor and weapons, try to use whatever cons blue or orange to you.

- Don't forget about bonus items that increase your base stats or resistances.
- Your chance to block arrows from a same-level archer with your shield is 30%. This is modified by Shield spec, quality and condition of the shield, and the Engage skill. You have a chance to block multiple archers with a larger shield.

Advanced Techniques:

- Spirit of the Hunt Ability. You shapeshift into a stag-headed huntsman with increased Hit Points (from +20% at 15th level up to +50% after 45th level). The ability lasts for 30 seconds. At the end of 30 seconds, your maximum Hit Points return to normal, and if your current HP are more than your normal pre-buffed max, your current HP are set back to match your normal max.

Hero Styles

Abbreviations. *Headers:* **F**atigue **C**ost / **B**onus **D**amage / **B**onus **t**o **H**it. *In table:* **L**ow / **M**edium / **H**igh / **V**ery **H**igh / **D**efensive **B**onus (for you, on next round) / **D**efensive **P**enalty (to you, on next round) / **A**ttack **S**peed **R**eduction / **M**ovement **R**eduction (for target)

Blades

Lvl	Style	FC	BD	BtH	Prerequisites / Other Notes
2	Shining Blade	H	M	–	
4	Return Blade	L	M	M	Prereq: blocked target / Low ASR
6	Taunting Blade	M	L	–	Attempt to taunt target; Med DP
8	Enervating Blade	M	–	–	Attempt to turn away target; Med DB
10	Glowing Blade	M	M	M	Prereq: beside target / Med MR
12	Lunging Blade	M	M	M	Prereq: Return Blade / Low Bleed; Low DB
15	Auroric Blade	L	M	M	Prereq: Glowing Blade / Low ASR
18	Fire Blade	H	M	L	Low DP
21	Horizon Blade	L	M	M	Prereq: blocked target / Low Stun; Low DB
25	Kinetic Blade	M	H	M	Prereq: Lunging Blade
29	Dancing Blade	L	M	H	Prereq: Horizon Blade / Med Bleed
34	Revenging Blade	M	M	M	Prereq: behind target / Med DP
39	Spectrum Blade	M	M	L	Prereq: Fire Blade / High ASR; Med DB
44	Prismatic Blade	L	H	M	Prereq: Kinetic Blade*
50	Brilliant Blade	M	H	VH	Prereq: target fumbled

*(may change to Prismatic Blade)

Celtic Spear

Lvl	Style	FC	BD	BtH	Prerequisites / Other Notes
2	Hunter's Spear	H	M	–	
4	Entrap	L	M	M	Prereq: evaded target / Low Bleed
6	Hunter's Boon	M	M	M	Prereq: behind target / Low MR; Med DP
8	Hunter's Barb	M	–	–	Attempt to turn away target; High DB
10	Forest Spear	M	L	M	Attempt to taunt target; Med DP
12	Hunter's Largess	M	M	M	Prereq: Entrap / Med ASR; Low DP
15	Hunter's Lance	H	M	M	Med DP
18	Javelin	M	M	M	Prereq: Hunter's Boon / Med Bleed
21	Tracking Spear	L	M	M	Prereq: evaded target / Med Stun; Low DB
25	Hunter's Gift	M	M	H	Prereq: Javelin / Med ASR; Low DB
29	Hawk's Talon	M	–	L	Prereq: Tracking Spear / Low DB
34	Eagle Talon	H	M	L	
39	Wyvern Talon	M	M	M	Prereq: Hawk's Talon / High Bleed
44	Dragon Talon	M	L	M	Prereq: beside target
50	Cuchulainn's	M	M	H	Prereq: Dragon Talon / High Bleed

Blunt

See the Blademaster's styles, page 146, for this style.

Piercing

See the Blademaster's styles, page 146, for this style.

Large Weapons

Lvl	Style	FC	BD	BtH	Prerequisites / Other Notes
2	Celtic Might	H	M	–	
4	Celtic Rage	L	H	M	Prereq: parried target / Low DB
6	Celtic Fury	M	L	M	Attempt to taunt target; Med DP
8	Hibernian Wrath	M	–	–	Attempt to turn away target; High DB
10	Hibernian Force	M	M	M	Prereq: beside target / Low Bleed; Low DP
12	Hibernian Vigor	M	M	M	Prereq: Celtic Rage / Low Stun; Low DB
15	Domination	H	M	L	Low DP
18	Obliteration	M	M	M	Prereq: Hibernian Force / Med ASR
21	Frontal Assault	H	M	M	Prereq: in front of target / Med MR
25	Gigantic Blow	L	VH	H	Prereq: Hibernian Vigor
29	Ultimate Recovery	M	H	M	Prereq: target parried you / Med Stun; Low DP
34	Demolish	M	M	H	Prereq: Obliteration / Med DB
39	Shatter	M	M	M	Prereq: target blocked you / High Bleed; Low DB
44	Devastate	L	M	M	Prereq: Ultimate Recovery / High ASR; large DB
50	Annihilation	M	M	VH	Prereq: behind target / High Stun; Med DP

Shields

Lvl	Style	FC	BD	BtH	Prerequisites / Other Notes
3	Numb	M	M	–	Low Stun
8	Stun	M	M	–	Prereq: blocked target / Low Stun
13	Disable	M	M	–	Prereq: beside target / Med Stun
18	Incapacitate	H	M	–	Prereq: blocked target / Med Stun; Med DB
23	Paralyze	M	M	–	Prereq: behind target / Med Stun
29	Bash	M	M	–	Prereq: blocked target / Med Stun
35	Mangle	M	M	–	Prereq: beside target / High Stun
42	Slam	VH	M	–	High Stun
50	Brutalize	L	M	–	Prereq: blocked target / High Stun

Champion

Races		Abilities	
Celt / Lurikeen / Elf		1	Staves
Skills		1	Cloth Armor
1	Blades	1	Leather Armor
1	Blunt	1	Small Shields
1	Piercing	1	Sprint
2	Parry	1	Reinforced Armor
4	Large Weaponry	2	Evade I
5	Valor (Magic)	4	Large Weapons
5	Shields	5	Medium Shields
Styles		15	Protect I
	Blades	18	Intercept
	Blunt	20	Scale Armor
	Piercing	20	Evade I
	Large Weaponry	25	Protect II

The Champion is a mix between a fighter and a mage, possessing both melee skills and some magical ability. This class's Valor line of spells includes Debuffs (STR/CON, DEX/QUI, and attack speed), a Nuke and Snare.

The Best Part: For anyone who enjoys something more than hack and slash, the Champion has many tools. It takes a bit more thought than to be a Champion than any other melee class. Additionally, it's the only melee class available to Elves and Lurikeens, and you get to carry a huge sword.

The Worst Part: Champions are much weaker than other melee classes, have fewer Hit Points and deliver less damage output. Unfortunately, Champions don't receive CON as a primary stat (like other melee classes). Therefore, it doesn't raise with leveling, and you have to rely on bonus equipment.

Race Choices:

Celtic. CON and STR is higher for this race than an Elf or a Lurikeen. However, DEX and QUI are not as high.

Elf. Most intelligent Champion race. QUI and DEX are higher as well. CON for this race is low, though. All Elves should put at least 10 points into this stat to compensate for the racial difference.

Lurikeen. Highest QUI and DEX for any available Champion race, and fairly intelligent as well. CON is low, so all Lurikeen Champions should put at least 10 points into this stat.

Stat Choices:

- *CON:* This is the most important stat for a Champion, since it is not innate and not granted as you progress in level. Since CON is vital for any melee class, put at least 10 points or more into it.
- *STR:* Your STR affects damage output. As a melee class, you'll find this stat very important as well. However, since it is raised automatically as you level, you might make better use of your points by putting them into QUI, especially if you're Celtic.

Weapon Choices: See Spec Paths.

Spec Paths: Basically, your path boils down to offense or defense, so figure out which playstyle suits you best.

- *Large Weapons:* Want to swing heavily and mightily? If you go with this, you have the skill points to fully spec Large Weapons as well as Valor, and enough left to boost Parry. This makes you a formidable damage dealer. However, your only defense is Parry, unless you group with a Shield-specialized Champion or hero. When you reach 50 in Large Weapons, you receive Annihilation, a Stun with a back positional component.
- *Shield/1-handed Weapon:* As a Champion specialized in Shield, you're much better at defense, but your damage output is less than desirable. Not only will the 1-handed weapon do less damage, but you also probably won't have the points available to fully specialize in your weapon. This can lower your damage output even more. However, Shield helps you block attacks and take less damage, as well as Guard other party members. The anytime Stun at 42 in Shield is very handy as well.

Big Mistakes to Avoid in Character Creation: The biggest mistake a Champion can make is not putting points into CON.

Deciding What You Want Your Role to Be: Kill things mightily and debuff your opponents. Or kill things, defend yourself and your groupmates, and debuff your opponents.

Plotting Your Future: The main decision you need to make during the first 10 Levels is whether to go with Large Weapons or a 1-handed weapon and Shield. Either way, put as many points as you can into Valor as you level to take advantage of more powerful Debuffs and damage spells.

Grouping:

- A Champion is rarely the primary tank for a group, though you can serve in that role if needed. You can serve as a great melee supporter, however, providing additional damage or protecting the primary tank with your shield.
- If you've spec'ed Shield, use Guard to protect another melee fighter in your party, or protect a caster by keeping mobs off of him or her.
- Guard enables you to try and block an attack for someone in your group. You must have a shield equipped, and the person you are guarding must be relatively close to you. Additionally, you cannot block someone behind you. Every time you block an attack, your Endurance suffers.
- Protect is a similar ability that allows you to take aggro away from a caster in your group. You can use it on a member of your party to attract the attention of the mob, relieving your caster. Typically, you'll use this mostly on healers (they generate the most aggro). You get Protect 1 at Level 15 and Protect 2 at Level 25.

Soloing:

- The most crucial element of soloing is your equipment. If your armor and weapons don't con yellow or orange, you can't solo yellows without difficulty. Even one blue piece of armor can be a risk while soloing yellow mobs.
- Pick your mobs carefully and stick to ones that yield a bonus to your weapon. If you're using blades, stick to furry creatures. For blunt weapons, fight skeletal or rock-based mobs.
- Avoid mobs that cast Debuffs or spells.
- Pick fights in which you have an advantage.
- One good method of hunting is to pull with a Nuke and then snare. This gives you time to reload and re-cast your Nuke.

Realm Versus Realm:

- A Champion that rushes headfirst into battle usually ends up in the dirt screaming for a Rez. You're really best suited for the outskirts of the battlefield. Hang out there and selectively take out opponents. Spellcasters and archers fall quickly, but you can have a difficult time with a melee class from another realm. Choosing opponents wisely is the key to playing a Champion effectively in RvR.
- Even if you pick Large Weapons, put at least 7 points into Shield to gain the Engage ability for fighting archers. This enables you to block about 90% of attacks from one opponent. You must have a shield, and you also forfeit all attacks while Engaging.
- If the mob takes damage, Engage fails.
- Each time you block an attack while Engaging, Endurance goes down.
- If an archer attempts to shoot you, block his arrows until you can get close enough to take him down with melee.

Beginner's Tips:

- When choosing your skills, it is best to decide on a weapon early on (Large Weapons or a 1-handed weapon and Shield). This lets you concentrate on your skill points. Spreading them too thinly can limit effectiveness.
- Put as many points as you can spare into Valor to take advantage of the strongest spells available to you.
- Unlike Albion, you do not need to put points into Blades or Blunt to be effective in large weapons. These skills are independent of one another. (Many players waste unnecessary points in Blade and/or Blunt weapons.)
- When you join a group, first thing you should do is make sure that you are guarding the primary melee fighter and/or protecting your healer or caster.

Advanced Techniques:

- Make good use of your combination styles. Positional styles are usually easy to accomplish, and the damage gained from them can be tremendous. Reactionary styles are very difficult to use, but when used successfully, can be very effective.
- Your chance to block arrows from a same-level archer with your shield is 30%. This is modified by Shield spec, quality and condition of the shield, and the Engage skill.

Champion Styles

Abbreviations. *Headers:* **F**atigue **C**ost / **B**onus **D**amage / **B**onus **t**o **H**it. *In table:* **L**ow / **M**edium / **H**igh / **V**ery **H**igh / **D**efensive **B**onus (for you, on next round) / **D**efensive **P**enalty (to you, on next round) / **A**ttack **S**peed **R**eduction / **M**ovement **R**eduction (for target)

Blades

See the Blademaster's styles, page 146, for this style.

Blunt

See the Blademaster's styles, page 146, for these styles.

Piercing

Lvl	Style	FC	BD	BtH	Prerequisites / Other Notes
2	Dragonfly	H	M	–	
4	Wasp's Sting	L	M	M	Prereq: behind target / Low Bleed
6	Bumblebee's Sting	M	L	M	Attempt to taunt target; High DP
8	Hornet's Sting	M	M	M	Prereq: Wasp's Sting / Low ASR
10	Scorpion	M	–	–	Attempt to turn away target; Med DB
12	Black Widow	H	M	L	Low DP
15	Tarantula	L	M	M	Prereq: blocked target / Med Bleed; Low DB
18	Sidewinder	M	M	M	Prereq: Black Widow
21	Copperhead	M	M	M	Prereq: beside target / Med MR; Low DP
25	Diamondback	L	M	M	Prereq: evaded target / Med Stun; Med DB
29	Viper's Bite	M	H	M	Prereq: Copperhead / Med DB
34	Asp's Bite	L	M	VH	Prereq: Tarantula / Med ASR; Med DB
39	Cobra's Bite	L	H	H	Prereq: Sidewinder / Low DB
44	Dragonspider	M	M	M	Prereq: Diamondback / High Bleed
50	Wyvern's Bite	M	VH	H	Prereq: Asp's Bite / High Bleed; Low DB

Large Weapons

Lvl	Style	FC	BD	BtH	Prerequisites / Other Notes
2	Celtic Might	H	M	–	
4	Celtic Rage	L	H	M	Prereq: parried target / Low DB
6	Celtic Fury	M	L	M	Attempt to taunt target; Med DP
8	Hibernian Wrath	M	–	–	Attempt to detaunt target; High DB
10	Hibernian Force	M	M	M	Prereq: beside target / Low Bleed; Low DP
12	Hibernian Vigor	M	M	M	Prereq: Celtic Rage / Low Stun; Low DB
15	Domination	H	M	L	Low DP
18	Obliteration	M	M	M	Prereq: Hibernian Force / Med ASR
21	Frontal Assault	H	M	M	Prereq: in front of target / Med MR
25	Gigantic Blow	L	VH	H	Prereq: Hibernian Vigor
29	Ultimate Recovery	M	H	M	Prereq: target parried you / Med Stun; Low DP
34	Demolish	M	M	H	Prereq: Obliteration / Med DB
39	Shatter	M	M	M	Prereq: target blocked you / High Bleed; Low DB
44	Devastate	L	M	M	Prereq: Ultimate Recovery / High ASR; large DB
50	Annihilation	M	M	VH	Prereq: behind target / High Stun; Med DP

Champion Spells

Valor

*STR/CON debuff. You must wait 20 seconds before casting one of these spells again. (This Debuff is **quadrupled** against Buffs, rather than just doubled.)*

Skill........................Valor Dmg Type...............Body
Casting Time ....Shout Range.....................1000
Duration ....60 sec.

Lvl	Spell	Cost	Debuff
2	Debility*	2P	6
6	Greater Debility*	4P	7.5
10	Atony*	6P	10
16	Greater Atony*	10P	12
24	Enervation*	15P	16
31	Greater Enervation*	19P	19
39	Infirmity*	25P	23
49	Greater Infirmity	32P	27.5

*DEX/QUI debuff. You must wait 20 seconds before casting one of these spells again. This Debuff is **quadrupled** against Buffs, rather than just doubled.)*

Skill........................Valor Dmg Type...............Body
Casting Time ....Shout Range.....................1000
Duration ....60 sec.

Lvl	Spell	Cost	Debuff
3	Submission*	3P	6.5
7	Greater Submission*	5P	8
11	Surrender*	7P	10
15	Greater Surrender*	9P	12
20	Capitulation*	12P	14.5
28	Greater Capitulation*	17P	18
37	Resignation*	23P	21.5
47	Greater Resignation	30P	26

Debuffs attack speed by (Debuff %). You must wait 20 seconds before casting one of these spells again.

Skill........................Valor Dmg Type...............Body
Casting Time ....Shout Range.....................1000
Duration ....60 sec.

Lvl	Spell	Cost	Debuff %
4	Minor Demoralization*	3P	6%
8	Lesser Demoralization*	5P	7%
13	Demoralization*	8P	8.5%
19	Major Demoralization*	12P	10.5%
27	Greater Demoralization*	17P	13%
36	Superior Demoralization*	23P	15.5%
48	Ultimate Demoralization	31P	19%

DD. You must wait 15 seconds before casting one of these spells again.

Skill........................Valor Dmg Type...............Body
Casting Time ....Shout Range.....................1500
Duration ....Inst.

Lvl	Spell	Cost	Dmg
1	Blast of Courage*	2P	4
5	Blast of Bravery*	4P	16
9	Blast of Boldness*	6P	27
14	Blast of Galliance*	9P	38
23	Blast of Defiance*	14P	61
30	Blast of Valiance*	19P	78
40	Blast of Heroism*	25P	103
50	Blast of the Champion	33P	129

Snare: Enemy's speed debuffed to 60% of original movement (see page 367 for PvE/RvR limitations). You must wait 20 seconds before casting one of these spells again.

Skill........................Valor Dmg Type..............Spirit
Casting Time ....Shout Range.....................1500

Lvl	Spell	Cost	Dur
12	Slowness*	8P	51 sec.
17	Languor*	10P	59 sec.
22	Lumber*	13P	68 sec.
32	Sluggishness*	20P	86 sec.
42	Crawl	27P	1.7 min.

Blademaster

Races	Abilities	
Celt / Firbolg	1	Staves
Skills	1	Cloth Armor
1 Blades	1	Leather Armor
1 Blunt	1	Sprint
1 Piercing	1	Small Shields
2 Parry	1	Reinforced Armor
5 Celtic Dual	2	Evade I
5 Shields	5	Medium Shields
Styles	10	Shortbows
Blades	10	Evade I
Blunt	15	Protect I
Piercing	15	Evade II
Celtic Dual	19	Intercept
Shields	20	Triple Wield
	23	Protect II
	25	Evade III
	32	Protect III

Blademasters are nimble on their feet, light and good with a blade. As easily as they can learn to dice up and evade enemies with a sword and shield, Blademasters can also choose to swing two weapons or draw a bow. This class is a true tank, skilled in the art of evasion and dedicated to protecting the magic-casting members of the group. If you're a Blademaster, you don't really need to concern yourself with the petty issues of encumbrance, Power or a lack of inventory space.

The Best Part: You're strong, and you take what you want. A Blademaster knows no fear, especially when backed by Buffs and Heals from others in the group. You can solo or group with ease.

The Worst Part: You don't get to play with magic at all, and the art of slicing and dicing can get tedious after a while. Plus, supporting your weapon and armor habit can get expensive. You're also limited to reinforced armor.

Race Choices:

Celtic. This is the average race of the realm, okay in all respects, but excellent at nothing. You'll need to boost the stats in which you want to shine.

Firbolg. This race is a bit larger (less desirable for RvR) and stronger. If you want to be the big brute on the PvE battlefield, you could go with a Firbolg.

Stat Choices: You have no magic, so INT, END and the other intangible stats really don't matter much to you. The one exception is CON, if you want to solo and are concerned about conserving HP in battle. What you choose here should really reflect what type of weapon you want to use.

- *STR:* Affects damage you do with your weapon, as well as your encumbrance. You probably don't have anything to worry about, especially as a Firbolg. Rises as you progress in level, but it's still a good idea to put in 10 points, especially if you're the weaker race.
- *CON:* Determines HP. Though you're more of a damage dealer than a damage sponge, you may want to put 10 points into this.
- *DEX:* Assists you in defending yourself; needed most when you're using a shield and want to dodge hits.
- *QUI:* Affects how fast you swing your weapon. If you're Dual Wielding, you'll need more points here (at least 10) to speed up your swing.

Weapon Choices:

- Get something that challenges your skills and get rid of it once you've mastered it (i.e., things that have conned blue for a while). Early on, this means buy weapons and armor that con orange to you. While they'll wear out more quickly and pose more risk than yellow items, you get more experience and you won't outgrow them quite as often.
- Always try to find a weapon that does the most damage, especially if you're a Blade and Shield player. Finally, remember that player-crafted weapons are of much better quality than NPC-sold weapons. You might even consider taking up Weaponcrafting in order to fund your habits.
- Going for Blade and Shield or Celtic Dual and Parry really boils down to whether you want to act more offensively or defensively. You really need to focus on one or the other to gain the full effect of specialization. Either way, try to always get the most bang for your buck from a weapon.

Spec Paths: You're going to want to spec heavily in one weapon skill in order to do the most damage that you can. That's your job. There are two main paths of thought — Blade and Shield, or Celtic Dual. Some Blademasters may also eventually put a few points into a ranged weapon, like a bow, for some form of ranged attack. Weapons are your life, and your means to a profitable career. You spend all day using them, and all night cleaning and polishing them. But, don't get in too much of a hurry to spend those spec points (wait at least until Level 5).

- *Celtic Dual:* Very, very important, as the ability to swing two 1-handed weapons at once delivers the most damage. Parrying along with this can create a damage-intensive Blademaster. You can put any 1-handed weapon in your main hand, but your other hand only takes certain ones.
- When deciding what weapons to put in each hand, keep in mind that weapons with more damage almost always swing less often, and vice versa.
- *Blade:* Obviously, this helps you swing a 1-handed bladed weapon. You're going to do less damage by concentrating on Blade and Shield instead of Celtic Dual, but you'll also be able to avert some damage.
- *Shield:* Helps you block hits for yourself as well as others.
- *Parry:* Helps you avoid hits during battle.

Big Mistakes to Avoid in Character Creation: Spending spec points right off the bat. Save them for Level 5.

Deciding What You Want Your Role to Be: You're pretty much assured of being a damage dealer on the front lines, although you will often serve as a damage-absorbing tank as well.

Plotting Your Future:

- Examine the different spec lines and figure out what special attacks you want later in life. Combat styles are going to be very important to you down the road, so choose wisely and develop your character so that you attain your goals.
- As far as gaining spec points, you receive twice your level in skill points for each level increase once you become a Blademaster. Eventually, you'll be able to fully spec two weapon skills, but probably not three. If you want more than two, at least make sure you put due emphasis on your main skill.

Grouping: Grouping for a Blademaster is not a problem. You're an offensive machine, even though you aren't really designed to sit there and take damage for the group. Your offense is better than your defense, so go out there and do some damage!

- Taunt enemies away from your casters and healers, and especially your rezzer. If they die, the group's in trouble.
- Finish off the enemies that have been weakened, and keep an eye on casters and healers who may need protection.
- If you run out of energy, keep slugging away with normal melee and yell for a Buff from your casting friends.

Soloing: Soloing may not be as exciting as PvE play in a group, but you get all of the experience when fighting alone.

- Look for blue cons, but don't attack mobs that will call for help from their friends.
- Whatever you do, don't attack monsters who can debuff your speed or mez you.

Realm Versus Realm:

- Get buffed up before wading into enemy territory, then try to disrupt enemy casters and healers. This works best if you've got your "own" healer who's hanging back and keeping you healthy.
- Enemy archers and casters present the most danger to your casters and healers. You often turn into the leader of an RvR group, so ensure that you (or someone you assign) is going after the ranged enemies.

Beginner's Tips:

- Gather as much loot as you can while soloing from Levels 1 through 5. There's no death penalty, and the more you can earn, the better weapon you'll be able to afford when you become a Blademaster.
- Go in swinging with your best combat styles first. You're not really a sprinting escape artist, so the quicker you can down or weaken the enemy mob, the better.

Advanced Techniques:

- In a group with other tanks, use your combat styles to control aggro without getting *too* much aggro. Figure out who's the main tank, and who's the backup. If you're the backup, take heat off the primary without taking over.
- If you can control your aggro, and your casters and healers are adequately covered by other tanks, concentrate on finishing off tough monsters that are already engaged with other tanks.
- Ability Triple Wield. You summon a magical sword that adds 50% to your damage for 30 seconds (assuming you hit your target, of course), and that can be used once every 30 minutes. Can you say, slice and dice?
- Your chance to block arrows from a same-level archer with your shield is 30%. This is modified by Shield spec, quality and condition of the shield, and the Engage skill. You have a chance to block multiple archers with a larger shield.

Blademaster Styles

Abbreviations. *Headers:* **F**atigue **C**ost / **B**onus **D**amage / **B**onus **t**o **H**it. *In table:* **L**ow / **M**edium / **H**igh / **V**ery **H**igh / **D**efensive **B**onus (for you, on next round) / **D**efensive **P**enalty (to you, on next round) / **A**ttack **S**peed **R**eduction / **M**ovement **R**eduction (for target)

Blades

Lvl	Style	FC	BD	BtH	Prerequisites / Other Notes
2	Shining Blade	H	M	–	
4	Return Blade	L	M	M	Prereq: blocked target / Low ASR
6	Taunting Blade	M	L	–	Attempt to taunt target; Med DP
8	Enervating Blade	M	–	–	Attempt to turn away target; Med DB
10	Glowing Blade	M	M	M	Prereq: beside target / Med MR
12	Lunging Blade	M	M	M	Prereq: Return Blade / Low Bleed; Low DB
15	Auroric Blade	L	M	M	Prereq: Glowing Blade / Low ASR
18	Fire Blade	H	M	L	Low DP
21	Horizon Blade	L	M	M	Prereq: blocked target / Low Stun; Low DB
25	Kinetic Blade	M	H	M	Prereq: Lunging Blade
29	Dancing Blade	L	M	H	Prereq: Horizon Blade / Med Bleed
34	Revenging Blade	M	M	M	Prereq: behind target / Med DP
39	Spectrum Blade	M	M	L	Prereq: Fire Blade / High ASR; Med DB
44	Prismatic Blade	L	H	M	Prereq: Spectrum Blade
50	Brilliant Blade	M	H	VH	Prereq: target fumbled

Blunt

Lvl	Style	FC	BD	BtH	Prerequisites / Other Notes
2	Contusions	H	M	–	
4	Bruiser	L	M	M	Prereq: blocked target / Low Stun
6	Blunt Trauma	M	–	–	Attempt to turn away target; Med DB
8	Slam	M	L	M	Attempt to taunt target; Med DP
10	Side Bash	M	M	L	Prereq: beside target; Low ASR
12	Impact	L	M	M	Prereq: Bruiser / Low Bleed; Low DP
15	Recovery	L	M	H	Prereq: you fumbled / Med Stun; Low DB
18	Force of Might	H	M	L	
21	Unstoppable Force	M	M	M	Prereq: Side Bash / Med MR; Low DB
25	Back Crush	M	H	M	Prereq: behind target / Med DP
29	Bone Crusher	L	M	M	Prereq: Recovery / Med Bleed; Low DB
34	Mauler	M	H	M	Prereq: Unstoppable Force / Med DB
39	Stunning Blow	L	M	M	Prereq: parried target / High ASR; Low DB
44	Crushing Blow	M	M	VH	Prereq: Back Crush / Low DB
50	Devastating Blow	M	M	M	Prereq: Stunning Blow / High Stun

Piercing

Lvl	Style	FC	BD	BtH	Prerequisites / Other Notes
2	Dragonfly	H	M	–	
4	Wasp's Sting	L	M	M	Prereq: behind target / Low Bleed
6	Bumblebee's Sting	M	L	M	Attempt to taunt target; High DP
8	Hornet's Sting	M	M	M	Prereq: Wasp's Sting / Low ASR
10	Scorpion	M	–	–	Attempt to turn away target; Med DB
12	Black Widow	H	M	L	Low DP
15	Tarantula	L	M	M	Prereq: blocked target / Med Bleed; Low DB
18	Sidewinder	M	M	M	Prereq: Black Widow
21	Copperhead	M	M	M	Prereq: beside target / Med MR; Low DP
25	Diamondback	L	M	M	Prereq: evaded target / Med Stun; Med DB
29	Viper's Bite	M	H	M	Prereq: Copperhead / Med DB
34	Asp's Bite	L	M	VH	Prereq: Tarantula / Med ASR; Med DB
39	Cobra's Bite	L	H	H	Prereq: Sidewinder / Low DB
44	Dragonspider	M	M	M	Prereq: Diamondback / High Bleed
50	Wyvern's Bite	M	VH	H	Prereq: Asp's Bite / High Bleed; Low DB

Celtic Dual

Lvl	Style	FC	BD	BtH	Prerequisites / Other Notes
2	Misty Gloom	H	M	–	
4	Blinding Rain	L	M	M	Prereq: evaded target / Low Bleed
6	Squall	M	L	L	Attempt to taunt target; Med DP
8	Snow Shower	M	H	M	Prereq: behind target / Low MR
10	Gale	L	M	M	Prereq: Snow Shower / Low Bleed; Low DP
12	Blizzard	L	H	M	Prereq: Blinding Rain / Med ASR
15	Thunderstorm	L	M	M	Prereq: Snow Shower / Attempt to taunt target; High DB
18	Ice Storm	M	M	M	Prereq: beside target / Low Stun
21	Hurricane	H	M	L	Med DP
25	Tornado	L	M	H	Prereq: parried target / High MR; Med DB
29	Tempest	M	M	M	Prereq: Ice Storm / Med Bleed
34	Meteor Shower	L	M	M	Prereq: Tornado / Low Stun
39	Solar Flare	M	H	L	Prereq: Hurricane / Low DB
44	Twin Star	M	M	M	Prereq: Meteor Shower / High Bleed
50	Supernova	M	VH	H	Prereq: Tempest / High ASR; Low DB

Shields

Lvl	Style	FC	BD	BtH	Prerequisites / Other Notes
3	Numb	M	M	–	Low Stun
8	Stun	M	M	–	Prereq: blocked target / Low Stun
13	Disable	M	M	–	Prereq: beside target / Med Stun
18	Incapacitate	H	M	–	Prereq: blocked target / Med Stun; Med DB
23	Paralyze	M	M	–	Prereq: behind target / Med Stun
29	Bash	M	M	–	Prereq: blocked target / Med Stun
35	Mangle	M	M	–	Prereq: beside target / High Stun
42	Slam	VH	M	–	High Stun
50	Brutalize	L	M	–	Prereq: blocked target / High Stun

Ranger

Races		Abilities	
Celt / Lurikeen / Elf		1	Staves
		1	Cloth Armor
Skills		1	Leather Armor
1	Stealth	1	Sprint
1	Piercing	1	Evade I
1	Blades	4	Recurve Bows
4	Pathfinding	5	Small Shields
5	Recurve Bow	10	Reinforced
10	Celtic Dual	12	Evade II
		25	Evade III
		Styles	
			Blades
			Piercing
			Celtic Dual

Rangers possess Dexterity, Stealth, proficient melee skills and deadly ranged skills. They can track enemy armies and creatures, or lay ambushes with unparalleled precision. The life of a Ranger requires cunning and a mental flexibility.

The Best Part: Being able to take every situation into your own hands. There is no situation for which you're unprepared. You are a survivor, rely on no one and are a deadly opponent. The ability to solo endlessly is a major attraction, and you dominate RvR.

The Worst Part: Finding a group and soloing. Rangers are versatile masters of many trades, but master of none that are group related. You're one of the least requested classes for a group.

Race Choices:

Elves. Naturally high DEX and QUI, but lower HP than Celtic. Good choice overall with higher DEX/QUI caps than Celtic, but lower than Lurikeen. Height may be a concern for RvR hiding.

Celtic. High HP, great Strength and melee ability. Substantially less DEX and QUI, and has lowest skill cap for those skills as well.

Lurikeen. Highest base DEX and QUI, as well as highest cap. Small stature makes it easy to hide in RVR. Very fast draw times, but few HP. Damage threshold is traded for good bow skill.

Stat Choices:

- *DEX:* Vital stat that affects bow damage and accuracy. Most Ranger-specific items revolve around this.
- *QUI:* Determines bow draw time. Very important in RvR, as the ability to shoot and run helps you live longer.
- *CON:* Gives HP. If you're a melee fighter, put points here.
- *STR:* Pretty important for carrying stuff.
- Starting stat choices make a difference for the first 30 levels. Never sink 15 points into one area; put points into DEX, QUI, STR and CON (in that order).
- For Celtics, put a few extra points into STR and CON.
- For Lurikeen, adding to DEX and QUI can only make your great bow skills even better.

Weapon Choices:

- *Bow:* Wide array of bows available, but only two with practical value — Recurve (less damage, faster) and Great Recurve (more damage, but slower).
- In RVR, the faster bow is often best for interrupting casters. But, Great Recurve could one-shot a caster.
- A group may kill a monster too fast for a second shot, so a faster bow might work best (but consumes more costly arrows).
- Recurve bows shoot slightly farther than Great Recurves. Change bows according to the situation.
- *Thrusting:* Natural choice, since Thrusting damage uses DEX and QUI. Low damage, but fast and ideal for Dual Wield.
- *Blades:* Slower than Thrusting weapons, but with substantially more damage. Finding blades is somewhat easier. Excellent choice for any Ranger, especially Celtic.
- *Celtic Dual:* A skill that can be employed with Thrusting and Blades. Few specialize past 20, unless they want specific styles. Most commonly, a Level 50 Ranger brings weapon skill to 20-30 and raises Celtic Dual high enough so that its action occurs often enough in battle.

Spec Paths:
See Weapon Choices, and add Stealth if you're so inclined.

Big Mistakes To Avoid In Character Creation:

- Don't put 15 points into any single area.
- Know what sort of Ranger you want so you don't have to recreate a character down the road.

Deciding What You Want Your Role To Be: To avoid character meltdown, consider what type of character you want to create early on. Know whether you want to solo, group, play RvR, or engage primarily in melee.

- *General Solo Ranger:* Prefers solitude. You can group, but generally go solo. Versatility, and no blaring weakness. You'll often explore remote regions without others' support. Usually Lurikeen or Elven. High emphasis on Bow, medium on Pathfinding and Blades, lower on Stealth, and least on Celtic Dual.
- *RvR-Focused Ranger:* Your skills are built around killing anything alien. Everything you do is just a means to get to RvR. Lurikeen is the most common race. High emphasis on Bow and Stealth, medium on Pathfinding and Thrusting, and least on Celtic Dual.
- *Melee-Focused Ranger:* You can drop the bow and wade into the thick of battle with a mage, tank or giant Tree. Celtics work best. Most emphasis on Bow and Blades, less on Pathfinding and Celtic Dual.

Plotting Your Future: Once you hit Level 5 and become a Ranger, start your career planning. Figure out where you want to be at Level 10, 20, and 30. You'll realize that you can't bring every skill to 100%. Think about where to cut back, depending on how you want to play.

Grouping: You found a group! Great! Hang on to it because you'll have a rough time finding another.

- Since you don't have specific group skills, you may pull. Often, you'll just sit back and shoot what comes at the group.
- Rangers work best with Rangers. Pull and time both critical shots.
- Distract monsters from casters by switching targets until tanks can arrive and take over aggro.
- Check with the group on what to pull/avoid. Make sure casters have enough Mana first and have them tell you when they need to rest.

Soloing: No one solos better! You can kill virtually anything you can hit, and it's really a matter of deciding what the fastest experience is over time, rather than on a per-kill basis. You'll like your life soloing.

- Hit Trees! Arrows have a strong bonus, and Trees don't usually bring friends. They're slow, and people tend to leave them alone because they're resistant to just about everything but arrows.
- Try both Recurve and Great Recurve bows on any creatures you fight.
- Seek Buffs from high level Druids/Bards/Wardens to improve damage and draw times.

Realm Versus Realm:

Beginner:

- Lay low and be cautious. Never let bloodlust take over.
- Never let a kill take more than five shots.
- Aim for mages, make your kill, and run!
- *Always* have a retreat path.

Intermediate:

- Emain is the biggest hotspot.
- Attack from strange angles — like on top of AMF. Rotate tactics and never attack from the same spot more than twice. Jump off the sides of AMF and figure out how to go up steps faster than anyone else.
- Carry only enough arrows to be 50 points under capacity. You'll move normally even when debuffed.
- Always have Bladeturn on. One shot, then head for the hills.
- Don't attack from a line with other Rangers. Try the side or flank to hit enemy archers.
- You cannot go into Stealth mode while carrying a Relic. In fact, you go visible as soon as you pick one up.

Professional:

- To kill a one-shot archer on the run, target the ground and draw your critical shot. The second he appears, fire.

- Instead of shooting one critical followed by normal shots, try aiming the critical shot, don't reload, and instead fire two criticals. Good mage-killing tactic.
- Get your blades poisoned.
- Use Bounty Point jewels.
- When running up stairs, master the switch to mouse control so you can turn on a dime and lose someone.

Beginner's Tips:

- Befriend a high level Ranger with extra bows and money.
- Group with another Ranger and master timed critical shots.
- When grouped, choose a slower bow to use fewer arrows.
- When grouping, have a strong friend carry your arrows.
- In dungeons, range is limited. Get high-accuracy, short-range arrows to save money.
- Attack from above to get in extra shots!
- Sacrifice a little Armor Factor for stats. Some leather or cloth armors have wonderful stat bonuses and minimal AF effects.
- A stealthed archer is visible once he fires his bow, and if he fails his Stealth skill check, he's visible once he nocks his arrow. Your Stealth spec % (-20% on Critical Shots) = your % chance to remain hidden.

Advanced Techniques:

- If you get a creature to 30% life, turn and run, then shoot. The creature will move slower than normal, allowing you to gain distance and more shots.
- Time speed boost so that it activates the second after being hit (for maximum retreat time).
- When you see a rogue character in RvR, stop, draw your shot and target nothing. When he finds you, press F8 to auto-target. The second you see him, face and fire to put him down 50-60%. Melee until well done.
- Ability Danger Sense. This lets you know when a scout monster has noticed your party. Handily enough, Danger Sense is always on. It has a prerequisite of 8 trains in Stealth.

Ranger's Spells

Pathfinding

Buffs Caster's DEX and QUI.

Skill ....Pathfinding Dmg Type...............Body
Casting Time ....3 sec. Range.....................1000
Duration.............10 min.

Lvl	Spell	Cost	Buff
6	Sharpened Senses*	10P	14
12	Keen Sight*	20P	19
19	Enhanced Senses*	30P	25
29	Honed Reflexes*	48P	33
40	Superior Coordination*	68P	42
48	Perfect Acuity	82P	48

Buffs Caster's speed by (Speed %); usable in combat. You must wait 10 minutes before casting one of these spells again.

Skill ....Pathfinding Dmg Type...............Body
Casting Time ....Shout

Lvl	Spell	Cost	Dur	Speed %
9	Forest Shadow*	16P	20 sec.	35%
16	Greater Forest Shadow*	26P	25 sec.	50%
25	Forest Spirit*	40P	35 sec.	65%
34	Greater Forest Spirit*	56P	45 sec.	80%
43	Forest Phantom	72P	50 sec.	95%

Buffs Caster's AF.

Skill ....Pathfinding Dmg Type...............Body
Casting Time ....3 sec. Duration.............10 min.

Lvl	Spell	Cost	Buff
2	Determination*	6P	12
4	Perserverance*	8P	14
8	Self Control*	14P	18
11	Iron Will*	18P	21
14	Resolution*	22P	24
18	Devotion*	30P	28
23	Steel Mind*	38P	33
31	Inner Strength*	50P	41
42	Invincibility	70P	52

Buffs Caster's STR.

Skill ....Pathfinding Dmg Type............Energy
Casting Time ....3 sec. Duration.............10 min.

Lvl	Spell	Cost	Buff
3	Vigorous Will*	3P	12
7	Strength of Will*	6P	15
13	Fortification of Will*	11P	20
20	Focus of Will*	16P	26
30	Power of Will*	25P	34
39	Force of Will*	33P	41
50	Sovereign Will	43P	50

Caster's damage/sec buffed (stacks as group 1).

Skill ....Pathfinding Dmg Type............Energy
Casting Time ....3 sec. Duration.............10 min.

Lvl	Spell	Cost	Dmg/Sec
5	Piercing Strike*	5P	1.4
10	Incisive Strike*	8P	1.8
15	Cutting Strike*	12P	2.9
21	Sharpened Strike*	17P	4.2
27	Precision Strike*	22P	5.4
36	Unerring Strike*	30P	7.3
46	Perfect Strike	39P	9.4

Ranger's Styles

Blades

Lvl	Style	FC	BD	BtH	Prerequisites / Other Notes
2	Shining Blade	H	M	–	
4	Return Blade	L	M	M	Prereq: blocked target / Low ASR
6	Taunting Blade	M	L	–	Attempt to taunt target; Med DP
8	Enervating Blade	M	–	–	Attempt to turn away target; Med DB
10	Glowing Blade	M	M	M	Prereq: beside target / Med MR
12	Lunging Blade	M	M	M	Prereq: Return Blade / Low Bleed; Low DB
15	Auroric Blade	L	M	M	Prereq: Glowing Blade / Low ASR
18	Fire Blade	H	M	L	Low DP
21	Horizon Blade	L	M	M	Prereq: blocked target / Low Stun; Low DB
25	Kinetic Blade	M	H	M	Prereq: Lunging Blade
29	Dancing Blade	L	M	H	Prereq: Horizon Blade / Med Bleed
34	Revenging Blade	M	M	M	Prereq: behind target / Med DP
39	Spectrum Blade	M	M	L	Prereq: Fire Blade / High ASR; Med DB
44	Prismatic Blade	L	H	M	Prereq: Spectrum Blade
50	Brilliant Blade	M	H	VH	Prereq: target fumbled

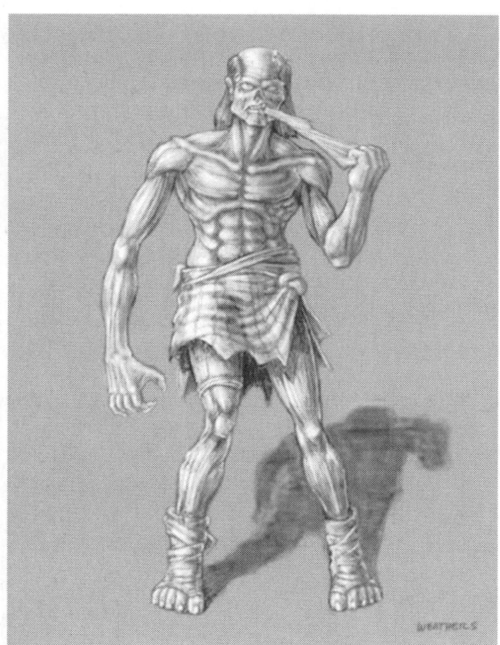

Piercing

Lvl	Style	FC	BD	BtH	Prerequisites / Other Notes
2	Dragonfly	H	M	–	
4	Wasp's Sting	L	M	M	Prereq: behind target / Low Bleed
6	Bumblebee's Sting	M	L	M	Attempt to taunt target; High DP
8	Hornet's Sting	M	M	M	Prereq: Wasp's Sting / Low ASR
10	Scorpion	M	–	–	Attempt to turn away target; Med DB
12	Black Widow	H	M	L	Low DP
15	Tarantula	L	M	M	Prereq: blocked target / Med Bleed; Low DB
18	Sidewinder	M	M	M	Prereq: Black Widow
21	Copperhead	M	M	M	Prereq: beside target / Med MR; Low DP
25	Diamondback	L	M	M	Prereq: evaded target / Med Stun; Med DB
29	Viper's Bite	M	H	M	Prereq: Copperhead / Med DB
34	Asp's Bite	L	M	VH	Prereq: Tarantula / Med ASR; Med DB
39	Cobra's Bite	L	H	H	Prereq: Sidewinder / Low DB
44	Dragonspider	M	M	M	Prereq: Diamondback / High Bleed
50	Wyvern's Bite	M	VH	H	Prereq: Asp's Bite / High Bleed; Low DB

Celtic Dual

Lvl	Style	FC	BD	BtH	Prerequisites / Other Notes
2	Misty Gloom	H	M	–	
4	Blinding Rain	L	M	M	Prereq: evaded target / Low Bleed
6	Squall	M	L	L	Attempt to taunt target; Med DP
8	Snow Shower	M	H	M	Prereq: behind target / Low MR
10	Gale	L	M	M	Prereq: Snow Shower / Low Bleed; Low DP
12	Blizzard	L	H	M	Prereq: Blinding Rain / Med ASR
15	Thunderstorm	L	M	M	Prereq: Snow Shower / Attempt to taunt target; High DB
18	Ice Storm	M	M	M	Prereq: beside target / Low Stun
21	Hurricane	H	M	L	Med DP
25	Tornado	L	M	H	Prereq: parried target / High MR; Med DB
29	Tempest	M	M	M	Prereq: Ice Storm / Med Bleed
34	Meteor Shower	L	M	M	Prereq: Tornado / Low Stun
39	Solar Flare	M	H	L	Prereq: Hurricane / Low DB
44	Twin Star	M	M	M	Prereq: Meteor Shower / High Bleed
50	Supernova	M	VH	H	Prereq: Tempest / High ASR; Low DB

Nightshade

Races		
Lurikeen / Elf		
Skills (& Styles)		
1	Stealth	
1	Piercing (& Styles)	
1	Blades (& Styles)	
4	Critical Strikes (& Styles)	
4	Celtic Dual (& Styles)	
5	Envenom	
5	Nightshade (Magic; automatic)	
Abilities		
1	Staves	
1	Cloth Armor	
1	Leather Armor	
1	Sprint	
1	Safe Fall IV	
1	Evade I	
4	Small Shields	
5	Evade II	
5	Distraction	
8	Danger Sense	
10	Evade III	
10	Safe Fall I	
16	Detect Hidden	
20	Evade IV	
20	Safe Fall II	
25	Climb Walls	
30	Evade V	
30	Safe Fall III	
40	Evade VI	
40	Safe Fall IV	
50	Evade VII	

Nightshades cause fear and confusion for most enemy parties. These assassins pop up in the middle of a party, wreak havoc, and then disappear as suddenly as they appeared!

The Best Part: Killing people indiscriminately. You can sneak into a well-armed group, pick and choose a target, and kill it.

The Worst Part: Most players shun you due to a lack of understanding about your abilities. Soloing is difficult, as is reaching a level at which your enemies truly fear you. You have a large number of skills you must focus on and decide between.

Race Choices:

Elf. Good for roleplaying, but that's it. Low DEX and QUI. Too tall and too hard to hide.

Lurikeen. Shorter, more DEX and more QUI.

Stat Choices:

- *DEX:* Helps with weapon damage.
- *QUI:* Helps you hit faster.
- *STR:* Affects carrying ability and melee damage, especially with bladed weapons.
- *CON:* Determines HP and Stamina. For meleeing, put at 15 or 20 points here.
- One combo is 10 STR and CON, and 5 DEX and QUI. This avoids any penalty for having anything below 50.
- Or, put 10 into QUI and forget boosting DEX. DEX rises with bonus items and level.

Weapon Choices:

- *Blades:* Larger selection, but slower. Usually more damaging, but misses are more costly.
- *Pierce:* Faster and more roguish. More frequent hits mean misses won't hurt too badly. (Pierce is the most popular, and most comments here assume you go that route.)

Spec Paths: Three basic routes exist.

- *Melee:* Focuses on melee skills, not Stealth. Get Piercing, Celtic Dual and Envenom to about two-thirds level so you excel in melee. Add remaining points into Critical Strike and/or Stealth — you won't use either one much. Most effective PvE profile for soloing.
- *Assassin:* More well rounded, and takes advantage of class skills. Concentrate on Stealth, Critical Strike (at about two-thirds level minimum apiece), Envenom, Pierce and Celtic Dual.
- *Super Scout/assassin:* Sacrifices Pierce and Critical Strike to max out Stealth. Stealthy, with a good opening shot, may die quickly. Best for sneaking into keeps or scouting.

Big Mistakes to Avoid in Character Creation: Failure to pick a template early on and distribute initial points accordingly. Also, thinking Stealth is your biggest skill. Stealth is less necessary in PvE, but essential for RvR. You can afford to wait, so develop combat skills first.

Deciding What You Want Your Role to Be: Are you going to be an assassin, super scout/assassin or melee fighter? Do you want to be well rounded, or an expert at one thing? You can experiment until Level 35 or so to see which template suits you best. One note — if melee really appeals to you, consider a Blademaster instead. They have basically the same skills, but better armor, more HP and a bow.

Plotting Your Future:

- A balanced template has Stealth, Critical Strike, Pierce and Envenom at about two-thirds your level. Most points should be put into Stealth and Critical Strike.
- Through the first 15 or 20 levels, specialize in the melee track to progress quickly to the battlegrounds and RvR. Stealth is useful, but not really your strong suit at these levels.
- Prior to level 40, each level awards plenty of points. Switch your focus around to find your preference.

- Don't raise Pierce above 29 unless you're going melee. You still get useful styles, and realm bonuses and items can get it higher.
- Keep Celtic Dual at around 18 unless you're a melee fighter. This is really the last level with a useful style for a while.
- Critical Strike is a worthwhile point expenditure for any assassin. You continue to get styles that can't be had from bonus items.
- With Envenom, poison isn't a style. Use bonuses for higher poisons instead of more points.
- As for Stealth, you get skills like Climb and Safe Fall with each level. You can find good Stealth bonus items as well.

Grouping: Nightshades sometimes have trouble finding a group, but are usually appreciated once they're accepted. Grouping is the fastest way to gain experience.

- The basic group tactic is to Envenom your dirks, stealthily sneak up, let the enemy come to the group's puller, then hit the mob with Critical Strike.
- Your group role is to poison and throw Critical Strikes! Toss in Direct Damage spells as often as you can.
- Group with classes that can pull from range and fight. They can draw the mob and keep its attention while you Perforate and Pierce.

Soloing:

- Soloing is not exactly easy. No Debuffs, and some of your best skills require help from others.
- When soloing, rely on Envenom as your primary skill. This helps you take down an enemy and survive.
- Use styles in Pierce and Celtic Dual that are based on Evade. They get better as you progress.
- You can use your Stealth to sneak up on a monster and deliver at least one Critical Strike, so Stealth is useful there. Try to come in at the monster from the back as well, so it has less of a chance of uncovering you.
- Best things to solo are animals! Any furry critter gives a damage bonus with piercing weapons. You should be able to handle blue and yellow con mobs.

Realm Versus Realm:

- This is where a Nightshade shines! In RvR, everyone appreciates the info they can provide.
- Against players, use your Disease poison and the best weakening poison you have.
- Don't stand still or hang out with a group of stealthers. That's how you get discovered.
- Pick your targets carefully! Never attempt to kill a tank that cons grey, and even then, stay away. Go for casters, other scouts, and anyone lower in level than you (except tanks).
- Communicate clearly. The "fog of war" is real, and a good plan can go down the drain quickly.
- You get the Climb ability at your 25th train in Stealth spec. Scale those keep walls!
- No Stealth mode while carrying a Relic.

Beginner's Tips:

- Every 3-5 levels, you tend to outgrow your equipment. Save your coins and take up a trade skill to earn money. Tailoring and Weaponcrafting are useful; you can try raising your skill to equip yourself.
- Perform killing tasks for the first 20 levels to get familiar with the land and earn experience.
- Grouping or RvR, to position yourself behind the enemy, /stick him, then use your strafe keys.
- Ability Danger Sense. Lets you know when a scout monster has noticed your party. Always on. Prereq: 8 trains in Stealth. Use it!
- Ability Detect Hidden. Increases range at which you can see hidden enemy players. Prereq: 16 trains in Stealth.
- Backstab "from hidden" styles take your Critical Strike spec into account, so you want to be highly trained in it.

Advanced Techniques:

- Use poisons! For NPCs and such, use the most lethal poison for damage and the best Disease poison you can. For monsters, sneak up and use Critical Strike in conjunction with your poisons. Throw in Direct Damage Shouts as often as possible.
- With DoT poison, and you can rehide and still do damage.
- You are a scout and assassin in RvR! You can keep an eye on enemy movements and even uncover enemy scouts, like archers. You can also sneak into enemy keeps to take out guards (good luck) or steal the relic (which makes you visible).

Nightshade Styles

Abbreviations. *Headers:* **F**atigue **C**ost / **B**onus **D**amage / **B**onus **t**o **H**it. *In table:* **L**ow / **M**edium / **H**igh / **V**ery **H**igh / **D**efensive **B**onus (for you, on next round) / **D**efensive **P**enalty (to you, on next round) / **A**ttack **S**peed **R**eduction / **M**ovement **R**eduction (for target)

Blades

Lvl	Style	FC	BD	BtH	Prerequisites / Other Notes
2	Shining Blade	H	M	–	
4	Return Blade	L	M	M	Prereq: blocked target / Low ASR
6	Taunting Blade	M	L	–	Attempt to taunt target; Med DP
8	Enervating Blade	M	–	–	Attempt to turn away target; Med DB
10	Glowing Blade	M	M	M	Prereq: beside target / Med MR
12	Lunging Blade	M	M	M	Prereq: Return Blade / Low Bleed; Low DB
15	Auroric Blade	L	M	M	Prereq: Glowing Blade / Low ASR
18	Fire Blade	H	M	L	Low DP
21	Horizon Blade	L	M	M	Prereq: blocked target / Low Stun; Low DB
25	Kinetic Blade	M	H	M	Prereq: Lunging Blade
29	Dancing Blade	L	M	H	Prereq: Horizon Blade / Med Bleed
34	Revenging Blade	M	M	M	Prereq: behind target / Med DP
39	Spectrum Blade	M	M	L	Prereq: Fire Blade / High ASR; Med DB
44	Prismatic Blade	L	H	M	Prereq: Spectrum Blade
50	Brilliant Blade	M	H	VH	Prereq: target fumbled

Piercing

Lvl	Style	FC	BD	BtH	Prerequisites / Other Notes
2	Dragonfly	H	M	–	
4	Wasp's Sting	L	M	M	Prereq: behind target / Low Bleed
6	Bumblebee's Sting	M	L	M	Attempt to taunt target; High DP
8	Hornet's Sting	M	M	M	Prereq: Wasp's Sting / Low ASR
10	Scorpion	M	–	–	Attempt to turn away target; Med DB
12	Black Widow	H	M	L	Low DP
15	Tarantula	L	M	M	Prereq: blocked target / Med Bleed; Low DB
18	Sidewinder	M	M	M	Prereq: Black Widow
21	Copperhead	M	M	M	Prereq: beside target / Med MR; Low DP
25	Diamondback	L	M	M	Prereq: evaded target / Med Stun; Med DB
29	Viper's Bite	M	H	M	Prereq: Copperhead / Med DB
34	Asp's Bite	L	M	VH	Prereq: Tarantula / Med ASR; Med DB
39	Cobra's Bite	L	H	H	Prereq: Sidewinder / Low DB
44	Dragonspider	M	M	M	Prereq: Diamondback / High Bleed
50	Wyvern's Bite	M	VH	H	Prereq: Asp's Bite / High Bleed; Low DB

Celtic Dual

Lvl	Style	FC	BD	BtH	Prerequisites / Other Notes
2	Misty Gloom	H	M	–	
4	Blinding Rain	L	M	M	Prereq: evaded target / Low Bleed
6	Squall	M	L	L	Attempt to taunt target; Med DP
8	Snow Shower	M	H	M	Prereq: behind target / Low MR
10	Gale	L	M	M	Prereq: Snow Shower / Low Bleed; Low DP
12	Blizzard	L	H	M	Prereq: Blinding Rain / Med ASR
15	Thunderstorm	L	M	M	Prereq: Snow Shower / Attempt to taunt target; High DB
18	Ice Storm	M	M	M	Prereq: beside target / Low Stun
21	Hurricane	H	M	L	Med DP
25	Tornado	L	M	H	Prereq: parried target / High MR; Med DB
29	Tempest	M	M	M	Prereq: Ice Storm / Med Bleed
34	Meteor Shower	L	M	M	Prereq: Tornado / Low Stun
39	Solar Flare	M	H	L	Prereq: Hurricane / Low DB
44	Twin Star	M	M	M	Prereq: Meteor Shower / High Bleed
50	Supernova	M	VH	H	Prereq: Tempest / High ASR; Low DB

Critical Strikes

Lvl	Style	FC	BD	BtH	Prerequisites / Other Notes
2	Backstab	M	M	M	Prereq: behind target, hidden / Med DP
4	Eviscerate	M	H	L	Prereq: Backstab / Low ASR; Low DP
6	Kidney Rupture	L	VH	L	Prereq: Eviscerate / Low Bleed; Med DP
8	Pincer	M	M	H	Prereq: beside target / High DP
10	Backstab 2	H	M	H	Prereq: behind target, hidden / Med DP
12	Hamstring	L	M	M	Prereq: evaded target / Med Bleed; Med DB
15	Thigh Cut	M	VH	M	Prereq: Backstab 2 / Low DP
18	Garrote	H	M	M	Med MR; Med DP
21	Perforate Artery	M	M	H	Prereq: in front of target, hidden / High Bleed; Med DP
25	Achilles Heel	M	H	M	Prereq: Garrote / High ASR
29	Leaper	L	M	H	Prereq: Hamstring / High Bleed; Low DB
34	Creeping Death	L	VH	H	Prereq: Perforate Artery / Med Stun
39	Stunning Stab	L	VH	VH	Prereq: Creeping Death / Low DB
44	Rib Separation	M	H	H	Prereq: Leaper / High MR
50	Ripper	M	VH	H	Prereq: Rib Separation/High Bleed; Low DB.

Nightshade Spells

Nightshade

DD.

Skill ....Nightshade Dmg Type................Cold
Casting Time ....3 sec. Range.....................1500
Duration.................Inst.

Lvl	Spell	Cost	Dmg
1	Lesser Dusk Strike*	2P	8
3	Dusk Strike*	3P	11
5	Lesser Twilight Strike*	4P	14
8	Twilight Strike*	5P	18
12	Lesser Gloaming Strike*	8P	24
16	Gloaming Strike*	10P	30
22	Lesser Nocturnal Strike*	13P	39
28	Nocturnal Strike*	17P	48
35	Lesser Midnight Strike*	22P	59
45	Midnight Strike	29P	74

DD. You must wait 20 seconds before casting one of these spells again.

Skill ....Nightshade Dmg Type................Cold
Casting Time ....Shout Range.......................700
Duration..................Inst.

Lvl	Spell	Cost	Dmg
6	Dart of Night*	4P	12
9	Dagger of Night*	6P	16
13	Knife of Night*	8P	20
18	Stiletto of Night*	11P	26
24	Arrow of Night*	15P	34
31	Rapier of Night*	19P	42
39	Spear of Night*	25P	52
48	Lance of Night	31P	62

Warden

Races		Abilities	
Celt / Firbolg		1	Staves
Skills		1	Cloth Armor
1	Nurture Magic	1	Leather Armor
1	Regrowth Magic	1	Sprint
5	Nurture Magic Spec.	1	Small Shields
5	Regrowth Magic Spec.	5	Medium Shields
5	Blades	7	Shortbows
5	Blunt	10	Reinforced Armor
15	Parry	20	Scale Armor
		Styles	
			Blades
			Blunt

The Warden is a jack of many trades, yet master of none. Strength comes through a combination of magic and melee. You can float between roles, providing aid where needed. You're not a primary role-filler for a group, but you are a welcome backup support unit. Your abilities include healing, buffing, fighting and chanting to increase battle effectiveness.

The Best Part: Variety is a perk. You can be a healer, buffer, tank, puller, support class, or supported class.

The Worst Part: You're spread pretty thinly and can't excel too much in any one area. You'll always depend on other classes to fill primary roles.

Race Choices:

Celtic. Middle-ground race for Hibernia, neither strong nor weak, nor overly agile. Even height is average. Celtics have an even stat spread, making a well-balanced Warden.

Firbolg. The powerhouse race, built for high damage, but at the cost of low agility. This race presents a tall target, bad for hiding in RvR.

Stat Choices:

- *STR:* Has a direct effect on damage; Celtics will dish out a bit less than high-STR Firbolgs due to this.
- *DEX:* Relates to defensive skills. The Celtic can Parry and Shield block more often due to higher DEX and QUI, an area in which Firbolgs suffer.
- Because of the nature of a Warden's magic, the effects of placing points in EMP are questionable. But, you can't go wrong with spending points in STR, CON, DEX or QUI. Play to your higher stats — i.e., for a Firbolg, you get better returns by boosting STR and CON, not QUI and DEX.

Weapon Choices: You can use a short bow, staff and shield, but cannot train in any of them. You can, however, train Blade, Blunt and Parry.

- *Blade:* Slash damage type, strong against leather armor and fleshy, furry creatures, tree/plant creatures, and Troll-like beings. Weak against magical and elemental creatures, as well as plate/scale armor, skin and soft creatures.
- *Blunt*: Crush damage type, strong against Undead, Earth/Ice Elementals, studded leather and plate armor and shelled creatures. Weakest against magical creatures, Air/Fire/Water Elementals, non-bony Undead and soft and Troll-like creatures.

Spec Paths: The Warden possesses two spell lines — Regrowth and Nurture.

- *Regrowth:* Includes minor, medium and major healing spells, minor and medium Resurrection, and self-only Health and Endurance regeneration Buffs.
- *Nurture:* Gives base Armor Factor, STR, DEX and CON Buffs, plus self-only haste Buff and several variations of Bladeturn.

Big Mistakes To Avoid In Character Creation: Don't waste spec points on useless spec lines. Also, CHA, PIE and INT are totally useless for your class, and any points are spent on these are lost.

Deciding What You Want Your Role To Be: It's very difficult for a Warden to pick a specific role. You work best as a group floater, helping others as needed.

Plotting Your Future: You can't break a character in only one level. If you make a mistake or spec in the wrong line, you can correct it in a few levels by training in a different line. Maxing out one line doesn't always carry benefits, so aim specifically for the spells or styles you want. Start your training at Level 5.

Grouping:

- With your versatility, you are a very valuable group member. Stay away from any primary roles, but you're fine as a secondary healer, tank, etc. You thrive symbiotically, working with others to accomplish a common goal. Other classes benefit from working with the Warden and the Warden benefits from working with other classes.
- Due to concentration limits, the best Druid buffer can't buff everyone. Take over casting base Nurture Buffs so that the Druid can concentrate on advanced Buffs. Your Damage Add Chant also works with the Druid and Ranger's self Damage Add spell to further increase damage output. Furthermore, your self-only combat haste Buff stacks with the Druid's Concentration-based haste Buff.

Soloing:

- With your Bladeturn and insta-cast Endurance Regeneration Chants, you can take some higher risks while soloing. The downside is low melee damage output. You must outlast the enemy in long, hard battles.
- You start in leather armor, progress to reinforced, and then on to scale.
- Start by soloing antisocial mobs that don't call for help. Then, look for mobs that match your strengths and weaknesses. If you have slow attacks, find an enemy that has slow attacks. If you use Blade or Blunt, fight an enemy weak to that damage type. Also, find enemies weak against your armor type.
- With Bladeturn Chants, the slower the enemy, the better your chances of blocking.
- With the Damage Add or Endurance Regeneration Chants, look for an enemy that is weaker than you, one that you can kill before it kills you.
- Never go into combat without buffing.
- Plan ahead — don't just rush in. Know the area and be watchful of scouts and mobs.

Realm Versus Realm:

- The Warden is growing into a stable RvR class. You can find usefulness and effectiveness within groups and by picking prey carefully. If you rush a Theurgist, you're toast. But if you go after a support class or other hybrid, you stand a better chance.
- RvR is all about teamwork. You lack high front-end damage and range, so group with realmmates.
- Help the tank by fighting, but watch the support classes and switch roles as needed.
- If things look bad, make sure you escape with the Group Run Speed Chant and the insta-cast self-only Endurance Regeneration Chant.
- Locking yourself into one role can get yourself or your group killed.
- Keep your group within Chant range, but not close enough to fall victim to AoE spells.
- With resist Buffs and high armor, you can often take time to kill, either by magic or melee. Act as a decoy and take a hit for the group, but make your escape as necessary.
- Be mindful of mobs. You can use them as a defensive wall. If you can pass a mob without attracting aggro, an enemy player may hesitate to follow in fear of a PvE death. If you attract the mob, sprint until you are out of melee range, and when the spell begins to pulse again, stop sprinting.

Beginner's Tips:

- Don't train until you choose a path. It is very possible to level from 1-5 without training.
- Complete as many trainer and guild quests as possible to help your character level while earning coins and enhanced items.

Advanced Techniques:

- If a mob is neutral or your attack is carefully planned, you can start a fight with a side or back positional style. If successfully done, they carry higher damage and effects, and a chain reaction of higher styles.
- There are mobs that stop to cast spells. If you use long-range arrows, you can do up to 25% damage to a mob before they enter melee range. Normally, with a short bow, you can nock and release faster than they can cast. The mob will try to cast 2-3 times before charging in a fight. Depending on level and the bow/arrows you use, you may be able to deal a decent amount of damage before they touch you.
- A stealthed archer is visible when he fires; when he nocks his arrow, if he fails his Stealth check. Stealth spec % (-20% on Critical Shots) = % chance to stay hidden.

Warden Styles

Abbreviations. *Headers:* **F**atigue **C**ost / **B**onus **D**amage / **B**onus **t**o **H**it. *In table:* **L**ow / **M**edium / **H**igh / **V**ery **H**igh / **D**efensive **B**onus (for you, on next round) / **D**efensive **P**enalty (to you, on next round) / **A**ttack **S**peed **R**eduction / **M**ovement **R**eduction (for target)

Blades

Lvl	Style	FC	BD	BtH	Prerequisites / Other Notes
2	Shining Blade	H	M	–	
4	Return Blade	L	M	M	Prereq: blocked target / Low ASR
6	Taunting Blade	M	L	–	Attempt to taunt target; Med DP
8	Enervating Blade	M	–	–	Attempt to turn away target; Med DB
10	Glowing Blade	M	M	M	Prereq: beside target / Med MR
12	Lunging Blade	M	M	M	Prereq: Return Blade / Low Bleed; Low DB
15	Auroric Blade	L	M	M	Prereq: Glowing Blade / Low ASR
18	Fire Blade	H	M	L	Low DP
21	Horizon Blade	L	M	M	Prereq: blocked target / Low Stun; Low DB
25	Kinetic Blade	M	H	M	Prereq: Lunging Blade
29	Dancing Blade	L	M	H	Prereq: Horizon Blade / Med Bleed
34	Revenging Blade	M	M	M	Prereq: behind target / Med DP
39	Spectrum Blade	M	M	L	Prereq: Fire Blade / High ASR; Med DB
44	Prismatic Blade	L	H	M	Prereq: Spectrum Blade
50	Brilliant Blade	M	H	VH	Prereq: target fumbled

Blunt

Lvl	Style	FC	BD	BtH	Prerequisites / Other Notes
2	Contusions	H	M	–	
4	Bruiser	L	M	M	Prereq: blocked target / Low Stun
6	Blunt Trauma	M	–	–	Attempt to turn away target; Med DB
8	Slam	M	L	M	Attempt to taunt target; Med DP
10	Side Bash	M	M	L	Prereq: beside target; Low ASR
12	Impact	L	M	M	Prereq: Bruiser / Low Bleed; Low DP
15	Recovery	L	M	H	Prereq: you fumbled / Med Stun; Low DB
18	Force of Might	H	M	L	
21	Unstoppable Force	M	M	M	Prereq: Side Bash / Med MR; Low DB
25	Back Crush	M	H	M	Prereq: behind target / Med DP
29	Bone Crusher	L	M	M	Prereq: Recovery / Med Bleed; Low DB
34	Mauler	M	H	M	Prereq: Unstoppable Force / Med DB
39	Stunning Blow	L	M	M	Prereq: parried target / High ASR; Low DB
44	Crushing Blow	M	M	VH	Prereq: Back Crush / Low DB
50	Devastating Blow	M	M	M	Prereq: Stunning Blow / High Stun

Warden Spells

Regrowth

Heals damage to Friend by (Heal) HP.
Skill................Regrowth Casting Time...2.25 sec.
Range....................1350 Duration.................Inst.

Lvl	Spell	Cost	Heal
1	Minor Revigoration*	1P	5
3	Minor Renewal*	2P	8
5	Minor Revivification*	3P	11
8	Minor Resurgance*	4P	16
11	Minor Revival*	6P	21
14	Minor Regeneration*	7P	26
18	Minor Regrowth*	9P	33
23	Minor Restoration*	11P	41
29	Minor Resuscitation*	14P	50
37	Minor Renascence*	19P	64
47	Minor Apotheosis	24P	80

Heals damage to Friend by (Heal) HP.
Skill................Regrowth Casting Time...2.75 sec.
Range....................1350 Duration.................Inst.

Lvl	Spell	Cost	Heal
4	Renewal*	5P	22
6	Revivification*	6P	30
9	Resurgance*	9P	42
12	Revival*	12P	54
16	Regeneration*	15P	71
21	Regrowth*	20P	91
27	Restoration*	26P	116
31	Resuscitation*	30P	132
36	Renascence*	36P	152
46	Apotheosis	47P	193

Resurrects corpse; target is resurrected with a percentage of its original Power and/or HP.
Skill................Regrowth Casting Time........4 sec.
Range....................1500 Duration.................Inst.
Cost............Based on corpse (see p. 368)

Lvl	Spell	Power	HP
10	Minor Reconstitution	No Power	10%

Warden's Regrowth

Heals damage to Friend by (Heal) HP.
Skill................Regrowth Casting Time.....3.5 sec.
Range....................1350 Duration.................Inst.

Lvl	Spell	Cost	Heal
5	Major Resurgance*	11P	50
8	Major Revival*	16P	75
11	Major Regeneration*	21P	99
15	Major Regrowth*	29P	132
20	Major Restoration*	38P	173
26	Major Resuscitation*	50P	222
33	Major Renascence*	65P	279
42	Major Apotheosis	84P	352

Buffs Caster's health regeneration by (Heal) every cycle.
Skill................Regrowth Cost........................8%P
Casting Time........3 sec. Duration..............6 min.

Lvl	Spell	Heal
6	Solar Conversion*	2
14	Solar Absorption*	4
25	Solar Regeneration*	5
35	Solar Regrowth*	7
45	Solar Resuscitation	8

Resurrects corpse; target is resurrected with a percentage of its original Power and/or HP.
Skill................Regrowth Casting Time........7 sec.
Range....................1500 Duration.................Inst.
Cost............Based on corpse (see p. 368)

Lvl	Spell	Power	HP
16	Lesser Reconstitution	10%	30%

Buffs Caster's fatigue regeneration every cycle.
Skill................Regrowth Cost......................2P/3s
Casting Time........Shout Duration.........Chant + 5

Lvl	Spell	Buff
2	Attack Unending	4

Reduces Caster's fatigue cost by (Bonus %).
Skill................Regrowth Cost......................10%P
Casting Time........3 sec. Duration............10 min.

Lvl	Spell	Bonus %
12	Attack Unfading*	10%
22	Attack Perpetual*	15%
32	Attack Unceasing*	20%
42	Attack Uninterrupted	25%

Nurture

Buffs Friend's STR.

Skill ....Nurture Casting Time ....3 sec.
Range.....................1000 Duration...........Concent.

Lvl	Spell	Cost	Buff
3	Strength of the Oak**	1C	12
7	Strength of the Redwood**	3C	15
14	Vigor of the Oak**	5C	21
20	Vigor of the Redwood**	7C	26
30	Force of the Oak**	11C	34
41	Force of the Redwood	15C	42
50	Might of the Redwood	19C	50

Buffs Friend's AF.

Skill ....Nurture Casting Time ....3 sec.
Range.....................1000 Duration...........Concent.

Lvl	Spell	Cost	Buff
2	Minor Bark Skin**	1C	12
4	Lesser Bark Skin**	2C	14
6	Bark Skin**	2C	16
9	Major Bark Skin**	3C	19
12	Greater Bark Skin**	4C	22
17	Superior Bark Skin**	6C	27
21	Skin of the Redwood**	7C	31
26	Greater Skin of the Redwood**	9C	36
32	Major Skin of the Redwood	11C	42
45	Superior Skin of the Redwood	16C	55

Buffs Friend's DEX.

Skill ....Nurture Casting Time ....3 sec.
Range.....................1000 Duration...........Concent.

Lvl	Spell	Cost	Buff
8	Dexterity of the Ferret**	3C	16
13	Dexterity of the Rabbit**	5C	20
19	Dexterity of the Badger**	7C	25
28	Dexterity of the Lynx**	10C	32
38	Dexterity of the Bear	14C	40
48	Dexterity of the Wolf	18C	48

Buffs Friend's CON.

Skill ....Nurture Casting Time ....3 sec.
Range.....................1000 Duration...........Concent.

Lvl	Spell	Cost	Buff
5	Oak's Stoutness**	2C	14
11	Oak's Stamina**	4C	18
15	Oak's Girth**	5C	22
24	Redwood's Stoutness**	8C	29
33	Redwood's Stamina	12C	36
43	Redwood's Girth	16C	44

Warden's Nurture

Buffs Caster's attack speed by (Speed %).

Skill ....Nurture Cost 15%P
Casting Time ....3 sec. Duration.............10 min.

Lvl	Spell	Speed %
3	Ferocity of Nature*	16%
8	Rage of Nature*	19%
13	Fury of Nature*	21%
21	Anger of Nature*	25%
30	Hostility of Nature*	30%
38	Aggression of Nature*	34%
47	Reckoning of Nature	38%

Groupmates' damage/sec buffed (stacks as group 2).

Skill ....Nurture Dmg Type...............Body
Cost...........................0P Casting Time ....Shout
Range.......................700 Duration ....Chant + 5

Lvl	Spell	Dmg/Sec
5	Nature's Revenge*	1.3
9	Nature's Vendetta*	1.9
14	Nature's Vengeance*	2.7
19	Nature's Retalliation*	3.4
25	Nature's Retribution*	4.3
35	Nature's Feud*	5.8
46	Nature's Reckoning	7.5

Bladeturn: Absorbs damage of single hit.

Skill ....Nurture Dmg Type............Matter
Casting Time ....4 sec.

Lvl Spell	Cost	Range	Dur	Target
Nature's ...				
2 Ward*	8%P	–	Until Hit	Self
10 Fend	8%P	1250	Until Hit	Friend
18 Shield	12%P	1250	Until Hit	Group
26 Guard*1	16P, 4P/10s	1250	Chant+10	Group
36 Barrier*2	23P, 5P/8s	1250	Chant+8	Group
45 Wall3	29P, 7P/6s	1250	Chant+6	Group

1 Absorbs first hit every 10 seconds.
2 Absorbs first hit every 8 seconds.
3 Absorbs first hit every 6 seconds.

Group Speed Buff by (Speed %).

Skill ....Nurture Dmg Type...............Body
Cost...........................0P Casting Time ....3 sec.
Range.....................2000 Duration ....Chant + 6

Lvl	Spell	Speed %
4	Guardian's Encouragement*	23%
15	Benefactor's Encouragement*	31%
24	Protector's Encouragement*	38%
34	Warden's Encouragement*	45%
44	Paragon's Encouragement	53%

Buffs Friend's Body resistance.

Skill ....Nurture Casting Time ....3 sec.
Range.....................1000 Duration...........Concent.

Lvl	Spell	Cost	Buff
22	Bolster Health**	8C	8
32	Bolster Resillience	11C	16
43	Bolster Heartiness	16C	24

Buffs Friend's Spirit resistance.

Skill ....Nurture Casting Time ....3 sec.
Range.....................1000 Duration...........Concent.

Lvl	Spell	Cost	Buff
23	Warden's Courage**	8C	8
33	Warden's Honor	12C	16
48	Warden's Spirit	18C	24

Buffs Friend's Energy resistance.

Skill ....Nurture Casting Time ....3 sec.
Range.....................1000 Duration...........Concent.

Lvl	Spell	Cost	Buff
27	Defy Thunder**	9C	8
37	Defy Storm	13C	16
49	Defy Lightning	18C	24

Bard

Races		Abilities	
Celt / Firbolg		1	Staves
Skills		1	Cloth Armor
1	Nurture Magic	1	Leather Armor
1	Regrowth Magic	1	Sprint
5	Music Magic	1	Small Shields
5	Nurture Magic Spec.	10	Evade I
5	Regrowth Magic Spec.	15	Reinforced Armor
5	Music Magic Spec.	25	Evade II
5	Blades		
5	Blunt		

Bards serve a support role very well. You can heal to a certain degree, you can mesmerize monsters and players, you can resurrect and you can support a party by regenerating Endurance and Power. Bards understand their power of song and use it selflessly to enhance the power of the group. This class is a blast to play — you may not slay many people, but you get plenty of face time in groups and guilds.

The Best Part: Mezzing that only lasts longer as you get better, and speed! You can help regen Endurance more quickly, lay out massive heals and mez mobs like nobody's business. You're popular with everyone, and an RvR natural.

The Worst Part: Okay, so there are times that you can't kill a mob that cons blue. Definitely, most definitely, this isn't a soloing class.

Race Choices:

Firbolgs: Great STR (good for weapons that can be used by this class, if you dare to waste points on weapons) and high EMP for spells. But, low DEX and QUI make this race a bit slower.

Celtic: Better physique and more balanced stats. No real standout stat, however.

Stat Choices: When you start out, EMP and CON are highlighted. Bards really don't need EMP as much as CHA, though. If you put too many points into EMP, you'll regret it later.

- *EMP:* Main casting stat, but don't start by putting points in it.
- *CHA:* Put 10 points here — it's your primary casting statistic.
- *DEX:* Your casting speed statistic. You'll want to put 10, if not 15, points into this.
- *CON:* Very good for HP, especially if you like to melee. Again, 10 points is a good investment. If you're in a good group with lots of protective tanks, you may not need as much CON.
- *STR*: Good for increasing weapon damage. If you're Celtic, put 10 points here to compensate for your race weakness. As a Firbolg, you can divert those points elsewhere.

Weapon Choices: Bards have the choice between Blunts or Blades. For best situational results, carry one of each and avoid developing them as skills. You won't do (or shouldn't be doing) much fighting since you're a support character, but a little defense may be necessary from time to time in the absence of a tank or other protective character.

Spec Paths: Your specialization path is a major individual decision. First, figure out what you want to do in the game. Then, figure out what you need to spec in to accomplish your goal. Also, make sure you understand how to support and heal a group.

- *Regrowth:* Nice skill line that gives various healing abilities. You get a group heal spell and a second Resurrect spell by investing points here.
- *Nurture:* Essential if you want to play a party support role. Three main things come from this line — Endurance regeneration, run speed, and Power regeneration.
- *Music:* This is *the* Bard skill to have, what with Area-Effect Mesmerize spells and damaging Shout spells. These can earn you some best friends in RvR.
- *Melee weapon:* Some players put a few points here, but honestly, these points are probably much better spent in spellcasting. Your songs are your bread and butter, not your melee weapon.
- A good point spread for a Bard raises Nurture and Music very high, at the cost of sacrificing either Regrowth or Melee skills, depending on your long-term goals.

Big Mistakes To Avoid In Character Creation: Make sure you understand what each stat does for your character type before dumping points into them. Whatever you do, don't put all 30 into any one thing, and don't spend spec points until Level 5. Don't put points into EMP.

Deciding What You Want Your Role To Be: Your spec points determine your role to a greater extent than most other classes. So, you'll find it hard to be useless as a Bard, no matter where you put points. If you invest mostly in Regrowth, you will make a great healer, with some Bard abilities tossed in for good measure. A lot of Nurturing? You make a wonderful party supporter. (Who doesn't love to run and regenerate Endurance super-fast?) Investing all your points in Music? You'll be the ruler of crowd control!

So, figure out what you want your end goal to be in the game and design your character and development accordingly. This is one of the most fun classes to play, so take advantage of your skills.

Plotting Your Future: Around Level 10, start putting points into your Nurture skill. Hopefully, you will have received your first Speed Song by then. Other points should be put into Regrowth, since big heals are really nice at lower levels.

Grouping: Everyone wants a Bard to balance out their group. The best combination, really, is to have two Druids (healers/buffers), two tanks (Hero, Champion, Blademaster, Ranger or Nightshade), one Bard, one Warden, and two chanters (Enchanter or Eldritch).

- A Bard's group role is often to prevent downtime. In battle, keep the Endurance Song playing. After the fight, play the Power Song to regain Mana and Power more quickly.
- A Bard and a Druid make a good team. The Bard can heal the Druid if he gets in trouble, or mesmerize/confuse the mob.
- Multiple Bards in a group stack well. With three Bards, the group can listen to Power, Endurance and Healing Chants all at once!
- Make sure that you keep rotating your Songs (a pain, but worth it), and also ensure that no mobs or reach the group without being mezzed first.

Soloing: Not really recommended for Bards. Some people will spec really high in a weapon to solo, but that comes at the expense of your other talents. If soloing is what you want, try a different class.

Realm Versus Realm: Fun, fun, fun in the realms!

- In RvR, it's generally your job to keep a 360-degree watch for invaders and stealthy opponents. Mesmerize over and over, and stay alive. You'll be a primary target for every offensive opponent out there!
- If you want to twist, yellow con instruments mean longer pulse lengths, and are considered better than gray con instruments.
- As with groups, prevent downtime by switching Songs and casting an occasional heal for your realmmates.
- Last but not least, find and resurrect any realmmates that need it.

Beginner's Tips:

- Mez invaders first!
- There's really no need to buy a more expensive instrument. A gray con one performs just as well as a yellow con one.
- Stay away from people who are always negative and don't be hasty about choosing a continuous group or guild.
- Always remember your end goal when you make important character decisions.
- You can drop instruments in your ranged weapons slot. It makes it easier to switch between them.
- Instruments have stat and skill bonuses. They also have condition and durability, and will degrade with use.

Advanced Techniques:

- As your character grows older, you'll figure out better techniques (like the fact that you can hold two instruments in your hands and switch at will).
- You've got eight Hotkey bars, so use them. Try putting your main healing Song on the first slot of each bar for quick access.

Bard's Spells/Songs

Regrowth

Heals damage to Friend by (Heal) HP.
Skill ....Regrowth Casting Time ...2.25 sec.
Range.....................1350 Duration..................Inst.

Lvl	Spell	Cost	Heal
1	Minor Revigoration*	1P	5
3	Minor Renewal*	2P	8
5	Minor Revivification*	3P	11
8	Minor Resurgance*	4P	16
11	Minor Revival*	6P	21
14	Minor Regeneration*	7P	26
18	Minor Regrowth*	9P	33
23	Minor Restoration*	11P	41
29	Minor Resuscitation*	14P	50
37	Minor Renascence*	19P	64
47	Minor Apotheosis	24P	80

Heals damage to Friend by (Heal) HP.
Skill ....Regrowth Casting Time ...2.75 sec.
Range.....................1350 Duration..................Inst.

Lvl	Spell	Cost	Heal
4	Renewal*	5P	22
6	Revivification*	6P	30
9	Resurgance*	9P	42
12	Revival*	12P	54
16	Regeneration*	15P	71
21	Regrowth*	20P	91
27	Restoration*	26P	116
31	Resuscitation*	30P	132
36	Renascence*	36P	152
46	Apotheosis	47P	193

Resurrects corpse; target is resurrected with a percentage of its original Power and/or HP.
Skill ....Regrowth Casting Time ....4 sec.
Range.....................1500 Duration..................Inst.
Cost ....Based on corpse (see p. 368)

Lvl	Spell	Power	HP
10	Minor Reconstitution	No Power	10%

Bard's Regrowth

Heals damage to Friend by (Heal) HP.
Skill ....Regrowth Casting Time .....3.5 sec.
Range.....................1350 Duration..................Inst.

Lvl	Spell	Cost	Heal
5	Major Resurgance*	11P	50
8	Major Revival*	16P	75
11	Major Regeneration*	21P	99
15	Major Regrowth*	29P	132
20	Major Restoration*	38P	173
26	Major Resuscitation*	50P	222
33	Major Renascence*	65P	279
42	Major Apotheosis	84P	352

Heals damage to Groupmates by (Heal) HP.
Skill ....Regrowth Casting Time ....4 sec.
Range.....................1350 Duration..................Inst.

Lvl	Spell	Cost	Heal
17	Tones of Health*	32P	75
27	Notes of Health*	52P	116
37	Tunes of Health*	73P	157
47	Chimes of Health	96P	197

Buffs groupmates' health regeneration by (Buff) every cycle; requires lute.
Skill ....Regrowth Cost............................0P
Casting Time ....3 sec. Range.....................1500
Duration ....Song + 6

Lvl	Spell	Buff
6	Chant of Healing*	5
14	Song of Healing*	6
25	Psalm of Healing*	7
35	Hymn of Healing*	8
45	Euphony of Healing	9

Resurrects corpse; target is resurrected with a percentage of its original Power and/or HP.
Skill ....Regrowth Casting Time ....7 sec.
Range.....................1500 Duration..................Inst.
Cost ....Based on corpse (see p. 368)

Lvl	Spell	Power	HP
16	Lesser Reconstitution	10%	30%

Nurture

Buffs Friend's STR.
Skill ....Nurture Casting Time ....3 sec.
Range.....................1000 Duration...........Concent.

Lvl	Spell	Cost	Buff
3	Strength of the Oak**	1C	12
7	Strength of the Redwood**	3C	15
14	Vigor of the Oak**	5C	21
20	Vigor of the Redwood**	7C	26
30	Force of the Oak**	11C	34
41	Force of the Redwood	15C	42
50	Might of the Redwood	19C	50

Buffs Friend's AF.
Skill ....Nurture Casting Time ....3 sec.
Range.....................1000 Duration...........Concent.

Lvl	Spell	Cost	Buff
2	Minor Bark Skin**	1C	12
4	Lesser Bark Skin**	2C	14
6	Bark Skin**	2C	16
9	Major Bark Skin**	3C	19
12	Greater Bark Skin**	4C	22
17	Superior Bark Skin**	6C	27
21	Skin of the Redwood**	7C	31
26	Greater Skin of the Redwood**	9C	36
32	Major Skin of the Redwood	11C	42
45	Superior Skin of the Redwood	16C	55

Buffs Friend's DEX.
Skill ....Nurture Casting Time ....3 sec.
Range.....................1000 Duration...........Concent.

Lvl	Spell	Cost	Buff
8	Dexterity of the Ferret**	3C	16
13	Dexterity of the Rabbit**	5C	20
19	Dexterity of the Badger**	7C	25
28	Dexterity of the Lynx**	10C	32
38	Dexterity of the Bear	14C	40
48	Dexterity of the Wolf	18C	48

Buffs Friend's CON.
Skill ....Nurture Casting Time ....3 sec.
Range.....................1000 Duration...........Concent.

Lvl	Spell	Cost	Buff
5	Oak's Stoutness**	2C	14
11	Oak's Stamina**	4C	18
15	Oak's Girth**	5C	22
24	Redwood's Stoutness**	8C	29
33	Redwood's Stamina	12C	36
43	Redwood's Girth	16C	44

Bard Nurture Spec

Group Speed Buff Song; buffs by (Speed %); requires lute.
Skill ....Nurture Cost............................0P
Casting Time ....3 sec. Range.....................2000
Duration ....Song + 6

Lvl	Spell	Speed %
3	Clear Path*	44%
13	Clear Trail*	59%
23	Clear Road*	74%
33	Clear Field*	89%
43	Clear Horizon	104%

Buffs Groupmates' fatigue regeneration by (Buff) every cycle; requires drum.
Skill ....Nurture Cost............................0P
Casting Time ....3 sec. Range.....................1000
Duration ....Song + 5

Lvl	Spell	Buff
2	Rhythm of Hibernia*	1
12	Rhythm of Earth*	2
22	Rhythm of Nature*	3
32	Rhythm of the World*	4
42	Rhythm of the Cosmos	5

Buffs Groupmates' power regeneration by (Buff) every cycle; requires flute.
Skill ....Nurture Cost............................0P
Casting Time ....3 sec. Range.....................1000
Duration ....Song + 6

Lvl	Spell	Buff
10	Rhyme of Earth*	1
21	Rhyme of Nature*	2
30	Rhyme of the World*	3
39	Rhyme of the Cosmos*	4
50	Rhyme of Creation	5

Music

Amnesia: Enemies in area have (Forget %) chance to forget they hate each person on their hate list. You must wait before casting one of these spells again (5 sec. for single target, 10 sec. for AoE).

Skill......Music Casting Time......Shout
Range......2300 Duration......Inst.

Lvl	Spell	Cost	Radius	Forget %
2	Minor Lullaby	2P	(1)	70%
12	Lesser Lullaby*	8P	100	77%
22	Lullaby*	13P	175	84%
32	Greater Lullaby*	20P	250	91%
42	Superior Lullaby	27P	325	100%

Mesmerize: target halts all movement and is unable to attack or cast spells; the effect breaks when the target is healed or takes damage (see page 367 for PvE/RvR limitations).

Skill......Music Casting Time......2.5 sec.
Range......1500

Lvl	Spell	Cost	Dur
1	Mesmerizing Melody*	2P	16 sec.
5	Entrancing Melody*	4P	21 sec.
10	Paralyzing Melody*	6P	28 sec.
16	Facinating Melody*	10P	35 sec.
21	Mesmerizing Hymn*	13P	42 sec.
28	Entrancing Hymn*	17P	51 sec.
36	Paralyzing Hymn*	23P	61 sec.
43	Facinating Hymn	27P	70 sec.

Spirits' Music

Confusion: (Switch %) chance to switch targets; (Ally %) chance to attack own ally (see page 367 for Pve/RvR limitations).

Skill......Music Dmg Type......Spirit
Casting Time......3.5 sec. Range......1350
Duration......60 sec.

Lvl	Spell	Cost	Switch %	Ally %
3	Confounding Cadence*	3P	70%	0%
8	Befuddling Cadence*	5P	85%	0%
14	Confusing Cadence*	9P	100%	0%
20	Mystifying Cadence*	12P	100%	15%
26	Confounding Ballad*	16P	100%	30%
32	Befuddling Ballad*	20P	100%	45%
38	Confusing Ballad*	24P	100%	60%
48	Mystifying Ballad	31P	100%	75%

DD. You must wait 10 seconds before casting one of these spells again.

Skill......Music Dmg Type......Body
Casting Time......Shout Range......700
Duration......Inst.

Lvl	Spell	Cost	Dmg
1	Concussive Shout*	2P	4
4	Concussive Bellow*	3P	13
7	Concussive Yell*	5P	21
12	Concussive Holler*	8P	33
18	Concussive Scream*	11P	50
25	Concussive Whoop*	15P	67
34	Concussive Shriek*	21P	89
44	Concussive Roar	28P	115

AoE Mesmerize: target halts all movement and is unable to attack or cast spells; the effect breaks when the target is healed or takes damage (see page 367 for PvE/RvR limitations).

Skill......Music Casting Time......3 sec.
Range......1500

Lvl	Spell	Cost	Dur	Radius
10	Captivate Audience*	6P	28 sec.	100
16	Captivate Crowd*	10P	35 sec.	150
21	Captivate Swarms*	13P	42 sec.	200
28	Captivate Multitude*	17P	51 sec.	250
36	Captivate Army*	23P	61 sec.	300
43	Captivate Legions	27P	70 sec.	350

Buffs Groupmates' Body resistance. You must wait 8 seconds before casting a Groupmate resistance buff spell again.

Skill......Music Cost......0P
Casting Time......Shout Range......1500
Duration......Chant + 5

Lvl	Spell	Buff
25	Hymn of Body Guarding*	10
44	Hymn of Body Protection	20

Buffs Groupmates' Spirit resistance. You must wait 8 seconds before casting a Groupmate resistance buff spell again.

Skill......Music Cost......0P
Casting Time......Shout Range......1500
Duration Chant + 5

Lvl	Spell	Buff
26	Hymn of Spirit Guarding*	10
45	Hymn of Spirit Protection	20

Buffs Groupmates' Energy resistance. You must wait 8 seconds before casting a Groupmate resistance buff spell again.

Skill......Music Cost......0P
Casting Time......Shout Range......1500
Duration......Chant + 5

Lvl	Spell	Buff
27	Hymn of Energy Guarding*	10
46	Hymn of Energy Protection	20

Buffs Groupmates' Heat resistance. You must wait 8 seconds before casting a Groupmate resistance buff spell again.

Skill......Music Cost......0P
Casting Time......Shout Range......1500
Duration......Chant + 5

Lvl	Spell	Buff
28	Hymn of Heat Guarding*	10
47	Hymn of Heat Protection	20

Buffs Groupmates' Cold resistance. You must wait 8 seconds before casting a Groupmate resistance buff spell again.

Skill......Music Cost......0P
Casting Time......Shout Range......1500
Duration......Chant + 5

Lvl	Spell	Buff
29	Hymn of Cold Guarding*	10
48	Hymn of Cold Protection	20

Buffs Groupmates' Matter resistance. You must wait 8 seconds before casting a Groupmate resistance buff spell again.

Skill......Music Cost......0P
Casting Time......Shout Range......1500
Duration......Chant + 5

Lvl	Spell	Buff
30	Hymn of Earth Guarding*	10
49	Hymn of Earth Protection	20

Druid

Races		Abilities	
Celt / Firbolg		1	Staves
Skills		1	Blunt Weapons
1	Nurture Magic	1	Cloth Armor
1	Regrowth Magic	1	Leather Armor
5	Nature Affinity Magic	1	Small Shields
5	Nurture Magic Spec.	1	Sprint
5	Regrowth Magic Spec.	1	Blades
5	Nature Affinity Magic Spec.	10	Reinforced Armor
		20	Scale Armor

The Druid is the premier Healer in the realm of Hibernia. As a Druid, you have three main specialization paths, which grant you the ability to heal, buff and resurrect group members and realmmates. You also get the not-so-common ability to call a pet if you need aid in battle.

The Best Part: Druids never have to look too far to find a group to adventure with. As the leading healer class for the realm, your Druid character will always be in demand. The abilities and the assorted beneficial spells that you acquire can be used to aid parties, assuring you a spot in most groups.

The Worst Part: Healing can cause the monsters to take a severe dislike to you, to the point they'll try to take you down first. Plus, your only defense is your armor, so you have to rely on your group for protection.

Race Choices:

Celtic. Celtics are the baseline race of Hibernia. They have an average aptitude in every class, and their starting statistics reflect this fact. While you can raise a Celtic's stats to favor the Druid's prime attributes – CON and EMP — your character can't easily match the natural characteristics of a Firbolg.

Firbolg. Firbolg characters start with a base EMP score of 70 and a base CON of 60. Since Empathy determines your maximum spell points for the Naturalist line, this race gives you an advantage from the start. However, you'll also find that Firbolg have reduced DEX and QUI.

Stat Choices: As mentioned above, the most important stats for a Druid are Constitution and Empathy. Of these two, EMP is by far the most important, as it affects your casting ability.

Weapon Choices: Your choice of weapon as a Druid is pretty much a personal decision. You can choose between Staves, Blunt weapons or Blades, so you have a fairly wide selection.

Druids don't spec their weapons. Many Druids, in fact, choose to carry both blunt and slash weapons with them — this lets them choose the particular attack to which a monster is vulnerable.

Spec Paths: Three main spec paths exist for the druid, the first two of which also belong to Bards and Wardens — Regrowth, Nurture and Naturalism.

- *Regrowth:* This spec line marks the path of a healer. In this specialty lies a number of healing spells, as well as the power of resurrection.
- *Nurture:* This spec line identifies the path of the support mage. All of your skill modification and Buff spells are found here.
- *Naturalist:* This path benefits any Druid that wants to be more then prepared to defend himself or herself. Here, you'll find the power to call forth a pet to do your bidding.

Big Mistakes to Avoid in Character Creation: Don't mistake your pet's role. Unlike other casters' pets, it's not meant to tank. They just "assist" like an animated DoT.

Deciding What You Want Your Role to Be: Healer, group supporter or petmaster? Solo or group? Once you make those two choices, things should fall into place.

Plotting Your Future:

- There isn't much advantage to grouping until around Level 5, when you start getting your more valuable spells. Until then, solo in the newbie areas, doing tasks and saving up for armor.
- Once you get a pet, go mostly solo hunting for another level or two, with a little grouping thrown in for experience.
- Once you hit around Level 5 or so, decide on your role and put the majority of your points in that spec path, with the rest into your chosen secondary line.

Grouping: In a group, the main role of a Druid is to keep the other members of your party healthy. The better you are at it, the longer they'll be able to hunt, and thus, the more experience you'll get to share.

- In group hunting, you should never have to engage in melee combat. Take up a position behind or to one side of your group and keep them healed as they fight.
- Before a heal, take note of your own Power level. There's little value in spending all of your Power to heal one person fully if it means you won't have the Power to heal others that may need it. Just know your group and the usual healing that's required for each person and keep everyone healthy enough to win the battle. Use downtime to help the group fully recover.
- Note that some of your Druid spells can't be stacked (cast simultaneously) with similar spells cast by other classes. If there are other casters in the group, talk about things beforehand and plan out who is going to maintain what Buffs, and on who.

Soloing:

Be aware that Druids are very much a Damage Over Time type of class. They don't wave their hands and suddenly something falls over dead. It takes patience, but they can stack their DoT, Pet, Damage Shield, Damage Add and Melee to be very effective at soloing monsters.

- Druids are far better off in solo play then many other healers. Not only do you get to use several weapon and armor types, but your pets can be a welcome aid to solo play.
- The Naturalist specialization line gives you pets, which you can use to initiate an attack against targets that fall into the yellow, or even orange, con range.
- Remember, your pet can't go anywhere that a normal player can't go.
- Your pet can weaken mobs to the point that you can easily finish them off. Without a pet, you'd better figure on hunting targets that con out as blue.

Realm Versus Realm:

- Druids in RvR are almost always expected to be healers. If you plan on doing a lot of RvR, that's probably the best role to concentrate on.
- Before your group goes out, make sure that everyone knows what role they're playing (especially if you're not a healing-spec'ed Druid!).
- Some people recommend looking more like a fighter in RvR if you can. It makes it harder for the enemy to figure out who to take down first.

Beginner's Tips:

- Your pet is 75% of your level. The peet levels three times for every four levels you make. Every fourth time you level, the pet will remain the same.
- Don't use a lot of healing on your pet in combat — it makes monsters aggro on you!
- When grouping, always let the fighters get in one or two hits before you do anything. Let the monsters aggro on *them*.
- If a monster aggros on you in group combat, stand there and let the fighter get it off you. If you run, it makes it much harder for your group to take care of the monster.

Advanced Techniques:

- In solo hunting, use your Wither spell. Then, as the creature advances, have your pet attack it. After your pet lands a few hits, wade in with your weapon. Then, if you're weak and it's getting too close, you can root it until you're ready to go again.
- Keep your group window out when grouping so that you can see who needs healing. Click on the person's name in the box and then cast heal.
- Your chance to block arrows from a same-level archer with your shield is 30%. This is modified by quality and condition of the shield.
- 20 and 32 spec pets ahve an AoE stun that can wake up mezzed mobs, so be sure to keep the pet away from mezzed monsters when you're in a group.

Druid's Spells

Regrowth

Heals damage to Friend by (Heal) HP.

Skill ....Regrowth Casting Time ...2.25 sec.
Range.....................1350 Duration..................Inst.

Lvl	Spell	Cost	Heal
1	Minor Revigoration*	1P	5
3	Minor Renewal*	2P	8
5	Minor Revivification*	3P	11
8	Minor Resurgance*	4P	16
11	Minor Revival*	6P	21
14	Minor Regeneration*	7P	26
18	Minor Regrowth*	9P	33
23	Minor Restoration*	11P	41
29	Minor Resuscitation*	14P	50
37	Minor Renascence*	19P	64
47	Minor Apotheosis	24P	80

Heals damage to Friend by (Heal) HP.

Skill ....Regrowth Casting Time ...2.75 sec.
Range.....................1350 Duration..................Inst.

Lvl	Spell	Cost	Heal
4	Renewal*	5P	22
6	Revivification*	6P	30
9	Resurgance*	9P	42
12	Revival*	12P	54
16	Regeneration*	15P	71
21	Regrowth*	20P	91
27	Restoration*	26P	116
31	Resuscitation*	30P	132
36	Renascence*	36P	152
46	Apotheosis	47P	193

Resurrects corpse; target is resurrected with a percentage of its original Power and/or HP.

Skill ....Regrowth Casting Time ....4 sec.
Range.....................1500 Duration..................Inst.
Cost..........Based on corpse (see p. 368)

Lvl	Spell	Power	HP
10	Minor Reconstitution	No Power	10%

Druid's Regrowth

Heals damage to Friend by (Heal) HP.

Skill ....Regrowth Casting Time ...3.25 sec.
Range.....................1350 Duration..................Inst.

Lvl	Spell	Cost	Heal
5	Major Resurgance*	11P	50
8	Major Revival*	16P	75
11	Major Regeneration*	21P	99
15	Major Regrowth*	29P	132
20	Major Restoration*	38P	173
26	Major Resuscitation*	50P	222
33	Major Renascence*	65P	279
42	Major Apotheosis	84P	352

Heals damage to Friend by (Heal) HP.

Skill ....Regrowth Casting Time ...3.75 sec.
Range.....................1350 Duration..................Inst.

Lvl	Spell	Cost	Heal
10	Greater Revival*	29P	136
14	Greater Regeneration*	40P	185
19	Greater Regrowth*	54P	246
25	Greater Restoration*	71P	319
32	Greater Resuscitation*	94P	405
41	Greater Renascence*	123P	515
50	Greater Apotheosis	154P	626

Cures Friend.

Skill ....Regrowth Casting Time .....3.2 sec.
Range.....................1000 Duration..................Inst.

Lvl	Spell	Cost
6	Cure Poison	6%P
7	Cure Disease	6%P

Resurrects corpse; target is resurrected with a percentage of its original Power and/or HP.

Skill ....Regrowth Range.....................1500
Duration..................Inst.
Cost..........Based on corpse (see p. 368)

Lvl	Spell	Cast	Power	HP
16	Lesser Reconstitution	7 sec.	10%	30%
24	Reconstitution	9 sec.	25%	50%
40	Greater Reconstitution	14 sec.	50%	100%

Heals damage to Friend by (Heal %) HP once every 15 min. You must wait 15 minutes before casting one of these spells again.

Skill ....Regrowth Cost............................0P
Casting Time ....Shout Range.....................1350
Duration..................Inst.

Lvl	Spell	Heal %
12	Nature's Appreciation*	33%
21	Nature's Blessing*	55%
31	Nature's Esteem*	75%
43	Nature's Sanction	100%

Heals damage to Groupmates by (Heal %) HP once every 20 min. You must wait 20 minutes before casting one of these spells again.

Skill ....Regrowth Cost............................0P
Casting Time ....Shout Range.....................1350
Duration..................Inst.

Lvl	Spell	Heal %
23	Bith's Benison*	50%
35	Bith's Acclamation*	75%
45	Bith's Benediction	100%

Heals damage to Groupmates by (Heal) HP.

Skill ....Regrowth Casting Time ....4 sec.
Range.....................1350 Duration..................Inst.

Lvl	Spell	Cost	Heal
13	Healing Conflux*	25P	57
22	Renewing Conflux*	42P	93
34	Restoring Conflux*	67P	141
44	Reviving Conflux	89P	181

Nurture

Buffs Friend's STR.

Skill ....Nurture Casting Time ....3 sec.
Range.....................1000 Duration...........Concent.

Lvl	Spell	Cost	Buff
3	Strength of the Oak**	1C	12
7	Strength of the Redwood**	3C	15
14	Vigor of the Oak**	5C	21
20	Vigor of the Redwood**	7C	26
30	Force of the Oak**	11C	34
41	Force of the Redwood	15C	42
50	Might of the Redwood	19C	50

Buffs Friend's AF.

Skill ....Nurture Casting Time ....3 sec.
Range.....................1000 Duration...........Concent.

Lvl	Spell	Cost	Buff
2	Minor Bark Skin**	1C	12
4	Lesser Bark Skin**	2C	14
6	Bark Skin**	2C	16
9	Major Bark Skin**	3C	19
12	Greater Bark Skin**	4C	22
17	Superior Bark Skin**	6C	27
21	Skin of the Redwood**	7C	31
26	Greater Skin of the Redwood**	9C	36
32	Major Skin of the Redwood	11C	42
45	Superior Skin of the Redwood	16C	55

Buffs Friend's DEX.

Skill ....Nurture Casting Time ....3 sec.
Range.....................1000 Duration...........Concent.

Lvl	Spell	Cost	Buff
8	Dexterity of the Ferret**	3C	16
13	Dexterity of the Rabbit**	5C	20
19	Dexterity of the Badger**	7C	25
28	Dexterity of the Lynx**	10C	32
38	Dexterity of the Bear	14C	40
48	Dexterity of the Wolf	18C	48

Buffs Friend's CON.

Skill ....Nurture Casting Time ....3 sec.
Range.....................1000 Duration...........Concent.

Lvl	Spell	Cost	Buff
5	Oak's Stoutness**	2C	14
11	Oak's Stamina**	4C	18
15	Oak's Girth**	5C	22
24	Redwood's Stoutness**	8C	29
33	Redwood's Stamina	12C	36
43	Redwood's Girth	16C	44

Druid's Nurture

Buffs friend's attack speed by (Speed %).
Skill ....Nurture Casting Time .....3.5 sec.
Range.....................1000 Duration...........Concent.

Lvl	Spell	Cost	Speed %
2	Hunter's Attack**	1C	8%
10	Hunter's Blow**	4C	10%
20	Hunter's Offense**	7C	12%
30	Hunter's Press**	11C	15%
40	Hunter's Strike	14C	17%
50	Hunter's Assault	19C	20%

Buffs Friend's STR and CON.
Skill ....Nurture Casting Time ....3 sec.
Range.....................1000 Duration...........Concent.

Lvl	Spell	Cost	Buff
5	Strength of the Tree**	4C	21
9	Strength of the Thicket**	6C	25
13	Strength of the Grove**	9C	30
18	Strength of the Orchard**	12C	36
25	Strength of the Wood**	17C	45
34	Strength of the Forest	24C	55
44	Strength of the Timberland	32C	67

Buffs Friend's DEX and QUI.
Skill ....Nurture Casting Time ....3 sec.
Range.....................1000 Duration...........Concent.

Lvl	Spell	Cost	Buff
7	Breeze's Dance**	5C	22
14	Gust's Dance**	9C	31
19	Squall's Dance**	13C	37
29	Storm's Dance**	20C	49
39	Tornado's Dance	28C	61
49	Zephyr's Dance	36C	73

Buffs Friend's INT, EMP and PIE.
Skill ....Nurture Casting Time ....3 sec.
Range.....................1000 Duration...........Concent.

Lvl	Spell	Cost	Buff
11	Nature's Sight**	4C	21
22	Nature's Wisdom**	8C	32
31	Nature's Sagacity	11C	41
42	Nature's Vision	15C	52

Buffs Friend's Heat resistance.
Skill ....Nurture Casting Time ....3 sec.
Range.....................1000 Duration...........Concent.

Lvl	Spell	Cost	Buff
23	Strength of the Sun**	8C	8
32	Resillience of the Sun	11C	16
43	Aura of the Sun	16C	24

Buffs Friend's Cold resistance.
Skill ....Nurture Casting Time ....3 sec.
Range.....................1000 Duration...........Concent.

Lvl	Spell	Cost	Buff
24	Warmth of the Badger**	8C	8
35	Warmth of the Wolf	12C	16
45	Warmth of the Bear	16C	24

Buffs Friend's Matter resistance.
Skill ....Nurture Casting Time ....3 sec.
Range.....................1000 Duration...........Concent.

Lvl	Spell	Cost	Buff
26	Earth Affinity**	9C	8
38	Earth Bond	14C	16
48	Earth Union	18C	24

Nature Magic

Root: Enemy speed debuffed to 1% of original movement.
Skill........Nature Affinity Dmg Type...............Body
Casting Time .....2.5 sec. Range.....................1500

Lvl	Spell	Cost	Dur
2	Grasping Vines*	2P	7 sec.
6	Bonding Vines*	4P	13 sec.
11	Webbing Vines*	7P	20 sec.
17	Clutching Vines*	10P	28 sec.
24	Holding Vines*	15P	38 sec.
30	Tangling Vines*	19P	47 sec.
37	Tenacious Vines*	23P	56 sec.
47	Detaining Vines	30P	70 sec.

Caster's damage/sec buffed (stacks as group 1).
Skill........Nature Affinity Dmg Type............Matter
Casting Time ....3 sec. Duration.............10 min.

Lvl	Spell	Cost	Dmg/Sec
1	Nails of the Wild*	2P	1
4	Claws of the Wild*	3P	1.6
9	Talons of the Wild*	6P	2.7
14	Teeth of the Wild*	9P	3.7
21	Fangs of the Wild*	13P	5.2
27	Pincers of Wild*	17P	6.5
36	Stingers of the Wild*	23P	8.4
46	Hooks of the Wild	30P	10.5

Spirits' Nature

Calls pet, up to 75% of Caster's level.
Skill........Nature Affinity Cost.......................25%P
Casting Time ....6 sec. Duration ....Until Neg.

Lvl	Spell	Max Lvl
1	Call Minor Nature Spirit*	7
7	Call Lesser Nature Spirit*	12
12	Call Nature Spirit*	20
20	Call Major Nature Spirit*	32
32	Call Greater Nature Spirit	50

DoT: inflicts (Dmg) every 5 seconds.
Skill........Nature Affinity Dmg Type...............Body
Casting Time ....3 sec. Range.....................1350
Duration ....30 sec.

Lvl	Spell	Cost	Dmg
5	Contamination*	4P	5
8	Pollution*	5P	9
11	Moldiness*	7P	14
15	Wither*	9P	19
19	Corruption*	12P	25
24	Blight*	15P	32
30	Dry Rot*	19P	41
35	Dilapidation*	22P	48
41	Degeneration*	26P	57
48	Defedation	31P	67

Damage Shield: On Friend; enemy damaged when hits Friend (stacks as group 1).
Skill........Nature Affinity Dmg Type............Matter
Casting Time ....4 sec. Range.....................1000
Duration...........Concent.

Lvl	Spell	Cost	Dmg/Sec
3	Briarsprout**	1C	0.9
6	Pricklesprout**	2C	1.2
13	Burrsprout**	5C	1.8
18	Thornsprout**	6C	2.2
25	Spursprout**	9C	2.9
34	Thistlesprout	12C	3.7
44	Spinesprout	16C	4.6

AoE Root: Enemy speed debuffed to 1% of original movement, radius of 350 wu.
Skill........Nature Affinity Dmg Type............Matter
Casting Time .....2.5 sec. Range.....................1500

Lvl	Spell	Cost	Dur
4	Patch of Ivy*	3P	15 sec.
10	Patch of Vines*	6P	23 sec.
16	Patch of Tangleweed*	10P	30 sec.
22	Field of Ivy*	13P	38 sec.
29	Field of Vines*	18P	47 sec.
39	Field of Tangleweed*	25P	60 sec.
49	Expanse of Tangleweed	32P	73 sec.

Eldritch

Races	Abilities
Lurikeen / Elf	1 Staves
Skills	1 Sprint
1 Mana Magic	1 Cloth Armor
1 Light Magic	5 QuickCast
5 Void Magic	
5 Mana Magic Spec.	
5 Light Magic Spec.	
5 Void Magic Spec.	

The Eldritch is an offense-based cloth caster. Some people may define this class as a pure damage dealer. In some respects, this is true, but you can do other things as an Eldritch. With a magical arsenal at your fingertips, you have the ability to deal out damage in a variety of ways, at a variety of ranges. You can even debuff opponents to some extent. With this class, you can develop a diverse caster who can deal damage in a variety of ways, or specialize to produce a massive damage output in a specifically tuned way.

The Best Part: Dishing out damage. You can usually decimate anything before it gets close to you.

The Worst Part: The tradeoff for such high damage output is a very weak defense. While you have some minor magical defenses, don't depend on them to save you. Most anything that gets its teeth in you will finish you off.

Race Choices: Elves and Lurikeen can choose only the Focus path, while Celtics may choose any path.

Elf. Has a high starting INT, which translates into a greater Power pool.

Lurikeen. Begins with high DEX, which improves casting time. Their smaller size also allows them to be less noticeable in RvR situations.

- Both races are inherently weak. If fortitude is a necessity, a well-rounded Celtic is probably your best choice.

Stat Choices: You'll find good availability for stat-enhancing items in the game, especially at later levels. Still, your starting stats can be very important. Splitting points evenly between DEX and INT is really the best way to go. Some players argue that extra CON is better, although it, too, can be boosted by game items. Every point you put initially into each stat means that your level cap for that stat is that much higher.

Weapon Choices: The Eldritch class is restricted to staves, but they play an important role with the Focus system and charges.

Spec Paths: As an Eldritch, you have three specialization paths.

- *Light:* Quick, powerful nukers, along with some minor Debuff spells.
- *Mana:* Gives you a powerful, point-blank, Area-Effect Nuke, as well as useful Debuffs.
- *Void:* Yields four pure damage-dealing spells. This includes two Bolt spells.

Big Mistakes To Avoid In Character Creation: Spending stat points at creation in the wrong area will have you cursing yourself later in the game. Even though QUI is listed as a tertiary stat, do not waste points in it. Stick to INT and DEX.

Deciding What You Want Your Role to Be: Determining your future is important, and the decisions you make in your first few levels will likely affect you throughout your entire career. So what do you want to be? Every specialization path has its own pros and cons.

- As a Light-spec'ed Eldritch, you will be able to cast off fast Nukes, as well as disable enemy spellcasters and archers from great distances. However, this path does its damage dealing at a closer range.
- If you choose the Mana path, you can eliminate tightly packed clusters of enemies. Proper tactics with these spells can make you the most feared enemy on the battlefield.
- If you're a Void-spec'ed Eldritch, you're all about damage. No fuss, no muss. You get two Bolts that deal damage from further away than any other damage spell, an Area-Effect Direct Damage spell for destroying groups of enemies, and a single-target Direct Damage spell for eliminating lone enemies.

Plotting Your Future: Once you have picked an appropriate path to follow, stay on it. Straying from your choices will often wind up with you wishing you had made better choices early on. Be consistent, and if you decide you don't like your character, create a new one and try something different.

Grouping:

- You are the primary magical damage dealer of any group. While groups can get by without you, you make a difficult fight seem almost too easy. Just don't get hit (i.e., find yourself a good tank protector).
- Eldritches are always an asset to a group, especially when teamed with support classes. A Mana Enchanter who can debuff your damage type always helps, as well as a Mentalist who can add Power regeneration spells to lower your downtime.
- In being all you can be, try to be aggressive, but not *too* aggressive. Drawing aggro in a group will get you killed before you know what's going on. Try and let the tanks establish a good hold on aggro before you nuke away. As well, try to use your debuff abilities if you have them. Every little bit counts.

Soloing:

- Despite a lack of self-defense skills, the Eldritch is the perfect soloing class. You can drop most mobs before they even reach you. Of course, the careful use of Stun and knowing the right moment to run are very important factors in soloing.
- The best things to solo are those monsters that are weak to your magic type. These monsters often display a notification field onscreen. Learn to identify these types of mobs, and try to avoid negative resistances. This can mean the difference between a relaxed solo career and certain death.
- Finally, don't be afraid to run! Save your Quickcast for when the mob is on top of you.

Realm Versus Realm: In RvR, lay waste to the Albion and Midgard classes. You're out there to do damage, so do it.

- As a rule, cloth casters are physically the weakest players on the battlefield. You're going to be eating dirt a lot, so get used to it.
- Try to always keep a pet tank around to manage any incoming bad guys. Your Stun often saves your life in that regard.
- Try at all costs to keep Bladeturn up; archers will have a field day with you if you forget about it.
- Never sit! Assassins get giddy when they find a sitting caster. It's a one-shot kill.
- You'll quickly learn what works for your particular specialization. Testing everything you've got is a much more effective way of discovering tactics than being fed strategies. Often, you can win simply by doing what your opponent *isn't* expecting you to do.

Beginner's Tips:

- Test every mob type out there and see what's weak to your magic. (Or, check out the monster chart on p. 347.)

Advanced Techniques:

- If you're having problems with resists, try using the second-highest spell in that particular spell line. This can greatly increase your chance to hit. Additionally, the more casters who cast upon a particular target, the greater your chance for a successful hit. If you can, bring buddies!
- A Mana Enchanter is your best friend. And a Void Eldritch is a Mana Enchanter's best friend. Work together to debuff both Cold and Energy, then use your respective AoE Nukes to take out hordes of enemies. Just be sure to watch aggro.
- Your chance to block arrows from a same-level archer with your shield is 30%. This is modified by quality and condition of the shield.

Eldritch Spells

Way of the Moon

Buffs Caster's AF.

Skill ....2/3 Spec Dmg Type............Energy
Casting Time ....3 sec. Duration.............15 min.

Lvl	Spell	Cost	Buff
1	Lesser Powerward	2P	13
3	Powerward	3P	22
5	Lesser Powerbarrier	4P	32
9	Powerbarrier	6P	51
13	Lesser Powerfield	8P	71
18	Powerfield	11P	95
24	Powershield	15P	124
31	Greater Powershield	19P	158
40	Greater Powerguard	25P	201
50	Supreme Powerguard	33P	250

Damage Shield: On Friend; enemy damaged when hits Friend (stacks as group 1).

Skill ....Mana Dmg Type............Energy
Casting Time ....4 sec. Range.....................1000
Duration.............10 min.

Lvl	Spell	Cost	Dmg/Sec
2	Aura of Turning	2P	0.8
4	Greater Aura of Turning	3P	1
8	Aura of Redirection	5P	1.3
14	Greater Aura of Redirection	9P	1.9
22	Aura of Reflection	13P	2.6
33	Greater Aura of Reflection	21P	3.6
44	Aura of Global Feedback	28P	4.6

Bladeturn: Absorbs damage of single hit.

Skill ....Mana Dmg Type............Energy
Casting Time ....4 sec. Duration.............10 min.

Lvl	Spell	Cost	Target
19	Barrier of Negation	8%P	Self

Non-magical damage to Caster reduced by (Bonus %).

Skill ....Mana Dmg Type............Energy
Casting Time ....3 sec. Duration.............15 min.

Lvl	Spell	Cost	Bonus %
30	Ward of Power	19P	5%
41	Barrier of Power	26P	10%

Vacuumancy

DD, Snare: enemy's speed debuffed to 60% of original movement.

Skill ....Mana Dmg Type................Cold
Casting Time ....3 sec. Range.....................1350
Duration ....30 sec.

Lvl	Spell	Cost	Dmg
1	Lesser Ensnaring Blast	2P	5
5	Ensnaring Blast	4P	21
9	Greater Ensnaring Blast	6P	37
13	Entangling Blast	8P	49
17	Greater Entangling Blast	10P	65
23	Webbing Blast	14P	85
33	Greater Webbing Blast	21P	120
41	Demobilizing Blast	26P	148
50	Greater Demobilizing Blast	33P	180

AoE DD, centered on Caster, radius 300.

Skill ....Mana Dmg Type................Cold
Casting Time ....3 sec. Duration..................Inst.

Lvl	Spell	Cost	Dmg
2	Lesser Mana Ripple	2P	16
7	Mana Ripple	5P	52
11	Mana Eddy	7P	74
15	Mana Splash	9P	104
20	Mana Burst	12P	134
26	Mana Flux	16P	177
32	Mana Billow	20P	215
39	Mana Surge	25P	265
48	Mana Flood	31P	325

Debuffs STR by 7.5% and movement speed by 15%; halves effect of any healing spell cast on target.

Skill ....Mana Dmg Type................Cold
Casting Time ....3 sec. Range.....................1500

Lvl	Spell	Cost	Dur	Radius
6	Entropic Affliction	4P	60 sec.	(1)
16	Entropic Sickness	10P	1.5 min.	250
27	Entropic Illness	17P	2 min.	300
37	Entropic Disease	23P	2.5 min.	350
47	Entropic Pestilence	30P	3 min.	400

STR/CON debuff.

Skill ....Mana Dmg Type................Cold
Range.....................1500 Duration ....60 sec.

Lvl	Spell	Cost	Cast	Debf.	Rad.
3	Lesser Strength Dispersal	3P	2 sec.	9	(1)
8	Disperse Strength	5P	2 sec.	12	(1)
12	Lesser Vigor Dispersal	8P	2 sec.	14	(1)
18	Disperse Vigor	11P	2 sec.	18	(1)
28	Lesser Health Dispersal	17P	3 sec.	24	200
38	Disperse Health	24P	3 sec.	30	275
49	Greater Vitality Dispersal	32P	3 sec.	36.5	350

AoE DD, Snare: debuffs attack speed by (Debuff %); radius 350 wu.

Skill ....Mana Dmg Type................Cold
Casting Time ....4 sec. Range.....................1500
Duration ....30 sec.

Lvl	Spell	Cost	Debuff%	Dmg
10	Lesser Kinetic Dispersal	8P	8%	29
14	Kinetic Dispersal	11P	9%	41
19	Lesser Kinetic Dampening	15P	10.5%	57
25	Kinetic Dampening	20P	12.5%	72
34	Lesser Kinetic Siphon	28P	15%	97
44	Kinetic Siphon	37P	18%	125

Way of the Sun

DD.

Skill........................Light Dmg Type ....Heat
Casting Time .....2.6 sec. Range.....................1500
Duration..................Inst.

Lvl	Spell	Cost	Dmg
1	Gleam Ray	2P	5
2	Gleam Streak	2P	9
3	Gleam Blast	3P	14
6	Moon Ray	4P	26
9	Moon Streak	6P	37
13	Moon Blast	8P	49
17	Sun Ray	10P	65
24	Sun Streak	15P	89
33	Sun Blast	21P	120
41	Aurora Ray	26P	148
50	Aurora Blast	33P	180

Stuns target, making him unable to move or perform actions (see page 367 for Pve/RvR limitations).

Skill........................Light Dmg Type ....Heat
Casting Time .....2.5 sec. Range.....................1500

Lvl	Spell	Cost	Dur
5	Prismatic Flare	4P	3 sec.
15	Prismatic Flash	9P	5 sec.
26	Prismatic Shimmer	16P	6 sec.
36	Prismatic Sheen	23P	8 sec.
46	Prismatic Strobe	30P	9 sec.

Shadow Control

DD.

Skill........................Light Dmg Type................Cold
Casting Time.....2.8 sec. Range.....................1500
Duration..................Inst.

Lvl	Spell	Cost	Dmg
1	Shadowburst	2P	5
5	Shadowblast	4P	26
8	Shadowcharge	5P	41
12	Shadowshock	8P	57
16	Shadowsmash	10P	77
22	Shadowcrash	13P	103
28	Shadowforce	17P	133
35	Shadowcrush	22P	164
45	Shadowdoom	29P	210

DEX/QUI debuff.

Skill........................Light Dmg Type................Cold
Casting Time........2 sec. Range.....................1500
Duration...............2 min.

Lvl	Spell	Cost	Debuff
3	Negate Coordination	2P	9
6	Nullify Coordination	3P	10.5
9	Obliviate Coordination	4P	12.5
13	Destroy Coordination	6P	15
18	Abrogate Coordination	8P	18
25	Blank Coordination	12P	22.5
36	Obliterate Coordination	18P	28.5
46	Extinguish Coordination	24P	34.5

AoE Mesmerize: target halts all movement and is unable to attack or cast spells; the effect breaks when the target is healed or takes damage; radius 350 wu (see page 367 for PvE/RvR limitations).

Skill........................Light Dmg Type................Cold
Casting Time........3 sec. Range.....................1500

Lvl	Spell	Cost	Dur
4	Paralyzing Wind	3P	10 sec.
15	Paralyzing Veil	9P	15 sec.
26	Paralyzing Cloak	16P	21 sec.
37	Paralyzing Sphere	23P	26 sec.
47	Paralyzing Cloud	30P	31 sec.

Reduces range on ranged attacks by (Debuff %).

Skill........................Light Dmg Type................Cold
Casting Time........2 sec. Range.....................2300
Duration...............2 min.

Lvl	Spell	Cost	Debuff %
10	Negate Sight	4P	25%
19	Nullify Sight	9P	35%
24	Obliviate Sight	12P	45%
32	Destroy Sight	16P	55%
40	Abrogate Sight	20P	65%

Way of the Eclipse

DD.

Skill........................Void Dmg Type................Cold
Casting Time........3 sec. Range.....................1500
Duration..................Inst.

Lvl	Spell	Cost	Dmg
3	Ethereal Concussion	3P	14
5	Major Ethereal Concussion	4P	21
7	Ethereal Blast	5P	29
10	Major Ethereal Blast	6P	37
13	Ethereal Detonation	8P	49
17	Major Ethereal Detonation	10P	65
23	Ethereal Explosion	14P	85
30	Major Ethereal Explosion	19P	108
37	Ethereal Devastation	23P	136
47	Major Ethereal Devastation	30P	172

Bolt (ranged DD). You must wait 20 seconds before casting one of these spells again.

Skill........................Void Dmg Type................Cold
Casting Time........4 sec. Range.....................1875
Duration..................Inst.

Lvl	Spell	Cost	Dmg
2	Void Slit	2P	13
4	Void Gap	3P	24
6	Void Break	4P	36
9	Void Cleave	6P	53
14	Void Rent	9P	75
18	Void Rift	11P	98
22	Void Fissure	13P	115
28	Void Gulf	17P	149
36	Void Chasm	23P	188
46	Void Abyss	30P	239

Void Mastery

Bolt (ranged DD). You must wait 20 seconds before casting one of these spells again.

Skill........................Void Dmg Type................Cold
Casting Time........4 sec. Range.....................1875
Duration..................Inst.

Lvl	Spell	Cost	Dmg
1	Nil Bolt	2P	8
4	Void Bolt	3P	30
7	Negative Bolt	5P	52
12	Abrogation Bolt	8P	82
17	Null Bolt	10P	118
24	Oblivion Bolt	15P	163
31	Annihilation Bolt	19P	207
38	Obliteration Bolt	24P	259
46	Bolt of Uncreation	30P	309

AoE DD, radius 350.

Skill........................Void Dmg Type................Cold
Casting Time........4 sec. Range.....................1500
Duration..................Inst.

Lvl	Spell	Cost	Dmg
3	Lesser Null Squall	3P	13
5	Null Squall	4P	20
8	Lesser Null Storm	5P	32
13	Null Storm	8P	48
18	Lesser Null Ebullition	11P	68
25	Null Ebullition	15P	92
32	Lesser Null Tempest	20P	116
44	Null Tempest	28P	159

Body resistance debuff.

Skill........................Void Casting Time........2 sec.
Range.....................1500 Duration.............30 sec.

Lvl	Spell	Cost	Debuff %
22	Nullify Hardiness	10P	7.5%
33	Negate Hardiness	16P	15%
45	Void Hardiness	23P	25%

Spirit resistance debuff.

Skill........................Void Casting Time........2 sec.
Range.....................1500 Duration.............30 sec.

Lvl	Spell	Cost	Debuff %
26	Nullify Spirit	12P	7.5%
35	Negate Spirit	17P	15%
48	Void Spirit	24P	25%

Energy resistance debuff.

Skill........................Void Casting Time........2 sec.
Range.....................1500 Duration.............30 sec.

Lvl	Spell	Cost	Debuff %
27	Nullify Dissipation	13P	7.5%
39	Negate Dissipation	20P	15%
49	Void Dissipation	25P	25%

Enchanter

Races	Abilities
Lurikeen / Elf	1 Staves
Skills	1 Sprint
1 Mana Magic	1 Cloth Armor
1 Light Magic	5 QuickCast
5 Enchantment Magic	
5 Mana Magic Spec.	
5 Light Magic Spec.	
5 Enchantment Magic Spec.	

Enchanters have the ability to summon a pet, provide weapon Buffs, a damage Shield, and in some cases, a boost to run speed. You function well in a solo setting, as well as in a group.

The Best Part: In early PvE levels, an Enchanter is probably the easiest and fastest class in which to solo. Your pet (and later, your wide choice of pets) gives you, for all intents and purposes, someone to help kill mobs faster.

The Worst Part: If you have any intention whatsoever of being the main tank in a group, the Enchanter class is not for you. Similarly, if you do not have the patience to be killed repeatedly by two or three hits, then the Enchanter is not for you. Finally, if you don't like being a major target in RvR, then stay away from an Enchanter.

Race Choices: Lurikeen and Elves are the only races who can become Enchanters.

Lurikeen. The number one reason for choosing the Lurikeen race is your small size. You'll be much harder for enemies to spot in RvR.

Elf. Elves also make powerful Enchanters.

- If you want to perform very well in RvR, then choose an Elven Mana/Light Enchanter.
- If you want to be very group-friendly and help people level, then choose a Lurikeen Enchantment Mastery Enchanter.

Stat Choices: The main statistics that define your Enchanter are DEX and INT.

- *DEX*: Determines how fast you can cast spells.
- *INT*: Affects how much Power you have.
- Due to the nature of the game and the items in the game, it is much more likely that your INT will be capped (raised to maximum allowed) with items in no time.
- Whatever race you choose, raise your INT to the highest level possible and put the rest of the points into DEX. Try to have your end character in mind when you create your Enchanter.

Weapon Choices: Weapons? What weapons?

Spec Paths:

You have three specialization lines:

- *Enchantment Mastery:* Gives you high-level pets and damage Buffs.
- *Mana:* Good AoE and Nuke spells.
- *Light:* Great DD attacks, as well as attack speed Debuffs. Makes you an efficient Enchanter.

Here are some common primary/secondary spec combinations:

- *Enchantment Mastery/Mana:* Full Enchantment Mastery Enchanters have the strongest pets in the game. You also receive the highest damage Buffs, and your secondary Mana specialization yields some impressive AoE spells. This combo is easy to solo, levels fast and is very group-friendly. However, in RvR, most enemy players ignore your pet and head straight for the master (you). This means you will burn a lot of Power casting your Nukes, since baseline DD spells are the only ones you will have.
- *Mana/Enchantment Mastery:* Fully specialized Mana Enchanters are the strongest nuking class in the game and have a fairly strong pet to boot. Your point-blank AoE spell does insane amounts of damage at higher levels. It does require a good group to use it effectively in PvE , but in RvR you can out-damage any other class in the game. You're also the fastest Enchanter since you have Run spells. But note that you will not level as fast or as easily with this template. The AoE in RvR battles is practically a death sentence if used too early.

ATYI MANA

• *Light/Enchantment Mastery:* Fully specialized Light Enchanters are probably the most efficient nukers, and like the previous template, have a fairly strong pet. You'll find that you have great DDs and some nice attack speed Debuffs. Light specialization helps you use less Power than the baseline DDs and helps you hit harder at high levels. (Note: Currently, attack speed Debuffs make monsters hit harder.) You will not level as fast or as easily as a full Enchantment Mastery Enchanter, but faster than a Mana-spec'ed Enchanter.

• *Light/Mana* or *Mana/Light:* Either combination gives you a pure endgame character. Your only goal is to be good at RvR combat. You will have a pet, but no pet Buffs. You'll also be a pure damage dealer, practically an Eldritch with a pet. This template really requires friends or a nice guild to get you leveled. To play this as your first Enchanter or solo Enchanter is only asking for a headache.

Big Mistakes to Avoid in Character Creation: Not knowing where you want to go with your Enchanter. Decide your role, then create your character.

Deciding What You Want Your Role To Be: Higher concentration on pets, Buffs or Nukes? More interested in soloing or grouping? Can't wait to get to RvR? Read through the spec paths and see what floats your boat.

Plotting Your Future: The guidelines for playing a low-level Enchanter are about the same as playing any other starting character class. Kill low level monsters as fast as you can so that you can progress to Level 5 and actually become an Enchanter. Remember, until Level 6, you don't incur any penalties for dying. After that point, you need to plan your battles a little more wisely.

Once you reach Level 5 and become an Enchanter, where do you go? The best templates develop full specialization in one line, with the rest of the points going into a secondary line. Spreading yourself thinly does not make you a more viable character — in fact, it does more harm than good.

Grouping:

• Enchanters make great grouping companions, especially since you bring another person (pet) to help the group kill mobs. Of course, the types of characters in your group should determine which pet you should use in any given situation. With tank-heavy groups, it's usually better to use your caster pet, since the Snare can come in handy. Groups with only one healer may ask you to summon your healing pet for the Health Regeneration spell.

• Get a feel for how your different pets react in different situations. Ultimately the decision on which pet to use is up to you.

• A group-friendly Enchanter is an Enchanter who levels fast.

Soloing: Solo combat for an Enchanter is a fairly simple process. You can either pull a mob with a Debuff or Nuke, and then sic your pet on it. Or, keep it even simpler and just send your pet at the mob. If you are hunting mobs which are not grouped, the second way is safest. Let your pet draw some aggro, debuff the mob if you can, then start nuking away.

Every Enchanter should be able to solo a yellow mob; most hunt orange mobs for better experience awards, since pets always absorb some XP. When an Enchanter solo hunts, the ideal pet is the tank pet.

Realm Versus Realm: The most significant thing to remember when RvR is that enemy players will ignore your pet 90% of the time. It is critical to keep this in mind, both in RvR and PvE. Find out the strengths and weaknesses of your different pets and use the most advantageous one for the situation.

Beginner's Tips:

• Before combat, call a pet. Buff your pet. Buff your friends. During combat, try to hit something.

• Before Level 3, go out around the towns and kill all the little monsters. Sticking to yellows is a good idea.

• Remember, it's OK to die until Level 5 — there's no penalty in experience or abilities.

- After reaching Level 3, buy a better weapon, do tasks, and kill yellows. Repeat until Level 5, when you need to decide on a spec path.
- The only reason to group at lower levels is to get experience grouping. If you don't need it, you don't need them taking a percentage of your XP for each kill.
- Remember, your pet can't go anywhere that a normal player can't go.

Advanced Techniques:

- You want to avoid multiple enemies, but the one-two punch of your pet and DD spells give you a good shot against high blues and yellows.
- Lesser Effervescence speed Buff in equipment can be extremely handy, and the extra party security it provides can be particularly crucial in RvR combat.

Enchanter Spells

Way of the Moon

Buffs Caster's AF.

Skill ....2/3 Spec Dmg Type ....Energy
Casting Time ....3 sec. Duration ....15 min.

Lvl	Spell	Cost	Buff
1	Lesser Powerward	2P	13
3	Powerward	3P	22
5	Lesser Powerbarrier	4P	32
9	Powerbarrier	6P	51
13	Lesser Powerfield	8P	71
18	Powerfield	11P	95
24	Powershield	15P	124
31	Greater Powershield	19P	158
40	Greater Powerguard	25P	201
50	Supreme Powerguard	33P	250

Damage Shield: On Friend; enemy damaged when hits Friend (stacks as group 1).

Skill ....Mana Dmg Type ....Energy
Casting Time ....4 sec. Range 1000
Duration ....10 min.

Lvl	Spell	Cost	Dmg/Sec
2	Aura of Turning	2P	0.8
4	Greater Aura of Turning	3P	1
8	Aura of Redirection	5P	1.3
14	Greater Aura of Redirection	9P	1.9
22	Aura of Reflection	13P	2.6
33	Greater Aura of Reflection	21P	3.6
44	Aura of Global Feedback	28P	4.6

Bladeturn: Absorbs damage of single hit.

Skill ....Mana Dmg Type ....Energy
Casting Time ....4 sec. Duration ....10 min.

Lvl	Spell	Cost	Target
19	Barrier of Negation	8%P	Self

Non-magical damage to Caster reduced by (Bonus %).

Skill ....Mana Dmg Type ....Energy
Casting Time ....3 sec. Duration ....15 min.

Lvl	Spell	Cost	Bonus %
30	Ward of Power	19P	5%
41	Barrier of Power	26P	10%

Empowerment

Pet Focus Damage Shield: On Pet; enemy damaged when hits Pet until Caster interrupted or out of power (stacks as group 2).

Skill ....Mana Dmg Type ....Energy
Casting Time ....4 sec. Range 1250
Duration ....Focus

Lvl	Spell	Cost	Dam/Sec
1	Aura of Echoing	1P/5s	0.7
6	Greater Aura of Echoing	3P/5s	1.2
9	Aura of Reflection	5P/5s	1.4
14	Greater Aura of Reflection	7P/5s	1.9
22	Aura of Resonation	11P/5s	2.6
30	Greater Aura of Resonation	15P/5s	3.3
40	Aura of Reverberation	20P/5s	4.2
50	Greater Aura of Reverberation	26P/5s	5.1

AoE DD, centered on Caster, radius 300.

Skill ....Mana Dmg Type ....Energy
Casting Time .....2.5 sec. Duration ....Inst.

Lvl	Spell	Cost	Dmg
7	Lesser Disenchanting Emanation	5P	52
11	Disenchanting Emanation	7P	74
16	Lesser Disenchanting Emission	10P	112
20	Disenchanting Emission	12P	134
26	Lesser Disenchanting Burst	16P	177
32	Disenchanting Burst	20P	215
39	Lesser Disenchanting Eruption	25P	265
48	Disenchanting Eruption	31P	325

Group Speed Buff by (Speed %).

Skill ....Mana Dmg Type ....Energy
Cost ....0P Casting Time ....3 sec.
Range ....2000 Duration ....Chant + 6

Lvl	Spell	Speed %
5	Lesser Effervescence	23%
15	Effervescence	31%
25	Greater Effervescence	38%
35	Superior Effervescence	46%
45	Maximum Effervescence	53%

Heat resistance debuff.

Skill ....Mana Casting Time ....2 sec.
Range ....1500 Duration ....30 sec.

Lvl	Spell	Cost	Debuff %
23	Amplify Heat	11P	7.5%
33	Endow Heat	16P	15%
44	Empower Heat	22P	25%

Cold resistance debuff.

Skill ....Mana Casting Time ....2 sec.
Range ....1500 Duration ....30 sec.

Lvl	Spell	Cost	Debuff %
24	Amplify Cold	12P	7.5%
34	Endow Cold	16P	15%
46	Empower Cold	24P	25%

Matter resistance debuff.

Skill ....Mana Casting Time ....2 sec.
Range ....1500 Duration ....30 sec.

Lvl	Spell	Cost	Debuff %
27	Amplify Matter	13P	7.5%
36	Endow Matter	18P	15%
49	Empower Matter	25P	25%

Way of the Sun

DD.

Skill........................Light Dmg Type...............Heat
Casting Time.....2.6 sec. Range.....................1500
Duration..................Inst.

Lvl	Spell	Cost	Dmg
1	Gleam Ray	2P	5
2	Gleam Streak	2P	9
3	Gleam Blast	3P	14
6	Moon Ray	4P	26
9	Moon Streak	6P	37
13	Moon Blast	8P	49
17	Sun Ray	10P	65
24	Sun Streak	15P	89
33	Sun Blast	21P	120
41	Aurora Ray	26P	148
50	Aurora Blast	33P	180

Stuns target, making him unable to move or perform actions (see page 367 for Pve/RvR limitations).

Skill........................Light Dmg Type...............Heat
Casting Time.....2.5 sec. Range.....................1500

Lvl	Spell	Cost	Dur
5	Prismatic Flare	4P	3 sec.
15	Prismatic Flash	9P	5 sec.
26	Prismatic Shimmer	16P	6 sec.
36	Prismatic Sheen	23P	8 sec.
46	Prismatic Strobe	30P	9 sec.

Bedazzlement

Debuffs attack speed by (Debuff %).

Skill........................Light Dmg Type...............Heat
Casting Time.....3.5 sec. Range.....................1500
Duration..............2 min.

Lvl	Spell	Cost	Debuff %
7	Distracting Scintillation	5P	7%
14	Soporific Scintillation	9P	9%
20	Blinding Scintillation	12P	11%
27	Disturbing Scintillation	17P	13%
36	Perturbing Scintillation	23P	15.5%
48	Agitating Scintillation	31P	19%

DD.

Skill........................Light Dmg Type...............Heat
Casting Time.....2.8 sec. Range.....................1500
Duration..................Inst.

Lvl	Spell	Cost	Dmg
1	Misleading Rapture	2P	5
5	Delusional Rapture	4P	26
8	Mystifying Rapture	5P	41
12	Duplicitous Rapture	8P	57
16	Illusory Rapture	10P	77
22	Deceiving Rapture	13P	103
28	Beguiling Rapture	17P	133
35	Phantom Rapture	22P	164
45	Insidious Rapture	29P	210

AoE Snare: Debuffs attack speed by (Debuff %); radius 350 wu.

Skill........................Light Dmg Type...............Heat
Casting Time.....3.5 sec. Range.....................1500
Duration...............2 min.

Lvl	Spell	Cost	Debuff %
17	Field of Scintillation	20P	10%
23	Array of Scintillation	28P	11.5%
29	Sea of Scintillation	36P	13.5%
37	Sky of Scintillation	46P	16%
46	Galaxy of Scintillation	60P	18.5%

Enchantment

Calls pet, up to 88% of Caster's level.

Skill.........Enchantments Cost.....................25%P
Casting Time........6 sec. Duration........Until Neg.

Lvl	Spell
1	Underhill Friend
7	Underhill Companion
12	Underhill Ally
20	Underhill Compatriot
32	Underhill Zealot

Heals damage to Pet by (Heal) HP.

Skill.........Enchantments Dmg Type..............Body
Casting Time........3 sec. Range.....................1350
Duration..................Inst.

Lvl	Spell	Cost	Heal
6	Assist Ally	4P	36
8	Support Ally	5P	46
11	Help Ally	7P	61
15	Invest Ally	9P	81
21	Reinforce Ally	13P	111
28	Infuse Ally	17P	146
35	Imbue Ally	22P	181
44	Succor Ally	28P	226

Enchantment Mastery

Friend's damage/sec buffed (stacks as group 2).

Skill.........Enchantments Dmg Type...............Body
Casting Time........3 sec. Range......................1000
Duration.............10 min.

Lvl	Spell	Cost	Dmg/Sec
4	Twinkling Arms	3P	1.6
8	Glossed Arms	5P	2.5
11	Shining Arms	7P	3.1
15	Shimmering Arms	9P	3.9
20	Glowing Arms	12P	5
26	Glittering Arms	16P	6.3
34	Brilliant Arms	21P	7.9
44	Splendorous Arms	28P	10

Buffs Pet's STR and CON.

Skill.........Enchantments Dmg Type..............Spirit
Casting Time........3 sec. Range......................1000
Duration.............10 min.

Lvl	Spell	Cost	Buff
3	Strength of the Underhill	3P	12
7	Vigor of the Underhill	6P	15
12	Zest of the Underhill	10P	19
18	Power of the Underhill	15P	24
24	Vim of the Underhill	19P	29
32	Force of the Underhill	26P	35
42	Fury of the Underhill	35P	43

Buffs Pet's DEX and QUI.

Skill.........Enchantments Dmg Type..............Spirit
Casting Time........3 sec. Range......................1000
Duration.............10 min.

Lvl	Spell	Cost	Buff
1	Craftiness	2P	10
5	Subtlety	5P	14
9	Cunning	8P	17
13	Slyness	11P	20
19	Trickiness	15P	25
25	Wiliness	20P	30
33	Guile	27P	36
43	Subdolosity	36P	44

Mentalist

Races		Skills	
Celt / Lurikeen / Elf		1	Mana Magic
Abilities		1	Light Magic
1	Staves	5	Mentalism Magic
1	Sprint	5	Mana Magic Spec.
1	Cloth Armor	5	Light Magic Spec.
5	QuickCast	5	Mentalism Magic Spec.

Mentalists are the Swiss army knives of casters. They have Direct Damage, Area Effect, Mesmerize, Heal, Damage-over-Time and Regeneration spells. Mentalists make an excellent support class for any group and thrive on being helpful to the group.

The Best Part: The best part about being a Mentalist is that people will want you in a group. You complement just about every other class. There will be little group down time with your skills and Power pool.

The Worst Part: You have very limited soloing potential after you rise in level. Like many classes, you can solo early, but must later stick to weaker monsters. You don't have the damage output or HP of some of the other support classes.

Race Choices: This is the only pure casting class that humans can join.

Elf. Highest INT (your source of Power), great DEX and QUI, but serious lack of STR and CON.

Lurikeen. Standard INT, great DEX and QUI, but also lacking in STR and CON.

Celtics. Baseline on all stats. Big disadvantage in DEX and QUI.

Stat Choices: Celtics are the easiest race; they can concentrate on main stats without having to worry about STR and CON. Try evenly splitting points between INT, DEX and QUI (in that order). This puts your Celtic on par with an Elf. Or, dump a few extra points into INT for some added Power.

Elves and Lurikeen both have STR and CON below 50, which penalizes HP, Stamina and encumbrance. If that bugs you, then put 10 points apiece into STR and CON, and the rest into INT. Or, dump a bunch of points into INT. Or, spread all points between INT, DEX and QUI (in that order).

- *STR:* Handy for carrying loot, but that's it. Be aware that many great +INT items also have -STR penalties.
- *CON:* Affects HP and Stamina. Not a strong suit for casters, but it helps to not be in the penalty range.
- *DEX:* Affects your casting time. Very important for casting as many spells as possible before an enemy disrupts you. Quite important in the long run.
- *QUI:* A tertiary stat for Mentalist.

Weapon Choices: You're a caster, what do you need a weapon for? Besides, you can only use a staff!

Weapons are generally used only to finish off something that is almost dead anyway. So, carry something, but don't worry about the quality and level of the weapon. Use whatever gives you the best stats.

Spec Paths: You have three paths of specialization.

- *Way of the Sun.* Basically, a damage and Charm line. You're a charmer and will normally travel with a pet.
- *Way of the Moon*: Gives you Buffs and DoT spells. You can wear mobs down slowly while powering the group.
- *Way of the Mind*: Yields healing, mezzing, and Confusion spells.

Big Mistakes to Avoid in Character Creation: Make sure you plan out what to do with your spec points! You only get one per level, while other classes get as many as two. They can afford to mix and match, but you need to hoard points until Level 40.5!

Deciding What You Want Your Role to Be: Your DD spells will never equal those of an Eldritch, and you don't have a pet to support you like an Enchanter does. So, you need to cater your character to a group for long-term benefits.

Plotting Your Future: This is where the debates rage on.

Highly recommended:

48 mana/09 Light/23 Mentalism

36 mana/35 Light/18 Mentalism

24 mana/45 Light/17 Mentalism

Also recommended:

- *41 Mind:* Healing is a nice side effect of spec'ing in this line, but the best part is mezzing or confusing monsters.
- *34 Moon:* Nice Buffs and DoTs. Your group will be asking for these spells, especially Power buffs and Hit Point Regeneration.
- *8 Sun:* Consumes any leftover points. Starting off with this lets you charm monsters, which may help you survive lower levels.

Grouping: Basically, you are well suited to group with just about any class. Get used to the dynamics and figure out what is expected of you in relation to each class.

- Make sure a monster is dead before it gets to you (if you are with another caster), or at least that it's mad at the other guy (if you are with a tank or light tank).
- To hold something still, stun it or mez it and then let the other guys shoot a few extra spells at it. This works well with melee fighters, since they can take aggro and you can heal them.
- Stick to attacks that don't require too many heals in order to avoid aggro, and use them along with Regens to lessen downtime.

Soloing:

- Don't get frustrated by the difficulty of soloing. For better soloing, be a Ranger.
- You are a caster, but not a big nuker. You can solo effectively up to about Level 20.
- Buff yourself whenever you can, since getting a heal off on yourself in battle usually doesn't work.
- Start off with a bang — a nice DD spell, then Stun. Put a DoT on a mob and then follow up with more DDs. (Remember, DoT ticks break mezzes and roots.) If the mob's not moving, go to max range again, rinse and repeat.

Realm Versus Realm:

- Other players hate mez! Therefore, this will be one of your most effective spells against another enemy caster or healer. They can't help their party if they aren't able to do anything but drool. You can even hit tanks with Insanity lines so they can't fight effectively.
- Your role is to create havoc. Mez, use Insane and apply DoTs at will.
- Hit assassin and stealth guys first with DoTs.
- Stay out of sight if you stand still (you can't Stealth, and sitting is an open invitation).
- Send Nightshades and archers ahead to scout for you.
- Don't /stick or /follow stealthers! Try to get up in a battlement or someplace high to observe the battlefield.

Beginner's Tips:

- Solo things that move slowly and put DoTs on them.
- Use AoE spells on tight groups, especially during attempts to siege a keep door.
- AoE spells are fun since you hit many people with one shot, but you won't kill this way.
- Remember, your pet can't go anywhere that a normal player can't go.
- You have an almost certain chance to charm / retain control of a creature your level or lower. The higher the level of the charmed creature compared to you, the greater the chance the monster has of breaking the charm.
- The higher your Light spec level, the greater your chance of charming and retaining control of a creature.
- If a charm breaks, you'll be the only thing on the released pet's aggro list!

Advanced Techniques:

- You are a support class. Heal tanks, give them damage Shields and do crowd control. Freeze monsters in place to give ranged attackers an extra shot at them. Put DoTs on critters to wear them down faster.
- You can do some of everything, so analyze the situation. Big damage spells may not be the best thing if DoTs work better. Or, you may want to mez a mob instead of paralyzing it.

Mentalist Spells

Way of the Moon

Buffs Caster's AF.

Skill ....2/3 Spec Dmg Type...........Energy
Casting Time ....3 sec. Duration............15 min.

Lvl	Spell	Cost	Buff
1	Lesser Powerward	2P	13
3	Powerward	3P	22
5	Lesser Powerbarrier	4P	32
9	Powerbarrier	6P	51
13	Lesser Powerfield	8P	71
18	Powerfield	11P	95
24	Powershield	15P	124
31	Greater Powershield	19P	158
40	Greater Powerguard	25P	201
50	Supreme Powerguard	33P	250

Damage Shield: On Friend; enemy damaged when hits Friend (stacks as group 1).

Skill ....Mana Dmg Type...........Energy
Casting Time ....4 sec. Range....................1000
Duration............10 min.

Lvl	Spell	Cost	Dmg/Sec
2	Aura of Turning	2P	0.8
4	Greater Aura of Turning	3P	1
8	Aura of Redirection	5P	1.3
14	Greater Aura of Redirection	9P	1.9
22	Aura of Reflection	13P	2.6
33	Greater Aura of Reflection	21P	3.6
44	Aura of Global Feedback	28P	4.6

Bladeturn: Absorbs damage of single hit.

Skill ....Mana Dmg Type...........Energy
Casting Time ....4 sec. Duration............10 min.

Lvl	Spell	Cost	Target
19	Barrier of Negation	8%P	Self

Non-magical damage to Caster reduced by (Bonus %).

Skill ....Mana Dmg Type...........Energy
Casting Time ....3 sec. Duration............15 min.

Lvl	Spell	Cost	Bonus %
30	Ward of Power	19P	5%
41	Barrier of Power	26P	10%

Holism

Buffs Friend's health regeneration by (Heal) HP every cycle.

Skill ....Mana Dmg Type.............Spirit
Casting Time ....3 sec. Range....................1350
Duration ....30 sec.

Lvl	Spell	Cost	Heal
10	Curative Trance	10P	33
21	Restorative Trance	20P	66
32	Healing Trance	32P	99
43	Sanative Trance	44P	132

DoT: inflicts (Dmg) every 4 seconds.

Skill ....Mana Dmg Type.............Spirit
Casting Time ....3 sec. Range....................1350
Duration ....24 sec.

Lvl	Spell	Cost	Dmg
1	Minor Mind Fade	2P	2
5	Lesser Mind Fade	4P	9
8	Mind Fade	5P	15
11	Lesser Mind Dissolution	7P	19
15	Mind Dissolution	9P	27
20	Greater Mind Dissolution	12P	35
25	Lesser Mind Melt	15P	45
30	Mind Melt	19P	53
35	Greater Mind Melt	22P	63
41	Mind Annihilation	26P	73
48	Complete Mind Annihilation	31P	87

Buffs Friend's power regeneration by (Buff) every cycle.

Skill ....Mana Dmg Type.............Spirit
Casting Time ....3 sec. Range....................1500
Duration............10 min.

Lvl	Spell	Cost	Buff
4	Empowering Unity	3P	1
14	Empowering Harmony	9P	2
24	Empowering Tranquility	15P	3
34	Empowering Concordance	21P	4
44	Empowering Perfection	28P	5

AoE DoT: inflicts (Dmg) every 5 seconds; radius 350 wu.

Skill ....Mana Dmg Type.............Spirit
Casting Time ....3 sec. Range....................1500
Duration ....20 sec.

Lvl	Spell	Cost	Dmg
17	Shroud of Madness	16P	31
23	Fog of Delirium	22P	41
29	Hallucinatory Winds	28P	53
36	Torrent of Dementia	36P	65
46	Storm of Insanity	47P	83

Way of the Sun

DD.

Skill.......................Light Dmg Type..............Heat
Casting Time .....2.6 sec. Range....................1500
Duration.................Inst.

Lvl	Spell	Cost	Dmg
1	Gleam Ray	2P	5
2	Gleam Streak	2P	9
3	Gleam Blast	3P	14
6	Moon Ray	4P	26
9	Moon Streak	6P	37
13	Moon Blast	8P	49
17	Sun Ray	10P	65
24	Sun Streak	15P	89
33	Sun Blast	21P	120
41	Aurora Ray	26P	148
50	Aurora Blast	33P	180

Stuns target, making him unable to move or perform actions (see page 367 for Pve/RvR limitations).

Skill.......................Light Dmg Type..............Heat
Casting Time .....2.5 sec. Range....................1500

Lvl	Spell	Cost	Dur
5	Prismatic Flare	4P	3 sec.
15	Prismatic Flash	9P	5 sec.
26	Prismatic Shimmer	16P	6 sec.
36	Prismatic Sheen	23P	8 sec.
46	Prismatic Strobe	30P	9 sec.

Illusions

DD.

Skill ....Light Dmg Type ....Heat
Casting Time .....2.8 sec. Range....................1500
Duration ....Inst.

Lvl	Spell	Cost	Dmg
1	Twinkling Visions	2P	5
5	Sparkling Visions	4P	26
8	Shimmering Visions	5P	41
12	Glimmering Visions	8P	57
16	Scintillating Visions	10P	77
22	Glittering Visions	13P	103
28	Radiant Visions	17P	133
35	Bedazzling Visions	22P	164
45	Coruscating Visions	29P	210

Charms creature for duration of spell up to 70-110% of Caster's level (depending on level of specialization); Caster can use weapons or cast another spell (not Chant or Song) on another target without breaking charm.

Skill ....Light Dmg Type ....Heat
Cost..................7%/4.5s Casting Time ....3 sec.
Range....................2000 Duration ....10 sec.

Lvl	Spell	Targets
4	Illusory Enemy	Human-like
10	Fabricated Enemy	Above + animals
17	Imaginary Enemy	Above + insects
25	Phantom Enemy	Above + magical creatures
33	Ghostly Enemy	Same as above
42	Dream Enemy	Same as above

AoE DD, radius 350.

Skill ....Light Dmg Type ....Heat
Casting Time ....4 sec. Range....................1500
Duration ....Inst.

Lvl	Spell	Cost	Dmg
3	Deluge of Illusion	3P	13
7	Flood of Illusion	5P	28
13	Sea of Illusion	8P	48
19	Rush of Illusion	12P	72
26	Flux of Illusion	16P	95
34	Inundation of Illusion	21P	123
44	Cataclysm of Illusion	28P	159

Mentalism

Heals damage to Friend by (Heal) HP.

Skill ....Mentalism Dmg Type ....Spirit
Casting Time ...2.75 sec. Range....................1350
Duration ....Inst.

Lvl	Spell	Cost	Heal
4	Somatic Reconstitution	5P	26
6	Somatic Renewal	6P	36
9	Somatic Reparation	9P	50
12	Somatic Revigoration	12P	65
16	Somatic Relief	15P	85
21	Somatic Rejuvenation	20P	109
27	Somatic Regeneration	26P	138
31	Somatic Rehabilitation	30P	158
36	Somatic Revival	36P	183
46	Somatic Resuscitation	47P	231

DoT: inflicts (Dmg) every 5 seconds.

Skill ....Mentalism Dmg Type ....Spirit
Casting Time ....3 sec. Range....................1350
Duration ....20 sec.

Lvl	Spell	Cost	Dmg
1	Illusory Ache	2P	2
5	Illusory Pains	4P	9
8	Illusory Cramps	5P	15
11	Illusory Anguish	7P	19
15	Illusory Spasms	9P	27
20	Illusory Convulsions	12P	35
25	Illusory Agony	15P	45
30	Illusory Lacerations	19P	53
35	Illusory Torture	22P	63
41	Illusory Excrutiation	26P	73
48	Illusory Neuralgia	31P	87

Mind Mastery

Heals damage to Friend by (Heal) HP.

Skill ....Mentalism Casting Time ...3.25 sec.
Range....................1350 Duration ....Inst.

Lvl	Spell	Cost	Heal
2	Major Somatic Renewal	5P	28
4	Major Somatic Reparation	9P	46
6	Major Somatic Revigoration	12P	64
9	Major Somatic Relief	17P	91
13	Major Somatic Rejuvenation	25P	127
18	Major Somatic Regeneration	34P	172
25	Major Somatic Rehabilitation	48P	235
33	Major Somatic Revival	65P	307
42	Major Somatic Resuscitation	84P	387

Confusion: (Switch %) chance to switch targets; (Ally %) chance to attack own ally (see page 367 for Pve/RvR limitations).

Skill ....Mentalism Dmg Type ....Spirit
Casting Time .....3.5 sec. Range....................1350

Lvl	Spell	Cost	Dur	Switch %	Ally %
3	Delusion	2P	16 sec.	50%	0%
8	Delirium	4P	26 sec.	65%	0%
12	Dementation	6P	34 sec.	80%	0%
17	Paranoia	8P	44 sec.	95%	0%
24	Eccentricity	12P	58 sec.	100%	10%
32	Madness	16P	74 sec.	100%	25%
40	Derangment	20P	1.5 min.	100%	40%
49	Insanity	25P	1.8 min.	100%	55%

Mesmerize: target halts all movement and is unable to attack or cast spells; the effect breaks when the target is healed or takes damage (see page 367 for PvE/RvR limitations).

Skill ....Mentalism Dmg Type ....Spirit
Casting Time ....3 sec. Range....................1500

Lvl	Spell	Cost	Dur
1	Enfeeble Mind	2P	16 sec.
5	Cripple Mind	3P	21 sec.
10	Incapacitate Mind	5P	28 sec.
15	Disable Mind	8P	34 sec.
23	Paralyze Mind	11P	44 sec.
31	Lock Mind	15P	55 sec.
41	Petrify Mind	19P	68 sec.
50	Unmake Mind	23P	80 sec.

Basic Racial Attributes

	Celt	Lurikeen	Firbolg	Elf
Strength	60	40	90	40
Constitution	60	40	60	40
Dexterity	60	80	40	75
Quickness	60	80	40	75
Intelligence	60	60	60	70
Charisma	60	60	60	60
Empathy	60	60	70	60
Piety	60	60	60	60

Innate Racial Resistances

	Celt	Lurikeen	Firbolg	Elf
Crushing	+2	+5	+3	–
Slashing	+3	–	+2	+2
Thrusting	–	–	–	+3
Energy	–	+5	–	–
Heat	–	–	+5	–
Spirit	+5	–	–	+5

Classes & Races

	Celt	Lurikeen	Firbolg	Elf
Hero (2x)	√		√	
Champion (2x)	√	√		√
Blademaster (2x)	√		√	
Ranger (2x)	√	√		√
Nightshade (2-2x)		√		√
Warden (1.5x)	√		√	
Bard (1.5x)	√		√	
Druid (1x)	√		√	
Eldritch (1x)		√		√
Enchanter (1x)		√		√
Mentalist (1x)	√	√		√

Classes & Paths

Way	*Path*	Essence	Harmony	Focus
Arms (Guardian)		Champion	Blademaster	Hero
Stealth (Stalker)		Nightshade		Ranger
Nature (Naturalist)		Bard	Druid	Warden
Magic (Magician)		Enchanter	Mentalist	Eldritch

Merchants

Armor/Clothing

Armor	
Tir na Nog	Cragen
	Gemma
Armor (Chitin)	
Tir na Nog	Nolan
Armor (High)	
Tir na Nog	Banyell
	Keya
	Sharon
	Taleai
Cloaks	
Ardagh	Moesen
Innis Carthaig	Feoras
Mag Mell	Oistin
Siopa	Murchach
Tir na Nog	Conary
Cloth (Woven)	
Ardee	Qunilan
Caille	Lysagh
Caonlla	Ronan
Mag Mell	Anice
Tir na mBeo	Duer
	Elith
Tir na Nog	Auliffe
	Eachann
	Kado
	Kinnat
Cloth (High)	
Tir na Nog	Lerena
Leather (Brea)	
Ardee	Fianait
Caonlla	Erskine
Mag Mell	Kylirean
Leather (Constaic)	
Basar	Neb
Howth	Kenna
Mardagh	Brody
Siopa	Caron
Tir na Nog	Vaughn
Leather (Cruaigh)	
Alainn Bin	Dympna
Basar	Arzhela
Innis Carthaig	Gorawen
Mardagh	Ebril
Tir na Nog	Tomas
Reinforced Leather	
Tir na Nog	Renny
Reinforced Leather (Cailocht)	
Alainn Bin	Cragen
Ardagh	Roise
Howth	Twm
Innis Carthaig	Mariota
Mardagh	Akira
Reinforced Leather (Nadurtha)	
Ardee	Evan
Basar	Anna
Howth	Bevin
Tir na mBeo	Boyd
Tir Urhost	Tavie
Reinforced Leather (Tacuil)	
Basar	Cubert
Howth	Kevain
Mardagh	Ardal
Robes	
Ardagh	Brisen
Ardee	Ailfrid
Caonlla	Sorcha
Innis Carthaig	Slaine
Mag Mell	Eluned
Siopa	Raghnall
Tir na mBeo	Kaenia
Tir na Nog	Cinnie
	Mada
	Nealcail
	Sissy
Scale	
Tir na Nog	Laurence
	Maxen
	Tristan
Scale (Cruanach)	
Alainn Bin	Finghin
Howth	Iain
Innis Carthaig	Kian
Tir na mBeo	Una
Tir Urhost	Mosby
Scale (Daingean)	
Basar	Cristin
Innis Carthaig	Talriese
Lough Gur	Una
Tir na mBeo	Teleri
Scale (Osnadurtha)	
Ardagh	Noreen
Caonlla	Colm
Lough Gur	Vivienne
Siopa	Devin
Tir na mBeo	Aidaila
Tir na Nog	Hywela

Weapons

Weapons (High)	
Tir na Nog	Deveryy
Arrows	
Alainn Bin	Liam
Ardagh	Celder
Basar	Tara
Caonlla	Edana
Howth	Blayne
Innis Carthaig	Dierdre
Mag Mell	Aillig
Mardagh	Calder
Tir na Nog	Connor
	Kelsi
Blades	
Ardagh	Ysbail
Ardee	Garnock
Caonlla	Eira
Howth	Ailbe
Innis Carthaig	Asthore
Mag Mell	Wony
Mardagh	Dirmyg
Blades (Swords)	
Siopa	Broc
Blunt Weapons	
Ardagh	Nyle
Ardee	Aideen
Basar	Deryn
Caonlla	Alun
Siopa	Alar
Tir na Nog	Franseza

Location	Merchant
Bows	
Alainn Bin	Maureen
Ardagh	Rhodry
Ardee	Rhona
Basar	Zinna
Caonlla	Kiara
Mag Mell	Mannix
Tir na Nog	Brianna
	Isibael
	Kenzia
Tir Urhost	Daracha
Celtic Spears	
Ardagh	Iaine
Ardee	Eleri
Caonlla	Marus
Howth	Cait
Lough Gur	Izold
Mardagh	Mearchian
Large Weapons	
Alainn Bin	Alaiina
Caonlla	Erwana
Howth	Ffion
Innis Carthaig	Drummond
Mardagh	Thady
Tir na mBeo	Achaius
Tir Urhost	Callough
Piercing Weapons	
Alainn Bin	Helori
Ardee	Mahon
Basar	Briac
Howth	Gaenor
Lough Gur	Yann
Mag Mell	Lachlan
Mardagh	Gaenor
Tir na Nog	Muirne
Staves	
Ardagh	Seana
Ardee	Ierna
Caonlla	Peadar
Howth	Anra
Innis Carthaig	Barra
Lough Gur	Fallon
Mag Mell	Sian
Mardagh	Muadhnait
Tir na mBeo	Anrai
Staves (High)	
Tir na Nog	Adrai

Shields

Location	Merchant
Shields	
Caonlla	Gavina
Howth	Blaez
Lough Gur	Wynda
Mag Mell	Cafell
Siopa	Morag
Tir Urhost	Yvon

Focus Items

Location	Merchant
Eldritch Staves	
Alainn Bin	Iama
Ardagh	Brenna
Ardee	Creirwy
Caille	Keir
Caonlla	Glyn
Innis Carthaig	Glennard
Tir na mBeo	Lavena
Enchanter Staves	
Alainn Bin	Aisling
Ardagh	Illaliel
	Torlan
Ardee	Daron
Caille	Brynn
Caonlla	Bryanna
Innis Carthaig	Crayg
Siopa	Emhyr
Tir na mBeo	Liadan
Mentalist Staves	
Ardee	Naomhan
Caille	Ariana
Caonlla	Edmyg
Innis Carthaig	Amynda
Mag Mell	Sedric
Focus Items	
Tir na Nog	Aghna
	Brianna, Kedric

Instruments

Location	Merchant
Bard Instruments	
Ardagh	Della
Caonlla	Edernola
Howth	Irksa
Mardagh	Edsoner
Tir na mBeo	Cian
Lutes, Flutes	
Tir na Nog	Fingal
	Rhosyn

Other Goods

Location	Merchant
Dyes	
Ardagh	Mabli, Reeni
Tir na Nog	Blanche, Cinnie
	Mada, Nealcail
Dyes (Enamel)	
Mardagh	Dilith
Tir na mBeo	Rhian
Dyes (Leather)	
Howth	Dyvyr, Tyree
Filidh	
Tir na Nog	Mona, Morven
Leathers (Low)	
Tir na Nog	Saffa
Ores (Low)	
Tir na Nog	Baran
Oreworking Equipment	
Innis Carthaig	Yealcha
Poisons	
Alainn Bin	Lirla
Ardee	Lexie
Caonlla	Kinney
Howth	Kalla
Innis Carthaig	Sarena
Tir na mBeo	Borlai
Tailoring Equipment	
Ardee	Arshan
Innis Carthaig	Macharan
Various expensive trade skill items	
Basar	Erech
Mag Mell	Jahan

Services

Location	Merchant
Enchanter	
Ardagh	Iola
Ardee	Eiral
Caille	Ainrebh
Caonlla	Eli
Innis Carthaig	Kern
Mag Mell	Dera
Tir na mBeo	Tangi
Tir na Nog	Caolan, Sadhbh
	Vaddon, Waljan
Tir Urhost	Cleary
Guardian	
Ardee	Flannery
Guild Emblemeer	
Tir na Nog	Ffhionbarr
Guild Registrar	
Tir na Nog	Filidh Fadywn
Harper	
Tir na Nog	Eibhilin
	Evelyn, Eveny
Healer	
Alainn Bin	Ceri
Ardagh	Fyrsil
Ardee	Llyn
Caonlla	Keagan
Howth	Gralon
Innis Carthaig	Blanche
Mag Mell	Epona
Mardagh	Beli
Siopa	Kerwin
Tir na mBeo	Ionhar
Smith	
Alainn Bin	Dalladva
Ardee	Criostoir
Caonlla	Sarff
Howth	Alwyn
Innis Carthaig	Siobhan
Lough Gur	Kyle
Mag Mell	Ilisa
Mardagh	Grizel
Tir na mBeo	Lainie

Trainers

Location	Merchant
Armorcraft Trainer	
Tir na Nog	Dunstan, Tegvan
Bard Trainer	
Caonlla	Dempsey
Howth	Maille
Tir na Nog	Selia
Blademaster Trainer	
Ardagh	Ea
Caonlla	Allistar
Tir na Nog	Luighseach
Champion Trainer	
Ardagh	Siodhachan
Caonlla	Cordelia
Tir na Nog	Lasairiona
Druid Trainer	
Howth	Bidelia
Tir na Nog	Daray
Eldritch Trainer	
Ardagh	Coman
Caonlla	Nainsi
Tir na Nog	Aodh
Enchanter Trainer	
Ardagh	Talaith
Caonlla	Eyslk
Tir na Nog	Anwar
Guardian Trainer	
Caonlla	Ailill
Howth	Kaley
Mag Mell	Meadghbh
Hero Trainer	
Caonlla	Searlas
Howth	Nevin
Tir na Nog	Riofach
Magician Trainer	
Ardee	Auliffe
Caonlla	Ennis
Howth	Adair
Mag Mell	Etain
Mentalist Trainer	
Ardagh	Aindreas
Caonlla	Treise
Tir na Nog	Ena
Naturalist Trainer	
Ardee	Caoimhe
Caonlla	Benen
Howth	Daibheid
Mag Mell	Breeda
Nightshade Trainer	
Ardagh	Leachlainn
Tir na Nog	Blathnaid
Ranger Trainer	
Ardagh	Teague
Caonlla	Sile
Tir na Nog	Mavelle
Stalker Trainer	
Ardee	Daithi
Caonlla	Bran
Howth	Damhnait
Mag Mell	Ula
Tailoring Trainer	
Tir na Nog	Armin
Warden Trainer	
Ardagh	Uilliam
Tir na Nog	Labhras
Weaponcraft Trainer	
Tir na Nog	Hendrika

Quests

Quests are only available once you've reached the appropriate level (**L**). When only specific races or classes can receive a quest, they are mentioned in the Restrictions column. Similarly, sometimes you must have finished a lower-level quest before you can advance to the next one; these prerequisite quests are also listed, in parentheses, in the Restrictions column.

L	Quest	Source / Restrictions
1	Way of Arms: Learn the Paths	Starting location: trainer / Guardian
1	Way of Magic: Learn the Paths	Starting location: trainer / Magician
1	Way of Nature: Learn the Paths	Starting location: trainer / Naturalist
1	Way of Stealth: Learn the Paths	Starting location: trainer / Stalker
1	Tadhg's Lost Treasure	Connla: Tadhg
2	Misdelivered Letter	Starting location: trainer
2	Please Deliver!	Starting location: varies
2	Troya's Research	Howth: Troya
3	Balance of Nature	Starting location: trainer / Naturalist
3	Balm Hunt	Howth: Kaylee / Guardian
3	Connla's Fever	Connla: trainer
3	Information Is the Key	Starting location: Maeve the Crone or trainer / Mag.
3	Kylieran's New Armor	Mag Mell: Kylieran
3	Mild Deception	Starting location: trainer / Stalker
4	Enchanted Bandit Hunt	Howth: Kaylee / Guardian
4	Sad Tale	Connla: trainer / Guardian
4	Slevin's Powder	Connla: trainer / Magician, Guardian, Stalker
4	Summoner Expulsion	Connla: trainer / Magician
4	Tale of Cad Goddeau	Connla: trainer / Naturalist
4	Track And Seek	Howth: Damhnait / Stalker
4	Wolf Infestation	Ardee: trainer / Naturalist
4	Youth Gone Wrong	Mag Mell: Mandra
6	Evan's Notes	Ardee: Evan
7	Cristin's Supplies	Basar: Cristin
9	Clik's Raids	Ardagh: Caitriona / Guardian, Warden
9	Gormghlaith's Tea	Ardee: Garnok
9	Little Wind	Tir Na mBeo: Reidie
10	Sad Fomorie	Ardagh: Reeni
10	Spinner's Cloak	Howth: Banba
10	Storyteller's Tale	Connla: Eira
11	Fagan's Wand	Ardee: Nyderra / Guardian, Naturalist, Stalker
11	Tyree's Dyes	Howth: Tyree
12	Keara's Enchantment	Ardee: Keara
12	Lochlain's Curse	Ardagh : Lochlain / Celt, Firbolg
13	Scuttle	Ardagh: Seana
13	The Hunt For Bristle	Basar: Eruvan
14	Beautiful Music	Tir Na mBeo: Tavie / Bard
15	Lesser of Two Evils	Tir na mBeo: Aidaila
16	Fearan	Ardagh: Fianait
16	Lysagh's Problems	Tir Na Nog: Gemma
16	Regional Distinctions	Tir na mBeo: Raine
17	Alastriona's Chest	Tir na Nog: east gate: Alastriona
17	Riona's Revenge	Mardagh: guard tower: Riona / Natur., Guard., Rang.
19	Freeing Osier	Ardagh: Odharnait
20	Criofan's Fish	Bridge in Shannon Estuary: Criofan / Magician, Stalker
20	Eoghan's Spell	Ardee: Eoghan
20	Seeking Glory	Tir na Nog: Loralye
20	The Feud	Howth: Lasrina / Magician
21	Treasure Hunt	Howth: Gaenor
22	Sheerie Mischief	Mag Mell: Anise / Naturalist
24	Bria's Savior	Tir na mBeo: Kaenia / Blademaster, Champion, Warden
24	Essence of Hostility	Tir Na mBeo: Guardian Andraste / Naturalist
24	Occupation of Lough Gur	Lough Derg island: Azilize
24	Sea Shell Sleeves	Tir na Nog: Kennocha / Naturalist
25	Sraoi's Heart	Tir na Nog: Labhaoise
27	Larylle's Necklace	Ardee: Larylle
27	Search For Nasco's Spear	Siabra island: Azilize
27	Sile's Sight	Connla: Oran O'Braonain / Guardian, Naturalist, Stalker
31	Returning For More	Howth: Banba
31	Returning to the Source	Ardagh: Reeni / (Returning for More)
31	The Anxious Healer	Tir Urphorst Tower: Cinead
31	Traces of Mad Changlings	eastern hill of Druim Cain: Tressa Gorrym'jiarg / (Returning for More)
36	Magic's Scar	Tir na mBeo: Tavie / Magician
38	Search For the Missing Smith	Tir na Nog: Ewen
38	The West Wind	Tir na Nog: Bairfhionn
40	The Touch of Amadan Dubh	Daingean: Flidh Martin
43	Missing Bard	Ardagh: Illaliel
50	Aid For Alainn Bin	Druim Cain: Oak Man / Magician
50	Piaras And Lhia	outside Howth: Piaras

Path (Guild) Track

You may only undertake the quests for your own path. You must complete each quest before undertaking the next.

Essence

L	Quest	Source
7	Strange Matters Indeed	varies: trainer
11	Roane Skin	Tir na Nog: trainer
15	Seek the Moonstone	Tir na Nog: trainer
20	Seek the Moonstone B	Ardee: The Crone
25	Seek the Moonstone C	Broken Tower of mBeo: Talking Wolves
30	Moonstone Quest	Tir na Nog: Fagan
40	Ilisa's Trade	Tir na Nog: trainer
43	The Moonstone Twin: 43,45,47,50	Tir na Nog: trainer

Focus

L	Quest	Source
7	Destructive Forces	varies: trainer
11	Connla's Well	Tir Na Nog: trainer
15	Stolen Ore A	Tir na Nog: trainer
20	Stolen Ore B	Howth: Chief of Howth
25	Secret of Nuada's Silver A	south of Innis Carthaig: Bran the Giant
30	Secret of Nuada's Silver B	Howth: Chieftan Pronnias
40	Lost Townsfolk of Bran Llyr	varies: trainer
43	Unnatural Powers: 43,45,47,50	Tir na Nog: trainer

Harmony

L	Quest	Source
7	Enchanting Willow	varies: trainer
7	Dying Favor (not required)	varies: trainer
11	Wug's Jug	Tir Na Nog: trainer
15	Cad Goddeau A	Tir na Nog: trainer
20	Cad Goddeau B	Siabra distorter camp: Druid Harkin
25	Cad Goddeau C	Howth: Cathbad
30	Cad Goddeau D	Innis Carthaig: Chieftain
40	Morven's Return	Tir na Nog: trainer
43	Last Heir: 43,45,47,50	Tir na Nog: trainer

Standard (Craftable) Weapons

Standard (craftable) weapons are sorted by the skill needed to wield them. For **Arrow** stats, see page 363. For unique weapons (including unique arrows), see page 84. For **Siege Equipment**, see page 324. For a general discussion of weapons and weapon stats, see page 361.

Headings. Delay = time between blows, in seconds / **Dam (M# 1)** = damage per hit, using a Material Level 1 weapon / **Incr**ement = additional damage per hit, with each improvement in Material / **Base DPS** = damage per second using a Material Level 1 weapon / **Wt.** = weight of the weapon / **Sec. Skill** = secondary skill that influences damage / **Range** = range of weapon, in world units / * = this weapon can be used as a second weapon with Albion's Dual Wield skill.

Standard (Craftable) Weapons

Blades

Lvl	Weapon	Delay (sec.)	Dam (M# 1)	Incr	Base DPS	Wt.
1	Short Sword *	2.5	3.7	3.7	1.5	1.8
2	Falcata *	2.8	5	4.2	1.8	1.8
3	Broadsword	3.2	6.7	4.8	2.1	2
4	Long Sword	3.5	8.5	5.3	2.4	2.3
5	Bastard Sword	4.1	11.1	6.2	2.7	3
6	Guarded Rapier	3.6	10.8	5.4	3.0	2.4
6	Sickle *	2.9	8.7	4.4	3.0	1.5
6	Crescent Sword *	3.1	9.3	4.7	3.0	1.8

Blunt

Lvl	Weapon	Delay (sec.)	Dam (M# 1)	Incr	Base DPS	Wt.
1	Club *	2.9	4.3	4.3	1.5	2.5
2	Mace *	3.3	5.9	4.9	1.8	3
3	Spiked Club	3.6	7.5	5.4	2.1	3.5
4	Hammer	3.9	9.3	5.8	2.4	4
5	Spiked Mace	4.3	11.6	6.4	2.7	4
6	Pick Hammer	3.8	11.4	5.7	3.0	3

Celtic Spear

Lvl	Weapon	Delay (sec.)	Dam (M# 1)	Incr	Base DPS	Wt.
1	Short Spear	3.4	5.1	5.1	1.5	3
2	Spear	4.0	7.2	6.0	1.8	3.5
3	Long Spear	4.6	9.7	6.9	2.1	4
4	War Spear	5.2	12.4	7.7	2.4	4.5
5	Barbed Spear	5.7	15.4	8.6	2.7	5
6	Hooked Spear	5.0	15	7.5	3.0	5

Large Weaponry

Lvl	Weapon	Delay (sec.)	Dam (M# 1)	Incr	Base DPS	Wt.	
1	Two-Handed Sword	4.6	6.9	6.9	1.5	4	Blades
2	Big Shillelagh	4.7	8.5	7.1	1.8	4	Blunt
3	Two Handed Spiked Mace	5.0	10.5	7.5	2.1	4.5	Blunt
4	Great Hammer	5.3	12.8	8.0	2.4	5	Blunt
5	Great Sword	5.3	14.3	7.9	2.7	5.5	Blades
6	Great Falcata	4.5	13.5	6.8	3.0	4.5	Blades
6	Sledge Hammer	5.4	16.2	8.1	3.0	5	Blunt

Piercing

Lvl	Weapon	Delay (sec.)	Dam (M# 1)	Incr	Base DPS	Wt.
1	Dirk *	2.3	3.5	3.5	1.5	0.9
2	Dagger *	2.6	4.6	3.8	1.8	1
3	Stiletto *	2.7	5.6	4.0	2.1	1
4	Rapier	2.7	7	4.1	2.6	1.5
5	Curved Dagger	2.7	7.5	4.1	2.8	1

Staff

Lvl	Weapon	Delay (sec.)	Dam (M# 1)	Incr	Base DPS	Wt.
1	Staff	4.5	6.7	6.8	1.5	4.5
1	Shod Staff	5	10.5	7.5	2.1	4.5
1	Focus Staff	4.5	6.7	6.7	1.5	4.5

Bow

Lvl	Weapon	Delay (sec.)	Dam (M# 1)	Incr	Base DPS	Wt.	Range
3	Short Bow	4.0	8.4	6.0	2.1	2.5	1200

Recurve Bow

Lvl	Weapon	Delay (sec.)	Dam (M# 1)	Incr	Base DPS	Wt.	Range
5	Short Recurve Bow	4.0	10.8	6.0	2.7	2.6	1600
5	Recurve Bow	4.7	12.7	7.1	2.7	3.1	1680
5	Great Recurve Bow	5.4	14.6	8.1	2.7	3.6	1600

Weapon Drops & Rewards

Abbreviations

Headings. PL = Power Level / **M#** = Material (M) and Material Level (#) / **Ql** = Quality / **Spd** = Speed, or weapon delay (the time between successive swings) / **Dam** = Damage with each hit / **DPS** = Damage per second / **Type** = Type of damage (**Cr**ush, **Sl**ash or **Thr**ust) / **Range** = basic range of the bow or crossbow, in world units (1 pace ≈ 60 world units ≈ 1 yard).

Stats. Resistance, Skill, **F**ocus / **Ch**arisma, **Con**stitution, **Emp**athy, **Dex**terity, **Int**elligence, **Pie**ty, **Qui**ckness, **Str**ength / **C**loth, **L**eather, **M**etal, **W**ood. The first positive percentage in any bonus indicates your increased chance to hit with the weapon.

* There is more than one weapon with this same name. This happens most often with casters' focus staffs, where up to four can have the same name, but significantly different stats.

Blades Skill (Axe, Bone, Claw, Falcata, Sickle, Sword)

Weapon	Bonus	PL	M#	Ql	Spd	Dam	DPS	Type	Generic
Training Sword		0	01	90	2.5	3	1.2	Sl	Sword
Granite Longsword	+1%; Blades S. +1	4	01	90	3.2	8	2.4	Sl	Sword
Spectral Long Sword	+1%; Blades S. +1	12	03	89	4.5	22	4.8	Sl	Axe
Richly Designed Broadsword		12	03	80	3.2	15	4.8	Sl	Sword
Jagged Bastard Sword	+5%; Str +7	13	03	90	4.3	22	5.1	Sl	Sword
Bloodstone Studded Falcata	+10%; Blades S. +1; Str +1	16	04	89	2.7	16	6.0	Sl	Falcata
Worn Dark Guardian Sword		16	04	80	2.5	15	6.0	Sl	Sword
Celestial Blade	+10%; Parry S. +1; Qui +1	17	04	89	3.4	21	6.3	Sl	Sword
Fury's Rage Blade	+10%; Blades S. +2; Int –4; HP +15	17	04	100	3.5	22	6.3	Sl	Sword
Draoi's Bastard Sword	+10%; Blades, Parry S. +1	20	04	89	4.1	30	7.2	Sl	Sword
Silver Blade	+10%; Blades S. +1; HP +12	21	05	90	2.5	19	7.5	Sl	Falcata
Rock Sword		21	05	80	2.5	19	7.5	Sl	Sword
Draoish Sickle	+10%; Blades, Parry S. +1; Con +1	22	05	89	2.9	23	7.8	Sl	Sickle
Silvermined Blade	+10%; Blades S. +1; Qui +1; Body R. +2; Power +1	22	05	89	2.4	19	7.8	Sl	Sword
Bloodied Bone	+10%; Parry S. +2; Energy R. +2	23	05	89	3.2	26	8.1	Sl	Bone
Fathomless Short Sword	+10%; Con +1; Celtic Dual, Blades S. +1	23	05	89	2.9	23	8.1	Sl	Sword
Soiagh Blade	+15%; Blades S. +1; Qui +1; Slash R. +2	24	05	89	3.5	29	8.4	Sl	Sword
Hedge Chopper	+5%; Blades S. +1; Body R. +2; Qui, Str +3	25	05	89	2.9	25	8.7	Sl	Falcata
Earthen Defender	+10%; Blades, Parry, Evade S. +1	25	05	89	2.8	24	8.7	Sl	Sword
Imperial Sword of the Depths	+10%; Blades S. +2	25	05	89	4	35	8.7	Sl	Sword
Fathomless Crescent Claw	+15%; Qui +4; Crush, Slash R. +2	26	06	89	3.4	31	9.0	Sl	Sword
Waylayer Short Sword	+15%; Celtic Dual S. +3	26	06	89	2.5	23	9.0	Sl	Sword
Sword of the Keeper	+10%; Blades S. +4; HP +12	27	06	100	2.4	22	9.3	Sl	Sword
Phantom Bastard Sword	+5%; Blades S. +2	28	06	89	3.6	35	9.6	Sl	Sword
Spined Razor Foreclaw	+15%; Qui +7	28	06	89	3.3	32	9.6	Sl	Sword
Spirit Searer	+5%; Spirit R. +6; Blades S. +1	28	06	89	3.7	36	9.6	Sl	Sword
Slicer	+15%; Qui +4; Blades S. +1; Heat R. +2	29	06	89	4.1	41	9.9	Sl	Sword
Pestilent Sickle	+15%; Blades, Celtic Dual S. +2; Qui +7	31	07	100	2.8	29	10.5	Sl	Sickle
Heavy Bastard Sword	+5%; Qui –2; Str +6	32	07	80	4.8	52	10.8	Sl	Sword
Glimmer Spirit Sword	+15%; Blades S. +2; Str +6	36	08	89	3	36	12.0	Sl	Sword
Flawed Asterite Falcata	+1%; Blades S. +1; HP +6	37	08	80	3	37	12.3	Sl	Falcata
Razor Edged Asterite Falcata	+20%; Blades S. +2; HP +12	37	08	89	3.8	47	12.3	Sl	Falcata
Sinister Alluvion Falcata	+20%; Qui +6; Slash R. +6	37	08	89	2.8	34	12.3	Sl	Falcata
Crescent Reaver	+20%; Parry S. +4; Qui +7; Str +3	37	08	100	2.8	34	12.3	Sl	Sword
Caustic Slicer	+15%; Blades S. +2; Qui +6	38	08	89	2.6	33	12.6	Sl	Sickle
Alluvion Sword	+20%; Str +6; Con +4	38	08	89	3.2	40	12.6	Sl	Sword
Crescent Razor	+20%; Dex, Str +4; Slash R. +2	38	08	89	2.9	37	12.6	Sl	Sword
Cliff Dweller Sword	+20%; Celtic Dual S. +2; Dex, Con +6	40	08	89	2.4	32	13.2	Sl	Sword
Gem Encrusted Claw	+20%; Blades, Celtic Dual, Parry S. +1; HP +15	41	08	90	3.1	42	13.5	Sl	Claw
Cathbad's Blade	+20%; Blades S. +4; Str +6; Heat R. +12	43	08	100	2.3	32	14.1	Sl	Falcata
Chieftain's Blade	+20%; Blades S. +4; Str +6; Matter R. +12	43	08	100	2.3	32	14.1	Sl	Falcata

Weapon	Bonus	PL	M#	QI	Spd	Dam	DPS	Type	Generic
Silvered Spellbound Falcata	+20%; Blades S. +4; Str +6; Heat R. +12	43	08	100	2.3	32	14.1	Sl	Falcata
Coruscating Truesilver Blade	+20%; Blades S. +2; Parry S. +1; Qui +6	45	08	89	3.5	51	14.7	Sl	Sword
Frosted Silverblade	+25%; Blades, Parry, Celtic Dual S. +1; Qui +6	48	08	89	2.4	37	15.6	Sl	Sword
Shadow Crystal Slicer	+25%; Blades, Parry S. +2; Qui +3	48	08	89	4.4	69	15.6	Sl	Sword
Antipodean Short Sword	+25%; Con, Qui +4; Slash, Cold R. +4	49	08	89	2.4	38	15.9	Sl	Sword
Midnight Vengeance Falcata	+25%; Celtic Dual, Blades S. +2; Str, Qui +6	50	08	90	2.5	41	16.2	Sl	Falcata
Harvester of Malign Doom	+25%; Blades S. +2; Str +9	50	08	89	3	49	16.2	Sl	Sickle
Luminescent Sickle of the Unicorn	+25%; Str, Qui +10; Dex +9; Blades S. +5	50	08	91	2.9	47	16.2	Sl	Sickle
Soul Reaver	+25%; Blades S. +3; Emp, Str +9	50	08	90	2.8	45	16.2	Sl	Sickle
Crescent of Light	+25%; Blades S. +3; Cha +6; Str, Qui +10	50	08	91	3.1	50	16.2	Sl	Sword
Glimmerspirit Sword	+25%; Blades S. +4; Str +7; Qui +3	50	08	90	4	65	16.2	Sl	Sword
Glistening Broadsword	+25%; Blades S. +2; Str, Qui +6	50	08	90	3	49	16.2	Sl	Sword
Spectral Manslayer	+25%; Celtic Dual S. +3; Str, Con +7	50	08	90	4.1	66	16.2	Sl	Sword

Blunt Skill (Club, Hammer, Mace, Paw)

Weapon	Bonus	PL	M#	QI	Spd	Dam	DPS	Type	Generic
Training Club		0	W1	90	4	5	1.2	Cr	Club
Thorny Club	+1%; Emp +3	4	01	90	3.4	8	2.4	Cr	Club
Blackthorn Club	+1%; Str, Qui +1	9	W2	89	3.8	15	3.9	Cr	Club
Pilfered Traveler's Mace	+5%; Power +1; HP +3	10	02	89	3.4	14	4.2	Cr	Mace
Richly Designed Spiked Club		12	03	80	3.7	18	4.8	Cr	Club
Ancient Granite Mace	+5%; Str, Emp +3	16	04	90	3.2	19	6.0	Cr	Mace
Gold Embossed Mace	+10%; Emp, Str, Con +1	16	04	89	4.3	26	6.0	Cr	Mace
Rage Sprite Club	+10%; Int, Emp, Con +1	18	04	89	3.6	24	6.6	Cr	Club
Forked Mephit Tail	+10%; Crush S. +1; HP +6	21	05	89	3.6	27	7.5	Cr	Club
Cracked Stone Mace		21	05	80	4.3	32	7.5	Cr	Mace
Imperial Golden Hammer	+15%; Emp +6	22	05	89	3.5	27	7.8	Cr	Hammer
Fathomless Mace	+10%; Celtic Dual, Blunt S. +1; Con +1	23	05	89	3	24	8.1	Cr	Mace
Briar Club	+5%; Blunt S. +1; Body R. +2; Emp, Cha +3	24	05	89	3.5	29	8.3	Cr	Club
Imperial Hammer of the Depths	+10%; Blunt S. +2	25	05	89	3.3	29	8.7	Cr	Hammer
Oaken Mallet	+5%; Emp +4; Regrowth S. +2	25	05	89	3.6	31	8.7	Cr	Hammer
Spined Granite Mace	+10%; Blunt S. +1; Str, Dex +3	25	05	89	4.3	37	8.7	Cr	Mace
Cruanach Crusher	+15%; Emp +4; Qui, Str +3	26	06	90	3.5	32	9.0	Cr	Club
Parthanon Fist	+15%; Blunt, Parry S. +1; Crush R. +2	26	W6	89	2.9	26	9.0	Cr	Club
Waylayer Hammer	+15%; Celtic Dual S. +3	26	06	89	3.9	35	9.0	Cr	Hammer
Waylayer Spiked Mace	+15%; Blunt S. +3	26	06	89	4.3	39	9.0	Cr	Mace
Blackened Feelion Paw	+15%; Spirit R. +4; Cold R. +2; Power +1	26	06	89	3.5	32	9.0	Cr	Paw
Etheric Bludgeoner	+5%; Power +5	27	06	89	3.5	33	9.3	Cr	Mace
Luch Paw	+15%; Parry S. +1; Slash R. +2; HP +3	27	06	89	3.3	31	9.3	Cr	Paw
Pluc	+15%; Blunt, Parry S. +1; Qui +1	28	W6	89	2.9	28	9.6	Cr	Club
Sentinel	+15%; Blunt, Parry S. +1; Energy R. +2	28	06	89	3.6	35	9.6	Cr	Club
Siog's Might	+15%; Blunt S. +1; Parry S. +2	31	07	89	3.3	35	10.5	Cr	Mace
Crude Club	+5%; Blunt S. +1	32	W7	80	2.9	31	10.8	Cr	Club
Muroi's Weighted Battlemace	+15%; Blunt S. +5; Crush R. +8	33	06	100	4	44	11.1	Cr	Mace
Sludge Covered Mace	+15%; Str, Emp +6	36	08	89	3	36	12.0	Cr	Mace
Alluvion Club	+20%; Str +13; Con +4	37	08	89	3.5	43	12.3	Cr	Club
Glimmer Spirit Club	+20%; Str, Qui, Emp +4	37	08	89	3.5	43	12.3	Cr	Club
Sinister Alluvion Club	+20%; Qui +6; Crush R. +6	37	08	89	3.5	43	12.3	Cr	Club
Flawed Asterite Hammer	+1%; Emp +3; HP +6	37	08	80	4.2	52	12.3	Cr	Hammer
Flawed Asterite Mace	+1%; Blunt S. +1; HP +6	37	08	80	3.9	48	12.3	Cr	Mace
Siabrian Crusher	+15%; Cha, Emp +6	38	08	100	3.8	48	12.6	Cr	Hammer
Balanced Asterite Hammer	+20%; Emp +6; HP +12	39	08	89	4	52	12.9	Cr	Hammer
Balanced Asterite Mace	+20%; Blunt S. +2; HP +12	39	08	89	3	39	12.9	Cr	Mace
Cliff Dweller Hammer	+20%; Celtic Dual S. +2; Str, Qui +6	40	08	89	3.9	51	13.2	Cr	Hammer
Fomorian's Betrayal	+20%; Blunt S. +4; Str +6; Spirit R. +12	43	08	100	4	56	14.1	Cr	Mace
Fomorian's Fist	+20%; Blunt S. +6; Str +3; Heat R. +12	43	08	100	4	56	14.1	Cr	Mace
Silver Spellbound Mace	+20%; Blunt S. +4; Str +6; Energy R. +12	43	08	100	4	56	14.1	Cr	Mace
Coruscating Spiked Club	+20%; Con, Emp +6; Cold R. +4	45	08	89	3.7	54	14.7	Cr	Club
Coruscating Truesilver Mace	+20%; Blunt S. +2; Qui +9	45	08	89	3.5	51	14.7	Cr	Mace
Crimson Crusher	+20%; Blunt S. +2; Emp, Con, Str +7	45	08	100	4.1	60	14.7	Cr	Mace
Antipodean Club	+25%; Con, Qui +4; Crush, Body R. +4	46	W8	89	2.9	44	15.0	Cr	Club
Fire Heatstone Stalagmite	+25%; Blunt S. +3; Con, Str +3	48	08	89	3.5	55	15.6	Cr	Club

Weapon	Bonus	PL	M#	QI	Spd	Dam	DPS	Type	Generic
Shadow Crystal Mace	+25%; Emp +9; Str +3; Crush, Body R. +2	48	08	89	4	62	15.6	Cr	Mace
Glistening Spiked Club	+25%; Blunt S. +2; Str, Qui +6	50	08	90	3.5	57	16.2	Cr	Club
Finliath Firebrand	+25%; Celtic Dual S. +4; Con, Qui +7	50	08	90	3.8	62	16.2	Cr	Hammer
Oghamist Pick Hammer	+25%; Dex, Emp +10; HP +30	50	08	91	3.8	62	16.2	Cr	Hammer
Spectral Crusher	+25%; Blunt S. +3; Str, Qui +7	50	08	90	3.8	62	16.2	Cr	Hammer
Glimmerstrike Crusher	+25%; Qui, Con +7; Celtic Dual S. +3	50	W8	90	2.8	45	16.2	Cr	Mace
Moondeath Mace	+25%; Str +9; Blunt S. +4; Qui +6	50	08	90	3.5	57	16.2	Cr	Mace
Moonstrike Mace	+25%; Nature Affinity, Nurture, Regrowth S. +2; Emp +9	50	08	90	3.5	57	16.2	Cr	Mace

Celtic Spear Skill (Spear)

Weapon	Bonus	PL	M#	QI	Spd	Dam	DPS	Type	Generic
Nasco's Spear		2	01	100	3.1	6	1.8	Thr	Spear
Well-Balanced Celtic Spear	+1%; Celtic Spear S. +1; Qui +1	7	02	90	3.8	13	3.3	Thr	Spear
Hunting Spear	+1%; Celtic Spear S. +1; HP +3	10	02	89	4	17	4.2	Thr	Spear
Richly Designed Short Spear		12	03	80	3.4	16	4.8	Thr	Spear
Finely Crafted Spear	+10%; Dex +4	16	04	89	5.7	34	6.0	Thr	Spear
Fire Hardened Irewood Spear	+10%; Dex +4	16	04	90	3.9	23	6.0	Thr	Spear
Crude Curmudgeon Spear		17	04	80	5.2	33	6.3	Thr	Spear
Cath Spear	+15%; Celtic Spear, Parry S. +1; Dex +1; Heat R. +2	21	05	89	4.6	35	7.5	Thr	Spear
Fathomless Spear	+10%; Celtic Spear S. +1; Con +4	23	05	89	3.8	31	8.1	Thr	Spear
Coral Spear	+10%; Celtic Spear S. +1; Dex +4	24	05	89	5.7	48	8.4	Thr	Spear
Worm Tipper	+10%; Celtic Spear S. +1; Dex +6	25	05	89	5.7	50	8.7	Thr	Spear
Bilk's Spear	+15%; Celtic Spear, Parry S. +1; Energy R. +2	26	06	89	4.6	41	9.0	Thr	Spear
Gilded Sea Spear	+15%; Celtic Spear S. +3; Energy R. +4; Qui +3	27	06	100	5.5	51	9.3	Thr	Spear
Spear of Elder Pearl	+15%; Celtic Spear S. +1; Con +4	27	06	89	5.4	50	9.3	Thr	Spear
Nasco's Barbed Spear	+10%; Celtic Spear S. +3; Cold R. +4	28	06	100	3.3	32	9.6	Thr	Spear
Crude Spear	+5%; Celtic Spear S. +1	32	07	80	4	43	10.8	Thr	Spear
Sidhe Spine Barbed Spear	+10%; Celtic Spear S. +3; Str +4	36	08	89	5.6	67	12.0	Thr	Spear
Virulent Darkened Spear	+15%; Celtic Spear S. +4	36	08	89	5	60	12.0	Thr	Spear
Alluvion Spear	+20%; Str +6; Dex +4	37	08	89	5.7	70	12.3	Thr	Spear
Flawed Asterite Spear	+1%; Celtic Spear S. +1; HP +6	37	08	80	3.7	46	12.3	Thr	Spear
Coruscating Truesilver Spear	+20%; Celtic Spear S. +2; Qui +6; Body R. +4	38	08	89	4.5	56	12.5	Thr	Spear
Balanced Asterite Spear	+20%; Celtic Spear S. +2; HP +12	39	08	89	3.5	45	12.9	Thr	Spear
Cathal's War Spear	+20%; Celtic Spear S. +2; Parry S. +4; Qui +9	43	08	100	5	71	14.1	Thr	Spear
Druidic Oaken Spear	+20%; Celtic Spear S. +4; Str +6; Energy R. +12	43	08	100	5	71	14.1	Thr	Spear
Heartwood Spear	+20%; Celtic Spear S. +4; Str +6; Cold R. +12	43	08	100	5	71	14.1	Thr	Spear
Infernal Bane	+20%; Celtic Spear S. +2; Parry S. +1; Heat R. +2; HP +6	43	08	89	5.7	80	14.1	Thr	Spear
Silvered Spellbound Spear	+20%; Celtic Spear S. +4; Str +6; Matter R. +12	43	08	100	5	71	14.1	Thr	Spear
Shadow Crystal Great Spear	+25%; Celtic Spear S. +2; Qui +9	48	08	89	5.4	84	15.6	Thr	Spear
Glimmer Geist Spear	+25%; Celtic Spear S. +4; Str, Dex, Qui +6	50	08	91	3.5	57	16.2	Thr	Spear
Glistening War Spear	+25%; Celtic Spear S. +2; Str, Dex +6	50	08	90	5	81	16.2	Thr	Spear
Spectral Impaler	+25%; Celtic Spear S. +3; Dex, Str +10	50	08	90	5.7	92	16.2	Thr	Spear
Wyvern Spear of Light	+25%; Celtic Spear S. +5; Str, Con, Dex +10	50	08	91	5	81	16.2	Thr	Spear

Large Weaponry Skill (Falcata, Hammer, Mace, Shillelagh, Sword, Tooth)

Weapon	Bonus	PL	M#	QI	Spd	Dam	DPS	Type	Generic
Spine-Breaker	+1%; Str +4	7	02	90	5.1	17	3.3	Cr	Mace
Well-Balanced Great Sword	+1%; Str +4	7	02	90	5	17	3.3	Sl	Sword
Richly Designed Sword		12	03	80	4.7	23	4.8	Sl	Sword
Long Thorned Tree Knot	+5%; Large Weaponry S. +1; Con +3	16	04	90	4.8	29	6.0	Cr	Mace
Silver Rune Hammer	+10%; Str +4	19	04	89	5.3	37	6.9	Cr	Hammer
Big Shillelagh		21	05	80	4.8	36	7.5	Cr	Shillelagh
Blunted Femur	+10%; Large Weaponry S. +2; Body R. +2	23	05	89	5.3	43	8.1	Cr	Hammer
Fathomless Great Hammer	+10%; Large Weaponry S. +1; Con +4	23	05	89	4.8	39	8.1	Cr	Hammer
Fathomless Great Sword	+10%; Large Weaponry S. +1; Con, Dex, Str +1	23	05	89	5	41	8.1	Sl	Sword
Giant Femur Cracker	+10%; Matter R. +6 or +9; Str +4	25	05	89	5.2	45	8.7	Cr	Hammer
Keeper's Friend	+10%; Large Weaponry S. +2; Str +1	25	05	89	4.7	41	8.7	Cr	Shillelagh
Will Shatterer	+15%; Str +3; Qui +4	26	06	89	5	45	9.0	Cr	Hammer
Waylayer Shillelagh	+15%; Large Weaponry S. +3	26	06	89	4.7	42	9.0	Cr	Shillelagh
Deathly Vindicator	+15%; Large Weaponry S. +2; Str +4	26	06	90	5.2	47	9.0	Sl	Sword
Sight Blighter	+15%; Str +4; Con +3	26	06	89	4.4	40	9.0	Sl	Sword
Waylayer Great Sword	+15%; Large Weaponry S. +3	26	06	89	5.3	48	9.0	Sl	Sword
Thumper	+15%; Large Weaponry S. +1; Crush R. +2; Qui +3	29	06	89	5.3	52	9.9	Cr	Hammer

Weapon	Bonus	PL	M#	Ql	Spd	Dam	DPS	Type	Generic
Windy Crusher	+5%; Spirit R. +3; Large Weaponry S. +1	29	06	89	4.3	43	9.9	Cr	Hammer
Lucky Striker	+15%; Large Weaponry S. +2; Body R. +4	30	06	89	5.3	54	10.2	Sl	Sword
Large Stone Mace	+5%; Emp +3	32	07	80	5	54	10.8	Cr	Mace
Heavy Great Sword	+5%; Qui –4; Str +9	32	07	80	5.7	62	10.8	Sl	Sword
Giant Swath-Cutter	+15%; Large Weaponry, Parry S. +2	36	08	89	4.8	58	12.0	Sl	Sword
Alluvion Great Hammer	+20%; Str +6; Qui +4	37	08	89	5.3	65	12.3	Cr	Hammer
Flawed Runic Shillelagh	+1%; Large Weaponry S. +1; HP +6	37	08	80	5.1	63	12.3	Cr	Shillelagh
Glistening Shillelagh	+25%; Large Weaponry S. +2; Str, Qui +6	37	08	90	4.7	58	12.3	Cr	Shillelagh
Alluvion Great Sword	+20%; Str +6; Qui +4	37	08	89	5.3	65	12.3	Sl	Sword
Flawed Asterite Sword	+1%; Large Weaponry S. +1; HP +6	37	08	80	5	62	12.3	Sl	Sword
Earth Shaker	+15%; Large Weaponry S. +1; Str +6; Con +3	39	08	89	5.3	68	12.9	Cr	Hammer
Runic Shillelagh	+20%; Large Weaponry S. +2; HP +12	39	08	89	5	65	12.9	Cr	Shillelagh
Imbedded Greatsword	+20%; Large Weaponry S. +5; Str +9	39	08	100	4.3	55	12.9	Sl	Sword
Razor Edged Asterite Sword	+20%; Large Weaponry S. +2; HP +12	39	08	89	4.8	62	12.9	Sl	Sword
Spine Splitter	+15%; Large Weaponry S. +2; Str +7	41	08	89	4.5	61	13.5	Cr	Shillelagh
Giant Gutter	+15%; Large Weaponry S. +2; Str +7	41	08	89	4.6	62	13.5	Sl	Sword
Infernal Edge	+20%; Large Weaponry S. +2; Qui, Con +1; Parry S. +1	42	08	89	5.3	74	13.9	Sl	Sword
War Blade of the Stoic	+20%; Large Weaponry S. +3; Slash, Thrust R. +6; Str +7	42	08	100	5.1	70	13.8	Sl	Sword
Boned Greatsword	+20%; Large Weaponry S. +4; Str +6; Cold R. +12	43	08	100	5.3	75	14.1	Sl	Sword
Fomorian's Bane	+20%; Large Weaponry S. +4; Str +6; Crush R. +12	43	08	100	5.3	75	14.1	Sl	Sword
Silvered Spellbound Greatsword	+20%; Large Weaponry S. +4; Str +6; Cold R. +12	43	08	100	5.3	75	14.1	Sl	Sword
Coruscating Truesilver Hammer	+20%; Large Weaponry S. +2; Con +3; Str +6	45	08	89	5.2	76	14.7	Cr	Hammer
Coruscating Truesilver Sword	+20%; Large Weaponry S. +3; Str +6	45	08	89	5	74	14.7	Sl	Sword
Shadow Crystal Great Mace	+25%; Large Weaponry S. +3; Str +6	48	08	89	5.3	83	15.6	Cr	Mace
Shadow Crystal Great Sword	+25%; Large Weaponry S. +3; Str +6	48	08	89	5.5	86	15.6	Sl	Sword
Sword of Valor	+25%; Large Weaponry S. +3; Parry S. +2; Power +1; Slash R. +6	48	08	89	4.2	66	15.6	Sl	Sword
Juggernaut Great Falcata	+25%; Large Weaponry S. +5; Str, Qui, Con +10	50	08	91	4.5	73	16.2	Sl	Falcata
Far Dorocha Devastator	+25%; Large Weaponry S. +3; Qui +7; Str +9	50	08	90	5.3	86	16.2	Cr	Hammer
Glimmer Wrath Great Hammer	+25%; Str +9; Qui +4; Large Weaponry S. +4	50	08	90	5.3	86	16.2	Cr	Hammer
Azure Avenger	+25%; Large Weaponry S. +4; Str +7; Con +6	50	08	90	5.3	86	16.2	Sl	Sword
Glistening Great Sword	+25%; Large Weaponry S. +2; Str, Qui +6	50	08	90	5.3	86	16.2	Sl	Sword
Sinach's Great Tooth	+20%; Large Weaponry S. +4; Parry S. +2	50	08	89	4	65	16.2	Sl	Tooth

Piercing Skill (Bone, Claw, Dagger, Dirk, Fang, Horn, Punch, Rapier, Stiletto, Tooth)

Weapon	Bonus	PL	M#	Ql	Spd	Dam	DPS	Type	Generic
Training Dirk		0	01	90	2.3	3	1.2	Thr	Dirk
Wavy Piercer	+1%; Piercing S. +1	4	01	90	2.7	6	2.4	Thr	Dagger
Pelt Punch	+1%; Piercing S. +1; Qui +1	10	02	89	2.8	12	4.2	Thr	Punch
Anger Sprite Dirk	+5%; Qui +4	11	03	89	2.3	10	4.5	Thr	Dirk
Red Hound Fang		11	03	100	2.3	10	4.5	Thr	Fang
Richly Designed Rapier		12	03	80	2.8	13	4.8	Thr	Rapier
Bristle's Fang	+5%; Piercing S. +2	13	03	100	2.2	11	5.1	Thr	Fang
Crystal Bleeder	+5%; Piercing S. +1; Dex +3	13	03	90	2.9	15	5.1	Thr	Rapier
Worn Dark Shadow Rapier		13	03	80	2.6	13	5.1	Thr	Rapier
Tiny Unicorn Horn	Parry, Piercing S. +1; HP +3	16	05	89	2.7	16	6.0	Thr	Horn
Adorned Stiletto	+10%; Piercing S. +1; Dex +1	16	04	89	2.6	16	6.0	Thr	Stiletto
Splintered Mephit Femur	+1%; Backstab S. +1; Dex +1; Cha –5	17	04	89	2.7	17	6.3	Thr	Bone
Celestial Piercer	+10%; Celtic Dual S. +1; Qui +1	17	04	89	2.4	15	6.3	Thr	Dirk
Rock Dagger		21	05	80	2.7	20	7.5	Thr	Dagger
Crystal Shard	+10%; Piercing S. +3	21	05	90	2.1	16	7.5	Thr	Dirk
Fanged Tooth	+10%; Celtic Dual S. +1; Qui +1; HP +3; Matter R. +2	22	05	89	2.6	20	7.8	Thr	Fang
Assailer's Curved Blade	+5%; Qui +6	23	05	89	2.4	19	8.1	Thr	Dagger
Fathomless Stiletto	+10%; Dex +1; Celtic Dual, Piercing S. +1	23	05	89	2.7	22	8.1	Thr	Stiletto
Cur Shaghey	+15%; Celtic Dual, Parry S. +1	24	05	89	2.7	23	8.4	Thr	Stiletto
Rib Tickler	+10%; Dex, Qui +4	25	05	89	2.3	20	8.7	Thr	Dirk
Imperial Rapier of the Depths	+10%; Piercing S. +2	25	05	89	3	26	8.7	Thr	Rapier
Oaken Impaler	+5%; Piercing S. +1; Heat R. +2; Dex, Qui +3	25	05	89	2.6	23	8.7	Thr	Stiletto
Kraken's Lost Tooth	+10%; Envenom S. +1; Body R. +2; Power +1	25	05	89	2.7	23	8.7	Thr	Tooth
Waylayer Dirk	+15%; Celtic Dual S. +3	26	06	89	2.3	21	9.0	Thr	Dirk
Waylayer Rapier	+15%; Piercing S. +3	26	06	89	2.7	24	9.0	Thr	Rapier
Twined Piercer	+15%; Celtic Dual S. +2; Qui +3	26	06	89	2.7	24	9.0	Thr	Stiletto
Feelion Razor	+15%; Matter R. +6; Parry S. +1	27	06	89	2.7	25	9.3	Thr	Rapier

Weapon	Bonus	PL	M#	Ql	Spd	Dam	DPS	Type	Generic
Pearl Rapier	+15%; Celtic Dual S. +2; Dex +3	27	06	89	3	28	9.3	Thr	Rapier
Spritely Stiletto	+15%; Piercing, Parry S. +1; Dex +3	29	06	89	2.7	27	9.9	Thr	Stiletto
Puinesean Fang	+15%; Envenom S. +1; Body R. +4; Qui +1; Thrust R. +2	30	06	89	2.7	28	10.2	Thr	Fang
Smiter	+15%; Piercing S. +1; Dex +3; Heat R. +4	31	07	89	2.5	26	10.5	Thr	Dagger
Razor-Sharp Lion Tooth	+15%; Piercing, Parry S. +2; Dex +7	31	07	100	2.4	25	10.5	Thr	Tooth
Carved Fang Dagger	+10% to hit	32	07	89	2.2	24	10.8	Thr	Dagger
Heavy Curved Dagger	+5%; Qui –2; Dex +6	32	07	80	3	32	10.8	Thr	Dagger
Deamhan Aeir Claw	+15%; Matter R. –4; Spirit R. +4; Piercing S. +1; Qui +3	35	07	89	2.3	27	11.7	Thr	Claw
Rapier of the Forsaken	+15%; Piercing S. +4; Parry S. +3	35	07	100	2.7	32	11.7	Thr	Rapier
Cliff Dweller Skewer	+20%; Celtic Dual S. +2; Dex, Qui +6	36	08	89	2.3	28	12.0	Thr	Dirk
Flawed Asterite Dirk	+1%; Piercing S. +1; HP +6	37	08	80	2.8	34	12.3	Thr	Dirk
Alluvion Rapier	+20%; Str +6; Con +4	37	08	89	2.7	33	12.3	Thr	Rapier
Sinister Alluvion Stiletto	+20%; Dex +6; Thrust R. +6	37	08	89	2.7	33	12.3	Thr	Stiletto
Ceremonial Black Dirk	+15%; Qui +9; Dex +3	38	08	89	2.2	28	12.6	Thr	Dirk
Rat Fang Stiletto	+20%; Piercing S. +1; Dex, Qui +6	38	08	90	2.7	34	12.6	Thr	Fang
Ailbe's Claw	+20%; Piercing, Parry S. +2; Dex, Qui +6	39	08	100	2.6	34	12.9	Thr	Claw
Balanced Asterite Dirk	+20%; Piercing S. +2; HP +12	39	08	89	2.5	32	12.9	Thr	Dirk
Cronsidhe Biter	+20%; Piercing S. +2; Qui +3; Body R. +2; HP +3	41	08	89	2.7	36	13.5	Thr	Tooth
Manganese Dagger	+20%; Piercing S. +4; Dex +6; Body R. +12	43	08	100	2.4	34	14.1	Thr	Dagger
Piercer	+20%; Piercing S. +6; Dex +3; Body R. +12	43	08	100	2.4	34	14.1	Thr	Dagger
Silvered Spellbound Dagger	+20%; Piercing S. +4; Dex +6; Body R. +12	43	08	100	2.4	34	14.1	Thr	Dagger
Glimmer Spirit Rapier	+20%; Piercing S. +2; Str +4; Dex +3	43	08	89	2.7	38	14.1	Thr	Rapier
Coruscating Truesilver Dagger	+20%; Piercing S. +3; Dex, Qui +3	45	08	89	2.7	40	14.7	Thr	Dagger
Wicked Thorn	+20%; Piercing S. +2; Qui +9	47	08	89	2.3	35	15.3	Thr	Dagger
Shadow Crystal Rapier	+25%; HP +24; Slash, Thrust R. +2	48	08	89	2.7	42	15.6	Thr	Rapier
Dob's Bloody Fang	+25%; Piercing, Parry S. +3; Dex, Qui +6	50	08	100	2.2	36	16.2	Thr	Fang
Deathmoon Rapier	+25%; Piercing S. +4; Str +9; Dex +7	50	08	91	2.8	45	16.2	Thr	Rapier
Shard of Light	+25%; Piercing S. +5; Dex, Qui +10	50	08	91	3.6	58	16.2	Thr	Rapier
Gehk Gouger	+25%; Celtic Dual S. +3; Dex +6	50	08	90	2.6	42	16.2	Thr	Stiletto
Glimmering Stiletto	+25%; Piercing, Celtic Dual S. +2; Qui +7; Dex +9	50	08	90	2.3	37	16.2	Thr	Stiletto
Glistening Stiletto	+25%; Piercing S. +2; Str, Dex +6	50	08	90	2.6	42	16.2	Thr	Stiletto
Granny's Needle	+25%; Piercing S. +3; Str, Dex +10	50	08	90	2.6	42	16.2	Thr	Stiletto

Staff Skill (Staff)

Weapon	Bonus	PL	M#	Ql	Spd	Dam	DPS	Type	Generic
Training Staff		0	W1	90	4.5	5	1.2	Cr	Staff
Ire Wood Sapling Staff		1	birch	71	4.5	7	1.5	Cr	Staff
Eldritch Staff of Light *	Light Magic F. +5; other Eldritch spells F. +2	6	W2	85	4.5	14	3.0	Cr	Staff
Eldritch Staff of Magic *	Eldritch spells F. +4	6	W2	85	4.5	14	3.0	Cr	Staff
Eldritch Staff of Mana *	Mana Magic F. +5; other Eldritch spells F. +2	6	W2	85	4.5	14	3.0	Cr	Staff
Eldritch Staff of Void *	Void Magic F. +5; other Eldritch spells F. +2	6	W2	85	4.5	14	3.0	Cr	Staff
Enchanter Staff of Enchantments *	Enchanter spells F. +5	6	W2	85	4.5	14	3.0	Cr	Staff
Enchanter Staff of Light *	Light Magic F. +5; other Enchanter spells F. +2	6	W2	85	4.5	14	3.0	Cr	Staff
Enchanter Staff of Magic *	Enchanter spells F. +4	6	W2	85	4.5	14	3.0	Cr	Staff
Enchanter Staff of Mana *	Mana Magic F. +5; other Enchanter spells F. +2	6	W2	85	4.5	14	3.0	Cr	Staff
Mentalist Staff of Light *	Light Magic F. +5; other Mentalist spells F. +2	6	W2	85	4.5	14	3.0	Cr	Staff
Mentalist Staff of Magic *	Mentalist spells F. +4	6	W2	85	4.5	14	3.0	Cr	Staff
Mentalist Staff of Mana *	Mana Magic F. +5; other Mentalist spells F. +2	6	W2	85	4.5	14	3.0	Cr	Staff
Mentalist Staff of Mentalism *	Mentalism F. +5; other Mentalist spells F. +2	6	W2	85	4.5	14	3.0	Cr	Staff
Staff of Insight	Eldritch spells Magic F. +4	6	W2	90	4.5	14	3.0	Cr	Staff
Staff of Mental Clarity	Mentalist spells F. +4	6	W2	90	4.5	14	3.0	Cr	Staff
Staff of Understanding	Enchanter spells F. +4	6	W2	90	4.5	14	3.0	Cr	Staff
Eldritch Staff of Channeling	+5%; Eldritch spells F. +8; Int +4	10	W2	90	4.8	20	4.2	Cr	Staff
Enchanter Staff of Channeling	+5%; Mentalist spells F. +8; Int +4	10	W2	90	4.8	20	4.2	Cr	Staff
Mentalist Staff of Channeling	+5%; Mentalist spells F. +8; Int +4	10	W2	90	4.8	20	4.2	Cr	Staff
Eldritch Staff of Light *	Light Magic F. +9; other Eldritch spells F. +5	11	W3	85	4.5	20	4.5	Cr	Staff
Eldritch Staff of Magic *	Eldritch spells F. +7	11	W3	85	4.5	20	4.5	Cr	Staff
Eldritch Staff of Mana *	Mana Magic F. +9; other Eldritch spells F. +5	11	W3	85	4.5	20	4.5	Cr	Staff
Eldritch Staff of Void *	Void Magic F. +9; other Eldritch spells F. +5	11	W3	85	4.5	20	4.5	Cr	Staff
Enchanter Staff of Enchantments *	Enchantments F. +9; other Ench. spells F. +5	11	W3	85	4.5	20	4.5	Cr	Staff
Enchanter Staff of Light *	Light Magic F. +9; other Enchanter spells F. +5	11	W3	85	4.5	20	4.5	Cr	Staff
Enchanter Staff of Magic *	Enchanter spells F. +7	11	W3	85	4.5	20	4.5	Cr	Staff

Weapon	Bonus	PL	M#	Ql	Spd	Dam	DPS	Type	Generic
Enchanter Staff of Mana *	Mana Magic F. +9; other Enchanter spells F. +5	11	W3	85	4.5	20	4.5	Cr	Staff
Mentalist Staff of Light *	Light Magic F. +9; other Mentalist spells F. +5	11	W3	85	4.5	20	4.5	Cr	Staff
Mentalist Staff of Magic *	Mentalist spells F. +7	11	W3	85	4.5	20	4.5	Cr	Staff
Mentalist Staff of Mana *	Mana Magic F. +9; other Mentalist spells F. +5	11	W3	85	4.5	20	4.5	Cr	Staff
Mentalist Staff of Mentalism *	Mentalism F. +9; other Mentalist spells F. +5	11	W3	85	4.5	20	4.5	Cr	Staff
Dergan Enchanter's Staff	+5%; Enchanter spells F. +9; HP +6	12	W3	89	4.5	22	4.8	Cr	Staff
Gaudy Enchantment Staff	Enchanter spells F. +8	12	W3	80	4.5	22	4.8	Cr	Staff
Gaudy Staff of Mentalism	Mentalist spells F. +8	12	W3	80	4.5	22	4.8	Cr	Staff
Gaudy Void Caster's Staff	Eldritch spells F. +8	12	W3	80	4.5	22	4.8	Cr	Staff
Staff of Inner Power	+5%; Eldritch spells F. +10; Power +3	12	W3	100	4.5	22	4.8	Cr	Staff
Studied Eldritch Staff	+5%; Eldritch spells F. +9; HP +6	12	W3	89	4.5	22	4.8	Cr	Staff
Studied Mentalist Staff	+5%; Mentalist spells F. +9; HP +6	12	W3	89	4.5	22	4.8	Cr	Staff
Eldritch Staff of Grandeur	+10%; Eldritch spells F. +12; Power +2	16	W4	89	4.5	27	6.0	Cr	Staff
Eldritch Staff of Light *	Light Magic F. +13; other Eldritch spells F. +7	16	W4	85	4.5	27	6.0	Cr	Staff
Eldritch Staff of Magic *	Eldritch spells F. +11	16	W4	85	4.5	27	6.0	Cr	Staff
Eldritch Staff of Mana *	Mana Magic F. +13; other Eldritch spells F. +7	16	W4	85	4.5	27	6.0	Cr	Staff
Eldritch Staff of Void *	Void Magic F. +13; other Eldritch spells F. +7	16	W4	85	4.5	27	6.0	Cr	Staff
Enchanter Staff of Enchantments *	Enchantments F. +13; other Ench. spells F. +7	16	W4	85	4.5	27	6.0	Cr	Staff
Enchanter Staff of Grandeur	+10%; Enchanter spells F. +10; Power +2	16	W4	89	4.5	27	6.0	Cr	Staff
Enchanter Staff of Light *	Light Magic F. +13; other Enchanter spells F. +7	16	W4	85	4.5	27	6.0	Cr	Staff
Enchanter Staff of Magic *	Enchanter spells F. +11	16	W4	85	4.5	27	6.0	Cr	Staff
Enchanter Staff of Mana *	Mana Magic F. +13; other Enchanter spells F. +7	16	W4	85	4.5	27	6.0	Cr	Staff
Mentalist Staff of Grandeur	+10%; Mentalist spells F. +10; Power +2	16	W4	89	4.5	27	6.0	Cr	Staff
Mentalist Staff of Light *	Light Magic F. +13; other Mentalist spells F. +7	16	W4	85	4.5	27	6.0	Cr	Staff
Mentalist Staff of Magic *	Mentalist spells F. +11	16	W4	85	4.5	27	6.0	Cr	Staff
Mentalist Staff of Mana *	Mana Magic F. +13; other Mentalist spells F. +7	16	W4	85	4.5	27	6.0	Cr	Staff
Mentalist Staff of Mentalism *	Mentalism F. +13; other Mentalist spells F. +7	16	W4	85	4.5	27	6.0	Cr	Staff
Kedger Staff of Enchantment	+10%; Enchanter spells F. +18; Int +7	18	W4	89	5	33	6.6	Cr	Staff
Kedger Staff of Mentalism	+10%; Mentalist spells F. +18; Int +7	18	W4	89	5	33	6.6	Cr	Staff
Kedger Staff of Void Magic	+10%; Eldritch spells F. +18; Int +7	18	W4	89	5	33	6.6	Cr	Staff
Aged Stone Staff *	+10%; Int +6; Light Magic, Mana Magic F. +14	20	W4	100	4.4	32	7.2	Cr	Staff
Aged Stone Staff *	+10%; Int +6; Eldritch spells F. +17	20	W4	100	4.4	32	7.2	Cr	Staff
Ancient Stone Staff	+10%; Int +6; Mentalist spells F. +17	20	W4	100	4.4	32	7.2	Cr	Staff
Runed Stone Staff	+10%; Int +6; Enchanter spells F. +17	20	W4	100	4.4	32	7.2	Cr	Staff
Eldritch Staff of Light *	Light Magic F. +18; other Eldritch spells F. +9	21	W5	85	4.5	34	7.5	Cr	Staff
Eldritch Staff of Magic *	Eldritch spells F. +14	21	W5	85	4.5	34	7.5	Cr	Staff
Eldritch Staff of Mana *	Mana Magic F. +18; other Eldritch spells F. +9	21	W5	85	4.5	34	7.5	Cr	Staff
Eldritch Staff of Void *	Void Magic F. +18; other Eldritch spells F. +9	21	W5	85	4.5	34	7.5	Cr	Staff
Eldritch Stone Staff	Eldritch spells F. +14	21	W5	80	4.5	34	7.5	Cr	Staff
Enchanter Staff of Enchantments *	Enchantments F. +18; other Ench. spells F. +9	21	W5	85	4.5	34	7.5	Cr	Staff
Enchanter Staff of Light *	Light Magic F. +18; other Enchanter spells F. +9	21	W5	85	4.5	34	7.5	Cr	Staff
Enchanter Staff of Magic *	Enchanter spells F. +14	21	W5	85	4.5	34	7.5	Cr	Staff
Enchanter Staff of Mana *	Mana Magic F. +18; other Enchanter spells F. +9	21	W5	85	4.5	34	7.5	Cr	Staff
Enchanter Stone Staff	Enchanter spells F. +14	21	W5	80	4.5	34	7.5	Cr	Staff
Mentalist Staff of Light *	Light Magic F. +18; other Mentalist spells F. +9	21	W5	85	4.5	34	7.5	Cr	Staff
Mentalist Staff of Magic *	Mentalist spells F. +14	21	W5	85	4.5	34	7.5	Cr	Staff
Mentalist Staff of Mana *	Mana Magic F. +18; other Mentalist spells F. +9	21	W5	85	4.5	34	7.5	Cr	Staff
Mentalist Staff of Mentalism *	Mentalism F. +18; other Mentalist spells F. +9	21	W5	85	4.5	34	7.5	Cr	Staff
Mentalist Stone Staff	Mentalist spells F. +14	21	W5	80	4.5	34	7.5	Cr	Staff
Deluged Carved Staff	+10%; Light Magic F. +23; Int +3; Power +2	23	W5	89	5	41	8.1	Cr	Staff
Imperial Staff of the Depths	+10%; Mentalism F. +23; Int +3; Power +2	23	W5	89	5	41	8.1	Cr	Staff
Shaped Watery Staff	+10%; Void Magic F. +23; Int +3; Power +2	23	W5	89	5	41	8.1	Cr	Staff
Twisted Coral Staff	+10%; Mana Magic F. +23; Int +3; Power +2	23	W5	89	5	41	8.1	Cr	Staff
Water Opal Staff	+10%; Enchantments F. +23; Int +3; Power +2	23	W5	89	5	41	8.1	Cr	Staff
Eldritch Etched Stone Staff	+10%; Eldritch spells F. +19; HP +18	25	W5	89	4.5	39	8.7	Cr	Staff
Enchanter Etched Stone Staff	+10%; Enchanter spells F. +19; HP +18	25	W5	89	4.5	39	8.7	Cr	Staff
Mentalist Etched Stone Staff	+10%; Mentalist spells F. +19; HP +18	25	W5	89	4.5	39	8.7	Cr	Staff
Dweomer Rifter	+15%; Enchantments F. +22; other Enchanter spells F. +14; Int +9	26	W6	90	4.4	39	8.9	Cr	Staff
Eldritch Staff of Light *	Light Magic F. +21; other Eldritch spells F. +11	26	W6	85	4.5	41	9.0	Cr	Staff
Eldritch Staff of Magic *	Eldritch spells F. +17	26	W6	85	4.5	41	9.0	Cr	Staff
Eldritch Staff of Mana *	Mana Magic F. +21; other Eldritch spells F. +11	26	W6	85	4.5	41	9.0	Cr	Staff
Eldritch Staff of Void *	Void Magic F. +21; other Eldritch spells F. +11	26	W6	85	4.5	41	9.0	Cr	Staff

Weapon	Bonus	PL	M#	Ql	Spd	Dam	DPS	Type	Generic
Enchanter Staff of Enchantments *	Enchantments F. +21; other Ench. spells F. +11	26	W6	85	4.5	41	9.0	Cr	Staff
Enchanter Staff of Light *	Light Magic F. +21; other Enchanter spells F. +11	26	W6	85	4.5	41	9.0	Cr	Staff
Enchanter Staff of Magic *	Enchanter spells F. +17	26	W6	85	4.5	41	9.0	Cr	Staff
Enchanter Staff of Mana *	Mana Magic F. +21; other Enchanter spells F. +11	26	W6	85	4.5	41	9.0	Cr	Staff
Mentalist Staff of Light *	Light Magic F. +21; other Mentalist spells F. +11	26	W6	85	4.5	41	9.0	Cr	Staff
Mentalist Staff of Magic *	Mentalist spells F. +17	26	W6	85	4.5	41	9.0	Cr	Staff
Mentalist Staff of Mana *	Mana Magic F. +21; other Mentalist spells F. +11	26	W6	85	4.5	41	9.0	Cr	Staff
Mentalist Staff of Mentalism *	Mentalism F. +21; other Mentalist spells F. +11	26	W6	85	4.5	41	9.0	Cr	Staff
Mind Rifter	+15%; Mentalism F. +22; other Mentalist spells F. +14; Int +9	26	W6	90	4.4	39	8.9	Cr	Staff
Staff of Mental Domination	+15%; Mental. F. +26; other Mental. spells F. +19; Int +12	26	W6	100	4.4	40	9.0	Cr	Staff
Void Rifter	+15%; Eldritch spells F. +14; Int +9	26	W6	90	4.4	39	8.9	Cr	Staff
Fagan's Staff	+15%; Enchanter spells F. +26; Int +9	31	W7	100	4.2	44	10.5	Cr	Staff
Silvered Staff	+15%; Eldritch spells F. +26; Int +10	31	M7	100	4	42	10.5	Cr	Staff
Ether Staff	+20%; Ench. F. +37; Energy R. +4; Ench. S. +2; HP +9	37	W8	89	4.6	57	12.3	Cr	Staff
Ether Staff of Light	+20%; Light Mg. F. +37; Energy R. +4; Light Mg. S. +2; HP +9	37	W8	89	4.6	57	12.3	Cr	Staff
Ether Staff of Thought	+20%; Mental. F. +37; Energy R. +4; Mental. S. +2; HP +9	37	W8	89	4.6	57	12.3	Cr	Staff
Flawed Mind Walkers Staff	+1%; Mentalist spells F. +24; HP +6	37	W8	80	4.8	59	12.3	Cr	Staff
Flawed Staff of the Underhill	+1%; Enchanter spells F. +24; HP +6	37	W8	80	4.8	59	12.3	Cr	Staff
Flawed Void Walkers Staff	+1%; Eldritch spells F. +24; HP +6	37	W8	80	4.8	59	12.3	Cr	Staff
Staff of Ominous Enchantment	+15%; Enchanter spells F. +28; Power +4	37	W8	89	4.8	59	12.3	Cr	Staff
Staff of Ominous Void	+15%; Eldritch spells F. +28; Power +4	37	W8	89	4.8	59	12.3	Cr	Staff
Staff of the Ominous Mind	+15%; Mentalist spells F. +28; Power +4	37	W8	89	4.8	59	12.3	Cr	Staff
Eldritch Staff of Magic *	+15%; Eldritch spells F. +29; Power +6	38	W8	89	4.3	54	12.6	Cr	Staff
Enchanter Staff of Power	+15%; Enchanter spells F. +29; Power +6	38	W8	89	4.3	54	12.6	Cr	Staff
Mentalist Staff of Power	+15%; Mentalist spells F. +29; Power +6	38	W8	89	4.3	54	12.6	Cr	Staff
Mind Walkers Staff	+20%; Mentalist spells F. +30; HP +18	39	W8	89	4.7	61	12.9	Cr	Staff
Staff of the Underhill	+20%; Enchanter spells F. +30; HP +18	39	W8	89	4.7	61	12.9	Cr	Staff
Void Walkers Staff	+20%; Eldritch spells F. +30; HP +18	39	W8	89	4.7	61	12.9	Cr	Staff
Petrified Staff of Destruction	+20%; Void Mg. F. +40; Cold R. +4; Light Mg. S. +2; Void Mg. S. +3	40	W8	89	4.4	58	13.2	Cr	Staff
Petrified Staff of Enchantments	+20%; Ench. F. +40; Spirit R. +4; Mana Mg. S. +2; Ench. S. +3	40	W8	89	4.4	58	13.2	Cr	Staff
Petrified Staff of Thought	+20%; Mental. F. +40; Heat R. +4; Mana Magic S. +2; Mental. S. +3	40	W8	89	4.4	58	13.2	Cr	Staff
Siabrian Staff of the Magi	+25%; Mana, Light Magic F. +38; Int +10; Power +5	40	W8	100	4.3	57	13.2	Cr	Staff
Aodh's Staff	+20%; Eldritch spells F. +37; Spirit R. +20	43	O8	100	4.2	59	14.1	Cr	Staff
Balor's Gift	+20%; Eldritch spells F. +37; Cold R. +20	43	O8	100	4.2	59	14.1	Cr	Staff
Elder's Staff of Light	+20%; Light Magic F. +43; Dex +4; HP +9; Power +3	43	W8	89	4.5	63	14.1	Cr	Staff
Elder's Staff of Mana	+20%; Mana Magic F. +43; Dex +4; HP +9; Power +3	43	W8	89	4.5	63	14.1	Cr	Staff
Elder's Staff of the Mind	+20%; Mentalism F. +43; Dex +4; HP +9; Power +3	43	W8	89	4.5	63	14.1	Cr	Staff
Elder's Staff of the Voided Land	+20%; Void Magic F. +43; Dex +4; HP +9; Power +3	43	W8	89	4.5	63	14.1	Cr	Staff
Elder's Staff of Thought	+20%; Enchantments F. +43; Dex +4; HP +9; Power +3	43	W8	89	4.5	63	14.1	Cr	Staff
Mindnumber	+20%; Mentalist spells F. +37; Energy R. +20	43	O8	100	4.2	59	14.1	Cr	Staff
Silvered Spellbound Enchanter Staff	+20%; Enchant. spells F. +37; Spirit R. +20	43	O8	100	4.2	59	14.1	Cr	Staff
Silvered Spellbound Mentalist Staff	+20%; Mental. spells F. +37; Matter R. +20	43	O8	100	4.2	59	14.1	Cr	Staff
Staff of the Enchantress	+20%; Enchanter spells F. +37; Matter R. +20	43	O8	100	4.2	59	14.1	Cr	Staff
Eldritch Staff of the Arcane	+20%; Eldritch spells F. +38; Power +10	45	W8	100	4	59	14.7	Cr	Staff
Enchanter Staff of the Arcane	+20%; Enchanter spells F. +38; Power +10	45	W8	100	4	59	14.7	Cr	Staff
Mentalist Staff of the Arcane	+20%; Mentalist spells F. +38; Power +10	45	W8	100	4	59	14.7	Cr	Staff
Truesilver Staff of Magic	+20%; Enchanter spells F. +34; Power +5	45	O8	89	5	74	14.7	Cr	Staff
Truesilver Staff of the Mind	+20%; Mentalist spells F. +34; Power +5	45	O8	89	5	74	14.7	Cr	Staff
Truesilver Staff of the Veil	+20%; Eldritch spells F. +34; Power +5	45	O8	89	5	74	14.7	Cr	Staff
Dark Shard of the Triumvirate	+25%; Eldritch spells F. +36; Int +12	48	W8	89	5	78	15.6	Cr	Staff
Dweomer Shard of the Triumvirate	+25%; Enchanter spells F. +36; Int +12	48	W8	89	5	78	15.6	Cr	Staff
Tali Shard of the Triumvirate	+25%; Mentalist spells F. +36; Int +12	48	W8	89	5	78	15.6	Cr	Staff
Fomorian Staff of Light	+25%; Light Magic F. +50; Int +6; Light Magic S. +3	50	W8	89	5	81	16.2	Cr	Staff
Fomorian Staff of Mana	+25%; Mana Magic F. +50; Int +6; Mana Magic S. +3	50	W8	89	5	81	16.2	Cr	Staff
Leprechaun's Staff of Enchantments	+25%; Ench. F. +50; Int +6; Ench. S. +3	50	W8	89	5	81	16.2	Cr	Staff
Leprechaun's Staff of Mentalism	+25%; Mental. F. +50; Int +6; Mental. S. +3	50	W8	89	5	81	16.2	Cr	Staff
Leprechaun's Staff of the Void	+25%; Void Magic F. +50; Int +6; Void Magic S. +3	50	W8	89	5	81	16.2	Cr	Staff
Staff of the Arch-Eldritch	+25%; Eldritch spells F. +44; Int +10	50	W8	90	4.4	71	16.2	Cr	Staff
Staff of the Arch-Enchanter	+25%; Enchanter spells F. +44; Int +10	50	W8	90	4.4	71	16.2	Cr	Staff
Staff of the Arch-Mentalist	+25%; Mentalist spells F. +44; Int +10	50	W8	90	4.4	71	16.2	Cr	Staff
Vindicator's Staff of Enchantments	+25%; Ench. F. +50; Int +9; Ench. S. +4; Dex +7	50	W8	90	5	81	16.2	Cr	Staff
Vindicator's Staff of Light	+25%; Light Mg. F. +50; Int +9; Light Mg. S. +4; Dex +7	50	W8	90	5	81	16.2	Cr	Staff

Weapon	Bonus	PL	M#	Ql	Spd	Dam	DPS	Type	Generic
Vindicator's Staff of Mana	+25%; Mana Mg. F. +50; Int +9; Mana Mg. S. +4; Dex +7	50	W8	90	5	81	16.2	Cr	Staff
Vindicator's Staff of Mentalism	+25%; Mental. F. +50; Int +9; Mental. S. +4; Dex +7	50	W8	90	5	81	16.2	Cr	Staff
Vindicator's Staff of the Void	+25%; Void Mg. F. +50; Int +9; Void Mg. S. +4; Dex +7	50	W8	90	5	81	16.2	Cr	Staff
Warshadow Staff of Enchantments	+25%; Ench. F. +50; Ench. S. +3; Int +12; Power +4	50	W8	90	5	81	16.2	Cr	Staff
Warshadow Staff of Mentalism	+25%; Mentalism F. +50; Mentalism S. +3; Int +12; Power +4	50	W8	90	5	81	16.2	Cr	Staff
Warshadow Staff of the Moon	+25%; Mana Magic F. +50; Mana Magic S. +3; Int +12; Power +4	50	W8	90	5	81	16.2	Cr	Staff
Warshadow Staff of the Sun	+25%; Light Magic F. +50; Light Magic S. +3; Int +12; Power +4	50	W8	90	5	81	16.2	Cr	Staff
Warshadow Staff of the Void	+25%; Void Magic F. +50; Void Magic S. +3; Int +12; Power +4	50	W8	90	5	81	16.2	Cr	Staff

Bow Skill (Bow)

Weapon	Bonus	PL	M#	Ql	Spd	Dam	DPS	Range	Generic
Ore Bow	+10%; Bow S. +2; Str +3	16	O4	100	4.2	25	6.0	1200	Bow
Kedger Short Bow	+10%; Bow S. +3	18	W4	89	4	26	6.6	1200	Bow
Hardened Short Bow	+10%; Bow S. +2; Qui +6	21	W5	100	4	30	7.5	1200	Bow
Ire Bow	+10%; Bow S. +3; Qui +4	21	W5	100	4.2	32	7.5	1200	Bow
Phantom Short Bow	+5% to hit	21	W5	89	4	30	7.5	1200	Bow
Water-Logged Short Bow	+10%; Dex +6	25	W5	89	4.4	38	8.7	1200	Bow
Flawed Runic Bow	+1%; Bow S. +1; HP +6	37	W8	80	4.5	55	12.3	1200	Bow
Runic Bow	+20%; Bow S. +2; HP +12	39	W8	89	4.3	55	12.9	1200	Bow
Truesilver Short Bow	+20%; Bow S. +5	45	O8	89	4	59	14.7	1200	Bow
Bow of the Silver Talon	+25%; Bow S. +2; Dex +9	48	O8	89	4.2	66	15.6	1200	Bow
Fomorian Short Bow	+25%; Bow S. +3; Dex +3; Cha +1	48	W8	89	4	62	15.6	1200	Bow
Glimmerspirit Short Bow	+25%; Dex, Str +10; Qui +9	50	W8	91	4	65	16.2	1200	Bow

Recurve Bow Skill (Bow)

Weapon	Bonus	PL	M#	Ql	Spd	Dam	DPS	Range	Generic
Elven Recurve Bow	Recurve Bow S. +1	6	W2	90	4.7	14	3.0	1680	Bow
Adorned Recurve Bow		12	W3	80	4.8	23	4.8	1680	Bow
Oaken Recurve Bow	+5%; Dex +3; Recurve Bow S. +1	13	W3	90	4.8	24	5.1	1680	Bow
Great Silver Rune Bow	+10%; Dex +4	16	W4	89	5.4	32	6.0	1600	Bow
Kedger Recurve Bow	+10%; Recurve Bow S. +3	18	W4	89	4.7	31	6.6	1680	Bow
Siabrian Recurve Bow	+5%; Recurve Bow S. +3; Dex, Qui +3	22	W5	100	4.6	36	7.8	1680	Bow
Abandoned Recurve Bow	+10%; Recurve Bow S. +1; Dex +3	25	W5	89	4.4	38	8.7	1680	Bow
Gilded Dark Bow	+15%; Recurve Bow S. +2; Dex +4; Qui +3	31	W7	100	4.9	51	10.5	1680	Bow
Silvered Recurve Bow	+15%; Recurve Bow S. +3; Dex +10	31	W7	100	4.9	51	10.5	1680	Bow
Thrall's Short Recurve Bow	+5%; Dex +3	34	W7	80	4.2	48	11.4	1600	Bow
Flawed Runic Recurve Bow	+1%; Recurve Bow S. +1; HP +6	37	W8	80	5.2	64	12.3	1600	Bow
Ursine Great Recurve Bow	+15%; Recurve Bow S. +2; Dex +6	38	W8	89	5.4	68	12.6	1600	Bow
Runic Recurve Bow	+20%; Recurve Bow S. +2; HP +12	39	W8	89	5	65	12.9	1680	Bow
Cliff Dweller Recurved Bow	+20%; Recurve Bow S. +2; Dex, Str +6	40	W8	89	4	53	13.2	1600	Bow
Spectral Flight	+20%; Recurve Bow S. +1; Matter R. +2; Str +6	40	W8	89	4.8	63	13.2	1680	Bow
Guardian's Bow	+20%; Recurve Bow S. +4; Str +3; Dex +9	41	W8	100	4.8	65	13.5	1680	Bow
Druidic Oaken Recurve Bow	+20%; Recurve Bow S. +4; Dex +6; Cold R. +12	43	W8	100	5.3	75	14.1	1600	Bow
Ruby Death Bringer	+20%; Dex +12	44	O8	100	4.7	68	14.5	1680	Bow
Truesilver Recurve Bow	+20%; Dex, Qui +7	45	O8	89	4.8	71	14.7	1680	Bow
Iontach Maraigh	+25%; Recurve Bow S. +4; Dex, Qui +7	46	W8	100	4.7	71	15.0	1680	Bow
Fomorian Recurve Bow	+25%; Recurve Bow S. +3; Dex +3; Qui +1	47	W8	89	5.4	83	15.3	1600	Bow
Shadow Walkers Great Bow	+25%; Recurve Bow S. +2; Dex +6; Qui +3	48	O8	89	5.5	86	15.6	1600	Bow
Empyreal Golden Reaver	+25%; Recurve Bow S. +3; Dex +11	50	O8	90	4.6	75	16.2	1680	Bow
Glimmerspirit Recurved Bow	+25%; Recurve Bow S. +4; Dex, Con, Str +6	50	W8	91	4.6	75	16.2	1680	Bow

Arrows

Weapon	Bonus	Ql	Dam	Type	Generic
Phantom Arrows	+5% to hit	89	x1.25	Sl	Arrow
Ranger's Last Flight	+15% to hit	89	x1	Thr	Arrow
Spectral Flight Arrows	+20% to hit	89	x1.25	Sl	Arrow

When firing an arrow or bolt, the speed of the bow determines how rapidly you can fire, and the shot's base damage. The arrow or bolt determines the type of damage (Crush, Slash or Thrust) and provides a multiplier to the base damage (indicated by "x1", "x1.25", and so forth).

Armor

For a brief discussion of how armor and armor stats work in *Dark Age of Camelot*, see page 362.

Abbreviations. Mat = Base Material / **Armor Factor** (per piece) / **ABS**orption / **Cl**oth / **L**ea**t**her / **S**tudded Leather / **C**hain / **Pl**ate.

Standard (Craftable) Armor Stats

Armor	Mat	Power Levels	AF	ABS
Woven	Cl	1,6,11, etc.	4,9,14, etc.	0%
Robe	Cl	1,6,11, etc.	4,9,14, etc.	0%
Brea	Lt	1,6,11, etc.	4,14,24, etc.	10%
Constaic	Lt	2,7,12, etc.	6,16,26, etc.	10%
Cruaigh	Lt	4,9,14, etc.	10,20,30, etc.	10%
Tacuil	Rn	1,6,11, etc.	4,14,24, etc.	19%
Nadurtha	Rn	2,7,12, etc.	6,16,26, etc.	19%
Cailiocht	Rn	4,9,14, etc.	10,20,30, etc.	19%
Cruanach	Sc	1,6,11, etc.	4,14,24, etc.	27%
Daingean	Sc	3,8,13, etc.	8,18,28, etc.	27%
Osnadurtha	Sc	5,10,15, etc.	12,22,32, etc.	27%

Armor Weights

Location	Cl	Lt	Rn	Sc
Cap/Helm	0.8	1.6	2.4	3.2
Vest/Jerkin	2.0	4.0	6.0	8.0
Sleeves	1.2	2.4	3.6	4.8
Gloves	0.8	1.6	2.4	3.2
Pants/Leggings	1.4	2.8	4.2	5.6
Boots	0.8	1.6	2.4	3.2
Robe	2.0			

Armor Drops & Rewards

Armor is sorted by type (Cloth, Leather, etc.), then by location (Head, Torso, Arms, Hands, Legs, Feet, Robes), then by Power Level.

Abbreviations

Headings. Power Level / Armor Factor / **M#** = Material (M) and Material Level (#) / Quality.

The first negative percentage in any bonus indicates your opponent's reduced chance of hitting you when you are wearing the item.

Stats. Resistance, **S**kill / **Cha**risma, **Con**stitution, **Emp**athy, **Dex**terity, **Int**elligence, **Pi**ety, **Qui**ckness, **Str**ength / **Cl**oth, **L**eather, **M**etal.

Cloth

Head

Item	Bonus	P	A	M	Q
Hood of the Forsaken	-1%; Int +1; Power +1	10	10	C3	89
Cap of the Mind	-5%; Mentalism S. +1; Int +6	11	11	C3	100
Dergan Enchanter's Cap		11	11	C3	80
Enchanter's Fine Cap	-5%; Power +2; Int +3	11	11	C3	90
Old Silk Cap		11	11	C3	80
Riven Silk Cap	-5%; Int +3; Power +1	13	13	C3	89
Regal Woven Cap	-10%; Power +1; Int +3	15	15	C4	89
Woven Crafter's Cap		15	15	C4	80
Woven Grass Helm	-10%; Power +2; Int +6	15	15	C4	100
Ambusher Cap	-10%; Int +6; Slash R. +4	18	18	C4	89
Dried Woven Root Cap		20	20	C5	80
Damp Shell Flecked Cap	-10%; HP +6; Dex, Int +3	21	21	C5	89
Earthen Woven Root Cap	-5%; Int +7; Light, Mana Mg. S. +1	24	24	C5	89
Woven Hedge Weed Cap	-5%; Int +7; Light, Mana Mg. S. +1	24	24	C5	89
Miss. Caster's Cap	-15%; Int +3; Light Mg. S. +1; HP +6; Spirit R. +2	25	25	C6	89
Runic Woven Cap	-15%; Spirit R. +4; Power +3; Int +7	25	25	C6	100
Sturdy Woven Cap	-15%; Light Magic, Mana Magic S. +1; Int +9	25	25	C6	90
Deamhan Circlet of Speed	-5%; Qui +9; Matter R. +2	25	25	C6	89
Crude Silk Cap	-5%; Int +3	31	31	C7	80
Mindlord's Cr. Cap	-15%; Light Mg., Mana Mg., Mental. S. +2; Int +6	31	31	C7	100
Eluvium Cap	-15%; Int +9; Dex +4; Crush R. +4	34	34	C7	89
Harden. Cl. Cap	-20%; Int +4; Power +2; HP +6; Light Mg. S. +2	35	35	C8	89
Spider Keeper's Cap	-15%; Power +2; Int +10	35	35	C8	89
Darkened Spirit Cap	-10%; Spirit R. +6; Int +12; Power +2	36	36	C8	89
Worn Jewel Dusted Cap	-1%; Power +1; Int +3	36	36	C8	80
Jewel Dusted Cap	-20%; Spirit R. +4; Int +9; Mind Magic S. +2	40	40	C8	89
Gh. Truesilver Cap	-20%; Light, Mana Mg. S. +1; Spirit R. +4; Int +9	44	44	C8	89
Odyllic Cap	-20%; Int +10; Dex +6; Str +4	44	44	C8	89
Unseelie Loyalist Cap	-25%; HP +21; Int +10	47	47	C8	89
Diabolical Fomorian Cap	-25%; Int, Dex +13; Con +7	49	49	C8	90
Manif. Terror Cap	-25%; HP +12; Int +12; Light, Mana Mg. S. +2	49	49	C8	90
Seolc Cap of Enchantment	-25%; Int +12; Dex +6; Enchant. S. +4	49	49	C8	90
Seolc Cap of Mentalism	-25%; Int +12; Dex +6; Mentalism S. +4	49	49	C8	90
Seolc Cap of the Void	-25%; Int +12; Dex +6; Void Magic S. +4	49	49	C8	90

Torso

Item	Bonus	P	A	M	Q
Sturdy Woven Vest	-1%; HP +12	6	6	C2	90
Dergan Enchanter's Vest		11	11	C3	80
Enchanter's Fine Vest	-5%; HP +6; Power +2	11	11	C3	90
Old Silk Vest		11	11	C3	80
Regal Woven Vest	-10%; HP +6; Int, Dex +1	15	15	C4	89
Woven Crafter's Vest	Power +1; HP +3	15	15	C4	80
Ambusher Vest	-10%; HP +12; Dex +3	18	18	C4	89
Dried Woven Root Vest		20	20	C5	80
Damp Shell Flecked Vest	-10%; Con, Dex +3; Cold R. +4	21	21	C5	89
Earthen Woven Root Vest	-5%; HP +9; Int, Con +4	24	24	C5	89
Woven Hedge Weed Vest	-5%; Int +6; HP +12; Slash R. +2	24	24	C5	89
Crude Silk Vest	-5%; HP +6	31	31	C7	80
Eluvium Vest	-15%; HP +24; Dex +4	34	34	C7	89
Spider Keeper's V.	-15%; Slash, Thr. R. +4 Or +6; Con +4; Int +6	35	35	C8	89
Darkened Spirit Vest	-10%; HP +9; Cold R. +6; Int +7; Dex +3	36	36	C8	89
Worn Jewel Dusted Vest	-1%; Body R. +4; Cold, Matter R. +2	36	36	C8	80
Hard. Cl. V.	-20%; Power +2; Void Mg. S. +3; Mana Mg. S. +1; Int +1	39	39	C8	89
Jewel Dusted Vest	-20%; HP +12; Light Magic, Mana Magic S. +2	40	40	C8	89

Item	Bonus	P	A	M	Q
Ghostly Truesilver Vest	-20%; HP +18; Power +2; Int +6	44	44	C8	89
Unseelie Loyalist V.	-25%; HP +12; Thr. R. +6; Body R. +4; Int +7	47	47	C8	89
Odyllic Vest	-25%; HP +24; Int +7; Str +3	48	48	C8	89
Diabolical Fomorian Vest	-25%; HP +45; Int +4; Dex +7	49	49	C8	90
Gossamer Seolc Vest	-25%; HP +39; Dex +6; Int +9	49	49	C8	90
Manifested Terror Vest	-25%; HP +24; Cold, Body R. +8; Int +10	49	49	C8	90

Arms

Item	Bonus	P	A	M	Q
Dergan Enchanter's Sleeves		11	11	C3	80
Enchanter's Fine Sleeves	-5%; HP +6; Str, Int +3	11	11	C3	90
Old Silk Sleeves		11	11	C3	80
Sturdy Woven Sleeves	-5%; Int, Str +3; Qui +1	12	12	C3	90
Riven Silk Sleeves	-5%; Str, Int +3	13	13	C3	89
Regal Woven Sleeves	-10%; Dex +3; Str, Int +1	15	15	C4	89
Woven Crafter's Sleeves		15	15	C4	80
Ambusher Sleeves	-10%; Str +3	18	18	C4	89
Dried Root Woven Sleeves		20	20	C5	80
Damp Shell Flecked Sleeves	-10%; Int +4; Power +2	21	21	C5	89
Earthen Woven Root Sleeves	-5%; Str +4; Dex, Qui, Int +3	24	24	C5	89
Woven Hedge Weed Sleeves	-5%; Str +4; Power +3	24	24	C5	89
Crude Silk Sleeves	-5%; Body R. +2 Or +3; HP +3	31	31	C7	80
Eluvium Sleeves	-15%; Str +3; Power +3	34	34	C7	89
Spider Keeper's Sl.	-15%; HP +9; Body R. +4 Or +6; Str, Int +4	35	35	C8	89
Darkened Spirit Sleeves	-10%; Power +3; Str +7; Int +3	36	36	C8	89
Worn Jewel Dusted Sleeves	-1%; Power +2	36	36	C8	80
Hardened Cloth Sleeves	-20%; Qui +7; HP +6; Str +6; Con +1	39	39	C8	89
Jewel Dusted Sl.	-20%; HP +12; Str, Int +3; Void Magic S. +2	40	40	C8	89
Odyllic Sleeves	-20%; Str, Int +7; Dex +6	43	43	C8	89
Ghostly Truesilver Sleeves	-20%; HP +12; Power +3; Int +3	44	44	C8	89
Unseelie Loyalist Sleeves	-25%; Str, Int +6; Body, Matter R. +6	47	47	C8	89
Diabolical Fomorian Sl.	-25%; Str +10; HP +15; Body, Heat R. +8	49	49	C8	90
Gossamer Seolc Sl.	-25%; Str +10; Int +10; Spirit, Energy R. +6	49	49	C8	90
Manif. Terror Sl.	-25%; Void Magic S. +3; Str, Int +10; Slash R. +8	49	49	C8	90

Hands

Item	Bonus	P	A	M	Q
Dergan Enchanter's Gloves		11	11	C3	80
Enchanter's Fine Gloves	-5%; Power +2; Slash, Cold R. +2	11	11	C3	90
Old Silk Gloves		11	11	C3	80
Riven Silk Gloves	-5%; Qui, Str +3	13	13	C3	89
Regal Woven Gloves	-10%; Int, Qui +3	15	15	C4	89
Sturdy Woven Gloves	-5%; Power +2; Int +4	15	15	C4	90
Woven Crafter's Gloves		15	15	C4	80
Skinner's Gloves	-10%; Body R. +8; Dex +6	16	16	C4	100
Ambusher Gloves	-10%; Qui +3; Light Magic, Mana Magic S. +1	18	18	C4	89
Dried Root Woven Gloves		20	20	C5	80
Damp Shell Flecked Gloves	-10%; HP +12; Dex +3	21	21	C5	89
Earthen Woven Root Gloves	-5%; Power +2; Dex +3; Int +4	24	24	C5	89
Woven Hedge Weed Gloves	-5%; Dex, Int +4; Slash R. +2	24	24	C5	89
Miss. Caster's Gl.	-15%; Dex +3; Mana Mg. S. +1; Body R. +2; HP +6	25	25	C6	89
Crude Silk Gloves	-5%; Dex +3	31	31	C7	80
Eluvium Gloves	-15%; Qui, Int +4; HP +15	34	34	C7	89
Spider Keeper's Gloves	-15%; Body R. +8 *or* +12; Dex +6; Int +4	35	35	C8	89
Darkened Spirit Gl.	-10%; Mana Mg., Light Mg. S. +2; Power +2	36	36	C8	89
Worn Jewel Dusted Gloves	-1%; Cold, Heat R. +2; HP +6	36	36	C8	80
Hard. Cloth Gl.	-20%; Dex, Qui +4; Mana Mg. S. +2; Cold R. +4	39	39	C8	89
Jewel Dusted Gl.	-20%; Dex, Int +4; Body R. +4; Enchant. S. +2	40	40	C8	89
Odyllic Gloves	-20%; Qui, Dex +6; Int +4	41	41	C8	89
Ghostly Truesilver Gloves	-20%; Dex, Str, Int +4; HP +15	44	44	C8	89
Unseelie Loyalist Gloves	-25%; HP +12; Power +3; Heat R. +8	47	47	C8	89
Diabolical Fomorian Gloves	-25%; Qui, Con +7; Dex, Int +9	49	49	C8	90
Gossamer Seolc Gl.	-25%; Qui +9; Light Mg., Mana Mg. S. +4	49	49	C8	90
Manif. Terror Gl.	-25%; Enchant. S. +3; Dex, Int +10; Cold R. +8	49	49	C8	90

Legs

Item	Bonus	P	A	M	Q
Sturdy Woven Pants	-5%; HP +6; Dex +3	9	9	C2	90
Dergan Enchanter's Pants		11	11	C3	80
Enchanter's Fine Pants	-5%; Con +3; Power +2	11	11	C3	90
Old Silk Pants		11	11	C3	80
Riven Silk Pants	-5%; Con +4; Crush R. +2	13	13	C3	89
Regal Woven Pants	-10%; HP +6; Con +3	15	15	C4	89
Woven Crafter's Pants		15	15	C4	80
Ambusher Pants	-10%; Con +7; Int +1	18	18	C4	89
Dried Woven Root Pants		20	20	C5	80
Damp Shell Flecked Pants	-10%; Con +3; Dex +1; Power +2	21	21	C5	89
Earthen Woven Root Pants	-5%; Con +4; Power +3	24	24	C5	89
Woven Hedge Weed Pants	-5%; Con +7; Power +2	24	24	C5	89
Crude Silk Pants	-5%; Power +1	31	31	C7	80
Eluvium Pants	-15%; Con +9; Str +3; Body R. +6	34	34	C7	89
Spider Keeper's Pants	-15%; HP +15; Con +9	35	35	C8	89
Darkened Spirit Pants	-10%; Body R. +6; Con +9; Dex, Int +3	36	36	C8	89
Worn Jewel Dusted Pants	-1%; HP +12	36	36	C8	80
Hardened Cloth Pants	-20%; Con +4; HP +15; Crush, Body R. +4	39	39	C8	89
Jewel Dusted Pants	-20%; Con +7; Power +4	40	40	C8	89
Ghostly Truesilver Pants	-20%; Con +12; Dex +6; Int +3	44	44	C8	89
Odyllic Pants	-25%; Con +10; Dex +4; Power +2	45	45	C8	89
Unseelie Loyalist P.	-25%; HP +15; Con +6; Power +2; Slash R. +2	47	47	C8	89
Diabolical Fomorian P.	-25%; Con +10; Dex +4; Crush, Cold R. +10	49	49	C8	90
Gossamer Seolc Pants	-25%; Con +10; Qui +4; Dex, Int +6	49	49	C8	90
Manif. Terror P.	-25%; Con, Dex +10; Matter R. +8; Mental. S. +3	49	49	C8	90

Feet

Item	Bonus	P	A	M	Q
Dergan Enchanter's Boots		11	11	C3	80
Enchanter's Fine Boots	-5%; Power +2; Dex +3	11	11	C3	90
Old Silk Boots		11	11	C3	80
Riven Silk Boots	-5%; Dex +3; HP +3; Qui +1	13	13	C3	89
Regal Woven Boots	-10%; Con, Dex +3	15	15	C4	89
Woven Crafter's Boots		15	15	C4	80
Ambusher Boots	-10%; Dex +6; Str +3	18	18	C4	89
Kedger's Quick Boots	-10%; Power +4; Dex +6	19	19	C4	100
Dried Woven Root Boots		20	20	C5	80
Sturdy Woven Boots	-10%; Con +4; Dex +9	20	20	C5	90
Damp Shell Flecked Boots	-10%; Con +4; Dex +3; Energy R. +2	21	21	C5	89
Earthen Woven Root Boots	-5%; Dex +4; Qui +3; Power +2	24	24	C5	89
Woven Hedge Weed Boots	-5%; Dex +9; HP +9	24	24	C5	89
Crude Silk Boots	-5%; Dex +3	31	31	C7	80
Eluvium Boots	-15%; Dex +7; Con +4; Body R. +6	34	34	C7	89
Spider Keeper's B.	-15%; Thrust, Body R. +4 Or +6; Dex +7; Qui +3	35	35	C8	89
Darkened Spirit Boots	-10%; Dex +9; Qui +3; Power +2	36	36	C8	89
Worn Jewel Dusted Boots	-1%; HP +6; Energy, Matter R. +2	36	36	C8	80
Hardened Cloth Boots	-20%; Dex +4; Cold, Spirit, Heat R. +6	39	39	C8	89
Jewel Dusted Boots	-20%; HP +12; Power +2; Dex +6	40	40	C8	89
Ghostly Truesilver Boots	-20%; Power +3; Dex, Con +6	44	44	C8	89
Odyllic Boots	-25%; Dex +9; Con, Qui +6	46	46	C8	89
Unseelie Loyalist Boots	-25%; HP +12; Dex +6; Cold, Spirit R. +6	47	47	C8	89
Diabolical Eldritch Boots	-25%; Dex, Int +10; Void Magic S. +3	49	49	C8	90
Diabolical Enchanter B.	-25%; Dex, Int +10; Enchantments S. +3	49	49	C8	90
Diabolical Mentalist Boots	-25%; Dex, Int +10; Mentalism S. +3	49	49	C8	90
Gossamer Seolc Boots	-25%; Dex +10; Power +4; Con +9	49	49	C8	90
Manifested Terror Boots	-25%; Dex, Qui +10; Power +4	49	49	C8	90

Robes

Item	Bonus	P	A	M	Q
Dergan Enchanter's Robe		11	11	C3	80
Enchanter's Fine Robe	-5%; HP +6; Power +2	11	11	C3	90
Riven Silk Robe	-5%; HP +3; Power +2	13	13	C3	89
Haur's Spectral Shroud	-10%; Slash R. +4; Power +1; HP +9	15	15	C4	100
Robes of the Arcane Order	-10%; Power +1; Int +1	17	17	C4	80
Empyrean Mist R.	-10%; Enchantments S. +3; Int +4; Power +2	20	20	C5	100

Item	Bonus	P	A	M	Q
Transfixing Robes	-10%; Crush R. +6; Dex, Int +6	20	20	C5	100
Damp Shell Flecked Robe	-10%; HP +12; Int +3	21	21	C5	89
Woven Hedge Weed Robe	-5%; Int +6; HP +12; Slash R. +2	24	24	C5	89
De'velyn's Fine Robes	-15%; Con +3; Int +9	25	25	C6	90
Robe of the Draoi	-15%; Int +4; Power +2; HP +12	27	27	C6	89
R. of Regalia	-15%; HP +27; Enchant., Void Mg., Mental. S. +2	30	30	C7	90
Mottled Dark Robes	-15%; HP +12; Slash R. +6; Dex +4; Int +9	31	31	C7	100
Spider Silk Robe	-15%; HP +18; Int +9	35	35	C8	89
Darkened Spirit Robe	-10%; HP +15; Power +3; Int +6	36	36	C8	89
Worn Jewel Dusted Robe	-1%; Body R. +4; Cold, Matter R. +2	36	36	C8	80
Ceremonial Robe	-15%; Crush, Slash R. +6; Int +9	37	37	C8	89
Ceremonial Robes	-15%; Crush, Slash R. +9; Int +9	37	37	C8	89
Gossamer Enchanted R.	-20%; Enchant. S. +3; Power +2; HP +3	37	37	C8	89
Gossamer Mentalist R.	-20%; Mentalism S. +3; Power +2; HP +3	37	37	C8	89
Gossamer Voided Robe	-20%; Void Magic S. +3; Power +2; HP +3	37	37	C8	89
Robes of the Maelstrom	-20%; Int +6; Dex +4; Power +4; HP +15	39	39	C8	100
Jewel Dusted Robe	-20%; HP +12; Light Magic, Mentalism S. +2	40	40	C8	89
Ghostly Truesilver Robe	-20%; HP +18; Power +2; Int +6	44	44	C8	89
Unseelie Loyalist R.	-25%; HP +12; Thr. R. +6; Body R. +4; Int +7	47	47	C8	89
Diabolical Fomorian Robe	-25%; HP +45; Int +4; Dex +7	49	49	C8	90
Gossamer Seolc Robe	-25%; HP +39; Dex +6; Int +9	49	49	C8	90
Manifested Terror Robe	-25%; HP +24; Cold, Body R. +8; Int +10	49	49	C8	90
Ruby Weave Robes	-25%; HP +21; Thrust R. +15; Dex +4; Int +13	49	49	C8	90
Yellow Silken R.	-25%; Thrust, Body R. +10; Int +10; Power +4	49	49	C8	100
Moonstruck Mire Robe	-25%; Int, Con +10; Spirit, Cold R. +10	50	50	C8	90

Leather

Head

Item	Bonus	P	A	M	Q
Patched Hide Helm		9	18	L2	80
Sewn Hide Helm	-5%; Cha, Emp +3	9	18	L2	90
Macabre Leather Helm		11	22	L3	80
Noble's Leather Helm	-10%; Qui +3; Stealth S. +1	15	30	L4	89
Siabrian Helm	-10%; Con, Str +3	15	30	L4	89
Worn Dark Shadow Helm		15	30	L4	80
Celestial Mist Helm	-10%; Body R. +6; Int +3	16	32	L4	89
Dried Molded Helmet		20	40	L5	80
Helm of Shadow Melding	-10%; Stealth S. +3; Dex +4	20	40	L5	90
Watery Shell Flecked Helm	-10%; Con, Dex, Qui +3	21	42	L5	89
Earth Crafted Molded Helm	-5%; Stealth S. +3; Dex +4	24	48	L5	89
Crude Leather Helm	-5%; Qui +3	31	62	L7	80
Glowing Guile Helm	-15%; Qui +9; Str +7	34	68	L7	89
Cath Helm	-20%; Power +2; Int +4; HP +9; Crush R. +4	36	72	L8	89
Silk Gatherer's Helm	-15%; Stealth S. +2; Qui +6; Dex +4	36	72	L8	89
Turbid Waters Helm	-20%; Str, Dex, Qui +3; HP +12	36	72	L8	89
Worn Jewel Pierced Helm	-1%; Spirit R. +4; HP +6	36	72	L8	80
Furtive Cavedweller Helm	-20%; Dex, Qui +6; Str +4	37	74	L8	89
Jeweled Rigid Helm	-20%; Con, Qui +6; Cold, Crush R. +4	40	80	L8	89
Ghostly Truesilver Helm	-20%; HP +24; Spirit, Body R. +6	44	88	L8	89
Imbued Unseelie Helm	-25%; Str +7; Crush, Cold, Spirit R. +6	47	94	L8	89
Dusk Dweller Helm	-25%; Qui, Dex, Con +7; Str +4	49	98	L8	90
Midnight Marauder Helm	-25%; Dex, Qui +10; HP +21	49	98	L8	90
Recondite Poacher H.	-25%; Dex, Qui +10; Str +9; Crit. Strike S. +1	49	98	L8	90

Torso

Item	Bonus	P	A	M	Q
Patched Hide Jerkin		9	18	L2	80
Sewn Hide Jerkin	-5%; HP +9; Body R. +2	9	18	L2	90
Macabre Leather Jerkin		11	22	L3	80
Noble's Leather Jerkin	-10%; HP +6; Dex +3	15	30	L4	89
Siabrian Jerkin	-10%; HP +12	15	30	L4	89
Worn Dark Shadow Jerkin	Dex, Qui +1	15	30	L4	80
Celestial Mist	-10%; Qui, Con +3; HP +3	16	32	L4	89
Dried Molded Jerkin		20	40	L5	80
Watery Shell Flecked Jerkin	-10%; HP +9; Dex +3; Str +1	21	42	L5	89
Earth Crafted Molded Jerkin	-5%; HP +15; Dex, Str +3	24	48	L5	89
Vest of Dislocation	-15%; Evade S. +2; Qui, Dex +4	25	50	L6	100
Ire-Wolf Hide Jerkin	-15%; HP +21; Dex, Str +6	29	58	L6	100
Crude Leather Jerkin	-5%; Dex, Str +1	31	62	L7	80
Mottled Dark Jerkin	-15%; HP +18; Dex, Qui, Str +4	31	62	L7	100
Silk Gatherer's Jerkin	-15%; Body R. +4 Or +6; HP +15; Qui +6	35	70	L8	89
Cath Jerkin	-20%; Dex +4; Matter, Slash R. +4; HP +12	36	72	L8	89
Pooka Hide Vest	-20%; Dex +7; HP +24; Body R. +10	36	72	L8	100
Turbid Waters Jerkin	-20%; HP +15; Str +4; Dex +3	36	72	L8	89
Worn Jewel Pierced Jerkin	-1%; HP +12	36	72	L8	80
Furtive Cavedweller Jerkin	-20%; HP +24; Dex +4	37	74	L8	89
Glowing Guile Jerkin	-20%; HP +27; Str +4	38	76	L8	89
Jeweled Rigid Jerkin	-20%; HP +36	40	80	L8	89
Ghostly Truesilver Jerkin	-20%; HP +24; Qui +6; Slash R. +4	44	88	L8	89
Imbued Unseelie Jerkin	-25%; Con +9; Dex, Qui +6	47	94	L8	89
Dusk Dweller Jerkin	-25%; HP +27; Str +4; Body, Cold R. +6	49	98	L8	90
Goblin Skin Tunic	-20%; Dex, Str +9; Body R. +10	49	98	L8	89
Leather Deo Jerkin	-25%; Thrust R. +6; Dex, Qui +7; HP +18	49	98	L8	91
Midnight Marauder Jerkin	-25%; HP +39; Str, Qui +7	49	98	L8	90
Recondite Poacher Jerkin	-25%; HP +45; Dex, Qui +6	49	98	L8	90
Moonstruck Mire Jerkin	-25%; Str, Qui +10; Spirit, Cold R. +10	50	100	L8	90

Arms

Item	Bonus	P	A	M	Q
Patched Hide Sleeves		9	18	L2	80
Sewn Hide Sleeves	-5%; HP +6; Str +3	9	18	L2	90
Sleeves of Might	-5%; Str +6	9	18	L2	90
Macabre Leather Sleeves		11	22	L3	80
Noble's Leather Sleeves	-10%; Str +4; Qui +1	15	30	L4	89
Siabrian Sleeves	-10%; Str +6	15	30	L4	89
Worn Dark Shadow Sleeves		15	30	L4	80
Celestial Mist Sleeves	-10%; Str +3; Cold, Body, Slash R. +2	16	32	L4	89
Dried Molded Sleeves		20	40	L5	80
Watery Shell Flecked Sleeves	-10%; Dex, Qui +4	21	42	L5	89
Earth Crafted Molded Sleeves	-5%; Dex +7; Qui +6	24	48	L5	89
Crude Leather Sleeves	-5%; Str +3	31	62	L7	80
Silk Gatherer's Sleeves	-15%; Str +10; Dex +6	35	70	L8	89
Cath Sl.	-20%; Qui +3; Celtic Dual S. +2; Body R. +2; Power +2	36	72	L8	89
Turbid Waters Sleeves	-20%; Str +6; HP +9; Heat R. +6	36	72	L8	89
Worn Jewel Pierced Sleeves	-1%; HP +6; Str +3	36	72	L8	80
Furtive Cavedweller Sleeves	-20%; Str +7; Qui +4; HP +9	37	74	L8	89
Glowing Guile Sleeves	-20%; Str +12; Con +4	37	74	L8	89
Jeweled Rigid Sleeves	-20%; Body, Matter R. +4; Str +9; Qui +3	40	80	L8	89
Ghostly Truesilver Sl.	-20%; Str +12; Con, Dex +3; Crush R. +4	44	88	L8	89
Imbued Unseelie Sleeves	-25%; HP +12; Str +10; Qui +4	47	94	L8	89
Dusk Dweller Sleeves	-25%; Str +12; HP +12; Body, Slash R. +6	49	98	L8	90
Midnight Marauder Sl.	-25%; Str +10; Con +7; Body, Spirit R. +6	49	98	L8	90
Recondite Poacher Sl.	-25%; Str +10; Qui +9; Thrust, Spirit R. +8	49	98	L8	90

Hands

Item	Bonus	P	A	M	Q
Blademaster Initiate Gloves	Qui +1	6	12	L2	90
Druid Initiate Gloves	Emp +1	6	12	L2	90
Patched Hide Gloves		9	18	L2	80
Sewn Hide Gloves	-5%; Qui, Emp +3	9	18	L2	90
Macabre Leather Gloves		11	22	L3	80
Gloves of Quickness	-5%; Qui +9	12	24	L3	90
Noble's Leather Gloves	-10%; Dex, Qui +3	15	30	L4	89
Siabrian Gloves	-1%; Body R. +3; Qui +4	15	30	L4	89
Worn Dark Shadow Gloves		15	30	L4	80
Celestial Mist Gloves	-10%; Qui +4; Celtic Dual S. +1	16	32	L4	89
Skinner's Gloves	-10%; Body R. +8; Dex +6	16	32	L4	100
Dried Molded Gloves		20	40	L5	80
Luminescent Gloves	-10%; Qui +3; Celtic Dual S. +2; Dex +1	21	42	L5	89
Watery Shell Flecked Gloves	-10%; Str +6; Qui +3	21	42	L5	89
Earth Crafted Molded Gloves	-5%; Str +9; Qui +4	24	48	L5	89

Item	Bonus	P	A	M	Q
Crude Leather Gloves	-5%; Dex, Str +1	31	62	L7	80
Fagan's Gloves of Poison	-15%; Dex, Qui +9; Body R. +8	31	62	L7	100
Glowing Guile Gloves	-20%; Qui, Dex +7	35	70	L8	89
Silk Gath's Gl.	-15%; Body R. +4 Or +6; Parry, Celt. Dl. S. +2; Qui +4	35	70	L8	89
Cath Gl.	-20%; Enven., Parry S. +2; Body R. +4; Crit. Strike S. +1	36	72	L8	89
Turbid Waters Gloves	-20%; Qui +6; Dex +3; HP +12	36	72	L8	89
Worn Jewel Pierced Gloves	-1%; Dex, Qui +3	36	72	L8	80
Furtive Cavedweller Gloves	-20%; Qui +7; Critical Strike S. +3	37	74	L8	89
Jeweled Rigid Gloves	-20%; Envenom S. +2; Dex +3; Qui +9	40	80	L8	89
Ghostly Trusilver Gloves	-20%; Qui +12; Envenom S. +3	44	88	L8	89
Imbued Unseelie Gl.	-25%; Envenom, Celtic Dual S. +2; Qui +9	47	94	L8	89
Dusk Dweller Gloves	-25%; Qui +12; Dex +6; Body, Thrust R. +6	49	98	L8	90
Midnight Marauder Gl.	-25%; Qui +13; Envenom S. +4; HP +15	49	98	L8	90
Rec. Poacher Gl.	-25%; Qui +10; Enven. S. +1; Heat R. +8; Str +9	49	98	L8	90

Legs

Item	Bonus	P	A	M	Q
Leggings of the Deft	-1%; Dex +4; Str +1	6	12	L2	90
Patched Hide Leggings		9	18	L2	80
Sewn Hide Leggings	-5%; Con +3; Dex, Cha +1	9	18	L2	90
Macabre Leather Leggings		11	22	L3	80
Noble's Leather Leggings	-10%; Con +4; Dex +1	15	30	L4	89
Siabrian Leggings	-10%; Con +4; Dex +1	15	30	L4	89
Worn Dark Shadow Leggings		15	30	L4	80
Celestial Mist Leggings	-10%; HP +3; Dex, Qui +3	16	32	L4	89
Dried Molded Leggings		20	40	L5	80
Dusty Leggings	-10%; Str +3; Cold R. +2; Qui +1; HP +6	21	42	L5	89
Watery Shell Flecked Leggings	-10%; Con, Dex +4	21	42	L5	89
Earth Crafted Molded Leggings	-5%; Con +9; Qui +4	24	48	L5	89
Crude Leather Leggings	-5%; Con +3	31	62	L7	80
Silk Gatherer's Leggings	-15%; Body R. +4 Or +6; HP +12; Con +7	35	70	L8	89
Cath Leggings	-20%; Str +6; Cold, Thrust R. +4; Con +4	36	72	L8	89
Turbid Waters Leggings	-20%; Con +10	36	72	L8	89
Worn Jewel Pierced Leggings	-1%; Con +6	36	72	L8	80
Furtive Cavedweller Leggings	-20%; Con +7; Str +4; Spirit R. +6	37	74	L8	89
Glowing Guile Leggings	-20%; Con +9; Dex, Qui +4	39	78	L8	89
Jeweled Rigid Leggings	-20%; HP +18; Body R. +8; Energy R. +4	40	80	L8	89
Ghostly Truesilver Leggings	-20%; Con +12; Dex, Qui +4	44	88	L8	89
Imbued Unseelie Leggings	-25%; Con +12; Str, Qui +3; Body R. +4	47	94	L8	89
Dusk Dweller Leg.	-25%; Con +12; Dex +6; Crush, Energy R. +6	49	98	L8	90
Midnight Marauder Leggings	-25%; Con +10; Str +7; Dex, Qui +6	49	98	L8	90
Recondite Poacher Leg.	-25%; Con +10; Str +7; Body, Spirit R. +8	49	98	L8	90

Feet

Item	Bonus	P	A	M	Q
Nightshade Initiate Boots	Dex +1	6	12	L2	90
Warden Initiate Boots	Qui +1	6	12	L2	90
Patched Hide Boots		9	18	L2	80
Sewn Hide Boots	-5%; HP +6; Dex +3	9	18	L2	90
Boots of the Wicked Evader	-5%; Evade S. +2; Qui +3	10	20	L3	100
Boots of Blending	-5%; Stealth S. +1; Dex +6	11	22	L3	100
Macabre Leather Boots		11	22	L3	80
Boots of Agile Movement	-5%; Dex +10	15	30	L4	90
Noble's Leather Boots	-10%; HP +6; Dex +3	15	30	L4	89
Siabrian Boots	-10%; Dex +4; Str +1	15	30	L4	89
Worn Dark Shadow Boots		15	30	L4	80
Celestial Mist Boots	-10%; Qui +3; Power +1; Matter R. +2	16	32	L4	89
Kedger's Gilded Boots	-10%; Evade S. +3; Qui +6	19	38	L4	100
Dried Molded Boots		20	40	L5	80
Luminescent Boots	-10%; Dex +3; Body R. +4; Power +1	21	42	L5	89
Watery Shell Flecked Boots	-10%; Dex +9	21	42	L5	89
Earth Crafted Molded Boots	-5%; Evade S. +2; Dex +7	24	48	L5	89
Crude Leather Boots	-5%; Dex +3	31	62	L7	80
Silk Gatherer's Boots	-15%; Stealth S. +2; Qui +10	35	70	L8	89
Cath Boots	-20%; Dex, Qui +4; Matter R. +4; HP +9	36	72	L8	89
Glowing Guile Boots	-20%; Dex +9; HP +15	36	72	L8	89
Turbid Waters Boots	-20%; Dex +6; Qui +4; HP +9	36	72	L8	89
Worn Jewel Pierced Boots	-1%; Body R. +2; Dex +4	36	72	L8	80
Furtive Cavedweller Boots	-20%; Dex +7; Con +3; Cold R. +6	37	74	L8	89
Jeweled Rigid Boots	-20%; Stealth S. +2; Dex +9; Matter R. +4	40	80	L8	89
Ghostly Truesil. B.	-20%; Stealth S. +2; Cold, Spirit R. +4; Dex +9	44	88	L8	89
Imbued Unseelie Boots	-25%; Stealth S. +2; Dex +12; Qui +3	47	94	L8	89
Dusk Dweller Boots	-25%; Dex +12; HP +12; Spirit, Thrust R. +6	49	98	L8	90
Midnight Marauder Boots	-25%; Dex +10; Str, Qui, Con +6	49	98	L8	90
Recondite Poacher B.	-25%; Dex +10; Con +9; Body, Matter R. +6	49	98	L8	90

Reinforced Leather

Head

Item	Bonus	P	A	M	Q
Blackthorn Helm		7	14	N2	80
Spiked Blackthorn Wreath	-5%; HP +3; Emp +3	7	14	N2	90
Blackthorn Wreath	-1%; HP +3; Emp +3	8	16	N2	89
Old Noble's Helm		11	22	N3	80
Sprite Vine Helm	-5%; Dex, Emp +3	11	22	N3	89
Imbued Helm	-5%; Emp +6; Cha +4	15	30	N4	90
Lavish Reinforced Helm	-10%; Emp, Dex +3	15	30	N4	89
Siabrian Bandit Helm	-10%; Dex, Qui +4	18	36	N4	89
Draoi Sentinel's H.	-10%; Emp +1; Cha +3; Valor, Nature Aff. S. +1	19	38	N4	89
Abandoned Crustacean Helm	-10%; Emp +6; Con +3	20	40	N5	89
Dried Root Reinforced Helm		20	40	N5	80
Lucky Failm	-10%; Int +1; Music S. +1; Power +2; Crush R. +2	22	44	N5	89
Coral Helm	-10%; Str, Con, Dex +3; Qui +1	23	46	N5	89
Earth Crafted Root Helm	-5%; Emp +6; Dex +3; HP +9	24	48	N5	89
Hollowed Crustacean Chitin	-15%; Str +6; Con +3; Thrust R. +2	25	50	N6	89
Spectral Helm	-15%; Regrowth, Nurture S. +2; HP +3	30	60	N7	89
Faded Spiderweave Helm	-5%; HP +6	33	66	N7	80
Worn Jewel Spiked Helm	-1%; Cold, Spirit R. +2; Emp +3	36	72	N8	80
Empyreal Helm	-20%; Regrowth S. +2; Power +3; Cha +4	37	74	N8	89
Mariner Helm	-20%; Con, Dex +6; Str +4	37	74	N8	89
Raider's Chitin Helm	-10%; Dex +7; Emp +10; Cold R. +2	37	74	N8	89
Silken Thr. Chitin H.	-15%; Spirit R. +4 Or +6; Emp +9; Dex, Qui +3	37	74	N8	89
Jewel Spiked Helm	-20%; Emp +9; Con, Str +3	40	80	N8	89
Mire Walker's Helm	-20%; Int +7; Qui +6; Slash, Body R. +4	42	84	N8	89
Reinforced Truemail Helm	-20%; Emp +7; Body R. +18	44	88	N8	89
Mischievious Greenbriar Helm	-15%; Emp, Cha +10; Cold R. +4	46	92	N8	89
Bladed Guardian Helm	-25%; Emp +7; Cha +4; Crush, Spirit R. +6	47	94	N8	89
Welkin Helm	-25%; Dex +9; Con, Str +6	48	96	N8	89
Lucent Spirit Helm	-25%; Emp, Cha, Str +7; Qui +4	49	98	N8	90
Mystical Moonglade Helm	-25%; Dex, Qui +10; HP +36	49	98	N8	91
Twisted Lusus Helm	-25%; Con +10; Str +12; Qui +10	49	98	N8	90
Twisted Melody Helm	-25%; Cha +10; Con +12; Qui +10	49	98	N8	90

Torso

Item	Bonus	P	A	M	Q
Blackthorn Vest		7	14	N2	80
Old Noble's Vest		11	22	N3	80
Spiked Blackthorn Vest	-5%; HP +9	13	26	N2	90
Lavish Reinforced Vest	-10%; HP +6; Emp, Str +1	15	30	N4	89
Abandoned Crustacean Vest	-10%; HP +18	20	40	N5	89
Dried Root Reinforced Vest		20	40	N5	80
Imbued Vest	-10%; HP +15; Str +6	20	40	N5	90
Coral Vest	-10%; Emp, Qui +6; HP +9	23	46	N5	89
Earth Crafted Root Vest	-5%; HP +15; Str +6	24	48	N5	89
Lucky Perree	-10%; Con, Cha +3; HP +6; Cold R. +4	24	48	N5	89
Hollowed Crustacean Carapace	-15%; Con +6; Dex +3; Cr. R. +2	25	50	N6	89
Bilk's Blue Vest	-15%; Cha +3; Con +1; HP +9; Slash R. +2	25	50	N6	89
Scarred Vest	-15%; HP +21; Con, Dex +4	25	50	N6	100
Spectral Tunic	-15%; Str, Con +4; Crush R. +4; HP +3	30	60	N7	89
Twilight Vest	-15%; Cha, Con +9; Heat R. +8	31	62	N6	100
Mottled Dark Vest	-15%; HP +15; Emp +6; Str +6; Dex +4	31	62	N7	100
Faded Spiderweave Vest	-5%; HP +6	33	66	N7	80

Item	Bonus	P	A	M	Q
Shape-Changer's Vest	-15%; HP +30; Dex +10	33	66	N7	100
Worn Jewel Spiked Vest	-1%; Emp, Con +3	36	72	N8	80
Empyreal Vest	-20%; Cha +4; Slash R. +2; Power +5	37	74	N8	89
Mariner Vest	-20%; HP +24; Qui +4	37	74	N8	89
Raider's Chitin Vest	-10%; Str +7; HP +21; Slash R. +2	37	74	N8	89
Silken Threaded Chitin Vest	-15%; HP +24; Qui +6	37	74	N8	89
Jewel Spiked Vest	-20%; HP +18; Qui +6; Emp +3	40	80	N8	89
Mire Walker's Vest	-20%; HP +15; Qui +6; Body, Cold R. +8	42	84	N8	89
Reinforced Truemail Vest	-20%; HP +42	44	88	N8	89
Mischievious Greenbriar Vest	-15%; Str +7; HP +27; Slash R. +4	46	92	N8	89
Bladed Guardian Vest	-25%; HP +30; Emp +6	47	94	N8	89
Welkin Vest	-25%; HP +30; Str +7	48	96	N8	89
Lucent Spirit Vest	-25%; HP +27; Dex +4; Body R. +12	49	98	N8	90
Mystical Moonglade Vest	-25%; HP +48; Str, Qui +7	49	98	N8	91
Reinforced Deo Vest	-25%; Emp +7; Cha, Qui +6; Power +4	49	98	N8	91
Twisted Lusus Vest	-25%; HP +45; Dex, Str +7	49	98	N8	90
Moonstruck Mire Vest	-25%; Str, Qui +10; Spirit, Cold R. +10	50	100	N8	90

Arms

Item	Bonus	P	A	M	Q
Blackthorn Sleeves		7	14	N2	80
Spiked Blackthorn Sleeves	-5%; Str +3; Emp +1	7	14	N2	90
Old Noble's Sleeves		11	22	N3	80
Lavish Reinforced Sleeves	-10%; HP +6; Str, Qui +1	15	30	N4	89
Abandoned Crustacean Sleeves	-10%; Str +6; Emp +3	20	40	N5	89
Dried Root Reinforced Arms		20	40	N5	80
Lucky Muinneelyn	-10%; Rec. Bow S. +1; Qui +3; HP +6; Thr. R. +2	22	44	N5	89
Coral Sleeves	-10%; Str +6; Qui +4	23	46	N5	89
Sea Shell Sleeves	-10%; Regrowth S. +3; Qui, Str +4	23	46	N5	100
Earth Crafted Root Sleeves	-5%; Str +6; Con +4; Emp +3	24	48	N5	89
Bilk's Blue Sleeves	-15%; Qui, Dex +3; HP +6; Crush R. +2	25	50	N6	89
Hollowed Crustacean Arms	-15%; Str +6; Qui +3; Body R. +2	25	50	N6	89
Archer's Sleeves	-15%; HP +12; Dex, Qui, Str +4	25	50	N6	100
Spectral Arms	-15%; Str +3; Slash R. +4; HP +15	28	56	N6	89
Faded Spiderweave Sleeves	-5%; HP +6	33	66	N7	80
Empyreal Sleeves	-20%; Qui +6; Body R. +4; HP +12	35	70	N8	89
Worn Jewel Spiked Sleeves	-1%; Str, Cha +3	36	72	N8	80
Mariner Sleeves	-20%; Str +9; Dex +4; Energy R. +4	37	74	N8	89
Radier's Chitin Sleeves	-10%; Str +10; Con +3; Slash R. +2	37	74	N8	89
Silken Thr. Chitin Arms	-15%; Body, Matter R. +4 Or +6; Str +12	37	74	N8	89
Jewel Spiked Sleeves	-20%; Str +9; Emp +6; Slash R. +4	40	80	N8	89
Mire Walker's Sleeves	Str +9; Con +4; Energy, Body R. +4	42	84	N8	89
Welkin Sleeves	-25%; Str +10; Dex, Qui +6	44	88	N8	89
Reinforced Truemail Sleeves	-20%; Str +10; Emp +6	44	88	N8	89
Mischievious Greenbriar Sl.	-15%; Str +10; Dex +6; Slash R. +4	46	92	N8	89
Bladed Guardian Sleeves	-25%; Str +12; Emp +6; Cold, Heat R. +2	47	94	N8	89
Lucent Spirit Sleeves	-25%; Str +12; Con +6; Cold, Body R. +6	49	98	N8	90
Myst. Moonglade Sl.	-25%; Str +18; Con +7; Matter, Heat R. +8	49	98	N8	91
Twisted Lusus Sleeves	-25%; Str +10; Dex +10; Cold, Spirit R. +8	49	98	N8	90

Hands

Item	Bonus	P	A	M	Q
Champion Initiate Gauntlets	Dex +1	6	12	N2	90
Hero Initiate Gauntlets	Str +1	6	12	N2	90
Blackthorn Gauntlets		7	14	N2	80
Spiked Blackthorn Gauntlets	-5%; Qui +3; HP +3	7	14	N2	90
Old Noble's Gauntlets		11	22	N3	80
Gloves of Agility	-5%; Dex +6; Qui +3	11	22	N3	100
Gloves of the Sure-Grip	-5%; Str, Dex +4	11	22	N3	100
Lavish Reinforced Gauntlets	-10%; Str, Qui +3	15	30	N4	89
Skinner's Gloves	-10%; Body R. +8; Dex +6	16	32	N4	100
Abandoned Crustacean Gauntlets	-10%; Emp +6; Qui +3	20	40	N5	89
Dried Root Reinforced Gloves		20	40	N5	80
Lucky Lauean	-10%; Dex +3; Celtic Dual S. +2; Thrust R. +2	22	44	N5	89
Coral Gauntlets	-10%; Qui +6; HP +12	23	46	N5	89
Earth Crafted Root Gauntlets	-5%; Str, Dex, Qui +4	24	48	N5	89
Bilk's Blue G.	-15%; Envenom, Celtic Dual S. +1; Dex +3; HP +3	25	50	N6	89
Hollowed Crustacean Claws	-15%; Str +6; Qui +3; Cold R. +2	25	50	N6	89
Spectral Gloves	-15%; Dex +4; Nurture S. +2; HP +9	28	56	N6	89
Resonant Gauntlets	-15%; Celtic Dual, Parry S. +2; Qui +6	31	62	N7	100
Faded Spiderweave Gauntlets	-5%; HP +6	33	66	N7	80
Empyreal Ranger G.	-20%; Rec. Bow S. +2; Dex +4; Thrust R. +6	35	70	N8	89
Silken Thr. Chitin Gl.	-15%; Body R. +4 Or +6; Emp +6; Str, Qui +4	36	72	N8	89
Worn Jewel Spiked Gloves	-1%; Crush R. +2; Qui +4	36	72	N8	80
Mariner Gauntlets	-20%; Qui +9; HP +9; Cold R. +4	37	74	N8	89
Raider's Chitin Gauntlets	-10%; Qui +12; Emp +4; Body R. +2	37	74	N8	89
Jewel Spiked Gauntlets	-20%; Qui +9; Heat, Body R. +6	40	80	N8	89
Mire Walker's G.	-20%; Qui +7; Dex +6; Body, Crush R. +4	42	84	N8	89
Reinforced Truemail Gauntlets	-20%; Qui +9; Emp +4; Con +7	44	88	N8	89
Welkin Gauntlets	-25%; Qui +10; Con, Str +6	44	88	N8	89
Mischvs. Greenbriar Gl.	-15%; Dex, Qui +6; Emp +9; Matter R. +4	46	92	N8	89
Bladed Guardian Gauntlets	-25%; HP +15; Qui +10; Str +3	47	94	N8	89
Lucent Spirit Gauntlets	-25%; Qui +12; HP +12; Cold, Crush R. +6	49	98	N8	90
Masterful Moonglade G.	-25%; Qui +12; Con +7; Parry S. +4	49	98	N8	90
Melodic Moonglade G.	-25%; Qui +10; Cha +10; Music S. +4	49	98	N8	90
Mossy Moonglade G.	-25%; Qui +12; Con +7; Recurve Bow S. +4	49	98	N8	90
Twisted Lusus G.	-25%; Qui +11; Dex +7; Crush, Cold R. +8	49	98	N8	90

Legs

Item	Bonus	P	A	M	Q
Blackthorn Leggings		7	14	N2	80
Spiked Blackthorn Leggings	-5%; Qui +1; Con +3	7	14	N2	90
Old Noble's Leggings		10	20	N3	80
Lavish Reinforced Leggings	-10%; HP +6; Con, Dex +1	15	30	N4	89
Abandoned Crustacean Leggings	-10%; Con +6; Emp +3	20	40	N5	89
Dried Root Reinforced Leggings		20	40	N5	80
Empyrean Mist Leggings	-10%; Con, Cha +6; Energy R. +6	20	40	N5	100
Coral Leggings	-10%; Con +7; Dex +3	23	46	N5	89
Earth Crafted Root Leggings	-5%; Con +9; Str +4	24	48	N5	89
Lucky Breechyn	-10%; Str +4; Thrust R. +4; Power +2	24	48	N5	89
Bilk's Blue Leggings	-15%; Str +3; Crush, Body R. +2; Power +2	25	50	N6	89
Hollowed Crustacean Legs	-15%; Con +6; Dex +3; Slash R. +2	25	50	N6	89
Imbued Leggings	-15%; Con +9; Qui, Dex +3	25	50	N6	90
Spectral Legs	-15%; Con +4; Slash R. +2; Power +3	28	56	N6	89
Faded Spiderweave Leggings	-5%; HP +6	33	66	N7	80
Empyreal Leggings	-20%; Qui +6; Body R. +4; HP +12	35	70	N8	89
Worn Jewel Spiked Leggings	-1%; HP +9; Cha +1	36	72	N8	80
Mariner Leggings	-20%; Con +9; Str +4; Body R. +4	37	74	N8	89
Raider's Chitin Leggings	-10%; Con +12; HP +12; Matter R. +2	37	74	N8	89
Silken Thr. Chitin Leg.	-15%; Energy, Cold R. +6 Or +9; Con +9	37	74	N8	89
Cliff Dweller's Leg.	-20%; Con +9; Cold, Matter R. +8; HP +21	40	80	N8	100
Jewel Spiked Leggings	-20%; Con +9; Cold, Heat R. +6	40	80	N8	89
Mire Walker's Leggings	-20%; Con +6; Str +4; Body, Heat R. +6	42	84	N8	89
Reinforced Truemail Leggings	-20%; Con +10; Cha +6	44	88	N8	89
Mischievious Greenbriar Leg.	-15%; Con +13; Qui +7; Energy R. +4	46	92	N8	89
Bladed Guardian Leggings	-25%; Con +10; Cha +6	47	94	N8	89
Twisted Lusus Leggings	-25%; Con +12; Qui +7; Body R. +16	48	96	N8	90
Welkin Leggings	-25%; Con +10; Str, Qui +6	48	96	N8	89
Goat Fur Leggings	-20%; Con +13; HP +24	49	98	N8	89
Lucent Spirit Leggings	-25%; Con +12; Qui +6; Body, Energy R. +6	49	98	N8	90
Mystical Moonglade Leggings	-25%; Con +10; Str, Qui, Dex +7	49	98	N8	91

Feet

Item	Bonus	P	A	M	Q
Blackthorn Boots		7	14	N2	80
Spiked Blackthorn Boots	-5%; Dex +3; HP +3	7	14	N2	90
Old Noble's Boots		11	22	N3	80
Boots of the Deft Strider	-10%; Dex, Qui +6	15	30	N4	100
Lavish Reinforced Boots	-10%; Dex, Qui +3	15	30	N4	89
Draoi Sentinel's B.	-10%; Dex +3; Matter R. +2; Power +2; HP +3	19	38	N4	89
Abandoned Crustacean Boots	-10%; Con, Dex +4	20	40	N5	89
Dried Root Reinforced Boots		20	40	N5	80

Item	Bonus	P	A	M	Q
Ire Boots	-10%; Dex +12; Energy R. +6	20	40	N5	100
Coral Boots	-10%; Dex +6; Str +3; Qui +1	23	46	N5	89
Earth Crafted Root Boots	-5%; Qui +9; Dex +4	24	48	N5	89
Lucky Bootsyn	-10%; Dex +3; Matter R. +4; HP +9; Cold R. +2	24	48	N5	89
Bilk's Blue Boots	-15%; Matter R. +4; HP +3; Power +2; Dex +1	25	50	N6	89
Hollowed Crustacn. Leg-Tips	-15%; Dex +6; Qui +3; Matter R. +2	25	50	N6	89
Spectral Boots	-15%; Dex +4; Matter R. +4; Str +3; HP +9	28	56	N6	89
Faded Spiderweave Boots	-5%; HP +6	33	66	N7	80
Empyreal Ranger Boots	-20%; Dex +6; HP +12; Matter R. +4	35	70	N8	89
Worn Jewel Spiked Boots	-1%; HP +12	36	72	N8	80
Mariner Boots	-20%; Dex +9; Con +4; Heat R. +4	37	74	N8	89
Raider's Chitin Boots	-10%; Dex +10; Qui +3; Energy R. +2	37	74	N8	89
Silken Threaded Chitin Boots	-15%; Matter R. +4 Or +6; Dex +10	37	74	N8	89
Jewel Spiked Boots	-20%; Dex +9; Energy, Spirit R. +6	40	80	N8	89
Mire Walker's Boots	-20%; Dex +7; Str +6; Cold, Heat R. +4	42	84	N8	89
Reinforced Truemail Boots	-20%; Dex +7; Cold, Heat, Spirit R. +6	44	88	N8	89
Mischvs. Greenbriar B.	-15%; Con +4; Dex +9; Qui +7; Energy R. +4	46	92	N8	89
Welkin Boots	-25%; Dex +10; Str +4; HP +12	46	92	N8	89
Bladed Guardian Boots	-25%; Dex +9; Con, Qui +6	47	94	N8	89
Lucent Spirit Boots	-25%; Dex +12; Qui +6; Heat, Slash R. +6	49	98	N8	90
Mystical Moonglade Boots	-25%; Dex +11; Str, Qui, Con +7	49	98	N8	91
Twist. Forestdweller B.	-25%; Dex +10; Con +6; Sl. R. +6; HP +21	49	98	N8	90
Twisted Lusus Boots	-25%; Dex +10; Qui +6; Slash R. +6; HP +21	49	98	N8	90
Twisted Melody B.	-25%; Dex +10; Cha +6; Slash R. +6; HP +21	49	98	N8	90

Scaled

Head

Item	Bonus	P	A	M	Q
Spendid Scale Coif	-10%; Emp +6	15	30	04	89
Worn Dark Guardian Coif		15	30	04	80
Dried Molded Scale Coif		20	40	05	80
Tidal Coif	-10%; Con, Dex +4	20	40	05	89
Kraken's Maw	-10%; Emp +3; Valor S. +1; HP +9	20	40	05	89
Draoi Helm	-10%; Emp +4; Slash R. +4; Power +2	21	42	05	89
Fathomless Deepscale Helm	-10%; Emp +4; Dex, Str +3	23	46	05	89
Earth Crafted Scale Coif	-5%; HP +9; Emp +6	24	48	05	89
Keeper's Quickhelm	-10%; Emp +6; HP +12	24	48	05	89
Twined Coif	-15%; Power +2; Emp +4	26	52	06	89
Nearahd Coif	-15%; Valor S. +1; Emp +3; Slash R. +2; HP +9	27	54	06	89
Fagan's Helm of Honor	-15%; Str, Qui +9; Crush R. +8	31	62	07	100
Thrall's Ruined Coif	-5%; Emp +3	33	66	07	80
Algae Covered Coral Helm	-10%; ; Emp +9; HP +12; Heat R. +4	34	68	07	89
Worn Loyalist Scale Coif	-1%; Power +1; Emp +3	36	72	08	80
Ursine Forged Scale C.	-15%; Cold R. +4 Or +6; Emp +10; Dex +4	37	74	08	89
Badg. Pelt H.	-20%; Emp +3; Nat. Aff. S. +1; Regr. S. +2; Mat. R. +4	39	78	08	89
Loyalist Scalemail Coif	-20%; Emp +9; Con, Str +4	40	80	08	89
Bog Strider Coif	-20%; Int +7; Str +6; Body, Cold R. +4	42	84	08	89
Silverhand Truemail Coif	-20%; HP +15; Emp +10; Spirit R. +4	44	88	08	89
Sable Drakescale Coif	-25%; Emp +10; Dex +3; Spirit R. +10	47	94	08	89
Shining Sheeroe Coif	-25%; Str, Con +6; Dex, Qui +4	47	94	08	89
Champion Burnished Shanshee C.	-25%; Con, Str +12; Valor S. +4	49	98	08	90
Dread Blackscale Coif	-25%; Emp +10; Dex +9; Spirit R. +8	49	98	08	90
Ensorcelled Explorer Coif	-25%; Emp, Str, Dex +7; Con +4	49	98	08	90
Heroic Burnished Shanshee C.	-25%; Con, Str +12; Celt. Sp. S. +4	49	98	08	90
Iridescent Sylph Coif	-25%; Emp +10; Power +4; Dex +6	49	98	08	90
Shagreen Coif	-25%; Emp, Con, Dex +10	49	98	08	90
Shagreen Fighter's Coif	-25%; Str, Con, Qui +10	49	98	08	90

Torso

Item	Bonus	P	A	M	Q
Smoldering Scale Hauberk	-10%; Heat R. +6; HP +12	15	30	04	90
Splendid Scale Hauberk	-10%; HP +12	15	30	04	89
Worn Dark Guardian Armor	Con, Str +1	15	30	04	80
Dergal's Runed Hauberk	-10%; HP +12; Str +3; Heat R. +4	16	32	04	100
Dergal's Runed Hauberk	-10%; HP +12; Str +4; Heat R. +4	17	34	04	100
Dried Molded Scale Hauberk		20	40	05	80
Empyrean Mist Hauberk	-10%; HP +12; Con +4; Dex +6	20	40	05	100
Tidal Hauberk	-10%; HP +12; Qui +3	20	40	05	89
Draoi Tunic	-10%; Emp +4; HP +12	21	42	05	89
Fathomless Deepscale Hauberk	-10%; Con +10	23	46	05	89
Earth Crafted Scale Hauberk	-10%; HP +12; Dex, Qui +3	24	48	05	89
Keeper's Hauberk	-10%; Str, Con +4; Crush R. +4	24	48	05	89
Charred Scale Hauberk	-15%; HP +21; Heat R. +4; Str +6	25	50	06	100
Forest Walker's Vest	-15%; HP +21; Emp, Str +4	25	50	06	100
Twined Hauberk	-15%; Emp +6; Power +2; Body R. +2	27	54	06	89
Nearahd Hbk.	-15%; Emp +3; Nat. Aff., Nurture S. +1; Power +2	29	58	06	89
Mottled Dark Hauberk	-15%; HP +24; Str +12	31	62	07	100
Tarnished Ancient Hauberk	-20%; HP +36; Str +7	32	64	07	100
Thrall's Ruined Hauberk	-5%; Emp +3	33	66	07	80
Algae Covered Coral Hbk.	-10%; HP +12; Cold R. +4; Str, Emp +4	35	70	08	89
Worn Loyalist Scalemail	-1%; Con, Dex, Qui, Str +1	36	72	08	80
Ursine Forged Scale Hauberk	-15%; HP +24; Dex, Str +3	37	74	08	89
Hauberk of Deceit	-20%; Stealth S. +2; Str, Qui +6; HP +24	39	78	08	100
Hauberk of Lies	-20%; Stealth S. +2; Str, Qui +6; HP +24	39	78	08	100
Loyalist's Scalemail Hauberk	-20%; HP +24; Str +6	40	80	08	89
Bog Strider Hauberk	-20%; HP +18; Dex +4; Cold, Heat R. +4	42	84	08	89
Silverhand Truemail Hbk.	-20%; HP +30; Cr., Sl., Thr. R. +2	44	88	08	89
Sable Drakescale Hauberk	-25%; HP +42	47	94	08	89
Valorous Hauberk	-25%; Valor S. +3; Str +6; Spirit, Body R. +4	47	94	08	89
Burnished Shanshee Hauberk	-25%; HP +42; Str +12; Qui +6	49	98	08	90
Deo Hauberk	-25%; Con, Str +7; Power +6; Crush R. +6	49	98	08	91
Dread Blackscale Hauberk	-25%; HP +30; Matter, Body R. +10	49	98	08	90
Ensorcelled Explorer Hbk.	-25%; HP +27; Qui +4; Body, Cr. R. +6	49	98	08	90
Iridescent Sylph Hauberk	-25%; HP +42; Con, Dex +7	49	98	08	90
Shagreen Hauberk	-25%; HP +45; Qui, Dex +6	49	98	08	90
Shining Sheeroe Hauberk	-25%; HP +30; Str, Qui +4	49	98	08	89
Moonstruck Mire Hauberk	-25%; Str, Qui +10; Spirit, Cold R. +10	50	100	08	90

Arms

Item	Bonus	P	A	M	Q
Imbued Sleeves	-1%; Emp, Str +3	6	12	02	90
Splendid Scale Sleeves	-10%; Str +6	15	30	04	89
Worn Dark Guardian Sleeves		15	30	04	80
Dried Molded Scale Sleeves		20	40	05	80
Tidal Sleeves	-10%; Str +6; HP +6	20	40	05	89
Draoi Sleeves	-10%; Con +3; HP +9; Nature Affinity S. +1	21	42	05	89
Fathomless Deepscale Sleeves	-10%; Str +7; Emp +3	23	46	05	89
Earth Crafted Scale Sleeves	-10%; Str +7; Emp +4	24	48	05	89
Keeper's Arms	-10%; Dex, Qui +4; Crush R. +4	24	48	05	89
Smoldering Scale Sleeves	-15%; Str +12	25	50	06	90
Nearahd Sleeves	-15%; Str +3; Energy R. +2; Cold R. +4; HP +9	27	54	06	89
Twined Sleeves	-15%; Str +4; Crush R. +2	27	54	06	89
Thrall's Ruined Sleeves	-5%; Str +3	33	66	07	80
Algae Covered Coral Sl.	-10%; Str +9; Dex, Qui +3; Heat R. +4	35	70	08	89
Worn Loyalist Scale Sleeves	-1%; Slash, Body R. +2; HP +6	36	72	08	80
Ursine Forged Scale Sleeves	-15%; Heat R. +4 Or +6; Str +10	37	74	08	89
Loyalist Scalemail Sleeves	-20%; HP +12; Str +9; Emp +3	40	80	08	89
Bog Strider Sl.	-20%; Str +7; Qui +6; Slash R. +4; Body R. +4	42	84	08	89
Silverhand Truemail Sleeves	-20%; Str +13; Emp +7	44	88	08	89
Sable Drakescale Sleeves	-25%; Str +18; Emp +3	47	94	08	89
Burnished Shanshee Sl.	-25%; Str +10; Con +10; Body R. +16	49	98	08	90
Dread Blackscale Sleeves	-25%; Str +18; Emp +9; Cold R. +4	49	98	08	90
Ensorcelled Explorer Sl.	-25%; Str +12; HP +12; Sl., Energy R. +6	49	98	08	90
Iridescent Sylph Sl.	-25%; Str +10; Emp +9; Cold, Energy R. +6	49	98	08	90
Shagreen Sleeves	-25%; Str +10; Qui +7; Spirit, Heat R. +8	49	98	08	90
Shining Sheeroe Sleeves	-25%; Str +10; HP +24	49	98	08	89

Hands

Item	Bonus	P	A	M	Q
Imbued Gloves	-5%; Dex, Str +3	9	18	02	90
Splendid Scale Gloves	-10%; Qui +6	15	30	04	89
Worn Dark Guardian Gloves		15	30	04	80
Skinner's Gloves	-10%; Body R. +8; Dex +6	16	32	04	100
Dried Molded Scale Gloves		20	40	05	80
Tidal Gloves	-10%; Qui +4; Str +1; Energy R. +4	20	40	05	89
Draoi Gauntlets	-10%; Nurture, Regrowth S. +1; Emp, Str +3	21	42	05	89
Keeper's Gloves	-10%; Str +3; Parry S. +3	22	44	05	89
Fathomless Deepscale G.	-10%; Dex, Qui, Str +3; Body R. +2	23	46	05	89
Earth Crafted Scale Gloves	-10%; Str, Dex +4; Emp +3	24	48	05	89
Earthen Scale Gloves	-15%; HP +12; Body R. +4; Emp +6; Dex +4	25	50	06	100
Twined Gloves	-15%; Valor S. +2; Str +4	25	50	06	89
Nearahd Gl.	-15%; Rec. Bow, Celt. Sp. S. +1; Dex +4; En. R. +2	27	54	06	89
Smoldering Scale Gloves	-15%; HP +9; Heat R. +6; Dex, Str +6	30	60	07	90
Silvered Gauntlets	-15%; Qui +4; Str +10; Parry S. +3	31	62	07	100
Thrall's Ruined Gloves	-5%; Qui +3	33	66	07	80
Algae Covered Coral Gauntlets	-10%; Dex, Qui +7; Heat R. +4	35	70	08	89
Worn Loyalist Scale Gloves	-1%; HP +6; Qui, Emp +1	36	72	08	80
Ursine Forged Scale Gloves	-15%; Body R. +4 Or +6; Emp, Qui +7	37	74	08	89
Gloves of Black Death	-20%; Str, Con +9; Dex +12	39	78	08	100
Loyalist Scalemail Gloves	-20%; Dex, Qui, Emp +6	40	80	08	89
Bog Strider Gloves	-20%; Qui +7; Con +6; Energy, Body R. +4	42	84	08	89
Silverhand Truemail Gloves	-20%; Qui +12; Str, Dex, Emp +3	44	88	08	89
Sable Drakescale Gloves	-25%; Qui, Emp +7; Energy R. +8	47	94	08	89
Shining Sheeroe Gloves	-25%; Qui +9; Con, Str +6	47	94	08	89
Burnished Shanshee Gloves	-25%; Qui +10; HP +18; Parry S. +4	49	98	08	90
Dread Blackscale Gloves	-25%; Str +9; Qui +12; Heat R. +4	49	98	08	90
Ensorcelled Explorer Gl.	-25%; Qui +12; Con +6; Spirit, Thr. R. +6	49	98	08	90
Iridescent Sylph Druid Gl.	-25%; Qui +11; Nat. Aff., Nurture S. +3	49	98	08	90
Iridescent Sylph Warden Gl.	-25%; Qui +11; Parry, Nurture S. +3	49	98	08	90
Shagreen Gloves	-25%; Qui +10; Dex +6; Energy, Body R. +8	49	98	08	90

Legs

Item	Bonus	P	A	M	Q
Splendid Scale Leggings	-10%; Con +6	15	30	04	89
Worn Dark Guardian Leggings		15	30	04	80
Dried Molded Scale Leggings		20	40	05	80
Smoldering Scale Leggings	-10%; Con +10; Qui +3	20	40	05	90
Tidal Leggings	-10%; Con +6; Dex +3	20	40	05	89
Draoi Leggings	-10%; Con +4; HP +9; Slash R. +2	21	42	05	89
Fathomless Deepscale Leggings	-10%; Con +6; Emp +4	23	46	05	89
Earth Crafted Scale Leggings	-10%; Con +9; Dex +3	24	48	05	89
Keeper's Legs	-10%; Str, Con +6	24	48	05	89
Twined Leggings	-15%; Con +6; Crush R. +6	26	52	06	89
Nearahd Leggings	-15%; Con, Str +3; Body R. +4; HP +9	29	58	06	89
Thrall's Ruined Leggings	-5%; Con +3	33	66	07	80
Algae Covered Coral Leggings	-10%; Con +12; Qui +3; Cold R. +4	35	70	08	89
Worn Loyalist Scale Legs	-1%; Con, Qui +1; HP +6	36	72	08	80
Ursine Forged Scale Leggings	-15%; Body R. +4 Or +6; Con +10	37	74	08	89
Reinforced Gr. of Might	-20%; Celtic Dual S. +6; Con +9; HP +18	39	78	08	100
Scale Greaves of Might	-20%; Str, Con +9; HP +18	39	78	08	100
Loyalist's Scalemail Leggings	-20%; Con +9; Power +3	40	80	08	89
Bog Strider Leggings	-20%; Con +7; Str +6; Body, Energy R. +4	42	84	08	89
Silverhand Truemail Leg.	-20%; Con +11; Mat., Ener., Body R. +2	44	88	08	89
Sable Drakescale Leggings	-25%; Con +12; Str +3	47	94	08	89
Burnished Shanshee Leg.	-25%; Con +10; Str +9; Qui, Dex +7	49	98	08	90
Dread Blackscale Greaves	-25%; Con +12; Str +9; Cold R. +4	49	98	08	90
Ensorcelled Expl. Leg.	-25%; Con +12; Qui +6; Energy, Heat R. +6	49	98	08	90
Iridescent Sylph Leggings	-25%; Con +12; Emp +9; Str, Dex +7	49	98	08	90
Shagreen Leggings	-25%; Con +10; Qui +7; Cold, Spirit R. +8	49	98	08	90
Shining Sheeroe Leggings	-25%; Con +12; Dex, Qui +6	49	98	08	89

Feet

Item	Bonus	P	A	M	Q
Imbued Boots	-5%; Dex, Qui +4	12	24	03	90
Splendid Scale Boots	-10%; Dex +6	15	30	04	89
Worn Dark Guardian Boots		15	30	04	80
Dried Molded Scale Boots		20	40	05	80
Tidal Boots	-10%; Dex +4; Qui +1; Cold R. +4	20	40	05	89
Draoi Boots	-10%; HP +9; Cold, Spirit R. +4	21	42	05	89
Fathomless Deepscale Boots	-10%; Con, Dex +4; Body R. +2	23	46	05	89
Earth Crafted Scale Boots	-10%; Dex, Qui +6	24	48	05	89
Keeper's Boots	-10%; Qui +6; HP +12	24	48	05	89
Twined Boots	-15%; Power +2; HP +9	26	52	06	89
Nearahd Boots	-15%; Dex +4; Crush, Cold R. +4; Qui +3	29	58	06	89
Thrall's Ruined Boots	-5%; Dex +3	33	66	07	80
Algae Covered Coral Boots	-10%; Dex, Qui +7; Cold R. +4	35	70	08	89
Worn Loyalist Scale Boots	-1%; Body, Energy R. +2; Dex +3	36	72	08	80
Shagreen Champion Boots	-25%; Dex +10; Valor S. +3; Con +6	37	74	08	90
Ursine Forged Scale Boots	-15%; Dex +12; Qui +6	37	74	08	89
Loyalist Scalemail Boots	-20%; Dex, Con +9	40	80	08	89
Bog Strider Boots	-20%; Dex +7; Str +6; Thrust, Body R. +4	42	84	08	89
Silverhand Truemail B.	-20%; Dex +10; Con +4; Mat., Spirit R. +4	44	88	08	89
Sable Drakescale Boots	-25%; Dex +9; Matter, Body R. +8	47	94	08	89
Burnished Shanshee Boots	-25%; Dex +10; Str, Qui +9; Con +4	49	98	08	90
Dread Blackscale Boots	-25%; Dex +12; Qui +9; Heat R. +4	49	98	08	90
Ensorcelled Expl. B.	-25%; Dex +12; Str +6; Spirit, Matter R. +6	49	98	08	90
Iridescent Sylph Boots	-25%; Dex +10; Str +10; Qui, Con +9	49	98	08	90
Shagreen Druid B.	-25%; Dex +10; Emp +7; Nature Affinity S. +3	49	98	08	90
Shagreen Hero Boots	-25%; Dex +10; Con, Str +7	49	98	08	90
Shagreen Warden Boots	-25%; Dex +10; Emp +7; Str +9	49	98	08	90
Shining Sheeroe Boots	-25%; Dex +10; Qui, Str +6	49	98	08	89

Miscellaneous Drops & Rewards

Item	Bonus	PL	QI
Stone: Expended Commanding Stone	Power +2	7	89
Soul: Cold Light Soul		8	100
Coin: Lucky Silver Coin	Emp +6	10	100
Skin: Selkie Skin	Cold R. +3; Qui +4	12	89
Totem: Nature Totem	Emp +4; Power +1	12	100
Shell: Scuttle's Glowing Tooth	Power +2; Int +3	14	100
Beads: Glowing Sherrie Beads	Power +2; Emp +1	18	89
Rock: Swirling Granite	Matter R. +6; Con +4	18	89
Beads: Rattling Sherrie Beads	HP +6; Str +3	21	89
Stone: Faerie Charm	Str +6; Qui +3	21	89
Coin: Mollachd Coin	Rec. Bow S. -1; Dex -1; Celt. Dl. S. +1; Str +3	23	89
Horn: Hollowed Unicorn Horn	Body R. +4; Nat. Aff. S. +1; Emp +1	23	89
Sac: Dark Crystalized Poison Sac	Envenom S. +2; Con +6	23	90
Ball: Odd Ball	Body, Crush, Slash R. +6	25	89
Coin: Lucky Rhusag	HP +6; Cha +1; Music S. +1; Spirit R. +4	25	89
Coin: Lucky Gold Coin	Dex +6; Qui, Con +4	26	100
Stone: Zephyr's Commanding Stone	Mana Magic S. +3; Power +4	32	89
Tooth: Aibill's Tooth	HP +6; Cha, Qui +4	35	89
Stone: Elemental Heatstone	HP +21; Matter, Heat R. +6	37	90
Skin: Selkie Skin	Power +3; Emp, Int +6	45	89
Flower: Netherworld Flower	Con, Str +4; Qui, Dex +6	48	89
Mane: Valorous Mane	Power +3; Valor S. +4; Str +3	48	89
Book: Bk. of Arc. Dealings	Matter, Cold, Heat R. +8; Power +4 *or* +6	50	90
Book: Siabr. Arc. Methods	Power +3; Int +9; Mana, Light Mg. S. +2	50	90
Head: Dullahan's Luminescent Head	Power +5; Int +12	50	90

Shield Drops & Rewards

For Standard (Craftable) Shields, see page 361.

For more information on what the various stats mean, see **Armor** (p. 362), **Weapons** (p. 361) and **Material** (p. 360).

Abbreviations

The first negative percentage in any bonus indicates your opponent's reduced chance of hitting you when you are wearing the item.

Headings. Power Level / **A**rmor Factor / **M#** = Material (M) and Material Level (#) / **Q**uality / **Sp**eed, or weapon delay (the time between bashes) / **D**amage with each hit / **DpS** = Damage per second.

The first positive percentage in any bonus indicates your increased chance to block with the shield and (if it can be used as a weapon), your increased chance to hit with it.

Stats. Resistance, **S**kill / **Cha**risma, **Con**stitution, **Emp**athy, **Dex**terity, **Pi**ety, **Qui**ckness, **Str**ength / **O**re.

Small

Shield	Bonus	P	A	M#	Q	Sp	D	DpS
Training Sh.		0	0	01	90	2.8	3	1.2
Resilient Oak Sh.	+1%; Str, Emp +1	4	8	01	90	2.9	7	2.4
Richly Designed Round Sh.		12	24	03	80	2.8	13	4.8
Sh. of the Decadent	+10%; Sh. S. +1; Con +3	16	32	04	89	2.8	17	6.0
Worn Dark Guardian Sh.		16	32	04	80	2.8	17	6.0
Imperial Small Sh.	+10%; Emp, Con +3; Energy R. +4	20	40	05	89	2.7	23	8.7
Round Slate Sh.		21	42	05	80	2.8	21	7.5
Draoi Sh.	+10%; Con, Emp +4; Crush R. +2	22	44	05	89	2.8	20	7.2
Jagged Sh.	+15%; Nurt., Regr., Nat. Aff. S. +2; Emp +6	31	62	07	100	2.8	29	10.5
Petrif. Wisen. Oak Sh.	+15%; HP +15; Emp +9; Dex +3	31	62	07	90	2.7	28	10.5
Wispy Sh.	+15%; HP +18; Cold R. +6; Emp, Qui +6	33	66	07	100	4	44	11.1
Rubigo Round Sh.	+20%; Str, Emp +7	36	72	08	89	2.8	34	12.3
Flawed Aster. Rd. Sh.	+1%; Sh. S. +1; Cold, Heat R. +2	37	74	08	80	3.1	38	12.3
Bal. Aster. Rd. Sh.	+20%; Sh. S. +1; Con +9; Ht., Cld. R. +6	39	78	08	89	3	39	12.9
Sol Protector	+20%; Sh. S. +3; Str +10; HP+27	43	86	08	100	4.5	53	11.7
Truesilver Rd. Sh.	+20%; HP +24; Mat., Spir., Heat R. +4	45	90	08	89	2.8	41	14.7
Fomor. Prot.	+25%; Emp +4; Dex +3; Nurt., Regr. S. +1	46	92	08	89	2.8	43	15.3
Earthen Protector	+25%; Emp, Str +7; Matter R. +8	48	96	08	89	4.3	67	15.6
Small Heatstone Prot.	+25%; Con, Qui +7; Heat R. +8	48	96	08	89	2.8	44	15.6
Obsidian Round Sh.	+25%; Con, Qui, Dex +6; Str +4	49	98	08	89	2.8	45	16.2
Glim'strike Sh.	+25%; Emp +9; Con +7; Cr., Body R. +6	50	100	08	90	2.8	45	16.2
Warshade Prot.	+25%; Str, Con +7; Crush, Heat R. +8	50	100	08	90	2.8	45	16.2

Medium

Shield	Bonus	P	A	M#	Q	Sp	D	DpS
Clik's Chitin	+5%; Sh. S. +1; Heat R. +2; HP +6	10	20	02	100	4.4	18	4.2
Richly Designed Kite Sh.		12	24	03	80	4.3	21	4.8
Imperial Kite Sh.	+10%; Con, Str +3; Cold R. +4	20	40	05	89	4.1	36	8.7
Stoic Defender	+10%; Sh. S. +1; Str, Con +3; Dex +4	20	40	05	90	4.3	32	7.5
Faerie Drake Hide Sh.	+10%; Crush R. +4; Emp, Str +7	24	48	05	100	4.3	36	8.4
Spritely Sh.	+15%; Sh. S. +1; Crush R. +4; Con +3	29	58	06	89	4.3	43	9.9
Silvered Sh.	+15%; Slash R. +8; Emp, Dex +9	32	64	07	100	4.3	45	10.5
Darkened Defender	+15%; Body R. +12 *or* +18; Dex +7	35	70	08	89	2.8	34	12.0
Crested Glow Worm Carapace	+20%; Emp, Con +6; Str, Qui +4	36	72	08	90	4	48	12.0
Rubigo Kite Sh.	+20%; Str +6; Dex, Qui +4	36	72	08	89	4.3	53	12.3
Badg. Pelt Sh.	+20%; Sh. S. +1; Con, Emp +3; Cr. R. +2	37	74	08	89	4.3	54	12.6
Flawed Aster. K. Sh.	+1%; Sh. S. +1; Body, Spir. R. +2	37	74	08	80	4.7	58	12.3
Siabrian Mystic Sh.	+15%; Sh. S. +2; Body R. +6; Heat, Spirit R. +4	38	76	08	100	4	50	12.6
Balanced Asterite Kite Sh.	+20%; Sh. S. +2; Qui +6; Body, Spirit R. +6	39	78	08	89	4.3	55	12.9
Blade Ward	+20%; Sh. S. +6; Str +9; Slash R. +8	43	86	08	100	4.5	63	14.1
Silver. Spellbd. Sh.	+20%; Sh. S. +6; Str +9; Sl. R. +8	43	86	08	100	4.5	63	14.1
Warding Sh.	+20%; Sh. S. +6; Str +9; Crush R. +8	43	86	08	100	4.5	63	14.1
Truesilver Kite Sh.	+20%; HP +24; Body R. +12	45	90	08	89	4	59	14.7
Obsidian Kite Sh.	+25%; Sh. S. +4; Qui +4; HP +12	49	98	08	89	4.3	70	16.2
Azure Defender	+25%; Sh. S. +4; Str +7; Con +6	50	100	08	90	3.8	62	16.2
Deathwatcher Ward	+25%; Sh. S. +4; Con +7; Str +4; Body R. +6	50	100	08	91	4.3	70	16.2

Large

Shield	Bonus	P	A	M#	Q	Sp	D	DpS
Gold Embossed Sh.	+10%; Sh. S. +1; Dex +3	16	32	04	89	4.5	27	6.0
Imperial Great Sh.	+10%; Con, Str, Dex +3	20	40	05	89	3.5	30	8.7
Earth Crafted Sh.	+10%; Sh. S. +1; Matter, Crush R. +4 *or* +6; Con +3	25	50	05	89	3.9	34	8.7
Guardian Sh. of the Keeper	+10%; Sh. S. +2; Str +4	25	50	05	89	4	35	8.7
Cath Sh.	+15%; Sh. S. +1; Crush R. +2; Con, Qui +1	27	54	06	89	4	37	9.3
Rubigo Heater Sh.	+20%; Sh. S. +2; Dex, Qui +4	36	72	08	89	3.8	47	12.3
Flawed Ast. Tower Sh.	+1%; Sh. S. +1; En., Spir. R. +2	37	74	08	80	4.8	59	12.3
Darkened Battle Sh.	+15%; Sh. S. +2; Crush, Slash R. +4 *or* +6; Str +6	38	76	08	89	4.2	53	12.6
Balanced Asterite Tower Sh.	+20%; Sh. S. +2; Str +6; Energy, Spirit R. +6	39	78	08	89	4.5	58	12.9
Truesilv. Htr. Sh.	+20%; HP +24; Cold R. +8; Spirit R. +4	45	90	08	89	3.8	44	11.7
Tower of the Mind Fortress	+25%; Sh. S. +2; Str +7; Spirit R. +10	48	96	08	89	4.5	70	15.6
Obsidian Tower Sh.	+25%; Sh. S. +4; Str +4; HP +12	49	98	08	89	4.5	73	16.2

Musical Instruments

Like most other items in the game, musical instruments vary in quality. All current instruments begin at Level 1 (which means that higher-grade instruments are available at levels 6, 11, 16, 21 and so forth). The higher the level of your instrument, the more effective your magical Songs. For recipes, see p. 362.

Abbreviations

Headings. Power Level / **M#** = Material (M) and Material Level (#) / Quality.

Abbreviations. S. = Skill / **R.** = Resistance / **Cha**risma, **Con**stitution, **Dex**terity, **Emp**athy, **Qui**ckness.

Drums (weight 2.0)

Instrument	Bonus	PL	M#	Ql
Drum (standard)		1,6,11, etc.	W	100
Kedger Drum	Music S. +1; Cha +1	16	W4	89
Shaped Coral Drum	HP +15	21	W5	89
Worm Round Drum	Music S. +1; Dex +6	21	W5	89
Feverish Runner	HP +27	31	W7	90
Bodb's Wailing Drum	Music S. +4; Cold, Crush, Matter R. +4	36	W8	91
Cath Drum	Music S. +2; Cold, Spirit, Matter R. +2	36	W8	89
Cliff Dweller Drum	Music S. +2; Cha, Dex +6	36	W8	89
Coruscat. Truesilver Drum	Music S. +4; Body, Matter, Spirit R. +4	36	O8	89
Drum of the Hollow Heart	Music S. +7	36	W8	89
Etched Drum	Music S. +3; HP +18	36	W8	89
Flawed Etched Drum	Music S. +1; HP +6	36	W8	80
Glimmerstrike Drum	Music S. +3; Cha, Con +4; Cold R. +6	36	W8	90
Granny's Kettle	Music S. +3; Cha +6	36	W8	89
Petrified Bardic Wonder	Music S. +4; Cold R. +12	36	W8	89

Flutes (weight 1.0)

Instrument	Bonus	PL	M#	Ql
Drum (standard)		1,6,11, etc.	**wd**	100
Melodic Flute	Music S. +1; Emp +7	11	W3	90
Kedger Flute	Music S. +1; Cha +1	16	W4	89
Flute of Shaped Shells	HP +15	21	W5	89
Hollow Root		21	W5	80
Bodb's Wailing Flute	Music S. +4; Body R. +8; Cold R. +4	36	W8	91
Carved Flute	Music S. +3; HP +18	36	W8	89
Coruscating Truesilver Flute	Music S. +4; Body R. +12	36	O8	89
Flawed Carved Flute	Music S. +1; HP +6	36	W8	80
Flute of Angus Og	Music S. +6; HP +21	36	W8	100
Flute of the Hollow Wind	Music S. +7	36	W8	89
Infernal Flute	Music S. +2; Cha +3; Spirit, Cold R. +2	36	W8	89
Pooka's Broken Horn	Music, Nurture, Regrowth S. +2; Cha +12	36	W8	90
Topaz Studded Shell Flute	Music S. +5; Cha, Qui +7	36	W8	89
Warshade Flute	Music S. +3; Cha, Con +6; Heat R. +6	36	W8	90

Lutes (weight 1.5)

Instrument	Bonus	PL	M#	Ql
Lute (standard)		1,6,11, etc.	**wd**	100
Bard Initiate Lute	Music S. +1; Cha +1	6	W2	90
Lute of the Sea	Music S. +2; Cha +4	11	W3	100
Kedger Lute	Music S. +1; Cha +1	16	W4	89
Fathomless Lute	HP +15	21	W5	89
Cath Lute	Music S. +1; Cha +3; Energy R. +2	26	W6	89
Badb's Wailing Lute	Music S. +7; Dex +10; Qui +7	36	W8	100
Bodb's Wailing Lute	Music S. +4; Heat, Cold, Spirit R. +4	36	W8	91
Cliff Dweller Lute	Music S. +2; Cha, Con +6	36	W8	89
Coruscat. Truesilver Lute	Music S. +4; Cold, Matter, Heat R. +4	36	O8	89
Cursed Lute	Music S. +3; Cha +6	36	W8	89
Deathwatcher Lute	Music S. +3; Cha, Con +6; Energy R. +8	36	W8	90
Embossed Lute	Music S. +3; HP +18	36	W8	89
Flawed Embossed Lute	Music S. +1; HP +6	36	W8	80
Lute of the Harpers	Nurture, Regrowth S. +3; Cha +6	36	W8	100
Lute of the Hollow Soul	Music S. +7	36	W8	89

Jewelry Drops & Rewards

Abbreviations

Headings. Power Level / Quality.

Stats. Resistance, Skill / **Cha**risma, **Con**stitution, **Emp**athy, **Dex**terity, **Int**elligence, Piety, **Qui**ckness, **Str**ength.

Item	Bonus	PL	Ql
Amulet			
Eagle Talon Amulet	Dex, Qui, Int +6; Spirit R. +8	50	89
Baldric			
Siabrian Sword Baldric	Dex +3; HP +6	15	89
Belts			
Sturdy Leather Belt	Con +3	7	90
Swordmans Belt	Dex, Qui, Str +1	8	100
Changeling Skin Belt	Int +3; HP +6	10	90
Bauble Studded Belt	HP +6; Emp +3	12	89
Belt of the Deranged	HP +15	16	89
Belt of Misdirection	Evade S. +2; Dex +3	16	89
Rage Sprite Belt	Str +4; Qui, Dex +1	18	89
Deepscale Belt	Con, Str +4	20	89
Fathomless Coral Wrap	Int, Dex +4	20	89
Aeiry Belt	Str +3; HP +6; Spirit, Energy R. +2	21	89
Crusty Old Work Belt	Slash R. +6 *or* +9; HP +9	21	89
Woven Belt	Str +6; Body R. +4; HP +6	21	100
Missing Caster's Belt	Power +1; Crush R. +2; Con +3; HP +9	25	89
Well Crafted Work Belt	Str +9; Dex +3	25	89
Wilde's Mane	Nurture S. +3; Emp +6	25	100
Eluvium Belt	Dex +7; HP +12	30	89
Smiter's Belt	Con, Str +4; Crush R. +2; Valor S. +1	30	89

Item	Bonus	PL	QI
Zephyr Belt	Str +7; HP +12	30	89
Belt of Spryness	Matter, Spirit, Energy R. +6; Dex +6	33	100
Feline's Tail	Power +4; HP +6; Dex +6	35	100
Braided Kelp Belt	Emp +10; Cold R. +8	36	89
Little Star's Braided Mane	Crush, Slash R. +4; Con, Str +7	36	100
Gem Covered Belt	HP +24; Crush, Slash, Thrust R. +2	38	89
Siabrian Belt	HP +33	38	89
Bladeturn Belt	Slash R. +8; Parry S. +3; Str +12	45	100
Dueler's Belt	Str +10; Parry S. +3; Slash R. +4	45	100
Lifter's Belt	Str +9; Valor S. +3; Body R. +4; HP +12	45	100
Crystal Flecked Belt	Enchant., Void Mg., Mental. S. +2; Power +5	46	89
Belt of Arcane Power	Power +6 *or* +8; HP +24	50	90
Belt of Resilience	Sl., Thr. R. +6 *or* +8; HP +18 *or* +12; Str +12	50	90
Braided Unicorn Mane	Dex, Str +10; HP +30	50	91
Stout Leather Belt	Str, Con +12; Spirit, Matter R. +6	50	90

Bracelets

Item	Bonus	PL	QI
Gem Encrusted Bracelet	Qui +3; Cha +1	8	100
Wind Formed Bracelet	Spirit R. +4; Int +3	9	100
Beaded Silk Bracelet	Dex, Int, Con +3	16	90
Ethereal Zephyr Bracelet	Valor S. +1; Con +4; Str +3	24	89
Braided Kelp Bracelet	Str +9; Thrust R. +10	36	89
Kelp Bracelet	Con +9; Cha +7	36	89
Bracelet of Enchanted Talent	Enchant. S. +3; Dex +6; Power +4	40	100
Bracelet of Thoughtful Talent	Mentalism S. +3; Dex +6; Power +4	40	100
Bracelet of Voided Talent	Void Magic S. +3; Dex +6; Power +4	40	100
Bracelet of Diem'ess Sidhe	Crush, Slash R. +6 *or* +8; Emp, Int +9	50	90
Horse Mane Bracelet	Con, Str +7; Body R. +8	50	89

Bracers (Br)

Item	Bonus	PL	QI
Banded Reed Bracer	Con +1	4	90
Woven Grass Bracer	Dex +1	4	90
Carved Wooden Bracer	Qui +3; Emp +1	8	100
Etched Bracer	Str +3; Con +1	8	100
Embossed Crystal Bracer	Emp, Int +3	10	90
Etched Crystal Bracer	Dex, Qui +3	10	90
Hardened Moss Bracer	Str, Dex +1; HP +3	10	89
Bracer of Station	Qui +3; Int +4	12	100
Gaudy Silver-Lined Bracer	Light Magic S. +1; Int +3	12	89
Hardened Grass Bracer	Int, Emp +3	13	89
Siabrian Bracer	Str +4; HP +6	15	89
Bracer of the Paranoid	Emp, Dex +3; Qui +1	16	89
Rough Hide Bracer	Slash, Body R. +3; HP +12	16	90
Rock Sherrie Bracer	Str +7	18	89
Banded Coral Bracer	Dex, Qui, Str +3	19	89
Chitinous Worm Round	HP +18	19	89
Opal Studded Bracer	Emp, Con, Str +3	19	89
Slimy Chitinous Worm Round	Parry S. +3	19	89
Cracked Earth Bracer	Emp, Int, Dex +3	21	89
Dried Earth Bracer	HP +9; Str +4	21	89
Mist Formed Bracer	Emp +7; Power +2	22	100
Slimed Bracer	Parry S. +1; Qui +3; Matter R. +2; HP +6	22	89
Cursed Stone Bracer	Matter R. +4; Str, Dex +1	24	100
Ick's Round	Dex, Emp +7	24	100
Stone Bracer	Matter R. +8; Str +6; Dex +3	24	100
Etched Stone Bracer	Int, Dex +6	25	89
Worked Stone Bracer	Emp, Str +6	25	89
Forged Earthen Bracer	Heat, Spirit R. +6; Str +9	26	100
Molded Magic Crystal Br.	Enchant., Mental, Void Mg. S. +3; Int +6	26	100
Bracer of Might	Str, Con +4; Body R. +2; Parry S. +1	30	89
Archer's Bracer	Recurve Bow, Celtic Dual S. +2; Dex +7	31	90
Bracer of the Honored Warrior	Blades, Blunt, Lg. Weap. S. +2; Str +7	31	90
Elite Mireguard Bracer	Parry, Celtic Dual S. +2; Dex +9	35	100
Glimmer Spirit Trammel	Cha +4; Str, Qui +6	35	89
Bracer of Tracelessness	Dex +7; Qui +3; Stealth S. +2	38	89
Left Bracer of Skill	Blades S. +2; Dex +7	38	89
Right Bracer of Skill	Piercing S. +2; Qui +7	38	89
Ursine Battle Bracer	HP +18; Str +7	38	89
Artist's Bracer	Parry S. +2; Power +4; Emp +7; Con +3	40	100
Bracer of Hidden Talent	Parry S. +2; Str, Con +7; Body R. +4	40	100
Bracer of the Unseelie	Emp, Con, Str +6	41	89
Leech Husk Bracer	Str, Dex +4; HP +12	41	89
Loyalist Observer's Bracer	HP +15; Rec. Bow S. +1; Dex, Str +4	42	89
Infernal Bracer	Parry S. +2; Con +6; Cold R. +4; Str +4	43	89
Bracer of the Silverhand	HP +15; Dex, Qui, Str +4	48	89
Bracer of the Triumvirate	HP +15; Power +2; Int, Emp +4	49	89
Acid-Etched Bracer	Dex, Qui +6; HP +12; Body R. +6	50	90
Bracer of Zo'arkat	Emp, Int, Dex, Qui +7	50	90
Deathshadow Bracer	Int +4; HP +36; Dex +4; Matter R. +8	50	90
Glimmershade Bracer	Emp +9; Dex +10; Body, Spirit R. +10	50	90
Mischievous Bracer	Qui, Dex +12; Spirit R. +14	50	91
Warshadow Bracer	Con, Qui +9; Matter, Cold R. +10	50	90

Charms

Item	Bonus	PL	QI
Bard Charm	HP +6; Cha +4	12	100
Blademaster *or* Champion Charm	HP +6; Qui +4	12	100
Druid Charm	Power +1; Emp +4	12	100
Eldritch *or* Enchanter Charm	Power +1; Int +4	12	100
Hero Charm	Str +4; HP +6	12	100
Mentalist Charm	Mentalism S. +1; Int +4	12	100
Nightshade, Ranger *or* Warden Charm	HP +6; Dex +4	12	100

Cloaks

Item	Bonus	PL	QI
Sheeries Fearsome Shroud	Con +4; Cha -9	5	80
Natures Shroud	Dex +3; Con +1	8	100
Spinner's Cloak	Energy R. +6	9	100
Sewn Cloak of Might	HP +3; Str +3	10	89
Ceremonial Cloak	Emp, Str +3	12	89
Protector's Cloak	Str +4; Dex +3	12	100
Tallulah's Cloak	Stealth S. +2; HP +3	13	100
Marvelous Cloak	HP +6; Emp +1; Int, Str +1	16	89
Silver Threaded Forest Cloak	Emp, Dex +4	16	100
Draoi Sentinel's Cloak	Emp, Dex +3; Slash, Crush R. +2	20	89
Empyrean Mist Cloak	Qui, Dex +6	21	100
Mantle of Regalia	Spirit R. +3; HP +6; Emp, Int +3	21	90
Spectral Shroud	Con -4; Emp, Int +3	22	89
Watery Kelp Cloak	Con +6; Dex +4	22	89
Keeper's Shade	Power +2; Cha +1	23	89
Manta Skin Cloak	Dex +4; Emp, Int +3	23	89
Mephit Wing	Qui +3; Slash R. +4; HP +6; Cha +1	23	89
Wolf Hide Cloak	Cold R. +4; Con +6; Qui +4	23	100
Cloak of the Oceanic Predator	Dex, Str +3; Qui +4	24	89
Faerie Saddle Cloak	Slash, Body R. +2; Dex +3; HP +9	24	89
Bilk's Blue Cloak	Sl. R. +4; Cha +4; Body R. +2; Mending S. +1	26	89
Darkened Earthen Cloak	Matter R. +6; Emp, Con +4; Str +3	28	100
Charred Earthen Cloak	Dex, Qui, Con, Qui +4	29	100
Ether Cloak	Valor S. +2; Emp, Cha +3; HP +3	29	89
Flowing Dark Earthen Cloak	Body R. +8; Power +2; Int +6	29	100
Nearahd Cloak	Body R. +4; Cha, Emp, Str +3	30	89
Cath Cloak	Body R. +2; Con +4; Body R. +4; HP +9	31	89
Cloak of Concealment	Stealth S. +2; Heat R. +6; Dex +7	31	90
Spectral Shadow	Dex, Qui +4; Body R. +2; Power +1	31	89
Fog Bound Cape	Power +2; Qui, Emp +3	32	89
Cloak of Obscurement	Stealth S. +2; Dex +7; Str +6	33	100
Spinner's Cloak	Energy, Heat R. +6; Con +10	33	100
Mantle of Forgotten Prowess	Dex, Emp +7	34	89
Sharkskin Cloak	HP +9; Emp, Int +4	35	89
Glimmer Spirit Cloak	Energy R. +4; Heat, Cold R. +6; Con +4	36	89
Vaporous Cloak	Void Mg., Mental., Enchant. S. +2; Dex +10	38	100
Badger Pelt Cloak	Cold R. +4; HP +6; Cha , Dex +3	40	89

Item	Bonus	PL	QI
Cloak of Broichan	Emp +9; Power +2; HP +15	40	100
Howling Shroud	HP -12; Power +5	40	89
Infernal Cloak	Energy, Heat R. +4; Power +4; Con +3	41	89
Empyrean Mist Cloak	Stealth S. +2; Dex +9; Qui +10	43	100
Mantle of Unseelie Skill	Parry, Celtic Dual S. +2; Dex, Qui +6	43	89
Cloak of Night	Dex, Con +9; Body, Slash R. +6	45	100
Emerald Threaded Forest Cloak	Dex +9; Cold, Cr. R. +6; HP +18	45	100
Badger Fur Cloak	HP +27; Dex, Str +7	48	100
Abysmal Cloak	Str, Qui +6; Heat R. +4	50	89
Calignous Shroud	Power +6; Con, Dex +9	50	91
Cloak of the Silverhand	Emp, Int, Str +7	50	89
Deleterious Pall	Str, Con, Dex, Qui +10	50	91
Granny's Shawl	Dex, Emp, Con +4; Power +2	50	89
Lurid Mantle	Str +13; Con, Qui +12	50	91
Paradisiacal Cloak	Emp, Int +6; Cold R. +4	50	89
Supernal Cloak	Str, Qui +6; Heat R. +4	50	89

Earrings

Item	Bonus	PL	QI
Madder Earring	Power +2; Valor S. +2; Spirit R. +2	29	89
Pooka's Tooth Earring	Matter, Body R. +4; Emp, Int +6	31	100

Eyes

Item	Bonus	PL	QI
Clouded White Eye	Emp +4; Cold R. +6 *or* +9	19	89
Slimy Clouded White Eye	Int +4; Cold R. +6 *or* +9	19	89
Faerie Drakes Eye	Cold R. +4; Dex +6	20	89
Bloodstone Left Eye	Power +3	22	89
Bloodstone Right Eye	HP +18	22	89
Mephit Eye	Con, Int +3; Mentalism S. +1; Cold R. +2	23	89
Caster's Missing Eye	Power +1; Enchant. S. +1; Int +3; Spirit R. +4	25	89
Silvered Eye	Int +3; Energy R. +2; Regrowth S. +2; HP +6	29	89
Eucail Eye	Body R. -2; Con -1; Mentalism S. +2; Power +2	30	89
Ollipheist Eye	HP +6; Power +4	34	89
Cronsidhe's Red Eye	Void Magic S. +3; Int -2; Cold R. +2; Str +4	41	89
Eye of Fire	Con, Dex, Str, Emp +10	50	91

Gems

Item	Bonus	PL	QI
Flawed Gem	HP -3; Spirit R. +2; Str +4; Valor S. +1	22	89
Perfect Gem	HP +6; Cold R. +2; Emp +3; Nature Affinity S. +1	22	89
Celestial Gem of the Sky	Int, Dex +7; HP +30	50	90
Ethereal Gem of the Sky	Emp, Dex +7; HP +36	50	90
Phantom Gem	Emp, Int, Str +6; Qui +4	50	89
Potent Gem of the Sky	Str, Qui +7; HP +33	50	90

Jewels & Jewelry

Item	Bonus	PL	QI
Heart of Oak	HP +8	7	90
Jewel of the Forest	Emp +3; Qui +1	8	100
Shadowy Gem	Dex +3; Qui +1	8	100
Jewel of Speed	Qui +7	12	100
Summoned Jewel	Mana Magic S. +1; Int +3	12	89
Fey Jewel	HP +6; Dex +4	13	90
Jewel of Madness	Stealth S. +1; Dex +4	16	89
Gem of the Restless Wind	Spirit R. +4; HP +18	20	100
Faerie Eye	Int +3; Power +2	22	89
Orb of Resistance	Cold, Spirit R. +2; Power +1; Int +4	23	89
Glowing Zephyr Gem	Dex +4; Cha, Str +3	24	89
Ageless Turquioise	Celtic Dual S. +2; Qui +6	25	89
Sraoi's Heart	Light Magic S. +9; HP +9; Int +6	26	100
Water Bound Gem	Parry S. +2; Str +6	26	89
Gem o.t. Watery Depths	Regrowth, Nat. Aff., Nurt. S. +1; Emp +3	27	89
Sraoi's Luminescent Heart	HP +18; Emp +4; Str +3	27	100
Empathetic Jewel	Emp +4; Power +3; Cold R. +2	28	89
Luminescent Water Opal	Enchant., Mental., Void Mg. S. +1; Int +9	28	89
Spider Gem	Light Magic, Mana Magic S. +2; Int +7	36	89
Truesilver Laced Jewel	Power +2; Int, Dex +6	39	89
Jewel of Intensity	HP +27; Int +4; Crush R. +2	43	89
Bard's Jewel	Emp +9; Music S. +3; HP +21	47	100
Blademaster's Jewel	Qui, Con +9; Crush R. +8; Slash R. +6	47	100
Champion's Jewel	Str, Con +9; Parry S. +2; Body R. +8	47	100
Druid's Jewel	Regrowth, Nurture S. +2; Emp +9; HP +15	47	100
Eldritch's Jewel	Light Magic, Mana Magic S. +2; Int +9; HP +15	47	100
Enchanter's Jewel	Light, Mana Magic S. +2; Int +9; Power +4	47	100
Hero's Jewel	Str, Con +9; HP +21	47	100
Mentalist's Jewel	Light Magic, Mana Magic S. +2; Int +9; HP +15	47	100
Nightshade's Jewel	Dex, Str +9; HP +15; Power +2	47	100
Ranger's Jewel	Dex +9; Recurve Bow S. +3; HP +21	47	100
Shadow Crystal Orb	Envenom, Stealth S. +2; HP +18	47	89
Warden's Jewel	Emp, Con +9; Power +2; HP +18	47	100
Bogeyman Crystalized Eye	Void Mg., Enchant., Mental. S. +3; Int +9	50	89

Mantles

Item	Bonus	PL	QI
Boogieman Mantle	Slash R. +4; Str, Dex +6	33	89
Eagle Mantle	Spirit R. +4; Int, Dex +6	33	89
Goatman Mantle	Body R. +4; Emp, Cha +6	33	89
Goblin Mantle	Cold R. +4; Dex, Emp +6	33	89
Horse Mantle	Cold R. +4; Qui, Con +6	33	89
Pooka Lord's Mantle	Cold, Heat R. +8; Stealth S. +2; Qui +11	50	100

Medal

Item	Bonus	PL	QI
Medal of Valor	Valor S. +3; Con, Str, Qui +7	50	90

Necklaces (N)

Item	Bonus	PL	QI
Braided Silver Necklace	Qui +1	4	90
Medialion of Warriors Spirit	Str +3; HP +3	8	100
Twisted Silver Choker	Int +3; Dex +1	8	100
Crystal-Threaded Necklace	Emp +3; Power +1	10	90
Glowing Rose Petal Chain	Con +3; HP +3	10	89
Gaudy Thin Necklace	Dex, Qui +3	12	89
Celestial Pearl Necklace	Int, Emp, Qui, Dex +1	13	89
Lavish Necklace	Emp +3; Int +4	16	89
Necklace of Energy	Mana Magic S. +2; Int +3	16	100
Ore Necklace	Int +3; Void Magic S. +2	16	100
Chain of Rage	Int, Emp +3; HP +3	18	89
Osier's Spectral Necklace	Enchantments S. +2; Cha +6	20	100
Fine Opal Pendant	Con, Qui +4	21	89
Green Vine Necklace	Regrowth S. +1; Power +3	21	100
Polished Stone Necklace	Mana Magic, Light Magic S. +1; Int +3	21	89
Strung Shell Necklace	Emp, Int +4	21	89
Polished Fire Opal Necklace	Con, Dex, Qui, Str +3	25	89
Master Bard's Necklace	Music, Blades, Blunt S. +1; HP +12	26	100
Master Champion's N.	Lg. Weap., Blades, Pierc. S. +1; Power +2	26	100
Master Enchanter's N.	Enchanter's spells S. +1; Power +2	26	100
Master Nightshade's N.	Evade, Blades, Piercing S. +1; Power +2	26	100
Badger Claw Necklace	Body, Crush, Slash R. +4; HP +15	27	100
Mist Necklace	Dex, Con +6	27	89
Mouse Lord's Tail	Emp +9; Str +7	27	100
Wraith Necklace	Str, Con +6	27	89
Wrathfully Righteous Beads	Emp +3; Power +2; HP +6	27	89
Fainne N.	Void Magic, Mentalism, Enchantments S. +1; Power +2	30	89
Cath Charms	Nurture S. +1; Emp +3; Power +2; HP +9	31	89
Lusmorebane's Jeweled Necklace	Mana Magic S. +3; Int +9	31	100
Scragger's Primitive Necklace	Body R. +12 *or* +18; Emp +6	32	89
Aotrom Pearls	Valor S. +2; Power +2; Con +1; HP +6	34	89
Badger Tooth Necklace	Power +2; Int +7; Emp +7	36	100
Braided Kelp Necklace	Light Magic, Mana Magic S. +2; Int +4	36	89
Shrunken Spider Necklace	HP +9; Body R. +6 *or* +9; Emp +7	36	89
Abrasive N.	Nature Affinity S. +2; Emp +3; Body R. +4; HP +12	37	89
Encrusted Truesilver Necklace	Power +3; Emp, Int +4	40	89
Elder's Pearl Strand	Dex, Str +6; Cold R. +4; HP +9	42	89
Emerald-Beaded Strand	Void Magic S. +3; Int +9; Heat, Body R. +6	45	100
Enchanted Gold Chain	Enchantments S. +3; Int, Dex +9	45	100
Entwined Silken Strand	Emp +6; Int +6; Con +9	45	89

Item	Bonus	PL	QI
String of Thoughts	Dex, Int +9; Mentalism S. +3	45	100
Empathic Deathwatcher Chain	Emp, Con +10; Spirit, Body R. +10	50	90
Necklace of the Arcane	Power +4; Int +10; HP +15	50	90
Necklace of Combat	HP +15; Int, Dex, Con +7	50	90
Pearlescent Necklace	Cha +6; Con, Str, Dex +9	50	90
Potent Deathwatcher Chain	Str, Con +10; Cold, Energy R. +10	50	90
Sorcerous Deathwatcher Chain	Int, Con +10; Body R. +8; Spirit R. +10	50	90
Stoney Links of Magic	Cha, Con, Str, Dex +10	50	91
Pelt			
Badger Pelt Cloak	HP +9; Cha +3; Cold, Matter R. +2	22	89
Pendants			
Sparrow Pendant	Dex +1	4	90
Apprentice Craftsman Pendant	Cha, Emp +1	9	89
Charm Locket	Cha +6	9	100
Fledgling Magi Pendant	Int, Dex +1	9	89
Footman Pendant	Str, Con +1	9	89
Rogue Petitioner Pendant	Dex, Qui +1	9	89
Apprentice Magi Pendant	Int +3; Dex +1	12	89
Infantryman Pendant	Str +3; Con +1	12	89
Neophyte Craftsman Pendant	Cha +3; Emp +1	12	89
Rogue Pendant	Dex +3; Qui +1	12	89
Captain Pendant	Str, Con +3	15	89
Journeyman Craftsman Pendant	Cha, Emp +3	15	89
Learned Magi Pendant	Int, Dex +3	15	89
Rogue Infiltrator Pendant	Dex, Qui +3	15	89
Adept Craftsman Pendant	Cha +4; Emp +3	18	89
Battlemaster Pendant	Str, Con +3; Slash R. +1	20	89
Rogue Captain Pendant	Dex, Qui +3; Stealth S. +1	20	89
Skillful Magi Pendant	Int, Dex +3; Power +1	20	89
Master Craftsman Pendant	Cha, Emp +4	21	89
Master Rogue Pendant	Dex, Qui +4; Stealth S. +1	25	89
Commander Pendant	Str +6; Con +4; Slash R. +1	30	89
Rogue Assassin Pendant	Dex +6; Qui +4; Envenom S. +1	30	89
Adroit Magi Pendant	Int, Dex +4; Power +2	35	89
General Pendant	Str +6; Con +4; Slash R. +2	35	89
Rogue Lord Pendant	Dex, Qui +6; Stealth S. +1	35	89
Master Assassin Pendant	Dex, Qui +6; Envenom S. +2	40	89
Masterful Magi Pendant	Int, Dex +6; Power +2	40	89
Noble Lord Pendant	Str +7; Con +6; Slash R. +2	40	89
Arch Magi Pendant	Int, Dex +7; Power +2	45	89
Rogue Overlord Pendant	Dex, Qui +7; Stealth, Envenom S. +1	45	89
Royal Guardian Pendant	Str, Con +7; Slash R. +2	45	89
Arch Magi Overlord Pendant	Int, Dex +9; Power +3	50	89
Noble Overlord Pendant	Str, Con +9; Slash R. +3	50	89
Pin			
Griffonhead Cloak Pin	Cha +3; Qui +6	18	89
Rings			
Ivy Ring	Emp +1	4	90
Quartz Ring	Int +1	4	90
Band of Twigs	Con +3	5	100
Ring of Faces	Dex +3	5	100
Ring of Staves	Int +3	5	100
Ring of Swords	Str +3	5	100
Hollowed Fingerbone Ring	Str +3	7	90
Mystical Metal Band	Int +3	7	90
Band of Woven Gold	Int +3; Dex +1	8	100
Band of Woven Twigs	Con +3; HP +3	8	100
Ring of Crossed Staves	Int +3; HP +3	8	100
Ring of Crossed Swords	Str +3; HP +3	8	100
Ring of Masked Faces	Dex +3; HP +3	8	100
Stone Loop	Int +3; Dex +1	8	100
Empyrean Ring	Power +2; HP +3	10	89

Item	Bonus	PL	QI
Gaudy Silver Ring	Blades S. +1; Str +3	12	89
Ring of Enchantments	Enchantments S. +1; Int +4	12	100
Ring of Song	Music S. +2; Cha +1	12	100
Sprite Ring	Emp +4; Dex +3	13	90
Twisted Silver Band	Int +4; Str +3	13	90
Fagan's Signet Ring	Int, Dex, Qui +3	16	100
Ore Ring	Celtic Dual S. +2; Qui +3	16	100
Ring of the Maddened	HP +9; Int +3	16	89
Ring of Nature Affinity	Nature Affinity S. +2; Emp +3	16	100
Fury Sprite's Ring	Power +2; Int +4	17	100
Mariner Ring	Con +4; Qui +3	17	89
Polished Coral Ring	Int +3; Dex +4	18	89
Sloithi's Ring of Fortitude	Str +6; Body R. +6	18	100
Water Opal Ring	Emp +3; Con +4	18	89
Pumice Ring	Heat R. +6; Qui +7	20	100
Carved Crome Diopside Ring	HP +18	21	89
Carved Sunstone Ring	Con +6; Power +1	21	89
Ring of Blades	Blades S. +1; Qui +3; Str +4	21	90
Ring of Blunts	Blunt S. +1; Emp +3; Str +4	21	90
Keeper's Ring	Music S. +2; Dex +4	23	89
Mineralized Ring	Power +2; Nature Affinity S. +1; Emp +1; HP +3	24	89
Zephyr's Band of Power	Con, Dex +3; Power +1	24	89
Carved Red Spinel R.	Power +3; Enchant., Mental., Void Mg. S. +1	25	89
Carved Sphene Ring	Celtic Spear, Blades, Blunt, Piercing S. +1	25	89
Ether Ring	Mana Magic S. +2; Body R. +2; HP +6; Int +1	26	89
Otherworldly Ring	Cold R. +8; Int, Str +4	27	100
Ring of the Amadan	Con, Cha -2; Int, Emp +6	29	89
Ring of Undead Might	Cha, Con -2; Str, Qui +6	29	89
Crystalline Band of Wind	Cha +3; Str +6; Con +4	30	89
Fagan's Signet Ring	Matter, Cold, Heat, Spirit R. +6	31	100
Ring of Earth	Matter R. +9; Power +2; Int +6	31	90
Ring of Ice	Cold R. +9; Power +2; Int +6	31	90
Blackthorn Ring	Light Magic, Mana Magic S. +2; Int +9	34	100
Screaming Ring	Valor S. +2; Body R. +4; Con +3; HP +12	35	89
Coral Ring	Con +7; Str +9	36	89
Gem Flecked Ring	Power +2; Int +4; Con +6	36	89
Ring of the Mental Fortress	Spirit R. +4; Body R. +6; Emp, Str +4	37	89
Sentinel's Ring	Int +4; Power +4; Heat R. +4	37	89
Band of Hidden Talent	Stealth S. +2; Con, Dex +9	40	100
Ring of Questions	Int +9; Power +3; Cold R. +12	40	100
Ring of the Elder	Int +6; Power +4; Cold R. +4	41	89
Glimmer Spirit Band	Spirit R. +12; Body R. +6; Qui +6	42	89
Heatstone Band	Cold, Spirit R. +6; Cha +4; Emp +6	44	89
Empathetic Ring	Con, Emp +9; Nature Affinity S. +3	45	100
Ring of Natures Song	Emp +6; Regrowth, Nurture S. +2; HP +18	45	100
Twisted Truesilver Ring	Body R. +12; Con, Str +6	45	89
Warder's Ring	Power +2; Emp +9; Nurture S. +2; Str +7	45	100
Glimmer Striker Ring	Str, Dex +7; Con +9; Slash R. +10	50	90
Revelin's Ring	HP +30; Crush, Cold R. +10	50	100
Ring of Delightful Deception	Mental. S. +4; Power +4; Spirit R. +8	50	90
Ring of Elements	Int, Con +7; Cold, Heat R. +10	50	91
Ring of Ench. Emanations	Enchant. S. +4; Power +4; Matter R. +8	50	90
Ring of Protection	Str +7; Con +6; Energy, Heat R. +6	50	90
Shadow Ring	Emp +7; Dex, Con +9; Thrust R. +10	50	90
Shadowstrike Ring	Int, Dex, Con +7; Crush R. +10	50	90
Void Formed Ring	Void Magic S. +4; Power +4 *or* +6; Cold R. +8	50	90
Sash			
Woven Sash	Int +4; Thrust R. +4; HP +3	21	100
Shackle			
Ghoulish Shackle	Str -2; Body, Spirit R. +4; Int +6	21	89
Talisman			
Bear Claw Talisman	Power +8; Str +9	50	89

Crafting Recipes

For a more detailed description of these stats, see **Crafting** (p. 364). For crafting other items: **Arrows**: p. 363. **Siege Equipment**: p. 324. **Instruments** and **Miscellaneous** items: p. 362.

Abbreviations

Time. Time to craft the item at 1st and 10th Material Levels.

Skills. **A**rmorcraft / **C**lothworking / **F**letching / **L**eatherworking / **M**etalworking / **T**ailoring / **Wd** = Woodworking / **Wp** = Weaponcraft.

Tools. **F** = Forge / **H** = Smith's Hammer / **K** = Sewing Kit / **L** = Lathe / **P** = Planing Tool.

Components. **b** = Ore Bars / **c** = Cloth squares / **l** = Leather / **t** = Thread / **w** = Wooden boards.

Costs. Costs are listed in Silver and Copper for Material Level 1. They're listed in Gold and Silver for Material Levels 5 and 10, rounded to the nearest Silver.

Crafting Armor & Clothing

Item	Time (sec.)	Skills	Tools	Components	1st (S.C)	5th (G.S)	10th (G.S)
Cloth (+ Secondary: C (all), L (gloves, cap, boots) at (-15))							
Woven Vest	7-75	T95	K	40c,10t	1.22	7.06	71.44
Pants	5-72	T65+	K	25c,5t	0.73	4.25	43.01
Sleeves	6-74	T80+	K	16c,4t	0.49	2.82	28.58
Gloves	1-69	T15+	K	4c,3t,2l	0.24	1.40	14.14
Boots	3-71	T45+	K	2c,2t,4l	0.24	1.41	14.29
Cap	2-70	T30+	K	16c,5t,6l	0.73	4.25	43.01
Dress Robe	1-69	T15+	K	44c,25t	1.66	9.58	96.96
Leather (+ Secondary: L, C at (-15))							
Brea Jerkin	7-75	T95+	K	20l,3t	0.81	4.71	47.68
Leggings	5-72	T65+	K	12l,2t	0.49	2.85	28.87
Sleeves	6-74	T80+	K	8l,1t	0.32	1.86	18.81
Gloves	1069	T15+	K	3l,2t	0.15	0.91	9.19
Boots	3-71	T45+	K	3l,2t	0.15	0.91	9.19
Helm	2-70	T30+	K	12l,2t	0.49	2.85	28.87
Constaic Jerkin	9-76	T115+	K	29l,3t	1.15	6.65	67.36
Leggings	6-74	T85+	K	17l,2t	0.68	3.93	39.80
Sleeves	8-75	T100+	K	11l,2t	0.45	2.64	26.68
Gloves	3-70	T35+	K	5l,2t	0.23	1.34	13.56
Boots	5-72	T65+	K	5l,2t	0.23	1.34	13.56
Helm	4-71	T50+	K	17l,2t	0.68	3.93	39.80
Cruaigh Jerkin	13-81	T175+	K	56l,8t	2.28	13.13	132.97
Leggings	11-78	T145+	K	34l,4t	1.36	7.86	79.61
Sleeves	12-79	T160+	K	22l,4t	0.91	5.27	53.36
Gloves	7-75	T95+	K	10l,4t	0.46	2.68	27.12
Boots	9-77	T125+	K	10l,4t	0.46	2.68	27.12
Helm	8-76	T110+	K	34l,4t	1.36	7.86	79.61

Item	Time (sec.)	Skills	Tools	Components	1st (S.C)	5th (G.S)	10th (G.S)
Reinforced Leather (+ Secondary: L, C at (-15))							
Tacuil Vest	7-75	A95+	S,H,F	19l,4t,5s	1.24	7.14	72.32
Leggings	5-72	A65+	S,H,F	12l,2t,3s	0.75	4.36	44.18
Sleeves	6-74	A80+	S,H,F	8l,1t,2s	0.49	2.87	29.01
Gauntlets	1-69	A15+	S,H,F	2l,4t,1s	0.25	1.45	14.73
Boots	3-71	A45+	S,H,F	2l,4t,1s	0.25	1.45	14.73
Helm	2-70	A30+	S,H,F	12l,2t,3s	0.75	4.36	44.18
Nadurtha Vest	9-76	A115+	S,H,F	25l,5t,8s	1.75	10.08	102.06
Leggings	6-74	A85+	S,H,F	12l,7t,5s	1.04	6.02	60.94
Sleeves	8-75	A100+	S,H,F	8l,2t,4s	0.69	4.00	40.53
Gauntlets	3-70	A35+	S,H,F	4l,5t,1s	0.35	2.02	20.41
Boots	5-72	A65+	S,H,F	4l,5t,1s	0.35	2.02	20.41
Helm	4-71	A50+	S,H,F	12l,7t,5s	1.04	6.02	60.94
Cailiocht Vest	12-79	A155+	S,H,F	50l,10t,16s	3.50	20.16	204.12
Leggings	9-77	A125+	S,H,F	24l,14t,10s	2.09	12.04	121.89
Sleeves	11-78	A140+	S,H,F	16l,4t,8s	1.39	8.01	81.06
Gauntlets	6-73	A75+	S,H,F	8l,10t,2s	0.70	4.03	40.82
Boots	8-76	A110+	S,H,F	8l,10t,2s	0.70	4.03	40.82
Helm	7-74	A90+	S,H,F	24l,14t,10s	2.09	12.04	121.89
Scale (+ Secondary: L, M (-15)) (sc = Scales; br., cn., cr. = matching piece of Brea, Constaic, Cruaigh armor)							
Scales	1-14	M0	H,F	20b	1.75	10.08	102.06
Cruanach Hauberk	7-75	A95+	H,F	15sc,br.	27.06	155.91	1578.58
Leggings	5-72	A65+	H,F	9sc,br.	16.24	93.57	947.41
Sleeves	6-74	A80+	H,F	6sc,br.	10.82	62.34	631.17
Gloves	1-69	A15+	H,F	3sc,br.	5.40	31.15	315.37
Boots	3-71	A45+	H,F	3sc,br.	5.40	31.15	315.37
Coif	2-70	A30+	H,F	9sc,br.	16.24	93.57	947.41
Daingean Hauberk	10-78	A135+	H,F	29sc,cn.	51.90	298.97	3027.10
Leggings	8-75	A105+	H,F	18sc,cn.	32.18	185.37	1876.88
Sleeves	9-77	A120+	H,F	12sc,cn.	21.45	123.60	1251.40
Gloves	4-72	A55+	H,F	6sc,cn.	10.73	61.82	625.92
Boots	6-74	A85+	H,F	6sc,cn.	10.73	61.82	625.92
Coif	5-73	A70+	H,F	17sc,cn.	30.43	175.29	1774.82
Osnadurtha Haubrk.	13-81	A175+	H,F	46sc,cr.	82.78	476.81	4827.73
Leggings	11-78	A145+	H,F	27sc,cr.	48.61	280.02	2835.23
Sleeves	12-80	A160+	H,F	18sc,cr.	32.41	186.71	1890.44
Gauntlets	7-75	A95+	H,F	9sc,cr.	16.21	93.40	945.66
Boots	9-77	A125+	H,F	9sc,cr.	16.21	93.40	945.66
Helm	8-76	A110+	H,F	27sc,cr.	48.61	280.02	2835.23

Crafting Weapons

+ Unless otherwise noted, completing a finished weapon also requires the skills necessary to craft its two component parts, minus 15. For example, when crafting a dagger at Material Level 2, your primary skill requirement is Weaponcraft 135, but you also must have Leatherworking and Metalworking at 120 (since the blade and hilt require those skills at 135).

(5+) None of the weapons that begin at Material Level 5 will ever be part of a consignment order.

Item	Time (sec.)	Skills	Tools	Components	1st (S.C)	5th (G.S)	10th (G.S)
Blades							
Short Sword	1-55	Wp15+	F,H	hilt,blade	0.98	5.69	57.59
Blade	1-14	M15	F,H	9b	0.78	4.54	45.93
Hilt	1-14	L15	F,H	1b,1w,2l	0.20	1.15	11.66
Falcata	2-56	Wp35+	F,H	hilt,blade	1.47	8.50	86.02
Blade	1-14	M35	F,H	14b	1.22	7.06	71.44
Hilt	1-14	L35	F,H	2b,1w,1l	0.25	1.44	14.58
Broadsword	3-57	Wp55+	F,H	hilt,blade	1.82	10.51	106.43
Blade	1-14	M55	F,H	18b	1.57	9.07	91.85
Hilt	1-14	L55	F,H	2b,1w,1l	0.25	1.44	14.58
Longsword	5-59	Wp75+	F,H	hilt,blade	2.47	14.26	144.34
Blade	1-15	M75	F,H	25b	2.18	12.60	127.58
Hilt	1-15	L75	F,H	2b,1w,2l	0.28	1.66	16.77
Bastard Sword	6-60	Wp95+	F,H	hilt,blade	2.96	17.06	172.77
Blade	1-15	M95	F,H	31b	2.71	15.62	158.19
Hilt	1-15	L95	F,H	2b,1w,1l	0.25	1.44	14.58
Crescent Sw. (5+)	31-61	Wp515+	F,H	hilt,blade	–	20.81	210.68
Blade	8-15	M515	F,H	38b	–	19.15	193.91
Hilt	8-15	L515	F,H	2b,1w,2l	–	1.66	16.77
Guarded Rapier (5+)	31-61	Wp515+	F,H	hilt,blade	–	19.80	200.48
Blade	8-15	M515	F,H	36b	–	18.14	183.71
Hilt	8-15	L515	F,H	2b,1w,2l	–	1.66	16.77
Sickle (5+)	31-61	Wp515+	F,H	hilt,blade	–	20.81	210.68
Blade	8-15	M515	F,H	38b	–	19.15	193.91
Hilt	8-15	L515	F,H	2b,1w,2l	–	1.66	16.77
Blunt							
Club	1-55	Wp15+	F,H	haft,head	0.97	5.62	56.86
Haft	1-14	Wd15	F,H,P	1b,19w	0.80	4.61	46.66
Head	1-14	M15	F,H	2b	0.17	1.01	10.21
Mace	2-56	Wp35+	F,H	haft,head	1.51	8.71	88.21
Haft	1-14	Wd35	F,H,P	1b,3w	0.20	1.15	11.66
Head	1-14	M35	F,H	15b	1.31	7.56	76.55
Spiked Club	3-57	Wp55+	F,H	haft,spikes	1.81	10.44	105.71
Haft	1-14	Wd55	F,H,P	1b,32w	1.28	7.42	75.09
Club Spikes	1-14	M55	F,H	6b	0.52	3.02	30.62
Hammer	5-59	Wp75+	F,H	haft,head	2.15	12.38	125.39
Haft	1-15	Wd75	F,H,P	2b,6w	0.40	2.30	23.33
Head	1-15	M75	F,H	20b	1.75	10.08	102.06
Spiked Mace	6-60	Wp95+	F,H	haft,head	2.85	16.42	166.21
Haft	1-15	Wd95	F,H,P	2b,6w	0.40	2.30	23.33
Head	1-15	M95	F,H	28b	2.45	14.11	142.88
Pick Hammer (5+)	31-61	Wp515+	F,H	haft,blade	–	19.37	196.10
Haft	6-14	Wd455	F,H,P	2b,8w	–	2.74	27.70
Head	8-15	M515	F,H	33b	–	16.63	168.40
Celtic Spear							
Short Spear	1-55	Wp15+	F,H	shaft,head	0.98	5.69	57.59
Shaft	1-14	Wd15	F,H,P	1b,10w	0.46	2.66	26.97
Spearhead	1-14	M15	F,H	6b	0.52	3.02	30.62
Spear	2-56	Wp35+	F,H	shaft,head	1.50	8.64	87.48
Shaft	1-14	Wd35	F,H,P	2b,12w	0.62	3.60	36.45
Spearhead	1-14	M35	F,H	10b	0.87	5.04	51.03
Long Spear	3-57	Wp55+	F,H	shaft,head	2.15	12.38	125.39
Shaft	1-14	Wd55	F,H,P	2b,13w	0.66	3.82	38.64
Spearhead	1-14	M55	F,H	17b	1.48	8.57	86.75
War Spear	5-59	Wp75+	F,H	shaft,head	2.46	14.18	143.61
Shaft	1-15	Wd75	F,H,P	2b,12w	0.62	3.60	36.45
Spearhead	1-15	M75	F,H	21b	1.83	10.58	107.16

Item	Time (sec.)	Skills	Tools	Components	1st (S.C)	5th (G.S)	10th (G.S)
Barbed Spear	6-60	Wp95+	F,H	shaft,head	2.81	16.20	164.03
Shaft	1-15	Wd95	F,H,P	2b,12w	0.62	3.60	36.45
Spearhead	1-15	M95	F,H	25b	2.18	12.60	127.58
Hooked Spear (5+)	31-61	Wp515+	F,H	shaft,blade	–	23.90	242.03
Haft	7-14	Wd455	F,H,P	2b,8w	–	2.74	27.70
Head	8-15	M515	F,H	42b	–	21.17	214.33
Large Weaponry							
Two Handed Sword	2-56	Wp35+	F,H	haft,head	1.82	10.51	106.43
Blade	1-14	M35	F,H	18b	1.57	9.07	91.85
Hilt	1-14	L35	F,H	2b,1w,1l	0.25	1.44	14.58
Big Shillelagh	2-56	Wp35+	F,H	haft,spikes	2.22	12.82	129.76
Shillelagh Haft	1-14	Wd35	F,H,P	2b,8w	0.47	2.74	27.70
Shillelagh Spikes	1-14	M35	F,H	20b	1.75	10.08	102.06
Two-H. Spkd. Mace	5-59	Wp75+	F,H	haft,head	2.92	16.85	170.59
Haft	1-15	Wd75	F,H,P	2b,8w	0.47	2.74	27.70
Head	1-15	M75	F,H	28b	2.45	14.11	142.88
Great Hammer	3-57	Wp55+	F,H	haft,head	3.10	17.86	180.79
Haft	1-14	Wd55	F,H,P	2b,8w	0.47	2.74	27.70
Head	1-14	M55	F,H	30b	2.62	15.12	153.09
Great Sword	6-60	Wp95+	F,H	hilt,blade	3.48	20.09	203.39
Blade	1-15	M95	F,H	37b	3.23	18.65	188.81
Hilt	1-15	L95	F,H	2b,1w,1l	0.25	1.44	14.58
Great Falcata (5+)	31-61	Wp515+	F,H	hilt,blade	–	24.34	246.40
Blade	8-15	M515	F,H	45b	–	22.68	229.64
Hilt	8-15	L515	F,H	2b,1w,2l	–	1.66	16.77
Sledge Ham. (5+)	31-61	Wp515+	F,H	haft,blade	-	23.90	242.03
Haft	7-14	Wd455	F,H,P	2b,8w	–	2.74	27.70
Head	8-15	M515	F,H	42b	–	21.17	214.33
Piercing							
Dirk	1-55	Wp15+	F,H	hilt,blade	0.81	4.68	47.39
Blade	1-14	M15	F,H	7b	0.61	3.53	35.72
Hilt	1-14	L15	F,H	1b,1w,2l	0.20	1.15	11.66
Dagger	2-56	Wp35+	F,H	hilt,blade	1.16	6.70	67.80
Blade	1-14	M35	F,H	10b	0.87	5.04	51.03
Hilt	1-14	L35	F,H	2b,1w,2l	0.28	1.66	16.77
Stiletto	3-57	Wp55+	F,H	hilt,blade	1.82	10.51	106.43
Blade	1-14	M55	F,H	18b	1.57	9.07	91.85
Hilt	1-14	L55	F,H	2b,1w,1l	0.25	1.44	14.58
Rapier	5-59	Wp75+	F,H	hilt,blade	2.17	12.53	126.85
Blade	1-15	M75	F,H	22b	1.92	11.09	112.27
Hilt	1-15	L75	F,H	2b,1w,1l	0.25	1.44	14.58
Curved Dagger	6-60	Wp95+	F,H	hilt,blade	2.78	16.06	162.57
Blade	1-15	M95	F,H	29b	2.53	14.62	147.99
Hilt	1-15	L95	F,H	2b,1w,1l	0.25	1.44	14.58
Staff (+ Secondary: M, Wd, L, all at 0)							
Staff	2-56	F40+	L,H,P	4b,25w,1l	1.32	7.63	77.27
Shod Staff	5-59	F80+	L,H,P	4b,38w,1l	1.81	10.44	105.71
Short Bow (+ Secondary: Wd, C, both at 30 below Primary)							
Short Bow	1-55	F15+	P,L	21w,2t	0.83	4.80	48.55
Recurve Bow (+ Secondary: Wd, C, both at 20 below Primary)							
Short Recurve Bow	2-56	F40+	P,L	24w,4t	0.99	5.70	57.74
Recurve Bow	4-58	F65+	P,L	32w,6t	1.33	7.69	77.86
Great Recurve Bow	5-59	F90+	P,L	44w,8t	1.83	10.54	106.73

Monsters

For more complete descriptions of what these stats describe, and a chart of which type of attack works best against each body type, see **Monster Stats**, p. 373.

Abbreviations

Speed. Slow, **M**edium, **F**ast, **2x**, **3x**, **4x** (two, three and four times faster than the average PC).

Aggr. (Aggression). **L**ow, **M**edium, **H**igh (with percent chance that it will attack).

Attack Type. Crush, **S**lash, **T**hrust. Information after a slash ("/") is type and percent chance of secondary attack.

Combat Modifier. Monster's modifier to hit / modifier to avoid being hit (defense) / modifier to hit points. When there is just one number, it modifies all three situations.

Social. Social monsters might group; **Call** means it is Social and might call for help.

Body Type. The body types are:

BU	Bony Undead	**EW**	Elemental Water	**Pl**	Plate
Ch	Chain	**FM**	Feeble-Minded	**Rp**	Reptile (Scaled)
Cl	Cloth	**FU**	Fleshy Undead	**Sh**	Shell (Chitin)
DV	Darkness/Void	**FA**	Furry Animal	**Soft**	Soft
EA	Elemental Air	**IU**	Incorporeal Undead	**St**	Studded Leather
EE	Elemental Earth	**Lr**	Leather	**TP**	Tree/Plant
EF	Elemental Fire	**LE**	Light Energy	**Tr**	Troll-like
EI	Elemental Ice	**ME**	Magical Energy		

Monster	Lvl	Body Type	Spd	Agg	Atk Spd	Atk Type	Ev %	Comb Mod	Soc. Call
Animal									
Aqueous Slug	23	Soft	S/145	H/99	3.8	S	–	–	Soc.
Badger	9-11	FA	M/170	L/5	3.5	S	–	–	Soc.
Badger Cub	0	FA	S/160	–	3.8	S	–	–	Soc.
Beach Rat	1-2	FA	S/150	–	3.8	T	–	-20/-20/-	–
Bird-Eating Frog	20-22	Soft	M/175	–	3.8	C	–	–	–
Black Badger	36-40	FA	M/188	–	3.6	S	–	–	–
Bog Frog	47-50	Soft	M/195	–	3.8	C	–	–	–
Bog Worm	30	Rp	M/188	–	3.8	S	–	–	–
Cave Toad	22	Soft	M/175	–	3.8	C	–	–	Soc.
Death Worm	14	Soft	S/165	H/99	3.8	S	–	–	–
Derg Monster	5	Rp	M/188	–	3.8	T	–	–	–
Faerie Badger	32-34	FA	M/188	–	3.8	S	–	–	–
Faerie Horse	18-23	FA	F/220	–	3.7	C	–	–	Call
Faerie Steed	19-24	FA	F/225	–	3.7	C	–	–	Call
Fee Lion	25-27	FA	M/190	M/30	3.5	S/S5	3	–	–
Fishing Bear	18-20	FA	M/180	–	3.8	T	1	–	Call
Fishing Bear Cub	11-12	FA	M/188	L/5	3.7	T	–	–	Soc.
Fishing Bear Forager	13-14	FA	M/175	–	3.8	T	1	–	Call
Fomorian Wolfbeast	46-49	FA	F/230	H/80	3.8	T/T1	–	–	Soc.
Glow Worm	36	LE	M/188	–	3.8	C	–	-10/-10/-	–
Gorge Rat	30-31	FA	M/190	L/5	3.6	T	–	–	–
Greater Luch	24-27	FA	M/190	–	3.8	T	3	–	–
Hill Hound	18-20	FA	M/195	–	3.5	T	1	–	–
Hill Toad	5-7	Soft	M/175	–	3.8	C	–	-20/-20/-	–
Horned Cave Toad	23	Soft	M/175	–	3.8	T/T2	–	–	Soc.
Horse	55	FA	3x/600	–	4.0	C	–	–	–
Ick Worm	17	Rp	S/165	–	3.8	S	–	–	Soc.
Ire Wolf	25-27	FA	M/210	M/50	3.5	T	1	–	Soc.
Juvenile Megafelid	35-38	FA	M/200	–	3.7	S/S1	–	–	–
Lair Worm	31-35	Rp	M/188	–	3.8	T	–	-10/-10/-	–
Large Frog	0-1	Soft	S/150	–	3.8	C	–	–	–
Large Luch	18-21	FA	M/190	–	3.8	T	1	–	–
Large Red Wolfhound	17-19	FA	M/200	–	3.7	T/S5	1	–	–
Levian	60-62	FA	M/200	M/30	3.8	S	–	–	–
Levian-Al	50-54	FA	M/200	M/30	3.8	S	–	–	–
Lough Wolf	7-9	FA	M/200	–	3.8	T	–	–	–
Lough Wolf Cadger	2-3	FA	M/200	–	3.8	T	–	–	–
Luch Catcher	25-28	FA	M/200	L/1	3.7	S/S3	1	–	–
Luch Hunter	31-34	FA	M/200	L/1	3.6	S/S8	1	–	–
Megafelid	39-42	FA	M/215	M/60	3.5	S/S5	–	–	–
Mindworm	57-59	Rp	M/175	M/30	3.8	C	–	–	–
Morass Leech	41-43	Rp	M/175	L/10	3.8	S	–	–	–
Poisonous Cave Toad	22	Soft	M/175	–	3.8	C	–	-20	Soc.
Rage Wolf	31-32	FA	F/220	H/80	3.5	T	1	–	Soc.
Red Wolfhound	10-13	FA	M/200	–	3.7	T/S5	1	–	–
Roan Stepper	29-32	FA	M/210	–	4.0	C	–	–	–
Root Worm	18-21	Rp	S/165	–	3.8	S	–	–	Soc.
Savage Fishing Bear	52-53	FA	M/188	H/80	3.3	T	3	–	–
Scourge Rat	10-23	FA	M/188	L/5	3.6	T	–	–	Soc.
Sett Dweller	27-31	FA	M/175	–	3.8	S	–	–	Call
Sett Matron	35-38	FA	M/178	–	3.7	S	–	–	Call
Sett Protector	32-33	FA	M/180	M/60	3.6	S/S3	–	–	Soc.
Sett Youngling	20-24	FA	M/172	–	3.8	S	–	–	Call
Shaft Rat	36	FA	M/188	L/5	3.3	T	–	-10/-10/-	–
Shock Aqueous Slug	24	Soft	S/145	H/99	3.8	S	–	–	Soc.
Silvermine Badger	22-23	FA	M/180	L/5	3.3	S/S4	–	–	–
Squabbler	28-30	FA	M/188	–	3.7	T	1	–	–
Swamp Hopper	43-44	Soft	M/188	–	3.8	C	–	–	–
Torc	34-37	FA	M/195	–	3.8	S	–	–	–
Torcan	31	FA	M/195	–	3.8	S	–	–	–
Umber Bear	42-45	FA	M/205	–	3.3	C/S1	–	–	–
Unearthed Cave Bear	49-51	FA	M/210	–	3.8	C/S4	–	–	–
Water Badger	21-23	FA	M/175	L/5	3.8	S	–	–	–
White Boar	40-41	FA	M/195	–	3.8	S	–	–	–
Wiggle Worm	0	Soft	S/150	–	3.8	C	–	–	–
Young Badger	7	FA	M/170	L/5	3.5	S	–	–	Soc.
Demon									
Abysmal	50	DV	M/188	H/80	2.9	S	–	–	–
Cruach Imp	33-35	ME	M/188	L/20	3.8	T	1	–	–
Cruiach Demon	55-57	DV	M/188	H/80	3.5	S/S5	–	-10	Soc.

Monster	Lvl	Body Type	Spd	Agg	Atk Spd	Atk Type	Ev %	Comb Mod	Soc. Call
Deamhan Aeir	34-37	EA	M/200	H/80	3.5	S/S7	5	-20	–
Deamhan Creig	17-18	EE	M/188	L/10	3.8	C	–	-10	–
Deamhan Hound	40-42	FA	M/205	M/50	3.3	T	–	-10	Soc.
Mountain Mephit	20-23	EE	M/188	M/30	3.8	C/C5	1	-5	–
Parthanan	17-18	EE	M/205	M/60	3.6	S	–	–	–
Tunnel Imp	38	DV	M/188	M/30	3.0	S	2	-10/-10/-	–

Dragon

Monster	Lvl	Body Type	Spd	Agg	Atk Spd	Atk Type	Ev %	Comb Mod	Soc. Call
Faerie Drake	20-22	Rp	M/188	–	3.5	T	1	-20	Soc.

Elemental

Monster	Lvl	Body Type	Spd	Agg	Atk Spd	Atk Type	Ev %	Comb Mod	Soc. Call
Bodachan Sabhaill	2-4	Cl	M/188	–	3.8	S	–	–	–
Chipstone Sheerie	21	EE	M/198	M/50	3.7	C	–	-10	Call
Clubmoss Sheerie	11	TP	M/188	H/80	3.8	S	1	-5	Soc.
Dew Sheerie	16-19	EW	M/188	H/70	3.8	S	–	-20	Soc.
Earth Sprite	24-26	EE	M/192	M/30	3.6	C	–	–	Soc.
Earthshaker	47-49	EE	M/179	L/1	3.9	C	–	-10	–
Gale	16-18	EA	M/215	M/30	3.5	S	2	-10	Soc.
Grass Sheerie	13-15	TP	M/188	H/80	3.8	S	1	-20	Soc.
Greater Zephyr	31-33	EA	M/205	L/1	3.7	S	2	-10	Soc.
Lesser Zephyr	23-24	EA	M/180	–	3.4	S	–	-20	–
Lode Protector	47-48	EE	M/188	H/80	4.2	C	–	–	–
Mist Sheerie	20-21	EW	M/188	H/70	3.8	S	–	-20	Soc.
Moss Monster	40-41	TP	M/179	–	3.9	C	–	-10/-10/-	–
Moss Sheerie	9-12	TP	M/188	H/80	3.8	S	1	-5	Soc.
Mudman	2-4	EE	M/170	–	3.8	C	–	–	–
Pit Boss	23-24	FA	M/188	L/10	3.8	S	–	–	Soc.
Pit Spraggon	20-22	FA	M/188	–	3.8	S	–	–	Soc.
Rock Golem	35-37	EE	M/180	–	3.8	C	–	–	Soc.
Rock Guardian	21-22	EE	M/188	–	3.8	C	–	-20	–
Rock Sheerie	18-21	EE	M/198	M/50	3.7	C	–	-10	Call
Rock Sprite	21-23	EE	M/175	–	4.0	S	–	–	Soc.
Rockbiter	37	EE	M/188	–	3.6	C	–	–	–
Sandman	2-4	EE	M/170	–	3.8	C	–	–	–
Scragger	30-32	Tr	M/180	L/5	3.8	C	–	–	Soc.
Small Walking Rock	2-3	EE	M/188	–	3.8	C	–	–	–
Spraggon	3-5	Cl	M/188	–	3.8	S	–	–	Call
Spraggon Cutter	23-25	FA	M/188	L/10	3.8	S	–	–	Soc.
Spraggon Runner	21-23	FA	M/188	L/10	3.7	S	–	–	–
Spraggon Springer	22-24	FA	M/188	M/30	3.7	S	–	–	Soc.
Spraggonale	21-23	Cl	M/188	L/10	3.7	S	–	–	Call
Spraggonite	5-6	Cl	M/188	L/10	3.8	S	–	–	Call
Spraggonix	25-26	FA	M/188	H/80	3.7	C	–	–	Soc.
Spraggonoll	7-9	Cl	M/188	L/10	3.8	S	–	–	Call
Spraggonote	24-25	FA	M/188	M/40	3.7	S	–	–	Soc.
Stone Sheerie	19-22	EE	M/198	M/50	3.7	C	–	-10	Call
Streaming Wisp	21-24	EA	M/200	–	3.8	S	4	-10	Soc.
Tidal Sheerie	35-39	EW	M/188	M/50	3.8	S	–	-10	Call
Vein Golem	49	EE	M/188	–	4.3	C	–	–	–
Walking Rock	24	EE	M/188	–	3.8	C	–	–	–

Giant

Monster	Lvl	Body Type	Spd	Agg	Atk Spd	Atk Type	Ev %	Comb Mod	Soc. Call
Fomorian Annag	55-56	FM	F/220	H/99	4.2	C	–	-/-/25	Call
Fomorian Cyclen	46-47	FM	F/220	H/99	3.9	C	–	-/-/5	Call
Fomorian Gehk	47-49	FA	F/220	H/99	3.9	C	–	-/-/5	Call
Fomorian Gleener	61-62	Sh	F/220	H/99	4.2	C	–	-/-/35	Call
Fomorian Goblern	49-50	FM	F/220	H/99	4.0	C	–	-/-/10	Call
Fomorian Grabeye	53-55	FM	F/220	H/99	4.1	C	–	-/-/20	Call
Fomorian Grencher	50-52	FU	F/220	H/99	4.1	C	–	-/-/15	Call
Fomorian Underling	37-38	FM	M/188	H/70	3.8	C	–	–	Soc.
Giant Lusus	58-61	Soft	M/179	M/30	3.8	C	–	–	–

Human-like

Monster	Lvl	Body Type	Spd	Agg	Atk Spd	Atk Type	Ev %	Comb Mod	Soc. Call
Amadan Touched	29-34	Cl	M/178	H/70	3.9	S	–	-10	–
Annoying Lucradan	0	Cl	M/188	–	3.8	S	–	-10	–
Azure Avenger	51-55	Cl	F/250	H/80	3.4	S/S5	–	–	Call
Azure Banisher	48-52	Cl	F/250	H/80	3.6	T/T1	–	–	Call
Azure Cleanser	45-49	Cl	F/250	H/80	3.8	C	–	–	Call
Azure Idolater	24-25	Cl	F/250	–	3.5	S/S5	–	–	Call
Bodach	31-32	Cl	M/188	H/80	3.8	C	–	–	Call
Boogie Man	34	Cl	M/188	M/30	3.8	C	–	–	–
Cliff Dweller	36-38	Cl	M/188	–	3.8	S	–	–	Call
Cliff Dweller Hunter	37-38	Pl	M/200	L/2	3.5	T/T2	1	–	Call
Cliff Dweller Spearman	38-40	Pl	M/188	L/10	3.5	T/T3	1	–	Call
Cluricaun	22-24	Cl	M/188	L/1	3.8	C	–	-5	–
Cluricaun Aquavitor	40	Cl	M/188	L/1	3.6	C	–	-20	–
Cluricaun Trip	7-9	Cl	M/188	L/5	3.8	C	1	-5	–
Coerced Groover	45	Cl	M/188	–	3.8	C	–	–	Soc.
Collared Gemgetter	38-39	Cl	M/188	–	3.8	C	–	–	Soc.
Corpan Side	39-41	Cl	M/188	M/60	3.8	T	–	–	–
Curm. Crab-Catcher	11	Lr	M/188	H/70	3.7	S	–	–	Call
Curmudgeon Fighter	16-18	St	M/188	H/70	3.6	S/T4	–	–	Call
Curm. Harvester	9-11	Lr	M/188	H/70	3.7	S	–	–	Call
Curmudgeon Poacher	15	Lr	M/188	H/70	3.7	T	2	–	Call
Curmudgeon Puggard	39-40	Lr	M/188	H/80	3.8	T	2	–	Call
Curmudgeon Ratoner	31-33	Lr	M/188	H/80	3.8	T	–	–	Call
Curm. Rockclimber	14-15	Lr	M/188	L/10	3.8	S	–	–	Call
Curmudgeon Scout	15-17	St	M/188	M/60	3.5	S/T2	2	–	Call
Curm. Scrapper	40-43	St	M/188	H/80	3.7	T	3	–	Call
Curmudgeon Skinner	10-11	Lr	M/188	H/70	3.7	S	–	–	Call
Curmudgeon Trapper	11-12	Lr	M/188	H/70	3.7	S	2	-8/-8/-	Call
Curmudgeon Wanter	34-35	Lr	M/188	H/80	3.8	T	–	–	Call
Dergan Enchanter	12	Cl	M/188	H/70	3.8	T	–	-20	Call
Dergan Fury	13-15	Cl	M/188	H/70	3.4	S/S3	–	–	Call
Dergan Tussler	14	St	M/188	M/60	3.6	T/S3	2	–	Call
Elfshot Madman	34-36	Cl	M/188	–	3.8	C	–	–	–
Enthralled Silvier	36-37	Cl	M/188	L/1	3.8	C	–	–	Soc.
Eriu Ambusher	19	Lr	M/188	H/80	3.7	T/S1	2	–	Soc.
Eriu Fiscere	13-15	Cl	M/188	L/5	3.8	T	–	–	Call
Eriu Henter	19-22	Cl	M/188	L/5	3.8	T	–	–	Call
Eriu Kedger	16-18	Cl	M/188	L/5	3.8	T	–	–	Call
Eriu Waylayer	26-27	Lr	M/188	H/80	3.7	T/S1	2	–	Soc.
Fachan	47-49	Cl	M/172	H/80	3.8	C	–	–	–
Feckless Lucragan	4	Cl	M/188	–	3.8	S	–	–	–
Forest Poacher	53-55	St	M/188	–	3.5	T	3	–	Soc.
Gan Ceanach	50-53	St	M/188	H/80	3.8	S	–	–	–
Geas-Bound Hewer	39	Cl	M/188	L/1	3.8	C	–	–	Soc.
Goborchend	46-49	Ch	M/195	H/80	3.8	C/C4	4	–	Call
Goborchend Gasher	52-55	Ch	M/195	H/80	3.8	S/S4	4	–	Call
Goborchend Piercer	50-53	Ch	M/195	H/80	3.8	T/T4	4	–	Call
Goborchend Wounder	54-56	Ch	M/195	H/80	3.6	T/T4	4	–	Call
Grogan	46-47	Cl	M/188	–	3.8	C	–	–	Call
Gurite Ambusher	19	Lr	M/188	H/80	3.7	T/S1	2	–	Soc.
Gurite Assailer	23-24	St	M/188	H/80	3.7	T/S2	–	–	Call
Gurite Footpad	16	St	M/188	H/80	3.7	T/T2	2	–	Soc.
Gurite Lookout	37	St	–	H/80	3.7	T	2	–	Call
Gurite Raider	37-39	St	M/188	H/80	3.4	T/S5	–	–	Call
Gurite Seeker	31	St	M/188	H/80	3.6	S/S4	4	–	Call
Gurite Tempriar	24	Ch	M/188	H/80	3.7	S/S2	–	–	Call
Gurite Waylayer	26-27	Lr	M/188	H/80	3.7	T/S1	2	–	Soc.
Koalinth Bouncer	20	EW	M/192	H/99	4.4	S	5	–	Soc.
Koalinth Castellan	26	EW	M/188	H/80	4.4	C	5	–	Soc.
Koalinth Elder	27	EW	M/188	H/80	4.4	C	–	–	Soc.

Monster	Lvl	Body Type	Spd	Agg	Atk Spd	Atk Type	Ev %	Comb Mod	Soc. Call
Koalinth Envoy	23-25	EW	M/192	H/99	4.4	S	5	–	–
Koalinth Guardian	24	EW	M/192	H/99	4.4	S	5	–	Soc.
Koalinth Sentinel	18-22	EW	M/192	H/99	4.4	S	5	–	Soc.
Koalinth Slinker	34-38	Rp	M/188	M/50	3.6	T/S1	–	–	Soc.
Koalinth Spectator	19	EW	M/192	H/99	4.4	S	5	–	–
Koalinth Warden	19	EW	M/192	H/99	4.4	S	5	–	Soc.
Koalinth Warder	20	EW	M/192	H/99	4.4	S	5	–	Soc.
Koalinth Wrestler	20	EW	M/192	H/99	4.4	S	5	–	–
Leprechaun	48-50	Cl	M/188	M/60	3.8	C	–	–	–
Loghery Man	46	Cl	M/188	–	3.8	C	–	-20	–
Lugradan	25	Cl	M/188	M/30	3.8	S	5	-5	–
Lugradan	27-30	Cl	M/188	M/30	3.8	S	5	-5	–
Lugradan Whelp	4-6	Cl	M/188	–	3.8	T	–	–	–
Luricaduane	6-8	Cl	M/188	L/5	3.8	S	1	-5	–
Merrow	20-22	Rp/Cl	M/180	–	3.8	C	–	–	Call
Moheran Distorter	17-19	Cl	M/188	H/80	3.8	S	–	-20	Call
Orchard Nipper	5-6	Cl	M/188	L/5	3.8	C	–	-5	–
Primrose	10	Cl	M/188	–	3.8	S	–	–	–
Raging Subverter	39-43	Lr	M/188	H/80	3.3	T/T3	–	–	–
Roane Maiden	12-13	Cl	M/188	–	3.8	C	–	–	Call
Rowdy	5-8	Lr	M/188	H/100	3.8	C	–	–	–
Sheevra Archer	14	St	M/188	M/60	3.5	T	2	–	Call
Sheevra Chieftain	15-16	St	M/188	M/60	3.5	S/S6	–	–	Call
Sheevra Miner	13-14	Lr	M/188	L/10	3.8	T	–	–	Call
Sheevra Skirmisher	13-15	St	M/188	M/60	3.6	T/S3	2	–	Call
Sheevra Swordsman	12-13	Lr	M/188	M/60	3.5	S	–	–	Call
Siabra Anchorite	41	Cl	M/188	H/80	3.8	S	–	-20/-20/-	Call
Siabra Archmagi	57-65	Cl	M/188	H/80	4.0	C	–	-20	Call
Siabra Guardian	56-64	Pl	M/188	H/80	3.2	S/T4	4	-10	Call
Siabra Lookout	47	St	–	H/80	3.7	T	2	–	Call
Siabra Mireguard	38	St	M/188	H/80	3.6	S	2	–	Call
Siabra Raider	37-39	St	M/188	H/80	3.4	T/S5	–	–	Call
Siabra Seeker	30-13	St	M/188	H/80	3.6	S/S4	4	–	Call
Siabra Venator	46-48	Ch	M/188	H/80	3.4	T	4	-10	Call
Siabra Waterwalker	49-52	Lr	M/188	H/80	4.0	C	–	-20	Call
Siabra Wayguard	43-44	St	M/188	H/80	3.5	S	2	–	Call
Silvermine Guard	45	St	M/188	H/80	3.2	S/S5	2	–	Soc.
Silvermine Knocker	36-37	Cl	M/188	L/1	3.8	C	2	–	–
Silvermine Sentry	39	St	M/188	H/80	3.2	S/S5	2	–	Soc.
Siog Footpad	15-16	St	M/188	H/80	3.7	T/T2	2	–	Soc.
Siog Piller	18-19	St	M/188	H/80	3.7	T/T3	2	–	Call
Siog Raider	37	St	M/188	H/80	3.4	T/S5	–	–	Call
Siog Seeker	28-31	St	M/188	H/80	3.6	S/S4	4	–	Call
Siog Waylayer	19	Lr	M/188	H/80	3.7	T/S1	2	–	Soc.
Tomb Creeper	9-16	Cl	M/188	H/99	3.7	S/T1	–	–	Soc.
Trammer	36	Cl	M/188	–	3.8	C	–	–	Soc.
Troglodyte	36-37	Rp	M/180	L/25	3.8	C	–	–	Soc.
Unseelie Overman	49	Ch	M/188	H/80	3.3	S	–	–	Call
Unseelie Underviewer	42	Lr	M/188	H/80	3.5	S/S1	2	–	Call
Unseelie Viewer	48	Ch	M/188	H/80	3.3	S	–	–	Call
Ursine Dweller	36	FA	M/205	M/50	3.8	S	–	–	Soc.
Ursine Patrol	37	FA	M/205	M/50	3.8	S	–	–	Soc.
Ursine Shaman	38	FA	M/205	M/50	3.8	S	–	-10/-15/-	Soc.
Ursine Sorcerer	39	FA	M/205	M/50	3.8	C	–	-15/-10/-	Soc.
Ursine Thrall	33-36	Cl	M/188	L/1	3.8	C	–	–	Soc.
Ursine Warrior	37	FA	M/205	M/50	3.8	C	–	–	Soc.
Villainous Youth	3-4	Lr	M/188	H/100	3.8	S	–	–	Call
Watery Escort	18	EW	M/192	H/99	4.4	S	5	–	Soc.
Wild Lucradan	9-10	Cl	M/188	L/20	3.6	S	–	-5	–
Insect									
Arachnid	37-39	Sh	M/200	M/50	3.8	T	–	–	Soc.
Arachnite	28-30	Sh	M/200	L/25	3.8	T	–	–	Soc.
Bloodletter	48-49	Sh	F/220	M/50	3.4	T/T5	–	-10	–
Bog Crawler	46-47	Sh	M/188	–	3.8	T	–	–	–
Bog Creeper	42-44	Sh	M/188	–	3.8	T	–	–	–
Carrion Scorpionida	15	Sh	S/165	H/99	3.8	S	–	–	Soc.
Cliff Beetle	31-37	Sh	M/188	L/5	3.8	T	–	–	–
Cliff Hanger	36-39	Sh	M/188	–	3.8	T	–	–	–
Crypt Spider	10-12	Sh	M/192	H/99	3.6	S	–	–	–
Dampwood Mite	22	Sh	M/188	L/10	3.6	T	–	–	Soc.
Detrital Crab	42	Sh	M/188	L/10	3.6	S/S3	–	–	–
Eirebug	4-5	Sh	S/165	–	3.9	T	–	–	–
Faerie Beetle	17	Sh	M/188	–	3.8	T	–	–	–
Forest Scourge Scorp.	57	Sh	M/190	–	3.5	C/T4	3	–	Soc.
Gemclicker	37-39	Sh	M/188	–	3.8	T	–	–	–
Gemclicker Horder	40	Sh	M/188	–	3.8	T	–	–	–
Giant Ant	21-24	Sh	M/180	–	3.8	T	–	–	Call
Giant Beetle	20-21	Sh	M/188	L/5	3.8	T	–	–	–
Large Eirebug	9-11	Sh	M/185	–	3.8	T	–	–	–
Larval Predator	36	Sh	M/188	M/65	2.1	T/S50	–	–	–
Malefic Forest Scorpion	61	Sh	M/190	–	3.5	C/T4	3	–	Soc.
Malevolent For. Scorp.	59	Sh	M/190	–	3.5	C/T4	3	–	Soc.
Pelagian Alliant	28	Sh	M/192	H/99	4.4	S	5	–	Soc.
Pelagian Crab	25-26	Sh	M/192	H/99	4.4	S	5	–	Soc.
Pelagian Guard	28	Sh	M/192	H/99	4.4	S	5	–	Soc.
Rock Clipper	21-23	Sh	M/185	–	3.8	T	–	–	–
Sand Crab	0-1	Sh	S/150	–	3.8	S	–	-20/-20/-	–
Small Freshwater Crab	4	Sh	S/165	–	3.8	T	–	–	–
Water Beetle	6-8	Sh	S/165	–	3.8	T	–	–	Soc.
Water Beetle Collector	4-5	Sh	S/165	–	3.8	T	–	–	Call
Water Beetle Larva	0-1	Sh	S/145	–	3.8	C	–	-20/-20/-	Soc.
Magical									
Alp Luachra	29-31	Cl	M/188	H/70	3.5	T	–	-10	–
Anger Sprite	11-13	Cl	M/192	H/90	3.7	S/S3	–	–	Soc.
Aughisky	31-33	FA	M/188	M/50	3.8	S	–	–	–
Barca	10-12	Cl	M/188	H/80	3.8	C	–	–	–
Bocaidhe	27-29	Cl	M/188	–	3.8	S	–	-20/-20/-	–
Breaker Roane Comp.	46-47	Rp	M/188	–	3.8	S	–	–	Call
Changeling	11	Cl	M/188	M/50	3.8	C	–	–	–
Empyrean Elder	41-44	St	M/188	–	3.9	C	–	-20/-20/-	Call
Empyrean Guardian	34-38	St	M/188	–	3.5	S/S9	6	–	Call
Empyrean Keeper	23-25	St	M/188	–	3.9	C	–	-20/-20/-	Call
Empyrean Orb	10	Cl	M/188	–	3.8	T	–	–	–
Empyrean Overseer	37-39	St	M/188	–	3.4	S/S10	8	–	Call
Empyrean Sentinel	25-29	St	M/188	–	3.9	C	–	-20/-20/-	Call
Empyrean Watcher	16-18	St	M/188	–	3.7	T/S3	2	–	Call
Empyrean Wisp	13-15	TP	M/190	–	3.8	T	–	-20/-20/-	–
Evanescer	33-35	FA	M/188	M/30	3.6	T	–	-20/-20/-	–
Far Darrig	46-48	Cl	M/188	M/60	3.8	C	–	-20/-20/-	–
Far Dorocha	50-55	Ch	M/210	H/80	3.1	T/T8	–	–	Soc.
Far Dorocha	53-62	IU/Ch	M/210	H/80	3.8	T/T8	–	–	–
Fear Dearc	46-47	Cl	M/188	M/60	3.8	S	–	–	–
Feccan	1-3	Cl	M/188	–	3.8	C	–	–	–
Fetch	15	Cl	M/188	M/30	3.8	C	–	-/-10/-	–
Fury Sprite	14-16	Cl	M/188	H/80	3.5	T/S2	–	–	Soc.
Glimmer Ardent	45-49	FU	F/250	H/80	3.8	S	–	-/-25/-	Call
Glimmer Avenger	65	Pl	3x/600	H/99	3.8	S	–	10/20/10	Soc.
Glimmer Deathwatcher	57-61	Pl	F/250	H/80	3.5	S	–	5/-5/-	Soc.
Glimmer Geist	60-62	FU	F/250	H/80	3.8	S	–	-/-25/-	Call

Monster	Lvl	Body Type	Spd	Agg	Atk Spd	Atk Type	Ev %	Comb Mod	Soc. Call
Glimmer Ghoul	39-43	FU	F/250	H/80	3.8	T	4	5/-5/-	Call
Glimmer Griever	48-52	FU	F/250	H/80	4.0	S	6	5/-5/-	Soc.
Glimmer Jinn	65	Pl	3x/600	H/99	3.8	S	–	30/-/-10	Soc.
Glimmer Knight	60-62	Pl	F/250	H/80	5.5	S/S3	–	5/-5/-	Soc.
Glimmer Messenger	50	Pl	2x/350	–	2.0	S	8	20/-/-	Soc.
Glimmer Prophet	65	Pl	3x/600	H/99	3.8	S	–	20/-/20	Soc.
Glimmer Striker	51-55	Pl	F/250	H/80	3.0	T	–	5/-5/-	Soc.
Glimmer Ward	42-46	Pl	F/250	H/80	3.6	C	–	5/-5/-	Call
Glimmer Warshade	54-58	Pl	F/250	H/80	5.0	C/C4	–	5/-5/-	Soc.
Glimmerling	36-40	FU	F/250	H/80	3.8	T	2	5/-5/-	Call
Grand Pooka	61-64	ME	M/210	M/50	3.4	C	–	-10	–
Graugach	32-33	FA/Cl	M/188	–	3.8	C	–	–	–
Hillock Changeling	35-37	Cl	M/188	M/30	3.8	C	–	–	–
Lhiannan-Sidhe	49	Cl	M/188	H/90	3.8	S	–	-20	–
Lunantishee	8-9	Cl	M/188	L/5	3.8	C	–	-30	Call
Mad Changeling	27-29	St	M/188	–	3.6	C/S5	4	–	Soc.
Merman	23-36	Rp	M/180	–	3.7	S/S1	–	–	Soc.
Minor Changeling	1-2	Soft	M/188	–	3.8	C	–	–	–
Pooka	52-57	FA	M/195	H/80	3.8	C/C2	5	-10	–
Pookha	33-35	FA	M/195	M/50	3.7	C	3	-10	–
Rage Sprite	18-20	Cl	M/188	H/80	3.5	T/S3	–	–	Soc.
Rat Boy	3	Soft	M/188	L/5	3.8	S	–	–	–
Roane Companion	12-13	Soft	M/188	–	3.8	S	–	–	Call
Silver-Mad. Werewolf	47	FA/Cl	M/188	H/80	2.3	S/S5	–	-10/-10/-	–
Vanisher	27-32	Cl	M/188	H/80	3.8	C	–	–	Call
Veil Wisp	11-13	Cl	M/190	–	3.8	T	–	–	–
Weewere	48-49	FA	M/188	L/20	3.0	S/S5	3	–	–
Wild Crouch	5-6	Cl	M/188	L/5	3.6	C	–	–	–
Wrath Sprite	27-28	Cl	M/188	H/80	3.4	T/S7	–	–	Soc.

Reptile

Monster	Lvl	Body Type	Spd	Agg	Atk Spd	Atk Type	Ev %	Comb Mod	Soc. Call
Ollipheist	34-37	Rp	M/195	H/80	3.8	S/C6	–	–	–
Sinach	49-51	Rp	M/188	H/70	3.8	S	–	–	–

Tree or Plant

Monster	Lvl	Body Type	Spd	Agg	Atk Spd	Atk Type	Ev %	Comb Mod	Soc. Call
Blackthorn	8-9	TP	M/180	L/5	4.2	C	–	-30	Call
Grovewood	38-40	TP	M/180	–	3.8	C	–	-10/-10/-20	Call
Haunted Driftwood	1	TP	S/150	–	3.8	C	–	–	–
Irewood	29-31	TP	M/180	H/80	3.8	C	–	-5	Soc.
Irewood Greenbark	40	TP	M/172	–	3.7	C/T5	–	–	Soc.
Irewood Sapling	21-22	TP	M/172	M/30	3.8	C/T5	–	-5	Soc.

Undead

Monster	Lvl	Body Type	Spd	Agg	Atk Spd	Atk Type	Ev %	Comb Mod	Soc. Call
Badh	46-47	IU/Cl	M/180	M/50	3.5	S	3	-5	Soc.
Bananach	40-41	IU	M/188	H/80	3.8	S	–	-20	–
Banshee	55-59	IU/Cl	M/195	H/70	3.7	S	1	-5/-5/-	Soc.
Bantam Spectre	15	IU	M/188	H/70	3.8	C	–	–	–
Bean Sidhe	39-41	IU/Cl	M/195	H/90	3.7	S	1	-10	–
Black Wraith	52-55	IU	M/200	M/60	3.3	T/S3	5	-5/-5/-	Soc.
Bocan	15	IU	M/188	H/70	3.8	C	–	–	–
Bocanach	46-48	IU	M/188	H/80	3.8	S	–	-20/-20/-	–
Corybantic Skeleton	46	BU	M/188	H/99	2.8	S/S3	–	–	–
Dullahan	48-51	IU/Ch	F/230	M/50	3.2	T/S4	3	–	–
Eidolon	58-64	IU/Cl	M/200	H/80	3.8	C	–	-20	Soc.
Faeghoul	34-36	FU	M/177	M/60	4.0	S	–	-5/-5/-	Soc.
Fallen Hib. Defender	45	IU	M/188	L/20	3.8	S	–	–	–
Far Liath	31-32	IU	M/180	H/80	3.2	C	–	-10	–
Finliath	58-60	FU	M/188	M/50	3.8	S	–	-20	–
Fog Phantom	21-23	IU	M/188	L/3	3.7	C	2	-10/-10/-	–
Fog Wraith	28-30	IU	M/188	M/60	3.7	T	2	-10/-10/-	–
Fuath	46-47	IU	M/188	H/80	3.8	S	–	–	–
Gem-Dusted Skeleton	37	BU	M/188	L/10	3.5	S	–	–	–
Ghastly Siabra	13-15	IU	M/188	H/80	3.8	S	–	–	–
Ghostly Midg. Invader	43	IU	F/240	L/20	3.8	S	–	–	–
Ghostly Siabra	11-12	IU	M/188	H/80	3.8	S	–	–	–
Ghoulie	20-22	FU/Cl	M/188	H/70	3.7	S/S5	–	–	Soc.
Granny	48-50	IU	M/188	L/5	3.8	S	–	–	–
Grass Spirit	1	IU	M/188	–	3.8	S	–	–	–
Gray Spectre	22-24	IU	M/205	H/90	3.3	S/S5	–	-20	–
Haunting Draft	49	EA	M/188	H/80	3.0	S	1	-10/-10/-	–
Lesser Banshee	36-37	IU/Cl	M/175	M/40	3.8	S	1	-10	Soc.
Mangled Troll Invader	45	IU	F/240	L/20	3.8	S	–	–	–
Mist Wraith	27-28	IU	M/188	M/30	3.7	T	2	-10/-10/-	–
Morghoul	33	FU	M/177	M/60	4.0	S	–	-5/-5/-	Soc.
Mummy Hag	11-13	BU	M/210	H/99	3.0	T	3	–	Soc.
Murkman	15-16	FU	S/165	H/99	3.8	S	–	–	Soc.
Pale Horse	50	IU	F/250	H/80	2.8	C	–	–	–
Phaeghoul	37-39	FU	M/177	M/60	4.0	S	–	-5/-5/-	Soc.
Phantom Miner	47	IU	M/188	H/80	3.8	C	–	–	–
Phantom Wickerman	28	IU	M/188	H/80	3.7	T	–	-5	–
Raven Wraith	58-64	IU	F/220	H/90	3.1	T/S7	8	-2/-2/-	Soc.
Shrieking Wraith	41-43	IU	F/220	H/90	3.1	T/S7	8	-2/-2/-	Call
Silver-Flecked Skeleton	47	BU	M/188	L/10	3.8	S	–	–	–
Skeletal Dwarf Invader	43	IU	M/188	L/20	3.8	S	–	–	–
Skeletal Minion	3-4	BU	M/180	–	3.8	S	–	–	–
Skeletal Pawn	1-2	BU	M/180	–	3.8	S	–	–	–
Spectral Briton Invader	43	IU	F/240	L/20	3.8	S	–	–	–
Spectral Manslayer	50-53	IU	M/188	H/99	3.8	T	2	-10/-10/-	–
Spectral Wickerman	14-17	IU	M/188	H/80	3.7	S/S1	–	-10	–
Speghoul	40-41	FU	M/177	M/60	4.0	S	–	-5/-5/-	Soc.
Suitor Spirit	14-15	IU	S/165	H/99	3.8	S	–	–	Soc.
Undead Briton Invader	44	IU	M/188	L/20	3.8	S	–	–	–
Undead Drudger	38-39	FU/Cl	M/188	H/80	3.8	C	–	–	–
Vindictive Bocan	20-22	IU	M/188	H/99	3.7	C/S1	–	–	Soc.
Wanshee	61-64	IU	M/188	H/80	3.8	S	–	-20	–
Wind Ghoul	7	IU	M/200	L/5	3.8	C	1	-10	–
Zephyr Wraith	29-32	IU	F/225	M/60	3.3	T/S3	8	-10	–

Tir na Nog

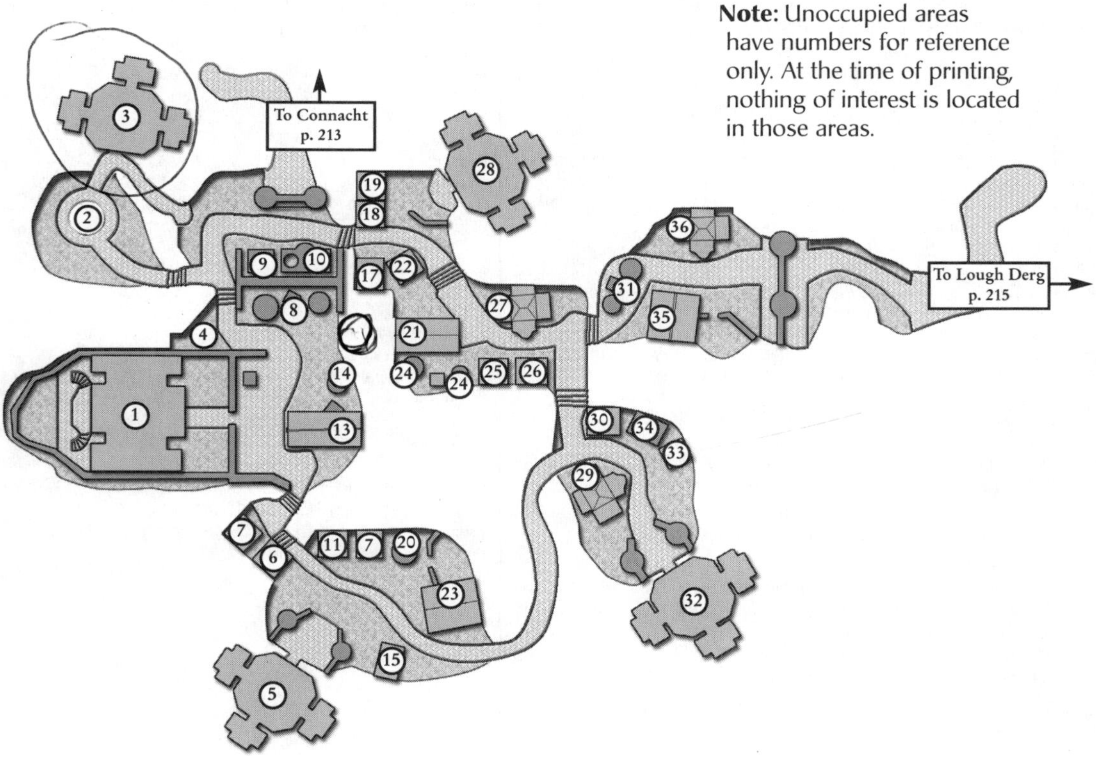
Note: Unoccupied areas have numbers for reference only. At the time of printing, nothing of interest is located in those areas.
To Connacht p. 213
To Lough Derg p. 215
1
2
3
4
5
6
7
8
9
10
11
7
13
14
15
17
18
19
20
21
22
23
24
24
25
26
27
28
29
30
31
32
33
34
35
36

1 **Aghaistin** Bounty Store - Crystals
1 **Bhreagar Hylvian** Vault Keeper
1 **Brigit**
1 **Caolan** Enchanter
1 **Ffhionbarr** Guild Emblemeer
1 **Filidh Fadwyn** Guild Registrar
1 **Filidh Filiara** Name Registrar
1 **Harper Eibhilin**
1 **Lauralaye**
1 **Lobais**
1 **Lovernios**
1 **Sentinel Liadin**
1 **Sentinel Llacheu**
1 **Vaddon** Healer
2 **Bard**
2 **Filidh Meilseior**
3 **Daray** Druid Trainer
3 **Grainne** Bounty Store - Crystals
3 **Labhras** Warden Trainer
3 **Selia** Bard Trainer
4 **Ffiara** Large weapons
4 **Geryn** Strips
5 **Antaine** Bounty Store - Crystals
5 **Lasairiona** Champion Trainer
5 **Luighseach** Blademaster Trainer
5 **Riofach** Hero Trainer
8 **Cedric** Boards
8 **Darcy** Tailoring equipment
8 **Ewen** Staff
8 **Hywela** Osnadurtha scale armor
8 **Saffa** Tailoring equipment
8 **Vaughn** Constaic leather armor
10 **Connor** Arrows
10 **Fingal** Bard instruments
10 **Guardian Daire**
10 **Guardian Sima**
10 **Jarlath**
10 **Jezza Blackfingers** Smith
10 **Jiskarr de'Mordan** Celtic spears
10 **Kenzia** Bows
10 **Waljan** Healer
12 **Arziqua** Fletching Master
12 **Izall** Fletching supplies (feathers)
13 **Deante** Poison
13 **Franseza** Blunt
13 **Jeanna** Green/brown/gray/orange/yellow leather dye
13 **Krianna** Blue/teal/red/purple leather dye
13 **Malior** Poison
13 **Tomas** Cruaigh leather armor
14 **Armin** Master Tailor
14 **Baran** Smithing equipment
14 **Dunstan** Armorcraft Master
14 **Hendrika** Weaponcraft Master
14 **Tegvan** Armorcraft Master
19 **Eavan**
19 **Tiarnan**
20 **Cristolia** Green/brown/grey/orange/yellow enamel dye
20 **Drumnail** Large weapons
20 **Kiam** Smith
20 **Kirsta** Blue/turq/teal/red/purple enamel dye
20 **Lulach** Blades
21 **Adrai** Staff
21 **Banyell** Reinforced armor
21 **Deverry** Carbide weapons
21 **Keya** Carbide scale armor
21 **Lerena** Sylvan woven armor
21 **Sharon** Embossed leather armor
21 **Taleai** Amber reinforced armor
24 **Briana** Bows
24 **Dierdra** Green/brown/grey/orange/yellow cloth dye
24 **Gemma** Cruaigh leather armor
24 **Kelsi** Arrows
24 **Laurence** Cruanach scale armor
24 **Sissy** Robes
27 **Banon** Smith
27 **Ermid** Brea leather armor
27 **Guardian Brighid**
27 **Guardian Teadoir**
27 **Romney** Celtic spears
27 **Seva** Blades
28 **Blathnaid** Nightshade Trainer
28 **Kiley** Bounty Store - Crystals
28 **Mavelle** Ranger Trainer
28 **Nona** Poison merchant
28 **Roibin** Poison merchant
29 **Bairfhionn**
29 **Blanche** Blue/teal/turq/red/purple cloth dye
29 **Harper Evelyn**
29 **Isibael** Bows
29 **Muirne** Piercers
29 **Seren** Arrows
29 **Tristan** Osnadurtha scale armor
31 **Cleit** Shields
31 **Cragen** Cailiocht reinforced armor
31 **Eachann** Woven armor
31 **Nolan** Cailiocht reinforced armor
31 **Renny** Nadurtha reinforced armor
31 **Sadhbh** Enchanter
31 **Sentinel Mada**
32 **Aghna** Enchanter staves
32 **Ailson** Bounty Store - Crystals
32 **Anwar** Enchanter Trainer
32 **Aodh** Eldritch Trainer
32 **Aulif** Woven armor
32 **Brianna** Mentalist staves
32 **Cinnie** Cheap cloth dye, robes
32 **Ena** Mentalist Trainer
32 **Kado** Woven armor
32 **Kedric** Eldritch staves
32 **Kinnat** Woven armor
32 **Madarl** Cheap cloth dye, robes
32 **Nealcail** Cheap cloth dye, robes
36 **Ailish**
36 **Bevan Clune**
36 **Conary**
36 **Conleth Cuagain**
36 **Fidelma Breen**
36 **Harper Eveny**
36 **Iarla Clune**
36 **Kieran Breen**
36 **Larla Clune**
36 **Maxen** Daingean scale armor
36 **Rhosyn** Bard instruments
36 **Somhairle Breen**
36 **Treasa Breen**
by 22 **Kennocha**
by 33 **Labhaoise**

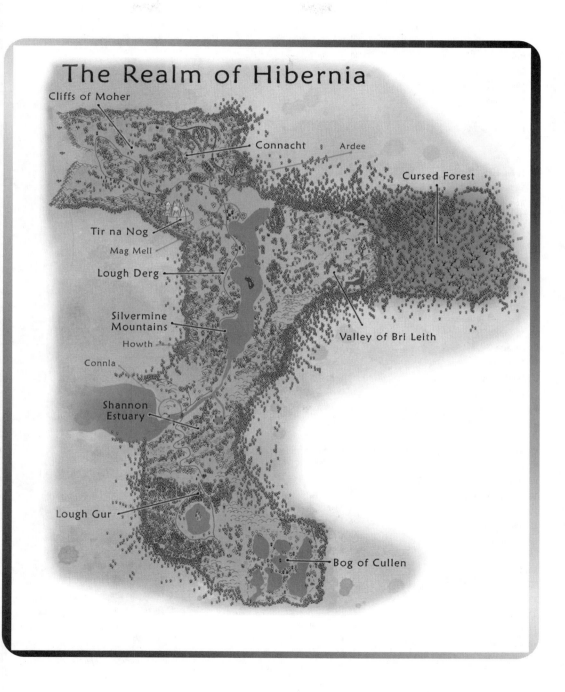

The Realm of Hibernia

Cliffs of Moher
Connacht
Ardee
Cursed Forest
Tir na Nog
Mag Mell
Lough Derg
Silvermine Mountains
Howth
Valley of Bri Leith
Connla
Shannon Estuary
Lough Gur
Bog of Cullen

BOG OF CULLEN

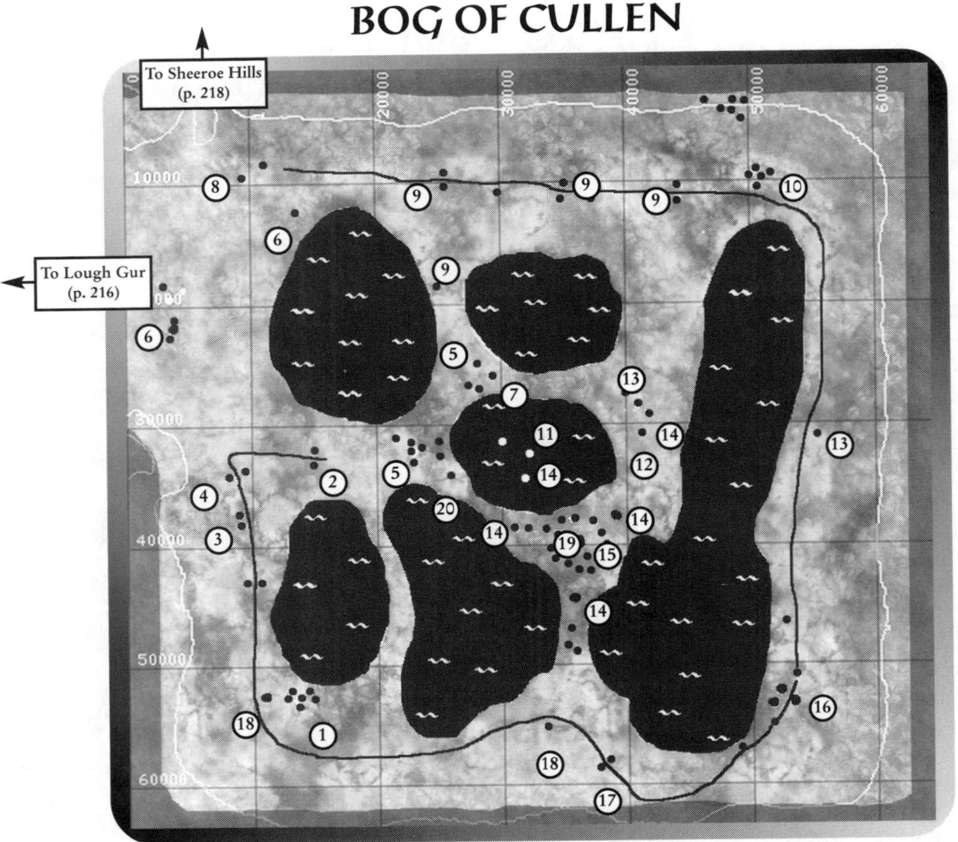

1 Siabra and Giant Mushrooms

2 Gold Glowing Gemstones

3 Siopa (p. 224)

4 Siabra Wayguard & Gold Glowing Gemstones

5 Siabra Guardian Lookout Tower

6 Giant Mushrooms and Gold Glowing Gemstones

7 Huts & Gold Glowing Gemstones

8 Siabra Guardian Treehouse Tower

9 Gold Glowing Gemstones

10 Giant Mushroom Circle

11 Gold Glowing Gemstones (Tower in Middle)

12 Huts

13 Gold Glowing Gemstone

14 Siabra Lookout Towers

15 Siabra Guardian Settlement

16 Alainn Bin (p. 221)

17 Gold Glowing Gemstones

18 Siabra Guardian Treehouse Tower

19 Central Siabra Lookout Tower

20 Siabra Guardian Huts & Gold Glowing Gemstones

CLIFFS OF MOHER

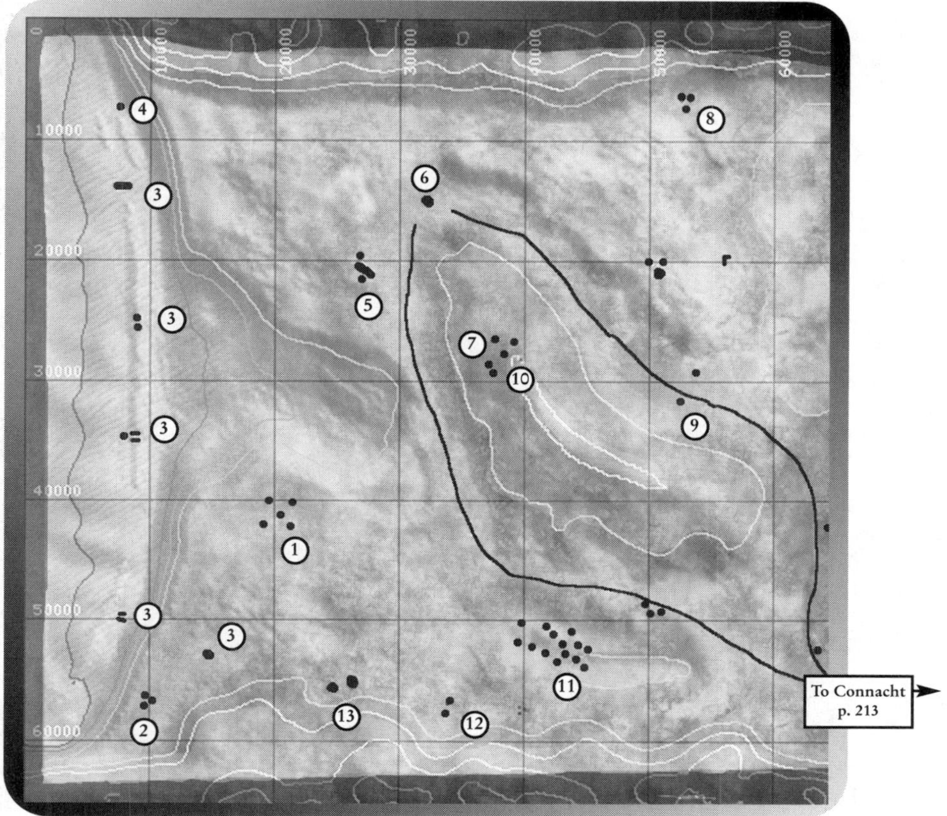

1 Vehement Guardian Stones
2 Phaegul Boulders
3 Cliff Dweller Camp & Kaolinth Tribal Caverns Dungeon (p.228)
4 Stone Beach House
5 Tir Urphost (p.225)
6 Tur Garda
7 Mushroom Pillars
8 Vindictive Bocan Camp
9 Gold Glowing Gemstone
10 Pillar
11 Summoned Urdrock Stones, 1 Gold Glowing Gemstone
12 Moheran Camp
13 Cliff Dweller Camp

CONNACHT

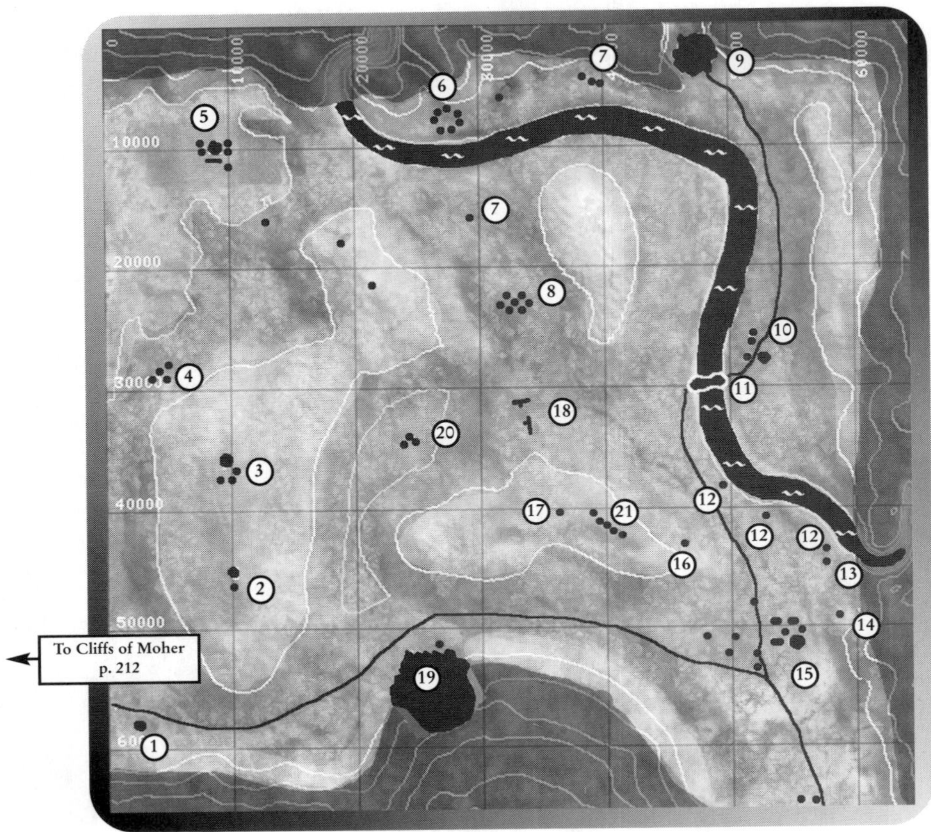

1 Tur Garda
2 Ghostly Siabra Store Circle
3 Cluricaun Settlement
4 Walking Rock Store Circle
5 Farm/Stable
6 Amure Stone Circle
7 Glowing Mushroom Circles
8 Sprite Camp
9 Druim Ligen
10 Basar (p. 222)
11 Ornate Bridge
12 Mudman Camp
13 Maeve the Crone's House
14 Mudman Camp
15 Ardee (p. 221)
16 Mudman Camp
17 Entrance to Muire Tomb Dungeon (p.227)
18 Rock Wall Ruins
19 Palace (entrance to Tir na Nog) (p. 208)
20 Ghostly Siabra Stone Circle
21 Spectre Stone Pillars

CURSED FOREST

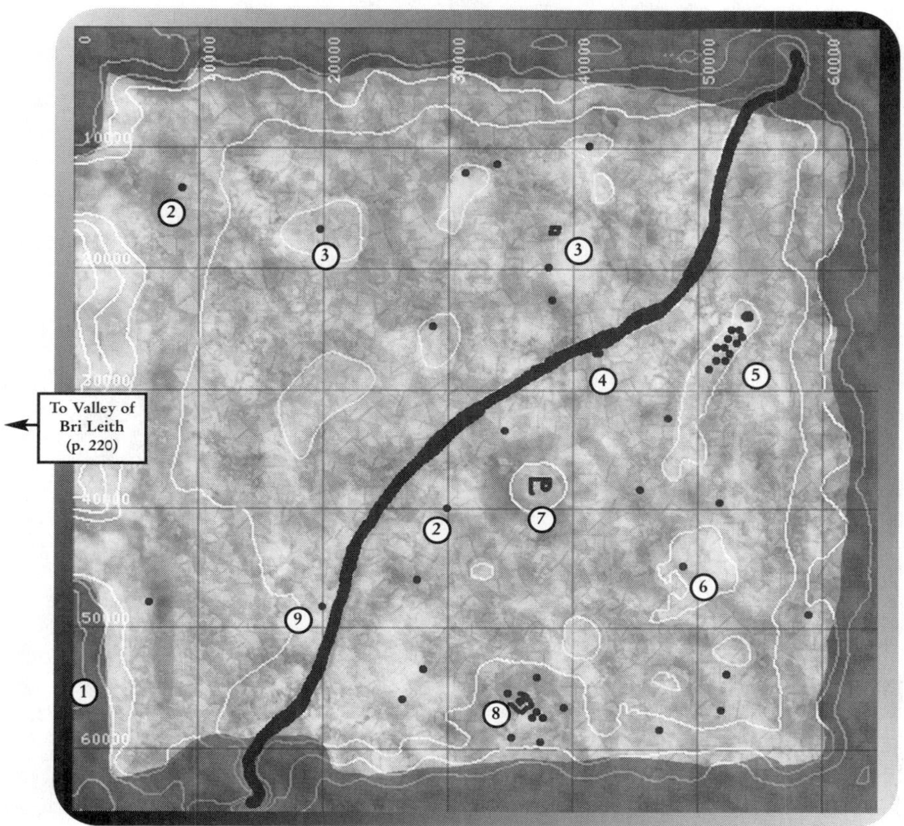

1 Moon Lake
2 Leprechaun Gold Glowing Gemstone
3 Gold Glowing Gemstone
4 Mushroom Circle
5 Queen's Nail Green Glowing Pillars
6 Gold Glowing Gemstone
7 Granny Fort
8 Goberchend Fort
9 Far Dorocha Mushroom Circle

LOUGH DERG

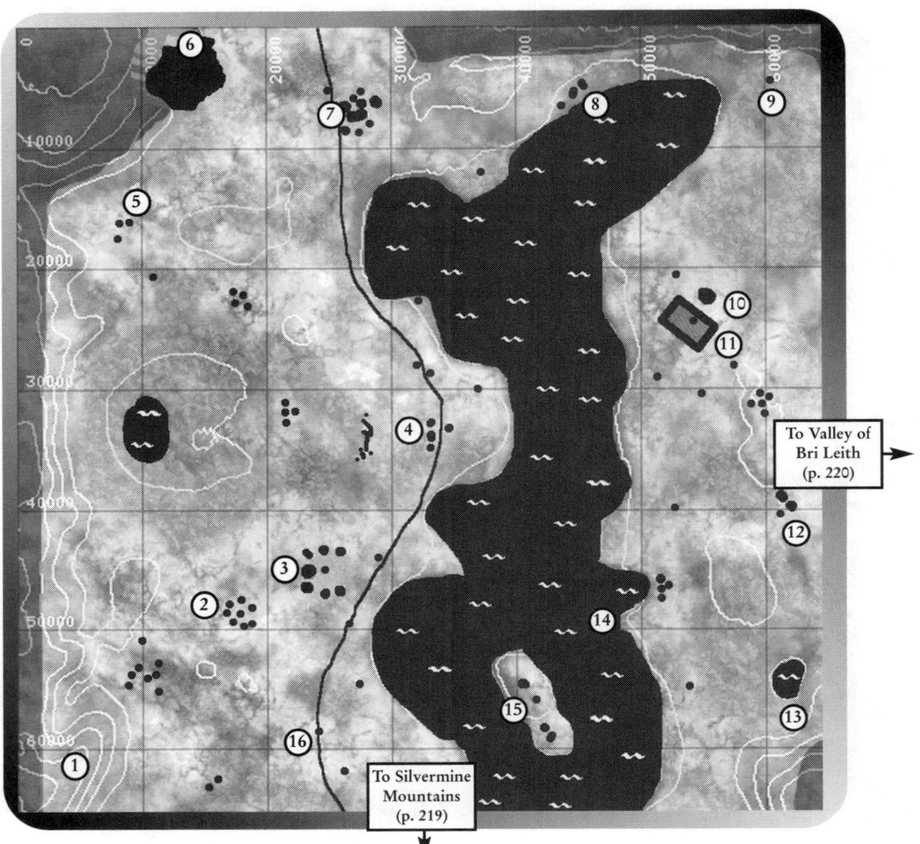

1 Siabra Stones
2 Wolfhound Stones
3 Tir na mBeo (p. 225)
4 Murdagh (p. 224)
5 Crystal Rock
6 Palace: Entrance to Tir na Nog (p. 208)
7 Mag Mell (p. 224)
8 Curmudgeon Camp
9 Dargon Ruin
10 Stable
11 Parthanan Farm Field
12 Curmudgeon Camp
13 Pond
14 Dock
15 Huts
16 Nessan's Land

LOUGH GUR

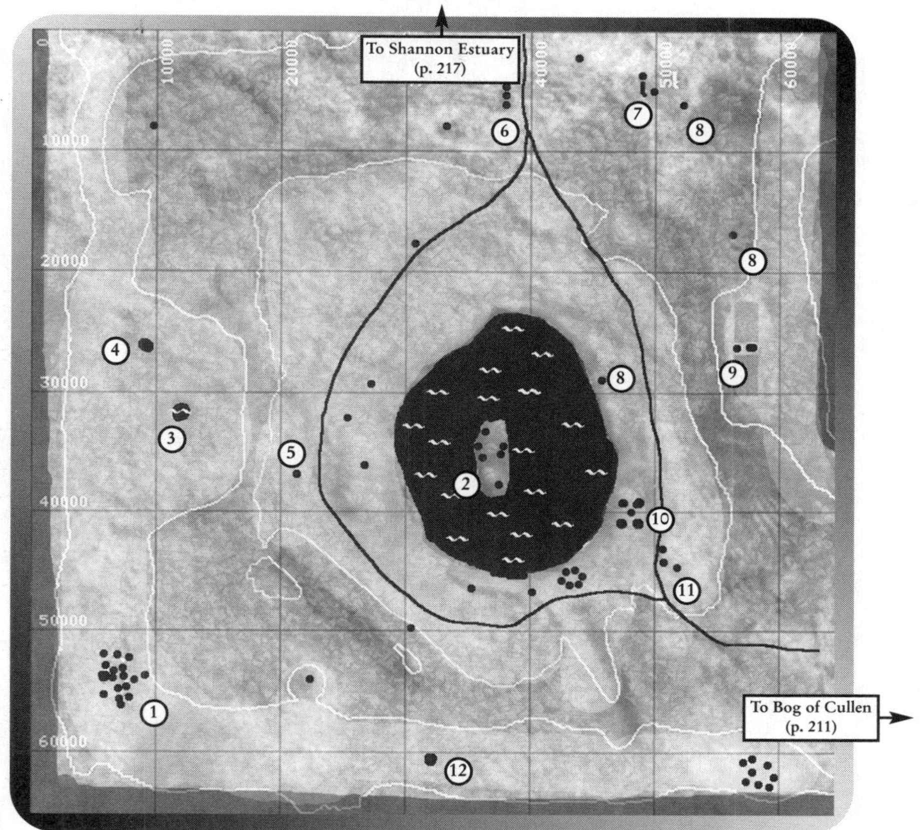

1 Gurite Settlement, Gold Glowing Gemstones, Giant Mushrooms
2 Faerie Horse Stores
3 Merucha Pond
4 Entrance to Treibh Caillte Dungeon (p. 228)
5 Gold Glowing Gemstone
6 Glowing Green Pillars
7 Rock Walls
8 Curmudgeon Camp
9 Parthanan Stable and Farm Fields
10 Innis Carthaig (p. 223)
11 Gold Glowing Gemstone
12 Deamhan Aeir Stone Building

SHANNON ESTUARY

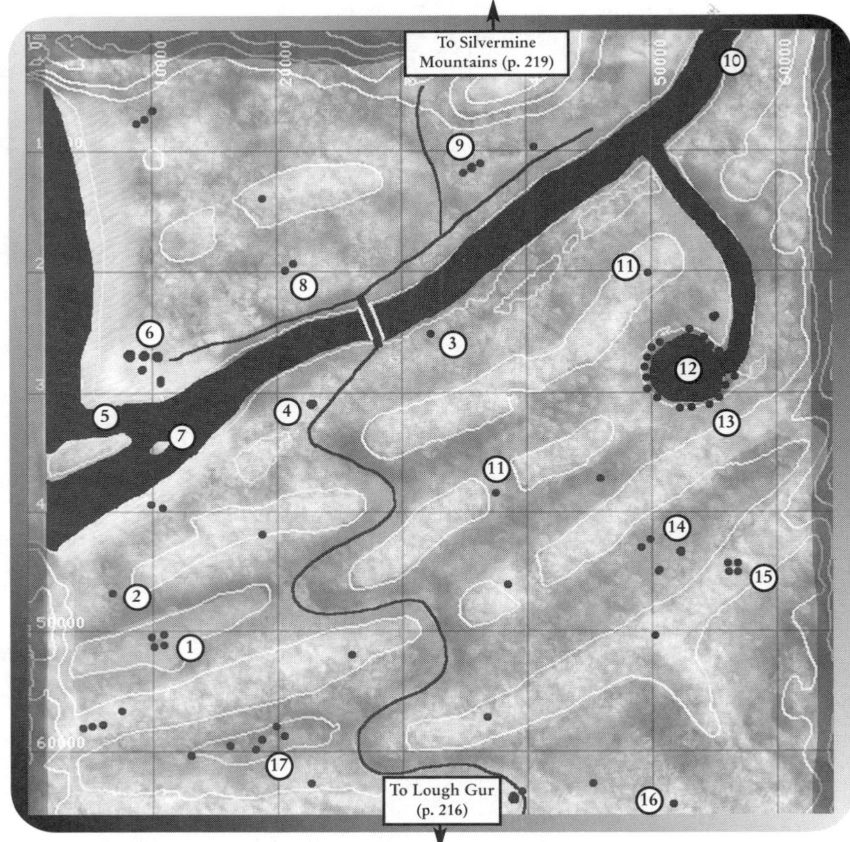

1 Spectral Wickerman Store Pillars
2 Camp
3 Gold Glowing Rock
4 Daingean (Tower) (p. 223)
5 Dock
6 Connia (p. 222)
7 Water Beetle Collector Sandbar Islands
8 Villainous Youth Camp
9 Rowdy Camp
10 Wooden Bridge
11 Giant Ants
12 Connla's Well
13 Stone Pillar Beach
14 Eriv Settlement
15 Stone Circle
16 Cennai
17 Olipheist Gold Glowing Rock

SHEEROE HILLS

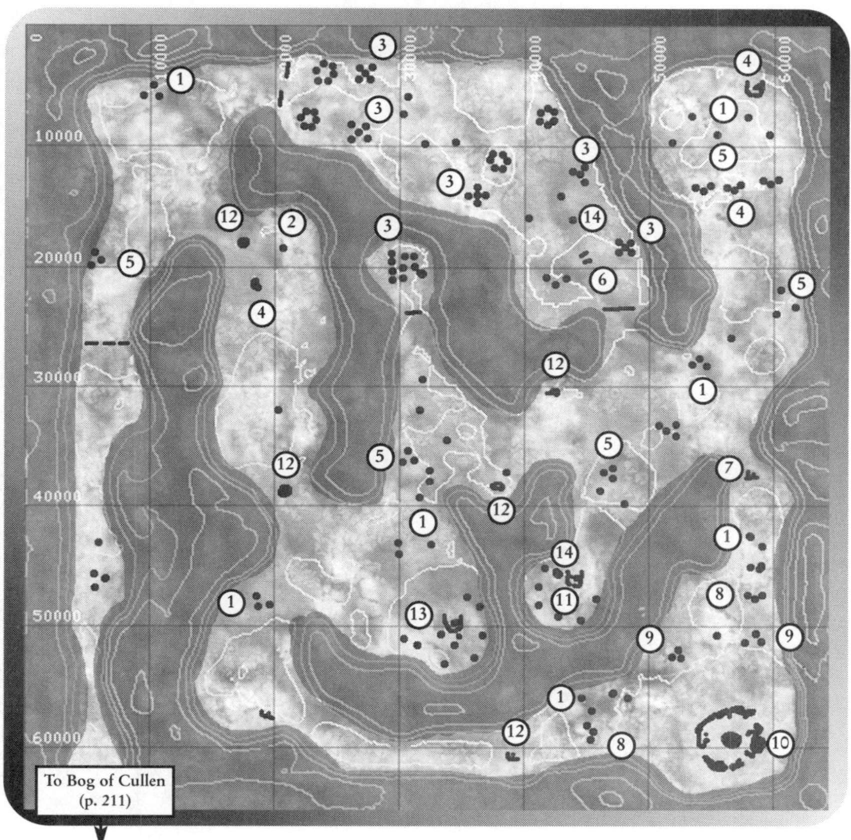

1 Yellow Glowing Gemstones
2 Mushroom Circle
3 Azure Cleanser Camp
4 Glimmer Fort Ruins
5 Purple Glowing Gemstones
6 Green Glowing Gemstones
7 Tower Ruin
8 Glimmer Geist Huts
9 Glimmer Knight
10 Cuuldurach Glimmer King Fortress
11 Glimmer Fort Ruins / Glowing Yellow Gemstones
12 Glimmer Tower Ruins
13 Glimmer Fort Ruins / Glowing Purple Gemstones
14 Gold Glowing Gemstone

SILVERMINE MOUNTAINS

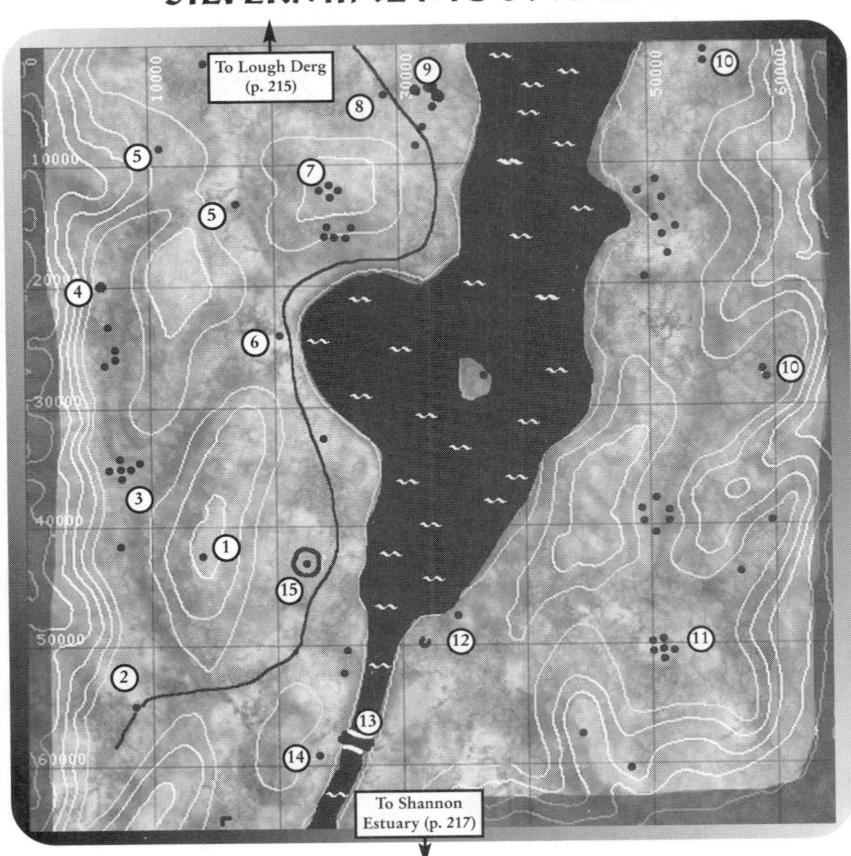

1 Merle the Old's House
2 Luricaduane Mushroom Circle
3 Mushroom Circle
4 Entrance to Spraggon Den Dungeon (p. 227)
5 Mushroom Circles
6 Guard Tower
7 Glom Stone Circle
8 Neasan's Land (Treehouse entrance)
9 Ardagh (p. 221)
10 Sheevra Hut
11 Camp with Gray Spectres
12 Mushroom Stone Circle
13 Boulder Bridge
14 Hut
15 Howth (p. 223)

VALLEY OF BRI LEITH

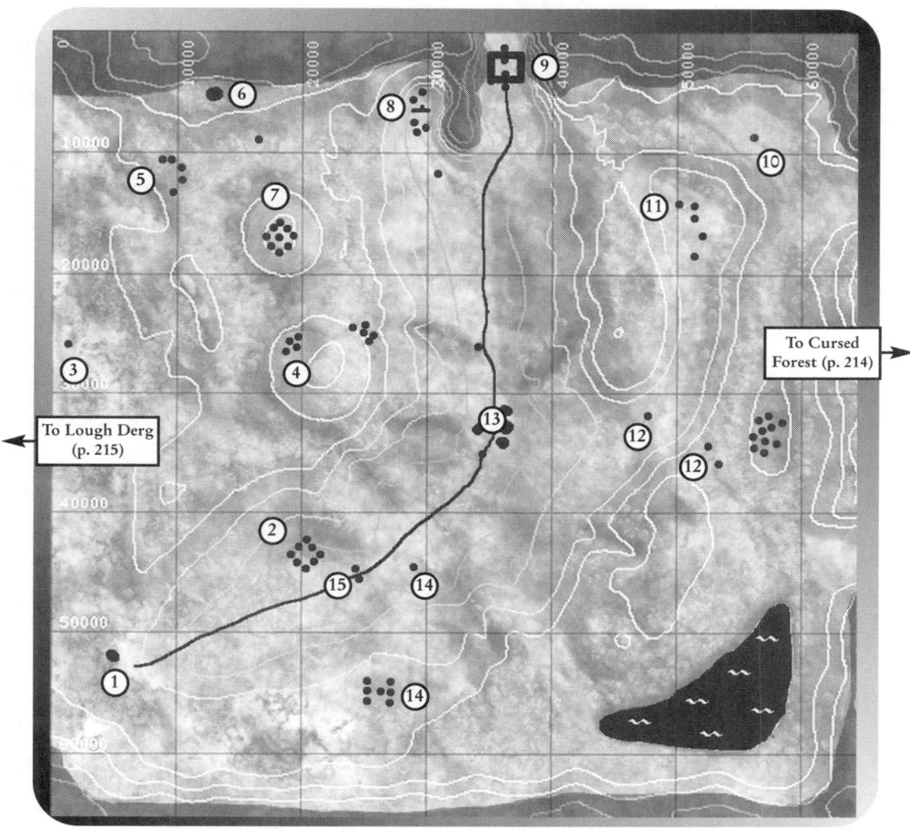

1 Tower
2 Stone Pillar Square
3 Stone Pillar
4 Siog Seeker Camp
5 Siog Settlement
6 Entrance to Coruscating Mines Dungeon (p. 226)
7 Druid Stone Circle
8 Siog Seeker Rock Wall
9 Druin Cain
10 Empyrean Well
11 Veeper Rasa's Huts
12 Mushroom Circle
13 Caille (p. 222)
14 Camp
15 Giant Mushrooms

Alainn Binn

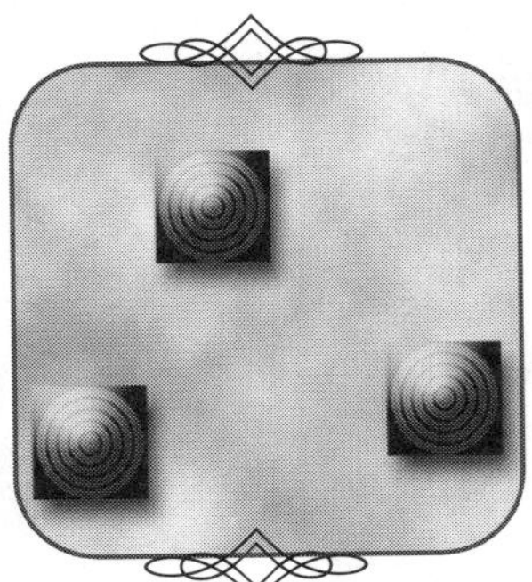

Chieftess Dana
Cragen Cailiocht reinforced armor
Alaiina Large weapons
Dympna Cruaigh leather armor
Liam Arrows
Lirla Poison
Iama Eldritch staves
Rois
Maureen Bows
Ceri Healer
Finghin Cruanach scale armor
Aisling Enchanter staves
Helori Piercing
Dalladva Smith

Ardagh

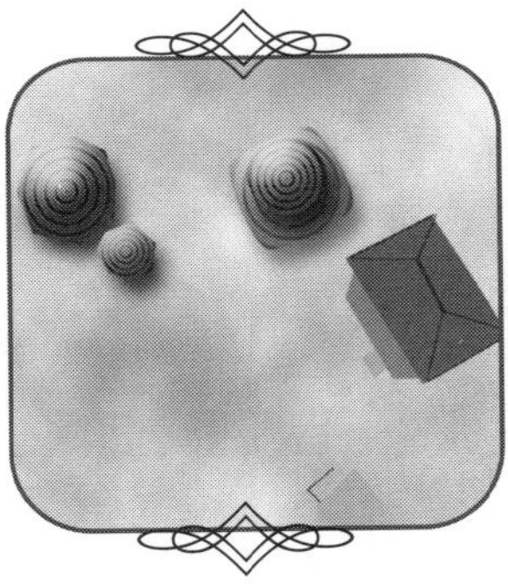

Edricar Stable Master
Ea Blademaster Trainer
Noreen Osnadurtha scale armor
Reeni Blue/teal/red/purple cloth dye
Roise Cailiocht reinforced armor
Nyle Blunt
Illaliel Enchanter staves
Della Bard instruments
Odharnait
Teague Ranger Trainer
Siodhachan Champion Trainer
Leachlainn Nightshade Trainer
Ysbail Blades
Iaine Celtic spears
Caitriona
Lochlain
Moesen Cloak
Brisen Robes
Brenna Eldritch staves
Talaith Enchanter Trainer
Coman Eldritch Trainer
Iola Enchanter
Torlan Enchanter staves
Mabli Green/brown/gray/orange/yellow cloth dye
Aindreas Mentalist Trainer
Uilliam Warden Trainer
Fyrsil Healer
Seana Staff
Rhodry Bows
Celder Arrows

Ardee

Caoimhe Naturalist Trainer
Auliffe Magician Trainer
Eiral Enchanter
Nyderra
Flannery Guardian
Mahon Piercing
Arshan Tailoring Equipment
Fianait Brea leather armor
Creirwy Eldritch staves
Naomhan Mentalist staves
Daron Enchanter staves
Near Forge
Aideen Blunt
Tira
Criostoir Smith
Evan Nadurtha reinforced armor
Garnock Blades
Lexie Poison
Tethra
Llyn Healer
Kiana
Larylle
Keara
Daithi Stalker Trainer
Freagus Stable Master
Eoghan
Lerna Staff
Ailfrid Robes
Qunilan Woven armor
Eleri Celtic spears
Rhona Bow

Basar

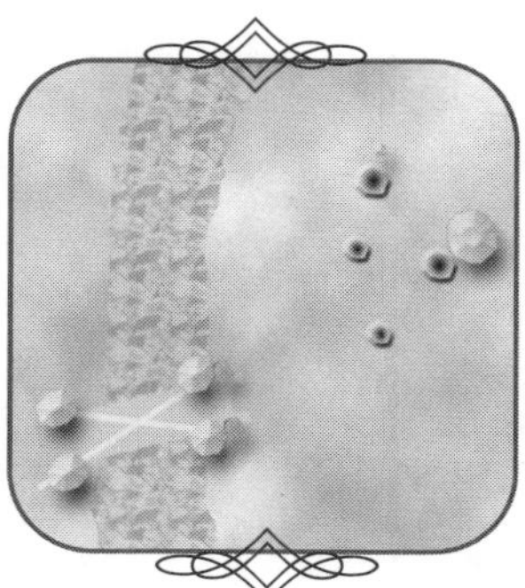

Erech Various expensive trade skill items
Neb Constaic leather armor
Anna Nadurtha reinforced armor
Tara Arrows
Zinna Bows
Arzhela Cruaigh leather armor
Deryn Blunt
Eruven
Briac Piercing
Cubert Tacuil reinforced armor
Cristin Daingean scale armor

Caille

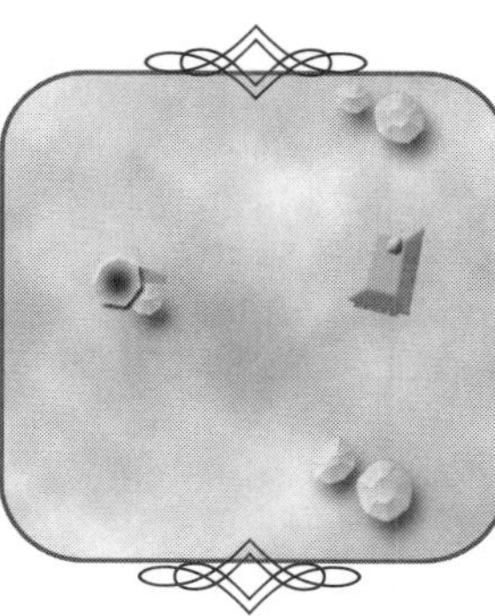

Olane
Empar
Ainrebh Enchanter
Keir Eldritch staves
Brynn Enchanter staves
Ariana Mentalist staves
Viola
Lysagh Woven armor

Connia

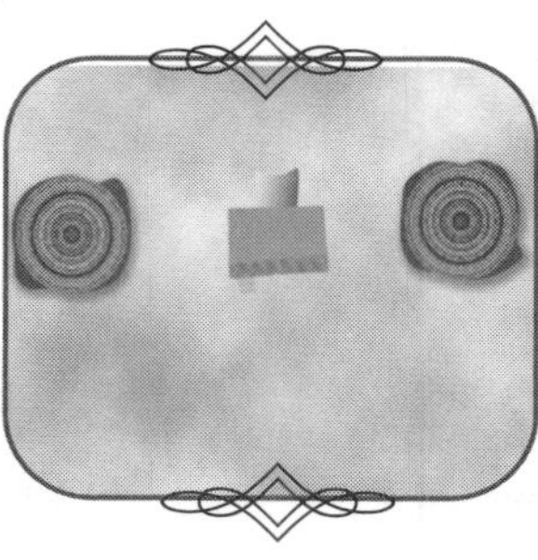

Cordelia Champion Trainer
Dempsey Bard Trainer
Harper Cadwr
Sile Ranger Trainer
Uisetan
Benen Naturalist Trainer
Aelerogh Stable Master
Searlas Hero Trainer
Colm Osnadurtha scale armor
Allistar Blademaster Trainer
Eli Enchanter
Eira Blades
Erwana Large weapons
Bryanna Enchanter staves
Tadhg
Bran Stalker Trainer
Kinney Poison
Maire
Kiara Bows
Ennis Magician Trainer
Alun Blunt
Marus Celtic spears
Sarff Smith
Erskine Brea leather armor
Edana Arrows
Glyn Eldritch staves
Gavina Shields
Edernola Bard instruments
Ailill Guardian Trainer
Peadar Staff
Ronan Woven armor
Sorcha Robes
Edmyg Mentalist staves
Treise Mentalist Trainer
Keagan Healer
Nainsi Eldritch Trainer
Eyslk Enchanter Trainer

Daingean

Slevin Shields
Torrance Druid Trainer
Rooney Nightshade Trainer
Iacob
Kaylee
Ghearic Chauchon Vault Keeper

Piaras
Gormghlaith
Pheuloc Stable Master
Maille Bard Trainer
Adair Magician Trainer
Kaley Guardian Trainer
Iain Cruanach scale armor
Keriann
Bidelia Druid Trainer
Nevin Hero Trainer
Gralon Healer
Chief Proinnsias
Cathbad
Kenna Constaic leather armor
Kevain Tacuil reinforced armor
Bevin Nadurtha reinforced armor
Tyree Leather dye
Dyvyr Leather dye
Damhnait Stalker Trainer
Irksa Bard instruments
Twm Cailiocht reinforced armor
Kalla Poison
Troya
Lasrina
Daibheid Naturalist Trainer
Anra Staff
Alwyn Smith
Gaenor Piercing
Blaez Shields
Ffion Large weapons
Blayne Arrows
Cait Celtic spears
Ailbe Blades
Mairona

Howth

Innis Carthaig

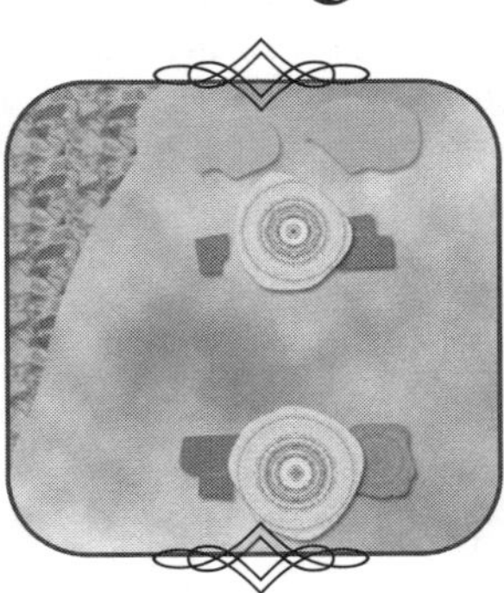

Macharan Tailoring equipment
Yealcha Metalworking equipment
Harper Brac
Chieftess Niamh
Feoras Cloak
Sarena Poison
Crayg Enchanter staves
Amynda Mentalist staves
Glennard Eldritch staves
Malachy
Breachus Stable Master
Asthore Blades
Barra Staff
Dierdre Arrows
Mariota Cailiocht reinforced armor
Drummond Large weapons
Talriese Daingean scale armor
Slaine Robes
Kern Enchanter
Siobhan Smith
Blanche Healer
Gorawen Cruaigh leather armor
Kian Cruanach scale armor

Mag Mell

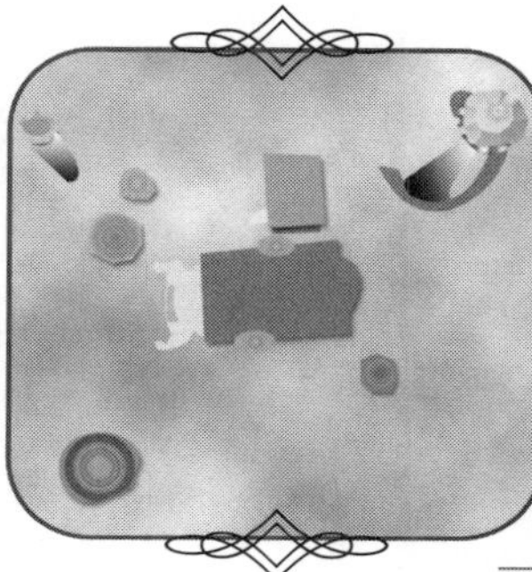

Wony Blades
Ilisa Smith
Cafell Shields
Kylirean Brea leather armor
Jahan Various expensive trade skill items
Sian Staff
Anice Woven armor
Dera Enchanter
Eluned Robes
Sedric Mentalist staves
By rocks
Breeda Naturalist Trainer
Etain Magician Trainer
Meadghbh Guardian Trainer
Epona Healer
Fagan
Harper Cara
Greagoir
Ula Stalker Trainer
Oistin Cloaks
Lachlan Piercing
Rumdor Stable Master
Mannix Bows
Aillig Arrows
Meara

Murdagh

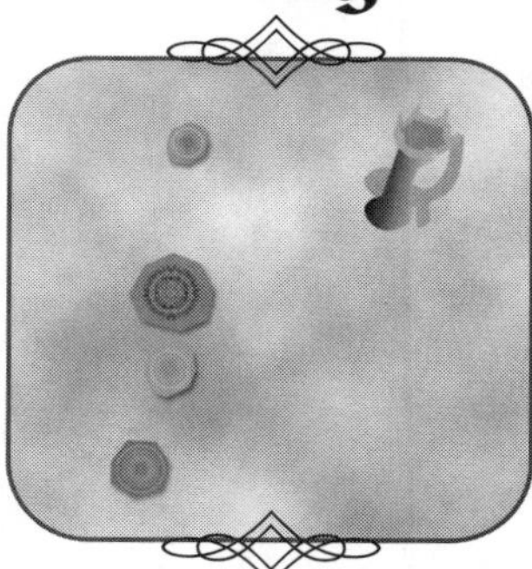

Dirmyg Blades
Dilith Enamel dye
Ebril Cruaigh leather armor
Ardal Tacuil reinforced armor
Thady Large weapons
Akira Cailiocht reinforced armor
Mearchian Celtic spears
Beli Healer
Grizel Smith
Muadhnait Staff
Edsoner Bard instruments
Gaenor Piercing
Brody Constaic leather armor
Calder Arrows
Riona Tower

Siopa

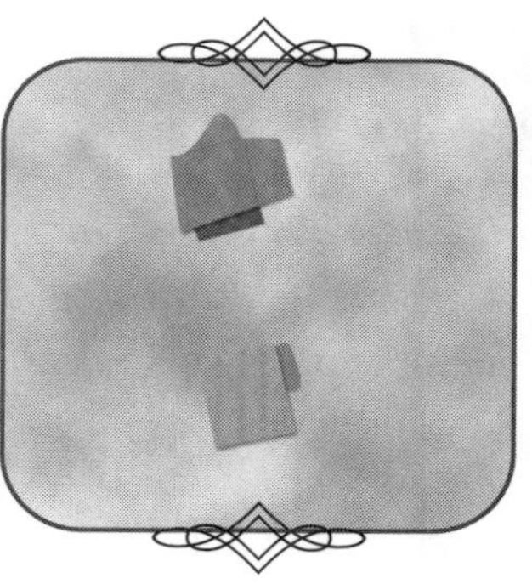

Murchach Cloak
Raghnall Robes
Emhyr Enchanter staves
Caron Constaic leather armor
Kerwin Healer
Devin Osnadurtha scale armor
Alar Blunt
Morag Shields
Broc Swords

Tir na mBeo

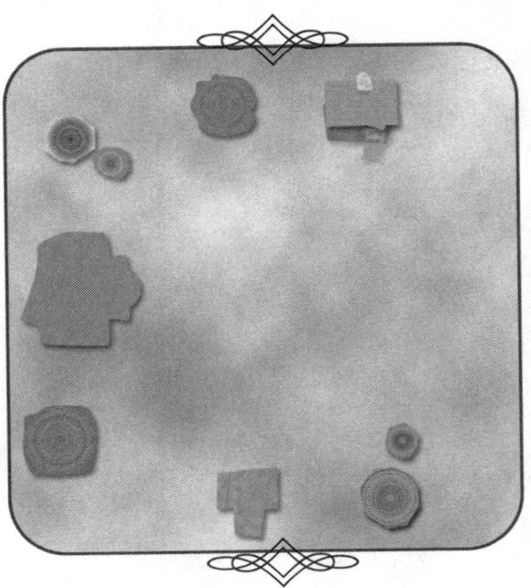

Ionhar Healer
Sentinel Ornora
Boyd Nadurtha reinforced armor
Cian Bard instruments
Harper Jocelin
Una Cruanach scale armor
Borlai Poison
Truichon Stable Master
Achaius Large weapons
Liadan Enchanter staves
Lainie Smith
Tangi Enchanter
Kaenia Robes
Filidh Morven
Tavie
Reidie
Teleri Daingean scale armor
Rhian enamel dye
Kean
Elith Woven armor
Anrai Staff
Duer Woven armor
Lavena Eldritch staves
Aidaila Osnadurtha scale armor

Tir Urphost

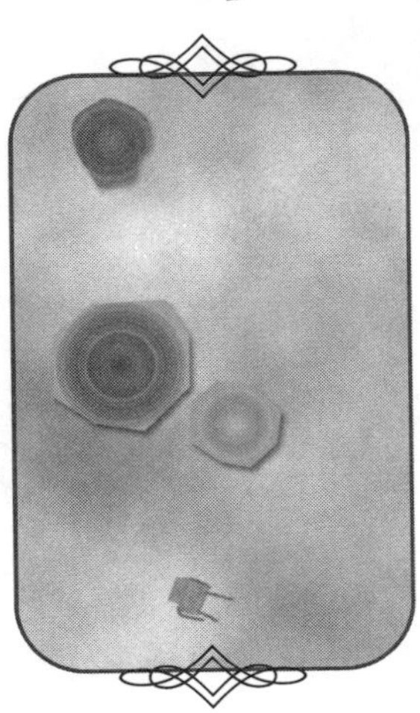

Cleary Enchanter
Leurgor Stable Master
Yvon Shields
Daracha Bows
Callough Large weapons
Tavie Nadurtha reinforced armor
Mosby Cruanach scale armor

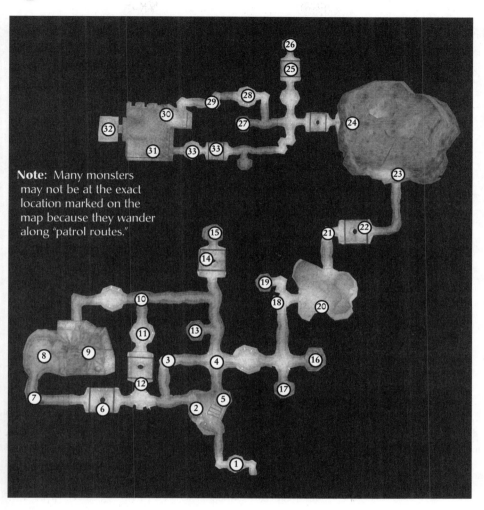

Note: Many monsters may not be at the exact location marked on the map because they wander along "patrol routes."

Coruscating Mines

1 Shaft Rat, Silvermine Knocker, Glow Worm
2 Enthralled Silvier, Rockbiter, Frit, Gemclicker
3 Larval Predator, Trammer, Gemclicker
4 Silvermine Knocker, Shaftrat
5 Rockbiter, Glow Worm
6 Gem Clicker, Gem-Dusted Skeleton
7 Rockbiter, Enthralled Silvier, Scratch
8 Geas-Bound Hewer, Silvermine Sentry, Collared Gemgetter
9 Silvermine Sentry, Unseelie Underviewer
10 Undead Drudger, Gemclicker, Tunnel Imp, Collared Gemgetter
11 Gemclicker
12 Larval Predator, Gemclicker, Gemclicker Hoarder
13 Enthralled Silvier
14 Collared Gemgetter
15 Enthralled Silvier
16 Undead Drudger, Collared Gemgetter, Geas-Bound Hewer
17 Enthralled Silvier, Collared Gemgetter
18 Gemclicker, Undead Drudger, Collared Gemgetter
19 Undead Drudger, Collared Gemgetter, Geas-Bound Hewer
20 Gemclicker, Geas-Bound Hewer, Silvermine Sentry, Unseelie Underviewer, Collared Gemgetter, Unseelie Overviewer
21 Silvermine Sentry, Undead Drudger
22 Collared Gemgetter, Gemclicker, Undead Drudger, Geas-Bound Hewer
23 Silvermine Guard, Coerced Groover
24 Lode Protector, Vein Golem
25 Troglodyte, Phantom Miner
26 Phantom Miner, Lode Protector, Casolith
27 Silver-Maddened Werewolf, Weewere
28 Weewere
29 Casolith, Haunting Draft, Phantom Miner, Silver-Maddened Werewolf
30 Unseelie Viewer, Coerced Groover, Unseelie Overman
31 Vein Golem, Coerced Groover, Lode Protector
32 Guardian of the Silver Hand, Overseer of the Silver Hand
33 Abysmal

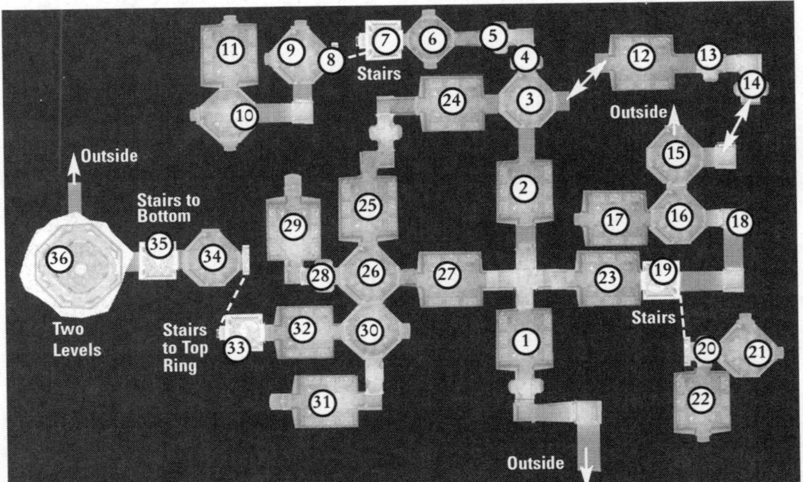

Muire Tomb

1 Crypt Spider, Mummy Hag
2 Crypt Spider
3 Mummy Hag, Tomb Creeper
4 Tomb Creeper
5 Tomb Creeper
6 Muire Man-at-arms, Conaire Muire, Muire Hero
7 Muire Champion
8 Muire Champion
9 Muire Hero, Mummy Hag Wizard, Muire Herbalist
10 Death Worm, Muire Champion
11 Muire Hero, Muire Herbalist, Mummy Hag Wizard, Shyene Muire
12 Murkman, Alsandair Muire
13 Tomb Creeper
14 Tomb Creeper
15 Tomb Creeper, Corpse Devourer
16 Tomb Creeper, Corpse Devourer
17 Crypt Spider, Tomb Dweller
18 Tomb Creeper
19 Tomb Creeper
20 Tomb Creeper, Corpse Devourer
21 Tomb Dweller, Corpse Devourer
22 Muire Lady-in-waiting, Corpse Devourer, Beare Muire
23 Mummy Hag, Crypt Spider
24 Murkman, Death Worm
25 Hellhag, Mummy Hag, Death Worm, Murkman
26 Hellhag, Death Worm, Mummy Hag
27 Crypt Spider, Mummy Hag
28 Tomb Creeper
29 Carrion Scorpionida, Scorpionida Regina
30 Suitor Spirit
31 Suitor Spirit, Muire Lady-in-waiting
32 Corpse Devourer, Muire Hero
33 Muire Champion, Muire Herbalist
34 Muire Hero, Muire Champion
35 Muire Hero, Muire Champion
36 Muire Champion, Muire Hero, Muire Herbalist, Quillan Muire

Spraggon Den

1 Root Worm
2 Rock Sprite
3 Spraggon Runner
4 Spraggon Cutter
5 Pit Spraggon, Spraggon Cutter
6 Rock Sprite, Pit Boss
7 Rock Sprite, Root Worm
8 Spraggonix
9 Spraggon Springer, Spraggonote
10 Root Worm, Yadda, Rock Sprite
11 Root Worm, Earth Sprite, Rock Sprite
12 Spraggonix
13 Pit Spraggon, Spraggon Springer, Rock Sprite
14 Spraggon Cutter, Spraggon Springer
15 Root Worm, Earth Sprite, Rock Sprite, Spraggon Runner
16 Root Worm
17 Spraggonote, Spraggon Springer
18 Spraggonote, Spraggonix
19 Spraggonote, Spraggonix
20 Spraggonix, Spriggit
21 Root Worm, Rock Sprite, Ruckus
22 Spraggonote

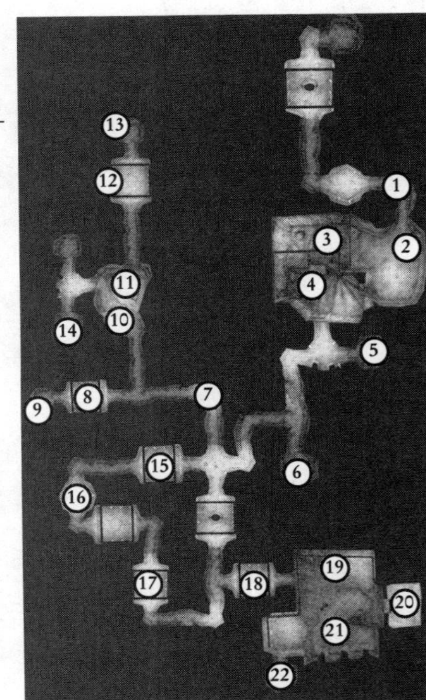

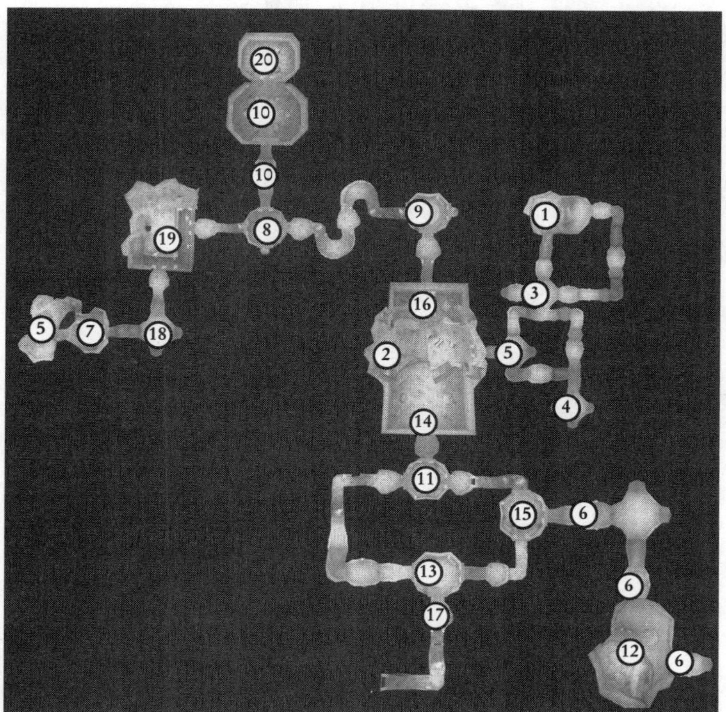

Koalinth Tribal Caverns

1 Aqueous Slug, Shock Aqueous Slug
2 Cave Toad
3 Cave Toad, Aqueous Slug
4 Cave Toad, Poisonous Cave Toad
5 Koa. Alliant, Koa. Guardian
6 Koa. Bouncer
7 Koa. Envoy, Koa. Diplomat, Pelagian Crab
8 Koa. Envoy, Koa. Guardian
9 Koa. Envoy, Koa. Sentinel
10 Koa. Guardian
11 Koa. Sentinel, Koa. Warden
12 Koa. Spectator, Koa. Wrestler
13 Koa. Warden
14 Koa. Warden, Koa. Watery Escort
15 Koa. Watery Escort, K. Sentinel, K. Warden
16 Koa. Watery Escort, Koa. Warder
17 Koalinth Sentinel
18 Pelagian Crab
19 Pelagian Crab, Koa. Castellan
20 Pelagian Crab, Koa. Elder

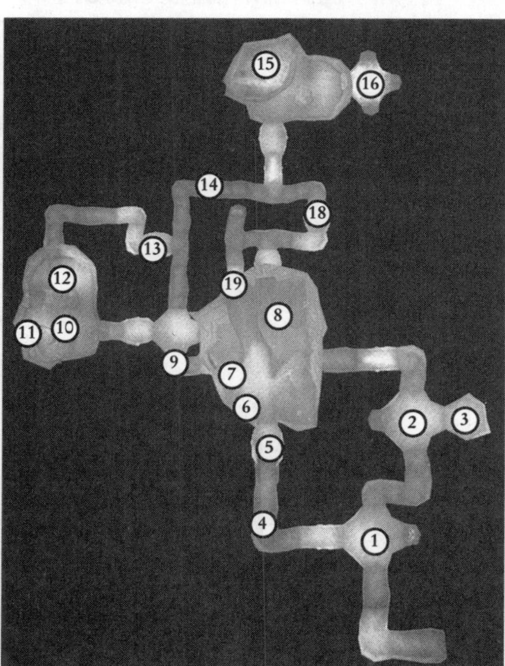

Treibh Caillte

1 Wolf Adult, Lairworm, Rock Golem
2 Scragger
3 Scragger, Scurry
4 Ursine Dweller, U. Savant
5 Rock Golem, Ursine Dweller, U. Patrol, U. Sorcerer
6 Ursine Thrall
7 Ursine Dweller, U. Patrol, U. Warrior, U. Shaman, U. Sorcerer, King Vian
8 Arachnid
9 Arachnid
10 Ursine Thrall
11 Webweaver
12 Lair Worm, Troglodyte, Thorg
13 Arachnid, Arachite
14 Arachnid, Arachite, Web Weaver
15 Lair Worm, Troglodyte, Helminth
16 Arachnid, Arachnite, Webweaver

Realm of Midgard

Midgard is a cold and harsh realm where friendships are forged in the face of adversity. The simplicity of the culture stands in counterpoint to the depth and generosity of its people.

Races & Classes

MYSTIC

Mystics are the spellcasters of the Realm of Midgard. You use the power given to you by your god to craft spells of great force. At fifth level, Mystics choose which god to follow: Odin or Hel. Followers of Odin become Runemasters, who use the power of runes to make Area-Effect spells. Hel's followers become Spiritmasters, who are able to call on the spirits of fallen Norse warriors who want to come back so they can die with honor protecting Midgard.

Trolls cannot become Mystics.

Kobold, Norse Mystics

As a Kobold or Norseman, you will make an average Mystic.

Well, actually that's the official line, but really Kobolds make excellent Runemasters. As for Spiritmasters, Kobolds and Norsemen rank about even.

Dwarven Mystic

At fifth level, Dwarven Mystics must join the House of Odin and become Runemasters, using the power of runes to cast Area-Effect spells.

As a Dwarf, you make an average Mystic.

By and large, it's a waste of time to make a Dwarf when you intend to go into the Mystic field. Their abilities tend more toward direct confrontation, in general.

ROGUE

Rogues are adept at hiding, sneaking and using their Dexterity and Quickness — experts in wielding weapons and masters at the arts of moving while unseen. At fifth level, Rogues choose which god they will follow: Loki or Skadi. Followers of Loki become Shadowblades, who mix their Roguish skills with spells of illusion. Followers of Skadi become Hunters, and learn tracking and bow skills. (Dwarves can only become Hunters.)

Trolls cannot become Rogues.

Kobold Rogue

As a Kobold Rogue, you will make a good Shadowblade and an good Hunter.

Keep in mind that Kobolds are small, which makes them harder to see, even when they are not moving with Stealth. This comes in extremely handy for any character you intend to take into Realm vs. Realm combat.

Norse Rogue

As a Norse Rogue, you will make a great Shadowblade and a good Hunter.

The extra CON and STR mean that a Norseman is a little handier to have in a group situation. Also, a Shadowblade's weapon are Strength-based, which gives the Norse an edge.

Dwarven Rogue

As a Dwarven Rogue, you may join the house of Skadi. You will make an good Hunter.

Dwarven Rogues are a rare choice, usually chosen only if the player has a good role-playing reason for making this choice.

SEER

Seers are highly sought after in groups, for a group with the protective magic of a Seer is much stronger than a group without one. At fifth level, Seers choose to follow either Ymir or Eir. Kobolds and Trolls become followers of Ymir — Shaman, wielding great magic to harm your enemies and care for your friends. Dwarves and Norsemen become followers of Eir — Healers, better than a Shaman at healing, and able to distract and delay your enemies.

Dwarven Seer

Dwarven Seers use the magical power of their gods to cast healing and other beneficial magic on their Realmmates. Because of hitpoint distribution and CON, plus bonuses from cloth armor, Dwarves are sturdy against archers, an advantage in RvR.

As a Dwarf, you may join the House of Eir at fifth level and become a Healer, with beneficial magic for all your Realmmates.

Because Dwarves have the native Strength required to wear chainmail, they have a longer life expectancy in combat.

Kobold Seer

As a Kobold, you may join the House of Ymir at fifth level and become a Shaman, with beneficial magic for all your Realmmates, as well your offensive spell ability (high DEX).

Kobolds Shaman are popular in groups since they can fulfill just about any need, including that of Healer. They are small, which means they are harder to see from a distance, and thus not so easily targeted in Realm vs. Realm combat. However they aren't able to take much direct damage; Kobolds are a rather fragile race.

Norse Seer

As a Norseman, you may join the House of Eir at fifth level and become a Healer, with beneficial magic for all your Realmmates.

Healers are always popular, plus Norsemen are harder to recognize as Healers in RvR (unless the staff is out).

Trollish Seer

As a Troll, you may join the House of Ymir at fifth level and become a Shaman, with beneficial magic for all your Realmmates, as well as some offensive spell ability.

Trolls have a naturally low Dexterity, which would need to be magically augmented before he could reach his full potential, but his high Strength and Constitution better enable him to survive direct conflict better than many other races.

VIKING

As a Viking you use the force of arms to vanquish your enemies and advance in level. At fifth level, you must choose which god to follow: Tyr (Warrior), Modi (Berserker), Thor (Thane), or Bragi (Skald). (Kobolds can only become Warriors or Skalds.) Warriors fight exclusively with weapons. Berserkers gain the ability to throw themselves into a battle rage, and at high levels to change into bear form. Thanes receive spellcasting abilities from Thor, and Skalds sing songs of heroism and bravery to help their groupmates fight better.

Trollish Viking

As a Troll, you will make a very good Warrior or Berserker, with the advantage of your brutish Strength. However, they are slow and non-dexterous.

Dwarven Viking

As a Dwarf, you will make a good Viking, with no advantages, but no disadvantages either.

A naturally high constitution is a definite advantage. You may wish to augment your relatively low Strength with magical items, which would be the trait most likely to stand you in good stead. Lack of height makes Dwarves a bit less likely to draw an attack in Realm vs. Realm.

Norse Viking

As a Norseman, you will make a good Viking, with no advantages, but no disadvantages either.

Because the Norse are actually well-balanced during the early stages, if this is your first Viking character you can feel comfortable waiting until Level 5 before you really know which type of Viking you'd like to be.

Kobold Viking

As a Kobold, you will make a good Viking, although they have relatively weak Strength and Constitution. Their small height is excellent for RvR, and their high Dex makes best use of a warrior's strongest suite: defensive skills. You may join either the House of Tyr or the House of Bragi.

Horse Routes

For a description of how to rent and ride a horse, see **Horse Routes**, page 372.

Stable	Stable Master	Tickets To
Audliten	Fraglock	Mularn
Fort Atla	Rundorik	Galplen Mularn
Fort Veldon	Arskar	Gna Faste
Galplen	Treflun	Fort Atla Vasudheim Gna Faste
Gna Faste	Wolgrun	Raumarik Fort Veldon Galplen Huginfel
Haggerfel	Yolafson	Vasudheim
Huginfel	Prulgar	Svasud Faste Gna Faste
Mularn	Gularg	Audliten Ft. Atla
Nalliten	Eryklan	Vindsaul Faste
Raumarik	Larsson	Gna Faste
Svasud Faste	Vorgar	Huginfel Vindsaul Faste
Vasudheim	Harlfug	Haggerfel Galplen
Vindsaul Faste	Ulufgar	Nalliten Svasud Faste

Thane

Races	Abilities	
Norseman / Troll / Dwarf	1	Staves
	1	Cloth Armor
	1	Leather Armor
	1	Studded Armor
	1	Sprint
	2	Small Shields
	10	Protect I
	12	Medium Shields
	12	Chain Armor
	15	Intercept
	20	Protect II

Skills	
1	Sword
1	Axe
1	Parry
1	Hammer
2	Shields
5	Stormcalling (Magic)

Styles
Axe
Hammer
Sword
Shields

As well-trained as a Warrior, you can handle most weapons and armor. You combine ranged and melee attacks — for instance, Stormcalling and Lightning from afar, and single or two-handed combat up close. Versatile and great for solo or group play.

The Best Part: You can play solo or grouped, using magic for pulling as a melee backup. You also get ranged spells for RvR, as well as self STR and weapon damage buffs, and Intercept.

The Worst Part: You can't heal yourself or buff others, and you don't do or take as much damage as a Warrior.

Race Choices:

Norseman. Human-like, with some resistance to Crush, Slash, Fire and Mana. Easy to impersonate Britons with hooded cloaks. Average race, average stats.

Dwarf. Get high CON, average QUI and DEX to start, plus some resistance to Slash, Thrust, Mind and Poison. Small size is good for RvR (easy to hide). Main drawback is low STR.

Troll. Very high STR, and some resistance to Slash, Thrust, Cold and Light. Extremely low QUI and DEX.

Stat Choices: You want STR, CON, DEX, QUI and PIE. DEX and QUI don't advance by level, so spend points on them. Norsemen may need CON, Dwarves STR, and Trolls QUI. Usually, about 10 points in the "weak" stat does it.

- *STR:* Helps determine damage and sets END for weapon styles. Increases with level.
- *CON:* Critical. Put some of your 30 points here. CON impacts HP, which determine damage you can take.
- *PIE:* Determines Mana/Power pool for casting. Place extra points here after tending to STR or CON.

Weapon Choices:

- Try 1- and 2-handed axes, hammers and swords. 2-handed weapons have more damage and delay, while 1-handed ones are quick with less punch. 1-handed weapons also let you hold a medium shield.
- Axes and swords give bonus hits on wood-like creatures, mammals, humanoid NPCs and wearers of studded or cloth armor. Hammers are good for Undead, Insects, Amphibians, and plate or scale armor.
- *Axes:* No need to train another skill in order to use the 2-handed version. Medium speed and damage compared to other 2-handed weapons.
- *Hammers:* Class gift. A damaging, but slow, 2-handed weapon.
- *Swords:* Fastest 1-handed or 2-handed weapon for this class. The 1-handed sword is the least damaging Thane weapon; for the 2-handed one, you don't need to train another skill.

Spec Paths: Spend skill points on weapon type (Axes, Hammers, Swords), Parry, Shield and Stormcalling. Become defensive, offensive or a mage/fighter (focused on Stormcalling). You get two times your level in skill points to spend when you level, so have no fear of being gimped by Level 50.

Big Mistakes to Avoid in Character Creation: Don't spend any points on INT, EMP or CHA.

Deciding What You Want Your Role to Be: You can play defensively, offensively or as a mage/fighter. Decide early and develop skills in that direction.

Plotting Your Future: You can change playing styles up into the 30s. Starting at Level 5, sculpt your playing style by spending skill points — always Stormcalling, your weapon and Parry. For a 1-handed weapon, focus on Shield as well.

- *Offensive:* The focus is on delivering damage, usually 2-handed. Carry a 1-handed weapon and shield for occasional battles (e.g., in RvR, use them until you engage in close melee, then switch to your 2-handed weapon).
- *Defensive:* Avoid combat hits and hold aggro in a fight using a 1-handed weapon and a shield. Skill points go into weapon, Shield, Parry and Stormcalling. This defensive path holds group aggro and helps defense. Use a 1-handed weapon for faster, more constant hits to keep a creature's attention. Shield styles can stun/hold a mob, as well as block.
- *Mage/Fighter:* Damage foes with Stormcalling and melee follow-up. Your arsenal includes spells, a 1-handed weapon and a shield. The higher Stormcalling, the sooner you get the next, more damaging spell.

Grouping: You're versatile and adaptable. You don't need Strength buffs from Shaman and Healers, and you can pull. With other pullers, you can be a tank. With other tanks, you can help Protect or Guard others or maintain aggro. Even two Thanes are not redundant.

- To hold your own as a main tank, hold aggro of the mob at hand while protecting susceptible classes. Be aware of mezzed, snared or rooted mobs and don't break them with an AE spell.
- As a secondary tank, assist the main tank. With Shield, you can stun critters in a non-mezzable mob until the group's ready. Just monitor Endurance (Shield drains it).
- You can also be a bodyguard and take hits for party members when you get Intercept at Level 15.
- Communication is key. Be flexible as best you can for any group, you will have a blast.

Soloing: You can solo the entire game with melee and spells since you can take a hit and survive longer in combat than most other classes. With good tactics, you can solo yellow and occasional orange mobs.

- Look for mobs that give a bonus to hit with your weapon and a minus to hit when they attack you.
- Find your mob, buff your STR and weapon damage, then cast a pulling spell (varies according to your Stormcalling skill level).
- Pull with spells on timers first. Later, use your insta-cast spells.
- When a mob closes on you, use your weapon of choice and beat the mob using weapon styles and Shield styles. You may want to use Shout spells if you get into trouble.
- Gray cons waste time (no experience). Green and blue con mobs give experience (green less than blue) and are pretty much a given victory. Yellow mobs are a good bit tougher and pose survivable encounters with some post-battle downtime. On a rare occasion, you can take on an orange con mob and live, but that is very rare. Red and purple mobs assure a quick trip back to your bind point.

Realm Versus Realm:

- Your role is similar to PvE — protect casters and inflict pain on enemies.
- Until you cast, opposing realms won't know your class, especially if you carry a shield.
- You get to use ranged damage in RvR, like Invoke Mjollnir spells (a great ability for keep raids). Also, you can use Thunder Shout at point blank range and engage in 2-handed weapon melee.
- Use /face if you get hit by a ranged attack to face the direction of your attacker. Use /stick in toe-to-toe combat to follow an enemy. Use /chat to plan RvR battle.

Beginner's Tips:

- Save skill points until Level 5, then train your chosen weapon skill. This lets you spend more on Stormcalling and Shield.
- Stay buffed whenever you're not in a city or town. Buffs are on a 10-minute timer, so keep your eye on them.
- Money is tight until the 30s. Try to get armor and weapons from mobs or quests. For more cash, solo blue and green con mobs at the beginning.

Advanced Techniques:

- Use caution with AoE spells, since you can break Mezzes and Roots. It's easier to kill foes one at a time.
- Stormcalling 16+ gives the Invoke Mjollnir line of spells, a distance Area Effect spell good for pulling. Use caution — you may get the attention of too many critters at once.
- Buff immediately before combat, open with a Bolt, follow with Toothgrinder's. Hit your opponent with Thunder Shout, then with your favorite weapon style, and finish them off with regular melee. Now, didn't that feel good?
- 30% chance of stopping arrows from a same-level archer with your shield. Modified by Shield spec, quality and condition of the shield, and Engage skill.

Thane Styles

Abbreviations. *Headers:* **F**atigue **C**ost / **B**onus **D**amage / **B**onus **t**o **H**it. *In table:* **L**ow / **M**edium / **H**igh / **V**ery **H**igh / **D**efensive **B**onus (for you, on next round) / **D**efensive **P**enalty (to you, on next round) / **A**ttack **S**peed **R**eduction / **M**ovement **R**eduction (for target)

Axe

Lvl	Style	FC	BD	BtH	Prerequisites / Other Notes
2	Splitter	H	M	–	
4	Cleave	L	M	M	Prereq: parried target / Low ASR
6	Plague	M	L	M	Attempt to taunt target; Med DP
8	Thrym's Strength	M	M	M	Prereq: Cleave / Low Stun
10	Pillage	M	M	L	Low ASR
12	Hoarfrost	M	–	L	Attempt to turn away target; Med DB
15	Evernight	L	H	M	Prereq: target fumbled / Med Bleed
18	Plunder	M	M	M	Prereq: Pillage / Low MR
21	Valkyrie's Shield	L	M	–	Prereq: target blocked by anyone / Med DB
25	Raider	L	H	–	Prereq: Pillage / Low Stun; Med penalty to hit; Med DP
29	Havoc	M	M	L	Prereq: in front of target / Low DP
34	Midnight Sun	M	M	H	Prereq: Valkyrie's Shield / Med Stun
39	Glacial Movement	M	M	M	Prereq: beside target / High ASR; Low DP
44	Arctic Rift	L	H	M	Prereq: Evernight
50	Tyr's Fury	M	H	H	Prereq: Havoc / High Bleed

Hammer

Lvl	Style	FC	BD	BtH	Prerequisites / Other Notes
2	Thor's Anvil	H	M	–	
4	Crushing Blow	L	M	M	Prereq: parried target / Low Stun
6	Placate	M	–	–	Attempt to turn away target; Med DB
8	Slam	M	M	M	Prereq: Crushing Blow / Low Bleed
10	Ruiner	M	H	L	
12	Frost Hammer	M	H	M	Prereq: beside target / Med MR
15	Provoke	M	L	M	Attempt to taunt target; Med DP
18	Demolish	H	M	L	Prereq: Ruiner / Low Stun
21	Revenge	L	M	M	Prereq: target is blocked by anyone / Med ASR; Low DP
25	Crumble	M	H	M	Prereq: Ruiner
29	Conquer	L	M	–	Prereq: behind target / Med MR; High DP
34	Thor's Answer	M	M	M	Prereq: Revenge / Med Stun
39	Lambast	L	M	M	Prereq: parried target / High Bleed; Low DB
44	Sledgehammer	M	H	H	Prereq: Conquer
50	Mjolnir's Fury	M	H	–	Prereq: Thor's Answer / High ASR; High DP

Sword

Lvl	Style	FC	BD	BtH	Prerequisites / Other Notes
2	Whirling Blade	H	M	–	
4	Frost Cut	L	M	L	Prereq: blocked target / Low Bleed
6	Draw Out	M	L	–	Attempt to taunt target; Med DP
8	Northern Lights	M	M	L	Prereq: beside target / Low ASR
10	Assault	M	M	M	
12	Temper	M	–	–	Attempt to turn away target; High DB
15	Aurora	M	H	M	Prereq: Northern Lights / Med MR
18	Baldur's Fury	H	M	M	Prereq: Assault / Low MR
21	Reinforcement	L	M	M	Prereq: target is parried by anyone / Low Bleed; Low DP
25	Ice Storm	M	H	M	Prereq: Assault
29	Rush	L	M	–	Prereq: Reinforcement / High ASR; Med DP
34	Polar Rift	H	M	L	
39	Niord's Fury	L	H	M	Prereq: target fumbled / Med Stun
44	Sif's Revenge	M	M	M	Prereq: Rush / High Bleed
50	Ragnarok	M	M	M	Prereq: behind target / High ASR; Low DP

Shields

Lvl	Style	FC	BD	BtH	Prerequisites / Other Notes
3	Numb	M	M	–	Low Stun
8	Stun	M	M	–	Prereq: blocked target / Low Stun
13	Disable	M	M	–	Prereq: beside target / Med Stun
18	Incapacitate	H	M	–	Prereq: blocked target / Med Stun; Med DB
23	Paralyze	M	M	–	Prereq: behind target / Med Stun
29	Bash	M	M	–	Prereq: blocked target / Med Stun
35	Mangle	M	M	–	Prereq: beside target / High Stun
42	Slam	VH	M	–	High Stun
50	Brutalize	L	M	–	Prereq: blocked target / High Stun

Thane Spells

Stormcalling

DD. You must wait 30 seconds before casting one of these spells again.

Skill ....Stormcalling　Dmg Type............Energy
Casting Time ....3 sec.　Range.....................1500
Duration..................Inst.

Lvl	Spell	Cost	Dmg
1	Thor's Minor Bolt*	2P	5
3	Thor's Lesser Bolt*	3P	12
6	Thor's Bolt*	5P	22
9	Thor's Greater Bolt*	8P	32
13	Thor's Major Bolt*	11P	42
17	Thor's Minor Lightning*	14P	56
23	Thor's Lesser Lightning*	19P	73
29	Thor's Lightning*	24P	93
38	Thor's Greater Lightning*	32P	120
48	Thor's Full Lightning	41P	151

Caster's damage/sec buffed (stacks as group 1).

Skill ....Stormcalling　Dmg Type............Energy
Casting Time ....3 sec.　Duration.............10 min.

Lvl	Spell	Cost	Dmg/Sec
4	Thunder's Bash*	4P	1.2
11	Thunder's Hammer*	9P	2.1
15	Thunder's Force*	12P	2.9
21	Thunder's Crush*	17P	4.2
27	Thunder's Strike*	22P	5.4
36	Thunder's Blow*	30P	7.3
46	Thunder's Rend	39P	9.4

AoE DD, centered on Caster, radius 250. You must wait 30 seconds before casting one of these spells again.

Skill ....Stormcalling　Dmg Type............Energy
Casting Time ....Shout　Duration..................Inst.

Lvl	Spell	Cost	Dmg
5	Thunder Shout*	5P	10
8	Greater Thunder Shout*	7P	15
10	Thunder Howl*	8P	17
12	Greater Thunder Howl*	10P	20
18	Thunder Bellow*	15P	30
25	Greater Thunder Bellow*	20P	40
34	Thunder Roar*	28P	54
44	Greater Thunder Roar	37P	69

Buffs Caster's STR.

Skill ....Stormcalling　Dmg Type............Energy
Casting Time ....3 sec.　Duration.............10 min.

Lvl	Spell	Cost	Buff
2	Thor's Vigor*	3P	11
7	Thor's Strength*	6P	15
14	Thor's Power*	11P	21
20	Thor's Might*	16P	26
30	Thor's Vitality*	25P	34
41	Thor's Fortification*	35P	42
50	Thor's Potence	43P	50

AoE DD.

Skill ....Stormcalling　Dmg Type............Energy
Casting Time ....4 sec.　Range.....................1500
Duration..................Inst.

Lvl	Spell	Cost	Dmg	Radius
16	Call Mjollnir*	13P	53	200
22	Invoke Mjollnir*	18P	69	250
35	Summon Mjollnir*	29P	110	300
45	Command Mjollnir	38P	141	350

DD. You must wait 20 seconds before casting one of these spells again.

Skill ....Stormcalling　Dmg Type............Energy
Casting Time ....Shout　Range.....................1500
Duration..................Inst.

Lvl	Spell	Cost	Dmg
5	Toothgrinders' Hoof*	5P	10
8	Toothgnasher's Hoof*	7P	15
10	Toothgrinder's Bite*	8P	17
12	Toothgnasher's Bite*	10P	20
18	Toothgrinder's Horn*	15P	30
25	Toothgnasher's Horn*	20P	40
34	Toothgrinder's Ram*	28P	54
44	Toothgnasher's Ram	37P	69

Warrior

Races		Abilities	
Norseman / Kobold / Troll / Dwarf		1	Staves
Skills		1	Cloth Armor
		1	Leather Armor
1	Sword	1	Studded Armor
1	Axe	1	Sprint
1	Parry	2	Small Shields
1	Hammer	5	Medium Shields
5	Shields	5	Thrown
5	Thrown	7	Protect I
Styles		10	Large Shields
	Axe	10	Chain Armor
	Hammer	13	Protect II
	Sword	15	Evade I
	Shields	18	Protect III

Warriors are tanks and use the heaviest armor and shields available. With no real ranged combat, they find themselves at the forefront of battle. Warriors deal damage, but are really defined by the ability to stay alive. Warriors tend to either protect casters or charge into melee combat.

The Best Part: Lots of HP at higher levels. Easy to learn, and desirable for groups.

The Worst Part: You must rely on others for heals and buffs and can't really pull. Little template variety.

Race Choices:

Troll. Most common race. High STR increases weapon skill, damage and carrying capacity. Their immense size makes Trolls easily identifiable targets.

Dwarf. Highest starting CON in the game (good for HP). Dwarves are less conspicuous than Trolls, though they may become even more of a target if mistaken for a Midgard Healer.

Norseman. Popular and well balanced, with no real drawbacks when it comes to starting attributes.

Kobold. Least common Warrior race due to low STR and CON, but with faster weapon attacks and defensive skills (Block, and Parry are affected by DEX, and Evade is Quickness and Dexterity). Kobold warriors do slightly less damage and have slightly fewer HP than the other races.

Stat Choices: CON is most important. Put other points into STR, DEX or QUI — whichever balances out a weakness of yours.

- *STR:* High level allows you carry more gear and directly affects melee weapon skill and damage. Put in 10 points at creation.
- *CON:* Directly affects max HP (more CON equals more HP). Put in 10 points at creation.
- *DEX:* Affects defensive skill activation rates. With more DEX, you block and parry more often.
- *QUI:* Removes some weapon delay. Hard stat to raise, with only one buff. Put 5 or 10 points in at creation.

Weapon Choices:

- You're restricted to either Slash (swords and axes) or Crush (hammers).
- Don't waste points on throwing weapons.
- Specialize in only one weapon, putting other points into Shield or Parry.
- Avoid equipment that cons green if possible; yellow or orange is best.
- Wear chainmail when you can (Level 10, or when you can afford it). Constantly upgrade by buying equipment or finding quests and drops. Repair constantly, as effectiveness varies with condition.

Spec Paths:

- *Swords:* Excellent availability, but suffer from player resists in RvR. Good against leather, but attacks on melee and healing classes come at a damage penalty.
- *Axes:* Give Slash damage and are subject to the same resists as swords (penalties to chain and scale armor). Exceptional availability later (Levels 40 through 50).
- *Hammers:* Do Crush and bonus damage against plate, scale and studded armor (worn by most enemy archers, tanks and healers). Provoke is well worth the wait — excellent bonus damage, a hit bonus, and low Endurance drain. Hammers damage and taunt more effectively than swords or axes.

  Also, Hammers can be a little harder to find, since so many people use them.

- *Parry:* Attempts to deflect incoming melee attacks, but not arrows, with your 1- or 2-handed weapon.
- *Shield:* Crucial to PvE and RvR. Helps block mob attacks against you or whoever you're Guarding. Guard is gained through specialization and lets you block shots for party members. At 42 Shield, you get Slam, which stuns, but costs Endurance. At 50, you get Brutalize, a very efficient style to have! All shield styles are useful against mobs and NPC guards.

Big Mistakes to Avoid in Character Creation: Warrior is pretty straightforward. some people thing it's a mistake to not place 10 points apiece into STR and CON.

Deciding What You Want Your Role To Be: You must either protect casters and healers or pursue enemy players in close combat. Short of stunning or killing, you can't really stop players from meleeing your realmmates. But, your Shield can effectively thwart archers.

Plotting Your Future: Fully specialize in your weapon of choice as fast as you can past Level 5 (when you choose a weapon type). Advance other skills evenly to achieve your plan. Shoot for 7 in Shield quickly, as it allows you to Engage targets (for a high block rate).

Grouping:

- All groups like smart and strong Warriors as a main or secondary tank.
- Shields help block archer attacks against Guarded members, important in fort or relic capture raids.
- As a main tank, maintain aggro with Taunting. Ask Dual Wielding or 2-handed melee fighters to hold back some styles so you can keep aggro.
- Taunt to get a mob's attention, but don't needlessly drain Endurance.
- If you're not the main tank, use Guard and Shield to block the main tank (saves your healer's Mana).

Soloing: With good equipment, soloing is a definite possibility, though downtime may make you want a Healer or Shaman.

- Avoid mobs that nuke in melee. If they only nuke at range they're usually weak in melee.
- Solo in areas with neutral mobs to avoid aggros during a fight.
- The best mobs are ones that use Slash attacks (if you're wearing chain) and are vulnerable to your damage type.
- If you have a good positional style, use it first.

Realm Versus Realm: Your role is two-fold — close in and engage the other realms' casters in direct melee, or protect your own vulnerable healers and casters, particularly from archers. Keep casters on the run.

- Spec'ing Shield makes you nearly immune to NPC archers — useful when ramming enemy keep doors.
- Defeat NPC guards at forts and relic keeps!
- Guard your party's healers or casters and have them stick close. Doors have a lower priority than NPC guards and attackers from the rear.
- Group with a Skald if possible for speed chants. Run around the sides and to the rear of the enemy force. Find a yellow or blue staff carrier and put him or her down. Land Shield stuns on casters to keep them still.
- Look for damaging targets, mainly those who mesmerize or cast DD spells. Identify by race, profile and spell effects.
- In Hibernia, Bards are the most important targets due to their Area Effect Mez, followed by robed casters. In Albion, target mage classes, Clerics and Minstrels.

Beginner's Tips:

- Get a Healer to stun targets you're about to engage.
- Attack one target at a time to minimize broken Mezzes.
- Learn what Buffs come from Healers and Shaman. If you can only have one, you are probably best off choosing Shaman Buffs for STR and CON.
- You have double your chance to block an arrow (compared to a melee attack). Remember, blocking rates are not affected by the quality/condition of the shield.

Advanced Techniques:

- Weapons with a 4.0+ delay have a damage bonus that increases faster than the delay. Slower weapons do more damage than faster ones, but are more vulnerable to the effects of Bladeturn.
- Smaller shields have a lower delay associated with them. Consider using a small shield to stun opponents and land more blows before the stun wears off.
- Side styles are not *supposed* to be an option once battle commences, but they can sometimes be pulled off while solo.

Warrior Styles

Abbreviations. *Headers:* **F**atigue **C**ost / **B**onus **D**amage / **B**onus **t**o **H**it. *In table:* **L**ow / **M**edium / **H**igh / **V**ery **H**igh / **D**efensive **B**onus (for you, on next round) / **D**efensive **P**enalty (to you, on next round) / **A**ttack **S**peed **R**eduction / **M**ovement **R**eduction (for target)

Axe

Lvl	Style	FC	BD	BtH	Prerequisites / Other Notes
2	Splitter	H	M	–	
4	Cleave	L	M	M	Prereq: parried target / Low ASR
6	Plague	M	L	M	Attempt to taunt target; Med DP
8	Thrym's Strength	M	M	M	Prereq: Cleave / Low Stun
10	Pillage	M	M	L	Low ASR
12	Hoarfrost	M	–	L	Attempt to turn away target; Med DB
15	Evernight	L	H	M	Prereq: target fumbled / Med Bleed
18	Plunder	M	M	M	Prereq: Pillage / Low MR
21	Valkyrie's Shield	L	M	–	Prereq: target blocked by anyone / Med DB
25	Raider	L	H	–	Prereq: Pillage / Low Stun; Med penalty to hit; Med DP
29	Havoc	M	M	L	Prereq: in front of target / Low DP
34	Midnight Sun	M	M	H	Prereq: Valkyrie's Shield / Med Stun
39	Glacial Movement	M	M	M	Prereq: beside target / High ASR; Low DP
44	Arctic Rift	L	H	M	Prereq: Evernight
50	Tyr's Fury	M	H	H	Prereq: Havoc / High Bleed

Shields

Lvl	Style	FC	BD	BtH	Prerequisites / Other Notes
3	Numb	M	M	–	Low Stun
8	Stun	M	M	–	Prereq: blocked target / Low Stun
13	Disable	M	M	–	Prereq: beside target / Med Stun
18	Incapacitate	H	M	–	Prereq: blocked target / Med Stun; Med DB
23	Paralyze	M	M	–	Prereq: behind target / Med Stun
29	Bash	M	M	–	Prereq: blocked target / Med Stun
35	Mangle	M	M	–	Prereq: beside target / High Stun
42	Slam	VH	M	–	High Stun
50	Brutalize	L	M	–	Prereq: blocked target / High Stun

Hammer

Lvl	Style	FC	BD	BtH	Prerequisites / Other Notes
2	Thor's Anvil	H	M	–	
4	Crushing Blow	L	M	M	Prereq: parried target / Low Stun
6	Placate	M	–	–	Attempt to turn away target; Med DB
8	Slam	M	M	M	Prereq: Crushing Blow / Low Bleed
10	Ruiner	M	H	L	
12	Frost Hammer	M	H	M	Prereq: beside target / Med MR
15	Provoke	M	L	M	Attempt to taunt target; Med DP
18	Demolish	H	M	L	Prereq: Ruiner / Low Stun
21	Revenge	L	M	M	Prereq: target is blocked by anyone / Med ASR; Low DP
25	Crumble	M	H	M	Prereq: Ruiner
29	Conquer	L	M	–	Prereq: behind target / Med MR; High DP
34	Thor's Answer	M	M	M	Prereq: Revenge / Med Stun
39	Lambast	L	M	M	Prereq: parried target / High Bleed; Low DB
44	Sledgehammer	M	H	H	Prereq: Conquer
50	Mjolnir's Fury	M	H	–	Prereq: Thor's Answer / High ASR; High DP

Sword

Lvl	Style	FC	BD	BtH	Prerequisites / Other Notes
2	Whirling Blade	H	M	–	
4	Frost Cut	L	M	L	Prereq: blocked target / Low Bleed
6	Draw Out	M	L	–	Attempt to taunt target; Med DP
8	Northern Lights	M	M	L	Prereq: beside target / Low ASR
10	Assault	M	M	M	
12	Temper	M	–	–	Attempt to turn away target; High DB
15	Aurora	M	H	M	Prereq: Northern Lights / Med MR
18	Baldur's Fury	H	M	M	Prereq: Assault / Low MR
21	Reinforcement	L	M	M	Prereq: target is parried by you / Low Bleed; Low DP
25	Ice Storm	M	H	M	Prereq: Assault
29	Rush	L	M	–	Prereq: Reinforcement / High ASR; Med DP
34	Polar Rift	H	M	L	
39	Niord's Fury	L	H	M	Prereq: target fumbled / Med Stun
44	Sif's Revenge	M	M	M	Prereq: Rush / High Bleed
50	Ragnarok	M	M	M	Prereq: behind target / High ASR; Low DP

Skald

Races		Abilities	
Norseman / Kobold / Troll / Dwarf		1	Staves
Skills		1	Cloth Armor
1	Sword	1	Leather Armor
1	Axe	1	Studded Armor
1	Parry	1	Sprint
1	Hammer	2	Small Shields
2	Shields	12	Protect I
5	Battlesongs (Magic)	19	Protect II
		20	Chain Armor
		20	Evade I

Skalds are the singer-fighters of Midgard. They're good at melee – although not as good as actual tanks – and have magical songs and chants to boot. It's a good, versatile class, perfect for anyone who gets tired of doing the same thing over and over again.

The Best Part: Skalds' travel songs give them the fastest travel time in the realm, other than horses. If you want to get out and see the world quickly (or outrun an enemy), a Skald is a good choice.

The Worst Part: If you try to use a Skald as a tank, you'll die. This class can't specialize in shield work, which only aggravates the problem. Finally, Skalds get fewer spec points per level than most other classes, and Shouts burn power and are on a timer.

Race Choices:

Norsemen. Lacking a little in STR.

Dwarves. Lacking a little in STR.

Trolls. Lacking a little in DEX and QUI.

Kobold. Lacking STR.

Stat Choices: Here's a good setup template for a Skald:

- *CHA:* Put 10 points into Charisma – this stat determines a Skald's Power, as well as damage for the Direct Damage Shouts.
- *CON:* Put 10 points in Constitution – this affects how many HP you receive at each level.
- The remaining 10 points depend on your race. If you're a Troll you might want to throw 10 points in DEX or QUI – Dexterity determines Shield Blocks, Parry and Evade rates. Quickness determines weapon speed. With any other race you might want to put the 10 points in Strength – a Skald's weapons use Strength to determine damage, and Strength also determines the amount of equipment and items you can carry.

Weapon Choices: Fewer spec points at each level means that Skalds don't specialize much in weapons. In turn, this means they do less damage and hit less often. You only need to specialize in one weapon, so pick one you're comfortable with long-term. Some people like a 2-handed weapon for the extra damage.

Spec Paths: Other than limited weapon specs, it's easy to allocate spec points. Whenever possible, put two-thirds of your points into your Songs, one-third into your primary weapon.

Big Mistakes to Avoid in Character Creation: Do basic combat for Levels 1 through 5, and don't spend any points training anything. After you reach Level 5, buy a better weapon of whatever kind you decide to specialize in, and spend enough points to raise Battlesongs to the current max level (5). If you have any points remaining, put them towards your weapon.

Deciding What You Want Your Role To Be:

- You can be a hit-and-run character, or someone who follows up a Song with Direct Damage.
- Whether solo or in a group, you will almost always lead off combat with your Song of Battle group damage Buff. After that, just wade in, casting your Direct Damage Songs as they become available.
- You're also the king of the quick getaway. Just sing Battleshout (your mesmerizing Song), immediately followed by Song of Travel to hike your speed. One thing to note, if the enemy has taken a lot of damage, your Mez will no longer be effective on them.

Plotting Your Future:

- When half-level points start kicking in at Level 40.5, start putting points into your weapon and Parry.
- Once you reach level 46, invest in Battlesongs one last time, and put all remaining points from levels 46.5 through 50 into weapons and Parry.

Grouping: Skalds are wonderful people to have in a group. They group well with every other class in Midgard. There is no downside; even two Skalds are good, although if a group has to choose between a second Skald and a tank, the tank would probably be the better addition.

- As a Skald, you have two primary duties in a group — quick charges and caster protection.
- A Skald's ability to travel faster than nearly anyone else means that if there's any hope of a melee character getting close and personal with an enemy caster or archer, it'll be a Skald. That's good, because magic and archery are usually interrupted by melee attacks. This saves your group from having to deal with whatever mischief the caster or archer was going to cause. This also gives your own casters a larger window for working up a good nuke barrage.
- Everyone loves your Better Speed Song. You are expected to be the last line of defense for the casters (letting the tanks take the really rough stuff). At the same time, you can help the group with one of your many Buffs. Song of Rest is great for increasing the healing rate during group downtime.

Soloing:

- Skalds are good enough to solo single creatures, but you should avoid casters and monsters that will bring a friend. Obviously, luring the target far enough away that it can't call for help is a good idea.
- A Skald can easily solo green and blue cons at all levels. Yellow con monsters should also be fairly easy for most levels. Starting at around Level 35, approach yellow cons with caution, and make sure you have an escape route if things get rough.

Realm Versus Realm:

- Being a Skald, you can move fast in order to get up close, and you're an excellent melee fighter once you get there. The bad news is that if there's anyone protecting the casters – and there almost always is – they're going to be all over you. If things grow too tense, try pulling back to your own tanks.
- Stay away from one-on-one combat with enemy tanks if possible, although if you're lucky, you could win a melee against a hardier person. It's not something to count on; it just means you aren't necessarily doomed if you're cornered by a bruiser.
- Make sure you protect your own casters, and be prepared to retreat if the encounter proves to be too damaging for the group.

Beginner's Tips:

- Don't invest in any skill points until Level 5.
- In early levels, invest as many points in Battlesongs as possible, put all remaining points in your weapon of choice.
- Only specialize in one weapon type.
- A Skald is not the same as music classes in other realms. It's most similar to Albion's Paladin, and Hibernia's Warden, as far as Strength and abilities go.

Advanced Techniques:

- In the borderlands, the Skald's specialization is "range hunting" and rapid group transport. When your group encounters an enemy group, look for telltale signs of a caster (no armor, a big staff, etc.). When one is found, put on a burst of speed and run over to the caster. Once in melee range, switch to Song of Battle (unless another Skald is already running it in your group), followed by both DD Shouts.
- If you do get caught in combat with an enemy tank, switch to a 2-handed weapon, especially if the enemy is using a 1-handed weapon with a shield. The 2-handed weapon deals more damage and you will benefit from your Damage Add Song, because the Song's Add increases as the attack rate increases.

Skald Spells

Battlesongs

Groupmates' damage/sec buffed (stacks as group 2). You must wait 8 seconds before casting a Groupmate buff spell again.

Skill............Battlesongs Dmg Type..............Body
Cost............................0P Casting Time ....Shout
Range.......................700 Duration ....Chant + 5

Lvl	Spell	Dmg/Sec
5	Chant of the Brawl*	1.3
9	Chant of the Fight*	1.9
14	Chant of the Charge*	2.7
19	Chant of the Battle*	3.4
25	Chant of the Siege*	4.3
35	Chant of the War*	5.8
46	Chant of Blood	7.5

Group Speed Buff by (Speed %). You must wait 8 seconds before casting a Groupmate buff spell again.

Skill............Battlesongs Cost............................0P
Casting Time ....Shout Range.....................2000
Duration ....Chant + 5

Lvl	Spell	Speed %
3	Simple Song of Travel*	44%
13	Song of Travel*	59%
23	Harmonic Song of Travel*	74%
33	Magnificent Song of Travel*	89%
43	Heavenly Song of Travel	104%

Buffs groupmates' health regeneration by (Heal) every cycle. You must wait 8 seconds before casting a Groupmate buff spell again.

Skill............Battlesongs Cost............................0P
Casting Time ....Shout Range.....................1500
Duration ....Chant + 5

Lvl	Spell	Heal
1	Simple Song of Rest*	2
10	Song of Rest*	4
20	Harmonic Song of Rest*	6
30	Magnificent Song of Rest*	8
40	Glorious Song of Rest*	10
50	Heavenly Song of Rest	12

DD. You must wait 20 seconds before casting one of these spells again.

Skill............Battlesongs Dmg Type..............Body
Casting Time ....Shout Range.......................700
Duration.................Inst.

Lvl	Spell	Cost	Dmg
2	Warcry*	3P	7
7	Warholler*	9P	21
18	Warshriek*	21P	50
34	Warbellow	41P	89

DD. You must wait 20 seconds before casting one of these spells again.

Skill............Battlesongs Dmg Type..............Body
Casting Time ....Shout Range.......................700
Duration.................Inst.

Lvl	Spell	Cost	Dmg
4	Battle Whoop*	5P	13
12	Battle Shout*	15P	33
26	Battle Scream*	31P	69
44	Battle Howl	55P	115

Mesmerize: target halts all movement and is unable to attack or cast spells; the effect breaks when the target is healed or takes damage (see page 367 for PvE/RvR limitations). You must wait 30 seconds before casting one of these spells again.

Skill............Battlesongs Dmg Type..............Body
Casting Time ....Shout Range.......................700

Lvl	Spell	Cost	Dur
6	Stunning Shout*	7P	11 sec.
15	Disabling Shout*	17P	15 sec.
21	Crippling Shout*	25P	18 sec.
32	Incapacitating Shout*	39P	24 sec.
42	Paralyzing Shout	53P	29 sec.

Snare: Enemy's speed debuffed to 60% of original movement (see page 367 for Pve/RvR limitations). You must wait 30 seconds before casting one of these spells again.

Skill............Battlesongs Dmg Type.............Spirit
Casting Time ....Shout Range.....................1500

Lvl	Spell	Cost	Dur
11	Compel Surrender*	7P	49 sec.
17	Compel Submission*	10P	59 sec.
22	Compel Resignation*	13P	68 sec.
31	Compel Captulation*	19P	84 sec.
41	Compel Defeat	26P	1.7 min.

Buffs Groupmates' Body resistance. You must wait 8 seconds before casting a Groupmate buff spell again.

Skill............Battlesongs Cost............................0P
Casting Time ....Shout Range.....................1500
Duration ....Chant + 5

Lvl	Spell	Buff
25	Body Bolstering Chant*	10
44	Body Bolstering Song	20

Buffs Groupmates' Spirit resistance. You must wait 8 seconds before casting a Groupmate buff spell again.

Skill............Battlesongs Cost............................0P
Casting Time ....Shout Range.....................1500
Duration ....Chant + 5

Lvl	Spell	Buff
26	Spirit Bolstering Chant*	10
45	Spirit Bolstering Song	20

Buffs Groupmates' Energy resistance. You must wait 8 seconds before casting a Groupmate buff spell again.

Skill............Battlesongs Cost............................0P
Casting Time ....Shout Range.....................1500
Duration ....Chant + 5

Lvl	Spell	Buff
27	Energy Diminishing Chant*	10
46	Energy Diminishing Song	20

Buffs Groupmates' Heat resistance. You must wait 8 seconds before casting a Groupmate buff spell again.

Skill............Battlesongs Cost............................0P
Casting Time ....Shout Range.....................1500
Duration ....Chant + 5

Lvl	Spell	Buff
28	Heat Diminishing Chant*	10
47	Heat Diminishing Song	20

Buffs Groupmates' Cold resistance. You must wait 8 seconds before casting a Groupmate buff spell again.

Skill............Battlesongs Cost............................0P
Casting Time ....Shout Range.....................1500
Duration ....Chant + 5

Lvl	Spell	Buff
29	Cold Diminishing Chant*	10
48	Cold Diminishing Song	20

Buffs Groupmates' Matter resistance. You must wait 8 seconds before casting a Groupmate buff spell again.

Skill............Battlesongs Cost............................0P
Casting Time ....Shout Range.....................1500
Duration ....Chant + 5

Lvl	Spell	Buff
30	Matter Diffusing Chant*	10
49	Matter Diffusing Song	20

Berserker

Races		Abilities	
Norseman / Troll / Dwarf		1	Staves
Skills		1	Cloth Armor
		1	Leather Armor
1	Sword	1	Studded Armor
1	Axe	1	Sprint
1	Parry	2	Small Shields
1	Hammer	4	Evade I
2	Shields	5	Berserk I
5	Left Axe	5	Left Axes
Styles		10	Evade II
	Axe	10	Berserk II
	Sword	10	Protect I
	Left Axe	15	Berserk III
		20	Evade III
		20	Berserk IV

Berserkers are one of Midgard's defining classes — well-rounded fighters with the highest damage output of any Midgard class. As a Berserker, you'll find yourself a welcome part of most groups, and you rank second only to Warriors in the ability to take damage. The lack of magic or ranged attacks is offset by your Vendo form, if you progress to level 25 or above.

The Best Part: At higher levels, you get to go Berserk and deliver massive damage as a half-human, half-bear or (word has it, to be implemented in the game later) as a bear.

The Worst Part: You lack casting or ranged attacks, and you're limited to light armor.

Race Choices: Dwarves, Norsemen and Trolls can be Berserkers.

Norsemen. This is the "average" race. Nothing to shout about, but no real hindrances.

Dwarves. This race sacrifices some initial STR for additional CON. But, Dwarves are better at taking damage and have more Endurance.

Trolls. Trolls trade DEX and QUI for a much higher STR. Therefore, this race tends to do more damage.

Stat Choices:

The prime statistics for Berserkers are STR, CON, and DEX. When allocating your starting points, be sure to put some of your points into Quickness, especially if you choose to play the Troll race. Quickness directly affects your attack speed, and it will not increase as you increase in level. This can be offset, however, by lots of magic items that will increase your QUI to a limited degree.

Strength will increase rather quickly as you level. So, you should also use your starting points to increase your CON (to give you as much Endurance as possible). Any remaining points should be spent to increase Dexterity, as that is the slowest attribute to grow as you level.

Weapon Choices:

- *Dual Wielding Axes:* Most common weapon combination. With it, you use two axes in combat. To use this effectively, spend points to increase your Axes, Left Axe, and Parry skills. This means you have to choose between having all three skills at two-thirds of your level, or having one at your level and two at half your level, or some other compromise.
- *Sword and Left Axe:* Using a Sword and Left Axe combination allows you to take advantage of the best of both worlds. One-handed swords do slightly more damage than equivalent axes, yet you still get to hack opponents apart with two weapons. To use this combination, spend points to increase your Swords, Left Axe and Parry skills. Again, this means you have to choose between having all three skills at two-thirds of your level, or having one at your level and two at half your level, or some other compromise.
- *2-Handed Axe:* The 2-Handed Axe is a much less common weapon choice, but it can let your Berserker swing a huge axe for massive amounts of damage. The drawback is that 2-handed weapons are much slower than equivalent 1-handed weapons (although not twice as slow). To use this combination effectively, spend points to increase your Axes and Parry skills. This means you can have both skills at your level.

Okay, now for the 2-handed vs. Dual Wield debate. Theoretically, a character wielding two 1-handed weapons will do more damage over time than a character wielding a single 2-handed weapon. Why? During combat, you will miss your opponent occasionally (at least). A fast-attacking, lower damage weapon therefore "loses" less damage from a miss than a slow, massive-damage, 2-handed weapon.

Proponents of the 2-handed axe Berserker argue that, since their skills are higher, they miss less often than their Dual Wielding brethren of equal level, and their damage output is therefore greater. They further argue that since their Parry skill is significantly higher than their Dual Wielding brethren, they take significantly less damage from their opponents.

In the end, don't get too fixated on the numbers game. Think about your character, and choose the style that fits the image you want to convey or pick the style that better fits your playing style.

Spec Paths:

- *Berserk:* Not really a specialization, Berserk is the basic ability behind this class. Using it, the Berserker can enter a killing frenzy at will (for 20 seconds, once every 7 minutes), dealing even more damage to opponents than usual. You Critical with every shot, with a bonus to hit, but lose all defensive skills. At Level 25, a character in a Berserk rage transforms into a half-human, half-bear form, called a Vendo. At a higher level, Berserkers will be able to transform completely into a bear when enraged (not yet implemented at the time of printing). Okay, there is one downside to going Berserk — you can't turn it off. You're forced to remain in a Berserk state until you zone away or die. (Note: You don't see your armor, but are still wearing it.)
- Left Axe skill is the ability to use an axe in your left hand. This is unique in that it allows you to Dual Wield weapons, and this ability is only available to Shadowblades and Berserkers. As expected, this has the potential to greatly increase your damage output. You'll find quite a few axes that can be used in your left hand, and many magical weapons and other items will increase your Left Axe skill.

Big Mistakes to Avoid in Character Creation: Berserkers earn 2x level in skill points at each level. Put them to good use by choosing your fighting style early on. This will help to minimize the number of skill points you spend on skills you don't use at higher levels. Otherwise, you end up wasting a lot of points. The most common combinations are Dual Wielding Axes, Sword and Axe, and 2-handed Axe.

Deciding What You Want Your Role To Be: You're the damage machine, pure and simple.

Plotting Your Future: See Big Mistakes and Weapon Choices.

Grouping:

- A Berserker's role in a group is to deal as much damage as possible in as short a time as possible. A good way to do this is to make sure that your weapon(s) are orange or red to you, unless you have a magical weapon that gives large bonuses to STR and your weapon skills.
- If you aren't the main "tank" of the group, then do not "off-tank" (steal the tank's target). Let the Warrior in heavier armor taunt your foes. Focus on taking down your target as quickly as possible, but be reasonable. If the Healer or Runecaster has several monsters, of course you should help the main tank taunt them off. But remember, you are better at dealing out damage, while the Warrior is better at taking it.

Soloing:

- The best armor you can wear is Studded Leather. A small inconvenience, but not insurmountable.
- You'll be able to use small shields, but you can't spend any skill points to gain Shield styles or increase blocking ability. You can, however learn and increase the Parry skill. And you can sometimes block arrows with your shield.
- Once you are within melee range, attack with the style that has the most damage and least delay. That first attack happens "instantly," and ignores the delay of your weapon and attack style. This is basically a "free hit," so use it effectively.

Realm Versus Realm:

- Kill their casters and/or protect your own.
- Sneak around and attack from behind. If there are bears in the area, the Bear form can be very useful here.
- You'll do much better with a group — especially if it includes a Skald (for Speed and Damage Add Songs), a Runecaster/Shaman (Damage Add spell), and/or a Healer.

Beginner's Tips:

- A wounded, even an "almost dead" opponent does just as much damage as a healthy one. Finish off any wounded opponents before attacking a healthy one.
- Since taking damage is not your forte, blue armor is acceptable, although yellow is preferred. Player-made weapons and armor are much better than store-bought and non-magical loot.

Advanced Techniques:

- When entering combat, don't go into attack mode and wait for your target to get close enough to hit. Target it, and when it's close enough, /stick to it. (Make a macro — "/macro Stick /stick" — and put it on your Hotkey bar.)
- Not having a pull ability and not being able to take on more than one critter at a time make the Berserker a better grouper than soloer at higher levels.

Berserker Styles

Abbreviations. *Headers:* **F**atigue **C**ost / **B**onus **D**amage / **B**onus **t**o **H**it. *In table:* **L**ow / **M**edium / **H**igh / **V**ery **H**igh / **D**efensive **B**onus (for you, on next round) / **D**efensive **P**enalty (to you, on next round) / **A**ttack **S**peed **R**eduction / **M**ovement **R**eduction (for target)

Axe

Lvl	Style	FC	BD	BtH	Prerequisites / Other Notes
2	Splitter	H	M	–	
4	Cleave	L	M	M	Prereq: parried target / Low ASR
6	Plague	M	L	M	Attempt to taunt target; Med DP
8	Thrym's Strength	M	M	M	Prereq: Cleave / Low Stun
10	Pillage	M	M	L	Low ASR
12	Hoarfrost	M	–	L	Attempt to turn away target; Med DB
15	Evernight	L	H	M	Prereq: target fumbled / Med Bleed
18	Plunder	M	M	M	Prereq: Pillage / Low MR
21	Valkyrie's Shield	L	M	–	Prereq: target blocked by anyone / Med DB
25	Raider	L	H	–	Prereq: Pillage / Low Stun; Med penalty to hit; Med DP
29	Havoc	M	M	L	Prereq: in front of target / Low DP
34	Midnight Sun	M	M	H	Prereq: Valkyrie's Shield / Med Stun
39	Glacial Movement	M	M	M	Prereq: beside target / High ASR; Low DP
44	Arctic Rift	L	H	M	Prereq: Evernight
50	Tyr's Fury	M	H	H	Prereq: Havoc / High Bleed

Left Axe

Lvl	Style	FC	BD	BtH	Prerequisites / Other Notes
2	Counter Slash	H	M	–	
4	Doubler	M	M	L	Prereq: behind target / Low Bleed; Low DP
6	Ravager	M	M	L	
8	Polar Light	L	M	H	Prereq: parried target / Low ASR; Low DB
10	Snowblind	M	L	L	Attempt to taunt target; Med DP
12	Atrophy	M	M	L	Prereq: Ravager / Med MR
15	Frost Shadow	M	H	M	Prereq: Polar Light / Low DB
18	Comeback	L	M	M	Prereq: target evaded by anyone
21	Scathing Blade	M	H	M	Prereq: Atrophy / High ASR; Med DP
25	Decaying Rage	L	M	M	Prereq: Atrophy / Strong attempt to turn away target; High DB
29	Snowsquall	M	H	M	Prereq: behind target
34	Doublefrost	H	M	L	
39	Frosty Gaze	M	M	M	Prereq: Comeback / Med Stun
44	Icy Brilliance	M	M	H	Prereq: Snowsquall / High Bleed
50	Aurora Borealis	L	H	H	Prereq: parried target / High ASR

Sword

Lvl	Style	FC	BD	BtH	Prerequisites / Other Notes
2	Whirling Blade	H	M	–	
4	Frost Cut	L	M	L	Prereq: blocked target / Low Bleed
6	Draw Out	M	L	–	Attempt to taunt target; Med DP
8	Northern Lights	M	M	L	Prereq: beside target / Low ASR
10	Assault	M	M	M	
12	Temper	M	–	–	Attempt to turn away target; High DB
15	Aurora	M	H	M	Prereq: Northern Lights / Med MR
18	Baldur's Fury	H	M	M	Prereq: Assault / Low MR
21	Reinforcement	L	M	M	Prereq: target is parried by anyone / Low Bleed; Low DP
25	Ice Storm	M	H	M	Prereq: Assault
29	Rush	L	M	–	Prereq: Reinforcement / High ASR; Med DP
34	Polar Rift	H	M	L	
39	Niord's Fury	L	H	M	Prereq: target fumbled / Med Stun
44	Sif's Revenge	M	M	M	Prereq: Rush / High Bleed
50	Ragnarok	M	M	M	Prereq: behind target / High ASR; Low DP

Hunter

Races		Abilities	
Norseman / Kobold / Dwarf		1	Staves
		1	Cloth Armor
		1	Leather Armor
		1	Studded Armor
		1	Sprint
		1	Evade I

Skills	
1	Sword
1	Stealth
5	Spear
5	Beastcraft (Magic)
5	Composite Bow

Styles
Spear
Sword

The Hunter's defining abilities are tied to nature, with the ability to charm animals, cast nature-based spells, use stealth and fire the best ranged weapons. The composite bow is good for range and damage. This is the only Midgard class that can use Spears, and the only one that gets both pets and Stealth. However, a Hunter is limited to light armor and can't use shields, making long-range attacks vital.

The Best Part: You get to use bows and spears, plus some magic. You are great at soloing, and you can deal massive damage in a group.

The Worst Part: With armor limitation and low HP, you can't take a lot of damage. If you can't half-kill a monster before it reaches you, you're in trouble. You also can't use a shield.

Race Choices:

Norseman. Good Hunters, especially in grouping.

Dwarf. Rare option, but good tank-hunters due to high CON and HP. Lack of height can be an advantage for avoiding detection.

Kobold. The most common race for Hunter, with high DEX and QUI for bow use. Melee, however, suffers greatly due to low STR. Again, being short is good for hiding.

Stat Choices: QUI and DEX are two stats to concentrate on, with STR a close third.

- *QUI:* Helps you shoot arrows faster.
- *DEX:* Assists you in hitting monsters with your spear.
- *STR:* Helps you carry arrows into battle if you use a bow.
- How you allocate starting points depends on your race. A Kobold's low STR puts a great limit on melee damage and encumbrance, and low CON increases vulnerability at low levels. Raising QUI gives a fast attack.
- Dwarves and Norsemen should spend more points on DEX and QUI. Try for balance.

Weapon Choices:

- *Spears:* Big, mean and unique to your class. For maximum benefit with this weapon, concentrate on STR and DEX.
- *Swords:* Popular, but you have to bicker with Warriors and Thanes over good sword drops.
- *Bows:* Very powerful. Bows put out more damage than spears because of arrow modifiers, so it is always better to deal damage with a bow than a spear. Note that there are no multiple damage arrows in RvR, because a thrusting arrow has less of a damage bonus than a slashing one, makeing them identical against chainmail.

Spec Paths:

- *Composite Bow:* Gives the Critical Shot style, good for massive ranged damage. For an archery emphasis, keep this ability as close to your level as possible. Spread other points between Spear and Beastcraft.
- *Spear*: If you love melee, buy a relatively high Spear skill. Otherwise, only spend enough points to develop this as a backup weapon.
- If you want to be a sneaky archer, forget Spear and put points into Stealth and Composite Bow. Your percentage spec in Stealth gives an equal chance of staying hidden while nocking your arrows (50% spec equals 50% chance of staying hidden). But, high Stealth has very little use outside of RvR.
- *Stealth:* Allows you sneak close to (or past) your foes, critical for scouting and sniping. Higher-level NPCs may see through you, as might PCs with high Stealth. Firing/taking arrows can break Stealth, as can casting or being hit by any offensive Area Effect spell cast by the enemy. You can't use Stealth again until ten combat seconds have elapsed.
- *Beastcraft:* Beastcraft is the Hunter's unique line of spells, enabling you to charm animals into pets. You can also temporarily buff a pet's Strength, as well as increase Armor Factor, QUI and DEX, and movement speed.

Big Mistakes to Avoid in Character Creation: Don't put all your skill points into one area. Spread them around between STR, QUI and DEX, with an emphasis on your weapon type.

Deciding What You Want Your Role to Be: If you hunt, you want to use the bow. Spears are okay, but best as a backup weapon. Choose your playing style early to minimize the number of points spent on skills not used at higher levels. The most common styles are snipers, soloists, and tanks.

Plotting Your Future:

- *Sniper:* A dreaded RvR character type. Focus on Stealth and Composite Bow so you can sneak into enemy territory. (However, snipers are routinely hunted down and killed by higher-level characters after a few kills.)
- *Soloist:* Well balanced, with equal emphasis on all abilities. Keep a pet at all times for protection and attack purposes. Use Stealth to locate prey and hide between combat encounters. Use Composite Bow to pull targets into melee range, and use Spear to finish off the target.
- *Tank-Hunter:* Rare, but a great benefit to groups. Focus on Spears and Composite Bow. Light armor and lack of Parry make this a poor choice for a group's tank, but you pull and play secondary tank.

Grouping:

- In a group, you're heavy artillery. If a battle gets difficult, put away the spear, step back and rely on your arrows.
- Never draw the mob's aggro; you'll upset your healers. Let the guys up front with swords and shiny armor take the hits. Support them as best you can.
- Even as a soloist, you can help a group. Having Pets and Spear increases the group's damage output, while Composite Bow and Stealth allow you to pull.
- If you over-pull or get attacked by something too big for the group, don't lead it back. Stand your ground and kill it, or let it kill you. Eventually, your group can find your corpse, and the Healer can resurrect you.

Soloing:

- Utilize your range. Attack from the maximum distance possible, and always with a critical shot followed by three or so normal shots. By that point, the mob should be at half Health and easy to finish off up close with the spear.
- Stick to hunting Animals or Insects. Humanoids can probably kill you. Always get a pet if you can find one.
- Never attack monsters that attract friends.
- If a fight goes badly, run. It's better to escape than visit your bind point.

Realm Versus Realm:

- Your role is to inflict as much damage to the enemy as possible, making the job of killing them easier for your tanks. Try splitting off from the group and disrupt the enemy forces whenever possible.
- Snipers are devastating in sieges and large RvR actions, as they can flank enemy forces and eliminate or interrupt healers and casters.
- No Stealth while carrying a Relic.

Beginner's Tips:

- Find a large group and ask to follow. Don't worry if you don't know them — the more, the merrier in RvR.
- Never take on an enemy player singly. You will likely lose, unless he hasn't seen you.
- Most Hunters start out with 120 to 160 arrows each time they go out. You can learn to make your own bows and arrows by developing the proper skills.
- Never equip a bow or a spear before you need to in a Frontier zone. They immediately identify you as a potential sniper to the enemy.
- Remember, your pet can't go anywhere that a normal player can't go.

Advanced Techniques:

- When a large group lays siege to a fort, fall back and keep lookout for incoming enemy forces. If you can give an early warning, you will save your side from being wiped out by a surprise attack.

- Always carry more than one arrow type. Slash damage broadhead arrows will not be as effective against chainmail-wearers in the enemy realm.
- A stealthed archer is visible when he fires; when he nocks his arrow, if he fails his Stealth check. Stealth spec % (-20% on Critical Shots) = % chance to stay hidden.

Hunter Styles

Abbreviations. *Headers:* **F**atigue **C**ost / **B**onus **D**amage / **B**onus **t**o **H**it. *In table:* **L**ow / **M**edium / **H**igh / **V**ery **H**igh / **D**efensive **B**onus (for you, on next round) / **D**efensive **P**enalty (to you, on next round) / **A**ttack **S**peed **R**eduction / **M**ovement **R**eduction (for target)

Spear

Lvl	Style	FC	BD	BtH	Prerequisites / Other Notes
2	Dazzling Spear	H	M	–	
4	Return Thrust	L	M	M	Prereq: evaded target / Low Bleed
6	Engage	M	L	M	Attempt to taunt target; Med DP
8	Extended Reach	L	M	L	Prereq: Return Thrust / Low ASR
10	Lancer	M	H	M	Small DP
12	Dismissal	M	–	–	Attempt to turn away target; High DB
15	Wounding Thrust	M	M	L	Prereq: Engage / Med MR
18	Stab	L	–	M	Prereq: Lancer / Med Bleed
21	Perforate	M	M	–	Prereq: beside target / High ASR; Med DP
25	Lunging Thrust	M	H	M	Prereq: Lance
29	Raze	M	L	M	Prereq: Stab / High Bleed
34	Whirling Spear	H	M	L	Low DP
39	Razor Edge	M	M	M	Prereq: behind target / Med Stun; Low DP
44	Odin's Wrath	L	H	H	Prereq: parried target / Low DB
50	Gungnir's Fury	M	M	M	Prereq: Perforation / High Bleed

Sword

Lvl	Style	FC	BD	BtH	Prerequisites / Other Notes
2	Whirling Blade	H	M	–	
4	Frost Cut	L	M	L	Prereq: blocked target / Low Bleed
6	Draw Out	M	L	–	Attempt to taunt target; Med DP
8	Northern Lights	M	M	L	Prereq: beside target / Low ASR
10	Assault	M	M	M	
12	Temper	M	–	–	Attempt to turn away target; High DB
15	Aurora	M	H	M	Prereq: Northern Lights / Med MR
18	Baldur's Fury	H	M	M	Prereq: Assault / Low MR
21	Reinforcement	L	M	M	Prereq: target is parried by anyone / Low Bleed; Low DP
25	Ice Storm	M	H	M	Prereq: Assault
29	Rush	L	M	–	Prereq: Reinforcement / High ASR; Med DP
34	Polar Rift	H	M	L	
39	Niord's Fury	L	H	M	Prereq: target fumbled / Med Stun
44	Sif's Revenge	M	M	M	Prereq: Rush / High Bleed
50	Ragnarok	M	M	M	Prereq: behind target / High ASR; Low DP

Hunter Spells

Beastcraft

Charms animals up to (% Cap) of Caster's level.

Skill ....Beastcraft Dmg Type ....Spirit
Cost ....25%P Casting Time ....4 sec.
Range.....................1200 Duration ....Until Neg.

Lvl	Spell	Max Lvl	% Cap
1	Minor Call of Gleipnir*	7	80%
7	Lesser Call of Gleipnir*	13	80%
13	Call of Gleipnir*	20	80%
20	Greater Call of Gleipnir*	32	80%
32	Superior Call of Gleipnir	50	82%

Buffs Caster's DEX and QUI.

Skill ....Beastcraft Dmg Type ....Body
Casting Time ....3 sec. Range.....................1000
Duration ....10 min.

Lvl	Spell	Cost	Buff
5	Nimbleness of the Lynx*	10P	14
12	Agility of the Lynx*	20P	19
21	Dexterity of the Lynx*	34P	26
30	Quickness of the Lynx*	50P	34
40	Alacrity of the Lynx*	68P	42
50	Heart of the Lynx	86P	50

Buffs Caster's speed by (Speed %); usable in combat. You must wait 10 minutes before casting one of these spells again.

Skill ....Beastcraft Dmg Type ....Body
Casting Time ....Shout

Lvl	Spell	Cost	Dur	Speed %
6	Speed of Prey*	10P	20 sec.	35%
16	Speed of Quarry*	26P	30 sec.	50%
25	Speed of the Chased*	40P	40 sec.	65%
34	Speed of the Pursued*	56P	50 sec.	80%
43	Speed of the Hunted	72P	60 sec.	95%

Buffs Caster's AF.

Skill ....Beastcraft Dmg Type ....Body
Casting Time ....3 sec. Duration ....10 min.

Lvl	Spell	Cost	Buff
2	Lynx's Pelt*	6P	12
4	Snake's Scales*	8P	14
8	Wolf's Hide*	14P	18
11	Turtle's Shell*	18P	21
14	Bear's Mantle*	22P	24
18	Crab's Shell*	30P	28
23	Drake's Hide*	38P	33
31	Wyvern's Scales*	50P	41
42	Arachite's Chitin	70P	52

Charms insects up to (% Cap) of Caster's level.

Skill ....Beastcraft Dmg Type ....Spirit
Cost ....25%P Casting Time ....4 sec.
Range.....................1200 Duration ....Until Neg.

Lvl	Spell	Max Lvl	% Cap
3	Influence Insect*	9	80%
9	Compel Insect*	15	80%
15	Charm Insect*	22	80%
22	Control Insect*	35	80%
35	Dominate Insect	50	82%

Buffs Pet's STR and CON.

Skill ....Beastcraft Dmg Type ....Body
Casting Time ....3 sec. Range.....................1000
Duration ....10 min.

Lvl	Spell	Cost	Buff
10	Wild Spirit*	16P	18
17	Feral Spirit*	28P	23
24	Furious Spirit*	38P	29
33	Raging Spirit*	54P	36
41	Frenzied Spirit	70P	42

Shadowblade

Races	
Norseman / Kobold	
Skills (& Styles)	
1	Sword (& Styles)
1	Stealth
4	Axe
4	Left Axe
5	Critical Strikes (& Styles)
5	Envenom
Abilities	
1	Staves
1	Cloth Armor
1	Leather Armor
1	Sprint
1	Safe Fall IV
1	Evade I
3	Evade II
4	Thrown
5	Small Shields
5	Left Axes
5	Distraction
8	Danger Sense
10	Evade III
10	Safe Fall I
16	Detect Hidden
20	Evade IV
20	Safe Fall II
25	Climb Walls
30	Evade V
30	Safe Fall III
40	Evade VI
40	Safe Fall IV
50	Evade VII

The Shadowblade is an assassin class, blessed with the ability of being able to sneak and hide, as well as learn deadly combat abilities. Here, the lithe Kobold comes into his own and excels (though Norsemen can also follow this path).

Shadowblades are assassin characters, separated from stereotypical rogues by their emphasis on big, Norse-like weapons such as the axe and 2-handed sword. Stealthy and silent, Shadowblades are more suited for solo play and can deliver quick, deadly attacks.

The Best Part: You excel at RvR combat, and playing a stealthy class for the "surprise" factor is a fun change of pace compared to playing the other classes.

The Worst Part: Groups aren't very quick to welcome you, and you're the classic paper tiger in combat... fragile and vulnerable.

Race Choices:

Kobolds. Smaller and harder to see, but definitely predisposed to DEX and QUI.

Norsemen. Bigger, with more STR and CON. Slightly more durability in combat.

Stat Choices:

- *STR:* Most important in Midgard, since weapons are STR-based.
- *CON:* Yields more HP.
- *DEX*: Not a lot of effect for this class, though dexterity is always good for stealthiness.

Weapon Choices:

- *Swords:* Great selection of weaponry, though your swords are entirely based on STR. If you plan to use 2-handed weapons exclusively, this is the way to go.
- *Axes:* Slightly less high-end selection, but plenty of STR-based axes to go around. If you want to incorporate Left Axe into your attacks, specializing in Axes yields an advantage. Your left axe will likely be a high damage-bonus axe.
- *Staves:* DEX-based staves can help avoid specialization, saving points that can be spent elsewhere. But it's hard to find high-level staves, and a staff won't do as much damage as a Critical Strike/Sword-specialized Shadowblade.

Spec Paths:

- *Stealth*: Makes you invisible to your enemies. The better your skill, the smaller your "stealth bubble" (distance at which enemies can locate you). Later, you get skills like Detect Hidden, Danger Sense, Safe Fall and Climbing.
- *Critical Strike:* Gives you high-damage multiplier styles, the most noteworthy being Backstab, Backstab II and Perforate Artery. These are your bread and butter.
- *Sword:* Increases your sword damage and gives you various styles to use.
- *Axe:* Increases axe damage and gives you various styles to use.
- *Envenom:* Provides ability to use Lethal, Enervating, Infectious and Crippling poisons.
- *Left Axe:* Raises damage when using two weapons and also has very nice styles.

Big Mistakes to Avoid in Character Creation: Avoid putting points into things other than STR, CON and DEX (preferably in that order).

Deciding What You Want Your Role to Be: Stealth is always important. Past that, do you want to put emphasis on two-weapon specialization, high damage multiplier styles, or poison?

Plotting Your Future: Your future depends on your spec paths. Early on, Stealth really doesn't need to be much more than half your level. Keep weapon specialization high so that you have the option to solo. By Level 15, you should have defined your path and started putting points toward your focused spec — for instance, Critical Strike, Left Axe, or Envenom.

Grouping: Your primary role in a group is damage add. You should help kill the monster, but without doing enough damage to gain aggro.

- Combine your Backstab II or Creeping Death Critical Strike skills with others' attacks. Certain attacks incorporate a stun element. For maximum efficiency, work out with healers when this will occur so that you can keep the monster stunned longer.
- Find groups with Skalds. Their Damage Add Song, combined with your Dual Wield with Left Axe, can add an impressive amount of damage during a fight.

Soloing: Soloing as a Shadowblade is difficult, though not impossible. Try to find non-aggressive (usually blue con) monsters that you can sneak up on and Backstab. By the time you get Perforate Artery, your soloing days are probably over.

- Look for anything that you have bonuses on damage against that have minuses on you, like wolves.
- Poison your weapons. Find a predictable enemy in a safe location, then Backstab him. If that fails, run away and try again.

Realm Versus Realm:

Working large battles: Rez killing ties up lots of Power and is easy, though not really rewarding. It does help your realm by keeping the dead, dead. Just watch for resurrected players, then run up and one-shot them with Perforate Artery.

You get the Climb ability at 25th train in Stealth. Scale those keep walls!

No Stealth while carrying a Relic.

Archer suppression: During a brawl, watch the edges of the fight for archers. One at a time they will unstealth as they pick targets. Sneak up and kill them as described above, preferably with a buddy.

Finishing off the wounded: This is probably the most rewarding, if not dangerous, tactic you will use. Place yourself right between your line of battle and theirs. Watch the casters and archers advance and cast or shoot at each other. When one caster/archer/tank takes a lot of damage and runs, follow him into the backfield. He usually sits down to recuperate, at which point you can strike for the kill and your share of Realm Points.

Beginner's Tips:

- One-shot kills are great, because if you can kill an enemy with a single Backstab, Backstab II or Perforate Artery, you stay invisible.
- It's easier to one-shot kill someone who's sitting.
- For fast enemies, use Disease poison to reduce their speed.
- Work in conjunction with a second Shadowblade if possible.
- Don't try soloing a tank.
- Have patience. Wait for the right target, and the right moment.
- Use DoT poison, and you can rehide and still do damage.
- Ability Danger Sense. Tells when a scout notices your party. Always on. Prerequisite: 8 trains in Stealth.
- Ability Detect Hidden. See hidden enemy players at increased range. Prerequisite: 16 trains in Stealth.

Advanced Techniques:

Killing an archer: Use Dual Wield, and don't worry much about landing a Perforate Artery or Backstab unless you have time to set one up. It is highly important you turn /stick on before you attack, because an archer will invariably run (or have someone coming to save him). On your Dual Wield, put Disease poison on one blade and Lethal on the other. The first slows him down, and the second makes it harder to cast speed escape spells. If he's loaded with arrows, you can substitute Enervating for Disease for better Snare, but this technique is hit and miss.

Killing a caster: Wait until he sits down; most casters do this. Pull out your biggest 2-handed sword or axe. Open with Perforate Artery or Backstab II. One shot may do it. If not, quickly switch to Dual Wield and keep hitting to interrupt casting. Better not try this in a group of enemies unless you can one-shot him. As for poison selection, Lethal and Disease poisons are a good combination to use in your attacks. They give added damage, reduced movement and reduced healing.

Killing Tanks: Find a friend and work out a plan ahead of time as to what poisons you are going to use. Ideally, one Shadowblade has Enervating and Lethal, the other Enervating and Disease. Look for lonely tanks in transit. Place one Shadowblade about 5 to 10 feet behind the first. Chain Perforate him as he runs through both of you. He probably won't react quickly enough to turn around, giving you better shots at landing Perforate Artery. Now, you can either melee him down or take turns kiting him while the other one hits.

Shadowblade Styles

Abbreviations. *Headers:* **F**atigue **C**ost / **B**onus **D**amage / **B**onus **t**o **H**it. *In table:* **L**ow / **M**edium / **H**igh / **V**ery **H**igh / **D**efensive **B**onus (for you, on next round) / **D**efensive **P**enalty (to you, on next round) / **A**ttack **S**peed **R**eduction / **M**ovement **R**eduction (for target)

Sword

Lvl	Style	FC	BD	BtH	Prerequisites / Other Notes
2	Whirling Blade	H	M	–	
4	Frost Cut	L	M	L	Prereq: blocked target / Low Bleed
6	Draw Out	M	L	–	Attempt to taunt target; Med DP
8	Northern Lights	M	M	L	Prereq: beside target / Low ASR
10	Assault	M	M	M	
12	Temper	M	–	–	Attempt to turn away target; High DB
15	Aurora	M	H	M	Prereq: Northern Lights / Med MR
18	Baldur's Fury	H	M	M	Prereq: Assault / Low MR
21	Reinforcement	L	M	M	Prereq: target is parried by anyone / Low Bleed; Low DP
25	Ice Storm	M	H	M	Prereq: Assault
29	Rush	L	M	–	Prereq: Reinforcement / High ASR; Med DP
34	Polar Rift	H	M	L	
39	Niord's Fury	L	H	M	Prereq: target fumbled / Med Stun
44	Sif's Revenge	M	M	M	Prereq: Rush / High Bleed
50	Ragnarok	M	M	M	Prereq: behind target / High ASR; Low DP

Critical Strikes

Lvl	Style	FC	BD	BtH	Prerequisites / Other Notes
2	Backstab	M	M	M	Prereq: behind target, hidden / Med DP
4	Eviscerate	M	H	L	Prereq: Backstab / Low ASR; Low DP
6	Kidney Rupture	L	VH	L	Prereq: Eviscerate / Low Bleed; Med DP
8	Pincer	M	M	H	Prereq: beside target / High DP
10	Backstab 2	H	M	H	Prereq: behind target, hidden / Med DP
12	Hamstring	L	M	M	Prereq: evaded target / Med Bleed; Med DB
15	Thigh Cut	M	VH	M	Prereq: Backstab 2 / Low DP
18	Garrote	H	M	M	Med MR; Med DP
21	Perforate Artery	M	M	H	Prereq: in front of target, hidden / High Bleed; Med DP
25	Achilles Heel	M	H	M	Prereq: Garrote / High ASR
29	Leaper	L	M	H	Prereq: Hamstring / High Bleed; Low DB
34	Creeping Death	L	VH	H	Prereq: Perforate Artery / Med Stun
39	Stunning Stab	L	VH	VH	Prereq: Creeping Death / Low DB
44	Rib Separation	M	H	H	Prereq: Leaper / High MR
50	Ripper	M	VH	H	Prereq: Rib Separation / High Bleed; Low DB

Shaman

Races	
Kobold / Troll	
Skills	
1	Mending (Magic)
1	Augmentation (Magic)
5	Cave Magic
5	Mending Spec.
5	Augmentation Spec.
5	Cave Magic Spec.

Abilities	
1	Staves
1	Cloth Armor
1	Leather Armor
1	Sprint
1	Hammers
1	Small Shields
10	Studded Armor
20	Chain Armor

Shaman are tribal mages blessed with magical ability. They can fill any open slot in a group and are willing to help in any way they can to assist other members. Shaman work best in small groups or in solo play.

The Best Part: You can buff stats and resistances for your group or realmmates, as well as heal, cure and resurrect. You're an adequate solo player with Buffs and low yellow/blue con mobs.

The Worst Part: You lack real combat skills and must cast constantly. Weapon skill is low, and you don't get Shield spec. Low damage, high aggro and your spells can be interrupted. With no styles and no instant effects, when a Shaman gets jumped it is often a death sentence.

Race Choices:

Kobold. High DEX, but low STR and CON keep you from being able to dish out or take much melee damage. Augmentation Buffs can supplement STR and CON.

Troll. Low DEX, but high STR and CON. DEX can be supplemented by Augmentation Buffs and specialized DEX/QUI spells.

Stat Choices: The primary class attribute is PIE, with DEX as the second most important one.

- *PIE:* Determines how much Power you have.
- *DEX:* Determines the bonus or hindrance to your casting speed, how many times your weapon procs, and your chance of being interrupted. Low DEX may not activate an item's ability, and casting times will not see a boost.
- *STR:* Determines damage output for both the hammer and staff.
- *CON:* Affects how many HP you have.
- Raising a stat by 1 costs 1 point for the first 10 raises, 2 points for the next 5 raises, and 3 points after that. Because of this, most players spend 10 points each in PIE, DEX, and either STR or CON, regardless of race.
- With a Kobold, consider raising STR or CON by 15 and PIE by 10.
- For a Troll, raise DEX by 15 and PIE by 10.

Weapon Choices:

- *Staff:* Not widely used (rare and less usable by this class), and no Focus Staves exist for Shaman. Less damage than a hammer. Must be wielded with two hands, so a shield is out.
- *Hammer:* High availability of 1- and 2-handed hammers. Good damage output and stat bonuses, but you can't hold a shield with a 2-handed hammer.
- You can wear leather armor at the start, studded leather at 10, and chain at 20.

Spec Paths: You share the Healer's path until Level 5 and have two base spell lines — Mending and Augmentation. Spec'ing in a path affects the outcome of spells in that path. Each spell has a healing, damage or success range. The closer you keep spec level to two-thirds Shaman level, the more dependable your spells become.

- *Mending:* Gives Healing spells and spells to keep your group alive and healthy. It's an okay primary path, but higher level spells don't last that long or do enough with a single casting. Mending makes a fine secondary line. Resurrect the group if a mob overcomes your party.
- *Augmentation:* Enhances friendly players' abilities and compensates for race weaknesses. Functions well as a primary or secondary spec line. The base Buffs (single-stat boost spells) stack with spec Buffs (combo-stat boost spells) and are desired by groups.
- Augmentation is a "cast-and-forget" line of spells that last until someone dies, zones or the Buff timer runs out. Currently, you can concentrate on a max of 20 Buffs at once.
- *Cave:* Weakest spec line, fine at early levels, but with little impact at higher levels without heavily investing in spec points.

Big Mistakes to Avoid in Character Creation: Investing in only one spec line, or — if you're a beginner Shaman — spec'ing in Cave. Cave can be rewarding, but it's difficult to maintain.

Deciding What You Want Your Role to Be: Healing or buffing? One of these will probably be your major role.

Plotting Your Future: It's good to put points into your primary specialization line until it reaches Level 5. Then, rotate by putting points into your primary/secondary line, and then your primary/tertiary line. Alternating keeps your primary line close to your character level and remains as close to two-thirds level as possible for maximum effect. Keep it up until you reach the maximum cap in any given line.

- Also, many Shaman try to obtain the next spell level in one line before putting points into the next line.
- Keeping spec at two-thirds of your level throughout your career yields the maximum effect for spells.

Grouping: Most group roles for a Shaman can also be filled by other classes — pulling, buffing and healing. You can also perform limited crowd control and issue Debuffs. There are also two Damage-over-Time spells in your arsenal that can wear away at opponents' HP. Smaller groups work best with this class.

- Casting group Friggs in combat is iffy, since groups separate quite easily and may move out of range.
- For group heals, stand away from combat to avoid monster aggro and get a head start in case of retreat.
- As the rezzer, it's your job to run if necessary and return when the coast is clear. Note that you should wait until after the monsters have left the area entirely. Rezzing can generate aggro even if after all the combatants are dead, so make sure you're in no danger.
- If you're the primary healer, designate a Warrior type as your protector. If he or she distracts a mob, step away from the group so you can heal/cast without redrawing aggro too quickly.
- If you get aggro, stand still! If you run, Warriors must first chase you and the mob down, and you'll probably die.

Soloing:

- Buff yourself before venturing out.
- Being jumped can kill you. Keep an eye on where you are and your surroundings. Knowing the pathing of mobs is helpful.
- Find a safe spot and pull with a Bolt at max range. While it's casting, hold down the Root spell. Once it's rooted, cast Disease. Cast Friggs on yourself, then Poison the mob. Throw one last Bolt at the mob if there's time. Finally, melee until the mob is dead.

Realm Versus Realm:

- In RvR, Mending (healing, curing and rezzing) is not prominent. Curing is done in a lull, and healing power doesn't keep up with RvR damage. Both healing and rezzing have line-of-sight restrictions. Mostly, you use Mending to resurrect and help players regenerate HP faster.
- Be aware of the AE vs. Mez dilemma. AE poison, Runemaster spears and Thane hammers can turn the tide of battle from defeat to victory *or* from victory to defeat. Groups should decide *before* battles whether they will be using AEs or crowd control. In small battles, crowd control is best. In large battles, AEs work better.
- You'll be kept busy casting Augmentation Buffs as players are resurrected or return from a /release.
- During keep defense or outright brawls in the middle of nowhere, the AoE Poison spell can come in handy, provided you can find a target.

Beginner's Tips:

- In early levels, right-click on people in towns to get quests. Completing trainer quests prior to Level 5 will net you money and other tangible rewards.
- While young, hunt monsters whose names con blue. You can also safely hunt greens, but yellow mobs will often kill you.
- Keep armor and weapons at blue, or better yet, at yellow and orange.
- Once you guild at Level 5, you get your third specialization line and any spec spells you were previously missing.
- If someone's pulling, root extra mobs to keep them still.
- Single-target and AoE Disease spells keep mobs or enemy players from regenerating Health.

Advanced Techniques:

- Set Buff priorities. Tanks generally need STR help, Hunters want DEX Buffs and Hastes, and casters want Acuity and DEX Buffs. Resistance Buffs and CON Buffs help everyone.
- Create a macro that says "OOM" or "OOP" (indicates that you're out of Mana/Power). Once Power drops under half, it regenerates more slowly.

Shaman Spells

Augmentation

Buffs Friend's AF.

Skill.........Augmentation Casting Time ....3 sec.
Range.....................1000 Duration...........Concent.

Lvl	Spell	Cost	Buff
1	Guardian's Lesser Ward**	1C	11
5	Guardian's Ward**	2C	15
10	Guardian's Lesser Shield**	4C	20
16	Guardian's Shield**	6C	26
22	Guardian's Lesser Barrier**	8C	32
31	Guardian's Barrier	11C	41
42	Guardian's Lesser Protection	15C	52

Buffs Friend's STR.

Skill.........Augmentation Casting Time ....3 sec.
Range.....................1000 Duration...........Concent.

Lvl	Spell	Cost	Buff
2	Lesser Strength of the Viking**	1C	11
4	Strength of the Viking**	2C	13
8	Lesser Vigor of the Viking**	3C	16
13	Vigor of the Viking**	5C	20
18	Lesser Power of the Viking**	6C	24
25	Power of the Viking**	9C	30
33	Lesser Might of the Viking	12C	36
43	Might of the Viking	16C	44

Buffs Friend's DEX.

Skill.........Augmentation Casting Time ....3 sec.
Range.....................1000 Duration...........Concent.

Lvl	Spell	Cost	Buff
11	Minor Evasion**	4C	18
15	Lesser Evasion**	5C	22
21	Evasion**	7C	26
28	Major Evasion**	10C	32
37	Greater Evasion	13C	39
48	Superior Evasion	18C	48

Buffs Friend's CON.

Skill.........Augmentation Casting Time ....3 sec.
Range.....................1000 Duration...........Concent.

Lvl	Spell	Cost	Buff
3	Augment Health**	1C	12
9	Increase Health**	3C	17
14	Enhance Health**	5C	21
20	Strengthen Health**	7C	26
29	Exaggerate Health**	10C	33
38	Intensify Health	14C	40
47	Amplify Health	17C	47

Touch of the Deep

Friend's damage/sec buffed (stacks as group 1).

Skill.........Augmentation Dmg Type............Matter
Casting Time ....3 sec. Range.....................1000
Duration.............10 min.

Lvl	Spell	Cost	Buff
1	Minor Force of the Deep*	2P	0.7
4	Lesser Force of the Deep*	3P	1
8	Force of the Deep*	5P	1.3
11	Major Force of the Deep*	7P	1.6
15	Greater Force of the Deep*	9P	2
20	Superior Force of the Deep*	12P	2.4
27	Mighty Force of the Deep*	17P	3
34	Supreme Force of the Deep*	21P	3.7
44	Ultimate Force of the Deep	28P	4.6

Buffs Friend's STR and CON.

Skill.........Augmentation Casting Time ....3 sec.
Range.....................1000 Duration...........Concent.

Lvl	Spell	Cost	Buff
2	Strength of the Deep**	2C	16
5	Vigor of the Deep**	4C	21
9	Energy of the Deep**	6C	25
13	Vitality of the Deep**	9C	30
19	Might of the Deep**	13C	37
26	Potence of the Deep**	18C	45
36	Fortification of the Deep	25C	57
46	Power of the Deep	33C	69

Buffs Friend's DEX and QUI.

Skill.........Augmentation Casting Time ....3 sec.
Range.....................1000 Duration...........Concent.

Lvl	Spell	Cost	Buff
3	Gloom's Guide**	2C	18
6	Gloom's Wisdom**	4C	21
10	Gloom's Enlightenment**	7C	27
14	Murk's Guide**	9C	31
21	Murk's Wisdom**	14C	39
28	Murk's Enlightenment**	19C	48
37	Shadow's Wisdom	26C	58
47	Shadow's Enlightenment	34C	70

Buffs Friend's INT, EMP and PIE.

Skill.........Augmentation Casting Time ....3 sec.
Range.....................1000 Duration...........Concent.

Lvl	Spell	Cost	Buff
12	Sight of the Deep**	4C	22
22	Wisdom of the Deep**	8C	32
31	Sagacity of the Deep	11C	41
42	Vision of the Deep	15C	52

Buffs Friend's Heat resistance.

Skill.........Augmentation Casting Time ....3 sec.
Range.....................1000 Duration...........Concent.

Lvl	Spell	Cost	Buff
23	Wrap of the Deep**	8C	8
30	Shroud of the Deep	11C	16
43	Caress of the Deep	16C	24

Buffs Friend's Cold resistance.

Skill.........Augmentation Casting Time ....3 sec.
Range.....................1000 Duration...........Concent.

Lvl	Spell	Cost	Buff
24	Warmth from Below**	8C	8
35	Heat from Below	12C	16
45	Fires from Below	16C	24

Buffs Friend's Matter resistance.

Skill.........Augmentation Casting Time ....3 sec.
Range.....................1000 Duration...........Concent.

Lvl	Spell	Cost	Buff
25	Rock Unity**	9C	8
38	Stone Unity	14C	16
48	Cavern Unity	18C	24

Mending

Heals damage by (Heal) HP to Friend.

Skill ....Mending Casting Time ...2.25 sec.
Range.....................1350 Duration..................Inst.

Lvl	Spell	Cost	Heal
1	Minor Mending*	1P	6
3	Minor Refinement*	2P	11
5	Minor Improvement*	3P	16
8	Minor Reconstitution*	4P	23
11	Minor Amelioration*	6P	31
14	Minor Purification*	7P	38
18	Minor Recovery*	9P	48
23	Minor Reparation*	11P	60
29	Minor Restoration*	14P	75
37	Minor Reconstruction*	19P	95
47	Minor Emendation	24P	119

Heals damage by (Heal) HP to Friend.

Skill ....Mending Casting Time ...2.75 sec.
Range.....................1350 Duration..................Inst.

Lvl	Spell	Cost	Heal
4	Refinement*	5P	26
6	Improvement*	6P	36
9	Reconstitution*	9P	50
12	Amelioration*	12P	65
16	Purification*	15P	85
21	Recovery*	20P	109
27	Reparation*	26P	138
31	Restoration*	30P	158
36	Reconstruction*	36P	183
46	Emendation	47P	231

Resurrects corpse; target is resurrected with a percentage of its original Power and/or HP.

Skill ....Mending CostPower cost based on corpse (see page 368)
Casting Time ....4 sec. Range.....................1500
Duration..................Inst.

Lvl	Spell	Power	HP
10	Arrival from Valhalla	No Power	10%

Deep Healing

Heals damage to Friend by (Heal) HP.

Skill ....Mending Casting Time ...3.25 sec.
Range....................1350 Duration ....Inst.

Lvl	Spell	Cost	Heal
5	Major Reconstitution*	11P	55
8	Major Amelioration*	16P	82
11	Major Purification*	21P	109
14	Major Recovery*	27P	136
18	Major Reparation*	34P	172
25	Major Restoration*	48P	235
33	Major Reconstruction*	65P	307
42	Major Emendation	84P	387

Buffs Friend's health regeneration by (Heal) every cycle.

Skill ....Mending Casting Time ....3 sec.
Range....................1350 Duration ....30 sec.

Lvl	Spell	Cost	Heal
9	Frigg's Antidote*	9P	30
12	Frigg's Medicant*	12P	39
16	Frigg's Cure*	15P	51
21	Frigg's Elixir*	20P	66
27	Frigg's Panacea*	26P	84
32	Frigg's Remedy*	32P	99
43	Frigg's Balm	44P	132

Resurrects corpse; target is resurrected with a percentage of its original Power and/or HP.

Skill ....Mending Duration ....Inst.
Casting Time ....7 sec. Range....................1500
Cost...............Power cost based on corpse (see p. 367)

Lvl	Spell	Power	HP
15	Reception from Valhalla	10%	30%

Cures Friend.

Skill ....Mending Casting Time ....3 sec.
Range....................1000 Duration ....Inst.

Lvl	Spell	Cost
6	Cure Disease	6%P
7	Cure Poison	6%P

Buffs Groupmates' health regeneration by (Heal) every cycle.

Skill ....Mending Casting Time ....4 sec.
Range....................1350 Duration ....30 sec.

Lvl	Spell	Cost	Heal
26	Fungal Rejuvenation*	50P	81
35	Fungal Regeneration*	70P	108
46	Fungal Restoration	94P	141

Subterranean Incantations

DoT: inflicts (Dmg) every 5 seconds.

Skill............Cave Magic Dmg Type...............Body
Casting Time ....3 sec. Range....................1500
Duration ....30 sec.

Lvl	Spell	Cost	Dmg
1	Fungal Dispersion*	2P	2
4	Fungal Deterioration*	3P	6
7	Fungal Decay*	5P	11
11	Fungal Solvent*	7P	16
15	Fungal Disintegration*	9P	22
20	Fungal Erosion*	12P	29
25	Fungal Degeneration*	15P	37
30	Fungal Devolution*	19P	43
35	Fungal Decrepitude*	22P	51
41	Fungal Dilapidation*	26P	59
48	Fungal Blight	31P	70

Debuffs STR by 7.5% and movement speed by 15%; halves effect of any healing spell cast on target.

Skill............Cave Magic Dmg Type...............Body
Casting Time ....3 sec. Range....................1500

Lvl	Spell	Cost	Dur	Radius
5	Sickening Spores	4P	60 sec.	(1)
16	Infectious Spores*	10P	1.5 min.	250
27	Fevering Spores*	17P	2 min.	300
37	Festering Spores*	23P	2.5 min.	350
47	Plague Spores	30P	3 min.	400

Root: Enemy speed debuffed to 1% of original movement (see page 367 for PvE/RvR limitations).

Skill............Cave Magic Dmg Type............Matter
Casting Time ....3 sec. Range....................1500

Lvl	Spell	Cost	Dur
2	Grasping Creepers*	2P	18 sec.
6	Bonding Creepers*	4P	24 sec.
10	Webbing Creepers*	6P	30 sec.
14	Clutching Creepers*	9P	36 sec.
19	Holding Creepers*	12P	43 sec.
26	Tangling Creepers*	16P	54 sec.
32	Tenacious Creepers*	20P	63 sec.
39	Detaining Creepers*	25P	73 sec.
46	Clenching Creepers	30P	84 sec.

Hand of the Deep

Damage Shield: On Friend; enemy damaged when hits Friend (stacks as group 1).

Skill............Cave Magic Dmg Type............Matter
Casting Time ....4 sec. Range....................1000
Duration...........Concent.

Lvl	Spell	Cost	Dmg/Sec
2	Fungal Covering**	1C	0.8
5	Fungal Pod**	2C	1.1
10	Fungal Case**	4C	1.5
16	Fungal Wrap**	6C	2.1
24	Fungal Coat**	8C	2.8
33	Fungal Sheath	12C	3.6
43	Fungal Husk	16C	4.5

Bolt (ranged DD). You must wait 20 seconds before casting one of these spells again.

Skill............Cave Magic Dmg Type............Matter
Casting Time ....4 sec. Range....................1875
Duration ....Inst.

Lvl	Spell	Cost	Dmg
1	Fungal Pin*	2P	8
4	Fungal Burr*	3P	26
7	Fungal Spike*	5P	45
11	Fungal Bramble*	7P	64
15	Fungal Spur*	9P	89
20	Fungal Thistle*	12P	114
25	Fungal Thorn*	15P	145
30	Fungal Needle*	19P	169
35	Fungal Barb*	22P	201
41	Fungal Spine	26P	232

AoE DoT: inflicts (Dmg) every 5 seconds, radius 350 wu.

Skill............Cave Magic Dmg Type............Matter
Casting Time ....3 sec. Range....................1500
Duration ....20 sec.

Lvl	Spell	Cost	Dmg
17	Spore Cloud*	16P	31
23	Spore Burst*	22P	41
29	Spore Explosion*	28P	53
36	Spore Storm*	36P	65
46	Spore Whirlwind	47P	83

AoE Root: Enemy speed debuffed to 1% of original movement; the effect breaks when the target is healed or takes damage; radius 350 wu. (These names are placeholders and will be changed once the spells become active.)

Skill........Nature Affinity Dmg Type............Matter
Casting Time .....2.5 sec. Range....................1500

Lvl	Spell	Cost	Dur
22	Vinefingers 1*	13P	38 sec.
31	Vinefingers 2*	19P	50 sec.
39	Vinefingers 3*	25P	60 sec.
49	Vinefingers 4	32P	73 sec.

Healer

Races		Abilities	
Norseman / Dwarf		1	Staves
Skills		1	Cloth Armor
1	Mending (Magic)	1	Leather Armor
1	Augmentation (Magic)	1	Hammers
5	Pacification (Magic)	1	Sprint
5	Mending Spec.	1	Small Shields
5	Augmentation Spec.	10	Studded Armor
5	Pacification Spec.	20	Chain Armor

Healers are a vital part of ensuring the Strength and Health of the realm. Whether in small or large groups, Healers are amazingly useful to partymates and the realm as a whole. Life can be filled with fun and frolic — as well as a bit of drama and excitement.

The Best Part: Most groups love good Healers. You get to be the life of the party, so to speak. Early on, during your "seer" Levels (5 and earlier), your combat abilities excel. It's a challenging role that lets you heal and buff your friends, as well as root or stun your enemies with instant spells, great for RvR combat. And you're the best mezzer in Midgard.

The Worst Part: You are very vulnerable, having developed offensive magic skills at the expense of defense. Your usefulness in groups may decline over time, and you can never solo or specialize in a weapon. Expect to die, and often.

Race Choices:

Dwarves. High CON, but low DEX and QUI. This race can usually wear chainmail later and survive longer in battle.

Norsemen. Also possess lower DEX and QUI, but higher STR and CON.

Stat Choices:

- *PIE:* Affects your Power. This is your primary stat.
- *DEX:* Helps determine your casting speed, weapon procs and interruptibility. This is your secondary stat.
- *STR:* Still important, since it affects your Hammer and Staff abilities.
- *CON:* Helps set your Hit Points.
- If you're a Norseman, you probably want to put 10 points into PIE, DEX and CON. For a Dwarven character, the most common places to put points are PIE, DEX and STR.

Weapon Choices:

- *Hammer:* Most prefer the 2-handed hammer for early soloing. Later, your weapon is meaningless against anything except non-aggressive green and gray mobs. At Level 3, buy the best 2-handed hammer or 1-handed hammer you can.
- Some like a 1-handed hammer and shield. The faster 1-handed swing rate is useful with a damage Buff, but shields mark you as a Healer in RvR.
- *Staff:* Few Healers use these, but you can.

Spec Paths: You get Mending, Augmentation and Pacification. Specialization determines what extra spells you get, and with Mending, improves spell efficiency.

- *Mending:* Mending yields the most effective healing spells. The closer Mending matches skill level, the more often you'll heal closer to the maximum allowed value. You'll use less Power than someone with lower Mending. Keep it between one-half and two-thirds of your current level. Mending also gives instant Healing and Group Healing spells. For a balanced Healer, consider a minimum of 32 (for the third Instant Heal spell) and a max of 35 (for the second Instant Group Heal spell).
- *Augmentation:* Not terribly common, but it gives self Damage Add, a haste Buff, a movement Buff and three resistance Buffs. Most Healers go for at least 15 in order to get the second movement Buff line spell. But, higher-level resistance Buffs don't kick in until Level 23, 24 and 27 – requiring a hefty point investment.
- *Pacification:* Helps control battle flow, enabling you to stun, mesmerize and root opponents. These spells make for great crowd control and provide access to Root, AoE Stun, AoE Mesmerize, a spiffy Power regeneration spell, and instant Stun and Mesmerize spells. Consider at least 29 in Pacification to get the first Instant Stun and Instant Mesmerize.

Big Mistakes to Avoid in Character Creation: Don't dump all of your points into a single area.

Deciding What You Want Your Role to Be: Consider the following things before deciding on your training path.

- Determine which spells you really want in each line and when you can get them.
- Revise what you want to reflect how much healing you want to do. For more healing, keep Mending higher. Try to balance specializations in all three areas. Many Healers give less to Augmentation and put points into Pacification or Mending almost exclusively.

Plotting Your Future:

- When you reach Level 5, wander into Jordheim, Myrkwood or the Yagdra frontier and talk to the Healer trainer to join the House of Eir. You get a gift and Power in a new line of spells.
- Level 5 is a good time to start spending points.

Grouping:

- Healers keep group members alive and use magic to stun, mesmerize and preoccupy enemies. You'll tend to become a battlefield general because you must pay attention to all things. You will also have to group once you progress a few levels, or you'll die.
- Identify the main tank early on and watch them. Know whether you're the main healer or backup healer.
- You need experience and intelligence playing this class; you're vital to the group's survival.
- Start buffing members as soon as you reach the combat area, especially haste for all tanks.
- Divide and conquer mobs with Pacification.
- If crowd control or healing efficiency aren't important, Augmentation can be strangely beneficial to a group. The higher level resistance Buffs are valuable, as is the haste Buff. Represent yourself accordingly, as Augmentation Healers are rare and people may assume you have other abilities.

Soloing: You really shouldn't solo at all, but you can until Level 4, when you really need a group. Early on, your weapon skill is decent, but you are highly vulnerable. Unless you are well equipped, stay away from the yellow, orange, red or purple con mobs.

Realm Versus Realm: You have many roles in RvR. Try Mesmerize for the first battle spell, as it divides and controls the enemy mob. Second, do your best to keep tanks healthy. Use Stun to help control mobs. At the same time, make sure you resurrect fallen comrades as quickly as possible. As time allows, buff your realmmates. Finally, don't save instant spells; RvR battles may end quickly.

- Try not to be obvious. Move around, and don't stand back and mark yourself as a target.
- If your realm group consistently kills monsters without dying, consider attacking green con mobs up through Level 2 and possibly 3.
- In RvR, armor benefits you immensely. You can wear leather armor immediately, graduating to studded at Level 10 and chain at 20. Try to wear the best armor you can.

Beginner's Tips:

- Seek items that improve CON, DEX, PIE, Power, resistances and Mending. Each raises something important, enabling you to survive longer, cast faster and heal more efficiently.
- Manage aggro carefully. Over-healing your party paints a target on you. Try to keep everyone at two-thirds Health or better, and stick to Minor Heals instead of large Heals.
- Stunning a monster at the start gives your party free hits and conserves Power.
- If the group's fate looks terrible, run away. Survive in order to resurrect your party.

Advanced Techniques:

- Don't forget about Wake Mindless — it clears the mob's aggro list! But, warn your party so another Healer doesn't throw a Greater Heal right after you clear the list.
- Sit down while trying to cast instants. If it's ready, you'll get a message saying you can't use it. If not, you'll find out how long you have to wait. (This keeps you from wasting an actual cast without knowing.)
- Watch for diseased party members and cure them before healing.
- Keep Healer Speed active. It's free and can help you escape battle.
- Rotate Pacification spells to keep duration penalties down.
- Watch how a monster attacks and try to stun just prior to an attack.

Healer Spells

Augmentation

Buffs Friend's AF.

Skill.........Augmentation Casting Time........3 sec.
Range.....................1000 Duration...........Concent.

Lvl	Spell	Cost	Buff
1	Guardian's Lesser Ward**	1C	11
5	Guardian's Ward**	2C	15
10	Guardian's Lesser Shield**	4C	20
16	Guardian's Shield**	6C	26
22	Guardian's Lesser Barrier**	8C	32
31	Guardian's Barrier	11C	41
42	Guardian's Lesser Protection	15C	52

Buffs Friend's STR.

Skill.........Augmentation Casting Time........3 sec.
Range.....................1000 Duration...........Concent.

Lvl	Spell	Cost	Buff
2	Lesser Strength of the Viking**	1C	11
4	Strength of the Viking**	2C	13
8	Lesser Vigor of the Viking**	3C	16
13	Vigor of the Viking**	5C	20
18	Lesser Power of the Viking**	6C	24
25	Power of the Viking**	9C	30
33	Lesser Might of the Viking	12C	36
43	Might of the Viking	16C	44

Buffs Friend's DEX.

Skill.........Augmentation Casting Time........3 sec.
Range.....................1000 Duration...........Concent.

Lvl	Spell	Cost	Buff
11	Minor Evasion**	4C	18
15	Lesser Evasion**	5C	22
21	Evasion**	7C	26
28	Major Evasion**	10C	32
37	Greater Evasion	13C	39
48	Superior Evasion	18C	48

Buffs Friend's CON.

Skill.........Augmentation Casting Time........3 sec.
Range.....................1000 Duration...........Concent.

Lvl	Spell	Cost	Buff
3	Augment Health**	1C	12
9	Increase Health**	3C	17
14	Enhance Health**	5C	21
20	Strengthen Health**	7C	26
29	Exaggerate Health**	10C	33
38	Intensify Health	14C	40
47	Amplify Health	17C	47

Valhalla's Touch

Caster's damage/sec buffed (stacks as group 1).

Skill.........Augmentation Dmg Type..............Spirit
Casting Time........3 sec. Duration...........Concent.

Lvl	Spell	Cost	Dam/Sec
1	Augmented Blow**	1C	1
4	Increased Blow**	2C	1.6
7	Enhanced Blow**	3C	2.3
11	Strengthen Blow**	4C	3.1
16	Exaggerated Blow**	6C	4.2
22	Intensified Blow**	8C	5.4
30	Amplified Blow**	11C	7.1
39	Burgeoned Blow	14C	9
49	Exalted Blow	18C	11.1

Buffs friend's attack speed by (Speed %).

Skill.........Augmentation Casting Time.....3.5 sec.
Range.....................1000 Duration...........Concent.

Lvl	Spell	Cost	Speed %
2	Lesser Purity of Attack**	1C	16%
10	Purity of Attack**	4C	20%
20	Lesser Purity of Offense**	7C	25%
31	Purity of Offense**	11C	30%
40	Lesser Purity of Aggression	14C	35%
50	Purity of Aggression	19C	40%

Group Speed Buff by (Speed %).

Skill.........Augmentation Cost............................0P
Casting Time........3 sec. Range.....................2000
Duration.........Chant + 6

Lvl	Spell	Speed %
5	Ease of Movement*	23%
15	Flow of Movement*	31%
25	Grace of Movement*	38%
35	Purity of Movement*	46%
45	Elegance of Movement	53%

Buffs Friend's Body resistance.

Skill.........Augmentation Casting Time........3 sec.
Range.....................1000 Duration...........Concent.

Lvl	Spell	Cost	Buff
23	Gods' Health**	8C	8
33	Gods' Vigor	12C	16
46	Gods' Potency	17C	24

Buffs Friend's Spirit resistance.

Skill.........Augmentation Casting Time........3 sec.
Range.....................1000 Duration...........Concent.

Lvl	Spell	Cost	Buff
24	Gods' Drive**	8C	8
36	Gods' Will	13C	16
47	Gods' Spirit	17C	24

Buffs Friend's Energy resistance.

Skill.........Augmentation Casting Time........3 sec.
Range.....................1000 Duration...........Concent.

Lvl	Spell	Cost	Buff
27	Thunder Affinity**	9C	8
37	Storm Affinity	13C	16
48	Lightning Affinity	18C	24

Mending

Heals damage to Friend by (Heal) HP.

Skill.................Mending Casting Time...2.25 sec.
Range.....................1350 Duration..................Inst.

Lvl	Spell	Cost	Buff
1	Minor Mending*	1P	6
3	Minor Refinement*	2P	11
5	Minor Improvement*	3P	16
8	Minor Reconstitution*	4P	23
11	Minor Amelioration*	6P	31
14	Minor Purification*	7P	38
18	Minor Recovery*	9P	48
23	Minor Reparation*	11P	60
29	Minor Restoration*	14P	75
37	Minor Reconstruction*	19P	95
47	Minor Emendation	24P	119

Heals damage to Friend by (Heal) HP.

Skill.................Mending Casting Time...2.75 sec.
Range.....................1350 Duration..................Inst.

Lvl	Spell	Cost	Buff
4	Refinement*	5P	26
6	Improvement*	6P	36
9	Reconstitution*	9P	50
12	Amelioration*	12P	65
16	Purification*	15P	85
21	Recovery*	20P	109
27	Reparation*	26P	138
31	Restoration*	30P	158
36	Reconstruction*	36P	183
46	Emendation	47P	231

Resurrects corpse; target is resurrected with a percentage of its original Power and/or HP.

Skill.................Mending Casting Time........4 sec.
Range.....................1500 Duration..................Inst.
Cost............Power cost based on corpse (see p. 368)

Lvl	Spell	Power	HP
10	Arrival from Valhalla	No Power	10% HP

Healing of Valhalla

Heals damage to Friend by (Heal) HP.

Skill.................Mending Casting Time...3.25 sec.
Range.....................1350 Duration..................Inst.

Lvl	Spell	Cost	Heal
5	Major Reconstitution*	11P	55
8	Major Amelioration*	16P	82
11	Major Purification*	21P	109
14	Major Recovery*	27P	136
18	Major Reparation*	34P	172
25	Major Restoration*	48P	235
33	Major Reconstruction*	65P	307
42	Major Emendation	84P	387

Heals damage to Friend by (Heal) HP.

Skill.................Mending Casting Time...3.75 sec.
Range.....................1350 Duration..................Inst.

Lvl	Spell	Cost	Buff
10	Greater Amelioration*	29P	145
13	Greater Purification*	37P	184
17	Greater Recovery*	48P	236
23	Greater Reparation*	65P	314
31	Greater Restoration*	90P	419
41	Greater Reconstruction*	123P	549
50	Greater Emendation	154P	667

Cures Friend.
Skill ....Mending   Casting Time .....3.2 sec.
Range....................1000   Duration.................Inst.

Lvl	Spell	Cost
6	Cure Disease	6%P
7	Cure Poison	6%P

Resurrects corpse; target is resurrected with a percentage of its original Power and/or HP.
Skill ....Mending   Range....................1500
Duration.................Inst.
Cost ....Power cost based on corpse (see p. 368)

Lvl	Spell	Cast	Power	HP
15	Reception from Valhalla	7 sec.	10%	30%
24	Welcome from Valhalla	9 sec.	25%	50%
40	Remigration from Valhalla	14 sec.	50%	100%

Heals damage to Friend by (Heal % HP) once every 15 min. You must wait 15 minutes before casting one of these spells again.
Skill ....Mending   Cost...........................0P
Casting Time ....Shout   Range....................1350
Duration.................Inst.

Lvl	Spell	Heal %
12	Favor from Eir*	33%
22	Boon from Eir*	55%
32	Dispensation from Eir*	75%
43	Tribute from Eir	100%

Heals damage to Groupmates by (Heal % HP) once every 20 min. You must wait 20 minutes before casting one of these spells again.
Skill ....Mending   Cost...........................0P
Casting Time ....Shout   Range....................1350
Duration.................Inst.

Lvl	Spell	Heal %
21	Eir's Glorious Touch*	50%
35	Eir's Magnificent Touch*	75%
45	Eir's Heavenly Touch	100%

Pacification

Mesmerize: target halts all movement and is unable to attack or cast spells; the effect breaks when the target is healed or takes damage (see page 367 for PvE/RvR limitations).
Skill ....Pacification   Casting Time .....2.5 sec.
Range....................1500

Lvl	Spell	Cost	Dur
1	Lull*	2P	16 sec.
5	Greater Lull*	4P	21 sec.
10	Diversion*	6P	28 sec.
16	Greater Diversion*	10P	35 sec.
22	Sedate*	13P	43 sec.
29	Greater Sedation*	18P	52 sec.
36	Entrance*	23P	61 sec.
43	Greater Entrancement	27P	70 sec.

Amnesia: Enemies in area have (Forget %) chance to forget they hate each person on their hate list.
Skill ....Pacification   Casting Time ....2 sec.
Range....................2300   Duration.................Inst.

Lvl	Spell	Cost	Radius	Forget %
4	Wake Senseless	3P	(1)	70%
14	Wake Forgetful*	9P	100	77%
24	Wake Ignorant*	15P	175	84%
34	Wake Mindless*	21P	250	91%
44	Wake Oblivious	28P	325	100%

Stuns target, making him unable to move or perform actions (see page 367 for PvE/RvR limitations).
Skill ....Pacification   Casting Time .....2.5 sec.
Range....................1500

Lvl	Spell	Cost	Dur
2	Halt Aggression*	2P	6 sec.
11	Halt Hostility*	7P	7 sec.
20	Halt Attack*	12P	8 sec.
32	Halt Offense*	20P	9 sec.
42	Halt Rally*	27P	10 sec.
50	Halt Invasion	33P	11 sec.

Calming Hand

Debuffs attack speed by (Debuff %).
Skill ....Pacification   Casting Time ....4 sec.
Range....................1500

Lvl	Spell	Cost	Dur	Debuff %
2	Hinder Spirit*	2P	44 sec.	8%
9	Harry Spirit*	6P	58 sec.	9.5%
21	Restrain Spirit*	13P	82 sec.	12.5%
31	Obstruct Spirit*	19P	1.7 min.	15%
40	Block Spirit*	25P	2 min.	17.5%
49	Impede Spirit	32P	2.3 min.	19.5%

Buffs Friend's power regeneration by (Buff) every cycle.
Skill ....Pacification   Casting Time ....3 sec.
Range....................1000   Duration..........Concent.

Lvl	Spell	Cost	Buff
4	Purity of Mind**	3C	1
15	Purity of Thought**	10C	2
25	Purity of Intellect**	17C	3
35	Purity of Contemplation	24C	4
45	Purity of Meditation	32C	5

AoE Mesmerize: target halts all movement and is unable to attack or cast spells; the effect breaks when the target is healed or takes damage (see page 367 for Pve/RvR limitations).
Skill ....Pacification   Casting Time ....3 sec.
Range....................1500

Lvl	Spell	Cost	Dur
6	Allay Area*	4P	16 sec.
13	Pacify Area*	8P	25 sec.
20	Conciliate Area*	12P	34 sec.
27	Placate Area*	17P	43 sec.
34	Harmonize Area*	21P	52 sec.
44	Tranquilize Area	28P	65 sec.

AoE Stuns target, making him unable to move or perform actions, radius 250 wu (see page 367 for Pve/RvR limitations).
Skill ....Pacification   Casting Time .....2.5 sec.
Range....................1500

Lvl	Spell	Cost	Dur
1	Suspend Charge*	2P	6 sec.
11	Halt Charge*	7P	7 sec.
32	Interrupt Charge*	20P	9 sec.
42	Nullify Charge*	27P	10 sec.
50	Cease Charge	33P	11 sec.

Root: Enemy speed debuffed to 1% of original movement.
Skill ....Pacification   Dmg Type..............Body
Casting Time .....2.5 sec.   Range....................1500

Lvl	Spell	Cost	Dur
3	Deny Movement*	2P	9 sec.
7	Repel Movement*	4P	14 sec.
12	Reject Movement*	6P	21 sec.
18	Negate Movement*	8P	30 sec.
24	Deny Advancement*	12P	38 sec.
30	Repel Advancement*	15P	47 sec.
37	Reject Advancement*	18P	56 sec.
46	Negate Advancement	24P	69 sec.

Mesmerize: target halts all movement and is unable to attack or cast spells; the effect breaks when the target is healed or takes damage. You must wait 10 minutes before casting one of these spells again. (There are no PvE/RvR limitations.)
Skill ....Pacification   Casting Time ....Shout
Range....................1500

Lvl	Spell	Cost	Dur	Radius
29	Pacifying Glance	18P	22 sec.	(1)
36	Pacifying Glare*	23P	26 sec.	150
47	Pacifying Gaze	30P	31 sec.	300

Stuns target, making him unable to move or perform actions. You must wait 10 minutes before casting one of these spells again.
Skill ....Pacification   Casting Time ....Shout
Range....................1500

Lvl	Spell	Cost	Dur	Buff
28	Paralyzing Glance	17P	8 sec.	(1)
38	Paralyzing Glare*	24P	9 sec.	150
48	Paralizing Gaze	31P	10 sec.	300

Runemaster

Races	Abilities
Norseman / Kobold / Dwarf	1 Staves
	1 Cloth Armor
	1 Sprint
	5 QuickCast

Skills	
1	Darkness (Magic)
1	Suppression (Magic)
5	Runecarving (Magic)
5	Darkness Spec.
5	Suppression Spec.
5	Runecarving Spec.

Synonymous with "nuker", Runemasters are the primary offensive mages of Midgard, masters of casting Direct Damage spells and magic Bolts (both ranged attacks). They also have powers based on Darkness, Suppression and Runecarving. Each has it's unique strength.

The Best Part: You can solo in PvE, and you're almost indispensable to groups with your group speed and Damage Add spells. Furthermore, you can cast Bolt spells — the longest-range and most damaging offensive spells in the game — and defend a comrade from taking damage. Group Pulsing Bladeturn is invaluable.

The Worst Part: Repeat after me — you are fragile! You desperately rely on Healers for Power regeneration spells, and you're the first to be targeted in RvR.

Race Choices:

Kobolds. Preferred race, with an impressive 70 starting DEX for a casting speed advantage. Low HP and an easy target in RvR, and this race can't carry much.

Dwarves. Come from hardier stock, but added HP from higher CON doesn't help much. Difference in casting speed is negligible.

Norsemen. Least desirable race; good only for looks.

Stat Choices: The three primary stats for Runemasters are PIE, DEX and QUI.

- *PIE:* Directly affects Power pool and damage output. Put at least 10 points in at the start (15 isn't out of the question).
- *DEX:* Directly affects casting speed. Again, put in 10 points, 15 if you're not a Kobold.
- *QUI:* Improves melee speed, but who cares. You shouldn't melee.
- *CON:* Determines HP. Every little bit helps — Kobolds should put in 10 points. Extra CON for Norseman/Dwarf is less important than extra DEX.
- *STR:* No real importance.

Most common builds are 10 PIE, DEX and CON for Kobolds; or 15 PIE and 10 DEX for the other races.

Weapon (and Equipment) Choices:

- *Staff:* Only available weapon, useless for melee. Focus staffs, though, help you cast spec spells in Darkness, Suppression and Runecarving. Spells cost 100% of Power, not 120%. A Focus staff indicates a certain level of performance for one or more paths. This level indicates that spells in that path (and beneath that level) only cost 80% power.
- Cloth armor is the only option for a Runemaster, but don't waste money buying any. Magical armor should be evaluated on stat, HP, and resist bonuses as opposed to Armor Factor.
- Best armor for a Runemaster is Ancient Bloodbound (Malmohus), Snow Crystal (Raumarik), epic or Darkness Falls … depending on your spec lines and individual stats.

Spec Paths: With each level, you get points equal to the new level, plus half your level in points at each half-level from 40 to 50. Keep spec level close to character level to ensure tight spell damage range (from 100-125%). Spec'ing too many things reduces your ability to maximize damage in one particular school. RVR is about fast, consistent damage, so pick a specialty and run with it.

- *Darkness:* Spell line for DD, Debuffing. Base spells are DEX Debuffs. DD spell has quick casting time. There is also a Debuffing damage spell, a Damage Add spell for melee and archer characters, and an AoE DD spell that lowers Cold resistance.
- *Suppression:* Most group-friendly path. Provides strength Debuff, a self Armor Factor Buff, armor absorption Buff, and single-target Root spell (your only crowd control). Gives Rune Fend and Pulsing Rune Shield, which high-level groups absolutely depend on.

- *Runecarving:* Class-defining path that provides access to the Rune lines of spells. Adds damage bonuses to spells from those paths. Bolt has a long range and high damage (good for RvR and solo play), a group running Chant, and Direct Damage spells, plus useful Debuffs.

Big Mistakes To Avoid In Character Creation: Stick to PIE, DEX and CON (in that order) when you make your Runemaster. Anything else is a mistake.

Deciding What You Want Your Role to Be: Suppression is group-friendly and handy for RvR. With Darkness, pay attention to recasting Damage Adds in a group setting. This requires more up-close-and-personal work in RvR due to range.

Grouping:

- Avoid aggro — wait till the mob is injured before nuking, and until then, debuff.
- In a healer-shy group, try chain-casting Rune Fend on the main tank to help out healers. Likewise, if you have Group Pulsing Bladeturn, chain-cast it to increase its frequency at a cheaper power cost than chain-casting single-target or group-effect static BT.
- If you have Pulsing Rune Shield Chant, keep it going and stay near your tanks.
- You can pull at long range with Nearsight and generate very little aggro.
- Your Area Effect spells break Mezzes.
- Bolts are useless in group PvE since they're easily blocked.
- No healer? Avoid nuking. Got a healer? Assist the main tank and nuke stunned mobs one by one.
- Help control "bring a friend" mobs with Root.
- When a Healer can't shake aggro, use the Hugin's Vex line of spells to confuse the mob.
- Got a Shaman or Healer? Get DEX and PIE Buffs for better damage and casting speed.
- A stacked Damage Add with a Skald's Add is impressive. All melee classes will thank you.

Soloing:

- Runecarvers can solo blues and yellows easily … even non-insta-nuking oranges!
- Ask a Healer to cast Purity for Power regeneration. Move to max range, then nuke/Bolt the monster. If the monster is tough, cast Root to stop it so you can reset your distance and resume nuking.
- Quickcast is essential for soloing and should be used wisely. Save it for a Root or a finishing spell.
- Casting-type monsters are the best targets — low HP, and you interrupt their casting. Avoid four-legged monsters (wolves, cats. etc.) because they're too fast.
- Start a Running Chant, cast Rune Fend on yourself. Armor Factor Buff and absorption Buff if you can. At max distance, cast a DD spell. If necessary, root, sprint, then damage again.

Realm Versus Realm: In RvR, follow a few guidelines for success. Deal damage from a distance. Don't get hit. Root tanks, and take out casters and rogues at a distance (Bolt/Quickcast/Bolt is good). Give Speed boosts if necessary. Give away Rune Fends freely.

- Keep Defense means ranged spells from enemy parapets.
- Target casters and archers with DD spells, then duck! Select your target by adjusting the camera angle before you actually have line of sight. Then, move into position, cast/quickcast/cast, then move out of sight.
- Having a Warrior or Thane team Guard you is invaluable.
- If your keep defense is failing, retreat to the Lord's Room when the second doors are around 10%. Prepare to Area-Effect the first target you see.
- For Milemarker defense, stay on the walls and cast at the incoming enemy as they pass through the gates. Target Milemarker doors to reveal Stealthed opponents who go through the gates. Finally, Nearsight renders enemy casters and archers ineffective — it greatly reduces enemy range and confuses enemy pets.
- On keep attack, your role is to help clear the enemy from the parapets, kill the guards that spawn, and watch for reinforcements trying to defend the keep.

- Open area warfare is the most common RvR engagement and also the fastest. When going into battle, have a general sense of what you want to do. Assist tanks, pick off casters, chase down retreaters, etc. The best way to know what to do is to have a rogue Scout tell you the position and number of the enemy.
- Don't be afraid to melee another caster if you're out of Power. You'll at least interrupt their casting.
- Don't ever stand still. Infiltrators and Nightshades are everywhere!

Beginner's Tips:

- Remember to attack from maximum range — don't give your target extra room to close in on you.
- Be friendly to Healers, since they provide Purity spells that increase your Power regen.
- Don't draw too much aggro. Use your damage spells in a group *after* the tank has gotten in a few swings.
- Don't ever buy armor, just use what you find. Save money for Focus staffs, cloth dyes, etc.

Advanced Techniques:

- Change your armor color every few days to keep the enemy guessing.
- Use the Hugin's Confuse line to solo bring-a-friend mobs (requires high Suppression).
- You can safely cast AE spells on low gray targets in the frontiers to find stealthers.
- Hugin's Confusion spells with a percent change to attack ally have been known to cause an enemy's pet to turn on him.

Runemaster Spells

Darkness

DD.

Skill................Darkness Dmg Type...............Cold
Casting Time.....2.6 sec. Range.....................1500
Duration.................Inst.

Lvl	Spell	Cost	Dmg
1	Minor Dusk Dart	2P	5
2	Dusk Dart	2P	9
3	Major Dusk Dart	3P	14
5	Greater Dusk Dart	4P	21
8	Minor Gloom Blast	5P	33
12	Gloom Blast	8P	45
15	Greater Gloom Blast	9P	57
20	Murk Blast	12P	73
26	Greater Murk Blast	16P	96
33	Shadow Blast	21P	120
43	Greater Shadow Blast	27P	156

DEX debuff.

Skill................Darkness Dmg Type..............Body
Casting Time........2 sec. Range.....................1500
Duration............60 sec.

Lvl	Spell	Cost	Debuff
4	Blanket of Darkness	3P	6.5
6	Screen of Darkness	4P	7
9	Envelope of Darkness	6P	8.5
13	Globe of Darkness	8P	10
18	Field of Darkness	11P	12
25	Wrap of Darkness	15P	15
36	Veil of Darkness	23P	19
46	Shroud of Darkness	30P	23

Runes of Darkness

Friend's damage/sec buffed (stacks as group 1).

Skill................Darkness Dmg Type..............Body
Casting Time........4 sec. Range.....................1000
Duration............10 min.

Lvl	Spell	Cost	Dmg
5	Rune of Discomfort	4P	1.3
11	Rune of Injury	7P	2.2
18	Rune of Hurt	11P	3.3
24	Rune of Pain	15P	4.2
31	Rune of Agony	19P	5.2
39	Rune of Misery	25P	6.4
49	Rune of Torment	32P	7.9

DD.

Skill................Darkness Dmg Type...............Cold
Casting Time.....2.8 sec. Range.....................1500
Duration.................Inst.

Lvl	Spell	Cost	Dmg
1	Rune of Dusk	2P	5
3	Greater Rune of Dusk	3P	16
6	Rune of Pitch	4P	32
10	Greater Rune of Pitch	6P	47
13	Rune of Murk	8P	62
17	Greater Rune of Murk	10P	82
23	Rune of Obscurity	14P	108
30	Greater Rune of Obscurity	19P	138
37	Rune of Shadow	23P	174
47	Greater Rune of Shadow	30P	220

Cold DD with 5% resistance debuff.

Skill................Darkness Dmg Type...............Cold
Casting Time........3 sec. Range.....................1500
Duration............60 sec.

Lvl	Spell	Cost	Dmg
4	Minor Raven Bolt	3P	16
8	Lesser Raven Bolt	5P	32
12	Raven Bolt	8P	44
16	Major Raven Bolt	10P	60
22	Greater Raven Bolt	13P	80
29	Superior Raven Bolt	18P	107
38	Munin's Claw	24P	139
48	Hugin's Claw	31P	175

AoE Cold DD with 5% resistance debuff; radius 350.

Skill................Darkness Dmg Type...............Cold
Casting Time........4 sec. Range.....................1500
Duration............60 sec.

Lvl	Spell	Cost	Dmg
9	Raven Drove	8P	29
14	Raven Flock	11P	41
19	Raven Horde	15P	57
25	Raven Throng	20P	72
32	Raven Host	26P	91
40	Raven Cloud	34P	112
50	Raven Legion	43P	140

Suppression

STR debuff.
Skill............Suppression Dmg Type...............Body
Casting Time........2 sec. Range.....................1500
Duration.............60 sec.

Lvl	Spell	Cost	Debuff
1	Lessen Strength	1P	5
5	Diffuse Strength	3P	7
8	Disperse Strength	4P	8
11	Suppress Strength	5P	9
17	Quell Strength	8P	11.5
25	Abolish Strength	12P	15
33	Extinguish Strength	16P	18
45	Annihilate Strength	23P	23

Buffs Caster's AF.
Skill.................2/3 Spec Dmg Type...............Body
Casting Time........3 sec. Duration.............15 min.

Lvl	Spell	Cost	Buff
2	Minor Magic Shield	2P	17
4	Lesser Magic Shield	3P	27
7	Magic Shield	5P	42
10	Major Magic Shield	6P	56
14	Greater Magic Shield	9P	75
18	Superior Magic Shield	11P	95
24	Major Suppressive Barrier	15P	124
32	Greater Suppressive Barrier	20P	162
42	Major Suppressive Barrier	27P	211
50	Major Suppressive Barrier	33P	250

Root: Enemy speed debuffed to 1% of original movement.
Skill............Suppression Dmg Type...............Body
Casting Time.....2.5 sec. Range.....................1500

Lvl	Spell	Cost	Dur
3	Lessen Movement	2P	9 sec.
6	Diffuse Movement	3P	13 sec.
13	Disperse Movement	6P	23 sec.
19	Suppress Movement	9P	31 sec.
26	Quell Movement	12P	41 sec.
31	Abolish Movement	15P	48 sec.
40	Extinguish Movement	20P	61 sec.
49	Annihilate Movement	25P	73 sec.

Non-magical damage to Caster reduced by (Bonus %).
Skill............Suppression Dmg Type...............Body
Casting Time........3 sec. Duration.............15 min.

Lvl	Spell	Cost	Bonus %
30	Magical Buffer	19P	5%
41	Suppressive Buffer	26P	10%

Runes of Suppression

DD, Snare: enemy's speed debuffed to 65% of original movement.
Skill............Suppression Dmg Type............Energy
Casting Time........3 sec. Range.....................1350
Duration.............30 sec.

Lvl	Spell	Cost	Dmg
1	Minor Entrapping Rune	2P	5
5	Lesser Entrapping Rune	4P	21
9	Entrapping Rune	6P	37
13	Lesser Tangling Rune	8P	49
17	Tangling Rune	10P	65
23	Lesser Snaring Rune	14P	85
33	Snaring Rune	21P	120
41	Lesser Rune of Mazing	26P	148
50	Rune of Mazing	33P	180

Confusion: (Switch %) chance to switch targets; (Ally %) chance to attack own ally.
Skill............Suppression Dmg Type............Energy
Casting Time.....3.5 sec. Range.....................1500
Duration.............60 sec.

Lvl	Spell	Cost	Switch %	Ally %
8	Hugin's Affliction	4P	70%	0%
12	Hugin's Malison	6P	85%	0%
18	Hugin's Curse	8P	100%	0%
24	Hugin's Vex	12P	100%	15%
28	Hugin's Damnation	13P	100%	30%
35	Hugin's Vilification	17P	100%	45%
45	Hugin's Malediction	23P	100%	60%

Bladeturn: Absorbs damage of single hit.
Skill............Suppression Dmg Type............Energy
Casting Time........4 sec.
Range..........1250 (except Lvl 2: Self)

Lvl	Spell	Cost	Dur	Targ
2	Runic Ward	8%P	Until Hit	Self
10	Runic Fend	8%P	Until Hit	Friend
16	Runic Shield	12%P	Until Hit	Group
26	Runic Guard[1]	16P, 4P/10s	Chant + 10	Group
34	Runic Barrier[2]	21P, 5P/8s	Chant + 8	Group
44	Runic Wall[3]	28P, 7P/6s	Chant + 6	Group

[1] Absorbs first hit every 10 sec.
[2] Absorbs first hit every 8 sec.
[3] Absorbs first hit every 6 sec.

Reduces range on ranged attacks by (Debuff %).
Skill............Suppression Dmg Type............Energy
Casting Time........2 sec. Range.....................2300
Duration...............2 min.

Lvl	Spell	Cost	Debuff %
11	Suppress Sight	5P	25%
19	Suppress Vision	9P	35%
25	Suppress View	12P	45%
32	Diminish Sight	16P	55%
40	Diminish Vision	20P	65%

AoE DD, Snare: enemy's speed debuffed to 65% of original movement, radius 350 wu.
Skill............Suppression Dmg Type............Energy
Casting Time........4 sec. Range.....................1350
Duration.............30 sec.

Lvl	Spell	Cost	Dmg
7	Field of Suppression	6P	22
14	Field of Slackening	11P	41
20	Field of Entrapping	16P	57
27	Field of Snaring	22P	78
36	Field of Tangling	30P	103
46	Field of Mazing	39P	131

Runecarving

Bolt (ranged DD). You must wait 20 seconds before casting one of these spells again.
Skill............Runecarving Dmg Type............Energy
Casting Time........4 sec. Range.....................1875
Duration..................Inst.

Lvl	Spell	Cost	Dmg
4	Simple Runebolt	3P	24
7	Minor Runebolt	5P	41
10	Lesser Runebolt	6P	53
13	Runebolt	8P	70
17	Major Runebolt	10P	92
22	Greater Runebolt	13P	115
28	Superior Runebolt	17P	149
36	Supreme Runebolt	23P	188
46	Sovereign Runebolt	30P	239

DD.
Skill............Runecarving Dmg Type............Energy
Casting Time........3 sec. Range.....................1500
Duration..................Inst.

Lvl	Spell	Cost	Dmg
6	Token of Destruction	4P	26
8	Stamp of Destruction	5P	33
11	Note of Destruction	7P	41
14	Mark of Destruction	9P	53
18	Insignia of Destruction	11P	69
23	Symbol of Destruction	14P	85
30	Seal of Destruction	19P	108
38	Signet of Destruction	24P	140
48	Rune of Destruction	31P	176

Group Speed Buff, by (Speed %).
Skill............Runecarving Dmg Type............Energy
Cost............................0P Casting Time........3 sec.
Range.....................2000 Duration.........Chant + 6

Lvl	Spell	Speed %
5	Token of Movement	23%
15	Mark of Movement	31%
25	Symbol of Movement	38%
35	Seal of Movement	46%
45	Rune of Movement	53%

Runes of Destruction

AoE DD, radius 350.

Skill............Runecarving Dmg Type............Energy
Casting Time........4 sec. Range.....................1500
Duration..................Inst.

Lvl	Spell	Cost	Dmg
2	Odin's Ire	2P	8
5	Odin's Grudge	4P	20
7	Odin's Anger	5P	28
12	Odin's Rage	8P	44
18	Odin's Frenzy	11P	68
24	Odin's Wrath	15P	88
32	Odin's Vengeance	20P	116
44	Odin's Hatred	28P	159

Bolt (ranged DD). You must wait 20 seconds before casting one of these spells again.

Skill............Runecarving Dmg Type............Energy
Casting Time........4 sec. Range.....................1875
Duration..................Inst.

Lvl	Spell	Cost	Buff
1	Lesser Sigil of Ruin	2P	8
3	Sigil of Ruin	3P	23
6	Lesser Sigil of Havoc	4P	46
10	Sigil of Havoc	6P	68
13	Lesser Sigil of Destruction	8P	90
17	Sigil of Destruction	10P	118
23	Lesser Sigil of Devastation	14P	156
30	Sigil of Devastation	19P	199
37	Lesser Sigil of Undoing	23P	251
47	Sigil of Undoing	30P	317

Heat resistance debuff.

Skill............Runecarving Casting Time........2 sec.
Range.....................1500 Duration.............15 sec.

Lvl	Spell	Cost	Debuff %
22	Vex of Heat	10P	7.5%
33	Vex of Fire	16P	15%
45	Vex of Flames	23P	25%

Cold resistance debuff.

Skill............Runecarving Casting Time........2 sec.
Range.....................1500 Duration.............15 sec.

Lvl	Spell	Cost	Debuff %
25	Vex of Cold	12P	7.5%
34	Vex of Frost	16P	15%
46	Vex of Ice	24P	25%

Matter resistance debuff.

Skill............Runecarving Casting Time........2 sec.
Range.....................1500 Duration.............15 sec.

Lvl	Spell	Cost	Debuff %
27	Vex of Soil	13P	7.5%
36	Vex of Dirt	18P	15%
48	Vex of Earth	24P	25%

Spiritmaster

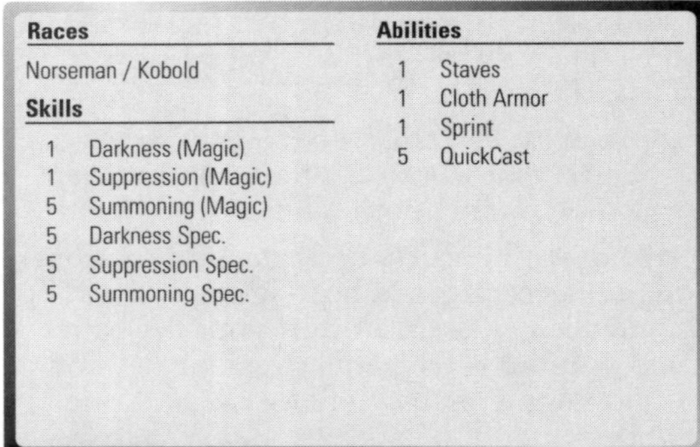

Races

Norseman / Kobold

Skills

1	Darkness (Magic)
1	Suppression (Magic)
5	Summoning (Magic)
5	Darkness Spec.
5	Suppression Spec.
5	Summoning Spec.

Abilities

1	Staves
1	Cloth Armor
1	Sprint
5	QuickCast

Spiritmasters, true to their name, can summon and control spirits. Control and tactics are of utmost importance — an efficient Spiritmaster always knows the next move. Although groupable, Spiritmasters love to solo. Basically, this is a cleric and mage rolled into one, with all the tools for survival at hand.

The Best Part: You can solo without help. You're an instant party with a renewable summoned fighter, and you can conquer most anything with your utility spells.

The Worst Part: You've got mage and cleric skills, but no unique abilities other than spirit calling. Plus, you're not a master at anything, and RvR can be difficult.

Race Choices:

Kobold. Small, wiry and dexterous, lithe, but not strong or hardy. High DEX, but STR and CON suffer a bit. Can cast faster than a Norseman.

Norseman. Basic race, average with no outstanding defects. Hardier and stronger, but slower casters.

Stat Choices:

- *PIE:* Vital stat. Sets Power and should be raised. Also adjusts damage.
- *DEX:* Also vital, since it defines how quickly you cast. High DEX can save up to 1.5 seconds per cast.
- *STR:* Important for carrying stuff. Boost or not, depending on how much you want to carry and how much you fear Debuffs.
- *CON:* More CON means more HP.

Most Spiritmasters add 10 to PIE and DEX, and 10 to STR or CON. Generally, put 10 Points into vital stats and distribute the rest to shore up race weaknesses.

Weapon Choices: Most Spiritmasters avoid melee combat, but carry Focus staves and steelshod staves. Your pet is your weapon.

Spec Paths:

- *Darkness:* This yields Direct Damage and DEX Debuff spells, as well as Spirit Dimming spells.
- *Suppression:* Gives crowd control spells, STR/CON/attack speed Debuffs, Shield spells, armor improvement spells and Protecting Spirit, as well as Mez and Root spells.
- *Summoning:* "Pet line" with summoned spirits, pet Buff/healing spells and Damage Shields. You get pets at Levels 5, 7, 12, 22 and 32.
- The best setup is to focus on Darkness, then Suppression, then Summoning.
- For RvR: 47 Darkness, 26 Suppression, the rest in Summoning. Hefty damage with Darkness and Lifetap spells. Suppression gives utility spells, but not a strong pet or pet healing ability.
- For balance: 37 Darkness, 37 Suppression and 13 Summoning. Good for PvE or RvR. Not a cold-blooded killer, but versatile.
- Each spec line has an associated spell line: Spirit Dimming for Darkness, Spirit Suppression for Suppression and Spirit Summoning for Summoning.

Big Mistakes to Avoid in Character Creation: Don't stuff points into Suppression or Summoning. For Suppression, you'll have utility and crowd control spells, but no damage capability. High Summoning limits your pet's damage at higher levels. You'll spend all your time casting Buffs and regenerating Power. RvR will be difficult.

Deciding What You Want Your Role to Be: Pure Darkness makes for a strong damager/nuker, but you'll often have to bail out your pet. Pure Summoning gives a strong pet, but hinders your damage ability. Pure Suppression is good for crowd control, Armor Factor and Debuffs, but weak for pets and damage/nukes.

Plotting Your Future:

- At Levels 1 through 3, kill yellow/blue targets and do training quests. At 3, buy a Spirit Darkness or Summoning staff. You can try getting a task from an NPC merchant if you get tired of hunting. By level 5, you're ready to go to Jordheim and start developing your character.
- In general, hunting con color ranges from green to red. Blue and green mobs award reduced experience.
- Past level 20, Muspelheim is a good place to fight fire-vulnerable mobs, but not Undead.

Grouping:

- As leader, you're probably most powerful and do the most damage. Attack things a bit higher than normal, relying on help from others.
- As follower, stay passive and only use your pet to save the group in times of need. Pets "steal" XP but can act as a valuable shield between a critter and someone who failed to mez or root it. Concentrate on DD via Darkblast and spend time Debuffing mobs.
- Optionally, ask tanks not to grab aggro. Your pet can work on a mob and keep aggro off, aiding both tanks and healers.
- Group with Healers or Shaman to take out higher level targets whose aggression can be controlled. A seer can Buff your pet better, and you can share pet healing duty. If you pull multiple mobs, the seer can mez one while you kill the other.

Soloing:

- You can attack things that make other players pale. And you'll be doing it almost constantly, barring regeneration rates.
- Kill Reptiles, Insects, some humanoids, and anything that's fire-based. Stay away from furry creatures, cold-based creatures and Undead.
- Travel and fight with a spirit, the highest type you can summon. Axe has quick little jabs, while Spear is slower but more damaging.

- Buff your pet and yourself before any fighting begins.
- Sit down to regenerate to full Power.
- Pick an orange or yellow target and Debuff it. Let it move within range, then sic your pet on it. After the pet draws aggro, Debuff the critter again. Let the pet melee until the mob is at 75% Health, and then DD it to death.

Realm Versus Realm:

- You're basically a weak mage with crowd control.
- Rule #1: Always buff. If a spell wears off, hide in the forest and rebuff. Protective spirit is your friend.
- Rule #2: Forget your pet. It's slow, doesn't do much damage and is frequently ignored in combat. At the most, have it attack archers or mages while you nuke something else.
- Use trees to hide, buff and rest in — but beware of assassins.
- Your chances of getting Realm Points are better in a group.
- Root and Mez are indispensable. You can mesmerize an entire party, and with your spirit, start on the mages and quickly decimate the group. Leave the tanks mezzed while you escape.
- Direct Damage is good, but Lifetap that you get at Level 47 is better — you get 90% of damage back as life.
- Never use a Focus spell in RvR, since it immobilizes you for up to 6 seconds.
- Never sit unless you're safe. Sitting makes you an easy, obvious target.
- Learn enemy ranges.
- You get pets at Levels 5, 7, 12, 22 and 32. Live them, learn them, love them.

Beginner's Tips:

- Keep mobs focused on killing the pet, not you. As a general rule, always do less damage than your pet.
- Don't heal your pet unless it's at 50% or less Health. Don't do it too often.
- Any aggressive acts towards a creature will aggro it onto you.
- Your pet won't attack until you tell it what to attack, or you're attacked.
- Debuffs draw less aggro, followed by nukes. Healing is the greatest aggro draw.
- There are several ways to pull mobs — a) debuff, mez or root the mob, retreat and then have your pet attack, b) nuke the mob, c) sic your pet on the mob then use the pet to pull the mob to you.
- Remember, your pet can't go anywhere that a normal player can't go.

Advanced Tips:

- At advanced levels, it takes longer to regenerate Power. If regen time is painful, bribe a Power regen spell from a healer.
- Currently, you can Quickcast with 0 Power, but only once.
- Try to get armor that increases stats, not Armor Factor. You'll see more effect from it.
- Focus staves are important!
- Crowd control is important! The Suppression line packs a basic Root and advanced Mesmerize spell.
- The Darkness line has point blank (AoE centered on caster), which mezzes an unlimited number of nearby targets.
- In PvE, Mez and Root spells operate on reduced duration. Each casting on the same mob lowers duration and effectiveness.
- Mez spells are broken by offensive actions but tend to be less costly than Root spells and last longer. Root spells are broken only by damage. Root a mob, then debuff the heck out of it. (But, a rooted mob can still attack and cast spells, so back up.).

Spiritmaster Spells

Darkness

DD.

Skill.................Darkness Dmg Type................Cold
Casting Time.....2.6 sec. Range.....................1500
Duration..................Inst.

Lvl	Spell	Cost	Dmg
1	Minor Dusk Dart	2P	5
2	Dusk Dart	2P	9
3	Major Dusk Dart	3P	14
5	Greater Dusk Dart	4P	21
8	Minor Gloom Blast	5P	33
12	Gloom Blast	8P	45
15	Greater Gloom Blast	9P	57
20	Murk Blast	12P	73
26	Greater Murk Blast	16P	96
33	Shadow Blast	21P	120
43	Greater Shadow Blast	27P	156

DEX debuff.

Skill.................Darkness Dmg Type...............Body
Casting Time........2 sec. Range.....................1500
Duration.............60 sec.

Lvl	Spell	Cost	Debuff
4	Blanket of Darkness	3P	6.5
6	Screen of Darkness	4P	7
9	Envelope of Darkness	6P	8.5
13	Globe of Darkness	8P	10
18	Field of Darkness	11P	12
25	Wrap of Darkness	15P	15
36	Veil of Darkness	23P	19
46	Shroud of Darkness	30P	23

Spirit Dimming

DD, with (Drain %) of damage drained from target to Caster.

Skill.................Darkness Dmg Type................Cold
Casting Time.....2.9 sec. Range.....................1500
Duration..................Inst.

Lvl	Spell	Cost	Dmg	Drain %
1	Dampen Lifeforce	2P	5	70%
3	Muffle Lifeforce	3P	14	70%
6	Smother Lifeforce	4P	26	70%
10	Mute Lifeforce	6P	39	70%
13	Stifle Lifeforce	8P	52	70%
17	Suppress Lifeforce	10P	68	70%
23	Silence Lifeforce	14P	90	70%
30	Hush Lifeforce	19P	115	80%
37	Stifle Lifeforce	23P	145	80%
47	Extinguish Lifeforce	30P	183	90%

AoE Mesmerize with Damage: target halts all movement and is unable to attack or cast spells; the effect breaks when the target is healed or takes damage; radius 300 wu (see page 367 for PvE/RvR limitations).

Skill.................Darkness Dmg Type................Cold
Casting Time........2 sec.

Lvl	Spell	Cost	Dur	Dmg
2	Gloom Wave	2P	9 sec.	8
4	Murk Wave	3P	10 sec.	16
7	Dusk Wave	5P	11 sec.	28
9	Shadow Wave	6P	12 sec.	36
14	Dark Wave	9P	15 sec.	52
18	Night Wave	11P	17 sec.	68
24	Black Wave	15P	20 sec.	88
32	Pitch Wave	20P	24 sec.	116
42	Umbral Wave	27P	29 sec.	151

AoE DEX/QUI debuff, radius 250 wu.

Skill.................Darkness Casting Time........2 sec.
Range.....................1500 Duration.............60 sec.

Lvl	Spell	Cost	Debuff
5	Cover Eyes	4P	10.5
8	Dull Sight	5P	12
15	Obscure View	9P	16.5
20	Darken Vision	12P	19.5
28	Ban Sight	17P	24
36	Curse of Blindness	23P	28.5
46	Greater Curse of Blindness	30P	34.5

Body resistance debuff.

Skill.................Darkness Casting Time........2 sec.
Range.....................1500 Duration.............15 sec.

Lvl	Spell	Cost	Debuff %
22	Dampen Health	10P	7.5%
33	Suppress Health	16P	15%
45	Extinguish Health	23P	25%

Spirit resistance debuff.

Skill.................Darkness Casting Time........2 sec.
Range.....................1500 Duration.............15 sec.

Lvl	Spell	Cost	Debuff %
25	Dampen Spirit	12P	7.5%
35	Suppress Spirit	17P	15%
48	Extinguish Spirit	24P	25%

Energy resistance debuff.

Skill.................Darkness Casting Time........2 sec.
Range.....................1500 Duration.............15 sec.

Lvl	Spell	Cost	Debuff %
27	Dampen Capacity	13P	7.5%
38	Suppress Capacity	19P	15%
49	Extinguish Capacity	25P	25%

Suppression

STR debuff.

Skill............Suppression Dmg Type...............Body
Casting Time........2 sec. Range.....................1500
Duration.............60 sec.

Lvl	Spell	Cost	Debuff
1	Lessen Strength	1P	5
5	Diffuse Strength	3P	7
8	Disperse Strength	4P	8
11	Suppress Strength	5P	9
17	Quell Strength	8P	11.5
25	Abolish Strength	12P	15
33	Extinguish Strength	16P	18
45	Annihilate Strength	23P	23

Buffs Caster's AF.

Skill.................2/3 Spec Dmg Type...............Body
Casting Time........3 sec. Duration.............15 min.

Lvl	Spell	Cost	Buff
2	Minor Magic Shield	2P	17
4	Lesser Magic Shield	3P	27
7	Magic Shield	5P	42
10	Major Magic Shield	6P	56
14	Greater Magic Shield	9P	75
18	Superior Magic Shield	11P	95
24	Major Suppressive Barrier	15P	124
32	Greater Suppressive Barrier	20P	162
42	Major Suppressive Barrier	27P	211
50	Major Suppressive Barrier	33P	250

Root: Enemy speed debuffed to 1% of original movement.

Skill............Suppression Dmg Type...............Body
Casting Time.....2.5 sec. Range.....................1500

Lvl	Spell	Cost	Dur
3	Lessen Movement	2P	9 sec.
6	Diffuse Movement	3P	13 sec.
13	Disperse Movement	6P	23 sec.
19	Suppress Movement	9P	31 sec.
26	Quell Movement	12P	41 sec.
31	Abolish Movement	15P	48 sec.
40	Extinguish Movement	20P	61 sec.
49	Annihilate Movement	25P	73 sec.

Non-magical damage to Caster reduced by (Bonus %).

Skill............Suppression Dmg Type...............Body
Casting Time........3 sec. Duration.............15 min.

Lvl	Spell	Cost	Bonus %
30	Magical Buffer	19P	5%
41	Suppressive Buffer	26P	10%

Spirit Suppression

Debuffs attack speed by (Debuff %).
Skill............Suppression Dmg Type..............Spirit
Casting Time........3 sec. Range.....................1500

Lvl	Spell	Cost	Dur	Debuff %
7	Scatter Fervor	4P	42 sec.	7%
9	Diffuse Fervor	4P	45 sec.	7.5%
12	Disperse Fervor	6P	51 sec.	8.5%
16	Dissipate Fervor	8P	58 sec.	9.5%
23	Scatter Zeal	11P	70 sec.	11.5%
30	Diffuse Zeal	15P	82 sec.	14%
38	Disperse Zeal	19P	1.6 min.	16%
48	Dissipate Zeal	24P	1.9 min.	19%

AoE STR/CON debuff, radius 400 wu.
Skill............Suppression Dmg Type..............Spirit
Casting Time........3 sec. Range.....................1500
Duration.............60 sec.

Lvl	Spell	Cost	Debuff
2	Weaken Strength	1P	8
6	Attenuate Strength	3P	10.5
13	Undermine Strength	6P	15
18	Enfeeble Strength	8P	18
25	Impair Strength	12P	22.5
33	Debilitate Strength	16P	27
43	Emasculate Strength	21P	33

Mesmerize: target halts all movement and is unable to attack or cast spells; the effect breaks when the target is healed or takes damage (see page 367 for PvE/RvR limitations).
Skill............Suppression Dmg Type..............Spirit
Casting Time........3 sec. Range.....................1500

Lvl	Spell	Cost	Dur
1	Cripple Spirit	2P	16 sec.
4	Hold Spirit	3P	20 sec.
10	Pin Spirit	6P	28 sec.
15	Lock Spirit	9P	34 sec.
24	Immobilize Spirit	15P	46 sec.
31	Disable Spirit	19P	55 sec.
40	Paralyze Spirit	25P	67 sec.
50	Petrify Spirit	33P	80 sec.

Transfers up to (Transfer HP) from Caster to Friend.
Skill............Suppression Casting Time........3 sec.
Range.....................1350 Duration.................Inst.

Lvl	Spell	Cost	Transfer
11	Spirit Flow	6P	50 (max)
17	Spirit Wave	8P	75 (max)
21	Spirit Flux	10P	91 (max)
27	Spirit Fount	13P	116 (max)
32	Spirit Flood	16P	136 (max)
37	Spirit Surge	19P	157 (max)
46	Spirit Confluence	24P	193 (max)

Summoning

Calls pet, up to 88% of Caster's level
Skill.............Summoning Dmg Type..............Spirit
Cost.......................25%P Casting Time........6 sec.
Duration........Until Neg.

Lvl	Spell
1	Summon Spirit Fighter
7	Summon Spirit Soldier
12	Summon Spirit Swordsman
20	Summon Spirit Warrior
32	Summon Spirit Champion

Heals damage by (Heal) HP to Pet.
Skill............Summoning Dmg Type..............Spirit
Casting Time........3 sec. Range.....................1350
Duration..................Inst.

Lvl	Spell	Cost	Heal
6	Renew Spirit	4P	36
8	Recover Spirit	5P	46
11	Refresh Spirit	7P	61
15	Reconstitute Spirit	9P	81
21	Replenish Spirit	13P	111
28	Rejuvenate Spirit	17P	146
35	Restore Spirit	22P	181
44	Regenerate Spirit	28P	226

Bladeturn: Absorbs damage of single hit.
Skill............Summoning Dmg Type..............Spirit
Casting Time........4 sec. Duration.............10 min.

Lvl	Spell	Cost	Target
19	Protecting Spirit	8%P	Self

Spirit Summoning

Pet Focus Dmg Shield: Pet's damage/sec buffed until Caster interrupted or out of power (stacks as group 2).
Skill............Summoning Dmg Type..............Spirit
Casting Time........4 sec. Range.....................1350
Duration................Focus

Lvl	Spell	Cost	Buff
2	Spirit's Revenge	2P/5s	0.8
6	Spirit's Vengeance	3P/5s	1.2
9	Spirit's Retaliation	5P/5s	1.4
15	Spirit's Vendetta	8P/5s	2
22	Spirit's Reckoning	11P/5s	2.6
30	Spirit's Retribution	15P/5s	3.3
40	Spirit's Vindication	20P/5s	4.2
50	Spirit's Justification	26P/5s	5.1

Buffs Pet's STR and CON.
Skill............Summoning Dmg Type..............Spirit
Casting Time........3 sec. Range.....................1000
Duration.............10 min.

Lvl	Spell	Cost	Buff
3	Vigor of Valhalla	3P	12
7	Strength of Valhalla	5P	15
12	Zest of Valhalla	8P	19
18	Energy of Valhalla	11P	24
24	Vitality of Valhalla	15P	29
32	Might of Valhalla	20P	35
42	Force of Valhalla	27P	43

Buffs Pet's DEX and QUI.
Skill............Summoning Dmg Type..............Spirit
Casting Time........3 sec. Range.....................1000
Duration.............10 min.

Lvl	Spell	Cost	Buff
1	Valkyrie's Agility	2P	10
5	Valkyrie's Nimbleness	4P	14
8	Valkyrie's Quickness	5P	16
13	Valkyrie's Vivacity	8P	20
19	Valkyrie's Spirit	12P	25
25	Valkyrie's Vigilance	15P	30
33	Valkyrie's Haste	21P	36
43	Valkyrie's Alacrity	27P	44

Damage Shield: On Self; enemy damaged when hits Caster (stacks as group 1).
Skill............Summoning Dmg Type................Cold
Casting Time........4 sec. Duration.............10 min.

Lvl	Spell	Cost	Dmg/Sec
4	Gift of the Fallen	3P	1.5
11	Blessing of the Fallen	7P	2.5
20	Boon of the Fallen	12P	3.9
29	Benison of the Fallen	18P	5.2
39	Imbuement of the Fallen	25P	6.7
49	Infusion of the Fallen	32P	8.2

Classes & Races

	Norseman	Kobold	Troll	Dwarf
Thane (1.5x)	√		√	√
Warrior (2x)	√	√	√	√
Skald (1.5x)	√	√	√	√
Berserker (2x)	√		√	√
Hunter (2x)	√	√		√
Shadowblade (2.2x)	√	√		
Shaman (1x)		√	√	
Healer (1x)	√			√
Runemaster (1x)	√	√		√
Spiritmaster (1x)	√	√		

Basic Racial Attributes

	Norseman	Kobold	Troll	Dwarf
Strength	70	50	100	60
Constitution	70	50	70	80
Dexterity	50	70	35	50
Quickness	50	70	35	50
Intelligence	60	60	60	60
Charisma	60	60	60	60
Empathy	60	60	60	60
Piety	60	60	60	60

Innate Racial Resistances

	Norseman	Kobold	Troll	Dwarf
Crushing	+2	+5	–	–
Slashing	+3	–	+3	+2
Thrusting	–	–	+2	+3
Body	–	–	–	+5
Cold	+5	–	–	–
Energy	–	+5	–	–
Matter	–	–	+5	–

Classes & Houses

Starting Class	Final Class	House
Viking	Berserker	Modi
	Skald	Bragi
	Thane	Thor
	Warrior	Tyr
Rogue	Hunter	Skadi
	Shadowblade	Loki
Seer	Healer	Eir
	Shaman	Ymir
Mystic	Runemaster	Odin
	Spiritmaster	Hel

Merchants

Armor/Clothing

Location	Merchant
Armor (Mithril)	
Jordheim	Hakan
Chain (Mithril)	
Jordheim	Tait
Chain (Pansarkedja)	
Audliten	Geirrid
Fort Atla	Ugg
Galplen	Thyra
Haggerfel	Den
Huginfell	Radgar
Jordheim	Njal
Mularn	Bein
Nalliten	Grungir
Vasudheim	Vidar
Chain (Starkakedja)	
Audliten	Deilf
	Pireda
Dvalin	Alfrig
Fort Veldon	Gerda
	Idona
	Kell
Huginfell	Wulfwer
Chain (Svarkedja)	
Audliten	Gruth
Mularn	Vers
Vasudheim	Krip
Cloth (Padded)	
Audliten	Tozur
Fort Atla	Pika
Galplen	Kaiti
Haggerfel	Culben
Huginfell	Aylarn
Jordheim	Torrad
Mularn	Asta
Nalliten	Moona
Vasudheim	Gunnar
Cloth (Padded (Sylvan))	
Jordheim	Uli
Leather (Embossed)	
Jordheim	Fjord
Leather (Mjuklaedar)	
Audliten	Olav
Fort Atla	Og
Jordheim	Im
Mularn	Lene
Vasudheim	Fianna
Leather (Starkalaedar)	
Dvalin	Tyrn
Jordheim	Morgen
Leather (Svarlaedar)	
Jordheim	Hodern
Studded Leather	
Jordheim	Hakan
Studded Leather (Starkaskodd)	
Audliten	Leim
Dvalin	Laed
Fort Veldon	Connor
	Darby
Huginfell	Enir
Studded Leather (Stelskodd)	
Audliten	Eigil
Fort Atla	Lagg
Jordheim	Keki
Mularn	Blyn
Vasudheim	Baldus
Studded Leather (Svarskodd)	
Audliten	Jordan
	Ragnar
Dvalin	Marianne
Dvalin	Rae
Fort Atla	Trunk
Galplen	Nyden
Haggerfel	Dritsa
	Erik
Nalliten	Dink
	Tig

Weapons

Location	Merchant
Weapons (One Handed (Mithril))	
Jordheim	Dala
Weapons (Two Handed)	
Jordheim	Kalf
	Saga
Weapons (Two Handed (Mithril))	
Jordheim	Tove
Arrows	
Audliten	Inga
Fort Atla	Sillis
Haggerfel	Takker
Huginfell	Dana
Jordheim	Asra
	Gerd
Mularn	Geir
Nalliten	Cragg
Vasudheim	Krisst
Axes	
Audliten	Armond
Dvalin	Svard
Fort Atla	Yop
Fort Veldon	Hlif
Galplen	Gestod
Haggerfel	Burr
Huginfell	Auda
Jordheim	Ema
	Gymir
Mularn	Hrolf
Vasudheim	Leik
Bows	
Audliten	Brede
Dvalin	Brok
Fort Atla	Krak
Fort Veldon	Bitta
Haggerfel	Mattie
Huginfell	Hakon
Jordheim	Ole
	Thir
Mularn	Linna
Vasudheim	Kerr
Hammers	
Audliten	Frey
Dvalin	Laran
Fort Atla	Stap
Fort Veldon	Olof
Galplen	Helga
Haggerfel	Cort
Huginfell	Lodin
Jordheim	Signy
Mularn	Gram
Vasudheim	Burl

Large Weapons

Location	Merchant
Fort Atla	Isleif
Galplen	Galena
Haggerfel	Sinmore

Spears

Location	Merchant
Audliten	Josli
Fort Atla	Freydis
Galplen	Gudrid
Haggerfel	Fuiren
Huginfell	Ivara
Jordheim	Hedin
	Synna
Vasudheim	Galagore

Staves

Location	Merchant
Audliten	Eirik
Fort Atla	Ruk
Galplen	Serilyna
Haggerfel	Eda
Huginfell	Svala
Jordheim	Borg
	Halla
	Magna
Mularn	Brik
Vasudheim	Mildri

Swords

Location	Merchant
Audliten	Pater
Dvalin	Vordn
Fort Atla	Harald
	Vifil
Fort Veldon	Liv
Galplen	Stein
Haggerfel	Armund
Huginfell	Orm
Jordheim	Flosi
	Hrapp
Mularn	Aren
Nalliten	Dalla
Vasudheim	Gyda

Throwing Weapons

Location	Merchant
Audliten	Delg
Fort Atla	Carl
Galplen	Aki
Haggerfel	Bodil
Huginfell	Ryden
Jordheim	Canute
	Harry
Mularn	Hild
Vasudheim	Hallfred

Shields

Shields

Location	Merchant
Audliten	Hulda
Dvalin	Aesirdia
Fort Atla	Klag
Fort Veldon	Avar
Galplen	Otkel
Haggerfel	Ime
Huginfell	Runolf
Jordheim	Aric
	Digby
Mularn	Marie
Vasudheim	Bothe

Focus Items

Runemaster Staves

Location	Merchant
Fort Atla	Niniver
Galplen	Ysunoic
Huginfell	Elengwen
Mularn	Raelyan
Vasudheim	Merwdda

Spiritmaster Staves

Location	Merchant
Fort Atla	Merarka
Galplen	Curka
Huginfell	Alyllyra
Mularn	Lyna
Vasudheim	Clena

Other Goods

Dyes

Location	Merchant
Fort Atla	Hrin
	Ullaria
Jordheim	Alleca
	Ella
	Greip
	Hyndla
	Ozur
	Solveig
Vasudheim	Gregor
	Thord

Dyes (Enamel)

Location	Merchant
Fort Veldon	Rulongia
	Seiml
Galplen	Ohar
	Tallya
Haggerfel	Gale
Huginfell	Arnlaug
	Ruloia

Dyes (Leather)

Location	Merchant
Audliten	Serath
Haggerfel	Belyria
Mularn	Cale
	Finn
Nalliten	Hallaya
	Rooka

Feathers

Location	Merchant
Jordheim	Darg

Poisons

Location	Merchant
Audliten	Jolgeir
	Osk
Fort Atla	Bersi
	Helja
Jordheim	Ander
	Oilibhear

Tailoring Equipment

Location	Merchant
Vasudheim	Ingerd

Various expensive trade equipment

Location	Merchant
Haggerfel	Frikk

Services

Enchanter

Location	Merchant
Fort Atla	Onund
Haggerfel	Pene
Huginfell	Raker
Jordheim	Amma
	Arve
Mularn	Elizabeth
Vasudheim	Ulf

Healer

Location	Merchant
Fort Atla	Kari
Galplen	Hord
Haggerfel	Gustav
Huginfell	Saydyn
Jordheim	Nanna
Mularn	Kalbin
Vasudheim	Aud

Metalworking

Location	Merchant
Jordheim	Om

Smith

Location	Merchant
Audliten	Dahn
Fort Atla	Eindridi
Galplen	Gord
Haggerfel	Genlu Edrill
	Hilde
Huginfell	Kol Smithir
Jordheim	Gris
	Kiarr
	M. Caan
Mularn	Vahn
Vasudheim	Arnfinn

Tailor

Location	Merchant
Jordheim	Dalla
	Gro

Trainers

Armorcraft Trainer

Location	Trainer
Jordheim	Gest

Berserker Trainer

Location	Trainer
Fort Atla	Kalli
Jordheim	Haaken
	Hodr

Fletcher Trainer

Location	Trainer
Jordheim	Gils

Healer Trainer

Location	Trainer
Fort Atla	Welgen
Jordheim	Per
	Rana

Hunter Trainer

Location	Trainer
Fort Atla	Budo
Jordheim	Hauk
	Singrid

Mystic Trainer

Location	Trainer
Fort Atla	Lycla
Mularn	Vigdis
Vasudheim	Ragna

Rogue Trainer

Location	Trainer
Fort Atla	Jucla
Haggerfel	Glum
Vasudheim	Hrut

Runemaster Trainer

Location	Trainer
Fort Atla	Thetus
Jordheim	Bera
	Signa

Seer Trainer

Location	Trainer
Fort Atla	Hyndia
Galplen	Canan
Haggerfel	Groa
Vasudheim	Tosti

Shadowblade Trainer

Location	Trainer
Fort Atla	Boidoc
Jordheim	Elin
	Hreidar

Shaman Trainer

Location	Trainer
Fort Atla	Korgan
Galplen	Bec
Jordheim	Dane
	Grimma

Skald Trainer

Location	Trainer
Fort Atla	Lalida
Galplen	Vanah
Jordheim	Leif
	Sven

Spiritmaster Trainer

Location	Trainer
Fort Atla	Sarry
Jordheim	Dyre
	Galn

Tailorcraft Trainer

Location	Trainer
Jordheim	Eskil

Thane Trainer

Location	Trainer
Fort Atla	Salma
Jordheim	Frode
	Katla

Viking Trainer

Location	Trainer
Galplen	Krek
Mularn	Skapi
Vasudheim	Saeunn

Warrior Trainer

Location	Trainer
Fort Atla	Halker
Jordheim	Osten
	Thordia

Weaponcraft Trainer

Location	Trainer
Jordheim	Aase

Quests

Quests are only available once you've reached the appropriate level. When only specific races or classes can receive a quest, they are mentioned in the Restrictions column. Similarly, sometimes you must have finished a lower-level quest before you can advance to the next one; these prerequisite quests are also listed, in parentheses, in the Restrictions column.

L	Quest	Source / Restrictions
1	Amora's Aid	Fort Atla: trainer
1	Bear Skins	Haggerfel: Helen
1	Learn the Hunt	starter town: Aegan
1	Sveabone Hilt Sword	Vasudheim: Greidash
1	Trappers Pride	Galplen: Wariel
1	Troubled Wild	Vasudheim: trainer
2	Copious Striders	Vasudheim: Alomali
2	Magnild's Cure	Fort Atla: Amora / (Amora's Aid)
2	Newfound Group	Trainers
3	Aegan's Letter To Helen	Mularn: Aegan
3	Letter To Sveck	Vasudheim: Saeunn
3	Trapper's Joy	Galplen: Wariel / (Newfound Group)
4	Brutal Chains	outside Vasudheim: Thrall Keeper
4	Knowledge of the Gods	starter town: trainer / Viking
4	Mystic Trainer	Haggerfel: Trustan / Mystic
4	Rogue Trainer	Varies: trainer / Rogue
4	Seer Trainer	Varies: trainer / Seer (Letter to Sveck)
4	Tric's Lost List	Vasudheim: Tric
4	Venture To Gotar	Galplen: Krek
5	Ghoul Hair Belt	Audliten: Lefur
5	Tomte Jerkin	Audliten: Gwaell
6	Hole of the Dead	Vasudheim: Frimeth / Dwarf
6	Svartmoln's Appetite	Vasudheim: Kyba
7	A Deed of Old	Audliten: Aleaniver
7	Simple Misgivings	Haggerfel: Hilde
8	Defeat the Hobgoblin Anklebiter	near Mularn: Carr
8	Mucking Through the Ick	Haggerfel: Yver Tiu
8	Sveawolf Guardian	S.E. of Huginfell: Elder Sveawolf
10	Minx Wiley	Huginfell: Hurg
10	Monstrous Beast	Vale of Mularn: Vic
10	Smyga's Raid	Mularn: Carr / (Defeat the Hobgoblin Anklebiter)
10	Spat the Wild Cat	Vale of Mularn: Vic / (Monstrous Beast)
11	Covet Wiley	Dvalin: Aesirdia
11	Klippa's Claw	Vasudheim: Alomali / (Copious Striders)
12	Hunting Party	Huginfell: Bork
12	Trustan's Belongings	Haggerfel: Trustan
14	Cape of the Mother Wolf	Tower N. of Audlitin: Sveck/Vk.,Rg. (Traveler's Way)
15	Evenings Empty Blessing	Mularn: Aegan
15	Lover's Circle	Huginfell: Sugnhild
15	Paranoid Guard	Huginfell: Agnor Crusher
15	Reach of the Shadow	Huginfell: Aylarn
16	Brack: Rollo's Story	Haggerfel: Hilde / Dwarf (Simple Misgivings)
16	Protect Huginfel	Huginfell: Gudlor
16	Waking of the Fallen	Huginfell: Saydyn
17	Protecting the Healer	Huginfell: Samlauf Kolsson
18	Family Business	Tower outside Mularn: Thrand
18	Fervent	SE of Huginfell: Elder Sveawolf
18	Gokstad: Wolves In Myrkwood	Jordheim: Singrid / Shadowblade
18	Gokstad's Jewel	Jordheim: Singrid / Hunter
18	Morana's Tunic	Gna Faste Tower: Sentry Dwarn / Mystic
19	The Creatures of Myrkwood	Gna Faste: Atzar
20	Bowyer's Draw	Huginfell: Hakon / Hunter
21	Living Warning	Huginfell: Gudlor
21	Widower Hunt	Haggerfel: Yver / Seer, Skald, Thane
22	Krrrck's Torment	Vasudheim: Arnlief / Mystic, Seer
22	Sugnhild's Revenge	Huginfell: Sunghild / (Living Warning)
22	Tale of Two Trolls	Fort Atla: Darrius / (Widower's Hunt)
23	Protecting Myrkwood: PM	Gna Faste: Serilyna
23	Silent Death	Huginfell: Bork
23	Sulphine's Demise	Haggerfel: Macalena / Viking
24	Foolish Dancers	Ft. Veldon: Cornelis / Seer, Viking
25	Stripe	Huginfell: Halla / Mystic, Seer
26	Nihm's Secret	Ft. Atla: Finni
29	Furf's Reward	Guard Tower near Nalliten: Dalla
30	Young Fire Wyrm Lord	Mularn: Bolli
35	Lord Laur's Wife	Nalliten: Dunfjall / (PM: Helping the Werewolves part)
35	Terje's Problem	Nalliten: Dunfjall / (PM: Helping the Svartalfs part)
35	Thraxia's Dilemma	Nalliten: Dunfjall / (PM: Helping the Arachites part)
35	Zrit-Zrit's Item	Nallitan: Gautr
38	Big Paw	Ft. Atla: Finna
40	Cargila's Blessing	Nallitan: Geiri
44	Price of Excellence	Yggdra Forest : Drunken Dwarf / Seer, Viking

Guild Track

You may only undertake the quests for your own path. You must complete each quest before undertaking the next.

Mystic

L	Quest	Source / Restrictions
7	Traveler's Way	Jordheim: trainer
11	Runes of Darkness	Jordheim: trainer / Runemaster
11	Prove Kobold Helen's Innocence	Jordheim: trainer / Spiritmaster
15	Grenlock Clan	Jordheim: trainer
20	Coplin's Spirit	Jordheim: Anrid
25	Fallen Warrior	Jordheim: Anrid
30	Forgotten Journey	Jordheim: Anrid
40	The Three Sisters	Jordheim: Anrid
43	Saving the Clan: 43,45,48,50	Jordheim: trainer

Rogue

L	Quest	Source / Restrictions
7	Traveler's Way	Jordheim: trainer
11	Hunt For Dorga	Jordheim: trainer / Hunter
11	Jewel Hunt	Fort Atla: Boidoc / Shadowblade
15	A War of Old: 15,20,25,30	Jordheim: trainer
40	The War Continues	Jordheim: trainer
43	War Concluded: 43,45,48,50	Jordheim: trainer

Seer

L	Quest	Source / Restrictions
7	Traveler's Way	Jordheim: trainer
11	Darksong's Dirge	Jordheim: trainer
15	Wisdom of Time	Jordheim: trainer
20	Visions of Darkness	Haggerfel: Inaksha
25	Decoding the Map	Haggerfel: Inaksha
30	Gashir	Haggerfel: Inaksha
40	Mimir's Protection	Haggerfel: Inaksha
43	The Desire of a God: 43,45,48,50	Jordheim: trainer

Guild Quests cont.: Viking

7 Traveler's Way	Jordheim: trainer
11 Hill Cat Hunt (Warrior) or Taldo's Amulet (Thane)	Jordheim: trainer
11 Rasczel's Bane (Berserker) or Rasczel's Nose (Skald)	Jordheim: trainer
15 The Red Dagger (15, 20, 25)	Jordheim: trainer
30 Thane's Blood	Jordheim: Gythja of Bragi
40 Blessed Enchantments	Mularn: Elizabeth
43 An End to the Daggers: 43,45,48,50	Jordheim: trainer

Standard (Craftable) Weapons

Standard (craftable) weapons are sorted by the skill needed to wield them. For **Arrow** stats, see page 278. For unique weapons (including unique arrows), see page 372. For **Siege Equipment**, see page 324. For a general discussion of weapons and stats, see page 361.

Headings. Delay = time between blows, in seconds / **Dam (M# 1)** = damage per hit, using a Material Level 1 weapon / **Incr**ement = additional damage per hit, with each improvement in Material / **Base DPS** = damage per second using a Material Level 1 weapon / **Wt.** = weight of the weapon / **Sec. Skill** = secondary skill that influences damage / **Range** = range of weapon, in world units / * = this weapon can be used as a second weapon with Midgard's Left Axe skill.

Standard (Craftable) Weapons

Axe (One Handed)

Lvl	Weapon	Delay (sec.)	Dam (M# 1)	Incr	Base DPS	Wt.
1	Hand Axe *	2.4	3.6	3.6	1.5	1.5
2	Bearded Axe *	2.7	4.9	4.1	1.8	2.5
3	War Axe *	3.2	6.7	4.8	2.1	3.5
4	Spiked Axe	3.7	8.9	5.6	2.4	4
5	Double Bladed Axe	4.3	11.5	6.4	2.7	5
6	Cleaver	4.0	12	6.0	3.0	3.5

Axe (Two Handed)

Lvl	Weapon	Delay (sec.)	Dam (M# 1)	Incr	Base DPS	Wt.
4	Large Axe	4.7	11.3	7.1	2.4	5.5
5	Great Axe	5.5	14.9	8.3	2.7	7.5
6	War Cleaver	5.3	16.2	8.0	3.1	5.5

Composite Bow

Lvl	Weapon	Delay (sec.)	Dam (M# 1)	Incr	Base DPS	Wt.	Range
5	Composite Bow	4.0	10.8	6.0	2.7	3.1	1600
5	Great Composite Bow	4.7	12.7	7.1	2.7	3.6	1600

Staff

Lvl	Weapon	Delay (sec.)	Dam (M# 1)	Incr	Base DPS	Wt.
1	Staff	4.5	6.7	6.8	1.5	4.5
1	Shod Staff	5	10.5	7.5	2.1	4.5
1	Focus Staff	4.5	6.7	6.7	1.5	4.5

Hammer (One Handed)

Lvl	Weapon	Delay (sec.)	Dam (M# 1)	Incr	Base DPS	Wt.
1	Small Hammer	2.8	4.2	4.2	1.5	2.4
2	Hammer	3.1	5.6	4.7	1.8	3.2
3	War Hammer	3.5	7.4	5.3	2.1	4
4	Pick Hammer	3.8	9.1	5.7	2.4	4.4
5	Battle Hammer	4.1	11.1	6.2	2.7	4.9
6	Spiked Hammer	4.1	12.3	6.2	3.0	3.5

Hammer (Two Handed)

Lvl	Weapon	Delay (sec.)	Dam (M# 1)	Incr	Base DPS	Wt.
4	Two Handed War Hammer	4.9	11.7	7.3	2.4	6.5
5	Great Hammer	5.4	14.5	8.1	2.7	7.5
6	Great Spiked Hammer	5.2	15.6	7.8	3.0	5.5

Spear

Lvl	Weapon	Delay (sec.)	Dam (M# 1)	Incr	Base DPS	Wt.
1	Spear	3.9	5.9	5.9	1.5	3
2	Long Spear	4.3	7.8	6.5	1.8	3.5
3	Trident	4.8	10	7.1	2.1	4
4	Bill Spear	5.3	12.6	7.9	2.4	4.5
5	Great Spear	5.0	13.5	7.5	2.7	5
6	Battle Spear	5.3	15.9	8.0	3.0	4

Sword (One Handed)

Lvl	Weapon	Delay (sec.)	Dam (M# 1)	Incr	Base DPS	Wt.
1	Dagger	2.3	3.5	3.5	1.5	1
2	Short Sword	2.5	4.5	3.8	1.8	1.5
3	Broadsword	3.1	6.6	4.7	2.1	2
4	Long Sword	3.7	8.8	5.5	2.4	2.5
5	Bastard Sword	4.2	11.3	6.3	2.7	3
6	Dwarven Short Sword	3.0	9	4.5	3.0	2.5

Sword (Two Handed)

Lvl	Weapon	Delay (sec.)	Dam (M# 1)	Incr	Base DPS	Wt.
4	Two-Handed Sword	4.7	11.2	7.0	2.4	5
5	Great Sword	5.5	14.8	8.2	2.7	6
6	Dwarven Great Sword	5.0	15	7.5	3.0	5

Thrown Weapons

Lvl	Weapon	Delay (sec.)	Dam (M# 1)	Incr	Base DPS	Wt.	Range
5	Weighted Throwing Axe	3.5	9.5	5.3	2.7	.15	1450
5	Weighted Throw. Hammer	4.0	10.8	6	2.7	.2	1450
5	Weighted Throwing Knife	3.0	8.1	4.5	2.7	.1	1450

There are up to 40 weapons in a stack.

Weapon Drops & Rewards

Abbreviations

Headings. PL = Power Level / **M#** = Material (M) and Material Level (#) / **Ql** = Quality / **Spd** = Speed, or weapon delay (the time between successive swings) / **Dam** = Damage with each hit / **DPS** = Damage per second / **Type** = Type of damage (**Cr**ush, **Sl**ash or **Thr**ust) / **Range** = basic range of the bow or crossbow, in world units (1 pace ≈ 60 world units ≈ 1 yard).

Stats. Resistance, Skill, **F**ocus / **Cha**risma, **Con**stitution, **Emp**athy, **Dex**terity, **Int**elligence, **Pi**ety, **Qui**ckness, **Str**ength / Cloth, **L**eather, **M**etal, **W**ood. The first positive percentage in any bonus indicates your increased chance to hit with the weapon.

* There is more than one weapon with this same name. This happens most often with casters' focus staffs, where up to four can have the same name but significantly different stats.

Axe Skill (Axe)

Weapon	Bonus	PL	M#	Ql	Spd	Dam	DPS	Type	Generic
Training Axe		0	M1	90	2.5	3	1.3	Sl	Axe
Huldu Axe	+1%; HP +3	4	M1	89	2.5	6	2.4	Sl	Axe
Wood Choppers Axe	+1%; Str +3	4	M1	90	4	10	2.4	Sl	Axe
Large Tomte Axe	+1% to hit	5	M1	89	4.9	13	2.7	Sl	Axe
Axe of Modi	Left Axe S. +1	6	M2	90	3.1	9	3.0	Sl	Axe
Gleaming Axe	+5%; Left Axe S. +1	7	M2	90	2.7	9	3.3	Sl	Axe
Thane's Blood	+3% to hit	7	M2	100	2.7	9	3.3	Sl	Axe
Treecutter	+5%; Axe S. +1	7	M2	90	4.7	16	3.3	Sl	Axe
Iron Skull Axe	+1%; HP +6	8	M2	89	4.8	17	3.6	Sl	Axe
Tomte War Axe		10	M2	80	3.2	13	4.2	Sl	Axe
Vendo Bone-Splitter	+5% to hit	11	M3	89	3.4	15	4.5	Sl	Axe
Mauler Claw Axe	+5%; Axe S. +1; Str +1	13	M3	89	3.2	16	5.1	Sl	Axe
War Rager's Axe	+5%; Axe S. +1; Str +3	13	M3	90	4	20	5.1	Sl	Axe
Brittle-Bone Great Axe	+5%; Axe S. +1; Str +1	14	M3	89	5.6	30	5.4	Sl	Axe
Brittle-Bone War Axe	+5%; Axe S. +1; Qui +1	14	M3	89	3.2	17	5.4	Sl	Axe
Brack Axe	+5%; Axe S. +3	18	M4	100	4.3	28	6.6	Sl	Axe
Brack Left Axe	+5%; Left Axe S. +3	18	M4	100	3.8	25	6.6	Sl	Axe
Bone-Handle Great Axe	+10%; Axe S. +1; Str +3	19	M4	89	5.5	38	6.9	Sl	Axe
Bone-Handle Axe	+20%; Axe S. +1; Str +3	20	M4	89	2.4	17	7.2	Sl	Axe
Bone-Handle War Axe	+10%; Left Axe S. +1; Str +3	20	M4	89	3.2	23	7.2	Sl	Axe
Mandible Headed Axe	+10%; Axe, Left Axe S. +1	20	M4	89	2.8	20	7.2	Sl	Axe
Noble Wanderer's Axe	+10%; Axe S. +2	20	M4	89	3	22	7.2	Sl	Axe
Vannsang Axe	+10%; Axe S. +1; Str +1	20	M4	89	4.3	31	7.2	Sl	Axe
Ashen Axe	+10%; Axe S. +2; Heat R. +2	22	M5	89	3.2	25	7.8	Sl	Axe
Smoking Sentry Axe	+10%; Axe S. +3; Qui +6	23	M5	100	2.7	22	8.1	Sl	Axe
Mourning Rage	+10%; Berzerk S. +3; Str +6	24	M5	100	6	50	8.4	Sl	Axe
Njessi Crossed Short Tooth Axe	+10%; Axe S. +4; Body R. +4	24	M5	100	4.3	36	8.4	Sl	Axe
Njessi Short Tooth Axe	+10%; Axe, Left Axe S. +2; Body R. +4	24	M5	100	3	25	8.4	Sl	Axe
Troika's Cursed Axe	+10%; Qui, Str, Con +3	24	M5	89	2.7	23	8.4	Sl	Axe
Charred Bone Axe	+10%; Axe S. +2; Str +3	25	M5	89	2.8	24	8.7	Sl	Axe
Draugr Commander Axe	+10%; Dex, Con, Str +3	25	M5	89	2.7	23	8.7	Sl	Axe
Hardened Stone Axe	+15%; Axe, Left Axe S. +2	26	M6	90	4	36	9.0	Sl	Axe
Rager's Axe	+15%; Axe S. +4	26	M6	90	5	45	9.0	Sl	Axe
Scapula Bone Axe	+15%; Axe, Left Axe S. +1; Dex +1	27	M6	89	2.8	26	9.3	Sl	Axe
Blazing Giant Axe	+15%; Axe S. +2; Spirit, Heat R. +2	29	M6	89	4.6	46	9.9	Sl	Axe
Seared Axe	+10%; Str +4; HP +9	29	M6	89	3.9	39	9.9	Sl	Axe
Vendo Berzerker Axe	+15%; Axe S. +1; Str, Qui +3	29	M6	89	3.6	36	9.9	Sl	Axe
Serrated Skull-Slicer	+15%; Left Axe S. +2; Axe S. +1; Str +10	31	M7	100	3.8	40	10.5	Sl	Axe
Garou Axe	+10%; Axe S. +3; Str +7	33	M7	89	3.3	37	11.1	Sl	Axe
Shibber's Shredder	+15%; Axe S. +3; Left Axe S. +2; Qui +4	33	M7	100	3.2	36	11.1	Sl	Axe

Weapon	Bonus	PL	M#	Ql	Spd	Dam	DPS	Type	Generic
Skull-Bone Axe	+15%; Axe S. +2; Con +4	33	M7	89	4.6	51	11.1	Sl	Axe
Feral Fiery Axe	+20%; Str +4; Qui +6	35	M7	89	2.7	32	11.7	Sl	Axe
Lupine Axe	+15%; Axe S. +2; Str +6	35	M7	89	2.4	28	11.7	Sl	Axe
Howl of the Moon	+20%; Axe S. +2; Str +4	36	M8	89	4.6	55	12.0	Sl	Axe
Wolf's Fang	+20%; Axe S. +2; Left Axe S. +1; Slash R. +2	36	M8	89	3	36	12.0	Sl	Axe
Dull Asterite Axe	+1%; Axe S. +1; Con +1	37	M8	80	2.8	34	12.3	Sl	Axe
Dull Asterite Large Axe	+1%; Axe S. +1; Str +1	37	M8	80	4.8	59	12.3	Sl	Axe
Giant Garou Axe	+20%; Axe S. +1; Str, Qui +4	38	M8	89	5.5	69	12.6	Sl	Axe
Gnarling Lupine Axe	+20%; Left Axe S. +2; Dex, Str +3	38	M8	89	2.4	30	12.6	Sl	Axe
Keen Asterite Axe	+20%; Left Axe S. +1; Qui +3; Str +4	38	M8	89	2.8	35	12.6	Sl	Axe
Keen Asterite Large Axe	+20%; Axe S. +2; Str +4	38	M8	89	4.8	60	12.6	Sl	Axe
Surveyor's Axe	+20%; Axe S. +7	39	M8	100	3.7	48	12.9	Sl	Axe
Forged Darksteel Spiked Axe	+20%; Axe S. +3; Heat R. +6	42	M8	89	3.4	47	13.8	Sl	Axe
Runic Clay Axe	+20%; Axe S. +2; Str +4; Qui +3	42	M8	89	3.3	46	13.8	Sl	Axe
Blessed Northern Axe	+20%; Axe S. +4; Con +6; HP +18	43	M8	100	3.5	49	14.1	Sl	Axe
Blessed Northern Great Axe	+20%; Axe S. +4; Energy R. +8; Str, Con +4	43	M8	100	5.6	79	14.1	Sl	Axe
Mischief Maker's Axe	+20%; Axe S. +4; HP +18; Qui +6	43	M8	100	4.3	61	14.1	Sl	Axe
Mischief Maker's Great Axe	+20%; Axe S. +4; Qui +6; HP +18	43	M8	100	4.6	65	14.1	Sl	Axe
Runed Clay Axe	+20%; Axe S. +3; Matter R. +4	45	M8	89	3.2	47	14.7	Sl	Axe
Screaming Ghastly Axe	+25%; Axe, Parry S. +2; Str, Qui +7	46	M8	100	5.4	81	15.0	Sl	Axe
Twilight Cleaver	+25%; Str +6; Qui +4; Slash R. +4	47	M8	89	5.5	84	15.3	Sl	Axe
Hooked Orm Claw	+25%; Battlesongs, Stormcalling S. +2; Qui +4; Str +3	48	M8	89	4	62	15.6	Sl	Axe
Ghastly Axe	+25%; Axe S. +2; Parry S. +2; Str, Qui +7	49	M8	100	5.6	89	15.9	Sl	Axe
Double-Bladed Ice Razor	+30%; Axe S. +5; Parry S. +2; Str +9; Cold R. +4	50	M8	93	4	65	16.2	Sl	Axe
Drakulv Militia Axe	+25%; Axe S. +2; HP +18	50	M8	89	3	49	16.2	Sl	Axe
Ebony Axe of Mindless Rage	+20%; Str +9; HP +15; Spirit R. +8; Int –10	50	M8	89	2.4	39	16.2	Sl	Axe
Fate Stealer	+25%; Axe S. +9	50	M8	90	5	81	16.2	Sl	Axe
Frozen Tree Splitter	+30%; Axe S. +6; Con +12; Cold R. +4	50	M8	93	5	81	16.2	Sl	Axe
Frozen Windswept Axe	+25%; Axe S. +5; Str +7	50	M8	90	3.6	58	16.2	Sl	Axe
Golden Alloy Axe	+25%; Axe S. +4; Left Axe, Parry S. +1; Str +9	50	M8	90	3.3	53	16.2	Sl	Axe
Immolated Dragonfire Cleaver	+25%; Axe S. +3; Qui +10; Heat R. +10	50	M8	90	4	65	16.2	Sl	Axe
Immolated Great Dragonfire Cleaver	+25%; Axe S. +5; Str +12	50	M8	90	5	81	16.2	Sl	Axe
Drakulv Militia Great Axe	+25%; Axe S. +2; Parry S. +1; Str +6	51	M8	89	4.6	76	16.5	Sl	Axe

Hammer Skill (Hammer)

Weapon	Bonus	PL	M#	Ql	Spd	Dam	DPS	Type	Generic
Training Hammer		0	M1	90	3.1	4	1.3	Cr	Hammer
Hobgoblin Hammer	+1%; HP +3	4	M1	89	2.9	7	2.4	Cr	Hammer
Hammer of Thor	Hammer S. +1	6	M2	90	3.1	9	3.0	Cr	Hammer
Old Smithy Hammer	+5%; Hammer S. +1	7	M2	90	3	10	3.3	Cr	Hammer
Iron Skull Hammer	+1%; HP +6	9	M2	89	4.5	18	3.9	Cr	Hammer
Tomte War Hammer		10	M2	80	3.5	15	4.2	Cr	Hammer
Decaying Hammer	+5%; Hammer S. +1	12	M3	89	3.5	17	4.8	Cr	Hammer
Red Bludgeoner	+5%; Hammer S. +2; Str +3	12	M3	100	4	19	4.8	Cr	Hammer
Blod Flekket Hammer	+5%; Str +1; HP +6	13	M3	89	5.2	27	5.1	Cr	Hammer
Hammer of Atonement	+5%; Hammer S. +1; Pie +3	13	M3	90	4	20	5.1	Cr	Hammer
Blodjeger Hammer	+5%; Hammer S. +1; Str +1	14	M3	89	4.1	22	5.4	Cr	Hammer
Brittle-Bone Great Hammer	+5%; Hammer S. +1; Con +1	14	M3	89	5.4	29	5.4	Cr	Hammer
Brittle-Bone War Hammer	+5%; Hammer S. +1; Pie +1	14	M3	89	4.1	22	5.4	Cr	Hammer
Brack Hammer	+5%; Hammer S. +3; Qui +3	18	M4	100	3	20	6.6	Cr	Hammer
Styring	+10%; Str +3; HP +6	20	M4	89	3.8	27	7.2	Cr	Hammer
Ancient Engraved Maul	+10%; Hammer S. +2; Str +3	21	M5	90	5.2	39	7.5	Cr	Hammer
Hammer of the Indomitable	+10%; Hammer S. +1; HP +9	23	M5	89	4.5	36	8.1	Cr	Hammer
Accursed Great Hammer	+10%; Pie +4; Con, Qui +3	24	M5	89	5.4	45	8.4	Cr	Hammer
Njessi Bone Hammer	+10%; Hammer S. +4; Crush R. +4	24	M5	100	3.5	29	8.4	Cr	Hammer
Njessi Skull Bone Hammer	+10%; Hammer S. +4; Crush R. +4	24	M5	100	3.7	31	8.4	Cr	Hammer
Vengeful Great Hammer	+10%; Hammer S. +2; Qui +4	24	M5	89	5.4	45	8.4	Cr	Hammer
Vengeful War Hammer	+10%; Hammer S. +2; Str +4	24	M5	89	3.5	29	8.4	Cr	Hammer
Accursed Hammer	+10%; Pie +6; Con +4	25	M5	89	3.5	30	8.7	Cr	Hammer
Charred Skull Hammer	+10%; Hammer S. +2; Con +3	25	M5	89	3.1	27	8.7	Cr	Hammer
Ashen Maul	+10%; Hammer S. +4; Qui +4	26	M6	100	4.2	38	9.0	Cr	Hammer
Blunted Fire Cat Tooth	+15%; Con +4; Str +3	26	M6	89	3.7	33	9.0	Cr	Hammer

Weapon	Bonus	PL	M#	QI	Spd	Dam	DPS	Type	Generic
Dread Lichess Demolisher	+10%; Con, Dex +4	26	M6	89	2.8	25	9.0	Cr	Hammer
Hammer of the Wildcrusher	+15%; Hammer S. +4	26	M6	90	4.3	39	9.0	Cr	Hammer
Fiery Giant Bone	+15%; Hammer S. +2; Str +1	27	M6	89	5.2	48	9.3	Cr	Hammer
Lava Scorched Hammer	+15%; Con, Pie +4	31	M6	89	5.2	55	10.5	Cr	Hammer
Skull-Bone Hammer	+15%; Hammer S. +1; Pie, Con, Str +3	33	M7	89	3.4	38	11.1	Cr	Hammer
Gagnrad's Icy Crusher	+15%; Hammer S. +3; Con, Pie, Str +4	35	M7	100	4.3	50	11.7	Cr	Hammer
Growling Garou Warhammer	+15%; Con, Dex, Qui, Pie +3	35	M7	89	3.5	41	11.7	Cr	Hammer
Dull Asterite Hammer	+1%; Hammer S. +1; Con +1	37	M8	80	3.7	46	12.3	Cr	Hammer
Dull Asterite Large Hammer	+1%; Hammer S. +1; Str +1	37	M8	80	4.6	57	12.3	Cr	Hammer
Forge Tender's Hammer	+15%; Str +12	37	M8	89	3.9	48	12.3	Cr	Hammer
Hammer of the Moon	+20%; Hammer S. +2; Str +3; Crush R. +2	37	M8	89	2.8	34	12.3	Cr	Hammer
Weighted Asterite Hammer	+20%; Hammer S. +1; Con +3; Str +4	38	M8	89	3.6	45	12.6	Cr	Hammer
Weighted Asterite Large Hammer	+20%; Hammer S. +2; Str +4	38	M8	89	4.5	57	12.6	Cr	Hammer
Wolf-Headed Hammer	+20%; Hammer S. +2; Qui +3; Heat R. –2	38	M8	89	4.8	60	12.6	Cr	Hammer
Ominous Moonstruck Hammer	+25%; Str +4; Qui +6	39	M8	89	3.5	45	12.9	Cr	Hammer
Garou Great Hammer	+20%; Hammer S. +2; Qui, Str +3	40	M8	89	5.4	71	13.2	Cr	Hammer
Forged Darksteel Pick Hammer	+20%; Hammer S. +3; Heat R. +6	42	M8	89	3.5	48	13.8	Cr	Hammer
Blessed Northern Great Hammer	+20%; Hammer S. +4; Con, Qui +7	43	M8	100	5	71	14.1	Cr	Hammer
Blessed Northern Hammer	+20%; Hammer S. +4; Str, Qui +7	43	M8	100	4.4	62	14.1	Cr	Hammer
Mimir's Hammer of Wisdom	+20%; HP +24; Pie, Con +7	43	M8	100	3	42	14.1	Cr	Hammer
Mimir's Large Hammer of Wisdom	+20%; HP +24; Pie, Str +7	43	M8	100	4.5	63	14.1	Cr	Hammer
Ulfgar's Hammer	+20%; Hammer S. +4; Str +7; HP +15	44	M8	100	5.4	78	14.4	Cr	Hammer
Drakulv Militia Great Hammer	+20%; Hammer S. +2; Str, Pie +4	45	M8	89	4.5	66	14.7	Cr	Hammer
Runed Clay War Hammer	+20%; Hammer S. +3; Str, Con +4	45	M8	89	3.9	57	14.7	Cr	Hammer
Hammer of Black Ice	+25%; Hammer S. +4; Str +7; HP +15	46	M8	100	5.4	81	15.0	Cr	Hammer
Runic Clay War Hammer	+25%; Hammer S. +2; Str +7	46	M8	89	3.8	57	15.0	Cr	Hammer
Twilight Battle Crasher	+25%; Con, Str +4; Cold R. +6	47	M8	89	5.2	80	15.3	Cr	Hammer
Drakulv Militia Hammer	+25%; Hammer S. +3; Con +4	48	M8	89	3	47	15.6	Cr	Hammer
Battle Scourge	+25%; Hammer S. +6; Parry S. +4	50	M8	91	4	65	16.2	Cr	Hammer
Celestial Storm Caller	+25%; Hammer S. +3; Stormcalling S. +2; Str +9	50	M8	90	4	65	16.2	Cr	Hammer
Frost Encrusted War Hammer	+25%; Hammer, Parry S. +3; Str +7	50	M8	90	3.4	55	16.2	Cr	Hammer
Golden Alloy Hammer	+25%; Mending, Augmentation, Pacification, Cave Magic S. +2	50	M8	90	3.4	55	16.2	Cr	Hammer
Great Ice Breaker	+30%; Hammer S. +6; Con, Str +6; Cold R. +6	50	M8	93	5	81	16.2	Cr	Hammer
Ice Breaker	+30%; Hammer S. +5; Con +13; Cold R. +8	50	M8	93	3.8	62	16.2	Cr	Hammer
Icebound War Hammer	+25%; Pie +9; Str +7; Power +4	50	M8	90	3.5	57	16.2	Cr	Hammer
Reincarnate Femur War Maul	+20%; Hammer S. +3; Str +7	50	M8	89	4.9	79	16.2	Cr	Hammer
Soul Forge	+25%; Hammer S. +6; Parry S. +4	50	M8	91	5.4	87	16.2	Cr	Hammer

Spear Skill (Bill, Bone, Spear, Trident)

Weapon	Bonus	PL	M#	QI	Spd	Dam	DPS	Type	Generic
Spear of the Initiate		4	M1	100	3.1	7	2.4	Thr	Spear
Brendig's Kneebiter	+5%; Spear S. +1	7	M2	90	4	13	3.3	Thr	Spear
Valorbound Spear	+5%; Spear S. +1; Cha +3	10	M2	90	5.2	22	4.2	Thr	Bill
Savage Iron Spear	+1% to hit	10	M2	89	4	17	4.2	Thr	Spear
Tomte Spear		10	M2	80	3.9	16	4.2	Thr	Spear
Brittle-Bone Trident	+5%; Spear S. +1; Qui +1	14	M3	89	4.8	26	5.4	Thr	Trident
Spined Spear	+10%; Spear S. +2	16	M4	89	5	30	6.0	Sl	Spear
Cinder Encrusted Spear	+10%; Spear S. +2; Cold R. +2	23	M5	89	3.9	32	8.1	Thr	Spear
Cursed Spirit Spear	+10%; Dex +3; Qui +4; Spear S. +1	23	M5	89	5	41	8.1	Sl	Spear
Spear of the Indomitable	+10%; Spear S. +1; Dex +3; Con +1	23	M5	89	4.4	36	8.1	Sl	Spear
Evanescent Long Spear	+10%; Spear S. +1; Qui +4	24	M5	89	4.3	36	8.4	Sl	Spear
Njessi Short Tooth Spear	+10%; Spear S. +4; Thrust R. +4	24	M5	100	5.3	45	8.4	Sl	Spear
Trademan's Heartfinder	+10%; Spear S. +3; Dex +6	24	W5	100	3.8	32	8.4	Thr	Spear
Serrated Bone Spear	+15%; Spear S. +4	26	M6	90	5.8	52	9.0	Thr	Spear
Eteki's Softskin Sticker	+15%; Spear S. +3; Dex +6; Qui +3	29	M6	100	4.8	48	9.9	Sl	Spear
Vendo Impaler	+15%; Spear S. +2; Dex +3	29	M6	89	4.6	46	9.9	Thr	Trident
Spear of the Elements	+15%; Spear S. +3; Heat, Cold, Spirit R. +4	30	W6	100	4	41	10.2	Thr	Spear
Skull-Bone Spear	+15%; HP +21	33	M7	89	4.9	54	11.1	Sl	Spear
Dull Asterite Spear	+1%; Spear S. +1; Dex +1	37	M8	80	4.1	50	12.3	Thr	Spear
Keen Asterite Spear	+20%; Spear S. +2; Dex +4	38	M8	89	4	50	12.6	Thr	Spear
Varulvhamn Spear	+20%; Spear S. +2; Qui, Str +3	38	M8	89	5	63	12.6	Sl	Spear
Squire's Practice Spear	+15%; Spear S. +5	39	M8	89	5	65	12.9	Sl	Spear

Weapon	Bonus	PL	M#	Ql	Spd	Dam	DPS	Type	Generic
Varulv Icy Spear	+25%; Str +6; Qui +4	39	M8	89	3.9	50	12.9	Thr	Spear
Seafarer's Trident	+20%; Spear S. +3; Dex +6	41	M8	89	4.5	61	13.5	Thr	Trident
Winter's Spear	+20%; Spear S. +4; HP +15; Dex +7	43	M8	100	4.3	61	14.1	Sl	Spear
Runed Clay Spear	+15%; Spear S. +3; Str +6	45	M8	89	5	74	14.7	Thr	Bill
Reincarnate Bone Shard	+20%; Spear S. +2; Qui +9	45	M8	89	4	59	14.7	Thr	Bone
Drakulv Milita Spear	+20%; Spear S. +5	45	M8	89	4	59	14.7	Thr	Trident
Twilight Impaler	+25%; Spear S. +2; Qui +7	47	M8	89	5	77	15.3	Thr	Spear
Golden Alloy Great Spear	+25%; Spear S. +6; Str, Qui +4	50	M8	90	4.7	76	16.2	Sl	Spear
Runic Clay Spear	+25%; Spear S. +2; Dex, Str +4	50	M8	89	5	81	16.2	Thr	Spear
Spirit of Prey	+30%; Spear S. +6; Dex, Str +6; Cold R. +6	50	M8	93	4	65	16.2	Sl	Spear

Staff Skill (Rod, Spine, Staff)

Weapon	Bonus	PL	M#	Ql	Spd	Dam	DPS	Type	Generic
Twisted Wood	+1%; Pie +3	4	W1	90	5	12	2.4	Cr	Staff
Runed Wanderer's Staff	+1%; Runemaster spells F. +5	6	W2	89	4.8	14	3.0	Cr	Staff
Runemaster Staff of Darkness *	Darkness F. +5; other Runemaster spells F. +2	6	W2	85	4.5	14	3.0	Cr	Staff
Runemaster Staff of Mysticism *	Runemaster spells F. +4	6	W2	85	4.5	14	3.0	Cr	Staff
Runemaster Staff of Runecarving *	Runecarving F. +5; other Runemaster spells F. +2	6	W2	85	4.5	14.	3.0	Cr	Staff
Runemaster Staff of Suppression *	Suppression F. +5; other Runemaster spells F. +2	6	W2	85	4.5	14	3.0	Cr	Staff
Runic Staff	Pie +3	6	W2	90	4.5	14	3.0	Cr	Staff
Spiritmaster Staff of Darkness *	Darkness F. +5; other Spiritmaster spells F. +2	6	W2	85	4.5	14	3.0	Cr	Staff
Spiritmaster Staff of Mysticism *	Spiritmaster spells F. +4	6	W2	85	4.5	14	3.0	Cr	Staff
Spiritmaster Staff of Summoning *	Summoning F. +5; other Spiritmaster spells F. +2	6	W2	85	4.5	14	3.0	Cr	Staff
Spiritmaster Staff of Suppression *	Suppression F. +5; other Spiritmaster spells F. +2	6	W2	85	4.5	14	3.0	Cr	Staff
Khertik's Staff	+5%; Mystic spells F. +5	7	W2	90	4.5	15	3.3	Cr	Staff
Wanderer's Spirit Staff	+1%; Spiritmaster spells F. +5	8	W2	89	4.8	17	3.6	Cr	Staff
Tomte Rune Staff	Runemaster spells F. +7	10	W2	80	4.5	19	4.2	Cr	Staff
Tomte Summoning Staff	Runemaster spells F. +7	10	W2	80	4.5	19	4.2	Cr	Staff
Runemaster Staff of Darkness *	Darkness F. +9; other Runemaster spells F. +5	11	W3	85	4.5	20	4.5	Cr	Staff
Runemaster Staff of Mysticism *	Runemaster spells F. +7	11	W3	85	4.5	20	4.5	Cr	Staff
Runemaster Staff of Runecarving *	Runecarving F. +9; other Runemaster spells F. +5	11	W3	85	4.5	20	4.5	Cr	Staff
Runemaster Staff of Suppression *	Suppression F. +9; other Runemaster spells F. +5	11	W3	85	4.5	20	4.5	Cr	Staff
Spirit Staff	+5%; Spiritmaster spells F. +10; Power +2	11	W3	100	4.5	20	4.5	Cr	Staff
Spiritmaster Staff of Darkness *	Darkness F. +9; other Spiritmaster spells F. +5	11	W3	85	4.5	20	4.5	Cr	Staff
Spiritmaster Staff of Mysticism *	Spiritmaster spells F. +7	11	W3	85	4.5	20	4.5	Cr	Staff
Spiritmaster Staff of Summoning *	Summoning F. +9; other Spiritmaster spells F. +5	11	W3	85	4.5	20	4.5	Cr	Staff
Spiritmaster Staff of Suppression *	Suppression F. +9; other Spiritmaster spells F. +5	11	W3	85	4.5	20	4.5	Cr	Staff
Weeping Runic Staff	+5%; Runemaster spells F. +10; Power +3	11	W3	100	4.5	20	4.5	Cr	Staff
Water Stained Staff	+5%; Darkness F. +13; Qui +3; Crush R. +2	13	W3	89	4.4	22	5.1	Cr	Staff
Wolfhead Totem Staff	+5%; Mystic spells F. +10	13	W3	90	4.5	23	5.1	Cr	Staff
Rigid Embossed Spine	+5%; Spiritmaster spells F. +11; Pie +4	14	W3	89	4.5	24	5.4	Cr	Staff
Rigid Runed Spine	+5%; Runemaster spells F. +11; Pie +4	14	W3	89	4.5	24	5.4	Cr	Staff
Runemaster Staff of Darkness *	Darkness F. +13; other Runemaster spells F. +7	16	W4	85	4.5	27	6.0	Cr	Staff
Runemaster Staff of Mysticism *	Runemaster spells F. +11	16	W4	85	4.5	27	6.0	Cr	Staff
Runemaster Staff of Runecarving *	Runecarving F. +13; other Runemaster spells F. +7	16	W4	85	4.5	27	6.0	Cr	Staff
Runemaster Staff of Suppression *	Suppression F. +13; other Runemaster spells F. +7	16	W4	85	4.5	27	6.0	Cr	Staff
Spiritmaster Staff of Darkness *	Darkness F. +13; other Spiritmaster spells F. +7	16	W4	85	4.5	27	6.0	Cr	Staff
Spiritmaster Staff of Mysticism *	Spiritmaster spells F. +11	16	W4	85	4.5	27	6.0	Cr	Staff
Spiritmaster Staff of Summoning *	Summoning F. +13; other Spiritmaster spells F. +7	16	W4	85	4.5	27	6.0	Cr	Staff
Spiritmaster Staff of Suppression *	Suppression F. +13; other Spiritmaster spells F. +7	16	W4	85	4.5	27	6.0	Cr	Staff
Vind Etset Staff	+10%; Summoning F. +17; Dex +1; HP +6	17	W4	89	4.4	28	6.3	Cr	Staff
Vind Pakket Staff	+10%; Runecarving F. +17; Dex +1; HP +6	17	W4	89	4.4	28	6.3	Cr	Staff
Brack Staff	+5%; Staff S. +3	18	M4	100	5	33	6.6	Cr	Staff
Driftwood Staff	+10%; Mystic spells F. +16	21	W5	90	4.3	32	7.5	Cr	Staff
Fire Flower Stalk	+10%; Summoning F. +21; Heat, Cold R. +4	21	W5	89	4	30	7.5	Cr	Staff
Runed Harvester Leg	+10%; Runecarving F. +21; Heat, Cold R. +4	21	W5	89	4	30	7.5	Cr	Staff
Runemaster Staff of Darkness *	Darkness F. +18; other Runemaster spells F. +9	21	W5	85	4.5	34	7.5	Cr	Staff
Runemaster Staff of Mysticism *	Runemaster spells F. +14	21	W5	85	4.5	34	7.5	Cr	Staff
Runemaster Staff of Runecarving *	Runecarving F. +18; other Runemaster spells F. +9	21	W5	85	4.5	34	7.5	Cr	Staff
Runemaster Staff of Suppression *	Suppression F. +18; other Runemaster spells F. +9	21	W5	85	4.5	34	7.5	Cr	Staff
Spiritmaster Staff of Darkness *	Darkness F. +18; other Spiritmaster spells F. +9	21	W5	85	4.5	34	7.5	Cr	Staff
Spiritmaster Staff of Mysticism *	Spiritmaster spells F. +14	21	W5	85	4.5	34	7.5	Cr	Staff

Weapon	Bonus	PL	M#	QI	Spd	Dam	DPS	Type	Generic
Spiritmaster Staff of Summoning *	Summoning F. +18; other Spiritmaster spells F. +9	21	W5	85	4.5	34	7.5	Cr	Staff
Spiritmaster Staff of Suppression *	Suppression F. +18; other Spiritmaster spells F. +9	21	W5	85	4.5	34	7.5	Cr	Staff
Mora Staff of Runecarving	+10%; Pie +4; Runecarving S. +1; Runecarving F. +23	23	W5	89	4.5	36	8.1	Cr	Staff
Mora Staff of Summoning	+10%; Pie +4; Summoning S. +1; Summoning F. +23	23	W5	89	4.5	36	8.1	Cr	Staff
Njessie Staff of Pure Thought	+5%; Runemaster or Spiritmaster spells F. +19; HP +24	23	W5	100	4.4	36	8.1	Cr	Staff
Rune Staff of the Indomitable	+10%; Runemaster spells F. +17; HP +15	23	W5	89	4	32	8.1	Cr	Staff
Spirit Staff of the Indomitable	+10%; Spiritmaster spells F. +17; HP +15	23	W5	89	4	32	8.0	Cr	Staff
Mora Staff of Darkness	+10%; Pie +4; Darkness S. +1; Darkness F. +24	24	W5	89	4.5	38	8.4	Cr	Staff
Mora Staff of Suppression	+10%; Pie +4; Suppression S. +1; Suppression F. +24	24	W5	89	4.5	38	8.4	Cr	Staff
Hearthwood Branch	+15%; Mystic spells F. +20	26	W6	90	4.3	39	9.0	Cr	Staff
Runemaster Staff of Darkness *	Darkness F. +21; other Runemaster spells F. +11	26	W6	85	4.5	41	9.0	Cr	Staff
Runemaster Staff of Mysticism *	Runemaster spells F. +17	26	W6	85	4.5	41	9.0	Cr	Staff
Runemaster Staff of Runecarving *	Runecarving F. +21; other Runemaster spells F. +11	26	W6	85	4.5	41	9.0	Cr	Staff
Runemaster Staff of Suppression *	Suppression F. +21; other Runemaster spells F. +11	26	W6	85	4.5	41	9.0	Cr	Staff
Spiritmaster Staff of Darkness *	Darkness F. +21; other Spiritmaster spells F. +11	26	W6	85	4.5	41	9.0	Cr	Staff
Spiritmaster Staff of Mysticism *	Spiritmaster spells F. +17	26	W6	85	4.5	41	9.0	Cr	Staff
Spiritmaster Staff of Summoning *	Summoning F. +21; other Spiritmaster spells F. +11	26	W6	85	4.5	41	9.0	Cr	Staff
Spiritmaster Staff of Suppression *	Suppression F. +21; other Spiritmaster spells F. +11	26	W6	85	4.5	41	9.0	Cr	Staff
Leaf Carved Staff	+15%; Suppression F. +27; Power +2; Qui +3	27	W6	89	4.3	40	9.3	Cr	Staff
Leaf Wrapped Staff	+15%; Darkness F. +27; Qui +3; Power +2	27	W6	89	4.3	40	9.3	Cr	Staff
Rune Skull-Bone Staff	+15%; Runemaster spells F. +25; HP +21	28	W6	89	4.2	40	9.6	Cr	Staff
Spirit Skull-Bone Staff	+15%; Spiritmaster spells F. +25; HP +21	28	W6	89	4.2	40	9.6	Cr	Staff
Wind Swept Staff	+15%; Runecarving F. +29; Power +2; Dex +3; Spirit R. +2	29	W6	89	4.3	43	9.9	Cr	Staff
Wind Wrapped Staff	+15%; Summoning F. +29; Power +2; Dex +3; Spirit R. +2	29	W6	89	4.3	43	9.9	Cr	Staff
Varulv Staff of Runecarving	+15%; Runecarving F. +35; Pie +6; Runecarving S. +2	31	W7	89	4.5	47	10.5	Cr	Staff
Varulv Staff of Spirit Magic	+15%; Summoning F. +35; Pie +6; Summoning S. +2	31	W7	89	4.5	47	10.5	Cr	Staff
Varulv Staff of Darkness	+20%; Darkness F. +38; Darkness S. +2; Pie +6	33	W7	89	4.5	50	11.1	Cr	Staff
Varulv Staff of Suppression	+20%; Suppression F. +38; Suppression S. +2; Pie +6	33	W7	89	4.5	50	11.1	Cr	Staff
Dark Bone Staff	+20%; Darkness F. +36; Power +3; Pie +4	36	W8	89	4.5	54	12.0	Cr	Staff
Dull Asterite Runed Staff	+1%; Runemaster spells F. +24; Power +2	37	M8	80	4.5	55	12.3	Cr	Staff
Dull Asterite Spirit Staff	+1%; Spiritmaster spells F. +24; Power +2	37	M8	80	4.5	55	12.3	Cr	Staff
Jaundiced Bone Staff	+20%; Suppression F. +38; Power +3; Pie +4	38	W8	89	4.3	54	12.6	Cr	Staff
Runemaster Ice-Forged Staff	+20%; Runemaster spells F. +32; Pie +10	38	W8	100	4	50	12.6	Cr	Staff
Spiritmaster Ice-Forged Staff	+20%; Spiritmaster spells F. +32; Pie +10	38	W8	100	4	50	12.5	Cr	Staff
Weighted Asterite Runed Staff	+20%; Runemaster spells F. +29; HP +21	38	M8	89	4.6	58	12.6	Cr	Staff
Weighted Asterite Spirit Staff	+20%; Spiritmaster spells F. +29; HP +21	38	M8	89	4.6	58	12.6	Cr	Staff
Runed Bone Staff	+20%; Runecarving F. +39; Power +3; Dex, Pie +3	39	W8	89	4.6	59	12.9	Cr	Staff
Spirit Bone Staff	+20%; Summoning F. +41; Power +3; Dex, Pie +3	41	W8	89	4.5	61	13.5	Cr	Staff
Forged Darksteel Runic Staff	+20%; Runemaster spells F. +32; Heat R. +10	42	M8	89	4.6	63	13.8	Cr	Staff
Forged Darksteel Spirit Staff	+20%; Spiritmaster spells F. +32; Heat R. +10	42	M8	89	4.6	63	13.8	Cr	Staff
Hagbui Runecarver's Staff	+20%; Runecarving F. +42; Power +4; Pie +6; Runecarving S. +2	42	W8	89	4	55	13.8	Cr	Staff
Hagbui Spiritmaster's Staff	+20%; Summoning F. +42; Power +4; Pie +6; Summoning S. +2	42	W8	89	4	55	13.8	Cr	Staff
Dark Staff of the Sisters	+20%; Darkness F. +43; other Runemaster spells F. +33; HP +36	43	W8	100	4	56	14.1	Cr	Staff
Darkened Staff of the Sisters	+20%; Darkness F. +43; other Spiritmaster spells F. +33; HP +36	43	W8	100	4	56	14.1	Cr	Staff
Mimir's Staff of Wisdom	+20%; HP +24; Pie, Con +7	43	W8	100	4.7	66	14.1	Cr	Staff
Runic Staff of the Sisters	+20%; Runecarving F. +43; other Runemaster spells F. +33; HP +36	43	W8	100	4	56	14.1	Cr	Staff
Staff of the Sisters	+20%; Summoning F. +43; other Spiritmaster spells F. +33; HP +36	43	W8	100	4	56	14.1	Cr	Staff
Suppressing Staff of the Sisters	+20%; Suppression F. +43; other Spiritmaster spells F. +33; HP +36	43	W8	100	4	56	14.1	Cr	Staff
Suppressive Staff of the Sisters	+20%; Suppression F. +43; other Runemaster spells F. +33; HP +36	43	W8	100	4	56	14.1	Cr	Staff
Frozen Soul-Shatterer	+25%; Spiritmaster spells F. +35; HP +27	47	M8	89	5	77	15.3	Cr	Staff
Runic Ember	+25%; Runemaster spells F. +35; HP +27	47	M8	89	5	77	15.3	Cr	Staff
Carved Orm Bone Staff	+20%; Spiritmaster spells F. +38; Pie +10	50	M8	89	4.4	71	16.2	Cr	Staff
Darkened Staff of Hoarfrost	+25%; Darkness F. +50; Darkness S. +3; Cold, Heat R. +10	50	W8	91	5	81	16.2	Cr	Staff
Elder Staff of Frozen Runes	+30%; Runecarving F. +50; Runecarving S. +4; Dex +10; Pie +7	50	W8	93	4	65	16.2	Cr	Staff
Elder Staff of Iceshadow	+30%; Darkness F. +50; Darkness S. +4; Dex +10; Pie +7	50	W8	93	4	65	16.2	Cr	Staff
Elder Staff of Icy Sundering	+30%; Suppression F. +50; Suppression S. +4; Dex +10; Pie +7	50	W8	93	4	65	16.2	Cr	Staff
Elder Staff of Windy Calling	+30%; Summoning F. +50; Summoning S. +4; Dex +10; Pie +7	50	W8	93	4	65	16.2	Cr	Staff
Prepared Long Ebony Rod	+25% to hit	50	M8	91	5	81	16.2	Cr	Rod
Runed Orm Bone Staff	+25%; Runemaster spells F. +38; Pie +10	50	M8	89	4.4	71	16.2	Cr	Staff
Runic Rigid Orm Sp.	+25%; Runecarving F. +43; other Runem. spells F. +28; Runecarving S. +6	50	M8	89	4	65	16.2	Cr	Spine
Snow Crystal Runecarver's Staff	+25%; Runecarving F. +50; Runecarving S. +3; Cold, Heat R. +10	50	W8	90	5	81	16.2	Cr	Staff
Snow Crystal Summoner's Staff	+25%; Summoning F. +50; Summoning S. +3; Cold, Heat R. +10	50	W8	90	5	81	16.2	Cr	Staff

Weapon	Bonus	PL	M#	Ql	Spd	Dam	DPS	Type	Generic
Suppressor's Staff of Hoarfrost	+25%; Suppression F. +50; Suppression S. +3; Cold, Heat R. +10	50	W8	91	5	81	16.2	Cr	Staff
Wispy Rigid Orm Sp.	+25%; Summoning F. +43; other Spiritm. spells F. +28; Summoning S. +6	50	M8	89	4	65	16.2	Cr	Spine
Black Diamond Staff	+25%; Darkness F. +50; Darkness S. +2; Pie +6; Power +4	51	W8	90	4.6	76	16.5	Cr	Staff
Blue Diamond Staff	+25%; Suppression F. +50; Suppression S. +2; Pie +6; Power +4	51	W8	90	4.6	76	16.5	Cr	Staff
Red Diamond Staff	+25%; Runecarving F. +50; Runecarving S. +3; Pie +6; Power +4	51	W8	90	4.6	76	16.5	Cr	Staff
Yellow Diamond Staff	+25%; Summoning F. +50; Summoning S. +3; Pie +6; Power +4	51	W8	90	4.6	76	16.5	Cr	Staff

Sword Skill (Fang, Leg, Sword, Tooth)

Weapon	Bonus	PL	M#	Ql	Spd	Dam	DPS	Type	Generic
Training Sword		0	M1	90	2.5	3	1.3	Sl	Sword
Sveabone Hilt Sword	Sword S. +1	3	M1	100	2.5	5	2.1	Sl	Sword
Spined Woodeater Leg	+1%; HP +3	4	M1	89	2.5	6	2.4	Sl	Leg
Kobold Forged Sword	+1%; Sword S. +1	4	M1	90	2.5	6	2.4	Sl	Sword
Iron Skull Sword	+1%; HP +6	7	M2	89	4.8	16	3.3	Sl	Sword
Tomte Long Sword		10	M2	80	3.7	16	4.2	Sl	Sword
Klippor	Sword, Parry S. +1	11	M3	100	2.5	11	4.5	Sl	Sword
Vendo Flesh-Flayer	+5% to hit	11	M3	89	4.3	19	4.5	Sl	Sword
Grass Viper Fang	+5%; Sword S. +1; HP +3	12	M3	89	2.7	13	4.8	Sl	Fang
Edskiver	+5%; Sword S. +2	12	M3	89	4.6	22	4.8	Sl	Sword
Golden Swathcutter	+5%; Sword S. +1; Qui +3	13	M3	90	4	20	5.1	Sl	Sword
Blodsverd	+5%; Sword S. +1; Str +1	14	M3	89	3	16	5.4	Sl	Sword
Brittle-Bone Bastard Sword	+5%; Sword S. +1; Str +1	14	M3	89	4.2	23	5.4	Sl	Sword
Brittle-Bone Great Sword	+5%; Sword S. +1; Qui +1	14	M3	89	5.5	30	5.4	Sl	Sword
Sword of Smack	+5%; Sword S. +3	14	M3	100	3.6	19	5.4	Sl	Sword
Firesteel	+10%; Battlesongs, Parry S. +1	16	M4	90	3.7	22	6.0	Sl	Sword
Forgotten Svartalf Sword	+10%; Sword S. +1; Str +1	16	M4	89	3.5	21	6.0	Sl	Sword
Traitors Bane	+10%; Sword S. +1; Slash R. +4	16	M4	90	4.6	28	6.0	Sl	Sword
Blodsnitt	+10%; Sword S. +1; Str +1	18	M4	89	4.1	27	6.6	Sl	Sword
Nightsworn	+5%; Sword S. +2; HP +15	19	M4	100	3.6	25	6.9	Sl	Sword
Tjen Og Adlyd	+10%; Sword S. +1; Str +3	20	M4	89	3.7	27	7.2	Sl	Sword
Fiery Sword	+10%; Sword S. +2	21	M5	89	3.1	23	7.5	Sl	Sword
N Battle-Chanter	+5%; Sword, Battlesongs S. +2	22	M5	100	3.5	27	7.8	Sl	Sword
Longsword of the Indomitable	+10%; Sword, Parry S. +1; Str +1	23	M5	89	3.7	30	8.1	Sl	Sword
Vengeful Great Sword	+10%; Sword S. +2; Qui +4	23	M5	89	5.5	45	8.1	Sl	Sword
Vengeful Sword	+10%; Sword S. +2; Qui +4	23	M5	89	3.7	30	8.1	Sl	Sword
Flameforged Sword	+10%; Sword S. +5	24	M5	100	2.5	21	8.4	Sl	Sword
Njessi Carved Fang	+10%; Sword S. +4; Slash R. +4	24	M5	100	4.3	36	8.4	Sl	Sword
Njessi Carved Short Fang	+10%; Sword S. +4; Slash R. +4	24	M5	100	3.3	28	8.4	Sl	Sword
Haggert's Bane	+10%; Str, Qui +4	25	M5	89	2.5	22	8.7	Sl	Sword
Razor-Edged Leg Bone	+15%; Sword S. +2; Str +1	26	M6	89	3.6	32	9.0	Sl	Sword
Svart-Alfar Forged Sword	+15%; Sword S. +4	26	M6	90	3	27	9.0	Sl	Sword
N Saga-Spinner	+15%; Sword, Battlesongs S. +3	27	M6	100	3.5	33	9.3	Sl	Sword
Engraved Wolf Blade	+15%; Sword S. +3; Str +3	29	M6	89	5.4	53	9.9	Sl	Sword
Inferno Sword	+15%; Sword S. +2; Str +3	29	M6	89	4.5	45	9.9	Sl	Sword
Vendo Flesh Reaver	+15%; Qui, Str +4	29	M6	89	4.5	45	9.9	Sl	Sword
Wolf Bone Blade	+15%; Sword S. +3; Qui +3	30	M6	89	2.9	30	10.2	Sl	Sword
Virulent Wyvern Fang	+15%; Sword S. +4; Qui +7	32	M7	100	3.4	37	10.8	Sl	Fang
Moonlit Sword	+15%; Sword S. +2; Heat R. +2; Dex +3	32	M7	89	3.6	39	10.8	Sl	Sword
Sword of the Wolf	+15%; Sword S. +2; Str +4	33	M7	89	4.6	51	11.1	Sl	Sword
Garou Sword	+15%; Sword S. +2; Str +6	35	M7	89	3.1	36	11.7	Sl	Sword
Ice-Cutter	+20%; Sword S. +3; Parry S. +4	36	M8	100	5.4	65	12.0	Sl	Sword
Lupine Lumen Longsword	+25%; Str +6; Qui +4	36	M8	89	3.7	44	12.0	Sl	Sword
Strength of the Wolf	+20%; Sword S. +2; HP +9	36	M8	89	5.3	64	12.0	Sl	Sword
Wolfpaw Sword	+20%; Sword S. +3; Parry S. +2; Matter R. +4	36	M8	89	3.1	37	12.0	Sl	Sword
Bloodied Coral Sword	+15%; Sword, Parry S. +2	37	M8	89	3.5	43	12.3	Sl	Sword
Dull Asterite Great Sword	+1%; Sword S. +1; Str +1	37	M8	80	5.6	69	12.3	Sl	Sword
Dull Asterite Sword	+1%; Sword S. +1; Con +1	37	M8	80	3.8	47	12.3	Sl	Sword
Long Gnarled Tooth	+20%; Sword S. +2; Qui +4	37	M8	89	2.8	34	12.3	Sl	Tooth
Serrated Black Tooth	+20%; Cha +4; Qui +3; Body R. +4	37	M8	89	3.5	43	12.3	Sl	Tooth
Gigantic Garou Sword	+20%; Sword S. +2; Qui, Str +3	38	M8	89	5.5	69	12.6	Sl	Sword
Keen Asterite Great Sword	+20%; Sword S. +2; Qui +4	38	M8	89	5.5	69	12.6	Sl	Sword
Keen Asterite Sword	+20%; Sword S. +1; Str +3; Qui +4	38	M8	89	3.7	47	12.6	Sl	Sword

Weapon	Bonus	PL	M#	QI	Spd	Dam	DPS	Type	Generic
Black Gnarled Tooth	+20%; Str +6; Qui +10	38	M8	90	2.9	37	12.6	Sl	Tooth
Forged Darksteel Bastard Sword	+20%; Sword S. +3; Heat R. +6	42	M8	89	4	55	13.8	Sl	Sword
Blessed Northern Great Sword	+20%; Sword S. +4; Str +6; HP +18	43	M8	100	5.5	78	14.1	Sl	Sword
Blessed Northern Sword	+20%; Sword S. +4; Cold R. +6; Str +6; Con +4	43	M8	100	4.6	65	14.1	Sl	Sword
Forest Viper Fang	+10%; Sword S. +3; Qui +7	43	M8	89	2.4	34	14.1	Sl	Sword
Sword of the Ice	+20%; Sword S. +4; Str +9; Qui +6	43	M8	100	4.5	63	14.1	Sl	Sword
Winter's Blade	+20%; Sword S. +4; Str, Qui +7	43	M8	100	3.1	44	14.1	Sl	Sword
Fell Cat's Razor Tooth	+20%; Sword S. +2; Parry S. +3	45	M8	89	2.5	37	14.7	Sl	Tooth
Shadow Razor	+25%; Parry S. +4; Str +7	45	M8	90	2.8	41	14.7	Sl	Tooth
Dark Frozen Eviscerator	+25%; Qui +6; HP +15; Cold, Spirit R. +4	46	M8	90	2.9	44	15.0	Sl	Tooth
Drakulv Militia Great Sword	+25%; Sword S. +2; Parry S. +1; Qui +4	47	M8	89	4.5	69	15.3	Sl	Sword
Twilight Soul Searer	+25%; Sword S. +2; Qui +7	47	M8	89	4.5	69	15.3	Sl	Sword
Carved Orm Fang Sword	+25%; Parry S. +1; Sword S. +3; Qui +4	50	M8	89	3.2	52	16.2	Sl	Sword
Drakulv Militia Sword	+25%; HP +21; Spirit R. +8	50	M8	89	3.3	53	16.2	Sl	Sword
Frozen Ice Claw	+30%; Sword S. +6; Str +12; Cold R. +4	50	M8	93	3	49	16.2	Sl	Sword
Golden Alloy Bastard Sword	+25%; Sword S. +4; Parry S. +2; Cha, Con +4	50	M8	90	4	65	16.2	Sl	Sword
Golden Alloy Great Sword	+25%; Sword S. +5; Parry S. +3; Qui +4	50	M8	90	5.3	86	16.2	Sl	Sword
Golden Alloy Short Sword	+25%; Sword S. +5; Cha +7	50	M8	90	2.4	39	16.2	Sl	Sword
Great Ice Claw	+30%; Sword S. +6; Con +12; Cold R. +4	50	M8	93	4.8	78	16.2	Sl	Sword
Runic Manslayer	+25%; Sword S. +3; HP +15	50	M8	89	4	65	16.2	Sl	Sword
Sword of the Fiery Heart	+25% to hit	50	M8	90	3.6	58	16.2	Sl	Sword

Thrown Skill (Axe)

Weapon	Bonus	PL	M#	QI	Spd	Dam	DPS	Type	Generic
Runic Throwing Axes (range 900)	+25% to hit	50	M8	90	3	49	16.2	Sl	Axe

Composite Bow Skill (Bow)

Weapon	Bonus	PL	M#	QI	Spd	Dam	DPS	Range	Generic
Bow of Winter	Comp. Bow S. +1	6	W2	90	4	12	3.0	1600	Bow
Stolen Hunting Bow		7	W2	89	4	13	3.3	1600	Bow
Tomte Bow		10	W2	80	4	17	4.2	1600	Bow
Brittle-Bone Bow	+5%; Comp. Bow S. +1; Dex +1	14	W3	89	4	22	5.4	1600	Bow
Silverleaf Bow	+5%; Comp. Bow S. +2	14	W3	90	4.3	23	5.4	1600	Bow
Bow of the Blodjeger	+5%; Comp. Bow S. +1; Qui, Dex +1	15	W3	89	3.9	22	5.7	1600	Bow
Willow Wind Bow	+5%; Dex, Qui +6	18	W4	100	3.9	26	6.6	1600	Bow
Moldy Tombdweller's Bow	+10%; Comp. Bow S. +1; Dex, Con +3	20	W4	89	4	29	7.2	1600	Bow
Bow of Flames	+10%; Comp. Bow S. +1; Cold R. +4	22	W5	89	4	31	7.8	1600	Bow
Bone Heart-Finder	+15%; Comp. Bow S. +2; Dex +3	29	W6	89	4.2	42	9.9	1600	Bow
Great Bone Heart-Finder	+15%; Comp. Bow S. +1; Dex, Qui +3	29	W6	89	4.8	48	9.9	1600	Bow
Heart-Piercer Bow	+15%; Comp. Bow S. +3; Dex +7; Qui +3	31	W7	100	3.8	40	10.5	1600	Bow
Skadi's Blessed Huntsman's Bow	+15%; Comp. Bow S. +2; Dex +4; Qui +3	31	W7	90	3.7	39	10.5	1600	Bow
Crescent Moon Bow	+15%; Comp. Bow S. +2; HP +9	34	W7	89	3.9	44	11.4	1600	Bow
Varulvhamn Bow	+15%; Comp. Bow S. +1; Dex +3; HP +12	35	W7	89	4	47	11.7	1600	Bow
Noble Hunting Bow	+20%; Comp. Bow S. +4; Dex +12	40	W8	100	4.2	55	13.2	1600	Bow
Crafted Darksteel Composite Bow	+20%; Comp. Bow S. +3; Qui +10	42	M8	89	4.2	58	13.8	1600	Bow
Bow of the North	+20%; Comp. Bow S. +4; Dex, Qui +4; HP +12	43	W8	100	3.9	55	14.1	1600	Bow
Drakulv Militia Composite Bow	+25%; Comp. Bow S. +3; Dex +4	46	W8	89	4.2	63	15.0	1600	Bow
Twilight Doombringer	+25%; Comp. Bow S. +3; Dex +4	47	M8	89	4.9	75	15.3	1600	Bow
Death Whisper	+25%; Comp. Bow S. +4; Dex +13	50	M8	90	4	65	16.2	1600	Bow
Golden Alloy Great Bow	+25%; Comp. Bow S. +4; Stealth S. +2; Dex +12	50	M8	91	4.8	78	16.2	1600	Bow
Ice Bone Prey Killer	+30%; Comp. Bow S. +5; Stealth S. +1; Dex +9; Qui +7	50	W8	93	4.4	71	16.2	1600	Bow
Runic Mystwood Bow	+25%; Comp. Bow S. +5; Dex +10	50	W8	90	4	65	16.2	1600	Bow

Arrows

Weapon	Bonus	QI	Dam	Type	Generic
Flameborn Arrows	+10% to hit	100	x1.25	Thr	Arrow
Tingler Arrows	+10% to hit	100	x1.25	Thr	Arrow

When firing an arrow or bolt, the speed of the bow determines how rapidly you can fire, and the shot's base damage. The arrow or bolt determines the type of damage (Crush, Slash or Thrust) and provides a multiplier to the base damage (indicated by "x1", "x1.25", and so forth).

Armor

For a brief discussion of how armor and armor stats work in *Dark Age of Camelot*, see page 362.

Abbreviations. Mat = Base Material / **Armor Factor** (per piece) / **ABS**orption / **Cl**oth / **L**ea**t**her / **St**udded Leather / **Ch**ain / **Pl**ate.

Standard (Craftable) Armor Stats

Armor	Mat	Power Levels	AF	ABS
Padded	Cl	1,6,11, etc.	4,9,14, etc.	0%
Mjuklaeder	Lt	1,6,11, etc.	4,14,24, etc.	10%
Svarlaeder	Lt	2,7,12, etc.	6,16,26, etc.	10%
Starkalaeder	Lt	4,9,14, etc.	10,20,30, etc.	10%
Stelskodd	St	1,6,11, etc.	4,14,24, etc.	19%
Svarskodd	St	2,7,12, etc.	6,16,26, etc.	19%
Starkaakodd	St	4,9,14, etc.	10,20,30, etc.	19%
Pansarkedja	Ch	1,6,11, etc.	4,14,24, etc.	27%
Svarkedja	Ch	2,7,12, etc.	6,16,26, etc.	27%
Starkakedja	Ch	5,10,15, etc.	12,22,32, etc.	27%

Armor Weights

Location	Cl	Lt	St	Ch
Cap/Helm	0.8	1.6	2.4	3.2
Vest/Jerkin	2.0	4.0	6.0	8.0
Sleeves	1.2	2.4	3.6	4.8
Gloves	0.8	1.6	2.4	3.2
Pants/Leggings	1.4	2.8	4.2	5.6
Boots	0.8	1.6	2.4	3.2

Armor Drops & Rewards

Armor is sorted by type (Cloth, Leather, etc.), then by location (Head, Torso, Arms, Hands, Legs, Feet, Robes), then by Power Level.

Abbreviations

Headings. Power Level / **A**rmor Factor / **M#** = Material (M) and Material Level (#) / **Q**uality.

The first negative percentage in any bonus indicates your opponent's reduced chance of hitting you when you are wearing the item.

Stats. Resistance, **S**kill / **Cha**risma, **Con**stitution, **Emp**athy, **Dex**terity, **Int**elligence, **Pie**ty, **Qui**ckness, **Str**ength / **C**loth, **L**eather, **M**etal.

Cloth

Head

Item	Bonus	P	A	M	Q
Tomte Padded Cap		5	5	C2	80
Cap of Mindbending	-5%; Pie +3; Power +1	7	7	C2	100
Cap of the Old Wanderer	-5%; Pie +3; Con +1	7	7	C2	90
Cap of the Wanderer		7	7	C2	80
Cap of the Malignant	-5%; Pie +4; Power +1	13	13	C3	89
Wind Tossed Cap	-5%; Pie +4; Spirit R. +4	14	14	C3	89
Svartalf Padded Cap	-10%; Dex, Pie +3	15	15	C4	89
Moldy Tombdweller Cap	-10%; Pie +6; Dex +3	18	18	C4	89
Soot Encrusted Cap	-10%; Pie +4; Power +2	20	20	C5	89
Crescent Crown	-10%; Pie +9; Power +2	20	40	C5	100
Woven Crescent Crown	-10%; Pie +9; Power +2	23	23	C5	100
Crusty Fur Cap		25	25	C6	80
Acorn Cap	-15%; Power +2; Pie +4; Spirit R. +4	26	26	C6	89
Stripe Hide Helm	-5%; Pie +9; Power +2; HP +12	26	26	C6	100
Cap of the Wisened Dead	-15%; Power +4; Pie +7	30	30	C7	90
Vaporous Crown	-15%; Int +4; Power +2; Spirit R. +4; Cold R. +2	30	30	C7	89
Grizzled Bear Fur Cap	-15%; Power +2; Pie +6; Con +3	32	32	C7	89
Lupine Lunatic Cap	-15%; Pie +7; Dex, Con +4	34	34	C7	89
Skullcap of Animation	-25%; HP +21; Power +7	35	35	C8	89
Faded Silksteel Cap	-1%; Power +2	36	36	C8	80
Woven Silksteel Cap	-20%; Pie +10; Darkness, Suppr. S. +1	37	37	C8	89
Muddied Frog Skin Cap	-15%; Pie +7; Runec., Summ. S. +4	39	39	C8	89
Ageless Luminary Cap	-20%; Con, Dex, Pie +6	40	40	C8	90
Woven Darksteel Cap	-20%; HP +15; Pie +12	41	41	C8	89
Cap of Twilight	-25%; Pie +13; Dex, Con +3; Spirit R. +2	46	46	C8	89
Ageless Bloodbound Cap	-25%; Power +4; Summ. S. +4; Pie +13	49	49	C8	90
Runed Bloodbound Cap	-25%; Power +4; Runec. S. +4; Pie +13	49	49	C8	90
Snow Crystal Cap	-25%; Drkns., Suppr. S. +2; Cr. R. +12; Pie +10	49	49	C8	90
Blood-Stained Tiara	-25%; HP +30; Pie +10; Power +5; Body R. -10	49	49	C8	91
Light Coral Crown	-25%; Runec., Summ. S. +3; Power +6; Pie +11	50	50	C8	91

Torso

Item	Bonus	P	A	M	Q
Tomte Tunic	-1%; HP +9	6	6	C2	100
Thickened Cloth Tunic	-5%; Power +1; Dex +1	6	6	C2	90
Vest of the Old Wanderer	-5%; HP +9	7	7	C2	90
Vest of the Wanderer		7	7	C2	80
Tomte Padded Vest		9	9	C2	80
Vest of the Malignant	-5%; HP +9; Pie +3	13	13	C3	89
Gold Stitched Tunic	-10%; Slash R. +6; Pie +4	15	15	C4	90
Svartalf Padded Vest	-10%; Power +3	15	15	C4	89
Vind Kalte Vest	-10%; Con +3; Slash R. +2; HP +3	16	16	C4	89
Dancing Silk	-5%; Emp +6; Power +3	19	19	C4	100
Moldy Tombdweller Vest	-10%; HP +18	19	19	C4	89
Fire Petal Vest	-10%; Pie, Int +3; HP +6	20	20	C5	89
Crusty Fur Vest		25	25	C6	80
Wind Swept Vest	-15%; Pie +3; Power +4; Spirit R. +2	28	28	C6	89
Vest of Living Flame	-15%; HP +12; Pie +4; Thrust R. +4	29	29	C6	89
Rune Embroidered Tunic	-15%; Power +2; HP +12; Pie +4; Con +3	30	30	C7	90
Runed Mystical Vest	-15%; HP +15; Crush, Slash R. +4; Pie +10	31	31	C7	100
Spirit-Dweller's Vest	-15%; HP +12; Power +2; Con, Pie +6	31	31	C7	100
Grizzled Bear Fur Vest	-15%; HP +9; Dex +4; Pie +6	32	32	C7	89
Lupine Lunatic Vest	-15%; HP +18; Dex +4; Body R. +4	34	34	C7	89
Frostbitten Tunic	-20%; HP +15; Cold R. +15; Pie +9; Dex +3	35	35	C8	100
Orb Weaver's Vest	-20%; Pie, Qui +12; Crush, Slash R. +16	35	35	C8	100
Faded Silksteel Vest	-1%; Power +2	36	36	C8	80

Item	Bonus	P	A	M	Q
Woven Silksteel Vest	-20%; Power +2; Pie +6; Con +4	37	37	C8	89
Supple Frog Skin Vest	-15%; HP +15; Pie +6; Power +2	39	39	C8	89
Woven Darksteel Vest	-20%; HP +15; Con, Pie +6	41	41	C8	89
Ageless Luminary Vest	-20%; HP +21; Power +2; Pie +4	42	42	C8	89
Vest of Twilight	-25%; HP +18; Pie +7; Str +4	46	46	C8	89
Ancient Bloodbound Vest	-25%; HP +30; Pie, Dex +9	49	49	C8	90
Snow Crystal Vest	-25%; HP +45; Body, Slash, Thrust R. +6	49	49	C8	90
Ancient Cobalt Vest	-25%; HP +30; Pie +10; Heat, Cold R. +10	50	50	C8	92

Arms

Item	Bonus	P	A	M	Q
Thickened Cloth Sleeves	-1%; Con +1; HP +3	3	3	C1	90
Sleeves of the Old Wanderer	-5%; Str, Dex, Pie +1	7	7	C2	90
Sleeves of the Wanderer		7	7	C2	80
Tomte Padded Sleeves		9	9	C2	80
Sleeves of the Malignant	-5%; Str +4; Pie +3	13	13	C3	89
Svartalf Padded Sleeves	-10%; Str, Pie +3	15	15	C4	89
Vind Kalte Sleeves	-10%; Dex, Pie +3; Crush R. +4	17	17	C4	89
Moldy Tombdweller Sleeves	-10%; Str +6; Dex, Con +3	18	18	C4	89
Fire Petal Sleeves	-10%; Str +3; HP +9; Cold R. +2	20	20	C5	89
Spirit-Dweller's Sleeves	-10%; Str +6; Pie +7; Slash R. +4	20	20	C5	100
Crusty Fur Sleeves		25	25	C6	80
Leaf-Embossed Sleeves	-15%; Con +4; Thrust R. +6; Pie +1	25	25	C6	89
Vaporous Sleeves	-15%; Dex +3; Crush R. +4; HP +15	30	30	C7	89
Grizzled Bear Fur Sleeves	-15%; Power +2; Str, Pie +4	32	32	C7	89
Lupine Lunatic Sleeves	-15%; Str +6; Pie +4; Heat, Cold R. +4	34	34	C7	89
Faded Silksteel Sleeves	-1%; Power +2	36	36	C8	80
Ageless Luminary Sleeves	-20%; HP +15; Str, Pie +4	37	37	C8	89
Woven Silksteel Sleeves	-20%; Str +6; Pie +4; Crush, Body R. +4	37	37	C8	89
Supple Frog Skin Sleeves	-15%; Power +4; Str +4; Dex +3	39	39	C8	89
Woven Darksteel Sleeves	-20%; Power +2; Str +6; Pie +4; Dex +3	41	41	C8	89
Sleeves of Twilight	-25%; Str +9; Pie +6; Heat, Energy R. +4	46	46	C8	89
Ancient Bloodbound Sl.	-25%; Drkns., Suppr. S. +2; Str +12; Pie +9	49	49	C8	90
Snow Crystal Sleeves	-25%; Con +10; Str, Pie +7; Matter R. +6	49	49	C8	90

Hands

Item	Bonus	P	A	M	Q
Gloves of the Eternal	-5%; Pie +7	7	7	C2	100
Gloves of the Old Wanderer	-5%; HP +3; Power +1	7	7	C2	90
Gloves of the Wanderer		7	7	C2	80
Tomte Padded Gloves		9	9	C2	80
Water Stained Gloves	-5%; Dex +3; Power +1	13	13	C3	89
Spirit-Dweller's Gl.	-10%; Summoning S. +2; Str +3; Power +1	15	15	C4	100
Svartalf Padded Gloves	-10%; Dex +3; Power +2	15	15	C4	89
Moldy Runecarving Gloves	-10%; Qui +6; Runecarving S. +1	18	18	C4	89
Moldy Summoner Gloves	-10%; Qui +6; Summoning S. +1	18	18	C4	89
Gold Stitched Gloves	-10%; Crush R. +8; Str +4; Pie +3	20	20	C5	90
Soot Encrusted Gloves	-10%; Dex +6; Cold R. +4	20	20	C5	89
Crusty Fur Gloves		25	25	C6	80
Leaf-Embossed Gloves	-15%; Dex +3; Matter R. +6; Slash R. +4	25	25	C6	89
Runed Mystical Gl.	-10%; Darkness, Suppression S. +2; Dex +9	25	25	C6	100
Living Flame Gloves	-15%; Dex +4; Body, Spirit R. +6	29	29	C6	100
Grizzled Bear Fur Gloves	-15%; Power +2; Pie, Dex +4	32	32	C7	89
Lupine Lunatic Gloves	-15%; Qui +7; Con +6; Matter R. +4	34	34	C7	89
Faded Silksteel Gloves	-1%; Power +2	36	36	C8	80
Woven Silksteel Gloves	-20%; Power +2; Str +4; Dex +6	37	37	C8	89
Ageless Luminary Gl.	-20%; HP +15; Cold R. +4; Pie +4; Dex +3	39	39	C8	89
Muddied Frog Skin Gloves	-15%; Body R. +6; Pie +4; Dex +6	39	39	C8	89
Woven Darksteel Gl.	-20%; Cold R. +6; Energy R. +4; Qui, Pie +6	41	41	C8	89
Gloves of Twilight	-25%; Qui, Pie +6; Cold, Heat R. +6	46	46	C8	89
Anc. Bloodbound Gl.	-25%; Power +5; Dex, Pie +7; Matter R. +10	49	49	C8	90
Snow Crystal Gl.	-25%; Runec., Summ. S. +2; Dex +12; Pie +10	49	49	C8	90

Legs

Item	Bonus	P	A	M	Q
Pants of the Old Wanderer	-5%; Con +3; Pie +1	7	7	C2	90
Pants of the Wanderer		7	7	C2	80
Thickened Cloth Pants	-5%; Power +1; Con +3	9	9	C2	90
Tomte Padded Pants		9	9	C2	80
Pants of the Malignant	-5%; Con +4; Power +1	13	13	C3	89
Gold Stitched Pants	-10%; Body R. +6; Con +4	15	15	C4	90
Svartalf Padded Pants	-10%; Con, Pie +3	15	15	C4	89
Vind Kalte Pants	-10%; Con +3; HP +12	17	17	C4	89
Moldy Tombdweller Pants	-10%; Con +6; Dex +3	19	19	C4	89
Fire Petal Leggings	-10%; HP +9; Power +2	20	20	C5	89
Runed Mystical Pants	-10%; Con +7; Cold R. +4; Power +2	20	20	C5	100
Crusty Fur Pants		25	25	C6	80
Spirit-Dweller's Pants	-15%; Con +10; Cold, Body R. +4	25	25	C6	100
Wind Swept Pants	-15%; Dex +4; HP +15	26	26	C6	89
Flame of the Earth P.	-15%; Qui +4; Slash, Body R. +4; Power +2	31	31	C7	89
Grizzled Bear Fur Pants	-15%; Con +7; Dex +4; Pie +3	32	32	C7	89
Lupine Lunatic Pants	-15%; Con +6; Dex +4; Energy, Spirit R. +4	34	34	C7	89
Faded Silksteel Pants	-1%; Power +2	36	36	C8	80
Woven Silksteel Pants	-20%; Con +10; Pie +3; Spirit R. +4	37	37	C8	89
Ageless Luminary Pants	-20%; Con +9; Dex +3; Power +2	38	38	C8	89
Supple Frog Skin Pants	-15%; HP +9; Con, Dex +7	39	39	C8	89
Woven Darksteel Pants	-20%; HP +12; Power +2; Body R. +10	41	41	C8	89
Pants of Twilight	-25%; Con +10; Pie +4; Crush, Slash R. +4	46	46	C8	89
Ancient Bloodbound P.	-25%; Con +12; Dex, Pie +6; Heat R. +10	49	49	C8	90
Snow Crystal Pants	-25%; HP +30; Dex +10; Cold, Heat R. +6	49	49	C8	90

Feet

Item	Bonus	P	A	M	Q
Boots of the Old Wanderer	-5%; HP +3; Dex +3	7	7	C2	90
Boots of the Wanderer		7	7	C2	80
Light Bear-Hide Boots	Qui +6	7	7	C2	100
Thickened Cloth Boots	-5%; Dex, Qui +3	9	9	C2	90
Water Stained Boots	-5%; Qui +3; Matter R. +4	12	12	C3	89
Runed Mystical Boots	-10%; Dex, Qui +4; Matter R. +4	15	15	C4	100
Svartalf Padded Boots	-10%; Dex +3; HP +6	15	15	C4	89
Slippers of Favor	-10%; Pie, Dex +3; HP +15	17	17	C4	100
Moldy Tombdweller Boots	-10%; Dex +6; Con +3	18	18	C4	89
Gold Stitched Boots	-10%; Matter R. +8; Dex +4; Qui +3	20	20	C5	90
Soot Encrusted Boots	-10%; Qui +3; Heat R. +2; Power +2	20	20	C5	89
Crusty Fur Boots		25	25	C6	80
Bark Edged Boots	-15%; Qui +4; Body R. +6; Con +3	26	26	C6	89
Flame o.t. Earth B.	-15%; Dex +3; Body R. +4; Power +2; HP +9	31	31	C7	89
Grizzled Bear Fur Boots	-15%; HP +9; Dex +7; Qui +3	32	32	C7	89
Lupine Lunatic Boots	-15%; Dex +7; Qui, Str +4	34	34	C7	89
Ageless Luminary Boots	-20%; HP +15; Dex +7	35	35	C8	89
Faded Silksteel Boots	-1%; Power +2	36	36	C8	80
Woven Silksteel Boots	-20%; Energy, Cold R. +6; Dex +7	37	37	C8	89
Muddied Frog Skin Boots	-15%; Qui +4; Dex +6; Matter R. +6	39	39	C8	89
Woven Darksteel Boots	-20%; Body R. +8; Spirit R. +4; Dex +10	41	41	C8	89
Boots of Twilight	-25%; Dex, Qui +7; Matter R. +8	46	46	C8	89
Anc. Bloodbound B.	-25%; HP +24; Dex +10; Energy, Cold R. +6	49	49	C8	90
Snow Crystal Boots	-25%; Con +10; Dex +12; Cold, Heat R. +8	49	49	C8	90

Leather

Head

Item	Bonus	P	A	M	Q
Eir's Circlet	Pie +3	6	12	L2	90
Supple Leather Helm	-5%; HP +9	7	14	L2	90
Tomte Leather Helm		7	14	L2	80
Helm of the Wolf	-1%; Pie +6	8	16	L2	100
Tomte Leather Helm		9	18	L2	80
Decaying Helm	-5%; Dex, Con +3	12	24	L3	89
Helm of Future Visions	-5%; Qui +3; Sword S. +1; Matter R. +2	13	26	L3	89
Mephitic Leather Helm	-5%; Stealth S. +2; Dex +1	13	26	L3	89
Bear Mask	-10%; Berzerk S. +3; Str +4; Con +3	20	40	L5	100
Muddied Hide Helm		22	44	L5	80

Item	Bonus	P	A	M	Q
Fire Charred Mask	-10%; Str +7; Stealth S. +1	22	44	L5	89
Rigid Crescent Crown	-10%; Qui, Dex +6; HP +12	23	46	M5	100
Flayed Hagbui Helm	-10%; Dex, Qui +4; Str, Con +3	24	48	L5	89
Wolf Skull Helm	-15%; Dex +3; Sword S. +2; Slash R. +4	27	54	L6	89
Cave Lurker's Helm	-15%; Dex, Qui, Str +4	28	56	L6	89
Feral Wulf Cap	-15%; Qui +7; Dex, Con +4	34	68	L7	89
Faded Silksteel Bound Helm	-1%; Dex +3; Pie, Qui +1	36	72	L8	80
Braided Silksteel Helm	-20%; Stealth S. +1; Dex, Str, Qui +4	37	74	L8	89
Braided Darksteel Helm	-20%; Stealth S. +3; Dex +4; Body R. +8	41	82	L8	89
Bandit King's Crown	-20%; HP +30; Str +10; Dex +9; Heat R. -10	43	86	L8	91
Runed Clay Helmet	-15%; Qui +10; Power +2; Stealth S. +2	44	88	L8	89
Runed Holl. Clay H.	-25%; HP +18; Stealth S. +2; Dex +3; Cr. R. +4	45	90	L8	89
Webbed Shadow Helm	-25%; Stealth S. +4; Dex, Qui +4	46	92	L8	89
Emerald Moonshone Helm	-25%; HP +30; Dex +7	48	96	L8	89
Hoarfrost Helm	-25%; Con, Dex, Str +9; Crush R. +10	49	98	L8	91
Timorous Drakulv Ebon H.	-25%; HP +27; Qui +9; Cr., Heat R. +8	49	98	L8	90
Coral Crown	Stealth S. +3; Dex, Qui +12; Thrust R. +6	50	100	L8	91

Torso

Item	Bonus	P	A	M	Q
Tomte Jerkin	-1%; HP +9	6	12	L2	100
Supple Leather Jerkin	-5%; HP +6; Dex +1	7	14	L2	90
Tomte Leather Jerkin		7	14	L2	80
Conditioned Leather Vest	-5%; HP +6; Dex +3	9	18	L2	90
Tomte Leather Jerkin		9	18	L2	80
Decaying Jerkin	-5%; HP +12	12	24	L3	89
Mephitic Leather Jerkin	-5%; HP +15	13	26	L3	89
Blodbror Jerkin	-5%; Con +4; Str +3	14	28	L3	89
Blackened Leather Jerkin	-10%; Dex +9; HP +9	20	40	L5	90
Fire Charred Jerkin	-10%; Con +3; HP +9; Cold R. +4	22	44	L5	89
Muddied Hide Jerkin		22	44	L5	80
Flayed Hagbui Jerkin	-10%; HP +24; Qui +3	24	48	L5	89
Shadowed Vest	-10%; HP +12; Qui +6; Dex +9	25	50	L6	100
Cave Lurker's Jerkin	-15%; HP +18; Dex +4	28	56	L6	89
Wolf Fur Jerkin	-15%; Con +4; HP +12; Slash R. +4	29	58	L6	89
Feral Wulf Jerkin	-15%; HP +18; Dex +4; Body R. +4	34	68	L7	89
Lynx Spider J.	-20%; Backstab S. +6; Envenom S. +3; Slash R. +6	35	70	L8	100
Faded Silksteel Bound Tunic	-1%; HP +12	36	72	L8	80
Forge Tender's Tunic	-15%; Heat R. +10; HP +21	36	72	L8	89
Braided Silksteel Jerkin	-20%; HP +18; Dex +7	37	74	L8	89
Braided Darksteel Jerkin	-20%; HP +21; Dex, Qui +4	41	82	L8	89
Runed Clay Jerkin	-15%; Dex +3; Qui +7; HP +24	44	88	L8	89
Runed Hollow Clay Jerkin	-25%; HP +30; Slash, Matter R. +4	45	90	L8	89
Webbed Shadow Jerkin	-25%; HP +21; Qui, Dex +4; Str +3	46	92	L8	89
Emerald Moonshone Jerkin	-25%; HP +30; Dex +7	48	96	L8	89
Hoarfrost Jerkin	-25%; Con, Dex, Str +10; Cold R. +6	49	98	L8	91
Timorous Drakulv Ebon Jerkin	-25%; Con +12; Dex, Qui, Str +7	49	98	L8	90
Ancient Cobalt Jerkin	-25%; HP +36; Dex, Qui +13	50	100	L8	92

Arms

Item	Bonus	P	A	M	Q
Supple Leather Sleeves	-5%; HP +3; Str +3	7	14	L2	90
Tomte Leather Sleeves		7	14	L2	80
Tomte Leather Sleeves		9	18	L2	80
Decaying Sleeves	-5%; Str +6	12	24	L3	89
Mephitic Leather Sleeves	-5%; Str +4; Qui +3	13	26	L3	89
Vannsang Sleeves	-10%; Dex, Str +3	15	30	L4	89
Flame Charred Sleeves	-10%; Str +7; Qui +3	22	44	L5	89
Muddied Hide Sleeves		22	44	L5	80
Flayed Hagbui Sleeves	-10%; Str +6; Dex, Qui +3	23	46	L5	89
Cave Lurker's Sleeves	-15%; Str +7; Qui +6	28	56	L6	89
Wolf Fur Sleeves	-15%; Str +4; Qui +3; Body, Spirit R. +4	28	56	L6	89
Feral Wulf Sleeves	-15%; Str +6; Qui +4; Heat, Cold R. +4	34	68	L7	89
Faded Silksteel Bound Sleeves	-1%; Con, Dex, Qui, Str +1	36	72	L8	80
Braided Silksteel Sleeves	-20%; Body R. +4; Str +9; Dex +4	37	74	L8	89
Braided Darksteel Sl.	-20%; Str +10; Con +3; Cold, Heat R. +4	41	82	L8	89
Runed Clay Sleeves	-15%; Str +13; Con, Dex +4	44	88	L8	89
Runed Hollow Clay Sleeves	-25%; Str +10; Dex +6	45	90	L8	89
Emerald Moonshone Sleeves	-25%; HP +15; Str +13	46	92	L8	89
Webbed Shadow Sleeves	-25%; Str +10; Qui +6; Dex +4	46	92	L8	89
Hoarfrost Sleeves	-25%; Str +18; Con +12; Cold R. +8	49	98	L8	91
Timorous Drakulv Ebon Sleeves	-25%; HP +24; Str, Dex +10	49	98	L8	90

Hands

Item	Bonus	P	A	M	Q
Bearclaw Gloves		1	2	L1	100
Blessed Tyr Gloves	Str +3	6	12	L2	90
Fishgutter's Gloves	-5%; Slash R. +2; Dex +3	6	12	L2	90
Supple Leather Gloves	-5%; Qui +4	7	14	L2	90
Tomte Leather Gloves		7	14	L2	80
Tomte Leather Gloves		9	18	L2	80
Decaying Gloves	-5%; Con, Qui +3	12	24	L3	89
Blodbror Gloves	-5%; Dex +3; Axe S. +1; Body R. +2	13	26	L3	89
Gloves of the Malignant	-5%; Power +1; Dex +4	13	26	L3	89
Mephitic Leather Gloves	-5%; HP +9; Qui +3	13	26	L3	89
Spirit-Dweller's Gl.	-10%; Summoning S. +2; Str +3; Power +1	15	30	L4	100
Gl. o.t. Spined Backpiercer	-5%; Critical Strike S. +3; Body R. +2	17	34	L4	100
Fire Charred Gloves	-10%; Qui +6; Envenom S. +1; Cold R. +2	22	44	L5	89
Muddied Hide Gloves		22	44	L5	80
Flayed Hagbui Gloves	-10%; Qui +6; Critical Strike S. +2	23	46	L5	89
Werewolf Paws	-15%; Envenom S. +1; Crit. Strike S. +2; Body R. +4	26	52	L6	89
Cave Lurker's Gloves	-15%; Envenom, Critical Strike S. +1; Dex +7	28	56	L6	89
Catgloves	-5%; Climb S. +3; Dex +6	29	58	L6	100
Gloves of Precision	-15%; Critical Strike S. +2; Dex +7; Qui +6	30	60	L7	90
Feral Wulf Gloves	-15%; Qui +7; Con +6; Matter R. +4	34	68	L7	89
Faded Silksteel Bound Gloves	-1%; Body R. +2; Dex +3; Qui +1	36	72	L8	80
Braided SS Gl.	-20%; Slash, Spirit R. +2; Qui +10; Crit. Strike S. +1	37	74	L8	89
Braided Darksteel Gloves	-20%; Left Axe S. +2; Dex +6; Qui +7	41	82	L8	89
Emerald Moonshone Gloves	-20%; Envenom S. +2; Qui +10	44	88	L8	89
Runed Clay Gloves	-15%; Envenom S. +2; Str, Qui +4; Dex +7	44	88	L8	89
Runed Hol. Clay Gl.	-25%; Envenom S. +2; Dex, Str +6; Body R. +4	45	90	L8	89
Webbed Shadow Gloves	-25%; Crush, Slash R. +4; Qui, Str +7	46	92	L8	89
Hoarfrost Gloves	-25%; Qui +13; Dex +12; Heat, Crush R. +6	49	98	L8	91
Timo. Drakulv Ebon Gl.	-25%; Left Axe, Env. S. +3; Dex +9; Str +7	49	98	L8	90

Legs

Item	Bonus	P	A	M	Q
Supple Leather Leggings	-5%; Con +3; Dex +1	7	14	L2	90
Tomte Leather Leggings		7	14	L2	80
Oiled Leather Leggings	-5%; Dex, Qui +3	9	18	L2	90
Tomte Leather Leggings		9	18	L2	80
Decaying Leggings	-5%; HP +12	12	24	L3	89
Mephitic Leather Leggings	-5%; Con +4; Dex +3	13	26	L3	89
Blodbror Leggings	-10%; Str +3; HP +6	15	30	L4	89
Shadowed Leggings	-10%; Dex, Con +6; Heat R. +6	20	40	L5	100
Fire Charred Leggings	-10%; Con +6; Dex +3; Heat R. +2	22	44	L5	89
Flayed Hagbui Leggings	-10%; Con +7; Dex +3	22	44	L5	89
Muddied Hide Leggings		22	44	L5	80
Wolf Fur Leggings	-15%; Str, Qui +4; Thrust R. +4	27	54	L6	89
Cave Lurker's Leggings	-15%; Con +7; Qui +6	28	56	L6	89
Feral Wulf Leggings	-15%; Con +6; Dex +4; Energy, Spirit R. +4	34	68	L7	89
Faded Silksteel Bound Leggings	-1%; Con +4; Dex +1	36	72	L8	80
Braided Silksteel Leg.	-20%; Cold, Heat R. +2; Con +9; Dex +4	37	74	L8	89
Braided Darksteel Leggings	-20%; Con +12; Dex +4; Qui +3	41	82	L8	89
Runed Clay Leggings	-15%; Con +13; Dex, Qui +4	44	88	L8	89
Runed Hollow Clay Leggings	-25%; Con +12; Str, Qui +4	45	90	L8	89
Emerald Moonshone Leggings	-25%; HP +18; Dex, Str +6	46	92	L8	89
Webbed Shadow Leggings	-25%; HP +12; Con +9; Dex +6	46	92	L8	89
Hoarfrost Leggings	-25%; Con +12; Qui +12; Cold R. +8	49	98	L8	91
Tim. Drakulv Ebon Legs	-25%; Con +12; Dex +7; Matter, Spirit R. +8	49	98	L8	90

Item	Bonus	P	A	M	Q
Feet					
Bearskin Boots		1	2	L1	100
Oiled Leather Boots	-1%; Dex +3	3	6	L1	90
Tomte Padded Boots		5	10	L2	80
Blessed Loki Boots	Qui +3	6	12	L2	90
Bear-Hide Boots	Qui +6	7	14	L2	100
Dwarven Boots of Air	-5%; Qui +7	7	14	L2	100
Supple Leather Boots	-5%; Dex +3; Qui +1	7	14	L2	90
Tomte Leather Boots		7	14	L2	80
Tomte Leather Boots		9	18	L2	80
Boots of Catlike Footing	-5%; Dex +6; Qui +3	10	20	L3	100
Wiley's Boots	-5%; Evade S. +2	11	22	L3	100
Decaying Boots	-5%; Dex +6	12	24	L3	89
Boots of the Malignant	-5%; Dex +4; Qui +3	13	26	L3	89
Mephitic Leather Boots	-5%; Dex +7	13	26	L3	89
Boots of the Agile Evader	-10%; Evade S. +1; Dex +6; Qui +3	15	30	L4	100
Blodbror Boots	-10%; Qui +3; Stealth S. +1; Body R. +2	16	32	L4	89
Boots of Favor	-10%; Con, Dex +3; HP +15	17	34	L4	100
Moccasins of Favor	-10%; Qui, Dex +3; HP +15	17	34	L4	100
Flame Charred Boots	-10%; Stealth S. +2; Heat R. +6	22	44	L5	89
Flayed Hagbui Boots	-10%; Dex +6; Qui +4	22	44	L5	89
Muddied Hide Boots		22	44	L5	80
Cave Lurker's Boots	-15%; Dex +10; Stealth S. +1	28	56	L6	89
Wolf Fur Boots	-15%; Stealth S. +2; Qui +4; Matter R. +4	28	56	L6	89
Boots of Loki	-15%; Dex +9; Evade, Stealth S. +3	32	64	L7	100
Feral Wulf Boots	-15%; Dex +7; Qui, Str +4	34	68	L7	89
Faded Silksteel Bound Boots	-1%; HP +6; Dex +3	36	72	L8	80
Br. Silksteel B.	-20%; Body, Matter R. +2; Stealth S. +1; Dex +10	37	74	L8	89
Dancing Evaders	-15%; Evade S. +5; Dex +10	39	78	L8	100
Braided Darksteel Boots	-20%; Stealth S. +2; Dex +10; Str +3	41	82	L8	89
Emerald Moonshone Boots	-20%; Dex, Qui +10	44	88	L8	89
Runed Clay Boots	-15%; Dex +10; Qui +6; Evade S. +2	44	88	L8	89
Runed Hollow Clay Boots	-25%; Dex, Qui +10	45	90	L8	89
Webbed Shadow Boots	-25%; ; Dex +13; Con +7	46	92	L8	89
Hoarfrost Boots	-25%; Dex +13; Qui +12; Matter, Heat R. +6	49	98	L8	91
Timorous Drakulv Ebon B.	-25%; Stealth S. +3; Dex +10; Str +7	49	98	L8	90

Studded Leather

Item	Bonus	P	A	M	Q
Head					
Tomte Studded Helm		9	18	M2	80
Jagged Bone Helm	-5%; Cold, Heat R. +2; HP +9	10	20	M3	90
Vendo Bone Studded Helm		10	20	M3	80
Smyga's Helm	-5%; Pie +7	11	22	M3	100
Mask of the Skogfru	-5%; Con +3; Spirit R. +4	12	24	M3	89
Blod Flekket Helm	-5%; Pie +3; Con +1; Body R. +4	13	26	M3	89
Malefic Studded Helm	-5%; Pie +6; Emp +1	13	26	M3	89
Noble Supple Helm	-10%; Con, Str +4	19	38	M4	89
Ant Skull Helm	-10%; Con +6; Spirit R. +6	21	42	M5	89
Bone Shard Helm		22	44	M5	80
Flame Helm	-10%; Heat R. +8; Dex, Qui +6	22	44	M5	100
Putrescent Helm	-10%; Str +4; Con, Dex, Qui +3	22	44	M5	89
Spiked Crescent Crown	-10%; Dex, Str +6; HP +12	23	46	M5	100
Crown of Insanity	-15%; Int, Cha -10; Str +10; Spirit R. +8	28	56	M6	100
Cave Prowler's Helm	-15%; HP +9; Qui, Con +4	28	56	M6	89
Wolf Moon Helm	-15%; Sword, Spear S. +2; Spirit R. +4	31	62	M7	89
Faded Studded Silksteel Helm	-1%; HP +12	36	72	M8	80
Serpent-Hide H.	-15%; Pie +6; Power +2; Body R. +2; Berz. S. +1	36	72	M8	89
Crafted Silksteel Helm	-20%; Spirit, Cold, Heat R. +4; Dex +7	37	74	M8	89
Vicious Varulv Helm	-20%; Str +7; Dex, Con +4	37	74	M8	89
Crafted Darksteel H.	-20%; HP +21; Thr., Body R. +2; Spirit R. +8	41	82	M8	89
Latticed Shadow Helm	-25%; HP +27; Spirit R. +10	46	92	M8	89
Helm of the Bloodwolf	-25%; HP +24; Body, Energy, Heat R. +6	47	94	M8	89
Crown of the Darkheart	-25%; HP +33; Str, Qui +10; Cold R. -10	49	98	M8	91
Soulbinder's Helm	-25%; HP +51; Body, Matter, Spirit R. +6	49	98	M8	91
Studded Furlined Helm	-25%; Con, Dex, Str +9; Body R. +10	49	98	M8	90
Studded Ormhide Helm	-25%; Con +4; Dex, Str, Qui +6	49	98	M8	89
Sup. Serp.-Hide H.	-25%; Pie +12; Heat R. +2; Sl. R. +4; Berz. S. +2	49	98	M8	90
Spiked Coral Crown	-25%; Con +12; Qui +10; Heat, Energy R. +10	50	100	M8	91
Torso					
Bone Studded Jerkin	-1%; HP +6	2	4	M1	90
Ruby Studded Jerkin	-5%; HP +6; Qui +3	7	14	M2	100
Pillager's Vest	-5%; Con, Str +4; Cha -4	9	18	M2	90
Tomte Studded Jerkin		9	18	M2	80
Jagged Bone Jerkin	-5%; HP +9; Qui +3	10	20	M3	90
Vendo Bone Studded Jerkin		10	20	M3	80
Malefic Studded Jerkin	-5%; HP +9; Dex +3	13	26	M3	89
Ornate Studded Vest	-5%; Cha, Con +4	14	28	M3	100
Sharpfang Jerkin	-5%; HP +30	17	34	M4	100
Wolftooth Studded Jerkin	-10%; Str +4; HP +9	18	36	M4	89
Blod Flekket Jerkin	-10%; Str +3; Con, Dex +1; Power +1	19	38	M4	89
Noble Supple Jerkin	-10%; HP +12; Cha +3	19	38	M4	89
Huntsman's Jerkin	-10%; Qui +9; HP +9	20	40	M5	90
Bone Shard Jerkin		22	44	M5	80
Putrescent Jerkin	-10%; HP +18; Str +4	22	44	M5	89
Ash Stained Jerkin	-10%; Str, Con +3; HP +9	23	46	M5	89
Cinder Stained Vest	-10%; Str +3; Beastcraft S. +1; HP +9	23	46	M5	89
Forest Hunter's Vest	-15%; Str, Qui +4; HP +21	25	50	M6	100
Cave Prowler's Vest	-15%; HP +15; Dex, Str +3	28	56	M6	89
Eir Blessed Tunic	-15%; Power +2; HP +12; Pie +7	30	60	M7	90
Note-Spun Tunic	-15%; HP +18; Cha +4; Str +6	30	60	M7	90
Frozen Studded Vest	-15%; HP +30; Cold, Spirit, Matter R. +6	31	62	M7	100
Wolf Moon Vest	-15%; HP +12; Con, Qui +4	32	64	M7	89
Faded Studded Silksteel Jerkin	-1%; Con, Str +3	36	72	M8	80
Serpent-Hide Vest	-15%; Dex, Qui +3; HP +18; Body R. +2	36	72	M8	89
Crafted Silksteel Vest	-20%; Con, Dex +6; Qui +4	37	74	M8	89
Vicious Varulv Vest	-20%; HP +18; Dex +4; Body R. +4	37	74	M8	89
Crab Spider Jerkin	-20%; HP +30; Con +7; Qui +9	38	76	M8	100
Crafted Darksteel Vest	-20%; HP +21; Matter, Heat, Spirit R. +4	41	82	M8	89
Latticed Shadow Vest	-25%; Dex, Qui +6; Cold, Body R. +6	46	92	M8	89
Soulbinder's Jerkin	-25%; HP +45; Dex, Str +12	49	98	M8	91
Studded Furlined Jerkin	-25%; Con, Str +13; Cold R. +10	49	98	M8	90
Studded Ormhide Vest	-25%; HP +45	49	98	M8	89
Supple Serpent-Hide Vest	-25%; Dex +9; HP +30; Heat R. +4	49	98	M8	90
Vest of the Bloodwolf	-25%; HP +42; Qui +10	49	98	M8	90
Dread Cobalt Vest	-25%; HP +39; Str +13; Qui +12	50	100	M8	92
Arms					
Studded Hide of Morra	-1%; Str +6	6	12	M2	100
Tomte Studded Sleeves		9	18	M2	80
Pillager's Sleeves	-5%; Str, Dex +3	9	18	M2	90
Jagged Bone Sleeves	-5%; Cold R. +2; Str +6	10	20	M3	90
Vendo Bone Studded Sleeves		10	20	M3	80
Blod Flekket Sleeves	-5%; Power +2; Pie +1	11	22	M3	89
Malefic Studded Sleeves	-5%; Str +6; Con +1	13	26	M3	89
Spirit of the Wood Sleeves	-5%; Dex +4; Str +1; Spirit R. +2	13	26	M3	89
Birk's Strength Sleeves	-5%; Str +9; HP +6	14	28	M3	100
Noble Supple Sleeves	-10%; Str +6; Qui +3	19	38	M4	89
Acid Etched Sleeves	-10%; Str +4; Heat, Body R. +4	21	42	M5	89
Bone Shard Sleeves		22	44	M5	80
Putrescent Sleeves	-10%; Str +7; Qui +3; HP +9	22	44	M5	89
Cave Prowler's Sleeves	-15%; Str +9; Dex +3; Qui +1	28	56	M6	89
Wolf Moon Studded Arms	-15%; Str +4; Axe S. +2; Body R. +4	30	60	M7	89
Hollowed Chitin Sleeves	-20%; Str, Qui +7	35	70	M8	89

Item	Bonus	P	A	M	Q
Faded Studded Silksteel Arms	-1%; Str, Con +3	36	72	M8	80
Serpent-Hide Sleeves	-15%; Str +12; Dex +3; Body R. +2	36	72	M8	89
Vicious Varulv Sleeves	-20%; Str +6; Qui +4; Heat, Cold R. +4	37	74	M8	89
Crafted Silksteel Sleeves	-20%; HP +9; Str +7; Qui +4	37	74	M8	89
Crafted Darksteel Sleeves	-20%; Str +13; Con, Dex +3	41	82	M8	89
Latticed Shadow Sl.	-25%; Str +10; Con +3; Cold, Heat R. +2	46	92	M8	89
Sleeves of the Bloodwolf	-25%; Str +10; Spirit, Energy R. +6	49	98	M8	89
Studded Furlined Arms	-25%; Con, Str +13; Thrust R. +10	49	98	M8	90
Studded Ormhide Sleeves	-25%; Str +13; Qui +6; Matter R. +4	49	98	M8	89
Soulbinder's Sleeves	-25%; Str +11; Qui +10; Spirit R. +10	49	98	M8	91
Supple Serpent-Hide Sleeves	-25%; Str +18; Con +6; Slash R. +4	49	98	M8	90

Hands

Item	Bonus	P	A	M	Q
Tomte Studded Gauntlets		9	18	M2	80
Jagged Bone Gauntlets	-5%; Heat R. +2; Qui +4; Str +1	10	20	M3	90
Vendo Bone Studded Gloves		10	20	M3	80
Blessed Warrior Gauntlets	-5%; Str +4; Dex +3	11	22	M3	100
Bowman's Gloves	-5%; Composite Bow S. +1; Dex +6	11	22	M3	100
Malefic Studded Gloves	-5%; Qui +6; Str +1	13	26	M3	89
Blod Flekket Gloves	-5%; Power +2; Pie +3	14	28	M3	89
Blodjeger Gloves	-10%; Qui +3; Parry S. +1	15	30	M4	89
Pillager's Gauntlets	-10%; Parry, Left Axe S. +1; Dex +3	15	30	M4	90
Berserker's Gloves of Skill	-10%; Left Axe S. +2; Str, Dex +3	15	30	M4	100
Noble Supple Gauntlets	-10%; Dex, Qui +4	19	38	M4	89
Putrescent Bowyer's Gloves	-10%; Qui +6; Composite Bow S. +1	20	40	M5	89
Acid Etched Gauntlets	-10%; Dex +4; Sword S. +2	21	42	M5	89
Putrescent Parrying Gloves	-10%; Qui +7; Parry S. +1	21	42	M5	89
Bone Shard Gloves		22	44	M5	80
Boned Gloves	-5%	22	44	M5	100
Cave Prowler's Gauntlets	-15%; Qui, Dex, Str +4	28	56	M6	89
Wolf Moon Gauntlets	-15%; Dex +3; Parry S. +1; HP +12	30	60	M7	89
Moon Studded G.	-15%; Composite Bow S. +1; Qui +6; HP +12	31	62	M7	89
Serpent-Hide G.	-15%; Qui +4; Dex +7; Body R. +2; Comp. Bow S. +1	36	72	M8	89
Faded Studded Silksteel Gloves	-1%; Str, Qui +3	36	72	M8	80
Crafted Silksteel Gauntlets	-20%; Dex, Str +6; Qui +4	37	74	M8	89
Vicious Varulv Gloves	-20%; Qui +7; Con +6; Matter R. +4	37	74	M8	89
Crafted Darksteel Gauntlets	-20%; Left Axe, Parry S. +2; Dex +7	41	82	M8	89
Latticed Shadow G.	-25%; Left Axe, Comp. Bow S. +3; Str, Qui +6	46	92	M8	89
Gauntlets of the Bloodwolf	-25%; Qui +14	47	94	M8	89
Soulpiercer's G.	-25%; Comp. Bow S. +4; HP +30; Qui, Dex +6	49	98	M8	91
Soulrager's Gauntlets	-25%; Left Axe S. +4; HP +21; Str, Qui +7	49	98	M8	91
Studded Furlined Gauntlets	-25%; Dex, Qui +13; Body R. +10	49	98	M8	90
Studded Ormhide Gauntlets	-25%; Body, Slash R. +4; Qui +11	49	98	M8	89
Sup. Serpent-H. G.	-25%; Dex, Qui +10; Sl. R. +2; Comp. Bow S. +2	49	98	M8	90

Legs

Item	Bonus	P	A	M	Q
Tomte Studded Leggings		9	18	M2	80
Jagged Bone Leggings	-5%; Con +6; Qui +1	10	20	M3	90
Vendo Bone Studded Leggings		10	20	M3	80
Malefic Studded Leggings	-5%; Con +6; Qui +1	13	26	M3	89
Blod Flekket Leggings	-5%; HP +9; Str +3	14	28	M3	89
Blodjeger Leggings	-5%; Str, Con +3; Slash R. +2	14	28	M3	89
Berbenet Leggings	-10%; Qui, Dex +4; Crush R. +6	18	36	M4	100
Noble Supple Leggings	-10%; Con +6; Cha +3	19	38	M4	89
Putrescent Leggings	-10%; Con +7; Str +3	21	42	M5	89
Bone Shard Leggings		22	44	M5	80
Acid Etched Leg.	-10%; Dex +4; Qui +3; Heat R. +4; Body R. +2	23	46	M5	89
Cave Prowler's Leggings	-15%; Con +9; Dex +3; Str +1	28	56	M6	89
Drakescale Leggings	-15%; Con +10; Dex +6	31	62	M7	100
Wolf Moon Legs	-15%; Str +4; HP +12; Dex +3; Crush R. +2	32	64	M7	89
Faded Studded Silksteel Leggings	-1%; Dex, Qui +3	36	72	M8	80
Serpent-Hide Leggings	-15%; Con +12; Qui +3; Body R. +2	36	72	M8	89
Crafted Silksteel Leggings	-20%; HP +9; Con +7; Qui +4	37	74	M8	89
Vicious Varulv Leg.	-20%; Con +6; Dex +4; Energy, Spirit R. +4	37	74	M8	89
Crafted Darksteel Leggings	-20%; Con +10; Qui +4	41	82	M8	89
Latticed Shadow Leggings	-25%; Con +10; Qui +3; Body R. +4	46	92	M8	89
Supple Serpent-Hide Leg.	-25%; Con +10; Qui +9; Slash R. +4	49	98	M8	90
Leggings of the Bloodwolf	-25%; HP +30; Dex +7	49	98	M8	89
Soulbinder's Legs	-25%; Con +10; Dex +12; Body, Matter R. +8	49	98	M8	91
Studded Furlined Legs	-25%; Dex, Qui +13; Cold R. +10	49	98	M8	90
Studded Ormhide Leggings	-25%; Con +11; Cold R. +8	49	98	M8	89

Feet

Item	Bonus	P	A	M	Q
Tomte Studded Boots		9	18	M2	80
Jagged Bone Boots	-5%; HP +6; Dex +3; Qui +1	10	20	M3	90
Vendo Bone Studded Boots		10	20	M3	80
Blod Flekket Boots	-5%; Con +3; Pie +1; Body R. +2	12	24	M3	89
Malefic Studded Boots	-5%; Dex +6; Qui +1	13	26	M3	89
Wolftooth Studded Boots	-10%; Dex +4; Stealth S. +1	17	34	M4	89
Noble Supple Boots	-10%; Dex +6; Con +3	19	38	M4	89
Forest Hunter's Boots	-10%; Evade, Stealth S. +2; Qui +4	20	40	M5	100
Pilllager's Boots	-10%; Evade S. +2; Qui +7	20	40	M5	90
Bone Shard Boots		22	44	M5	80
Ash Stained Boots	-10%; Qui +4; Dex +3; Stealth S. +1	23	46	M5	89
Putrescent Boots	-10%; Dex +6; Qui +3	23	46	M5	89
Cave Prowler's Boots	-15%; HP +9; Dex +9	28	56	M6	89
B. o.t. Frenzied Bear	-15%; Evade, Berzerk S. +1; Qui +6; Dex +7	30	60	M7	90
Moon Studded Boots	-15%; Stealth S. +3; Qui +4; Matter R. +4	33	66	M7	89
Wolf Moon Boots	-15%; Dex +7; Con +4; Matter R. +6	33	66	M7	89
Faded Studded Silksteel Boots	-1%; Dex, Qui +3	36	72	M8	80
Serpent-Hide Boots	-15%; Dex +6; Qui +9; Body R. +2	36	72	M8	89
Crafted Silksteel Boots	-20%; Dex +9; Qui +7	37	74	M8	89
Vicious Varulv Boots	-20%; Dex +7; Qui, Str +4	37	74	M8	89
Crafted Darksteel Boots	-20%; Stealth S. +3; Dex +10	41	82	M8	89
Latticed Shadow Boots	-25%; Dex +10; Qui +3; Body R. +4	46	92	M8	89
Boots of the Bloodwolf	-25%; Stealth S. +2; Con +4; Dex, Qui +6	49	98	M8	89
Soulbinder's Boots	-25%; Dex +15; Body R. +20	49	98	M8	91
Studded Furlined Boots	-25%; Con, Dex +13; Matter R. +10	49	98	M8	90
Studded Ormhide Boots	-25%; HP +21; Dex +12	49	98	M8	89
Supple Serpent-Hide B.	-25%; Dex, Qui +9; HP +12; Evade S. +2	49	98	M8	90

Chain

Head

Item	Bonus	P	A	M	Q
Tomte Chain Coif		9	18	M2	80
Edbrottsjo Helm	-5%; Sword, Axe S. +1	11	22	M3	89
Miscreant's Helm	-5%; HP +9; Dex +3	13	26	M3	89
Lashed Web Helm	-10%; Con, Pie +3	15	30	M4	89
Helm of the Aki	-5%; Qui +6; Cha +4	17	34	M4	100
Blighted Chain Coif	-10%; Pie +6; Dex +3	18	36	M4	89
Bloddarlig Helm	-10%; Axe, Hammer, Sword S. +1	18	36	M4	89
Woeful Chain Coif	-10%; Str, Qui +4	19	38	M4	89
Barbed Crescent Crown	-10%; Con, Str +6; HP +12	23	46	M5	100
Thick Crescent Crown	-10%; Pie +9; Power +2	23	46	M5	100
Lava Forged Coif	-10%; Pie +4; Power +2; Heat R. +4	24	48	M5	89
Rusted Ringmail Coif		25	50	M6	80
Giant Skull Helm	-15%; Con +3; HP +12; Crush R. +6	29	58	M6	89
Moonshone Helm	-15%; HP +12; Power +2; Heat R. +4; Pie +9	30	60	M7	100
Primordial Skull Helm	-15%; Cold R. +4; Con +6; Pie +10	30	60	M7	90
Cerus	-15%; Heat R. +10; Cha, Qui +9	32	64	M7	100
Ursine Ringmail Coif	-15%; Pie +10; Str +4	32	64	M7	89
Claw Forged H.	-15%; Con, Pie +4; Cold R. +2; Augm. S. +2	33	66	M7	89
Faded Chain Silksteel Coif	-1%; HP +12	36	72	M8	80
Crazed Lupine Coif	-20%; Con, Str +4; Spirit R. -4; Cold R. +6	37	74	M8	89
Gnarling Garou Coif	-20%; Pie +7; Dex, Con +4	37	74	M8	89

Item	Bonus	P	A	M	Q
Growling Garou Coif	-20%; Str +7; Dex, Con +4	37	74	M8	89
Ringed Silksteel Coif	-20%; Pie +9; Qui +4; Dex +3	37	74	M8	89
Ringed Darksteel H.	-20%; Heat, Energy R. +4; Pie +10; Cha +3	41	82	M8	89
Blood Crystal Helm	-20%; Cha +9; Con +10	42	84	M8	89
Jet Bloodletter's Helm	-25%; Cha, Pie +10	45	90	M8	89
Twilight-Mail Coif	-25%; Pie +13; Qui +4; Cold R. +4	46	92	M8	89
Ageless Dragon Etched Coif	-25%; Cave Magic S. +4; Power +4; Pie +12; Crush R. +4	49	98	M8	90
Anc. Drag. Etch. C.	-25%; Pacif. S. +4; Power +4; Pie +12; Cr. R. +4	49	98	M8	90
Barbed Ebon Coif	-25%; Con, Str +13; Crush, Slash R. +8	49	98	M8	91
Chilllsome Icebound Helm	-25%; HP +30; Qui +9; Spirit R. +6	49	98	M8	90
Crackling Ebon C.	-25%; Stormcall. S. +4; Qui +12; Cr., Spir. R. +8	49	98	M8	90
Dragon Singed Ebon Coif	-25%; Cha +12; Qui +12; Heat R. +8	49	98	M8	90
Forlorn Icebound Helm	-25%; HP +30; Dex, Pie +9; Crush R. +6	49	98	M8	90
Jotun Blackorm Coif	-25%; Pie +12; Cha +9; Power +2	49	98	M8	89
Shrunken Orm Skull	-25%; Pie +10; Spirit, Body R. +10	49	98	M8	90
Black Golden-Embossed Hood	-25%; HP +60; Str +22; Cha -20	49	98	M8	91
Heavy Coral Crown	-25%; Cha, Pie +10; Con +9; Spirit R. +10	50	100	M8	91

Torso

Item	Bonus	P	A	M	Q
Tomte Chain Hauberk		9	18	M2	80
Amber Hauberk	-5%; HP +5	10	20	M3	100
Edbrottsjo Hauberk	-5%; Con +3; HP +6	11	22	M3	89
Blazing Hauberk	-5%; Con, Str, Cha +3	12	24	M3	90
Miscreant's Hauberk	-5%; Con +4; Str +3	13	26	M3	89
Gokstad's Hauberk		15	30	M4	100
Lashed Web Hauberk	-10%; HP +12	15	30	M4	89
Riva	HP +22	15	30	M4	100
Strengthened Hauberk	-10%; HP +15; Str +4	15	30	M4	100
Blighted Chain Hauberk	-10%; HP +15; Pie +1	19	38	M4	89
Woeful Chain Hauberk	-10%; HP +18; Str +3	23	46	M5	89
Lava Etched Hauberk	-10%; Con +3; HP +12; Augm. S. +1	24	48	M5	89
Rabid Bearhide Hauberk	-15%; HP +24; Str +7	25	50	M6	100
Rune Etched Hauberk	-15%; HP +9; Power +2; Pie, Str +4	25	50	M6	100
Rusted Ringmail Hauberk		25	50	M6	80
Saga-Spinner's Protector	-15%; Battlesg. S. +2; Con, Str, Dex +4	25	50	M6	100
Stormriders Hauberk	-15%; HP +21; Con, Str +4	25	50	M6	100
Hroderk's Chain	-15%; HP +15; Dex, Qui +4	26	52	M6	100
Brimstone Breastplate	-10%; HP +45	27	54	M6	100
Obsidian Hauberk	-15%; Con +4; HP +18	29	58	M6	89
War Ravager's Hauberk	-15%; HP +27; Str +6; Con +4	31	62	M7	100
Ursine Ringmail	-15%; HP +12; Str, Qui +4	32	64	M7	89
Askafroa's Chain Hbk.	-15%; Crush, Slash, Thrust R. +4; HP +36	34	68	M7	100
Wolfsclaw Hbk.	-20%; Cave Magic S. +3; Augm., Mending S. +1	35	70	M8	89
Wolftooth Hbk.	-20%; Pacification S. +3; Augm., Mending S. +1	35	70	M8	89
Crazed Lupine Hauberk	-20%; Dex, Str +7	36	72	M8	89
Faded Chain Silksteel Hauberk	-1%; HP +12	36	72	M8	80
Growling Garou Hauberk	-20%; HP +18; Dex +4; Body R. +4	37	74	M8	89
Ringed Silksteel Hauberk	-20%; Str, Pie +6; Con +4	37	74	M8	89
Scaffold Web Hauberk	-20%; Crush, Slash, Thrust R. +8; Str +13	39	78	M8	100
Ringed Darksteel Hauberk	-20%; HP +27; Str +6	41	82	M8	89
Blood Crystal Hauberk	-20%; HP +24; Cha +7	42	84	M8	89
Jet Bloodletter's Hauberk	-20%; Con, Str +7; Pie +4	42	84	M8	89
Soulsong's Hauberk	-20%; HP +33; Pie, Dex, Str +6	44	88	M8	100
Twilight-Mail Hauberk	-25%; Con, Str +7; Pie +6	46	92	M8	89
Chillsome Icebound Hauberk	-25%; HP +60	49	98	M8	90
Dragon Etched Hauberk	-25%; HP +30; Pie, Str +7; Thrust R. +8	49	98	M8	90
Dragon Singed Ebon Hauberk	-25%; HP +48; Str, Qui +6	49	98	M8	91
Forlorn Icebound Hauberk	-25%; Con +10; Str, Pie +9; Cold R. +6	49	98	M8	91
Jotun Black Orm Hauberk	-25%; Pie +4; Heat R. +8; HP +33	49	98	M8	90
Dread Cobalt Hauberk	-25%; HP +42; Str +10; Pie +6; Slash R. +4	50	100	M8	92

Arms

Item	Bonus	P	A	M	Q
Tomte Chain Sleeves		9	18	M2	80
Mauler Claw Sleeves	-5%; Pie, Dex +3	11	22	M3	89
Miscreant's Sleeves	-5%; Str +7	13	26	M3	89
Lashed Web Sleeves	-10%; Str, Dex +3	15	30	M4	89
Blighted Chain Sleeves	-10%; Str, Dex +4	18	36	M4	89
Blazing Sleeves	-10%; Str +10; Heat R. +4	20	40	M5	90
Rabid Bearhide Sleeves	-10%; Qui +6; Con, Str +4	20	40	M5	100
War Ravager's Sleeves	-10%; Str +13; Dex +3	20	40	M5	100
Woeful Chain Sleeves	-10%; Str +6; Dex +3	20	40	M5	89
Lava Etched Sleeves	-10%; Dex +4; Heat R. +6; Pie +3	24	48	M5	89
Rusted Ringmail Sleeves		25	50	M6	80
Impervious Sleeves	-15%; Cold, Spirit R. +4; Str +9; Qui +4	26	52	M6	100
Smoldering Sl.	-15%; Sword S. +1; Dex +3; Body, Crush R. +4	27	54	M6	89
Sleeves of the Dauntless	-15%; Cold, Heat R. +6; Con +4; Str +6	30	60	M7	90
Wyrm Sleeves	-15%; Str +18; Heat R. +8	31	62	M7	100
Ursine Ringmail Sleeves	-15%; Str +12; Pie +3	32	64	M7	89
Claw Forged Sleeves	-15%; Con +4; HP +12; Mending S. +2	34	68	M7	89
Dark Moon Lupine Sl.	-20%; Stormcall. S. +3; Pie +4; Body R. -2	35	70	M8	89
Moon-Struck Lupine Sleeves	-20%; Con +4; Str +9; Body R. -2	35	70	M8	89
New Moon Lupine Sl.	-20%; Dex +4; Battlesg. S. +3; Body R. -2	35	70	M8	89
Faded Chain Silksteel Sleeves	-1%; HP +12	36	72	M8	80
Growling Garou Sleeves	-20%; Str +6	37	74	M8	89
Ringed Silksteel Sleeves	-20%; Str +13; Body, Cold R. +2	37	74	M8	89
Jet Bloodletter's Sl.	-20%; Str +10; Matter R. +4; Thrust R. +2	41	82	M8	89
Ringed Darksteel Sleeves	-20%; Str +10; Pie +3; Slash R. +2	41	82	M8	89
Blood Crystal Sleeves	-20%; Battlesongs S. +2; Str +13	42	84	M8	89
Twilight-Mail Sleeves	-25%; HP +12; Str +12; Qui +3	46	92	M8	89
Dragon Singed Ebon Arms	-25%; Str +22; Body, Matter R. +10	49	98	M8	90
Chillsome Icebound Sleeves	-25%; Str +14; Heat R. +10	49	98	M8	90
Dragon Etched Sleeves	-25%; Str +10; Pie +12; Matter R. +10	49	98	M8	90
Forlorn Icebound Sleeves	-25%; St, Pie +12; Crush, Slash R. +8	49	98	M8	90
Jotun Black Orm Sleeves	-25%; Str +14; Heat R. +8	49	98	M8	90
Thunder Embossed Sl.	-25%; Str +22; Cr. R. +6; Stormcall. S. +2	49	98	M8	90

Hands

Item	Bonus	P	A	M	Q
Tomte Chain Gloves		9	18	M2	80
Blazing Gauntlets	-5%; Parry S. +1; Dex, Qui +3	12	24	M3	90
Mauler Claw Gloves	-5%; Dex +3; Parry S. +1	12	24	M3	89
Miscreant's Gloves	-5%; Qui +7	13	26	M3	89
Thunderous Gauntlets	-10%; Stormcalling S. +2; Str, Dex +3	15	30	M4	100
Lashed Web Gloves	-10%; Parry S. +1; Str +3	15	30	M4	89
Blighted Chain Gloves	-10%; Qui, Dex +3; Cave Magic S. +1	18	36	M4	89
Blighted Keeper Chain Gloves	-10%; Qui, Dex +3; Mending S. +1	18	36	M4	89
Woeful Melody Gloves	-10%; Qui +6; Emp +3	18	36	M4	89
Woeful Chain Gloves	-10%; Qui +6; Str +3	19	38	M4	89
Note-Spinners Gauntlets	-10%; Crush R. +4; Dex, Qui, Str +4	20	40	M5	100
Stormcaller Woeful Gloves	-10%; Qui +6; Stormcalling S. +1	20	40	M5	89
Gauntlets of the Redhand	-10%; Dex +6; Matter R. +8; Qui +3	23	46	M5	100
Brimstone Gloves	-10%; Dex +9; Str +7	24	48	M5	100
Lava Etched Gloves	-10%; Str +7; Mending, Pacification S. +1	24	48	M5	89
Lava Forged Gloves	-10%; Str +7; Mending, Cave Magic S. +1	24	48	M5	89
War Ravager's G.	-15%; Parry S. +2; Spirit R. +6; Str +6; Qui +3	25	50	M6	100
Moonshone Gloves	-15%; Power +2; Energy R. +6; Pie +9	25	50	M6	100
Rusted Ringmail Gloves		25	50	M6	80
Singed Gloves	-15%; Dex +3; Parry S. +2; Heat R. +4	27	54	M6	89
Gauntlets of Stormrage	-15%; Stormcall. S. +2; Str, Dex, Con +4	30	60	M7	90
G. o.t. Tempest	-15%; Stormcalling S. +2; Str +12; Qui +6	31	62	M7	100
Rune Etched Gloves	-15%; Power +3; Pie +9; Str +6	31	62	M7	100
Ursine Ringmail Gloves	-15%; Qui +9; Pie +3; Parry S. +1	32	64	M7	89
Claw Forged Gloves	-15%; Pie +4; Power +4; Body R. +4	33	66	M7	89

Item	Bonus	P	A	M	Q
Crazed Lupine Gloves	-20%; Parry, Shield S. +2; Qui +3	35	70	M8	89
Faded Chain Silksteel Gloves	-1%; HP +12	36	72	M8	80
Growling Garou Gloves	-20%; Qui +7; Con +6; Matter R. +4	37	74	M8	89
Ringed Silksteel Gloves	-20%; Str, Pie +6; Dex +4	37	74	M8	89
Jet Bloodletter's Gloves	-20%; HP +12; Qui, Pie +6	38	76	M8	89
Ringed Darksteel Gl.	-20%; Axe, Hammer, Sword S. +1; Qui +10	41	82	M8	89
Blood Crystal Gloves	-20%; Sword, Hammer, Axe S. +1; Qui +10	42	84	M8	89
Twilight-Mail Gloves	-25%; Str, Pie, Qui +6; Heat R. +8	46	92	M8	89
Jotun Black Orm Gauntlets	-25%; Str +9; Dex, Qui +6; Parry S. +2	49	98	M8	90
Barbed Ebon Gl.	-25%; Parry S. +4; Sword, Axe, Hammer S. +3	49	98	M8	91
Chillsome Icebound Gloves	-25%; HP +30; Str +9; Heat R. +6	49	98	M8	90
Crackling Eb. Gl.	-25%; Stormcall., Shield S. +2; Str +12; Body R. +8	49	98	M8	90
Dragon Etched Gl.	-25%; Mending, Augm. S. +3; Qui +9; Pie +7	49	98	M8	90
Forlorn Icebound Gloves	-25%; HP +30; Dex, Pie +9	49	98	M8	90
Hymn-Wvr's Eb. Gl.	-25%; Battlesg. S. +3; Cha, Qui +10; Body R. +8	49	98	M8	90

Legs

Item	Bonus	P	A	M	Q
Tomte Chain Leggings		9	18	M2	80
Edbrottsjo Leggings	-5%; Str +4	10	20	M3	89
Miscreant's Leggings	-5%; Con +7	13	26	M3	89
Lashed Web Legs	-10%; HP +12	15	30	M4	89
Gokstad's Leggings		16	32	M4	100
Blighted Chain Leggings	-10%; Con +6; Str +3	18	36	M4	89
Thunder-Striders Leg.	-10%; Con +12; Body, Spirit, Energy R. +2	20	40	M5	100
Woeful Chain Leggings	-10%; Con +7; Str +4	23	46	M5	89
Rusted Ringmail Leggings		25	50	M6	80
Lava Forged Leggings	-15%; Str +3; HP +9; Power +2	26	52	M6	89
Impervious Leggings	-15%; Con +10; Dex +3	27	54	M6	100
Flaming Leggings	-15%; Cha, Str +4; Heat R. +6	29	58	M6	89
Scorched Leggings	-15%; Con, Str +4; Heat R. +6	29	58	M6	89
Smoldering Leggings	-15%; Pie, Str +4; Heat R. +6	29	58	M6	89
Ursine Ringmail Leggings	-15%; Con +12; Str +3	32	64	M7	89
Askafroa's Chain Leg.	-15%; Cold, Heat, Matter R. +4; Con +12	34	68	M7	100
Claw Forged Legs	-15%; Str +4; HP +18; Body R. +4	34	68	M7	89
Crazed Lupine Legs	-20%; Str +4; HP +18; Dex +3	35	70	M8	89
Faded Chain Silksteel Leggings	-1%; HP +12	36	72	M8	80
Growling Garou Leg.	-20%; Con +6; Dex +4; Energy, Spirit R. +4	37	74	M8	89
Ringed Silksteel Leg.	-20%; Con +9; Str +4; Matter, Slash R. +2	37	74	M8	89
Ringed Darksteel Leggings	-20%; Con +10; Str +3; Crush R. +2	41	82	M8	89
Blood Crystal Leggings	-20%; Con +10; Cha +4	42	84	M8	89
Jet Bloodletter's Leggings	-20%; ; Energy, Cold R. +4	43	86	M8	89
Twilight-Mail Leggings	-25%; HP +18; Dex, Qui +6	46	92	M8	89
Chillsome Icebound Legs	-25%; Con, Cha +10	49	98	M8	90
Dragon Etched Legs	-25%; Con +12; Pie +6; Body R. +12	49	98	M8	90
Dragon Singed Ebon Legs	-25%; Con +16; Cold R. +16	49	98	M8	90
Forlorn Icebound Legs	-25%; Con +11; Dex +9; Cold, Heat R. +6	49	98	M8	90
Jotun Blackorm Leggings	-25%; Con +14; Heat R. +4	49	98	M8	89

Feet

Item	Bonus	P	A	M	Q
Tomte Chain Boots		9	18	M2	80
Mauler Claw Boots	-5%; Dex +3; HP +15	13	26	M3	89
Miscreant's Boots	-5%; Dex +4; Qui +3	13	26	M3	89
Blazing Boots	-10%; Evade S. +1; Qui +6	15	30	M4	90
Lashed Web Boots	-10%; Con, Qui +3	15	30	M4	89
Lightfoot Boots	-5%; Qui +7; Dex +1	15	30	M4	90
Heavy Boots of Favor	-10%; Str, Dex +3; HP +15	17	34	M4	100
Blighted Chain Boots	-10%; Dex +6; Con +3	18	36	M4	89
Woeful Chain Boots	-10%; Dex +6; Con +3	19	38	M4	89
Rusted Ringmail Boots		25	50	M6	80
Lava Forged Boots	-15%; Qui +4; Cold R. +6; Mending S. +1	26	52	M6	89
Flaming Boots	-15%; Dex +3; Qui +4; Str, Pie +1	27	54	M6	89
Claw Forged Boots	-15%; Str, Qui +4; Heat, Body R. -4	32	64	M7	89
Ursine Ringmail Boots	-15%; Dex +9; Qui, Con +3	32	64	M7	89
Crazed Lupine Boots	-20%; Dex, Qui +4; Heat, Cold R. +4	35	70	M8	89
Faded Chain Silksteel Boots	-1%; HP +12	36	72	M8	80
Growling Garou Boots	-20%; Dex +7; Qui, Str +4	37	74	M8	89
Ringed Silksteel Boots	-20%; Qui +7; Dex +6; Matter R. +4	37	74	M8	89
Jet Bloodletter's Boots	-20%; Con, Dex +9	40	80	M8	89
Ringed Darksteel Boots	-20%; Dex +10; Str +4; Matter R. +6	41	82	M8	89
Blood Crystal Boots	-20%; HP +15; Dex, Qui +6	42	84	M8	89
Twilight-Mail Boots	-25%; Con, Dex +9; Qui +3; Energy R. +4	46	92	M8	89
Chillsome Icebound Boots	-25%; Con, Dex +9; Cold, Matter R. +6	49	98	M8	90
Dragon Etched Boots	-25%; Dex +12; Matter, Body R. +10	49	98	M8	90
Dragon Singed Ebon B.	-25%; Con, Dex +12; Matter, Cold R. +8	49	98	M8	90
Forlorn Icebound Boots	-25%; Con, Dex +10; Cold, Heat R. +6	49	98	M8	90
Jotun Black Orm Boots	-25%; Dex, Qui +10; Evade S. +2	49	98	M8	90

Shield Drops & Rewards

For Standard (Craftable) Shields, see page 361.

For more information on what the various stats mean, see **Armor** (p. 362), **Weapons** (p. 361) and **Material** (p. 360).

Abbreviations

The first negative percentage in any bonus indicates your opponent's reduced chance of hitting you when you are wearing the item.

Headings. Power Level / **A**rmor Factor / **M#** = Material (M) and Material Level (#) / **Q**uality / **Sp**eed, or weapon delay (the time between bashes) / **D**amage with each hit / **DpS** = Damage per second.

The first positive percentage in any bonus indicates your increased chance to block with the shield and (if it can be used as a weapon), your increased chance to hit with it.

Stats. Resistance, **S**kill / **Cha**risma, **Con**stitution, **Dex**terity, **Pie**ty, **Qui**ckness, **Str**ength / **Met**al.

Small

Shield	Bonus	P	A	M#	Q	Sp	D	DpS
Small Training Sh.		0	0	M1	100			
Tomte Round Sh.		10	20	M2	80	2.8	12	4.2
Berolig	+5%; Pacification S. +2	13	26	M3	89	2.8	14	5.1
Sangsbrottsjo Sh.	+5%; Battlesongs S. +1; Str +3	13	26	M3	89	2.8	14	5.1
Sh. of the Forest Spirit	+5%; Sh. S. +1; Str +1	13	26	M3	89	2.8	14	5.1
Ville Dyr	+5%; Cave Magic S. +2	13	26	M3	89	2.8	14	5.1
Brittle-Bone Round Sh.	+5%; Sh. S. +1; Qui +4	14	28	M3	89	2.9	16	5.4
Flaming Sh.	+10%; Sh. S. +2; Heat R. +4	21	42	M5	89	2.8	20	7.2
Sh. of the Indomitable	+10%; Sh. S. +1; Str +4; Con +3	23	46	M5	89	2.8	23	8.1
Widower Sh.	+10%; Sh. S. +2; Pie, Str +4	23	46	M5	100	2.8	23	8.1
Accursed Sh.	+10%; Sh. S. +1; Con +4; Qui +3	24	48	M5	89	2.8	23	8.1
Vengeance Sh.	+10%; Str, Pie +3; Con +4	24	48	M5	89	2.8	23	8.1
Fiery Sh.	+10%; Sh. S. +2; Heat R. +4; Pie +6; Str +4	25	50	M5	100	2.7	23	8.7
Scorched Bone Sh.	+15%; Sh. S. +2; Battlesongs S. +1; Heat R. +2	26	52	M6	89	2.8	25	9.0
Burnt Ember Sh.	+15%; Mend., Augm., Pacific. S. +1	30	60	M6	89	2.8	29	10.2
Glow. Emb. Sh.	+15%; Mend., Augm., Cave Mg. S. +1	30	60	M6	89	2.8	29	10.2
Wolf Engrvd. Sh.	+15%; Dex, Con +4; Sl. R. +2; Thr. R. +4	30	60	M6	89	2.7	28	10.2
Wolf Mn. Sh.	+15%; Axe, Par. S. +1; Con +6; Body R. +4	33	66	M7	89	2.7	30	11.1
Feral Protector	+15%; HP +12; Qui +3; Sh. S. +1	34	68	M7	89	3.8	44	11.7
Varulv Sh.	+20%; Dex, Con +6	37	74	M8	89	2.8	35	12.6
Reinforced Chitin Sh.	+20%; HP +15; Pie, Qui +4	38	76	M8	89	3	38	12.6
Skycaller's Prot.	+20%; Stormcall., Sh. S. +2; Str +6	39	78	M8	89	4.3	55	12.9
Drakulv Small Sh.	+20%; Con, Pie +7; Thrust R. +6	42	84	M8	89	3	41	13.8
Drakulv Sh.	+20%; HP +18; Cold, Heat, Spirit R. +6	43	86	M8	89	2.8	39	14.1
Gridelin Guard	+20%; Pie, Con +10; Energy, Body R. +8	43	86	M8	100	2.8	33	11.7
Runed Clay Sh.	+20%; HP +24; Power +3	43	86	M8	89	3.4	50	14.7
Icebound Buckler	+30%; Power +6; Con +13; Pie +12; Heat R. +10	50	100	M8	93	3	49	16.2
Icebound Protector	+30%; Sh. S. +5; Con, Str, Qui +10	50	100	M8	93	4	65	16.2
Orm Skullcap Sh.	+25%; Sh. S. +3; Pie +12; HP +27	50	100	M8	90	5	81	16.2
Runed Clay Bckl.	+25%; Mat., Ht., Cold R. +4; HP +24	50	100	M8	89	3	49	16.2
Soulbinder's Sh.	+25%; Con, Pie +10; Thrust R. +10	50	100	M8	91	2.5	41	16.2

Medium

Shield	Bonus	P	A	M#	Q	Sp	D	DpS
Focium		0	0	M1	100			
Regnbrottsjo Sh.	+5%; Stormcalling S. +1; Pie +1	11	22	M3	89	4.3	19	4.5
Brack Sh.	+5%; Sh. S. +3; Dex +6	18	36	M4	100	4.3	28	6.6
Evanescent Kite Sh.	+10%; Sh. S. +2; Str +3	19	38	M4	89	4.3	30	6.9
Charred Rib Cage Sh.	+15%; Sh. S. +2; Stormcalling S. +1; Heat R. +4	27	54	M6	89	3.6	33	9.3
Garou Defender	+15%; Sh. S. +1; HP +12; Str +3	30	60	M7	89	4.5	53	11.7
Skull-Bone Sh.	+15%; Sh. S. +2; Dex +3; Str +6	33	66	M7	89	3.8	42	11.1
Forged Darksteel Kite Sh.	+20%; Cr. R. +4; Ht. R. +6; Str +6; Sh. S. +2	42	84	M8	89	4.2	58	13.8
Beryl Bulwark	+20%; Qui, Str +10; Cold, Energy R. +8	43	86	M8	100	3.8	44	11.7
Midnight Def.	+20%; Qui, Str +10; Cold, Heat R. +8	43	86	M8	100	2.8	33	11.7
Runed Clay Battle-Sh.	+25%; Stormcalling S. +2; HP +18; Matter, Body R. +4	46	92	M8	89	4	60	15.0
Gold. Alloy K. Sh.	+25%; Sh., Stormcall. S. +4; Con +9	50	100	M8	90	4	65	16.2

Large

Shield	Bonus	P	A	M#	Q	Sp	D	DpS
Edbrottsjo Sh.	+5%; Sh. S. +1; Dex +1	10	20	M2	89	4.4	18	4.2
Tomte Large Sh.		10	20	M2	80	4.3	18	4.2
Brittle-Bone Tower Sh.	+5%; Sh. S. +1; Str +4	15	30	M3	89	4.5	24	5.4
Accursed Tower Sh.	+10%; Sh. S. +2; Con +3; Str +4	23	46	M5	89	4.5	36	8.1
Vendo Bl. Blocker	+15%; Sh. S. +1; Con, Dex, Qui +3	25	50	M6	89	4	40	9.9
Charred Bone Sh.	+15%; Sh. S. +2; Qui +3; Cr. R. +2	27	54	M6	89	4.5	42	9.3
Drakulv Great Sh.	+20%; Con, Str, Qui +6	41	82	M8	89	4.5	61	13.5
Runed Clay War-Sh.	+20%; Sh. S. +2; HP +15; Matter, Cold R. +4	42	84	M8	89	4.5	62	13.8
Bedlam Bladest.	+20%; Str, Qui +10; Body, Spir. R. +8	43	86	M8	100	4.5	53	11.7
Twilght. Blade-Stop.	+25%; Sl., Thr. R. +4; Con, Dex +6	47	94	M8	89	4	61	15.3
Blk. Orm Sc. Sh.	+25%; Sh. S. +6; Ht., Cd. R. +6; Str +7	50	100	M8	90	4	65	16.2
Icebound Warshield	+30%; Sh. S. +7; Con, Str +13	50	100	M8	94	4	65	16.2
Smoldering Ebon Sh.	+25%; HP +24; Sh. S. +4; Heat, Energy R. +8	50	100	M8	91	4	65	16.2

Jewelry Drops & Rewards

Abbreviations

Headings. Power Level / Quality.

Stats. Resistance, Skill / Charisma, Constitution, Empathy, Dexterity, Intelligence, Piety, Quickness, Strength.

Item	Bonus	PL	Ql
Amber			
Piece of Amber	Str, Pie +1	6	89
Amulet			
Taldos' Amulet	Str +4; Dex +3; HP +3	12	100
Badge			
Badge of Courage	Parry S. +3; Con +7; Str, Dex +6	47	100
Belts			
Oiled Leather Belt	Dex +1	4	90
Ghoul Hair Belt	HP +6	6	100
Belt of Health	HP +6	8	100
Bone Belt o.t. Wild	Pie +3; HP +3	10	89
Edbrottsjo Belt	Con +3; Str +1	10	89
Hardened Silkstrand Belt	HP +12	10	100
Silkstrand Belt	Power +2	10	100
Brendig's Belt	HP +9; Evade S. +1	13	90
Trustan's Embroidered Belt	Pie, Dex, Qui +3	14	100
Trustan's Hand Embossed Belt	Pie, Con, Str +3	14	100
Trustan's Handmade Belt	Str, Con, Dex +3	14	100
Trustan's Handwoven Belt	Dex, Qui, Str +3	14	100
Vannsang Belt	Stealth S. +2; Thrust R. +2	16	89
Toe Bone Belt	Con, Str, Qui +3	17	100
Mildewed Leather Belt	Qui, Str +4	20	89
Moldy Leather Belt	HP +9; Power +1	20	89
Bear-Hide Belt	Crush R. +3; Spear, Hammer S. +1; Con +3	24	89
Dread Lichess Belt	Con, Dex +6	26	89
Dwarf-Skin Belt	Matter, Body R. +6; Con +7	30	89
Poor Sod's Belt	HP +12; Power +2; Qui +4	32	89
Sigum's Belt of Warmth	Cold R. +15; Con, Str +6	32	100
Flayed Wolfskin Belt	HP +15; Qui +6; Matter R. +4	35	89
Ceremonial Belt	HP +15; Dex +9	37	89
Wolfskin Belt	HP +15; Pie +6; Matter R. +4	38	89
Band of Chitin	HP +12; Dex, Qui +6	39	89
Drakulv Defender's Belt	Con, Dex, Qui +6	39	89
Wicked Wulf Belt	Qui +7; Energy, Matter R. +6	39	89
Enslaved Orm's Collar	Spirit R. -6; Qui, Str, Dex +7	40	89
Svartalf Crafted Belt	HP +24; Matter, Body R. +4	40	89
Manoi Belt	Power +2; HP +15; Pie +4; Str +6	41	100
Belt of Mischief	Critical Strike S. +3; Dex, Con +9	45	100
Belt of Thunder	Parry S. +3; Str +9; HP +18	45	100
Fungus Covered Belt	Cave Magic S. +3; Pie +12; Dex +6	45	100
Modi's Belt of Bravery	Left Axe S. +3; Str +10; HP +15	45	100
Shadowsteel Belt	Con, Str +10	46	89
Belt of Glacial Might	Con +13; Str +10; Crush, Slash R. +6	50	93
Flame Wrought Belt	HP +45; Power +5	50	91
Furlined Hunter's Belt	HP +27; Str, Dex +6	50	90
Mystical Golden Scale Belt	Runec., Summ. S. +2; Dex +12; Pie +6	50	90
Soulbinder's Belt	HP +36; Spirit, Cold R. +10	50	91

Item	Bonus	PL	Ql
Bracelets			
Initiate's Bracelet			100
Tail of Morra	Sword S. +1; Str +1	8	100
Tomb Priestess Bracelet	Power +1; Con, Str +3	23	89
Flame-Wrought Bracelet	Heat R. +4; Str +6	31	100
Agile Defender	Parry S. +3; Slash R. +4; Str, Dex +4	36	100
Giant Green Sapphire Ring	Cha +4; Con, Str +3; HP +15	37	89
Bracelet of Defense	Parry S. +3; Body R. +8; Qui +9	39	100
Embossed Hagbui Bracelet	Power +4; Heat R. +8	40	89
Giant Yellow Tourmaline Ring	Pie, Con, Str +6	40	89
Etched Hagbui Bracelet	Pie +6; Power +4; HP +12	42	89
Giant Pink Sapphire Ring	Dex, Qui +4; Power +2; HP +9	43	89
Giant Alexandrite Ring	Pie +7; Energy, Body R. +8	46	89
Giant Black Sapphire Ring	Str, Dex +7; HP +15	50	89
Bracers			
Engraved Bracer	HP +3	4	90
Crusty Old Bracer	Dex +3	6	89
Iron Skull Bracer	Str +3	7	89
Bracer o.t. Lost Soul	Pie +3; Summoning S. +1	10	90
Bracer of Malevolence	Pie +3; Con +1	10	89
Icebound Bracer	Cold R. +2; Con +1; HP +6	10	90
Blodjeger Bracer	Left Axe S. +1; Con +3	14	89
Runed Hollow Bone Bracer	HP +6; Str +3	14	89
Skogfru Skin Bracer	Beastcraft S. +1; Qui +3	14	89
Beastfriends Bracer	Beastcraft S. +2; Con +3	16	100
Blessed Bone Bracer	Augmentation, Mending, Cave Magic S. +1	16	100
Bracer of Valor	Dex, Qui, Cha +3	16	90
Jeweled Bracer	Cha +3; Str +4	16	89
Ornate Bracer	Cha +3; Dex +4	16	89
The Healer's Defender	HP +9; Pie +4; Body, Slash R. +2	19	100
Flame Wrought Bracer	Str, Dex +3; Cold R. +4	20	89
Bracer of Pacification	Pacification S. +2; Pie +6	21	100
Bear-Hide Bracer	Thrust R. +3; Axe, Sword S. +1; Str +3	23	89
Svart-Alfar Battlebracer	Axe, Hammer S. +1; HP +15	26	90
Trollish Stone Bracer	Sword, Spear S. +1; HP +15	26	90
Troll-Skin Bracer	Str +7; Con +6	29	89
Hardened Viper Skin Bracer	Crush R. +4; Con, Str +6	34	89
Hardened Viper Skin Bracer	Slash R. +4; Dex, Qui +6	34	89
Skin-Flayer's Bracer	HP +12; Dex +6; Qui +3	35	89
Wolfskin Bracer	Energy R. +4; Con, Pie, Dex +4	35	89
Missionary's Bracer	Power +3; Dex +4; Body R. +4	36	89
Twisted Ice Bracer	Darkness, Mend. S. +4; Suppr., Augm. S. +3	36	100
Hollow Chitin	Matter, Body R. +6; Qui +7	37	89
Silksteel Lattice	Slash, Crush R. +2; Str +7; HP +12	37	89
Silksteel Lattice	Thrust, Body R. +2; Dex +7; HP +12	37	89
Svartalf Crafted Bracer	Power +2; Con +4; Pie +6	37	89
Flayed Wolfskin Bracer	Energy R. +4; Con, Str, Dex +4	38	89
Singed Hollow Chitin	Heat, Spirit R. +6; Cha +7	38	89
Darksteel Bracer	Composite Bow S. +2; Dex +7; Str +6	43	89
Twisted Darksteel Bracer	Darkness, Suppression S. +2; Pie +7	44	89
Viper Spine Wrist Wrap	HP +21; Body, Matter, Spirit R. +4	44	89
Shadowsteel Lattice	Cha, Dex +6; Qui +9	48	89
Twisted Shadowsteel Lattice	HP +21; Power +4	49	89
Ancient Ebon Bracer	HP +24; Dex +9; Cha +6	50	90
Bracer of Embodiment	Mending, Augmentation S. +2; Power +9	50	91
Dragon Etched Bracer	HP +21; Str +6; Parry, Composite Bow S. +2	50	90
Rigid Wight Claw	Cold, Matter R. +6; Con, Str +9	50	90
Skrunken Ribcage	Body, Matter R. +6; Con +13; Pie +10	50	93

Item	Bonus	PL	QI
Brooches			
Skullbone Brooch of Morra	Con +4	8	100
Willow Heart	Con +9	15	100
Cape			
Cape o.t. Mother Wolf	Qui +6; Str +3	15	100
Clasp			
Webclasp	Dex +10	18	100
Cloaks			
Black Night Cloak	Qui +9; Evade S. +1		95
Huldu Mantle of Obscurity	Dex +1	4	89
Battlesingers Cloak	Battlesongs S. +1	6	90
Windswept Cloak	Dex +3	6	89
Traveler's Cloak	Dex +6	8	100
Dwarf-Skin Cloak	Con +4	10	89
Huntsman's Cloak	Dex +3; Qui +1; HP +3	10	90
Fine Norse Cloak	Stealth S. +1; Dex +4; Qui +3	12	100
Wind Filled Cloak	Dex +3; Spirit R. +2; Pie +1	14	89
Wretched Cloak	Dex +6	14	89
Driftspirit Cloak	Spirit R. +4; Pie, Dex +3	15	100
Vannsang Cloak	Stealth S. +1; Dex +3; Heat R. +2	15	89
Cloak of Fire Resistance	Heat R. +6; Dex, Qui +3	18	100
Blod Flekket Cloak	Augmentation, Mending S. +1; Body R. +4	19	89
Molten Lava Cloak		21	89
Glimmering Mantle	Cha +7; Qui +3	24	89
Shrouded Hagbui Mantle	Con +4; Dex, Qui +3	24	89
Shrouded Hagbui Pall	Con +4; Dex, Pie +3	24	89
Haggert's Shroud of Death	Con, Dex +6	25	89
Bear-Skin Mantle	Energy, Heat R. +3; Cha +3; Qui +6	27	89
Firecloak	Heat R. +8; HP +12; Pie +4	27	100
Fur Edged Cloak	Stealth S. +2; Dex +3; Energy R. +2; Cold R. +4	28	89
Mantle o.t. Valhallan	Heat, Cold R. +4; Con, Str +6	31	100
Moonshadow Cloak	Critical Strike, Stealth S. +1; Qui +7; Dex +6	31	100
Royal Teal NPC Cool Cloak	Crit. Strk., Stealth S. +1; Qui +7; Dex +6	31	100
Grizzly Skin Cloak	Cold R. +6; Battlesongs S. +1; Str +3; Pie +6	33	89
Wild Wulf Cloak	Con +7; Str +6; Heat R. +4	35	89
Wicked Wulf Cloak	HP +15; Dex +6	36	89
Seafarer's Death Shroud	Body R. +8; Con +4	37	89
Lunatic Lupine Cloak	Dex +7; Pie +6; Heat R. +4	38	89
Herald's Furlined Cloak	Spirit, Cold R. +6; Str +9	39	89
Black Silksteel Cloak	Cold R. +8; Con, Str +6	40	89
Dispositional Cloak	Dex, Qui +12	40	100
Crab Spider Cloak	Cold R. +16; Con, Qui +6	41	100
Lynx Spider Cloak	Heat, Matter R. +8; Dex, Qui +6	41	100
Orb Weaver's Cloak	Crush, Slash R. +8; Pie, Dex +6	41	100
Scaffold Web Cloak	Cold, Heat, Body R. +8; Con +6	41	100
Cloak o.t. Bloodwolf	Stealth S. +2; Cha +3; Dex, Qui +6	45	89
Cloak o.t. Unseen Stalker	Con +9; Cha, Pie +6	45	89
Ghostly Cloak	Stealth, Battlesongs S. +4; Dex, Qui +7	46	100
Jade Moonshone Cloak	Con +6; Slash, Crush R. +4; Cold R. +12	48	89
Cloak o.t. Dragonwolf	Cha, Con, Str +7; Spirit R. +10	50	90
Ebony Flecked Shimmering Cloak	Power +6; Pie +9; Cr., Sl. R. +4	50	90
Flame Wrought Cloak	Dex +14; Heat R. +12	50	90
Frozen Tundra Walker's Mantle	Con, Str +13; Heat, Cold R. +8	50	93
Lichen Covered Seal-Skin Cloak	Str, Pie +13	50	90
Collars			
Hel's Collar	Pie +3	6	90
Collar of Wind	Power +2; Thrust R. +2	15	89
Lavastone Collar	Con +3; Body, Matter R. +4	22	89
Collar o.t. Dead	HP +15; Str, Int, Pie +4	35	100
Earrings			
Ashmonger Eye Earring	Cha +3; HP +12	20	89
Planar Earring	Con +9; HP +9	23	100

Item	Bonus	PL	QI
Eyes			
Red Crystal Eye	Pie +1	4	90
Mystical Beast Eye	Qui +4	9	89
Red Eye	Power +3	15	100
Bulbous Eye	Pie +6; Body, Matter R. +6	24	100
Glowing Black Eye	Con, Pie +6; Power +2	40	89
Crystalized Viper Eye Necklace	Body R. +8; Con +7; Pie +6	42	89
Frozen Cyclops Eye	HP +33; Comp. Bow, Enven. S. +2; Str +10	50	91
Reincarnate Orm Eye	HP +45	50	89
Gems			
Fiery Jewel	Pie +4; Power +1	13	90
Jewel of Augmentation	Augmentation S. +2; Pie +3	16	90
Ghastly Gem	HP +15; Pie *or* Str +3	22	89
Marodor Gem	Envenom S. +2; Left Axe S. +1; Str +9	39	89
Jewels & Jewelry			
Pulsing Jewel of Anger	Qui +4	10	89
Shrunken Jeweled Skull	HP +6; Qui +3	14	89
Incandescent Black Jewel	Pie, Dex +4; Qui +3	26	89
Shrunken Bear Skull	Beastcraft S. +2; Con, Str +4	32	89
Varulvhamn Gem	HP +9; Body R. +4; Pie, Str +4	35	89
Scryer's Jewel of Ice	Cold, Heat R. +6; Str +9; Pie +3	36	100
J. of Venern Swamp	Runec., Summ., Cave Magic, Pacif. S. +4	37	89
Wulf Gem	HP +9; Body R. +4; Qui, Str +4	38	89
Wicked Wulf Gem	Body, Spirit R. +6; Dex +7	39	89
Facetted Insect Eye	Stealth, Parry S. +3; Qui +9	40	89
Shadowsteel Orb	Pie +12; HP +18	47	89
Bloodbound Totem	Con, Dex, Qui +7; Cha +6	50	90
Jewel of Venom	Envenom S. +3; Dex, Qui, Str +6	50	90
Medal			
Rusty Draugr Commander Medal	Dex +3; Con, Str +4	25	89
Necklaces			
Necklace of Purification	Pie +3	7	90
Tomte Necklace of Agitation	HP +9	10	89
Berserker Strength Necklace	Str +4; HP +6	12	100
Skald's Mediallion	Battlesongs S. +1; Cha +3; Str +1	12	100
Windchimes	Spirit R. +4; Qui +4	12	100
Spiritist Amulet	Pie +6	13	90
Blood Stained Bead Necklace	Slash R. +4; Dex +3	14	89
Necklace of Solid Darkness	Darkness S. +1; Pie +6	16	90
Blodbror Necklace	Left Axe S. +2; Body R. +2	17	89
Wanestone Jewel Necklace	Str +4; Dex, Qui +3	18	100
Ghastly Chain	Dex, Pie +4	20	89
Ghostly Chain	Qui, Str +4	20	89
Dancing Flame Necklace	Dex +3; Parry S. +2; Body R. +4	21	89
Necklace of Shamanic Magic	Cave Magic S. +2; Pie +6	21	100
Jeweled Wolf Eye Necklace	Power +2; Pie +6	22	100
Bevard's Ghastly Chain	Str *or* Dex +4; Heat, Matter R. +4	24	89
Bear-Totem Necklace	Body R. +6; Con, Pie +4	25	100
Bear-Tooth Necklace	HP +9; Dex, Str +4	31	89
Scyer's Necklace	HP +15; Qui, Dex +6	32	100
Lycanthropic Necklace	Power +2; Spirit R. +4; Pie +4	35	89
Wicked Wulf Chain	Con +9; Qui, Dex +3	35	89
Luminescent Choker	Pie +6; Power +4; HP +9	38	100
Lycanthrope's Necklace	HP +18; Spirit R. +2; Str +4	38	89
Svartalf Crafted Necklace	Axe, Sword, Hammer S. +2	39	89
Twisted Silksteel Necklace	Dex, Qui, Str, Pie +4	39	89
Spider Silk Necklace	Slash R. +4; Dex +3	41	89
Breath of Winter	Cold R. +6; Power +2; Pie +9; Con +6	43	100
Arrowhead Necklace	Stealth S. +3; Dex +9; HP +18	45	100
Darksteel Necklace	Stealth, Battlesongs S. +2; Con, Str +7	45	89
Eye of Odin Necklace	Summoning S. +3; Pie +12; Dex +6	45	100
Healer's Touch Necklace	Pacification S. +3; Pie +12; Str +6	45	100

Item	Bonus	PL	QI
Necklace of Runes	Runecarving S. +3; Pie +12; Dex +6	45	100
Tyr's Hand Necklace	Shield S. +3; Str +9; HP +21	45	100
Voice of Bragi	Parry S. +3; Str +9; HP +18	45	100
Drakulv Crescent Talisman	Str, Con, Dex +7	48	89
Frozen Icespine Necklace	Power +4; Energy, Heat R. +8; Pie +12	50	90
Luminescent Diamond Necklace	Pie +12; Con +7; Cold R. +12	50	90
Necklace of Hoarfrost	HP +78	50	94
Shadowsteel Necklace	Heat, Cold R. +6; Qui +7; Con +3	50	89
Soulbound Necklace	Pacific., Cave Mg. S. +2; Pie +12; Spirit R. +10	50	91
Pendant			
Eir Blessed Pendant	Mending, Augmentation, Pacification S. +1	16	100
Pins			
Fervent Jewel	Con +7; Dex +3	18	100
Crystalized Fire Flower Pin	Heat R. +4; Matter R. +2; Power +2	21	89
Crystalized Musical Note	Battlesongs S. +3; Con +10; Str +9	47	100
Crystalized Snowflake Pin	Composite Bow S. +3; Dex +10; Str +9	47	100
Dancing Flame	Stealth S. +3; Dex +10; Str +9	47	100
Hand-Shaped Pin	Parry S. +3; Dex +9; Str +10	47	100
Healing Hand Pin	Mending, Augmentation S. +2; Con +7; Pie +9	47	100
Lightning Bolt Pin	Stormcalling S. +3; Con +10; Str +9	47	100
Rune Carved Pin	Darkness, Suppression S. +2; Con +7; Pie +9	47	100
Twin Ravens Pin	Darkness, Suppression S. +2; Con +7; Pie +9	47	100
World Engraved Pin	Mending, Augmentation S. +2; Con +7; Pie +9	47	100
Rings			
Ring of Redhands	HP +3; Qui +1	4	89
Wooden Band	Pie +1	4	90
Boneclaw Ring of Morra	Pie +7	5	100
Dead Master's Signet Ring	Con +3	7	89
Dwarven Glima Ring	Dex +4	7	100
Ring o.t. Quickening	Qui +3	7	90
Ring of Surefooting	Dex +3	7	90
Ring of Health	Con, Pie +3	8	100
Ring o.t. Stealthy	Stealth S. +1; Dex +3	8	100
Ring of Hatred	Str +3; Dex +1	10	89
Ring of Wisdom	Pie +6	10	100
Decayed Bone Ring	Str +4	12	89
Fimx	Dex +7	12	100
Pious Ring	Pie +4; Power +1	12	100
Vendo Bone Ring	Str +3	12	80
Carved Hollow Bone Ring	Pie, Con +3	14	89
Soothsayer's Ring	Critical Strike, Envenom S. +1	14	89
Watery Ring	Power +2; HP +3	14	89
Ring o.t. Stalwart Soul	Con +6; Body R. +4	16	90
Song-Spun Ring	Str, Qui +4	16	100
Watercast Ring	Matter, Cold R. +4; Con +4	17	100
Ring of Illbane	Body R. +4; Mending S. +1; Pie +4	18	100
Blodstein Ring	Power +2; Cave Magic S. +9	19	89
Boar's Head Ring	Con +6; HP +9	21	90
Kobold Bone Ring	Sl. R. +3; Critical Strike, Stealth S. +1; Dex +3	22	89
Lavastone Ring	Parry, Axe S. +1; Body R. +2; Str +3	23	89
Baneful Mora Ring	Dex, Con +3; Pie +4	24	89
Cursed Mora Ring	Dex, Con +3; Str +4	24	89
Troika's Enchanted Ring	Dex +3; Con +4; Body, Cold R. +2	24	89
Lightbound Ring	Con, Str, Pie +4	26	90
Shadowformed Ring	Pie +7; Power +2	26	90
Flamecast Ring	Cold R. +6; Power +4	27	100
Bear-Shaman's Ring	Power +2; Pie +6	28	89
Ring of Fire	Hammer, Axe, Sword S. +1; Cold R. +6	29	89
Ring of Possession	Spirit, Body R. +6; Pie +9; Con +3	29	100
Mistring	Power +2; Str, Con +6	31	100
Ancient Bear Shaped Ring	Darkness, Suppr. S. +1; Con +4; Pie +4	34	89
Carved Bone Ring	Dex +7; Qui +6; Cold R. +4	35	89
Coldfoot's Wretched Ring	Dex, Qui, Con +6; Slash R. +6	35	100
Retainer's Ceremonial Ring	Darkness, Suppression S. +2; Pie +4	37	89
Retainers Signet Ring	Augmentation, Pacification S. +2; Pie +4	37	89
Horned Silksteel Ring	Power +3; Con *or* Pie +7	38	89
Svartalf Crafted Ring	Slash R. +4; HP +12; Str +7	38	89
Werewolf Bone Ring	Dex +7; Pie +6; Cold R. +4	38	89
Serpent Bone Ring	Power +4; Pie +6	40	89
Darksteel Ring	Energy, Heat, Cold R. +4; HP +18	41	89
Drakulv Mightcaller	HP +15; Str +12	42	89
Twisted Darksteel Ring	Critical Strike S. +2; Dex +7; Qui +6	42	89
Ring of Spun Silk	HP +21; Crush, Matter R. +10; Con +3	48	100
Ancient Ebon Ring	Con, Str, Qui +7; Cha +6	50	90
Band of Ice	Cold, Heat, Spirit R. +6; Con +13	50	90
Flame Wrought Ring	Heat, Spirit R. +8; Dex, Qui +9	50	90
Ring of Glacial Might	Str, Con +10; Cold, Body R. +6	50	90
Ring of Hoarfrost	Cha, Con, Pie, Str +9	50	93
Ring o.t. Mindwall	Spirit R. +12; Power +4; Pie +7; Cha +6	50	91
Sash			
Fine Sash	Power +3; Con, Qui +4	30	100
Shackles			
Cursed Spirit Shackle	Qui, Con, Str +3	20	89
Trapped Spirit Shackle	Power +2	20	89

Miscellaneous Drops & Rewards

Item	Bonus	PL	QI
Hide: Black Orm Hide			80
Stone: Ymir's Stone	Con +3	6	90
Paw: Paw of Morra	Con +4	8	100
Stone: Stone o.t. Pious	Pie +7; Con +3	17	100
Figurine: Small Warrior Figurine	Str +4; Dex, Qui +3	21	90
Stone: Stone of Coldfire	Cold R. +6; Dex, Qui +6	27	100
Stone: Nimh's Curse	Pie -10; Cold, Energy R. +6; Dex +7	27	100
Scroll: Elder Runed Scroll	Heat, Cold, Matter R. +2; Pie +9	40	89
Wrap: Enslvd. Biter's Muz. Wrap	Cha, Qui +7; Sl. R. +4; Thr. R. +2	44	89
Book: Icebound Spellbook	Power +4; Dex, Pie +10	50	90
Book: Bloodbound Book	Pie +13; Body, Spirit, Cold R. +6	50	90
Vial: Glowing Vial of Swamp Water	Power +5; Pie +7	50	89
Vial: Vial of Brackish Water	HP +30; Power +5	50	89
Vial: Vial of Fetid Bog Water	Body R. +18; HP +21	50	89

Crafting Recipes

For a more detailed description of these stats, see **Crafting**, page 364. For **Arrow** crafting, see page 363. For **Siege Equipment** crafting, see page 324. For miscellaneous craftable items, see page 362.

Abbreviations

Time. Time to craft the item at 1st and 10th Material Levels.

Skills. **A**rmorcraft / **C**lothworking / **F**letching / **L**eatherworking / **M**etalworking / **T**ailoring / **Wd** = Woodworking / **Wp** = Weaponcraft.

Tools. F = Forge / **H** = Smith's Hammer / **K** = Sewing Kit / **L** = Lathe / **P** = Planing Tool.

Components. b = Metal Bars / **c** = Cloth squares / **l** = Leather / **t** = Thread / **w** = Wooden boards.

Costs. Costs are listed in Silver and Copper for Material Level 1. They're listed in Gold and Silver for Material Levels 5 and 10, rounded to the nearest Silver.

Crafting Armor & Clothing

Item	Time (sec.)	Skills	Tools	Components	1st (S.C)	5th (G.S)	10th (G.S)
Cloth (+ Secondary: C (all but vest), L (gloves, cap, boots) at (-15))							
Padded Vest	7-75	T95	K	40c,10t	1.22	7.06	71.44
Pants	5-72	T65+	K	25c,5t	0.73	4.25	43.01
Sleeves	6-74	T80+	K	16c,4t	0.49	2.82	28.58
Gloves	1-69	T15+	K	4c,3t,2l	0.24	1.40	14.14
Cap	2-70	T30+	K	16c,5t,6l	0.73	4.25	43.01
Boots	3-71	T45+	K	2c,2t,4l	0.24	1.41	14.29
Leather (+ Secondary: L, C at (-15))							
Mjuklaedar Jerkin	7-75	T95+	K	20l,3t	0.81	4.71	47.68
Leggings	5-72	T65+	K	12l,2t	0.49	2.85	28.87
Sleeves	6-74	T80+	K	8l,1t	0.32	1.86	18.81
Boots	3-71	T45+	K	3l,2t	0.15	0.91	9.19
Gloves	1-69	T15+	K	3l,2t	0.15	0.91	9.19
Cap	2-70	T30+	K	12l,2t	0.49	2.85	28.87
Svarlaedar Jerkin	9-76	T115+	K	29l,3t	1.15	6.65	67.36
Leggings	6-74	T85+	K	17l,2t	0.68	3.93	39.80
Sleeves	8-75	T100+	K	11l,2t	0.45	2.64	26.68
Boots	5-72	T65+	K	5l,2t	0.23	1.34	13.56
Gloves	3-70	T35+	K	5l,2t	0.23	1.34	13.56
Cap	4-71	T50+	K	17l,2t	0.68	3.93	39.80
Starklaedar Jerkin	13-81	T175+	K	56l,8t	2.28	13.13	132.97
Leggings	11-78	T145+	K	34l,4t	1.36	7.86	79.61
Sleeves	12-79	T160+	K	22l,4t	0.91	5.27	53.36
Boots	9-77	T125+	K	10l,4t	0.46	2.68	27.12
Gloves	7-75	T95+	K	10l,4t	0.46	2.68	27.12
Cap	8-76	T110+	K	34l,4t	1.36	7.86	79.61

Item	Time (sec.)	Skills	Tools	Components	1st (S.C)	5th (G.S)	10th (G.S)
Studded Leather (+ Secondary: L, C, M (-15)) (st = studs)							
Stelskodd Jerkin	7-75	A95+	S,H,F	19l,4t,5st	9.55	55.02	557.10
Leggings	5-72	A65+	S,H,F	12l,2t,3st	5.74	33.09	335.05
Sleeves	6-74	A80+	S,H,F	8l,1t,2st	3.82	22.02	222.93
Boots	3-71	A45+	S,H,F	2l,4t,1st	1.91	11.03	111.68
Gloves	1-69	A15+	S,H,F	2l,4t,1st	1.91	11.03	111.68
Helm	2-70	A30+	S,H,F	12l,2t,3st	5.74	33.09	335.05
Svarskodd Jerkin	9-76	A115+	S,H,F	25l,5t,8st	15.05	86.69	877.72
Leggings	6-74	A85+	S,H,F	12l,7t,5st	9.35	53.90	545.73
Sleeves	8-75	A100+	S,H,F	8l,2t,4st	7.34	42.31	428.36
Boots	5-72	A65+	S,H,F	4l,5t,1st	2.01	11.59	117.37
Gloves	3-70	A35+	S,H,F	4l,5t,1st	2.01	11.59	117.37
Helm	4-71	A50+	S,H,F	12l,7t,5st	9.35	53.90	545.73
Starkaskodd Jerkin	12-79	A155+	S,H,F	50l,10t,16st	30.10	173.38	1755.43
Leggings	9-77	A125+	S,H,F	24l,14t,10st	18.71	107.80	1091.46
Sleeves	11-78	A140+	S,H,F	16l,4t,8st	14.69	84.61	856.72
Boots	8-75	A105+	S,H,F	8l,10t,2st	4.02	23.18	234.74
Gloves	6-73	A75+	S,H,F	8l,10t,2st	4.02	23.18	234.74
Helm	7-74	A90+	S,H,F	24l,14t,10st	18.71	107.80	1091.46
Chain (+ Secondary: M, L (-15)) (wr = wire, mj., sv., st. = matching piece of mjuklaedar, svarlaedar, starklaedar armor)							
Pansarkedja Hauberk	7-74	A95+	H,F	15 wr,mj.	27.06	155.91	1578.58
Leggings	5-72	A65+	H,F	9 wr,mj.	16.24	93.57	947.41
Sleeves	6-74	A80+	H,F	6 wr,mj.	10.82	62.34	631.17
Boots	3-71	A45+	H,F	3 wr,mj.	5.40	31.15	315.37
Gloves	1-69	A15+	H,F	3 wr,mj.	5.40	31.15	315.37
Helm	2-70	A30+	H,F	9 wr,mj.	16.24	93.57	947.41
Svarkedja Hauberk	10-78	A135+	H,F	29 wr,sv.	51.90	298.97	3027.10
Leggings	8-75	A105+	H,F	18 wr,sv.	32.18	185.37	1876.88
Sleeves	9-77	A120+	H,F	12 wr,sv.	21.45	123.60	1251.40
Boots	6-74	A85+	H,F	6 wr,sv.	10.73	61.82	625.92
Gloves	4-72	A55+	H,F	6 wr,sv.	10.73	61.82	625.92
Helm	5-73	A70+	H,F	17 wr,sv.	30.43	175.29	1774.82
Starkakedja Hauberk	13-81	A175+	H,F	46 wr,st.	82.78	476.81	4827.73
Leggings	11-78	A145+	H,F	27 wr,st.	48.61	280.02	2835.23
Sleeves	12-80	A160+	H,F	18 wr,st.	32.41	186.71	1890.44
Boots	9-77	A125+	H,F	9 wr,st.	16.21	93.40	945.66
Gloves	7-75	A95+	H,F	9 wr,st.	16.21	93.40	945.66
Helm	8-76	A110+	H,F	27 wr,st.	48.61	280.02	2835.23

Crafting Weapons

+ Unless otherwise noted, completing a finished weapon also requires the skills necessary to craft its two component parts, minus 15. For example, when crafting a dagger at Material Level 2, your primary skill requirement is Weaponcraft 115, but you also must have Leatherworking and Metalworking at 100 (since the blade and hilt require those skills at 115).

(5+) None of the weapons that begin at Material Level 5 will ever be part of a consignment order.

One Handed Sword

Item	Time (sec.)	Skills	Tools	Components	1st (S.C)	5th (G.S)	10th (G.S)
Dagger	1-55	Wp15+	F,H	hilt,blade	0.98	5.69	57.59
Blade	1-14	M15	F,H	9b	0.78	4.54	45.93
Hilt	1-14	L15	F,H	1b,1w,2l	0.20	1.15	11.66
Short Sword	2-56	Wp35+	F,H	hilt,blade	1.30	7.49	75.82
Blade	1-14	M35	F,H	13b	1.13	6.55	66.34
Hilt	1-14	L35	F,H	1b,1w,1l	0.16	0.94	9.48
Broadsword	3-57	Wp55+	F,H	hilt,blade	1.91	11.02	111.54
Blade	1-14	M55	F,H	19b	1.66	9.58	96.96
Hilt	1-14	L55	F,H	2b,1w,1l	0.25	1.44	14.58
Long Sword	5-59	Wp75+	F,H	hilt,blade	2.52	14.54	147.26
Blade	1-15	M75	F,H	26b	2.27	13.10	132.68
Hilt	1-15	L75	F,H	2b,1w,1l	0.25	1.44	14.58
Bastard Sword	6-60	Wp95+	F,H	hilt,blade	3.05	17.57	177.88
Blade	1-15	M95	F,H	32b	2.80	16.13	163.30
Hilt	1-15	L95	F,H	2b,1w,1l	0.25	1.44	14.58
Dwarv. Sht. Sw. (5+)	31-61	Wp515+	F,H	hilt,blade	–	21.10	213.60
Blade	8-15	M515	F,H	39b	–	19.66	199.02
Hilt	8-15	L515	F,H	2b,1w,1l	0.25	1.44	14.58

Two Handed Sword

Item	Time (sec.)	Skills	Tools	Components	1st (S.C)	5th (G.S)	10th (G.S)
Two Handed Sword	7-61	Wp115+	F,H	hilt,blade	2.87	16.56	167.67
Blade	2-15	M115	F,H	30b	2.62	15.12	153.09
Hilt	2-15	L115	F,H	2b,1w,1l	0.25	1.44	14.58
Great Sword	8-62	Wp135+	F,H	hilt,blade	3.40	19.58	198.29
Blade	2-16	M135	F,H	36b	3.15	18.14	183.71
Hilt	2-16	L135	F,H	2b,1w,1l	0.25	1.44	14.58
Dwrv. Grt. Sw. (5+)	32-62	Wp535+	F,H	hilt,blade	–	24.12	244.22
Blade	8-16	M535	F,H	45b	–	22.68	229.64
Hilt	8-16	L535	F,H	2b,1w,1l	0.25	1.44	14.58

One Handed Axe

Item	Time (sec.)	Skills	Tools	Components	1st (S.C)	5th (G.S)	10th (G.S)
Hand Axe	1-55	Wp15+	F,H	haft,head	0.98	5.69	57.59
Haft	1-14	Wd15	F,H,P	1b,3w	0.20	1.15	11.66
Head	1-14	M15	F,H	9b	0.78	4.54	45.93
Bearded Axe	2-56	Wp35+	F,H	haft,head	1.51	8.71	88.21
Haft	1-14	Wd35	F,H,P	2b,3w	0.28	1.66	16.77
Head	1-14	M35	F,H	14b	1.22	7.06	71.44
War Axe	3-57	Wp55+	F,H	haft,head	1.98	11.45	115.91
Haft	1-14	Wd55	F,H,P	2b,4w	0.32	1.87	18.95
Head	1-14	M55	F,H	19b	1.66	9.58	96.96
Spiked Axe	5-59	Wp75+	F,H	haft,head	2.50	14.40	145.80
Haft	1-15	Wd75	F,H,P	2b,6w	0.40	2.30	23.33
Head	1-15	M75	F,H	24b	2.10	12.10	122.47
Double Bladed Axe	6-60	Wp95+	F,H	haft,head	3.02	17.42	176.42
Haft	1-15	Wd95	F,H,P	2b,6w	0.40	2.30	23.33
Head	1-15	M95	F,H	30b	2.62	15.12	153.09
Cleaver (5+)	31-61	Wp515+	F,H	haft,head	–	20.74	209.95
Haft	8-15	Wd515	F,H,P	2b,12w	–	3.60	36.45
Head	8-15	M515	F,H	34b	–	17.14	173.50

Two Handed Axe

Item	Time (sec.)	Skills	Tools	Components	1st (S.C)	5th (G.S)	10th (G.S)
Large Axe	7-61	Wp115+	F,H	haft,head	3.02	17.42	176.42
Haft	2-15	Wd115	F,H,P	2b,6w	0.40	2.30	23.33
Head	2-15	M115	F,H	30b	2.62	15.12	153.09
Great Axe	8-62	Wp135+	F,H	haft,head	3.46	19.94	201.93
Haft	2-16	Wd135	F,H,P	2b,6w	0.40	2.30	23.33
Head	2-16	M135	F,H	35b	3.06	17.64	178.61
War Cleaver (5+)	31-61	Wp535+	F,H	haft,head	–	24.77	250.78
Haft	8-15	Wd515	F,H,P	2b,12w	–	3.60	36.45
Head	8-15	M535	F,H	42b	–	21.17	214.33

Hammer

Item	Time (sec.)	Skills	Tools	Components	1st (S.C)	5th (G.S)	10th (G.S)
Small Hammer	1-55	Wp15+	F,H	haft,head	0.98	5.69	57.59
Haft	1-14	Wd15	F,H,P	1b,3w	0.20	1.15	11.66
Head	1-14	M15	F,H	9b	0.78	4.54	45.93
Hammer	2-56	Wp35+	F,H	haft,head	1.55	8.93	90.40
Haft	1-14	Wd35	F,H,P	1b,4w	0.23	1.37	13.85
Head	1-14	M35	F,H	15b	1.31	7.56	76.55
War Hammer	3-57	Wp55+	F,H	haft,head	1.98	11.45	115.91
Haft	1-14	Wd55	F,H,P	2b,4w	0.32	1.87	18.95
Head	1-14	M55	F,H	19b	1.66	9.58	96.96
Pick Hammer	5-59	Wp75+	F,H	haft,head	2.68	15.48	156.74
Haft	1-15	Wd75	F,H,P	2b,4w	0.32	1.87	18.95
Head	1-15	M75	F,H	27b	2.36	13.61	137.78
Battle Hammer	6-60	Wp95+	F,H	haft,head	3.33	19.22	194.64
Haft	1-15	Wd95	F,H,P	2b,5w	0.36	2.09	21.14
Head	1-15	M95	F,H	34b	2.97	17.14	173.50
Spiked Ham. (5+)	31-61	Wp515+	F,H	haft,head	–	21.24	215.06
Haft	8-15	Wd515	F,H,P	2b,12w	–	3.60	36.45
Head	8-15	M515	F,H	35b	–	17.64	178.61

Two Handed Hammer

Item	Time (sec.)	Skills	Tools	Components	1st (S.C)	5th (G.S)	10th (G.S)
Two H. War Ham.	7-61	Wp115+	F,H	haft,head	2.86	16.49	166.94
Haft	2-15	Wd115	F,H,P	2b,4w	0.32	1.87	18.95
Head	2-15	M115	F,H	29b	2.53	14.62	147.99
Great Hammer	8-62	Wp135+	F,H	haft,head	3.33	19.22	194.64
Haft	2-16	Wd135	F,H,P	2b,5w	0.36	2.09	21.14
Head	2-16	M135	F,H	34b	2.97	17.14	173.50
Grt. Spkd. Ham. (5+)	32-62	Wp535+	F,H	haft,head	–	22.75	230.36
Haft	8-16	Wd535	F,H,P	2b,12w	–	3.60	36.45
Head	8-16	M535	F,H	38b	–	19.15	193.91

Spear

Item	Time (sec.)	Skills	Tools	Components	1st (S.C)	5th (G.S)	10th (G.S)
Spear	1-55	Wp15+	F,H	shaft,head	1.32	7.63	77.27
Shaft	1-14	Wd15	F,H,P	1b,12w	0.53	3.10	31.35
Spearhead	1-14	M15	F,H	9b	0.78	4.54	45.93
Long Spear	2-56	Wp35+	F,H	shaft,head	1.67	9.65	97.69
Shaft	1-14	Wd35	F,H,P	2b,12w	0.62	3.60	36.45
Spearhead	1-14	M35	F,H	12b	1.05	6.05	61.24
Trident	3-57	Wp55+	F,H	shaft,head	1.93	11.16	113.00
Head	1-14	M55	F,H	15b	1.31	7.56	76.55
Shaft	1-14	Wd55	F,H,P	2b,12w	0.62	3.60	36.45
Lugged Spear	5-59	Wp75+	F,H	shaft,head	2.63	15.19	153.82
Shaft	1-15	Wd75	F,H,P	2b,12w	0.62	3.60	36.45
Spearhead	1-15	M75	F,H	23b	2.01	11.59	117.37
Great Spear	6-60	Wp95+	F,H	shaft,head	3.42	19.73	199.75
Shaft	1-15	Wd95	F,H,P	2b,12w	0.62	3.60	36.45
Spearhead	1-15	M95	F,H	32b	2.80	16.13	163.30
Battle Spear (5+)	31-61	Wp515+	F,H	shaft,head	–	24.26	245.67
Head	8-15	M515	F,H	41b	–	20.66	209.22
Shaft	8-15	Wd515	F,H,P	2b,12w	–	3.60	36.45

Staff (+ Secondary: M, Wd, L, all at 0)

Item	Time (sec.)	Skills	Tools	Components	1st (S.C)	5th (G.S)	10th (G.S)
Staff	2-56	F40+	L,H,P	4b,25w,1l	1.32	7.63	77.27
Shod Staff	5-59	F80+	L,H,P	4b,38w,1l	1.81	10.44	105.71

Thrown Weapon

Item	Time (sec.)	Skills	Tools	Components	1st (S.C)	5th (G.S)	10th (G.S)
Throwing Axe	3-57	F55	F,H,P	1b,1w,1l	.16	.94	9.48
Throwing Hammer	3-57	F55	F,H,P	1b,1w,1l	.16	.94	9.48
Throwing Knife	3-57	F55	F,H,P	1b,1w,1l	.16	.94	9.48

Composite Bow (+ Secondary: Wd, C, both at 30 below Primary)

Item	Time (sec.)	Skills	Tools	Components	1st (S.C)	5th (G.S)	10th (G.S)
Composite Bow	1-55	F15+	P,L	24w,4t	0.99	5.70	57.74
Great Comp. Bow	4-58	F65+	P,L	32w,6t	1.33	7.69	77.86

Monsters

For more complete descriptions of what these stats describe, and a chart of which type of attack works best against each body type, see **Monster Stats**, p. 373.

Abbreviations

Speed. Slow, Medium, Fast, **2x**, **3x**, **4x** (two, three and four times faster than the average PC).

Aggr. (Aggression). Low, Medium, High (with percent chance that it will attack).

Attack Type. Crush, Slash, Thrust. Information after a slash ("/") is type and percent chance of secondary attack.

Combat Modifier. Monster's modifier to hit / modifier to avoid being hit (defense) / modifier to hit points. When there is just one number, it modifies all three situations.

Social. Social monsters might group; **Call** means it is Social and might call for help.

Body Type. The body types are:

BU	Bony Undead	**EW**	Elemental Water	**Pl**	Plate
Ch	Chain	**FM**	Feeble-Minded	**Rp**	Reptile (Scaled)
Cl	Cloth	**FU**	Fleshy Undead	**Sh**	Shell (Chitin)
DV	Darkness/Void	**FA**	Furry Animal	**Soft**	Soft
EA	Elemental Air	**IU**	Incorporeal Undead	**St**	Studded Leather
EE	Elemental Earth	**Lr**	Leather	**TP**	Tree/Plant
EF	Elemental Fire	**LE**	Light Energy	**Tr**	Troll-like
EI	Elemental Ice	**ME**	Magical Energy		

Monster	Lvl	Body Type	Spd	Agg	Atk Spd	Atk Type	Ev %	Comb Mod	Soc. Call
Animal									
Albino Cave Mauler	25	FA	M/192	H/70	3.7	S	–	–	–
Battle-Scar. Mauler	34-35	FA	M/200	M/40	3.6	C/C6	–	–	–
Black Mauler	12-14	FA	F/225	L/10	3.6	C/C5	–	–	–
Black Mauler Cub	0	FA	S/160	–	4.1	C	–	–	–
Black Mauler Juvenile	5	FA	M/180	–	3.7	C	–	–	–
Blodfelag Warhound	10	FA	M/200	H/85	3.3	T	1	–	Soc.
Blood Rat	19-21	FA	M/188	L/5	3.6	T	–	–	–
Bloodthirsty She-Wolf	12	FA	M/210	L/20	3.3	T	2	–	Soc.
Brush Cat	25-27	FA	M/188	M/30	3.6	T	2	–	–
Callow Wolverine	30-31	FA	M/178	H/80	3.3	S/S6	–	–	Call
Cave Bear	20-23	FA	M/192	H/70	3.8	S	–	–	–
Cave Mauler	20-22	FA	M/192	H/70	3.7	S	–	–	–
Coastal Wolf	3	FA	M/190	–	3.8	T	–	–	–
Dark Hound	17-18	FA	M/215	H/90	3.3	T	2	–	–
Dire Wolverine	58	FA	M/195	H/80	2.1	S/S4	–	–	–
Draugr Hound	22-24	FA	M/188	L/15	3.8	T	–	–	Soc.
Elder Sveawolf	13	FA	M/210	–	3.3	S	2	–	–
Enhorning	48-51	FA	F/230	L/1	4.0	C/T1	–	–	Soc.
Fell Cat	45	FA	M/200	M/50	3.8	S	–	–	–
Fire Toad	27	Rp	M/188	–	3.8	C	–	-20	–
Firecat	24	Rp	F/220	H/80	3.5	S/S2	2	–	–
Frost Bound Bear	47-50	FA	M/200	H/80	3.8	C	–	–	–
Frost Hound	30-31	FA	M/205	L/5	3.7	T	–	–	–
Frost Stallion	54-55	FA	F/230	L/25	4.0	C	–	–	Soc.
Frosty Colt	20	FA	F/230	–	4.0	C	–	–	Soc.
Frothing Sveawolf	19	FA	M/210	H/99	3.2	T	–	–	Soc.
Fylgja	50-52	IU	F/230	–	3.5	S/S3	–	–	–
Giant Bull Frog	1	Soft	M/175	–	3.8	T	–	–	–
Giant Tree Frog	20-21	Soft	M/175	–	3.8	C	–	–	–
Glacial Mauler	44-45	FA	M/200	H/80	3.8	C	–	–	–
Grass Cat	11-12	FA	F/230	–	3.5	S/S1	3	–	–
Gray Worg	10	FA	M/210	M/50	3.6	T/S5	3	–	Soc.
Great Lynx	39-42	FA	M/210	–	3.5	S/S3	–	–	–
Grizzled Sveawolf	13	FA	M/210	M/50	3.3	T	2	–	Soc.
Hallaratta	36-38	FA	M/195	L/10	3.8	T	–	–	–
Hill Cat	10	FA	M/200	L/20	3.7	S	2	–	–
Icebreaker	48	Rp	M/177	–	3.9	C	–	-/-/50	–
Icemuncher	28	Rp	M/177	–	3.9	C	–	–	–
Kopparorm	49	Rp	M/183	–	3.8	T	–	–	–
Large Sveawolf	11	FA	M/210	M/50	3.3	T	2	–	Soc.
Lupine Gnawer	0	FA	M/200	–	3.8	T	–	–	–
Lupine Snarler	2	FA	M/200	–	3.8	T	–	–	–
Mad Rat	20-22	FA	M/188	L/13	3.8	T	–	–	–
Mud Frog	30-36	Soft	M/192	–	3.5	C	–	–	–
Myrkcat	3	FA	M/180	–	3.7	S	–	–	–
Nocuous Hound	29	Rp	F/225	H/80	3.3	T	3	-20	–
Noxious Hound	24	Rp	M/210	H/80	3.5	T	1	-20/-20/-	Soc.
Rabid Sveawolf	18	FA	M/210	H/99	3.2	T	–	–	–
Rabid Wolfhound	11	FA	M/200	H/99	3.7	T/S5	–	-/15/-10	–
Ribbon Toad	12-13	Soft	M/170	–	3.8	C	–	–	–
Ridgeback Worg	11-13	FA	M/210	H/70	3.6	T/S5	3	–	Soc.
Rugged Dwarven Pony	4	FA	M/210	–	3.8	C	–	–	–
Savage Lynx	15-16	FA	M/210	H/99	3.0	S/S5	7	–	–
Savage Winterwolf	51-55	FA	F/225	L/1	3.4	T	–	–	Soc.
Scaled Retriever	50	FA-Rp	2x/350	M/50	2.0	S	8	20/-/-	–
Scaled Varg Snarler	34-36	FA-Rp	F/224	H/80	3.8	C	–	–	–
Scaled Varg Yearling	25-31	FA-Rp	F/220	H/80	3.3	T/T1	1	–	–
Scavenger	1	FA	S/150	–	3.8	T	–	–	–
Sharpfang Worg	12-14	FA	M/210	H/90	3.5	T/S5	3	–	Soc.
Sleigh Horse	30	FA	F/270	–	4.0	C	–	–	–
Sleipneirsson	55-56	FA	F/230	–	4.0	C	–	–	–
Small Cave Mauler	18-19	FA	M/192	H/70	3.8	S	–	–	–
Small Hill Cat	7	FA	M/210	H/70	3.0	S/S3	10	–	–
Smiera-Gatto	4	FA	F/220	L/1	3.8	S	2	–	–
Sveawolf	3	FA	M/200	–	3.8	T	–	–	Soc.
Sveawolf Cub	0	FA	S/140	–	3.8	T	–	–	Soc.
Sveawolf Mother	5	FA	M/200	–	3.8	T	–	–	Soc.
Sveawolf Packleader	14	FA	M/210	M/50	3.3	T	2	–	Soc.
Taiga Cat	32-33	FA	M/200	–	3.6	S/S3	–	–	–
Tawny Lynx	8	FA	M/205	L/5	3.6	S/S1	5	–	–

Monster	Lvl	Body Type	Spd	Agg	Atk Spd	Atk Type	Ev %	Comb Mod	Soc. Call
Tawny Lynx Cub	0	FA	F/220	–	3.8	S	1	–	–
Timber Cat	36-37	FA	M/201	–	3.5	S/S9	3	–	–
Timberland Badger	32-33	FA	M/180	L/10	3.7	S/T3	–	–	–
Tomte Warhound	9	FA	M/200	H/85	3.3	T	1	–	Soc.
Torpor Worm	37	Rp	M/177	L/2	3.9	C	–	-20	–
Wee Wolf	5	FA	M/200	L/10	3.5	T	1	–	–
White Wolf	27-31	FA	M/215	–	3.6	T	–	–	Soc.
Wild Hog	2	FA	M/188	–	3.8	S	–	–	–
Winter Wolf	42-46	FA	F/225	L/1	3.4	T	–	–	Soc.
Wolf Nipper	0	FA	S/150	–	3.8	T	–	–	–
Wolfhound	6	FA	M/205	L/10	3.8	T	2	–	Soc.
Wolverine	39-40	FA	M/190	H/90	3.0	S/S2	2	–	Soc.
Wood Rat	24-25	FA	M/188	M/30	3.7	T	2	–	–
Woodland Badger	22-23	FA	M/175	L/1	3.7	S/T2	–	–	–
Wounded Sveawolf	11	FA	M/210	–	3.3	S	2	–	–
Young Lynx	2	FA	F/220	–	3.8	S	1	–	–
Young Sveawolf	1	FA	S/160	–	3.8	T	–	–	Soc.
Young Wolverine	28-29	FA	M/170	H/70	3.3	S/S4	–	–	Call

Demon

Monster	Lvl	Body Type	Spd	Agg	Atk Spd	Atk Type	Ev %	Comb Mod	Soc. Call
Flaming Raukomaz	30	EF	M/200	H/80	3.1	S/S5	6	-20	Call
Nip Mephit	23-25	EI	M/188	L/1	3.8	S	–	-10	–
Pine Imp	6	TP	M/190	M/50	3.6	C/T2	1	-20	–
Pine Mephit	23	TP	M/188	M/50	3.6	C/T5	5	-10	–
Snow Imp	20-22	EI	M/188	L/1	3.8	S	–	-/-5/-5	–
Wood Imp	5	TP	M/190	M/50	3.6	C/T5	1	-20	–
Wood Mephit	22	TP	M/188	M/50	3.6	C/T5	5	-10	–

Dragon

Monster	Lvl	Body Type	Spd	Agg	Atk Spd	Atk Type	Ev %	Comb Mod	Soc. Call
Cinder Drake	28	Rp	F/220	–	3.2	S/S1	2	-20	–
Envy Drakeling	9	Rp	F/240	M/50	3.6	T/S2	–	-30	Call
Mature Wyvern	54-57	Rp	M/188	L/5	3.3	T	–	-10/-10/-	Soc.
Savage Wyvern	45-48	Rp	M/188	H/90	3.1	T	–	-10/-10/-	Soc.
Silverscale Drakeling	9	Rp	F/240	–	3.6	T	12	-30	Call
Spawn Of Gjalpinulva	37	FA-Rp	F/275	H/100	3.0	T/S4	–	-/30/-	Soc.
Wyvern	36-39	Rp	M/188	L/15	3.5	T	–	-10/-10/-	Soc.
Young Envy Drake	20-22	Rp	F/240	H/90	3.6	T/S5	5	-10	Soc.
Yg. Silverscale Drake	22	Rp	F/240	–	3.7	T	12	-5	Call
Young Wyvern	28-30	Rp	M/188	L/2	3.6	T	–	-10	Soc.

Elemental

Monster	Lvl	Body Type	Spd	Agg	Atk Spd	Atk Type	Ev %	Comb Mod	Soc. Call
Biting Wind	29-33	EA	M/188	L/20	3.2	S/S1	–	-10	–
Block Of Ice	36-37	EI	M/188	–	4.3	C	–	–	–
Crusher	48-50	EE	M/175	L/1	4.0	C	–	–	–
Dryad Blossom	20	CI	M/188	M/50	3.8	T	–	-10	Call
Dryad Greenthumb	21	CI	M/188	M/50	3.8	T	–	-10	Call
Dryad Sprig	4	Soft	M/188	–	3.8	T	–	-10	Call
Dryad Sprout	3	Soft	M/188	–	3.8	T	–	-10	Call
Flame Spout	25	EF	M/188	H/80	3.7	S	–	-20	–
Flame Thrower	21-23	EF	M/188	M/30	3.8	S	–	-20	Soc.
Flurry	23	EA	M/188	L/20	3.3	S	–	-5	–
Gelid Mass	35	EI	M/188	–	4.1	C	–	–	–
Hailer	28	EI	M/188	M/50	3.8	C	–	–	Soc.
Hailstone	20	EI	M/188	–	3.0	C	–	-20/50/-	Soc.
Host Of The Earth	6	EE	F/220	–	4.3	C/C5	–	-10/-10/-	Soc.
Host Of The Wind	7	EA	F/220	–	3.5	S	4	-10	Soc.
Iceberg	41-42	EI	M/188	–	3.9	C	–	–	–
Lava Monster	28	EF	M/188	H/80	4.0	C	–	-20	–
Maghemoth	30	EF	M/188	H/80	4.2	C	–	-5	–
Nacken	8	EI	M/188	H/80	3.8	S	–	-10	–
Ra Of Oak	30	CI	M/188	L/20	3.8	T	–	–	Soc.
Ra Of Pine	29	CI	M/188	L/20	3.8	T	–	–	Soc.
Ra Of Willow	31	CI	M/188	L/20	3.8	T	–	–	Soc.
Shard Golem	42	EI	M/188	L/5	3.8	C	–	-3	–
Sidhe Gaoite	35-36	EA	M/188	–	3.8	C	–	-10	Soc.
Tree Spirit	27	TP	M/188	–	3.8	C	–	-10/-10/-	Call
Twister	29	EA	M/188	L/20	3.3	S	–	-40	–
Water Sprite	13-14	EW	M/188	M/30	3.8	C	–	-10	Soc.
Whirlwind	6	EA	M/210	L/10	4.0	S	7	-20	–
Wind Spirit	27-28	EA	M/188	–	3.8	C	–	-10	Call
Wind Sprite	14-15	EA	M/188	M/30	3.8	S	–	-10	Soc.
Wind Wisp	9	EA	F/220	–	3.5	S/S2	6	-10	Soc.

Giant

Monster	Lvl	Body Type	Spd	Agg	Atk Spd	Atk Type	Ev %	Comb Mod	Soc. Call
Broken Jotun	54-57	St	M/192	L/20	3.4	C/S15	–	–	Soc.
Clay Jotun	40-42	St	M/200	L/20	2.5	C/S15	–	–	Soc.
Clay Jotun Guard	44	St	M/200	L/20	2.5	C/S15	–	20	Soc.
Clay Jotun Hunter	50	St	M/200	L/20	3.4	C/S15	–	–	Soc.
Clay Jotun Retainer	46	St	M/200	L/20	2.5	C/S15	–	–	Soc.
Clay Jotun Runner	48	St	F/250	L/20	2.5	C/S15	–	–	Soc.
Crippled Jotun	50-53	St	S/100	L/20	3.4	C/S15	–	–	Soc.
Fire Giant Guard	30	St	M/200	H/80	4.2	C	–	-10/-10/-	Call
Fire Giant Lookout	27	St	M/200	H/80	4.2	C	–	-10/-10/-	Call
Fire Giant Scout	28	St	M/200	H/80	4.2	C	–	-10/-10/-	Call
Fire Giant Spirit	40	IU	M/200	H/80	4.2	C/C20	–	-10/-10/-	–
Fire Giant Watchman	29	St	M/200	H/80	4.2	C	–	-10/-10/-	Call
Frost Cyclops	61-62	EI/CI	F/260	H/70	4.5	C	–	-10/-/-	Soc.
Frost Giant	37-39	EI/CI	F/260	L/10	4.4	C	–	-10/10/-	–
Ice Giant	33-36	EI/CI	F/230	L/10	4.2	C	–	-10/10/-	–
Ice Scrag	33-34	EI	M/178	H/80	3.7	C	–	–	–
Jotun Despot	61	St	F/250	L/20	2.1	C/S15	–	–	Soc.
Jotun Outcast	58-59	St	M/192	L/20	3.4	C/S15	–	–	Soc.
Jotun Overlord	62	St	F/250	L/20	2.1	C/S15	–	–	Soc.
Jotun Warchief	60	St	F/250	L/20	2.1	C/S15	–	–	Soc.
Snow Giant	30-33	EI/CI	M/200	L/10	4.0	C	–	-10/10/-	–

Human-like

Monster	Lvl	Body Type	Spd	Agg	Atk Spd	Atk Type	Ev %	Comb Mod	Soc. Call
Abomin. Snowman	27-30	CI	M/188	H/80	3.8	C	–	–	–
Ashmonger	23-25	Rp	M/195	H/80	3.7	C	1	–	Soc.
Backwoods Marodor	39-43	St	M/188	H/80	3.3	S/S3	4	–	–
Blodfelag Captive	10	CI	M/188	–	4.5	C	–	-5/-5/-	–
Blodfelag Dreng	14-16	St	M/188	H/85	3.6	S/S4	–	–	Soc.
Blodfelag Haxa	19-20	CI	M/188	H/85	4.0	C	–	-20	Soc.
Blodfelag Henchman	12-13	Lr	M/188	H/85	3.3	S/S3	–	–	Soc.
Blodfelag Livvakt	20	Ch	M/188	H/85	3.0	S/T3	–	–	Soc.
Blodfelag Oathbreaker	10-12	St	M/188	H/85	3.8	C	–	–	Soc.
Blodfelag Partisan	13-15	CI	M/188	H/85	3.6	S	–	–	Soc.
Blodfelag Soothsayer	14	CI	M/188	H/85	4.0	C	–	-20	Soc.
Blodfelag Svard	16-17	St	M/188	H/85	3.5	S/S4	1	–	Soc.
Blodfelag Thralldriver	14-15	CI	M/188	H/85	3.8	S	–	-20/-20/-	Soc.
Blodfelag Tormentor	19-20	St	M/188	H/85	3.5	S	–	–	Soc.
Blodfelag Windcaller	17-18	CI	M/188	H/85	4.0	C	–	-20	Soc.
Blodfelag Wolfwarrior	18-19	Ch	M/188	H/85	3.0	S/T5	5	–	Soc.
Bone-Eater Clanmother	42	CI	M/188	H/80	3.8	S	–	-20	Soc.
B-E. Eviscerater	41-42	Ch	M/188	H/80	3.0	S/S5	–	–	Soc.
Bone-Eater Oracle	39-41	CI	M/188	H/80	3.9	C	–	-20	Soc.
Bone-Eater Slayer	37-38	Ch	M/188	H/80	3.5	S/S2	–	–	Soc.
B-E. Spine-Ripper	39-40	Ch	M/188	H/80	3.4	S/S3	–	–	Soc.
Bone-Eater Warleader	45	Ch	M/188	H/80	3.4	S/S4	–	–	Soc.
Bounty Hunter	55	Lr	M/188	H/80	3.7	S	–	–	Call
Bounty Hunter Leader	57	Lr	M/188	H/80	3.7	S	–	–	Call
Cave Ogre	29-30	Lr	M/192	H/70	3.7	S	–	–	Soc.
Cave Trow	47	CI	M/188	L/10	3.8	S	–	–	Soc.
Cave Trow Trollkarl	48	CI	M/188	L/10	3.8	C	–	-20	Soc.
Duegar Tjuv	37	Lr	M/188	L/3	3.8	T	3	–	–

Monster	Lvl	Body Type	Spd	Agg	Atk Spd	Atk Type	Ev %	Comb Mod	Soc. Call
Dverge Crackler	28	St	M/188	M/50	3.6	T/C15	5	-20	Call
Dverge Fire-Eater	30	St	M/188	H/80	3.6	T/C20	7	-20	Call
Dverge Igniter	25	St	M/188	H/75	3.6	C/S5	1	-20/-20/-	Call
Dverge Sparker	24	St	M/188	H/75	3.6	C/S5	1	-20/-20/-	Call
Elder Skogsfru	32	Cl	M/188	H/80	3.8	S	–	–	Call
Escaped Thrall	3	Cl	M/188	M/30	3.8	C	–	–	–
Fossegrim	29-31	Cl	M/185	–	3.8	C	–	–	–
Frostbite Wildling	27-29	FA	M/185	L/1	3.8	S	–	-/-5/-5	–
Goblin Guard	25-27	Ch	M/192	H/70	3.7	S	–	–	–
Gotawitch	9	Cl	M/175	H/80	4.0	C	–	-20/-20/-	–
Half-Frozen Madman	25	Cl	M/180	H/80	4.1	C	–	–	–
Hill Person	6	Cl	M/188	M/40	3.8	C	–	–	Call
Hobgoblin Biter	6	Cl	M/188	M/60	3.8	S	–	–	Soc.
Hobgoblin Fish-Catcher	0	Cl	M/188	–	3.8	S	–	–	Soc.
Hobgoblin Pincher	4	Cl	M/188	M/40	3.8	T	–	–	Soc.
Hobgoblin Prankster	3	Cl	M/188	–	3.8	S	–	–	Soc.
Hobgoblin Prowler	8	Cl	M/188	H/80	3.7	S/T1	–	–	Soc.
Hobgoblin Snagger	2	Cl	M/188	–	3.8	S	–	–	Soc.
Hobgoblin Snake-Finder	1	Cl	M/188	–	3.8	S	–	–	Soc.
Huldu Hunter	4	Cl	M/188	L/5	3.8	T	–	–	Soc.
Huldu Lurker	2	Cl	M/188	L/5	3.8	T	–	–	Soc.
Huldu Outcast	1	Cl	M/188	–	3.8	T	–	–	–
Huldu Stalker	5	Cl	M/188	M/30	3.8	T	–	–	Soc.
Isalf Abider	30	Lr	M/188	–	3.8	C	–	–	Soc.
Isalf Blinder	34-35	Lr	M/188	L/5	4.0	C	–	-20/-20/-	Soc.
Isalf Forayer	44	Ch	M/188	L/5	2.5	S/S2	–	–	Call
Isalf Icemage	32-34	Lr	M/188	L/5	4.0	C	–	-20	Soc.
Isalf Scryer	33	Lr	M/188	L/5	4.0	C	–	-20	Soc.
Isalf Snowtracker	35	St	M/188	L/5	3.6	T/S1	–	–	Soc.
Isalf Surveyor	32-33	St	M/188	L/5	3.8	T	–	–	Soc.
Isalf Warrior	35-36	Ch	M/188	L/5	3.3	S/S2	–	–	Soc.
Lair Guard	10-11	Lr	M/175	H/90	3.7	S	–	–	–
Lair Patrol	9	Lr	M/175	H/90	3.7	S	–	–	–
Little Water Goblin	2	Cl	S/150	–	3.8	S	–	–	–
Mad Kobold	42	Cl	M/188	L/25	3.8	C	–	–	–
Mindless Thrall	10	Cl	M/188	H/85	3.8	C	–	–	–
Minor Fideal	15-16	EW	M/188	H/80	3.8	S	–	-10/-10/-	–
Moss Maiden	24-25	Cl	M/188	H/80	3.8	S	–	-5	–
Nordic Yeti	33-36	FA	M/188	H/80	3.8	C	–	–	–
Northern Ettin	25-27	Cl	M/188	H/80	3.8	C	–	–	–
Perfidious Pook	10	Cl	M/188	H/80	3.3	S	7	–	–
Prisoner	0	Cl	2x/400	–	3.9	S	–	–	Soc.
Red Rager	10	Cl	M/180	H/99	3.3	C/S2	–	–	–
Roaming Thrall	7	Cl	M/188	H/70	3.8	C	–	–	–
Savage Wildling	10	FA	M/188	H/90	3.5	S/S2	–	–	–
Seithkona Initiate	5	Cl	M/188	H/80	4.0	C	–	-20/-20/-	Call
Seithkona Laering	10	Cl	M/188	H/80	4.0	C	–	-20/-20/-	Call
Sharktooth Whelp	1	Cl	S/150	–	3.8	T	–	–	–
Sidhe Draoi	36-38	Cl	M/188	L/10	4.0	C	–	-20	Call
Skogsfru	13-14	Cl	M/188	H/80	3.8	S	–	-10/-10/-	Call
Snowshoe Bandit	30-35	St	M/188	H/80	3.7	S	–	–	Soc.
Snowsh. Band. Mage	32-33	Cl	M/188	H/80	3.8	C	–	-20	Soc.
Stromkarl	38-40	Cl	M/185	L/5	3.8	C	–	–	–
Svartalf Arbetare	37	Cl	M/188	–	3.8	C	–	–	Call
Svartalf Bloodbinder	51-55	Lr	F/225	H/80	3.4	T/T5	–	–	Call
Svartalf Chanter	14-15	DV/Lr	M/188	H/85	3.8	C	–	-20	Call
Svartalf Foister	48-52	Lr	M/195	H/80	3.6	T/T1	–	–	Call
Svartalf Foreman	39	Cl	M/188	–	3.8	C	–	–	Call
Svartalf Guard	10	Cl	M/188	H/80	3.6	S/S15	2	-/-/10	Soc.
Svartalf Hunter	14-15	DV/Lr	M/188	H/85	3.3	T	1	–	Soc.
Svartalf Infiltrator	45-49	Lr	M/192	H/80	3.8	T	–	–	Call
Svartalf Merchant	6	Cl	M/188	H/80	3.7	S	2	–	Call
Svartalf Outcast	8	Cl	M/188	H/80	3.7	S	2	–	Soc.
Svartalf Predator	16	DV/St	M/190	H/90	3.1	S/T3	8	–	Call
Svartalf Smith	6	Cl	M/188	H/80	3.7	S	2	–	Call
Svartalf Sorcerer	15	DV/Cl	M/188	H/90	4.0	C	–	-20	Call
Svartalf Thrall	36	Cl	M/188	–	3.8	C	–	–	Call
Svartalf Watcher	13	DV/Lr	M/190	H/90	3.5	S/T2	3	–	Call
Svartskogsfru	17	DV/Cl	M/192	H/80	3.7	S	–	–	Soc.
Svendo	31-34	FA/Cl	M/192	H/70	3.7	S	–	–	Soc.
Thrall	3	Cl	M/188	–	3.8	S	–	–	–
Tomte Aggressor	9	Lr	M/175	H/90	3.7	S	–	–	Call
Tomte Caitiff	17	FA	M/188	H/80	3.5	S/S30	–	–	Call
Tomte Captor	12	FA	M/175	H/99	3.7	S	3	–	Call
Tomte Cutthroat	8	FA	M/175	H/80	3.7	S	3	–	–
Tomte Guard	16	FA	M/188	H/80	3.5	S/S30	–	–	–
Tomte Guard	17	FA	M/188	H/80	3.5	S/S30	–	–	Soc.
Tomte Handler	10	FA	M/175	H/90	3.7	S	–	–	Call
Tomte Hoodoo	13	FA	M/188	H/80	4.4	C	–	-20	Soc.
Tomte Jager	15	FA	M/188	H/80	3.5	S/S30	–	–	Soc.
Tomte Pillager	8	Lr	M/175	H/80	3.7	S	3	–	Call
Tomte Plunderer	10	Lr	M/175	H/99	3.7	S	3	–	Call
Tomte Protector	13	FA	M/175	H/90	3.7	S	–	–	–
Tomte Runner	13	FA	M/175	H/90	3.7	S	–	–	–
Tomte Seer	18	FA	M/188	H/80	3.5	S/S30	–	–	Call
Tomte Shaman	10	FA	M/188	H/80	4.4	C	–	-20	–
Tomte Skirmisher	7	Lr	M/175	H/70	3.8	S	3	–	Call
Tomte Thug	5	Lr	M/175	M/50	3.8	C	–	–	Call
Tomte Zealot	16	FA	M/188	H/80	3.5	S/S30	–	–	Soc.
Vendo Bone-Collector	13	FA	M/188	H/80	4.4	C	–	-20	Soc.
Vendo Flayer	15	FA	M/188	H/80	3.5	S/S3	–	–	Soc.
Vendo Frightener	14	FA	M/188	H/80	3.5	S	3	–	Soc.
Vendo Guard	22-25	Ch	M/192	H/70	3.7	S	–	–	Soc.
Vendo Reaver	24-30	St	M/192	H/70	3.8	S	–	–	Soc.
Vendo Savager	32-35	Pl	M/192	M/60	3.6	S	–	–	Soc.
Vendo Shaman	10	FA	M/188	H/80	4.4	C	–	-20	Soc.
Vendo Stalker	12	FA	M/188	H/80	3.6	T/S5	2	–	Soc.
Vendo Warrior	11	FA	M/188	H/80	3.6	S/C2	–	-/-/20	Soc.
Vendo Yowler	28-31	Lr	M/192	H/70	3.8	S	–	–	Soc.
Wild Thrall	10	Cl	M/188	H/99	3.5	C	–	–	–
Wildling	0	FA	M/188	–	3.8	S	–	–	–

Insect

Monster	Lvl	Body Type	Spd	Agg	Atk Spd	Atk Type	Ev %	Comb Mod	Soc. Call
Arachite Greensilk	5	Sh	M/190	L/10	3.8	T	–	–	Soc.
Arachite Grymherre	42	Sh	M/195	H/80	2.5	T/T8	–	20/20/-	Call
Arachite Hatchling	1	Sh	M/170	–	3.8	T	–	–	Soc.
Arachite Husker	38-39	Sh	M/195	H/80	3.3	T	–	-10/-10/-	Call
Arachite Impaler	37-39	Sh	M/195	H/80	3.0	T/T1	–	–	Call
Arachite Krigare	40	Sh	M/195	H/80	3.0	T/T5	–	–	Call
Arachite Prelate	39-40	Sh	M/195	H/80	3.3	T	–	-20	Call
Arachite Priest	15-16	Sh	M/190	H/75	3.7	T	–	-20	Call
Arach. Shadowslinker	13-15	Sh	M/190	M/50	3.6	T/T1	2	-10	Call
Arachite Tunnelhost	36-37	Sh	M/195	H/80	3.3	T	–	–	Call
Arachite Vakt	37-38	Sh	M/195	H/80	3.0	T/T1	–	–	Call
Arachite Weblasher	14-16	Sh	M/190	H/80	3.6	T/T5	2	-10	Call
Army Ant Soldier	8	Sh	M/175	H/70	3.6	T/T4	–	-/-/20	Soc.
Army Ant Worker	6	Sh	M/175	–	3.8	T	–	–	Call
Carrion Crawler	6	Sh	M/170	–	3.7	T/S10	–	–	–
Carrion Eater	7	Sh	M/170	–	3.7	T/S10	–	–	–
Cave Crab	19-21	Sh	M/188	–	3.8	T/S20	–	–	–
Cave Spider	13-14	Sh	M/192	H/75	3.6	S	–	-10	–
Chiseler	20-24	Sh	M/188	–	3.8	T	–	–	–

Monster	Lvl	Body Type	Spd	Agg	Atk Spd	Atk Type	Ev %	Comb Mod	Soc. Call
Corpse Crawler	21-23	Sh	M/188	M/50	3.7	S	–	–	–
Corpse Eater	11-13	Sh	M/188	–	3.7	S	–	–	–
Cursed Thulian	47	Sh	M/188	L/5	3.0	T	–	–	–
Death Spider	18	Sh	M/190	H/80	3.5	T/T2	5	-10	–
Deeplurk Dissembler	47-49	Sh	M/195	H/80	3.0	T	–	–	Soc.
Deeplurk Feeder	47	Sh	M/195	H/80	3.8	T	–	–	Soc.
Deeplurk Manslayer	47-48	Sh	M/195	H/80	3.0	T/T3	–	–	Soc.
Djupt Odjur	49	Sh	M/195	H/80	2.6	T/T3	–	–	Soc.
Djupt Usling	48	Sh	M/195	H/80	2.6	T/T3	–	–	Soc.
Djupt Vivunder	50	Sh	M/195	H/80	2.6	T/T3	–	–	Soc.
Duegarhunter	36	Sh	M/200	L/1	3.8	T	–	–	–
Dungeon Chitin	22-23	Sh	M/195	L/20	3.5	T	–	–	–
Dungeon Crab	20-22	Sh	M/188	–	3.8	S/S20	–	–	–
Ekyps Gunstling	45	Sh	M/195	–	3.0	T	–	–	Soc.
Ekyps Scavenger	42	Sh	M/195	–	3.5	T	–	–	–
Fire Ant Gatherer	21	Sh	M/188	L/10	3.8	T	–	-20/-20/-	Soc.
Fire Ant Scavenger	20	Sh	M/188	L/10	3.8	T	–	-20/-20/-	Soc.
Fire Ant Worker	22	Sh	M/188	L/10	3.8	T	–	-20/-20/-	Soc.
Forest Spider	50-52	Sh	M/192	L/20	2.0	S	–	–	–
Forest Spider Queen	55	Sh	M/192	L/20	2.0	S	–	–	–
Forest Spider Runner	53	Sh	M/210	L/20	2.0	S	–	–	–
Frenetic Wolfspider	38	Sh	M/188	L/20	3.5	T/T3	–	-5	–
Frosty Scuttlebug	23-24	Sh	M/188	–	3.8	S	–	–	–
Giant Snowcrab	33-34	Sh	M/188	–	3.8	S/S1	–	–	–
Giant Water Strider	5	Sh	M/175	M/65	3.8	T	–	–	Call
Great Tingler	16-18	Sh	M/190	M/30	3.6	T	–	–	Soc.
Harvestman	3	Sh	M/180	–	3.8	T	–	–	–
Husk	10	Soft	M/195	–	3.8	S	–	–	–
Icestrider Chiller	43-45	Sh	M/188	H/80	3.3	T	–	–	Soc.
Icestr. Frostweaver	44-46	Sh	M/188	H/80	3.8	C	–	-20	Soc.
Icestrider Interceptor	47-51	Sh	M/188	H/80	3.1	T/T4	–	–	Soc.
Large Wolfspider	28	Sh	M/188	–	3.5	T	–	–	–
Mud Crab	35	Sh	M/192	L/20	3.5	S	–	–	Soc.
Mud Crab Warrior	36	Sh	M/192	L/20	3.5	S	–	–	Soc.
Poisonous Cave Spider	15	Sh	M/192	H/75	3.6	S	–	-10/-10/-20	–
Poisonous Cave Spider	23	Sh	M/192	H/75	3.6	T	–	-10/-10/-20	–
Rock Crab	7	Sh	M/190	L/10	4.5	S/S5	5	–	–
Soft-Shelled Crab	1	Soft	M/190	–	3.8	S	3	–	–
Soot Harvester	20-22	Sh	M/170	L/10	3.8	T/S2	–	–	–
Spider	25-28	Sh	M/192	H/70	3.8	S	–	–	–
Spindel	37	Sh	M/195	–	3.7	T	–	-10/-10/-	Soc.
Spindel Layer	41	Sh	M/195	–	3.7	T	–	-10/-10/-	Call
Spindel Silkster	39	Sh	M/195	–	3.7	T	–	-10/-10/-	Soc.
Spindly Rock Crab	9	Sh	M/190	L/5	4.0	S/S3	15	–	–
Stinger	37-39	Sh	M/190	L/5	3.3	S/T6	–	-10/-10/-	–
Sulphur Crab	20-22	Sh	M/170	L/10	3.8	T/S2	–	–	–
Terra Crab	38-40	Sh	M/185	–	3.3	S/S4	–	–	–
Tingler	12	Sh	M/190	L/20	3.7	T	–	–	Soc.
Vein Spider	5	Sh	M/170	–	3.8	T	–	–	–
Vein Spiderling	0	Sh	S/130	–	3.8	T	–	–	–
Venomous Tree Crawler	55	Sh	F/250	H/100	0.0	–	10	-75/-/-	–
Water Strider	1	Sh	M/188	–	3.8	T	–	–	Soc.
Wolfspider	25	Sh	M/188	–	3.5	T	–	-5	–
Wood-Eater	3	Sh	M/188	–	3.8	T	–	–	Call
Wood-Eater Alate	7	Sh	M/210	–	3.8	T	5	–	Call
Wood-Eater Hunter	5	Sh	M/188	–	3.5	T	2	–	Call
Wood-Eater King	15	Sh	M/200	L/10	3.6	T/T20	–	10	Call
Wood-Eater Queen	8	Sh	S/160	–	4.3	T	–	-10/-10/20	Call
Wood-Eater Royal Grd.	16	Sh	M/210	–	3.8	T	5	–	Soc.
Wood-Eater Soldier	6	Sh	M/188	L/10	3.6	T/T20	–	10	Soc.
Wood-Eater Worker	4	Sh	M/188	–	3.8	T	–	–	Call

Magical

Monster	Lvl	Body Type	Spd	Agg	Atk Spd	Atk Type	Ev %	Comb Mod	Soc. Call
Aurora	41-47	LE	M/188	–	3.8	S	–	-20/-20/-	–
Cold Light	20-25	LE	M/188	–	3.8	S	–	-20	–
Crazed Lycantic	34	Cl	M/188	M/50	3.0	S/S1	–	–	Soc.
Drakulv Armguard	42-46	FA-Rp	M/192	H/80	4.4	S	–	-10/5/5	Call
Drakulv Attendant	51-55	FA-Rp	M/192	H/80	4.8	S	–	-10/5/5	Soc.
Drakulv Axehand	48-52	FA-Rp	F/220	H/80	4.6	S	–	-10/5/5	Soc.
Drakulv Disciple	62-64	FA-Rp	F/250	H/80	5.4	S/C3	–	-10/5/5	Call
Drakulv Executioner	57-61	FA-Rp	F/245	H/80	5.2	S	–	-10/5/5	Soc.
Drakulv Klok	65	FA-Rp	3x/600	H/99	3.8	S	–	30/-/10	Soc.
Drakulv Missionary	36-40	FA-Rp	F/250	H/80	4.0	S	–	-10/5/5	Call
Drakulv Prast	65	FA-Rp	3x/600	H/99	3.8	S	–	20/-/20	Soc.
Drakulv Protector	54-58	FA-Rp	F/220	H/80	5.0	S/C4	–	-10/5/5	Call
Drakulv Riddare	65	FA-Rp	3x/600	H/99	3.8	S	–	10/20/10	Soc.
Drakulv Sacrificer	45-49	FA-Rp	M/195	H/80	4.4	S	–	-25/-/-	Call
Drakulv Soultrapper	62-64	FA-Rp	F/248	H/80	5.2	S	–	-25/-/-	Call
Fenrir Guard	45	FA/Lr	M/188	H/80	3.6	S	–	–	Call
Fenrir Mystic	57-60	FA/Lr	M/188	H/80	3.3	S/S3	–	–	Call
Fenrir Prime	49	FA/Lr	M/188	H/80	3.3	S/S3	–	–	Call
Fenrir Prophet	44-45	FA/Cl	M/188	H/80	4.0	S	–	-20	Call
Fenrir Shredder	45-46	FA/Lr	M/188	H/80	2.1	S/S10	–	–	Call
Fenrir Snowscout	36-38	FA/Lr	M/188	H/80	3.5	T/S1	1	–	Call
Fenrir Soldier	58	FA/Lr	M/188	H/80	3.3	S/S3	–	–	Call
Fenrir Tracker	40-42	FA/Lr	M/188	H/80	3.6	T/S1	1	–	Call
Ghost Light	7	LE	F/220	–	3.5	S	–	-10	–
Greater Fenrir	59-62	FA/Lr	M/188	H/80	3.3	S/S3	–	–	Call
Icy Wisp	28-33	El	M/188	–	3.8	S	–	-20/-20/-	–
Minor Werewolf Noble	19-21	FA/Lr	M/192	H/90	3.3	S/S3	5	10	Call
Mora Dancer	14-16	DV/Cl	M/195	H/80	3.4	S	3	–	Soc.
Mora Rider	15	DV/Cl	M/195	H/80	3.4	S	3	–	Soc.
Northern Light	25-30	LE	M/188	–	3.8	S	–	-20	–
Patrolling Drakulv	39-43	FA-Rp	F/265	H/80	4.2	S	–	-10/5/5	Call
Seithr Orb	9	ME	F/220	–	3.3	S	–	-10	Soc.
Shadow	10-11	DV	M/205	H/90	3.2	S	1	-10/-10/-	–
Soul Sinker	16	DV	M/192	H/90	3.4	C/C1	–	-10	Soc.
Werewolf	17	FA/Lr	M/192	H/90	3.3	S/S3	5	–	Call
Werewolf Bodyguard	37	FA/Lr	M/188	M/50	3.3	S/S2	3	–	Soc.
Werewolf Captain	37-38	FA/Lr	M/195	H/90	3.2	S/S16	6	–	Soc.
Werewolf Churl	34	FA/Lr	M/188	–	3.8	S	–	–	Soc.
Werewolf Commander	36	FA/Lr	M/195	H/90	3.2	S/S14	6	–	Soc.
Werewolf Courier	27-28	FA/Lr	M/200	H/90	3.2	S/S1	6	–	Call
Werewolf Grimnought	39	FA/Lr	M/188	L/25	2.9	S/S5	–	25/25/-	Soc.
Werewolf Guard	31-33	FA/Lr	M/195	H/90	3.2	S/S10	6	–	Soc.
Werewolf Lieutenant	33-34	FA/Lr	M/195	H/90	3.2	S/S12	6	–	Soc.
Werewolf Noble	38	FA/Lr	M/188	L/20	3.6	S/S2	1	–	Soc.
Werewolf Runner	21-22	FA/Lr	M/200	H/90	3.2	S/S2	6	–	Call
Werewolf Scruff	35	FA/Lr	M/188	M/30	3.8	S	–	–	Soc.
Werewolf Skulker	23-25	FA/Lr	M/195	H/90	3.2	S/S4	6	–	Soc.
Werewolf Warder	27-30	FA/Lr	M/195	H/90	3.2	S/S6	6	–	Call
Wolfaur Headsman	33-36	FA/Lr	M/195	H/90	3.2	S/S8	6	–	Soc.
Wolfaur Lunarian	39	FA/Lr	M/188	L/1	3.8	S	–	-20	Call
Wolfaur Pragmatic	35	FA/Lr	M/188	–	3.6	S	–	-5	Call
Wolfaur Quixot	37	FA/Lr	M/188	L/1	3.4	S/S3	3	-/20/-	Soc.

Reptile

Monster	Lvl	Body Type	Spd	Agg	Atk Spd	Atk Type	Ev %	Comb Mod	Soc. Call
Aged Boreal Cockatrice	49	Rp	M/188	L/5	3.5	S	–	-10/-10/-	–
Alpine Cockatrice	32-33	Rp	M/188	L/5	3.5	S	–	-10/-10/-	–
Black Orm	36-38	Rp	M/192	M/50	3.0	T/T15	–	–	Soc.
Blindsnake	37-38	Rp	M/180	–	3.8	T	–	–	–
Boreal Cockatrice	24-27	Rp	M/188	L/5	3.5	S	–	-10/-10/-	–
Carrion Lizard	3	Rp	M/210	–	3.7	S	–	–	–
Cave Crawler	16-22	Rp	M/192	H/70	3.8	S	–	-10	–

Monster	Lvl	Body Type	Spd	Agg	Atk Spd	Atk Type	Ev %	Comb Mod	Soc. Call
Cave Viper	25	Rp	M/192	H/70	3.8	S	–	–	–
Enslaved Orm	40	Rp	M/192	M/50	3.0	T/T15	–	–	Soc.
Enslaved Orm Biter	44	Rp	M/192	M/50	3.0	T/T15	–	–	Soc.
Enslaved Orm Runner	42	Rp	M/212	M/50	3.0	T/T15	–	–	Soc.
Forest Viper	40-44	Rp	M/192	L/20	3.5	S	–	–	–
Frost Orm	35	Rp	M/188	L/15	3.8	T	–	-20/-20/-	–
Grass Viper	12	Rp	M/175	H/80	3.8	T	–	–	–
Green Orm	38-40	Rp	M/188	M/60	4.6	S	–	–	–
Green Serpent	2	Rp	S/165	–	3.8	T	–	–	–
Hog-Nose Slither	0	Rp	M/170	–	3.8	T	–	–	–
Ice Lizard	32-34	Rp	M/188	–	3.6	T	–	–	–
Lake Serpent	10-11	Rp	M/175	–	3.8	T	–	–	–
Large Enslaved Orm	48-50	Rp	M/192	M/50	3.0	T/T15	–	–	Soc.
Lg. Ensl. Orm Runner	48	Rp	M/212	M/50	3.0	T/T15	–	–	Soc.
Lava Lizard	22	Rp	M/188	–	4.0	T	–	–	–
Mud Snake	0	Rp	S/130	–	3.7	T	–	–	–
Reincarnate Orm	45-55	Rp	M/192	M/50	2.5	T/T25	–	–	Soc.
Small Black Orm	35	Rp	M/192	M/50	3.0	T/T15	–	–	Soc.
Venomspitter	11-13	Rp	M/180	H/90	3.2	S	3	-10	–
Water Snake	0	Rp	M/180	–	3.8	T	–	–	–
Young Fire Wyrm	25-27	Rp	M/200	L/10	4.0	S/S10	–	-20	–
Young Grendelorm	7	Rp	M/180	L/20	3.6	S	–	–	–

Tree or Plant

Monster	Lvl	Body Type	Spd	Agg	Atk Spd	Atk Type	Ev %	Comb Mod	Soc. Call
Fire Flower	20-22	TP	M/170	L/10	4.0	S	–	-20/-20/-	Soc.
Frigid Broadleaf	57	TP	2x/350	H/99	3.8	C/S6	–	–	Soc.
Sapherd	5	TP	S/160	M/50	4.1	C	–	-20	Call
Shrieking Willow	18	TP	M/185	M/35	3.9	S	–	-5	–
Treekeep	22	TP	M/188	M/50	4.0	C	–	-10	Call
Weeping Willow	12	TP	M/185	L/5	3.9	S	–	-30	–
Whispering Willow	33-34	TP	M/188	–	4.2	T	–	–	–

Undead

Monster	Lvl	Body Type	Spd	Agg	Atk Spd	Atk Type	Ev %	Comb Mod	Soc. Call
Acrid Ghoul	29	FU	M/188	H/80	3.6	C	–	–	–
Ashen Spirit	21-23	IU	M/170	L/10	3.8	C	–	–	–
Brittle Skeleton	0	BU	M/170	–	3.8	S	–	–	–
Burnt Skeletal Sentry	21	BU	M/170	M/30	3.7	T	–	–	Call
Charred Skel. Warr.	23-25	BU	M/170	H/80	3.7	S/T10	4	–	Call
Chattering Skeleton	32	BU	M/188	–	3.8	S	–	–	–
Chillsome Wight	51-52	FU	M/178	H/99	3.7	S	–	-10/-10/-	–
Cursed Mora	23-24	IU	M/210	L/20	3.0	T	3	-15/-20/-	Call
Cursed Mora Dancer	25	IU	M/210	L/15	3.2	T	3	-15/-20/-20	Call
Cursed Mora Weeper	25	IU	M/210	L/15	3.2	T	3	-10/-20/-20	Call
Cursed Spirit	19-20	IU	M/188	M/50	3.8	C	–	–	Soc.
Decaying Norseman	11	FU	M/175	M/30	3.8	C/C5	–	-10/-10/-	–
Decaying Troll	10	FU	M/175	M/30	3.8	C	–	-10/-10/-	–
Dishonored Hagbui	23-24	FU	M/188	H/80	3.8	S	–	–	Soc.
Draugr Warrior	21-23	FU/Lr	M/188	H/80	3.8	C	–	–	Soc.
Drifting Spirit	12-14	IU	M/170	L/10	3.7	S	–	–	–
Drowned Soul	3	IU	M/175	–	3.8	C	–	–	–
Dwarf Bone Skeleton	5	BU	M/192	H/85	4.5	C	–	–	Soc.
Enraged Mara	50	Rp	F/226	H/80	2.8	S	–	–	–
Entrancing Dirge	21	IU	M/170	M/60	3.8	C	–	-20	–
Fallen Troll	44-45	FU	M/188	L/20	3.8	C	–	–	–
Fire Phantom	25	IU	M/188	H/80	3.7	S	–	-20	–
Fragile Skeleton	3	BU	M/170	–	3.8	S	–	–	–
Frore Lich	55-57	FU	M/175	H/99	3.7	S	–	-20	Soc.
Frost Spectre	45-46	IU	M/188	H/80	3.8	S	–	-20/-20/-	–
Ghastly Alb. Invader	42-43	IU	M/188	L/20	3.8	S	–	–	–
Ghostly Hib. Invader	42-43	IU	M/188	L/20	3.8	S	–	–	–
Ghoulish Warrior	44-45	FU	M/188	L/20	3.8	S	–	–	–
Hagbui Berserker	50-51	IU/Lr	M/192	M/60	3.2	S	–	–	Soc.
Hagbui Forge Tender	37	FU/Lr	M/192	–	2.1	S	–	–	–
Hagbui Guard	40-42	FU/Lr	M/192	M/60	3.2	S	–	–	Soc.
Hagbui Herald	38	FU/Lr	M/192	–	2.1	S	–	–	–
Hagbui Page	36	FU/Lr	M/192	–	2.1	S	–	–	–
Hagbui Runemaster	42	IU/Lr	M/192	M/60	3.2	S	–	-/-/-20	Soc.
Hagbui Shaman	40	IU/Lr	M/192	M/60	3.2	S	–	-/-/-20	Soc.
Hagbui Spiritmaster	43	IU/Lr	M/192	M/60	3.2	S	–	-/-/-20	Soc.
Hagbui Squire	39	FU/Lr	M/192	–	2.1	S	–	–	–
Hagbui Swordbearer	35	FU/Lr	M/192	–	2.1	S	–	–	–
Hagbui Thane	53	IU/Lr	M/192	M/60	3.2	S	–	–	Soc.
Haunt	7	IU	M/190	L/15	3.9	C	–	–	–
Icy Skeleton	25	BU	M/188	–	3.8	S	–	–	–
Lost Hagbui	42	FU/Cl	M/175	H/80	3.8	C	–	-10/-10/-	Soc.
Lost Spirit	19	IU	M/188	–	3.8	S	–	–	–
Magmatasm	29-31	IU	M/188	H/80	3.3	C	–	-20	–
Meandering Spirit	1	IU	S/150	–	3.8	S	–	–	–
Mephitic Ghoul	25-28	IU	M/188	H/80	3.7	S	–	-20	–
Miserable Zombie	28-32	FU	M/175	L/1	4.0	S	–	-10/-10/-	–
Nordic Dirge	6	IU	S/150	M/60	3.8	C	–	-20/-20/-	–
Phantom Hound	3	IU	M/200	–	3.8	T	–	–	–
Phantom Wolf	17-19	FU	M/210	H/99	3.0	T	3	–	–
Plasmatasm	23-25	IU	M/188	H/80	3.5	C	–	-20	–
Pyrophantom	28-30	IU	M/188	H/80	3.4	S	–	-20	–
Pyrotasm	35-42	IU	M/188	H/80	3.5	C/S5	–	-20	–
Rattling Skeleton	1	BU	M/170	–	3.8	S	–	–	–
Roaming Corpse	19-21	FU	M/174	–	3.8	C	–	–	–
Roaming Dirge	8	IU	S/150	H/80	3.8	C	–	-20/-20/-	–
Sanguinite Ghoul	13-14	FU	M/170	H/80	3.8	T	–	-3/-3/-	–
Seared Skeleton	27-29	BU	M/175	H/80	3.6	T	–	–	–
Shivering Presence	32-33	IU	M/190	L/1	3.8	S	–	–	–
Skeletal Oarsman	5	BU	M/175	–	3.8	S/T5	–	–	–
Skeletal Seafarer	4	BU	M/175	–	3.8	S	–	–	–
Spectral Bayer	13	IU	M/200	H/90	3.3	S	2	–	–
Spectral Hog	2	IU	M/170	–	3.8	S	–	–	–
Spook	6	IU	M/188	L/15	3.9	C	–	–	–
Sulphuric Ghoul	22	FU	M/188	H/80	3.7	S	–	-20	–
Sveawolf Spirit	11	IU	M/210	M/50	3.3	T	2	–	Soc.
Thawing Corpse	31	FU	M/170	H/99	3.8	C	–	–	–
Tomb Sentry	19-20	BU	M/188	H/75	3.8	C	–	–	–
Trapped Thrall	19-20	IU	M/170	–	3.8	C	–	–	–
Undead Explorer	3	FU	M/170	–	3.8	C	–	–	–
Undead Troll Warrior	47	FU/Ch	M/188	L/20	3.8	C/C5	–	–	–
Undead Viking	44-45	FU	M/188	L/20	3.8	C	–	–	–
Undead Woodcarver	4	FU	M/188	–	3.8	C	–	–	–
Vapor Wraith	30	IU	F/240	H/80	3.0	T/S30	9	–	–
Vengeful Ghoul	23-24	FU	M/175	M/60	3.4	S	–	–	Call
Way Keeper	19-20	BU	M/188	H/75	3.8	C	–	–	–
Wayward Ghoul	4	FU	M/170	–	3.8	S	–	–	–
Windswept Wraith	50-53	IU	M/200	H/80	3.3	S	–	–	Soc.
Wintery Dirge	40-42	IU	M/188	H/80	3.8	S	–	-20	–

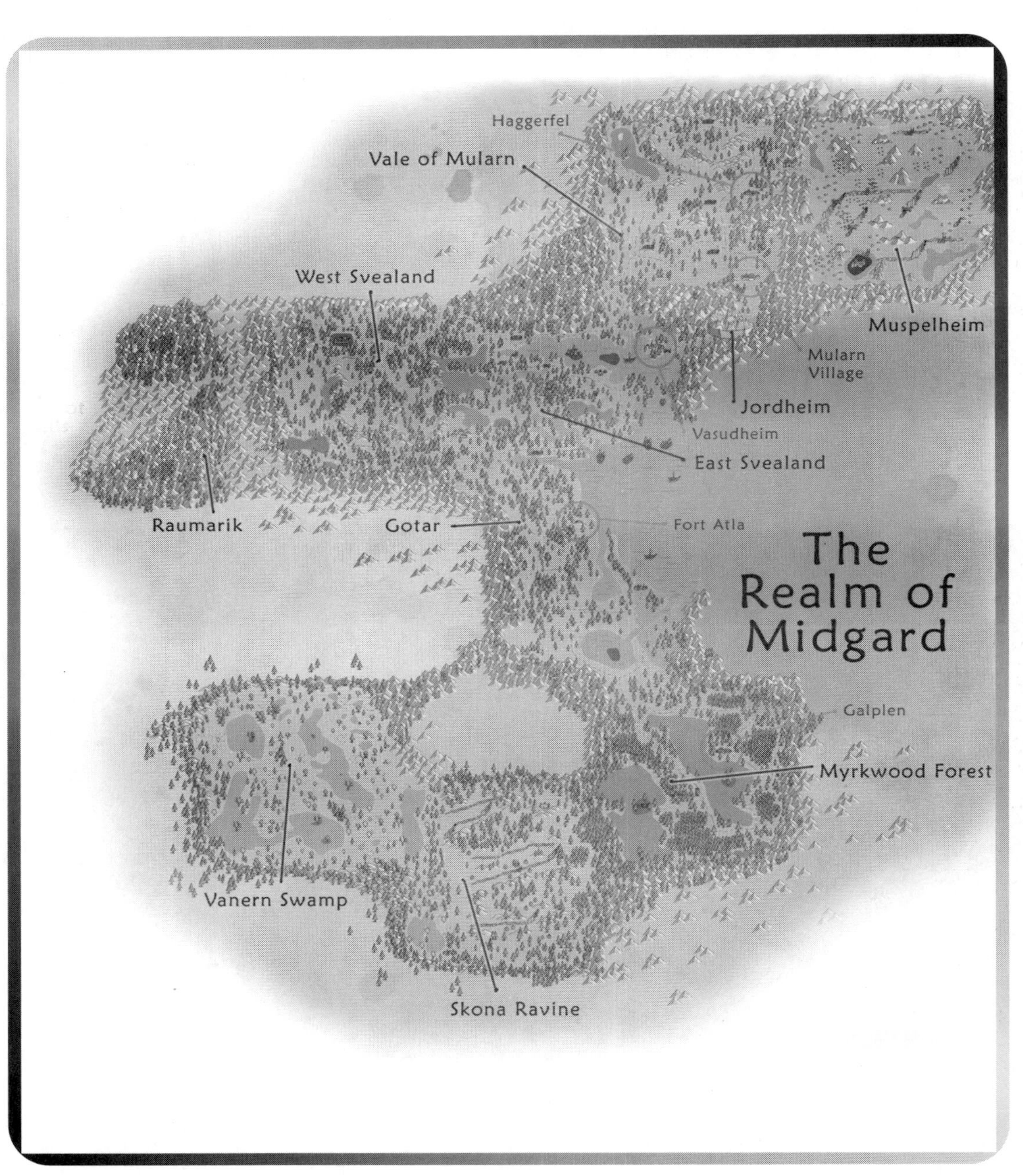
Haggerfel
Vale of Mularn
West Svealand
Muspelheim
Mularn
Village
Jordheim
Vasudheim
East Svealand
Raumarik
Gotar
Fort Atla
The
Realm of
Midgard
Galplen
Myrkwood Forest
Vanern Swamp
Skona Ravine

Jordheim

Note: Unoccupied areas have numbers for reference only. At the time of printing, nothing of interest is located in those areas.

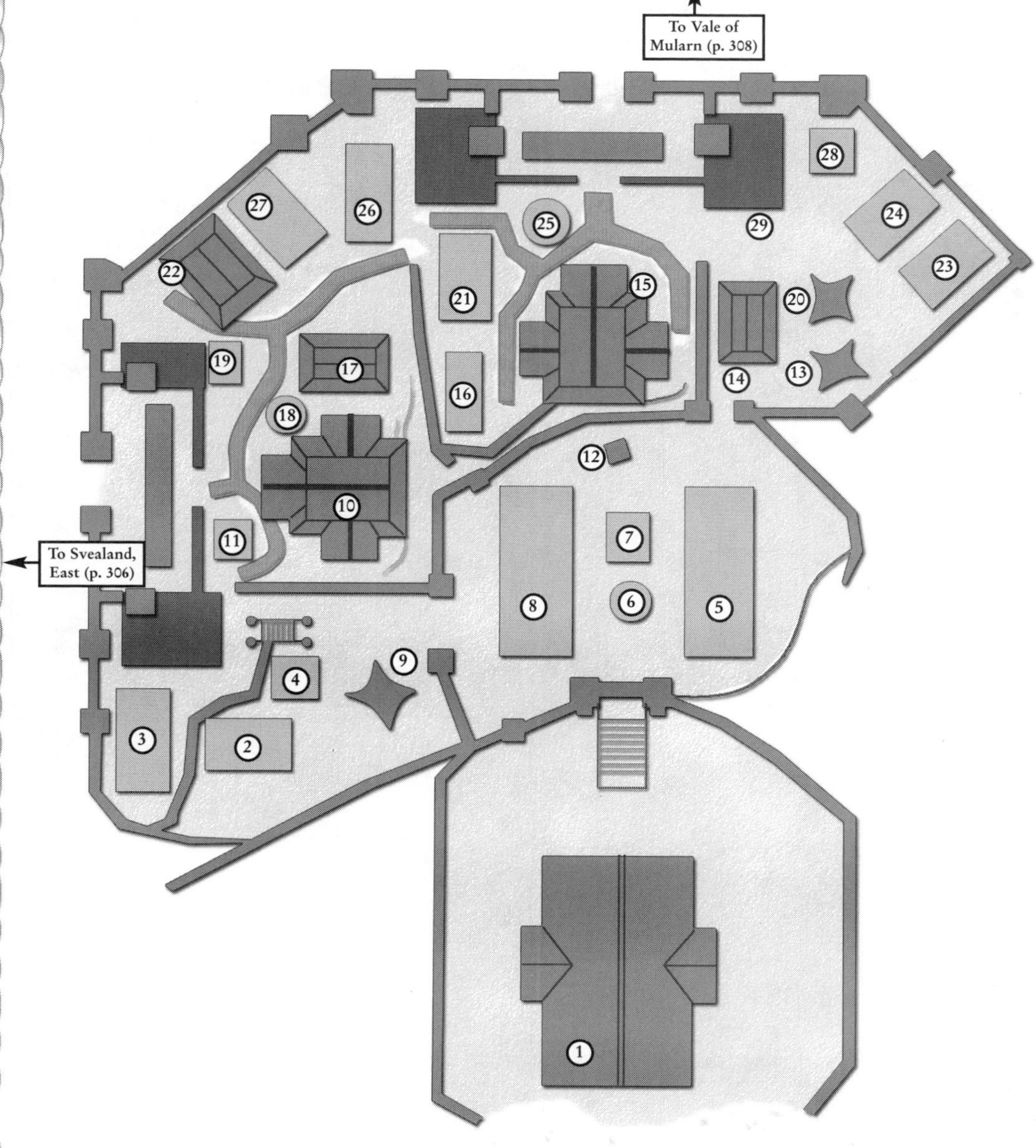
To Vale of Mularn (p. 308)
To Svealand, East (p. 306)
1
2
3
4
5
6
7
8
9
10
11
12
13
14
15
16
17
18
19
20
21
22
23
24
25
26
27
28
29

1 **Tora** Bounty Store - Crystals
1 **Aesa**
1 **Karis** Guild Emblemeer
1 **Jarl Uffenlong** Name Registrar
1 **Jarl Yuliwyf** Vault Keeper
1 **Brit** Guild Registrar
2 **Tait** Mithril chain armor
2 **Hakan** Mithril studded armor
2 **Flosi** Blades
2 **Ema** Axes
2 **Signy** Hammers
2 **Ole** Bows
2 **Aric** Shields
2 **Hedin** Spears
2 **Fiora** Embossed leather armor
4 **Nanna** Healer
4 **Anya** Runemaster staves
4 **Magna** Spiritmaster staves
5 **Per** Healer Trainer
5 **Solveig** Green/brown/grey/orange/ yellow enamel dye
5 **Grimma** Shaman Trainer
5 **Falla** Tailoring Equipment
5 **Miri**
6 **Gungir** Healer
7 **Gest** Armorcraft Master
7 **Aase** Weaponscraft Master
8 **Dane** Shaman Trainer
8 **Greip** Blue/turq/teal/red/purple enamel dye
8 **Rana** Healer Trainer
8 **Om** Smithing equipment
9 **Tove** Mithril large weapons
9 **Kalf** Large weapons
9 **Harry** Throwing weapons
9 **Asra** Arrows
9 **Morgen** Starklaedar leather armor
10 **Elli** Bounty Store - Crystals
11 **Ander** Poison
11 **Oilibhear** Poison
12 **Kiarr** Smith
13 **Im** Mjuklaeder leather armor
13 **Keki** Stelskodd studded armor
13 **Njal** Pansarkedja chain armor
14 **Leif** Skald Trainer
15 **Royd** Bounty Store - Crystals
16 **Gris** Smith
16 **Morlin Caan** Smith
18 **Amma** Enchanter
19 **Uli** Sylvan padded armor
19 **Ozur** Green/brown/grey/orange/ yellow leather dye
19 **Ella** Blue/turquoise/teal/red/purple leather dye
20 **Gerd** Arrows
20 **Synna** Spears
20 **Saga** Large weapons
20 **Canute** Throwing weapons
20 **Hodern** Svarlaeder leather armor
20 **Frode** Thane Trainer
20 **Hrapp** Blades
20 **Borg** Staff
20 **Digby** Shields
20 **Thir** Bows
20 **Gymir** Axes
21 **Barkeep Prugar**
21 **Barkeep Banak**
21 **Anrid**
22 **Hauk** Hunter Trainer
22 **Singrid** Hunter Trainer
22 **Hreidar** Shadowblade Trainer
22 **Elin** Shadowblade Trainer
23 **Eskil** Tailoring Master
23 **Sven** Skald Trainer
23 **Osten** Warrior Trainer
23 **Katla** Thane Trainer
23 **Hodr** Berserker Trainer
25 **Arve** Enchanter
25 **Ottar** Woodworking equipment
26 **Dyre** Spiritmaster Trainer
26 **Signa** Runemaster Trainer
26 **Bera** Runemaster Trainer
26 **Galn** Spiritmaster Trainer
27 **Darg** Fletching equipment (feathers)
27 **Gils** Fletching Master
27 **Dala** Mithril weapons
28 **Thordia** Warrior Trainer
28 **Torrad** Padded armor
28 **Gro** Tailoring equipment
28 **Alleca** Blue/turq/teal/red/purple cloth dye
28 **Hyndla** Green/brown/grey/orange/ yellow cloth dye
29 **Haaken** Berserker Trainer

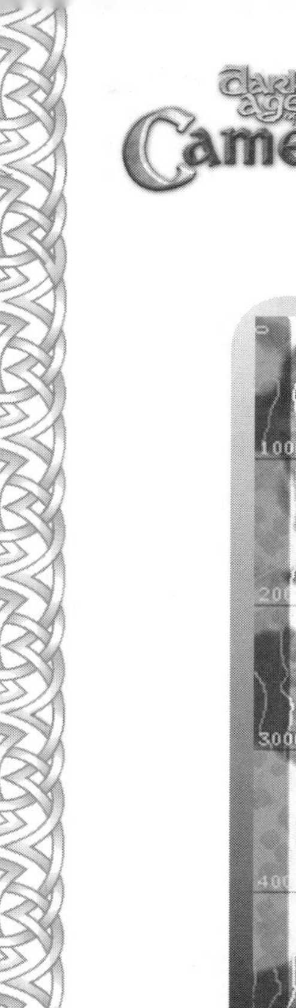

GOTAR

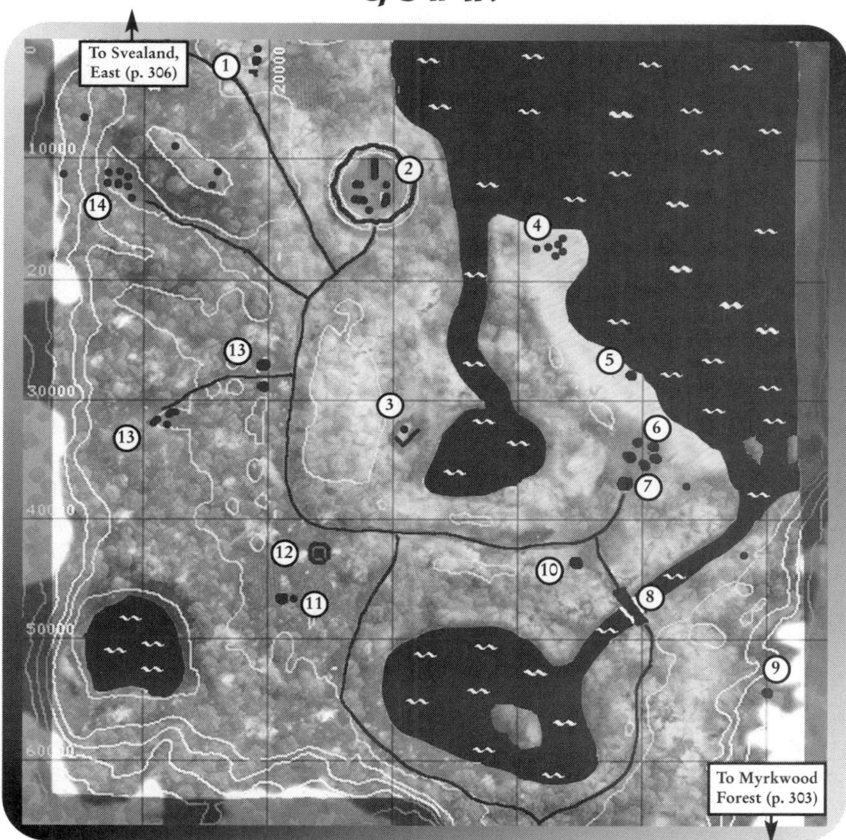

1 Hobgoblin Farmhouse
2 Fort Atla (p. 310)
3 Stone House Ruins (Meandering Ruins)
4 Muldo Stone Foundations
5 Boat
6 Nalliten (p. 313)
7 Arced Claw Arch
8 Arced Claw Bridge
9 Entrance to Cursed Tomb Dungeon (p. 316)
10 Stone Lookout Tower
11 Most of the Earch Farmhouse
12 Fort
13 Svartalf Settlement
14 Camp

MALMOHUS

1 Drakulv Camp
2 Large Svartolf Settlement
3 Svartolf Camp
4 Drakulv Sacrificial Stone Formations
5 Gjalpinulva's Fortress (Dragon)
6 Drakulv Settlement

MUSPELHEIM

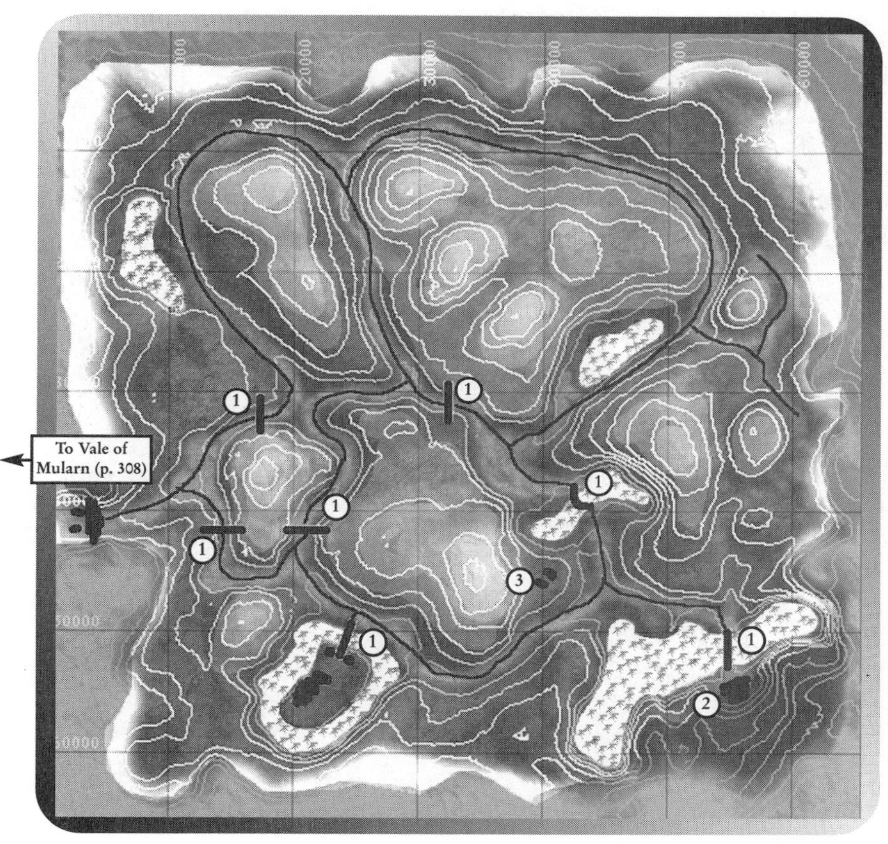

1 Bridge
2 Drerge Forge
3 Charred Skeletal Stone Formation

MYRKWOOD FOREST

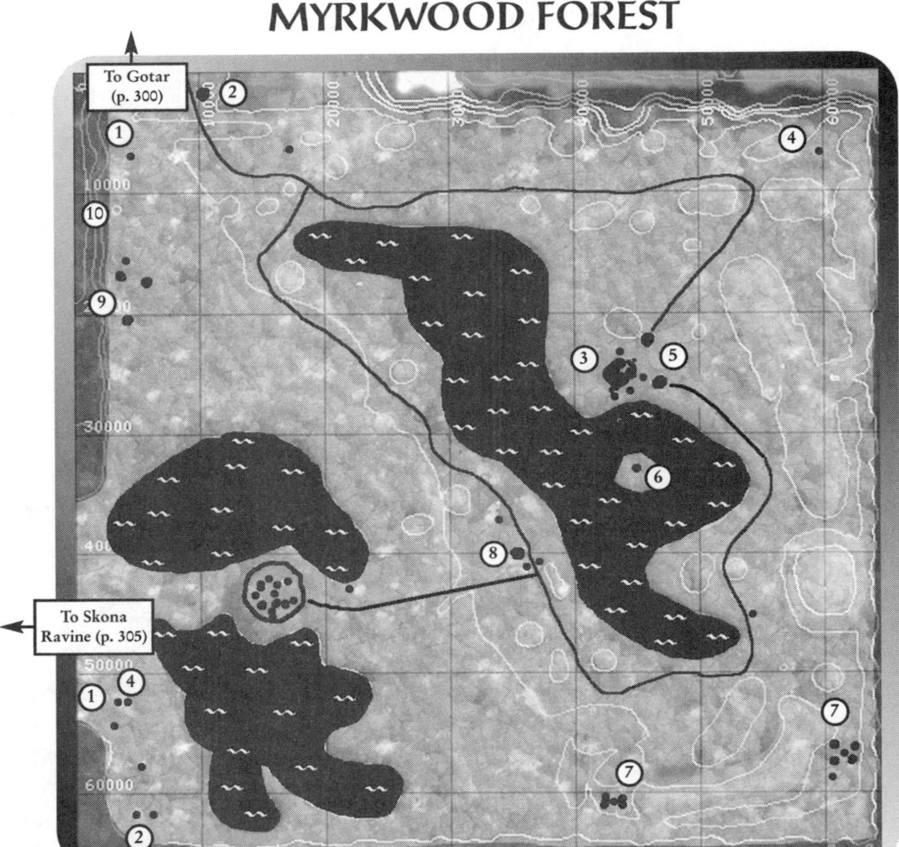

1 Skull-cracking Stone
2 Stone Sentry Tower
3 Galplen (p. 311)
4 Skeletal Remains
5 Claw Arches
6 Storehouse Ruins
7 Svartalf Settlement
8 Gna Faste (p. 311)
9 Abandoned Wooden Gem Towers
10 Entrance to Spindelhalla Dungeon (p. 314)

RAUMARIK

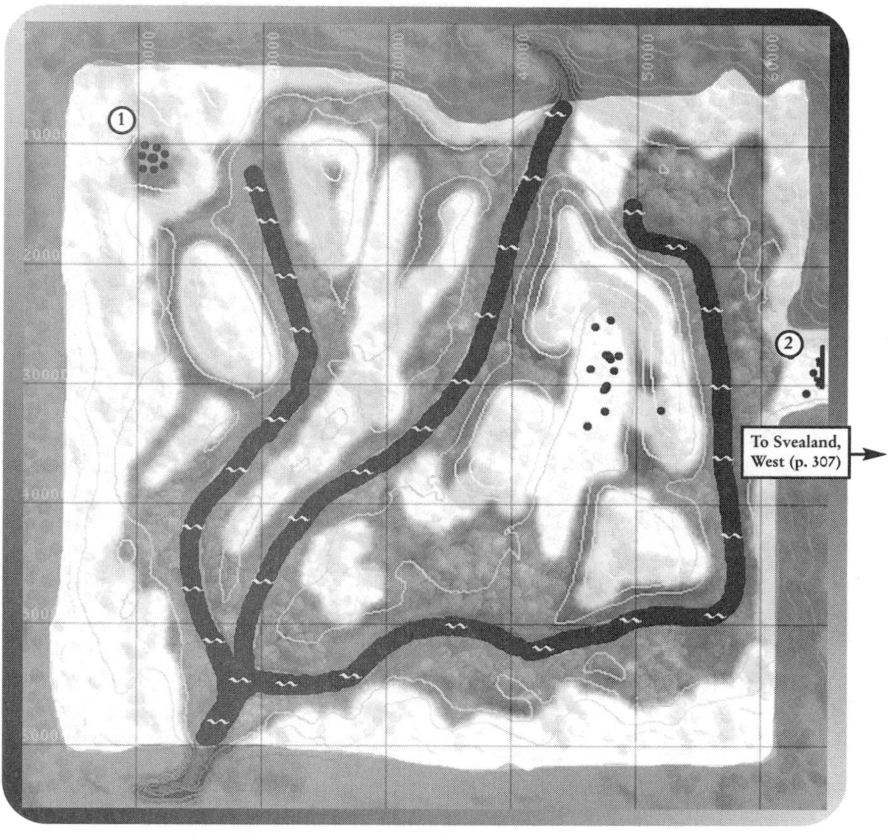

1 Undead Fortress (Ruins)

2 Lookout Towers

SKONA RAVINE

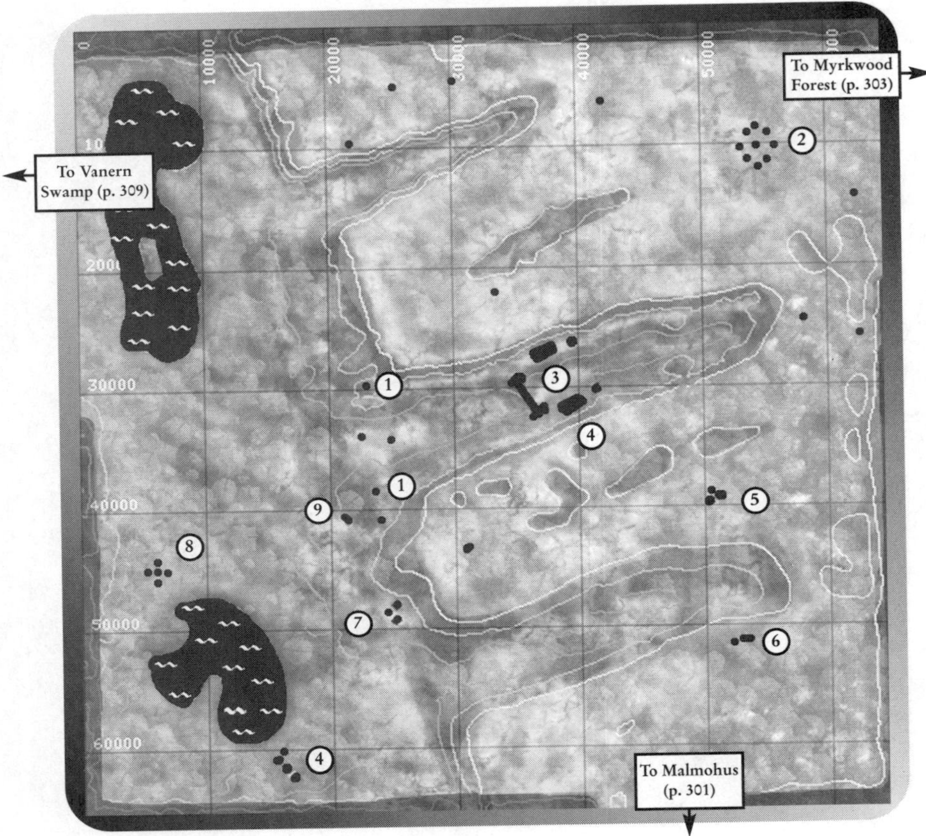

1 Werewolf Lookout Tower
2 Seithkona Stone Pillar Circle
3 Wooden Bridge
4 Werewolf Settlement
5 Camp
6 Werewolf Settlement with Tower
7 Werewolf Camp
8 Sidhe Draoi Camp
9 Entrance to Varulvhamn Dungeon (p. 316)

SVEALAND: EAST SVEALAND

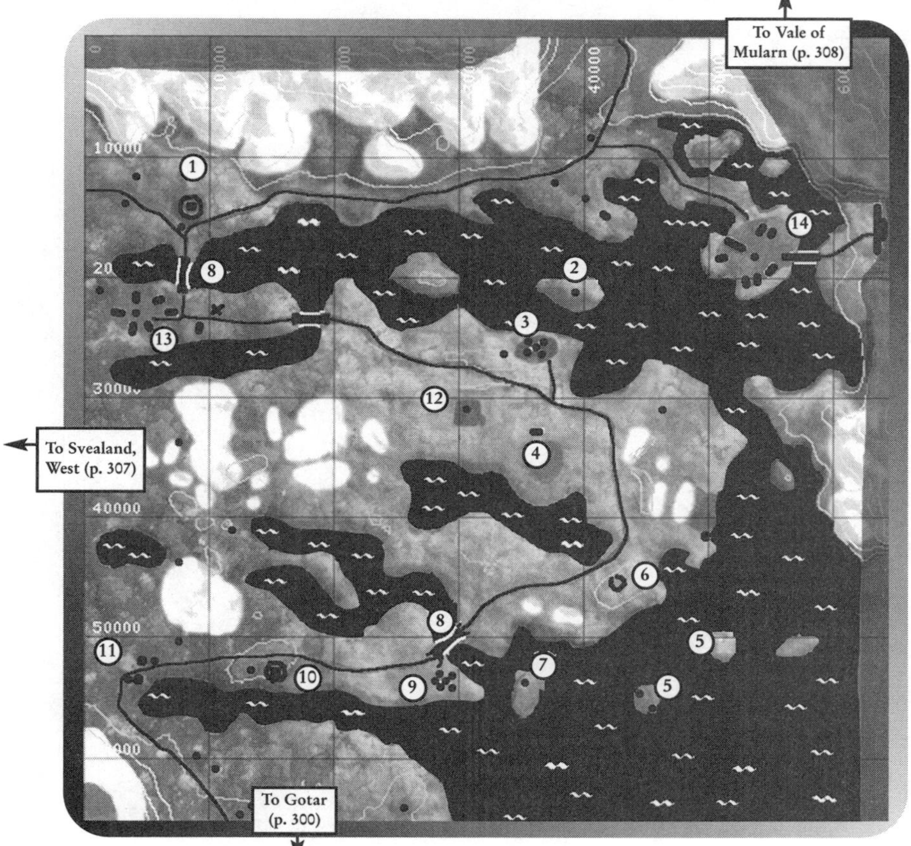

1 Viking Drang Fortress
2 Lynnleigh & Engraved Stone
3 Tomte Camp
4 Kasan's Grave / Farmhouse
5 Engraved Stone
6 Tomte Fort
7 Entrance to Nisse's Lair Dungeon (p.315)
8 Bridge
9 Tomte Camp
10 Fort
11 Dvalin (p. 310)
12 Tomte Lookout Tower
13 Audliten (p. 310)
14 Vasudheim (p. 313)

SVEALAND: WEST SVEALAND

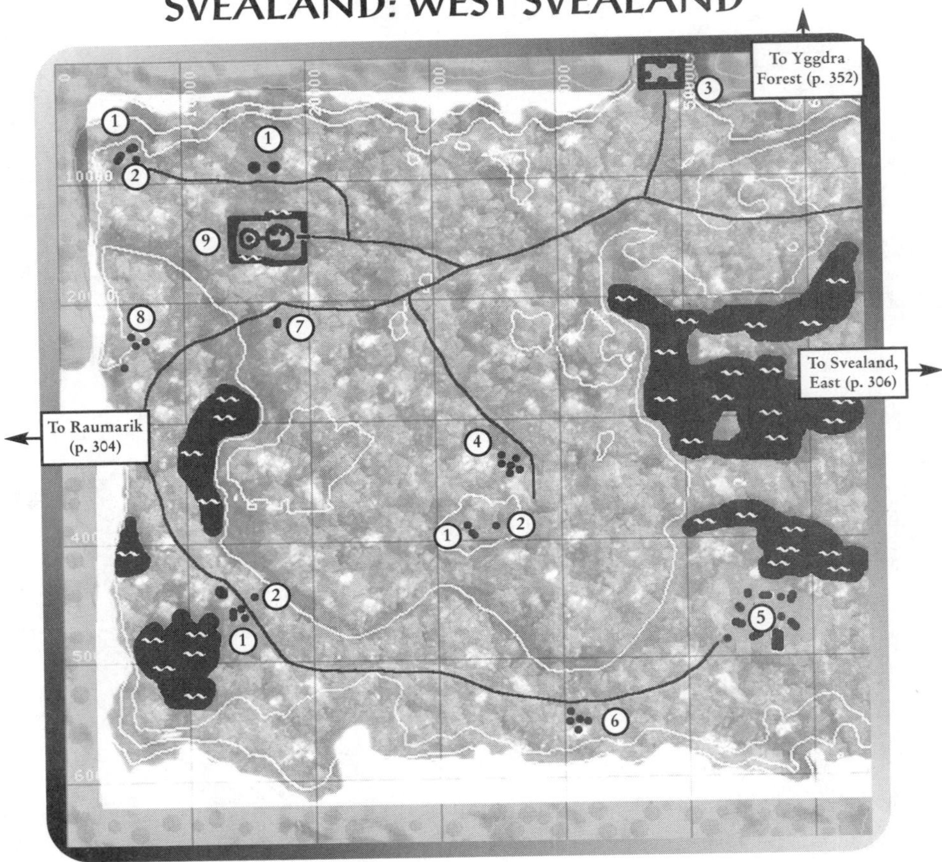

1 Blodfelag Settlement
2 Blodfelag Lookout Tower
3 Vindsaul Faste
4 Blodfelag Camp
5 Huginfel (p. 312)
6 Svartolf Camp
7 Blodfelag Meeting Hall
8 Blodfelag Camp Windcaller
9 Blodfelag Fortress

VALE OF MULARN

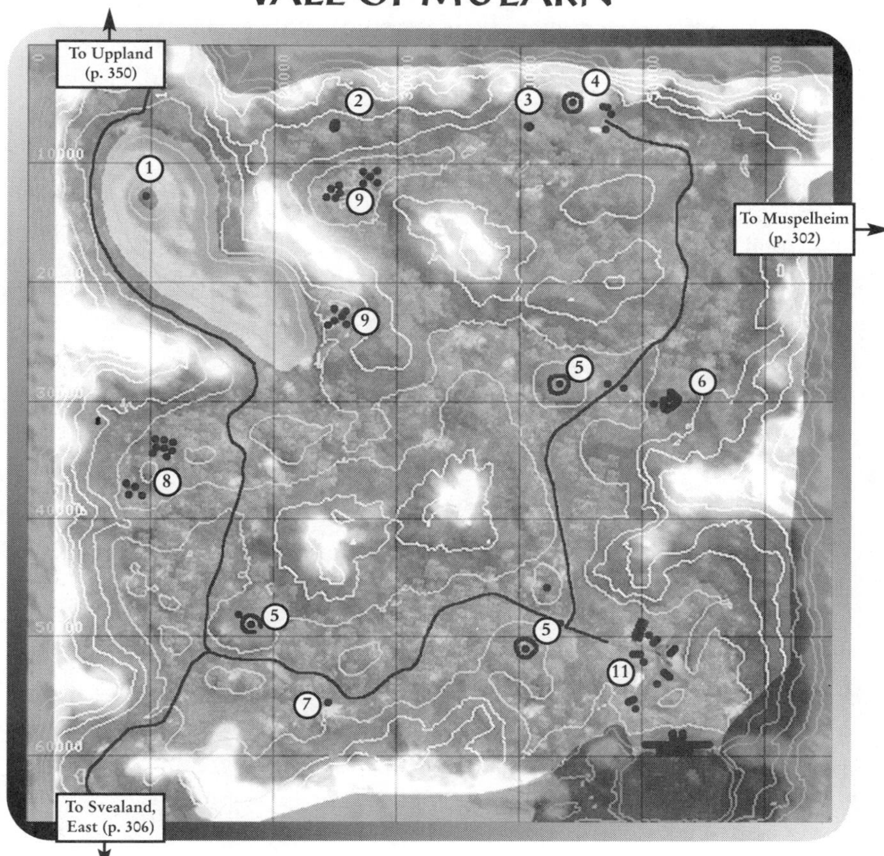

1 Engraved Stone
2 Entrance to Vendo Caverns Dungeon (p. 316)
3 Stone House Ruins
4 Fort Veldon (p. 311)
5 Viking Fort / Lookout Tower
6 Haggerfel (p. 312)
7 Viking Weaponsmith's Wagon
8 Huldu Camp
9 Vendo Camp
10 Demon Teleporter
11 Mularn Village

VANERN SWAMP

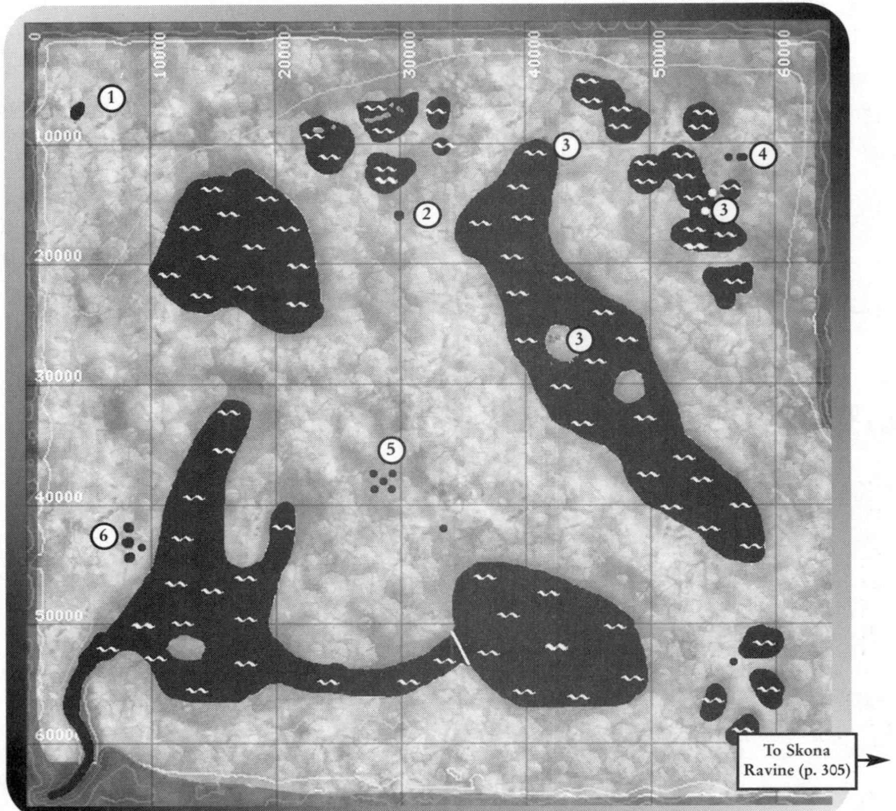

1 Hagbui Farmhouse
2 Stone House Ruins
3 Lookout Tower
4 Settlement
5 Clay Jotun Camp
6 Hagbui Settlement

Audliten

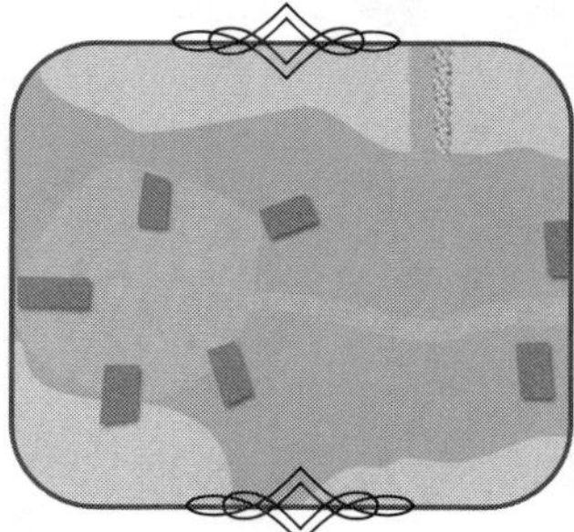

Aleaniver
Inga Arrows
Brede Bows
Gorne
Gruth Svarkedja chain armor
Deilf Starkakedja chain armor
Olav Mjuklaedar leather armor
Eigil Stelskodd studded armor
May
Leim Starkaskodd studded armor
Pireda Starklaedar leather armor
Jordan Svarlaedar leather armor
Ragnar Svarskodd studded armor
Lefur
Dahn Smith
Jolgeir Poisons
Osk Poisons
Hulda Shields
Gwaell
Serath leather dye
Tozur Padded cloth armor
Eirik Staves
Fraglock Stable Master
Armond Axes
Trapper Jora
Josli Spears
Delg Throwing weapons
Pater Swords
Frey Hammers
Geirrid Pansarkedja chain armor

Dvalin

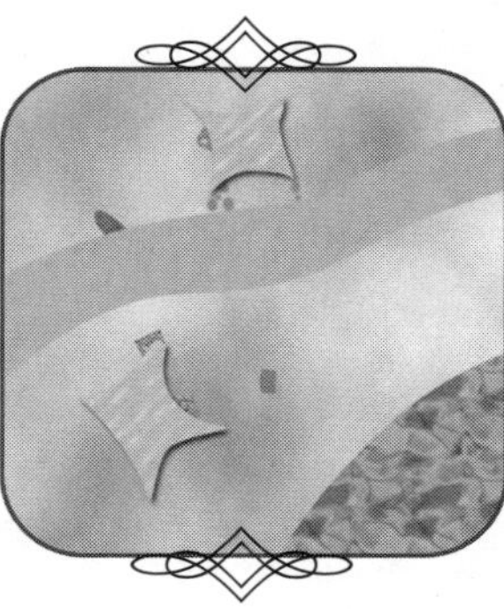

Laran Hammers
Marianne Svarskodd studded armor
Rae Svarlaedar leather armor
Alfrig Starkakedja chain armor
Svard Axes
Vordn Swords
Aesirdia Shields
Laed Starkaskodd studded armor
Tyrn Starkalaedar leather armor
Brok Bows

Fort Atla

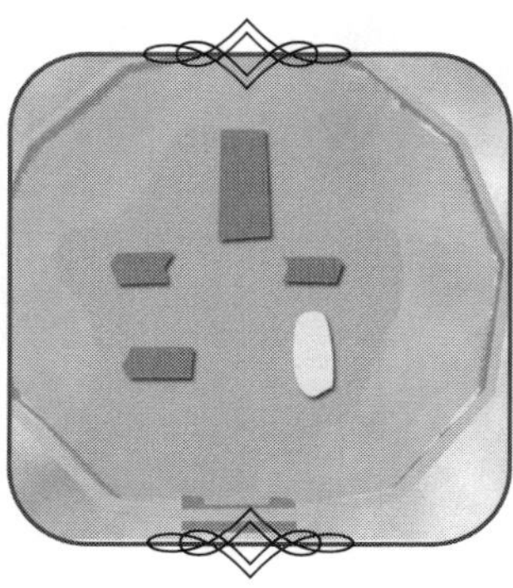

Sillis Arrows
Korgan Shaman Trainer
Jucla Rogue Trainer
Ullaria Cloth dye
Ruk Staff
Og Mjuklaedar leather armor
Hrin Cloth dye
Hyndia Seer Trainer
Finna
Pika Padded cloth
Isleif Large weapons
Halker Warrior Trainer
Trunk Svarskodd studded armor
Lalida Skald Trainer
Budo Hunter Trainer
Amora
Magnild
Lycla Mystic Trainer
Welgen Healer Trainer
Barkeep Tesin
Kari Healer
Vifil Swords
Onund Enchanter
Lagg Stelskodd studded armor
Bersi Poisons
Masri
Helja Poisons
Thetus Runemaster Trainer
Ugg Pansarkedja chain armor
Niniver Runemaster staves
Rundorik Stable Master
Boidoc Shadowblade Trainer
Kalli Berserker Trainer
Finni
Sarry Spiritmaster Trainer
Merarka Spiritmaster staves
Salma Thane Trainer
Yop Axes
Carl Throwing weapons
Krak Bows
Freydis Spears
Eindridi Smith
Stap Hammers
Harald Swords
Klag Shields

Fort Veldon

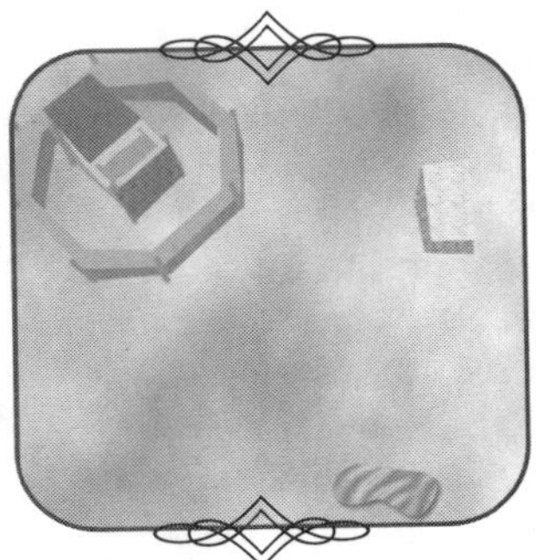

Seiml Enamel dye
Liv Swords
Hlif Axes
Olof Hammers
Darby Starkaskodd studded armor
Idona Starklaedar leather armor
Rulongia Enamel dye
Sydney
Viking Oddnaug
Connor Starkaskodd studded armor
Kell Starkakedja chain armor
Bitta Bows
Avar Shields
Gerda Starklaedar leather armor
Arskar Stable Master

Galplen

Treflun Stable Master
Galena Large weapons
Vanah Skald Trainer
Ohar Enamel dye
Tallya Enamel dye
Kaiti Padded cloth armor
Ysunoic Runemaster staves
Curka Spiritmaster staves
Bec Shaman Trainer
Otkel Shields
Serilyna Staff
Krek Viking Trainer
Stein Swords
Gestod Axes
Helga Hammers
Aki Throwing weapons
Gord Smith
Gudrid Spears
Barkeep Yseniver
Hord Healer
Nyden Svarlaedar leather armor
Thyra Pansarkedja chain armor
Canan Seer Trainer

Gna Faste

Khelad Warrior Trainer
Halldis Enchanter
Itesta Healer Trainer
Zalerik Berserker Trainer
Ulwatyl Smithing/tailoring supplies
Jytal Tailoring/fletching supplies
Aphriodora Thane Trainer
Ingrid Arrows
Kedin Bows
Wolgrun Stable Master

Haggerfel

Yolafson Stable Master
Groa Seer Trainer
Culben Padded cloth armor
Helen
Genlu Edrill Smith
Frikk Various expensive trade equipment
Hilde Smith
Fuiren Spears
Burr Axes
Ime Shields
Arnkatla
Cort Hammers
Armund Swords
Mattie Bows
Takker Arrows
Glum Rogue Trainer
Inaksha
Gustav Healer
Pene Enchanter
Macalena
Eda Staff
Den Pansarkedja chain armor
Dritsa Svarlaedar leather armor
Erik Svarskodd studded armor
Bodil Throwing weapons
Gale Enamel dye
Sinmore Large weapons
Belyria Leather dye
Kran
Yver Tiu

Huginfel

Raker Enchanter
Saydyn Healer
Alyllyra Spiritmaster staves
Elengwen Runemaster staves
Aylarn Padded cloth armor
Enir Starkaskodd studded armor
Runolf Shields
Wulfwer Starklaedar leather armor
Dail
Svala Staff
Samlauf Kolsson
Olgara
Ryden Throwing weapons
Ivara Spears
Dana Arrows
Auda Axes
Lodin Hammers
Kol Smithir Smith
Orm Swords
Radgar Pansarkedja chain armor
Hakon Bows
Arnlaug Enamel dye
Ruloia Enamel dye
Hurg
Thora
Gudlor
Sugnhild
Barkeep Alaka
Corath
Ljot
Valgard
Halla
Prulgar Stable Master
Virge
Bork

Mularn Village

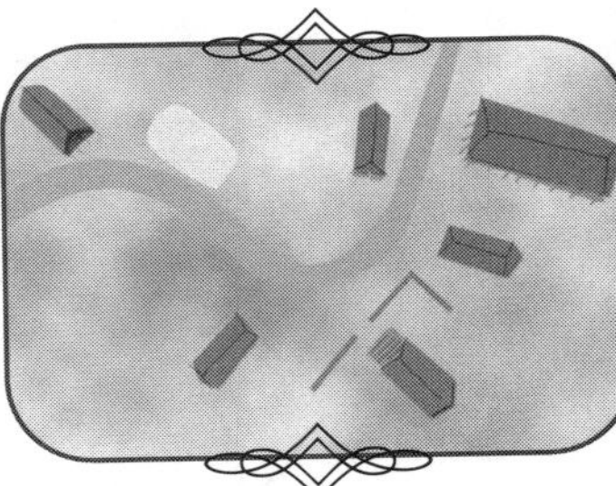

Bolli
Gularg Stable Master
Barkeep Nognar
Brik Staff
Denise
Viking Kreimhilde
Gordin Tuhan
Skapi Viking Trainer
Asta Padded cloth armor
Vigdis Mystic Trainer
Hild Throwing weapons
Elizabeth Enchanter
Kalbin Healer
Cale Leather dye
Lene Mjuklaedar leather armor
Blyn Stelskodd studded armor
Hrolf Axes
Gram Hammers
Vahn Smith
Bein Pansarkedja chain armor
Linna Bows
Marie Shields
Geir Arrows
Aren Swords
Finn Leather dye
Oslin
Aegen
Vers Svarkedja chain armor
Lyna Spiritmaster staves
Raelyan Runemaster staves
Carr

Nalliten

Dink Svarskodd studded armor
Tig Svarlaedar leather armor
Gautr
Rooka Leather dye
Hallaya Leather dye
Cragg Arrows
Eryklan Stable Master
Moona Padded cloth armor
Grungir Pansarkedja chain armor
Geiri
Dalla Swords

Vasudheim

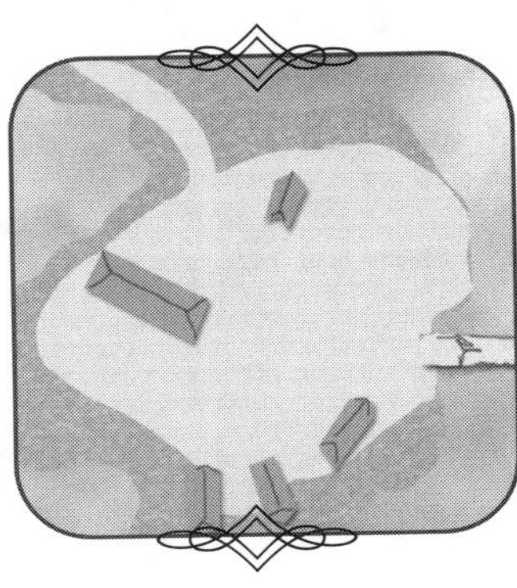

Saeunn Viking Trainer
Kerr Bows
Krisst Arrows
Tric
Ragna Mystic Trainer
Daga
Frimeth
Karl Gat
Gyda Swords
Burl Hammers
Baldus Stelskodd studded armor
Ingerd Tailoring equipment
Leik Axes
Galagore Spears
Arnfinn Smith
Vidar Pansarkedja chain armor
Hallfred Throwing weapons
Fianna Mjuklaedar leather armor
Mildri Staff
Ulf Enchanter
Kjell
Aud Healer
Gunnar Padded cloth armor
Hrut Rogue Trainer
Kyba
Merwdda Runemaster staves
Clena Spiritmaster staves
Alomali
Bothe Shields
Erekith
Arnleif
Tosti Seer Trainer
Krip Svarkedja chain armor
Barkeep Kanar
Thord Blue/teal/red/purple cloth dye
Gregor Green/brown/gray/orange/yellow cloth dye
Yosef Angor
Geoffrey Krath
Kristen
Harlfug Stable Master
Gridash

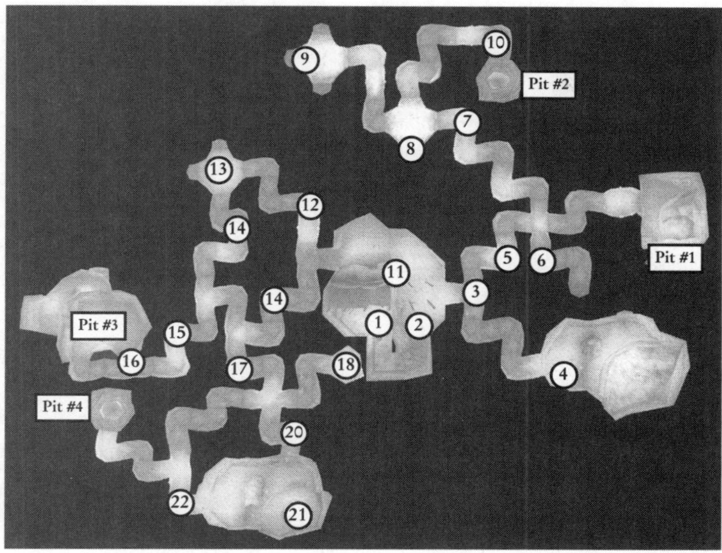

Spindelhalla

1 Blindsnake, Svartalf thrall
2 Svartalf Thrall
3 Svartalf Thrall, Svartalf Arbetare, Terra Crab
4 Stinger, Terra Crab
5 Stinger, Blindsnake, Svartalf Thrall, Terra Crab, Te'Bui
6 Stinger, Terra Crab
7 Spindel, Spindel Silkster, Duegar Hunter
8 Husk
9 Spindel, Husk, Arachite Husker, Spindel Silkster
10 Spindel Silkster, Ara. Husker
11 Svartalf Arbetare, Svartalf Thrall, Svartalf Foreman
12 Ara. Tunnelhost
13 Hallaratta, Ara. Tunnelhost, Ara. Vakt
14 Ara. Impaler, Ara. Tunnelhost
15 Blindsnake, Ara. Tunnelhost
16 Duegar Tjuv
17 Ara. Impaler
18 Ara. Krigare, Ara. Prelate
19 Ara. Tunnelhost
20 Ara. Vakt
21 Ara. Prelate, Ara. Grymherre
22 Ara. Krigare
23 Ara. Krigare

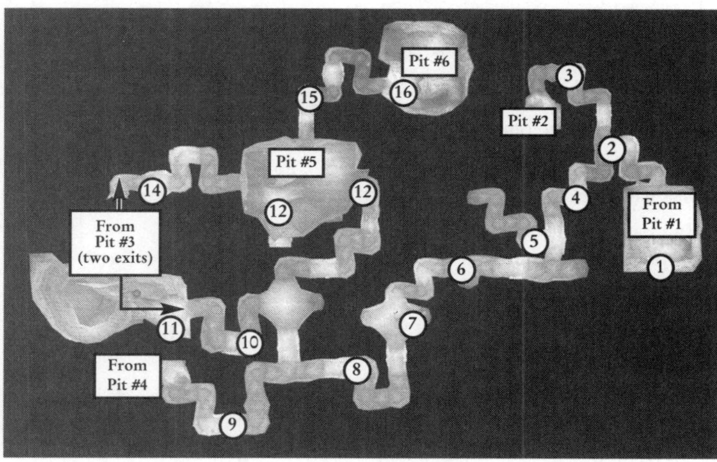

(Spindelhalla Level 2)

1 Terra Crab
2 Terra Crab
3 Ekyps Scavenger, Mad Kobold
4 Ekyps Scav., Terra Crab
5 Ekyps Scav., Mad Kobold
6 Fell Cat, Ekyps Gunstling
7 Ekyps Gunstling, Fell Cat, Stor Ekyps, Djupt Vivunde
8 Ekyps Gunstling
9 Djupt Odjur, Ekyps Gunstling, Ekyps Scav.
10 Cursed Thulian, Undead Troll Warrior
11 Cave Trow
12 Ekyps Scav., Mad Kobold
13 Ekyps Scav., Deeplurk Feeder
14 Ekyps Scav.
15 Cursed Thalion, Undead Troll Warrior
16 Cave Trow

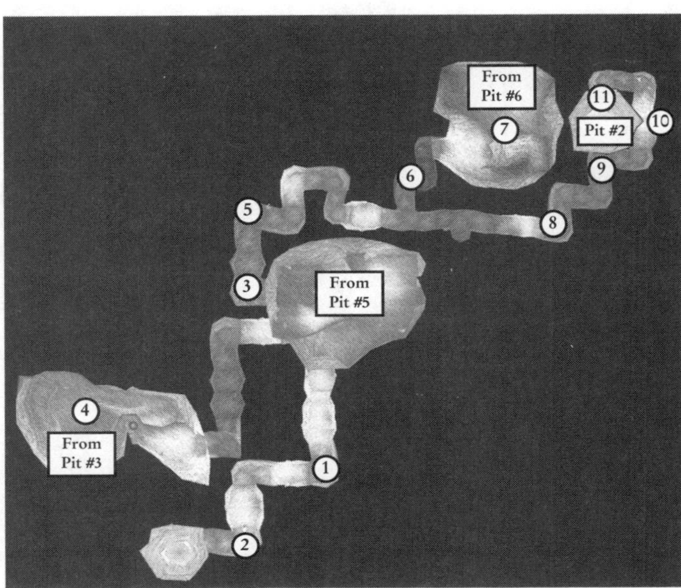

(Spindelhalla Level 3)

1 Djupt Usling
2 Djupt Usling
3 Crusher, Cave Trow, Cave Troll Trollkarl
4 Cave Troll Trollkarl
5 Deeplurk Manslayer, Kopparorm
6 Deeplurk Feeder
7 Crusher, Cave Troll Trollkarl, Cave Trow, Igo
8 Deeplurk Manslayer, Deeplurk Feeder
9 Deeplurk Dissembler, Deeplurk Manslayer
10 Deeplurk Dissembler
11 Ond
12 Djupt Usling, Kopparorm

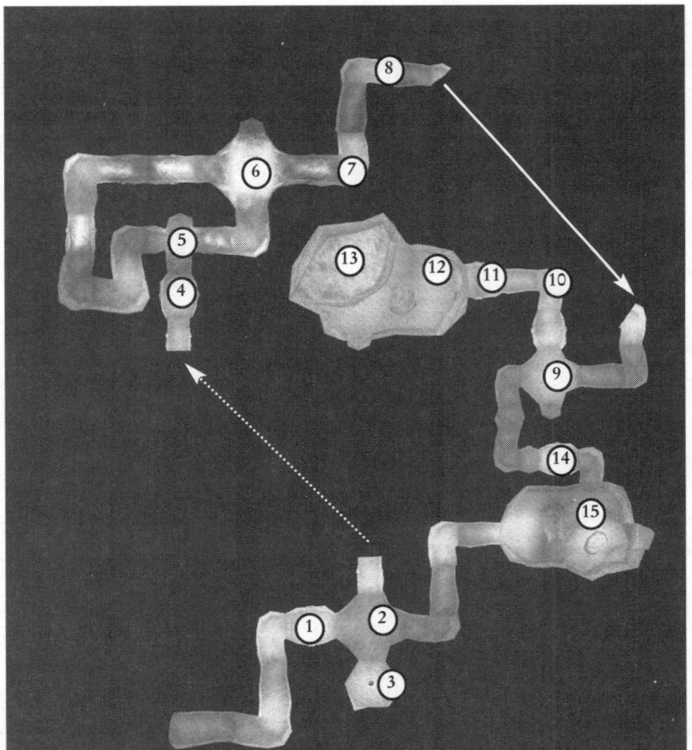

Nisse's Lair

1 Tomte Cutthroat
2 T. Cutthroat, Lair Patrol
3 T. Warhound, T. Handler
4 Lair Guard, T. Shaman
5 Cave Spider, Haunt
6 Cave Spider
7 Poisonous Cave Spider
8 T. Runner
9 T. Hoodoo, T. Jagger, T. Runner, T. Caitiff
10 T. Guard
11 T. Guard
12 T. Zealot, T. Seer
13 T. Guard, Nisse
14 T. Hoodoo, T. Proctector
15 T. Captor, Executioner, Prisoner, T. Guard

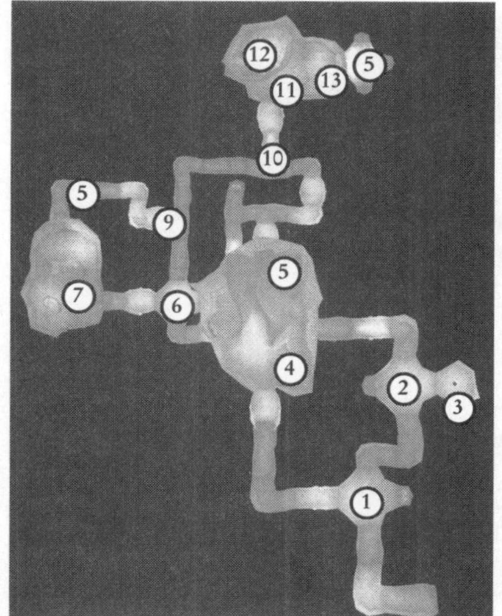

Varulvhamn

1 Werewolf Churl
2 Were. Churl, Crazed Lycantic
3 Crazed Lycantic, Were. Churl, Ffaz
4 Were. Churl, Crazed Lycantic
5 Were. Churl
6 Wolfspider, Large Wolfspider, Were. Churl, Wolfaur Pragmatic, Wolfaur Quixot
7 Wolfaur Q., Wolfaur Pragmatic, Thelod
8 Wolfaur Q.
9 Wolfaur Pragmatic, Wolfaur Q.
10 W. Bodyguard, W. Noble
11 W. Grimnought, Lord Ungar, Lord Grym, Lord Brumma, Lord Vild, Lord Gifttand, Lord Huggleand
12 W. Bodyguard
13 Frenetic Wolfspider
14 Wolfaur Q.
15 Wolfaur Q., Wolfaur Lunarian
16 Wolfaur Lunarian, Wolfaur Q.
17 Frenetic Wolfspider
18 Wolfaur Q.
19 Frenetic Wolfspider

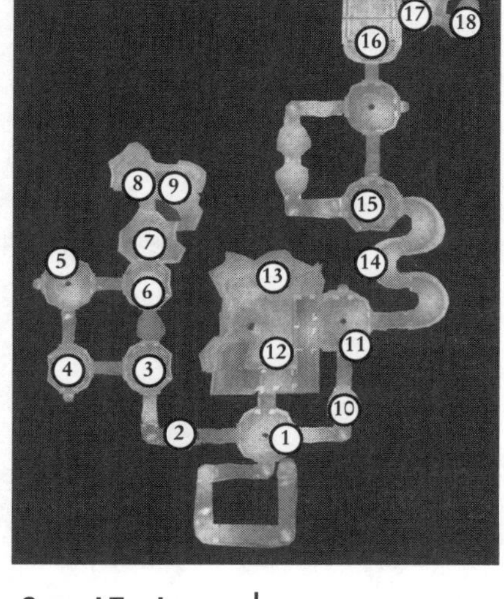

Cursed Tomb

1 Cave Crab, Tomb Sentry
2 Draugr Warrior, Corpse Crawler
3 Draugr Warrior, Vengeful Ghoul, Mad Rat, Corpse Crawler
4 Dungeon Chitin, Cursed Mora, Poisonous Cave Spider, Vengeful Ghoul
5 Vengeful Ghoul
6 Draugr Hound
7 Dungeon Chitin, Roaming Corpse
8 Roaming Corpse, Dungeon Crab, Dungeon Chitin, Corpse Crawler
9 Dungeon Crab
10 Tomb Sentry, Roaming Corpse, Cave Crab
11 Tomb Sentry
12 Tomb Sentry, Cursed Spirit, Corpse Crawler, Cave Crab
13 Cursed Spirit, Tomb Priestess
14 Mad Rat, Poisonous Cave Spider, Cave Crab
15 Corpse Crawler, Mad Rat, Poisonous Cave Spider, Cave Crab
16 Dishonored Hagbui, Bevard
17 Draugr Warrior, Corpse Crawler
18 Rotting Corpse, Corpse Crawler
19 Cursed Mora, Cursed Mora Dancer, Cursed Mora Weeper, Troika

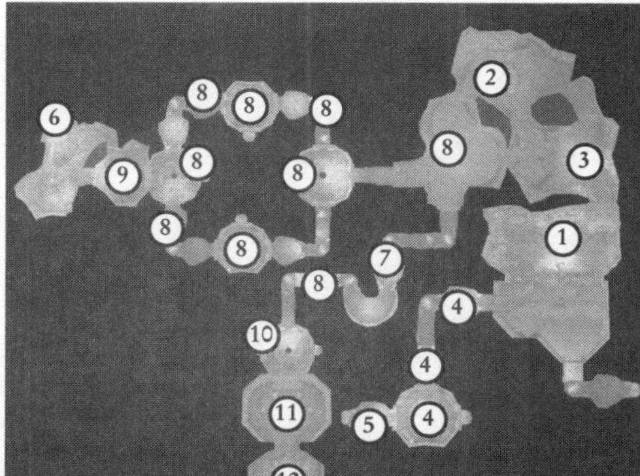

Vendo Cave

1 Cave Crawler, Goblin Guard, Small Cave Bear, Spider
2 Cave Crawler, Vendo Snake Charmer
3 Cave Mauler, Cave Bear, Grjotguard
4 Goblin Guard
5 Goblin Guard, Goblin Advisor
6 Spider
7 Spider, Vendo guard
8 Vendo Guard
9 Vendo Guard, Spider
10 Vendo Yowler
11 Vendo Yowler, Svendo, Cave Ogre
12 Vendo Yowler, Vendo Savager

Realm vs. Realm

Mythic has designed Dark Age of Camelot *to be the best of both worlds. There are plenty of places to go and things to do without putting yourself in danger of being "player killed." Sure, you can be killed just as dead by a monster, but you'll always know what you're facing (as long as you have this strategy guide handy). As long as you're safe within the walls of your realm, no one can kill you out of malice or spite.*

However, after a while you may get to feeling like facing The Greatest Enemy — players from other realms. This is really the meat of the DAoC *experience. Try it and see if you like it.*

Basics

zKill … but be nice. Please remember that while RvR is a game where it's a good thing to kill people … it's really not okay to try to hurt people's feelings. You can have a good time, and slaughter people by the dozens, while still being mature and appropriate to the situation.

Don't stalk. Killing the same people over and over isn't fun, it's griefing.

Gating

In *DAoC*, you can't "accidentally" wander into enemy Realm (RvR) territory. It's not over the hill, or through the door, or even on the other side of a gate. It takes a spell … and it's arranged so that you'll see this spell coming.

1) Your character should be at least Level 15. Newbies can't play with the big kids, that's just the way it is.
2) You must go to the special area.

Albion	Castle Sauvage
Hibernia	Connacht border keep
Midgard	Uppland border keep

   Inside the castle/keep, off to the side a bit, is a raised platform ... but that comes in later.

3) Purchase a Medallion of Passage to your chosen destination from the vendor nearby. Put on the medallion. (The vendor is very helpful, and will tell you what to do with the medallion, and how to prepare for the gating ceremony.)

   Gating eats up all your medallions … don't buy more than one!

4) About every fifteen minutes, half a dozen casters will come out and stand around the platform. At this time you have one minute to get on the platform, medallion in place. Once the spell begins, you can't "jump in." You'll have to wait for the next gating ceremony.

Tada! You're in enemy territory.

You'll need another medallion to gate back.

Keep Claiming (and Maintenance)

Claiming. Checklist for claiming a keep is:

* You must claim permission (assigned to your current rank).
* You must be in a full group (i.e., have 8 members of your guild grouped).
* Your guild must have at least 500 Guild Bounty Points.
* You must be standing next to the Keep Lord of the keep you wish to claim.
* It cannot be owned by a group friendly to yours.
* Your guild must not own any other keep.

If all conditions are met, type **/gc claim**.

A message goes out realm-wide (to whichever realm controls the outpost) when it is claimed or released. Everyone who belongs to the pertinent guild is notified, as well as realm members of realm level 10 or higher.

Fees. There is a cost associated with owning a keep — 50 Guild Bounty Points per hour, per level of keep (a keep starts off at Level 1).

When your guild runs out of bounty points, your claim on the keep is released. If you miss the rent, you're out.

Upgrade. A guild can upgrade a keep — this upgrades the keep's NPCs.

Anyone who has Upgrade permission can **/gc upgrade** to bump up the keep's level. Each keep will have an "upgrade" level from 1 to 10. The higher the keep's level, the stronger (combat strength) the guards, archers, patrollers and Keep Lord are. Since each additional level costs 50 GBPs, a Level 1 keep costs 50 an hour, a maximum level (Level 10) keep costs 500 GBPs per hour.

Release. To release a claim on a keep, a guild member who is of a rank that has Release privileges can use the **/gc release** command (from anywhere in the game). This releases your claim on the keep, stops the hourly charge of Guild Bounty Points, and allows you to claim a new keep.

Keep Raids

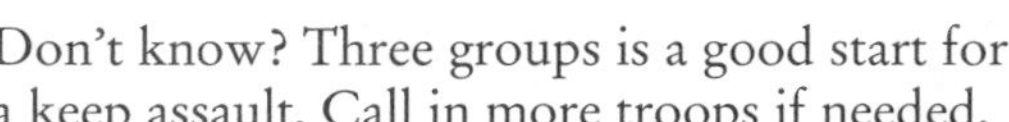

Special thanks to Nate "Stylean" Nieman

Who do you take? The size of your keep raiding force is entirely dependant upon how many defenders you expect to be inside the keep. No defenders? No problem — you can do it with 8, possibly fewer, depending upon how coordinated your folks are. As the number of defenders increases, so should the number of your keep raid force.

This number depends upon the class composition of both you and them. A good rule of thumb is for every three or four defenders, you should add *another group* to the assault force. Yes, another group! Three or four people can defend a keep against sixteen attackers, if they have a good class composition.

Don't know? Three groups is a good start for a keep assault. Call in more troops if needed.

Pick off the guards. Okay, so you've got your raid party together.

First, set up your raid force on the perimeter of the keep's guards — in other words, stay out of aggro range of the static guards.

Now eliminate the roaming patrols while your raid force is set up here. The standard place to set this up is facing the keep's main door, although sneaky attack forces will hit from the side or rear.

Once the roamers are dealt with, send in one person to start pulling the static guards out to the raid force. This can be done by walking toward a static guard until he reacts, and

then running back. Classes with Speed Songs excel at this … but *not casters* (even if they have Speed Songs) because they don't have the Hit Points to survive the archers' attacks. Continue to pull the NPC melee guards until they're all gone from the front of the keep.

Clear the door. Now, send 1 person up to the door, and have them play "tag" on the door. In other words, run at the door until you collide with it, then turn around and run back to the raid party. This is because there are often more melee-type guards inside the keep that are not visible, who will aggro on anyone standing near the door. Kill 'em. This is a good way to get them out of the way before the main force heads up to the door.

Rush the door. Now that all the melee guards are dealt with, move the raid force up to the door. Have your tanks lead the rush, so that NPC archers lock onto them first. The tanks should deploy shields and engage the archers, removing them from the fight. Make sure the tanks have healer support to keep them up and running. Meanwhile, have casters take out archers on the ramparts.

The full-out battle. At this point PC defenders are going to start making your life miserable. Be ready for massive AoE attacks near the gate, snipers shooting at you from the ramparts, and melee-types porting out of the keep to wreak havoc in your frontlines. Remember, stun and mez don't go away just because the defenders are inside the keep, so be ready for those as well.

Retreat as needed. If the defenders are doing too much damage to the raid force (i.e., you're getting your butts kicked), pull back and rest, and then go and do it again. Don't stay near the gate if your force is getting hammered, as guard "repopping" at the wrong time can destroy your raid force.

Equipment. Siege equipment is essential when dealing with a well-defended keep. Get rams up and running on the door, and keep them running *at all costs*. Abandoning a ram at a door costs time — and you can bet the defenders are using that extra time to repair the door, rez the dead inside the keep, and call for help.

Rogues. Assassin-types who can climb should be used to deal with threats inside the keep. Door-repair people and AoE casters should be #1 priority. A defended keep with key personnel can become vulnerable by simply removing 2 or 3 of those people. Don't remove them, and your job becomes 100 times harder to accomplish.

Getting in. Knocking down the doors can take any amount of time, based on the sizes of the armies clashing. Keep assaults have run more than eight hours before they were resolved. Remember, sometimes you just can't win. If you think you're in that situation, and you can't pull in more troops, you're going to have to retreat. (The only other option is to split off a small group to go assault an undefended keep while the main army keeps the defenders here busy.) If you can't take the keep, don't fight. The defenders have the stronger position. If you *can't* win, they'll make you suffer in the end.

The final push. Assuming you gain access to the keep, kill all remaining PC defenders on the ground floor and the ramparts first. Then remove the archers from the ramparts, if any are remaining, and proceed up to the Lord's room. Attack him — while paying close attention to what's going on around you. Be ready for guard repops, possible NPC archers shooting you through walls, etc.

Be prepared for PCs helping the Lord. *Always* kill players before NPCs. A healer focused on a Lord can cause a lot of damage to a raid force indirectly, just by healing the Lord.

Celebrate your job well done!

RvR Combat

Also with special thanks to Nate Nieman

Before you enter your first RvR battle, you must understand that it can be vicious. You may think that some of the monsters you've battled were tough and fast, but they are nothing compared to a gang of PCs who might well be not only tougher, but also more experienced and better organized than you are. There is only one way to long-term success in the RvR lands, and that's to be better than most of the enemies you meet there. There is no magic formula in RvR which will allow any ordinary player to prosper once they learn it. RvR is an intensely competitive activity that has to be practiced to be mastered.

In RvR, the party is everything. Random, just-for-fun, "pick-up" parties can win the day on occasion, but in general, they don't last long in RvR expeditions. As mentioned, there's no way to tell whether the next group you meet is going to be tougher or more powerful than you are, but the one thing you can control in RvR is to make sure your party knows itself thoroughly, and will react with maximum unity and efficiency. The secret to winning RvR combat on a regular basis is making the whole (the party) greater than the sum of the parts.

There are no shortcuts. On a winning RvR team everybody knows their own capabilities, the capabilities of everybody else on the team, their expected function in combat, and exactly how the game works. And when we say everybody, we do mean *everybody*. One clueless member, even if they're the weakest and least-important member of the group, can send the whole fight south for everybody with one false move. How do you avoid this? Easy. Talk to your team members, pay attention, and practice.

One other thing: the goal of RvR combat is not to amass Realm Points. The only goal of RvR is to *survive*. If you can do that, the Realm Points will come.

Who's In Charge Here? Always remember, "teamwork" does not equal "democracy." A successful RvR party will have a leader who leads, while the rest of the party follows. A strong leader who knows the game and knows how to communicate on the battlefield is probably the single most powerful edge a party can have in RvR.

The group leader has two major responsibilities in combat. The first is to physically lead the group — take point, be in front. Since RvR situations develop and resolve so fast, there's no time to pass along information. It has to be acted on as soon as it's perceived. The group leader should be the member of the team best able to assess and react to a hostile engagement instantly.

This leads directly to the leader's second responsibility, to "trigger" the group. When a situation develops, the group leader decides whether to engage, or to take off. Fight or flight. When the group leader changes direction, the rest of the party needs to be able to instantly follow, no questions asked. There's no time in RvR to type, "Run away!" or even "Charge!" There's just time to do it. (Autofollow, however, is *not* recommended in RvR combat. It allows the player to go along without thinking where he's going or paying attention to the surroundings, both very fatal mistakes in RvR combat.)

There's no one class that makes the best team leaders, but as the first person to engage the enemy, the team leader is naturally suited to being either a front-line fighter (the one that actually charges the enemy), or a "crowd-control" caster: that is, the one with the most and best mez spells. (See "Party Time," below.)

Raid Lead. If you're leading multiple parties in a large strike force, the leader's job becomes quite different. For a Raid Leader, communication is all important. You have to know where you're going before you start out, and make sure everybody in your force knows it too – multiple parties will not follow a single player indefinitely with no destination. You also have to keep your force focused on the primary goal. If three or four players scamper off after some random troll, that significantly undermines your force, and if that happens three or four times, you probably don't have a force left any more. Once the battle is joined, you'll actually have some time to give orders. Perhaps the best thing you can do during an actual battle is to make sure the less experienced players know what they're supposed to be doing, so they don't screw it up for everybody.

Move it Move it Move it!! One thing to always keep in mind during an RvR expedition … Keep moving. Call as few halts as possible, and try to be moving again within a minute. Confusion – the *enemy's* confusion – is your friend. Ideally he'll never know you're in his space until you're either jumping down his throat, or long gone.

Use the Terrain. This is an important but much-neglected survival skill in RvR.

Stay off the roads. You're much less likely to run into an enemy army that way.

Staying behind a treeline is a good way to ensure that you can see an enemy before he sees you. However, archers like to set up ambushes in forested areas. If you're in the treeline and you start taking fire, particularly from multiple directions, head out for an open space as quickly as possible. That way the snipers have to expose themselves if they want to continue the fight.

Use the elevations. You can see much further in all directions from the heights, allowing you to pick your targets and plan your assaults better. You can also be seen on the heights, but only if the enemy remembers to look up as they move past. This brings us to the converse of this rule: always remember to look up, down and behind you when moving in enemy territory. Nothing is more embarrassing than having a horde of screaming bad guys descend on your rear because your party forgot to check the top of the hill they were sitting on.

Is Chivalry Dead? Let's say you're a fully-packed RvR party, and you happen across one or two enemies out killing monsters for experience. Let's say the enemy is right in the middle of their fight. Do you ..

A. Let them finish the monster before piling on. They aren't a real danger, and they might as well get the experience from the monsters before you send them off to the next world. Plus, if you kill them while they're engaged, they'll take an experience hit when they rez, adding insult to injury.

B. Take them out fast and hard. Who says they aren't a real danger? Everybody in enemy territory is a "real danger." Anyway, that's what they get for monster-hunting in an RvR area anyway. Evolution in action.

The question remains open, with vehement defenders on both sides. On the one hand, letting the enemy have their kill earns you definite style points, and you might find yourself on the other side of the situation some day. On the other hand, eventually it's going to bite you in the butt. Your call, based on the way your party chooses to roleplay.

Fighters' Blues. One sad but irrefutable fact about RvR combat (as this book goes to press) is that front-line fighters are seriously nerfed. Right now, the fighter's function in combat is, at best, to get nuked by their nuker while your nuker nukes their nuker instead of their nuker nuking your nuker.

In short, you're a rather fragile and not particularly convincing decoy. Plus, you don't get any Realm Points if you're dead, no matter how heroic your sacrifice.

The problem is not just that fighters' damage lags far behind casters' (although it does), it's that it's darn near impossible to get to a caster with your offensive potential intact. Between Roots, Stuns, Mezzes and combat Debuffs, it's going to take you way too long to close with a nuker, and once you get there you'll probably be at a fraction of your full offensive potential.

As plans to revamp RvR combat go forward, expect this discrepancy to be addressed. However, it will probably remain true for some time that mages will dominate player vs. player combat, while fighters remain in more of a support role.

Healing Blues. Healers don't play the same central role in RvR combat that they do in fights against monsters. They're still important both before the fight (Buffs) and after (resurrections & healings). However, because RvR combat is so quick and vicious, there's just not time for a healer to do much during the actual combat. At best, expect to get off one instant heal on an individual, and one more on the party before it's all over but the shouting. Of course, getting these two heals off at just the right time may well mean the difference between victory and defeat. And when you're creating a healer, don't forget that you've got other abilities besides healing. Put some points and effort into those other abilities, and you'll find yourself a lot more useful in RvR.

Oil and Water. If your party relies heavily on Mez spells to get the drop on the enemy, don't use any Area of Effect spells. Once you have a significant chunk of the enemy force mezzed, an AoE spell is like Mr. Grenade after the pin is pulled. It's No Longer Your Friend.

Disclaimer. We're saying that AoE spells are a bad idea if you're relying on a mez-heavy strategy. We are not saying that AoE is always a bad idea in RvR combat. There are potentially effective strategies that rely very heavily on AoE spells. It's just the combination of AoE and Mez that should be avoided.

PARTY TIME

There are a lot of potential strategies for RvR combat, and a different ideal party composition for each one. The example we give you here is a party based on a battle-tested strategy built on the concept of mezzing as many enemies as quickly as possible.

This party concept has six "core" slots and two "open" slots. (It's always better to have a full eight characters in a party than to have fewer … always assuming, of course, that all eight know what they're doing.) The "core" functions are:

Crowd Control. This is the mage that does the mezzing. The idea is to get the entire enemy force mezzed as quickly as possible, then let the fighters and nukers take them out one or two at a time. Crowd Control needs to be able to analyze and react to a situation almost instantaneously, making for a natural overlap between this slot and the team leader's job. Best classes for this post are Sorcerer, Mentalist and Spiritmaster.

Commando. This is a pure fighter whose job is to engage the enemy directly, causing as much chaos as possible. If you and the rest of your party are very, very good, you will eventually come to a point where you sometimes survive the battle. This is a thankless job, but absolutely essential. Any heavily combat-based class can fulfill this function. Polearms work particularly well.

Tank. This is the back-up, defensive fighter. He may move in with the commando, or he may hang back to intercept enemy commandos, or he may work the flanks, taking out archers and casters on the outskirts of the main group. This is also a good task for the leader, since it requires sizing up each situation and reacting instantly for best effect. Any well-armored fighter class can do this.

Medic. This is somebody to dish out the Heals and the Rezzes. During combat, the Medic should always zero in on the commando to keep him alive, so your nuker and crowd control have more time to take enemy forces out of commission. Clerics, Druids and Healers are your primary medics.

Nuker. Your main offensive spellcaster. Actually does most of the damage to the enemy. Theurgists, Mentalists or Runemasters are the classes to look to.

Speed. Three words: Group Speed Buff. High mobility is your primary defensive asset in enemy territory. (See Move it Move it Move it!! above.) Do not even try to make it in RvR without the ability to move in (and out) of combat at supernatural speed. You're looking for Minstrels, Bards and Skalds here.

Open Slots. That leaves two more slots to fill. You want the characters in your "core" slots to be as optimized as possible for their function, so this is where you can put those less-focused, more-rounded hybrid classes, as well as specialists like thief-types and archers. Probably the single most useful type to have in an open slot is a back-up healer, with rez ability if possible. Back-up nukers are good, but avoid casters heavily specialized in AoE spells, as discussed under "Oil and Water," above. A really experienced AoE caster, though, who's good at analyzing situations in combat, can still be a good addition to your party.

You can add a "Blitzkrieg" class — someone who will break through the front lines and wreak havoc. Assassins and scouts fit this description.

Another useful and very versatile option is the stealther. This is either an archer-type or rogue-type character with high Stealth skill. The stealther's duty is to guard the nukers and healers against enemy stealthers, and feed the group info about enemy locations. Once he's reasonably sure that there are no enemy stealthers, he can wait for the group to engage, then move in under cover and try to take out or disrupt the enemy any way he can from close quarters.

The Venus Flytrap

Alternative, Stealth-Based RvR concept

Thanks to "Bilal the Rat"

They call this strategy "The Venus Flytrap," because it looks very inviting until you're inside it.

The basic party makeup is:

1 Healer (with Crowd Control potential)

1 Speed

3 Archers

3 Rogues/Assassins

Find an open area and put the Speed and the Healer in the middle. Then they just stand there. The Stealthers deploy and hide so that they're guarding access points to the exposed characters. Eventually, an enemy party will wander along and think, "Aha, two suckers out monster-hunting. Let's get 'em!"

When this happens, the Stealthers pop up and take on the attackers. The Healer supports them by mezzing as best he can, while the Speed stands by to defend the Healer. If the battle starts to go bad, the Speed grabs the Healer and takes off, while the Stealthers hide and slink off. Eventually, everybody meets up at a pre-arranged fall-back point to regroup.

Don't forget that *everything* is subjective. There may be times in RvR where 6 AoE'ers going off nonstop can be more powerful than 6 mezzers. Conversely, 1 mezzer can be more powerful than 10 AoE'ers in the right situation.

Each engagement is unique, and must be evaluated as such. Everything relies on the individual situation, and that's part of what makes RvR so much fun!

Siege Equipment

Using Siege Weapons

Siege Weapons are a vital element of RvR warfare, and are made by players with Siegecrafting.

There are three types of Siege Weapons.

Rams. This is the up-close-and-personal device for bashing anything big and heavy. Keep doors and gates are usual targets.

Ballistae. These are mostly used to destroy other siege weapons, only from a much safer distance than a ram.

Catapults. This is used against the enemy fortifications, and often even against the enemy themselves.

There are four steps in using Ballistae and Catapults.

Target. Select the target to be destroyed.

Arm. The machine must be readied. This takes a while.

Load. Put the materials you've been lugging around into the machine's inventory window, then select the specific material to load for the next shot.

Fire. The weapon fires its load at the target.

Components

The final stage of crafting siege equipment provides the only exception to the rule that you must have all components in your inventory. When crafting siege equipment, the final components do not have to be in your inventory. However, you have to own them and they must be within 512 world units (about nine paces) of where you're standing.

Siege Equipment Recipes

Abbreviations

Time. Time to craft the item, in seconds.
Skills. **A**rmorcraft / **C**lothworking / **F**letching / **L**eatherworking / **M**etalworking / **S**iegecraft / **T**ailoring / **Wd** = Woodworking / **Wp** = Weaponcraft.
Tools. **F** = Forge / **H** = Smith's Hammer / **K** = Sewing Kit / **P** = Planing Tool.
Components. **B** = Metal or Ore Bars / **C**loth Squares / **L**eather / **T**hread / **W**ooden Boards.
Costs. Costs are listed in **G**old and **S**ilver, rounded to the nearest Silver.

Siege Equipment

Item	Time	Skills	Tools	Components	Cost (G.S)
Small Ram	6	S1/M,L,Wd0	K,H,P	cladding, ram beak, 2 swing harnesses, 300 elm W	27.37
Scorpion	6	S1/M,C,Wd0	K,H,P	gimbal, 2 torsion cables, spring arm, trigger, 400 elm W	80.32
Onager	6	S1/Wd,L,M0	K,H,P	bucket, cushion, winding crank, counterweight, pivot, 600 elm W	117.60
Ram	6	S1/M,L,Wd0	K,H,P	cladding, ram beak, 2 swing harnesses, 300 oaken W	32.77
Ballista	6	S1/M,C,Wd0	K,H,P	gimbal, 2 torsion cables, spring arm, trigger, 400 oaken W	87.52
Catapult	6	S1/Wd,L,M0	K,H,P	bucket, cushion, winding crank, counterweight, pivot, 600 oaken W	128.40
Siege Ram	6	S1/M,L,Wd0	K,H,P	cladding, ram beak, 2 swing harnesses, 300 ironwood W	47.17
Palintone	6	S1/M,C,Wd0	K,H,P	gimbal, 2 torsion cables, spring arm, trigger, 400 ironwood W	106.72
Trebuchet	6	S1/Wd,L,M0	K,H,P	bucket, cushion, winding crank, counterweight, pivot, 600 ironwood W	157.20

Siege Components

Item	Time	Skills	Tools	Components	Cost (G.S)
Arm Cushion*	38	T500/M,L,C200	K,H	100 iron/ferrite B, 400 tanned L, 400 linen C	5.40
Ballista Trigger*	38	T500/M,L,C200	K,H	100 iron/ferrite B, 300 tanned L, 450 linen C	5.00
Bucket*	38	A500/M200	F,H	400 iron/ferrite B	5.60
Counterweight*	38	A500/M200	F,H	400 iron/ferrite B	5.60
Gimbal*	38	A500/M200	F,H	400 iron/ferrite B	5.60
Pivot*	30	Wp500/M200	F,H	450 iron/ferrite B	6.30
Ram Beak*	30	Wp500/M200	F,H	140 iron/ferrite B	1.96
Ram Cladding*	38	A500/M200	F,H	140 iron/ferrite B	1.96
Spring Arms*	30	Wp500/L,M200	K,H,F	100 tanned L, 300 iron/ferrite B	4.80
Swing Harness*	38	T500/M,L,C200	K,H	36 iron/ferrite B, 110 tanned L, 20 linen T	1.24
Torsion Cables*	30	F500/L,C485	F,H	100 tanned L, 400 linen T	2.04
Winding Crank*	30	Wp500/M200	F,H	400 iron/ferrite B	5.60

** Siege components will never be part of a consignment order.*

Realm Abilities

As this guide went to press, Mythic released a draft version of the new Realm Abilities system. Even though we know parts of this system will change, we believe that it will be more useful for you to have it (even with bits of out-of-date material) than to omit it completely.

The purpose of this system is to give higher-level players new abilities that you can attain by engaging in RvR combat. A secondary benefit is to give classes more abilities that can help them during RvR battles — for example, one of the Realm Abilities open to melee classes is to gain an increased resistance to Stun/Mez spells. Please note that this system will require lots of testing, and many of the abilities listed here will probably change at least a little based on tester feedback. Mythic may also add new abilities, or shuffle existing ones around during the testing process.

Please remember that there are Realm Ranks and Realm Levels. There are 100 Realm Levels, which are divided into 10 Realm Ranks. For the Realm Ability system, you will receive one Realm Skill Point for each Realm Level attained, giving you a maximum of about 100 points to spend on these new abilities.

In order to "spend" Realm Ability Points on a skill, go to your standard class trainer. The Realm Abilities available to your class will be listed there. Please note that you do not have to have a high number of Realm Levels to be able to take advantage of these new abilities — in almost all cases, a character that has even a few Realm L<None>levels can purchase at least a couple of new abilities.

There are two types of Realm Abilities: Passive and Active. Passive Realm Abilities are always on, and can affect your character in small ways, generally 3% per level (high levels of passive Realm Abilities grant substantial bonuses, however). Active abilities have re-use timers between 5 and 30 minutes, and are either instant effects or duration effects lasting between 30 and 60 seconds. Each class has a list of abilities tailored to it, and each class has an ability unique to it.

Some Realm Abilities have multiple levels, and each level will add a higher bonus. For example, the Augmented Strength Realm Ability awards 6 Strength points per level of the ability purchased, and there are five levels. So, in our example, a Level 3 Augmented Strength would give +18 Strength to a character.

The costs for each level of ability, as well as the costs for advanced abilities, increase with the level you are trying to attain. Also, please note that some Realm Abilities have prerequisites that must be purchased beforehand. Prerequisite skills may have to be purchased to a given level before an advanced skill can be trained.

Without further ado, here are the new Abilities, both listed (pp. 326-27) and charted by class (pp. 328-29). In general, the most common Abilities are listed earlier, with the single-class Abilities at the end of the list. The Augmented Stat Abilities are listed first (with their dependent Abilities).

Realm Ability Descriptions

Pre-Req Ability. An abbreviation for the prerequisite Ability (if any), plus the required level in that Ability. Abilities with prerequisites are indented and listed below their prereq Ability.

Type / Re-Use. Passive Abilities are always "on." They don't have to be cast. You must wait 15 minutes between each use of a Combat Style, indicated by **Style (15)**. All other Abilities are Active, and the time you must wait before using it again is listed for each Active Ability.

Training Costs. You can learn up to five levels for each Ability (although some Abilities have just one level). For each possible level, the Realm Point cost is listed in these columns.

Ability	Pre-Req Ability	Type / Re-Use	L1	L2	L3	L4	L5	Description
Augmented Strength (AS)	–	Passive	1	3	6	10	14	Increased Strength. (+6/level)
Mastery of Arms	AS 3	Passive	1	3	6	10	14	Increased attack speed with melee weapons. (+3%/level)
Augmented Constitution (AC)	–	Passive	1	3	6	10	14	Increased Constitution. (+6/level)
Second Wind	AC 3	15 min.	6	10	14	–	–	Complete Fatigue recovery.
Avoid Pain	AC 3	15 min.	3	6	10	–	–	1-minute boost to physical damage absorption. (+5%/level; caster)
Armor of Faith	AC 3	15 min.	3	6	10	–	–	1-minute boost to Armor Factor. (+5%/level; caster)
Battle Yell	AC 3	15 min.	3	6	10	–	–	Point-blank, Area-Effect taunt (350 wu radius); does no damage but draws monster aggro.
Augmented Dexterity (AD)	–	Passive	1	3	6	10	14	Increased Dexterity. (+6/level)
Mastery of Blocking	AD 2	Passive	1	3	6	10	14	Increased chance to block. (+3%/level)
Mastery of Pain	AD 2	Passive	1	3	6	10	14	Increased chance to critical hit with melee attacks. (+5%/level)
Hail of Blows	AD 3	15 min.	3	6	10	–	–	1-minute boost to attack speed. (+5%/level; caster)
Falcon's Eye	AD 2	Passive	1	3	6	10	14	Increased chance to critical hit with archery attacks. (+3%/level)
Mastery of Archery	AD 3	Passive	1	3	6	10	14	Increased attack speed when firing bows/crossbows. (+3%/level)
Dualist's Reflexes	AD 2	Passive	1	3	6	10	14	Increased chance for Dual Wield damage. (+3%/level)
Whirling Dervish	AD 3	15 min.	3	6	10	–	–	Short boost to Dual Wield chance/Left Axe damage. (+5%/level)
Bladedance	AD 3	30 min.	14	–	–	–	–	Point-blank, Area-Effect attack.(150 damage; 350 wu radius)
Augmented Quickness (AQ)	–	Passive	1	3	6	10	14	Increased Quickness. (+6/level)
Mastery of Parrying	AQ 2	Passive	1	3	6	10	14	Increased chance to parry. (+3%/level)
Dodger	AQ 2	Passive	1	3	6	10	14	Increased chance to evade. (+3%/level)
Mastery of Stealth	AQ 2	Passive	1	3	6	10	14	Increased movement speed while stealthy. (+3%/level)
Augmented Acuity (AA)	–	Passive	1	3	6	10	14	Increased casting stat: either Intelligence, Piety, Empathy or Charisma, based on class. (+6/level)
Serenity (Ser)	AA 2	Passive	1	3	6	10	14	Increased Power regeneration. (+1/level (per cycle))
Ethereal Bond	Ser 2	Passive	1	3	6	10	14	Increased maximum Power. (+3%/level)
Mastery of the Arcane	AA 3	Passive	1	3	6	10	14	Increased effectiveness of duration-based spells. (+3%/level)
Mastery of Concentration	AA 3	30 min.	14	–	–	–	–	Reduces chance of casting interruption by 50% for 1 minute. (caster)
Majesty of Magery	AA 3	30 min.	6	10	14	–	–	1-minute reduction to chance of magic being resisted. (-10%/level; caster)
Mastery of the Art	AA 3	Passive	1	3	6	10	14	Increased attack speed when casting spells. (+3%/level)
Mastery of Magery	AA 3	Passive	1	3	6	10	14	Increased effectiveness of magical damage spells. (+3%/level)
Wild Arcana	AA 2	Passive	1	3	6	10	14	Increased chance to crit (up to double effect) with duration-based magic. (+5%/level)
Concentration	AA 3	15 min.	10	–	–	–	–	Resets Quickcast timer to allow for a second Quickcast.
Wild Power	AA 2	Passive	1	3	6	10	14	Increased chance to critical hit with damage spells. (+5%/level)
Wild Minion (WM)	AA 2	Passive	1	3	6	10	14	Increased chance for a pet to critical hit. (+5%/level)
Minion Control	WM 1	Passive	1	3	6	10	14	Reduced experience taken by pets. (-3%/level)
Mastery of Healing	AA 3	Passive	1	3	6	10	14	Increased effectiveness of Heal spells. (+3%/level)
Wild Healing	AA 2	Passive	1	3	6	10	14	Increased chance to crit (up to double effect) with healing magic. (+5%/level)
Long Wind	–	Passive	1	3	6	10	14	Reduced Fatigue cost of sprinting. (-20%/level)
Tireless	–	Passive	1	3	6	10	14	Increased Fatigue regeneration, even during combat. (+1/level)
Regeneration	–	Passive	1	3	6	10	14	Increased HP regeneration. (+1/level (per cycle))
Toughness	–	Passive	1	3	6	10	14	Increased maximum Health. (+3%/level)
Mastery of Water	–	Passive	1	3	6	10	14	Increased swim speed. (+3%/level)
Avoidance of Magic	–	Passive	1	3	6	10	14	Increased magic resistance to all types of magic. (+3%/level)
Lifter	–	Passive	1	3	6	10	14	Increased maximum carrying capacity. (+20%/level)
Veil Recovery	–	Passive	1	3	6	10	14	Reduced duration of resurrection sickness. (-10%/level)
Purge	–	30 min.	10	–	–	–	–	Dispels all negative spell effects. (caster)
The Empty Mind	–	30 min.	6	10	14	–	–	1-minute boost to all magic resistances. (+15%/level; caster)

Ability	Pre-Req Ability	Type / Re-Use	L1	L2	L3	L4	L5	Description
			Training Costs					
Mystic Crystal Lore (MCL)	–	5 min.	3	6	10	–	–	Minor self-only boost to Power. (+10%/level)
Raging Power	MCL 2	30 min.	6	10	14	–	–	Big boost to Power, usable in combat. (+15%/level; caster)
First Aid (FA)	–	15 min.	3	6	10	–	–	Minor self-heal that cannot be used in combat. (+10%/level)
Ignore Pain	FA 2	30 min.	14	–	–	–	–	In-combat self-heal. (+15%)
Rain of Fire	–	15 min.	3	6	10	–	–	Adds heat damage to non-magical attacks for 1 minute. (+5%/level)
Rain of Ice	–	15 min.	3	6	10	–	–	Adds cold damage to non-magical attacks for 1 minute. (+5%/level)
Rain of Annihilation	–	15 min.	3	6	10	–	–	Adds spirit damage to non-magical attacks for 1 minute. (+5%/level)
Trip	–	15 min.	3	6	10	–	–	Point-blank, small radius, Area-Effect Snare.
Grapple	Trip 1	30 min.	14	–	–	–	–	Point-blank, small radius, Area-Effect Root.
Determination	–	Passive	1	3	6	10	14	Decreases duration of Mesmerize, Stun, and Snare effects. (-15%/level)
Arrow Salvaging	–	Passive	1	3	6	10	14	Increased chance to not expend arrow on firing. (+10%/level)
See Hidden	–	Passive	8	–	–	–	–	Detects stealthy characters that don't have the "Detect Hidden" ability.
Soldier's Barricade	–	30 min.	10	–	–	–	–	50% bonus to group's Armor Factor for 30 seconds.
Void	–	Style (15)	10	–	–	–	–	Powerful combat style.
Faith Healing	–	30 min.	14	–	–	–	–	Substantial group Heal.
Volley	–	30 min.	6	10	14	–	–	Area-targeted attack that fires successive arrows at multiple targets in the area. (2/3/4 arrows)
Speed of Sound	–	30 min.	10	–	–	–	–	30-second boost to group run speed that doesn't break in combat.
Vanish	–	30 min.	14	–	–	–	–	Immediately hides, regardless of action state.
Reflex Attack	–	30 min.	14	–	–	–	–	For a short duration, automatically counter-attacks any melee attack.
Bunker of Faith	–	30 min.	10	–	–	–	–	Large bonus (50) to group's melee absorption for 30 seconds.
Siege Bolt	–	15 min.	10	–	–	–	–	Powerful Bolt usable only on doors and siege engines. (3000 damage)
Volcanic Pillar	–	15 min.	14	–	–	–	–	Area-Effect Bolt. (1875 wu range; 350 wu radius; Heat)
Corporeal Disintegration	–	30 min.	14	–	–	–	–	Area-Effect DoT; stacks with other DoT lines. (every 3 seconds for 30 seconds; 1500 wu range; 350 wu radius)
Juggernaut	–	30 min.	14	–	–	–	–	Summons powerful pet for 4 minutes.
Static Tempest	–	30 min.	14	–	–	–	–	30-second Area-Effect (on a location) that stuns anyone who moves through it. (1500 wu range; 350 wu radius)
Doombringer	–	Style (15)	10	–	–	–	–	Powerful combat style.
Fury of the Gods	–	30 min.	14	–	–	–	–	30-second Damage-Add that stacks on top of other Damage-Add effects. (group)
Tundra	–	Style (15)	10	–	–	–	–	Powerful combat style.
True Sight	–	30 min.	10	–	–	–	–	Detects all hidden characters for a short duration.
Shadow Run	–	30 min.	10	–	–	–	–	Short boost to run speed while stealthy.
Ichor of the Deep	–	15 min.	14	–	–	–	–	30-second Area-Effect damage and Root.
Perfect Recovery	–	30 min.	14	–	–	–	–	Resurrects with high HP and no resurrection side-effects. (1500 wu range)
Rune of Decimation	–	15 min.	14	–	–	–	–	8-minute Area-Effect (on a location) that damages anyone who moves through it. (350 wu radius)
Whip of Encouragement	–	30 min.	6	–	–	–	–	1-minute boost to pet run speed. (2000 wu range)
Excited Frenzy	–	30 min.	6	–	–	–	–	30-second boost to pet attack speed. (1500 wu range)
Razorback	–	Style (15)	10	–	–	–	–	Powerful combat style.
Wrath of the Champion	–	15 min.	10	–	–	–	–	Point-blank Area-Effect Direct Damage. (350 wu radius)
Winter Moon	–	Style (15)	10	–	–	–	–	Powerful combat style.
Longshot	–	15 min.	10	–	–	–	–	Critical Shot that works only on long distance targets.
Viper	–	30 min.	14	–	–	–	–	Doubles damage of all DoT poisons for its duration.
Thornweed Field	–	30 min.	14	–	–	–	–	Area-Effect spell (on a location) that damages and snares anyone who moves through it. (30 seconds; 700 wu radius; doesn't break when snared target is hit)
Ameliorating Melodies	–	30 min.	14	–	–	–	–	30-second boost to group's Health regeneration. (1500 wu range)
Group Purge	–	30 min.	14	–	–	–	–	Purges all negative effects from group.
Negative Maelstrom	–	30 min.	14	–	–	–	–	30-second Area-Effect spell (on a location) that damages anyone who moves through it. (1500 wu range; 350 wu radius)
Brilliant Aura of Deflection	–	30 min.	14	–	–	–	–	Short boost to all magical resistance. (group; 1500 wu range)
Severing the Tether	–	15 min.	14	–	–	–	–	Dispels all Summon and Charm effects. (30 seconds; 1875 wu range; 1000 wu radius)

Classes for Each Realm Ability

Ability	Albion Classes: Armsman (AM)	Mercenary (MC)	Paladin (PL)	Scout (ST)	Minstrel (MI)	Infiltrator (IN)	Friar (FR)	Cleric (CL)	Theurgist (TR)	Wizard (WZ)	Sorcerer (SR)	Cabalist (CB)	Midgard Classes: Thane (TN)	Warrior (WR)	Skald (SK)	Berserker (BS)	Hunter (HN)	Shadowblade (SB)	Shaman (SN)	Healer (HL)	Runemaster (RM)	Spiritmaster (SP)	Hibernia Classes: Hero (HO)	Champion (CH)	Blademaster (BM)	Ranger (RG)	Nightshade (NS)	Warden (WD)	Bard (BD)	Druid (DR)	Eldritch (ED)	Enchanter (EN)	Mentalist (MT)
Ability	**AM**	**MC**	**PL**	**ST**	**MI**	**IN**	**FR**	**CL**	**TR**	**WZ**	**SR**	**CB**	**TN**	**WR**	**SK**	**BS**	**HN**	**SB**	**SN**	**HL**	**RM**	**SP**	**HO**	**CH**	**BM**	**RG**	**NS**	**WD**	**BD**	**DR**	**ED**	**EN**	**MT**
Augmented Strength	AM	MC	PL	ST	MI	IN	FR	CL	TR	WZ	SR	CB	TN	WR	SK	BS	HN	SB	SN	HL	RM	SP	HO	CH	BM	RG	NS	WD	BD	DR	ED	EN	MT
Mastery of Arms	AM	MC	PL		MI	IN	FR						TN	WR	SK	BS	HN	SB					HO	CH	BM	RG		WD	BD	DR			
Augmented Constitution	AM	MC	PL	ST	MI	IN	FR	CL	TR	WZ	SR	CB	TN	WR	SK	BS	HN	SB	SN	HL	RM	SP	HO	CH	BM	RG	NS	WD	BD	DR	ED	EN	MT
Second Wind	AM	MC	PL	ST	MI	IN	FR	CL	TR	WZ	SR	CB	TN	WR	SK	BS	HN	SB	SN	HL	RM	SP	HO	CH	BM	RG	NS	WD	BD	DR	ED	EN	MT
Avoid Pain	AM		PL		MI			CL						WR	SK	BS	HN						HO	CH		RG	NS						
Armor of Faith			PL				FR	CL					TN		SK				SN	HL			HO					WD	BD	DR			
Battle Yell	AM		PL											WR									HO					WD					
Augmented Dexterity	AM	MC	PL	ST	MI	IN	FR	CL	TR	WZ	SR	CB	TN	WR	SK	BS	HN	SB	SN	HL	RM	SP	HO	CH	BM	RG	NS	WD	BD	DR	ED	EN	MT
Mastery of Blocking	AM		PL	ST	MI								TN	WR	SK				SN	HL			HO	CH					BD	DR			
Mastery of Pain	AM	MC	PL	ST	MI	IN	FR						TN	WR	SK	BS	HN	SB					HO	CH	BM	RG	NS	WD	BD				
Hail of Blows	AM	MC	PL	ST	MI		FR						TN	WR			HN	SB					HO	CH	BM		NS						
Falcon's Eye				ST													HN									RG							
Mastery of Archery				ST													HN									RG							
Dualist's Reflexes		MC				IN										BS		SB							BM		NS						
Whirling Dervish		MC				IN										BS		SB							BM	RG	NS						
Bladedance		MC				IN										BS		SB							BM	RG	NS						
Augmented Quickness	AM	MC	PL	ST	MI	IN	FR	CL	TR	WZ	SR	CB	TN	WR	SK	BS	HN	SB	SN	HL	RM	SP	HO	CH	BM	RG	NS	WD	BD	DR	ED	EN	MT
Mastery of Parrying	AM	MC	PL				FR						TN	WR	SK	BS							HO	CH	BM			WD					
Dodger		MC		ST	MI	IN	FR									BS	HN	SB							BM	RG	NS						
Mastery of Stealth				ST		IN												SB									NS						
Augmented Acuity			PL		MI		FR	CL	TR	WZ	SR	CB	TN		SK		HN		SN	HL	RM	SP		CH		RG	NS	WD	BD	DR	ED	EN	MT
Serenity					MI		FR	CL	TR	WZ	SR	CB	TN						SN	HL	RM	SP						WD	BD	DR	ED	EN	MT
Ethereal Bond								CL	TR	WZ	SR	CB	TN						SN	HL	RM	SP						WD	BD	DR	ED	EN	MT
Mastery of the Arcane			PL		MI		FR	CL	TR	WZ	SR	CB			SK		HN		SN	HL	RM	SP		CH		RG		WD	BD	DR	ED	EN	MT
Mastery of Concentration							FR	CL	TR	WZ	SR	CB								HL	RM	SP									ED	EN	MT
Majesty of Magery								CL	TR	WZ	SR	CB									RM	SP									ED	EN	MT
Mastery of the Art								CL	TR	WZ	SR	CB							SN	HL	RM	SP							BD	DR	ED	EN	MT
Mastery of Magery								CL	TR	WZ	SR	CB									RM	SP									ED	EN	MT
Wild Arcana									TR	WZ	SR	CB							SN	HL	RM	SP		CH		RG	NS				ED		MT
Concentration									TR	WZ	SR	CB									RM	SP									ED	EN	MT
Wild Power									TR	WZ	SR										RM										ED	EN	MT
Wild Minion											SR	CB					HN					SP								DR		EN	
Minion Control												CB					HN					SP								DR		EN	
Mastery of Healing							FR	CL											SN	HL									BD	DR			MT
Wild Healing							FR	CL											SN	HL									BD	DR			MT
Long Wind	AM	MC	PL	ST	MI	IN	FR	CL	TR	WZ	SR	CB	TN	WR	SK	BS	HN	SB	SN	HL	RM	SP	HO	CH	BM	RG	NS	WD	BD	DR	ED	EN	MT
Tireless	AM	MC	PL	ST	MI	IN	FR	CL	TR	WZ	SR	CB	TN	WR	SK	BS	HN	SB	SN	HL	RM	SP	HO	CH	BM	RG	NS	WD	BD	DR	ED	EN	MT
Regeneration	AM	MC	PL	ST	MI	IN	FR	CL	TR	WZ	SR	CB	TN	WR	SK	BS	HN	SB	SN	HL	RM	SP	HO	CH	BM	RG	NS	WD	BD	DR	ED	EN	MT
Toughness	AM	MC	PL	ST	MI	IN	FR	CL	TR	WZ	SR	CB	TN	WR	SK	BS	HN	SB	SN	HL	RM	SP	HO	CH	BM	RG	NS	WD	BD	DR	ED	EN	MT
Mastery of Water	AM	MC	PL	ST	MI	IN	FR	CL	TR	WZ	SR	CB	TN	WR	SK	BS	HN	SB	SN	HL	RM	SP	HO	CH	BM	RG	NS	WD	BD	DR	ED	EN	MT
Avoidance of Magic	AM	MC	PL	ST	MI	IN	FR	CL	TR	WZ	SR	CB	TN	WR	SK	BS	HN	SB	SN	HL	RM	SP	HO	CH	BM	RG	NS	WD	BD	DR	ED	EN	MT
Lifter	AM	MC	PL	ST	MI	IN	FR	CL	TR	WZ	SR	CB	TN	WR	SK	BS	HN	SB	SN	HL	RM	SP	HO	CH	BM	RG	NS	WD	BD	DR	ED	EN	MT
Veil Recovery	AM	MC	PL	ST	MI	IN	FR	CL	TR	WZ	SR	CB	TN	WR	SK	BS	HN	SB	SN	HL	RM	SP	HO	CH	BM	RG	NS	WD	BD	DR	ED	EN	MT
Purge	AM	MC	PL	ST	MI	IN	FR	CL	TR	WZ	SR	CB	TN	WR	SK	BS	HN	SB	SN	HL	RM	SP	HO	CH	BM	RG	NS	WD	BD	DR	ED	EN	MT
The Empty Mind	AM	MC	PL	ST	MI	IN	FR	CL	TR	WZ	SR	CB	TN	WR	SK	BS	HN	SB	SN	HL	RM	SP	HO	CH	BM	RG	NS	WD	BD	DR	ED	EN	MT

	Albion Classes												Midgard Classes										Hibernia Classes										
	Armsman (AM)	Mercenary (MC)	Paladin (PL)	Scout (ST)	Minstrel (MI)	Infiltrator (IN)	Friar (FR)	Cleric (CL)	Theurgist (TR)	Wizard (WZ)	Sorcerer (SR)	Cabalist (CB)	Thane (TN)	Warrior (WR)	Skald (SK)	Berserker (BS)	Hunter (HN)	Shadowblade (SB)	Shaman (SN)	Healer (HL)	Runemaster (RM)	Spiritmaster (SP)	Hero (HO)	Champion (CH)	Blademaster (BM)	Ranger (RG)	Nightshade (NS)	Warden (WD)	Bard (BD)	Druid (DR)	Eldritch (ED)	Enchanter (EN)	Mentalist (MT)
Ability	**AM**	**MC**	**PL**	**ST**	**MI**	**IN**	**FR**	**CL**	**TR**	**WZ**	**SR**	**CB**	**TN**	**WR**	**SK**	**BS**	**HN**	**SB**	**SN**	**HL**	**RM**	**SP**	**HO**	**CH**	**BM**	**RG**	**NS**	**WD**	**BD**	**DR**	**ED**	**EN**	**MT**
Mystic Crystal Lore							FR	CL	TR	WZ	SR	CB			SK				SN	HL	RM	SP		CH				WD	BD	DR	ED	EN	MT
Raging Power							FR	CL	TR	WZ	SR	CB			SK				SN	HL	RM	SP		CH				WD	BD	DR	ED	EN	MT
First Aid	AM	MC	PL	ST	MI	IN			TR	WZ			TN	WR	SK	BS	HN	SB	SN		RM		HO	CH	BM	RG	NS	WD			ED	EN	
Ignore Pain	AM	MC	PL	ST	MI	IN							TN	WR	SK	BS	HN	SB	SN				HO	CH	BM		NS	WD					
Rain of Fire	AM	MC	PL	ST	MI	IN							TN	WR	SK	BS		SB					HO	CH	BM		NS	WD					
Rain of Ice	AM	MC	PL	ST	MI	IN							TN	WR	SK	BS		SB					HO	CH	BM		NS	WD					
Rain of Annihilation	AM	MC	PL	ST	MI	IN							TN	WR	SK	BS		SB					HO	CH	BM		NS	WD					
Trip	AM	MC	PL				FR							WR		BS							HO		BM								
Grapple	AM	MC	PL											WR		BS							HO		BM								
Determination	AM	MC												WR		BS							HO		BM								
Arrow Salvaging				ST													HN									RG							
See Hidden						IN												SB									NS						
Soldier's Barricade	AM																																
Void		MC																															
Faith Healing			PL																														
Volley				ST																													
Speed of Sound					MI																												
Vanish						IN																											
Reflex Attack							FR																										
Bunker of Faith								CL																									
Siege Bolt									TR																								
Volcanic Pillar										WZ																							
Corporeal Disintegration											SR																						
Juggernaut												CB																					
Static Tempest													TN																				
Doombringer														WR																			
Fury of the Gods															SK																		
Tundra																BS																	
True Sight																	HN																
Shadow Run																		SB															
Ichor of the Deep																			SN														
Perfect Recovery																				HL													
Rune of Decimation																					RM												
Whip of Encouragement																						SP											
Excited Frenzy																						SP											
Razorback																							HO										
Wrath of the Champion																								CH									
Winter Moon																									BM								
Longshot																										RG							
Viper																											NS						
Thornweed Field																												WD					
Ameliorating Melodies																													BD				
Group Purge																														DR			
Negative Maelstrom																															ED		
Brilliant Aura of Deflection																																EN	
Severing the Tether																																	MT

Monsters

For more complete descriptions of what these stats describe, and a chart of which types of attack works best against each body type, see **Monster Stats**, p. 373.

Abbreviations

Speed. Slow, **M**edium, **F**ast, **2x**, **3x**, **4x** (two, three and four times faster than the average PC).

Aggr. (Aggression). **L**ow, **M**edium, **H**igh (with percent chance that it will attack).

Attack Type. **C**rush, **S**lash, **T**hrust. Information after a slash ("/") is type and percent chance of secondary attack.

Combat Modifier. Monster's modifier to hit / modifier to avoid being hit (defense) / modifier to hit points. When there is just one number, it modifies all three situations.

Social. Social monsters might group; **Call** means it is Social and might call for help.

Body Type. The body types are:

BU	Bony Undead	**EW**	Elemental Water	**Pl**	Plate
Ch	Chain	**FM**	Feeble-Minded	**Rp**	Reptile (Scaled)
Cl	Cloth	**FU**	Fleshy Undead	**Sh**	Shell (Chitin)
DV	Darkness/Void	**FA**	Furry Animal	**Soft**	Soft
EA	Elemental Air	**IU**	Incorporeal Undead	**St**	Studded Leather
EE	Elemental Earth	**Lr**	Leather	**TP**	Tree/Plant
EF	Elemental Fire	**LE**	Light Energy	**Tr**	Troll-like
EI	Elemental Ice	**ME**	Magical Energy		

Monster	Lvl	Body Type	Spd	Agg	Atk Spd	Atk Type	Ev %	Comb Mod	Soc. Call
Animal									
Demoniac Familiar (Boar)	27	FA	F/220	L/1	3.5	S	1	–	–
Demoniac Familiar (Cat)	21	FA	F/220	L/1	3.5	S	1	–	–
Demoniac Familiar (Dog)	33	FA	F/220	L/1	3.5	C	1	–	–
Demoniac Familiar (Lynx)	36	FA	F/220	L/1	3.5	S	1	–	–
Demoniac Familiar (Rat)	15	FA	F/220	L/1	3.5	T	1	–	–
Demon									
Ambassador Mannam	65	Lr	2x/450	H/80	4.0	S	–	–	Soc.
Avernal Quasit	32-34	Rp	M/200	H/80	3.9	T	3	–	Soc.
Cambion	52-54	Cl	F/315	H/80	3.0	S	–	–	Soc.
Chaosian	55	Rp	2x/385	H/80	3.8	S	–	–	Soc.
Chthonian Crawler	60	Sh	2x/440	H/80	4.2	T	–	–	Soc.
Chthonic Knight Absax	70	Pl	2x/500	H/80	4.1	S	–	-/-15/15	Soc.
Chthonic Knight Aciel	62	Pl	2x/500	H/80	4.1	S	–	-/-15/15	Soc.
Chthonic Knight Ain	62	Pl	2x/500	H/80	4.1	S	–	-/-15/15	Soc.
Chthonic Knight Azea	70	Pl	2x/500	H/80	4.1	S	–	-/-15/15	Soc.
Chthonic Knight Babyzu	62	Pl	2x/500	H/80	4.1	S	–	-/-15/15	Soc.
Chthonic Kn. Carnivon	64	Pl	2x/500	H/80	4.1	S	–	-/-15/15	Soc.
Chthonic Knight Exal	68	Pl	2x/500	H/80	4.1	S	–	-/-15/15	Soc.
Chthonic Knight Exte	60	Pl	2x/500	H/80	4.1	S	–	-/-15/15	Soc.
Chthonic Knight Ezpeth	66	Pl	2x/500	H/80	4.1	S	–	-/-15/15	Soc.
Chthonic Knight Fonath	74	Pl	2x/500	H/80	4.1	S	–	-/-15/15	Soc.
Chthonic Kn. Gaapoler	72	Pl	2x/500	H/80	4.1	S	–	-/-15/15	Soc.
Chthonic Knight Haag	72	Pl	2x/500	H/80	4.1	S	–	-/-15/15	Soc.
Chthonic Knight Ibeko	60	Pl	2x/500	H/80	4.1	S	–	-/-15/15	Soc.
Chthonic Knight Marbos	68	Pl	2x/500	H/80	4.1	S	–	-/-15/15	Soc.
Chthonic Knight Obarus	60	Pl	2x/500	H/80	4.1	S	–	-/-15/15	Soc.
Chthonic Knight Olov	74	Pl	2x/500	H/80	4.1	S	–	-/-15/15	Soc.
Chthonic Knight Prosel	64	Pl	2x/500	H/80	4.1	S	–	-/-15/15	Soc.
Chthonic Knight Ronoro	66	Pl	2x/500	H/80	4.1	S	–	-/-15/15	Soc.
Chthonic Knight Tamuel	74	Pl	2x/500	H/80	4.1	S	–	-/-15/15	Soc.
Chthonic Knight Ukobat	66	Pl	2x/500	H/80	4.1	S	–	-/-15/15	Soc.
Chthonic Knight Vosoes	72	Pl	2x/500	H/80	4.1	S	–	-/-15/15	Soc.
Chthonic Knight Zaeber	68	Pl	2x/500	H/80	4.1	S	–	-/-15/15	Soc.
Chthonic Knight Zafan	64	Pl	2x/500	H/80	4.1	S	–	-/-15/15	Soc.
Chthonic Knight Zagal	70	Pl	2x/500	H/80	4.1	S	–	-/-15/15	Soc.
Commander Abgar	61	Pl	2x/480	H/80	3.5	S/S1	–	-5/15/-	Soc.
Deamhaness	32-34	Rp	F/225	H/80	3.7	S	2	–	Soc.
Duke Alloc	75	FA	3x/600	H/80	3.2	S/S5	5	8	Soc.
Duke Aypol	75	Lr	3x/600	H/80	3.1	S	–	8	Soc.
Duke Bimure	75	Lr	3x/600	H/80	3.0	S	–	8	Soc.
Duke Eligar	75	Pl	3x/600	H/80	3.8	S/T1	–	8	Soc.
Duke Harboris	75	Lr	3x/600	H/80	2.5	S	–	8	Soc.
Duke Sallis	75	Pl	3x/600	H/80	3.4	S	–	8	Soc.
Duke Satori	75	Rp	3x/600	H/80	3.9	T	2	8	Soc.
Duke Zepor	75	Pl	3x/600	H/80	3.5	T	–	8	Soc.
Earl Amagin	71	Lr	2x/550	H/80	4.0	S	–	6	Soc.
Earl Fenex	71	Lr	2x/550	H/80	4.3	C	–	6	Soc.
Earl Glassalab	71	Rp	2x/550	H/80	3.8	S	2	6	Soc.
Earl Ipostian	71	Rp	2x/550	H/80	3.0	S/S5	5	6	Soc.
Earl Mercur	71	Rp	2x/550	H/80	3.9	S	–	6	Soc.
Earl Mermer	71	Pl	2x/550	H/80	3.5	S	–	6	Soc.
Earl Oraxus	71	FA	2x/550	H/80	2.6	S/S5	5	6	Soc.
Earl Vone	71	FA	2x/550	H/80	2.8	S/S5	5	6	Soc.
Essence Shredder	54-56	Rp	F/335	H/80	2.3	T/S3	–	–	Soc.
Field Marshal Nebir	70	Lr	2x/500	H/80	3.1	S	–	5	Soc.
Inquisitor Asil	66	Cl	2x/500	H/80	3.2	T/T1	–	15/-8/-7	Soc.
Inquisitor Bor	70	Cl	2x/500	H/80	3.2	T/T1	–	15/-8/-7	Soc.
Inquisitor Eciraum	66	Lr	2x/500	H/80	3.2	T/T1	3	15/-8/-7	Soc.
Inquisitor Factol	70	Lr	2x/500	H/80	3.2	T/T1	3	15/-8/-7	Soc.
Inquisitor Famuel	74	Cl	2x/500	H/80	3.2	T/T1	–	15/-8/-7	Soc.
Inquisitor Haap	72	Cl	2x/500	H/80	3.2	T/T1	–	15/-8/-7	Soc.
Inquisitor Hadis	64	Cl	2x/500	H/80	3.2	T/T1	–	15/-8/-7	Soc.
Inquisitor Haimir	68	Cl	2x/500	H/80	3.2	T/T1	–	15/-8/-7	Soc.
Inquisitor Hellos	62	Lr	2x/500	H/80	3.2	T/T1	3	15/-8/-7	Soc.
Inquisitor Irawn	60	Lr	2x/500	H/80	3.2	T/T1	3	15/-8/-7	Soc.
Inquisitor Kireasil	74	Lr	2x/500	H/80	3.2	T/T1	3	15/-8/-7	Soc.
Inquisitor Lokis	60	Cl	2x/500	H/80	3.2	T/T1	–	15/-8/-7	Soc.
Inquisitor Medebo	60	Cl	2x/500	H/80	3.2	T/T1	–	15/-8/-7	Soc.
Inquisitor Morg	62	Lr	2x/500	H/80	3.2	T/T1	3	15/-8/-7	Soc.

Monster	Lvl	Body Type	Spd	Agg	Atk Spd	Atk Type	Ev %	Comb Mod	Soc. Call
Inquisitor Morrian	62	Lr	2x/500	H/80	3.2	T/T1	3	15/-8/-7	Soc.
Inquisitor Mucifen	64	Lr	2x/500	H/80	3.2	T/T1	3	15/-8/-7	Soc.
Inquisitor Nej	68	Cl	2x/500	H/80	3.2	T/T1	–	15/-8/-7	Soc.
Inquisitor Nifil	64	Cl	2x/500	H/80	3.2	T/T1	–	15/-8/-7	Soc.
Inquisitor Niloc	66	Lr	2x/500	H/80	3.2	T/T1	3	15/-8/-7	Soc.
Inquisitor Tlaw	70	Lr	2x/500	H/80	3.2	T/T1	3	15/-8/-7	Soc.
Inquisitor Yonzael	74	Lr	2x/500	H/80	3.2	T/T1	3	15/-8/-7	Soc.
Inquisitor Yor	68	Lr	2x/500	H/80	3.2	T/T1	3	15/-8/-7	Soc.
Inquisitor Zaviben	72	Cl	2x/500	H/80	3.2	T/T1	–	15/-8/-7	Soc.
Inquisitor Zazinol	72	Lr	2x/500	H/80	3.2	T/T1	3	15/-8/-7	Soc.
Lieutenant Gargantan	68	Lr	2x/475	H/80	2.9	S	–	-/15/-10	Soc.
Lieutenant Loran	68	Lr	2x/475	H/80	3.7	S	–	15/-10/-	Soc.
Lieutenant Persun	68	FA	2x/475	H/80	3.3	S/S5	5	-10/-/15	Soc.
Lilispawn	29-31	Pl	F/220	H/80	4.0	C	–	–	Soc.
Mahr	55	Soft	F/350	H/80	3.8	S	2	–	Soc.
Marquis Almen	73	FA-Rp	3x/575	H/80	2.3	T	2	7	Soc.
Marquis Chaosmar	73	FA-Rp	3x/575	H/80	3.3	T	2	7	Soc.
Marquis Dortaleon	73	Lr	3x/575	H/80	3.0	S	–	7	Soc.
Marquis Focalleste	73	Rp	3x/575	H/80	4.0	S	2	7	Soc.
Marquis Haurian	73	Rp	3x/575	H/80	4.2	T	2	7	Soc.
Marquis Sabonach	73	FA	3x/575	H/80	3.2	S/S5	5	7	Soc.
Marquis Scottiax	73	Lr	3x/575	H/80	3.9	S	–	7	Soc.
Marquis Valupa	73	FA	3x/575	H/80	3.8	S	2	7	Soc.
Molochian Tempter	40-42	Rp	2x/400	H/80	4.0	C	–	–	Soc.
Mutilator Axa'Al	70	St	2x/500	H/80	2.5	C/C5	1	-10/15/-5	Soc.
Mutilator Axalnam	68	St	2x/500	H/80	2.5	C/C5	1	-10/15/-5	Soc.
Mutilator Axtanax	60	St	2x/500	H/80	2.5	C/C5	1	-10/15/-5	Soc.
Mutilator Konapher	74	Ch	2x/500	H/80	2.5	C/C5	–	-10/15/-5	Soc.
Mutilator Laicanroth	62	St	2x/500	H/80	2.5	C/C5	1	-10/15/-5	Soc.
Mutilator Lazorous	64	Ch	2x/500	H/80	2.5	C/C5	–	-10/15/-5	Soc.
Mutilator Marbozer	68	St	2x/500	H/80	2.5	C/C5	1	-10/15/-5	Soc.
Mutilator Nianax	62	Ch	2x/500	H/80	2.5	C/C5	–	-10/15/-5	Soc.
Mutilator Novinrac	64	St	2x/500	H/80	2.5	C/C5	1	-10/15/-5	Soc.
Mutilator Okabi	60	St	2x/500	H/80	2.5	C/C5	1	-10/15/-5	Soc.
Mutilator Oprionach	74	Ch	2x/500	H/80	2.5	C/C5	–	-10/15/-5	Soc.
Mutilator Oronor	66	St	2x/500	H/80	2.5	C/C5	1	-10/15/-5	Soc.
Mutilator Phaxazis	66	Ch	2x/500	H/80	2.5	C/C5	–	-10/15/-5	Soc.
Mutilator Samiol	74	St	2x/500	H/80	2.5	C/C5	1	-10/15/-5	Soc.
Mutilator Taboku	66	Ch	2x/500	H/80	2.5	C/C5	–	-10/15/-5	Soc.
Mutilator Uxybab	62	Ch	2x/500	H/80	2.5	C/C5	–	-10/15/-5	Soc.
Mutilator Vorazax	72	St	2x/500	H/80	2.5	C/C5	1	-10/15/-5	Soc.
Mutilator Vozoaz	72	Ch	2x/500	H/80	2.5	C/C5	–	-10/15/-5	Soc.
Mutilator Xaabaro	68	Ch	2x/500	H/80	2.5	C/C5	–	-10/15/-5	Soc.
Mutilator Xagalith	70	Ch	2x/500	H/80	2.5	C/C5	–	-10/15/-5	Soc.
Mutilator Xakanos	64	St	2x/500	H/80	2.5	C/C5	1	-10/15/-5	Soc.
Mutilator Xazbalor	70	Ch	2x/500	H/80	2.5	C/C5	–	-10/15/-5	Soc.
Mutilator Yooginroth	72	St	2x/500	H/80	2.5	C/C5	1	-10/15/-5	Soc.
Mutilator Zurabo	60	Ch	2x/500	H/80	2.5	C/C5	–	-10/15/-5	Soc.
Naburite Drinker	47-51	Rp	2x/300	H/80	4.0	T	–	–	Soc.
Nightmare	61	Soft	2x/425	H/80	2.4	S	2	–	Soc.
Pale Guardian	72	IU	2x/500	H/80	4.6	C	–	–	Soc.
Plated Fiend	25-27	Pl	F/220	H/80	3.8	C	–	–	Soc.
Rocot	36-38	Lr	F/250	H/80	3.5	S/T1	–	–	Soc.
Soult. A. Alerion Knight	43	IU	M/188	L/5	3.6	T	–	–	–
Soult. A. Dragon Knight	50	IU	M/188	L/5	3.6	T	–	–	–
Soult. A. Eagle Knight	38	IU	M/188	L/5	3.6	C	–	–	–
Soult. A. Gryphon Knight	35	IU	M/188	L/5	3.6	T	–	–	–
Soult. A. Guardian	28	IU	M/188	L/5	3.6	T	–	–	–
Soult. A. Lion Knight	48	IU	M/188	L/5	3.6	S	–	–	–
Soult. A. Myrmidon	33	IU	M/188	L/5	3.6	S	–	–	–
Soult. A. Phoenix Knight	40	IU	M/188	L/5	3.6	S	–	–	–

Monster	Lvl	Body Type	Spd	Agg	Atk Spd	Atk Type	Ev %	Comb Mod	Soc. Call
Soult. A. Protector	25	IU	M/188	L/5	3.6	S	–	–	–
Soult. A. Unicorn Knight	45	IU	M/188	L/5	3.6	C	–	–	–
Soult. A. Warder	30	IU	M/188	L/5	3.6	C	–	–	–
Soult. H. Brehon	33	IU	M/188	L/5	3.6	T	–	–	–
Soult. H. Cosantoir	30	IU	M/188	L/5	3.6	S	–	–	–
Soult. H. Emerald Ridere	50	IU	M/188	L/5	3.6	C	–	–	–
Soult. H. Gilded Spear	45	IU	M/188	L/5	3.6	S	–	–	–
Soult. H. Grove Protecter	35	IU	M/188	L/5	3.6	C	–	–	–
Soult. H. Raven Ardent	38	IU	M/188	L/5	3.6	S	–	–	–
Soult. H. Savant	28	IU	M/188	L/5	3.6	C	–	–	–
Soult. H. Silver Hand	40	IU	M/188	L/5	3.6	T	–	–	–
Soult. H. Thunderer	43	IU	M/188	L/5	3.6	C	–	–	–
Soult. H. Tiarna	48	IU	M/188	L/5	3.6	T	–	–	–
Soult. H. Wayfarer	25	IU	M/188	L/5	3.6	T	–	–	–
Soult. N. Einherjar	50	IU	M/188	L/5	3.6	S	–	–	–
Soult. N. Elding Herra	45	IU	M/188	L/5	3.6	T	–	–	–
Soult. N. Elding Vakten	35	IU	M/188	L/5	3.6	S	–	–	–
Soult. N. Flammen Herra	43	IU	M/188	L/5	3.6	S	–	–	–
Soult. N. Flammen Vakten	33	IU	M/188	L/5	3.6	C	–	–	–
Soult. N. Isen Herra	40	IU	M/188	L/5	3.6	C	–	–	–
Soult. N. Isen Vakten	30	IU	M/188	L/5	3.6	T	–	–	–
Soult. N. Skiltvakten	28	IU	M/188	L/5	3.6	S	–	–	–
Soult. N. Stormur Herra	48	IU	M/188	L/5	3.6	C	–	–	–
Soult. N. Stormur Vakten	38	IU	M/188	L/5	3.6	T	–	–	–
Soult. N. Vakten	25	IU	M/188	L/5	3.6	C	–	–	–
Succubus	57	Cl	2x/400	H/80	3.1	S	2	–	Soc.
Umbral Aegis	63	Sh	2x/440	H/80	4.2	S	–	–	Soc.
Umbral Hulk	65	Pl	2x/455	H/80	4.0	C	–	–	Soc.
Umbrood Warrior	59	Rp	2x/415	H/80	3.3	S	–	–	Soc.
Human-like									
Apprent. Necyomancer	18	Cl	M/188	L/1	3.8	S	1	–	–
Apprent. Necyomancer	21	Cl	M/188	L/1	3.8	T	1	–	–
Condemn. Necyomancer	48	Cl	M/188	L/1	3.8	T	1	–	–
Cursed Necyomancer	42	Cl	M/188	L/1	3.8	C	1	–	–
Cursed Necyomancer	45	Cl	M/188	L/1	3.8	S	1	–	–
Experien. Necyomancer	36	Cl	M/188	L/1	3.8	S	1	–	–
Experien. Necyomancer	39	Cl	M/188	L/1	3.8	T	1	–	–
Necyomancer	30	Cl	M/188	L/1	3.8	T	1	–	–
Necyomancer	33	Cl	M/188	L/1	3.8	C	1	–	–
Torment. Necyomancer	50	Cl	M/188	L/1	3.8	C	1	–	–
Young Necyomancer	24	Cl	M/188	L/1	3.8	C	1	–	–
Young Necyomancer	27	Cl	M/188	L/1	3.8	S	1	–	–
Insect									
Demoniac Familiar (Ant)	18	Sh	F/220	L/1	3.5	T	1	–	–
Demon. Fam. (Scorpion)	24	Sh	F/220	L/1	3.5	T	1	–	–
Demoniac Fam. (Spider)	30	Sh	F/220	L/1	3.5	T	1	–	–

Special thanks go to Ethan "Esis" Kidhardt for risking life, limb and sanity in the investigation of the most dangerous realms in the game!

Cruachan Gorge

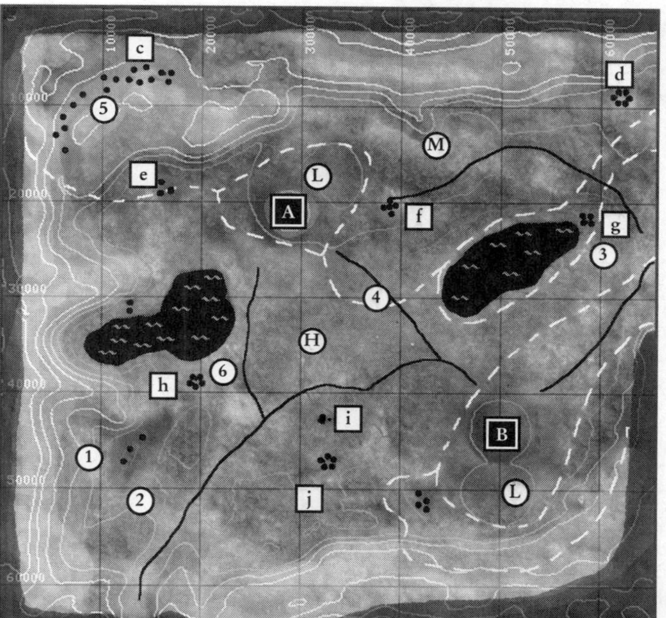

Key Explanation

- A Keep or Outpost
- e Significant Feature
- L Invader risk
- 4 Tip Reference (see tips for each map)

Map Key

A. Dun Lamfhota & Spear Relic
B. Dun Ailinne
c. Curmudgeon Stones
d. Empyrean Elder Stones
e. Cluricaun Fairy Rings
f. Stones
g. Daughters of Medb & Cruachan Warriors
h. Mist Wraith Stones
i. Formorians
j. Empyrean Guardian Stones
L Low Invader Risk
M Medium Invader Risk
H High Invader Risk

At the northern tip of Hibernia lies Druim Ligen, Hibernia's most active realm gate. Directly outside the doors is Cruachan Gorge, which is constantly under siege by invaders. Cruachan Gorge comprises rolling hills and grassy valleys with the occasional lake harboring gigantic crabs. The "Gorge" as it's known, sports a variety of creatures, the lowest of which is around 20, and the highest in the high 40's ; however, generally speaking it's almost entirely populated by Level 20-35 creatures. Although some of the creatures might be fierce, the real worry here is invaders. The hunting spots can be lucrative, but with the likelihood of invaders, most of this zone falls into a "High Risk" category.

1. Ant Valley

Virtually dead north from the Ligen gate lies Ant Valley. The pit that these Ants sit in makes them natural targets for archers; just watch out when they call for friends.

Location	12, 47
Invader Risk	8
Terrain Type	These Ants are situated in a deep valley, great for ranged attackers.
Level Range	21-24
Behaviors	Generally docile, they are non aggro but call on friends when in trouble.

2. Gray Specters Woods

These Gray Specters cast spells and have decent melee to boot. Word has it that they drop some magical items too. Save invaders, this is a decent hunting spot. For low 20th levels.

Location 8, 45
Invader Risk 8 High
Level Range 22-24
Quantity Roughly 10
Personality Aggressive, they rarely stop moving so you have to pick your target quickly to keep it in range
Terrain Type Woods and sloping hill

3. Greenbark Grove

Greenbark Grove is usually hunted thoroughly by solo Rangers, but often a large group can be found here gaining experience. While the loot isn't so wonderful, recently they have been dropping magical cloth armor frequently. Pretty dangerous unless you're in a group: for Levels 35+. Perfect for archers from 38-48!

Location 51, 32
Invader Risk 7 High
Level Range 40-44
Quantity 20+
Terrain Type Sloping hill for increased range
Magic Drop Level 30'ish Hardened Cloth Armor

4. Corybantic Skeletons

These skinny fellas aren't too friendly, but thankfully they're not on any public road. They don't cast spells, and make for pretty good hunting if you have a group in the low 40's — at the time this book printed — cash drop!

Location 38, 21
Invader Risk 5 Mid/Low
Level Range 46
Quantity Roughly 8
Personality Aggressive, but no BAF
Terrain Type Top of a knoll

5. Curmudgeon Valley

These wandering oafs may be aggressive depending on your faction with them. In this particular spot, they wander along a valley, and since they're spread out, you don't have to worry about pulling too many at once. If you're looking for a spot most people haven't been to, this is the place. It is particularly good for solo archers.

Location 8, 8
Invader Risk 8 High
Level Range 34
Quantity 12-15
Personality Faction based, these guys rarely stop to smell the flowers but archers can take advantage of the terrain. They are often grouped and may come in pairs.
Terrain Type These Curmudgeons patrol a valley near the border. No other enemies to worry about nearby.

5. Beetle Log

One can always find a group of newbies beating up beetles at this spot. However, due to that specific reason, invaders always stop here. So, if you plan on hunting, expect to be killed. The beetles are dense and there's plenty of them, so dive in!

Location 24, 41
Invader Risk 8.5 Very High
Level Range 20-21
Quantity 5-10
Personality Slow moving in a concentrated area. Wide-open fields would make this a great spot if not for the danger of invaders.
Terrain Type Wide open field on all sides, no threat of other creatures nearby.

6. Mist Wraiths

They spawn only at night, but it's a popular spot for a group in their low 20's. These Wraiths are known to drop some valuable magic items. The spot is decent, but beware invaders!

Location 20, 39
Invader Risk 8.5 Very High
Level Range 27-28
Quantity 5-10
Personality Nighttime spawn only. Aggressive.
Terrain Type Open field without anything dangerous nearby.

Emain Macha

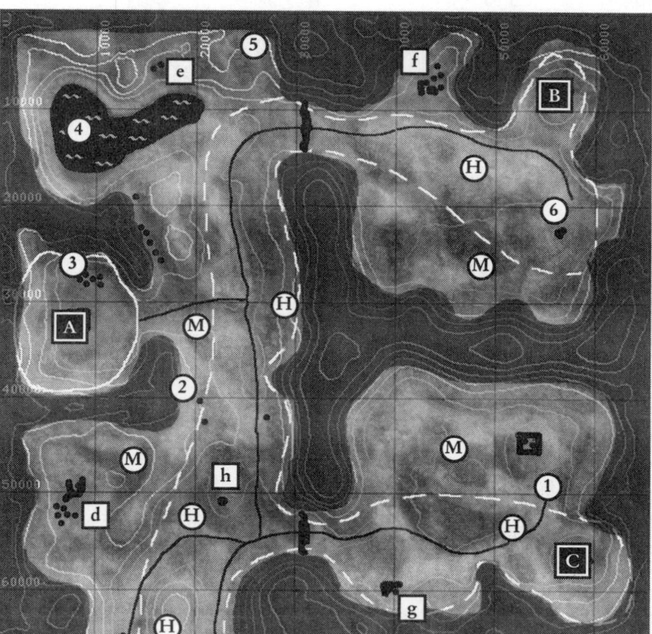

Map Key

A. Dun Cruachon
B. Midgard Outpost
C. Albion Outpost
d. Granny Stones & Ruins
e. Mindworm Holes
f. Ruins & Granny Stones
g. Ruins
h. Stone Tower
(L) Low Invader Risk
(M) Medium Invader Risk
(H) High Invader Risk

Emain Macha is the world's most active RvR area. In all the realms, there is no single other zone that rivals the massive battles that continually happen here. Hunting for experience is not the most lucrative venture; however, if you want to be where the action is, and still get experience, this isn't a bad spot—that is, if you're willing to take the risk. The average creature level is around 35 ranging from high 20's to high 50's. Generally speaking, due to the RvR traffic, there are few to no wandering creaturse to hassle those looking to find some RvR action.

1. Faeghoul Graveyard

This is perhaps where some fallen invaders make their home. This graveyard sits beside the Albion Portal Fort, and it is not a bad spot for hunting, other than that Hibernian defenders regularly scour the area.

Location	54, 44
Invader Risk	10 Highest
Quantity	8-12
Terrain Type	Small graveyard, various Undead creatures.

2. Grogan Grove

This spot is near a crossroad that marks perhaps the world's most busy RvR spot. The XP is great, but the risk is tremendous. For those interested in RvR and XP at the same time, here's your spot.

Location	19, 34
Invader Rsk	10 Highest
Quantity	8-12
Terrain Type	On a flat near a zone wall, massive RVR risk.

3. Granny Stones

For whoever owns Castle Cruachan, this spot is great for any high level group. Its right beside a castle and in guards range. Only a foolish few would tangle with someone here.

Location	9, 27
Invader Risk	4 Low
Quantity	8-12
Terrain Type	Right beside a castle at the bottom of a hill. Great spot.

4. Giant Lusus Lake

If you've never seen a Lusus, they've evidently been beaten with the ugly stick. They're ugly, they're strong and don't like visitors. On the other hand, few RvR's wander to this spot, so it's a decent mix of RvR and XP.

Location	7, 10
Invader Risk	5 Average
Quantity	8-10 spread out over a lake
Terrain Type	Lake with hills on one side, near a border. No wandering creatures.

5. Grogan Grove

Near the Midgard Milefort gate, this group of Grogans is generally unknown to most players. It's situated on a depression on a hill at a zone side with trees blocking the view from any wandering RvR'ers. Great place and unknown to most.

Location	19, 4
Invader Risk	6
Quantity	12-15
Terrain Type	Side of a zone hill. Remote, relatively unknown spot.

6. Bean Sidhe Cemetery

Occasionally you'll see some players out here contending with the undead Bean Sidhe, but more often than not, it's empty. For a solo or duo group, it's a great spot that keeps you near the action.

Location	56, 22
Invader Risk	6
Quantity	6
Terrain Type	Open area surrounded by fields, densely packed.

Breifine

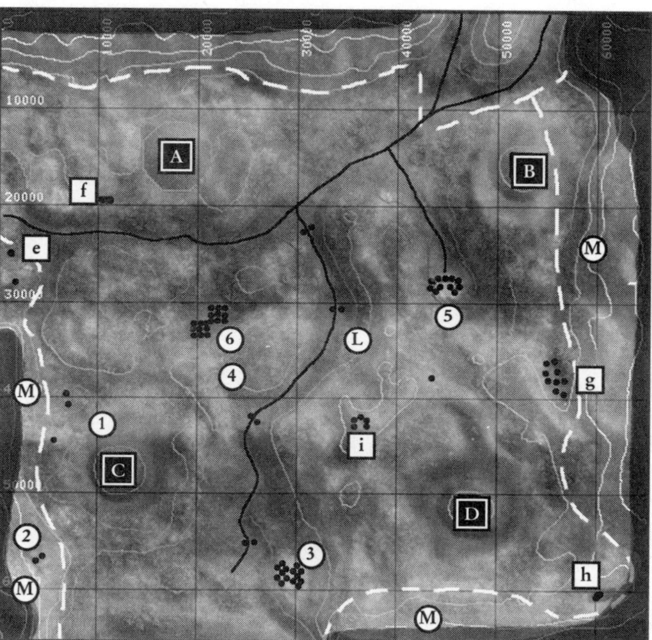

Map Key

- A. Dun Bolg
- B. Dun Crimthainn
- C. Dun na nGed
- D. Dun da Behnn
- e. Stone Tower
- f. Ruins
- g. Formorian Stones
- h. Earthshaker Quarry
- i. Corybantic Stones
- (L) Low Invader Risk
- (M) Medium Invader Risk
- (H) High Invader Risk

Breifine is hardly a friendly retreat; you'll find no vacationers here. Other than in one of the nearby castles, there is virtually no safe spot; even the roads are spotted with highly aggressive creatures. The average creature level is around 45 with creatures that go down to 35 or so, and up to 65. The landscape is similar to the rest of the Hibernian RvR areas, rolling hills, spotted with forests and even the occasional lake. For the brave and foolish alike, Breifine is home to what are perhaps Hibernia's most powerful denizens.

1. Bocanach

Though few travelers come here for business, this spot is rather decent if you want to avoid the crowd. They're humanoid and have lots of hit points, but they're beside a castle with a good amount of space. Find a group and pay a visit, the Invader Risk is fairly low.

Location	7.5, 39
Invader Risk	3 Low
Quantity	Roughly 13
Terrain Type	bottom of a bowl surrounded by hills. Plenty of safe spots with occasional other wandering creatures.

2. Formorian Camp

These one-eyed creatures don't like visitors. There aren't too many of them, but they pack a wallop. Other than their gigantic single eye, the other notable attribute is the jet thrusters they must have installed somewhere in their boots, because you'll not outrun these guys without a bard!

Location 4, 56
Invader Risk 3Low
Quantity 4 + One named "Morc"
Personality Very aggressive. They run faster than you can sprint, so stay away unless you're ready for them.
Terrain Type Top of a knoll. Fairly safe surrounding area though.

3. Empyrean's Stones

These are generally pleasant ghostly folk who have made these standing stones their home. They don't move a whole lot, and they've been known to drop some magic loot. There are plenty of them here if you bring a group, but beware the wandering Undead. They are faction based, so if you kill them and ruin your faction, go kill some Siabra to raise it again.

Location 29, 58
Invader Risk 2 Very Low
Level Range 34-48
Quantity 10-15
Personality Faction based. They're in a medium sized area and stand still frequently.
Terrain Type Open field with hill on one side, frequented by wandering higher-level creatures,

4. Corybantic Skeletons

These guys are just giant skeletons that sit between two castles. The area is decent for hunting, but supplies are hard to come by if needed and the nearest shop is a long run. If you want a spot that is very unlikely to be camped, head over this way. Just be careful of the horrible monsters en route to the spot.

Location 38, 21
Invader Risk 5 Mid/Low
Quantity Roughly 8
Terrain Type Top of a knoll with an occasional wandering creature; not a bad spot!

5. Wraith Drakes

These Wraith Drakes look like gigantic evil chameleons. These guys are *tough*, as in level 65 (yes, that's 65). This basically means 'look but don't touch' — unless you're looking for a quick trip back to town. I would imagine they're worth a whole lot of experience, but not many living have ever killed one.

Location 44, 28
Invader Risk 4 Low
Quantity Around 4
Terrain Type Bottom of a small valley surrounded by other level 50'ish creatures.

6. Cruiach Demon Stones

These demons are as strong as they are ugly. This is an obviously dangerous spot with wandering high-level creatures ambling by frequently. If you're in the area, take a look. They're impressive, with one 'boss' demon towering above the rest; don't try to feed them though.

Location 20, 31
Invader Risk 3 Very Low
Level Range: 55-57
Quantity 8-10
Terrain Type Open fields with lots of wandering aggro. Avoid!

Mt. Collory

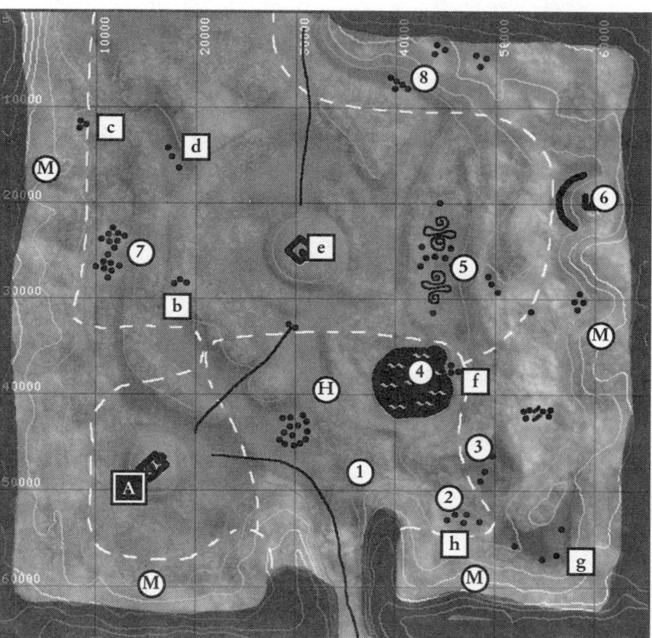

Map Key

A. Dun Dagda & Cauldron relic
b. Curmudgeons
c. Underlings
d. Sett Stones
e. Don Scathaig
f. Siabra
g. Sett Stones
h. Empyrean Stones
(L) Low Invader Risk
(M) Medium Invader Risk
(H) High Invader Risk

Wide open, grassy plains with occasional dense woods characterize Mt. Collory. For Hibernia, Mt. Collory holds many experience opportunities due to the quantity of camps. To invaders, the wide-open fields make finding someone relatively easy. The zone itself is relatively safe with a typical setup of monsters; the farther away you wander from the entrance, the more difficult and aggressive they become. Overall though, this zone would almost be considered friendly if it weren't for the quantity of medium-level aggressive creatures.

1. Grovewoods

These Grovewoods are easy to find, they don't move, and there are plenty of them. That, however, doesn't mean they're easy. They cast Root spells and bring friends. A small group might find this spot perfect for them, but the looming presence of invaders may be a deterrent.

Location	36,46
Invader Risk	7
Quantity	10-15
Terrain Type	Open field on one side, mountains & lake on the other, no wandering creatures.

2. Irewoods

There is no shortage of evil Trees in Mt. Collory. These Trees look just like normal trees, except that they have gaping maws and they want to eat you. These Trees make an excellent hunt spot for virtually anyone. Wandering creatures and invaders are the biggest risk here.

Location 42, 46
Invader Risk 7
Quantity 15-25
Terrain Type These Trees line a small mountain ridge.

3. Sett Dwellers

A duo might find this spot to be beneficial due to the quantity and personality of these creatures. They wander enough so a group wouldn't pull the entire camp, and only some of them are naturally aggressive.

Location 49, 46
Invader Risk 7
Quantity 10-15
Terrain Type Small dip in a field, no wandering enemies. Fairly safe.

4. Aughisky Shores

This may be the most popular spot in Mt. Collory. Groups have taken a fancy to these black stallions. Few horses can swim, but these swim like fish and the area around the lake is clear from wandering creatures, making it a popular spot for a couple of groups at a time.

Location 40, 41
Invader Risk 7
Quantity 8-12
Terrain Type spread out along the shores of a lake.

5. Empyrean Elders

These Empyrean Elders don't move much, but are in tight groups standing on top of strange crop formations in the grass. They're not very personable and there are some evil leprechauns nearby to deter visitors.

Location 43, 30
Invader Risk 4
Quantity 6
Terrain Type Large open field, hill on one side. No wandering enemies. Two groups of 6 spread out

6. Curmudgeon Bastion

Somehow, the forces of Hibernia have allowed these Curmudgeons to set up a stronghold in the northeastern corner of Mt. Collory. There are a good quantity of these here inside buildings, and when attacked, they generally respond as one force. It's a bit far away from home, but other than that, there's a variety of them here that need to be exterminated!

Location 59, 20
Invader Risk 4
Quantity 8-12
Terrain Type Top of a hill with wooden spikes. Various Curmudgeons, mostly Scrappers and Puggards.

7. Phaeghoul Stones

Two large areas of standing stones seem to attract the undead variety of housing applicants. These Phaeghouls don't move much and when they do, they amble slowly. There is a slight Invader Risk here, but otherwise there are many clear angles to sit a party or two.

Location 10, 26
Invader *Risk* 6
Quantity 20+
Personality Slowly wandering, spread out.
Terrain Type These guys are at the bottom of a small valley, like the bottom of a hot-dog bun, hills on two sides.

8. Fuath Camp

These Fuaths are densely packed and rarely move around. There is a slight risk of invaders but otherwise this is a safe spot with plenty of areas to camp around them. The only drawback is the distance it takes to get here, although you can be sure this is an un-camped and relatively unknown spot.

Location 44, 6
Invader Risk 5
Quantity 7-10
Terrain Type On the side of a hill in a small pit. They don't wander much; very safe spot.

Pennine Mountains

Map Key

- A. Caer Sursbrook
- B. Caer Erasleigh
- C. Caer Berkstead
- D. Caer Boldiam
- (L) Low Invader Risk
- (M) Medium Invader Risk
- (H) High Invader Risk

No single zone in the entire world even remotely compares to the dangers that the Pennine Mountains hold. This zone is laced with extremely high level and aggressive creatures; it's a death trap for any explorer. The Pennine Mountains, as the name implies, is a zone full of sharp rocky peaks and very deep ravines, all of which are covered with horrible monsters of every sort. For a large group, this place may be heaven as the creature spots are endless, and there are named spawns all over the place. The average creature level here is around 50, or possibly higher.

1. Gnarled Fellwood Grove

These Trees are situated very near to Hadrian Wall border and are densely packed together. They're gigantic gray Trees with gaping maws; not the sort of tree you'd make a lean-to out of. The area is surprisingly safe in the local vicinity; although, the Invader Risk factor is relatively high. Great spot for archers.

Location	53, 3
Invader Risk	7 Medium
Quantity	10-14
Terrain Type	Hillside near Road; sedentary; no roaming creatures.

2. Tylwyth Teg Ranger Valley

These Rangers seem to be the 'filler' for every spot in Pennine that doesn't contain some outrageously powerful creature. Be warned that they shoot from a long distance, and they have scouts that you may not see, which could bring the entire group running at you. One of the

safer spots; by safer I mean safer than sitting inside a dragon's mouth.

Location 36, 18
Invader Risk 4 Slim
Quantity 9-12
Terrain Type Steep hills, creatures spread over large area with large detection range, some wandering creatures.

3. Draco's Pit (Draco Magnificens)

This big guy looks like a house-sized chameleon inside a massive stone structure. He resides in a pit that is surrounded by lesser powerful, but by no means weak, creatures. On the hills surrounding him, you'll find Young Brown Drakes and larger and meaner versions. This is not a place to set up camp; it's not even a good place to visit unless you're looking to slay this giant.

Location 41, 29
Invader Risk 3 Slim
Quantity 1 Draco, 4-5 Young Brown Drakes
Terrain Type This guy sits in a huge stone hut in a large barren pit surrounded by mountains. Tons of drakes

4. Knotted/Gnarled Fellwood Grove

Luckily, these mean old trees don't have territorial instincts. They're all in close proximity to each other and don't move at all, unless provoked. Like their cousins, they're large gray trees with pulsing red eyes. If you get to this spot alive, you're lucky; there are wandering creatures everywhere.

Location 54, 38
Invader Risk 4 Slim
Quantity 8-13
Terrain Type Rocky hillside, few normal trees around. Many wandering creatures.

5. Ravenclan Giant Peak

Beside an Albion keep lies this enormous mountain where on top sits a large group of Ravenclan Giants. Amidst them is what looks to be their boss, named "Belgrik". They really are giants too. They run fast, they hit hard, and they don't like visitors. There is virtually no Invader Risk here due to the monsters and close proximity of a castle.

One named "Belgrik" is here.

Location 10,42
Invader Risk 3 Very Slim
Quantity 8-12
Terrain Type Top of a huge mountain! Wandering creatures everywhere. Unsafe

6. Ellyll Village

In the broadest and deepest valley of Pennine sits an array of miniature folk. The Ellyll may look like little munchkins, but they're all around Level 50 and they're social deviants. On the outskirts of their castle is this spot, small huts and mushrooms are their homes, and they move slowly in groups of 3-4. There is one little fella named "Champion Merendon".

Location 14, 50
Invader Risk 3 extremely low
Quantity 20-30 Spread out, one named "Champion Merendon."
Terrain Type Large rocky barren hills around, some wandering creatures. These wander only slightly.

7. Ellyll Castle

If somehow you make it through the Ellyll Village, you'll come upon the ruined castle of the Ellylls. No spot in the entire world has more high-level creatures densely packed together. In two broken down rooms, there are roughly 40 of these little guys all vying for breathing room. Don't be fooled, they're all extremely powerful, and have some pets as allies to boot. If you make it through this small city of them, their boss, "Lord Elidyn" awaits you in one of the back rooms. Good luck.

7. Ellyll Castle (continued)

Location 3, 52
Invader Risk 2 Extremely Low
Quantity 40+
Terrain Type Castle ruins with a massive amount of these wandering around. One named Lord Elidyn at the bottom of an enormous pit.

8. Ravenclan Giant Ravine

It looks as though a good portion of the Ravenclan Giants have fallen into this pit. They don't move, but they're highly aggressive to any wanderer. If you manage to fall into this pit, it's mostly likely the end of the road for you. There are many ways in, but one way out–and it's past those giants. It may be a great spot for ranged attackers.

Location 5, 37
Invader Risk 4 Low
Quantity 10+
Terrain Type Bottom of a deep pit. They're close together and wander little. Castle guards frequent the area.

9. Saffron, named Cockatrice

What wonders this armored chicken may hold is a mystery. The area is rife with violent and ugly creatures, so be careful where you step.

Location 11, 26
Invader Risk 4 Low
Quantity 1
Terrain Type Mountainside near Rangers, wandering creatures everywhere.

10. Hill Scrag Lair

If for some reason you're still alive and wandering around for a decent hunting spot, here you'll find a large group of Hill Scrags for the picking; this is one of the few spots where there aren't wandering creatures. If you live to make it here, it might be a lucrative endeavor.

Location 4, 21
Invader Risk 5 Small
Quantity 10-20
Terrain Type Zone border on barren hill, no trees and no wandering enemies.

11. Cyhraeth Mountain

If Hill Giants, Armored Chickens, Brown Drakes, and Ellylls aren't enough, there is a mighty mountain peak covered with Cyraeths. Not only are they spread out and aggressive, but they're virtually invisible. They look like ghosts, and if you're not paying complete attention, you'll run right into them. Avoid this place if you can.

Location 28, 46
Invader Risk 2 Slim
Quantity 20-30 Spread out and translucent.
Terrain Type Spread out over a huge hill. Extremely Dangerous.

12. Cliff Crawler Mountain

Every mountain in Pennine has inhabitants. This particular one is covered with lots of gigantic spiders. They move frequently and cover an enormous amount of territory. Tread carefully. This may be a great spot, if you can find a safe place for your party to sit.

Location 36, 62
Invader Risk 6 Medium
Quantity 10-20
Terrain Type Huge barren hill covered with these huge spiders.

13. Corryn

Corryn is the named Cliff Crawler. He's big, ugly and meaner than the other spiders, but he may drop something nice.

Location 36, 62
Invader Risk 6 Medium
Quantity 1
Terrain Type Spider-covered barren hill. This is a named Cliff Crawler.

Snowdonia

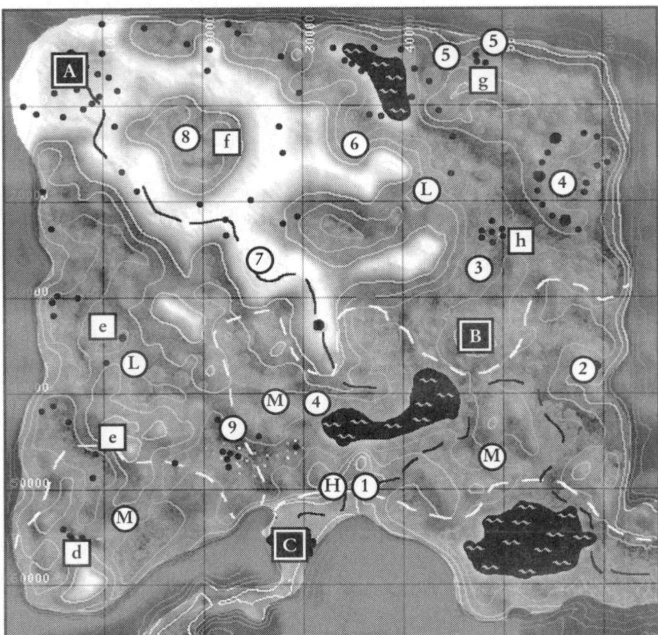

Map Key

A. Castle Myrddin
B. Caer Hurbury
C. Snowdonia Fortress
d. Arawnites
e. Stone Hut
f. Bwcas
g. Tylwyths
h. Hollow Men Stones
(L) Low Invader Risk
(M) Medium Invader Risk
(H) High Invader Risk

Snowdonia, despite what the name says, is mostly snow free. Only in the northwestern regions will one find snow at higher altitudes. Otherwise, it's a zone comprised of steep rocky barren hills with valleys of dense trees and an occasional vicious creature. Realm invaders here near the gate are a constant risk, but farther to the north, it is generally safe. There are few wandering creatures here intent on the traveler's doom, but there is a unique quantity of small fortifications by large groups of rogue creatures. Snowdonia is an impressive realm of the world's highest peaks and lowest rocky valleys.

1. Arawnite Camp

Due to the close proximity of the Snowdonia border fortress, this spot is generally popular. However, due to its easy access and low danger, invaders will certainly stop here to check if Albions are hunting. The creatures here don't move much and there are no wandering threats.

Location	36, 50
Invader Risk	8 High
Quantity	8
Terrain Type	Side of a steep hill right beside Snowdonia border gate.

2. Ravenclan Giants

It seems some of the Ravenclan Giants from the Pennine Mountains have moved north! Here you'll find a medium-sized group looking to intercept any invader that might pass his way. As the name suggests, they're huge and can crush you pretty quickly. Fortunately, they are

2. Ravenclan Giants (continued)

spread out, allowing an attacker to take them down one at a time.

Location 59, 37
Invader Risk 6 Medium
Quantity 5-8
Terrain Type Spread over a wide area of rocky sparsely treed terrain, they do not wander far.

3. Hollow Man's Stones

These Hollow Men are ugly creatures near the heart of Snowdonia. There is a small Invader Risk here and they wander occasionally without any other wandering threats nearby. There are enough that a small group could make some good experience while staying relatively safe.

Location 48, 23
Invader Risk 5, Low
Quantity 8-10
Terrain Type Open rolling hills with occasional trees, they wander slightly, but not far.

4. Arawnite Headhunter/Cyclops Stronghold

It seems that each realm has allowed a single large stronghold to exist of enemy creatures. This one is in a bit more shambles than the other realms'; there is an effective combination of Cyclops and Arawnites that comb a large area of land. The Arawnites look like they've employed the Cyclops as mean scouts. Those looking to hunt here will find plenty to fight; just be wary of getting in over your head.

Location 56, 18
Invader Risk 5 Low
Quantity 15-25
Terrain Type Many large rock and wooden outposts over a substantial area; wandering Cyclops.

5. Tylwyth Teg Rover Camps

These rangers seem to be the aggressive space fillers for the entire Albion frontier. They look like friendly Scouts dressed in green, but don't be fooled, they often stand behind trees to mask their presence, and by the time they attack, you're going to be in bad shape due to their longbow range.

Location 47, 5 and at 42, 7
Invader Risk 4 Slim
Quantity 5
Terrain Type Open area beside a hill with occasional trees. Most don't move, with the exception of a couple scouts.

6. Sprawling Arachnid Pit

Albion gets to claim the largest quantity of spiders in the entire world. Not only are there many of them, but they're huge! These aren't the kinds that make pretty webs in your barn; these are the kinds that eat the horses. There are enough here for a full group. They don't move much and they move only slowly. It seems they've claimed a pit all to themselves.

Location 35, 12
Invader Risk 4 Slim
Quantity 10
Terrain Type Beside a lake in a barren pit with no trees around. Wandering guards for protection; no other wandering creatures. These move only slightly and slowly.

7. Tylwyth Teg Rover Camp

Similar to the other camps, these Rangers populate areas that might catch travelers offguard. However, if you're looking to attack some creatures that use ranged attack, this is a good place.

Location 26, 29
Invader Risk 3 Slim
Quantity 6-8
Terrain Type Small unmoving group in a wooded valley with scouts wandering around them.

8. Angry Bwca Pit

And boy are they angry! They'll chase you all around if you're not careful. Located in a small recess from the snowy portion of Snowdonia, the Bwca are little rodent-looking fellas that walk on two legs. The only risk is that they travel a lot and cover a great deal of land.

Location 19, 13
Invader Risk 3 Slim
Quantity 5-10
Terrain Type A wide recess in the snow which is filled by Angry Bwcas wandering around randomly. Very spread out.

9. Arawnite Camp

The Arawnite have made quite a home of Snowdonia. This is one of their camps that might be a safer bet than the larger one to the northeast. There seem to be many sedentary Arawnites with the occasional Cyclops, but not nearly as many as their other larger camp/stronghold. Aside from the ugly Cyclops, there are no wandering threats.

Location 20, 44
Invader Risk 4 Slim
Quantity 10-12
Terrain Type Open hilly area with wandering Cyclops, otherwise clear from wandering aggros.

Hadrian's Wall

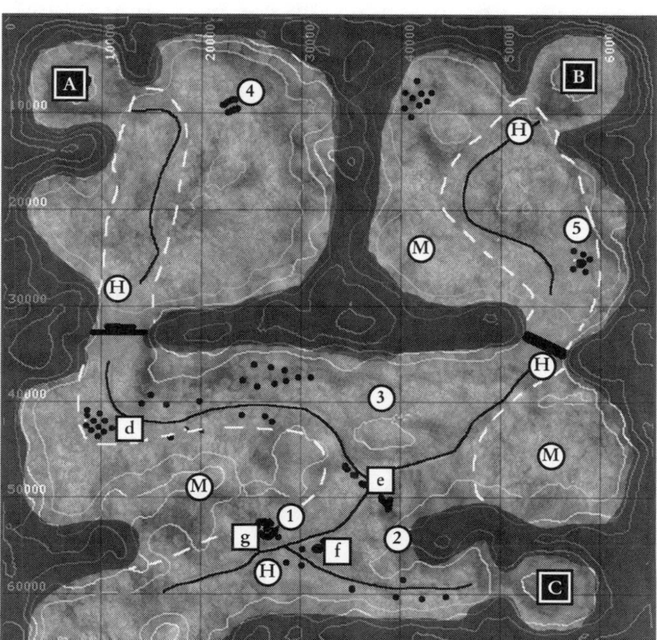

Map Key

A. Hibernia Outpost
B. Midgard Outpost
C. Caer Benowyc
d. Colonnade Ruins
e. Ruined Aqueduct
f. Tower Ruins
g. Legionnaires
(L) Low Invader Risk
(M) Medium Invader Risk
(H) High Invader Risk

Hadrian's Wall is where Hibernians and the Midgard armies come to invade Albion territory. The terrain is a mostly grassy knoll with some rugged hills among a variety of trees. It's often sunny and rather picturesque, and except for the massive amount of bloodshed here, it's a generally pleasant place to visit. There aren't too many hunting spots, but there are a variety of places to ambush other players from. Hadrian's Wall is home to an occasional strong group of creatures, but is mostly filled with monsters that are there to pester people. Where exactly is the 'wall' for which this zone was named? Well, no one is really sure ....

1. Legionnaire's Camp

The Legionnaire's Camp is one of the most dangerous areas you can enter due to the RvR traffic. It sits at a common intersection heading towards the dangerous Pennine Mountains, but one might be able to sneak a few kills here and there, Notably, there is a named spawn here. Some candidly refer to this spot as "Taco Bell" because it almost looks like a typical Bell building.

Location	27, 54
Invader Risk	8 High
Quantity	5-8, one named "Legionnaire Commander"
Terrain Type	Destroyed building harboring Undead Legionnaires. No wandering monster risk.

2. Cave Fairy Corner

Cave Fairies are nothing to scoff at. They're small and really mean. Don't get too close, they do bite. The area around them is benign, and for those who own the castle nearby, it's a bit more safe than if you didn't. This is a very high RvR risk area, and not a place to dally.

Location	48, 55
Invader Risk	8 Very High
Quantity	5-6
Terrain Type	Side of a hill beside a road leading to a castle. Close to guards, but high danger from invaders.

3. Waylayer Knoll

Between the Midgard and Hibernian roads, there is a hill. And for anyone who wishes to cut across this hill to get at the other, they will run smack into Midgard and Hibernian Waylayers. This isn't exactly a hunting spot, but it's a spot of interest to avoid, and maybe if you're in the mood for a little danger, you can bring a group here. They wander frequently but there is little else here of interest.

Location	39, 41
Invader Risk	8 High
Quantity	6-10
Terrain Type	A knoll! They're spread out, they wander, and they're not friendly.

4. Templar's Ruins

These "Templars" look like fallen warriors. They have shiny armor and appear well prepared for an onslaught. If someone is actually looking to gain experience in this zone, this is one of the better spots. Other than the wandering they do themselves, the area is relatively safe.

Location	22, 9
Invader Risk	6 Medium
Quantity	13
Terrain Type	Near zone wall at a ruin with open treed fields on all sides but one. Templars wander slightly, but no other wandering enemies nearby.

5. Cait Sidhe Ruins

This is a dangerous spot due to the RvR risks; however, there is a decent quantity of these creatures and there is little danger other than this, so if you have a group who wants to stick in the action but still gain experience while you are waiting, this is not a bad spot.

Location	58, 26
Invader Risk	8 Very High
Quantity	10
Terrain Type	Near a road in an open area. They are translucent , no wandering creatures nearby.

Forest Sauvage

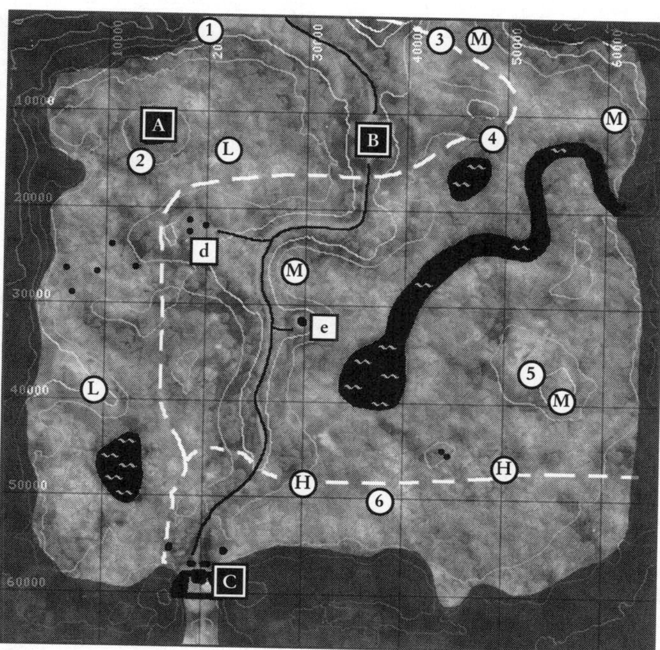

Map Key

A. Caer Renaris
B. Castle Excalibur & Scabbard Relic
C. Castle Sauvage
d. Skeletons
e. Guard Tower
Ⓛ Low Invader Risk
Ⓜ Medium Invader Risk
Ⓗ High Invader Risk

Forest Sauvage is truly a forest of as many trees that move as don't move. This zone takes the cake as the most friendly realm zone where monsters are concerned due to the wide-open forests with sporadic friendly creatures. Relic Fort Excaliber sits at the northern end along friendly roads where the only worry is from invaders. Along the eastern side the woods become slightly swampy and there seems to be a misty haze covering the lowest areas. Small lakes and rivers wind through the eastern side, but the western area is virtually empty of creature variety and is mostly just a foggy woodland. The average creature level here is around 27 with highs in the 30's and lows in the 20's. In the daylight, Forest Sauvage is one of the most beautiful and scenic places in the world.

1. Knotted Fellwood Grove

These are probably Sauvage's most formidable creatures, likely because they're near the Pennine Mountains. Sitting right on the border, these are gigantic gray Trees with an appetite for travelers. These creatures don't move at all and there are no wandering creatures nearby, making this a decent spot.

Location	20, 1
Invader Risk	3 Slim
Quantity	10-15
Terrain Type	Aside from some Trees, a barren rocky hillside. No wandering creatures. These don't move.

2. Roaming Fellwoods (Aspen/Downy/Hornbeam)

This spot encompasses virtually the entire western area of Sauvage. For a massive area, there are only groups of Trees blindly wandering around. Occasionally there are some snakes and large cats, but it's otherwise a simple flat expanse of wandering Fellwoods.

Location	8, 11
Invader Risk	2 Very Slim
Quantity	40-50 Spread over massive area.
Terrain *Type*	Dense woods/swamp. These Trees wander constantly and are spread out. Otherwise, no other creatures.

3. Forest Giant Woods

These are some of the more powerful creatures in Sauvage, yet there aren't enough of them to constitute a serious warning. However, consider it your civic duty to rid the world of these enormous and green creatures. They wander a great deal, but there is nothing else to worry about in the vicinity.

Location	45, 3
Invader Risk	4 Slim
Quantity	5-8
Terrain Type	A generally flat, almost swampy area, these guys wander a lot. No other wandering dangers, though.

4. Forest Ettin Woods

Forest Ettins take the cake as the strangest creatures to walk the land in Albion territory. They look like a bad genetic experiment, a green two-headed Frankenstein creature with ripped pants. They seem to move frequently in small groups of 2 or 3, with one parent figure followed by a couple of younger ones. The area around is very safe with only a slight risk of invaders.

Location	50, 18
Invader Risk	5 Small
Quantity	20+
Terrain Type	In groups of 3-4, spread out over a misty woods. They wander frequently, but there are no other wandering creatures.

5. Ashen/Oaken Fellwood Grove

These are another strange group of creatures. They're similar to their cousins to the western part of Sauvage; they are small trees that congregate and move like small flocks of birds. Looks like good hunting material, and the area is very safe with a medium risk of invaders.

Location	46, 31
Invader Risk	6 Medium
Quantity	15-30
Terrain Type	Open, misty woods. They move in packs of 3-4 over a large area.

6. Forest Giant Woods

This spot is a popular Albion attraction for a variety of players. They are huge green Giants with one eye, but not quite a Cyclops. They are located close to the realm gate for easy access, but invader probability is likely. A very safe area for any player.

Location	39, 50
Invader Risk	6 Medium
Quantity	10-20
Terrain Type	Misty wooden area, almost swamp on zone border. Huge wandering giants.

Uppland

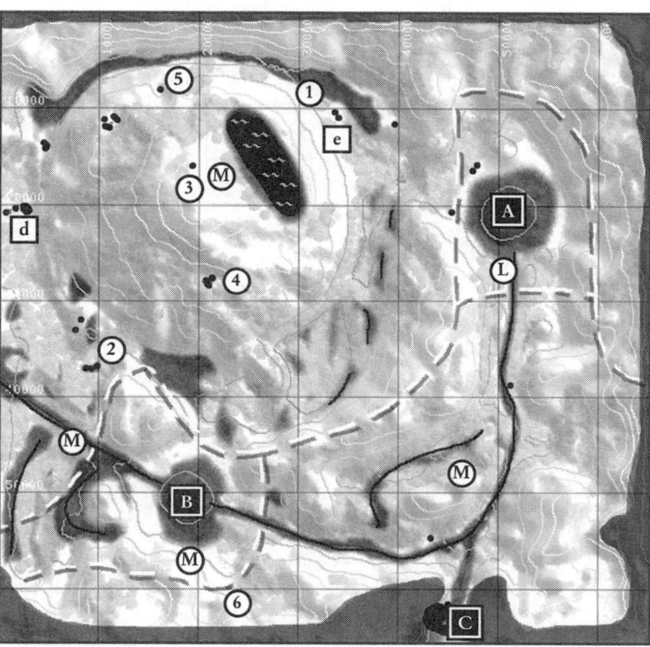

Map Key

A. Mjollner Faste & Hammer Relic
B. Fensalir Faste
C. Svasud Faste
d. Fenrir Camp
e. Snowshoe Bandits
(L) Low Invader Risk
(M) Medium Invader Risk
(H) High Invader Risk

Typical of Midgard territory, Uppland is a snowy mountainous region with gigantic pine trees everywhere. The creatures here are mostly mid to low level and hunting spots are spread out well with few wandering creatures to hassle explorers. To the northern end of this zone, the creatures become more powerful, but generally speaking, along the roads you can find a decent variet. Just beware invaders. Be sure to bring a hat! It gets cold.

1. Snowshoe Bandit Camp

This Snowshoe Bandit camp is in the northern reaches of Uppland. There is a relatively low risk of invaders, and other than a few wandering scouts, this hunting spot is a good choice if you're looking to get away from the crowds.

Location	33, 11
Invader Risk	5 Medium
Quantity	12-15
Terrain Type	In a small ravine, plenty of room for a party here.

2. Isalf Camp

This is another good spot for a group of adventurers with an eye for something different. Most of the Isalfs stay within their camp area, but beware the scouts! They wander about freely and will hightail it back to their friends when they see you.

Location	9, 37
Invader Risk	5 Medium
Quantity	6-8
Terrain Type	A dense wood, many wandering scouts.

3. Fenrir Camp

Located in the heart of Uppland, this is a decent hunting spot for anyone in their level range. There are few to no wandering creatures to hassle a party, including invaders, and there are large flat open areas around the camp to keep an eye on anything.

Location	17, 21
Invader Risk	4 Low
Quantity	7-12
Terrain Type	Snowy flat area with large open areas. Few/No wandering creatures.

4. Bone-Eater Camp

As is usually the case, these Bone-Eaters have made a camp on the sloping side of a hill and are simply waiting to be attacked. Other than a couple of scouts that they send out, it's a relatively safe area with few other creatures to interfere, low risk of RvR encounters to boot.

Location	21,28
Invader Risk	4, Low
Quantity	8-12
Personality	They stand still, with a couple scouts.
Terrain Type	Side of a hill with trees. Very good spot.

5. Icestrider Frostweaver Pit

Every realm has their "Ugly" creature; this is perhaps Midgard's most ugly. It happens to be that the most scary creatures are often the most powerful as well, and this is the case with these Icestriders. They're situated along a broken road that goes through a valley. Think of a hot dog bun–these guys sit where the hot dog would be.

Location	17, 5
Invader Risk	6 Medium
Quantity	11
Terrain Type	They line the bottom of a valley and up two sides. Very good spot for the brave!

6. Young Wyvern Mountain

Not far off the road from a castle, these Wyverns don't move very much and allow archers to have a good range on them. Unfortunately, many invaders follow the Zone wall to reach the gates at Uppland, and this is where they lay. Other than the Invader Risk, this is a decent spot for those looking to duo, or solo.

Location	21, 62
Invader Risk	7 High
Quantity	8
Personality	They move, but not very far.
Terrain Type	Zone side, Mountainside.

Yggdra Forest

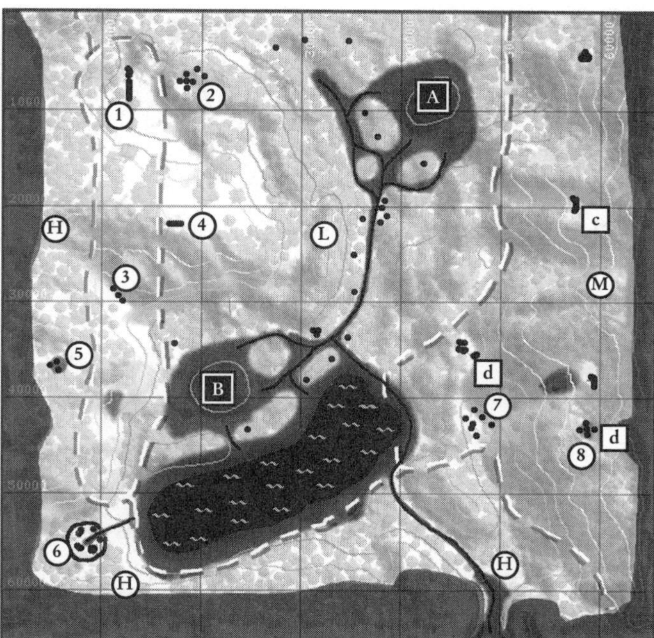

Map Key

A. Arvakr
B. Grallarhorn Faste & Horn relic
c. Bone Eaters
d. Isalfs
(L) Low Invader Risk
(M) Medium Invader Risk
(H) High Invader Risk

Yggdra Forest is one of the most popular, and thus dangerous, RvR zones in the world. There are plenty of mountains, and as the name suggests, it's a dense and often deadly forest. There are two castles here, but due to the lack of manpower, there aren't enough guards to prevent all the invaders from terrorizing the locals. Yggdra Forest has many excellent hunting spots, but with its known history for invaders, it is a high-risk area. The creatures here are generally unfriendly once you step off the road and there are a surprising amount of mid-level aggressive and scout-type creatures to harry explorers; the creatures range from the low 20's to the high 40's.

1. Ghastly Albion Invader Wall

It appears that finding good real estate is hard to find in the underworld, and so these Ghastly Invaders have made this their home. There are a good quantity of them here for a medium-sized group, and they don't move a whole lot. The area is flat around them for good positioning and there is no threat from wandering creatures.

Location 12,8
Invader Risk 6, Medium
Quantity 9
Personality They move only slightly.
Terrain Type Flat area around this wall; no wandering creatures.

2. Icestrider Chiller Pit

These Icestrider Chillers keep the same good looks as their cousins over in Uppland. They're densely packed in one sunken area, which would make them a good target if not for the

wandering creatures around waiting to assault an explorer.

Location 18, 7
Invader Risk 4 Low
Quantity 10-12
Terrain Type Dip on top of a hill; they don't move, but wandering creatures are around.

3. Wintery Dirge Stones

These ugly folks are situated near a zone border on a hillside. The risk of invaders is average, but there are plenty of these to go around; they move only small distances but are otherwise grouped together with few other wandering creatures to bother you.

Location 11,29
Invader Risk 7 High
Quantity 10
Personality They wander small distances.
Terrain Type Steep hills on two sides.

4. BoneEater Oracle Camp

The Bone Eater Oracle Camp is near the zone border where invaders frequently travel by; they're packed together tightly and only wander slightly. A short distance away are some mean aggressive creatures, but otherwise this is a popular archer spot and a great place to gain experience.

Location 16, 21
Invader Risk 8 High
Quantity 12
Personality They wander slightly.
Terrain Type Flat clearing on top of a hill.

5. Bone Eater Camp

Only the brave hunt her;, the cautious need not apply. This camp has a variety of Bone Eaters, and as the name suggests, they're not friendly and want to eat your bones. While the variety here is dangerous, the real danger is that it lies in the path of every invader coming into Yggdra Forest. The benefit here is that you'll never find people camping, but on the other side, you won't be alive very long.

Location 5, 36
Invader Risk 8 High
Quantity 10
Personality Sedentary.
Terrain Type Dense trees on a hillside, zone wall.

6. Fenrir Fort

How the armies of Midgard missed this spot is unknown. The Fenrir have made this their stronghold and it has become the size of a small town. There are guards, there are scouts and there are some mean individuals inside if you manage to make it past the first two. It's an easy-to-reach destination with few interruptions along the way, but the risk of invaders is very high.

Location 9, 55
Invader Risk 8 High
Quantity 20+
Personality Scouts.
Terrain Type Inside an open fort, various Fenrir types.

7. Undead Camp

This area is widely hunted for experience due to its close proximity to the realm gate. However, also due to the popularity of the spot, invaders constantly frequent here. This is a typical high risk area—great experience and lots of creatures, but at the price of safety.

Location 47, 42
Invader Risk 8 Very High
Quantity 20+
Personality Miserable Zombies, Shivering Presences, Thawing Corpses—all in a dense area.
Terrain Type Broad depression, woods on all sides.

8. Isalf Camp

Many adventurers have met their doom while wandering these slopes. The Isalf are legendary for their aggravating scouts, which can shoot you from a disturbing distance. Once you get by the scouts however, there is some good hunting that can be found here with only a relatively small risk of invasion.

Location 58, 43
Invader Risk 5 Low
Quantity 10
Personality Scouts, with majority being sedentary.
Terrain Type Side of a slowly sloping mountain in a wooded area.

Odin's Gate

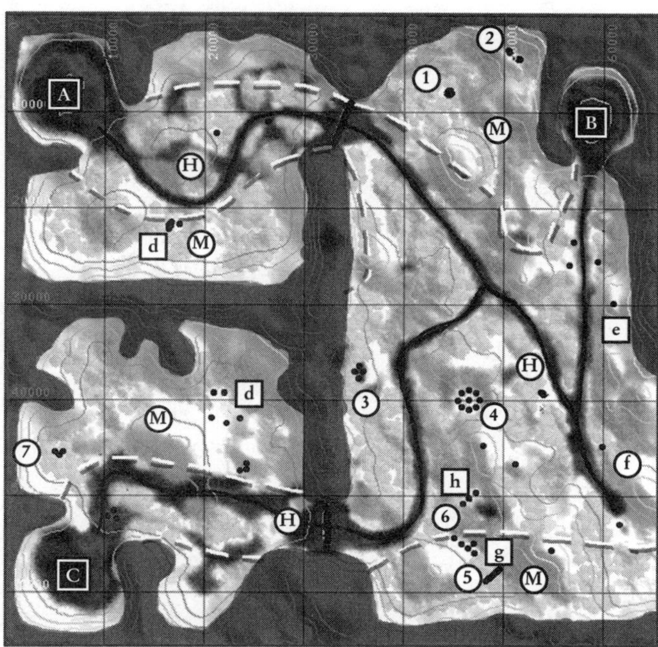

Map Key

- A. Hibernia Outpost
- B. Bledmeer Faste
- C. Albion Outpost
- d. Isalfs
- e. Wooden Tower
- f. Giant
- v. Undead Soldiers
- h. Icestrider Stones
- (L) Low Invader Risk
- (M) Medium Invader Risk
- (H) High Invader Risk

5

Odin's Gate is the entry point for Albion and Hibernia to invade Midgard frontier areas. It is generally considered unsafe to do anything but hunt enemy forces, although, for those who wish to spice up their lives with danger, this is a good place to do it. Odin's Gate is covered entirely with snow, large mountains, and occasionally dense forest. There aren't many decent hunting spots here, but there are plenty of creatures close to the roads which are rather powerful. Creature levels here range from low 30's to high 60's.

6

1. Isalf Forayer Hut

The Isalf apparently have some decent construction workers among them because they've made themselves a rather large and comfortable-looking log cabin. This is out of the way for any invader, so it may be a decent spot to find some experience–no wandering creatures to hassle you.

Location	44, 8
Invader Risk	5 Low
Quantity	8
Terrain Type	Small hut in the middle of a snowy flat. No wandering creatures; these are sedentary.

2. Fenrir Guard Post

The Fenrir must have been working hard to stake claim to this remote and mostly useless portion of land. It is situated on a hill at the zone border, but they seem to like it plenty. Invader Risk is low due to its locale, and there are a good amount here for a solo, duo or group looking to find some experience.

Location 50, 4
Invader Risk 4 Low
Quantity 8
Terrain Type Near zone border on side of mountain. Guards and Prophets inside two buildings.

3. Snowshoe Bandit Camp

This is a small camp on a hill beside the path of incoming Albion invaders. The reason to note this spot is the named spawn "Melechan Vezian". This spot is dangerous to camp and easily visible from the road; no wandering creatures.

Location 35, 37
Invader Risk 5 Low
Quantity 4, named spawn "Melechan Vezian"
Terrain Type Near road on the side of a small hill, a couple of tents and a fireplace.

4. Icestrider Frostweaver Stone

They're strong ugly and mean. This group of monsters is placed to prevent Albions from crossing through the woods safely. This isn't a particularly good hunting spot, but definitely one to avoid; wandering creatures abound!

Location 46 39
Invader Risk 7 High
Quantity 5
Terrain Type On a flat in a small depression with a single stone in the middle.

5. Undead Soldiers

Some poor soldiers became Undead and now haunt a single stone. The important part here is that a named soldier, "General Albanus" makes this spot home. While this spot may not be wonderful for experience, the General might give you something nice.

Location 47, 56
Invader Risk Low
Quantity 2 regular, one named "General Albanus".
Terrain Type They stand still, with some dangerous wandering creatures in a snowy plain with trees.

6. Icestrider Interceptor Totem

As their name implies, they are 'interceptors'. They're less hunting fodder than they are to keep people on the road. They're well hidden on top of a snowy peak, ready to descend upon an errant traveler. They move only slightly, but there are plenty of other creatures in the local vicinity to cause worry.

Location 46, 50
Invader Risk 5, low
Quantity 5
Terrain Type Top of a snowy hill. They slowly wander over a short distance, with few other wandering creatures.

7. Wintery Dirge Outpost

This is located within visible distance of the Albion portal fort. It's not a bad spot by any means, and the only real drawback is the Invader Risk. They sit in an open area around a small fort and slowly wander around.

Location 6, 45
Invader Risk 8 Very High
Quantity 6
Terrain Type Near Albion Portal Fort, open area with no wandering creatures. Dirges move only slowly.

Jamtdland Mountains

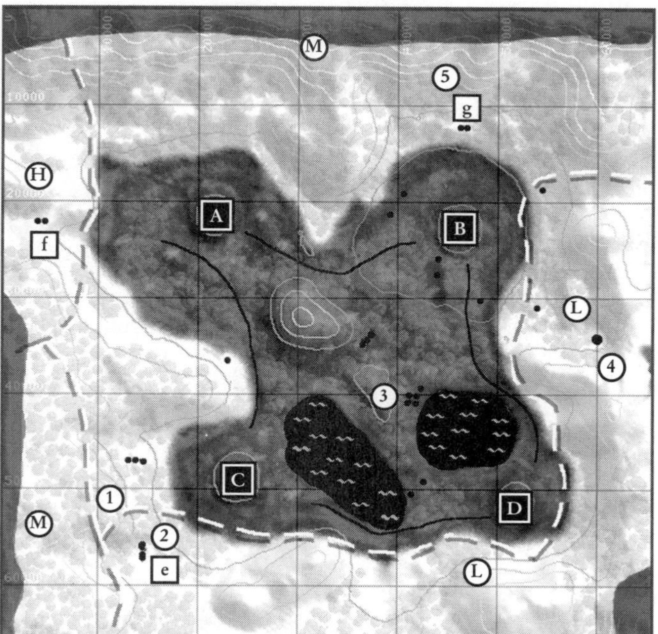

Map Key

A. Nottmoor Faste
B. Blendrake Faste
C. Hledskiaff Faste
D. Glenlock Faste
e. Fenrir
f. Stones
g. Wraiths

(L) Low Invader Risk
(M) Medium Invader Risk
(H) High Invader Risk

The Jamtland Mountains are probably the least mountainous of all the Midgard zones and make claim to the largest snow-free spots of the entire Midgard frontier. There are four large castles in the corners of this zone and it's mostly flat with occasional rolling hills and mountains that meet the zone borders. The creatures here are relatively tame with few exceptions, the highest being around Level 48 and the lowest in the low 30's. Roads connect the castles, and large dirt swaths ensure someone won't likely get lost. With so many castles around, a Midgard player is protected by guards virtually all the time.

1. Wraith Stones

These Wraiths are near the zone border and are a good run from the nearest realm gate, so if you're looking for solitude and likely a monst likely un-camped spot, this might be a decent place to hunt.

Location	13, 46
Invader Risk	6 Medium
Quantity	6
Terrain Type	Bottom end of a hill with a castle in sight. They move occasionally with no wandering creatures around.

2. Fenrir Shredder Cabins

The Fenrir have set up shop and are waiting to be hunted. The area around this spot is relatively flat with no wandering creatures to hassle you. Good spot for a solo or duo, although it's a bit far from home.

Location	13, 57
Invader Risk	6 Medium
Quantity	10
Terrain Type	Snowy, woodsy, wide-open, flat area with no wandering creatures.

3. Fenrir Guard/Prophet Camp

The Fenrir here have constructed a lean-to log cabin for some reason, yet it's the only area around without snow. Situated beside a lake and near four castles, this spot is very safe from invaders.

Location	41, 40
Invader Risk	4 Slim
Quantity	6
Terrain Type	Snow free! Beside a lake with plenty of guard protection from nearby castles.

4. Fenrir Hide Out

Now this place is a little more impressive than the Fenrir lean-to. They managed to construct a circular log cabin with all the amenities. There are a good amount of them here, with a variety of types including Fenrir Prophets. There are protective castles in plain view.

Location	59, 34
Invader Risk	4 Slim
Quantity	10
Terrain Type	Mostly inside a medium-sized building with some outside on a hill; no wandering creatures.

5. Windswept Wraith Outpost

These ugly invisible folk are towards the northern border of this zone and are in a good spot to intercept invaders. A friendly castle is in direct sight, and there are plenty of these to go around. Unfortunately, they help define the word 'ugly' and they have a personality to match their looks. They like to move a good deal, and there are some aggressive wandering creatures nearby.

Location	45, 12
Invader Risk	6 Medium
Quantity	9
Personality	They like to move frequently.
Terrain Type	Snowy hillside near a castle; wandering creatures around them.

Darkness Falls Dungeon

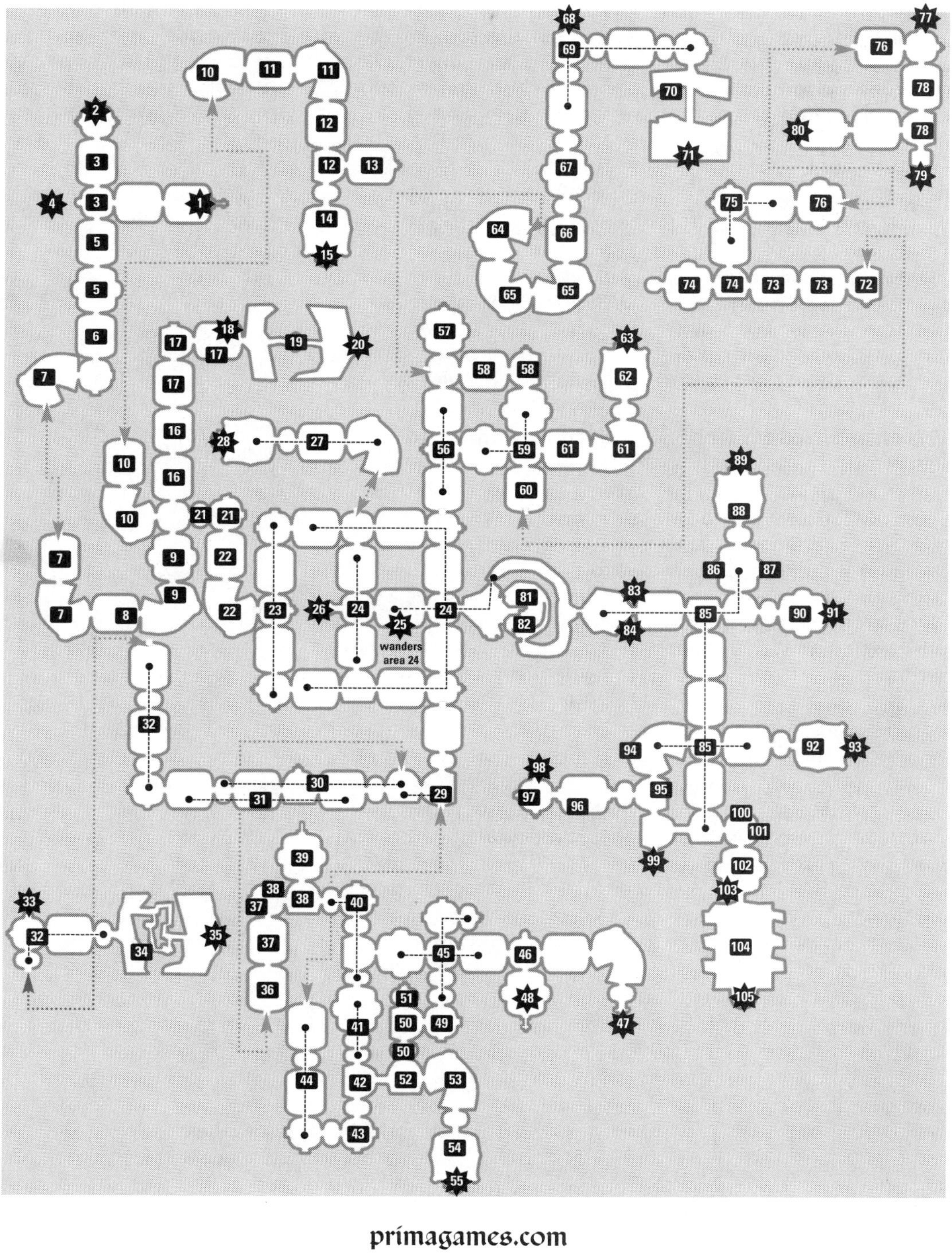

1 **Midgard Entrance (M)**
2 **Midgard Stores**
3 Demoniac Familiar (rat)
4 **Portal (P)**
5 Plated Fiend
6 Apprentice Necyomancer, Plated Fiend
7 Demoniac Familar (scorpion), Soultorn, Avernal Quasit
8 Demoniac Familiar (boar), Young Necyomancer, Soultorn
9 Lilispawn, Demoniac Familiar (spider, scorpion)
10 Deamhaness, Demoniac Familiar (wolf)
11 Soultorn
12 Rocot
13 Experienced Necyomancer, Demoniac Familiar (cat, scorpion, boar)
14 Soultorn, Molochian Tempter
15 **Lecherous Gress**
16 Umbrood Warrior
17 Chthonic Knights
18 **Commander Abgar, Lieutenant Persun**
19 Chthonic Knights, Pale Guardian, Umbral Aegis, Chaosian, Umbrood Warrior, Essence Shredder (in pit), Earl Glassalab
20 **Prince Abdin**
21 Molochian Tempter, Naburite Drinker, Cursed Necyomancer
22 Cambion, Soultorn, Demoniac Familiar (scorpion, boar, wolf, lynx), Naburite Drinker, Cursed Necyomancer
23 Essence Shredder, Condemned Necyomancer, Tormented Necyomancer
24 Mahr, Succubus, Nightmare, Chthonian Crawler
25 **Director Kobil** (wanders)
26 **Portal (P)**
27 Succubus, Nightmare
28 **Princess Nahemah**
29 Cambion
30 Mahr, Cursed Necyomancer, Condemned Necyomancer, Tormented Necyomancer
31 Essence Shredder
32 Mutilator
33 **Portal (P)**
34 Mutilator, Chaosian, Umbral Aegis, Pale Guardian, Earl Ipostian, Essence Shredder (in pit)
35 **Prince Asmoien**
36 Rocot
37 Apprentice Necyomancer, Demoniac Familiar (lynx, wolf, spider)
38 Soultorn, Demoniac Familiar (lynx)
39 Rocot
40 Avernal Quasit, Soultorn, Young Necyomancer
41 Young Necyomancer, Avernal Quasit, Demoniac Familiar (cat, scorpion, boar)
42 Necyomancer, Young Necyomancer, Soultorn
43 Experienced Necyomancer, Cursed Necyomancer, Molochian Tempter
44 Naburite Drinker
45 Apprentice Necyomancer, Demoniac Familiar, Plated Fiend, Soultorn
46 Demoniac Familiar (rat)
47 **Hibernia Entrance (H)**
48 **Hibernia Stores**
49 Lilispawn
50 Soultorn
51 Deamhaness, Necyomancer
52 Ricot
53 Experienced Necyomancer, Soultorn, Rocot
54 Molochian Tempter, Soultorn
55 **Archivist Borath**
56 Essence Shredder, Tormented Necyomancer, Condemned Necyomancer
57 Rocot, Deamhaness
58 Soultorn, Experienced Necyomancer, Demoniac Familiar (lynx), Rocot
59 Deamhaness, Lilispawn, Necyomancer, Soultorn
60 Lilispawn, Soultorn, Young Necyomancer
61 Rocot, Experienced Necyomancer, Soultorn
62 Molochian Tempter, Soultorn
63 **Malrock the Cook**
64 Cursed Necyomancer, Molochian Tempter
65 Cursed Necyomancer, Naburite Drinker, Soultorn, Demoniac Familiar (wolf, lynx)
66 Cursed Necyomancer, Condemned Necyomancer, Demoniac Familiar (lynx)
67 Tormented Necyomancer, Condemned Necyomancer, Essence Shredder, Cambion, Demoniac Familiar (spider, wolf, lynx)
68 **Portal (P)**
69 Inquisitors
70 Umbrood Warrior, Pale Guardian, Inquisitor, Earl Mermer, Chaosian, Essence Shredder (in pit), Umbral Aegis (in pit)
71 **Prince Ba'alorien**
72 Lilispawn, Soultorn, Young Necyomancer
73 Young Necyomancer, Plated Fiend, Deamhaness, Avernal Quasit, Demoniac Familiar (boar)
74 Avernal Quasit, Young Necyomancer, Demoniac Familiar (cat, scorpion), Soultorn
75 Plated Fiends, Apprentice Necyomancer, Demoniac Familiar (ant, cat)
76 Plated Fiend, Apprentice Necyomancer, Demoniac Familiar (ant)
77 **Albion Stores**
78 Demoniac Familiar (rat)
79 **Portal (P)**
80 **Albion Entrance (A)**
81 Center
82 Umbral Hulk
83 Gate Room
84 **Gatekeeper Dommel**
85 Umbral Aegis, Succubus, Inquisitors, Mutilators, Chthonic Knights, Chthonian Crawler, Nightmare
86 Duke Bimure
87 Marquis Scottiax
88 Duke Sallis, Marquis Sabonach, Earl Mercur
89 **High Lord Oro**
90 Marquis Focallaste, Duke Harboris, Earl Fenex
91 **High Lord Baelerdoth**
92 Duke Zepor, Marquis Almen, Earl Oraxus
93 **High Lord Saeor**
94 Duke Eligar
95 Marquis Dortaleon
96 Duke Aypol
97 Marquis Chaosmar, Duke Alloc, Earl Amagin
98 **High Lord Bain**
99 Portal
100 Duke Satori
101 Marquis Valupa
102 Chthonic Knights, Mutilators, Inquisitors, Earl Vone
103 **Grand Chancellor Adremal**
104 The Chamberlain, Pale Guardian, Chaosian, Marquis Haurian, Inquisitors, Mutilators, Chthonic Knights, Umbrood Warrior, Behemoth
105 **Legion**

Appendix A: Explanations

Materials

Most standard items in *Dark Age of Camelot* are made from one of a series of materials. For each kind of material (Cloth, Leather, Metal, Natural, Ore and Wood), there are increasingly better qualities. In general, each better grade of material raises the level (and value) of an item by 5. For example, the first two grades of metal are bronze and iron. An iron item tends to be 5 levels better than a corresponding bronze item.

The grades of various kinds of material are:

Levels	Cloth	Leather	Metal	Natural	Ore	Wood
0-5	Woolen	Rawhide	Bronze	Leaf	None	Rowan
6-10	Linen	Tanned	Iron	Bone	Ferrite	Elm
11-15	Brocade	Cured	Steel	Vine	Quartz	Oaken
16-20	Silk	Hard	Alloy	Shell	Dolomite	Ironwood
21-25	Gossamer	Rigid	Fine Alloy	Fossil	Cobalt	Heartwood
26-30	Sylvan	Embossed	Mithril	Amber	Carbide	Runewood
31-35	Seamist	Imbued	Adamantium	Coral	Sapphire	Stonewood
36-40	Nightshade	Runed	Asterite	Chitin	Diamond	Ebonwood
41-45	Wyvernskin	Eldritch	Netherium	Petrified	Netherite	Dyrwood
46-50	Silksteel	Tempered	Arcanium	Crystalized	Arcanite	Duskwood

QUALITY

All weapons, armor and jewelry items in the game have a Quality — how well the item was made when it was crafted. In general, Qualities range from 70 to 100. 70 is extremely poor. Common drop items range from 70 to 80 in Quality. Store bought items have Quality 85. Rare items have Quality 89 to 93 (almost all rare items that come from monsters below level 50 have Quality 89). The rare items exceed that as the monsters surpass level 50. Very rare items have Quality 90. Trade items and PC-crafted items have Qualities that range from 90 to 100. Quest items pretty much all have Quality 100.

Quality is important for weapons and armor; it is a direct multiplier to the effectiveness of the armor or weapon. A weapon will only deliver its listed damage if it has Quality 100; a weapon with Quality 90 inflicts only 90% of the listed damage. The Armor Factor listed for a piece of armor only applies if the armor has Quality 100; a piece of armor with Quality 80 has only 80% of the listed AF. As an item deteriorates, it loses more and more of its usefulness, until it is completely worthless. That's why it's important to keep your equipment in good repair. (This deterioration also significantly affects the usefulness of items whose Power Level is higher than your own level — the higher it is, the more quickly it deteriorates.)

Because an item's usefulness depends on both its initial Quality and its current state of repair, this book doesn't try to give you the maximum effective stats for any item; it gives the stats as though all items begin at Quality 100, even though some can never be that good. However, from that starting point, it's easier to figure out a weapon's current effectiveness, based on its Quality and its current state of repair.

Weapons

For standard weapons and unique weapons, see pages 83 and 84 (Albion), pages 181 and 182 (Hibernia) and pages 271 and 272 (Midgard). For **Siege Equipment**, see page 324. For **Arrows**, see page 363.

Each standard weapon in *Dark Age of Camelot* can be found in a variety of metals (or woods, ores, and other weapons, of course). A weapon's material, and its corresponding level, are both crucial when determining how much damage it can do and how quickly you can strike with it.

The better the material used to make a weapon, the higher its Power Level, and the greater damage it can inflict — when wielded by a character who at least matches its level. While a better, higher-level weapon can usually inflict more damage with each attack, a lower-level character's damage is capped by his own level.

It should be no surprise that, on average, the most efficient damage output is achieved with a weapon that matches your character's level.

Each higher quality material improves the quality of a weapon by five "levels" — since a bronze dagger is level 1, then an iron dagger is level 6, a steel dagger is level 11, an alloy dagger is level 16, a fine alloy dagger is level 21, a mithril dagger is level 26 and so forth.

Other weapons follow exactly the same pattern.

Each weapons table sorts weapons first by the skill needed to use them, then by Power Level. Remember that the stats given are base values, assuming an average wielder at the same level as the weapon's level. In particular, if you wield a weapon whose Power Level is higher than your own level, its DPS (Damage per Second) — and thus your damage with each swing — is decreased to the norm for your lower level.

Shields

A shield's usual purpose is to fend off attackers; the four standard types of shield available in all three realms accomplish that. However, these and most other shields can also become weapons, using the Shield skill. As with other weapons, a shield's damage depends on its material and level (see **Weapons**, above). A shield whose Power Level matches your level is the most efficient shield for your purposes.

Standard shields at Material Level 1 (M#1: bronze, copper and so forth) have Armor Factor 2 and Power Level 1 (AF 2 and PL 1). At Material Level 2 (Iron and Ferrite), a standard shield has AF 12 and PL 6. Each higher Material Level after that results in +10 AF and +5 PL. Therefore, a standard Alloy or Dolomite shield (Material Level 4) has AF 32 and PL 16.

Standard shields that can be used as crushing weapons have 1.2 DPS at Material Level 1. They gain 1.5 DPS at each higher Material Level. (For example, a standard Material Level 3 shield has 4.2 DPS (1.2 + 1.5 + 1.5).)

For a more detailed explanation of a shield's defensive and offensive stats, see **Armor** (p. 362) and **Weapons** (above).

Levels	Size	Shield	AF	Delay (sec.)	Dmg (M#1)	Increment	Base DPS	Weight	Notes
1,6,11, etc.	Small	Round Shield	2,12,22,etc.	2.8	3.4	4.2	1.2	3.1	defends against 1 foe
1,6,11, etc.	Medium	Kite Shield	2,12,22,etc.	4.3	5.2	6.5	1.2	3.5	defends against 2 foes
1,6,11, etc.	Large	Heater Shield	2,12,22,etc.	3.8	4.6	5.7	1.2	3.8	defends against 3 foes
1,6,11, etc.	Large	Tower Shield	2,12,22,etc.	4.5	5.4	6.8	1.2	4.1	defends against 3 foes

Shield Recipes (all realms)

Shield	Time (sec.)	Skills	Tools	Components	1st (S.C)	5th (G.S)	10th (G.S)
Heater Shield	6-60	Wp95+	F,H	body,facing	0.58	3.38	34.26
Body	1-15	Wd95	F,H,P	1b,3w,1l	0.23	1.37	13.85
Facing	1-15	M95	F,H	4b	0.35	2.02	20.41
Kite Shield	6-60	Wp95+	F,H	body,facing	0.41	2.38	24.06
Body	1-15	Wd95	F,H,P	1b,3w,1l	0.23	1.37	13.85
Facing	1-15	M95	F,H	2b	0.17	1.01	10.21
Round Shield	6-60	Wp95+	F,H	body,fittings	0.33	1.94	19.68
Body	1-15	Wd95	F,H,P	1b,2w	0.16	0.94	9.48
Fittings	1-15	M95	F,H	2b	0.17	1.01	10.21
Tower Shield	6-60	Wp95+	F,H	body,facing	0.50	2.88	29.16
Body	1-15	Wd95	F,H,P	1b,3w,1l	0.23	1.37	13.85
Facing	1-15	M95	F,H	3b	0.26	1.51	15.31

See **Crafting** *(p. 364) for explanations of abbreviations and column headings.*

Miscellaneous Recipes (all realms)

Shield	Time (sec.)	Skills	Tools	Components	1st (S.C)	5th (G.S)	10th (G.S)
Bracket	1-14	M0	H,F	1b	0.08	0.50	5.10
Breadboard	1-14	Wd0	P	2w	0.07	0.43	4.37
Bridle	1-14	L0	S,H	1b,1l,1t	0.14	0.85	8.60
Curio Box	1-14	Wd50	P	2w	0.07	0.43	4.37
Doll	1-14	C0	K	2c,1t	0.07	0.42	4.23
Hinge	1-14	M50	H,F	2b	0.17	1.01	10.21
Puppet	1-14	C50	K	1c,1t,1w	0.08	0.49	4.96
Riding Crop	1-14	L50	S,H	1b,1l,1t	0.14	0.85	8.60
Scales (Hib.)	1-14	M0	H,F	20b	1.75	10.08	102.06
Strapping (Straps)	1-14	L0	H,F	2b,20l,2t	0.97	5.59	56.57
Studs (not in Hib.)	1-14	M0	H,F	20b	1.75	10.08	102.06
Wire (not in Hib.)	1-14	M0	H,F	20b	1.75	10.08	102.06
Cloak * *or* Hooded Cloak *	1	T15/C0	K	5 woolen c, 2 woolen t	1.70 (Material Lvl 2)		
Drum, Flute, Lute (not in Midgard)	2-56	F25/ Wd,C,L5	P,L	18w,4t,6l	.99	5.70	57.74

** Cloaks will never be part of a consignment.*

Armor

For standard armor and unique armor, see page 95 (Albion), page 190 (Hibernia), and pages 279 (Midgard).

Armor and other clothing are available across all three realms, in a variety of Qualities. A few (like robes) are one-piece items. However, most armor and clothing covers a specific part of your body — head (caps, helmets and helms), torso (vests, jerkins, hauberks and breastplates), arms (sleeves), hands (gloves and gauntlets), legs (pants and leggings) or feet (boots).

Each piece protects you from the forces arrayed against you. (Well, most of them do. The lower-Quality cloth items provide little, if any, protection.) When you're hit, a hit location is determined and a check is made to see what armor (if any) is protecting you there. Without going into the complicated formulas, both your total armor (all the armor you're wearing) and your specific armor (the armor protecting the specific place you were hit) affect how much damage you actually take from the hit.

You can see two numbers displayed for each piece of armor you're wearing. One is labelled "AF" (Armor Factor) and the other "ABS" (which stands for absorption, but doesn't really mean absorption). ABS is always the same for a given type of armor — 10% for Leather, 19% for Reinforced Leather, and so forth. (Cloth, at the lowest end of the scale, is actually a bit funky about its ABS value, but it's near 0%.)

AF is directly related to the Quality of the material. Albion's Rawhide Cymric Leather is Level 2 and AF 6. Tanned Cymric Leather (one step up from rawhide), is five levels better and 10 AF better: Level 7, AF 16. In general, each step of Quality improvement improves any type of armor by 5 levels and 10 AF. (Again, Cloth is odd, with AF improvement progressing more slowly than for other materials.)

Unfortunately, neither the ABS number nor the AF number (nor the two combined) tell you directly how much damage your armor will protect against. Larger pieces of armor (particularly your torso armor) affect this result much more than smaller pieces (for example, gloves and footwear). Price is not always a good indicator of relative protection — helms tend to be more expensive than gloves, but don't affect your overall AF as much.

Just as a weapon's ability to inflict damage improves as its Quality improves, so does armor's ability to deflect and absorb damage as its Quality improves.

Arrows & Bolts

For bows and/or crossbows, see p. 93 (Albion), p. 189 (Hibernia) and p. 278 (Midgard).

For unique arrows and bolts, see p. 94 (Albion), p. 189 (Hibernia) and p. 278 (Midgard).

Bow (and crossbow) damages are listed in the Weapon Table for each realm. However, which arrow you use also affects your shot. Standard arrows and bolts are the same across all three realms. They are crafted from three types of heads, three types of shafts, and three types of fletchings. The three heads are called "blunt," "bodkin" and "broadhead." The three shafts are "clout," average (with no special name) and "flight." The three fletchings are "rough," average (no name) and "footed."

The head affects your damage — blunt and bodkin heads inflict low and average thrust damage, respectively. A broadhead inflicts heavier slash damage.

The shaft affects how far you can shoot — clout shafts are relatively short-ranged, while flight shafts are relatively long-ranged.

The fletching affects your accuracy — rough fletching makes an arrow inaccurate except at very short range, while a footed arrow can split an apple on a boy's head at 100 paces. But that's another story.

Of course, the better the arrow, the more you'll pay for it. Expect to pay nine times as much for an arrow with a flight shaft as you'll pay for an arrow with a clout shaft. Expect to pay nine times as much for a broadhead arrow as for a blunt arrow. And expect to pay over six times as much for a footed arrow as for a rough arrow. (Yes, the most expensive arrows tend to cost more than several hundred times the cost of the cheapest arrow, and that's before you start adding in any magical effects or other bells and whistles.)

Effects

Type	Effect	Cost Multiple (approx.)
Head		
Blunt	-15% bow's damage (Thrust)	x1
Bodkin	bow's normal damage (Thrust)	x3
Broadhead	+25% bow's damage (Slash)	x9
Fletching		
Rough	-15% accuracy	x1
(Average)	normal accuracy	x2
Footed	+25% accuracy	x6
Shaft		
Clout	-15% bow's range	x1
(Average)	bow's normal range	x3
Flight	+25% bow's range	x9

Recipes

(+ Secondary: Wd (all three), M (Bodkin, Broadhead); both at 15 below Primary)

All arrows take 5 seconds to make.

Arrow Fletching	Shaft	Skls	Tls	Wood	Feather	Metal/Ore	Cost (S.C)
Blunt (Head)							
Rough	Clout *	F10+	P	1 rowan	1 crow		.06
Rough	(Average)	F45+	P	3 rowan	1 hawk		.21
Rough	Flight	F115+	P	2 rowan	1 gull		.58
(Average)	Clout	F80+	P	2 rowan	2 hawk		.28
(Average)	(Average)	F150+	P	3 rowan	1 gull		.61
(Average)	Flight	F220+	P,L	2 elm	1 gull		1.70
Footed	Clout	F185+	P,L	1 elm	2 hawk		.80
Footed	(Average)	F255+	P,L	2 elm	1 gull		1.70
Footed	Flight	F290+	P,L	1 oaken	1 cockatrice		4.90
Bodkin (Head)							
Rough	Clout	F110+	P	3 rowan	1 hawk	1 bronze/copper	.30
Rough	(Average)	F145+	P	2 rowan	3 hawk	2 bronze/copper	.55
Rough	Flight	F215+	P,L	2 elm	1 gull	2 bronze/copper	1.88
(Average)	Clout	F180+	P	1 elm	1 hawk	2 bronze/copper	.88
(Average)	(Average)	F250+	P	2 elm	1 gull	2 bronze/copper	1.88
(Average)	Flight	F320+	P,L	1 oaken	2 gull	1 iron/ferrite	4.80
Footed	Clout	F285+	P,L	2 elm	2 hawk	1 iron/ferrite	2.80
Footed	(Average)	F355+	P,L	1 oaken	2 gull	1 iron/ferrite	4.80
Footed	Flight	F390+	P,L	1 ironwood	1 cockatrice	1 steel/quartz	15.30
Broadhead							
Rough	Clout	F210+	P	1 elm	1 hawk	2 bronze/copper	.88
Rough	(Average)	F245+	P	2 elm	3 hawk	2 bronze/copper	1.68
Rough	Flight	F315+	P,L	1 oaken	3 gull	1 iron/ferrite	5.30
(Average)	Clout	F280+	P	2 elm	2 hawk	1 iron/ferrite	2.80
(Average)	(Average)	F350+	P	1 oaken	2 gull	1 iron/ferrite	4.80
(Average)	Flight	F420+	P,L	1 ironwood	1 cockatrice	1 steel/quartz	15.30
Footed	Clout	F385+	P,L	1 oaken	1 cockatrice	2 iron/ferrite	7.70
Footed	(Average)	F455+	P,L	1 ironwood	1 cockatrice	1 steel/quartz	15.30
Footed	Flight	F490+	P,L	1 heartwood	1 phoenix	1 alloy/dolomite	48.40

** Rough clout blunt arrows will never be part of a consignment.*

Crafting

For **Siege Equipment** Crafting, see page 324.

For **Arrow** Crafting, see page 363.

For **Shield** Crafting and recipes for other **Miscellaneous** items that can be crafted in all realms, see pages 361-362.

For other **Albion Weapons** and **Armor Crafting**, see page 106.

For other **Midgard Weapons** and **Armor Crafting**, see page 202.

For other **Hibernia Weapons** and **Armor Crafting**, see pages 290.

Required Skills and Chance of Success

If your craft skill exactly matches the skill level listed for the item you're crafting, you have a 50% chance of making the item, and a 50% chance of failing to make the item.

For every additional point you have, your chance of success shifts 1% in your favor. For example, if you're crafting something 25 points below your skill level, you have a 75% chance to make the item (and a 25% chance to fail). Similarly, for every point below the listed item skill, you have a 1% greater chance of failure.

Critical failures can apply when you try to make something that is above your skill. For each point that your skill is below the listed skill, there's another 1% critical failure chance. For example, if you're trying to make something that is 25 points above your skill, you have a 25% chance of success and a 75% chance of failure (split into 50% normal failure and 25% critical failure).

If you fail normally when attempting to craft an item, nothing happens — the item is simply not made. If you critically fail, you lose at least one ingredient. Your chance of losing each individual component (for example, each metal bar, rather than the entire stack of bars) is equal to your chance of critical failure. For example, if your chance of critical failure was 37%, then there is a 37% chance for each component that you might lose that component. If you get lucky and lose nothing this way, you still lose the first listed component (or one of them, if it's a stack).

A few items can only be crafted at Material Level 5 or better. For those items, the listed skill levels are for level 5, not level 1.

Chance of Skill Improvement

Roughly speaking, your chance to improve a skill is equal to your chance of failure. However, your chance of improvement is twice as good at lower levels, and only half as good at higher levels. Your chance of improvement actually matches your chance of failure in the neighborhood of skill level 400-500.

Secondary Skills

"+" Unless otherwise noted, completing a finished shield also requires the skills necessary to craft its two component parts, minus 15. For example, when crafting a heater shield at Material Level 1, your primary skill requirement is Weaponcraft 95, but you also must have Woodworking and Metalworking at 80 (since the body and facing require those skills at 95).

For each item, the skill levels listed are those to craft it at Material Level 1. To craft the same item with better materials, add 100 levels to each skill listed. For example, a rawhide bridle (Material Level 1, p. 362) requires Leatherworking 0. Therefore, a tanned bridle (Material Level 2) requires Leatherworking 100, Level 3 requires 200, and so forth.

If a secondary skill is listed as "(-15)", that means that crafting the item at Material Level 1 requires the minimum possible skill (0).

Crafting the item at Material Level 2 requires 85 skill (-15 + 100), Material Level 3 requires 185, and so forth.

Tools

There are currently five "tools" to help you craft items: Sewing Kit (K), Planing Tool (P), Smith's Hammer (H), Forge (F) and Lathe (L). Three can be carried — the Sewing Kit, Planing Tool and Smith's Hammer. You must have any of these in your inventory to use it. The other two (the Forge and Lathe) cannot be carried. You must be within 512 World Units (about nine yards) of one of these to use it.

Time

Time listed is always in seconds and lists two values — the time to craft the item at Material Level 1, and the time to craft it at Material Level 10. (For those items that can only be crafted at Material Level 5 and above, the first number is the time to craft it at Level 5.)

Base Components and Costs

You must always have the exact components in your inventory to craft an item. (Actually, there are a few exceptions when crafting siege equipment; see page 324.) If the recipe requires Elm (Level 2 Wood), you must have Elm, not Rowan (Level 1) or Oaken (Level 3). Most items can be crafted at any of ten Material Levels. To craft an item at any Material Level, all components must match that level.

All prices have been calculated using the following base component costs. In case of fractional results, the final prices are rounded down to the nearest copper:

Material Level: *Component*	1st	5th	10th
Metal or Ore Bar (b)	8.75 cop.	5040 cop. (50S,40C)	51030 cop. (5G,10S,30C)
Strips (s)	8.75 cop.	5040 cop. (50S,40C)	51030 cop. (5G,10S,30C)
Wooden Board (w)	3.75 cop.	2160 cop. (21S,60C)	21750 cop. (2G,17S,50C)
Leather Square (l)	3.75 cop.	2160 cop. (21S,60C)	21750 cop. (2G,17S,50C)
Cloth Square (c)	2.50 cop.	1440 cop. (14S,60C)	14580 cop. (1G,45S,80C)
Heavy Thread (t)	2.25 cop.	1296 cop. (12S,96C)	13050 cop. (1G,30S,50C)

Material Level Multipliers

In the various tables, costs are only listed for finished products at Material Levels 1, 5 and 10 (only Material Levels 5 and 10 for items that can't be crafted before that level). To get the costs for other material levels, find the cost for the 1st, 5th or 10th level and use the following multiples or divisions:

Material Lvl: *Base Lvl*	1st	2nd	3rd	4th	5th	6th	7th	8th	9th	10th
1st	1x	16x	64x	192x						
5th		x/36	x/9	x/3	1x	2x	3x	4.5x	6.75x	
10th								x/2.25	x/1.5	1x

Bear in mind that these are the base costs to craft the item if you make it from scratch. Buying the various intermediate components, or buying the finished piece itself, can often result in significantly different prices.

Crafting Stat Abbreviations

The following abbreviations are used for all crafting tables in this guide:

Time. Time to craft the item at 1st and 10th Material Levels (in seconds).

Skills. **C** = Clothworking / **L** = Leatherworking / **M** = Metalworking / **T** = Tailoring / **Wd** = Woodworking / **Wp** = Weaponcraft.

Tools. **F** = Forge / **P** = Planing Tool / **H** = Smith's Hammer / **K** = Sewing Kit / L = Lathe.

Components. **b** = Metal or Ore Bars / **c** = Cloth Squares / **l** = Leather Squares / **s** = Strips / **t** = Heavy Thread / **w** = Wooden Boards.

Costs. Costs are listed in Silver and Copper for Material Level 1. They're listed in Gold and Silver for Material Levels 5 and 10, rounded to the nearest Silver.

Spells

SPELL RESULTS

The listed spell results (for duration, damage, Buffs, Debuffs and so forth) are actually just "benchmark" values. The better you are at casting a spell, the better your personal results.

In general, the effect of a spell ranges between 75% and 125% of the listed ("benchmark") values for that spell. (Direct Damage spells range from 25% to 125%.) The higher your ability with the skill that governs that spell, the higher your personal results. A spell never produces an effect higher than 125% of the benchmark value, but you can pull the low end up from 75% to better than 100% if you improve the related skill. The skill for each list of spells is given with that list, in the description at the top of the table.

Specialized spells compare your level of specialization to the level of the spell you're casting. If your level of specialization is no better than half the spell level, you'll tend to get results at the lower end of the range.

When you acquire a spell (whether early or late) has no effect on the spell's power (although the earlier you get it, the weaker you'll probably be with it, until you gain a few more levels/spend a few more specialization points).

To get information about one of your spells, right click on it. You can also get information about spells cast on your character by using the Shift-I key. The BONUSES button on your character sheet shows your resistances, along with realm and outpost bonuses.

Spellcasts cannot be interrupted by resisted spells, missed Bolt spells or arrows, or bladeturned arrows.

SPELL LIST ABBREVIATIONS

Distances (range and radius) are measured in world units (wu). World units are the units of measurement you see on your screen during the game. To get a visual idea of how long a world unit might be, it takes about 60 world units to equal a character's "pace" distance in the game, and a human pace equals about one yard.

AF. Armor Factor.

AoE. Area of Effect. Indicates a spell that has an effect over a wide radius, rather than on a single target. These spells are centered on a target unless they specify, "Centered on Caster," which indicates a "point blank" spell. Damage is reduced for anyone farther from the center with AoE spells.

Atk. Attack, usually used as Atk Spd, or attack speed.

Concent. Concentrate. Indicates that the Caster must keep his attention on the spell to keep it activated.

C. Concentration points.

DD. Direct Damage.

Dmg. Damage.

DoT. Damage over Time. DoT spells inflict the listed damage at impact, and then the same damage every few seconds (listed in the spell description) until the spell's duration expires.

HP. Hit Points.

Inst. Instantaneous. Spells with an Instantaneous casting time have an immediate effect on their target.

Lvl. Level.

Mes. Mesmerize.

Neg. Negated. Spells with a duration of "Until Negated" remain in effect until the Caster stops them or the called creature is killed.

P. Power Points.

Sec. and Min. Seconds and Minutes.

Spd. Speed.

Spec. Specialization.

STR, DEX, QUI, PIE, INT, CON, EMP, CHA. Abbreviations for the main character attributes. STR = Strength, DEX = Dexterity, QUI = Quickness, PIE = Piety, INT = Intelligence, CON = Constitution, EMP = Empathy and CHA = Charisma.

STATISTICS

Statistics vary a bit from spell group to spell group. Any statistics that apply to the whole spell series (such as the general description) appear at the top of the series listing. Statistics that change from spell to spell within the group are listed in columns in the table.

Possible statistics include:

Description. Each spell list begins with a short description of what that group of spells does. There are several different types of spells available.

Some spells can be stacked, meaning that you can cast them more than once on the same target, or can cast two different spells on a single target at the same time. If a spell "stacks as group 1", it can be stacked with a group 2 spell. If a spell "stacks as group 2", it can be stacked with a group 1 spell, but its duration will be halved.

All Snare, Root, Stun and Mesmerize spells have limitations if you cast them on a target that you've already Snared, Rooted or Mesmerized. When you're in PvE, stacking a second spell (of the same type) doesn't overlap the duration of the first spell, but it does cut the duration of the second spell in half. The duration of the third stacked spell (again, of the same type) is only one quarter as long, and so forth. In RvR, these spells can't be stacked. In fact, you have to wait a full minute after the effect of the first spell wears off before you can cast another spell of the same type.

All current Confusion spells (those that cause an enemy to change targets at random) are also subject to these limitations, but future spells of this sort might not be.

Chants and Songs that are not affected by the above stacking limitations do not stack at all. Hitting the button to recast the spell cancels the spell rather than stacking it.

Most continuing spells that regenerate Health, Power or Fatigue points do so every "cycle". What is a cycle? It's the same period of time that you use to regain any of these stats normally (without spells). The length of a cycle depends on what you're doing. If you're fighting, you regain points much more slowly than when you're resting. Periods for regeneration are:

	In Combat	Not in Combat (on your feet)	Not in Combat (sitting)
Fatigue Cycle	none	1 sec.	.25 sec.
Health Cycle	14 sec.	6 sec.	3 sec.
Power Cycle	14 sec.	6 sec.	3 sec.

You normally regain a point every cycle. Regeneration Buffs increase the amount you regenerate each cycle.

Skill. Skill required to have the spell. Note that all spells that require the Instrument skill do not necessarily require an instrument to cast. For those spells that don't require an instrument, you're assumed to be "singing".

A few spells have their skill listed as "2/3 spec". In those cases, the skill value checked, instead of being the value of a specific skill (which is how most spells work), is the value of whatever spell skill you're spec'ed in. Two-thirds of that value is used to determine the efficacy of the cast spell.

Dmg Type. Type of damage the spell does.

Lvl. The level number for a base spell is the level at which you acquire the spell. Base spells are free. You also get the first specialization spell in each of your available lists at no charge, but you do have to pay for further specialization spells on that list. The level number for a specialization spell indicates both the level at which you can acquire the spell and the cost for acquiring the spell. The more points you spend on a specialization, the higher the level of spell you have in it. (See **Specialization**, p. 14.)

Spell. Name of the spell. Some spells are grouped together so that when you get a higher level spell in the same "line," you lose lower level spells. If a spell's name is followed by an asterisk (*), that spell will be lost to you when you learn the next higher spell in that list. If the name is followed by two asterisks, you will lose that spell when you learn two higher spells in that list. (These spells are in the spell lists for Paladins, Minstrels, Clerics, Friars, Healers, Shamans, Thanes, Skalds, Hunters, Bards, Druids, Wardens, Champions, Rangers and Nightshades.)

Cost. What the Caster has to spend at the time of casting for the spell to be cast. When there is a cost, it will either be in Power Points (P), a percentage of the Caster's Power (%P), or Concentration Points (C).

When figuring a Power percentage, the game bases its calculation on the full Power of a normal character at your level. For example, if a normal character of your level has 80 Power, casting a spell that charges 25% Power will cost you 20 Power. Now, if you've boosted your max Power up to 120 (with magic items and the like), but you've spent all but 15 of your Power, casting this spell will still cost 20 Power, so you've got to regain another 5 Power to cast it.

If the spell has a duration of "Focus," it costs a certain amount of Power every few seconds (xP/y sec.).

Resurrection spell costs are based on the level of your target, relative to your own level. If you're resurrecting someone who has the same level as you, it costs 50% of your Power. If you're resurrecting someone whose level is less than half of yours, it costs 25% of your Power. If you're resurrecting someone whose level is 50% higher than yours, it costs you your full Power. If you're resurrecting someone in between those points, the cost is scaled based on the two levels, relative to each other. Note that you can actually resurrect someone whose level is even higher than 50% above your own, if you have more Power available than normal.

A few spells (generally Songs, Chants and Shouts) cost nothing to cast, but you must wait a few seconds (or even a few minutes) to cast the spell again.

Casting Time. How long it takes for the spell to cast (from the time the Caster casts it to the time the effect actually occurs). For most spells, this is a time in seconds. Some spells take no extra time to cast, and have a casting time of "Shout." Shouts can be cast in or out of combat, regardless of movement, and cannot be interrupted.

Casting time is modified by the Caster's Dexterity. Casting speed can be as much as 25% faster if you're max-buffed and have a high DEX.

Range. How far the spell can be "thrown," from the Caster to the target. Range is expressed in world units. A good guideline (which you can adjust to your preference) is that up to 1200 wu (world units) is "short range," 1200-1700 wu is "medium range," and over 1700 wu is "long range."

Duration. How long the spell's effect lasts. This is usually expressed in seconds or minutes.

Spells with an Instantaneous duration simply "fire," immediately causing the listed effect.

Songs, Chants, Concentration and Focus spells last as long as the Caster is devoting time and energy to them (and has any of the right kind of points left to spend on them). Actually, though, they "recharge" every few seconds, when the game checks again to see if you're still maintaining the spell. (Songs and Chants with a "+" to their duration last the length of the Song or Chant — or until your friends get out of range of the Song or Chant — plus up to that extra number of seconds. In other words, a Song with a duration of Song + 6 lasts the length of the Song, plus from 0 to 6 extra seconds, until the game again makes its check.)

You may move, fight and cast other spells while Chanting. You cannot maintain two Chants at once.

You may move, fight and cast other spells while Concentrating. You can only cast a maximum of 16 Concentration spells on your friends at one time.

You may move and cast other spells (but not fight) while Singing. You cannot maintain two Songs at once.

You may not move, fight or cast other spells while Focused. Focus spells can be interrupted.

(Note that most spells require you to be standing still and not in melee combat.)

Some spells continue to buff your friends as long as you keep the spell going. These spells require your friends to stay within the spell's range. If one of them leaves, he loses the buff, but he regains it if he gets close enough to you again. As a matter of fact, these spells don't require your friends to *always* stay within range; they only have to be close by when the spell "recharges" and buffs everyone who is in range at that moment. That means a friend can step out of range for a few seconds (while still benefitting from your buff), and if he's lucky, he can get back within range before the spell recharges again. Most recharge cycles are only about 4 to 6 seconds long, so don't be gone for long!

Area. Radius of an Area Effect spell in world units. Occasionally, the first spell in an AoE series is single target only, indicated by (1).

Bonus. Bonus value used to plug into the description for the effect.

Buff. If the spell is a kind of Buff (adding to the Attributes, speed, AF, etc. of the Caster, a Friend, his Pet or his Groupmates), this entry shows how much the original value is buffed.

Base Buffs and spec Buffs can stack with each other and with item Buffs, and all are capped separately, so a combination of all three gives the most bang for the buck. Buffs that elevate more than one stat stack on top of normal Buffs. Characters can have a total of 16 Buffs on them at any one time.

Players can have a stat buffed up to 10 points or their level, whichever is higher.

Debuff. Where Buffs improve, Debuffs take away. A Debuff spell subtracts from the listed stat, resistance, speed or other attribute. If the listed attribute is already Buffed, a Debuff is twice as good — for example, a 10 Debuff will cancel out a 20 Buff. Once the Buff is eliminated, the Debuff goes back to regular strength. For example, a 15 Debuff will both cancel out a 20 Buff (using the first 10 points of the Debuff) and subtract another 5 from the now unbuffed attribute.

A few Debuffs — particularly movement Debuffs (Snares, Roots and so forth) and range Debuffs — do not have this doubling effect. On the other hand, the Champion's stat-debuff lines have a *quadrupled* effectiveness against Buffs.

Note that attack speed Debuffs only slow down the target's attacks. They don't keep the target from evading or blocking.

Dmg Healed. For Healing spells, this shows how many HP are returned to the target.

Dmg. If the spell does damage, this entry shows how many HP it takes away from the target(s).

Dmg/Time. For a spell that repeatedly does damage over a period of time (DoT), this shows how much damage is done and how often.

Effect. Effect of the spell, if it can't be described by using the other column types.

HP. How many Hit Points the spell can add, subtract, transfer, or (for a corpse) return during resurrection.

Max lvl. Maximum level of the creature that can be called.

Power. How much Power is returned to the corpse during resurrection.

Resist. How often the target has a chance of trying to resist the effects of the spell.

Speed. Change in speed due to the spell.

Target. Target of the spell. This can be "Self" (the Caster), "Friend" (any Realmmate), "Pet" (controlled creature), or "Groupmate" (anyone currently grouped with you). Target is assumed to be an Enemy or Enemies when the spell does damage or Debuffs.

NOTES

Line of Sight. You must be able to see your target (or target location, for Area-Effect spells) to cast an offensive spell. Defensive spells (friend-buffs) don't require you to *facing* your target, but if that there is an unobstructed line from your head to your target..

Safe! The offensive spells you cast (even Area-Effect spells) do not affect your friends. (This may change in future versions of the game, especially in RvR situations.)

Speed Buffs cast on you (Run Speed Buffs) are dispelled when you take a hit or when you enter combat. If you've buffed several friends with one spell, only those who start fighting lose the buff.

Strength Buffs and **Debuffs** cast on an encumbered character immediately affect encumbrance and, so, movement rate. They also affect offensive skill.

Dexterity Buffs and **Debuffs** affect defensive skills and, for players, casting time.

Quickness Buffs and **Debuffs** affect attack speed.

Constitution Buffs and **Debuffs** affect HP for players and damage absorption for monsters.

Damage Buffs are stated as buffing a certain amount of damage per second. That means that you get the same total damage bonus, whether your weapon strikes every second or every three seconds. For example, a damage buff of 2 per second adds 4 damage (2 x 2) to a weapon that can strike every two seconds. It adds 6 damage (2 x 3) to a weapon that can strike every three seconds.

That doesn't mean you can hold back your strike, "storing up" a higher and higher damage bonus. The damage bonus for a specific weapon is calculated on its base strike time, not on how long it's been since you've attacked with it.

Damage Shield Buffs work much like damage Buffs, except they are based on the attack speed of your attacker. When you have a Damage Shield Buff, every time someone hits you, *he* takes damage equal to the Buff multiplied by his attack speed.

Mesmerized targets cannot move, cast spells or fight until the spell expires or the target takes damage. They also cannot equip or unequip items, use charged items, or enter Stealth mode. Targets whose Health is below 90% cannot be mesmerized — they're too distracted by their pain (and the ones who caused it!).

Stuns have the same effect, but do not break when the target is hit or healed.

Drain spells inflict the listed damage, while transferring a percentage of that damage (also listed) to the Caster.

Resurrect spells target a corpse and bring it back to life at the Caster's feet, with no CON loss or /release experience penalty for the target.

When you get a dialog box prompting you for resurrection, you must acknowledge it within 15 seconds or the spell will have to be recast.

If you resurrect a character while the monster who killed him is still in combat, you're added to the monster's "hate list" and have a chance of being targeted.

Heal spells cannot be cast on dead player bodies.

Bolts are ranged Direct Damage spells. They can be blocked by shields and armor and are *not* effective in melee combat. Outside of melee, they hit about 85% of the time.

Bladeturn spells nullify a single attack and work against all non-magical attacks, including arrows. The chance of a Bladeturn deflecting a higher-level attack is approximately Caster's level / attacker's level.

Confusion spells cannot cause a monster to aggro on other monsters more than one color higher in level than they are.

Charm spells turn their targets into pets you can control. Charmed targets will obey you until you damage them. When the charm breaks (or the Caster releases the Pet), the Pet will immediately aggro on the Caster. You cannot charm other players.

Temporary Pets have been described as fire-and-forget Elementals. You must target an enemy to cast any of these spells, which summon an Elemental for a few seconds who is totally devoted to hurting your target.

Pet Buffs. Pet Buffs are shown in the Pet control window.

When figuring Pet bonuses, use the monster bonuses.

You can only buff your own Pet.

Delving

Delving gives you stats about spells and items. Usually, the numbers are the same numbers used in this guide, but there is one somewhat complicated exception.

Remember that most Debuffs work at double strength against Buffs (see **Debuffs**, p. 369).

When delving a spell, the Debuff is listed at its doubled strength (if it can be doubled). The stats in this guide reflect each Debuff's normal strength, since most Debuff targets aren't already Buffed. Note that fractional modifiers (either Buffs or Debuffs) are rounded down.

GL 20

Poisons

Infiltrators, Shadowblades and Nightshades can inflict poison, using any poison that has a level equal to or lower than your Envenom specialization. (Poisons can be bought at stores; their level is listed below, and displayed in the object information window.) Pick a poison out of inventory and click it on an equipped weapon. That weapon is now "poisoned." On the next hit with that weapon, there's a chance your target will be poisoned. A resistance check compares your level vs. the defender's level; in an even fight, the poison has about an 85% chance of sticking.

You cannot reapply poison to a weapon during combat. However, you can de-equip weapons that have poisons; they retain the poison effect on them even if not equipped. That means you can prep multiple weapons with different poisons, and switch during a fight for best effect.

These poison stats use the same format as spell stats; see **Spells** (p. 366) for an explanation of any stats that are unfamiliar. All current poisons inflict Body damage. **Cost** is the cost for 10 doses, and is given in Silver and Copper (S.C).

DoT: inflicts (Dmg) every 3.9 seconds.
Duration . . . .20 sec

Lvl	Poison	Dmg	Cost (S.C)
1	Minor Lethal Poison	9	.20
5	Lesser Lethal Poison	12	.70
10	Lethal Poison	16	3.15
15	Major Lethal Poison	21	6.65
20	Greater Lethal Poison	26	14.00
25	Minor Lethal Venom	31	23.20
30	Lesser Lethal Venom	37	38.45
35	Major Lethal Venom	43	63.75
40	Greater Lethal Venom	50	86.10
45	Insidious Lethal Venom	57	116.35
50	Lifebane	64	157.15

STR Debuff.
Duration . . . .60 sec

Lvl	Poison	Debuff	Cost (S.C)
2	Minor Weakening Poison	5.5	.30
6	Lesser Weakening Poison	7	.95
11	Major Weakening Poison	9	3.70
17	Greater Weakening Poison	11.5	8.95

Disease: Debuffs STR, speed and healing rate.

Lvl	Poison	Dur	Debuff	Cost (S.C)
4	Minor Infect. Serum	60 sec	5	.55
16	Lesser Infect. Serum	90 sec	7.5	7.70
26	Infectious Serum	2 min	10	25.65
38	Major Infect. Serum	2.5 min	12.5	76.35
48	Greater Infect. Serum	3 min	15	139.35

Snare: enemy's speed debuffed to 60% of original movement.

Lvl	Poison	Dur	Cost (S.C)
3	Minor Imbalance Poison	35 sec	.40
8	Lesser Imbalance Poison	44 sec	1.75
13	Major Imbalance Poison	52 sec	4.95
18	Greater Imbalance Poison	61 sec	10.40
23	Minor Crippling Poison	70 sec	18.95
27	Lesser Crippling Poison	77 sec	28.40
31	Major Crippling Poison	84 sec	42.55
42	Greater Crippling Poison	103 sec	97.15

STR and CON Debuff.
Duration . . . .60 sec

Lvl	Poison	Debuff	Cost (S.C)
22	Minor Enervating Poison	13.5	17.10
29	Lesser Enervating Poison	16.5	34.75
37	Major Enervating Poison	19.5	71.90
47	Greater Enervating Poison	23.5	131.20

Horse Routes

Horse routes are listed on page 37 (Albion), 137 (Hibernia) and 231 (Midgard).

Stable masters are stationed throughout each Realm. They sell tickets to various pre-determined horse routes. All trips cost 5 silver.

Each stable master has a different selection of routes available.

When you buy a ticket from the Stable Master a horse is created, with you automatically astride.

The horse then runs along its route at a speed that is considerably faster than even the fastest player can run. Just sit back and enjoy the scenery. The horses move along roads or through relatively safe areas and move too fast for most monsters to attack you. If you want to get off the horse before you reach your destination, hit the "jump" key (A by default) and you'll safely dismount — while the horse continues to run along the route without you (or anyone else) on its back.

Note that the horse doesn't wait for you to get back on. if you jump off mid-route you have to walk to the nearest stable to get another horse.

Monsters

This guide lists most of the Monsters in *Dark Age of Camelot*. Note that even as you read this book more Monsters are being added to the game, so there's always a chance that you'll run into something you don't find listed here. However, this chapter includes nearly anything you'll find, and gives you a good idea of the different kinds of Monsters you might encounter in your adventures. In particular, Quest or special "named" Monsters are not included in this list.

Type. Each Monster is part of a general category. A Monster's type generally determines which charming classes can charm it (for example, some classes can charm "animals") or if it is vulnerable to certain weapon types (for example, a "Giant" Monster is vulnerable to the Sword of Giant Slaying). The types are as follows:

Animal	Giant	Magical
Demon	Human-like	Reptile
Dragon	Insect	Tree or Plant
Elemental	(& spider)	Undead

Within each realm, the Monster list is organized by type of Monster. (For example, all of each realm's Giants are listed together, as are all of the Reptiles, and so forth.) If you have any trouble finding a specific Monster in this list, find its name in the alphabetical Monster Cross-Reference (p. 375) to look up its Monster Type.

Name. Obvious.

Level. A Monster's level determines its Hit Points, Strength, experience and other typical combat stats. This column lists each Monster's base level. However, any Monster over Level 5 has a 25% chance to gain a level when it spawns, and the stats for any Monster may vary from the base values by up to 5%.

Body. This indicates the Monster's skin (or whatever ...). For example, a lion is a "furry animal" ("FA"). Common sense suggests that a "furry animal" is vulnerable to fire but resistant to cold. Some creatures (especially Human-likes) wear armor, in which case the type of armor is also listed, after a slash. (For example, a Moor Boogey (Albion Human-like) has "Tr/Ch," which means it has a troll-like skin, protected by chain armor.) The body types are:

BU	Bony Undead	**IU**	Incorporeal Undead
Ch	Chain	**Lr**	Leather
Cl	Cloth	**LE**	Light Energy
DV	Darkness/Void	**ME**	Magical Energy
EA	Elemental Air	**Pl**	Plate
EE	Elemental Earth	**Rp**	Reptile (Scaled)
EF	Elemental Fire	**Sh**	Shell (Chitin)
EI	Elemental Ice	**Soft**	Soft
EW	Elemental Water	**St**	Studded Leather
FM	Feeble-Minded	**TP**	Tree/Plant
FU	Fleshy Undead	**Tr**	Troll-like
FA	Furry Animal		

Speed. The speed at which the Monster runs: Slow, Medium, Fast, 2x, 3x, 4x (two, three and four times faster than the average PC). For perspective, an unenhanced player character runs at speed 192. (The number in parentheses is the actual speed, in world units.)

Aggression (Aggr). Low, Medium, High. (The number in parentheses is the actual percent chance that a Monster will attack you if you're within its aggression radius.)

Attack Speed (Atk Sp). How often a Monster can attack (in seconds).

Attack. Up to three stats are included in the next column:

Primary Attack. The type of damage that a Monster's primary melee attack inflicts.

Secondary Attack. If a Monster can make a second attack in the same attack round, the secondary attack determines the type of melee damage that this second attack inflicts.

Secondary Attack Chance. This is the percent chance (per round) that a Monster will make two attacks. A Monster's level may increase its chance to make two attacks.

Evade. This is the base percent chance that the Monster can evade your attack. A Monster's chance to evade may increase as its level increases.

Combat Modifier. This determines the bonus or penalty a Monster receives in its melee combat. Most (though not all) Monsters that cast spells or have some sort of special ability will be offset by having a melee penalty.

These three numbers are: *Monster's modifier to hit / modifier to avoid being hit (defense) / modifier to Hit Points*. Positive numbers are good for the monster in each case. When there is just one number, it modifies all three situations.

Social. This is where it gets a little tricky, unfortunately. If a Monster is Social, it may be found with other Monsters, and it might respond to another Monster's "Bring a Friend" or "Call for Help." Some Social Monsters might Call for Help if their Health drops below 50%; if within hearing range, other Monsters of the attacked Monster's group may come to help. However, since only Social Monsters might Call for Help, this column lists "**Call (S)**" (Monsters that are Social and might Call for Help), "**Social**" (Monsters that are Social but won't Call for Help) or "**–**" (Monsters that aren't Social).

Vulnerabilities and Resistances

An observant person will notice early on that some types of weapons or spells work especially well against certain types of creatures. Usually it makes sense. Stabbing a skeleton, for instance, does less damage than hitting it with a hammer. That's because of its body type.

You can usually tell what kind of body type a creature has just by looking at it. However, in the Monster list — starting on the next page — every Monster has its body type listed. If the creature always wears a certain kind of armor, then that counts as part of its body type, too.

Some body types are more vulnerable to certain kinds of attacks, so an attack by that weapon or spell will do a certain percent more damage. The extra percent of damage is listed as a positive number in the list below. Some body types are resistant to certain kinds of attacks, and the percent less damage a weapon or spell will give is listed as a negative number.

Abbreviations: Crush / **Sl**ash / **Thr**ust / **Mat**ter / **Sp**irit / **En**ergy.

Attack Type:	**Cr**	**Sl**	**Thr**	**Heat**	**Cold**	**Mat**	**Body**	**Sp**	**En**
Body Type									
Bony Undead	20	–	-20	5	-15	–	–	30	–
Chain	–	-15	15	-10	–	–	–	–	10
Cloth	–	–	–	–	–	–	–	–	–
Darkness/Void	–	–	–	–	–	-20	–	10	–
Drakulv (Furry Animal)	–	-5	15	–	15	–	–	–	–
Elemental: Air	-10	-10	-10	10	-10	–	–	30	-5
Elemental: Earth	15	-10	-15	-10	10	–	–	30	–
Elemental: Fire	-10	-10	-10	-20	20	–	–	30	–
Elemental: Ice	10	-10	10	20	-20	–	–	30	10
Elemental: Water	-15	-10	-10	15	10	–	–	–	10
Feeble-Minded	–	–	–	–	–	–	–	–	–
Fleshy Undead	-10	15	15	10	-10	–	–	30	–
Furry Animal	–	10	10	15	-5	–	5	–	–
Incorporeal Undead	-15	-15	-15	10	10	–	-20	30	–
Leather	–	15	-15	15	-10	–	–	–	–
Light Energy	-15	-15	-15	–	–	-20	–	–	–
Magical Energy	-15	-15	-15	–	–	–	–	10	–
Plate	10	-5	–	-10	10	–	–	–	10
Reptile (Scaled)	–	-15	15	–	15	–	–	–	–
Shell (Chitin)	15	–	–	-10	10	–	–	–	–
Soft	–	–	–	–	–	–	–	–	–
Studded Leather	10	–	-10	-10	5	–	–	–	5
Tree/Plant	–	20	-15	20	–	–	-15	–	-10
Troll-like	-15	10	10	25	-15	–	-5	–	15

Monster Cross-Reference

To find the stats for a particular monster, find its realm and type, below. **Albion Monsters** begin on page 108. **Hibernia Monsters** begin on page 204. **Midgard Monsters** begin on page 292. "**Realm vs. Realm**" monsters (those that can be encountered during RvR play) begin on page 330.

Realm Abbreviations. **A**lbion, **H**ibernia, **M**idgard, **R**ealm (RvR).

Type Abbreviations. **An**imal, **Dm** (Demon), **Dr**agon, **El**emental, **Gi**ant, **Hu**man-like, **In**sect, **Mg** (Magical), **Rp** (Reptile), **TP** (Tree or Plant), **Un**dead.

Monster	Realm / Type
Abominable Snowman	M Hu
Abysmal	H Dm
Acrid Ghoul	M Un
Actarius	A Un
Adder	A Rp
Afanc Hatchling	A Rp
Aged Basilisk	A Rp
Aged Boreal Cockatrice	M Rp
Albino Cave Mauler	M An
Albion Waylayer	A Hu
Alp Luachra	H Mg
Alpine Cockatrice	M Rp
Amadan Touched	H Hu
Ambassador Mannam	R Dm
Ancient Basilisk	A Rp
Anger Sprite	H Mg
Angler	A In
Angry Bwca	A Hu
Annoying Lucradan	H Hu
Ant Drone	A In
Apprentice Beastmaster	A Hu
Apprentice Necyomancer	R Hu
Aqueous Slug	H An
Aquilifer	A Un
Arachite Greensilk	M In
Arachite Grymherre	M In
Arachite Hatchling	M In
Arachite Husker	M In
Arachite Impaler	M In
Arachite Krigare	M In
Arachite Prelate	M In
Arachite Priest	M In
Arachite Shadowslinker	M In
Arachite Tunnelhost	M In
Arachite Vakt	M In
Arachite Weblasher	M In
Arachnid	H In
Arachnite	H In
Arawnite Headhunter	A Hu
Arawnite Shamaness	A Hu
Arawnite Warrior	A Hu
Archer	A Un
Army Ant Soldier	M In
Army Ant Worker	M In
Ashen Fellwood	A TP
Ashen Spirit	M Un
Ashmonger	M Hu
Aspen Fellwood	A TP
Aughisky	H Mg
Aurora	M Mg
Avernal Quasit	R Dm
Azure Avenger	H Hu
Azure Banisher	H Hu
Azure Cleanser	H Hu
Azure Idolater	H Hu
Backwoods Marodor	M Hu
Badger	H An
Badger Cub	H An
Badh	H Un
Bananach	H Un
Bandit	A Hu
Bandit Henchman	A Hu
Bandit Leader	A Hu
Bandit Lieutenant	A Hu
Bandit Messenger	A Hu
Bandit Thaumaturge	A Hu
Banshee	H Un
Bantam Spectre	H Un
Barca	H Mg
Barguest	A Un
Barrow Wight	A Un
Basilisk	A Rp
Battle-Scarred Mauler	M An
Beach Rat	H An
Bean Sidhe	H Un
Bean-Nighe	A Un
Bear	A An
Bear Cub	A An
Bearded Gorger	A Mg
Bird-Eating Frog	H An
Biting Wind	M El
Black Badger	H An
Black Bear	A An
Black Dog	A An
Black Lion	A An
Black Lioness	A An
Black Mauler	M An
Black Mauler Cub	M An
Black Mauler Juvenile	M An
Black Orm	M Rp
Black Poplar Fellwood	A TP
Black Willow Fellwood	A TP
Black Wolf	A An
Black Wolf Pup	A An
Black Wraith	H Un
Blackthorn	H TP
Bleeder	A Un
Blindsnake	M Rp
Bloated Spider	A In
Block Of Ice	M El
Blodfelag Captive	M Hu
Blodfelag Dreng	M Hu
Blodfelag Haxa	M Hu
Blodfelag Henchman	M Hu
Blodfelag Livvakt	M Hu
Blodfelag Oathbreaker	M Hu
Blodfelag Partisan	M Hu
Blodfelag Soothsayer	M Hu
Blodfelag Svard	M Hu
Blodfelag Thralldriver	M Hu
Blodfelag Tormentor	M Hu
Blodfelag Warhound	M An
Blodfelag Windcaller	M Hu
Blodfelag Wolfwarrior	M Hu
Blood Rat	M An
Bloodletter	H In
Bloodthirsty She-Wolf	M An
Bloody-Bones	A Un
Boar Piglet	A An
Bocaidhe	H Mg
Bocan	H Un
Bocanach	H Un
Bodach	H Hu
Bodachan Sabhaill	H El
Bog Crawler	H In
Bog Creeper	H In
Bog Frog	H An
Bog Worm	H An
Boggart	A Hu
Bogman	A Hu
Bogman Fisher	A Hu
Bogman Gatherer	A Hu
Bogman Grappler	A Hu
Bogman Hunter	A Hu
Bogman Trapper	A Hu
Bone Snapper	A In
Bone-Eater Clanmother	M Hu
Bone-Eater Eviscerater	M Hu
Bone-Eater Oracle	M Hu
Bone-Eater Slayer	M Hu
Bone-Eater Spine-Ripper	M Hu
Bone-Eater Warleader	M Hu
Boogie Man	H Hu
Boreal Cockatrice	M Rp
Botched Sacrifice	A Un
Boulder Imp	A Dm
Boulderling	A El
Bounty Hunter	M Hu
Bounty Hunter Leader	M Hu
Breaker Roane Companion	H Mg
Brittle Skeleton	M Un
Broken Jotun	M Gi
Brown Bear	A An
Brown Drakeling	A Dr
Brownie	A Hu
Brownie Grassrunner	A Hu
Brownie Nomad	A Hu
Brownie Rover	A Hu
Brush Cat	M An
Bucca	A Hu
Bullyboy	A Hu
Burnt Skeletal Sentry	M Un
Bwca	A Hu
Bwgan	A Hu
Bwgan Elder	A Hu
Bwgan Fisherman	A Hu
Bwgan Horde	A Hu
Bwgan Horde Leader	A Hu
Bwgan Hunter	A Hu
Bwgwl	A Un
Cailleach Guard	A Mg
Cailleach Priest	A Mg
Cait Sidhe	A Un
Callow Wolverine	M An
Cambion	R Dm
Carrion Crab	A In
Carrion Crawler	M In
Carrion Drake	A Dr
Carrion Eater	M In
Carrion Lizard	M Rp
Carrion Scorpionida	H In
Cart Horse	A An
Cave Bear	A An
Cave Bear	M An

Monster	Realm / Type
Cave Bear Cub	A An
Cave Crab	M In
Cave Crawler	M Rp
Cave Fairy	A Mg
Cave Fisher	A In
Cave Hound	A An
Cave Lion	A An
Cave Mauler	M An
Cave Ogre	M Hu
Cave Spider	M In
Cave Toad	H An
Cave Trow	M Hu
Cave Trow Trollkarl	M Hu
Cave Viper	M Rp
Celtic Lich	A Un
Celtic Sepulchre Chieftain	A Un
Celtic Sepulchre Warrior	A Un
Centurio Manipularis	A Un
Centurio Pilus Posterior	A Un
Centurio Primus Ordines	A Un
Centurio Primus Pilus	A Un
Changeling	H Mg
Chaosian	R Dm
Charred Skeletal Warrior	M Un
Chattering Skeleton	M Un
Chilled Presence	A Un
Chillsome Wight	M Un
Chipstone Sheerie	H El
Chiseler	M In
Cthonian Crawler	R Dm
Chthonic Knight Absax	R Dm
Chthonic Knight Aciel	R Dm
Chthonic Knight Ain	R Dm
Chthonic Knight Azea	R Dm
Chthonic Knight Babyzu	R Dm
Chthonic Knight Carnivon	R Dm
Chthonic Knight Exal	R Dm
Chthonic Knight Exte	R Dm
Chthonic Knight Ezpeth	R Dm
Chthonic Knight Fonath	R Dm
Chthonic Knight Gaapoler	R Dm
Chthonic Knight Haag	R Dm
Chthonic Knight Ibeko	R Dm
Chthonic Knight Marbos	R Dm
Chthonic Knight Obarus	R Dm
Chthonic Knight Olov	R Dm
Chthonic Knight Prosel	R Dm
Chthonic Knight Ronoro	R Dm
Chthonic Knight Tamuel	R Dm
Chthonic Knight Ukobat	R Dm
Chthonic Knight Vosoes	R Dm
Chthonic Knight Zaeber	R Dm
Chthonic Knight Zafan	R Dm
Chthonic Knight Zagal	R Dm
Cinder Drake	M Dr
Clay Jotun	M Gi
Clay Jotun Guard	M Gi
Clay Jotun Hunter	M Gi
Clay Jotun Retainer	M Gi
Clay Jotun Runner	M Gi
Clergyman	A Un
Cliff Beetle	H In

Monster	Realm / Type
Cliff Crawler	A In
Cliff Dweller	H Hu
Cliff Dweller Hunter	H Hu
Cliff Dweller Spearman	H Hu
Cliff Hanger	H In
Cliff Spider	A In
Cliff Spiderling	A In
Clubmoss Sheerie	H El
Cluricaun	H Hu
Cluricaun Aquavitor	H Hu
Cluricaun Trip	H Hu
Coastal Wolf	M An
Cockatrice	A Rp
Coerced Groover	H Hu
Cohorstalis	A Un
Cold Light	M Mg
Collared Gemgetter	H Hu
Commander Abgar	R Dm
Condemned Necyomancer	R Hu
Cornish Frog	A An
Cornish Giant	A Gi
Cornish Hen	A Rp
Cornwall Drake	A Dr
Cornwall Hunter	A Hu
Cornwall Leader	A Hu
Corpan Side	H Hu
Corpse Crawler	M In
Corpse Eater	M In
Corpse-Eating Sow	A An
Corybantic Skeleton	H Un
Crazed Lycantic	M Mg
Creeping Crud	A TP
Creeping Ooze	A Un
Crippled Jotun	M Gi
Cruach Imp	H Dm
Cruiach Demon	H Dm
Crusher	M El
Crypt Spider	H In
Curmudgeon Crab-Catcher	H Hu
Curmudgeon Fighter	H Hu
Curmudgeon Harvester	H Hu
Curmudgeon Poacher	H Hu
Curmudgeon Puggard	H Hu
Curmudgeon Ratoner	H Hu
Curmudgeon Rockclimber	H Hu
Curmudgeon Scout	H Hu
Curmudgeon Scrapper	H Hu
Curmudgeon Skinner	H Hu
Curmudgeon Trapper	H Hu
Curmudgeon Wanter	H Hu
Cursed Believer	A Un
Cursed Mora	M Un
Cursed Mora Dancer	M Un
Cursed Mora Weeper	M Un
Cursed Necyomancer	R Hu
Cursed Spirit	M Un
Cursed Thulian	M In
Cutpurse	A Hu
Cwn Annwn	A An
Cyclops	A Gi
Cyclops Scout	A Gi
Cyhraeth	A Un

Monster	Realm / Type
Cythraul	A Un
Dampwood Mite	H In
Danaoin Clerk	A Un
Danaoin Commander	A Un
Danaoin Farmer	A Un
Danaoin Fisherman	A Un
Danaoin Lieutenant	A Un
Danaoin Priest	A Un
Danaoin Sailor	A Un
Danaoin Soldier	A Un
Dappled Lynx	A An
Dappled Lynx Cub	A An
Dark Fire	A Un
Dark Hound	M An
Dartmoor Pony	A An
Deamhan Aeir	H Dm
Deamhan Creig	H Dm
Deamhan Hound	H Dm
Deamhaness	R Dm
Death Grip Vines	A TP
Death Spider	M In
Death Stalker	A An
Death Worm	H An
Decayed Barbarian	A Un
Decayed Barbarian Chieftain	A Un
Decayed Zombie	A Un
Decaying Norseman	M Un
Decaying Spirit	A Un
Decaying Tomb Raider	A Un
Decaying Troll	M Un
Decurion	A Un
Deep Goblin	A Hu
Deep Goblin Blighter	A Hu
Deeplurk Dissembler	M In
Deeplurk Feeder	M In
Deeplurk Manslayer	M In
Demoniac Familiar (Ant)	R In
Demoniac Familiar (Boar)	R An
Demoniac Familiar (Cat)	R An
Demoniac Familiar (Dog)	R An
Demoniac Familiar (Horse)	R An
Demoniac Familiar (Lynx)	R An
Demoniac Familiar (Rat)	R An
Dem. Familiar (Scorpion)	R In
Demoniac Familiar (Spider)	R In
Derg Monster	H An
Dergan Enchanter	H Hu
Dergan Fury	H Hu
Dergan Tussler	H Hu
Detrital Crab	H In
Devout Filidh	A Hu
Devout Follower	A Un
Dew Sheerie	H El
Diamondback Toad	A An
Dire Wolverine	M An
Diseased Rat	A An
Dishonored Hagbui	M Un
Disturbed Presence	A Un
Djupt Odjur	M In
Djupt Usling	M In
Djupt Vivunder	M In
Doomed Minion	A Un

Monster	Realm / Type
Downy Fellwood	A TP
Draconarius	A Un
Draconic Ancilla	A Dr
Dragon Ant Drone	A In
Dragon Ant Queen	A In
Dragon Ant Soldier	A In
Dragon Ant Worker	A In
Drakulv Armguard	M Mg
Drakulv Attendant	M Mg
Drakulv Axehand	M Mg
Drakulv Disciple	M Mg
Drakulv Executioner	M Mg
Drakulv Klok	M Mg
Drakulv Missionary	M Mg
Drakulv Prast	M Mg
Drakulv Protector	M Mg
Drakulv Riddare	M Mg
Drakulv Sacrificer	M Mg
Drakulv Soultrapper	M Mg
Draugr Hound	M An
Draugr Warrior	M Un
Dreadful Cadaver	A Un
Drifting Spirit	M Un
Drowned Soul	M Un
Druid	A Hu
Druid Sacrificer	A Hu
Druid Seer	A Hu
Druidic Spirit	A Un
Dryad	A El
Dryad Blossom	M El
Dryad Greenthumb	M El
Dryad Invert	A El
Dryad Sprig	M El
Dryad Sprout	M El
Dryad Twig	A El
Duegar Tjuv	M Hu
Duegarhunter	M In
Duke Alloc	R Dm
Duke Aypol	R Dm
Duke Bimure	R Dm
Duke Eligar	R Dm
Duke Harboris	R Dm
Duke Sallis	R Dm
Duke Satori	R Dm
Duke Zepor	R Dm
Dullahan	H Un
Dungeon Chitin	M In
Dungeon Crab	M In
Dunter	A Un
Dux	A Un
Dverge Crackler	M Hu
Dverge Fire-Eater	M Hu
Dverge Igniter	M Hu
Dverge Sparker	M Hu
Dwarf Bone Skeleton	M Un
Dwarf Brawler	A Hu
Dwarf Pillager	A Hu
Dwarf Raider	A Hu
Earl Amagin	R Dm
Earl Fenex	R Dm
Earl Glassalab	R Dm
Earl Ipostian	R Dm

Monster	Realm / Type
Earl Mercur	R Dm
Earl Mermer	R Dm
Earl Oraxus	R Dm
Earl Vone	R Dm
Earth Sprite	H El
Earthshaker	H El
Ebony Fellwood	A TP
Echo Of Life	A Un
Ectoplasm	A Un
Eel	A An
Eidolon	H Un
Eirebug	H In
Ekyps Gunstling	M In
Ekyps Scavenger	M In
Elder Beech	A TP
Elder Skogsfru	M Hu
Elder Sveawolf	M An
Elfshot Madman	H Hu
Ellyll Champion	A Hu
Ellyll Froglord	A Hu
Ellyll Guard	A Hu
Ellyll Sage	A Hu
Ellyll Seer	A Hu
Ellyll Villager	A Hu
Ellyll Windchaser	A Hu
Emerald Snake	A Rp
Empyrean Elder	H Mg
Empyrean Guardian	H Mg
Empyrean Keeper	H Mg
Empyrean Orb	H Mg
Empyrean Overseer	H Mg
Empyrean Sentinel	H Mg
Empyrean Watcher	H Mg
Empyrean Wisp	H Mg
Endless Sorrow	A Un
Enhorning	M An
Enraged Cockatrice	A Rp
Enraged Mara	M Un
Enslaved Orm	M Rp
Enslaved Orm Biter	M Rp
Enslaved Orm Runner	M Rp
Enthralled Silvier	H Hu
Entrancing Dirge	M Un
Envy Drakeling	M Dr
Eriu Ambusher	H Hu
Eriu Fiscere	H Hu
Eriu Henter	H Hu
Eriu Kedger	H Hu
Eriu Waylayer	H Hu
Escaped Bandit	A Hu
Escaped Bandit Leader	A Hu
Escaped Thrall	M Hu
Essence Shredder	R Dm
Eternal Scream	A Un
Ettin Shaman	A Gi
Evanescer	H Mg
Experienced Necyomancer	R Hu
Fachan	H Hu
Fading Spirit	A Un
Faeghoul	H Un
Faerie Badger	H An
Faerie Beetle	H In

Monster	Realm / Type
Faerie Bell-Wether	A El
Faerie Drake	H Dr
Faerie Frog	A An
Faerie Horse	H An
Faerie Mischief-Maker	A El
Faerie Steed	H An
Faerie Wolf-Crier	A El
Faint Grim	A Un
Fallen Cleric	A Un
Fallen Hibernian Defender	H Un
Fallen Paladin	A Un
Fallen Troll	M Un
Fallen Warrior	A Un
Far Darrig	H Mg
Far Dorocha	H Mg
Far Liath	H Un
Fear Dearc	H Mg
Feccan	H Mg
Feckless Lucragan	H Hu
Fee Lion	H An
Fell Cat	M An
Fenrir Guard	M Mg
Fenrir Mystic	M Mg
Fenrir Prime	M Mg
Fenrir Prophet	M Mg
Fenrir Shredder	M Mg
Fenrir Snowscout	M Mg
Fenrir Soldier	M Mg
Fenrir Tracker	M Mg
Fetch	H Mg
Field Marshal Nebir	R Dm
Fiery Fiend	A Dm
Filidh	A Hu
Filidh Sacrificer	A Hu
Finliath	H Un
Fire Ant Gatherer	M In
Fire Ant Scavenger	M In
Fire Ant Worker	M In
Fire Flower	M TP
Fire Giant Guard	M Gi
Fire Giant Lookout	M Gi
Fire Giant Scout	M Gi
Fire Giant Spirit	M Gi
Fire Giant Watchman	M Gi
Fire Phantom	M Un
Fire Toad	M An
Firecat	M An
Fisher Hatchling	A In
Fishing Bear	H An
Fishing Bear Cub	H An
Fishing Bear Forager	H An
Fitful Bwca	A Hu
Flame Spout	M El
Flame Thrower	M El
Flaming Raukomaz	M Dm
Flurry	M El
Fog Phantom	H Un
Fog Wraith	H Un
Fomorian Annag	H Gi
Fomorian Cyclen	H Gi
Fomorian Gehk	H Gi
Fomorian Gleener	H Gi

Monster	Realm / Type
Fomorian Goblern	H Gi
Fomorian Grabeye	H Gi
Fomorian Grencher	H Gi
Fomorian Underling	H Gi
Fomorian Wolfbeast	H An
Footman	A Un
Forest Adder	A Rp
Forest Bear	A An
Forest Bear Cub	A An
Forest Cat	A An
Forest Chief	A Hu
Forest Ettin	A Gi
Forest Giant	A Gi
Forest Hunter	A Hu
Forest Lion	A An
Forest Messenger	A Hu
Forest Poacher	H Hu
Forest Runner	A Hu
Forest Scourge Scorpion	H In
Forest Smuggler	A Hu
Forest Snake	A Rp
Forest Spider	M In
Forest Spider Queen	M In
Forest Spider Runner	M In
Forest Stalker	A Hu
Forest Tracker	A Hu
Forest Viper	M Rp
Forester	A Hu
Forester Merchant	A Hu
Forgotten Emperor	A Un
Forgotten Promise	A Un
Fossegrim	M Hu
Fragile Skeleton	M Un
Frenetic Wolfspider	M In
Frenzied Feeder	A Mg
Freybug	A Hu
Frigid Broadleaf	M TP
Frore Lich	M Un
Frost Bound Bear	M An
Frost Cyclops	M Gi
Frost Giant	M Gi
Frost Hound	M An
Frost Orm	M Rp
Frost Spectre	M Un
Frost Stallion	M An
Frostbite Wildling	M Hu
Frosty Colt	M An
Frosty Scuttlebug	M In
Frothing Sveawolf	M An
Fuath	H Un
Fury Sprite	H Mg
Fylgja	M An
Gabriel Hound	A Dm
Gale	H El
Gan Ceanach	H Hu
Geas-Bound Hewer	H Hu
Gelid Mass	M El
Gem-Dusted Skeleton	H Un
Gemclicker	H In
Gemclicker Horder	H In
Ghastly Albion Invader	M Un
Ghastly Siabra	H Un

Monster	Realm / Type
Ghost Light	M Mg
Ghost Miner	A Un
Ghost Wolf	A Un
Ghostly Cleric	A Un
Ghostly Hibernian Invader	M Un
Ghostly Knight	A Un
Ghostly Midgard Invader	H Un
Ghostly Paladin	A Un
Ghostly Siabra	H Un
Ghoul Footman	A Un
Ghoul Knight	A Un
Ghoul Lord	A Un
Ghoulic Viper	A Un
Ghoulie	H Un
Ghoulish Warrior	M Un
Giant Ant	H In
Giant Beetle	H In
Giant Boar	A An
Giant Bull Frog	M An
Giant Frog	A An
Giant Lizard	A Rp
Giant Lusus	H Gi
Giant Rooter	A An
Giant Skeleton	A Un
Giant Snowcrab	M In
Giant Spider	A In
Giant Tree Frog	M An
Giant Water Leaper	A An
Giant Water Strider	M In
Giant Wolf	A An
Glacial Mauler	M An
Glimmer Ardent	H Mg
Glimmer Avenger	H Mg
Glimmer Deathwatcher	H Mg
Glimmer Geist	H Mg
Glimmer Ghoul	H Mg
Glimmer Griever	H Mg
Glimmer Jinn	H Mg
Glimmer Knight	H Mg
Glimmer Messenger	H Mg
Glimmer Prophet	H Mg
Glimmer Striker	H Mg
Glimmer Ward	H Mg
Glimmer Warshade	H Mg
Glimmerling	H Mg
Glow Worm	H An
Glowing Goo	A Un
Gnarled Fellwood	A TP
Goblin	A Hu
Goblin Apprentice	A Hu
Goblin Beastmaster	A Hu
Goblin Cleaner	A Hu
Goblin Crawler	A Hu
Goblin Fisherman	A Hu
Goblin Guard	M Hu
Goblin Imperator	A Hu
Goblin Lookout	A Hu
Goblin Lord	A Hu
Goblin Monitor	A Hu
Goblin Patrol Leader	A Hu
Goblin Scout	A Hu
Goblin Shaman	A Hu

Monster	Realm / Type
Goblin Snatcher	A Hu
Goblin Warrior	A Hu
Goblin Watcher	A Hu
Goblin Whip	A Hu
Goborchend	H Hu
Goborchend Gasher	H Hu
Goborchend Piercer	H Hu
Goborchend Wounder	H Hu
Gold Oaken Fellwood	A TP
Gorge Rat	H An
Gotawitch	M Hu
Grand Pooka	H Mg
Granite Giant	A Gi
Granite Giant Earthmagi	A Gi
Granite Giant Elder	A Gi
Granite Giant Gatherer	A Gi
Granite Giant Herdsman	A Gi
Granite Giant Oracle	A Gi
Granite Giant Outlooker	A Gi
Granite Giant Pounder	A Gi
Granite Giant Reinforcer	A Gi
Granite Giant Stonecaller	A Gi
Granite Giant Stonelord	A Gi
Granite Giant Stonemender	A Gi
Granite Giant Stoneshaper	A Gi
Granite Knocker	A Hu
Granny	H Un
Grass Cat	M An
Grass Sheerie	H El
Grass Snake	A Rp
Grass Spirit	H Un
Grass Viper	M Rp
Graugach	H Mg
Grave Goblin	A Hu
Grave Goblin Crueler	A Hu
Grave Goblin Shaman	A Hu
Grave Goblin Whelp	A Hu
Gray Spectre	H Un
Gray Warg	A An
Gray Wolf	A An
Gray Wolf Pup	A An
Gray Worg	M An
Great Boar	A An
Great Brown Drake	A Dr
Great Lynx	M An
Great Tingler	M In
Greater Boogey	A Hu
Greater Fenrir	M Mg
Greater Luch	H An
Greater Telamon	A Mg
Greater Zephyr	H El
Green Ghast	A Un
Green Orm	M Rp
Green Serpent	M Rp
Green Snake	A Rp
Greenhorn Poacher	A Hu
Gremlin	A Hu
Grimwood	A TP
Grimwood Keeper	A Un
Grizzled Sveawolf	M An
Grogan	H Hu
Grove Nymph	A Hu

Monster	Realm / Type
Grovewood	H TP
Grumoz Demon	A Dm
Guardsman	A Un
Gurite Ambusher	H Hu
Gurite Assailer	H Hu
Gurite Footpad	H Hu
Gurite Lookout	H Hu
Gurite Raider	H Hu
Gurite Seeker	H Hu
Gurite Tempriar	H Hu
Gurite Waylayer	H Hu
Gwr-Drwgiaid	A Un
Gytrash	A Un
Hagbui Berserker	M Un
Hagbui Forge Tender	M Un
Hagbui Guard	M Un
Hagbui Herald	M Un
Hagbui Page	M Un
Hagbui Runemaster	M Un
Hagbui Shaman	M Un
Hagbui Spiritmaster	M Un
Hagbui Squire	M Un
Hagbui Swordbearer	M Un
Hagbui Thane	M Un
Hailer	M El
Hailstone	M El
Half-Frozen Madman	M Hu
Hallaratta	M An
Hamadryad	A TP
Harvestman	M In
Haunt	M Un
Haunted Driftwood	H TP
Haunting Draft	H Un
Haunting Gloom	A Un
Heretical Hermit	A Hu
Hibernian Waylayer	A Hu
Highwayman	A Hu
Hill Avenger	A Hu
Hill Cat	M An
Hill Chief	A Hu
Hill Guard	A Hu
Hill Hound	H An
Hill Person	M Hu
Hill Scrag	A Hu
Hill Shaman	A Hu
Hill Toad	H An
Hill Warrior	A Hu
Hillock Changeling	H Mg
Hoary Worm	A Rp
Hobgoblin Biter	M Hu
Hobgoblin Fish-Catcher	M Hu
Hobgoblin Pincher	M Hu
Hobgoblin Prankster	M Hu
Hobgoblin Prowler	M Hu
Hobgoblin Snagger	M Hu
Hobgoblin Snake-Finder	M Hu
Hog-Nose Slither	M Rp
Hollow Man	A Hu
Hornbeam Fellwood	A TP
Horned Cave Toad	H An
Horse	H An
Host Of The Earth	M El

Monster	Realm / Type
Host Of The Wind	M El
Howling Knifeman	A Hu
Howling Maiden	A Hu
Huge Boar	A An
Huldu Hunter	M Hu
Huldu Lurker	M Hu
Huldu Outcast	M Hu
Huldu Stalker	M Hu
Husk	M In
Ice Giant	M Gi
Ice Lizard	M Rp
Ice Scrag	M Gi
Iceberg	M El
Icebreaker	M An
Icemuncher	M An
Icestrider Chiller	M In
Icestrider Frostweaver	M In
Icestrider Interceptor	M In
Ick Worm	H An
Icy Skeleton	M Un
Icy Wisp	M Mg
Imaginifer	A Un
Immunis	A Un
Impling	A Dm
Inquisitor Asil	R Dm
Inquisitor Bor	R Dm
Inquisitor Eciraum	R Dm
Inquisitor Factol	R Dm
Inquisitor Famuel	R Dm
Inquisitor Haap	R Dm
Inquisitor Hadis	R Dm
Inquisitor Haimir	R Dm
Inquisitor Hellos	R Dm
Inquisitor Irawn	R Dm
Inquisitor Kireasil	R Dm
Inquisitor Lokis	R Dm
Inquisitor Medebo	R Dm
Inquisitor Morg	R Dm
Inquisitor Morrian	R Dm
Inquisitor Mucifen	R Dm
Inquisitor Nej	R Dm
Inquisitor Nifil	R Dm
Inquisitor Niloc	R Dm
Inquisitor Tlaw	R Dm
Inquisitor Yonzael	R Dm
Inquisitor Yor	R Dm
Inquisitor Zaviben	R Dm
Inquisitor Zazinol	R Dm
Insidious Whisper	A Un
Ire Wolf	H An
Irewood	H TP
Irewood Greenbark	H TP
Irewood Sapling	H TP
Isalf Abider	M Hu
Isalf Blinder	M Hu
Isalf Forayer	M Hu
Isalf Icemage	M Hu
Isalf Scryer	M Hu
Isalf Snowtracker	M Hu
Isalf Surveyor	M Hu
Isalf Warrior	M Hu
Isolationist Armsman	A Hu

Monster	Realm / Type
Isolationist Cleric	A Hu
Isolationist Courier	A Hu
Isolationist Mercenary	A Hu
Isolationist Paladin	A Hu
Isolationist Scout	A Hu
Isolationist Sorcerer	A Hu
Isolationist Wizardess	A Hu
Jotun Despot	M Gi
Jotun Outcast	M Gi
Jotun Overlord	M Gi
Jotun Warchief	M Gi
Juvenile Megafelid	H An
Keltoi Banisher	A Hu
Keltoi Eremite	A Hu
Keltoi Familiar	A An
Keltoi Initiate	A Hu
Keltoi Recluse	A Hu
Keltoi Ritualist	A Hu
Keltoi Spiritualist	A Hu
Keltoi Visionary	A Hu
King's Wight	A Un
Knight	A Un
Knotted Fellwood	A TP
Koalinth Bouncer	H Hu
Koalinth Castellan	H Hu
Koalinth Elder	H Hu
Koalinth Envoy	H Hu
Koalinth Guardian	H Hu
Koalinth Sentinel	H Hu
Koalinth Slinker	H Hu
Koalinth Spectator	H Hu
Koalinth Warden	H Hu
Koalinth Warder	H Hu
Koalinth Wrestler	H Hu
Kopparorm	M An
Lair Guard	M Hu
Lair Patrol	M Hu
Lair Worm	H An
Lake Adder	A Rp
Lake Serpent	M Rp
Large Ant	A In
Large Boulderling	A El
Large Eirebug	H In
Large Enslaved Orm	M Rp
Large Enslaved Orm Runner	M Rp
Large Frog	H An
Large Luch	H An
Large Red Wolfhound	H An
Large Rock Bounder	A An
Large Skeleton	A Un
Large Sveawolf	M An
Large Wolfspider	M In
Larval Predator	H In
Last Breath	A Un
Lava Lizard	M Rp
Lava Monster	M El
Legatio	A Un
Legionarius	A Un
Legionnaire	A Un
Leprechaun	H Hu
Lesser Banshee	H Un
Lesser Telamon	A Mg

Monster	Realm / Type
Lesser Zephyr	H El
Levian	H An
Levian-Al	H An
Lhiannan-Sidhe	H Mg
Lieutenant Gargantan	R Dm
Lieutenant Loran	R Dm
Lieutenant Persun	R Dm
Lilispawn	R Dm
Lingering Shade	A Un
Little Water Goblin	M Hu
Living Entombed	A Un
Lode Protector	H El
Loghery Man	H Hu
Lone Wolf	A An
Lost Hagbui	M Un
Lost Spirit	M Un
Lough Wolf	H An
Lough Wolf Cadger	H An
Luch Catcher	H An
Luch Hunter	H An
Lugradan	H Hu
Lugradan Whelp	H Hu
Lunantishee	H Mg
Lupine Gnawer	M An
Lupine Snarler	M An
Luricaduane	H Hu
Mad Changeling	H Mg
Mad Kobold	M Hu
Mad Rat	M An
Maghemoth	M El
Magister	A Un
Magmatasm	M Un
Mahr	R Dm
Malefic Forest Scorpion	H In
Malefic Phantom	A Un
Malevolent Disciple	A Un
Malevolent Forest Scorpion	H In
Manes Demon	A Dm
Mangled Troll Invader	H Un
Manipularis	A Un
Marquis Almen	R Dm
Marquis Chaosmar	R Dm
Marquis Dortaleon	R Dm
Marquis Focalleste	R Dm
Marquis Haurian	R Dm
Marquis Sabonach	R Dm
Marquis Scottiax	R Dm
Marquis Valupa	R Dm
Marrow Leech	A An
Marsh Scrag	A Gi
Marsh Worm	A An
Master Hunter	A Hu
Mature Wyvern	M Dr
Meandering Spirit	M Un
Medial Telamon	A Mg
Megafelid	H An
Megalith Wight	A Un
Megalithic Terror	A Un
Menacing Presence	A Un
Mephitic Ghoul	M Un
Mercenary Tomb Raider	A Hu
Merman	H Mg
Merrow	H Hu
Midgard Waylayer	A Hu
Mindless Minion	A Hu
Mindless Thrall	M Hu
Mindworm	H An
Mineshaft Juggernaut	A Mg
Minor Changeling	H Mg
Minor Fideal	M Hu
Minor Werewolf Noble	M Mg
Miserable Zombie	M Un
Mist Monster	A El
Mist Sheerie	H El
Mist Sprite	A El
Mist Wraith	H Un
Moheran Distorter	H Hu
Moldy Skeleton	A Un
Molochian Tempter	R Dm
Moor Boogey	A Hu
Moor Den Mother	A An
Moor Pack Leader	A An
Moor Wolf	A An
Moorlich	A Un
Mora Dancer	M Mg
Mora Rider	M Mg
Morass Leech	H An
Morghoul	H Un
Moss Maiden	M Hu
Moss Monster	H El
Moss Sheerie	H El
Mouldering Corpse	A Un
Mountain Grim	A Un
Mountain Mephit	H Dm
Muck Snake	A Rp
Mud Crab	M In
Mud Crab Warrior	M In
Mud Frog	M An
Mud Golem	A El
Mud Snake	M Rp
Mud Worm	A An
Mudman	H El
Mummy Hag	H Un
Murkman	H Un
Muryan	A Mg
Muryan Emmisary	A Mg
Muryan Trickster	A Mg
Mutilator Axa'Al	R Dm
Mutilator Axalnam	R Dm
Mutilator Axtanax	R Dm
Mutilator Konapher	R Dm
Mutilator Laicanroth	R Dm
Mutilator Lazorous	R Dm
Mutilator Marbozer	R Dm
Mutilator Nianax	R Dm
Mutilator Novinrac	R Dm
Mutilator Okabi	R Dm
Mutilator Oprionach	R Dm
Mutilator Oronor	R Dm
Mutilator Phaxazis	R Dm
Mutilator Samiol	R Dm
Mutilator Taboku	R Dm
Mutilator Uxybab	R Dm
Mutilator Vorazax	R Dm
Mutilator Vozoaz	R Dm
Mutilator Xaabaro	R Dm
Mutilator Xagalith	R Dm
Mutilator Xakanos	R Dm
Mutilator Xazbalor	R Dm
Mutilator Yooginroth	R Dm
Mutilator Zurabo	R Dm
Myrkcat	M An
Naburite Drinker	R Dm
Nacken	M El
Nain Dwarf	A Hu
Necyomancer	R Hu
Needletooth Devourer	A Mg
Nightmare	R Dm
Nip Mephit	M Dm
Nocuous Hound	M An
Nordic Dirge	M Un
Nordic Yeti	M Hu
Northern Ettin	M Hu
Northern Light	M Mg
Noxious Hound	M An
Oak Man	A TP
Oaken Fellwood	A TP
Ollipheist	H Rp
Optio	A Un
Orchard Nipper	H Hu
Ossuary Guardian	A Un
Outcast Rogue	A Hu
Padfoot	A Un
Pale Guardian	R Dm
Pale Horse	H Un
Parthanan	H Dm
Patrolling Drakulv	M Mg
Peallaidh	A Hu
Pelagian Alliant	H In
Pelagian Crab	H In
Pelagian Guard	H In
Pendragon Ardent	A Un
Pendrake	A Un
Perfidious Pook	M Hu
Petrified Grovewood	A Un
Phaeghoul	H Un
Phantom	A Un
Phantom Hound	M Un
Phantom Miner	H Un
Phantom Page	A Un
Phantom Squire	A Un
Phantom Wickerman	H Un
Phantom Wolf	M Un
Pictish Druid	A Hu
Pictish Warrior	A Hu
Pikeman	A Un
Pine Imp	M Dm
Pine Mephit	M Dm
Piper Fairy	A Mg
Pit Boss	H El
Pit Spraggon	H El
Pixie	A El
Pixie Imp	A El
Pixie Scout	A El
Plague Spider	A In
Plasmatasm	M Un
Plated Fiend	R Dm
Poacher	A Hu
Poacher Leader	A Hu
Pogson	A Gi
Poisonous Cave Spider	M In
Poisonous Cave Toad	H An
Pooka	H Mg
Pookha	H Mg
Praefectus	A Un
Praetor	A Un
Praetorian Guard	A Un
Priestess	A Hu
Primrose	H Hu
Princep	A Un
Prisoner	M Hu
Pseudo Basilisk	A Rp
Puny Skeleton	A Un
Putrid Sacrificer	A Un
Putrid Zombie	A Un
Pygmy Goblin	A Hu
Pygmy Goblin Bombardier	A Gi
Pygmy Goblin Tangler	A Hu
Pyrophantom	M Un
Pyrotasm	M Un
Quicksand	A El
Ra Of Oak	M El
Ra Of Pine	M El
Ra Of Willow	M El
Rabid Sveawolf	M An
Rabid Wolfhound	M An
Rage Sprite	H Mg
Rage Wolf	H An
Raging Subverter	H Hu
Rat Boy	H Mg
Rattling Skeleton	M Un
Raven Wraith	H Un
Ravenclan Giant	A Gi
Reanimated Foe	A Un
Red Adder	A Rp
Red Dwarf Bandit	A Hu
Red Dwarf Chief	A Hu
Red Dwarf Matron	A Hu
Red Dwarf Thief	A Hu
Red Dwarf Youth (Female)	A Hu
Red Dwarf Youth (Male)	A Hu
Red Lion	A An
Red Rager	M Hu
Red Wolfhound	H An
Redbone Skeleton	A Un
Reincarnate Orm	M Rp
Renegade Guard	A Hu
Repentant Follower	A Un
Ribbon Toad	M An
Ridgeback Worg	M An
River Drake Hatchling	A Dr
River Drakeling	A Dr
River Racer	A Rp
River Sprite	A El
River Spriteling	A El
Roaming Corpse	M Un
Roaming Dirge	M Un
Roaming Thrall	M Hu

Monster	Realm / Type
Roan Stepper	H An
Roane Companion	H Mg
Roane Maiden	H Hu
Rock Clipper	H In
Rock Crab	M In
Rock Elemental	A El
Rock Golem	H El
Rock Guardian	H El
Rock Imp	A Dm
Rock Sheerie	H El
Rock Sprite	H El
Rockbiter	H El
Rocot	R Dm
Roman Ghost	A Un
Roman Spirit	A Un
Root Worm	H An
Rot Worm	A An
Rotting Skeleton	A Un
Rotting Tombraider	A Un
Rotting Zombie	A Un
Rowdy	H Hu
Rugged Dwarven Pony	M An
Ruthless Brigand	A Hu
Sacrificed Slave	A Un
Sacrificial Soul	A Un
Salisbury Giant	A Gi
Sand Crab	H In
Sandman	H El
Sanguinite Ghoul	M Un
Sapherd	M TP
Savage Fishing Bear	H An
Savage Lynx	M An
Savage Wildling	M Hu
Savage Winterwolf	M An
Savage Wyvern	M Dr
Saxonbone Skeleton	A Un
Scaled Fiend	A Dm
Scaled Retriever	M An
Scaled Varg Snarler	M An
Scaled Varg Yearling	M An
Scavenger	M An
Scorned Bwca	A Hu
Scourge Rat	H An
Scrag	A Gi
Scragger	H El
Scragling	A Gi
Scrawny Bogman	A Hu
Scrawny Red Lion	A An
Scum Toad	A An
Seared Skeleton	M Un
Seithkona Initiate	M Hu
Seithkona Laering	M Hu
Seithr Orb	M Mg
Sett Dweller	H An
Sett Matron	H An
Sett Protector	H An
Sett Youngling	H An
Shadow	M Mg
Shadowhunter	A An
Shadowhunter She-Wolf	A An
Shaft Rat	H An
Shambler	A TP
Shard Golem	M El
Sharktooth Whelp	M Hu
Sharpfang Worg	M An
Sheevra Archer	H Hu
Sheevra Chieftain	H Hu
Sheevra Miner	H Hu
Sheevra Skirmisher	H Hu
Sheevra Swordsman	H Hu
Shepherd	A Un
Shivering Presence	M Un
Shock Aqueous Slug	H An
Shrieking Willow	M TP
Shrieking Wraith	H Un
Siabra Anchorite	H Hu
Siabra Archmagi	H Hu
Siabra Guardian	H Hu
Siabra Lookout	H Hu
Siabra Mireguard	H Hu
Siabra Raider	H Hu
Siabra Seeker	H Hu
Siabra Venator	H Hu
Siabra Waterwalker	H Hu
Siabra Wayguard	H Hu
Sidhe Draoi	M Hu
Sidhe Gaoite	M El
Signifier	A Un
Silver Oaken Fellwood	A TP
Silver-Flecked Skeleton	H Un
Silver-Maddened Werewolf	H Mg
Silvermine Badger	H An
Silvermine Guard	H Hu
Silvermine Knocker	H Hu
Silvermine Sentry	H Hu
Silverscale Drakeling	M Dr
Sinach	H Rp
Singular	A Un
Siog Footpad	H Hu
Siog Piller	H Hu
Siog Raider	H Hu
Siog Seeker	H Hu
Siog Waylayer	H Hu
Skeletal Centurion	A Un
Skeletal Druid	A Un
Skeletal Druidess	A Un
Skeletal Dwarf Invader	H Un
Skeletal High Priestess	A Un
Skeletal Legionnaire	A Un
Skeletal Minion	H Un
Skeletal Oarsman	M Un
Skeletal Pawn	H Un
Skeletal Seafarer	M Un
Skeleton	A Un
Skogsfru	M Hu
Slave	A Hu
Slave Master	A Hu
Slave Master Bodyguard	A Hu
Slaver	A Hu
Sleigh Horse	M An
Sleipneirsson	M An
Slime Lizard	A Rp
Slith Broodling	A Rp
Slough Serpent	A Rp
Small Bear	A An
Small Black Orm	M Rp
Small Cave Mauler	M An
Small Freshwater Crab	H In
Small Gray Wolf	A An
Small Hill Cat	M An
Small Rock Bounder	A An
Small Skeletal Centurion	A Un
Small Skeletal Legionnaire	A Un
Small Snake	A Rp
Small Walking Rock	H El
Smiera-Gatto	M An
Snake	A Rp
Snow Giant	M Gi
Snow Imp	M Dm
Snowdon Grim	A Un
Snowshoe Bandit	M Hu
Snowshoe Bandit Mage	M Hu
Soft-Shelled Crab	M In
Soot Harvester	M In
Soul Harvester	A Un
Soul Sinker	M Mg
Soultorn A. Alerion Knight	R Dm
Soultorn A. Dragon Knight	R Dm
Soultorn A. Eagle Knight	R Dm
Soultorn A. Gryphon Knight	R Dm
Soultorn A. Guardian	R Dm
Soultorn A. Lion Knight	R Dm
Soultorn A. Myrmidon	R Dm
Soultorn A. Phoenix Knight	R Dm
Soultorn A. Protector	R Dm
Soultorn A. Unicorn Knight	R Dm
Soultorn A. Warder	R Dm
Soultorn H. Brehon	R Dm
Soultorn H. Cosantoir	R Dm
Soultorn H. Emerald Ridere	R Dm
Soultorn H. Gilded Spear	R Dm
Soultorn H. Grove Protecter	R Dm
Soultorn H. Raven Ardent	R Dm
Soultorn H. Savant	R Dm
Soultorn H. Silver Hand	R Dm
Soultorn H. Thunderer	R Dm
Soultorn H. Tiarna	R Dm
Soultorn H. Wayfarer	R Dm
Soultorn N. Einherjar	R Dm
Soultorn N. Elding Herra	R Dm
Soultorn N. Elding Vakten	R Dm
Soultorn N. Flammen Herra	R Dm
Soultorn N. Flammen Vakten	R Dm
Soultorn N. Isen Herra	R Dm
Soultorn N. Isen Vakten	R Dm
Soultorn N. Skiltvakten	R Dm
Soultorn N. Stormur Herra	R Dm
Soultorn N. Stormur Vakten	R Dm
Soultorn N. Vakten	R Dm
Spawn Of Gjalpinulva	M Dr
Spectral Bayer	M Un
Spectral Briton Invader	H Un
Spectral Essence	A Un
Spectral Hog	M Un
Spectral Manslayer	H Un
Spectral Wickerman	H Un
Spectral Wizard	A Un
Speghoul	H Un
Spider	M In
Spindel	M In
Spindel Layer	M In
Spindel Silkster	M In
Spindly Rock Crab	M In
Spiny Eel	A An
Spirit	A Un
Spirit Hound	A Un
Spiritual Advisor	A Un
Spiteful Wraith	A Un
Spook	M Un
Spraggon	H El
Spraggon Cutter	H El
Spraggon Runner	H El
Spraggon Springer	H El
Spraggonale	H El
Spraggonite	H El
Spraggonix	H El
Spraggonoll	H El
Spraggonote	H El
Sprawling Arachnid	A In
Spriggarn	A El
Spriggarn Ambusher	A El
Spriggarn Elder	A El
Spriggarn Howler	A El
Spriggarn Waylayer	A El
Squabbler	H An
Stalker	A In
Stinger	M In
Stone Sentinel	A El
Stone Sheerie	H El
Stonecrush Demolisher	A Gi
Stonecrush Excavator	A Gi
Stonecrush Rockgrinder	A Gi
Streaming Wisp	H El
Stromkarl	M Hu
Succubus	R Dm
Suffering Apparition	A Un
Suitor Spirit	H Un
Sulphur Crab	M In
Sulphuric Ghoul	M Un
Svartalf Arbetare	M Hu
Svartalf Bloodbinder	M Hu
Svartalf Chanter	M Hu
Svartalf Foister	M Hu
Svartalf Foreman	M Hu
Svartalf Guard	M Hu
Svartalf Hunter	M Hu
Svartalf Infiltrator	M Hu
Svartalf Merchant	M Hu
Svartalf Outcast	M Hu
Svartalf Predator	M Hu
Svartalf Smith	M Hu
Svartalf Sorcerer	M Hu
Svartalf Thrall	M Hu
Svartalf Watcher	M Hu
Svartskogsfru	M Hu
Sveawolf	M An
Sveawolf Cub	M An
Sveawolf Mother	M An

Monster	Realm / Type
Sveawolf Packleader	M An
Sveawolf Spirit	M Un
Svendo	M Hu
Swamp Hopper	H An
Swamp Rat	A An
Swamp Slime	A TP
Sylvan Goblin	A Hu
Sylvan Goblin Chief	A Hu
Sylvan Goblin Hunter	A Hu
Sylvan Goblin Magician	A Hu
Sylvan Goblin Warrior	A Hu
Sylvan Goblin Whelp	A Hu
Taiga Cat	M An
Tawny Lynx	M An
Tawny Lynx Cub	M An
Templar	A Hu
Terra Crab	M In
Thawing Corpse	M Un
Thrall	M Hu
Tidal Sheerie	H El
Timber Cat	M An
Timberland Badger	M An
Tingler	M In
Tomb Creeper	H Hu
Tomb Keeper	A Un
Tomb Raider	A Hu
Tomb Raider Commander	A Hu
Tomb Raider Digger	A Hu
Tomb Raider Scout	A Hu
Tomb Sentry	M Un
Tomb Wight	A Un
Tomte Aggressor	M Hu
Tomte Caitiff	M Hu
Tomte Captor	M Hu
Tomte Cutthroat	M Hu
Tomte Guard	M Hu
Tomte Handler	M Hu
Tomte Hoodoo	M Hu
Tomte Jager	M Hu
Tomte Pillager	M Hu
Tomte Plunderer	M Hu
Tomte Protector	M Hu
Tomte Runner	M Hu
Tomte Seer	M Hu
Tomte Shaman	M Hu
Tomte Skirmisher	M Hu
Tomte Thug	M Hu
Tomte Warhound	M An
Tomte Zealot	M Hu
Torc	H An
Torcan	H An
Tormented Necyomancer	R Hu
Torpor Worm	M An
Tortured Soul	A Un
Townsman	A Un
Trammer	H Hu
Trapped Thrall	M Un
Tree Snake	A Rp
Tree Spider	A In
Tree Spirit	A Un
Tree Spirit	M El
Treekeep	M TP
Tribune	A Un
Tribunus Laticlavicus	A Un
Trimbeak	A Rp
Troglodyte	H Hu
Tunnel Imp	H Dm
Tunneler	A Rp
Twister	M El
Tylwyth Teg Huntress	A Hu
Tylwyth Teg Ranger	A Hu
Tylwyth Teg Rover	A Hu
Umber Bear	H An
Umbral Aegis	R Dm
Umbral Hulk	R Dm
Umbrood Warrior	R Dm
Undead Briton Invader	H Un
Undead Builder	A Un
Undead Drudger	H Un
Undead Druid	A Un
Undead Explorer	M Un
Undead Filidh	A Un
Undead Goblin Chief	A Un
Undead Goblin Fisherman	A Un
Undead Goblin Warrior	A Un
Undead Guardsman	A Un
Undead Miner	A Un
Undead Monk	A Un
Undead Poacher	A Un
Undead Retainer	A Un
Undead Troll Warrior	M Un
Undead Viking	M Un
Undead Woodcarver	M Un
Unearthed Cave Bear	H An
Unfortunate Pragmatic	A Un
Unseelie Overman	H Hu
Unseelie Underviewer	H Hu
Unseelie Viewer	H Hu
Ursine Dweller	H Hu
Ursine Patrol	H Hu
Ursine Shaman	H Hu
Ursine Sorcerer	H Hu
Ursine Thrall	H Hu
Ursine Warrior	H Hu
Vanisher	H Mg
Vapor Wraith	M Un
Veil Wisp	H Mg
Vein Golem	H El
Vein Spider	M In
Vein Spiderling	M In
Vendo Bone-Collector	M Hu
Vendo Flayer	M Hu
Vendo Frightener	M Hu
Vendo Guard	M Hu
Vendo Reaver	M Hu
Vendo Savager	M Hu
Vendo Shaman	M Hu
Vendo Stalker	M Hu
Vendo Warrior	M Hu
Vendo Yowler	M Hu
Vengeful Ghoul	M Un
Venomous Tree Crawler	M In
Venomspitter	M Rp
Vigilant Soul	A Un
Vigilis	A Un
Villainous Youth	H Hu
Vindictive Bocan	H Un
Walking Rock	H El
Wandering Spirit	A Un
Wanshee	H Un
Warrior Ant	A In
Water Badger	H An
Water Beetle	H In
Water Beetle Collector	H In
Water Beetle Larva	H In
Water Leaper	A An
Water Snake	A Rp
Water Snake	M Rp
Water Sprite	M El
Water Strider	M In
Watery Escort	H Hu
Way Keeper	M Un
Wayward Ghoul	M Un
Weak Skeleton	A Un
Wee Wolf	M An
Weeping Willow	M TP
Weewere	H Mg
Welsh Hobgoblin	A Hu
Welsh Hobgoblin Chief	A Hu
Werewolf	M Mg
Werewolf Bodyguard	M Mg
Werewolf Captain	M Mg
Werewolf Churl	M Mg
Werewolf Commander	M Mg
Werewolf Courier	M Mg
Werewolf Grimnought	M Mg
Werewolf Guard	M Mg
Werewolf Lieutenant	M Mg
Werewolf Noble	M Mg
Werewolf Runner	M Mg
Werewolf Scruff	M Mg
Werewolf Skulker	M Mg
Werewolf Warder	M Mg
Western Basilisk	A Rp
Whirlwind	M El
Whispering Willow	M TP
White Boar	H An
White Willow Fellwood	A TP
White Wolf	M An
Wicked Cythraul	A Un
Wiggle Worm	H An
Wight	A Un
Wild Boar	A An
Wild Crouch	H Mg
Wild Hog	M An
Wild Lucradan	H Hu
Wild Mare	A An
Wild Sow	A An
Wild Stallion	A An
Wild Thrall	M Hu
Wildling	M Hu
Will O' Wisp	A Mg
Wind Ghoul	H Un
Wind Mephit	A Dm
Wind Spirit	M El
Wind Sprite	M El
Wind Wisp	M El
Windswept Wraith	M Un
Winter Wolf	M An
Wintery Dirge	M Un
Wisp Ghoul	A Un
Witherwoode	A TP
Wolf Nipper	M An
Wolfaur Headsman	M Mg
Wolfaur Lunarian	M Mg
Wolfaur Pragmatic	M Mg
Wolfaur Quixot	M Mg
Wolfhound	M An
Wolfspider	M In
Wolverine	M An
Wood Imp	M Dm
Wood Mephit	M Dm
Wood Ogre Berserker	A Gi
Wood Ogre Lord	A Gi
Wood Ogre Mystic	A Gi
Wood Ogre Scourge	A Gi
Wood Ogre Seer	A Gi
Wood Rat	M An
Wood-Eater	M In
Wood-Eater Alate	M In
Wood-Eater Hunter	M In
Wood-Eater King	M In
Wood-Eater Queen	M In
Wood-Eater Royal Guard	M In
Wood-Eater Soldier	M In
Wood-Eater Worker	M In
Woodeworm	A An
Woodland Badger	M An
Worker Ant	A In
Worm	A Rp
Wounded Sveawolf	M An
Wrath Sprite	H Mg
Wyvern	M Dr
Yell Hound	A An
Young Badger	H An
Young Boar	A An
Young Brown Bear	A An
Young Brown Drake	A Dr
Young Cutpurse	A Hu
Young Envy Drake	M Dr
Young Fire Wyrm	M Rp
Young Forest Runner	A Hu
Young Grendelorm	M Rp
Young Lynx	M An
Young Necyomancer	R Hu
Young Poacher	A Hu
Young Silverscale Drake	M Dr
Young Sveawolf	M An
Young Wolverine	M An
Young Wyvern	M Dr
Zephyr Wraith	H Un
Zombie Boar	A Un
Zombie Farmer	A Un
Zombie Sow	A Un

Appendix B: Crafting Basics

Learning a craft is a good break from constantly going off to combat, recuperating from combat and (the old standby) ... talking about combat. It adds different challenges to the *DAoC* experience, it gives a sense of accomplishment, and it's another way to be useful to your friends and allies. Siegecrafting, in particular, is invaluable in advanced RvR play.

Those are the reasons why you should do it.

There are also reasons not to do it: it's expensive in money and time, at least in the early stages. You'll spend more time completing tasks or consignments to get the money to afford to practice than you would spend completing other tasks that give you enough money to just buy the items.

Also, unfortunately, most craftwork has to be done near a forge or lathe, so you can't make use of your "downtime" between battles.

In the end, the question is: do you want to do it? If you think you might, give it a try and see if you like it.

Crafting Skills

There are currently five Trade Skills:

- Armorcrafting
- Fletching
- Siegecrafting
- Tailoring
- Weaponcrafting

There are four Material Skills:

- Metalworking
- Leatherworking
- Clothworking
- Woodworking

To craft, you must choose a primary Trade Skill. Your ability to craft with other skills is capped, based on what craft you take as your primary craft. Other crafts are restricted to a certain percentage of your primary crafting skill, loosely based on which crafts are more alike or dissimilar:

Other Skill	Arm	Fle	Tai	Wea	Sieg
Primary Skill					
Armor	—	40%	75%	75%	40%
Fletch	40%	—	40%	75%	75%
Tailor	40%	75%	—	40%	40%
Weapon	75%	40%	40%	—	75%

ARMORCRAFTING

Creates studded, chain or plate armor.

Useful Material Skills	Metalworking Leatherworking
Useful Trade Skill	Tailoring

FLETCHING

Makes bows, arrows, crossbows, bolts and staves.

Useful Material Skill	Woodworking

SIEGECRAFTING

Makes ballistas, battering rams, catapults and so forth.

Useful Material Skills	All
Useful Trade Skills	All

TAILORING

Creates cloth and leather armors, plus cloaks and robes.

Useful Material Skills	Clothworking Leatherworking

WEAPONCRAFTING

Makes swords, axes, maces and other weapons.

Useful Material Skills	Metalworking Leatherworking

Money

The first thing you're going to need in order to make items is cold, hard cash. There are three ways to make money in *DAoC*.

One way is to make goods to sell. Well, you're just starting off on that one, so it won't help you yet. Later, you'll be able to make a profit on the things you create and will be able to "stay in business" on consignment profits alone.

Other ways to make money? If you have a brand new character, a good way to get started is to perform the tasks that are offered around town. It takes a while, but it won't be too long before you can at least start trying out the basics of the trade skill you want to learn.

If you have a character capable of solo combat (even if you are very low-level), you should ask around until you get a "kill task" — a task where a named guard (that's a guard who has an actual name visible when you see him) asks you to go kill something. That pays really well if you're up to it. Of course another way to make money is to rely on the gold and loot you get during combat — but that takes a while to stockpile, especially if you need to buy armor as you level up.

Master Trainers

Next you must decide what Order you want to join, and go talk to the master of that Order.

This is not a trivial thing! Each character can only belong to one Order. You can always do other things, but you'll never be master of them. In fact, all other trade skills will always be less than your primary, "official" skill. So if you choose Armorcrafting, and you never practice crafting armor to get good at it, no matter how often you make arrows you'll never be better than 40% as good as you are at making armor. The moral of this story is to choose right the first time, because you (currently) can't change your mind later.

Trade Skill	Master Trainer
Albion (Camelot)	
Armorcraft	Loraine Elgen
Tailoring	Arliss Eadig
Weaponcraft	Hephas Elgen
Midgard (Jordheim)	
Armorcraft	Gest
Tailoring	Eskil
Weaponcraft	Aase
Hibernia (Tir na Nog)	
Armorcraft	Dunstan, Tegvan
Tailoring	Armin
Weaponcraft	Hendrika

Making Something

First you're going to have to prepare.

1) Open your Skills menu. It's the one that looks like a hand.
2) Look at the list of skills available to you.
3) Open a new Hotkey bar. This bar will be devoted to your new abilities.
4) Drag the icon that represents your new skill from the open window. (For instance, the Armorcrafting icon looks like a helmet.)
5) Click on the icon in your Hotkey Bar to see the list of what is available for you to make. There are different "kinds" of each item. Notice that the items are color-coordinated, just like Monsters. Some are green, some blue, some yellow and so forth. As you could guess, the items that are green are fairly easy for you to make, while the red items are impossible. The more you successfully make items, the better you become, the more complicated recipes will become available.

Red Item is at least 20 points above your skill level. You'll almost certainly fail, probably losing the item entirely.

Orange Item is 1-20 points above your skill level. You'll likely fail, possibly losing the item.

Yellow Item is approximately your skill level. 50% chance of success, no loss of ingredients if you fail.

White Item is exactly your skill level.

Blue Item is 10-30 points below your skill level. Good chance of success, no loss of ingredients.

Green Item is at least 30 points below your skill level. You'll probably succeed, no loss of ingredients.

Gray Item is at least 50 points below your skill level. You'll always succeed.

You get more XP for making yellow items than you do for blues or greens, but you don't get that much more for making something orange than you do for making something yellow. The best tradeoff of experience for materials lost is yellow — if you stick to making yellow items, you'll improve the fastest. The best tradeoff of experience for money spent is blue — if you stick to blue items you'll get points and only rarely flub an item.

6) Drag the icon of an item that is blue or yellow to you or to your Hotkey Bar, under your primary trade skill icon.

7) Right-click on the Item icon on your Hotkey Bar. It shows you what you need to have to make that item. Some are things you need to purchase (if you don't already have them); some may be things you can make. We'll call these things "prerequisite" items.

   Note: Most raw product comes already packed in batches of 20. Don't buy multiples of basic items! Buy one and see if it's "stacked" in your inventory — you might not need more than one stack to begin.

7a) If you need to make something else, go and grab that icon from the appropriate skills window and drag its icon up onto your Hotkey Bar. You may have to open a Material Skill window (such as Woodworking for Fletching) to find the appropriate icon.

7b) Check (by right-clicking on the item) what you need to make any prerequisite items.

8) Go shopping or hunting and get the items you need. If you're going to make multiples — either for practice or because you need them — buy a batch of 20 or more. Stack them in your backpack to save room.

9) If you need to be in a certain place (a forge for Armorcrafting or Weaponcrafting, or a lathe for Fletching), go there. You need to be close enough to target it (within about nine paces).

10) Make an item. Click on the icon of the item you want to make. (You don't have to click on the ingredients, just have them in your backpack.) If you have to craft a prerequisite item, you'll need to do that one first. (You don't need to click on any tools, such as a hammer. You just need to have the proper tools in your inventory.)

BREAKING SOMETHING

If you're making things for the experience, you can speed the process up a little by salvaging some of the materials of the item you just made. Drop the item on the ground, type **/salvage** and click on the dropped item. You'll get back some of the basic ingredients. In fact, if you decide to do this, it's a good idea to assign a macro to **/salvage**. (See **Assigning a Slash Command to a Hotkey** in the manual.)

Keep Your Skills Up

Don't let your Material Skills fall behind. You'll need to make trinkets (small things like hinges, breadboards or puppets) in order to keep your skills up. Don't forget to salvage the materials!

For practice, make the things that take the least amount of materials.

*Note: **http://www.lindenhall.com / rothwell/guides/tradeskills.htm** is a very useful resource.*

Falaanla's Tailoring Guide

Being a tailor is simple. There are only a few things you really need to do to get started:

- Have about 1 gold piece handy; it'll be more than enough to get you started.
- Talk to the Master Tailor in your realm's main city. He or she will likely be hanging out near all the other trade masters.

Then you need to start tailoring! To get started, do the following:

1) Click the Hand icon.
2) In the bottom window you'll see a Needle icon, with the word "Tailoring" by it. That's the icon you'll use to make your various tailored items.
3) Go to a Hotkey Bar you haven't used yet. You'll probably fill up more than one bar by the time you're done with trade skills — but for now, one will be sufficient.
4) Drag the Tailoring icon to this bar's top slot. Click the icon, and you'll see a large list, with various possible items to make. You should see the three different levels of leather armor listed.
5) Click the first one, and select "Boots."
6) Drag this icon next to your Tailoring icon on your new Hotkey Bar.
7) Find the vendor that sells tailoring supplies and buy the following: 1 sewing kit, 1 stack of rawhide leather squares, and 1 stack of heavy woven thread.
8) Make boots. Start by clicking the Boot icon. You will now attempt to make the boots. If successful, the boots will appear in your inventory. If not … that only means you have to try again. The materials you bought will last you for several projects.

   Successfully creating items will increase your skill, unless they were too easy for your skill level. If you keep making orange items, you'll rapidly raise your skill level (but also check out the pros and cons of yellow and blue items, on page 383).

   As your skill increases, other items become available to you. You'll want to make boots and gloves until you have 100 Tailoring skill, since they're the cheapest to make.

   If the gloves/boots you're making are no longer of "orange" difficulty to make — check this by opening your tailoring menu and looking at the Boot icon — then move up to the next type of gloves and boots.
9) Once you have a skill of 100, talk to the Master Tailor and ask for help, to be able to go to the next level of accomplishment. (In fact, you're going to do this so often in your tailoring career you might want to make an "ask for help" macro — type **/macro /whisper help**.) It doesn't have to be a whisper, but it's a polite thing to do. The Master Tailor will give you a task to make something and deliver it to an NPC in the city.

Tasks. Completing tasks means that your skill level will rise more slowly — you're going to be spending time delivering the goods, of course — but you'll be making a profit instead of losing all your money buying materials.

Going public. You can also make armor for other players. Of course, to make things easier, make a "selling" macro with the particulars of what you're making, and how much you want for it: **/broadcast Selling <what type> armor for <cost>**. Click this while you're working on your skill. If you end up with someone that wants to purchase your armor, that's wonderful!

By selling to players, you get six chances to raise your skill, and you get to make a profit. Check the appropriate craft recipe chart (for Albion, on page 106; Hibernia, page 202; and Midgard, page 290) to see what the raw material cost is for each item; mark that price up 10% to 20% to get your selling price to players.

And that's it! You're now well on your way to becoming a skilled tailor! Good luck, and enjoy!

Appendix C: Roles

Archery 101 – The Basics

Basic Lessons — and more — by Jim Rothwell can be found at http://www.rothwellhome.org/camelot.html.

Quick-key. To be most effective with your bow (or crossbow), you should put your bow, any bow special abilities, your melee weapon, your shield, and any melee combat styles on your quick-key bar.

Get close, target and shoot. When you spot prey that you want to hunt, creep within range, being quiet so as not to alert your prey. Click the bow icon on your quick-key bar to strip your bow out of its oilskin and string it. Click the bow a second time to select an arrow from the first bundle in your supplies, nock, and draw it. Depending on your quickness, you will need to take about 5 seconds to line up your shot. When you feel that you have everything lined up perfectly (there will be a message in your combat window), click again to loose the arrow. If the opponent was far enough away, you can rapidly click again to draw another arrow, aim, and loose it before the charging foe is close enough that you need to switch over to your melee combat gear. This is why you should have your melee weapon and shield on the quick-key bar also, as it makes drawing your sword and donning your shield much faster. Don't forget to take your combat stance as well.

Auto-release. Also note that if you click the bow quick-key before you are ready to release your shot, it will auto-release as soon as the draw time runs out. If you click it again before you are ready to loose the arrow, it will auto-release the arrow and then automatically redraw for the next shot. If you click the bow quick-key a third time before you are ready to loose the arrow, it will once again wait for a manual release.

Arrow order. At the moment, the arrows first encountered in your packs are the arrows you will shoot. As an advanced technique, line up your initial shot (probably a critical shot) with a flight arrow. While your character is aiming, switch to your normal arrows by swapping the position of your arrow bundles in your packs. Release the first shot and draw the next with the double click described above, and the monster should charge into the normal arrow range by the time you are ready to loose the second arrow. This will allow you to use cheaper arrows most of the time, but still be able to attack at the furthest range possible.

Doh! It moved! Should your target move out of range, you may quickly change targets by selecting a different opponent that is in view, and attempt to loose at it. Should there be no other opponents in front of you, you may turn to try to find something else, but if you move your feet, your will need to draw again. You have about 15 seconds of holding time while you attempt to find another target before you must relax your draw.

Melee. The primary archers all have the option of standing back from a melee and

firing at your foes in melee. This is a recommended tactic for scouts because their melee damage is usually less than their bow damage, but rangers and hunters may prefer melee over archery when group melee begins. Keep in mind that each arrow you shoot costs money, so using the cheaper clout arrows is recommended if you plan on firing into melee.

Retreat. Also, be ready to run when using archery to encourage opponents to chase you into an ambush. Many creatures are intelligent, and call for help if they are wounded too severely. The first call for help usually occurs when the mob reaches half health, but sometimes occurs before that. Some creatures also like to bring friends when they are attacked, and they sense that you are leading them to an ambush.

Practice. I recommend that new archers find some gray-con mobs to practice upon until they feel proficient. Please search for an area that is not being utilized by those less skilled than yourself, as they need their own practice with melee and magical skills. Only by working together can we defend our realm against those who would seek to invade us, and the youngster you help advance today could be your shieldmate tomorrow. Every time you begin to use a longer range arrow, spend about half a bundle checking the range against gray-con creatures also, so that you find the limits of your new arrows' range, and can determine that approximate range when sneaking up on prey.

Coordinate with others. It is possible for several archers to coordinate their fire. Generally, you should signal to each other which opponent you are choosing to fire upon before drawing your arrows, and whether you will all fire normally or use a special ability. The designated commander will then call for everyone to ready their bow if someone still has their melee weapon out, draw, and loose. This takes significant practice, and should again be practiced until all are proficient in the correct timing. The commander must follow his own commands slightly after giving them in order to match the timing of everyone else in the unit.

If your unit can coordinate fire, every arrow hitting a stationary target will receive a bonus to hit for their lack of vigilance, as well as the cumulative effects of being turned into a sudden pincushion. It is difficult to say, but it appears that the opponent also suffers the multiple opponents penalty to their defense. If the target happens to be sitting, your arrows will automatically do maximum damage.

Archery 102 – Specialization

There is some continuing confusion over how archery specialization affects characters after the recent changes. This information is provided so that players can make some informed decisions as to how to specialize.

Raising your bow spec has an effect on the damage done by your normal shots, exactly the same way melee specialization has on melee skills. If your modified bow specialization is half of your level, damage will be 50% to 100% (average 75%) of the "standard" amount. If your modified bow specialization is two-thirds of your level, damage will be 75% to 125% (average 100%) of the "standard" amount. If your modified bow specialization is equal or over your level, damage will be 100% to 150% (average 125%) of the "standard" amount. This

"standard" amount is based on the item's DPS and delay, and the targets ABS.

Skills — but most noteably archery and Stealth — benefit from "overspeccing" through items and Realm Points.Raising your bow spec also grants you higher critical shot styles:

Critical Shot	# Train	Draw Time (x normal)
I	3rd	2.0
II	6th	1.9
III	9th	1.8
IV	12th	1.7
V	15th	1.6
VI	18th	1.5
VII	21st	1.4
VIII	24th	1.3
IX	27th	1.2

Despite the persistent rumor that is still making the rounds, Critical Shot X does not exist and has never existed.

The damage multiplier for critical shot used to be based on your bow specialization, which is why most archers kept their bow skills at or over max. Now it is based on your level, and is determined by the difference between your level and the targets level, indicated by the target's con. The multiplier is a maximum of 2.0 and a minimum of 1.1. As a broad generalization which does not take the continuous curve nature of this into account, you will do 2.0 times normal damage to all targets that con grey, green, blue, or yellow. You will do approximately 1.7 times normal damage to high-orange targets, 1.4 times normal damage to high-red targets, and 1.1 times normal damage to purple targets.

Please note that critical shot will work against targets that are: sitting (automatic max damage), standing still (which includes standing in combat mode but not actively swinging at something), walking, moving backwards, strafing, or casting a spell.

Critical shot will not work against targets that are: running, in active combat (swinging at something), stunned, or mezzed. Also note that if the target has a shield or are being guarded by someone with a shield, and the one holding the shield is facing the archer and is in combat mode (actively swinging or not), their block rate against arrows is *doubled*. If they are using engage against you, you'll only get past their defenses about 5% of the time.

Archers will eventually be getting bow styles like longshot and volley, and perhaps some special styles on top of that. Sorry, but we have no idea how many trains in bow will be necessary to get these skills. Longshot will be used to extend the range of a normal shot at the drawback of not being able to choose a specific target. Volley is an ability that has the same functionality as longshot, but increases the number of arrows shot. As I recall, it will be individual arrows (three or five - I've heard both) that you fire in rapid succession, each of which has normal chances to hit a random target in an area around where you placed your ground target. It is AOE in that you don't select a specific target, but it does not do equal damage to everyone in the area.

There are other suggestions for improving the class that Mythic has not yet commented on, but which have enough popular support among players that they may be implemented sometime in the future. Many players would like to augment the current design plans with some specialty shots. The primary suggestions are for a leg-shot (movment speed reduction), arm-shot (attack speed reduction), head-shot (critical hit), attention-shot (pulling mobs with no damage, still interrupts, chance to avoid BAF), gut shot (increased aggro useful when duoing with classes apt to get aggro

quickly that you don't want to get it – like robed casters), rapid-shot (60% draw time at 60% damage), and coordinated fire (slave firing to a leader's command). Each of these would be a separate ability icon like critical shot, longshot, and volley, preventing you from using these other skills. All of these are suggested for all primary archers, with the exception of rapid-shot as that skill is designed to allow scouts with their very large draw time to have a way to match the interrupt-power of buffed hunters and rangers by sacrificing the extra damage we do.

There has also been a very popular suggestion for a way for the game interface to help primary archers perform Coordinated Fire — this would allow an archer to pass choice of target, type of shot, and loose control over to another archer. The lead scout would pick a target, what type of shot, and when to release. All scouts following his direction will draw when the leader does and release at that time or as soon as their draw time has ended if they are on different timers and the lead released before their draw time was done. Again, Mythic has not commented on this skill, but it has wide popular support and may be implemented at some future point.

Stealth 101

Assassin classes that have trained to 16th level in stealth have the ability "detect hidden". They have a minimum detection distance of 250 /loc units against archers and minstrels, who can stealth but don't have the detect hidden ability, and 125 /loc units against other assassins. In either case the range is extended another 50 /loc units for every experience level they have over the hidden character's stealth specialization. Please note that 125 /loc units is approximately the length of a "human-ridable" horse.

Border Fort and Portal Fort guards also have detect hidden, and function exactly like assassins. However, they apparently also automatically see through stealth as if the hidden character were not stealthed at all within approximately 2500 /loc units. This conclusion is based on their ability to attack assassins even though the assassin should be out of detection range, and yet archers can get into bow range and not be attacked until they drop stealth to shoot.

Mob scouts also have detect hidden, and function exactly like assassins.

All other classes and mobs (including assassins without detect hidden, archers, minstrels, normal keep guards, and wandering frontier guards) have a minimum detection distance of 125 /loc units, which is extended another 20 /loc units for every experience level they have over the hidden character's stealth specialization.

Note that the minimum detection distance means that anyone within that radius, player character or mob, can see the stealthed character. Characters must attack the hidden character in order to uncover them, unfriendly mobs can uncover hidden characters without doing damage. Characters that can be seen while stealthed appear as shadowy outlines, those that are uncovered are forced back into full visibility.

Speed while stealthed varies from slower than a walk to about the average of a walk and normal run speeds. The actual speed while stealthed is determined by the ratio of the character's stealth specialization to their experience level.

As was mentioned in Archery 102, skills — and most noteably archery and Stealth — benefit from "overspeccing" through items and Realm Points.

Pulling

If you are either a solo player or the designated puller in a group, your goal is to pull one and only one Monster. Of course it's more exciting to pull half a dozen, but that's the kind of excitement you can live without.

In *DAoC* many creatures have an aggro (aggression) range. The edge is fuzzy: if you're outside the aggro range, the Monster will ignore your existence. If you're near the line, it may chase you, it may not. The closer you get, the more likely it becomes that the Monster will begin to chase you. It's the fuzzy border area that's so important in pulling, because that's where you need to be to insure you only pull one Monster at a time from a group.

How to Pull

1) Find the local monsters. (Be aware of where *all* the nearby Monsters are, you don't want to have one walk up behind you while you're concentrating on his friend.) Pick the one that you want to pull. If there's one that's a bit farther away from the rest, that's a good one.

2) Approach the Monster directly. You want to keep your chosen Monster between you and any others.

3) Get near your target Monster. About 9 running paces away should be safe. Hold your position for a few seconds to see if it notices you. If not, good! You want to be able to slowly approach until that one, and not the others, react to your presence.

If the monster reacts, you've got your pull.

4) Slowly step closer, one pace at a time. Be patient. When you cross over the "aggro line" the Monster will start to run toward you.

4b) If you are pulling with a spell or a bow — *and you are fighting solo* — stand at the maximum range possible. Shoot the monster as often as possible, so it's weaker when the fight actually starts.

If you are fighting with a group, you'll want to shoot the monster with your very lightest shot — and only once if possible. If you use a high damage attack, or hit multiple times, your tanks will be unable to get aggro away from you before you are hacked to pieces.

4c) You can pull with a pet by commanding it to attack in defense mode. Let it hit the monster, then switch it to passive mode and it will come toward you. When the monster is at the desired distance, command your pet to attack (defense mode).

5) Turn and run. Make sure you do not run toward any other Monsters and find a place far enough away that your quarry won't get help from friends or neighbors.

6) When pulling for a group, don't do so much damage that it makes it difficult for the tank to get the aggro.

7) Be aware that some monsters will just not follow you to camp if it is too far. Also, when a monster sees you and starts to run back to its own camp, it's a monster scout. (It will usually shout something.) If it's a high con, the best thing to do is run away from it.

BAF. If you pull a monster, and more than one comes, run like mad. Monsters are sometimes linked — these travel in tight packs. Bringing more monsters than expected can kill your group. Run away until you're out of their range, and they give up.

BAF monsters are usually humanoid or pack-style monsters, but only rarely undead. True BAF monsters adjust the size of *their* pack based on the size of *your* group.

Appendix D: Glossary

Massive online games are a culture unto themselves. There is a certain amount of "common" jargon that has evolved over time ... words, phrases and abbreviations make communicating via keyboard a little more convenient. More than that there are words that refer to things unique to Dark Age of Camelot. All in all, it can be confusing to anyone new to the game, and utterly mystifying to someone who's never played the genre at all. Below is a list of words and their definitions that may help you to more quickly understand your new language. Trust us, it doesn't take long at all to become fluent!

+ or - Relative level. Shows an item's or creature's level in relation to yours. See Hints and Tips: Relative Level, p. 97.

10-20-30-etc. % power. When stated by a caster in the group, tells the group what percentage of mana that caster has left.

Level number. A number in front of a person or place will refer to its level. A 28 Hero is a level 28 Hero, for instance.

add A new creature. Warns others in your group that a new Monster is about to enter the current combat, probably either in response to your current target's Call for Help or just because it's aggressive.

aoe/ae Area of Effect. Some spells or effects will affect the area around a target, rather than just the target itself. It's good to know what spells are AoE: sometimes it's handy to hurt the target's buddies, and sometimes you really don't want to affect what's nearby. Remember, even unintentional attacks will wake up a mesmerized Monster.

af Armor Factor. Describes how much protection a piece of armor gives.

afaik As Far As I Know. Indicates you're not certain you are correct, but you have no reason to believe you are wrong.

afk Away From Keyboard. AFK warns your friends that your character is going to stand still and unresponsive for a minute while you go find another bag of chips, pull the puppy out of the toilet, or do whatever other short term project that needs doing. "AFK broom" means the person is taking a bathroom break.

aggress Be aggressive. Lesser-used phrase. See Aggro.

aggro Be aggressive. When a Monster attacks, it "aggros" on its target. Monsters tend to aggro on the person who hits it first, hits it hardest, or casts spells on it. Controlling who the Monster aggros on is an important skill.

apple Red creature. A creature who "cons" red and is a tricky kill.

ai Artificial Intelligence. The people and creatures in the game are controlled by the Artificial Intelligence — in other words, the programming. There is usually only one response to a certain situation, although the situation might be more complex than you realize.

baf Bring A Friend. The more intelligent creatures will enlist the aid of their cohorts when fighting a group.

bait Monster bait. Someone who goes out to lure a Monster back to the group is "Monster bait."

bind Reset your home point. When you die, your character resurrects at your bind point — a bindstone, actually. It is possible to bind to another bindstone by standing near the new stone and typing /bind.

bladeturns No-hit spell. Bladeturns are spells that nullify the first hit, or the first hit every few seconds.

blue (Creature) Ideal solo target. When you target a Monster, its name will appear in a box along with some basic information. Blue gives you the most experience points while being a likely kill. (Item) A good item for your experience level.

brb Be Right Back. Tells your group that you will go away, but not for very long.

broadcast Shout. Broadcast a message for all in your town or city to hear.

brt Be Right There. This tells your group that you are going to rejoin them as quickly as possible.

btw By The Way. This is an acronym that has come across from Email Quickspeak.

bubble/bub Status bar section. The segmented bar looks like a string of beads or bubbles. It indicates how far along you are in achieving the next level. Each segment represents 10% of the total. When you have nine segments filled, you could say you are "one bubble" from leveling up.

buff/buffing Magical enhancement. Some spells increase certain stats of its (friendly) target: making it stronger, faster, etc. These are "buffing" spells, and someone so enhanced is said to be "buffed."

camp (1) Wait. If you think that someone or something might happen in an area, characters may just stand around, waiting for the event. This is called "camping" the event. This is a problem in some other multiplayer games, but less so in DAoC.

camp (2) Monster site. A camp can refer to a stationary spawn of more than one creature.

camp (3) End a playing session. Sometimes the word "camp" is used to indicate quitting for a while, as in "I'm going to camp for the night."

caster One who casts magic. Any magic user can be called a caster, but this mainly refers to those whose primary talent is spellcasting.

cfh Call For Help. Some creatures won't "Bring a Friend" to a fight; instead they'll try defeat you by themselves. If things turn against them, they may Call For Help, summoning nearby friends to come to their aid.

chicken Basilisk. A silly nickname for a dangerous beast.

cob Chant Of Battle. A continuing spell from a "music-based" caster that is useful during battle situations.

con (1) Short for constitution. If someone says he had to "buy back his con" he means he had to pay a Healer to bring his constitution level back to normal.

con (2) Relative level. When you target a creature or item, you "consider" its level in relation to yours. If a creature "cons gray," it's not dangerous at all (unless, of course, there are so many that they seriously outnumber you). If an item "cons gray," it's so low to you it's worthless.

conc Concentration. When people capable of casting long-term buffs cast them, they use up concentration points (Conc). They may sometimes be asked if they have enough Conc for a buff. If they don't, they're "conced out."

cu/cya See you (see ya). This is a quick way to say goodbye.

dd Direct Damage. Some spells do a set amount of immediate damage, and are called Direct Damage (DD) spells. These are distinguished from the spells that do Damage over Time. These are debuffing spells.

debuff Reduce attributes. Some spells decrease the stats of its (enemy) target: making it slower, weaker, etc.

ding Go up a level. There is a (realm-based) sound that you hear when you go up a level – but frequently players will type "ding" to let the other players know they just acquired the necessary experience points to "level up."

dot Damage over Time. Some spells do a certain amount of damage immediately, then continue to do damage over a set period of time. These are called DoTs.

drain Health transference spell. A spell that absorbs life from the target and gives it to the caster.

end Endurance. Endurance is required for important acts such as combat styles and out-running enemies.

fatigue Less endurance. Fatigue is the other side of the Endurance coin. When your Endurance is low, you have high fatigue.

fetch Lure creature. A character (usually physically strong) will try to get a creature to attack him or her, and then lure ("fetch") the creature back to the group for combat.

focus Spell enhancement. An item or spell that facilitates more efficient spell casting. While focusing via magic, a caster cannot move at all.

fop/fp Full Of Power. A caster has enough power to use his spells. In combat situations it is important that casters avoid a Monster until they are ready to cast.

fom/fm Full Of Mana. Mana is another term for magical power … but not officially used in DAoC. See FOP/FP.

fyi For Your Information. This is an acronym to let people know that the information is not immediately important, but that it may be useful at some later time.

gank Beat up/defeat. Ganked implies that not only was someone beaten in combat, but that the winner didn't even work up a sweat.

gimp Cripple. To be gimped is to be rendered weaker than you should be, often by a poor allocation of specialization points.

grape Purple creature. A creature who "cons" purple is a nearly impossible kill.

gray (Creature) Certain victory. A ridiculously easy creature for you to kill, unless you are seriously outnumbered. It gives no experience points. (Item) An item far too basic for you to be using.

green/greenie (Creature) Easy opponent. A certain win … unless they seriously outnumber you. (Item) An item that's far too basic for your experience level, but you can get some use out of it.

griefer Troublemaker. There are some people whose goal in playing a MOG is simply to annoy the other players.

gtg (1) Good To Go. An acronym to let your group know that you are ready to do whatever needs to be done: to fight, to leave, etc.

gtg (2) Got To Go. Some people use this acronym to mean they have to leave immediately.

hibby Hibernia.

imho In My Humble Opinion. This lets the audience know the speaker is stating a personal belief, but does not want to offend anyone who might believe differently. It is an acronym that has come across from Email Quickspeak.

imo In My Opinion. This lets the audience know that the speaker is stating a personal belief. It is an acronym from Email Quickspeak.

inc Incoming. This warns the group that an aggressive Monster is heading toward them.

irl In Real Life. In real life, as opposed to something in the game.

jk or **j/k** Just Kidding. This acronym lets the audience know that the previous statement was meant to be humorous, and was not meant to be taken seriously.

k Short for OK. Means you agree with the latest suggestion.

kill stealing/ks Unwelcome help. When someone jumps into a combat (uninvited) that has been initiated by someone else, and does more damage than the first fighter, it can be called Kill Stealing.

kos Kill On Sight. A kill on sight reaction means that there is no way to avoid combat with that person/Monster/race/class. There is some KOS reaction in DAoC, but not as much as in some other games. Most Monsters will gauge whether to attack determined based on level. Only Realm Guards will attack regardless of level.

lag Slow connection. The symptom of lag is that a character's reaction is erratic, and will continue to react to things after the situation is no longer applicable (for example, swinging at a Monster that has already moved somewhere else).

lamo Stupid. When someone makes a blunder, it was a lamo mistake.

ld Link Dead. Linkdeath is when a player's connection to the game is lost. Other players will see the character disappear or continue following the last command (such as walking forward) until he or she blinks out (disappears). The player who was disconnected will receive a message to that effect.

leeching Unwelcome "help." If you damage a creature that is currently fighting someone else, you can steal or "leech" a lot of the experience from the original fighter (usually without the danger that it will turn and attack you), plus if you hurt it enough you may be awarded the loot drop. You can also stop lower levels from getting experience if the creature they are fighting is gray to you and you damage it.

level up Increase character level. When a character has accumulated enough points to achieve the next level. "I'm about to level up."

lol Laughing Out Loud. Indicates that the speaker thinks the last thing said is funny enough to cause laughter. It's an acronym that has come across from Email Quickspeak.

lop/lom Low On Power/Low On Mana. Casters warn their team that they are running out of magical power and will need to rest soon.

loot Creature inventory. Anything received from a fallen foe is loot. (You only get loot from a Monster of high enough level that it would give you experience points.) It is possible to interrupt another character's combat, doing so much more damage than the original fighter that you get their loot. This is not considered fair play.

los Line Of Sight. Some spells can only be cast on targets that the caster can actually see. These are called Line of Sight spells.

lowbie Low-level, but not new, character. Someone level 15-25 might be considered a lowbie.

mana Power. Some other games refer to magical power as mana. DAoC refers to it as Power, but it's a hard habit for some players to break.

med Meditate. It's actually no different than what another sort of character would do … it's just sitting and resting. (Some people refer to resting to recover power as Mana Pause.)

mez Mesmerize. When an enemy is magically stunned and unable to move or initiate attack, it is mezzed.

mob Monster (MOBile object). A Monster or any sort of non-player aggressor is frequently called a MOB.

nerf Programmed to be less effective. In order to keep the game balanced between classes, it is sometimes necessary that the developers decrease the effectiveness of an item or spell. Because Nerf is the name of a line of foam toys that do not hurt when they hit you, an item that does less damage is said to have been Nerfed.

newbie Newly created character. Newbie usually refers to a character of level 5 or below, but can also refer to a player who has not been in DAoC for very long.

newbie zone/garden Area with lots of low-level Monsters. The areas near where new characters start are crawling with easily killed critters.

np No Problem. Either a response to thanks (similar to "you're welcome"), or to let someone know that a requested action will be performed.

npc	Non-Player-Character. A character that is a part of DAoC and controlled by a computer, not a live person.
nuke	Powerful destructive spell. Spells that do a lot of damage, specifically a lot of physical damage, are called nukes.
omg	Oh My God (Gosh). When a player is impressed or surprised, the response might be OMG.
omw	On My Way. Signals that the sender will be joining the person or group as soon as possible.
ooc	Out Of Character. When someone in the game says something that has nothing to do with the game.
ooe	Out Of Endurance. A common phrase for melee fighters. When a melee fighter is out of endurance, she cannot use her valuable combat styles.
oop/oom	Out Of Power/Out Of Mana. When magic users run out of magical energy.
owned	Defeated. A very casual (and non-role play) way of saying an opponent was defeated without any trouble.
oot	Out Of Time. A general all-purpose phrase for being … well, out of time.
orange	(Creature) Difficult opponent. A creature that will be difficult for you to kill solo, but is an easy group kill. (Item) An item that is far enough advanced for your skill level that you'll use it inexpertly for a while, but you should "grow into it."
otm	On the move. Means someone or something is changing location. This is usually used by the group leader to let the others know that they should follow her, but sometimes (usually clear by the context) means the monster target is moving.
otw	On The Way. Signals that the sender will be joining the person or group as soon as possible.
pc	Player-character. A character that is being controlled by a live player and not by the computer.
pet	Monster servant. Some magic users can summon a creature that will fight enemy creatures for them. These summoned creatures are called "pets" … but does not imply any emotional bonding.
pk	Player-Killer. A player character who kills other player characters.
pom	Purity of Mind (In Midgard). Purity of Mind is a popular buff among magic users. (Sometimes Purity of Movement.)
pop	Creature has spawned. Typing pop lets your group know that a creature has appeared nearby.
power-leveling	(Also, **pl'ing**)Playing just to gain levels as fast as possible. This is sometimes done by a higher-level player taking a lower-level player to places where he'd get max experience points per kill with much less risk than if the low-level player went alone.

	Also, you can "Power level" in crafting skills by spending a lot of money to gain experience, rather than relying on consignments or sales to fund your practice.
proc	PROCess an action. This is an unintuitive word that means "do something." It's usually used in regards to an item which has a special, usually beneficial effect. Each time this effect occurs, it "procs."
pull	Lure creature. A character (usually physically strong) will try to get a creature to attack him or her, and then lure ("pull") the creature back to the group for combat.
puppy	Wolf. A nickname for any wolf-type monster.
purple	(Creature) A nearly impossible win. A creature that registers as purple when you target it would be a challenge even for your group. (Item) An item far too advanced for you. Sell or trade it.
ptm	Purple to me. Means a monster cons as purple, and is a nearly impossible kill.
pve	Player Versus Environment. Describes combat where the enemy is a Monster (rather than another player).
pvp/rvr	Player Versus Player/Realm vs Realm. This refers to a player-character attacking another player character. In DAoC, characters from one realm can kill characters from another realm, but cannot attack characters from their own realm.
pwned	Similar to "ganked," meaning someone was easily beaten in combat. May have evolved from a common mis-typing of "owned", or perhaps stands for "pure ownage."
quest item	Rare item. An item that can only be acquired through the fulfillment of a quest.
rdy/r	Ready.
realm points	In-game "scoring" points. Finishing quests, or participating in the capture or defense of a relic will earn Realm Points for a character.
red	(Creature) An impossible solo win. A creature that registers as red should only be attacked when you are part of a group. (Item) An item that is too good for your abilities. You can use it, but you would cause it to degrade quickly.
release	Return to life. If there is no option to be resurrected via magic, you can type /release and be returned to your bindstone, with full res sickness and an extra 5% experience and constitution loss.
relic	Holy item. There are a certain number of relics in the game, usually well-defended in shrines in the frontier zones of a Realm. When a relic is taken from its realm, all the people of that realm suffer a reduction in stats. When a relic is placed within a realm's shrine, all the people of that realm receive stat bonuses.

res/rez	Resurrected. Returning to life by someone with a resurrection spell. You are returned to life at the place where you died, with less experience and constitution loss than if you simply released yourself.
res sickness	Temporarily lowered stats. After a player-character dies, he or she will come back with a temporary reduction in stats (res sickness) and a loss of experience (for the total required of that level). The usual loss of experience is eliminated (you only lose 5% of your experience) if your are brought back via magic.
rfp	Ready For Pull. Indicates that your group has recovered from the last battle and is ready to fight again.
rhfs	Rest Here For a Second. Tells your groupmates that you need to stop for a moment.
rl	Real Life. To differentiate between DAoC and something outside the game.
rofl	Rolling On Floor Laughing. Means that something just said or done is very funny.
roflmao	Rolling On Floor Laughing My Ass Off. Means that something just said or done is hilarious.
root	Immobilization spell. A spell that keeps the enemy from walking or running. Note that root spells do not stop the target from attacking, it just keeps them from moving.
rp	(1) Realm points. People may ask "how many RPs do you have?" referring to your realm point accumulation.
rp	(2) Rally Point. A Realm vs. Realm term used to call the group back to its Rally Point. This is usually a relatively safe location with a distinguishing landmark.
rp/rp'ing	(3) Role Playing. Having your character speak and react as though he or she were a real fighter, caster, etc., and not just "in a game."
rtm	Red to me. Means a monster cons as red, and is a difficult kill.
snare	Slow spell. A spell that slows the target's movement.
social	Creatures that defend each other. When you attack a social creature, more creatures may join the fight.
sor	Song Of Rest. A spell from a "music-based" magic user that allows group members to recuperate faster.
spam	Message to everyone. An Internet term: to send a message to as many people as possible. It can sometimes mean rapidly sending multiple messages to one person.
spawn	Creature creation. When a creature pops into existence, it is said to have spawned.
spec	Specialization. A chosen specialization or career path.
stun	Paralysis spell. A spell that immobilizes the target and keeps it from attacking. It's usually a short-term spell, but handy for giving you a few safe hits.

tank/tanking Overwhelming defense and strength. A Tank is a character whose main attribute is his ability to take and deal direct physical damage. To tank is to use melee attacks on an opponent, usually in order to keep it away from the weaker magic users.

taunt Enrage. Creatures will attack the character they feel is doing them the most harm. Usually that will be a magic user. However, since a magic user is often physically weak, stronger player-characters will use special skills to keep the target distracted away from the weaker members of the party.

These styles can either "protect" your friend by distracting the enemy, or "guard" your friend – if close enough – by arranging that you take the hit instead of the weaker person.

tpw/tgw Total Party Wipeout/Total Group Wipeout. Everyone in the party died.

train Creatures following a target. The image of a player-character running away from, and being followed by, several hostile creatures is similar to a train engine being followed by several train cars.

tree A nickname for any tree-form monster.

ttfn Ta Ta For Now. A casual way of saying "goodbye until we meet again."

ts Terra Strike. A popular Albion melee buff.

twinking Giving high-level equipment to low-level characters. In some games, this may give a new character an unfair advantage. In DAoC, it's just a waste of excellent equipment – low-level characters wear out high-level equipment quickly, and don't get much of a bonus to their attack.

warp Lag recovery. When lag (or whatever) causes a character or Monster to run past the point where it actually stops, then "warps" back to that location.

wb Welcome Back. A common greeting to someone you know well.

woot! Verbal reaction to something good. An exclamation like "Great!" or "Congratulations!"

wtb Want To Buy. Signals that someone needs a specific item, usually one that can only be purchased from another player-character.

wts Want To Sell. Signals that someone has something he wants to sell to another player-character.

wtt Want To Trade. A little less common than WTB or WTS, it signals that someone wants to trade (usually rare) items.

xp/exp/ep Experience Points. Experience points are a way of keeping track of your combat accomplishments. Accumulated experience points are what raise a character's level.

yellow (Creature) Tough kill. A difficult creature for you to kill, but valuable in terms of the experience points you'll get if you succeed. (Item) An item that is a little advanced for your skill level, but still good for you.

Appendix E: Slash Commands

While some commands may be set up using quick keys (see Configure Keyboard), others require the use of "/" commands. To use the following commands, simply type "/" in the command line followed by the appropriate command.

When a word appears in <brackets>, that word should be substituted with the appropriate name/place/etc. You should not type in the brackets. For instance, if you're looking for the NPC called Frip, instead of typing **/where <name>**, you should type in **/where frip**.

GAME TALK

Be aware that characters from one realm cannot understand words spoken by another realm.

/em or **/emote**	Describe an action that isn't immediately available in the game.
/group or **/g**	Send a message only to members of your party.
/say or **/s**	Send a message to those in the immediate vicinity.
/send	Send a private message to another character. For instance, you could /send john hi and only John would see your greeting.
/whisper	Send a message to a targeted player who is standing nearby.
/yell	Send a message to people in a broad range.
/gu	Send a message to everyone in your guild who is logged on.
/oc	Send a message to other officers in your guild.
/as	Send a message to everyone in your alliance who is logged on.
/b	Send a message to everyone in the city or town you're in.

GROUP COMMANDS

/invite	Invites a targeted person into your group.
/disband	Disbands a group or allows you to remove yourself from a group
/join	Join a person who has invited you into their group.
/autosplit	By Group leader, toggles whether group is automatically splitting all loot and coins.
/autosplit coins	By Group leader, toggles whether group is automatically splitting coins.
/autosplit loot	By Group leader, toggles whether group is automatically splitting items.
/autosplit objects	By Group leader, toggles whether group is automatically splitting items.
/autosplit self	Toggles whether or not you are on the item autosplit list for your group. Use this if you decide that you don't want any more items.

HELP

/advice List players who have signed up as advisors.

/advice <advisor name> <question> Send a question to the named advisor.

/advisor List yourself as an advisor. Your character must have have 15 hours of experience hours to be an advisor.

/appeal <request> Request help from the in-game support staff (during business hours).

/cancelappeal Deletes your appeal from the queue.

/filter Toggles the bad word filter on and off. Saved by character. On by default.

/stuck Relog your character if you become stuck, and moves you to the previous valid position. In cities you are moved to the center of the city.

ACTION

/bind Bind your character to a bind stone where it will resurrect in the event of death.

/control Take control of a siege engine.

/face Auto-face your target. This is excellent for archers and magic users.

/follow Follow the targeted character.

/macro <text> Assigns <text> to the cursor. Click on an empty slot on the Quick Bar to assign it to a hotkey. Works with slash commands, too.

/pray or /pr Recover experience. With your character's gravestone targeted, /pray allows you to recover some of the experience lost due to a death.

/quit or /q Quit the game.

/release or /re In case of death, type /release to return to life.

/repair Repair the selected item. If you are stealthed, repairing an item will cause you to reveal yourself.

/rest or /r Recover Hit Points, Endurance and Power. Rest is used to allow your character to sit and recuperate. The rate of resting Hit Point regeneration is approximately twice that of the standing rate.

/sit Same as /rest.

/stand Make your character stand up. Or use forward or backward arrows.

/stick Follow the target. /stick will break if the target gets too far away, but is excellent to use in cities or tight dungeons.

INFORMATION

/dir or /d	Show the direction you are facing.
/effects all	Shows all spell effects.
/effects none	Shows no spell effects.
/effects self	Shows spell effects that you have cast.
/help	Display help system.
/quest	Display the details of the quests you are on and/or have completed. You can also open the Journal on the Player Sheet panel to see current quests only.
/keyboard	Lists what keys are mapped to what commands.
/loc	Gives your location, for stuck points and other bug reports.
/realm	Gives keep information.
/relic	Gives relic information.
/task	Display information about any current tasks you have accepted.
/time	Show the current game time.
/where <name>	Locate <name>. Target a guard and use this command to find out where another NPC <name> is located.
/who <#>	List up to 25 players (on that server) of specified level.
/who <class>	List up to 25 players (on that server) of specified class.
/who <location>	List up to 25 players (on that server) in specified area.
/who <name>	List up to 25 players whose location or name includes <name>. Example: **/who Got** 1) Scriba, Level 24 Hunter in Gotar 2) Gottadie, Level 1 Mystic in Myrkwood.
/who all	List up to 25 players on the server, their class, level and location.
/who csr	List up to 25 Customer Service Representatives currently online.
/who help	List possible /who options.
/who	List the number of active players.

EMOTE ANIMATIONS

Emotes are commands you can type to have your character perform an action. They add another level of "believability" to the grouping adventure.

/bang	Bang on your shield.
/beckon	Wave someone over to your location.
/blush	Slightly embarrassed, "aw shucks" motion.
/bow	Character bows/greets.
/cheer	Way to go!

/clap	Clap in support.
/cry	You are feeling sad.
/curtsey	Character bows/greets.
/dance	Show your dancing skills.
/flex	Flex your muscles, macho-style.
/kiss	One of the most wonderful things.
/laugh	Now that was funny.
/point	Point in a direction.
/salute	Character salutes/greets.
/victory	Raise your hands in victory.
/wave	Wave goodbye or hello.

FRIEND CHAT

/friends	Shows your current friends list in a popup window.
/friends add <name>	Add someone to your Friends list. Your Friends list is by character basis, saved on the server. A friend must be logged in for you to add them to the list. You get text notifications when a friend logs in and out. If your window does not update, just type **/friends** again.
/friends remove <name>	Remove friend from your Friends list.
/cg invite <name>	Invite a player to join a chat group. If player's character is targeted, you do not need to type in the name. You can invite multiple people at once, if you like.
/cg join	Join a chat group when invited.
/cg decline	Decline an invitation to join a chat group.
/cg leave	Remove yourself from a chat group.
/cg remove <name>	Remove a player from a chat group.
/cg who	Lists all members of the chat group.
/cg disband	Disband the chat group.
/chat	Send messages to members of your chat group (or use the Friends tab).

GUILD AND ALLIANCE COMMANDS

See **Player Guilds**, page 29.

Appendix F: Websites

Internet websites are incredibly useful to the online gamer. Of course there's nothing better than a good ol' strategy guide to use as a reference when you're actually in the game: it's handy, it's immediate and you don't have to log out when you want a quick look at a map or list of spells. Still, a game that's played over the Internet means there are a lot of Internet-savvy people who are more than happy to share the benefits of their experiences. These are some that our panel of experts thought were particularly good.

Official Sites

Dark Age of Camelot

www.darkageofcamelot.com

The official home page. Good info, great links.

Camelot Herald

www.camelotherald.com

The official information site, with updates, patch information and server activity.

Official Camelot Support

http://support.darkageofcamelot.com/

Where to go when something's gone wrong.

General Sites

Camelot Vault

http://camelotvault.ign.com/

The longest-running Camelot news site on the Internet.

Grail News

http://www.grailbrotherhood.info/

DAoC and Galahad server news, and a good DAoC links resource.

Camelot Castle

http://cam-castle.com

Definitely something for everyone here!

Camelot Stratics

http://camelot.stratics.com/

The folks at Stratics take their game websites seriously. This is a great site for thorough game information.

Camelot Warcry

http://daoc.warcry.com/

Daily updates, with a friendly attitude. Nice guides for quests.

Of Camelot

http://ofcamelot.com/

Good forums. You must have a paid account to access some of the more valuable features.

Game Banshee

http://gamebanshee.com/darkageofcamelot/

Good nuts-and-bolts information, and useful databases.

Camelot Lore

http://camelot.rpglore.com/

A good all-purpose site for the non-newbie player.

CritShot

http://www.critshot.com/forums/index.php

Good forums, general and spec'ed for archers.

Camelot Outpost

http://www.camelotoutpost.com/

Good for newbies and players who are interested in communication.

Dark Age of Camelot Guides

http://www.rothwellhome.org/camelot.html

Usual set of news, gameplay, class, and realm links, plus the history and mythology of the realms. Guides on specialization, tradeskills, understanding the death penalty, and various class guides have been submitted by the beta test class leads. Great links page!

DAOC Catacombs

http://daoc.catacombs.com/index.cfm

Daily news plus a Character Builder that helps you see how spending your points will impact your character. Has an "emblem preview" that lets you view guild colors along with patterns and emblems.

Camelot Guild

http://gameznet.com/camelot/index.shtml

Game news. Equipment, quests, beast, etc.

RPG Market

http://www.rpgmarket.net/

Forums for crafters and traders with items for sale in-game.

The Messenger of Albion

http://www.albionmessenger.com/index.php

Nicely done site, especially for new players.

Allakhazam's Magical Realm

http://camelot.allakhazam.com

Great for guides, items, and useful stuff.

Sterling Order of Knights

http://www.sok.org

Bedevere Hibernia Guild

Specialized Sites

Dark Age of Camelot – The Maps

www.daatlas.com

Maps, maps and more maps. Muse has a long history of shedding blood and ink to draw up maps of interest to bold travelers, intrepid cave-crawlers and even the lady-about-town. Check it out; check it frequently.

http://www.rps.net/mojo/daoc/index.shtml

High-quality maps with a hunt list.

Tarnished Dagger

http://www.tarnished-dagger.com/

An excellent site for Rogues.

Defenders of Order

www.defendersoforder.com

The Defenders of Order is a multi-game guild now living in Albion. There's still nuts-and-bolts information to be found, plus it's a good example of why joining a guild can be fun and useful.

The Shaman Guide

http://www.daoc-shaman.com

An excellent site for Shamans.

Dark Age of Camelot Tradeskills

http://www.daoctradeskills.com

For those who are interested in building a career around tradeskills, this is a useful site.

Sanctum Arcanum

http://www.pub66.ezboard.com/bdaocelementalists

Major message board for all Wizards and Theurgists.

Hall of Valor

http://www.hallofvalor.com

Champion dedicated website

Appendix G: Panel Gallery

We wanted to run an entire gallery of *all* of our panelists, but these were the only ones we could chase down. As for the rest of them, they must have been very Stealthy. Or, perhaps they were all off gallivanting about the realm, lopping off heads and manipulating bodies and souls.

Ellyndria Dracaneco

Jubal Kinseeker

Oakleif

So ugly we broke the camera

Kronk

Grimsong

Mindeater Petmaster
Mindeater Petmaster
<Carnage>
Prior Tuck
Prior Tuck
<Amberforce>
Maia
Larian LeQuella
Larian LeQuella
<Armyn ab Treanid>
Varnarock
Varnarok Wolfbane
<MoX>